2009

Guidebook to CALIFORNIA TAXES

Includes Personal Income Tax Return Preparation Guide

Bruce A. Daigh
Christopher A. Whitney

Contributing Editors

CCH Editorial Staff

Editors .... Carolyn Kwock, Sandy Weiner
Production Coordinator .... Michelle Alvarado
Production .... Linda Barnich

ISBN 978-0-8080-1928-2

4025 W. Peterson Ave.
Chicago, IL 60646-6085
1 800 248 3248

www.CCHGroup.com

Printed in the United States of America

PREFACE

This *Guidebook* gives a general picture of the taxes imposed by the state of California and the general property tax levied by the local governments. All 2008 legislative amendments received as of press time are reflected, and references to California and federal laws are to the laws as of the date of publication of this book.

The emphasis is on the law applicable to the filing of income tax returns in 2009 for the 2008 tax year. However, if legislation has made changes effective after 2008, we have tried to note this also, with an indication of the effective date to avoid confusion.

The taxes of major interest—income and sales and use—are discussed in detail. Other California taxes, including estate taxes, are summarized, with particular emphasis on application, exemptions, returns, and payment.

Throughout the *Guidebook,* tax tips are highlighted to help practitioners avoid pitfalls and use the tax laws to their best advantage.

The *Guidebook* is designed as a quick reference work, describing the general provisions of the various tax laws, regulations, and administrative practices. It is useful to tax practitioners, businesspersons, and others who prepare or file California returns or who are required to deal with California taxes.

The *Guidebook* is not designed to eliminate the necessity of referring to the law and regulations for answers to complicated problems, nor is it intended to take the place of detailed reference works such as the CCH CALIFORNIA TAX REPORTS. With this in mind, specific references to the publisher's California tax product are inserted in most paragraphs. By assuming some knowledge of federal taxes, the *Guidebook* is able to provide a concise, readable treatment of California taxes that will supply a complete answer to most questions and will serve as a time-saving aid where it does not provide the complete answer.

With the 1987 edition, Mr. Russell S. Bock relinquished his role as primary author of the *Guidebook to California Taxes,* but continued in close association as a valued consultant for over 15 years thereafter.

In this edition, the *Guidebook* includes materials from two Contributing Editors: Bruce Daigh and Chris Whitney. These well-known practitioners provide practitioner comments throughout the book providing key insights into complex and controversial areas of tax law.

SCOPE OF THE BOOK

This *Guidebook* is designed to do four things:

1. Provide a quick step-by-step guide to the preparation of individual resident, nonresident, and part-year resident income tax returns.

2. Give a general picture of the impact and pattern of all taxes levied by the state of California and the general property tax levied by local governmental units.

3. Provide a readable quick-reference work for the personal income tax and the tax on corporate income. As such, it explains briefly what the California law provides and indicates whether the California provision is the same as federal law.

4. Analyze and explain the differences, in most cases, between California and federal law.

HOW TO USE THE BOOK

1. If you know the section number of the comparable federal law on the point in which you are interested, consult the Federal-California Cross-Reference Table and Index at the beginning of the portion of the book devoted to the tax involved.

2. If you know the section number of the California law, consult the California-Federal Cross-Reference Table and Index.

HOW TO USE THE RETURN PREPARATION GUIDE

1. Information can easily be found by consulting the Table of Contents to the *Guidebook* for residents' returns at page 41, or for nonresidents' and part-year residents' returns at page 61.

2. Explanations relating to specific lines on the residents' return can be found by consulting the cross-reference chart at page 42.

HIGHLIGHTS OF 2008 CALIFORNIA TAX CHANGES

The most important 2008 California tax changes received by press time are noted in the "Highlights of 2008 California Tax Changes" section of the *Guidebook,* beginning on page 9. This useful reference gives the practitioner up-to-the-minute information on changes in tax legislation.

FINDERS

The practitioner may find the information wanted by consulting the general Table of Contents at the beginning of the *Guidebook,* the Table of Contents at the beginning of each chapter, the Topical Index, the Table of Cases Cited, the Table of Franchise Tax Board Legal Rulings, or the Summary of Principal Items of 2008 Legislation.

The Topical Index is a useful tool. Specific taxes and information on rates, allocations, credits, exemptions, returns, payments, collection, penalties, and remedies are thoroughly indexed and cross-referenced to paragraph numbers in the *Guidebook.*

November 2008

ABOUT THE EDITORS

Bruce A. Daigh

Bruce Daigh is a partner in the New York office of PricewaterhouseCoopers LLP specializing in California taxation. Mr. Daigh has over 25 years of experience in California taxation, 18 of which were in PricewaterhouseCoopers' California offices. Key areas of his practice include combined reporting, state tax implications of mergers and acquisitions, state taxation of foreign earnings, state taxation of partnerships and water's edge issues. Mr. Daigh is a nationally recognized lecturer and instructor on state taxation. Among the many courses he instructs is the Center for State and Local Taxation's Annual Summer Institute at the University of California at Davis which he has instructed for 15 years. Mr. Daigh has also testified as an expert witness on several key state tax decisions. He is an Editorial Consultant for CCH Incorporated's California Tax Analysis: Corporation Tax, and has authored several articles on a variety of California and state and local taxation issues.

Christopher A. Whitney

Christopher A. Whitney is a partner with PricewaterhouseCoopers LLP, based in Orange County, California. Mr. Whitney specializes in state and local tax, with a particular emphasis on California tax matters. Key areas of his practice include combined reporting and California water's edge issues as well as state tax implications of mergers and acquisitions. Mr. Whitney is a frequent speaker at local and national tax conferences and has authored several articles on a variety of state and local taxation issues. He is also an Editorial Consultant for CCH Incorporated's California Tax Analysis: Corporation Tax publication.

CONTENTS

HIGHLIGHTS OF 2008 CALIFORNIA TAX CHANGES

Highlights of the 2008 California tax changes are noted below.

Multiple Taxes

• *Net operating losses suspended; conformity to NOL carryovers and carrybacks enacted*

With the exception of small businesses, taxpayers are prohibited from claiming a net operating loss (NOL) deduction during the 2008 and 2009 taxable years. However, the carryover period is extended from 10 years to 20 years, commencing with NOLs incurred during the 2008 taxable year. In addition, a 2-year NOL carryback is being phased in beginning with NOLs incurred in 2011. See ¶309, ¶1024. (Ch. 763 (A.B. 1452), Laws 2008)

• *Temporary business credit limitations enacted*

The amount of business credits against corporation franchise and income and personal income taxes and business credit carryovers that may be claimed by taxpayers are limited to 50% of a taxpayer's tax during the 2008 and 2009 tax years. Thereafter, the credits may be claimed in full. Small businesses are exempt from the credit limitations. See ¶125, ¶818. (Ch. 763 (A.B. 1452), Laws 2008)

• *Former LLC fee calculation declared unconstitutional*

Two California courts of appeal have held that the former limited liability company (LLC) fee, that was based on an LLC's worldwide income, was an unconstitutional unapportioned tax. One court held that the LLC fee scheme was unconstitutional as applied to an out-of-state LLC that had registered as an LLC with the California Secretary of State's office but that had no income from activities. (*Northwest Energetic Services, LLC v. California Franchise Tax Board,* (2008) 159 Cal.App. 4th 841) The court ordered a full refund of the tax and the Franchise Tax Board (FTB) is refunding the fee to all qualified similarly situated taxpayers (*FTB Notice 2008-2*). The other court held that the tax was unconstitutional as applied to a taxpayer with income from both inside and outside California and that the proper remedy to be applied to the unapportioned tax was to refund the difference between the amount of the fee paid by the taxpayer and the amount of the fee that would have been required had the fee been fairly apportioned. (*Ventas Finance I, LLC v. California Franchise Tax Board,* (2008) 165 Cal.App.4th 1207, petition for review denied, California Supreme Court, November 13, 2008). See ¶625.

• *Estimated tax installment amounts revised*

Applicable to installments due for each taxable year beginning after 2008, the amount of the estimated corporation franchise and income tax and estimated personal income tax installment payments is increased from 25% to 30% of the amount of annual tax due for the first and second installments and decreased from 25% to 20% for the third and fourth installments. See ¶111, ¶811. (Ch. 1 (S.B. 28), Laws 2008, First Special Session; Ch. 305 (A.B. 3078), Laws 2008)

• *Estimated LLC fee payment requirement enacted*

Beginning with the 2009 taxable year, LLCs are required to make an estimated LLC fee payment by the 15th day of the sixth month of the current taxable year. See ¶625. (Ch. 763 (A.B. 1452), Laws 2008; Ch. 1 (SB 28), Laws 2008, First Special Session)

• *Tax relief available for 2007/2008 California disasters*

Taxpayers that incurred disaster losses stemming from qualified disasters throughout California in 2007 and 2008 may carryover the losses on their California personal income tax or corporation franchise or income tax returns for up to 15 years. See ¶307, ¶1007. (Ch. 386 (S.B. 1064), Laws 2008)

• *Real estate withholding provisions expanded and revised*

Applicable to real property sales occurring after 2008, out-of-state partnerships are subject to the withholding at source requirements for sales of California real estate, the withholding rate applicable to S corporations is increased, and the treatment of withholding on installment sales of real property is revised. See ¶716. (Ch. 305 (A.B. 3078), Laws 2008)

• *Farmworker housing credit made part of low-income housing credit*

Beginning with the 2009 taxable year, the farmworker housing credit is repealed, but at least $500,000 per year must be set aside under the low-income housing credit to support farmworker housing projects. See ¶137, ¶138, ¶818. (Ch. 521 (S.B. 1247), Laws 2008)

• *Eligibility requirements for nonresident group returns eased*

Applicable to returns filed after 2009, for taxable years beginning after 2008, a nonresident group return may be filed by partnerships and S corporations on behalf of a single nonresident partner or shareholder and the return may also include nonresidents who are subject to the additional 1% mental health personal income tax imposed on the portion of a taxpayer's income in excess of $1 million. See ¶619. (Ch. 751 (A.B. 1389), Laws 2008)

• *Taxpayers' Rights Advocate authorized to abate penalties and interest*

Applicable to requests for advocate consideration that are received after 2008, the FTB's Taxpayers' Rights Advocate may abate any penalties, fees, additions to tax, or interest assessed against a taxpayer under specified circumstances. See ¶712. (Ch. 305 (A.B. 3078), Laws 2008)

• *FTB implements LLC suspension/forfeiture program*

The FTB will begin to suspend/forfeit the rights, powers, and privileges of LLCs for nonpayment of taxes, penalties, or interest, and/or failure to file a return. The program will commence early in 2009. See ¶625. (*Tax News*, California Franchise Tax Board, October 2008)

• *SBE's offer-in-compromise program expanded*

During the 2009 through 2012 calendar years, the State Board of Equalization (SBE) may accept offers in compromise from qualified businesses even if those businesses are still operating, for liabilities relating to sales and use, cigarette, use fuel, diesel fuel, and alcoholic beverage taxes, as well as for a variety of fees and surcharges. See ¶1512. (Ch. 222 (A.B. 2047), Laws 2008)

Personal Income Taxes

• *Partial conformity to Mortgage Forgiveness Debt Relief Act enacted*

California allows a limited exclusion from gross income for discharge of an individual's qualified principal residence indebtedness discharged in the 2007 and 2008 calendar years. See ¶221. (Ch. 282 (S.B. 1055), Laws 2008)

• *Estimated tax payment threshold increased*

The personal income estimated tax payment threshold is increased from $200 to $500 (from $100 to $250 for married taxpayers filing separately), beginning with the 2009 taxable year. See ¶111. (Ch. 1 (SB 28), Laws 2008, First Special Session; Ch. 305 (A.B. 3078), Laws 2008)

• *Prior year's tax estimated tax safe harbor repealed for high-income taxpayers*

Applicable to installments due for each taxable year beginning after 2008, the safe harbor provision from the estimated tax underpayment penalty for individuals who pay 110% of their prior year's tax liability will no longer be available to individuals with adjusted gross incomes for the taxable year that equal or exceed $1 million ($500,000 in the case of a married individual filing a separate return). See ¶111. (Ch. 1 (SB 28), Laws 2008, First Special Session)

• *Electronic payment requirements enacted*

Applicable to all installments due after 2008, personal income taxpayers are required to make their tax payments electronically if their estimated personal income tax installment payment or extension request payment exceeds $20,000 or if their total annual post-2008 tax liability exceeds $80,000. See ¶110. (Ch. 751 (A.B. 1389), Laws 2008)

• *Same-sex married couples treated as spouses*

Same-sex couple marriages performed in California between June 16, 2008, and November 5, 2008, have been recognized as valid marriages for California purposes. However, at the time this book went to press, the FTB had not yet announced whether such same-sex married couples (SSMCs) married during this period would be treated as spouses for Revenue and Taxation purposes. Should SSMCs be treated as spouses for California income tax purposes, numerous adjustments to federal taxable income would be required to determine a SSMC's California tax liability. See ¶119.

• *Refund limitations period for taxes paid to other state extended*

Applicable to taxes paid to another state after 2008, taxpayers may file claims for refund or credit for taxes paid to other states within one year from the date the tax is paid to the other state even if the standard statute of limitations period has lapsed. See ¶719. (Ch. 305 (A.B. 3078), Laws 2008)

Corporation Franchise and Income Taxes

• *Assignment of credits among unitary group authorized*

Beginning with the 2010 taxable year, members of a unitary group included in a combined report may assign tax credits to other eligible group members, applicable to any credit earned by the taxpayer in a taxable year beginning after 2007 or any credit earned in any taxable year beginning before July 1, 2008, that is eligible to be carried forward to the taxpayer's first taxable year beginning after June 30, 2008. See ¶1310. (Ch. 763 (A.B. 1452), Laws 2008)

• *Unitary group intercompany dividend elimination deduction modified*

Modifications to the intercompany dividend elimination deduction available to members of a combined reporting group clarify that (1) as long as certain conditions are satisfied, the deduction is available even if the income is earned by members of a group who are not California taxpayers or who were not included in the combined report at the time the income was earned, and (2) the deduction is also available if the payee was formed after the income was earned. Additional amendments authorize the FTB to disallow the deduction if the transaction was undertaken for purposes of tax evasion, beginning with the 2009 taxable year. See ¶1310. (Ch. 305 (A.B. 3078), Laws 2008)

• *FTB adopts regulation excluding treasury function income from apportionment formula sales factor*

The FTB has adopted a regulatory amendment that excludes "treasury function" income and receipts from the apportionment formula sales factor. The exclusion applies, beginning with the 2007 taxable year, to interest and dividends from intangible assets held in connection with a treasury function of the taxpayer's unitary business, as well as to the gross receipts and overall net gains from the maturity, redemption, sale, exchange or other disposition of such intangible assets. See ¶1309. (Reg. 25137(c)(1)(D), 18 CCR)

• *New large corporate tax underpayment penalty enacted*

Business entities that underpay their corporate tax liability by more than $1 million (computed on a unitary group basis) for any taxable year are subject to a new 20% underpayment penalty, in addition to any other penalty that may be imposed. The penalty applies retroactively to each taxable year beginning after 2002, for which the statute of limitations on assessment has not expired. However, taxpayers will have until March 1, 2009, to report and pay outstanding taxes in order to avoid the imposition of this penalty. See ¶1411. (Ch. 1 (SB 28), Laws 2008, First Special Session)

Sales and Use Taxes

• *Presumption for use of vehicle, vessel, or aircraft in state expanded*

The presumption that a vehicle shipped or brought into the state within 90 days from the date of its purchase was purchased from a retailer for storage, use, or other consumption in California has been expanded to apply to a vehicle, vessel, or aircraft brought into California within 12 months from the date of its purchase, provided specified conditions are satisfied. See ¶1505. (Ch. 763 (A.B. 1452), Laws 2008)

• *Barnes & Noble.com disputes resolved*

On May 29, 2008, the SBE approved a global settlement with Barnes & Noble.com that resolved all disputes between Barnes & Noble.com and the State of California for sales and use taxes. See ¶1505. (*Form 10-Q Quarterly Report*, Barnes & Noble, Inc., filed with the Securities and Exchange Commission on September 11, 2008)

• *Voluntary use tax reporting program reinstated*

The voluntary use tax reporting program that was in effect from January 1, 2004, through January 1, 2008, has been reinstated. The period of time for which the SBE may issue a determination is reduced from eight years to three years when unregistered in-state purchasers voluntarily report to the SBE purchases subject to use tax. See ¶1512. (Ch. 306 (A.B. 3079), Laws 2008)

• *Managed audit program extended*

The Managed Audit Program, under which taxpayers can perform an audit of their own books and records with limited guidance from the SBE, has been extended indefinitely. See ¶1512. (Ch. 306 (A.B. 3079), Laws 2008)

• *Limitations periods provided for deficiencies of corporate officers*

Effective January 1, 2009, limitations periods are provided for the issuance of deficiency determinations against corporate officers and other responsible persons liable for the unpaid sales and use taxes of a business. See ¶1512. (Ch. 24 (A.B. 1895), Laws 2008)

Property Taxes

• *Homeowners and renters assistance program unfunded for 2008 claims*

The California budget approved for the 2008/2009 fiscal year deleted funding for property tax assistance payments under the Homeowner and Renter Assistance Program. Consequently, 2008 claims cannot be paid. See ¶1705. (*Important Update*, California Franchise Tax Board, September 2008)

• *Selection process for business audits amended*

Effective January 1, 2009, county assessors must annually conduct a significant number of audits of the books and records of nonexempt business taxpayers with taxable property in the county. Under the new process, 50% of the audits required annually must be performed on taxpayers selected from a pool of those taxpayers that have the largest assessments of trade fixtures and business tangible personal property in the county. Each taxpayer in the pool must be audited at least once every four years. See ¶1707. (Ch. 297 (A.B. 550), Laws 2008)

• *New construction reassessment exclusion for solar energy systems expanded, extended*

The exclusion from new construction reassessment for active solar energy systems is expanded and extended through the 2015-2016 fiscal year. See ¶1702. (Ch. 538 (A.B. 1451), Laws 2008)

• *Time limitation set for refund claims*

Effective January 1, 2009, if a qualifying application has been filed for a reduction in property tax assessment and the applicant does not state that the application is intended to constitute a claim for a refund, the applicant must request a refund within one year of the earlier of (1) the county notifying the applicant of an assessment reduction without advising the applicant to seek a refund or (2) if the time period for the county to make a final determination expires. If an applicant is notified of both a reduction in assessment and the right to file a claim for refund, the applicant will have six months within which to file the claim. See ¶1711. (Ch. 329 (A.B. 2411), Laws 2008)

Miscellaneous Taxes

• *Tax return preparer signature requirements clarified*

Effective June 23, 2008, returns that are prepared by an employee of a tax preparer who is exempt from the California Tax Education Council (CTEC) registration requirements must be signed by a California certified public accountant, attorney, enrolled agent, or a tax preparer who is registered with the CTEC. See ¶701. (Ch. 33 (S.B. 797), Laws 2008)

SUMMARY OF PRINCIPAL ITEMS OF 2008 LEGISLATION AFFECTING CALIFORNIA PERSONAL INCOME TAX AND TAXES ON CORPORATE INCOME

Law Section	Comparable Federal	Summary of Change
PERSONAL INCOME TAX:		
17039.2	None	Limits amount of business credits and credit carryovers that may be claimed during 2008 and 2009 taxable years
17053.14	None	Repeals farmworker housing credit beginning with 2009 taxable year
17058	42	Creates low-income housing credit set-aside for farmworker housing and revises partnership allocation rules
17144.5	108	Partially conforms to gross income exclusion for discharge of qualified principal residence indebtedness
17207	165	Extends special carryover loss treatment to losses resulting from specified disasters occurring in 2007 and 2008
17276	172	Authorizes phase-in of net operating loss (NOL) carryback
17276.9	172	Suspends NOL deduction for 2008 and 2009 taxable years
17276.10	172	Conforms to federal NOL carryover and carryback periods
17942	None	Enacts estimated LLC fee payment requirement
ADMINISTRATION		
18535	None	Eases eligibility requirements for filing of nonresident group partnership return
18536	None	Eases eligibility requirements for filing of group return for nonresident S corporation shareholders
18662	None	Revises real estate withholding at source requirements for partnerships, S corporations, and installment sales
18668	None	Extends withholding liability provisions to employers who fail to timely remit withholding taxes
19011.5	None	Enacts electronic payment requirements for specified individuals
19025	None	Revises corporation franchise estimated tax installment amounts

Law Section	Comparable Federal	Summary of Change
19136	6654	Increases personal income estimated tax payment threshold amounts
19136.1	6654	Revises personal income estimated tax installment amounts
19136.3	6654	Repeals estimated tax prior year safe harbor provision for high-income taxpayers
19138	...	Enacts new large corporate tax underpayment penalty
19311.5	None	Extends limitations period for refunds attributable to taxes paid to another state
19551-51.5	None	Establishes reciprocal information exchange program between FTB and California cities imposing a business license tax
21004	None	Authorizes Taxpayers' Rights Advocate to abate interest and penalties under specified circumstances
TAXES ON CORPORATE INCOME:		
23036.2	None	Limits amount of business credits and credit carryovers that may be claimed during 2008 and 2009 taxable years
23608.2	None	Repeals farmworker housing credit beginning with 2009 taxable year
23608.3	None	Repeals farmworker housing financing credit beginning with 2009 taxable year
23610.5	42	Creates low-income housing credit set-aside for farmworker housing projects and revises partnership allocation rules
23663	None	Authorizes assignment of credits among unitary group members
24347.5	165	Extends special carryover loss treatment to losses resulting from specified disasters occurring in 2007 and 2008
24416	172	Authorizes phase-in of NOL carryback
24416.9	172	Suspends NOL deduction for 2008 and 2009 taxable years
24416.10	172	Conforms to federal NOL carryover and carryback periods
25106	None	Clarifies eligibility for intercompany dividends elimination deduction

TAX CALENDAR

The following table lists significant dates of interest to California taxpayers and tax practitioners.

ANNUALLY RECURRING DATES

January

1st—Annual withholding reconciliation returns due
Property tax assessment date; property tax liens attach
Property tax on race horses due

31st—Employers must furnish W-2 Form to each employee subject to withholding of personal income tax, state disability insurance, or voluntary disability insurance
Annual withholding reconciliation returns delinquent
Persons required to file information returns concerning patronage dividend, rebate, or refund payments; employee group life insurance costs; transfers of stock pursuant to a stock option plan; brokerage services; renumeration of fishing boat crew members; or dividends, interest, or distributions out of earnings or profits must furnish a statement to each person named in a return

February

1st—Second installment of real property tax due
Second installment of oil and gas producers' tax delinquent

15th—Property tax on race horses delinquent

March

1st—Insurance tax liens attach
Surplus line brokers annual return due
Property tax assessment date; property tax liens attach
Oil and gas producers' annual reports due

15th—Affidavits due for cemetery, college, exhibition, welfare, free public library, free museum, veterans' organizations, and public school property tax exemptions
Calendar-year taxpayers' corporate income and franchise tax returns due

31st—Affidavits due for church and religious property tax exemptions
Affidavits due for historically significant aircraft property tax exemption

April

1st—Insurers' (other than ocean marine insurers and surplus line brokers) returns and tax due
Affidavits due for documented vessel classification

10th—Second installment of real property tax delinquent

15th—Calendar-year taxpayers' personal income tax returns and tax due
Affidavits due for homeowners' and veterans' property tax exemptions

30th—Property tax reports on private railroad cars due

May

15th—Calendar-year exempt organizations' information returns due
Senior citizens' property tax assistance claims due

Last Friday—Property statements due

June

15th—Ocean marine insurers' returns and tax due

July

1st—Oil and gas producers' tax due

August

15th—First installment of oil and gas producers' tax delinquent

31st—Tax on unsecured property delinquent

November

1st—Personal property tax and first installment of real property tax due

December

10th—Personal property tax and first installment of real property tax delinquent

Property tax on private railroad cars due

MONTHLY RECURRING DATES

1st—Common carriers' distilled spirits monthly reports and tax due

15th—Beer and wine manufacturers', growers', importers', and sellers' monthly reports and tax due

Distilled spirits agents', manufacturers', rectifiers', wholesalers', and sellers' monthly reports and tax due

25th—Motor fuel distributors', producers', and brokers' monthly reports and tax due

Aircraft jet fuel monthly reports and tax due

Cigarette monthly reports or returns and tax due

Last day—Oil and gas producers' monthly reports due

QUARTERLY RECURRING DATES

Jan., April, July, and Oct.

Last day—Quarterly reports and payment of withheld personal income tax due

Use fuel vendors and users reports and tax due

Quarterly returns and payment of sales and use tax due

Quarterly returns and payment of timber yield tax due

April, June, Sept., and Jan.

15th—Estimated tax installments for personal income taxpayers due

Fourth, Sixth, Ninth, and 12th Month of Income Year

15th—Estimated tax installments exceeding $800 for corporate income taxpayers due

PART I

TAX RATE SCHEDULES AND TABLES

¶1 Personal Income Tax Tables for 2008

The Tax Tables for 2008 Personal Income Tax start on the following page.

2008 California Tax Table

To Find Your Tax:

- Read down the column labeled "If Your Taxable Income Is . . ." to find the range that includes your taxable income from Form 540/540A, line 19.
- Read across the columns labeled "The Tax For Filing Status" until you find the tax that applies for your taxable income and filing status.

Filing status: 1 or 3 (Single; Married/RDP Filing Separately) 2 or 5 (Married/RDP Filing Jointly; Qualifying Widow(er)) 4 (Head of Household)

If Your Taxable Income Is ...		The Tax For Filing Status			If Your Taxable Income Is ...		The Tax For Filing Status			If Your Taxable Income Is ...		The Tax For Filing Status		
At Least	But Not Over	1 Or 3 Is	2 Or 5 Is	4 Is	At Least	But Not Over	1 Or 3 Is	2 Or 5 Is	4 Is	At Least	But Not Over	1 Or 3 Is	2 Or 5 Is	4 Is
$1	$50	$0	$0	$0	6,451	6,550	65	65	65	12,951	13,050	188	130	130
51	150	1	1	1	6,551	6,650	66	66	66	13,051	13,150	190	131	131
151	250	2	2	2	6,651	6,750	67	67	67	13,151	13,250	192	132	132
251	350	3	3	3	6,751	6,850	68	68	68	13,251	13,350	194	133	133
351	450	4	4	4	6,851	6,950	69	69	69	13,351	13,450	196	134	134
451	550	5	5	5	6,951	7,050	70	70	70	13,451	13,550	198	135	135
551	650	6	6	6	7,051	7,150	71	71	71	13,551	13,650	200	136	136
651	750	7	7	7	7,151	7,250	72	72	72	13,651	13,750	202	137	137
751	850	8	8	8	7,251	7,350	74	73	73	13,751	13,850	204	138	138
851	950	9	9	9	7,351	7,450	76	74	74	13,851	13,950	206	139	139
951	1,050	10	10	10	7,451	7,550	78	75	75	13,951	14,050	208	140	140
1,051	1,150	11	11	11	7,551	7,650	80	76	76	14,051	14,150	210	141	141
1,151	1,250	12	12	12	7,651	7,750	82	77	77	14,151	14,250	212	142	142
1,251	1,350	13	13	13	7,751	7,850	84	78	78	14,251	14,350	214	143	143
1,351	1,450	14	14	14	7,851	7,950	86	79	79	14,351	14,450	216	145	145
1,451	1,550	15	15	15	7,951	8,050	88	80	80	14,451	14,550	218	147	147
1,551	1,650	16	16	16	8,051	8,150	90	81	81	14,551	14,650	220	149	149
1,651	1,750	17	17	17	8,151	8,250	92	82	82	14,651	14,750	222	151	151
1,751	1,850	18	18	18	8,251	8,350	94	83	83	14,751	14,850	224	153	153
1,851	1,950	19	19	19	8,351	8,450	96	84	84	14,851	14,950	226	155	155
1,951	2,050	20	20	20	8,451	8,550	98	85	85	14,951	15,050	228	157	157
2,051	2,150	21	21	21	8,551	8,650	100	86	86	15,051	15,150	230	159	159
2,151	2,250	22	22	22	8,651	8,750	102	87	87	15,151	15,250	232	161	161
2,251	2,350	23	23	23	8,751	8,850	104	88	88	15,251	15,350	234	163	163
2,351	2,450	24	24	24	8,851	8,950	106	89	89	15,351	15,450	236	165	165
2,451	2,550	25	25	25	8,951	9,050	108	90	90	15,451	15,550	238	167	167
2,551	2,650	26	26	26	9,051	9,150	110	91	91	15,551	15,650	240	169	169
2,651	2,750	27	27	27	9,151	9,250	112	92	92	15,651	15,750	242	171	171
2,751	2,850	28	28	28	9,251	9,350	114	93	93	15,751	15,850	244	173	173
2,851	2,950	29	29	29	9,351	9,450	116	94	94	15,851	15,950	246	175	175
2,951	3,050	30	30	30	9,451	9,550	118	95	95	15,951	16,050	248	177	177
3,051	3,150	31	31	31	9,551	9,650	120	96	96	16,051	16,150	250	179	179
3,151	3,250	32	32	32	9,651	9,750	122	97	97	16,151	16,250	252	181	181
3,251	3,350	33	33	33	9,751	9,850	124	98	98	16,251	16,350	254	183	183
3,351	3,450	34	34	34	9,851	9,950	126	99	99	16,351	16,450	256	185	185
3,451	3,550	35	35	35	9,951	10,050	128	100	100	16,451	16,550	258	187	187
3,551	3,650	36	36	36	10,051	10,150	130	101	101	16,551	16,650	260	189	189
3,651	3,750	37	37	37	10,151	10,250	132	102	102	16,651	16,750	262	191	191
3,751	3,850	38	38	38	10,251	10,350	134	103	103	16,751	16,850	264	193	193
3,851	3,950	39	39	39	10,351	10,450	136	104	104	16,851	16,950	266	195	195
3,951	4,050	40	40	40	10,451	10,550	138	105	105	16,951	17,050	268	197	197
4,051	4,150	41	41	41	10,551	10,650	140	106	106	17,051	17,150	272	199	199
4,151	4,250	42	42	42	10,651	10,750	142	107	107	17,151	17,250	276	201	201
4,251	4,350	43	43	43	10,751	10,850	144	108	108	17,251	17,350	280	203	203
4,351	4,450	44	44	44	10,851	10,950	146	109	109	17,351	17,450	284	205	205
4,451	4,550	45	45	45	10,951	11,050	148	110	110	17,451	17,550	288	207	207
4,551	4,650	46	46	46	11,051	11,150	150	111	111	17,551	17,650	292	209	209
4,651	4,750	47	47	47	11,151	11,250	152	112	112	17,651	17,750	296	211	211
4,751	4,850	48	48	48	11,251	11,350	154	113	113	17,751	17,850	300	213	213
4,851	4,950	49	49	49	11,351	11,450	156	114	114	17,851	17,950	304	215	215
4,951	5,050	50	50	50	11,451	11,550	158	115	115	17,951	18,050	308	217	217
5,051	5,150	51	51	51	11,551	11,650	160	116	116	18,051	18,150	312	219	219
5,151	5,250	52	52	52	11,651	11,750	162	117	117	18,151	18,250	316	221	221
5,251	5,350	53	53	53	11,751	11,850	164	118	118	18,251	18,350	320	223	223
5,351	5,450	54	54	54	11,851	11,950	166	119	119	18,351	18,450	324	225	225
5,451	5,550	55	55	55	11,951	12,050	168	120	120	18,451	18,550	328	227	227
5,551	5,650	56	56	56	12,051	12,150	170	121	121	18,551	18,650	332	229	229
5,651	5,750	57	57	57	12,151	12,250	172	122	122	18,651	18,750	336	231	231
5,751	5,850	58	58	58	12,251	12,350	174	123	123	18,751	18,850	340	233	233
5,851	5,950	59	59	59	12,351	12,450	176	124	124	18,851	18,950	344	235	235
5,951	6,050	60	60	60	12,451	12,550	178	125	125	18,951	19,050	348	237	237
6,051	6,150	61	61	61	12,551	12,650	180	126	126	19,051	19,150	352	239	239
6,151	6,250	62	62	62	12,651	12,750	182	127	127	19,151	19,250	356	241	241
6,251	6,350	63	63	63	12,751	12,850	184	128	128	19,251	19,350	360	243	243
6,351	6,450	64	64	64	12,851	12,950	186	129	129	19,351	19,450	364	245	245

Continued on next page.

2008 California Tax Table - Continued

Filing status: 1 or 3 (Single; Married/RDP Filing Separately) 2 or 5 (Married/RDP Filing Jointly; Qualifying Widow(er)) 4 (Head of Household)

If Your Taxable Income Is ...		The Tax For Filing Status			If Your Taxable Income Is ...		The Tax For Filing Status			If Your Taxable Income Is ...		The Tax For Filing Status		
At Least	But Not Over	1 Or 3 Is	2 Or 5 Is	4 Is	At Least	But Not Over	1 Or 3 Is	2 Or 5 Is	4 Is	At Least	But Not Over	1 Or 3 Is	2 Or 5 Is	4 Is
19,451	19,550	368	247	247	26,451	26,550	648	387	387	33,451	33,550	1,062	527	527
19,551	19,650	372	249	249	26,551	26,650	652	389	389	33,551	33,650	1,068	529	529
19,651	19,750	376	251	251	26,651	26,750	656	391	391	33,651	33,750	1,074	531	531
19,751	19,850	380	253	253	26,751	26,850	660	393	393	33,751	33,850	1,080	533	533
19,851	19,950	384	255	255	26,851	26,950	666	395	395	33,851	33,950	1,086	535	535
19,951	20,050	388	257	257	26,951	27,050	672	397	397	33,951	34,050	1,092	537	537
20,051	20,150	392	259	259	27,051	27,150	678	399	399	34,051	34,150	1,098	541	541
20,151	20,250	396	261	261	27,151	27,250	684	401	401	34,151	34,250	1,104	545	545
20,251	20,350	400	263	263	27,251	27,350	690	403	403	34,251	34,350	1,110	549	549
20,351	20,450	404	265	265	27,351	27,450	696	405	405	34,351	34,450	1,116	553	553
20,451	20,550	408	267	267	27,451	27,550	702	407	407	34,451	34,550	1,122	557	557
20,551	20,650	412	269	269	27,551	27,650	708	409	409	34,551	34,650	1,128	561	561
20,651	20,750	416	271	271	27,651	27,750	714	411	411	34,651	34,750	1,134	565	565
20,751	20,850	420	273	273	27,751	27,850	720	413	413	34,751	34,850	1,140	569	569
20,851	20,950	424	275	275	27,851	27,950	726	415	415	34,851	34,950	1,146	573	573
20,951	21,050	428	277	277	27,951	28,050	732	417	417	34,951	35,050	1,152	577	577
21,051	21,150	432	279	279	28,051	28,150	738	419	419	35,051	35,150	1,158	581	581
21,151	21,250	436	281	281	28,151	28,250	744	421	421	35,151	35,250	1,164	585	585
21,251	21,350	440	283	283	28,251	28,350	750	423	423	35,251	35,350	1,170	589	589
21,351	21,450	444	285	285	28,351	28,450	756	425	425	35,351	35,450	1,176	593	593
21,451	21,550	448	287	287	28,451	28,550	762	427	427	35,451	35,550	1,182	597	597
21,551	21,650	452	289	289	28,551	28,650	768	429	429	35,551	35,650	1,188	601	601
21,651	21,750	456	291	291	28,651	28,750	774	431	431	35,651	35,750	1,194	605	605
21,751	21,850	460	293	293	28,751	28,850	780	433	433	35,751	35,850	1,200	609	609
21,851	21,950	464	295	295	28,851	28,950	786	435	435	35,851	35,950	1,206	613	613
21,951	22,050	468	297	297	28,951	29,050	792	437	437	35,951	36,050	1,212	617	617
22,051	22,150	472	299	299	29,051	29,150	798	439	439	36,051	36,150	1,218	621	621
22,151	22,250	476	301	301	29,151	29,250	804	441	441	36,151	36,250	1,224	625	625
22,251	22,350	480	303	303	29,251	29,350	810	443	443	36,251	36,350	1,230	629	629
22,351	22,450	484	305	305	29,351	29,450	816	445	445	36,351	36,450	1,236	633	633
22,451	22,550	488	307	307	29,451	29,550	822	447	447	36,451	36,550	1,242	637	637
22,551	22,650	492	309	309	29,551	29,650	828	449	449	36,551	36,650	1,248	641	641
22,651	22,750	496	311	311	29,651	29,750	834	451	451	36,651	36,750	1,254	645	645
22,751	22,850	500	313	313	29,751	29,850	840	453	453	36,751	36,850	1,260	649	649
22,851	22,950	504	315	315	29,851	29,950	846	455	455	36,851	36,950	1,266	653	653
22,951	23,050	508	317	317	29,951	30,050	852	457	457	36,951	37,050	1,272	657	657
23,051	23,150	512	319	319	30,051	30,150	858	459	459	37,051	37,150	1,278	661	661
23,151	23,250	516	321	321	30,151	30,250	864	461	461	37,151	37,250	1,284	665	665
23,251	23,350	520	323	323	30,251	30,350	870	463	463	37,251	37,350	1,291	669	669
23,351	23,450	524	325	325	30,351	30,450	876	465	465	37,351	37,450	1,299	673	673
23,451	23,550	528	327	327	30,451	30,550	882	467	467	37,451	37,550	1,307	677	677
23,551	23,650	532	329	329	30,551	30,650	888	469	469	37,551	37,650	1,315	681	681
23,651	23,750	536	331	331	30,651	30,750	894	471	471	37,651	37,750	1,323	685	685
23,751	23,850	540	333	333	30,751	30,850	900	473	473	37,751	37,850	1,331	689	689
23,851	23,950	544	335	335	30,851	30,950	906	475	475	37,851	37,950	1,339	693	693
23,951	24,050	548	337	337	30,951	31,050	912	477	477	37,951	38,050	1,347	697	697
24,051	24,150	552	339	339	31,051	31,150	918	479	479	38,051	38,150	1,355	701	701
24,151	24,250	556	341	341	31,151	31,250	924	481	481	38,151	38,250	1,363	705	705
24,251	24,350	560	343	343	31,251	31,350	930	483	483	38,251	38,350	1,371	709	709
24,351	24,450	564	345	345	31,351	31,450	936	485	485	38,351	38,450	1,379	713	713
24,451	24,550	568	347	347	31,451	31,550	942	487	487	38,451	38,550	1,387	717	717
24,551	24,650	572	349	349	31,551	31,650	948	489	489	38,551	38,650	1,395	721	721
24,651	24,750	576	351	351	31,651	31,750	954	491	491	38,651	38,750	1,403	725	725
24,751	24,850	580	353	353	31,751	31,850	960	493	493	38,751	38,850	1,411	729	729
24,851	24,950	584	355	355	31,851	31,950	966	495	495	38,851	38,950	1,419	733	733
24,951	25,050	588	357	357	31,951	32,050	972	497	497	38,951	39,050	1,427	737	737
25,051	25,150	592	359	359	32,051	32,150	978	499	499	39,051	39,150	1,435	741	741
25,151	25,250	596	361	361	32,151	32,250	984	501	501	39,151	39,250	1,443	745	745
25,251	25,350	600	363	363	32,251	32,350	990	503	503	39,251	39,350	1,451	749	749
25,351	25,450	604	365	365	32,351	32,450	996	505	505	39,351	39,450	1,459	753	753
25,451	25,550	608	367	367	32,451	32,550	1,002	507	507	39,451	39,550	1,467	757	757
25,551	25,650	612	369	369	32,551	32,650	1,008	509	509	39,551	39,650	1,475	761	761
25,651	25,750	616	371	371	32,651	32,750	1,014	511	511	39,651	39,750	1,483	765	765
25,751	25,850	620	373	373	32,751	32,850	1,020	513	513	39,751	39,850	1,491	769	769
25,851	25,950	624	375	375	32,851	32,950	1,026	515	515	39,851	39,950	1,499	773	773
25,951	26,050	628	377	377	32,951	33,050	1,032	517	517	39,951	40,050	1,507	777	777
26,051	26,150	632	379	379	33,051	33,150	1,038	519	519	40,051	40,150	1,515	781	781
26,151	26,250	636	381	381	33,151	33,250	1,044	521	521	40,151	40,250	1,523	785	785
26,251	26,350	640	383	383	33,251	33,350	1,050	523	523	40,251	40,350	1,531	789	789
26,351	26,450	644	385	385	33,351	33,450	1,056	525	525	40,351	40,450	1,539	793	793

Continued on next page.

2008 California Tax Table – Continued

Filing status: 1 or 3 (Single; Married/RDP Filing Separately) 2 or 5 (Married/RDP Filing Jointly; Qualifying Widow(er)) 4 (Head of Household)

If Your Taxable Income Is ...		The Tax For Filing Status			If Your Taxable Income Is ...		The Tax For Filing Status			If Your Taxable Income Is ...		The Tax For Filing Status		
At Least	But Not Over	1 Or 3 Is	2 Or 5 Is	4 Is	At Least	But Not Over	1 Or 3 Is	2 Or 5 Is	4 Is	At Least	But Not Over	1 Or 3 Is	2 Or 5 Is	4 Is
40,451	40,550	1,547	797	797	47,451	47,550	2,113	1,077	1,150	54,451	54,550	2,764	1,374	1,576
40,551	40,650	1,555	801	801	47,551	47,650	2,122	1,081	1,156	54,551	54,650	2,773	1,380	1,584
40,651	40,750	1,563	805	805	47,651	47,750	2,132	1,085	1,162	54,651	54,750	2,783	1,386	1,592
40,751	40,850	1,571	809	809	47,751	47,850	2,141	1,089	1,168	54,751	54,850	2,792	1,392	1,600
40,851	40,950	1,579	813	813	47,851	47,950	2,150	1,093	1,174	54,851	54,950	2,801	1,398	1,608
40,951	41,050	1,587	817	817	47,951	48,050	2,160	1,097	1,180	54,951	55,050	2,811	1,404	1,616
41,051	41,150	1,595	821	821	48,051	48,150	2,169	1,101	1,186	55,051	55,150	2,820	1,410	1,624
41,151	41,250	1,603	825	825	48,151	48,250	2,178	1,105	1,192	55,151	55,250	2,829	1,416	1,632
41,251	41,350	1,611	829	829	48,251	48,350	2,188	1,109	1,198	55,251	55,350	2,839	1,422	1,640
41,351	41,450	1,619	833	833	48,351	48,450	2,197	1,113	1,204	55,351	55,450	2,848	1,428	1,648
41,451	41,550	1,627	837	837	48,451	48,550	2,206	1,117	1,210	55,451	55,550	2,857	1,434	1,656
41,551	41,650	1,635	841	841	48,551	48,650	2,215	1,121	1,216	55,551	55,650	2,866	1,440	1,664
41,651	41,750	1,643	845	845	48,651	48,750	2,225	1,125	1,222	55,651	55,750	2,876	1,446	1,672
41,751	41,850	1,651	849	849	48,751	48,850	2,234	1,129	1,228	55,751	55,850	2,885	1,452	1,680
41,851	41,950	1,659	853	853	48,851	48,950	2,243	1,133	1,234	55,851	55,950	2,894	1,458	1,688
41,951	42,050	1,667	857	857	48,951	49,050	2,253	1,137	1,240	55,951	56,050	2,904	1,464	1,696
42,051	42,150	1,675	861	861	49,051	49,150	2,262	1,141	1,246	56,051	56,150	2,913	1,470	1,704
42,151	42,250	1,683	865	865	49,151	49,250	2,271	1,145	1,252	56,151	56,250	2,922	1,476	1,712
42,251	42,350	1,691	869	869	49,251	49,350	2,281	1,149	1,258	56,251	56,350	2,932	1,482	1,720
42,351	42,450	1,699	873	873	49,351	49,450	2,290	1,153	1,264	56,351	56,450	2,941	1,488	1,728
42,451	42,550	1,707	877	877	49,451	49,550	2,299	1,157	1,270	56,451	56,550	2,950	1,494	1,736
42,551	42,650	1,715	881	881	49,551	49,650	2,308	1,161	1,276	56,551	56,650	2,959	1,500	1,744
42,651	42,750	1,723	885	885	49,651	49,750	2,318	1,165	1,282	56,651	56,750	2,969	1,506	1,752
42,751	42,850	1,731	889	889	49,751	49,850	2,327	1,169	1,288	56,751	56,850	2,978	1,512	1,760
42,851	42,950	1,739	893	893	49,851	49,950	2,336	1,173	1,294	56,851	56,950	2,987	1,518	1,768
42,951	43,050	1,747	897	897	49,951	50,050	2,346	1,177	1,300	56,951	57,050	2,997	1,524	1,776
43,051	43,150	1,755	901	901	50,051	50,150	2,355	1,181	1,306	57,051	57,150	3,006	1,530	1,784
43,151	43,250	1,763	905	905	50,151	50,250	2,364	1,185	1,312	57,151	57,250	3,015	1,536	1,792
43,251	43,350	1,771	909	909	50,251	50,350	2,374	1,189	1,318	57,251	57,350	3,025	1,542	1,800
43,351	43,450	1,779	913	913	50,351	50,450	2,383	1,193	1,324	57,351	57,450	3,034	1,548	1,808
43,451	43,550	1,787	917	917	50,451	50,550	2,392	1,197	1,330	57,451	57,550	3,043	1,554	1,816
43,551	43,650	1,795	921	921	50,551	50,650	2,401	1,201	1,336	57,551	57,650	3,052	1,560	1,824
43,651	43,750	1,803	925	925	50,651	50,750	2,411	1,205	1,342	57,651	57,750	3,062	1,566	1,832
43,751	43,850	1,811	929	929	50,751	50,850	2,420	1,209	1,348	57,751	57,850	3,071	1,572	1,840
43,851	43,950	1,819	933	934	50,851	50,950	2,429	1,213	1,354	57,851	57,950	3,080	1,578	1,848
43,951	44,050	1,827	937	940	50,951	51,050	2,439	1,217	1,360	57,951	58,050	3,090	1,584	1,856
44,051	44,150	1,835	941	946	51,051	51,150	2,448	1,221	1,366	58,051	58,150	3,099	1,590	1,864
44,151	44,250	1,843	945	952	51,151	51,250	2,457	1,225	1,372	58,151	58,250	3,108	1,596	1,872
44,251	44,350	1,851	949	958	51,251	51,350	2,467	1,229	1,378	58,251	58,350	3,118	1,602	1,880
44,351	44,450	1,859	953	964	51,351	51,450	2,476	1,233	1,384	58,351	58,450	3,127	1,608	1,888
44,451	44,550	1,867	957	970	51,451	51,550	2,485	1,237	1,390	58,451	58,550	3,136	1,614	1,896
44,551	44,650	1,875	961	976	51,551	51,650	2,494	1,241	1,396	58,551	58,650	3,145	1,620	1,904
44,651	44,750	1,883	965	982	51,651	51,750	2,504	1,245	1,402	58,651	58,750	3,155	1,626	1,912
44,751	44,850	1,891	969	988	51,751	51,850	2,513	1,249	1,408	58,751	58,850	3,164	1,632	1,920
44,851	44,950	1,899	973	994	51,851	51,950	2,522	1,253	1,414	58,851	58,950	3,173	1,638	1,928
44,951	45,050	1,907	977	1,000	51,951	52,050	2,532	1,257	1,420	58,951	59,050	3,183	1,644	1,936
45,051	45,150	1,915	981	1,006	52,051	52,150	2,541	1,261	1,426	59,051	59,150	3,192	1,650	1,944
45,151	45,250	1,923	985	1,012	52,151	52,250	2,550	1,265	1,432	59,151	59,250	3,201	1,656	1,952
45,251	45,350	1,931	989	1,018	52,251	52,350	2,560	1,269	1,438	59,251	59,350	3,211	1,662	1,960
45,351	45,450	1,939	993	1,024	52,351	52,450	2,569	1,273	1,444	59,351	59,450	3,220	1,668	1,968
45,451	45,550	1,947	997	1,030	52,451	52,550	2,578	1,277	1,450	59,451	59,550	3,229	1,674	1,976
45,551	45,650	1,955	1,001	1,036	52,551	52,650	2,587	1,281	1,456	59,551	59,650	3,238	1,680	1,984
45,651	45,750	1,963	1,005	1,042	52,651	52,750	2,597	1,285	1,462	59,651	59,750	3,248	1,686	1,992
45,751	45,850	1,971	1,009	1,048	52,751	52,850	2,606	1,289	1,468	59,751	59,850	3,257	1,692	2,000
45,851	45,950	1,979	1,013	1,054	52,851	52,950	2,615	1,293	1,474	59,851	59,950	3,266	1,698	2,008
45,951	46,050	1,987	1,017	1,060	52,951	53,050	2,625	1,297	1,480	59,951	60,050	3,276	1,704	2,016
46,051	46,150	1,995	1,021	1,066	53,051	53,150	2,634	1,301	1,486	60,051	60,150	3,285	1,710	2,024
46,151	46,250	2,003	1,025	1,072	53,151	53,250	2,643	1,305	1,492	60,151	60,250	3,294	1,716	2,032
46,251	46,350	2,011	1,029	1,078	53,251	53,350	2,653	1,309	1,498	60,251	60,350	3,304	1,722	2,040
46,351	46,450	2,019	1,033	1,084	53,351	53,450	2,662	1,313	1,504	60,351	60,450	3,313	1,728	2,048
46,451	46,550	2,027	1,037	1,090	53,451	53,550	2,671	1,317	1,510	60,451	60,550	3,322	1,734	2,056
46,551	46,650	2,035	1,041	1,096	53,551	53,650	2,680	1,321	1,516	60,551	60,650	3,331	1,740	2,064
46,651	46,750	2,043	1,045	1,102	53,651	53,750	2,690	1,326	1,522	60,651	60,750	3,341	1,746	2,072
46,751	46,850	2,051	1,049	1,108	53,751	53,850	2,699	1,332	1,528	60,751	60,850	3,350	1,752	2,080
46,851	46,950	2,059	1,053	1,114	53,851	53,950	2,708	1,338	1,534	60,851	60,950	3,359	1,758	2,088
46,951	47,050	2,067	1,057	1,120	53,951	54,050	2,718	1,344	1,540	60,951	61,050	3,369	1,764	2,096
47,051	47,150	2,076	1,061	1,126	54,051	54,150	2,727	1,350	1,546	61,051	61,150	3,378	1,770	2,104
47,151	47,250	2,085	1,065	1,132	54,151	54,250	2,736	1,356	1,552	61,151	61,250	3,387	1,776	2,112
47,251	47,350	2,095	1,069	1,138	54,251	54,350	2,746	1,362	1,560	61,251	61,350	3,397	1,782	2,120
47,351	47,450	2,104	1,073	1,144	54,351	54,450	2,755	1,368	1,568	61,351	61,450	3,406	1,788	2,128

Continued on next page.

2008 California Tax Table – Continued

Filing status: 1 or 3 (Single; Married/RDP Filing Separately) 2 or 5 (Married/RDP Filing Jointly; Qualifying Widow(er)) 4 (Head of Household)

If Your Taxable Income Is ...		The Tax For Filing Status			If Your Taxable Income Is ...		The Tax For Filing Status			If Your Taxable Income Is ...		The Tax For Filing Status		
At Least	But Not Over	1 Or 3 Is	2 Or 5 Is	4 Is	At Least	But Not Over	1 Or 3 Is	2 Or 5 Is	4 Is	At Least	But Not Over	1 Or 3 Is	2 Or 5 Is	4 Is
61,451	61,550	3,415	1,794	2,136	68,451	68,550	4,066	2,214	2,754	75,451	75,550	4,717	2,655	3,405
61,551	61,650	3,424	1,800	2,144	68,551	68,650	4,075	2,220	2,763	75,551	75,650	4,726	2,663	3,414
61,651	61,750	3,434	1,806	2,152	68,651	68,750	4,085	2,226	2,772	75,651	75,750	4,736	2,671	3,423
61,751	61,850	3,443	1,812	2,160	68,751	68,850	4,094	2,232	2,782	75,751	75,850	4,745	2,679	3,433
61,851	61,950	3,452	1,818	2,168	68,851	68,950	4,103	2,238	2,791	75,851	75,950	4,754	2,687	3,442
61,951	62,050	3,462	1,824	2,176	68,951	69,050	4,113	2,244	2,800	75,951	76,050	4,764	2,695	3,451
62,051	62,150	3,471	1,830	2,184	69,051	69,150	4,122	2,250	2,810	76,051	76,150	4,773	2,703	3,461
62,151	62,250	3,480	1,836	2,192	69,151	69,250	4,131	2,256	2,819	76,151	76,250	4,782	2,711	3,470
62,251	62,350	3,490	1,842	2,200	69,251	69,350	4,141	2,262	2,828	76,251	76,350	4,792	2,719	3,479
62,351	62,450	3,499	1,848	2,208	69,351	69,450	4,150	2,268	2,838	76,351	76,450	4,801	2,727	3,489
62,451	62,550	3,508	1,854	2,216	69,451	69,550	4,159	2,274	2,847	76,451	76,550	4,810	2,735	3,498
62,551	62,650	3,517	1,860	2,224	69,551	69,650	4,168	2,280	2,856	76,551	76,650	4,819	2,743	3,507
62,651	62,750	3,527	1,866	2,232	69,651	69,750	4,178	2,286	2,865	76,651	76,750	4,829	2,751	3,516
62,751	62,850	3,536	1,872	2,240	69,751	69,850	4,187	2,292	2,875	76,751	76,850	4,838	2,759	3,526
62,851	62,950	3,545	1,878	2,248	69,851	69,950	4,196	2,298	2,884	76,851	76,950	4,847	2,767	3,535
62,951	63,050	3,555	1,884	2,256	69,951	70,050	4,206	2,304	2,893	76,951	77,050	4,857	2,775	3,544
63,051	63,150	3,564	1,890	2,264	70,051	70,150	4,215	2,310	2,903	77,051	77,150	4,866	2,783	3,554
63,151	63,250	3,573	1,896	2,272	70,151	70,250	4,224	2,316	2,912	77,151	77,250	4,875	2,791	3,563
63,251	63,350	3,583	1,902	2,280	70,251	70,350	4,234	2,322	2,921	77,251	77,350	4,885	2,799	3,572
63,351	63,450	3,592	1,908	2,288	70,351	70,450	4,243	2,328	2,931	77,351	77,450	4,894	2,807	3,582
63,451	63,550	3,601	1,914	2,296	70,451	70,550	4,252	2,334	2,940	77,451	77,550	4,903	2,815	3,591
63,551	63,650	3,610	1,920	2,304	70,551	70,650	4,261	2,340	2,949	77,551	77,650	4,912	2,823	3,600
63,651	63,750	3,620	1,926	2,312	70,651	70,750	4,271	2,346	2,958	77,651	77,750	4,922	2,831	3,609
63,751	63,850	3,629	1,932	2,320	70,751	70,850	4,280	2,352	2,968	77,751	77,850	4,931	2,839	3,619
63,851	63,950	3,638	1,938	2,328	70,851	70,950	4,289	2,358	2,977	77,851	77,950	4,940	2,847	3,628
63,951	64,050	3,648	1,944	2,336	70,951	71,050	4,299	2,364	2,986	77,951	78,050	4,950	2,855	3,637
64,051	64,150	3,657	1,950	2,345	71,051	71,150	4,308	2,370	2,996	78,051	78,150	4,959	2,863	3,647
64,151	64,250	3,666	1,956	2,354	71,151	71,250	4,317	2,376	3,005	78,151	78,250	4,968	2,871	3,656
64,251	64,350	3,676	1,962	2,363	71,251	71,350	4,327	2,382	3,014	78,251	78,350	4,978	2,879	3,665
64,351	64,450	3,685	1,968	2,373	71,351	71,450	4,336	2,388	3,024	78,351	78,450	4,987	2,887	3,675
64,451	64,550	3,694	1,974	2,382	71,451	71,550	4,345	2,394	3,033	78,451	78,550	4,996	2,895	3,684
64,551	64,650	3,703	1,980	2,391	71,551	71,650	4,354	2,400	3,042	78,551	78,650	5,005	2,903	3,693
64,651	64,750	3,713	1,986	2,400	71,651	71,750	4,364	2,406	3,051	78,651	78,750	5,015	2,911	3,702
64,751	64,850	3,722	1,992	2,410	71,751	71,850	4,373	2,412	3,061	78,751	78,850	5,024	2,919	3,712
64,851	64,950	3,731	1,998	2,419	71,851	71,950	4,382	2,418	3,070	78,851	78,950	5,033	2,927	3,721
64,951	65,050	3,741	2,004	2,428	71,951	72,050	4,392	2,424	3,079	78,951	79,050	5,043	2,935	3,730
65,051	65,150	3,750	2,010	2,438	72,051	72,150	4,401	2,430	3,089	79,051	79,150	5,052	2,943	3,740
65,151	65,250	3,759	2,016	2,447	72,151	72,250	4,410	2,436	3,098	79,151	79,250	5,061	2,951	3,749
65,251	65,350	3,769	2,022	2,456	72,251	72,350	4,420	2,442	3,107	79,251	79,350	5,071	2,959	3,758
65,351	65,450	3,778	2,028	2,466	72,351	72,450	4,429	2,448	3,117	79,351	79,450	5,080	2,967	3,768
65,451	65,550	3,787	2,034	2,475	72,451	72,550	4,438	2,454	3,126	79,451	79,550	5,089	2,975	3,777
65,551	65,650	3,796	2,040	2,484	72,551	72,650	4,447	2,460	3,135	79,551	79,650	5,098	2,983	3,786
65,651	65,750	3,806	2,046	2,493	72,651	72,750	4,457	2,466	3,144	79,651	79,750	5,108	2,991	3,795
65,751	65,850	3,815	2,052	2,503	72,751	72,850	4,466	2,472	3,154	79,751	79,850	5,117	2,999	3,805
65,851	65,950	3,824	2,058	2,512	72,851	72,950	4,475	2,478	3,163	79,851	79,950	5,126	3,007	3,814
65,951	66,050	3,834	2,064	2,521	72,951	73,050	4,485	2,484	3,172	79,951	80,050	5,136	3,015	3,823
66,051	66,150	3,843	2,070	2,531	73,051	73,150	4,494	2,490	3,182	80,051	80,150	5,145	3,023	3,833
66,151	66,250	3,852	2,076	2,540	73,151	73,250	4,503	2,496	3,191	80,151	80,250	5,154	3,031	3,842
66,251	66,350	3,862	2,082	2,549	73,251	73,350	4,513	2,502	3,200	80,251	80,350	5,164	3,039	3,851
66,351	66,450	3,871	2,088	2,559	73,351	73,450	4,522	2,508	3,210	80,351	80,450	5,173	3,047	3,861
66,451	66,550	3,880	2,094	2,568	73,451	73,550	4,531	2,514	3,219	80,451	80,550	5,182	3,055	3,870
66,551	66,650	3,889	2,100	2,577	73,551	73,650	4,540	2,520	3,228	80,551	80,650	5,191	3,063	3,879
66,651	66,750	3,899	2,106	2,586	73,651	73,750	4,550	2,526	3,237	80,651	80,750	5,201	3,071	3,888
66,751	66,850	3,908	2,112	2,596	73,751	73,850	4,559	2,532	3,247	80,751	80,850	5,210	3,079	3,898
66,851	66,950	3,917	2,118	2,605	73,851	73,950	4,568	2,538	3,256	80,851	80,950	5,219	3,087	3,907
66,951	67,050	3,927	2,124	2,614	73,951	74,050	4,578	2,544	3,265	80,951	81,050	5,229	3,095	3,916
67,051	67,150	3,936	2,130	2,624	74,051	74,150	4,587	2,550	3,275	81,051	81,150	5,238	3,103	3,926
67,151	67,250	3,945	2,136	2,633	74,151	74,250	4,596	2,556	3,284	81,151	81,250	5,247	3,111	3,935
67,251	67,350	3,955	2,142	2,642	74,251	74,350	4,606	2,562	3,293	81,251	81,350	5,257	3,119	3,944
67,351	67,450	3,964	2,148	2,652	74,351	74,450	4,615	2,568	3,303	81,351	81,450	5,266	3,127	3,954
67,451	67,550	3,973	2,154	2,661	74,451	74,550	4,624	2,575	3,312	81,451	81,550	5,275	3,135	3,963
67,551	67,650	3,982	2,160	2,670	74,551	74,650	4,633	2,583	3,321	81,551	81,650	5,284	3,143	3,972
67,651	67,750	3,992	2,166	2,679	74,651	74,750	4,643	2,591	3,330	81,651	81,750	5,294	3,151	3,981
67,751	67,850	4,001	2,172	2,689	74,751	74,850	4,652	2,599	3,340	81,751	81,850	5,303	3,159	3,991
67,851	67,950	4,010	2,178	2,698	74,851	74,950	4,661	2,607	3,349	81,851	81,950	5,312	3,167	4,000
67,951	68,050	4,020	2,184	2,707	74,951	75,050	4,671	2,615	3,358	81,951	82,050	5,322	3,175	4,009
68,051	68,150	4,029	2,190	2,717	75,051	75,150	4,680	2,623	3,368	82,051	82,150	5,331	3,183	4,019
68,151	68,250	4,038	2,196	2,726	75,151	75,250	4,689	2,631	3,377	82,151	82,250	5,340	3,191	4,028
68,251	68,350	4,048	2,202	2,735	75,251	75,350	4,699	2,639	3,386	82,251	82,350	5,350	3,199	4,037
68,351	68,450	4,057	2,208	2,745	75,351	75,450	4,708	2,647	3,396	82,351	82,450	5,359	3,207	4,047

Continued on next page.

2008 California Tax Table – Continued

Filing status: 1 or 3 (Single; Married/RDP Filing Separately) 2 or 5 (Married/RDP Filing Jointly; Qualifying Widow(er)) 4 (Head of Household)

If Your Taxable Income Is ...		The Tax For Filing Status			If Your Taxable Income Is ...		The Tax For Filing Status			If Your Taxable Income Is ...		The Tax For Filing Status		
At Least	But Not Over	1 Or 3 Is	2 Or 5 Is	4 Is	At Least	But Not Over	1 Or 3 Is	2 Or 5 Is	4 Is	At Least	But Not Over	1 Or 3 Is	2 Or 5 Is	4 Is
82,451	82,550	5,368	3,215	4,056	88,951	89,050	5,973	3,735	4,660	95,451	95,550	6,577	4,273	5,265
82,551	82,650	5,377	3,223	4,065	89,051	89,150	5,982	3,743	4,670	95,551	95,650	6,586	4,282	5,274
82,651	82,750	5,387	3,231	4,074	89,151	89,250	5,991	3,751	4,679	95,651	95,750	6,596	4,291	5,283
82,751	82,850	5,396	3,239	4,084	89,251	89,350	6,001	3,759	4,688	95,751	95,850	6,605	4,301	5,293
82,851	82,950	5,405	3,247	4,093	89,351	89,450	6,010	3,767	4,698	95,851	95,950	6,614	4,310	5,302
82,951	83,050	5,415	3,255	4,102	89,451	89,550	6,019	3,775	4,707	95,951	96,050	6,624	4,319	5,311
83,051	83,150	5,424	3,263	4,112	89,551	89,650	6,028	3,783	4,716	96,051	96,150	6,633	4,329	5,321
83,151	83,250	5,433	3,271	4,121	89,651	89,750	6,038	3,791	4,725	96,151	96,250	6,642	4,338	5,330
83,251	83,350	5,443	3,279	4,130	89,751	89,850	6,047	3,799	4,735	96,251	96,350	6,652	4,347	5,339
83,351	83,450	5,452	3,287	4,140	89,851	89,950	6,056	3,807	4,744	96,351	96,450	6,661	4,356	5,349
83,451	83,550	5,461	3,295	4,149	89,951	90,050	6,066	3,815	4,753	96,451	96,550	6,670	4,366	5,358
83,551	83,650	5,470	3,303	4,158	90,051	90,150	6,075	3,823	4,763	96,551	96,650	6,679	4,375	5,367
83,651	83,750	5,480	3,311	4,167	90,151	90,250	6,084	3,831	4,772	96,651	96,750	6,689	4,384	5,376
83,751	83,850	5,489	3,319	4,177	90,251	90,350	6,094	3,839	4,781	96,751	96,850	6,698	4,394	5,386
83,851	83,950	5,498	3,327	4,186	90,351	90,450	6,103	3,847	4,791	96,851	96,950	6,707	4,403	5,395
83,951	84,050	5,508	3,335	4,195	90,451	90,550	6,112	3,855	4,800	96,951	97,050	6,717	4,412	5,404
84,051	84,150	5,517	3,343	4,205	90,551	90,650	6,121	3,863	4,809	97,051	97,150	6,726	4,422	5,414
84,151	84,250	5,526	3,351	4,214	90,651	90,750	6,131	3,871	4,818	97,151	97,250	6,735	4,431	5,423
84,251	84,350	5,536	3,359	4,223	90,751	90,850	6,140	3,879	4,828	97,251	97,350	6,745	4,440	5,432
84,351	84,450	5,545	3,367	4,233	90,851	90,950	6,149	3,887	4,837	97,351	97,450	6,754	4,449	5,442
84,451	84,550	5,554	3,375	4,242	90,951	91,050	6,159	3,895	4,846	97,451	97,550	6,763	4,459	5,451
84,551	84,650	5,563	3,383	4,251	91,051	91,150	6,168	3,903	4,856	97,551	97,650	6,772	4,468	5,460
84,651	84,750	5,573	3,391	4,260	91,151	91,250	6,177	3,911	4,865	97,651	97,750	6,782	4,477	5,469
84,751	84,850	5,582	3,399	4,270	91,251	91,350	6,187	3,919	4,874	97,751	97,850	6,791	4,487	5,479
84,851	84,950	5,591	3,407	4,279	91,351	91,450	6,196	3,927	4,884	97,851	97,950	6,800	4,496	5,488
84,951	85,050	5,601	3,415	4,288	91,451	91,550	6,205	3,935	4,893	97,951	98,050	6,810	4,505	5,497
85,051	85,150	5,610	3,423	4,298	91,551	91,650	6,214	3,943	4,902	98,051	98,150	6,819	4,515	5,507
85,151	85,250	5,619	3,431	4,307	91,651	91,750	6,224	3,951	4,911	98,151	98,250	6,828	4,524	5,516
85,251	85,350	5,629	3,439	4,316	91,751	91,850	6,233	3,959	4,921	98,251	98,350	6,838	4,533	5,525
85,351	85,450	5,638	3,447	4,326	91,851	91,950	6,242	3,967	4,930	98,351	98,450	6,847	4,542	5,535
85,451	85,550	5,647	3,455	4,335	91,951	92,050	6,252	3,975	4,939	98,451	98,550	6,856	4,552	5,544
85,551	85,650	5,656	3,463	4,344	92,051	92,150	6,261	3,983	4,949	98,551	98,650	6,865	4,561	5,553
85,651	85,750	5,666	3,471	4,353	92,151	92,250	6,270	3,991	4,958	98,651	98,750	6,875	4,570	5,562
85,751	85,850	5,675	3,479	4,363	92,251	92,350	6,280	3,999	4,967	98,751	98,850	6,884	4,580	5,572
85,851	85,950	5,684	3,487	4,372	92,351	92,450	6,289	4,007	4,977	98,851	98,950	6,893	4,589	5,581
85,951	86,050	5,694	3,495	4,381	92,451	92,550	6,298	4,015	4,986	98,951	99,050	6,903	4,598	5,590
86,051	86,150	5,703	3,503	4,391	92,551	92,650	6,307	4,023	4,995	99,051	99,150	6,912	4,608	5,600
86,151	86,250	5,712	3,511	4,400	92,651	92,750	6,317	4,031	5,004	99,151	99,250	6,921	4,617	5,609
86,251	86,350	5,722	3,519	4,409	92,751	92,850	6,326	4,039	5,014	99,251	99,350	6,931	4,626	5,618
86,351	86,450	5,731	3,527	4,419	92,851	92,950	6,335	4,047	5,023	99,351	99,450	6,940	4,635	5,628
86,451	86,550	5,740	3,535	4,428	92,951	93,050	6,345	4,055	5,032	99,451	99,550	6,949	4,645	5,637
86,551	86,650	5,749	3,543	4,437	93,051	93,150	6,354	4,063	5,042	99,551	99,650	6,958	4,654	5,646
86,651	86,750	5,759	3,551	4,446	93,151	93,250	6,363	4,071	5,051	99,651	99,750	6,968	4,663	5,655
86,751	86,850	5,768	3,559	4,456	93,251	93,350	6,373	4,079	5,060	99,751	99,850	6,977	4,673	5,665
86,851	86,950	5,777	3,567	4,465	93,351	93,450	6,382	4,087	5,070	99,851	99,950	6,986	4,682	5,674
86,951	87,050	5,787	3,575	4,474	93,451	93,550	6,391	4,095	5,079	99,951	100,000	6,993	4,689	5,681
87,051	87,150	5,796	3,583	4,484	93,551	93,650	6,400	4,103	5,088					
87,151	87,250	5,805	3,591	4,493	93,651	93,750	6,410	4,111	5,097	OVER $100.000 YOU MUST COMPUTE YOUR TAX USING THE TAX RATE SCHEDULES.				
87,251	87,350	5,815	3,599	4,502	93,751	93,850	6,419	4,119	5,107					
87,351	87,450	5,824	3,607	4,512	93,851	93,950	6,428	4,127	5,116					
87,451	87,550	5,833	3,615	4,521	93,951	94,050	6,438	4,135	5,125					
87,551	87,650	5,842	3,623	4,530	94,051	94,150	6,447	4,143	5,135					
87,651	87,750	5,852	3,631	4,539	94,151	94,250	6,456	4,152	5,144					
87,751	87,850	5,861	3,639	4,549	94,251	94,350	6,466	4,161	5,153					
87,851	87,950	5,870	3,647	4,558	94,351	94,450	6,475	4,170	5,163					
87,951	88,050	5,880	3,655	4,567	94,451	94,550	6,484	4,180	5,172					
88,051	88,150	5,889	3,663	4,577	94,551	94,650	6,493	4,189	5,181					
88,151	88,250	5,898	3,671	4,586	94,651	94,750	6,503	4,198	5,190					
88,251	88,350	5,908	3,679	4,595	94,751	94,850	6,512	4,208	5,200					
88,351	88,450	5,917	3,687	4,605	94,851	94,950	6,521	4,217	5,209					
88,451	88,550	5,926	3,695	4,614	94,951	95,050	6,531	4,226	5,218					
88,551	88,650	5,935	3,703	4,623	95,051	95,150	6,540	4,236	5,228					
88,651	88,750	5,945	3,711	4,632	95,151	95,250	6,549	4,245	5,237					
88,751	88,850	5,954	3,719	4,642	95,251	95,350	6,559	4,254	5,246					
88,851	88,950	5,963	3,727	4,651	95,351	95,450	6,568	4,263	5,256					

¶2 Alternative Minimum Tax

The tentative minimum tax rate is 7% (¶117).

¶3 Personal Income Tax Rate Schedules for 2008

These are the official rate schedules on which the tax tables that follow are based. These schedules *must* be used if taxable income is more than $100,000. For taxable income of $100,000 or less, the tax must be determined using the tax tables. Taxpayer filing Form 540 2EZ must use the tax tables in the 2008 California Form 540 2EZ Tax Booklet.

2008 CALIFORNIA TAX RATE SCHEDULES
SCHEDULE X
SINGLE, MARRIED/RDP FILING SEPARATE AND FIDUCIARY TAXPAYERS

IF THE TAXABLE INCOME IS		COMPUTED TAX IS			
OVER	BUT NOT OVER				OF THE AMOUNT OVER
$0	$7,168	$0.00	PLUS	1.0%	$0
$7,168	$16,994	$71.68	PLUS	2.0%	$7,168
$16,994	$26,821	$268.20	PLUS	4.0%	$16,994
$26,821	$37,233	$661.28	PLUS	6.0%	$26,821
$37,233	$47,055	$1,286.00	PLUS	8.0%	$37,233
$47,055	AND OVER	$2,071.76	PLUS	9.3%	$47,055

SCHEDULE Y MARRIED/RDP FILING JOINT / QUALIFYING WIDOW(ER) WITH DEPENDENT CHILD

IF THE TAXABLE INCOME IS		COMPUTED TAX IS			
OVER	BUT NOT OVER				OF THE AMOUNT OVER
$0	$14,336	$0.00	PLUS	1.0%	$0
$14,336	$33,988	$143.36	PLUS	2.0%	$14,336
$33,988	$53,642	$536.40	PLUS	4.0%	$33,988
$53,642	$74,466	$1,322.56	PLUS	6.0%	$53,642
$74,466	$94,110	$2,572.00	PLUS	8.0%	$74,466
$94,110	AND OVER	$4,143.52	PLUS	9.3%	$94,110

SCHEDULE Z HEAD OF HOUSEHOLD TAXPAYERS

IF THE TAXABLE INCOME IS		COMPUTED TAX IS			
OVER	BUT NOT OVER				OF THE AMOUNT OVER
$0	$14,345	$0.00	PLUS	1.0%	$0
$14,345	$33,989	$143.45	PLUS	2.0%	$14,345
$33,989	$43,814	$536.33	PLUS	4.0%	$33,989
$43,814	$54,225	$929.33	PLUS	6.0%	$43,814
$54,225	$64,050	$1,553.99	PLUS	8.0%	$54,225
$64,050	AND OVER	$2,339.99	PLUS	9.3%	$64,050

Franchise Tax and Corporation Income Tax Rates

¶10 Bank and Corporation Franchise Tax

Corporations, other than banks and financial institutions, are taxed at the rate of 8.84% (¶816).

For the rate on banks and financial institutions, see ¶816.

For the rate on S corporations, see ¶806.

The minimum franchise tax is $800 for existing corporations (¶816).

Corporations are exempt from the minimum franchise tax for their first taxable year, see ¶816.

¶11 Corporation Income Tax

The rate is the same as the franchise tax on corporations other than banks and financial institutions (see above and ¶816).

¶12 Alternative Minimum Tax

The alternative minimum tax rate is 6.65% (¶817).

FEDERAL/STATE KEY FEATURE COMPARISONS

¶13 Personal Income Tax Comparison of Federal/State Key Features

The following is a comparison of key features of federal income tax laws that have been enacted as of October 3, 2008, and California personal income tax laws. California adjusted gross income (AGI) is based on federal AGI. The California personal income tax combines unique state provisions with subchapters and individual provisions of the Internal Revenue Code that are incorporated by reference as amended through a specified date and modified for California purposes (¶101, 103, 201, 202). State modifications to federal adjusted gross income required by law differences are discussed beginning at ¶201. Special attention should be paid to adjustments required for same-sex married individuals and registered domestic partners (¶119) who are required to use the joint or married filing separately filing status.

Nonresidents and part-year residents.—California taxes its residents on their entire income, regardless of its source, while nonresidents are taxed only on income derived from California. A part-year resident must include in California AGI his or her income from any source for the part of the tax year when he or she resided in the state and income received from California sources during the portion of the year he or she was a nonresident (see ¶60, 61).

Except for military personnel, a nonresident's or part-year resident's tax liability is determined by first computing tax on total taxable income, as though the taxpayer were a full-year California resident for the taxable year and for all prior taxable years for any carryover items, deferred income, suspended losses, or suspended deductions, and dividing that tax by the income that the tax was calculated upon, to arrive at the tax rate. This rate is then applied to the California source taxable income of the nonresident or part-year resident to determine the nonresident's or part-year resident's tax liability (¶116).

• *Alternative minimum tax (IRC Sec. 55—IRC Sec. 59)*

California imposes an alternative minimum tax (AMT) that is a modified version of the federal AMT (IRC Sec. 55—IRC Sec. 59) (¶117).

• *Asset expense election (IRC Sec. 179)*

California allows an asset expense election (IRC Sec. 179) for personal income tax purposes that is limited to $25,000. California does not allow an expanded asset expense election (IRC Sec. 179(e), IRC Sec. 1400N) for purchases of qualified disaster assistance property or for qualified hurricane and tornado disaster victims (see ¶311).

• *Bad debts (IRC Sec. 166)*

California's treatment of bad debts is the same as federal because IRC Sec. 166 is incorporated by reference (see ¶308).

• *Business deductions (IRC Sec. 162)*

California conforms to federal law regarding business deductions (IRC Sec. 162), except that California denies the deduction of business expenses incurred at private clubs that discriminate on the basis of age, sex, race, or religion, and has not adopted the federal provision that limits the deduction for executive compensation paid to executives of financial institutions participating in the troubled asset relief program (¶301, 302, 329, 343).

• *Capital gains and capital losses (IRC Sec. 1(h), IRC Sec. 1211, and IRC Sec. 1212)*

California generally determines capital gains and losses in the same manner as federal law (IRC Sec. 1(h), IRC Sec. 1211 and IRC Sec. 1212). However, unlike federal law (1) California law treats capital gains as ordinary income and the amount of tax is not dependent on the holding period, (2) California does not permit capital loss carrybacks, and (3) California law does not provide for any special tax rates for capital gains (see ¶526). California does not adopt the federal amendments to IRC Sec. 1221 that allow a taxpayer to elect to treat as a sale or exchange of a capital asset, the sale or exchange of musical compositions or copyrights in musical works created by the taxpayer's personal efforts (or having a basis determined by reference to the basis in the hands of the taxpayer whose personal efforts created the composition or copyrights).

• *Charitable contributions (IRC Sec. 170)*

The California charitable contribution deduction is generally the same as the federal deduction (IRC Sec. 170) (see ¶321). However, California does not conform to federal provisions that increase the standard mileage rate for charitable use of a vehicle and exempt from gross income mileage reimbursement received if the vehicle was used for hurricane, tornado, or Midwestern storm relief purposes. Nor did California conform to federal provisions that (1) waived the 50% income limitation for all cash donations through the end of 2005, and exempted them from the phase-out of itemized deductions for high AGI taxpayers and (2) increased the substantiation requirements for donations of motor vehicles, boats, and airplanes. California also does not conform to other federal amendments to IRC Sec. 170, including required substantiation of all cash contributions, the disallowance of a deduction for used clothing or household goods that are not in "good" condition, and changes in the rules regarding donations of fractional interests in tangible personal property.

California does not conform to the federal provisions that (1) require recapture of charitable deductions if the donated property is disposed of within three years and the donee does not certify exempt use, (2) prohibit a charitable contribution deduction for amounts excluded from income for payments provided by a state or local government for the expenses of performing volunteer services, and (3) allow an enhanced deduction for donations of wholesome food inventory made by businesses prior to 2010 and waive the 10% limitation applicable to food inventory donations for contributions made by qualified farmers and ranchers after October 2, 2008, and before 2009.

California also does not allow deductions for contributions of real property for conservation purposes (see ¶321). However, California does offer a credit for donations of real property for conservation purposes (see ¶143). California also allows a credit for the costs of transporting donated agricultural products to nonprofit charitable organizations (see ¶141).

• *Child care credit (IRC Sec. 45F)*

California does not incorporate the federal child care credit (IRC Sec. 45F), but allows an employer two separate credits for employee child care expenses: one for a portion of the costs of establishing a child care program or contributing to child care referral services and another for contributions to a qualified employee child care plan (see ¶134).

• *Civil rights deduction (IRC Sec. 62)*

California incorporates the federal civil rights deduction (IRC Sec. 62) (see ¶202).

• *Dependents (IRC Sec. 152)*

California generally conforms to the federal definition of "dependent." However, California does not adopt federal provisions that beginning with the 2009 taxable year (1) require that a qualifying child be younger than the taxpayer, (2) with specified exceptions, prohibit the filing of a joint return by a qualifying child, and (3) clarify the tie-breaker rules that apply when more than one taxpayer can claim the same qualifying child (IRC Sec. 152) (see ¶115).

• *Depreciation (IRC Sec. 167 and IRC Sec. 168)*

California adopts federal depreciation provisions (IRC Sec. 167 and IRC Sec. 168) for personal income tax purposes (see ¶310). However, California does not conform to the 30% or optional 50% "bonus" depreciation allowed under IRC Sec. 168(k). Nor does California incorporate the federal accelerated write-off for qualified property used in renewal communities. In addition, California does not incorporate the shortened recovery periods for leasehold improvements, restaurant property, retail improvement property, smart electric meters, smart grid systems, qualified farm machinery and equipment, and, for property placed in service during 2009 and 2010, motorsports entertainment complexes.

Nor does California follow the accelerated MACRS recovery periods for Indian reservation property; the special federal depreciation treatment for participations and residuals, or the shortened recovery period for young racehorses placed in service after 2008 and before 2014. California also does not conform to federal provisions relating to geological and geophysical expenses, electric transmission property, and natural gas lines. California does not allow five-year amortization of expenses paid or incurred in creating or acquiring a musical composition or a copyright to a musical composition and require certain major integrated oil companies to amortize geological and geophysical expenditures over a five-year or seven-year period instead of a 24-month period. In addition, California does not allow a 50% additional depreciation allowance for qualified cellulosic biomass ethanol plant property, qualified cellulosic biofuel facilities, qualified reuse and recycling property, and qualified disaster assistance property (see ¶310).

• *Earned income credit (IRC Sec. 32)*

California has no equivalent to the federal earned income tax credit (IRC Sec. 32), but requires employers to inform employees of their potential eligibility for the federal credit (see ¶125).

• *Educational assistance benefits (IRC Sec. 62(a)(2)(D); IRC Sec. 127; IRC Sec. 221; IRC Sec. 222)*

California law is generally the same as federal law concerning employee educational assistance benefits (IRC Sec. 127) and the above-the-line deduction for interest on student loans (IRC Sec. 221) (see ¶242, ¶305). However, California does not allow the federal above-the-line deduction for qualified tuition and related expenses (IRC Sec. 222). Nor does California allow the above-the-line deduction for teacher's expenses (IRC Sec. 62(a)(2)(D)) (see ¶344, ¶202).

• *Extraterritorial income/domestic production deduction (IRC Sec. 114 and IRC Sec. 199)*

California had no personal income tax provision comparable to IRC Sec. 114, which excluded extraterritorial income from gross income. Any amount so excluded for federal purposes had to be added back to federal AGI for California purposes (see ¶201). IRC Sec. 114 is repealed by the AJCA, effective for tax years after 2006.

• *Foreign earned income (IRC Sec. 911 and IRC Sec. 912)*

The federal provision allowing an exemption for income earned by U.S. citizens living abroad is not applicable in California (IRC Sec. 911); therefore, amounts excluded from federal AGI must be added back for California personal income tax purposes. Presumably, amounts excluded under IRC Sec. 912, providing an exemption for certain allowances paid to civilian employees of the U.S. working abroad, also have to be added back (see ¶231, ¶235).

• *Health insurance and medical expenses; Health savings accounts (HSAs) (IRC Sec. 106(e); IRC Sec. 162(l); IRC Sec. 223)*

California law is the same as federal law concerning health insurance premiums for self-employed individuals because IRC Sec. 162(l) is incorporated by reference without modification. In addition, self-employed individuals may also claim a deduction for health insurance costs paid for a registered domestic partner and the domestic partner's dependents (see ¶301). California does not recognize health savings accounts (HSAs). Consequently, an addition adjustment is required for contributions to and earnings on HSAs. However, California personal income taxpayers may subtract any nonqualified distributions from an HSA included in federal taxable income (see ¶219, ¶247).

• *Indebtedness (IRC Sec. 108 and IRC Sec. 163)*

Generally, California incorporates IRC Sec. 108 by reference, with some modifications; however, California does not adopt federal provisions excluding from taxable income cancellation of a personal debt by individuals affected by Hurricane Katrina (see ¶221). California only partially conforms to federal provisions that exclude from federal gross income, income from the discharge of qualified principal residence indebtedness which occurs after 2006 and before 2013. California's treatment of interest on indebtedness is generally the same as federal because IRC Sec. 163 is incorporated by reference; however, certain modifications regarding original issue discount (OID) instruments, mortgage interest, investment interest, and interest from loans made to enterprise zone businesses apply (see ¶217, ¶237, ¶305).

• *Interest on federal obligations (IRC Sec. 61)*

Generally, California does not tax interest received from obligations of the United States and its political subdivisions (IRC Sec. 61). The interest from these bonds is subtracted from federal AGI in computing California AGI (see ¶217). The FTB has ruled that interest from certain specified federal agency obligations is not taxable, whereas the interest from other federal agency obligations is taxable (see ¶217).

• *Interest on state and local obligations (IRC Sec. 103)*

Interest on obligations of state and local governments, other than from obligations of California and its political subdivisions, must be added to federal adjusted gross income in determining California taxable income (see ¶217).

• *Losses not otherwise compensated (IRC Sec. 165)*

The California deduction for business losses, casualty and disaster losses, and theft losses is generally the same as the federal deduction for such losses (IRC Sec. 165) (see ¶307). California, but not federal, law also allows 100% of any excess loss resulting from specified disasters to be carried forward to the next succeeding 15 years. In addition, California has not adopted federal provisions that lift the 10% of AGI and $100 floor limitations for casualty losses attributable to federally declared disasters occurring in 2008 or 2009 or that arose in a hurricane, tornado, or Midwest storm disaster area and that were attributable to those hurricanes, tornadoes, or storms (see ¶307).

• *Net operating losses (IRC Sec. 172 and 1400N)*

California allows a deduction for net operating losses (NOLs) that is patterned on the federal NOL deduction provision (IRC Sec. 172), with some modifications. With the exception of certain small businesses, California suspends the NOL deduction for the 2008 and 2009 taxable years. California does not allow NOL carrybacks prior to the 2011 taxable year, but phases in a two-year carryback period beginning with the 2011 taxable year. California did not conform to the federal 20-year carryover period until 2008. Also, special rules apply to taxpayers located in certain economic development areas and to taxpayers residing in California for less than the entire tax year in which a NOL is incurred (see ¶309). California does not follow the federal expanded NOL (IRC Sec. 1400N) for qualified hurricane, tornado, or Midwest storm disaster victims or the extended NOL carryback for NOLs attributable to federally declared disasters.

• *Personal residence (IRC Sec. 121, IRC Sec. 163(h)(3), and IRC Sec. 1033)*

California incorporates, with modifications, the federal provision regarding the gross income exclusion of income from the sale of a personal residence (IRC Sec. 121) (see ¶229) and the federal provision regarding nonrecognition of gain when property is involuntarily converted (IRC Sec. 1033). However, California does not incorporate federal provisions that (1) extend the replacement period to five years for business and residential property involuntarily converted by specific hurricane or tornado victims (see ¶503), (2) extend the requirement that a personal residence acquired in a like-kind exchange be held for at least five years in order to be eligible for the exclusion to apply to transferees of the property; or (3) suspend the five-year test period for specified intelligence community employees serving on extended foreign duty or Peace Corps volunteers serving outside the U.S. (although California does have special provisions that relate to Peace Corps volunteers); or (4) allow an unmarried surviving spouse the $500,000 exclusion available to joint filers if the principal residence is sold or exchanged within two years of the spouse's death, for sales or exchanges after 2007. California also does not conform to the federal provision that provides that gain from the sale of a principal residence that is allocable to periods of nonqualified use is not excluded from the taxpayer's income, effective for sales and exchanges after 2008 (see¶229).

California also does not conform to a federal amendment to IRC Sec. 163 that treats qualified premiums paid for mortgage insurance as deductible interest (see ¶305).

• *Retirement plans (IRC Sec. 401—IRC Sec. 424, IRC Sec. 457 and IRC Sec. 457A)*

California generally conforms to the federal provisions, as amended to date, regarding retirement plans (IRC Sec. 401—IRC Sec. 420, IRC Sec. 457) (see ¶206, 330, 607). California also incorporates the federal provisions concerning employment stock options (IRC Sec. 421—IRC Sec. 424) and also extends the favorable treatment provided by federal law to incentive and employee stock options to California qualified stock options (see ¶207). Although California generally conforms to federal deferred compensation provisions as amended to date, because California does not recognize health savings accounts (HSAs) it does not conform to an amendment made to IRC Sec. 408 that authorizes a one-time tax-free distribution from an IRA to an HSA, effective for tax years beginning after 2006 (see ¶206). In addition, California has not incorporated the federal provision that requires the current inclusion in income of some deferred compensation paid by foreign corporations when there is no substantial risk of forfeiture of the rights to the compensation (IRC Sec. 457A)

• *Start-up expenses (IRC Sec. 195)*

California's treatment of start-up expenditures is the same as IRC Sec. 195, because IRC Sec. 195 is incorporated by reference (see ¶334).

• *Taxes paid (IRC Sec. 164)*

Although California incorporates IRC Sec. 164 by reference, California does not allow the federal deductions for state, local, and foreign income taxes; state disability insurance; foreign real property taxes; or state or local sales and use taxes. These disallowed federal tax deductions must be subtracted from federal itemized deductions in computing California itemized deductions (see ¶303, 306). California permits credits for net income taxes paid to other states, the District of Columbia, or U.S. possessions (but not to the United States or to foreign countries) on income that is also taxed by California (see ¶127). Such credits are available to residents (see ¶128), nonresidents (see ¶129), estates and trusts (see ¶130), partners (see ¶131), S corporation shareholders (see ¶131), limited liability company members (see ¶131), and estate and trust beneficiaries (see ¶130).

California does not incorporate federal provisions that prohibit a deduction for taxes for which qualified state and local tax benefits (reduction or rebate of real property, personal property, or income taxes) were provided to a member of a qualified volunteer emergency response organization. California also does not incorporate the federal provision that allows nonitemizers an additional standard deduction in 2008 for property taxes.

¶14 Corporate Income Tax Comparison of Federal/State Key Features

The following is a comparison of key features of federal income tax laws that have been enacted as of October 3, 2008, and California corporation tax law. California incorporates by reference numerous Internal Revenue Code (IRC) provisions (see ¶803, 901). Some federal provisions are incorporated by reference with specific modifications, while others are incorporated without any modifications. State modifications to federal taxable income required by law differences are discussed beginning at ¶901.

• *IRC Sec. 27 foreign tax credit*

California has no equivalent to the federal foreign tax credit (IRC Sec. 27).

• *IRC Sec. 29 fuel from nonconventional source credit*

California has no equivalent to the federal fuel from nonconventional source credit (IRC Sec. 29).

• *IRC Sec. 30 qualified electric vehicle credit*

California has no equivalent to the federal qualified electric vehicles credit (IRC Sec. 30). However, California does incorporate the federal provision allowing more favorable depreciation for electric vehicles (IRC Sec. 280F) (see ¶1011).

• *IRC Sec. 40 alcohol fuel credit*

California has no equivalent to the federal alcohol fuel credit (IRC Sec. 40).

• *IRC Sec. 41 incremental research expenditures credit*

California allows a credit for incremental research expenditures that is generally based on the federal credit (IRC Sec. 41) (see ¶818). However, California's credit is available indefinitely and California does not adopt federal provisions that (1) increase the credit for amounts paid to eligible small businesses, universities, and federal laboratories, (2) allow a credit for amounts paid to a research consortium for energy research, (3) increase the rates used to compute the alternative incremental credit (AIC) and allow taxpayers to elect to compute the credit under a third method, the alternative simplified credit, generally effective in tax years ending after 2006, and (4) repeal the AIC for taxable years beginning after 2008. California incorporates the IRC Sec. 280C provision that disallows a deduction for that portion of qualified research expenses or basic research expenses that equals the credit amount allowed for such expenses under IRC Sec. 41 (see ¶1023).

• *IRC Sec. 42 low-income housing*

California allows a low-income housing credit that is generally based on the federal credit (IRC Sec. 42) (see ¶818).

• *IRC Sec. 44 disabled access expenditures credit*

California allows a disabled access expenditures credit that is generally based on the federal credit (IRC Sec. 44) (see ¶818).

• *IRC Sec. 45A Indian employment credit*

California has no equivalent to the Indian employment credit (IRC Sec. 45A). Taxpayers may deduct expenses for which a federal Indian employment credit was claimed, as California does not incorporate the applicable IRC Sec. 280C provision (see ¶1023). California allows credits to employers in certain areas for wages paid to qualified employees, among whom are members of a federally recognized Indian tribe, band, or other group of Native American descent (see ¶818).

• *IRC Sec. 45B employer social security credit*

California has no equivalent to the employer social security credit (IRC Sec. 45B).

• *IRC Sec. 45C orphan drug credit*

California has no equivalent to the orphan drug credit (IRC Sec. 45C). California incorporates the IRC Sec. 280C provision that disallows a deduction for the portion of qualified clinical testing expenses for which a credit is claimed under IRC Sec. 45C (see ¶1023).

• *IRC Sec. 45D new markets credit*

California has no equivalent to the new markets credit (IRC Sec. 45D). However, California does provide a credit for deposits made to certain community development financial institutions (see ¶818).

• *IRC Sec. 45E small business pension start-up costs credit*

California has no equivalent to the small employer pension plan start-up costs credit (IRC Sec. 45E).

• *IRC Sec. 45F employer-provided child care credit*

California allows a credit for a portion of the start-up costs associated with starting a child care program or constructing a child care facility and for payments made to child care programs or providers on behalf of qualifying employee dependents (see ¶818).

• *IRC Sec. 45K fuel from nonconventional source credit*

California has no equivalent to the federal fuel-from-nonconventional-source credit (IRC Sec. 45K).

• *IRC Sec. 46—IRC Sec. 49 investment credit (former law)*

California has no equivalent to the former federal investment credit (repealed effective for property placed in service after 1985) or to the current federal investment credits (IRC Sec. 47, IRC Sec. 48, IRC Sec. 48A, and IRC Sec. 48B).

• *IRC Sec. 51—IRC Sec. 52 (and IRC Sec. 1396, IRC Sec. 1400R) wage credits*

California has no equivalent to the federal work opportunity credits (IRC Sec. 51—IRC Sec. 52), the empowerment zone employment credit (IRC Sec. 1396), or the employee retention credit applicable to employees hired in specific hurricane, tornado, or Midwestern storm disaster areas (IRC Sec. 1400R). However, California allows a deduction for wages disallowed under IRC Sec. 280C when the federal credits are claimed (see ¶1023). California also allows credits to employers in certain areas for wages paid to qualified employees (see ¶818).

• *IRC Sec. 55—IRC Sec. 59 alternative minimum tax*

California imposes an alternative minimum tax (AMT) that is a modified version of the federal AMT (IRC Sec. 55—IRC Sec. 59) (see ¶817).

• *IRC Sec. 78 deemed dividends*

California allows a deduction from gross income for the amount of dividend gross-up included in federal gross income (IRC Sec. 78) when a corporation claims a federal foreign tax credit (see ¶909).

• *Interest on federal obligations*

Interest on federal obligations is taxable under the California franchise tax, but exempt under the corporate income tax (see ¶910).

• *IRC Sec. 103 interest on state obligations*

Under the franchise tax, all state and municipal bond interest, including that of California, is taxable and must be added back to federal taxable income. California bond interest is exempt under the corporate income tax and may be subtracted from federal taxable income (see ¶910).

• *IRC Sec. 114 extraterritorial income*

California had no equivalent to the federal exclusion for extraterritorial income (IRC Sec. 114). Amounts excluded under IRC Sec. 114 were required to be added back to the California taxable income base (see ¶925). IRC Sec. 114 was repealed, effective for tax years after 2006.

• *IRC Sec. 163 interest on indebtedness*

Generally, California's treatment of interest on indebtedness is the same as the federal treatment because IRC Sec. 163 is incorporated by reference. California does not conform to the federal earnings stripping rules that provide that a corporate partner's interest and expenses for purposes of the limitation on the interest expense deduction for disqualified interest is to be treated as that of the corporation and not the partnership (see ¶1004).

• *IRC Sec. 164 income and franchise tax deductions*

California does not allow a subtraction for state, federal, or foreign taxes on or measured by income (see ¶1006).

• *IRC Sec. 165 losses*

Generally, California's treatment of losses is the same as federal because IRC Sec. 165 is incorporated by reference (see ¶1007, 1010). In addition, California allows an expanded deduction for qualified disaster losses.

• *IRC Sec. 166 bad debts*

California's treatment of bad debts is the same as federal because IRC Sec. 166 is incorporated by reference (see ¶1009).

• *IRC Sec. 167 and IRC Sec. 168 depreciation*

California does not follow federal ACRS or MACRS depreciation with respect to corporate taxpayers (IRC Sec. 167 and IRC Sec. 168). Consequently, neither the IRC Sec. 168(k) bonus depreciation deduction, nor the limits placed on sales-in, lease out (SILO) transactions or the shortened recovery periods for leasehold improvements, restaurant property, and retail improvement property apply in California. Although California does allow the income forecast method of depreciation, it has not incorporated the special federal treatment provided to distribution costs and participations and residuals. California also does not adopt federal provisions that require two-year amortization of geological and geophysical expenses and specified recovery periods for electric transmission property and natural gas lines. California also does not conform to federal law allowing five-year amortization of expenses paid or incurred in creating or acquiring a musical composition or a copyright to a musical composition. Nor does California adopt federal provisions relating to (1) amortization of geological and geophysical expenses, electric transmission property, and natural gas lines and (2) the shortening of the recovery period for young racehorses placed in service after 2008 and before 2014 and smart electric meter and electric grid systems, and (3) bonus depreciation for reuse and recycling property and qualified disaster assistance property (see ¶1011).

• *IRC Sec. 168(f) safe harbor leasing (pre-1984 leases)*

California recognizes safe harbor leases under former IRC Sec. 168(f) (see ¶1011).

• *IRC Sec. 169 pollution control facilities amortization*

California's treatment of pollution control facilities is the same as federal (IRC Sec. 169) because the IRC is incorporated by reference, except that the facility must be located in California (see ¶1011).

• *IRC Sec. 170 charitable contributions*

California and federal laws are generally parallel. However, there are differences in the (1) income from which the contributions are deducted, (2) types of contributions eligible for the deduction, and (3) treatment of appreciated property. California does not follow federal law allowing an augmented deduction for donations of computer technology and scientific property. In addition, California does not follow federal provisions that limit the charitable contribution deduction for patents and most other intellectual property, increase the substantiation requirements for donations of $500 or more, and limit the deductions for donations of vehicles, boats, and aircraft while simultaneously increasing the substantiation requirements. California also has not conformed to federal provisions that (1) allow enhanced deductions for donations of food and book inventory; (2) waive the 10% income limitation for cash donations related to specified hurricanes, tornadoes, or Midwest storms; (3) require substantiation of all cash contributions; (4) change the rules regarding donations of fractional interests in tangible personal property; (5) recapture charitable deductions, if the donated property is disposed of within three years and the donee does not certify exempt use; and (6) allow deductions for contributions of real property for conservation purposes. However, California does offer a credit for donations of real property for conservation purposes (see ¶818, ¶1014, ¶1312). California allows a credit for the costs of transporting donated agricultural products to nonprofit charitable organizations (see ¶818).

• *IRC Sec. 171 amortizable bond premium*

The California provisions are generally the same as federal law (IRC Sec. 171). However, a rule in the California provision for computing the amount of amortizable bond premium for the year in which a bond having a call date is actually called differs from the federal rule (see ¶1015).

• *IRC Sec. 172 net operating loss (and IRC Sec. 1400N) net operating loss*

California permits the deduction of an apportioned and allocated NOL, generally in accord with the federal provisions (IRC Sec. 172), except that (1) California suspends the NOL deduction for the 2008 and 2009 taxable years; (2) there is no California carryback allowed prior to the 2011 taxable year; (3) the California carryforward period is limited to 10 years prior to the 2008 taxable year; (4) California does not follow the federal expanded NOL (IRC Sec. 1400N) for qualified hurricane, tornado, and Midwestern storm disaster victims; and (5) for losses incurred prior to 2004, only a specified percentage of a net loss may be carried over (an exception is provided for losses of businesses located in economic incentive areas and certain new businesses and small businesses) (see ¶1024).

• *IRC Sec. 174 research and experimental expenditures*

California's treatment of research and experimental expenditures is the same as federal because IRC Sec. 174 is incorporated by reference (see ¶1011).

• *IRC Sec. 179 asset expense election*

California allows an asset expense election (IRC Sec. 179) for corporation franchise and income tax purposes that is limited to $25,000. California does not allow an expanded asset expense election (IRC Sec. 1400N) for qualified hurricane and tornado disaster victims (see ¶1011).

• *IRC Sec. 179A clean-fuel vehicles*

California did not incorporate the federal provisions regarding clean-fuel vehicles (IRC Sec. 179A) (see ¶1011). The federal provision was eliminated by the ETIA for property placed in service after 2005.

• *IRC Sec. 179D energy efficient commercial building deduction*

California does not incorporate the federal provisions allowing qualified taxpayers to claim a deduction for energy efficiency improvements installed on U.S. commercial property (IRC Sec. 179D) (see ¶1027).

• *IRC Sec. 190 deduction for barriers removal*

The California provision is generally the same as the federal provision (IRC Sec. 190), except that under California law, but not federal law, the deduction is extended to cover the costs of installing a qualified emergency exit/safe area refuge system (see ¶1001).

• *IRC Sec. 195 start-up expenses*

California's treatment of start-up expenditures is the same as federal because IRC Sec. 195 is incorporated by reference (see ¶1018).

• *IRC Sec. 197 amortization of intangibles*

California's treatment of amortization of intangibles is the same as federal because IRC Sec. 197 is incorporated by reference (see ¶1011).

• *IRC Sec. 198 (and IRC Sec. 1400N) environmental remediation costs*

California does not incorporate the federal provisions regarding environmental remediation costs (IRC Sec. 198, IRC Sec. 1400N) (see ¶1011).

• *IRC Sec. 198A qualified disaster expenses*

California does not incorporate the federal provision that allows taxpayers to currently expense qualified disaster expenses (IRC Sec. 198A).

• *IRC Sec. 199 domestic production deduction*

California does not allow the domestic production activities deduction (IRC Sec. 199) (see ¶925).

• *IRC Sec. 243—IRC Sec. 245 dividends received deduction*

California does not incorporate the federal dividends received deduction (IRC Sec. 243—IRC Sec. 245), but does allow a deduction for intercompany dividends and a deduction for dividends received from an insurance company subsidiary (see ¶909).

• *IRC Sec. 248 organizational expenditures*

California law is similar, but not identical to the federal provision (IRC Sec. 248) regarding the treatment of organizational expenditures (see ¶1011).

• *IRC Sec. 301—IRC Sec. 385 corporate distributions and adjustments*

Generally, California's treatment of corporate distributions and adjustments is the same as federal (IRC Sec. 301—IRC Sec. 385) with minor modifications (see ¶1211 et seq.). However, California has not incorporated federal amendments to IRC Sec. 312(k) that deal with the treatment of new federal energy credits in determining a corporation's earnings and profits or amendments to IRC Sec. 355 that modify the active business test for tax-free distributions of controlled corporation stock (later amended to delete "the substantially all" requirement of the active business test) and disallow tax-free distribution treatment with regard to disqualified investment corporations (see ¶1214 and ¶1215).

• *IRC Sec. 401—IRC Sec. 424 deferred compensation plans*

Generally, California's treatment of deferred compensation plans is the same as federal because IRC Sec. 401—IRC Sec. 420 are generally incorporated by reference as amended to date (see ¶1016 and ¶1017). IRC Sec. 421—IRC Sec. 424, regarding certain stock options, are incorporated only as of California's current conformity date.

• *IRC Sec. 441—IRC Sec. 483 accounting periods and methods*

Generally, California's accounting periods and methods are the same as federal because IRC Sec. 441—IRC Sec. 483 are incorporated by reference (see ¶1100 et seq.). However, California does not incorporate IRC Sec. 451(i), which allows a taxpayer to elect to recognize qualified gain from a qualifying electric transmission transaction over an eight-year period for transactions before 2008 (2010 for qualified electric utilities) and has not incorporated amendments made to IRC Sec. 468A, regarding accounting rules for nuclear decommissioning costs. California also does not adopt the amendment to IRC Sec. 468B that exempts from federal income tax certain escrow accounts and settlement funds established to resolve claims brought under the Comprehensive Environmental Response, Compensation, and Liability Act of 1980 (CERCLA) (P.L. 96-510) by designating that these funds are beneficially owned by the U.S. (see ¶807) In addition, California does not incorporate amendments to IRC Sec. 470 that retroactively make the loss deferral rules for property leased to tax-exempt entities inapplicable to partnerships unless specified conditions are satisfied. Nor does California incorporate a federal amendment to IRC Sec. 461 that limits the amount of net farm losses that can be claimed for any tax year after 2009 in which a taxpayer, other than a C corporation, has received certain subsidies (see ¶1106).

The incorporation of IRC Sec. 482 gives the state tax agency the authority to allocate income and deductions among related taxpayers to avoid evasion of tax or to clearly reflect income (see ¶1110).

• *IRC Sec. 501—IRC Sec. 530 exempt organizations*

The California provisions are similar, but not identical to the federal provisions (IRC Sec. 501—IRC Sec. 530). California incorporates the federal provisions regarding taxation of unrelated business income (IRC Sec. 512—IRC Sec. 514) with modifications (see ¶808 , ¶809). California does not conform to the federal amendment to IRC Sec. 512, which specifies that only excess qualifying specified payments from a controlled entity are included in an exempt organization's unrelated business taxable income.

• *IRC Sec. 531—IRC Sec. 547 corporations used to avoid shareholder taxation*

California has no provisions comparable to the federal provisions regarding corporations used to avoid shareholder taxation (IRC Sec. 531—IRC Sec. 558). California does not impose a tax on accumulated earnings or on personal holding companies.

• *IRC Sec. 581—IRC Sec. 597 banking institutions*

California incorporates IRC Sec. 582, regarding bad debts, gains and losses involving securities or bonds. California has some provisions regarding financial institutions that are similar to the federal provisions but, in some instances, California has no comparable provisions (see ¶1009).

• *IRC Sec. 611—IRC Sec. 638 natural resources*

California's treatment of natural resources is generally the same as federal because IRC Sec. 611—IRC Sec. 638 are incorporated by reference. However, California does not incorporate the IRC Sec. 613A suspension of the 100% taxable income limit on percentage depletion deductions for oil and gas production from marginal properties or the modifications to the depletion deduction refinery exemption for independent producers (see ¶1012, ¶1013, ¶1250).

• *IRC Sec. 801—IRC Sec. 848 insurance companies*

There is no equivalent to the federal provisions relating to insurance companies (IRC Sec. 801—IRC Sec. 848). A gross premiums tax is imposed on foreign and domestic insurers in lieu of the corporation income tax (see ¶1902).

• *IRC Sec. 851—IRC Sec. 860L RICs, REITs, REMICs, and FASITs*

California incorporates, with certain exceptions, the federal provisions on RICs, REITs, REMICs, and FASITs (see ¶805). However, California, unlike federal law, does not provide for a reduced tax rate for dividends passed on by RICs, REITs, or other investment entities.

In addition, California does not adopt the federal amendments that expand the Foreign Investment in Real Property Tax Act (FIRPTA) distribution rules, extend the regularly traded securities exception to publicly traded RIC U.S. Real Property Holding Corporations (USRPHCs), modify the RIC termination date, require withholding on RIC USRPHC distributions, and treat certain RIC capital gain distributions as dividends.

Because a federal REIT election, or lack thereof, or termination of a REIT, is automatically recognized for California corporation tax purposes, California incorporates IRC Sec. 856 provisions that impact REIT eligibility, elections, and terminations, as amended to date.

• *IRC Sec. 861—IRC Sec. 865 foreign source income*

California does not follow the foreign sourcing rules (IRC Sec. 861—IRC Sec.865). Multistate and international businesses that conduct business both inside and outside California utilize the state's allocation (see ¶1303) and apportionment rules (see ¶1302) for determining whether income is attributable to state sources. California allows a subtraction from taxable income for income derived from the operation of aircraft or ships by a foreign corporation (see ¶916).

• *IRC Sec. 901—IRC Sec. 908 foreign tax credit*

California has no provisions comparable to those relating to the foreign tax credit (IRC Sec. 901—IRC Sec. 908).

• *IRC Sec. 965 temporary dividends received deduction*

California has no provision comparable to the federal temporary dividends received deduction (IRC Sec. 965). California does allow water's-edge taxpayers to exclude certain foreign corporation dividends (see ¶909, ¶1309, ¶1311).

• *IRC Sec. 1001—IRC Sec. 1092 gain or loss on disposition of property*

California specifically incorporates several federal provisions; has some provisions that are similar to the federal provisions; and, in some cases, has no comparable provisions (see ¶1201 et seq.). However, California does not incorporate federal amendments that require basis adjustments in relation to the new federal energy credits or that extend the IRC Sec. 1033 replacement period for nonrecognition of gain as a result of an involuntary conversion of business property from two years to five years for property converted by Hurricane Katrina, the 2007 Kansas tornadoes, or the Midwestern 2008 summer storms (see ¶1202). California does not incorporate the repeal of IRC Sec. 1081—IRC Sec. 1083, relating to special rules for determining basis and gains or losses in connection with exchanges and distributions pursuant to SEC ordered reorganizations of public utility holding companies (see ¶1205).

California also does not adopt (1) the amendment to IRC Sec. 1035 to provide for the nonrecognition of gain from the exchange of certain long-term care contracts after 2009 (see ¶1207), or (2) amendments to IRC Sec. 1012 that require that the determination of the basis of securities is to be done on an account by account basis, Nor does, California incorporate the amendments to the IRC Sec. 1092 straddle rules governing basis adjustments and identification requirements. California also does not incorporate amendments to IRC Sec. 1031, which provide that an exchange of certain mutual ditch, reservoir or irrigation company stock completed after May 22, 2008, qualifies as a like-kind exchange.

• *IRC Sec. 1201 alternative capital gains tax*

California does not provide for an alternative tax rate on capital gains.

• *IRC Sec. 1211 and IRC Sec. 1212 capital losses*

California's treatment of capital loss carryovers is the same as federal because IRC Sec. 1211 and IRC Sec. 1212 are incorporated by reference. However, California does not allow capital loss carrybacks (see ¶1222).

• *IRC Sec. 1221—IRC Sec. 1260 determining capital gains and losses*

Generally, California's determination of capital gains and losses is the same as federal because IRC Sec. 1221—IRC Sec. 1260 are incorporated by reference (see ¶1222 et seq.). However, California does not require recapture under IRC Sec. 1245(a) on disposal of multiple IRC Sec. 197 assets; therefore, gain or loss on the sale of such assets may differ for federal and state purposes.

California also does not adopt the federal amendments to IRC Sec. 1221 that allow a taxpayer to elect to treat as a sale or exchange of a capital asset, the sale or exchange of musical compositions or copyrights in musical works created by the taxpayer's personal efforts (or having a basis determined by reference to the basis in the hands of the taxpayer whose personal efforts created the composition or copyrights).

• *IRC Sec. 1361—IRC Sec. 1379 S corporations*

California adopts federal treatment of S corporations and their shareholders (IRC Sec. 1361—IRC Sec. 1379), but imposes a 1.5% tax on S corporation net income prior to its pass-through to shareholders. However, California does not adopt the federal amendments to IRC Sec. 1367, regarding the basis reduction in stock of a shareholder as the result of a charitable contribution made in 2006 through 2008, or amendments that changed this rule so that the basis reduction does not apply to a charitable contribution of appreciated property to the extent that the shareholder's pro rata share of the contribution exceeds the shareholder's pro rata share of the adjusted basis of the property. California conforms to federal amendments made to IRC Sec. 1361 and IRC Sec. 1362 that impact eligibility, elections, and terminations, but does not conform to other federal amendments made to those provisions (see ¶806).

• *IRC Sec. 1391—IRC Sec. 1400J empowerment zones and renewal communities*

Although California has no provisions directly comparable to the federal provisions regarding empowerment zones and renewal communities (IRC Sec. 1391—IRC Sec. 1400J), California's provisions regarding manufacturing enhancement areas apply to businesses located in federally designated empowerment zones (see ¶818). California provides incentives for targeted tax areas, enterprise zones, and local agency military base recovery areas (see ¶818). Taxpayers may deduct expenses for which a federal empowerment zone employment credit was claimed, as California does not incorporate the applicable IRC Sec. 280C provision (see ¶1023).

• *IRC Sec. 1400M—IRC Sec. 1400T Gulf Opportunity Zones*

California does not incorporate GOZA provisions that, among other things: allow a current deduction for 50% of any qualified GO Zone clean-up costs and allow GO Zone public utility disaster losses resulting from Hurricane Katrina to be deducted in the fifth tax year preceding the loss. California also does not incorporate the federal extension of these benefits to victims of the 2007 Kansas tornadoes or the Midwestern storms in the summer of 2008.

• *IRC Sec. 1501—IRC Sec. 1504 consolidated returns*

Except for certain affiliated groups of railroad corporations, California does not incorporate the federal provisions allowing affiliated corporations to file consolidated returns (see ¶812).

Business Incentives and Credits

¶15 Introduction

California has created a number of tax incentives designed to attract business to the state, stimulate expansion, and/or encourage certain economic activity. These incentives are listed below, by tax, with a brief description and a cross-reference to the paragraph at which they are discussed in greater detail. Most exemptions and deductions, which are too numerous to be fully included below, are discussed under the taxes to which they apply (see the Table of Contents or the Topical Index).

¶16 Corporate Franchise and Income Taxes

The amount of credits and credit carryovers that may be claimed by taxpayers on a corporation franchise and income tax return are limited to 50% of a taxpayer's tax during the 2008 and 2009 tax years, see ¶818 for details.

• *Research and development credit*

California provides a credit for research and development expenditures that is generally the same as that allowed under federal law (Sec. 41), with some differences in the areas of rates and percentages. The qualifying research must be conducted in California (¶818).

• *Community development investment credit*

For taxable years beginning before 2012, California allows a credit equal to 20% of each qualified investment made into a community development financial institution (¶818).

• *Child care credits*

In taxable years beginning before 2012, credits are available to employers for establishing child care programs or facilities, for contributing to child care information and referral services, and for contributions to qualified child care plans (¶818).

• *Enhanced oil recovery credit*

California allows certain independent oil producers an enhanced oil recovery credit equal to one third of the federal credit allowed under IRC Sec. 43, provided the costs for which the credit is claimed are attributable to projects located within California (¶818). However, this credit is unavailable during the 2008 taxable year.

• *Disabled access expenditures credit*

California allows eligible small businesses a credit for 50% of up to $250 of the disabled access expenditures paid or incurred by those businesses to comply with the federal Americans with Disabilities Act (¶818).

• *Transportation of donated agricultural products credit*

California allows a credit against net tax for 50% of the costs paid or incurred in connection with the transportation of agricultural products donated to nonprofit charitable organizations (¶818).

• *Low-income housing credit*

Corporations may qualify for a low-income housing credit, generally based upon federal law (IRC Sec. 42) (¶818).

• *Farmworker housing credit*

Prior to the 2009 taxable year California allows a credit for certain qualified costs associated with the construction or rehabilitation of farmworker housing located in California. In addition, banks and financial institutions may claim a credit for low-interest loans made to finance qualified expenditures associated with construction or rehabilitation of farmworker housing (¶818). Beginning with the 2009 taxable year, the low-income housing credit is modified to require an allocation set-aside to support farmworker housing projects.

• *Prison inmate job credit*

Employers may claim a credit equal to 10% of the wages paid to each prison inmate hired under a program established by the Director of Corrections (¶818).

• *Natural heritage preservation credit*

A taxpayer may claim a credit equal to 55% of the fair market value of qualified real property donated before July 1, 2008, for conservation to the California Resources Agency (CRA), a local government, or a nonprofit land and water conservation organization designated by the CRA or local government to accept donations (¶818).

• *Ultra-low sulfur diesel fuel production credit*

A credit is available for ultra low-sulfur diesel fuel produced by a qualified small refiner at a California facility (¶818).

¶17 Sales and Use Taxes

See ¶1509 et seq. for a listing of the major exemptions from sales and use taxes.

¶18 Property Taxes

• *Solar energy construction*

Through the 2015-2016 fiscal year property tax lien dates, active solar energy system construction or additions do not constitute new construction for purposes of required valuation reassessment (¶1702).

• *Economic revitalization rebate*

Any city, county, or special district (except for school districts) is authorized to rebate property tax revenues derived from economic revitalization manufacturing property. In addition to a property component, the use of the property must also create new jobs in the taxing jurisdiction (¶1711).

• *Capital investment rebate*

The governing body of any city, city and county, or county may implement a capital investment incentive program and rebate certain tax revenues derived from taxation of an assessed value in excess of $150 million for any qualified manufacturing facility (¶1711).

¶19 Enterprise Zones

Incentives, including credits and deductions, are allowed against corporate franchise and corporate and personal income taxes for taxpayers located in enterprise zones, Local Agency Military Base Recovery Areas (LAMBRA), targeted tax areas, and manufacturing enhancement areas (¶104).

PART II

RETURN PREPARATION GUIDE

RESIDENTS: PREPARING INDIVIDUAL FORM 540

¶25 How Residents Are Taxed

The computation of tax on a resident return (Form 540) begins with federal adjusted gross income. Modifications (¶30) are made for law differences, then modified itemized deductions (¶31) or the standard deduction (¶29) are subtracted to arrive at "taxable income." Special rules apply to registered domestic partners (¶119).

After the tax liability is determined, personal exemption and dependent exemption credits (¶28) are subtracted. Various other special credits are also allowed (¶33).

Special California rate provisions (¶32) deal with (1) the alternative minimum tax, (2) the penalty or recapture tax on premature distributions of IRAs, Keogh plans, or other qualified retirement plans, (3) the penalty on nonqualified distributions from Coverdell education savings accounts and qualified tuition programs, (4) the penalty tax on nonexempt withdrawals from medical savings accounts, (5) the separate tax on lump-sum distributions, and (6) the tax on minor children's unearned income ("kiddie tax").

The deadline for filing the 2008 Form 540 and paying the tax is the same as the federal deadline—April 15, 2009, for calendar-year taxpayers (¶34). California grants an automatic extension of time to file to October 15, 2009.

Paragraph references throughout this discussion are to explanations in the *Guidebook.* The CCH CALIFORNIA STATE TAX REPORTER should also be consulted for further details on any point.

• *Tax form outline*

The following chart illustrates the steps that an individual must follow in completing a 2008 California return.

CALIFORNIA RESIDENT

References to page numbers and line numbers below are to pages and lines of California Form 540 or Schedule CA(540). References to paragraph numbers are to the paragraphs of this discussion.

	FILING STATUS	
p. 1, lines 1-5	Single; Married/RDP filing jointly; Married/RDP filing separately; Head-of-household; Qualifying widow(er)	Par. 27

p. 1, line 13	Federal adjusted gross income (AGI)	Par. 25
	[+] or [–]	
p. 1, Sch. CA(540), lines 7-37	CA adjustments to fed. AGI	Par. 30
	[–]	
p. 1, line 18 p. 1, Sch. CA(540) lines 38-44	Standard deduction or CA itemized deductions (adjusted federal deductions)	Par. 29 Par. 31
	[=]	
p. 1, line 19	CA taxable income	Par. 25
	[×]	
p. 1, line 20	Tax rate	Par. 32
	[–]	
p. 1, lines 21, 25-33	Credits	Par. 28, 33
	[=]	
p. 2, lines 47, 48	Tax liability or refund	Par. 34

¶26 Return Filing Requirements

California Forms: Forms 540 (California Resident Income Tax Return), 540A (California Resident Income Tax Return), 540 2EZ (California Resident Income Tax Return).

The following filing levels apply in 2008 (¶106):

2008 Filing Thresholds

On 12/31/08, the taxpayer's filing status was:	**and on 12/31/08, the taxpayer's age was[6]:**	California Gross Income[1]			California Adjusted Gross Income[2]		
		Dependents			Dependents		
		0	1	2 or more	0	1	2 or more
Single or Head of household[3]	Under 65	14,845	25,145	32,870	11,876	22,176	29,901
	65 or older	19,795	27,520	33,700	16,826	24,551	30,731
Married/RDP filing jointly or filing separately[4]	Under 65 (both spouses/RDPs)	29,690	39,990	47,715	23,752	34,052	41,777
	65 or older (one spouse/RDP)	34,640	42,365	48,545	28,702	36,427	42,607
	65 or older (both spouses/RDPs)	39,590	47,315	53,495	33,652	41,377	47,557
Qualifying widow(er)[3]	Under 65		25,145	32,870		22,176	29,901
	65 or older		27,520	33,700		24,551	30,731
Dependent of another person Any filing status	Any age	More than your standard deduction[5]					

[1] **California gross income** is all income received from all sources in the form of money, goods, property, and services that are not exempt from tax. Gross income does not include any adjustments or deductions.

[2] **California adjusted gross income** is federal adjusted gross income from all sources reduced or increased by all California income adjustments.

[3]See ¶15-320.

[4]The income of both spouses or registered domestic partners (RDPs) must be combined; both spouses or RDPs may be required to file a return even if only one spouse or RDP had income over the amounts listed.

[5]Use the California Standard Deduction Worksheet for Dependents in the 2008 California Resident Booklet to compute the standard deduction.

[6]If the taxpayer's 65th birthday is on January 1, 2009, she or he is considered to be age 65 on December 31, 2008.

Income filing levels are determined by reference to federal gross and adjusted gross income.

For purposes of the filing thresholds (1) single persons include taxpayers filing as heads of households and qualifying widowers and (2) married couples and RDPs include taxpayers filing either jointly or separately.

Special filing levels apply for the filing of a separate return by a dependent (¶106).

For information regarding which taxpayers may file Forms 540A and 540 2EZ, see ¶106.

See ¶105 for a discussion as to who is considered a "resident" of the state.

• *Military personnel*

Members of the U.S. Armed Forces who are residents stationed in California are subject to the same return filing requirement amounts as other taxpayers (¶105).

¶27 Filing Status

With the exceptions noted below, a taxpayer's filing status on the California return is generally the same as his or her filing status on the federal Form 1040 (¶114).

Military: Spouses who file a joint federal return and who had different states of residence at any time during the year have the option of filing separate California returns if one spouse was an active member of the Armed Forces (Form 540). The tax should be figured both jointly and separately in order to determine the more favorable filing status.

Part-year residents and nonresidents: This exception is discussed at ¶63.

Registered domestic partners: Registered domestic partners must file California personal income tax returns jointly or separately by applying the same standards as are applied to married taxpayers under federal income tax law, see ¶114.

Same-sex married couples: See ¶114 for a discussion of the filing status for same-sex married couples.

Factors in determining which filing status is advantageous are discussed at ¶114.

¶28 Personal and Dependent Exemptions

California provides credits against the tax for personal and dependent exemptions in lieu of deductions from income (¶113).

The 2008 tax credit amounts are as follows:

Single	$99
Married/registered domestic partnership (RDP), separate return	99
Married/RDP, joint return	198
Head of household	99
Surviving spouse	198
Dependent	309
Visually impaired person (additional)	99
Elderly person aged 65 and over (additional)	99

A physician's statement must be filed with the first return on which the visually impaired exemption credit is claimed (Instructions to Form 540).

The exemption dependent credits must be reduced for taxpayers whose federal adjusted gross income exceeds the threshold amounts specified for the taxpayer's filing status (¶113).

¶29 Standard Deduction

The election of a California taxpayer to itemize or to claim a standard deduction is independent of the federal election (¶303). Taxpayers may choose the more favorable tax treatment.

The California standard deduction amounts for 2008 are as follows:

Filing status	*Amount*
Single	$3,692
Married/RDP filing jointly	7,384
Married/RDP filing separately	3,692
Head of household	7,384
Qualifying widow(er)	7,384

The above amounts are not increased (as under federal law) if the taxpayer is elderly or blind.

The standard deduction amount for dependents is limited to the greater of (1) $900 or (2) the individual's earned income plus $300.

See ¶335 for more details.

¶30 Modifications to Federal Adjusted Gross Income

California Forms: Sch. CA (540) (California Adjustments - Residents), Sch. D (California Capital Gain or Loss Adjustment), Sch. D-1 (Sales of Business Property), FTB 3801 (Passive Activity Loss Limitations), FTB 3805V (Net Operating Loss (NOL) Computation and NOL and Disaster Loss Limitations - Individuals, Estates, and Trusts), FTB 3805Z (Enterprise Zone Deduction and Credit Summary), FTB 3806 (Los Angeles Revitalization Zone Deduction and Credit Summary), FTB 3807 (Local Agency Military Base Recovery Area Deduction and Credit Summary), FTB 3809 (Targeted Tax Area Deduction and Credit Summary), FTB 3885A (Depreciation and Amortization Adjustments).

The computation on Form 540 starts with federal adjusted gross income (AGI); modification adjustments are listed to reflect federal/state law differences. The adjustments are grouped as subtractions and as additions on California Schedule CA (540). They are aggregated and then netted before entry on Form 540.

The California Schedule CA (540) has two parts. Part I reports the subtractions and additions to federal adjusted gross income. Part II reports the modified federal itemized deductions. Part II adjustments are explained at ¶31.

Practice Note: Registered Domestic Partners and Same-Sex Married Couples

Registered domestic partners (RDPs) must make additional adjustments to reconcile the differences that arise from using a different filing status on their California tax returns than their federal income tax returns. These adjustments may be made by completing a pro forma federal return or by utilizing the worksheets provided in FTB Pub. 737, Tax Information for Registered Domestic Partnerships. For more information concerning RDPs, see the discussion at ¶119.

At the time this book went to press, the Franchise Tax Board had not made a determination as to the tax treatment of same-sex individuals who were married in California prior to the passage of Proposition 8, which repealed the right of same-sex individuals to legally marry. If it is determined that such couples should be treated as spouses for California Revenue and Taxation Code purposes, adjustments similar to those required by RDPs must be made, see ¶119 for details.

The most commonly made modifications to adjusted gross income (AGI) are discussed in the following paragraphs. Other modifications are discussed in FTB Pub. 1001, 2008 Supplemental Guidelines to California Adjustments.

Interest on state obligations (¶217): Interest on bonds of states other than California or on obligations issued by municipalities of other states is added back to federal adjusted gross income.

Notes:

— Interest from investment in an enterprise zone is deductible under California, but not federal, law (¶240).

— Interest on Community Energy Authority bonds issued in California is deductible under California, but not federal, law (¶201).

Interest on federal obligations (¶217): Interest on federal obligations is exempt and, consequently, is subtracted from federal AGI. See also ¶217 for the pass-through of tax-exempt interest from a mutual fund.

Interest income from Federal Farm Credit banks, Federal Home Loan banks, the Student Loan Marketing Association (SLMA), the Resolution Funding Corporation, the Production Credit Association, the Commodity Credit Corporation, Certificates of

Accrual on Treasury Securities (CATS), and Treasury Investment Growth Receipts (TIGRS) is also exempt interest that is subtracted from federal adjusted gross income; however, interest from Fannie Maes, Ginnie Maes, or FHLMC securities is taxable in California and, therefore, no modification is made to federal AGI for interest from these instruments.

Childrens' interest and dividend income (¶217, ¶226): California law, unlike federal law, limits the election for parents to include interest and dividend income of children on the parents return to such income of children under the age of 14. Parents that included dividend and interest income of children between the ages of 14 and 24 on their federal return must subtract such income from the amount included in their federal AGI.

Depreciation (¶310, 311): California depreciation is generally the same as federal depreciation (the "modified accelerated cost recovery system" under IRC Sec. 168) for assets placed in service after 1986. However, California does not incorporate the additional 50% first-year bonus depreciation available under IRC Sec. 168(k) for property placed in service in 2008, and did not incorporate the additional 30%/50% first-year bonus depreciation available for qualified property purchased after September 10, 2001, and before 2005. Nor has California incorporated the additional first-year bonus depreciation deduction allowed for qualified New York Liberty Zone property or the accelerated write-off for qualified property located in a renewal community.

For taxable years beginning after 2002 and before 2011, federal law allows taxpayers to currently expense higher amounts under IRC Sec. 179 than is allowed under California law. Also, if the maximum IRC Sec. 179 deduction was taken for property placed in service in tax years beginning after 1992 and before 1999, the federal and California amounts will differ; see ¶311 for a detailed discussion. In addition, California has not conformed to additional federal amendments that increase the amount at which the phase-out of the IRC Sec. 179 deduction begins and that allow the deduction to be claimed for off-the-shelf computer software.

California adopts the federal 39-year depreciation recovery period for nonresidential real property acquired after May 12, 1993, but only for property placed in service after 1996 in taxable years beginning after 1996. Thus, for California purposes, nonresidential real property placed in service before 1997 in taxable years beginning before 1997 continues to be depreciated over a 31.5-year recovery period.

California has also not conformed to post-2004 federal amendments that

— classify qualified leasehold improvements, qualified restaurant property, and qualified retail improvement property as 15-year recovery property and require the use of the straight-line method;

— provide special depreciation treatment for participations and residuals;

— revise the depreciation deduction for geological and geophysical expenses, electric transmission property, and natural gas lines;

— allow five-year amortization of expenses paid or incurred in creating or acquiring a musical composition or a copyright to a musical composition;

— require certain major integrated oil companies to amortize geological and geophysical expenditures over a five-year or seven-year period instead of a 24-month period;

— allow a 50% additional depreciation allowance for qualified cellulosic biomass ethanol and qualified cellulosic biofuel plant property, qualified reuse and recycling property, and qualified disaster assistance property;

— extend the shortened MACRS recovery periods for qualified Indian reservation property to apply to qualified property placed in service prior to 2010;

— provide shortened recovery periods for qualified smart electric meters and smart grid systems, qualified farming machinery and equipment, motorsports entertainment complexes, and young race horses; and

— ease the current expense allowance qualifying criteria for film production expenses.

Further differences in the amount of depreciation claimed for federal and California purposes may arise due to California provisions that allow taxpayers operating in specified depressed areas to claim accelerated write-offs for certain property (¶316) and federal provisions that allow accelerated writeoffs for small film production costs (¶311) and reforestation expenditures (¶315).

ACRS is allowed federally for assets placed in service after 1980 and before 1987. However, for California purposes, assets placed in service before 1987 are depreciated over the period of useful life, or guideline periods established in the appropriate federal Revenue Procedure, using sum-of-the-years digits, declining balance, straight-line, or other pre-ACRS federal method.

Note: The differences between federal and California deductions are adjusted on FTB 3885A. The net adjustment may be an addition or a subtraction.

Capital gains and losses (¶523): California law and federal law prior to the 1997 tax year treat all capital gains realized after 1986 as ordinary income. However, for tax years beginning after 1996, federal law subjects long-term capital gains to a lower tax rate.

Differences between the amount of capital gain or loss recognized for California and federal purposes can occur both in the year a gain or loss is recognized and also in loss carryover years. For the 2008 taxable year, differences can occur between the gain or loss allowed for federal and California purposes because of the following:

— California does not permit capital loss carrybacks (¶526);

— California, but not federal, law excludes gain on the sale or disposition of qualified assisted housing developments (¶505);

— California requires certain adjustments to basis not required by federal law and makes certain federal adjustments inapplicable (¶559);

— California has not incorporated federal law that limits the amount of long-term capital gain that a taxpayer can recognize from constructive ownership contracts involving pass-through entities (¶525);

— different basis may apply to property for which an additional first-year bonus depreciation was claimed for federal, but not California, purposes (¶310);

— different basis may apply as a result of the different amounts that may be claimed as an IRC Sec. 179 deduction (¶311);

— California does not incorporate federal provisions that allow capital gains treatment for sales or exchanges of qualified musical compositions or copyrights in musical works (¶526).

Differences between pre-1987 California and federal laws that can affect the reporting of capital gain and loss include the following:

— A difference in capital loss carryover (¶526).

— The pre-1987 holding periods and taxable percentages of capital gains for California were different from the federal.

— The California adjustment to capital gains computed for purposes of the investment interest expense deduction was different from the federal adjustment.

— Dividends from mutual funds were treated as ordinary income for California purposes.

— Because of the various differences between California and federal law mentioned above, the California basis may not always be the same as the federal basis of the property. Examples of such situations are as follows:

(a) valuation of property acquired by inheritance (¶546);
(b) depreciation of business property (¶310, 311);
(c) basis adjustment of property for moves into California (¶504);
(d) basis adjustments for California and federal credits (¶142 , 151); and
(e) basis in the stock of an S corporation (¶233).

Schedule D, Form 540, is used to calculate the differences, and the appropriate modification is carried to California Schedule CA (540).

See ¶523 —541 for further details.

State income tax refund (¶201): Any California income tax refunds included in federal AGI are subtracted.

Unemployment compensation (¶201): Unemployment compensation included on the federal return is not taxed by California and is subtracted from federal AGI.

Paid family leave (¶201): Paid family leave included on the federal return is not taxed by California and is subtracted from federal AGI.

Social security benefits (¶201): California does not tax Social Security benefits. Any Social Security benefits included in federal AGI are subtracted.

Railroad retirement benefits (¶201, 205): Both tier 1 and tier 2 railroad retirement benefits, including ridesharing benefits and sick pay, received under the Federal Insurance Contributions and Railroad Retirement Act are subtracted from federal AGI.

California lottery winnings (¶201): Any California lottery winnings included in federal AGI, including amounts received pursuant to an assignment, are subtracted.

IRA and Keogh distributions (¶330): The California and federal deductible dollar limits are generally the same for post-1986 tax years. For pre-1987 tax years, the amounts differed; consequently, the amount taxable on a distribution will differ. Differences may also arise if the taxpayer changed residence during the time he or she made contributions to the IRA or Keogh plan.

A worksheet to compute differences in the tax treatment of distributions for federal and California purposes is included in FTB Pub. 1005, Pension and Annuity Guidelines.

Net operating loss (NOL) (¶309): With the exception of the suspension of the NOL deduction for losses incurred or carried over in the 2008 and 2009 and 2002 and 2003 taxable years, the California NOL is determined under the same rules as the federal NOL except that prior to 2011, no carrybacks are allowed (including the extended NOL carryback enacted by the Job Creation and Worker Assistance Act) and for pre-2004 losses the amount of loss eligible for carryover to future years is generally limited to a specified percentage of the California net operating loss dependent on the year the loss was incurred. In addition, California limits NOL carrybacks for 2011 to 50% of the NOL and for 2012 to 75% of the NOL. Furthermore, applicable to NOLs incurred prior to the 2008 taxable year, an NOL may be carried forward for California purposes for only 10 years (five years for losses incurred in taxable years prior to 2000) rather than the 20 years permitted under federal law (15 years for losses incurred in tax years beginning before August 6, 1997). Commencing with the 2008 taxable year, California NOLs may be carried over for 20 years. The NOL carryover period is extended for losses suspended during the 2008, 2009, 2002 and 2003 taxable years.

Special rules apply for taxpayers operating in enterprise zones, the former Los Angeles Revitalization Zone (LARZ), local agency military base recovery areas (LAMBRAs), or targeted tax areas. For taxable years beginning after 2000 and before

2003, special provisions also applied to farming businesses directly impacted by Pierce's disease.

Calculation of the California NOL is made on FTB 3805V and the appropriate adjustment is entered on California Schedule CA (540). The order in which net operating losses are absorbed is computed on a separate worksheet (which is not filed with the return). Calculation of the NOL for enterprise zone businesses is made on FTB 3805Z. FTB 3806 is used to calculate the NOL for taxpayers who operated in the former LARZ, FTB 3807 is used to calculate the NOL for taxpayers operating in LAMBRAs, and FTB 3809 is used to calculate the NOL for taxpayers operating in targeted tax areas.

Recycling revenues (¶201): The income received by a taxpayer for recycling empty beverage containers is exempt for California purposes and is subtracted if included in federal AGI.

Expenses related to tax-exempt income (¶305): Expenses related to federally tax-exempt income that were disallowed as a deduction in computing federal AGI are subtracted for California purposes. Expenses incurred to purchase or carry obligations that are tax-exempt under California but not federal law are added to federal AGI.

Note: These modifications, to the extent not business-related, are made to federal itemized deductions.

Income from exercising California qualified stock options (¶207): Compensation received from exercising a California qualified stock option is excluded from California gross income and may be subtracted if the compensation was included in federal AGI.

Ridesharing and employee commuter deductions (¶241): An exclusion from gross income is available to an employee for amounts received from his or her employer for certain ridesharing or commuting arrangements. Because California does not place a limit on the monthly benefits that may be excluded and allows for more excludable ridesharing/commuter options, a subtraction from federal AGI may be allowed.

Pensions and annuities (¶205, 206): California rules for taxing pensions and annuities are basically the same as federal; however, the taxable amount may differ because of federal/California differences in the years when contributions were made. For further information see FTB Pub. 1005, Pension and Annuity Guidelines.

Passive activity loss (¶340): California generally adopts federal rules for computing the limitation on deducting passive activity losses. However, California does not conform to the federal passive activity loss rules relating to rental real estate losses suffered by certain taxpayers who materially participate in real property trades or businesses. Differences may also exist because the amount of passive income and loss may differ. Taxpayers must segregate California adjustments that relate to passive activities from California adjustments that relate to nonpassive items (¶340). This calculation is made on FTB 3801, Passive Activity Loss Limitations.

Other gains or losses (¶503, ¶537): Although California law on the computation of gain from sales of business property and certain involuntary conversions is generally the same as federal, the amount of gain or loss may differ because of federal/California basis differences. An addition adjustment may be required because California does not incorporate federal amendments that extend the two-year replacement period (four years for residential property in a federally declared disaster area) to five years for property converted by Hurricane Katrina or other specified disasters, as long as the replacement property purchased is located in the disaster area. These amounts are reported on Schedule D-1.

Other adjustments may arise as a result of transfers between same-sex spouses and registered domestic partners, in which no gain is recognized for California purposes (see ¶119). Federal law requires that gain or loss be recognized in such transactions, see ¶502.

Alimony (¶204): Alimony received by a nonresident alien that was not included in the taxpayer's federal gross income is treated as an addition on Schedule CA (540).

Income from specially treated sources: See the indicated paragraphs for possible federal/California differences in the taxation of the following items: (1) noncash patronage dividends from farmers' cooperatives or mutual associations (¶232), and (2) interest income from investment in enterprise zones (¶240).

Claim of right adjustment (¶415): A claim of right adjustment may be claimed as either a deduction or a credit. A taxpayer that claims a credit for repayment amount on his or her federal return may claim a deduction on his or her California personal income tax return. Deductions of $3,000 or less are subject to the 2% floor for miscellaneous itemized deductions. A taxpayer that claims a deduction on his or her federal return, may claim a credit for the repayment amount on his or her California personal income tax return.

Income from S corporations (¶233): Shareholders of California S corporations add or subtract, as appropriate, the difference between their distributive shares of federal and California S corporation income or loss.

Income from partnerships and limited liability partnerships (¶616, 623): Partners add or subtract, as appropriate, the difference between their distributive shares of federal and California partnership income or loss.

Income from limited liability companies (¶625): Members and persons with economic interests in an LLC add or subtract, as appropriate, the difference between their shares of federal and California LLC income in the same manner as partners must include their distributive shares of partnership income in their taxable income.

Income from trusts and estates (¶605): Trust or estate beneficiaries add or subtract, as appropriate, the difference between their shares of federal and California trust or estate income or loss.

Business expenses incurred in discriminatory clubs (¶301, 336): California prohibits a business expense deduction for expenditures at a club that restricts membership or use on the basis of age, sex, race, religion, color, ancestry, national origin, or beginning with the 2008 taxable year, ethnic group identification, sexual orientation, or disability. There is no similar federal prohibition.

Wages (¶201): If there is a difference in wages because of an employee's fringe benefits, also reported on the W-2, an adjustment must be made because California does not adopt the federal rules; the amount of federal wages reported on the W-2 is subtracted and the amount reported as California wages is added.

Crime hotline rewards (¶246): Any rewards received from a government authorized crime hotline are excluded from gross income.

Water conservation rebates/vouchers (¶244): California excludes from gross income specified water conservation rebates/vouchers received from local water and energy agencies or suppliers.

Conservation and environmental cost-share payments (¶243): Certain cost-share payments received by forest landowners from the Department of Forestry and Fire Protection are subtracted from federal gross income.

Reparation payments (¶248): An exclusion from gross income is provided for amounts received as reparation payments for individuals who were required to perform forced or slave labor during World War II, Canadian government reparation payments paid to persons of Japanese ancestry interned in Canada during World War II, and Armenian genocide settlement payments.

Wrongful conviction compensation (¶201): Amounts paid by the state of California to compensate an individual for wrongful conviction and incarceration are subtracted from federal AGI.

Energy-efficient home improvement grants (¶245): Energy-efficient home improvement grants awarded by the State Energy Resources Conservation and Development Commission to low-income individuals are subtracted from federal AGI (¶245).

Medical expenses (¶219, 301, 325): California taxpayers may subtract from federal AGI amounts received from employer-provided accident, health insurance, and medical expense reimbursements and self-employed health insurance payments associated with expenses for the taxpayer's registered domestic partner and the domestic partner's dependents. This subtraction may also apply to same-sex married couples (see ¶119.

Health savings accounts (¶247): California does not allow an above-the-line deduction for contributions to a health savings account. Amounts deducted on a taxpayer's federal return should be added back to federal AGI.

Energy efficient commercial building costs (¶345): California does not incorporate federal law allowing taxpayers to currently deduct a portion of the costs of installing energy efficient systems in commercial buildings. Such amounts must be added back to federal AGI and an increased California depreciation deduction may be claimed.

Teacher expenses (¶202): Unreimbursed expenses incurred by eligible elementary and secondary school educators for books, supplies, equipment, and material used in the classroom, to the extent deductible under federal law, but not California law, are added back to federal AGI.

Tuition and education expenses (¶344): California requires an addition adjustment for qualified tuition and related expenses deducted on a taxpayer's federal income tax return.

Environmental remediation expenses (¶346): California requires an addition adjustment and depreciation adjustment for environmental remediation costs currently expensed on a taxpayer's federal return.

Disaster costs (¶347): California requires an addition adjustment and depreciation adjustment for qualified disaster costs currently expensed on a taxpayer's federal return.

¶31 Itemized Deductions

California Form: Sch. CA (540) (California Adjustments - Residents).

California itemized deductions are based on federal itemized deductions, with the modifications discussed below. These modifications are independent of the adjustments to federal adjusted gross income (AGI) discussed at ¶30, even though both are calculated on Schedule CA (540).

Taxpayers may elect either the standard deduction or itemized deductions for California purposes, regardless of which was elected for federal purposes (¶29). A federal Schedule A must be completed if the taxpayer did not itemize federally but chooses to itemize on the California return. A copy of the federal Form 1040 and all supporting federal forms and schedules must be attached to Form 540 if the taxpayer filed federal schedules other than Schedules A and B.

Practice Note: Registered Domestic Partners and Same-Sex Married Couples

Registered domestic partners (RDPs) must make additional adjustments to itemized deductions to reconcile the differences that arise as a result of using a different filing status on their California tax returns than their federal income tax returns. These adjustments may be made by completing a pro forma federal return or by utilizing the worksheets provided in FTB Pub. 737, Tax Information for Registered Domestic Partnerships. For more information concerning RDPs, see the discussion at ¶119.

At the time this book went to press, the Franchise Tax Board had not made a determination as to the tax treatment of same-sex individuals who were married in California prior to the passage of Proposition 8, which repealed the right of same-sex individuals to legally marry. If it is determined that such couples should be treated as spouses for California Revenue and Taxation Code purposes, adjustments similar to those required by RDPs must be made, see ¶119 for details.

The adjustments are as follows:

— *Taxes* (¶306): State, local, and foreign income taxes (including state disability insurance—SDI) and sales and use taxes claimed on federal Schedule A are not allowable deductions for California purposes and are subtracted from federal itemized deductions.

— *California Lottery losses* (¶336): California Lottery losses are not deductible for California purposes. The amount of such losses, as shown on federal Schedule A, must be subtracted from federal itemized deductions.

— *Federal obligation expense* (¶305): Because California does not tax interest from federal obligations, any expenses relating to such interest that have been deducted for federal purposes on Schedule A should be subtracted from federal itemized deductions.

— *State obligation expense* (¶305): Because California taxes interest from state or local obligations of states other than California, which is exempt for federal purposes, any expenses related to this interest that were not entered on federal Schedule A may be added to federal itemized deductions.

— *Employee business expense deduction for depreciation* (¶310): If the employee business expense deduction claimed federally included depreciation of assets placed in service prior to 1987, the depreciation component is recomputed for California purposes because business property was depreciated under a different method for California and federal purposes prior to 1987. For taxable years beginning after 2002 and before 2011, federal law allows taxpayers to currently expense higher amounts under IRC Sec. 179 than is allowed under California law. Also, if the maximum IRC Sec. 179 deduction was taken for property placed in service in tax years beginning after 1992 and before 1999, the federal and California amounts will differ (¶311). Finally, differences will result if a taxpayer claimed the additional 30%/50% first-year bonus depreciation deduction that was available for federal, but not California, purposes for qualified property purchased after September 10, 2001, but before 2005, or for purchases of qualified New York Liberty Zone property (¶310). Additional differences may arise as a result of the shortened federal recovery periods for leasehold, restaurant property, and retail improvement property and the accelerated write-off allowed on the federal return for qualified property located in a renewal community. All these differences must be accounted for in computing California's deduction.

— *Adoption-related expenses* (¶139): California allows a credit for specified adoption-related expenses. If the taxpayer claims the California adoption costs credit for the same amounts deducted on the federal Schedule A, these amounts must be subtracted on California Schedule CA (540).

— *Investment interest expense* (¶305): This item is generally treated the same for California as for federal purposes. However, taxpayers filing federal Form 4952 must file the corresponding California FTB 3526. Differences, if any, are reported on Schedule CA (540). Differences may occur because of the capital gain component in computing pre-1987 investment interest expense; the pre-1987 holding period and taxable percentages of capital gains were different under California law.

— *Federal mortgage interest credit:* California does not have a credit comparable to the federal mortgage interest credit. If federal miscellaneous itemized deductions on Schedule A were reduced by the amount of this credit, California itemized deductions may be increased by the same amount on Schedule CA (540).

— *Limitation for high-income taxpayers* (¶303): The itemized deductions of taxpayers with adjusted gross incomes over a threshold amount must be reduced by the lesser of (1) 6% (3% under federal law) of the excess of adjusted gross income over the threshold amount or (2) 80% of the amount of the itemized deductions otherwise allowable for the tax year. A worksheet is provided in the Schedule CA (540) Instructions for calculation of the adjustment.

— *Federal estate and generation-skipping transfer taxes:* California does not allow deductions for federal tax paid on income with respect to a decedent or for tax paid on generation-skipping transfers. Accordingly, amounts deducted on federal Schedule A for these items must be subtracted on California Schedule CA (540).

— *Legislators' travel expenses* (¶301): California does not follow the federal rule allowing legislators to deduct expenses for every legislative day. California allows legislators to deduct only those expenses incurred on days that the legislators are actually away from their districts overnight. Amounts deducted for federal purposes on Schedule A that do not qualify for California purposes must be subtracted from federal itemized deductions.

— *Interest on public utility-financed loans for energy conservation* (¶305): California allows taxpayers to claim a deduction, not subject to the 2% floor limit, for interest on public utility-financed loans used to obtain energy efficient equipment for California residences.

— *Charitable contributions* (¶321): California has not adopted post-2004 federal amendments. Consequently differences may arise in the treatment of contributions as a result of California's nonconformity with these amendments.

¶32 Tax Rates

California Forms: Sch. P (540) (Alternative Minimum Tax and Credit Limitations - Residents), Sch. G-1 (Tax on Lump-Sum Distributions), FTB 3800 (Tax Computation for Children Under Age 14 with Investment Income), FTB 3803 (Parents' Election to Report Child's Interest and Dividends), FTB 3805P (Additional Taxes on Qualified Plans (Including IRAs) and Other Tax-Favored Accounts).

The tax rates are progressive, ranging from 1% to 9.3% of taxable income (¶116). The tax tables are reproduced at ¶3. The tax rate schedules are reproduced at ¶1. An additional tax is also imposed on the portion of a taxpayer's income in excess of $1 million (¶116).

• *Alternative minimum tax*

The California alternative minimum tax is imposed at the rate of 7%. It is generally calculated in the same manner as for federal purposes, but there are differences (¶117).

The California AMT is computed on Schedule P (540).

California incorporates the IRC Sec. 53 credit for "prior year minimum tax" (¶33).

• *Tax on premature distributions of IRAs, Keogh plans, annuities, and life insurance contracts*

Both California and federal law impose a penalty tax on premature distributions from IRAs, Keogh plans, other self-employed plans, annuity plans, and "modified endowment contracts," to the extent the distribution is included in income (¶206). The amount of the premature distribution includible in income for California purposes may differ from that allowed federally because of differences in deductibility of contributions in pre-1987 tax years and because California, but not federal law, treats rollovers from an IRA to a health savings account as a premature distribution (¶206, ¶330).

The California penalty is 2.5%.

Form FTB 3805P is used to make the computation.

• *Tax on nonqualified distributions from educational savings accounts*

Both California and federal law impose a penalty tax on distributions from Coverdell education savings accounts and qualified tuition programs that are not used for qualified educational expenses (¶206, 250). The California penalty is 2.5% and is reported on FTB 3805P.

• *Tax on nonexempt withdrawals from medical savings accounts*

Distributions from a medical savings account for nonmedical purposes are subject to a 10% penalty tax (15% under federal law). California law, unlike federal law, imposes the penalty on rollovers from medical savings accounts to health savings accounts. For further information see ¶247. Form FTB 3805P is used to make the computation.

• *Separate tax on lump-sum distributions*

Taxpayers with lump-sum distributions of retirement income compute and pay a separate tax on these distributions if they elected to pay the separate federal tax (¶206). The California tax, which is computed on Schedule G-1, is determined under the same rules as the federal tax. The tax is transferred from Schedule G-1 to Form 540 and is added to the regular tax.

• *Tax on minor child's unearned income ("kiddie tax")*

California incorporates the federal "kiddie tax" provisions prior to amendment by the Tax Increase Prevention and Reconciliation Act of 2005, the Small Business and Work Opportunity Tax Act of 2007, and the Emergency Economic Stabilization Act of 2008, applicable when a child who is not yet 14 by the close of the tax year and who has a parent living at such time has unearned income in excess of $1,800 (¶118). The tax is computed on FTB 3800, which parallels federal Form 8615.

Under certain circumstances, a parent may elect to include the unearned income of a child on the parent's return. If the parent elects to exercise this option, FTB 3803 must accompany the parent's return.

• *Tax rates for servicemembers domiciled outside California*

Military compensation of servicemembers domiciled outside California, and their spouses, may not be included in gross income for purposes of determining the tax rate on nonmilitary income; see ¶225.

¶33 Credits Against the Tax

California Forms: Form 540 (California Resident Income Tax Return), Form 540A (California Resident Income Tax Return), Sch. P (540) (Alternative Minimum Tax and Credit Limitations - Residents), Sch. S (Other State Tax Credit), FTB 3501 (Employer Child Care Program/Contribution Credit), FTB 3506 (Child and Dependent Care Expenses Credit), FTB 3507 (Prison Inmate Labor Credit), FTB 3508 (Solar Energy System Credit), FTB 3510 (Credit for Prior Year Alternative Minimum Tax - Individuals or Fiduciaries), FTB 3521 (Low Income Housing Credit), FTB 3523 (Research Credit), FTB 3540 (Credit Carryover Summary), FTB 3546 (Enhanced Oil Recovery Credit), FTB 3547 (Donated Agricultural Products Transportation Credit), FTB 3548 (Disabled Access Credit for Eligible Small Businesses), FTB 3553 (Enterprise Zone Employee Credit), FTB 3805Z (Enterprise Zone Deduction and Credit Summary), FTB 3807 (Local Agency Military Base Recovery Area Deduction and Credit Summary), FTB 3808 (Manufacturing Enhancement Area Credit Summary), FTB 3809 (Targeted Tax Area Deduction and Credit Summary).

The order of using the various tax credits is specified in the instructions to the California 540 return, with each credit identified by a code number. If there are more than three credits claimed, the taxpayer must attach the appropriate credit form and summarize each credit on California Schedule P (540).

Business credits and business credit carryovers that may be claimed by taxpayers are limited to 50% of a taxpayer's tax during the 2008 and 2009 tax years, see ¶125.

The following is a brief description of the allowable credits:

1. **Child care expense credits** (¶125): Tax credits are allowed for employers who construct child care facilities, establish child care programs, contribute to child care information and referral services, or contribute to qualified child care plans. These credits are claimed on Form 3501. Unused credit may be carried over until exhausted.

2. **Renter's credit** (¶133): A nonrefundable credit is available to qualified renters. For the 2008 taxable year, the amount of the credit is (1) $120 for married couples and registered domestic partners filing joint returns, heads of households, and surviving spouses, provided adjusted gross income is $69,872 or less, and (2) $60 for other individuals, provided adjusted gross income is $34,936 or less. Unused credits may not be carried over.

3. **Joint custody head-of-household, dependent parent credits** (¶136): For the 2008 taxable year, these credits, which cover both dependent children and dependent parents, equal the lesser of 30% of the California tax liability or $393. A worksheet is provided in the Instructions to Form 540 for computation purposes. Qualifications that must be met in order to claim the credits are discussed at ¶136. Unused credit may not be carried over.

4. **Research and development credit** (¶150): California generally allows the federal credit for increasing research activities with the following changes:

— the California credit is available indefinitely, whereas the federal credit does not apply to amounts paid or incurred after 2009;

— research must be conducted within California to qualify;

— the applicable California credit percentage is 15% of the excess of qualified research expenses for the tax year over the "base amount";

— California modifies the formula used by those taxpayers that elect to compute the amount of the credit using an alternative method;

— California has not conformed to post-2004 federal amendments that authorize the use of a third method, the alternative simplified credit, generally effective for federal purposes in tax years ending after 2006, and that repeal the alternative incremental method for tax years beginning after 2008;

— California does not allow a credit against personal income tax for basic research payments;

— California limits the "gross receipts" that may be taken into account for purposes of calculating the base amount;

— the California credit may be carried over while the federal credit is part of the general business credit subject to the limitations of IRC Sec. 38;

— California law disallows the credit for expenses incurred to purchase property for which a sales and use tax exemption for teleproduction or other postproduction property is claimed;

— California does not incorporate post-2004 federal amendments that allow a taxpayer to claim 20% of amounts paid or incurred by the taxpayer during the tax year to an energy research consortium and that repeal the limitation on contract research expenses paid to eligible small businesses, universities and federal laboratories for qualified energy research; and

— California did not incorporate the federal suspension periods of July 1, 1999—September 30, 2000, and October 1, 2000—September 30, 2001, that were enacted by the Tax Relief Extension Act of 1999.

A married couple or registered domestic partnership filing separately has the option of one spouse or partner taking the full credit or of dividing it equally between them.

FTB 3523 is used to compute the credit. Unused credit from nonpassive activities may be carried over until exhausted.

5. **Credit for income taxes paid to other states** (¶128): A credit is allowed for income taxes paid to certain states and possessions, but no credit is allowed for income taxes paid to any city, the federal government, or a foreign country. A list of the states and possessions for which the credit is allowed appears at ¶128.

The credit for income taxes paid to other states is available only for net income taxes (excluding any kind of alternative minimum tax or other tax on preference items) paid to another state on income with its source in the other state that is also taxed by California. The latter requirement rules out the credit for tax paid on income from intangible property because such income is deemed under California law to be attributable to California as the state of residence. The amount of the credit is limited to that proportion of the total California tax payable as the double-taxed income bears to the total income taxed by California.

Schedule S, showing computation of the credit, must be attached to the California return along with a copy of the other state's tax return.

There is no carryover of this credit.

6. **Excess state disability insurance credit** (¶132): Excess employee contributions for California disability insurance are treated as a refundable income tax credit. For 2008, the credit amount is the amount contributed in excess of $693.58. Excess contributions may occur when a taxpayer works for more than one employer during the tax year. The amount of the credit is calculated on a worksheet included in the Instructions to Form 540.

Note: If more than the maximum was withheld by a single employer, or at a higher rate, the excess amount must be claimed as a refund from the employer rather than as a tax credit.

7. **Personal exemption credits** (¶113): Credits are allowed for personal and dependency exemptions (¶28).

8. **Disabled access expenditures credit** (¶140): California allows eligible small businesses a credit for 50% of up to $250 of the disabled access expenditures paid or incurred by those businesses to comply with the federal Americans with Disabilities Act. Except for the amount, the credit is similar to the federal credit allowed under IRC Sec. 44. The credit is computed on FTB 3548. Unused credit may be carried over until exhausted.

9. **Farmworker housing credit** (¶137): Prior to the 2009 taxable year, California allows a nonrefundable credit for the lesser of (1) up to 50% of qualified amounts paid or incurred for the construction or rehabilitation of farmworker housing in California or (2) the amount certified by the Tax Credit Allocation Committee. Unused credit may be carried over until exhausted.

10. **Low-income housing credit** (¶138): California allows a low-income housing credit for owners of residential rental projects that provide low-income housing located in California. The credit is similar to the federal credit computed under IRC Sec. 42, but also provides a set-aside for promotion of farmworker housing projects for taxable years after 2008. The California Tax Credit Allocation Committee certifies to the taxpayer on Form 3521A the amount of the credit for each year in the credit period.

The credit is computed on FTB 3521. A copy of Form 3521A must be provided to the FTB upon request. Unused credit may be carried over until exhausted.

11. **Enterprise zone credit for wages earned** (¶146): The California credit is 5% of qualified wages received from an enterprise zone business. For each dollar of income in excess of qualified wages, the credit is reduced by 9¢. The credit is nonrefundable. There is no carryover of unused credits. Designated zones are listed at ¶104.

FTB 3553 is used to calculate the amount of the credit.

12. **Enterprise zone hiring and sales tax credits** (¶144 , 145): The amount of the California hiring credit is 50% of qualified wages paid to a qualified employee in his or her first year of employment, 40% in the second year, 30% in the third year, 20% in the fourth year, and 10% in the fifth year. The credit is limited to tax attributable to income from the enterprise zone. An employer's deduction for salaries and wages must be offset by the amount of the credit. California enterprise zones are listed at ¶104 as well as in FTB 3805Z. Unused amounts may be carried over.

The amount of sales or use tax paid on the purchase of machinery or parts used in an enterprise zone may also be claimed as a credit against tax. Unused credit may be carried over to future years.

The enterprise zone credits are computed on FTB 3805Z. A separate FTB 3805Z must be attached to the taxpayer's return for each enterprise zone in which the business area invests.

13. **Local agency military base recovery area (LAMBRA) hiring and sales tax credits** (¶144, 147): Hiring and sales tax credits substantially similar to enterprise zone credits are available to qualified LAMBRA businesses.

The credits are computed on FTB 3807. The amount claimed by a taxpayer for both of the LAMBRA credits combined may not exceed the amount of tax attributable to LAMBRA income. Unused credit may be carried over to succeeding taxable years and applied to tax on income from the area.

14. **Targeted tax area hiring and sales and use tax credits** (¶144, 148): Tax credits are provided for employers who hire certain disadvantaged individuals within a targeted tax area. A tax credit is also available for businesses that purchase machinery or equipment to be used within the area. The credits are similar to those available to enterprise zone businesses and are computed on FTB 3809.

15. **Manufacturing enhancement area hiring credit** (¶149): A hiring credit substantially similar to the credit available to enterprise zone businesses may be claimed by qualified manufacturing enhancement area businesses. The credit is computed on FTB 3808.

16. **Credit for prior year minimum tax** (¶152): California incorporates the IRC Sec. 53 credit for alternative minimum tax paid in a prior year by a taxpayer who is not liable for the AMT in the current year. The credit is based on preference items that defer tax liability rather than permanently reduce the tax. The amount allowable as a credit in any tax year is limited to the regular California personal income tax for the year, less (a) the refundable credits that have no carryover provisions and (b) the credit for taxes paid to other states. Unused credit may be carried over. The credit is computed on FTB 3510.

17. **Enhanced oil recovery credit** (¶153): California allows certain independent oil producers an enhanced oil recovery credit equal to 1/3 of the federal credit allowed under IRC Sec. 43, provided the costs for which the credit is claimed are attributable to projects located within California. FTB 3546 is used to compute the credit. Unused credit may be carried forward for up to 15 years. The credit is not available during the 2008 taxable year.

18. **Senior head-of-household credit** (¶135): A credit is available to qualified seniors. A worksheet to compute the credit is included in the Instructions to Form 540.

19. **Prison inmate labor credit** (¶154): A credit is available to employers for 10% of the wages paid to certain prison inmates. FTB 3507 is used to calculate the credit. There is no carryover of this credit.

20. **Adoption costs credit** (¶139): A credit is available for up to 50% of the costs directly related to the adoption of a U.S. citizen or legal resident minor child who was in the custody of a state or county public agency. A worksheet is provided in the Form 540 Instructions to compute the credit. Unused credit may be carried over until exhausted. The credit is similar to the federal credit allowed under IRC Sec. 23.

21. **Credit for costs of transporting donated agricultural products** (¶141): California allows a credit against net tax for 50% of the costs paid or incurred in connection with the transportation of agricultural products donated to nonprofit charitable organizations. FTB 3547 is used to compute the credit. Unused credit may be carried over until exhausted.

22. **Credit for community development investments** (¶156): For taxable years beginning before 2012, California allows a credit equal to 20% of each qualified deposit that is made into a community development financial institution and certified by the California Organized Investment Network.

23. **Natural heritage preservation credit** (¶143): Taxpayers may claim a nonrefundable credit equal to 55% of the fair market value of real property donated before July 1, 2008, for qualified conservation purposes to the California Resources Agency (CRA), a local government, or an exempt nonprofit land and water conservation organization designated by the CRA or a local government to accept donations.

24. **Household and dependent care expense credit** (¶142): A refundable credit for employment-related household and dependent care expenses is allowed in an amount that is a percentage of the allowable federal credit.

25. **Ultra-low sulfur diesel fuel production credit** (¶151): An environmental tax credit may be claimed for ultra-low sulfur diesel fuel produced by a qualified small refiner at a California facility. The credit is computed on FTB 3511.

• *Carryover credits*

Other credits for which carryovers may still exist (and the years for which they were available) include the following:

1. water conservation credit (1980—1982);
2. solar pump (agricultural) credit (1981—1983);
3. solar energy installation credit (1985—1988);
4. energy conservation credit (1981—1986);
5. ridesharing credits (1981—1986 and 1989—1995);
6. commercial solar energy credit (1987—1988);
7. political contributions credit (1987—1991);
8. residential rental and farm sales credit (1987—1991);
9. agricultural products credit (1989—1991);
10. orphan drug research credit (1987—1992);
11. qualified parent's infant care credit (1991—1993);
12. commercial solar electric system credit (1990—1993);
13. recycling equipment credit (1989—1995);
14. low-emission vehicle credit (1991—1995);
15. Los Angeles Revitalization Zone hiring and sales and use tax credits (1992—1997);

16. salmon and steelhead trout habitat credit (1995—1999);
17. manufacturers' investment credit (1994—2003);
18. joint strike fighter property credit (2001—2005);
19. joint strike fighter wage credit (2001—2005);
20. solar and wind energy systems credit (2001—2005); and
21. rice straw credit (1997-2007).

All of the above credit carryovers may be claimed on FTB 3540. See prior editions of the *Guidebook* for details about these credits.

¶34 When and Where to File and Pay Tax

The due date for filing California Form 540 and paying the tax is the same as the federal due date—April 15, 2009, for calendar-year taxpayers (¶108, 110). Returns made by fiscal year taxpayers are due on or before the 15th day of the fourth month after the close of the fiscal year. Returns made by mail are considered timely if properly addressed and postmarked on or before the due date.

Returns are filed with the Franchise Tax Board (FTB). However, the address to which they are sent differs depending on (1) whether an amount is due or a refund is expected and (2) the type of form used.

Refund requests made on Forms 540, 540A, 540 2EZ, 540NR (Long and Short), 540X, and 541 are sent to P.O. Box 942840, Sacramento, CA 94240-0002. Refund requests made on scannable Forms 540 and 540A are sent to P.O. Box 942840, Sacramento, CA 94240-0009.

Regular returns for which an amount is due are sent to P.O. Box 942867, Sacramento, CA 94267-0001. Scannable returns for which an amount is due are sent to P.O. Box 942867, Sacramento, CA 94267-0009. For all other forms, the appropriate address is noted on the return.

Checks or money orders should be made payable to the "Franchise Tax Board" with the taxpayer's social security number written on the check or money order.

• *E-file*

The FTB also accepts electronic filing of returns through the e-file program. Tax return preparers who prepare and file more than 100 timely original California personal income tax returns during any calendar year and who prepare at least one personal income tax return using tax preparation software in the current calendar year must file all personal income tax returns for the current calendar year and subsequent calendar years using electronic technology (unless the taxpayer elects to file a paper return). Detailed information concerning the mandatory e-file program is available at the FTB's Web site at http://www.ftb.ca.gov/professionals/efile/m_e_file.shtml.

• *Electronic payments*

Beginning with installments due after 2008, personal income taxpayers must make their tax payments electronically if their estimated personal income tax installment payment or extension request payment exceeds $20,000 or if their total annual post-2008 tax liability exceeds $80,000, see ¶110.

• *Military personnel*

The due date for returns by members of the armed forces is the same as for other taxpayers, except that it may be postponed in certain cases (*i.e.*, duty outside the United States, service in a combat zone) (¶109).

¶35 Extensions

California Forms: FTB 3519 (Payment Voucher for Automatic Extension for Individuals), FTB 3537 (Payment Voucher for Automatic Extension for Limited Liability Companies), FTB 3538 (Payment Voucher for Automatic Extension for Limited Liability

Partnerships, LLPs, and REMICs), FTB 3563 (Payment Voucher for Automatic Extension for Fiduciaries).

The Franchise Tax Board (FTB) will allow an automatic six-month extension to file if the return is filed within six months of the original due date. No written request is required. The automatic extension does not extend the time for paying the tax. Tax payments must be accompanied by the appropriate form: FTB 3519 (Payment Voucher for Automatic Extension for Individuals); FTB 3537 (Payment Voucher for Automatic Extension for Limited Liability Companies); FTB 3538 (Payment Voucher for Automatic Extension for Limited Partnerships, LLPs, and REMICS); or FTB 3563 (Payment Voucher for Automatic Extension for Fiduciaries).

Taxpayers should send FTB 3519 or FTB 3563 to the FTB at P.O. Box 942867, Sacramento, CA 94267-0051. FTB 3537 and FTB 3538 are sent to the FTB at P.O. Box 942857, Sacramento, CA 94257-0651.

Payment extensions may be granted for a reasonable period by the FTB (¶110). There is no prescribed form. Extensions of up to one year are also available to disaster victims or victims of terroristic or militaristic actions (¶110).

Taxpayers abroad: Taxpayers who are outside the United States on the return due date are automatically granted an additional two-month extension of time to file (¶109). Consequently, the extended due date for such taxpayers is December 15. However, interest accrues on any unpaid tax from the original due date of the return. Any additional extensions must be applied for in writing with a letter of explanation.

¶36 Estimated Tax

California Forms: 540-ES (Estimated Tax for Individuals).

For the 2009 taxable year, estimated tax payments are generally due if (1) the 2008 or 2009 California tax (less withholding and allowable credits) exceeds $500 ($250 for married persons filing separately) or (2) more than 10% of the taxpayer's 2008 or 2009 tax will not be paid by withholding. Prior to the 2009 taxable year, the estimated tax payment threshold was $200 ($100 for married persons filing separately).

The California alternative minimum tax (¶32) is included in determining any required estimated tax payments.

Estimated tax is paid in quarterly installments on the same dates as federal payments: April 15, June 15, September 15, and January 15. The January 15 installment need not be made if the taxpayer files a tax return and pays the balance of tax due by February 1. When a due date falls on a Saturday, Sunday, or other legal holiday, payments are due on the next business day.

Generally, each payment is based on 25% of net income, multiplied by the applicable estimated tax rate. However, applicable to installments due for each taxable year beginning after 2008, the amount due is increased to 30% of estimated tax for the first and second installments and decreased to 20% of estimated tax for the third and fourth installments, see ¶111.

Married couples and registered domestic partners (RDPs) may file separate or joint estimated tax payment vouchers, but no joint Form 540-ES can be made if the spouses/RDPs have different tax years or are legally separated.

Form 540-ES is used for paying estimated tax.

¶37 State Tax Assistance

The Franchise Tax Board (FTB) offers various taxpayer assistance programs ranging from providing trained volunteers to assist taxpayers at no cost in completing their tax returns to in-state toll-free telephone assistance. The toll-free numbers are included in the Instructions to Form 540.

In addition, the FTB has several district offices located in principal cities throughout the state. These offices and their addresses are printed in the 540 Instruction booklet.

CCH Comment: ReadyReturn Program

Under the ReadyReturn program, the FTB will complete a qualified personal income taxpayer's return utilizing withholding and wage information received from employers. Taxpayers may then accept the calculation and sign the completed return or elect to complete their own return.

¶38 Forms

Forms may be ordered directly from the state at the following address:

Franchise Tax Board
Tax Forms Development and Distribution Unit
P.O. Box 1468
Sacramento, CA 95812-1468

California income tax forms and publications may also be downloaded from the Internet or obtained through automated telephones. The Internet address and telephone numbers are listed in the Form 540 Instruction booklet.

¶39 Interest

The California rate of interest on underpayments and overpayments of tax is based on the federal underpayment rate (¶711). The interest rate is redetermined semiannually and is as follows:

January 1, 2006—June 30, 2006	6%
July 1, 2006—December 31, 2006	7%
January 1, 2007—June 30, 2007	8%
July 1, 2007—December 31, 2007	8%
January 1, 2008—June 30, 2008	8%
July 1, 2008—December 31, 2008	7%
January 1, 2009—June 30, 2009	5%

¶40 Penalties

A penalty of 5% per month, up to a maximum of 25%, is imposed for failure without reasonable cause to file a return. If the failure to file is fraudulent, the penalty is 15% per month, up to a maximum of 75%.

The penalty for failure to pay income tax when it is due is 5% of the unpaid amount plus 1/2% per month. If the penalties for failure to file and failure to pay are both applicable, the penalty imposed is the higher of (1) the penalty for failure to pay or (2) the total of the penalty for failure to file and the penalty for failure to furnish information.

A minimum penalty of the lesser of $100 or 100% of the tax liability is imposed if the return is not filed within 60 days of the due date.

Other penalties are discussed at ¶712.

NONRESIDENTS AND PART-YEAR RESIDENTS:

PREPARING RETURN FORM 540NR

¶60 How Nonresidents Are Taxed

Nonresidents compute California tax as if they were California residents, then the applicable tax rate is applied to the nonresident's California-source taxable income (¶116).

The computation of taxable income on a nonresident return (Form 540NR) begins with federal adjusted gross income (AGI). Modifications (¶67) are made for law differences, then modified itemized deductions (¶68) or the standard deduction (¶65) are subtracted to arrive at "taxable income." Special rules apply to registered domestic partners (¶119).

After tax liability is determined, personal exemption and dependent exemption credits (¶64) are subtracted. The resulting amount is prorated to determine California tax liability. A nonresident's taxable income is multiplied by the ratio of (1) the tax on the nonresident's entire taxable income, computed as if the nonresident was a California resident for the taxable year and for all prior taxable years for purposes of any carryover items, deferred income, suspended losses, or suspended deductions over (2) the nonresident's total taxable income (¶116). Special rules apply to military compensation and income earned or received by Native Americans.

Further reduction to California tax is available by way of various other special credits (¶70).

Special California rate provisions (¶32) deal with

— the alternative minimum tax,

— the penalty or recapture tax on premature distributions of IRAs, Keogh plans, or other qualified retirement plans,

— the penalty on nonqualified distributions from Coverdell education savings accounts and qualified tuition programs,

— the penalty tax on nonexempt withdrawals from medical savings accounts,

— the separate tax on lump-sum distributions, and

— the tax on minor children's unearned income ("kiddie tax").

Paragraph references throughout are to explanations in the *Guidebook*. The CCH CALIFORNIA STATE TAX REPORTER should also be consulted for further details on any point.

¶61 How Part-Year Residents Are Taxed

A part-year resident is taxed on income received while residing in California and, except for retirement income received for services performed while residing in California (¶405), on income derived from sources in California during any period of nonresidency.

Computation of income for part-year residents, as for nonresidents, begins with federal adjusted gross income (AGI). Part-year residents use the same form (Form 540NR) as nonresidents and execute the same computational steps, as follows: California adjustments to federal AGI are made (¶67), followed by subtraction of modified itemized deductions (¶68) or the standard deduction (¶65). After tax liability is determined, personal exemption and dependent exemption credits are subtracted (¶64) and the result is prorated to determine California tax.

A part-year resident's taxable income is multiplied by the ratio of (1) the part-year resident's entire taxable income computed as if the part-year resident was a California resident for the taxable year and for all prior taxable years for purposes of any carryover items, deferred income, suspended losses, or suspended deductions over (2) the part-year resident's total taxable income; see ¶116. Different rules apply to military compensation.

Various other "special" credits reduce the California tax base. These special credits include prorated credits, credits that are taken in full, and carryover credits (¶70).

Special California rate provisions (¶32) deal with

— the alternative minimum tax,

— the penalty or recapture tax on premature distributions of IRAs, Keogh plans, or other qualified retirement plans,

— the penalty on nonqualified distributions from Coverdell education savings accounts and qualified tuition programs,

— the penalty tax on nonexempt withdrawals from medical savings accounts,

— the separate tax on lump-sum distributions, and

— the tax on minor children's unearned income ("kiddie tax").

Paragraph references throughout are to explanations in the *Guidebook*. The CCH CALIFORNIA STATE TAX REPORTER should also be consulted for further details on any tax point.

¶62 Return Filing Requirements

California Form: Form 540NR (California Nonresident or Part-Year Resident Income).

Nonresidents: Nonresident taxpayers must file California returns if they have income from California sources and at least the following federal gross or adjusted gross income amounts, which are the same as for residents (¶106):

2008 Filing Thresholds

On 12/31/08, the taxpayer's filing status was:	and on 12/31/08, the taxpayer's age was[6]:	California Gross Income[1]			California Adjusted Gross Income[2]		
		Dependents			Dependents		
		0	1	2 or more	0	1	2 or more
Single or Head of household[3]	Under 65	14,845	25,145	32,870	11,876	22,176	29,901
	65 or older	19,795	27,520	33,700	16,826	24,551	30,731
Married/RDP filing jointly or filing separately[4]	Under 65 (both spouses/RDPs)	29,690	39,990	47,715	23,752	34,052	41,777
	65 or older (one spouse/RDP)	34,640	42,365	48,545	28,702	36,427	42,607
	65 or older (both spouses/RDPs)	39,590	47,315	53,495	33,652	41,377	47,557
Qualifying widow(er)[3]	Under 65		25,145	32,870		22,176	29,901
	65 or older		27,520	33,700		24,551	30,731
Dependent of another person Any filing status	Any age	More than your standard deduction[5]					

[1] **California gross income** is all income received from all sources in the form of money, goods, property, and services that are not exempt from tax. Gross income does not include any adjustments or deductions.

[2] **California adjusted gross income** is federal adjusted gross income from all sources reduced or increased by all California income adjustments.

[3]See ¶15-320.

[4]The income of both spouses or registered domestic partners (RDPs) must be combined; both spouses or RDPs may be required to file a return even if only one spouse or RDP had income over the amounts listed.

[5]Use the California Standard Deduction Worksheet for Dependents in the 2007 California Resident Booklet to compute the standard deduction.

[6]If the taxpayer's 65th birthday is on January 1, 2009, she or he is considered to be age 65 on December 31, 2008.

Regardless of the above threshold amounts, a return must be filed for any tax liability of $1 or more. This may occur, for example, if California adjustments to federal income (*e.g.*, non-California municipal bond interest) cause California taxable income to be higher than federal.

For purposes of the filing thresholds (1) single persons include taxpayers filing as heads of households and qualifying widowers and (2) married couples or registered domestic partners include taxpayers filing either jointly or separately.

A "nonresident" is an individual who is not a resident. Case law dealing with the question of residency is found at ¶105.

Part-year residents: Part-year residents are subject to the same income filing-level requirements as nonresidents.

A "part-year resident" is informally defined as an individual who moves into or out of California during the taxable year.

• *Military personnel*

Nonresidents stationed in California under military orders are not considered residents. Consequently, their military pay is not subject to California taxation (¶105). However, servicepersons are taxed on all other income derived from California sources.

A California resident stationed outside California under permanent military orders is considered a nonresident.

The spouses of military personnel who come to California are California residents if they are here for other than "temporary or transitory purposes."

• *Attachment of federal return*

A copy of the taxpayer's federal return and all supporting documents must be attached to the Form 540NR.

¶63 Filing Status

Unmarried taxpayers: Single taxpayers are generally required to use their federal filing status. However, beginning with the 2007 taxable year, registered domestic partners must file California personal income tax returns jointly or separately by applying the same standards as are applied to married taxpayers under federal income tax law (see ¶114). Also see ¶114 for a discussion of the filing status for same-sex married couples.

Married taxpayers: If a husband and wife file a joint federal income tax return, one of the spouses was a California resident for the entire year, and the other spouse was a nonresident for all or any portion of the taxable year, a joint nonresident return (Form 540NR) must be filed. There are two exceptions to this rule. A couple filing a joint federal income tax return may file either separate returns or a single joint return in California if

— either spouse was an active member of the military during the taxable year or

— either spouse was a nonresident of California for the entire taxable year and had no income from a California source during the taxable year.

If one of these exceptions applies, the tax should be figured both jointly and separately to determine the more favorable status.

¶64 Personal and Dependent Exemptions

California provides tax credits for personal and dependent exemptions in lieu of deductions from income as provided under federal law (¶113).

The 2008 credit amounts are:

Single	$ 99
Married/registered domestic partner (RDP), separate return	99
Married/RDP, joint return	198
Head of household	99
Surviving spouse	198
Dependent	309
Visually impaired person (additional)	99
Elderly aged 65 and over (additional)	99

A doctor's statement verifying a visual impairment must be attached to the first 540NR return on which the exemption credit is claimed (Instructions to Form 540).

The exemption credits must be reduced for taxpayers whose federal adjusted gross income exceeds the threshold amounts specified for the taxpayer's filing status (¶113).

¶65 Standard Deduction

The election of a nonresident or part-year resident to itemize or to claim a standard deduction is independent of the federal election (¶303). Taxpayers may choose the more favorable tax treatment.

The California standard deduction amounts for 2008 are:

Filing status	*Amount*
Single	$3,692
Married/RDP, joint return	7,384
Married/RDP, separate return	3,692
Head of household	7,384
Surviving spouse	7,384

The above amounts are not increased (as under federal law) if the taxpayer is elderly or blind.

Individuals who can be claimed on another's tax return are limited to the greater of (1) $900 or (2) the amount of earned income plus $300.

See ¶335 for more details.

¶66 Income Attributable to California

California Form: Sch. CA (540NR) (California Adjustments - Nonresidents or Part-Year Residents).

Nonresidents: Nonresidents are generally taxed on California-source adjusted gross income (¶231).

Part-year residents: Generally, part-year residents must include in adjusted gross income (AGI) for California purposes income from all sources attributable to any part of the tax year during which they resided in California, and income from California sources for that portion of the year during which they resided elsewhere (¶231).

• *Attribution rules*

The rules of attribution for various types of income are discussed in the following paragraphs (see also ¶231). The details are reported on Schedule CA (540NR).

• *Income from trade or business*

Business income of a nonresident is attributed in full to California if the nonresident's trade or business is carried on entirely in California (¶231). On the other hand, if the nonresident's trade or business is conducted entirely outside of California, none of the income is attributed to California.

Where a trade or business is partly within California and partly in other states, the manner in which the income is attributed depends on the relationship of the segments of the taxpayer's business. If the California business activity is separate and distinct from that carried on elsewhere (*e.g.*, a California hotel but an out-of-state manufacturing activity), only the income from the California portion is reported to California. On the other hand, if the in-state and out-of-state portions are integral parts of a single trade or business (*i.e.*, "unitary"), business income is apportioned by a formula as discussed below.

The term "business income" means all income that arises from the conduct of the business operations of a taxpayer. Typically it includes those items reported on federal Schedules C or C-EZ. "Nonbusiness income" is all other income. Nonbusiness income is allocated, rather than apportioned, by rules described in the following paragraphs.

Formula: The apportionment formula prescribed is the same as the one generally used for the California corporation franchise tax: the average ratio of California property, payroll, and sales (double-weighted) to total property, payroll, and sales. For a discussion of formula apportionment and rules regarding its application, see Chapter 13 of the *Guidebook.*

• *Compensation for personal services*

Nonresidents: Nonresidents are taxed on compensation for personal services performed in California (¶231). The attribution rules for a number of specific occupations are as follows:

Salespersons: Nonresident salespersons determine the portion of commission income attributable to California by the ratio of sales volume in California to total sales volume.

Performers/athletes: Nonresident performers or athletes include gross amounts received for performances or athletic events in California.

Professionals: Fees received by nonresident professionals (*e.g.*, doctors, lawyers, accountants) for services performed in California are taxable.

Employees: Nonresident employees, excluding sales personnel, include total compensation for any period during which they are continuously employed in California.

Transportation workers: Nonresident transportation employees may prorate compensation on whatever basis is used by their employers to measure services. For example, proration may be based on the number of days worked or the number of miles traveled in California compared to days or miles everywhere. Federal law, incorporated by California, prohibits California from taxing income of certain interstate transportation workers; see ¶231 for details.

Part-year residents: All compensation received by part-year residents during the period of residency is taxable and attributed in full to California. Such income received during nonresidency is attributed under the rules applicable to nonresidents.

Military personnel: Federal law prohibits the taxation of military pay of nonresident servicemen while they are stationed in California, even though such income would be considered taxable to a nonresident under the regular rules (¶225). Also exempt from tax is pay of a nonresident military person that is attributed to a resident spouse by the community property laws.

Native Americans: Federal law prohibits the taxation of specified income received by Native Americans from Indian country sources (¶254).

• *Interest, dividend, rent, and royalty income*

Nonresidents: A nonresident's income from interest or dividends that is not related to a trade or business is not taxed by California unless the nonresident buys the stock or obligations in California or places orders with brokers in California so regularly as to constitute doing business, in which case the income is California-source AGI and must be reported in full (¶231). Special rules apply for purposes of determining whether a nonresident's interest and dividends from qualifying investment securities are California-source income (¶231).

Royalty income from intangibles such as patents or franchises is taxable only if the intangible has a business situs in California. A business situs in California is established when (1) the property is employed as capital or (2) control of the property is localized in connection with a business in California so that its use becomes an asset of the business.

Rental income received by a nonresident from real estate or from tangible personal property located in California is California-source AGI regardless of whether it is related to a trade or business.

The source of gains and losses from the sale or other disposition of intangible personal property is determined at the time of the sale or disposition of that property.

Part-year residents: All income, of whatever kind, received by part-year residents during the period of residency is taxable and allocable to California. Such income received during nonresidency is attributed under the rules applicable to nonresidents.

• *Pensions and annuities*

Nonresidents: Nonresidents' retirement income is not subject to California income tax even if the income is received for services performed in California (¶231, 405).

Part-year residents: Part-year residents who move into California are taxed on pension income from non-California sources received after the taxpayer becomes a California resident. Part-year residents who move out of California are subject to California income tax only on their retirement income received during the period of their California residency (¶405).

• *Gains or losses from disposition of property*

Nonresidents: Gain or loss from the sale of real or tangible personal property in California is California-source income whether or not related to business activities (¶231).

Gain or loss from stock and bond sales made by a nonresident is not attributable to California unless the nonresident buys such property in California or places orders in California so regularly so as to constitute doing business in California, in which case the profits from such transactions would be considered California-source income. Special rules apply for purposes of determining whether gain or loss from the sale of qualifying investment securities by a nonresident is California-source income (¶231).

Part-year residents: Gains and losses derived from any source during the period of residency are California-source income to part-year residents. Such income received during nonresidency is attributed under the rules applicable to nonresidents.

• *Income from trusts and estates*

Nonresidents: The information needed to complete the beneficiary's 540NR return, including the portion attributable to California and the character of each item, is shown on Schedule K-1 (Form 541).

A nonresident beneficiary is taxed on the portion of the beneficiary's distributive share of the trust's or estate's modified federal taxable income from sources in California (¶605). Income or loss has the same character when passed through to a beneficiary as it had to the trust or estate. Dividends and interest from estate or trust stocks and bonds is not income from sources within the state and is not taxable to a nonresident unless the property is used by the estate or trust so as to acquire a business situs in California. The source of a nonresident's income from other trust or estate property that has not acquired a business situs in the state is determined by the fiduciaries under the general rules for allocation and apportionment (see Chapter 13).

Part-year residents: The information needed to complete the beneficiary's 540NR return, including the portion attributable to California and the character of each item, is shown on Schedule K-1 (Form 541).

A part-year resident beneficiary's distributive share of certain trust income is taxed based on the beneficiary's period of residency and nonresidency during the trust's taxable year (¶605). The allocation of income between the period of residency and the period of nonresidency must be made in a manner that reflects the actual date of realization. In the absence of information that reflects the actual date of realization, the annual amount of trust income must be allocated on a proportional basis between the two periods, using a daily pro rata method. Income or loss has the same character when passed through to the beneficiaries as it had to the trust or estate.

Part-year residents qualify for a credit for tax paid to other states on their income from trusts or estates that is also taxed by California (¶130).

• *Income from partnerships and limited liability partnerships*

Nonresidents: The information needed to complete the partner's 540NR return is shown on Schedule K-1 (Form 565). Amounts allocated outside California are shown as differences between California income and income reported on the federal return.

Nonresident partners are taxed on the part of their distributive shares of partnership income or loss derived from California sources (¶619).

Nonresident partners qualify for a credit for tax paid to certain states of residence on partnership income that is also taxed by California (¶131).

Part-year residents: A part-year resident partner's distributive share of partnership income is taxed based on the partner's period of residency and nonresidency during the partnership's taxable year (¶619). The allocation of income between the period of residency and the period of nonresidency must be made in a manner that reflects the actual date of realization. In the absence of information that reflects the actual date of realization, the annual amount of partnership income must be allocated on a proportional basis between the two periods, using a daily pro rata method.

Part-year resident partners qualify for a credit for tax paid to other states on partnership income taxed by California (¶131).

• *Income from S corporations*

Nonresidents: Nonresidents apply the S corporation apportionment percentage to their distributive shares of S corporation income to determine their portion taxable to California. The percentage is reported on Schedule K-1 (Form 100S), which is sent to the shareholders by the S corporation.

Nonresidents qualify for a credit for taxes paid to certain states of residence on their S corporation income taxed by California (¶131).

Part-year residents: A part-year resident shareholder's distributive share of S corporation income is taxed based on the shareholder's period of residency and nonresidency during the S corporation's taxable year (¶233). The allocation of income between the period of residency and the period of nonresidency must be made in a manner that reflects the actual date of realization. In the absence of information that reflects the actual date of realization, the annual amount of S corporation income must be on a proportional basis between the two periods, using a daily pro rata method.

Part-year resident shareholders qualify for a credit for taxes paid to other states on S corporation income taxed by California (¶131).

• *Alimony income*

Alimony received by a part-year resident during the period of California residence is attributed to California.

Alimony paid by a California resident to a nonresident is not taxable to the recipient (¶204, ¶323). Alimony paid either by a nonresident or part-year resident during a period of nonresidency is deductible on a prorated basis equal to the ratio that California adjusted gross income for the entire year bears to the total adjusted gross income (computed without regard to the alimony deduction).

¶67 Modifications to Federal Adjusted Gross Income

California Forms: Sch. CA (540NR) (California Adjustments - Nonresidents or Part-Year Residents), Sch. D (Capital Gain and Loss), Sch. D-1 (Sales of Business Property), FTB 3801 (Passive Activity Loss Limitations), FTB 3805V (Net Operating Loss (NOL) Computation and NOL and Disaster Loss Limitations - Individuals, Estates, and Trusts), FTB 3805Z (Enterprise Zone Deduction and Credit Summary), FTB 3806 (Los Angeles Revitalization Zone Deduction and Credit Summary), FTB 3807 (Local Agency Military Base Recovery Area Deduction and Credit Summary), FTB 3808 (Manufacturing Enhancement Area Business Booklet), FTB 3809 (Targeted Tax Area Deduction and Credit Summary), FTB 3885A (Corporation Depreciation and Amortization).

Nonresidents and part-year residents make the following three kinds of California modification adjustments on Schedule CA (540NR):

(1) addition and subtraction modifications to federal adjusted gross income (AGI) to arrive at total adjusted gross income (AGI) from all sources using California law;

(2) adjustments to determine the portion of total AGI that is subject to California tax (either because it is California source income or because it is attributable to the taxpayer's period of residency); and

(3) adjustments to federal itemized deductions, should the taxpayer itemize for California purposes (¶68 for such adjustments).

The adjustments under (2), above, are computed in accordance with the rules for attributing income to California (¶66).

The most common adjustments under (1), above, are discussed in the following paragraphs. Other adjustments are discussed in FTB Pub. 1001, Supplemental Guidelines to California Adjustments.

Practice Note: Registered Domestic Partners and Same-Sex Married Couples

Registered domestic partners (RDPs) must make additional adjustments to reconcile the differences that arise from using a different filing status on their California tax returns than their federal income tax returns. These adjustments may be made by completing a pro forma federal return or by utilizing the worksheets provided in FTB Pub. 737, Tax Information for Registered Domestic Partnerships. For more information concerning RDPs, see the discussion at ¶119.

At the time this book went to press, the Franchise Tax Board had not made a determination as to the tax treatment of same-sex individuals who were married in California prior to the passage of Proposition 8, which repealed the right of same-sex individuals to legally marry, see ¶119 for details.

Interest on state obligations (¶217): Interest earned on bonds issued by states other than California or on obligations issued by municipalities of other states is taxed by California and is added back to federal AGI. State bond interest (other than from California obligations) that passes through from S corporations, trusts, partnerships, limited liability companies, and limited and mutual funds is also treated as an addition.

Interest paid by California in conjunction with the refund of the smog impact fee is deductible under California, but not federal, law if the taxpayer was not allowed to deduct the fee when it was paid (¶201).

Interest on federal obligations (¶217): Interest on federal obligations is tax-exempt and, consequently, is subtracted from federal AGI. See also ¶217 for the pass-through of tax-exempt interest from a mutual fund.

Interest income from Federal Farm Credit banks, Federal Home Loan banks, the Student Loan Marketing Association (SLMA), the Resolution Funding Corporation, the Production Credit Association, the Commodity Credit Corporation, Certificates of Accrual on Treasury Securities (CATS), and Treasury Investment Growth Receipts (TIGRS) is also exempt and is subtracted from federal adjusted gross income. However, interest from Fannie Maes, Ginnie Maes, or FHLMC securities is taxable by California and, therefore, no modification is made to federal adjusted gross income for interest from these instruments.

Childrens' interest and dividend income (¶217, ¶226): California law, unlike federal law, limits the election for parents to include interest and dividend income of children on the parents return to such income of children under the age of 14. Parents that included dividend and interest income of children between the ages of 14 and 19 (24 for qualified full-time students) on their federal return must subtract such income from the amount included in their federal AGI.

Depreciation (¶310): Because nonresidents and part-year residents, in computing their California tax liability on Form 540NR, first compute a taxable income figure in the same manner as full-year residents, they must make the same California depreciation modifications required of resident taxpayers, even for assets not located in California (¶310).

California depreciation is generally the same as federal (the "modified accelerated cost recovery system" under IRC Sec. 168) for assets placed in service after 1986. However, California does not conform to the IRC Sec. 168(k) bonus depreciation deduction for qualified property placed in service in 2008 and did not incorporate the additional 30%/50% first-year bonus depreciation for qualified property purchased after September 10, 2001, and before 2005. Nor does California incorporate the additional first-year bonus depreciation deduction allowed for qualified New York

Liberty Zone property or the accelerated write-off for qualified property utilized in a renewal community.

For taxable years beginning after 2002 and before 2011, and after 1992 and before 1999, the maximum allowable IRC Sec. 179 deduction for California purposes is lower than that allowed under federal law; see ¶311 for a detailed discussion. In addition, California does not conform to federal amendments that increase the amount at which the phase-out of the IRC Sec. 179 deduction begins and that allow the deduction to be claimed for off-the-shelf computer software.

California adopts the federal 39-year depreciation recovery period for nonresidential real property acquired after May 12, 1993, but only for property placed in service after 1996 in taxable years beginning after 1996. Thus, for California purposes, nonresidential real property placed in service before 1997 in taxable years beginning before 1997 continues to be depreciated over a 31.5-year recovery period.

California has also not conformed to post-2004 federal amendments that

— classify qualified leasehold improvements, qualified restaurant property, and qualified retail improvement property as 15-year recovery property and require the use of the straight-line method,

— provide special depreciation treatment for participations and residuals;

— revise the depreciation deduction for geological and geophysical expenses, electric transmission property, and natural gas lines;

— allow five-year amortization of expenses paid or incurred in creating or acquiring a musical composition or a copyright to a musical composition;

— require certain major integrated oil companies to amortize geological and geophysical expenditures over a five-year or seven-year period instead of a 24-month period;

— allow a 50% additional depreciation allowance for qualified cellulosic biomass ethanol and qualified cellulosic biofuel plant property;

— extend the shortened MACRS recovery periods for qualified Indian reservation property to apply to qualified property placed in service prior to 2010;

— provide shortened recovery periods for qualified smart electric meters and smart grid systems, qualified farming machinery and equipment, motorsports entertainment complexes, and young race horses; and

— ease the current expense allowance qualifying criteria for film production expenses.

Further differences in the amount of depreciation claimed for federal and California purposes may arise due to California provisions that allow taxpayers operating in specified depressed areas to claim accelerated write-offs for certain property (¶316) and federal provisions that allow accelerated write offs for small film production costs (¶310) and allow current deductions for reforestation expenditures (¶315).

Note: The differences between federal and California deductions are adjusted on FTB 3885A. The net adjustment may be an addition or a subtraction.

Capital gains and losses (¶523): California law, unlike federal law, treats all capital gains as ordinary income after 1986. In contrast, federal law subjects long-term capital gains to a lower tax rate.

Differences between the amount of capital gain or loss recognized for California and federal purposes can occur both in the year a gain or loss is recognized and in carryover years.

The following differences may occur for 2008 between the gain or loss recognized for federal and California purposes because

— California does not permit capital loss carrybacks (¶526);

— California, but not federal, law excludes gain on the sale or disposition of qualified assisted housing developments (¶505);

— California requires certain adjustments to basis not required by federal law and makes certain federal adjustments inapplicable (¶559);

— California has not incorporated federal law that limits the amount of long-term capital gain that a taxpayer can recognize from constructive ownership contracts involving pass-through entities (¶525);

— the basis may be different due to different depreciation deductions (¶310) or asset expense deductions (¶311); and

— California does not incorporate federal provisions that allow capital gains treatment for sales or exchanges of qualified musical compositions or copyrights in musical works (¶526).

Differences between pre-1987 California and federal laws that can affect the reporting of capital gain and loss include the following:

— A capital loss carryover may be different for California purposes than for federal purposes.

— The pre-1987 holding periods and taxable percentages of capital gains for California were different than federal.

— The California adjustment to capital gains computed for purposes of the investment interest expense deduction was different from the federal adjustment.

— For years prior to 1987, the federal 50% limitation on long-term capital loss deductions did not apply for California.

— Dividends from mutual funds were treated as ordinary income for California.

— Gain or loss may be reported in different tax years for California purposes because changes to the federal law affecting the computation of gain or loss were not generally adopted by California until subsequent years.

California Schedule D is used to calculate the differences, and the appropriate modification is carried to California Schedule CA (540NR).

— The California and federal basis of certain assets may be different at the time of disposition because of prior and current differences between California and federal law (¶542 and following). Examples of such situations are

(a) valuation of property acquired by inheritance (¶546),

(b) depreciation of business property (¶310, 311),

(c) basis adjustments for California and federal credits (¶144),

(d) basis of the stock of an S corporation (¶233), and

(e) basis adjustment of property for moves into California (¶504).

Calculation of capital gain and loss adjustments is made on California FTB 3885A.

State income tax refunds (¶201): Any California income tax refunds included in federal AGI are subtracted.

Unemployment compensation (¶201): The amount of unemployment compensation included on the federal return is subtracted from federal AGI.

Paid family leave (¶201): Paid family leave included on the federal return is not taxed by California and is subtracted from federal AGI.

Social Security benefits (¶201): The amount of Social Security benefits included in federal AGI is subtracted because California does not tax social security benefits.

Railroad retirement benefits, ridesharing benefits, and sick pay (¶205): Tier 1 and tier 2 railroad retirement benefits, including ridesharing benefits and sick pay, received under the Federal Insurance Contributions and Railroad Retirement Act are subtracted from federal AGI.

California lottery winnings (¶201): Any California lottery winnings included in federal AGI are subtracted.

IRA and Keogh distributions (¶330): The California and federal deductible dollar amounts are generally the same for post-1986 tax years. However, for pre-1987 tax years, the amounts differed; consequently, the amount taxable on a distribution will differ. Differences may also arise if the taxpayer changed residence during the time he or she made contributions to the IRA or Keogh plan.

A worksheet to compute differences in the tax treatment of distributions for federal and California purposes is included in FTB Pub. 1005, Pension and Annuity Guidelines.

Net operating loss (NOL) (¶309): With the exception of the suspension of the NOL deduction for California income tax purposes for losses incurred or carried over in 2008 and 2009 and the 2002 and 2003 taxable years, California's treatment of NOLs is like federal treatment except that prior to 2011 no carrybacks are allowed, and for losses incurred prior to 2004 the amount of loss eligible for carryover to future years is generally limited to a specified percentage of the net operating loss dependent on the year the loss was incurred. In addition, California limits NOL carrybacks for 2011 to 50% of the NOL and for 2012 to 75% of the NOl. Furthermore, applicable to NOLs incurred prior to the 2008 taxable year, a California NOL may be carried forward for only 10 years (five years for losses incurred prior to the 2000 taxable year) rather than the 20 years permitted under federal law (15 years for losses incurred in tax years beginning before August 6, 1997). Commencing with the 2008 taxable year, California NOLs may be carried over for 20 years. The NOL carryover period is extended for NOLs suspended during the 2008, 2009, 2002 and 2003 taxable years.

Special rules apply to taxpayers operating in enterprise zones, the former Los Angeles Revitalization Zone (LARZ), local agency military base recovery areas (LAMBRAs), or targeted tax areas. For taxable years beginning after 2000 and before 2003, special provisions also applied to farming businesses directly impacted by Pierce's disease.

Calculation of the California NOL is on FTB 3805V and the appropriate adjustment entered on California Schedule CA (540NR). The NOL for enterprise zone businesses is calculated on FTB 3805Z, for former LARZ businesses is calculated on FTB 3806, for LAMBRA businesses is calculated on FTB 3807, and for targeted tax area businesses is calculated on FTB 3809.

Recycling revenues (¶201): The income received by a taxpayer for recycling empty beverage containers is exempt for California purposes and is subtracted if included in federal adjusted gross income.

Expenses related to tax-exempt income (¶305): Expenses related to federally tax-exempt income that were disallowed as a deduction in computing federal AGI are subtracted for California. Expenses incurred to purchase or carry obligations that are tax-exempt under California but not federal law are added to federal AGI.

Note: These modifications, to the extent not business-related, are made to federal itemized deductions (¶68).

Income from exercising California qualified stock option (¶207): Compensation received from exercising a California qualified stock option is excluded from California gross income and may be subtracted if the compensation was included in federal AGI.

Ridesharing and employee commuter deductions (¶241): An exclusion from gross income is available to an employee for amounts received from his or her employer for qualifying ridesharing or commuter arrangements. Because California does not place a limit on the monthly benefits that may be excluded and allows for more excludable ridesharing/commuter options, a subtraction from federal AGI may be allowed.

Pensions and annuities (¶206): California rules for taxing pensions and annuities are the same as federal; however, the taxable amount may differ because of federal/California differences in the years when contributions were made. For further information see FTB Pub. 1005, Pension and Annuity Guidelines.

Passive activity loss (¶340): California generally adopts federal rules for computing the limitation on deducting passive activity losses. However, California does not conform to the passive activity loss rules relating to rental real estate losses suffered by certain taxpayers who materially participate in a real property trade or business. Differences may also exist because the amount of passive income and loss may differ. Taxpayers must segregate California adjustments that relate to passive-activity items from California adjustments that relate to nonpassive items. This calculation is made on FTB 3801, Passive Activity Loss Limitations.

Other gains or losses (¶537): Although California law on the computation of gain from sales of business property and certain involuntary conversions is the same as federal, the amount of gain or loss may differ because of federal/California basis differences. These amounts are reported on Schedule D-1.

Other adjustments may arise as a result of transfers between same-sex spouses and registered domestic partners, in which no gain is recognized for California purposes. Federal law requires that gain or loss be recognized in such transactions, see ¶502.

Alimony (¶204): Alimony received by a nonresident alien that was not included in the taxpayer's federal gross income is treated as an addition on Schedule CA (540).

Income from specially treated sources: See the indicated paragraphs for possible federal/California differences in the taxation of the following items: (1) noncash patronage dividends from farmers' cooperatives or mutual associations (¶232); and (2) interest income from investment in enterprise zones (¶240).

Claim of right adjustment (¶415): A claim of right adjustment may be claimed as either a deduction or a credit. A taxpayer that claims a credit for repayment amount on his or her federal return may claim a deduction on his or her California personal income tax return. Deductions of $3,000 or less are subject to the 2% floor for miscellaneous itemized deductions. A taxpayer that claims a deduction on his or her federal return, may claim a credit for the repayment amount on his or her California personal income tax return. Nonresidents may only claim an adjustment for income that was attributable to California sources.

Income from S corporations (¶66, 233): Nonresident shareholders of California S corporations add or subtract, as appropriate, the difference between their distributive shares of federal and California S corporation income or loss.

Income from partnerships and limited liability partnerships (¶66, 616, 623): Partners add or subtract, as appropriate, the difference between their distributive shares of federal and California partnership income or loss.

Income from limited liability companies (¶625): Members and persons with economic interests in an LLC add or subtract, as appropriate, the difference between their shares of federal and California LLC income in the same manner as partners must include their distributive shares of partnership income in their taxable income.

Income from trusts and estates (¶66, 605): Trust or estate beneficiaries add or subtract, as appropriate, the difference between their shares of federal and California trust or estate income or loss.

Business expenses incurred in discriminatory clubs (¶301, 336): California prohibits a business expense deduction for expenditures at a club which restricts membership or use on the basis of age, sex, race, religion, color, ancestry, national origin, or beginning with the 2008 taxable year, ethnic group identification, sexual orientation, or disability. There is no similar federal prohibition.

Wages (¶201): If there is a difference in wages because of an employee's fringe benefits, also reported on the W-2, an adjustment must be made because California does not adopt the federal rules; the amount of federal wages reported on the W-2 is subtracted and the amount reported as California wages is added.

Crime hotline rewards (¶246): Any rewards received from a government authorized crime hotline are excluded from gross income.

Water conservation rebates/vouchers (¶244): California excludes from gross income specified water conservation rebates/vouchers received from local water and energy agencies or suppliers.

Conservation and environmental cost-share payments (¶243): Certain cost-share payments received by forest landowners from the Department of Forestry and Fire Protection are subtracted from federal gross income.

Reparation payments (¶248): An exclusion is available for amounts received as reparation payments for individuals who were required to perform forced or slave labor during World War II, Canadian reparation payments made to individuals of Japanese ancestry interned during World War II, and Armenian genocide settlement payments.

Wrongful conviction compensation (¶201): Amounts paid by the state of California to compensate an individual for wrongful conviction and incarceration are subtracted from federal AGI.

Energy-efficient home improvement grants (¶245): Energy-efficient home improvement grants awarded by the State Energy Resources Conservation and Development Commission to low-income individuals are subtracted from federal AGI.

Medical expenses (¶219, 301, 325): California taxpayers may subtract from federal AGI amounts received from employer-provided accident, health insurance, and medical expense reimbursements and self-employed health insurance payments associated with expenses for the taxpayer's registered domestic partner (RDP) and the RDP's dependents.

Health savings accounts (¶246, 326): California does not recognize health savings accounts. Amounts deducted on a taxpayer's federal return should be added back to federal AGI.

Energy efficient commercial building costs (¶345): California does not incorporate federal law allowing taxpayers to currently deduct a portion of the costs of installing energy efficient systems in commercial buildings. Such amounts must be added back to federal AGI and an increased California depreciation deduction may be claimed.

Teacher expenses (¶202): Unreimbursed expenses incurred by eligible elementary and secondary school educators for books, supplies, equipment, and material used in the classroom, to the extent deductible under federal law, but not California law, are added back to federal AGI.

Tuition and education expenses (¶344): California requires an addition adjustment for qualified tuition and related expenses deducted on a taxpayer's federal income tax return.

Environmental remediation expenses (¶346): California requires an addition adjustment and depreciation adjustment for environmental remediation costs currently expensed on a taxpayer's federal return.

Qualified disaster expenses (¶347): California requires an addition adjustment and depreciation adjustment for qualified disaster costs currently expensed on a taxpayer's federal return.

¶68 Itemized Deductions

California Forms: Sch. CA (540NR) (California Adjustments - Nonresidents or Part-Year Residents), FTB 3526 (Investment Interest Expense Deduction), FTB 3885A (540NR) (Depreciation and Amortization).

California itemized deductions are based on federal itemized deductions shown on federal Schedule A, with the modifications discussed below. These modifications are independent of the adjustments to federal adjusted gross income (AGI) discussed at ¶67.

Practice Note: Registered Domestic Partners and Same-Sex Married Couples

Registered domestic partners (RDPs) must make additional modifications to reconcile the differences that arise from using a different filing status on their California tax returns than their federal income tax returns. These adjustments may be made by completing a pro forma federal return or by utilizing the worksheets provided in FTB Pub. 737, Tax Information for Registered Domestic Partnerships. For more information concerning RDPs, see the discussion at ¶119.

At the time this book went to press, the Franchise Tax Board had not made a determination as to the tax treatment of same-sex individuals who were married in California prior to the passage of Proposition 8, which repealed the right of same-sex individuals to legally marry, see ¶119 for details.

Taxpayers may elect either the standard deduction or itemized deductions for California purposes, regardless of which was elected for federal purposes (¶65). However, if itemized deductions are elected for California purposes, federal Schedule A must be attached to the California Form 540NR. The adjustments to federal itemized deductions are computed in Part III of California Schedule CA (540NR) ("California Adjustments—Nonresidents or Part-Year Residents").

The adjustments are as follows:

— *Taxes* (¶306): State, local, and foreign income taxes (including state disability insurance—"SDI"), sales and use taxes, federal estate tax, and generation-skipping transfer taxes claimed on federal Schedule A are not allowable deductions for California purposes and are subtracted from federal itemized deductions.

— *California Lottery losses* (¶336): California Lottery losses are not deductible for California purposes. The amount of such losses, as shown on federal Schedule A, must be subtracted from federal itemized deductions.

— *Federal obligation expense* (¶305): Because California does not tax interest from federal obligations, any expenses relating to such interest that have been deducted for federal purposes on Schedule A are subtracted from federal itemized deductions for California purposes.

— *State obligation expense* (¶305): Because, unlike federal law, California taxes interest from state or local obligations of states, other than California, any expenses related to this interest that were not entered on federal Schedule A should be added to federal itemized deductions for California purposes.

— *Employee business expense deduction for depreciation* (¶310): If the employee business expense deduction claimed federally included depreciation of assets placed in service prior to 1987, the depreciation component is recomputed for California purposes because of California/federal differences in depreciation methods prior to 1987. For taxable years beginning after 2002 and before 2011, federal law allows taxpayers to currently expense higher amounts under IRC Sec. 179 than is allowed under California law (¶311). Finally, adjustments may be required if the taxpayer claimed the IRC Sec. 168(k) first-year bonus depreciation deduction on his or her tax return for property purchased during 2008 or after September 10, 2001, but before 2005, or for purchases of qualified New York

Liberty Zone property. Additional differences may arise as a result of the shortened recovery periods for leasehold, restaurant property, and retail improvement property and the accelerated write-off for qualified property used in a renewal community that are allowed under federal law. Use FTB 3885A for computing the differences.

— *Adoption-related expenses* (¶139): California allows a credit for specified adoption-related expenses. If the taxpayer claims the California adoption costs credit for amounts deducted on the federal Schedule A, these amounts must be subtracted on California Schedule CA (540NR).

— *Investment expense* (¶305): This item is generally treated the same as under federal law. Taxpayers filing federal form 4952 must file the corresponding California FTB 3526. Differences, if any, are reported on Schedule CA (540NR). Differences may occur because of the capital gain component in computing pre-1987 investment interest expense; the pre-1987 holding period and taxable percentages of capital gains were different under California law (¶525).

— *Limitation for high-income taxpayers* (¶303): The itemized deductions of taxpayers with adjusted gross incomes over a threshold amount must be reduced by the lesser of (1) 6% (3% under federal law) of the excess of adjusted gross income over the threshold amount or (2) 80% of the amount of the itemized deductions otherwise allowable for the tax year. A worksheet is provided in the Schedule CA (540NR) Instructions to calculate the adjustment.

— *Federal mortgage interest credit:* California does not have a credit comparable to the federal mortgage interest credit. If federal miscellaneous itemized deductions on Schedule A were reduced by the amount of this credit, California itemized deductions may be increased by the same amount on Schedule CA (540NR).

— *Legislators' travel expenses* (¶301): California does not follow the federal rule allowing legislators to deduct expenses for every legislative day. California allows legislators to deduct only those expenses incurred on days that they are actually away from their districts overnight. Amounts deducted for federal purposes on Schedule A that do not qualify for California purposes must be subtracted from federal itemized deductions.

— *Interest on public utility-financed loans for energy conservation* (¶305): California allows taxpayers to claim a deduction, not subject to the 2% floor limit, for interest on public utility-financed loans used to obtain energy-efficient equipment for California residences.

— *Charitable contributions* (¶321): California has not adopted post-2004 federal amendments to the charitable contributions deduction. Consequently, differences may arise in the treatment of contributions as a result of California's nonconformity with these amendments

¶69 Tax Rates

California Forms: Sch. G-1 (Tax on Lump-Sum Distributions), Sch. P (540NR) (Alternative Minimum Tax and Credit Limitations - Nonresidents or Part-Year Residents), FTB 3800 (Tax Computation for Children Under Age 14 with Investment Income), FTB 3803 (Parents' Election to Report Child's Interest and Dividends), FTB 3805P (Additional Taxes on Qualified Plans (Including IRAs) and Other Tax-Favored Accounts).

Nonresidents and part-year residents pay tax at rates applied to their total income (California income plus other income) of the taxpayer. The rates are progressive, ranging from 1% to 9.3% of taxable income. An additional 1% tax is also imposed on taxable income in excess of $1 million. Total tax is then prorated, for nonresidents and part-year residents, on the basis of California taxable income (¶116).

The tax tables are reproduced at ¶3. The tax rate schedules are reproduced at ¶1.

• *Alternative minimum tax*

Nonresidents and part-year residents are subject to the alternative minimum tax in the same manner as residents, except that the tax is computed on the basis of prorated taxable income (¶117).

The California alternative minimum tax is imposed at the rate of 7%. It is generally computed the same as for federal purposes, but there are differences (¶117). The alternative minimum tax is computed on Schedule P (540NR).

California incorporates the IRC Sec. 53 "credit for prior year minimum tax" (¶70).

• *Tax on premature distributions of retirement plans and life insurance plans*

Nonresidents and part-year residents are liable in the same manner as residents for the penalty or recapture tax on premature distributions from IRAs, Keogh plans, annuities, and "modified endowment contracts," to the extent the distribution is included in California-source income (¶206 , 405). The amount included for California purposes may differ from that required to be included federally because California, but not federal law, treats rollovers from an IRA to a health savings account as a premature distribution and because of differences in the deductibility of contributions in years prior to 1987.

The California penalty is 2.5%.

Form FTB 3805P is used to make the tax computation.

• *Tax on nonqualified distributions from educational savings accounts*

Both California and federal law impose a penalty tax on distributions from Coverdell education savings accounts and qualified tuition programs that are not used for qualified educational expenses (¶206, 250). The California penalty is 2.5% and is reported on FTB 3805P.

• *Tax on nonexempt withdrawals from medical savings accounts*

Distributions from a medical savings account for nonmedical purposes are subject to a 10% penalty tax (15% under federal law). California law, unlike federal law, imposes the penalty on rollovers from medical savings accounts to health savings accounts. For further information see ¶247. Form FTB 3805P is used to make the computation.

• *Separate tax on lump-sum distributions*

Nonresidents and part-year residents with lump-sum distributions of retirement income attributable to California sources compute and pay a separate tax on these distributions if they elected to pay the separate federal tax (¶206, 405). The California tax, which is computed on Schedule G-1, is determined under the same rules as the federal tax. The tax is transferred from Schedule G-1 to Form 540NR and is added to the prorated tax on total taxable income.

• *Tax on minor child's unearned income ("kiddie tax")*

California incorporates the federal "kiddie tax" provisions prior to their amendment by the Tax Increase Prevention and Reconciliation Act of 2005, the Small Business and Work Opportunity Tax Act of 2007, and the Emergency Economic Stabilization Act of 2008, that are applicable to a child who is not yet 14 by the close of the tax year and who has a parent living at such time has unearned income in excess of $1,800 (¶118). The tax is computed on FTB 3800, which parallels federal Form 8615. For nonresidents and part-year residents, the amounts needed to complete FTB 3800 come from the corresponding federal Form 8615 and from both the parent's and the child's Form 540NR (including California adjusted gross income amounts from Schedule CA (540NR). The tax is subject to proration.

Under certain circumstances, a parent may elect to include the unearned income of a child on the parent's return. If the parent elects to exercise this option, FTB 3803 must accompany the parent's return.

• *Tax rates for servicemembers domiciled outside California*

Military compensation of servicemembers domiciled outside California, and their spouses, may not be included in gross income for purposes of determining the tax rate on nonmilitary income; see ¶ 225.

¶70 Credits Against Tax

California Forms: Form 540NR (California Nonresident or Part-Year Resident Income Tax Return), Sch. P (540NR) (Alternative Minimum Tax and Credit Limitations - Nonresidents or Part-Year Residents), Sch. S (Other State Tax Credit), FTB 3501 (Employer Child Care Program/Contribution Credit), FTB 3507 (Prison Inmate Labor Credit), FTB 3508 (Solar Energy System Credit), FTB 3510 (Credit for Prior Year Alternative Minimum Tax - Individuals or Fiduciaries), FTB 3521 (Low Income Housing Credit), FTB 3523 (Research Credit), FTB 3540 (Credit Carryover Summary), FTB 3546 (Enhanced Oil Recovery Credit), FTB 3547 (Donated Agricultural Products Transportation Credit), FTB 3548 (Disabled Access Credit for Eligible Small Businesses), FTB 3553 (Enterprise Zone Employee Credit), FTB 3805Z (Enterprise Zone Deduction and Credit Summary), FTB 3807 (Local Agency Military Base Recovery Area Deduction and Credit Summary), FTB 3808 (Manufacturing Enhancement Area Credit Summary), FTB 3809 (Targeted Tax Area Deduction and Credit Summary).

Credits available to nonresidents and part-year residents are generally divided into the following two categories: (1) those that are prorated by the percentage of California taxable income to total taxable income; and (2) those that are taken in full because they are based upon a California transaction.

If there are more than three credits claimed, the taxpayer must attach the appropriate credit form and summarize them on California Schedule P (540NR).

Major credits are treated individually in the following paragraphs, and those credits that affect only a few taxpayers are treated together at the end of ¶ 70.

The amount of business credits and business credit carryovers that may be claimed by taxpayers are limited to 50% of a taxpayer's tax during the 2008 and 2009 tax years, see ¶ 125.

1. Exemption credits (¶ 113): Nonresidents and part-year residents are entitled to the same credits for personal or dependent exemptions as are residents. The amounts of these credits are at ¶ 64.

2. Child care expense credits (¶ 134): Tax credits are available to employers for a percentage of the costs of establishing child care programs or facilities, contributing to child care information and referral services, or contributing to qualified child care plans. These credits are computed on FTB 3501. Unused credit may be carried over until exhausted.

3. Renter's credit (¶ 133): Nonresidents cannot claim this credit.

Part-year residents who qualify for the credit are allowed a $^{1}/_{12}$ credit for each full month of California residence during the year.

4. Joint custody head-of-household, dependent parent credits (¶ 136): For the 2008 tax year, these credits, which cover both dependent children and dependent parents, equal the lesser of 30% of the California liability or $393. Qualifications that must be met in order to claim the credit are discussed at ¶ 136. A worksheet is provided in the Instructions to Form 540NR to compute the credit. There is no carryover of this credit.

5. Research and development credit (¶ 150): Nonresidents and part-year residents may generally take the same research and development credit as that provided by federal law, except the following:

— the California credit is available indefinitely, whereas the federal credit does not apply to amounts paid or incurred after 2009;

— research must be conducted in California to qualify;

— the applicable California credit percentage is 15% of the excess of qualified research expenses for the tax year over the "base amount;"

— California modifies the formula used by those taxpayers that elect to compute the amount of the credit using an alternative incremental method and has not conformed to the federal repeal of the alternative incremental method for taxable years beginning after 2008;

— California has not conformed to post-2004 federal amendments that authorize the use of a third method, the alternative simplified credit, generally effective for federal purposes in tax years ending after 2006;

— California does not allow a credit against personal income tax for basic research payments;

— California limits the "gross receipts" that may be taken into account for purposes of calculating the base amount;

— the California credit may be carried over, while the federal credit is part of the general business credit subject to the limitations of IRC Sec. 38.

— California disallows the credit for expenses incurred to purchase property for which a sales and use exemption for teleproduction or other postproduction property is claimed;

— California does not incorporate post-2004 federal amendments that allow a taxpayer to claim 20% of amounts paid or incurred by the taxpayer during the tax year to an energy research consortium and (2) repeal the limitation on contract research expenses paid to eligible small businesses, universities and federal laboratories for qualified energy research; and

— California did not incorporate the federal suspension periods of July 1, 1999—September 30, 2000, and October 1, 2000—September 30, 2001, that were enacted by the Tax Relief Extension Act of 1999.

A married couple or registered domestic partners filing separately may take the full credit or divide it equally between the spouses or partners.

FTB 3523 is used to compute the credit.

6. Credit for prior-year minimum tax (¶152): California incorporates the IRC Sec. 53 credit for alternative minimum tax paid in a prior year by a taxpayer who is not liable for the AMT in the current year. The credit is based on preference items that defer tax liability rather than permanently reduce the tax. The amount allowable as a credit in any tax year is limited to the regular California personal income tax for the year less the refundable credits that have no carryover provisions and the credit for taxes paid to other states. The credit is computed on FTB 3510.

7. Credit for income taxes paid other states (nonresidents) (¶129): The credit for income taxes paid other states is available for net income taxes paid to another state or possession on income also taxed by California when the state or possession of residence is one of the following: Arizona, Guam, Indiana, Oregon, and Virginia. Net tax does not include any tax comparable to the California AMT or preference tax (¶69) or any tax not based on net income.

There are the following two limitations: (1) the credit is limited to the same proportion of the total tax paid to the state of residence as the income taxed in both states bears to the total income taxed by the state of residence; and (2) it is similarly limited to the same proportion of the total California tax as the income taxed in both states bears to the total income taxed by California.

Schedule S is used to compute the credit.

8. Credit for income taxes paid other states (part-year residents) (¶128): For the period of time that part-year residents are residents of California, they are entitled to credit for net income taxes paid to other states. A listing of the states and possessions for which credit is allowed appears at ¶128. The amount of the credit is limited to the same proportion of the total California tax as the income taxed in both states bears to the total income taxed by California. See ¶128 for a discussion of the credit and an example of the credit calculation.

For the period of time that the part-year resident is a nonresident of California, he/she is entitled to the credit available to nonresidents as discussed above. Because the states for which credit is allowed are mutually exclusive as to treatment of residents or nonresidents, a two-step computation is required only when California-source adjusted gross income is received while a nonresident.

Schedule S is used to compute the credit. There is no carryover of this credit.

9. Excess state disability insurance credit (¶132): Excess employee contributions for California disability insurance are treated as a refundable credit against the income tax. For 2008, the credit amount is the excess of the amount contributed over $693.58. Excess contributions may occur when a taxpayer works for more than one employer during the tax year. The amount of the credit can be calculated on a worksheet included in the Instructions to Form 540NR.

Note: If more than the maximum was withheld by a single employer, or at a higher rate, the excess amount must be claimed as a refund from the employer rather than as a tax credit.

• *Other credits*

Farmworker housing credit (¶137): Prior to the 2009 taxable year, California allows a nonrefundable credit for the lesser of (1) up to 50% of qualified amounts paid or incurred for the construction or rehabilitation of farmworker housing in California, or (2) the amount certified by the California Tax Credit Allocation Committee. Unused credit may be carried over until exhausted.

Low-income housing credit (¶138): California allows a credit to owners of residential rental projects that provide low-income housing located in California. The credit is similar to the federal credit computed under IRC Sec. 42, however the California credit allocates a specified set-aside of funds to support farmworker housing projects for taxable years after 2008. The California Tax Credit Allocation Committee certifies to the taxpayer on FTB 3521A the amount of the credit for each year in the credit period.

The credit is computed on FTB 3521. A copy of FTB 3521A must be provided to the FTB upon request. Unused credit may be carried over until exhausted.

Enterprise zone hiring and sales tax credits (¶144, 145): Tax credits are provided for employers who pay wages to qualified individuals in an enterprise zone (attach FTB 3805Z) and for business operators who purchase machinery or parts in an enterprise zone (attach FTB 3805Z). Unused credit may be carried over to succeeding tax years.

Enterprise zone credit for wages earned (¶146): A credit is available for qualified wages paid to specified enterprise zone employees (computation of the credit is on FTB 3553). There is no carryover of unused credit.

Local agency area military base recovery area (LAMBRA) hiring and sales tax credits (¶144, 147): A hiring credit and a sales tax credit substantially similar to those available to enterprise zone businesses may be claimed by qualified LAMBRA businesses.

The credits are computed on FTB 3807. The amount that may be claimed by a taxpayer for both LAMBRA credits is limited to the amount of tax attributable to LAMBRA income. Unused credit may be carried over and applied to tax on income from the area in succeeding tax years.

Targeted tax area hiring and sales and use tax credits (¶144, 148): Tax credits are provided for employers who hire certain disadvantaged individuals within the targeted tax area. A tax credit is also available for businesses that purchase machinery or equipment to be used within the area. The credits are computed on FTB 3809. Unused credit may be carried over and applied to tax on income from the area in succeeding tax years.

Manufacturing enhancement area hiring credit (¶149): A hiring tax credit substantially similar to the credit available to enterprise zone businesses may be claimed by qualified manufacturing enhancement area businesses. The credit is computed on FTB 3808. Unused credit may be carried over and applied to tax on income from the area in succeeding tax years.

Senior head-of-household credit (¶135): A credit is available to qualified seniors. A worksheet to compute the credit is included in the Instructions to Form 540NR.

Prison inmate labor credit (¶154): A credit is available to employers for 10% of the wages paid to certain prison inmates (FTB 3507). There is no carryover of this credit.

Adoption costs credit (¶139): A credit is available for costs directly related to the adoption of a U.S. citizen or legal resident minor child who was in the custody of a state or county public agency. A worksheet is provided in the Form 540NR Instructions to compute the credit. Unused credit may be carried over until exhausted.

Disabled access expenditures credit (¶140): California allows eligible small businesses a credit for 50% of up to $250 of the disabled access expenditures paid or incurred by those businesses to comply with the federal Americans with Disabilities Act. Except for the amount of the credit, the credit is similar to the federal credit allowed under IRC Sec. 44. The credit is computed on FTB 3548. Unused credit may be carried over until exhausted.

Enhanced oil recovery credit (¶153): California allows certain independent oil producers an enhanced oil recovery credit equal to 1/3 of the federal credit allowed under IRC Sec. 43, provided the costs for which the credit is claimed are attributable to projects located within California. FTB 3546 is used to compute the credit. Unused credit may be carried forward for up to 15 years. The credit is not available during the 2008 taxable year.

Credit for costs of transporting donated agricultural products (¶141): California allows a credit against net tax for 50% of the costs paid or incurred in connection with the transportation of agricultural products donated to nonprofit charitable organizations. FTB 3547 is used to compute the credit. Unused credit may be carried over until exhausted.

Credit for community development investments (¶156): For taxable years beginning before 2012, California allows a credit equal to 20% of each qualified deposit that is made into a community development financial institution and certified by the California Organized Investment Network.

Natural heritage preservation credit (¶143): Taxpayers may claim a nonrefundable credit equal to 55% of the fair market value of real property donated before July 1, 2008, for qualified conservation purposes to the California Resources Agency (CRA), a local government, or an exempt nonprofit land and water conservation organization designated by the CRA or a local government to accept donations.

Household and dependent care expense credit (¶142): A refundable credit for employment-related household and dependent care expenses is allowed against California personal income tax in an amount that is a percentage of the allowable federal credit.

Ultra-low sulfur diesel fuel production credit (¶151): An environmental tax credit may be claimed for ultra-low sulfur diesel fuel produced by a qualified small refiner at a California facility. The credit is computed on FTB 3511.

• *Carryover credits*

Nonresidents and part-year residents may apply carryovers of certain credits that are no longer available. The credits for which such carryovers may still exist (and the years for which the credits were available) are as follows:

1. water conservation credit (1980—1982);
2. solar pump (agricultural) credit (1981—1983);
3. solar energy installation credit (1985—1988);
4. energy conservation credit (1981—1986);
5. ridesharing credits (1981—1986 and 1989—1995);
6. political contributions credit (1987—1991);
7. commercial solar energy credit (1987—1988);
8. residential rental and farm sales credit (1987—1991);
9. credit for donation of agricultural products (1989—1991);
10. orphan drug research credit (1987—1992);
11. qualified parent's infant care credit (1991—1993);
12. commercial solar electric system credit (1990—1993);
13. recycling equipment credit (1989—1995);
14. low emission vehicle credit (1991—1995);
15. Los Angeles Revitalization Zone hiring and sales and use tax credits (1992—1997);
16. salmon and steelhead trout habitat credit (1995—1999);
17. manufacturers' investment credit (1994—2003);
18. joint strike fighter property credit (2001—2005);
19. joint strike fighter wage credit (2001—2005);
20. solar and wind energy systems credit (2001—2005); and
21. rice straw credit (1997—2007).

All of the above credit carryovers may be claimed on FTB 3540. See prior editions of the *Guidebook* for details about these credits.

¶71 When and Where to File and Pay Tax

The due date for filing Form 540NR and payment of the tax is April 15, 2009, for calendar-year taxpayers (¶108, 110). Returns made by fiscal-year taxpayers are due on or before the 15th day of the fourth month after the close of the fiscal year. Returns made by mail are considered timely if properly addressed and postmarked on or before the due date.

Returns are filed with the Franchise Tax Board (FTB). However, the address to which they are sent differs depending upon whether an amount is due or a refund is expected. Refund requests are sent to P.O. Box 942840, Sacramento, CA 94240-0002. Returns for which an amount is due are sent to P.O. Box 942867, Sacramento, CA 94267-0001.

Checks or money orders are payable to the "Franchise Tax Board" with the social security number written on the check or money order.

• *E-file*

The FTB also accepts electronic filing of returns through the e-file program. Tax return preparers who prepare and file more than 100 timely original California personal income tax returns during any calendar year and who prepare at least one personal income tax return using tax preparation software in the current calendar year must file all personal income tax returns for the current calendar year and subsequent calendar years using electronic technology (unless the taxpayer elects to file a paper return). Detailed information concerning the mandatory e-file program is available at the FTB's Web site at http://www.ftb.ca.gov/professionals/efile/m_e_file.shtml.

• *Electronic payments*

Beginning with installments due after 2008, personal income taxpayers must make their tax payments electronically, including utilizing a pay by phone option, if their estimated personal income tax installment payment or extension request payment exceeds $20,000 or if their total annual post-2008 tax liability exceeds $80,000, see ¶110.

• *Military personnel*

The due date for returns by members of the Armed Forces is the same as for civilians except that it may be postponed in certain cases, such as duty outside the U.S. or service in a combat zone (¶109).

¶72 Extensions

California Forms: FTB 3519 (Payment Voucher for Automatic Extension for Individuals), FTB 3537 (Payment Voucher for Automatic Extension for Limited Liability Companies), FTB 3538 (Payment Voucher for Automatic Extension for Limited Partnerships, LLPs and REMICs), or FTB 3563 (Payment Voucher for Automatic Extension for Fiduciaries).

The Franchise Tax Board (FTB) will allow an automatic six-month extension to file if the return is filed within six months of the original due date. No written request is required. The automatic extension does not extend the time for paying the tax. Tax payments must be accompanied by the appropriate form: FTB 3519 (Payment Voucher for Automatic Extension for Individuals); FTB 3537 (Payment Voucher for Automatic Extension for Limited Liability Companies); FTB 3538 (Payment Voucher for Automatic Extension for Limited Partnerships, LLPs and REMICs); or FTB 3563 (Payment Voucher for Automatic Extension for Fiduciaries). Taxpayers should send FTB 3519 or FTB 3563 to the FTB at P.O. Box 942867, Sacramento, CA 94267-0051. FTB 3537 and FTB 3538 are sent to the FTB at P.O. Box 942857, Sacramento, CA 94257-0651.

Payment extensions may be granted for a reasonable period by the FTB. There is no prescribed form; presumably a letter of explanation may be used for this purpose. Extensions of up to one year are also available to disaster victims and victims of terroristic or militaristic actions (¶110).

Taxpayers abroad: An additional automatic two-month extension of time to file a return is granted to a taxpayer traveling or residing abroad on the due date (¶109). Consequently, the extended due date for such taxpayers is December 15. However, interest accrues on any unpaid tax from the original due date of the return. Any additional extensions must be applied for in writing with a letter of explanation.

¶73 Estimated Tax

California Form: 540-ES (Estimated Tax for Individuals).

Nonresidents or part-year residents are required to pay estimated taxes in the same manner as residents (¶36, 111).

The California alternative minimum tax (¶117) is included in determining any required estimated tax payments.

The estimated tax is paid in quarterly installments on the same dates as federal payments: April 15, June 15, September 15, and January 15. The January 15 installment need not be made if the taxpayer files the tax return and pays the balance of tax before February 1. When the due date falls on a Saturday, Sunday, or other legal holiday, payment may be made on the next business day.

Married couples may file separate or joint estimated tax payment vouchers, but no joint payments can be made if the spouses have different tax years, or if the spouses are legally separated.

Form 540-ES is used for paying estimated tax. This form consists of a four-part payment voucher, with the due date on each voucher.

¶74 State Tax Assistance

The Franchise Tax Board (FTB) offers various taxpayer assistance programs ranging from providing trained volunteers to assist taxpayers at no cost in completing their tax returns to toll-free telephone assistance. The toll-free telephone numbers are included in the instruction booklet for Form 540NR.

In addition, the FTB has several district offices located in principal cities throughout the state. These offices and their addresses are printed in the 540NR Instruction booklet.

¶75 Forms

Forms may be ordered directly from the state at the following address:

Franchise Tax Board
Tax Forms Development and Distribution Unit
P.O. Box 1468
Sacramento, CA 95812-1468

California income tax forms and publications may also be downloaded from the Internet. The Internet address and telephone numbers are listed in the Form 540NR Instruction booklet.

¶76 Interest

The California rate of interest on underpayments and overpayments of tax is based on the federal underpayment rate (¶711). The interest rate is redetermined semiannually and is as follows:

January 1, 2006—June 30, 2006	6%
July 1, 2006—December 31, 2006	7%
January 1, 2007—June 30, 2007	8%
July 1, 2007—December 31, 2007	8%
January 1, 2008—June 30, 2008	8%
July 1, 2008—December 31, 2008	7%
January 1, 2009—June 30, 2009	5%

¶77 Penalties

A penalty of 5% per month, up to a maximum of 25%, is imposed for failure without reasonable cause to file a return. If the failure to file is fraudulent, the penalty is 15% per month, up to a maximum of 75%.

The penalty for failure to pay the income tax when it is due is 5% of the unpaid amount plus 1/2% per month. If the penalties for failure to file and failure to pay are both applicable, the penalty imposed is the higher of (1) the penalty for failure to pay or (2) the total of the penalty for failure to file and the penalty for failure to furnish information.

A minimum penalty of the lesser of $100 or 100% of the tax liability is imposed if the return is not filed within 60 days of the due date.

Other penalties are discussed at ¶712.

PART III

PERSONAL INCOME TAX

FEDERAL-CALIFORNIA CROSS-REFERENCE TABLE AND INDEX

Showing Sections of California Personal Income Tax Law (Revenue and Taxation Code) Comparable to Sections of Federal Law (1986 Internal Revenue Code)

Federal	California	Subject	Paragraph
IRC Sec. 1	Secs. 17041, 17048	Tax Rates and Tables	¶116, ¶118
IRC Sec. 2(a)	Secs. 17046, 17142.5	"Surviving Spouse" Defined	¶107
IRC Secs. 2(b), 2(c)	Sec. 17042	"Head of Household" Defined	¶114
IRC Sec. 15	Sec. 17034	Effect of Changes	¶406
IRC Sec. 21	Sec. 17052.6	Credit—Child Care	¶142
IRC Sec. 23	Sec. 17052.25	Adoption Costs Credit	¶139
IRC Secs. 25-30A	Sec. 17039	Credits—Various	. . .
IRC Sec. 31	Sec. 19002	Credit—Tax Withheld	¶715
IRC Secs. 32-34	. . .	Credits—Various	. . .
IRC Sec. 38	Sec. 17053.57	Community Development Investment Credit	¶155
IRC Secs. 39-40	. . .	Credits—Various	. . .
IRC Sec. 41	Sec. 17052.12	Research Expenditures Credit	¶150
IRC Sec. 42	Secs. 17057.5, 17058	Low-income Housing Credit	¶138
IRC Sec. 43	Sec. 17052.8	Enhanced Oil Recovery Credit	¶153
IRC Sec. 44	Sec. 17053.42	Disabled Access Credit	¶140
IRC Sec. 45	...	Solar and Wind Energy Systems Credits	...
IRC Sec. 45C	. . .	Clinical Testing Credit	. . .
IRC Sec. 45D	. . .	New Markets Tax Credit	. . .
IRC Sec. 45E	. . .	Credit for Small Employer Pension Plan Startup Costs	. . .
IRC Sec. 45F	Sec. 17052.17	Employer-Provided Child Care Credit	¶134
IRC Sec. 45G	. . .	Railroad Track Maintenance Credit	. . .
IRC Sec. 45H	Sec. 17053.62	Low Sulfur Diesel Fuel Production Credit	151
IRC Sec. 45I	. . .	Marginal Well Production Credit	. . .
IRC Sec. 48	...	Energy Credit; Reforestation Credit	...
IRC Secs. 51-52	Sec. 17053.7	Work Opportunity Credit	. . .
IRC Sec. 53	Sec. 17063	Minimum Tax Credit	¶152
IRC Secs. 55-59	Secs. 17062, 17062.3, 17062.5	Alternative Minimum Tax	¶117, ¶331
IRC Sec. 61	Secs. 17071, 17087.6, 17090, 17131, 17133, 17133.5, 17135, 17136, 17138, 17140.5, 17147.7, 17149, 17153.5, 17555	"Gross Income" defined	¶201
IRC Sec. 62	Sec. 17072	"Adjusted Gross Income" defined	¶201, ¶202, ¶329
IRC Sec. 63	Secs. 17073, 17073.5, 17301, 17304	Standard Deduction	¶112, ¶203, ¶303, ¶335
IRC Sec. 64	Sec. 17074	"Ordinary Income" defined	. . .
IRC Sec. 65	Sec. 17075	"Ordinary Loss" defined	. . .
IRC Sec. 66	Sec. 18534	Income Where Spouses Living Apart	¶107, ¶239
IRC Sec. 67	Sec. 17076	2% Floor on Itemized Deductions	¶303, ¶329, ¶604
IRC Sec. 68	Sec. 17077	6% Floor on Itemized Deductions	¶303, ¶329
IRC Sec. 71	Sec. 17081	Spousal and Child Support Payments	Various
IRC Sec. 72	Secs. 17081, 17085, 17085.7, 17087	Annuities	¶205, ¶206, ¶214, ¶215
IRC Sec. 73	Sec. 17081	Services of Child	¶208
IRC Sec. 74	Sec. 17081	Prizes and Awards	¶209
IRC Sec. 75	Sec. 17081	Dealers in Tax-Exempt Securities	¶210
IRC Sec. 77	Sec. 17081	Commodity Credit Corp. Loans	¶211
IRC Sec. 79	Sec. 17081	Group Term Life Insurance	¶212
IRC Sec. 80	Sec. 17081	Restoration of Value of Certain Securities	. . .
IRC Sec. 82	Sec. 17081	Moving Expense Reimbursement	¶238
IRC Sec. 83	Sec. 17081	Property Transferred to Employee	¶207
IRC Sec. 84	Sec. 17081	Transfers to Political Organizations	¶201, ¶544
IRC Sec. 85	Secs. 17081, 17083	Unemployment Compensation	¶201
IRC Sec. 86	Secs. 17081, 17087	Social Security Benefits, etc.	¶201
IRC Sec. 88	Sec. 17081	Nuclear Plant Expenses	¶201
IRC Sec. 90	Sec. 17081	Illegal Irrigation Subsidies	¶201
IRC Sec. 101	Secs. 17131, 17132.5	Death Benefits	¶213, ¶215
IRC Sec. 102	Sec. 17131	Gifts and Inheritances	¶216

Federal	California	Subject	Paragraph
IRC Sec. 103	Secs. 17131, 17133, 17143	Interest on Government Bonds	¶217
IRC Sec. 104	Secs. 17131, 17132.7	Compensation—Injury or Sickness	¶218
IRC Sec. 105	Secs. 17131, 17087	Accident and Health Plans—Amounts Received	¶219
IRC Sec. 106	Secs. 17131, 17131.4	Accident and Health Plans—Employer Contributions	¶219 , ¶247
IRC Sec. 107	Secs. 17131, 17131.6	Rental Value of Parsonages	¶220, ¶247
IRC Sec. 108	Secs. 17131, 17134, 17144, 17144.5	Income from Discharge of Indebtedness	¶221
IRC Sec. 109	Sec. 17131	Improvements by Lessee	¶222
IRC Sec. 110	Sec. 17131	Short-Term Lease Construction Allowances	¶223
IRC Sec. 111	Secs. 17131, 17142	Recovery of Bad Debts and Prior Taxes	¶224
IRC Sec. 112	Secs. 17131, 17142.5	Combat Pay of Members of Armed Forces	¶225
IRC Sec. 114	Sec. 17132	Extraterritorial Income	¶201
IRC Sec. 115	Sec. 17131	Income of States and Municipalities	. . .
IRC Sec. 117	Sec. 17131	Scholarship and Fellowship Grants	¶227
IRC Sec. 119	Sec. 17131	Employer-Furnished Meals and Lodging	¶228
IRC Sec. 120	Sec. 17131	Employer Contributions to Legal Services Plan	¶201 , ¶244
IRC Sec. 121	Secs. 17131, 17152	Exclusion for Primary Residence Sale	¶229 , ¶504
IRC Sec. 122	Sec. 17131	Reduced Uniformed Services Retirement Pay	¶205 , ¶225
IRC Sec. 123	Sec. 17131	Living Expenses Paid by Insurance	¶238
IRC Sec. 125	Secs. 17131, 17131.5	Employer Contributions to "Cafeteria" Plans	¶201, ¶346
IRC Sec. 126	Secs. 17131, 17135.5	Government Payments for Environmental Conservation	¶201 , ¶243
IRC Sec. 127	Secs. 17131, 17151	Educational Assistance Programs	¶242
IRC Sec. 129	Sec. 17131	Dependent Care Assistance Programs	¶201
IRC Sec. 130	Sec. 17131	Personal Injury Assignments	¶201
IRC Sec. 131	Sec. 17131	Foster Care Payments	¶201
IRC Sec. 132	Secs. 17131, 17154	Fringe Benefits	¶201 , ¶238 , ¶241
IRC Sec. 134	Sec. 17131	Military Benefits	¶201 , ¶225
IRC Sec. 135	Sec. 17151	Bond Income Used for Higher Education	. . .
IRC Sec. 136	Sec. 17131	Energy Conservation Subsidies	¶201 , ¶245
IRC Sec. 137	Sec. 17131	Adoption Assistance Programs	¶249
IRC Sec. 138	Sec. 17201	Medicare Advantage MSA	¶247
IRC Sec. 139	Sec. 17131	Disaster Relief Payments	¶201 , ¶251
IRC Sec. 139A	Sec. 17139.6	Federal Subsidies for Prescription Drug Plans	¶252
IRC Sec. 139B	...	Exclusion of volunteer firefighter benefits	¶251
IRC Sec. 140	Sec. 17131	Miscellaneous Non-IRC Federal Exemptions	. . .
IRC Secs. 141-50	Sec. 17143	Private Activity Bonds	¶217
IRC Sec. 151	Secs. 17054, 17054.1	Deductions for Personal and Dependent Exemptions	¶113
IRC Sec. 152	Sec. 17056	Dependents	¶115
IRC Sec. 161	Secs. 17201, 17202.5, 17274, 17275, 17278, 17299.8, 17299.9	Allowance of Deductions	¶300
IRC Sec. 162	Secs. 17201, 17202, 17269, 17270, 17273, 17273.1, 17286	Trade or Business Expense	Various
IRC Sec. 163	Secs. 17201, 17224, 17230, 17235	Interest	¶237 , ¶303 , ¶305
IRC Sec. 164	Secs. 17201, 17220, 17222	Taxes—Deductions	¶303 , ¶306
IRC Sec. 165	Secs. 17201, 17207 17207.4	Losses—Deductions	¶303 , ¶307 , ¶407
IRC Sec. 166	Sec. 17201	Bad Debts—Deductions	¶308
IRC Sec. 167	Secs. 17201, 17250.5	Depreciation	¶310 , ¶332 , ¶562
IRC Sec. 168	Secs. 17201, 17250	Accelerated Cost Recovery System	¶310
IRC Sec. 169	Secs. 17201, 17250	Amortization of Pollution Control Facilities	¶314
IRC Sec. 170	Secs. 17201, 17275.5	Charitable Contributions	¶302 , ¶321
IRC Sec. 171	Sec. 17201	Amortization of Bond Premium	¶324
IRC Sec. 172	Secs. 17201, 17276-76.10	Net Operating Loss Carryover	¶309
IRC Sec. 173	Sec. 17201	Circulation Expenditures	¶303 , ¶342
IRC Sec. 174	Sec. 17201	Research and Experimental Expenditures	¶331
IRC Sec. 175	Sec. 17201	Soil and Water Conservation Expenditures	¶302 , ¶341
IRC Sec. 178	Sec. 17201	Depreciation or Amortization of Cost of Acquiring a Lease	¶313
IRC Sec. 179	Secs. 17201, 17255, 17268	Election to Expense Depreciable Assets	¶311
IRC Sec. 179B	Secs. 17201.4, 17255.5	Refiners' Sulfur Rules Compliance Costs	¶318
IRC Sec. 179C	...	Expensing of Qualified Refinery Property	¶301
IRC Sec. 179D	...	Energy Efficient Commercial Building Costs	¶345
IRC Sec. 179E	...	Election to Expense Mining Safety Equipment	¶301
IRC Sec. 180	Sec. 17201	Farm Fertilizer Expenses	¶302 , ¶341

Federal	California	Subject	Paragraph
IRC Sec. 181	Sec. 17201.5	Qualified Film and Television Productions	¶310
IRC Sec. 183	Sec. 17201	Hobby Losses	¶336, ¶338
IRC Sec. 186	Sec. 17201	Recovery of Antitrust Damages	. . .
IRC Sec. 190	Sec. 17201	Facilities for Handicapped	¶301
IRC Sec. 192	Sec. 17201	Contributions to Black Lung Benefit Trust	. . .
IRC Sec. 193	Secs. 17201, 17260	Tertiary Injectants	¶320
IRC Sec. 194	Secs. 17201, 17278.5	Amortization of Reforestation Expenses	¶315
IRC Sec. 194A	Sec. 17201	Contributions to Employer Liability Trusts	¶330
IRC Sec. 195	Sec. 17201	Start-Up Expenditures	¶334
IRC Sec. 196	Sec. 17024.5	Unused Business Credits—Deduction	. . .
IRC Sec. 197	Sec. 17279	Amortization of Goodwill	¶310, ¶333
IRC Sec. 198	Sec. 17279.4	Environmental Remediation Costs	¶346
IRC Sec. 199	Sec. 17201.6	Domestic Production Deduction	¶317
IRC Sec. 211	Sec. 17201	Additional Allowance of Deductions	. . .
IRC Sec. 212	Sec. 17201	Expenses for Production of Income	¶304
IRC Sec. 213	Sec. 17201	Medical Expenses	¶325
IRC Sec. 215	Secs. 17201, 17302	Spousal Support	¶323
IRC Sec. 216	Sec. 17201	Taxes and Interest Paid to Cooperative Housing Corporation	¶327
IRC Sec. 217	Sec. 17201	Moving Expenses	¶328
IRC Sec. 219	Secs. 17201, 17507.6	Retirement Savings	¶330
IRC Sec. 220	Secs. 17201, 17215, 17215.1	Archer MSAs	¶247, ¶326
IRC Sec. 221	Secs. 17201, 17204	Interest on Education Loans	¶305
IRC Sec. 222	Secs. 17204.7	Qualified Tuition and Related Expenses Deduction	¶344
IRC Sec. 223	Sec. 17215.4	Health Savings Accounts	¶326
IRC Sec. 224	...	Cross Reference	...
IRC Sec. 261	Sec. 17201	Disallowance of Deductions	¶300, ¶336
IRC Sec. 262	Sec. 17201	Personal Living and Family Expenses	¶336
IRC Sec. 263	Secs. 17201, 17260	Capital Expenditures	¶320, ¶336
IRC Sec. 263A	Sec. 17201	Inventory Capitalization Rules	¶336, ¶407, ¶409, ¶416
IRC Sec. 264	Sec. 17201	Amounts Paid in Connection with Insurance Contracts	¶305, ¶336
IRC Sec. 265	Sec. 17280	Tax Exempt Income—Interest and Expenses	¶305, ¶336
IRC Sec. 266	Sec. 17201	Carrying Charges	¶336
IRC Sec. 267	Sec. 17201	Transactions Between Related Individuals	¶336
IRC Sec. 268	Sec. 17201	Sale of Land with Unharvested Crop	¶336
IRC Sec. 269	Sec. 17201	Acquisition Made to Avoid Income Tax	. . .
IRC Sec. 269A	Secs. 17201, 17287	Personal Service Corporations	¶412
IRC Sec. 269B	Sec. 17201	Stapled Stock	¶412
IRC Sec. 271	Sec. 17201	Debts Owed by Political Parties	¶308
IRC Sec. 272	Sec. 17201	Disposal of Coal or Domestic Iron Ore	. . .
IRC Sec. 273	Sec. 17201	Holders of Terminable Interest	¶336
IRC Sec. 274	Sec. 17201	Entertainment, Travel and Gift Expenses	¶302, ¶329, ¶336
IRC Sec. 275	Sec. 17222	Withheld Taxes	¶306
IRC Sec. 276	Sec. 17201	Indirect Political Contributions	¶336
IRC Sec. 277	Sec. 17201	Expenses by Membership Organizations	. . .
IRC Sec. 280A	Sec. 17201	Disallowance of Business Expenses of Home, Vacation Rentals	¶301, ¶336
IRC Sec. 280B	Sec. 17201	Demolition of Historic Structures	¶336
IRC Sec. 280C	Secs. 17201, 17270	Federal Credits	¶336
IRC Sec. 280E	Secs. 17201, 17281, 17282	Illegal Drug Sales	¶336
IRC Sec. 280F	Sec. 17201	Luxury Cars, etc.	¶310
IRC Sec. 280G	Sec. 17201	"Golden Parachute" Payments	¶336
IRC Sec. 280H	Sec. 17201	Salaries of Shareholder/Owners of Personal Service Corp.	. . .
IRC Sec. 301	Sec. 17321	Corporate Distributions of Property	¶226
IRC Sec. 302	Secs. 17321-22	Distributions in Redemption of Stock	¶226
IRC Sec. 303	Sec. 17321	Distributions in Redemption of Stock to Pay Death Taxes	¶226
IRC Sec. 304	Sec. 17321	Redemption Through Use of Related Corporations	¶226
IRC Sec. 305	Sec. 17321	Distributions of Stock and Rights	¶226
IRC Sec. 306	Sec. 17321	Dispositions of "306" Stock	¶226
IRC Sec. 307	Sec. 17321	Basis of Stock and Rights of Distribution	¶226, ¶558
IRC Sec. 312	Sec. 17321	Effect on Earnings and Profits	¶226
IRC Sec. 316	Sec. 17321	"Dividend" Defined	¶226
IRC Sec. 317	Sec. 17321	"Property," "Redemption" Defined	¶226
IRC Sec. 318	Sec. 17321	Constructive Ownership of Stock	¶226
IRC Sec. 331	Sec. 17321	Gain or Loss in Corporate Liquidations	¶226, ¶522
IRC Sec. 334	Sec. 17321	Basis of Property Received in Liquidation	¶226, ¶522, ¶548

Federal	California	Subject	Paragraph
IRC Sec. 346	Sec. 17321	"Partial Liquidation" Defined	¶226, ¶522
IRC Sec. 351	Sec. 17321	Corporate Organizations—Transfer to Controlled Corporation	¶512
IRC Sec. 354	Sec. 17321	Exchange of Stock in Reorganization	¶516
IRC Sec. 355	Sec. 17321	Reorganizations—Distributions by Controlled Corporation	¶517
IRC Sec. 356	Sec. 17321	Receipt of Additional Consideration	¶518
IRC Sec. 357	Sec. 17321	Assumption of Liability	. . .
IRC Sec. 358	Sec. 17321	Basis to Distributees	¶547, ¶549
IRC Sec. 367	Sec. 17321	Transfers to Foreign Corporations	¶519
IRC Sec. 368	Sec. 17321	Corporate Reorganizations—Definitions	¶516
IRC Sec. 382	Sec. 17321	Discharge of Indebtedness	¶221
IRC Sec. 385	Sec. 17321	Treatment of Corporate Interests as Stock or Indebtedness	. . .
IRC Sec. 401	Sec. 17501	Pension, Profit-Sharing, Stock Bonus Plans	¶206, ¶607
IRC Sec. 402	Secs. 17501, 17504	Taxability of Beneficiary of Employees' Trust	¶206, ¶330, ¶607
IRC Sec. 403	Secs. 17501, 17506	Taxability of Employee Annuities	¶206, ¶607
IRC Sec. 404	Secs. 17203, 17501	Deduction for Employer's Contributions to Employee Pension, Profit-Sharing, and Stock Bonus Plans	¶330, ¶607
IRC Sec. 404A	Secs. 17501, 17563.5	Foreign Deferred Compensation Plans	¶330, ¶607
IRC Sec. 406	Sec. 17501	Employees of Foreign Subsidiaries	¶330, ¶607
IRC Sec. 407	Sec. 17501	Employees of Domestic Subsidiaries	¶330, ¶607
IRC Sec. 408	Secs. 17507, 17508	Individual Retirement Accounts	¶206, ¶330
IRC Sec. 408A	Sec. 17507.6	Roth IRAs	¶206, ¶330
IRC Sec. 409	Sec. 17501	Employee Stock Ownership Plans	¶330
IRC Sec. 409A	Sec. 17501	Treatment of Nonqualified Deferred Compensation Plans	¶206
IRC Sec. 410	Sec. 17501	Minimum Participation Standards	¶330
IRC Sec. 411	Sec. 17501	Minimum Vesting Standards	¶330
IRC Sec. 412	Sec. 17501	Minimum Funding Standards	¶330
IRC Sec. 413	Secs. 17501, 17509	Collectively Bargained Plans	¶330
IRC Sec. 414	Sec. 17501	Definitions and Special Rules—Plans	¶206, ¶330
IRC Sec. 415	Sec. 17501	Limitations on Benefits and Contributions	¶206, ¶330
IRC Sec. 416	Sec. 17501	Top-Heavy Plans	¶330
IRC Sec. 417	Sec. 17501	Minimum Survivor Annuity Requirements	¶330
IRC Secs. 418-18E	Sec. 17501	Pension Plan Reorganizations	¶330
IRC Sec. 419	Sec. 17501	Welfare Benefit Plans	¶330
IRC Sec. 419A	Sec. 17501	Qualified Asset Account; Limitation on Additions to Account	¶330
IRC Sec. 420	Sec. 17501	Transfers of Excess Pension Assets to Retiree Health Accounts	¶206
IRC Sec. 421	Secs. 17501, 17502	Employee Stock Options—Employer Deductions	¶207
IRC Sec. 422	Sec. 17501	Incentive Stock Options	¶207
IRC Sec. 423	Sec. 17501	Employee Stock Purchase Plan	¶207
IRC Sec. 424	Sec. 17501	Stock Options—Definitions and Special Rules	¶207
IRC Sec. 441	Secs. 17551, 17656	Accounting Periods—Generally	¶400, ¶401
IRC Sec. 442	Secs. 17551, 17556	Accounting—Change of Period	¶400, ¶402
IRC Sec. 443	Secs. 17551-52	Accounting—Short Period Returns	¶400, ¶403, ¶404
IRC Sec. 444	Sec. 17551	Election to Keep Same Tax Year—Partnerships	¶400, ¶401, ¶616
IRC Sec. 446	Sec. 17551	Methods of Accounting—General Rule	¶400, ¶407
IRC Sec. 447	Sec. 17551	Accounting—Corporations Engaged in Farming	¶400, ¶407
IRC Sec. 448	Sec. 17551	Restriction on Use of Cash Method	¶400, ¶407
IRC Sec. 451	Secs. 17551, 17552.3	Taxable Year of Inclusion	¶400, ¶407
IRC Sec. 453	Secs. 17551, 17560	Installment Method	¶400, ¶411
IRC Sec. 453A	Secs. 17551, 17560	Installment Method—Dealers in Personal Property	¶400, ¶411
IRC Sec. 453B	Sec. 17551	Gain or Loss Disposition of Installment Obligations	¶400, ¶411
IRC Sec. 454	Secs. 17551, 17553	Obligations Issued at Discount	¶400, ¶408
IRC Sec. 455	Sec. 17551	Prepaid Subscription Income	¶400, ¶407
IRC Sec. 456	Sec. 17551	Prepaid Dues Income	¶400, ¶407
IRC Sec. 457	Secs. 17501.5, 17501.7, 17551	State Deferred Compensation Plans	¶206, ¶330, ¶400
IRC Sec. 457A	...	Nonqualified Deferred Compensation From Certain Tax Indifferent Parties	¶206
IRC Sec. 458	Sec. 17551	Returned Magazines	¶400, ¶407
IRC Sec. 460	Secs. 17551, 17564	Long-Term Contracts	¶400, ¶407
IRC Sec. 461	Sec. 17551	Taxable Year of Deduction	¶400, ¶407

Federal	California	Subject	Paragraph
IRC Sec. 464	Sec. 17551	Deduction Limitation—Farming Syndicates	¶400, ¶407
IRC Sec. 465	Sec. 17551	At-Risk Limitation	¶339, ¶400
IRC Sec. 467	Sec. 17551	Deferred Rental Payments	¶400, ¶407
IRC Sec. 468	Sec. 17551	Waste Disposal Costs	¶400, ¶407
IRC Sec. 468A	Sec. 17551	Nuclear Plant Expenses	¶400, ¶407
IRC Sec. 468B	Sec. 17551	Settlement Funds	¶400, ¶407
IRC Sec. 469	Secs. 17551, 17561	Passive Loss Limits	¶340, ¶400
IRC Sec. 470	Secs. 17551	Limitations on Deductions Allocable to Tax-Exempt Property	¶307
IRC Sec. 471	Sec. 17551	Inventories	¶400, ¶409
IRC Sec. 472	Sec. 17551	LIFO Inventories	¶400, ¶410
IRC Sec. 473	Sec. 17551	Liquidation of LIFO Inventories	¶400, ¶410
IRC Sec. 474	Sec. 17551	Dollar-Value LIFO Method	¶400, ¶410
IRC Sec. 475	Secs. 17551, 17570	Mark-to-Market Accounting	¶400, ¶409, ¶533
IRC Sec. 481	Sec. 17551	Adjustments	¶400, ¶407
IRC Sec. 482	Sec. 17551	Allocation of Income Among Taxpayers	¶400, ¶412
IRC Sec. 483	Sec. 17551	Imputed Interest	¶400, ¶414
IRC Sec. 501	Secs. 17631, 17632	Exempt Organizations and Trusts	¶321, ¶606, ¶607
IRC Sec. 503	Secs. 17635-40	Requirements for Exemption	¶607
IRC Secs. 511-14	Sec. 17651	Unrelated Business Income	¶607
IRC Sec. 529	Secs. 17140, 17140.3	Qualified Tuition Programs	¶250
IRC Secs. 530, 531	Sec. 23712	Coverdell Education Savings Accounts	¶206, ¶250, ¶330
IRC Secs. 541-58	Sec. 17024.5	Personal Holding Companies	. . .
IRC Sec. 584	Sec. 17671	Common Trust Funds	¶614
IRC Sec. 611	Sec. 17681	Depletion—Deduction	¶319
IRC Sec. 612	Sec. 17681	Basis for Cost Depletion	¶319, ¶562
IRC Sec. 613	Sec. 17681	Percentage Depletion	¶319
IRC Sec. 613A	Secs. 17681, 17734.6	Limitations on Depletion—Oil, Gas and Geothermal Wells	¶319, ¶562
IRC Sec. 614	Sec. 17681	"Property" Defined	¶319
IRC Sec. 616	Sec. 17681	Mine Development Expenses	¶320
IRC Sec. 617	Sec. 17681	Mine Exploration Expenses	¶320
IRC Sec. 631	Sec. 17681	Gain or Loss in Case of Timber, Coal or Iron	¶540
IRC Sec. 636	Sec. 17681	Mineral Production Payments	¶319
IRC Sec. 638	Sec. 17681	Continental Shelf Areas	¶319
IRC Sec. 641	Secs. 17731, 17731.5, 17734, 17742-45.1	Estates and Trusts—Imposition of Tax	¶601, ¶604, ¶606
IRC Sec. 642	Secs. 17731-33, 17736	Special Rules for Credits and Deductions	¶604, ¶605, ¶606
IRC Sec. 643	Secs. 17731, 17750	Estates and Trusts—Definitions	¶601, ¶604
IRC Sec. 644	Sec. 17731	Taxable Year of Trusts	¶601, ¶604
IRC Sec. 645	Secs. 17731, 17751	Certain Revocable Trusts Treated as Part of Estate	¶401, ¶604
IRC Sec. 646	. . .	Alaska Native Settlement Trusts	¶601
IRC Sec. 651	Sec. 17731	Simple Trusts	¶604
IRC Sec. 652	Sec. 17731	Beneficiaries of Simple Trusts	¶605
IRC Sec. 661	Secs. 17731, 17735	Complex Trusts—Deductions	¶604
IRC Sec. 662	Sec. 17731	Beneficiaries of Complex Trusts	¶605
IRC Sec. 663	Secs. 17731, 17752	Special Rules Applicable to §§661 and 662	¶605
IRC Sec. 664	Sec. 17731	Charitable Remainder Trusts	¶605, ¶606
IRC Sec. 665	Secs. 17731, 17779	Excess Distributions by Trusts—Definitions	¶601, ¶605
IRC Sec. 666	Secs. 17731, 17779	Accumulation Distribution Allocation	¶605
IRC Sec. 667	Secs. 17731, 17779	Amounts Distributed in Preceding Years	¶605
IRC Sec. 668	Secs. 17731, 17779	Interest on Accumulation from Foreign Trusts	¶605
IRC Sec. 671	Sec. 17731	Grantor Trusts—Trust Income	¶608
IRC Sec. 672	Sec. 17731	Grantor Trusts—Definitions	¶608
IRC Sec. 673	Sec. 17731	Reversionary Interests	¶608
IRC Sec. 674	Sec. 17731	Power to Control Beneficial Enjoyment	¶608
IRC Sec. 675	Sec. 17731	Administrative Powers	¶608
IRC Sec. 676	Sec. 17731	Power to Revoke	¶608
IRC Sec. 677	Sec. 17731	Income for Benefit of Grantor	¶608
IRC Sec. 678	Sec. 17731	Person Other Than Grantor Treated as Owner	¶608
IRC Sec. 679	Secs. 17024.5, 17731	Foreign Trusts with U.S. Beneficiaries	¶608
IRC Sec. 681	Sec. 17731	Limitation on Charitable Deduction—Unrelated Business Income	¶606
IRC Sec. 682	Secs. 17731, 17737	Income in Case of Divorce	¶611
IRC Sec. 683	Sec. 17731	Use of Trust as Exchange Fund	¶516
IRC Sec. 684	Secs. 17731, 17760	Gain on Transfers to Foreign Trusts and Estates	¶520
IRC Sec. 685	Secs. 17731, 17760.5	Funeral Trusts	¶608

Federal	California	Subject	Paragraph
IRC Sec. 691	Sec. 17731	Income in Respect of Decedents	¶413
IRC Sec. 692	Secs. 17731, 17142.5	Income Taxes of Armed Forces Members on Death	¶225
IRC Sec. 701	Secs. 17851, 17851.5	Partners, Not Partnership, Subject to Tax	¶616
IRC Sec. 702	Sec. 17851	Income and Credits of Partner	¶620
IRC Sec. 703	Secs. 17851, 17853	Partnership Computations	¶620
IRC Sec. 704	Secs. 17851, 17858	Partner's Distributive Share	¶617, ¶620
IRC Sec. 705	Sec. 17851	Determination of Basis of Partner's Interest	¶555, ¶618
IRC Sec. 706	Sec. 17851	Taxable Years of Partner and Partnership	¶621
IRC Sec. 707	Secs. 17851, 17854	Transactions Between Partner and Partnership	¶617, ¶620
IRC Sec. 708	Sec. 17851	Continuation of Partnership	¶621
IRC Sec. 709	Sec. 17851	Organization and Syndication Fees	¶620
IRC Sec. 721	Sec. 17851	Recognition of Gain or Loss Contribution	¶617
IRC Sec. 722	Sec. 17851	Basis of Contributing Partner's Interest	¶555, ¶617
IRC Sec. 723	Sec. 17851	Basis of Property Contributed to Partnership	¶555, ¶617
IRC Sec. 724	Sec. 17851	Disposition of Contributed Property	¶617
IRC Sec. 731	Sec. 17851	Recognition of Gain or Loss on Distribution	¶617
IRC Sec. 732	Sec. 17851	Basis of Distributed Property	¶555
IRC Sec. 733	Sec. 17851	Basis of Distributee Partner's Interest	¶555
IRC Sec. 734	Sec. 17851	Optional Adjustment to Basis of Undistributed Property	¶555
IRC Sec. 735	Sec. 17851	Character of Gain or Loss on Disposition of Distributed Property	¶617
IRC Sec. 736	Sec. 17851	Payments to Retiring Partner or Deceased Partner's Successor	¶617, ¶618
IRC Sec. 737	Sec. 17851	Precontribution Gain From Partnership Distributions	¶618
IRC Sec. 741	Sec. 17851	Gain or Loss on Sale or Exchange	¶618
IRC Sec. 742	Sec. 17851	Basis of Transferee Partner's Interest	¶555
IRC Sec. 743	Sec. 17851	Optional Adjustment to Basis of Property	¶555
IRC Sec. 751	Secs. 17851, 17855-57	Unrealized Receivables and Inventory Items	¶618
IRC Sec. 752	Sec. 17851	Treatment of Certain Liabilities	¶618
IRC Sec. 753	Sec. 17851	Partner Receiving Income in Respect of Decedent	¶618
IRC Sec. 754	Sec. 17851	Electing Optional Adjustment to Basis of Partnership Property	¶555, ¶618
IRC Sec. 755	Sec. 17851	Rules for Allocation of Basis	¶555, ¶618
IRC Sec. 761	Sec. 17851	Terms Defined	¶616
IRC Secs. 771-77	Secs. 17851, 17865	Special Rules for Electing Large Partnerships	¶624
IRC Sec. 851	Sec. 17088	Regulated Investment Company	¶226
IRC Sec. 852	Secs. 17088, 17145	Dividends to Shareholders of Certain Mutual Funds	¶217
IRC Sec. 853	Sec. 17024.5	Foreign Tax Credit for Shareholders	¶226
IRC Secs. 854-55	Sec. 17088	Dividends of Regulated Investment Company	¶217, ¶226, ¶559
IRC Secs. 856-60	Sec. 17088	Real Estate Investment Trusts	¶226, ¶609
IRC Secs. 860A-860G	Sec. 17088	Real Estate Mortgage Investment Conduits	¶615
IRC Secs. 860H-860L	Sec. 17088	Financial Asset Securatization Trusts	¶610
IRC Secs. 861-65	Secs. 17951-54	Sources of Income	¶201, ¶231
IRC Secs. 871-79	. . .	Nonresident Aliens	¶239
IRC Sec. 893	Sec. 17146	Employees of Foreign Country	¶230
IRC Secs. 901-05	. . .	Income from Sources Outside U.S.	¶127, Various
IRC Sec. 911	Sec. 17024.5	Foreign Income Exclusion	¶231, ¶235
IRC Sec. 912	. . .	Income from Sources Within U.S. Possessions	¶231, ¶235
IRC Sec. 941	. . .	Qualifying Foreign Trade Income	. . .
IRC Sec. 942	. . .	Foreign Trading Gross Receipts	. . .
IRC Sec. 943	. . .	Other Foreign Property	. . .
IRC Secs. 951-52	. . .	Controlled Foreign Corporations—Shareholders	¶226
IRC Sec. 988	Sec. 17078	Foreign Currency Transactions	¶521
IRC Secs. 991-99	Sec. 17024.5	Domestic International Sales Corp. (DISC)	. . .
IRC Sec. 995	. . .	Taxation of DISC Income to Shareholders	¶226
IRC Sec. 1001	Secs. 18031, 18041.5	Determination of Gain or Loss	¶501
IRC Sec. 1011	Sec. 18031	Adjusted Basis for Determining Gain or Loss	¶559
IRC Sec. 1012	Sec. 18031	Basis of Property	¶542
IRC Sec. 1013	Sec. 18031	Basis of Property Included in Inventory	¶543
IRC Sec. 1014	Secs. 18031, 18035.6	Basis of Property Acquired from Decedent	¶546
IRC Sec. 1015	Sec. 18031	Basis of Property Acquired by Gift and Transfers in Trust	¶544, ¶545
IRC Sec. 1016	Secs. 18031, 18036, 18036.5	Adjustments to Basis	¶559, ¶560
IRC Sec. 1017	Sec. 18031	Discharge of Indebtedness	¶221, ¶559
IRC Sec. 1019	Sec. 18031	Property on Which Lessee Has Made Improvements	¶559, 561
IRC Sec. 1021	Sec. 18031	Sale of Annuity Contract	¶559

Federal	California	Subject	Paragraph
IRC Sec. 1022	Sec. 18036.6	Basis of Property Acquired from Post-2009 Decedent	¶546
IRC Sec. 1031	Sec. 18031	Exchange of Property Held for Productive Use or Investment	¶507
IRC Sec. 1033	Secs. 18031, 18037	Involuntary Conversions	¶503, ¶550
IRC Sec. 1035	Sec. 18031	Exchange of Insurance Policies	¶508
IRC Sec. 1036	Sec. 18031	Exchange of Stock	¶509
IRC Sec. 1037	Sec. 18031	Exchanges of U.S. Obligations	¶510
IRC Sec. 1038	Sec. 18031	Reacquisition of Real Property	¶511
IRC Sec. 1040	Secs. 18031, 18038	Transfer of Certain Real Property	¶604
IRC Sec. 1041	Sec. 18031	Inter-Spousal Transfers	¶502
IRC Sec. 1042	Secs. 18031, 18042	Securities Sales to ESOPs	¶501, ¶514
IRC Sec. 1043	Sec. 18031	Sale of Property to Comply with Conflict of Interest Requirements	. . .
IRC Sec. 1044	Secs. 18031, 18049	Rollover of Publicly Traded Securities	¶501
IRC Sec. 1045	Secs. 18038.4, 18038.5	Rollover of Gain from Small Business Stock	¶515
IRC Sec. 1052	Secs. 18031, 18039	Basis Provisions from Prior Codes	¶554
IRC Sec. 1053	Sec. 18031	Basis of Property Acquired Before March 1913	¶556
IRC Sec. 1054	Sec. 18031	Basis of Stock Issued by FNMA	¶551
IRC Sec. 1055	Sec. 18031	Redeemable Ground Rents	¶552
IRC Sec. 1056	Sec. 18031	Basis Limitations for Player Contracts	¶563
IRC Sec. 1058	Sec. 18031	Transfer of Securities Under Loan Agreement	. . .
IRC Sec. 1059A	Sec. 18031	Basis or Inventor Costs on Imports	¶542
IRC Sec. 1060	Sec. 18031	Allocation of Transferred Business Assets	¶564
IRC Sec. 1081	Sec. 18031	Exchanges in Obedience to Orders of S.E.C.	¶506
IRC Sec. 1082	Sec. 18031	Basis for Determining Gain or Loss	¶557
IRC Sec. 1083	Sec. 18031	Definitions	. . .
IRC Sec. 1091	Sec. 18031	Wash Sales of Stock or Securities	¶527, ¶553
IRC Sec. 1092	Sec. 18031	Straddle Losses	¶532
IRC Sec. 1202	Secs. 18152, 18152.5	Small Business Stock	¶525
IRC Secs. 1211-12	Secs. 18151, 18155	Limitation on Capital Losses	¶523, ¶526
IRC Sec. 1221	Sec. 18151	"Capital Asset" Defined	¶504, ¶524
IRC Sec. 1222	Sec. 18151	Other Terms Relating to Capital Gains and Losses	¶525
IRC Sec. 1223	Secs. 18151, 18155.5	Holding Period of Property	¶528
IRC Sec. 1231	Sec. 18151	Sale of Business Property and Involuntary Conversions	¶537
IRC Sec. 1233	Sec. 18151	Gains and Losses from Short Sales	¶529
IRC Sec. 1234	Sec. 18151	Options to Buy and Sell	¶532
IRC Sec. 1234A	Sec. 18151	Gain or Loss from Certain Terminations	¶523
IRC Sec. 1234B	Sec. 18151	Gain or Loss from Securities Futures Contracts	¶523
IRC Sec. 1235	Sec. 18151	Sale or Exchange of Patents	¶530
IRC Sec. 1236	Sec. 18151	Dealers in Securities	¶533
IRC Sec. 1237	Sec. 18151	Real Property Subdivided for Sale	¶536
IRC Sec. 1239	Sec. 18151	Gain on Depreciable Property Transferred Between Related Taxpayers	¶537, ¶539
IRC Sec. 1241	Sec. 18151	Cancellation of Lease or Distributor's Agreement	¶541
IRC Sec. 1242	Sec. 18151	Losses on Small Business Investment Company Stock	¶307
IRC Sec. 1243	Sec. 18151	Stock Received Pursuant to Conversion Privilege	¶307
IRC Sec. 1244	Sec. 18151	Losses on Small Business Stock	¶307
IRC Sec. 1245	Secs. 18151, 18165	Recapture of Depreciation on Personal Property	¶539
IRC Sec. 1246	Sec. 17024.5	Gain on Foreign Investment Company Stock	¶538
IRC Secs. 1247-48	Secs. 17024.5, 18151	Special Rules on Foreign Investment Company Stock	¶538
IRC Sec. 1249	Secs. 17024.5, 18151	Patents Sold to Foreign Corporation	¶530, 538
IRC Sec. 1250	Secs. 18151, 18171, 18171.5	Recapture of Depreciation on Real Property	¶539
IRC Sec. 1252	Sec. 18151	Recapture of Soil and Water Conservation Expenditures	¶539
IRC Sec. 1253	Sec. 18151	Transfers of Franchises, Trademarks and Trade Names	¶332, ¶531, ¶539
IRC Sec. 1254	Sec. 18151	Recapture of Intangible Drilling Costs	¶539
IRC Sec. 1255	Sec. 18151	Certain Cost-Sharing Payments	¶539
IRC Sec. 1256	Sec. 18151	Regulated Futures Contracts	¶532
IRC Sec. 1257	Sec. 18151	Wetlands or Erodible Croplands	¶523
IRC Sec. 1258	Sec. 18151	Recharacterization of Gain from Certain Financial Transactions	. . .
IRC Sec. 1259	Sec. 18151	Constructive Sales Treatment for Appreciated Financial Positions	¶534

Federal	California	Subject	Paragraph
IRC Sec. 1260	. . .	Recharacterization of Derivative Contract Gains	¶523, 525
IRC Secs. 1271-88	Secs. 18151, 18177, 18178	Income from Discount Bonds, etc.	¶217, ¶237, ¶535
IRC Secs. 1291-1298	Sec. 18181	Treatment of Passive Investment Companies	¶523
IRC Secs. 1311-14	Secs. 19057-67	Mitigation of Effect of Limitations	¶710, ¶719
IRC Sec. 1341	Sec. 17049	Repayment of Amounts Received Under Claim of Right	¶415
IRC Secs. 1361-79	Secs. 17087.5, 18006	Subchapter S Corporations	¶233
IRC Secs. 1381-83	. . .	Tax Treatment of Cooperatives	¶232
IRC Sec. 1385	Sec. 17086	Amounts Includible in Patron's Gross Income	¶232
IRC Sec. 1396	Sec. 17053.74	Empowerment Zone Employment Credit	¶145
IRC Sec. 1445	Secs. 18662, 18668	Withholding—Disposition of Real Estate	¶714, ¶716
IRC Sec. 1446	Sec. 18666	Withholding—Amounts Paid to Foreign Partners	¶714
IRC Secs. 1491-94	. . .	Transfers of Property to Avoid Tax	. . .
IRC Secs. 3401-05	Secs. 18551, 18661-63, 18667, 18668	Withholding	¶715
IRC Sec. 3406	. . .	Backup Withholding	¶713
IRC Secs. 3501-05	Sec. 18677	Collection of Withholding Tax	¶715
IRC Secs. 4940-48	. . .	Private Foundations	¶606
IRC Secs. 4971-75	. . .	Pension Plans, etc.	¶206, ¶607
IRC Sec. 4980A	. . .	Excess Distributions from Qualified Plans	¶206
IRC Sec. 4980B	. . .	Excise Tax on Failure to Meet Health Care Continuous Coverage	. . .
IRC Sec. 6011	Secs. 18407, 18408, 18409	General Return Requirements/Abusive Tax Shelters	¶622, ¶715, ¶727
IRC Sec. 6012	Secs. 18501, 18503-9, 18601	Returns Required	¶106
IRC Sec. 6013	Secs. 18521-33, 19006	Joint Returns	¶106, ¶107, ¶709, ¶712
IRC Sec. 6014	..	Tax Not Computed by Taxpayer	¶106
IRC Sec. 6015	Sec. 18533	Innocent Spouse Relief	¶107
IRC Sec. 6031	Secs. 18535, 18633-33.5	Return of Partnership Income	¶622
IRC Sec. 6034	Sec. 18635	Information from Charitable Trust	¶606
IRC Sec. 6034A	Secs. 18505, 18635.5	Information to Beneficiaries	¶106, ¶601
IRC Sec. 6036	Sec. 19089	Notice of Executor's Qualification	. . .
IRC Sec. 6039	Sec. 18631	Returns for Stock Transfers	¶713
IRC Sec. 6039C	Sec. 18631	Returns by Foreign Persons	¶713
IRC Sec. 6039D	. . .	Fringe Benefit Plans Return	¶713
IRC Sec. 6041	Secs. 18631, 18661	Reporting Requirements	¶713
IRC Sec. 6041A	Sec. 18631	Reporting Certain Payments	¶713
IRC Sec. 6042	Secs. 18631, 18639	Returns for Dividends	¶713
IRC Sec. 6043	. . .	Returns for Dividends on Liquidation	¶713
IRC Sec. 6044	Sec. 18640	Returns by Cooperatives	¶713
IRC Sec. 6045	Sec. 18631	Reporting by Brokers	¶713
IRC Sec. 6046A	. . .	Foreign Partnership Return	¶713
IRC Sec. 6047	Sec. 19518	Information Returns	¶607, ¶713
IRC Sec. 6048	Sec. 18505	Consistency Rule	¶601, ¶711
IRC Sec. 6049	Secs. 18631, 18639	Returns for Interest	¶713
IRC Sec. 6050A	Sec. 18644	Fishing Boat Operators—Reporting Requirements	¶713
IRC Sec. 6050B	. . .	Reporting Unemployment Compensation	. . .
IRC Sec. 6050E	. . .	Reporting Tax Refunds	¶713
IRC Sec. 6050H-S	Sec. 18631	Information Returns	¶713
IRC Sec. 6051	. . .	Receipts for Employees	¶715
IRC Sec. 6052	Sec. 18631	Returns for Group-Term Life Insurance	¶713
IRC Sec. 6053	UI Code	Reporting Tips	¶713, ¶715
IRC Sec. 6060	. . .	Tax Preparer Information Returns	¶701
IRC Sec. 6072	Secs. 18566, 18601	Time for Filing Returns	¶108
IRC Sec. 6081	Secs. 18567, 18604	Extension of Time	¶108, ¶109
IRC Sec. 6091	Sec. 18621	Form of Return	¶108
IRC Sec. 6102	Sec. 18623	Fractional Dollar Calculations	¶106
IRC Secs. 6103-10	Secs. 19542-64	Secrecy and Disclosure of Returns	¶701, ¶704, ¶721
IRC Secs. 6111-12	Secs. 18628, 18648, 19182	Reportable and Listed Transactions	¶712, ¶713
IRC Sec. 6115	Sec. 18648.5	Disclosure Related to Quid Pro Quo Contributions	. . .
IRC Sec. 6151	Secs. 19001-06	Payment of Tax	¶107
IRC Sec. 6161	. . .	Extensions of Time for Payment	¶107
IRC Sec. 6201	Secs. 19054, 21024	Assessment Authority	¶208, ¶704
IRC Sec. 6211	Sec. 19043	"Deficiency" Defined	¶704, ¶705
IRC Sec. 6212	Secs. 19031-36, 19049, 19050	Notice of Deficiency	¶704
IRC Sec. 6213	Secs. 19041-48, 19051, 19332-34	Restrictions Applicable to Deficiencies	¶704 -06
IRC Sec. 6225	Sec. 19063	SOL for Partnership Related Deficiencies	¶710

Federal	California	Subject	Paragraph
IRC Sec. 6233	...	Partnership Audits	...
IRC Sec. 6302	Sec. 19011	Electronic Funds Transfer	¶110
IRC Sec. 6311	Sec. 19222	Payment by Check or Money Order	¶110
IRC Sec. 6313	...	Fractional Dollar Calculations	¶110
IRC Sec. 6315	Sec. 19007	Payments of Estimated Taxes	¶111
IRC Sec. 6321	Sec. 19221	Lien on Tax	¶612
IRC Sec. 6322	Sec. 19221	Period of Lien	...
IRC Sec. 6323	Secs. 19253, 21016	Priority of Lien	...
IRC Sec. 6325	Secs. 19206-09, 19226	Release of Lien	...
IRC Sec. 6331	Secs. 19231, 19236, 19262, 21019	Levy to Collect Tax	...
IRC Sec. 6343	Sec. 21016	Release of Levy	¶702
IRC Sec. 6401	Secs. 19107, 19349, 19354	Excess of Tax Withheld	¶717, ¶718
IRC Sec. 6402	Secs. 19301, 19323, 19362, 19363	Credits and Refunds	¶706, ¶717, ¶718
IRC Sec. 6403	...	Overpayment of Installment	¶110
IRC Sec. 6404	Secs. 19104, 19109, 19116, 19431	Abatements	¶703, ¶711, ¶712
IRC Sec. 6428	...	Acceleration of 2001 10% Income Tax Bracket	...
IRC Secs. 6501-04	Secs. 19057, 19058, 19065-67, 19087, 19371	Limitations on Assessment	¶613, ¶710
IRC Sec. 6511	Secs. 19306-16	Limitation on Refunds	¶719
IRC Sec. 6513	Sec. 19002	Time Return Filed and Tax Paid	¶108
IRC Sec. 6531	Sec. 19704	Statute of Limitations—Criminal Actions	...
IRC Sec. 6532	Secs. 19381-85, 19388-89	Suits for Refund	¶720, ¶726
IRC Sec. 6601	Secs. 19101-14	Interest on Tax Due	¶110, ¶711
IRC Sec. 6602	Sec. 19411	Interest on Erroneous Refund	¶726
IRC Sec. 6603	Secs. 19041.5	Deposits to Stop the Running of Interest	¶719, ¶720
IRC Sec. 6611	Secs. 19325, 19340-51	Interest on Overpayments	¶722
IRC Sec. 6621	Sec. 19521	Interest Rate	¶711
IRC Sec. 6622	Sec. 19521	Compounding of Interest	¶711
IRC Sec. 6631	Sec. 19117	Notice of Interest Charges	¶711
IRC Sec. 6651	Secs. 19131-32.5	Penalty—Failure to Make Return	¶712
IRC Sec. 6652	Sec. 19133.5	Penalty—Certain Information Returns	¶712
IRC Sec. 6653	...	Penalty—Failure to Pay Stamp Tax	¶712
IRC Sec. 6654	Secs. 19136-36.6	Underpayment of Estimated Tax	¶111
IRC Sec. 6657	Secs. 19005, 19134	Bad Checks	¶712
IRC Sec. 6658	Sec. 19161	Timely Payment During Bankruptcy	¶712
IRC Secs. 6662-63	Secs. 19164, 19164.5, 19772-74	Penalty for Substantial Understatement	¶712, ¶727
IRC Sec. 6672	Sec. 19708	Penalty—Failure to Collect and Pay Tax	¶712
IRC Sec. 6673	Sec. 19714	Penalty for Delay	¶712
IRC Sec. 6674	UI Code	Penalty—Fraudulent Statement	¶712
IRC Sec. 6682	Sec. 19176	Penalty—False Withholding Information	¶712
IRC Sec. 6690	...	Penalty—Fraudulent Statement to Pension Plan Participant	...
IRC Sec. 6693	Sec. 19184	Penalty—Failure to Properly Report IRA	¶712
IRC Sec. 6694	Sec. 19166	Understatement by Preparer	¶701, ¶712
IRC Secs. 6695-96	Secs. 19166-69, 19712	Penalties—Tax Preparers	¶701, ¶712
IRC Sec. 6698	Sec. 19172	Penalty—Partnership Returns	¶622, ¶712
IRC Sec. 6700	Secs. 19174, 19177	Penalty for Promoting Abusive Tax Shelters	¶727
IRC Sec. 6701	Sec. 19178	Penalty for Aiding and Abetting Understatement	¶712
IRC Sec. 6702	Sec. 19179	Penalty for Frivolous Returns	¶712
IRC Sec. 6703	Sec. 19180	Rules for Penalties	¶712
IRC Sec. 6704	...	Penalty—Failure to Keep Records	...
IRC Sec. 6705	...	Penalty—Broker's Failure to Notify Payors	...
IRC Sec. 6706	Secs. 18649, 19181	OID Information	¶237, ¶712
IRC Sec. 6707	Sec. 19182	Penalty—Tax Shelters	¶727
IRC Sec. 6707A	Sec. 19772	Reportable Transaction Nonreporting Penalty	¶727
IRC Sec. 6708	Sec. 19173	Tax Shelters	...
IRC Sec. 6714	Sec. 19182.5	Penalty; Failure to Disclose Quid Pro Quo Information	...
IRC Secs. 6721-24	Sec. 19183	Penalty—Failure to File Information Returns	¶712
IRC Sec. 6751	Sec. 19187	Procedures for Penalties	¶712
IRC Sec. 6861	Secs. 19081, 19086, 19092	Jeopardy Assessments	¶707
IRC Sec. 6863	Secs. 19083-85	Jeopardy Assessments—Stay of Collection	¶707
IRC Sec. 6867	Sec. 19093	Unexplained Cash	¶707
IRC Sec. 6871	Secs. 19088-90	Assessment in Receivership	¶708
IRC Sec. 6872	Sec. 19089	Suspension of Period of Assessment	¶708
IRC Sec. 6873	Sec. 19091	Unpaid Claims	¶708
IRC Sec. 6901	Secs. 19071-74	Liability of Transferees and Fiduciaries	¶613, ¶709
IRC Sec. 6903	Sec. 19512	Notice of Fiduciary Relationship	¶613, ¶709
IRC Sec. 6905	Sec. 19516	Discharge of Liability for Decedent's Taxes	¶613
IRC Sec. 7121	Sec. 19441	Closing Agreements	¶723
IRC Sec. 7122	Sec. 19702	Compromises	¶724

Federal	California	Subject	Paragraph
IRC Sec. 7201	Secs. 19701, 19708	Evasion of Tax	¶712
IRC Sec. 7202	Secs. 19708-09	Failure to Remit Withheld Tax	¶712
IRC Sec. 7203	Secs. 19701, 19706	Violation—Failure to File Return	¶712
IRC Sec. 7206	Secs. 19701, 19705	False Statements—Fraud	¶712
IRC Sec. 7207	Secs. 19701, 19706	Violation—Fraudulent Returns, Statements, or Other Documents	¶712
IRC Secs. 7213-16	Secs. 19542, 19542.3, 19552, 19713	Unauthorized Disclosure of Information	¶721
IRC Sec. 7403	Sec. 19371	Suit for Tax	...
IRC Sec. 7405	Sec. 19411	Recovery of Erroneous Refunds	¶726
IRC Sec. 7408	Sec. 19715	Injunctive Relief	¶712
IRC Sec. 7421	Sec. 19381	Suits to Restrain Collection Prohibited	¶701, ¶720
IRC Sec. 7422	Secs. 19381-83, 19387-89	Actions for Refunds	¶720
IRC Sec. 7429	Sec. 19084	Jeopardy Assessment Review	¶707
IRC Sec. 7430	Secs. 19717, 21013	Recovery of Litigation Costs	¶701
IRC Sec. 7502	Sec. 21027	Mailing	¶108
IRC Sec. 7503	Gov. Code	Due Date—Holiday	¶108
IRC Sec. 7508	Secs. 17142.5, 18570, 18571	Extension—Members of Armed Forces	¶109
IRC Sec. 7508A	Sec. 18572	Extensions for Disaster Victims	¶108, ¶110, ¶710, ¶719
IRC Sec. 7512	Sec. 19009	Separate Accounting for Certain Collected Taxes, etc.	¶715
IRC Sec. 7518	Sec. 17088.3	Capital Construction Funds for Vessels	¶234
IRC Sec. 7602	Sec. 19504.7	Notice of Contact of Third Parties	¶701
IRC Sec. 7612	Sec. 19504.5	Software Trade Secrets	¶720
IRC Sec. 7701	Various	Definitions	¶212, ¶607, ¶616
IRC Sec. 7702B	Sec. 17020.6	Qualified Long-Term Care Insurance	¶219
IRC Sec. 7703	Sec. 17021.5	Marital Status	¶114
IRC Sec. 7704	Sec. 17008.5	Publicly Traded Partnerships	¶616
IRC Sec. 7811	Secs. 21001-26	Taxpayers' Bill of Rights	¶701, ¶702, ¶703
IRC Sec. 7872	Sec. 18180	Loans with Below-Market Interest Rates	¶414

CALIFORNIA-FEDERAL CROSS-REFERENCE TABLE AND INDEX

Showing Sections of Federal Law (1986 Internal Revenue Code) Comparable to Sections of California Personal Income Tax Law (Revenue and Taxation Code)

California	Federal	Subject	Paragraph
Sec. 17002	IRC Sec. 7806	Definitions	. . .
Sec. 17003	IRC Sec. 7701(a)(11)	"Franchise Tax Board" defined	. . .
Sec. 17004	IRC Sec. 7701(a)(1), (14)	"Taxpayer" defined	. . .
Sec. 17005	. . .	"Individual" defined	. . .
Sec. 17006	IRC Sec. 7701(a)(6)	"Fiduciary" defined	. . .
Sec. 17007	IRC Sec. 7701(a)(1)	"Person" defined	. . .
Sec. 17008	IRC Sec. 7701(a)(2)	"Partnership" defined	¶616
Sec. 17008.5	IRC Sec. 7704	Publicly-traded partnerships	¶616
Sec. 17009	IRC Sec. 7701(a)(3)	"Corporation" defined	¶606
Sec. 17010	IRC Sec. 7701(a)(23)	"Taxable year" defined	. . .
Sec. 17011	IRC Sec. 7701(a)(24)	"Fiscal year" defined	. . .
Sec. 17012	IRC Sec. 7701(a)(25)	"Paid or incurred" defined	. . .
Sec. 17014	. . .	"Resident" defined	¶105
Sec. 17015	. . .	"Nonresident" defined	¶105
Sec. 17015.5	. . .	"Part-year resident" defined	¶105
Sec. 17016	. . .	Presumption of residence	¶105
Sec. 17017	IRC Sec. 7701(a)(9)	"United States" defined	. . .
Sec. 17018	IRC Sec. 7701(a)(10)	"State" defined	. . .
Sec. 17019	. . .	"Foreign country" defined	. . .
Sec. 17020	IRC Sec. 7701(a)(26)	"Trade or business" defined	. . .
Sec. 17020.1	IRC Sec. 7701(a)(42)	Substituted basis property	. . .
Sec. 17020.2	IRC Sec. 7701(a)(43)	Transferred basis property	. . .
Sec. 17020.3	IRC Sec. 7701(a)(44)	Exchanged basis property	. . .
Sec. 17020.4	IRC Sec. 7701(a)(45)	Nonrecognition transaction	. . .
Sec. 17020.5	IRC Sec. 7701(g)	Determination of gain or loss	. . .
Sec. 17020.6	IRC Sec. 7702-02B	"Life insurance contract" defined	. . .
Sec. 17020.7	IRC Sec. 7701(a)(46)	Collective bargaining agreement	. . .
Sec. 17020.8	IRC Sec. 7701(e)	Contracts for services	. . .
Sec. 17020.9	IRC Sec. 7701(a)(19)	Domestic building & loan association	. . .
Sec. 17020.11	IRC Sec. 7701(h)	Motor vehicle operating leases	. . .
Sec. 17020.12	IRC Sec. 7701(a)(20)	"Employee" defined	¶212
Sec. 17020.13	IRC Sec. 7701(k)	Treatment of amounts paid to charity	. . .
Sec. 17021	IRC Sec. 7701(a)(17)	"Husband" and "Wife" defined	. . .
Sec. 17021.5	IRC Sec. 7703	Marital status	¶114
Sec. 17021.7	. . .	Treatment of domestic parnter	¶119, ¶206, ¶219, ¶247, ¶253¶301, ¶325
Sec. 17022	IRC Sec. 7701(a)(15)	"Armed Forces" defined	. . .
Sec. 17023	IRC Sec. 7801	"Franchise Tax Board" defined	. . .
Sec. 17024	IRC Sec. 7701(a)(29)	"Personal Income Tax Law of 1954" defined	. . .
Sec. 17024.5	IRC Secs. 196, 541-47, 551-58, 679, 853, 911, 991-99, 1246, 1551-3322, 7806	Federal conformity program	Various
Sec. 17024.7	IRC Sec. 222	Tuition and related expenses deduction	¶344
Sec. 17026	IRC Sec. 7851	Application of act	. . .
Sec. 17028	IRC Sec. 7807	Construction of code	. . .
Sec. 17029	IRC Sec. 7807	Rights and liabilities under prior code	. . .
Sec. 17029.5	. . .	Basis adjustments and carryovers	. . .
Sec. 17030	IRC Sec. 7807	Reference to corresponding law	. . .
Sec. 17031	IRC Sec. 7807	Reference to prior period	. . .
Sec. 17033	IRC Sec. 7852	Severability of law	. . .
Sec. 17034	IRC Sec. 15	Effect of law changes	¶406
Sec. 17035	IRC Sec. 7701(a)(16)	"Withholding agent" defined	. . .
Sec. 17036	. . .	Service of notice	. . .
Sec. 17038	. . .	"Consumer price index" defined	. . .
Sec. 17039	IRC Sec. 26	"Net tax" defined	¶117, ¶125, ¶126, ¶132
Sec. 17039.1	. . .	Natural heritage preservation credit	¶117
Sec. 17039.2	. . .	Temporary limits on business credits	¶125
Sec. 17041	IRC Sec. 1(g)	Rate of tax	¶60, ¶61, ¶116, ¶118, ¶309
Sec. 17041.5	. . .	Local income tax	¶101

California	Federal	Subject	Paragraph
Sec. 17042	IRC Sec. 2(b), (c)	"Head of household" defined	¶114
Sec. 17043	...	Additional tax on millionaires	¶116, ¶125
Sec. 17045	...	Joint return tax rate	¶107
Sec. 17046	IRC Sec. 2(a)	"Surviving spouse" defined	¶107
Sec. 17048	IRC Sec. 3	Tax table	¶116
Sec. 17049	IRC Sec. 1341	Claim of right adjustment	¶415
Sec. 17052.6	IRC Sec. 21	Household and dependent care expense credit	¶142
Sec. 17052.8	IRC Sec. 43	Enhanced oil recovery credit	¶153
Sec. 17052.10	...	Rice straw credit	¶155¶125
Sec. 17052.12	IRC Sec. 41	Research & development credit	¶150
Sec. 17052.17	IRC Sec. 45F	Child care facility credit	¶134
Sec. 17052.18	...	Credit for contributions to child care plan	¶134
Sec. 17052.25	IRC Sec. 23	Adoption costs credit	¶139
Sec. 17053.5	...	Renter's credit	¶133
Sec. 17053.6	...	Prison inmate labor credit	¶154
Sec. 17053.7	IRC Sec. 51	Jobs tax credit	¶154
Sec. 17053.12	...	Credit for transportation of donated agricultural products	¶141
Sec. 17053.14	...	Farmworker Housing Credit	¶137
Sec. 17053.30	...	Natural heritage preservation credit	¶143
Sec. 17053.33	...	Sales tax credit	¶144
Sec. 17053.34	...	Targeted tax area employers'credit	¶148
Sec. 17053.42	IRC Sec. 44	Disabled access credit	¶140
Sec. 17053.45	...	LAMBRA credit, sales tax equivalent	¶144
Sec. 17053.46	...	LAMBRA credit, employers	¶147
Sec. 17053.47	...	Manufacturing enhancement area employers' credit	¶149
Sec. 17053.57	IRC Sec. 38	Community development investment credit	¶156¶155
Sec. 17053.62	IRC Sec. 45H	Low-Sulfur Diesel Fuel Production Credit	¶160
Sec. 17053.70	...	Enterprise zone sales taxcredit	¶144
Sec. 17053.74	IRC Sec. 1396	Enterprise zone employer'scredit	¶145
Sec. 17053.75	...	Enterprise zone employee's credit	¶146
Sec. 17054	IRC Sec. 151(c)	Credits for personal and dependent exemptions	¶113
Sec. 17054.1	IRC Sec. 151(d)	Credit reduction for high-income taxpayers	¶113
Sec. 17054.5	...	Joint custody head of household, dependent parent credits	¶136
Sec. 17054.7	...	Senior head of household credit	¶135
Sec. 17055	...	Credits for nonresidents, part-year residents	¶125
Sec. 17056	IRC Sec. 152(a)	"Dependent" defined	¶113, ¶115
Sec. 17057.5	IRC Sec. 42	Low-income housing credit	¶138
Sec. 17058	IRC Sec. 42	Low-income housing credit	¶138
Sec. 17061	...	Credit for excess SDI contributions	¶132
Sec. 17062	IRC Secs. 55-59	Alternative minimum tax	¶117
Sec. 17062.3	IRC Sec. 56(g)	Extraterritorial income AMT modification inapplicable	¶117
Sec. 17062.5	IRC Sec. 55(b)	Federal noncorporate AMT tax rate inapplicable	¶117
Sec. 17063	IRC Sec. 53	Minimum tax credit	¶152
Sec. 17071	IRC Sec. 61	"Gross income" defined	¶201
Sec. 17072	IRC Sec. 62	"Adjusted gross income" defined	¶202, ¶305, ¶328, ¶329
Sec. 17072.5	IRC Sec. 62(a)(2)(E)	National guard/reservists travel expenses	¶201
Sec. 17073	IRC Sec. 63	"Taxable income" defined	¶112, ¶203, ¶303
Sec. 17073.5	IRC Sec. 63	Standard deduction	¶203, ¶335
Sec. 17074	IRC Sec. 64	"Ordinary income" defined	...
Sec. 17075	IRC Sec. 65	"Ordinary loss" defined	...
Sec. 17076	IRC Sec. 67	2% floor on miscellaneous itemized deductions	¶303, ¶328, ¶329, ¶604
Sec. 17077	IRC Sec. 68	6% limit on itemized deductions	¶303
Sec. 17078	IRC Sec. 988	Foreign currency transactions	¶521
Sec. 17081	IRC Secs. 71-90	Items in gross income	Various
Sec. 17081	IRC Sec. 72	Annuities, endowments, and life insurance proceeds	¶205
Sec. 17081	IRC Sec. 83	Property transfers in connection with services	¶207

California	Federal	Subject	Paragraph
Sec. 17083	IRC Sec. 85	Unemployment compensation	¶201
Sec. 17085	IRC Sec. 72	Lump-sum distributions	¶205, ¶206, ¶214
Sec. 17085.7	IRC Sec. 72	Levies on retirement plans and IRAs	¶206
Sec. 17086	IRC Sec. 1385	Patronage allocations	¶232
Sec. 17087	IRC Secs. 72(r), 86, 105(i)	Social security benefits, etc.	¶201, ¶219
Sec. 17087.5	IRC Secs. 1361-79	S corporation shareholders	¶233
Sec. 17087.6	IRC Sec. 61	Limited liability companies	¶625
Sec. 17088	IRC Secs. 851-60L	RICs, REITs, REMICs, and FASITs	¶217, ¶226, ¶559, ¶609, ¶610, ¶615
Sec. 17088.3	IRC Sec. 7518	Capital construction funds for vessels	¶234
Sec. 17090	IRC Sec. 61	Subsidized employee parking	¶241
Sec. 17131	IRC Secs. 101-40	Exclusions—gross income	Various
Sec. 17131.1	Act Sec. 803 (P.L. 107-16)	Holocaust reparation exclusion	¶248
Sec. 17131.2	. . .	Armenian genocide settlement payments	¶248
Sec. 17131.4	IRC Sec. 106(d)	Employer contributions to health savings accounts	¶219, ¶247
Sec. 17131.5	IRC Sec. 125(d)	Employer contributions to health savings accounts	¶223, ¶247
Sec. 17131.6	IRC Sec. 107	Rental value of parsonage	¶220
Sec. 17132	IRC Sec. 114	Extraterritorial income exclusion	...
Sec. 17132.4	. . .	California national guard/ reservists death benefit exclusion	¶225
Sec. 17132.5	IRC Sec. 101	Certain death benefits	¶213
Sec. 17132.6	IRC Sec. 104(a)	Ricky Ray Hemophilia Relief Fund	¶213
Sec. 17132.7	IRC Sec. 104(a)	Exempt damages	¶218
Sec. 17133	IRC Sec. 61	Constitutional prohibition	¶201, ¶217, ¶324
Sec. 17133.5	IRC Sec. 61	Gain or loss from exempt bonds	¶201, ¶513
Sec. 17134	IRC Sec. 108	Discharge of student loans	¶221
Sec. 17135	IRC Secs. 61, 132, 274	Automobile expenses of federal or state taxing authority agents	¶201
Sec. 17135.5	IRC Sec. 126	Cost-share payments received by forest landowners	¶201, ¶243
Sec. 17136	IRC Sec. 61	Forest Service payments	¶201
Sec. 17138	IRC Sec. 61	Water conservation rebates	¶244
Sec. 17138.1	IRC Sec. 136	Energy conservation subsidy exclusion	¶245
Sec. 17139.5	. . .	Interest on smog impact fee refund	...
Sec. 17139.6	IRC Sec. 139A	Federal subsidies for prescription drugs	¶252
Sec. 17140	IRC Sec. 529	Golden State Scholarshare Trust	¶250
Sec. 17140.3	IRC Sec. 529	Qualified tuition programs	¶250
Sec. 17140.5	IRC Sec. 61	Military compensation	¶225
Sec. 17141	. . .	Community Energy Authority	¶201
Sec. 17142	IRC Sec. 111	Credits, credit carryovers	¶224
Sec. 17142.5	IRC Secs. 112, 692, 7508	Military combat pay	¶109, ¶225
Sec. 17143	IRC Secs. 103, 141-50	Exempt interest	¶217
Sec. 17144	IRC Sec. 108	Exclusion for income from discharge of indebtedness	¶221
Sec. 17144.5	IRC Sec. 108	Discharge of qualified residential property indebtedness	¶221
Sec. 17145	IRC Sec. 852	Exempt distributions from RICs	¶217
Sec. 17146	IRC Sec. 893	Employees of foreign countries	¶230
Sec. 17147.7	IRC Sec. 61	Crime hotline rewards	¶201, ¶246
Sec. 17149	IRC Secs. 61, 132	Subsidized commuter expense	¶241
Sec. 17151	IRC Sec. 127	Educational assistance	¶201, ¶242
Sec. 17152	IRC Sec. 121	Exclusion of gain from primary residence sale	¶229
Sec. 17153.5	IRC Sec. 61	Recycling income	¶201
Sec. 17154	IRC Sec. 132	Taxable education or training benefits	¶201
Sec. 17155	U.S.-Federal Republic of Germany Income Tax Convention	Holocaust victim compensation	¶248
Sec. 17155.5	. . .	WWII slave labor reparations	¶248
Sec. 17156.5	. . .	Japanese internment reparations	¶248
Sec. 17157	. . .	Wrongful conviction compensation	¶201
Sec. 17201	IRC Secs. 161-222, 261-280H	Allowance of deductions	Various
Sec. 17201	IRC Sec. 215	Alimony payments	¶323
Sec. 17201	IRC Sec. 280G	"Golden parachute" payments	¶336
Sec. 17201	IRC Sec. 179	Asset expense election	¶311
Sec. 17201.4	IRC Sec. 179B	EPA sulfur compliance costs	¶318
Sec. 17201.5	IRC Sec. 181	Film and production expenses	¶301, ¶310

California	Federal	Subject	Paragraph
Sec. 17201.6	IRC Sec. 199	Domestic production activities deduction	¶317
Sec. 17202	IRC Sec. 162	Employee parking cash-out programs	¶343
Sec. 17202.5	IRC Sec. 161(a)(2)	National guard/reservists travel expenses	¶202
Sec. 17203	IRC Secs. 162, 219, 404	"Compensation" or "earned income"	¶301, ¶330
Sec. 17204	IRC Sec. 221	Interest on student loans	¶305
Sec. 17204.7	IRC Sec. 222	Tuition and related expenses	¶344
Sec. 17206	IRC Sec. 170	Tsunami relief donations	¶321
Secs. 17207, 17207.4	IRC Sec. 165	Disaster losses	¶303, ¶307, ¶407
Sec. 17208.1	...	Energy-efficient equipment loan interest	¶305
Sec. 17215	IRC Sec. 220	Archer MSAs	¶247, ¶326
Sec. 17215.1	IRC Sec. 220	Rollover from MSA to HSA	¶247
Sec. 17215.4	IRC Sec. 223	Health savings accounts	¶247, ¶326
Sec. 17220	IRC Sec. 164	Deduction for taxes	¶303, ¶306
Sec. 17222	IRC Sec. 275	Withheld taxes	¶306
Sec. 17224	IRC Sec. 163(e)	Income from OIDs	¶237, ¶305
Sec. 17230	IRC Sec. 163	Buy-down mortgage fees	¶305
Sec. 17235	IRC Sec. 163	Interest deduction—depressed areas	¶240
Sec. 17250	IRC Secs. 168, 169	ACRS depreciation	¶310, ¶314
Sec. 17250.5	IRC Secs. 167(g), 168	Depreciation under income forecast method	¶310
Sec. 17255	IRC Sec. 179	Expense election dollar limitation	¶311
Sec. 17255.5	IRC Sec. 179B	Sulfur regulation compliance costs	¶318
Sec. 17256	IRC Sec. 179A	Clean fuel vehicles deduction	...
Sec. 17260(a)	IRC Sec. 193	Tertiary injectant expenses	¶320
Sec. 17260(b)	IRC Sec. 263	Capital expenditures	¶201, ¶322
Sec. 17267.6	...	Election to expense targeted tax area property	¶316
Sec. 17268	IRC Sec. 179	Accelerated write-off	¶316
Sec. 17269	IRC Sec. 162	No deductions for expenditures at discriminatory clubs	¶301, ¶336
Sec. 17270(a)	IRC Sec. 162	Trade and business expenses	¶301, ¶322
Sec. 17270(b)	IRC Sec. 280C(c)	Targeted employment credit(s)	¶336
Sec. 17270(c)	IRC Sec. 280C(a)	Legislators' expenses	¶301
Sec. 17273	IRC Sec. 162(l)	Trade or business expense	¶301
Sec. 17274	IRC Sec. 161	Expenses of substandard housing	¶336
Sec. 17275	IRC Sec. 161	Abandonment and recoupment fees	¶336
Sec. 17275.5	IRC Sec. 170(f)(8), (9)	Charitable contributions	¶321
Secs. 17276-76.710	IRC Sec. 172	Net operating loss	¶309
Sec. 17278	IRC Secs. 161, 1031	Interindemnity payments	¶301
Sec. 17278.5	IRC Sec. 194	Amortization of forestation expenditures	¶315
Sec. 17279	IRC Sec. 197	Amortization of goodwill	¶333
Sec. 17279.4	IRC Sec. 198	Amortization of goodwill	¶346
Sec. 17280	IRC Sec. 265	Expenses of tax-exempt income	¶305, ¶336
Secs. 17281-82	IRC Sec. 280E	Expenses of illegal activities	¶336
Sec. 17286	IRC Sec. 162	Illegal payments to foreign officials, etc.	¶336
Sec. 17287	IRC Sec. 269A	Personal service corporation formed to avoid/evade income tax	¶412
Secs. 17299.8-99.9	IRC Sec. 161	Deductions disallowed	¶336, ¶712
Secs. 17301-02	IRC Sec. 63	Deductions of nonresidents	¶323, ¶337
Secs. 17302	IRC Sec. 215	Alimony deduction for nonresidents	¶323
Sec. 17304	IRC Sec. 63	Itemized deductions for nonresidents/part-year residents	¶337
Secs. 17306-07	...	Nonresident deductions	¶337
Sec. 17321	IRC Secs. 301-85	Corporate distributions, etc.	Various
Sec. 17322	IRC Sec. 302	Limitation periods	¶226
Sec. 17501	IRC Secs. 401-24	Deferred compensation	Various
Sec. 17501.5	Various	Government pension plan rollovers	¶206
Sec. 17501.7	IRC Secs. 403, 457	Purchases of service credits	¶206
Sec. 17502	IRC Sec. 421	California qualified stock options	¶207
Sec. 17504	IRC Sec. 402(a)	Lump-sum distributions	¶206, ¶330, ¶607
		Beneficiaries of exempt trusts	¶206, ¶330, ¶607
Sec. 17506	IRC Sec. 403(a)	Employee annuities	¶206, ¶330
Sec. 17507	IRC Sec. 408	Individual retirement accounts	¶330
Sec. 17507.6	IRC Secs. 219, 408A	Roth IRAs	¶206, ¶330

California	Federal	Subject	Paragraph
Sec. 17508	IRC Sec. 408(o)	Nondeductible contributions to IRAs	¶318
Sec. 17509	IRC Sec. 413	Liability for funding tax	¶330
Sec. 17510	IRC Sec. 7701(j)	Federal thrift savings funds	¶607
Sec. 17551	IRC Secs. 280H, 441-83	Accounting periods and methods	Various
Sec. 17552	IRC Sec. 443	Short-period returns	¶403
Sec. 17552.3	IRC Sec. 451	Farm production flexibility contract	¶407
Sec. 17553	IRC Sec. 454	Obligations issued at discount	¶408
Sec. 17555	IRC Sec. 61	Allocation of income—spouses	¶412
Sec. 17556	IRC Sec. 442	Change accounting period—estates	¶402
Sec. 17560	IRC Secs. 453, 453A	Allocable installment indebtedness	¶411
Sec. 17561	IRC Sec. 469	Passive activity losses and credits	¶340
Sec. 17563.5	IRC Sec. 404(a)(11)	Accrued vacation	¶330
Sec. 17564	IRC Sec. 460	Long-term contracts	¶407
Sec. 17565	IRC Sec. 441	Taxable year	¶401
Sec. 17570	IRC Sec. 475	Mark-to-market accounting	¶400, ¶409
Sec. 17631	IRC Sec. 501(a)	Exemption for employee trusts	¶607
Sec. 17632	IRC Sec. 501(b)	Exempt organizations—unrelated income	¶607
Sec. 17635	IRC Sec. 503(a)	Prohibited transactions	¶607
Sec. 17636	IRC Sec. 503(a)	Application to Sec. 17501	¶607
Sec. 17637	IRC Sec. 503(b)	"Prohibited transactions" defined	¶607
Sec. 17638	IRC Sec. 503(c)	Claim for exemption	¶607
Sec. 17639	IRC Sec. 503(e)	Security for loan	¶607
Sec. 17640	IRC Sec. 503(f)	Trust loan to employer	¶607
Sec. 17651	IRC Secs. 511, 512	Unrelated business income	¶607
Sec. 17671	IRC Sec. 584	Common trust funds	¶614
Sec. 17677	IRC Secs. 584, 6032	Return for common trust	¶614
Sec. 17681	IRC Secs. 611-38	Taxation of natural resources	¶319, ¶320, ¶540
Sec. 17681.6	IRC Secs. 613A	Depletion limitation for marginal properties	¶319
		Basis for cost depletion	¶562
Sec. 17731	IRC Secs. 641-92	Taxation of estates and trusts	Various
Sec. 17731.5	IRC Sec. 641	Determining rates and special credits	¶604
Sec. 17732	IRC Sec. 642	No deduction personal exemptions	. . .
Sec. 17733	IRC Sec. 642	Exemption credits	¶113
Sec. 17734	IRC Sec. 641	Nonresident beneficiaries	¶605
Sec. 17734.6	IRC Sec. 646	Alaska Native Settlement trusts	¶601
Sec. 17735	IRC Sec. 661	Distributions to nonresidents	¶604
Sec. 17736	IRC Sec. 642	Modification I.R.C. Sec. 642	¶604
Sec. 17737	IRC Sec. 682	Alimony trusts	¶611
Secs. 17742-45.1	IRC Sec. 641	Effect of residence upon taxability	¶105, ¶602, ¶603
Sec. 17750	IRC Sec. 643	Estates and trusts—election	¶604
Sec. 17751	IRC Sec. 645	Certain revocable trusts treated as part of estate	¶604
Sec. 17752	IRC Sec. 663	Special rules applicable to IRC Secs. 661 and 662	¶605
Sec. 17760	IRC Sec. 684	Gain on transfers to foreign trusts	...
Sec. 17760.5	IRC Sec. 685	Funeral trusts	¶608
Sec. 17779	IRC Secs. 665-68	Accumulation distributions	¶605
Sec. 17851	IRC Secs. 701-61	Partners and partnerships	Various
Sec. 17851.5	. . .	Taxation of partnerships	¶620
Sec. 17853	IRC Sec. 703	Deductions not allowed	¶620
Sec. 17854	IRC Sec. 707	Guaranteed payments	¶620
Secs. 17855-57	IRC Sec. 751	Transfer of partnership interest	¶618
Sec. 17858	IRC Sec. 704	Depreciation election by partnership	¶620
Sec. 17865	IRC Secs. 771—777	Electing large partnerships	¶624
Secs. 17935—37	. . .	Tax on limited partnerships	¶116, ¶616
Secs. 17941—46	. . .	LLC taxes and fees	¶116, ¶625
Secs. 17948-48.3	. . .	LLP minimum tax	¶623
Sec. 17951	. . .	Income of nonresidents	¶231, ¶233, ¶619
Sec. 17952	. . .	Income of nonresidents from intangibles	¶231
Sec. 17952.5	. . .	California source retirement income	. . .
Sec. 17953	. . .	Income to nonresident beneficiaries	¶231
Sec. 17954	. . .	Allocation of income of nonresidents	¶231
Sec. 17955	. . .	Nonresident income from qualifying investment securities	¶231

California	Federal	Subject	Paragraph
Sec. 18001	. . .	Taxes paid by resident to other state—credit	¶127, ¶128
Sec. 18002	. . .	Taxes paid by nonresident to other state—credit	¶127, ¶129
Sec. 18003	. . .	Residence of estate or trust	¶127, ¶130
Sec. 18004	. . .	Estate or trust—credit for taxes paid another state	¶127, ¶130
Sec. 18005	. . .	Resident beneficiary credit	¶127, ¶130
Sec. 18006	. . .	Resident and nonresident S corporation shareholders and partners—credit for taxes paid another state by entity	¶127, ¶128, ¶129, ¶131, ¶233
Sec. 18007	. . .	Report of other state tax credit	¶127
Sec. 18008	. . .	Tax due on other state credit	¶127
Sec. 18009	. . .	Interest on credit	¶127
Sec. 18011	. . .	Discrimination resulting from taxes paid to other state	¶127
Sec. 18031	IRC Sec. 1041	Inter-spousal transfers	¶502
Sec. 18031	IRC Sec. 1001-92	Determination of gain or loss	¶501
Sec. 18031	IRC Sec. 1014	Basis of property acquired from decedent	Various
Sec. 18031	IRC Sec. 1015	Basis of property acquired by transfer in trust	¶546
Sec. 18031	IRC Sec. 1060	Allocation of transferred business assets	¶564
Sec. 18035.6	IRC Sec. 1014	Basis of property acquired from a decedent	¶546
Sec. 18036	IRC Sec. 1016	Adjustments to basis	¶316, ¶559
Sec. 18036.5	IRC Sec. 1016	Basis adjustment for sale of small business stock	¶559
Sec. 18036.6	IRC Sec. 1022	Basis of property acquired from a decedent	¶546
Sec. 18037	IRC Sec. 1033	Certain involuntary conversions	¶503, ¶550
Sec. 18038	IRC Sec. 1040	Transfer of certain real property	¶604
Sec. 18038.4	IRC Sec. 1045	Rollover of gain from small business stock	¶515
Sec. 18038.5	IRC Sec. 1045	Rollover of gain from small business stock	¶515
Sec. 18039	IRC Sec. 1052	Basis established by prior law	¶554
Sec. 18041.5	IRC Sec. 1001	Gain from sale of assisted housing	¶505
Sec. 18042	IRC Sec. 1042	Sales to ESOP's	¶501, ¶514
Sec. 18044	IRC Sec. 1044	Rollover of publicly traded securities	¶501
Sec. 18151	IRC Secs. 1201-98	Capital gains and losses	Various
Sec. 18152	IRC Sec. 1202	Small business stock	¶525
Sec. 18152.5	IRC Sec. 1202	Small business stock	¶523, ¶525
Sec. 18155	IRC Sec. 1212	Carryovers and carrybacks	¶523, ¶526
Sec. 18155.5	IRC Sec. 1223	Holding period for small business stock	¶528
Sec. 18165	IRC Sec. 1245	Recapture of depreciation on personal property	¶539
Sec. 18171	IRC Sec. 1250	Depreciation adjustments	¶523, ¶539
Sec. 18171.5	IRC Sec. 1250	IRC Sec. 1250(a) modified	¶539
Sec. 18177	IRC Sec. 1275	Tax-exempt obligations	. . .
Sec. 18178	IRC Sec. 1272	Original issue discount	¶236, ¶237, ¶512
Sec. 18180	IRC Sec. 7872	Loans with below-market interest rates	¶414
Sec. 18181	IRC Secs. 1291-98	Treatment of passive foreign investment companies	¶523
Secs. 18401-03	. . .	General application of administrative provisions	. . .
Sec. 18405	. . .	Relief upon noncompliance with new provisions	. . .
Sec. 18407	IRC Sec. 6011	Reporting abusive tax shelters	¶727
Sec. 18408	IRC Sec. 6011(b)	Information, i.e. taxpayer	¶715
Sec. 18409	IRC Sec. 6011	Returns on magnetic media	¶622
Secs. 18412-17	IRC Sec. 7807	Continuity of provisions with prior law	. . .
Secs. 18416	...	Last known address	¶704
Sec. 18501	IRC Sec. 6012(a)	Returns required	¶106
Sec. 18505	IRC Sec. 6012(b)	Returns filed by fiduciary	¶106, ¶601
Sec. 18505.3	IRC Sec. 6012(b)(1)	Return of deceased individual	¶106
Sec. 18505.6	IRC Sec. 6012(b)	Agent for making return	¶106
Sec. 18506	IRC Sec. 6012(b)	Exempt trust—unrelated business income	¶106, ¶607

California	Federal	Subject	Paragraph
Sec. 18508	IRC Sec. 6012	Returns filed by joint fiduciaries	¶106
Sec. 18509	IRC Sec. 6012	Fiduciary as individual	¶106
Sec. 18510	. . .	Payment of qualified use taxes	¶108
Sec. 18521	IRC Sec. 6013	Filing of returns	¶106 , ¶107 , ¶114 , ¶601
Sec. 18522	IRC Sec. 6013(b)	Joint return after filing separate return	¶107
Sec. 18523	IRC Sec. 6013(b)(1)	Elections made in separate returns	¶106 , ¶107
Sec. 18524	IRC Sec. 6013(b)(1)	Death of spouse	¶106 , ¶107
Sec. 18526	IRC Sec. 6013(b)(2)	Time limitation	¶106 , ¶107
Sec. 18527	IRC Sec. 6013(b)(3)	Credit or refund periods	¶106 , ¶107
Sec. 18528	IRC Sec. 6013(b)(3)	When return deemed filed	¶106 , ¶107
Sec. 18529	IRC Sec. 6013(b)(4)	Assessment period extended	¶106 , ¶107 , ¶710
Sec. 18530	IRC Sec. 6013(b)(5)	Additions to tax, penalties	¶106 , ¶107 , ¶712
Sec. 18531	IRC Sec. 6013(b)(5)	Returns, criminal penalty	¶106
Sec. 18531.5	IRC Sec. 6013(c)	Death of one spouse	¶107
Sec. 18532	IRC Sec. 6013(d)	Marital status determined	¶106 , ¶114
Sec. 18533	IRC Secs. 6013(e), 6015	Liability of spouse	¶107
Sec. 18534	IRC Sec. 66	Liability for community income	¶106 , ¶107
Sec. 18535	IRC Sec. 6031	Returns by pass-through entities	¶233 , ¶619 , ¶622 , ¶625
Sec. 18536	...	Group returns for nonresident corporate directors	¶714
Sec. 18542	. . .	Reporting of charitable contributions	. . .
Sec. 18551	IRC Sec. 3402(a)	Filing withholding return	¶715
Sec. 18566	IRC Sec. 6072	Time for filing returns	¶108
Sec. 18567	IRC Sec. 6081(a)	Extension of time	¶108 , ¶109 , ¶110
Sec. 18570	IRC Sec. 7508	Members of armed forces	¶109
Sec. 18571	IRC Sec. 7508	Extension—service in combat zone	¶109
Sec. 18572	IRC Sec. 7508A	Extensions for disaster victims	¶108 , ¶110 , ¶710 , ¶719
Sec. 18601	IRC Secs. 6012(a), 6037, 6072	Filing of returns; due dates	. . .
Sec. 18604	IRC Sec. 6081	Extension of time for filing returns	. . .
Sec. 18606	IRC Secs. 6012(a), 6065	Filing of returns by receiver, trustee, or assignee of bankrupt taxpayer	. . .
Sec. 18621	IRC Secs. 6065, 6091	Form of return	¶105
Sec. 18621.5	. . .	Electronic filing	¶108
Sec. 18621.7	. . .	Electronic proprietary software	...
Sec. 18621.9	. . .	Mandatory electronic filing	¶108
Sec. 18622	. . .	Amendment of return after federal changes	¶106
Sec. 18623	IRC Sec. 6102(a)	Fractional dollar calculations	¶106
Sec. 18624	IRC Sec. 6109	Identifying numbers	¶701
Sec. 18625	IRC Sec. 6107	Copy to taxpayer	¶701
Sec. 18626	. . .	Return defined	. . .
Sec. 18628	IRC Sec. 6111	Reportable transactions	¶727
Sec. 18631	IRC Secs. 6034A, 6039, 6039C, 6041, 6041A, 6042, 6045, 6049, 6050H-S, 6052	Information returns	¶713
Sec. 18631.7	. . .	Check cashing business information return	¶712 , ¶713
Sec. 18632	. . .	Administration of withholding	¶713
Sec. 18633	IRC Sec. 6031	Returns by partnerships	¶622
Sec. 18633.5	IRC Sec. 6031	Returns by LLCs	¶625
Sec. 18635	IRC Secs. 6013(a), 6034	Information from charitable trust	¶606
Sec. 18635.5	IRC Sec. 6034A	Information to beneficiaries	¶106
Sec. 18639	IRC Secs. 6042, 6049	Returns for interest, dividends, collections	¶713
Sec. 18640	IRC Sec. 6044	Returns by cooperatives	¶713
Sec. 18642	IRC Sec. 6045	Reporting—property owners	¶713
Sec. 18644	IRC Sec. 6050A	Fishing boat operators—reporting requirements	¶713
Sec. 18646	IRC Sec. 6050M	State agency head—reporting requirements	¶713
Sec. 18648	IRC Sec. 6112	Listed transactions	¶713
Sec. 18648.5	IRC Sec. 6115	Disclosure related to quid pro quo contributions	. . .
Sec. 18649	IRC Sec. 1275	Original issue discount reporting	¶713
Sec. 18661	IRC Secs. 3402, 6041(c)	Recipient of income	¶713

California	Federal	Subject	Paragraph
Sec. 18662	IRC Secs. 1445, 3402	Withholding of tax—nonresidents	¶625, ¶714, ¶715, ¶716
Sec. 18663	IRC Sec. 3402(a)	Withholding	¶715
Sec. 18665	. . .	Change in withholding due to legislative enactments	¶714, ¶715
Sec. 18666	IRC Sec. 1446	Withholding exemption certificates	¶625, ¶714, ¶715
Sec. 18667	IRC Sec. 3402	Withholding—foreign partners	¶714, ¶715
Sec. 18668	IRC Sec. 3403	Withholding penalties	¶714, ¶716
Sec. 18669	. . .	Sale, transfer, or disposition of business	¶714
Sec. 18670	. . .	Withholding notice—delinquency	¶714
Sec. 18670.5	. . .	Electronic notice to withhold	...
Sec. 18671	. . .	Withholding—state agencies	¶714
Sec. 18672	. . .	Liability for failure to withhold	¶714
Sec. 18673	. . .	Employee relief from liability	¶715
Sec. 18674	. . .	Person required to withhold—compliance	¶714
Sec. 18675	IRC Sec. 6414	Remedies on taxes withheld	¶714
Sec. 18676	. . .	Withholding notice to state agencies	¶712
Sec. 18677	IRC Sec. 3505	Lender, surety or other person liable	¶714
Secs. 18711-18865	. . .	Designated contributions	¶322
Sec. 19001	IRC Sec. 6151	Date tax due	¶110
Sec. 19002	IRC Secs. 31(a), 6513	Credit for tax withheld	¶714, ¶715
Sec. 19004	IRC Secs. 6151, 6655	Payment prior to due date	¶110
Sec. 19005	IRC Sec. 6151	Remittance to FTB	¶110, ¶712
Sec. 19006	IRC Sec. 6151	Joint return liability	¶107, ¶709
Sec. 19007	IRC Sec. 6315	Payments of estimated taxes	¶111
Sec. 19008	IRC Sec. 6159	Installment payment of tax	¶110
Sec. 19009	IRC Sec. 7512	Failure to pay collected taxes	¶715
Sec. 19010	IRC Sec. 6655	Assessing delinquent estimated taxes	¶110
Sec. 19011	IRC Sec. 6302	Electronic funds transfer	¶110, ¶712
Sec. 19011.5	...	Electronic payment requirements	¶110, ¶111
Sec. 19031	IRC Sec. 6212	Deficiency assessments—FTB authority	¶704
Sec. 19032	IRC Sec. 6212	Examination of return	¶704
Sec. 19033	IRC Sec. 6212(a)	Notice of deficiency	¶704
Sec. 19034	. . .	Details of notice	¶704
Sec. 19035	IRC Sec. 6212	Joint return notice	¶704
Sec. 19036	IRC Sec. 6212	Addition to tax as deficiency	¶704
Sec. 19041	IRC Sec. 6213	Protest to assessment	¶704
Sec. 19041.5	6603	Treatment of deposits	¶719, ¶720
Sec. 19042	IRC Sec. 6213	Final decision if no protest	¶704, ¶706
Sec. 19043	IRC Sec. 6211	"Deficiency and rebate" defined	¶704
Sec. 19043.5	. . .	Carryforward adjustments	¶704
Sec. 19044	IRC Sec. 6213	Reconsideration of assessment	¶702
Sec. 19045	. . .	Appeal from FTB's action	¶705
Sec. 19046	IRC Sec. 6213	Mailing of appeal	¶705
Sec. 19047	IRC Sec. 6213	Notice of SBE's determination	¶705
Sec. 19048	IRC Sec. 6213	Petition for rehearing	¶705
Sec. 19049	IRC Sec. 6212	Notice and demand for payment	¶706
Sec. 19050	IRC Sec. 6212	Evidence of assessment	¶704
Sec. 19051	IRC Sec. 6213	Mathematical error in return	¶704
Sec. 19052	. . .	Limitations period for refund adjustments	¶719
Sec. 19054	IRC Sec. 6201	Overstatement of credit	¶726
Sec. 19057	IRC Sec. 6501	Limitation period on assessment	¶710
Sec. 19058	IRC Sec. 6501(e)	Limitation period extended	¶710
Sec. 19059	. . .	Limitation period after amended return	¶710
Sec. 19060	. . .	Limitation period following federal adjustment	¶710
Sec. 19061	IRC Secs. 1032, 1033(a)(2)(A)-(D)	Limitation period—involuntary conversion	¶710
Sec. 19063	IRC Secs. 6225, 6501(a)	Items of federally registered partnership	¶710
Sec. 19064	IRC Sec. 7609	Motion to quash subpoena	¶710
Sec. 19065	IRC Sec. 6501(c)	Agreement to extend period	¶710
Sec. 19066	IRC Sec. 6501(b)	Time return deemed filed	¶710, ¶719
Sec. 19067	IRC Sec. 6501(c)	Extension by agreement	¶710
Sec. 19071	IRC Sec. 6901	Assessments against persons secondarily liable	¶613, ¶709

California	Federal	Subject	Paragraph
Sec. 19072	IRC Sec. 6901	Collection from person secondarily liable	¶613 , ¶709
Sec. 19073	IRC Sec. 6901	Assessment and collection from transferees and fiduciaries	¶613 , ¶709
Sec. 19074	IRC Sec. 6901	Limitations period for assessment of transferee or fiduciary	¶613 , ¶709
Sec. 19081	IRC Sec. 6861	Jeopardy assessment	¶707
Sec. 19082	IRC Sec. 6862	Taxable period terminated	¶707
Sec. 19083	IRC Secs. 6861, 6863	Collection of jeopardy assessment; bond	¶707
Sec. 19084	IRC Secs. 6213, 6863	Hearing	¶707
Sec. 19085	IRC Sec. 6863	Appeal	¶707
Sec. 19086	IRC Sec. 6861	Evidence of jeopardy	¶707
Sec. 19087	IRC Sec. 6501(c)	Fraudulent or no return	¶710
Sec. 19088	IRC Sec. 6871	Assessments in bankruptcy or receivership	¶708
Sec. 19089	IRC Secs. 6036, 6872	Notice; suspension of period	¶708
Sec. 19090	IRC Sec. 6871	Deficiency claims	¶708
Sec. 19091	IRC Sec. 6873	Unpaid claim	¶708
Sec. 19092	IRC Sec. 6861	Regulations	. . .
Sec. 19093	IRC Sec. 6867	Unexplained cash	¶707
Sec. 19101	IRC Sec. 6601	Interest on tax due	¶711
Sec. 19104	IRC Sec. 6404	Interest on deficiency	¶711
Sec. 19105	IRC Sec. 6601	No interest period	¶711
Sec. 19107	. . .	Overpayment applied to spouse's deficiency	¶711
Sec. 19108	. . .	Overpayment applied to another year's deficiency	¶709
Sec. 19109	. . .	Abatement of interest	¶710
Sec. 19110	. . .	Overpayment—estate or trust	¶110 , ¶710
Sec. 19112	. . .	Interest waived	¶711
Sec. 19113	IRC Sec. 6601(f)	Satisfaction by credit	¶711
Sec. 19114	IRC Sec. 6601(g)	When interest may be collected	¶711
Sec. 19116	IRC Sec. 6404(g)	Suspension of interest and penalties	¶711 , ¶712
Sec. 19117	IRC Sec. 6631	Notice of interest charges	¶711
Sec. 19120	. . .	Interest on erroneous refund	¶711
Sec. 19131	IRC Sec. 6651	Penalty—failure to make return	¶712
Sec. 19132	IRC Sec. 6651	Penalty for tax not paid	¶712
Sec. 19132.5	IRC Sec. 6651	Waiver of penalties for victims of Northridge earthquake	. . .
Sec. 19133	. . .	Penalty—failure to furnish information	¶704 , ¶712
Sec. 19133.5	IRC Sec. 6652	Penalty—failure to report small business stock gain	¶712
Sec. 19134	IRC Sec. 6657	Bad check penalty	¶712
Sec. 19136	IRC Sec. 6654	Penalty—payments estimated tax	¶111
Sec. 19136.1	IRC Sec. 6654	Estimated payment installment percentages	¶111
Sec. 19136.2-36.13	. . .	Estimated tax penalty abatement	¶111
Sec. 19161	IRC Sec. 6658	Timely payment during bankruptcy	¶712
Sec. 19164	IRC Secs. 6662-65	Accuracy-related penalty	¶712
Sec. 19164.5	IRC Secs. 6662A	Accuracy-related penalty on reportable transactions	¶727
Sec. 19166	IRC Sec. 6694	Penalty—preparer understatement	¶712
Sec. 19167	IRC Sec. 6695	Penalties—tax preparers	¶712
Sec. 19168	IRC Sec. 6696	Penalties—tax preparers	¶712
Sec. 19169	IRC Sec. 6695(f)	Penalty—negotiating client's refund check	¶712
Sec. 19170	. . .	Penalty—electronic returns	¶712
Sec. 19172	IRC Sec. 6698	Penalty—partnership returns	¶622 , ¶625 , ¶712
Sec. 19173	IRC Sec. 6708	Penalty—tax shelters	¶712
Sec. 19174	IRC Sec. 6700	Penalty—tax shelters	¶712
Sec. 19175	. . .	Penalty—information returns	¶712 , ¶713
Sec. 19176	IRC Sec. 6682	Penalty—false withholding information	¶712
Sec. 19177	IRC Sec. 6700	Penalty—abusive tax shelters	¶712
Sec. 19178	IRC Sec. 6701	Penalty—aiding and abetting tax understatement	¶712
Sec. 19179	IRC Sec. 6702	Penalty—frivolous return	¶710
Sec. 19180	IRC Sec. 6703	Penalty—burden of proof	. . .
Sec. 19181	IRC Sec. 6706	Penalty—original issue discount reporting	¶710
Sec. 19182	IRC Secs. 6111, 6707	Penalty—tax shelters	¶712 , ¶713

California	Federal	Subject	Paragraph
Sec. 19182.5	IRC Sec. 6174	Penalty—failure to disclose quid pro quo information	. . .
Sec. 19183	IRC Secs. 6652, 6721-24	Penalty—certain information returns	¶712
Sec. 19184	IRC Sec. 6693	Penalty—failure to properly report IRA	¶712
Sec. 19187	IRC Sec. 6751	Procedures for penalties	¶712
Secs. 19191-94	. . .	Voluntary disclosure agreements	¶725
Secs. 19195	. . .	Public disclosure of large delinquent taxpayers	¶721
Sec. 19201	. . .	Judgment for tax	. . .
Sec. 19202	. . .	Entry of judgment	. . .
Sec. 19203	. . .	Abstract as lien	. . .
Sec. 19204	. . .	Extension of lien	. . .
Sec. 19205	. . .	Execution of judgment	. . .
Sec. 19206	IRC Sec. 6325	Release of lien	. . .
Sec. 19207	IRC Sec. 6325	Release of unenforceable lien	. . .
Sec. 19208	IRC Sec. 6325	Certificate of release	. . .
Sec. 19209	IRC Sec. 6325	Cost for certificate	. . .
Sec. 19221	IRC Sec. 6321	Lien on tax	¶612
Sec. 19222	IRC Sec. 6311	Lien for dishonored checks	[illegible]
Sec. 19223	. . .	Lien against trust	[illegible]12
Sec. 19224	. . .	Service of notice of fiduciar[illegible]	[illegible]12
Sec. 19225	. . .	Administrative review	¶702
Sec. 19226	IRC Sec. 6325	Release of third-party liens	. . .
Sec. 19231	IRC Sec. 6331	Warrant to collect tax	. . .
Sec. 19232	. . .	Warrant as writ of execution	. . .
Sec. 19233	. . .	Fees for warrant	. . .
Secs. 19234-35	. . .	Fees as obligation of taxpayer	. . .
Sec. 19236	IRC Sec. 6331	Seizure of property	. . .
Sec. 19251	. . .	Remedies are cumulative	. . .
Sec. 19252	. . .	FTB as representative	. . .
Sec. 19253	IRC Sec. 6323	Priority of lien	. . .
Sec. 19254	. . .	Collection and filing enforcement fees	¶712
Sec. 19255	IRC Sec. 6502	Limitations period for collections	¶710
Sec. 19256	IRC Sec. 7504	Fractional dollar amount	. . .
Sec. 19262	IRC Secs. 6331, 6335	Seizure and sale of personal property	. . .
Sec. 19263	IRC Secs. 6338, 6342	Bill of sale; disposition of excess	. . .
Sec. 19264	. . .	Earnings withholding tax order	. . .
Sec. 19271	. . .	Child support delinquency	. . .
Sec. 19271.6	. . .	Financial Institution Match System	. . .
Sec. 19301	IRC Sec. 6402	Credit for overpayment	¶717
Sec. 19302	. . .	Credit and refund approval	¶717
Sec. 19306	IRC Sec. 6511(a)	Time limit for refund	¶719
Sec. 19307	. . .	Return as claim for refund	¶717, ¶719
Sec. 19308	IRC Sec. 6511(c)	Effect of assessment extension	¶717
Sec. 19309	IRC Sec. 6511(c)	Claims filed before assessment extension	¶719
Sec. 19311	IRC Sec. 6511	Time limit following federal adjusted return	¶719
Sec. 19311.5	...	Limitations period for refund of taxes paid to other state	¶719
Sec. 19312	IRC Sec. 6511(d)	Time limit where bad debts or worthless securities	¶719
Sec. 19313	IRC Sec. 6511(g)	Federally registered partnerships	¶719
Sec. 19314	. . .	Overpayment used as offset	¶719
Sec. 19316	IRC Sec. 6511(h)	Financially disabled individuals	¶719
Sec. 19321	. . .	Final action	¶717
Sec. 19322	. . .	Claim for refund	¶717
Sec. 19322.1	. . .	Informal refund claims	¶719
Sec. 19323	IRC Sec. 6402	Disallowance of claim	¶717
Sec. 19324	. . .	Appeal from FTB's action	¶718
Sec. 19325	. . .	Refunds resulting from federal law	¶718, ¶722
Sec. 19331	. . .	Failure to mail notice	¶718
Sec. 19332	IRC Sec. 6213	Mailing of appeals	¶718
Sec. 19333	IRC Sec. 6213	SBE determination	¶718
Sec. 19334	IRC Sec. 6213	Petition for rehearing	¶718
Sec. 19335	. . .	Payment of tax protested	¶718
Sec. 19340	IRC Sec. 6611(b)	Interest on overpayments	¶722
Sec. 19341	IRC Sec. 6611(e)	Refunds made within certain time	¶722
Sec. 19342	. . .	Notice of disallowance	¶722

California	Federal	Subject	Paragraph
Sec. 19343	. . .	Finality of notice	¶722
Sec. 19344	. . .	Appeal to SBE	¶722
Sec. 19345	. . .	Hearing	¶722
Sec. 19346	. . .	Finality of determination	¶722
Sec. 19347	. . .	Suit to recover interest	¶722
Sec. 19348	. . .	Failure of FTB to give notice	¶722
Sec. 19349	IRC Sec. 6401	Payments not entitled to interest	¶722
Sec. 19350	. . .	No interest on barred claim	¶722
Sec. 19351	IRC Sec. 6611(b)	Payment deemed made on due date	¶722
Sec. 19354	IRC Sec. 6401(b)	Excess of tax withheld	. . .
Sec. 19355	. . .	Refunding excess	. . .
Sec. 19361	IRC Sec. 6414	Employer's overpayment	. . .
Sec. 19362	IRC Sec. 6402	Credits against estimated tax	. . .
Sec. 19363	IRC Sec. 6402	Interest on overpayments of estimated tax	¶722
Sec. 19364	...	Estimated tax overpayment carryover	...
Sec. 19365	. . .	Transfers of S corporation tax payments	¶806
Sec. 19368	. . .	Erroneous refund	¶726
Sec. 19371	IRC Secs. 6502, 7403	Suit for tax	¶710
Sec. 19372	. . .	Prosecution of suit	. . .
Sec. 19373	. . .	Writ of attachment	. . .
Sec. 19374	. . .	Evidence of delinquency	. . .
Sec. 19375	. . .	Suit in any court	. . .
Sec. 19376	. . .	Collection of tax	. . .
Sec. 19377	IRC Sec. 6301	Agreements with collection agencies	. . .
Sec. 19378	IRC Sec. 6301	Collection and transfer of funds	. . .
Sec. 19381	IRC Sec. 7421	Injunction actions prohibited	¶720
Sec. 19382	IRC Sec. 7422	Action to recover void tax	¶720
Sec. 19383	IRC Sec. 7422	Credit for overpayment	¶720
Sec. 19384	IRC Sec. 6532	Time for filing	¶720
Sec. 19385	IRC Sec. 6532	No FTB notice of action	¶720
Sec. 19387	IRC Sec. 7422	Service of summons and complaint	¶720
Sec. 19388	IRC Secs. 6532, 7422(f)	Location of trial	¶720
Sec. 19389	IRC Sec. 6532	Defense of action	¶720
Sec. 19390	. . .	Failure to sue within time limit	¶720
Sec. 19391	IRC Sec. 6612	Interest on judgment	¶720
Sec. 19392	. . .	Judgment against FTB	¶720
Sec. 19394	. . .	Refund of unconstitutional LLC fee	¶625
Sec. 19411	IRC Secs. 6602, 7405	Recovery of erroneous refunds	¶726
Sec. 19412	. . .	Court of trial	¶726
Sec. 19413	. . .	Prosecution of suit	¶726
Sec. 19431	IRC Sec. 6404	Illegal levy	. . .
Sec. 19441	IRC Secs. 7121-23	Closing agreements	¶723
Sec. 19442	. . .	Settlement of tax disputes	¶723
Sec. 19443	. . .	Offers in compromise	¶724
Sec. 19444	. . .	Amnesty	¶710, ¶712
Sec. 19501	IRC Sec. 7621(a)	FTB—administering the law	¶701
Sec. 19502	IRC Sec. 7621(b)	FTB—establishment of districts	¶701
Sec. 19503	IRC Sec. 7805	FTB regulations	¶701
Sec. 19504	IRC Sec. 7602	FTB's powers	¶701
Sec. 19504.5	IRC Sec. 7612	Software trade secrets	¶701, ¶721
Sec. 19504.7	IRC Sec. 7602	Notice of contact of third parties	¶701
Sec. 19505	IRC Sec. 7803	FTB—appointment and removal	¶701
Sec. 19506	. . .	FTB deputies	¶701
Sec. 19507	. . .	FTB—temporary appointments	¶701
Sec. 19508	. . .	FTB—salaries	¶701
Sec. 19509	. . .	FTB—bond	¶701
Sec. 19511	IRC Sec. 7622	FTB—oath	¶701
Sec. 19512	IRC Sec. 6903	Fiduciary assuming taxpayer's duties	¶613
Sec. 19513	. . .	Tax clearance on estate	¶613
Sec. 19514	. . .	FTB action on certificate	¶613
Sec. 19515	. . .	No release from liability	¶613
Sec. 19516	IRC Sec. 6905	Fiduciary personally liable	¶613
Sec. 19517	. . .	FTB assessment of tax	¶613
Sec. 19518	IRC Sec. 6047	Information returns—self-employed retirement trusts	¶607
Sec. 19519	. . .	Disability insurance—refund or credit	. . .

California	Federal	Subject	Paragraph
Sec. 19520	. . .	Tax enforcement definition	. . .
Sec. 19521	IRC Secs. 6621-22	Current interest rate for deficiencies and refunds	¶711
Sec. 19522	. . .	Federal tax changes	¶103
Sec. 19523	. . .	Disqualification of appraiser	¶712
Sec. 19523.5	. . .	Tax practitioner disbarment/ suspension	...
Sec. 19525	IRC Sec. 7623	Rewards for informers	¶701
Sec. 19526	. . .	Taxpayer cross-reference file	. . .
Sec. 19528	. . .	Information on state licensees	. . .
Sec. 19530	. . .	Preserving tax returns	¶721
Sec. 19532	. . .	Priority for application of collected amounts	. . .
Sec. 19533	. . .	Priority of payments	. . .
Sec. 19542	IRC Secs. 6103, 7213	Secrecy of returns	¶717
Secs. 19542.1-42.3	IRC Sec. 7213	Illegal disclosures	. . .
Sec. 19543	IRC Sec. 6103(b)	"Business affairs" defined	. . .
Sec. 19544	IRC Sec. 6103(b)	Nondisclosure of audit methods	¶721
Sec. 19545	IRC Sec. 6103(h)	Disclosure—judicial order	¶721
Secs. 19546-46.5	IRC Sec. 6103(f)	Disclosure to legislative committee	¶717
Sec. 19547	IRC Sec. 6103(h)	Disclosure to Attorney General	¶721
Sec. 19548	. . .	Disclosure to Calif. Parent Locator Service	¶721
Sec. 19549	IRC Sec. 6103(b)	"Return" defined	¶721
Sec. 19550	...	Address of people from whome there is an outstanding warrant	...
Sec. 19551	IRC Sec. 6103(d)	Disclosure to proper authorities	¶721
Sec. 19551.5	...	Reciprocal information exchange program with cities	¶721
Sec. 19552	IRC Secs. 6103, 7213	Unwarranted disclosure	¶721
Sec. 19553	IRC Sec. 6103	Disclosure to Director of Social Services	¶721
Sec. 19554	IRC Sec. 6103	Locating owners of unclaimed property	¶721
Sec. 19555	IRC Sec. 6103	Unearned income information	¶721
Sec. 19556	. . .	Disclosure in FTB proceedings	¶721
Sec. 19557	IRC Sec. 6103	Student loan applicants	¶721
Sec. 19558	. . .	Disclosure to Public Employees' Retirement System	¶721
Sec. 19559	. . .	Disclosure for national security purposes	¶721
Sec. 19561	. . .	Fee for copies of returns	¶721
Sec. 19562	IRC Sec. 6103	Charge for reasonable cost	¶721
Sec. 19563	IRC Sec. 6108	Publication of statistics	¶721
Sec. 19564	IRC Sec. 6108	High income taxpayer report	¶721
Sec. 19565	IRC Sec. 6104	Disclosure of information	¶721
Sec. 19566	...	Information obtained by FTB	...
Sec. 19581	. . .	Use of federal forms	Specimen return
Sec. 19582	. . .	Simplification of tax forms	. . .
Sec. 19582.5	. . .	Form 540 2EZ income limits	¶106
Sec. 19583	. . .	Forging spouse's signature	¶712
Secs. 19590-92	. . .	Tax service fees	. . .
Sec. 19701	IRC Secs. 7203, 7206	Violation—failure to file return	¶712
Sec. 19701.5	. . .	Forging spouse's signature	¶712
Sec. 19702	. . .	Prosecutor's compromise	¶712
Sec. 19703	. . .	Evidence of failure to file	¶712
Sec. 19704	IRC Sec. 6531	Statute of limitations—violations	¶712
Sec. 19705	IRC Sec. 7206	False statements—fraud	¶712
Sec. 19706	IRC Sec. 7203	Failure to file return	¶712
Sec. 19707	. . .	Venue	. . .
Sec. 19708	IRC Sec. 7202	Failure to remit withheld tax	¶712
Sec. 19709	IRC Sec. 7202	Failure to withhold tax as misdemeanor	¶712
Sec. 19710	. . .	Writ of mandate	
Sec. 19711	IRC Sec. 7205	Penalties—employees	¶712
Sec. 19712	IRC Sec. 6695	Misdemeanor conviction for endorsing client's refund check	¶712
Sec. 19713	IRC Sec. 7215	Failure to set up withholding account	¶712
Sec. 19714	IRC Sec. 6673	Delay tactics	¶712
Sec. 19715	IRC Sec. 7408	Penalties—injunctive relief	¶712
Sec. 19717	IRC Sec. 7430	Recovery of litigation costs	¶701
Sec. 19718	. . .	Wage statements for immigrants	. . .
Secs. 19720-21	. . .	Penalty for fraudulently obtaining refunds	¶712
Secs. 19730-38	. . .	Amnesty	¶712

California	Federal	Subject	Paragraph
Secs. 19751-54	. . .	Abusive tax shelter voluntary compliance	¶727
Sec. 19755	. . .	Abusive tax shelter limitations period	¶710
Sec. 19772	6707A	Penalty—reportable transaction omission	¶727
Sec. 19774	6662, 6663	Penalty—noneconomic substance transaction understament	¶712 , ¶727
Sec. 19777	. . .	Interest-based penalty—abusive tax shelter deficiency	¶727
Sec. 19777.5	. . .	Amnesty enhanced interest penalty	¶711 , ¶712
Sec. 19778	. . .	Interest—reportable transaction understatement	¶712
Sec. 19850-19854	. . .	EITC information provided by employer	¶125 , ¶715
Secs. 21001-14	IRC Secs. 6404(f), 7430, 7521, 7811	Taxpayers' bill of rights	¶701 , ¶702 , ¶703
Sec. 21015	. . .	Relief from penalties	¶701 , ¶712
Sec. 21015.5	. . .	Tax lien and levy protections	¶702
Secs. 21016-28	IRC Secs. 6103(e)(8), 6201(d)(4), 6331, 7433, 7435, 7502, 7524, 7811	Taxpayer's bill of rights	¶108 , ¶702 , ¶703

PERSONAL INCOME TAX

CHAPTER 1
IMPOSITION OF TAX, RATES, EXEMPTIONS, RETURNS

¶101 Overview of Personal Income Tax

The California personal income tax was first enacted in 1935 and has been amended on numerous occasions since then. It constitutes Part 10 of Division 2 of the Revenue and Taxation Code. Administrative provisions applicable to both personal income and corporate franchise and income taxpayers are encompassed by Part 10.2 of Division 2 of the Revenue and Taxation Code.

The law is administered by the Franchise Tax Board, composed of the State Controller, the Director of the Department of Finance, and the Chair of the State Board of Equalization.

California's personal income tax is generally patterned after the federal income tax. Moreover, interpretations of federal income tax law by the Internal Revenue Service and the courts have typically been followed in the administration of analogous provisions of California law. However, there remain significant differences between federal and California income tax laws. See ¶103 for an explanation of the federal conformity program established in 1983.

Personal income tax is imposed on the entire taxable income of California residents and on the taxable income of nonresidents derived from sources within California. It applies to individuals, estates, and trusts. Tax is computed on a graduated scale, at rates ranging from 1% to 10.3% (¶116). Under certain circumstances, tax is reduced by a credit for tax paid to another state or by various other credits (¶125 et seq.).

• *No local income tax*

California law specifically prohibits the imposition of an income tax by any city, county, or other local jurisdiction, and also prohibits local jurisdictions from imposing a tax on the earnings of nonresident employees unless the same tax is imposed on resident employees.

In *County of Alameda, County of Contra Costa, County of Santa Clara v. City and County of San Francisco* (1971) (CCH CALIFORNIA TAX REPORTS ¶204-550), the California Court of Appeal held that a San Francisco nonresident commuter tax was unconstitutional. However, in *Weekes, et al. v. City of Oakland, et al.* (1978) (CCH CALIFORNIA TAX REPORTS ¶205-861), the California Supreme Court upheld the validity of a 1% tax imposed on employee compensation by the City of Oakland. The Court held that the tax was a license tax rather than an income tax.

¶102 Scope of Chapter

This chapter discusses the questions of who is subject to the tax and who qualifies as a "resident," requirements for filing returns and payment of tax, the base upon which tax is imposed, and the rates of tax.

¶103 Federal Conformity Program

Law: Secs. 17024.5, 19522 (CCH CALIFORNIA TAX REPORTS ¶15-515).

Prior to 1983, California personal income tax law was wholly self-contained. However, California statutes duplicated many provisions of federal law. This situation was remedied in 1983 when California law was completely restructured to incorporate much of the federal law by reference to Internal Revenue Code subchapters and provisions and to concentrate primarily on the *differences* between California and federal law.

Beginning with the 2005 taxable year, California conforms to the IRC provisions it incorporates as the provisions were amended on January 1, 2005. (Sec. 17024.5, Rev. & Tax. Code) Consequently, at the time this book went to press, California had not conformed to amendments made by the Energy Tax Incentives Act of 2005, the Hurricane Katrina Emergency Tax Relief Act of 2005, the Gulf Opportunity Zone Act of 2005, the Tax Increase Prevention and Reconciliation Act of 2005, the Tax Relief and Health Care Act of 2006, the U.S. Troop Readiness, Veterans' Care, Katrina Recovery, and Iraq Accountability Appropriations Act of 2007, the Energy Independence & Security Act of 2007, the Tax Increase Prevention Act of 2007, the Tax Technical Corrections Act of 2007, the Economic Stimulus Act of 2008, the Heartland, Habitat, Harvest, and Horticulture Act of 2008, the Heroes Earnings Assistance and Relief Tax Act of 2008, the Housing Assistance Tax Act of 2008, and the Emergency Economic Stimulus Act of 2008.

In addition, California does not incorporate many of the amendments made by the Pension Protection Act of 2006 (PPA), the Small Business and Work Opportunity Tax Act of 2007, and the Mortgage Forgiveness Debt Relief Act of 2007 (MFDRA). However, because California incorporates most IRC provisions relating to deferred compensation and retirement plans and to S corporation qualifications, elections, and terminations as the provisions are currently amended (¶330), California does incorporate numerous amendments made by the PPA and the Small Business and Work Opportunity Tax Act and some of the amendments made by the MFDRA.

Beginning with the 2005 taxable year, California incorporates most of the amendments made by the following federal Acts:

— Economic Growth and Tax Relief Reconciliation Act of 2001 (P.L. 107-16);

— Victims of Terrorism Tax Relief Act of 2001 (P.L. 107-134) (most of these amendments were previously incorporated);

— Job Creation and Worker Assistance Act of 2002 (P.L. 107-147);

— Jobs and Growth Tax Relief Reconciliation Act of 2003 (P.L. 108-27);

— Military Family Tax Relief Act of 2003 (P.L. 108-121) (most of these amendments were previously incorporated);

— Medicare Prescription Drug, Improvement, and Modernization Act of 2003 (P.L. 108-173);

— Working Families Tax Relief Act of 2004 (P.L. 108-311); and

— American Jobs Creation Act of 2004 (P.L. 108-357).

Planning Note: EGTRRA Sunset Provisions Incorporated

California incorporates the federal provision of the Economic Growth and Tax Relief Reconciliation Act of 2001 that provides that all provisions of, and amendments made by, the 2001 Act will not apply to taxable, plan, or limitation years beginning after 2010. However, to the extent that any of these provisions are extended or the sunset date repealed, California will incorporate the extension of these amendments, whether the extension is temporary or permanent. (Sec. 17024.5(a)(2)(B), Rev. & Tax. Code)

Any federal provisions that have not been incorporated—with the corresponding impact on the filing of the California personal income tax return—are discussed at appropriate paragraphs in the *Guidebook*.

Because of the extent of the state conformity to federal law, the state income tax return has been designed to reflect a modification format. The computation of income begins with federal adjusted gross income, to which state modifications are then made. Accordingly, the *Guidebook* includes a guide to aid in the preparation of California individual income tax returns (¶25 et seq.).

• *Recent federal incorporation history*

In 2002, California conformed to most of the amendments made by the Transportation Equity Act for the 21st Century, the Tax and Trade Relief Extension Act of 1998, the Internal Revenue Service Restructuring and Reform Act of 1998, the Miscellaneous Trade and Technical Corrections Act of 1999, the Tax Relief Extension Act of 1999, the FSC Repeal and Extraterritorial Income Exclusion Act of 2000, the Community Renewal Tax Relief Act of 2000, and the Installment Tax Correction Act of 2000.

For taxable years beginning after 2001, California incorporated much of the Internal Revenue Code as in effect on January 1, 2001. In addition, California incorporated many of the amendments concerning pensions, retirement benefits, discharges of indebtedness by S corporations, and qualified tuition programs enacted by the Economic Growth and Tax Relief Reconciliation Act of 2001 and the Job Creation and Worker Assistance Act of 2002, and all of the changes made by the Military Family Tax Relief Act of 2003 and the Servicemembers Civil Relief Act of 2003. California also incorporated many of the expanded disaster relief provisions enacted by the Victims of Terrorism Tax Relief Act of 2001.

• *Federal regulations apply to California*

When federal law has been incorporated into California law, as explained above, federal regulations issued under the law in both temporary and final form are applicable for California purposes unless they conflict with California law or California regulations. (Sec. 17024.5(h), Rev. & Tax. Code)

• *Federal elections apply to California*

In most cases, federal conformity relieves a taxpayer from making a separate election for California purposes when an election is required. California law provides that a proper federal election is deemed to be a proper election for California purposes unless otherwise provided in California law or regulations. A copy of the federal election must be furnished to the Franchise Tax Board (FTB) upon request. (Sec. 17024.5(e), Rev. & Tax. Code)

A taxpayer may make an election for federal purposes and not for California purposes, or vice versa, when the law permits a choice. In such cases, the taxpayer must file a proper election or timely statement with the FTB setting forth relevant information and clearly expressing an intent to make a different election for California purposes. This rule does not apply where a California regulation has requirements that are substantially different from the federal requirements. (Sec. 17024.5(e), Rev. & Tax. Code)

Federal income tax elections, or lack thereof, made before becoming a California taxpayer are binding for California personal income tax purposes, unless a separate election is specifically authorized by a California law or regulation. (Sec. 17024.5(e), Rev. & Tax. Code)

Practitioner Comment: FTB's Pre-California Election Treatment Codified

Prior to the enactment of Ch. 486 (S.B. 1065) Laws 2003, California law generally provided that a federal election was deemed to be a proper election for California purposes unless the taxpayer "elected out" of the federal election. However, the law did not address what happened if the federal election was made before a taxpayer entered the state and became a "taxpayer."

The FTB's internal position has long been that a corporation that did not have nexus and was not a California taxpayer was not entitled to make elections in California, thus prohibiting such a corporation from making a state-only election to get treatment different from a federal election. Accordingly, when a taxpayer entered the state it was bound by its federal elections that it made prior to becoming a taxpayer. Senate Bill 1065 simply codified this internal FTB position, applicable to post-2003 taxable years.

Bruce Daigh, Chris Whitney, Contributing Editors

• *Federal approval applies to California*

Federal conformity also simplifies the requirement of obtaining approval from taxing authorities when such approval is required. Whenever a taxpayer is required to file an application or seek consent, proper action taken for federal purposes is deemed to be effective for California purposes, unless otherwise provided by California law or regulations. A copy of any such application must be furnished to the FTB upon request. (Sec. 17024.5(h), Rev. & Tax. Code)

A taxpayer may take certain actions for federal purposes and not for California purposes, or vice versa, when the law permits a choice and approval or consent is required. The rules discussed above, relating to elections, apply with equal force to these situations.

¶104 Special Programs for Economic Incentives

California Forms: FTB 3805Z (Enterprise Zone Deduction and Credit Summary), FTB 3806 (Los Angeles Revitalization Zone Deduction and Credit Summary), FTB 3807 (Local Agency Military Base Recovery Area Deduction and Credit Summary), FTB 3808 (Manufacturing Enhancement Area Credit Summary), FTB 3809 (Target Tax Area Deduction and Credit Summary).

A geographically-targeted economic development area (G-TEDA) is an area designated as an enterprise zone, a manufacturing enhancement area, a targeted tax area, or a local agency military base recovery area. (Sec. 7072, Govt. Code) G-TEDAs designated prior to January 1, 2007, were generally required to update their goals and objectives by April 15, 2008. G-TEDAs that failed to obtain their approved goals and objectives by April 15, 2008, were dedesignated, effective July 1, 2008.

The G-TEDA programs are administered by the California Department of Housing and Community Development (HCD). G-TEDAs are subject to audit at least once every five years. If a G-TEDA fails to successfully comply with a corrective plan after receiving a failing grade, the zone loses its designation. However, businesses located in a zone that loses its designation may continue to receive tax incentives for the remaining life of the zone. (Sec. 7076.1, Govt. Code)

• *Enterprise zones*

The enterprise zone program provides special tax incentives and other benefits for businesses established in designated depressed areas. The tax incentives are as follows:

— Income tax credits for sales or use tax paid on purchases of certain machinery and equipment (¶144).

— Income tax credits to employers for certain wages paid to disadvantaged individuals (¶145).

— Income tax credits to employees who are disadvantaged individuals (¶146).

— Tax-exemption of income from investments in enterprise zones (¶240).

— Accelerated write-off of certain machinery and equipment costs (¶316).

— Carryover of 100% of net operating losses for up to 15 years (¶309).

The special tax incentives available to businesses operating within enterprise zones may be claimed only for costs paid or incurred after the zone is designated and before the designation expires (Instructions to Form 3805Z). The effective date of the original designation for former enterprise zones and program areas remains the original designation date for the "new" enterprise zones.

The various enterprise zone deductions and credits are reported on FTB 3805Z.

The following enterprise zones received final designation in 2007 and 2008: Calexico, Coachella Valley, Compton, Eureka, Fresno City, Fresno County, Long Beach, Los Angeles—Hollywood, Oroville, Pasadena, San Jose, Santa Clarita, Shasta Metro, and Southgate—Lynwood. Before filing for any of the enterprise zone credits, check hcd.ca.gov and search for "EDA" for updated information.

Also, at the time this book went to press, the following areas had conditional designation as enterprise zones: Arvin, Delano, Kings County, Los Angeles—East, Merced, Northern Sacramento, Oakland, Richmond, Salinas Valley, San Bernardino, San Diego, San Francisco, San Joaquin County, Santa Ana, Siskiyou County, West Sacramento, and Yuba Sutter. Taxpayers located in a conditionally designated enterprise zone that had previously been designated as an enterprise zone can claim the zone incentives while HCD completes the designation process. However, taxpayers located in a brand new zone that has received conditional designation can only begin to claim the enterprise zone incentives once the zone has received final designation. These new zones include the city of Arvin, and Salinas Valley. (*FTB Tax News*, November 2007; *Press Release*, California Governor Arnold Schwarzenegger, January 31, 2008)

Numerous zones have expired. Unless a zone receives a new conditional designation, once a zone expires, no new credits or deductions may be generated. However, credits or deductions accrued prior to the expiration date may still be carried over. The following zones have expired, with the zone expiration dates indicated:

— Altadena/Pasadena (April 9, 2007)

— Bakersfield/Kern (SE Bakersfield) (October 14, 2006)

— Calexico (October 14, 2006)

— Coachella Valley (November 10, 2006)

— Delano (December 16, 2006)

— Eureka (October 14, 2006)

— Fresno (October 14, 2006)

— Long Beach (January 7, 2007)
— Los Angeles (Central City) (October 14, 2006)
— Los Angeles (Mid-Alameda Corridor) (October 14, 2006)
— Los Angeles (Northeast Valley) (October 14, 2006)
— Merced/Atwater (December 16, 2006)
— Oroville (November 5, 2006)
— Pittsburgh (January 10, 2008)
— Porterville (October 14, 2006)
— Redding/Anderson (Shasta/Metro) (November 5, 2006)
— Richmond (March 1, 2007)
— Sacramento (Northgate) (October 14, 2006)
— San Bernardino/Riverside (Agua Mansa) (October 14, 2006)
— San Diego (Metro) (October 14, 2006)
— San Diego (South Bay) (January 27, 2007)
— San Francisco (May 27, 2007)
— San Jose (December 31, 2006)
— Yuba/Sutter (October 14, 2006)

(Instructions, 2007 FTB 3805Z, Enterprise Zone Deduction and Credit Summary; *Tax News*, Franchise Tax Board, November 2007, CCH CALIFORNIA TAX REPORTS ¶404-487)

Comment: Local Zone Managers

Local zone managers, who are available to answer business eligibility and zone related information, are listed on the State's official zone Web site at www.hcd.ca.gov/fa/cdbg/ez.

• *Local agency military base recovery areas*

As a means of stimulating business and industrial growth to offset revenue losses occasioned by military base closures, a number of income tax incentives are available to businesses conducted within designated local agency military base recovery areas (LAMBRAs), provided those businesses increase their number of employees by one or more during the first two taxable years after commencing business within the LAMBRA. Deductions and credits applicable to LAMBRAs are reported on FTB 3807.

The following LAMBRAs have been designated: Alameda Naval Air Station, Castle Air Force Base, Mare Island Naval Base, Mather Field/McClellan Park, San Bernardino International Airport and Trade Center (Norton Airforce Base), San Diego NTC Liberty Station, Southern California Logistic Airport (George Airforce Base), and Tustin Marine Corps Air Station.

Income tax incentives provided for businesses conducted within a designated local agency military base recovery area include the following:

— Income tax credits for sales and use tax paid or incurred for certain equipment, components, and depreciable property (¶144).

— Income tax credits for wages paid to disadvantaged individuals or displaced employees (¶147).

— Accelerated write-off of the cost of certain depreciable business assets (¶316).

— Carryover of 100% of net operating losses for up to 15 years (¶309).

• *Targeted tax area*

To encourage private investment and employment within a targeted tax area, special tax incentives are available to eligible businesses located in the area. All of the incorporated cities and portions of the unincorporated areas of Tulare County have been designated as the targeted tax area. Deductions and credits applicable to the targeted tax area are reported on FTB 3809.

Income tax incentives provided for businesses conducted within a targeted tax area include the following:

— Income tax credits for sales and use tax paid or incurred for certain equipment, machinery, and parts (¶144).

— Income tax credits for wages paid to disadvantaged individuals (¶148).

— Accelerated write-off of the cost of certain depreciable business assets (¶316).

— Carryover of 100% of net operating losses for up to 15 years (¶309).

• *Manufacturing enhancement area*

Finally, businesses conducted within manufacturing enhancement areas are eligible for an employer's credit for certain wages paid to disadvantaged individuals. The cities of Brawley and Calexico in Imperial County are designated as manufacturing enhancement areas. The credit is reported on FTB 3808.

• *Los Angeles Revitalization Zone*

In addition to the economic incentives available in enterprise zones, special tax incentives were provided for taxable years beginning after 1991 and before 1998 to encourage investment, employment, and rebuilding in areas constituting the Los Angeles Revitalization Zone (LARZ). Credit carryovers are reported on FTB 3540 and FTB 3806 and deductions applicable to the LARZ are reported on FTB 3806.

The following special tax incentives for investment, employment, and rebuilding apply to the Los Angeles Revitalization Zone (LARZ):

— For taxable years beginning prior to 1998, income tax credits for sales or use tax paid on purchases of certain building materials, equipment, and machinery (¶125).

— For taxable years beginning prior to 1998, income tax credits for wages paid to certain individuals.

— Tax exemption of income from LARZ investments earned prior to December 1, 1998.

— Accelerated write-off of certain property purchased prior to December 1, 1998, for LARZ use (¶316).

— Carryover for up to 15 years of 100% of net operating losses incurred prior to the 1998 taxable year (¶309).

¶105 Who Is a Resident

Law: Secs. 17014-16, 17745 (CCH CALIFORNIA TAX REPORTS ¶15-110).

Comparable Federal: None.

California law defines "resident" to include the following:

— Every individual who is in the state for other than a temporary or transitory purpose. (As explained below, it does not matter whether such an individual's domicile, or permanent home, is in California or elsewhere.)

— Every individual who is domiciled in the state but who is outside the state for a temporary or transitory purpose. (Sec. 17014, Rev. & Tax. Code)

All individuals who are not "residents," as defined above, are "nonresidents." (Sec. 17015, Rev. & Tax. Code)

• *Temporary or transitory purpose*

A regulation (Reg. 17014) containing several examples of "temporary or transitory purpose" indicates: "the underlying theory . . . is that the state with which a person has the closest connection during the taxable year is the state of his residence."

California law specifically provides that an individual whose permanent home is in California, but who is absent from the state for an uninterrupted period of at least 546 days under an employment-related contract, will generally be considered to be outside the state for other than a temporary or transitory purpose and, therefore, will not be treated as a resident subject to California tax. A return to California for not more than 45 days during a taxable year will not affect the nonresident status of such an individual. However, the individual will be considered a resident if the individual has intangible income exceeding $200,000 in any taxable year during which the employment-related contract is in effect, or if the principal purpose of the individual's absence from the state is to avoid California personal income tax. The same rules will apply to a spouse who accompanies such an individual. (Sec. 17014, Rev. & Tax. Code)

• *Effect of domicile*

"Residency" is not the same as "domicile," which is an individual's permanent home, the place to which the individual, whenever absent, intends to return. One may be domiciled outside California, and still be considered a California resident by remaining in the state for other than temporary or transitory purposes. Conversely, California domiciliaries may be considered nonresidents if they remain outside the state for purposes that are neither temporary nor transitory. (Reg. 17014, 18 CCR) It is not necessary to demonstrate residency in any particular foreign state or country to avoid being considered a California resident—see the *Vohs* case, discussed below under "Seamen not California residents."

Certain U.S. officials who are domiciled in California are classified as "residents" for income tax purposes. This applies to elected officials, congressional staff members, and presidential appointees subject to Senate confirmation, other than military and foreign service career appointees. (Sec. 17014(b), Rev. & Tax Code)

• *Nine-month presumption*

California law provides that "every individual who spends in the aggregate more than nine months of the taxable year within this state shall be presumed to be a resident." The nine-month presumption is not conclusive and may be overcome by satisfactory evidence. (Sec. 17016, Rev. & Tax. Code)

Conversely, presence within the state for less than nine months does not necessarily mean that the individual is not a resident. This point was made in *Appeal of Raymond T. and Ann B. Stefani* (1984) (CCH CALIFORNIA TAX REPORTS ¶15-110.782), involving a California professor who taught at a school in Switzerland while on sabbatical leave from his California position. Additionally, a regulation (Reg. 17016, 18 CCR) provides that "a person may be a resident even though not in the state during any portion of the year."

• *Nine-month presumption overcome*

The presumption based on nine-months' residence, described above, was overcome by the taxpayer in *Appeal of Edgar Montillion Woolley* (1951) (CCH CALIFORNIA TAX REPORTS ¶200-134). The taxpayer, a well-known actor, maintained his permanent home in New York State. He was in California continuously for a period of a little over a year in 1944 and 1945, including over nine months in 1945. During that time he made two motion pictures and appeared in radio broadcasts. While in California, he lived in a hotel on a weekly basis. His departure was delayed because of illness and a studio strike. The State Board of Equalization (SBE) held that he was in California only for a temporary or transitory purpose and, therefore, was not a resident.

Another case in which the nine-month presumption was overcome is *Appeal of Joseph and Rebecca Peskin* (1962) (CCH CALIFORNIA TAX REPORTS ¶15-110.734). Over a period of several years the taxpayer spent from six to ten months in California each year. He engaged in extensive business activities and owned property in California. He overcame the presumption of residence by showing that he was more closely connected with Illinois than with California.

• *Nine-month presumption upheld*

The presumption based on nine-months' residence was upheld in *Appeal of Ralph V. and Marvelle J. Currier* (1969) (CCH CALIFORNIA TAX REPORTS ¶15-110.262). The taxpayer was employed in a job that required him to move frequently in the course of his employment, but he lived with his family in California for 2$^1/_2$ years. The SBE decided that the taxpayer was domiciled in Arizona but that, because his stay in California was for an indefinite period, he was a California resident.

• *Less than nine months in California*

In *Appeal of Morgan C. and Ann M. Jones* (1972) (CCH CALIFORNIA TAX REPORTS ¶15-110.736), the taxpayers argued unsuccessfully that a presumption of nonresidency arises from living in California for a period of less than nine months. However, although the taxpayers were registered to vote in Texas, had Texas drivers' licenses, and Texas automobile registration plates, the SBE held that the taxpayers were California residents in 1961, when they lived in the state for eight months, and in 1962, when they lived in the state for only five months.

• *Military personnel—In general*

Military personnel are subject to special treatment with respect to residency. Under Legal Ruling No. 300 (CCH CALIFORNIA TAX REPORTS ¶15-175.30), issued by the Franchise Tax Board (FTB) in 1965, California military personnel are treated as nonresidents when they leave the state under permanent military orders to serve at out-of-state posts of duty. If the serviceperson retains a California domicile and has a spouse who remains a California resident, the resident spouse is taxable on one-half of their community income. Out-of-state military personnel serving at posts of duty in California are treated as nonresidents unless California domicile is adopted. If California domicile is adopted, California will tax the entire income received during the period of residence. Declarations filed with military service branches showing California as the state of legal residence are treated as presumptive evidence of California residence. The 1965 ruling resulted from a 1963 decision of the SBE: *Appeal of Harold L. and Miriam J. Naylor* (CCH CALIFORNIA TAX REPORTS ¶15-175.25). See also ¶225.

FTB Pub. 1032 (Tax Information For Military Personnel) also provides information on determining resident status for military personnel.

• *Effect of temporary military assignment*

In *Appeal of Cecil L. and Bonai G. Sanders* (1971) (CCH CALIFORNIA TAX REPORTS ¶15-175.301), the SBE declined to follow the *Naylor* case, discussed above, where a serviceman spent most of the year outside California under military orders designating a "permanent change of station." Instead, the SBE held that the taxpayer's out-of-state duty was clearly "temporary rather than permanent or indefinite."

• *Civil employees of military*

The special rules for military personnel do not apply to civilian employees of the military. See *Appeal of Ronald L. and Joyce E. Surette* (1983) (CCH CALIFORNIA TAX REPORTS ¶15-110.3312), where a civilian employee of the U.S. Army and his wife spent three years in West Germany on an Army assignment. They continued to own a California home and maintained California driver's licenses and voter registrations in California. The SBE held that they were California residents throughout the three-year period.

In *Appeal of Dennis W. and Emiko Leggett* (1984) (CCH CALIFORNIA TAX REPORTS ¶400-671), the taxpayer, a civilian employee of the U.S. Navy, spent at least ten months a year aboard ships. His wife lived in California and reported one-half of his income as her share of community income. The SBE held that he was a California resident and that his entire income was taxable.

• *Business assignments outside California—In general*

Several decisions of the SBE have involved taxpayers whose domicile admittedly was California, but who claimed nonresident status when they were out of the state on business assignments or projects for varying periods. The cases turn largely on the extent to which the taxpayers sever their ties to California and establish connections elsewhere, and the extent to which out-of-state activities appear to require long or indefinite periods of time to accomplish.

• *Business assignment cases favorable to taxpayer*

In *Appeal of Richard H. and Doris J. May* (1987) (CCH CALIFORNIA TAX REPORTS ¶15-115.751), the taxpayer was employed by a Washington wholesaler to service sales areas in Washington and Oregon. The taxpayer and his wife had all of their business interests in Washington, maintained most bank accounts in Washington and Oregon, were registered Washington voters, had Washington drivers' licenses, and had all their legal, accounting, and medical needs met by Washington and Oregon professionals. In holding that the taxpayer and his wife were Washington residents, the SBE held that the fact that they erroneously claimed residency for purposes of the California homeowners property tax exemption on their California condominium and for the federal exclusion of gain from the sale of a personal residence were factors to consider but were not conclusive with respect to residence.

In Appeal of Berry Gordy, Jr. (1986) (CCH CALIFORNIA TAX REPORTS ¶15-110.42), where the taxpayer filed a 1969 California part-year resident return, the SBE held that the state with which a person has the closest connections is the state of residence, and that the taxpayer had the closest connections with Michigan, where he owned several houses, had the majority of his business interests, registered and licensed his cars, and voted, and where his attorney, accountant, physician, dentist, and insurance agent were all located.

In *Appeal of Jeffrey L. and Donna S. Egeberg* (1985) (CCH CALIFORNIA TAX REPORTS ¶15-110.3381), the taxpayer was an engineer employed by a nuclear engineering firm in California. He spent 17 months in Europe on an assignment that was expected to last at least three years. The family and household goods were moved to Europe, memberships in California were terminated, and other ties with California were severed. Despite retention of some important California relationships, the SBE held that the taxpayer and his wife were not California residents during their absence from the state.

In *Appeal of Robert C. and Grace L. Weaver* (1985) (CCH CALIFORNIA TAX REPORTS ¶15-110.88), the taxpayer was an engineer employed by an aircraft manufacturer in California. He spent two years on Kwajalein Island on a "long-term foreign assignment" that was described as "more than one year and indefinite in nature." The taxpayer and his wife took an active part in social activities on Kwajalein, their minor daughter attended school there, and they established other connections there. However, they retained ownership of a home, stored an automobile and other possessions, and maintained some financial connections in California. The SBE held that their absence from California was for other than a temporary or transitory purpose, and concluded that they were not California residents during their absence from the state.

In *Appeal of Tommy H. and Leila J. Thomas* (1983) (CCH CALIFORNIA TAX REPORTS ¶15-110.338), the taxpayer made a commitment in 1977 to move to Iran for two or three years. He kept his home in California, maintained some other connections with the state, and left two daughters in school in California, but severed other connections. Due to the political unrest in Iran, the taxpayer's commitment was canceled and he returned to California after about a year overseas. The SBE held that he was not a California resident during his absence from the state.

In *Appeal of James E. Duncan* (1982) (CCH CALIFORNIA TAX REPORTS ¶15-110.507), the taxpayer moved to Texas to accept an executive position with the intention of remaining indefinitely. Although he left the Texas position and returned to California after only seven months, the SBE held that he acquired a new domicile in Texas during his employment there and that, therefore, he was not a California resident during the relevant period.

In *Appeal of David A. and Frances W. Stevenson* (1977) (CCH CALIFORNIA TAX REPORTS ¶15-110.506), the taxpayer was an untenured professor at a California university. He spent a period of 14 months in Europe working for most of that time under a research grant from the Fulbright Commission. The SBE accepted the taxpayer's contention that he intended to remain in Europe for at least two years and, consequently, held that he was not a California resident while he was absent from the state.

In *Appeal of Christopher T. and Hoda A. Rand* (1976) (CCH CALIFORNIA TAX REPORTS ¶15-110.482), the taxpayer was a specialist in Near Eastern affairs and was fluent in Arabic and Persian. He had traveled widely in the Near East and elsewhere, and was married to an Egyptian national. He lived in California for several years, beginning in 1966, and was assumed to be domiciled in California. He moved to Libya in July 1970 to take a job there, but moved back to California four months later because he lost the job. The SBE held that the taxpayer was a nonresident for the four months that he was in Libya because he "intended and expected to remain in the Near East either permanently or indefinitely."

In *Appeal of Richards L. and Kathleen K. Hardman* (1975) (CCH CALIFORNIA TAX REPORTS ¶15-110.481), a professional writer was held to be a nonresident in 1969 when he spent most of the year in England, even though his absence from the state in 1969 and 1970 lasted only 13 months. The taxpayer and his wife severed most of their connections with California before their departure, and it appeared that they originally expected to stay in England for several years.

• *Business assignment cases unfavorable to taxpayer*

In *Appeal of David A. Abbott* (1986) (CCH CALIFORNIA TAX REPORTS ¶15-110.3143), the taxpayer was held by the SBE to be a California resident during his seven-month employment in Maryland because his absence was for a temporary or transitory purpose. His wife and two children remained in their California home while he lived in a hotel for his entire stay outside the state. He owned other property in California and also retained his driver's license, automobile registration, and bank accounts in California.

In *Appeal of Frank J. Milos* (1984) (CCH CALIFORNIA TAX REPORTS ¶15-110.317), the taxpayer spent four years working as an engineer on Johnson Island. His wife and children remained in California and he retained other connections with California. He contended that he was no longer domiciled in California because he could not find employment in the state. The SBE held that he retained his California domicile and was a California resident during the entire period. For another case involving employment on Johnson Island, with somewhat similar facts and the same result, see *Appeal of John A. Purkins* (1984) (CCH CALIFORNIA TAX REPORTS ¶15-110.331).

In *Appeal of Albert L. and Anna D. Tambini* (1984) (CCH CALIFORNIA TAX REPORTS ¶15-110.339), the taxpayer spent about a year on an assignment of "indefinite" duration in Spain, with an agreement that his employer would transfer him back to California upon completion of the assignment. The SBE held that he was a California resident during the period involved.

In *Appeal of Harold L. and Wanda G. Benedict* (1982) (CCH CALIFORNIA TAX REPORTS ¶15-110.339), the taxpayer was an airline flight engineer. He was transferred by his employer to an Australian base station, where he remained for about ten months and then returned to California. Although he retained close connections with California, he contended that he was no longer a California resident because he did not intend to return to California. The SBE held that he was a California resident throughout the period involved.

In *Appeal of Nelson and Doris DeAmicis* (1982) (CCH CALIFORNIA TAX REPORTS ¶15-110.89), the taxpayer worked on Ascension Island for a year in 1976 and 1977. He argued that he had established residence there after he and his wife had agreed to a trial separation. However, he did not sever his principal personal and family California connections and he did not establish connections with Ascension Island. The SBE held that he was a California resident during the period involved.

In *Appeal of Pierre E.G. and Nicole Salinger* (1980) (CCH CALIFORNIA TAX REPORTS ¶15-110.333), the taxpayer spent about a year on a business assignment in Europe, but maintained many close connections with California. The SBE cited some of the cases discussed above, and held that the taxpayer remained a California resident during the period involved. Also, to the same effect, see *Appeal of David C. and Livia P. Wensley* (1981) (CCH CALIFORNIA TAX REPORTS ¶15-110.864); in this case the taxpayer spent 18 months on a business assignment in Germany, in a situation generally similar to the *Salinger* case. See also *Appeal of Robert J. Addington, Jr.* (1982) (CCH CALIFORNIA TAX REPORTS ¶15-110.867), involving a one-year stay in England on an assignment that was expected to last for two or three years. Also, see *Appeal of Russell R. Stephens, Jr.* (1985) (CCH CALIFORNIA TAX REPORTS ¶15-110.3351), where the taxpayer spent 18 months on a work assignment in Saudi Arabia.

In *Appeal of Robert J. and Kyung Y. Olsen* (1980) (CCH CALIFORNIA TAX REPORTS ¶15-110.382), the taxpayer had a work assignment in Iran from December 1974 to December 1976. His wife and five children stayed in their California home while he was away. Although he spent 90% of the year 1976 in Iran, the SBE held that he was outside the state for temporary or transitory purposes and was a California resident throughout the period.

In *Appeal of Alexander B. and Margaret E. Salton* (1977) (CCH CALIFORNIA TAX REPORTS ¶15-110.336), the taxpayer spent about two years on a job assignment in Japan. The SBE cited the *Broadhurst* case, discussed below, at some length, and held that the taxpayer was a California resident throughout the period involved.

In *Appeal of William and Mary Louise Oberholtzer* (1976) (CCH CALIFORNIA TAX REPORTS ¶15-110.38), the taxpayer was a California engineer who worked in France for approximately eighteen months under a contract with his employer for that period. He kept a home and a car in California, and left a daughter there to finish her schooling. Although he was treated as a resident of France under French law, the SBE held that he was a California resident during the years in question.

In *Appeal of David J. and Amanda Broadhurst* (1976) (CCH CALIFORNIA TAX REPORTS ¶15-110.335), the taxpayer worked for the United Nations in Argentina from April 1971 to December 1972. His family stayed in the house they owned in California. The SBE cited some of the cases discussed above and held that he remained a California resident in 1971. To the same effect, see *Appeal of Wilbert L. and Doris Penfold* (1986) (CCH CALIFORNIA TAX REPORTS ¶15-110.318); in this case the taxpayer worked at numerous locations outside California for 30 years, usually remaining at each site for approximately one year.

In *Appeal of Malcolm A. Coffman* (1976) (CCH CALIFORNIA TAX REPORTS ¶15-110.381), the taxpayer spent five months in Australia in 1970 on a short-term assignment with the idea of possibly returning later for a long-term assignment. He arranged for a long-term assignment shortly after his return to California, and went to Australia again early in 1971. The SBE held that he was a California resident throughout 1970.

In *Appeal of Anthony V. and Beverly Zupanovich* (1976) (CCH CALIFORNIA TAX REPORTS ¶15-110.334), the taxpayer worked from December 1967 to February 1971 as a tugboat seaman in the Vietnam war zone. The SBE held that he was a California resident in 1968 and 1969, noting that, "although appellant's absence turned out to be rather lengthy, his family life, his social life, and much of his financial life remained centered in California throughout the years in question." The SBE's opinion discusses the significance of "connections," and indicates that the connections maintained by a taxpayer "are important both as a measure of the benefits and protection that the taxpayer has received from the laws and government of California, and also as an objective indication of whether the taxpayer entered or left this state for temporary or transitory purposes."

In *Appeal of John B. and Beverly A. Simpson* (1975) (CCH CALIFORNIA TAX REPORTS ¶15-110.332), an engineer was held to be a resident in 1971 although he spent the period from October 1970 to May 1972 on an assignment in Australia. In this case, the taxpayer's family stayed in California, and his assignment was originally scheduled for only one year.

• *Mixed residence of spouses/registered domestic partners—Community income*

When one spouse/registered domestic partner (RDP) is domiciled in California, works outside the state, and establishes nonresident status, while the other spouse/RDP remains a California resident, the resident spouse/RDP may be taxable on one-half of the nonresident spouse's/RDP's income because it is deemed to be community income. See cases to this effect cited at ¶239. (However, as explained at ¶239, in case of a permanent separation of the spouses/RDPs, their earnings are separate income; in this event the resident spouse/RDP would not be required to report any of the nonresident spouse's/RDP's earnings.)

• *Seamen held to be California residents*

In *Appeal of Charles F. Varn* (1977) (CCH CALIFORNIA TAX REPORTS ¶15-110.708), the taxpayer was a merchant seaman on a ship that never called at California ports. On June 8, 1971, he married a California resident who continued to live in California and who filed a separate California income tax return for 1971. The SBE held that the taxpayer acquired a California domicile when he married, and that he was a California resident for the remainder of the year.

In *Appeal of Olav Valderhaug* (1954) (CCH CALIFORNIA TAX REPORTS ¶15-110.26), the SBE held that a seaman who was in a California port three months of the year was a resident because California was the state with which he had the closest connection during the year. The seaman's wife and children lived in California for the full year. See also cases involving similar situations of merchant seamen decided by the SBE in later years, particularly *Appeal of Fernandez* (1971) (CCH CALIFORNIA TAX REPORTS ¶15-110.70), *Appeal of Haring* (1975) (CCH CALIFORNIA TAX REPORTS ¶15-110.703), *Appeal of Miller* (1975) (CCH CALIFORNIA TAX REPORTS ¶15-110.704), *Appeal of Laude* (1976) (CCH CALIFORNIA TAX REPORTS ¶15-110.707), and *Appeal of Estill William Fairchild* (1983) CCH CALIFORNIA TAX REPORTS ¶15-110.7092); the SBE held in each case that the taxpayer was domiciled in California and was outside the state for only a temporary or transitory purpose.

• *Seamen not California residents*

In *Appeal of John Jacobs* (1985) (CCH CALIFORNIA TAX REPORTS ¶15-115.653), the taxpayer was an unmarried sea captain who was assigned by his employer to operations in the Persian Gulf. Although he had a California driver's license and some other connections with California, he had no home or business interests in the state. The SBE held that he was not a California resident, because his connections with California were insignificant, even though he had closer connections with California than elsewhere.

Another case holding that a merchant seaman was *not* a California resident was *Appeal of Thomas J. Tuppein* (1976) (CCH CALIFORNIA TAX REPORTS ¶15-115.652). The taxpayer worked exclusively for California shipping companies, and was assumed to be domiciled in California. Although he was in California frequently for a few days between voyages, he spent a total of less than one month a year in the state. On the other hand, he spent longer periods in foreign countries and in Hawaii, and he maintained bank accounts and owned real estate in such locations. The SBE concluded that his closest connections were not with California and that he did not receive "sufficient benefits from the laws and government of California to warrant his classification as a resident."

In *Appeal of Richard W. Vohs* (1973) (CCH CALIFORNIA TAX REPORTS ¶15-115.651), the SBE held that a merchant seaman was *not* a California resident despite the fact that his closest connections were with California. The taxpayer had been born and raised in California, was domiciled in the state, voted in the state, had a California driver's license, and had other connections in the state. The SBE held that the taxpayer was outside California for other than a temporary or transitory purpose, and commented that "a taxpayer need not establish that he became a resident of any particular state or country in order to sustain his position that he was not a resident of California."

• *Resident though domiciled elsewhere*

In *Appeal of German A. Posada* (1987) (CCH CALIFORNIA TAX REPORTS ¶15-110.453), the taxpayer was apparently a Colombian domiciliary, but was found to be a California resident for jeopardy assessment purposes. The taxpayer spent considerable time in California during the years at issue, obtaining a California driver's license, registering a car and boat there, and, after living for a time with friends in the state, prepaying six months rent on a California apartment. The SBE conceded that the taxpayer had "few contacts" with California, and that many of the usual indicia of residency, such as voter registration and bank accounts, were lacking, but concluded that this was evidence of the taxpayer's "nomadic nature" rather than of nonresidency in California.

In *Appeal of George D. Yaron* (1976) (CCH CALIFORNIA TAX REPORTS ¶205-567), the taxpayer had substantial business interests and other connections in both California and Vietnam. Although he was considered a resident of Vietnam under the laws of that country and was assumed not to be domiciled in California, the SBE held that he was a California resident.

In *Appeal of Mary G. Steiner* (1954) (CCH CALIFORNIA TAX REPORTS ¶15-110.26), the SBE held that an individual who resided in California for a substantial portion of the year was a California resident although it appeared that her domicile was in Florida. The individual involved owned property in Utah, had bank accounts in Utah and Florida, voted in Florida, paid property taxes there under a "resident" classification, and contributed to a church there. She rented a furnished apartment in California on a month-to-month basis and spent about half her time in the state.

A somewhat similar situation was involved in *Appeal of Lucille F. Betts* (1954) (CCH CALIFORNIA TAX REPORTS ¶15-110.26). The individual in this case was a widow who claimed residence in New Jersey, where she owned property, maintained bank accounts, voted, etc. She lived in a hotel in California and, because of transportation difficulties, did not return to New Jersey for a period of years during World War II.

The SBE held that she was a California resident, relying on the nine-month presumption discussed above.

• *Substantial connections with California*

In *Appeal of Beldon R. and Mildred Katleman* (1980) (CCH CALIFORNIA TAX REPORTS ¶ 15-110.401), the taxpayer owned and managed a Las Vegas hotel and casino for several years until it burned down in 1960. From 1960 to 1970 he was engaged in efforts to reconstruct or develop the property. In 1962 he purchased a large home in California. Thereafter he spent a considerable amount of time and developed substantial connections in California. Although he maintained important connections in Nevada throughout the years involved, the SBE held that he was a California resident in 1962 and subsequent years.

In *Appeal of Jerald L. and Joan Katleman* (1976) (CCH CALIFORNIA TAX REPORTS ¶ 15-110.223), the taxpayer had important ties with Illinois, including voting and filing state income tax returns there. The SBE held that he was a California resident, on the basis of a closer connection with California and also upon the fact the he "enjoyed substantial benefits and protection from the laws and government of California."

In *George and Elia Whittell v. Franchise Tax Board* (1964) (CCH CALIFORNIA TAX REPORTS ¶ 15-110.261), decided by the California Court of Appeal, it was held that the taxpayers were California residents, even though they had a large home in Nevada, voted there, filed federal tax returns there, and had many other connections with that state. The taxpayers spent most of their time in California and had important family and business connections in the state.

In *Appeal of Ada E. Wrigley* (1955) (CCH CALIFORNIA TAX REPORTS ¶ 15-110.26), the SBE held that the taxpayer was a resident of California despite these factors: important business interests in Chicago; maintenance of a home and club membership there; exercise of her voting privilege there; principal banking activity there; and maintenance of three other large homes outside of California. The SBE indicated: "Long continued preference for (spending her time in) California, when coupled with her extensive and long continued financial interests within the state, the burial of her husband in California, the retention of two large homes within the state and the exchange of her large apartment in Chicago for smaller quarters there, convinces us that . . . California had become her principal place of abode."

• *Nonresidency found despite substantial California connections*

In *Appeal of Stephen D. Bragg* (2003) (CCH CALIFORNIA TAX REPORTS ¶ 15-110.266) the taxpayer had homes and business activities in both California and Arizona, had personal bank accounts in California, had vehicles registered in California, and obtained all of his professional services in California. In spite of these substantial contacts with California, the SBE determined that the taxpayer was a resident of Arizona, as he spent the majority of his time during the taxable year at his residence in Arizona, conducted the majority of his business and full-time employment in Arizona, and had no real intent to return to California to reside.

In *Corbett v. Franchise Tax Board* (1985) (CCH CALIFORNIA TAX REPORTS ¶ 15-110.607), the taxpayers maintained important business, social, and other connections with Illinois, including voter registration and drivers' licenses there. Nonetheless, the SBE held that they were California residents because in the years involved they spent $6^1/_2$ to $8^1/_2$ months of each year in California, owned a substantial California home, and had important social and family connections with the state. However, a court of appeal reversed the SBE's decision, and held that the taxpayers were not California residents.

In *Fred C. Klemp v. Franchise Tax Board* (1975) (CCH CALIFORNIA TAX REPORTS ¶ 15-110.557), the California Court of Appeal overruled the SBE and held that the taxpayers were not California residents, despite the fact that they owned a home in

California and spent more time in California than they spent in the state of their domicile, Illinois. The court mentioned several factors that showed a closer connection with Illinois than with California. These included: voter registration, automobile registration, drivers' licenses, business offices and accounting, investment counselor, doctor, dentist, church affiliation, safe deposit box, all in Illinois.

• *Importance of supporting evidence*

In *Appeal of Raymond H. and Margaret R. Berner* (2001) (CCH CALIFORNIA TAX REPORTS ¶15-115.75), the SBE overturned an FTB determination that the taxpayers were California residents on the basis of affidavits and declarations of friends, family, and Nevada professionals stating that the taxpayers changed their domicile from California to Nevada. The taxpayers owned homes in both Nevada and California, and appeals in previous years had resulted in determinations that the taxpayers were California residents. The FTB determined that the taxpayers were California residents during the tax years at issue on the basis of the taxpayers' California country club memberships, credit card records, California doctors' office visits, weekly home maintenance service records for their California home, and bank records. However, the SBE determined that the affidavits and declarations from friends, family, and Nevada professionals (including the postmaster for the Nevada town of residence) were sufficient to overcome the FTB's evidence.

In *Appeal of C.I. Schermer* (1961) (CCH CALIFORNIA TAX REPORTS ¶15-110.604), the SBE sustained the findings of the FTB that the taxpayer became a resident in 1952, on the basis of bank accounts opened, credit applications filed, and the renting of an apartment. Taxpayer offered oral argument in opposition, but failed to supply affidavits of business associates or relatives concerning the amount of time spent in California. Since the taxpayer was an attorney, the SBE noted that it was reasonable to assume he would have maintained detailed records of his time as a basis for charging clients, and he failed to introduce these records in support of his position.

• *Indefinite intentions regarding California stay*

Appeal of George W. and Gertrude S. Davis (1964) (CCH CALIFORNIA TAX REPORTS ¶15-110.505) involved the intent of the taxpayers as a factor in determining residence. When the taxpayers initially came to California, they were uncertain whether, or when, they would depart. Accordingly, they were considered to have come for an indefinite period and were held to be residents for purposes of the California income tax.

• *"Nonresident alien" was California resident*

In *Appeal of Riad Ghali* (1971) (CCH CALIFORNIA TAX REPORTS ¶15-110.263), an Egyptian citizen was held to be a California resident despite the fact that he was classified as a nonresident alien for federal tax purposes. During the period in question, the taxpayer had no lawfully permanent status in the United States but was allowed to remain in this country because he was in disfavor with the Egyptian government and was afraid to return to that country. Nevertheless, he was held to be a California resident on the basis of his continued residence in the state over a period of years and, accordingly, was taxed on gain from sale of oil and gas leases in Mexico.

• *Professors on out-of-state assignments*

In *Appeal of Thomas K. and Gail G. Boehme* (1985) (CCH CALIFORNIA TAX REPORTS ¶15-110.783), the SBE held that a California university professor and his wife remained California residents throughout a 22-month assignment to a university study center in Egypt. The taxpayers rented out their California home on a month-to-month rather than a long-term basis, continued to claim the California homeowner's property tax exemption for it, left their family car in California, kept various California bank and charge accounts, and maintained a number of other contacts with California during their stay in Egypt. To the same effect, see *Appeal of Mortimer and Catherine*

Chambers (1987) (CCH CALIFORNIA TAX REPORTS ¶15-110.783), involving a university professor who taught in Germany for two years.

Appeal of William F. and June A. Massy (1972) (CCH CALIFORNIA TAX REPORTS ¶204-755) involved the residence status of a Stanford University professor who spent a year in Pennsylvania as a visiting professor. The taxpayer moved to Pennsylvania with the understanding that a permanent position would become available there. The SBE held that the taxpayer was not a California resident during the period in question.

• *Airline pilots transferred to California*

Appeal of Warren L. and Marlys A. Christianson (1972) (CCH CALIFORNIA TAX REPORTS ¶15-110.20) involved the residence status of an airline pilot (and family) in 1967 and 1968. He was transferred in 1966 from Texas to California to fly on military charter flights from California to Southeast Asia. Although he bought a home in California, he maintained business interests in Texas and other ties to that state. He argued that his presence in California was temporary because it was related to the uncertain duration of the Vietnam conflict. The SBE held that the taxpayer was a resident of California, although still domiciled in Texas. The SBE's opinion discusses the distinction between "residence" and "domicile," and comments that, "oftentimes in our mobile society they are not the same." See also the 1972 and 1973 decisions of the SBE in *Appeal of Donald E. and Betty J. MacInnes* (CCH CALIFORNIA TAX REPORTS ¶15-110.201) and *Appeal of Henry C. Berger* (CCH CALIFORNIA TAX REPORTS ¶15-110.202), involving other pilots transferred to California during the same time period; these taxpayers were also held to be California residents, although they were registered voters in other states and had other ties to those states.

• *Federal civil service employees*

In *Appeal of Paul Peringer* (1980) (CCH CALIFORNIA TAX REPORTS ¶15-110.265), the taxpayer was a federal civil service employee who had been transferred several times during his government career. Although he had been stationed in California for several years before and during the taxable years, he argued that his job location was not "permanent" and also challenged California's constitutional power to tax a federal employee domiciled in another state. The SBE's holding that he was a California resident, and this was affirmed by the California Court of Appeal. To the same effect, see *Appeal of George M. and Georgia M. Webster* (1977) (CCH CALIFORNIA TAX REPORTS ¶15-110.264), involving a taxpayer who had been a federal employee in California for 16 years.

• *Professional sports*

In *Appeal of Jimmy J. Childs* (1983) (CCH CALIFORNIA TAX REPORTS ¶15-110.211), the taxpayer was a professional football player with the St. Louis Cardinals. During the year in question (1979), he spent eight months in Missouri and four months in California, where he stayed with his parents during the off-season. He filed a nonresident Missouri return, in which he stated that his home address was in California. The SBE held that he was a resident of California.

Appeal of Richard and Carolyn Selma (1977) (CCH CALIFORNIA TAX REPORTS ¶15-110.212) involved a native Californian, admittedly domiciled in California, who played baseball for the Philadelphia Phillies. During the off-season he worked in California as a part-time bartender. He filed nonresident Pennsylvania tax returns in which he stated that he was a California resident and had numerous connections with California. The SBE held that he was a California resident. To the same effect, see *Appeal of Robert D. and Susan Owchinko* (1985) (CCH CALIFORNIA TAX REPORTS ¶15-110.213); in this case the taxpayer played for the Cleveland Indians in the year involved and also played winter baseball in Puerto Rico. See also *Appeal of Joe and Gloria Morgan* (1985) (CCH CALIFORNIA TAX REPORTS ¶15-110.213), in which the taxpayer played for the Houston Astros and kept a house or apartment in Houston.

• *Effect of homeowner's property tax exemption*

In *Appeal of Robert and Nancy D. Hanley* (1981) (CCH CALIFORNIA TAX REPORTS ¶15-110.863), the taxpayer-husband spent about eight months in Florida and only 137 days in California during the year involved. He owned a home in Florida and managed a business there. However, his wife remained in California, where the couple also had business and other interests and where they claimed a California home as their permanent residence for purposes of the homeowner's property tax exemption. The SBE held that they were California residents.

• *Factors affecting residency*

As the illustrative cases summarized above indicate, there is no easy rule of thumb for determining when an individual is a California resident. All of the surrounding circumstances must be considered in making a residency determination. An FTB publication entitled "Guidelines for Determining Resident Status—2008" (FTB Pub. 1031) provides the following list of some factors that should be considered, with a cautionary note that the list is only a partial one:

— the amount of time you spend in California versus amount of time you spend outside California;

— the location(s) of your spouse and children;

— the location of your principal residence;

— where you were issued your driver's license;

— where your vehicles are registered;

— where you maintain your professional licenses;

— where you are registered to vote;

— the locations of banks where you maintain accounts;

— the locations of your doctors, dentists, accountants, and attorneys;

— the locations of the church, temple, or mosque, professional associations, and social and country clubs of which you are a member;

— the locations of your real property and investments;

— the permanence of your work assignments in California; and

— the location of your social ties.

The State Board of Equalization has provided an even more extensive list of factors in *Appeal of Stephen D. Bragg* (2003) (CCH CALIFORNIA TAX REPORTS ¶15-110.266).

• *Court action to determine residence status*

A person who is alleged to be a California resident can obtain a determination of the fact of his or her residence by the Superior Court by first protesting a notice of proposed deficiency issued by the FTB (¶704). If the action of the FTB is unfavorable, he or she must then appeal to the SBE (¶705). If the SBE also rules unfavorably, an action must then be brought in the Superior Court to determine the issue of residency. All of this can be done without first paying the underlying tax.

• *Special rule for trust beneficiaries*

A resident beneficiary of a trust is presumed to continue to be a resident when he or she receives an accumulation distribution from the trust within 12 months after leaving the state and returns to the state within 12 months after receiving the distribution (¶605). (Sec. 17745, Rev. & Tax. Code)

• *California-federal comparison*

Although in some respects the California rules relating to residence are similar to federal provisions regarding resident aliens, the two laws deal with quite different situations. Therefore, no attempt is made here to compare them.

¶106 Returns—Who Required to File—Forms

Law: Secs. 18409, 18501-34, 18622-23, 18635.5, 19582.5; Reg. 19524, 18 CCR (CCH CALIFORNIA TAX REPORTS ¶15-260, 15-265, 15-270, 15-275, 89-102, 89-112).

Comparable Federal: Secs. 6011-14, 6034A, 6102 (CCH U.S. MASTER TAX GUIDE ¶510, 2501).

California Forms: Form 540 (California Resident Income Tax Return), Form 540A (California Resident Income Tax Return), Form 540 2EZ (California Resident Income Tax Return), Form 540NR (California Nonresident or Part-Year Resident Income Tax Return), Form 540X (Amended Individual Income Tax Return), Form 541 (California Fiduciary Income Tax Return), Form 565 (Partnership Return of Income), Form 568 (Limited Liability Company Return of Income).

For the 2008 tax year, California law requires that an income tax return be filed for every individual who has income in excess of the following amounts (Sec. 18501, Rev. & Tax. Code):

2008 Filing Thresholds

On 12/31/08, the taxpayer's filing status was:	**and on 12/31/08, the taxpayer's age was[6]:**	California Gross Income[1]			California Adjusted Gross Income[2]		
		Dependents			Dependents		
		0	1	2 or more	0	1	2 or more
Single or Head of household[3]	Under 65	14,845	25,145	32,870	11,876	22,176	29,901
	65 or older	19,795	27,520	33,700	16,826	24,551	30,731
Married/RDP filing jointly or filing separately[4]	Under 65 (both spouses/RDPs)	29,690	39,990	47,715	23,752	34,052	41,777
	65 or older (one spouse/RDP)	34,640	42,365	48,545	28,702	36,427	42,607
	65 or older (both spouses/RDPs)	39,590	47,315	53,495	33,652	41,377	47,557
Qualifying widow(er)[3]	Under 65		25,145	32,870		22,176	29,901
	65 or older		27,520	33,700		24,551	30,731
Dependent of another person Any filing status	Any age	More than your standard deduction[5]					

[1] **California gross income** is all income received from all sources in the form of money, goods, property, and services that are not exempt from tax. Gross income does not include any adjustments or deductions.

[2] **California adjusted gross income** is federal adjusted gross income from all sources reduced or increased by all California income adjustments.

[3] See ¶15-320.

[4] The income of both spouses or registered domestic partners (RDPs) must be combined; both spouses or RDPs may be required to file a return even if only one spouse or RDP had income over the amounts listed.

[5] Use the California Standard Deduction Worksheet for Dependents in the 2008 California Resident Booklet to compute the standard deduction.

[6] If the taxpayer's 65th birthday is on January 1, 2009, she or he is considered to be age 65 on December 31, 2008.

For filing threshold purposes (1) single persons include taxpayers filing as heads of households and qualifying widowers and (2) married couples/registered domestic partners (RDPs) include couples and RDPs filing either jointly or separately. (Sec. 18501, Rev. & Tax. Code)

CCH Comment: Tax Liability Threshold Distinguished

While filing requirements are triggered at the levels set forth above, tax liability is incurred at lower income levels than the thresholds. For the 2008 tax year, tax liability is incurred if the AGI of a single or married filing separate taxpayer is $12,226 or more, or if the AGI of a married filing joint, surviving spouse, or head of household taxpayer is $24,452 or more. (*News Release*, California Franchise Tax Board, October 3, 2008)

Form 540 must also be filed if any of the following taxes are due:

— a tax on lump-sum distributions (¶206);

— a tax on a qualified retirement plan, including IRAs (¶206) or Archer MSAs (¶247);

— a tax for children under age 14 with investment income in excess of $1,800 (¶118);

— alternative minimum tax (¶117);

— recapture taxes;

— deferred tax on certain installment obligations; and

— a tax on an accumulation distribution from a trust (¶605). (Instructions, 2008 Form 540)

Certain fiduciaries (except for fiduciaries acting on behalf of certain grantor trusts—see ¶608) must file a California return. A fiduciary acting on behalf of an individual must file if:

— the individual is single and has adjusted gross income over $8,000,

— the individual is married and has adjusted gross income over $16,000, or

— the gross income of the individual exceeds $10,000 ($20,000, if married). (Sec. 18505, Rev. & Tax. Code)

A fiduciary acting on behalf of an estate or trust must file if:

— the estate or trust owes alternative minimum tax,

— the estate has net income from all sources over $1,000,

— the trust has net income from all sources over $100, or

— the gross income from all sources of the estate or trust exceeds $10,000. (Sec. 18506, Rev. & Tax. Code)

A fiduciary must also file a California return for *every* decedent for the year of death, and for all prior years in which the decedent should have filed returns but failed to do so. (Reg. 18505-4, 18 CCR) The return must be made by the decedent's executor, administrator, or other person charged with the property of the decedent. (Sec. 18505.3, Rev. & Tax. Code)

An individual for whom a federal dependent exemption may be claimed must file a separate state income tax return if the individual's gross income from all sources exceeds the amount of the basic standard deduction allowed to the individual under federal law. (Sec. 18501, Rev. & Tax. Code)

Married couples, and registered domestic partners (RDPs) (see ¶114, ¶119) may elect to file separate returns or a joint return. (Sec. 18521, Rev. & Tax. Code) For a discussion of joint returns, see ¶107.

Although partnerships are not taxed as such, they are required to file returns in some cases (¶622). A charitable trust is subject to special reporting requirements (¶606). See ¶607 regarding returns of employees' trusts.

Every common trust fund for which a trust company acts must file a return, regardless of the amount of gross or net income. (Sec. 17677, Rev. & Tax. Code) The fiduciary return form (Form 541) is used for this purpose.

• *ReadyReturn pilot program*

Under the ReadyReturn program, the FTB will complete a qualified personal income taxpayer's return utilizing withholding and wage information received from employers. Taxpayers may then accept the calculation and sign the completed return or elect to complete their own return. (*Tax News*, California Franchise Tax Board, January 2007)

• *Return forms*

The principal return forms are as follows:

Resident individuals	540, 540A, 540 2EZ
Nonresident and part-year residents	540NR, 540NR Short
Amended individual return	540X
Estates and trusts	541
Partnerships	565
Limited liability companies (LLCs) classified as partnerships and single member LLCs that are disregarded and treated as a sole proprietorship	568

A copy of the federal return and schedules must accompany the 540NR. It must also accompany the 540 if the taxpayer attached any federal schedules other than Schedule A or B to the federal return.

CCH Practice Tip: Protective Claims for Refund

Taxpayers filing a claim for refund on Form 540X for a tax year for which litigation or a final determination by the IRS is pending must write "PROTECTIVE CLAIM" in red ink at the top of their Form 540X. In addition, they must specify the pending litigation or reference the federal determination on Side 2, Part II, of Form 540X, so that the Franchise Tax Board can properly process their claims.

Caution Note: Attaching Letters to Forms Inadvisable

The FTB advises tax practitioners against attaching letters to their clients' income tax returns, stating that in most cases tax practitioners will get faster results by calling the FTB's Tax Practitioner Hotline at (916) 845-7057 to ask specific questions regarding their clients' tax returns or other issues requiring timely action. The Tax Practitioner Hotline is open from 8 a.m. to 5 p.m., Monday through Friday. Questions may also be sent by fax to (916) 845-6377, 24 hours a day, seven days a week.

Often letters attached to returns are not answered until they have traveled through the FTB's entire return processing system and are ultimately rerouted to the FTB's Taxpayer Service Center for a reply, which may take many weeks. Also, letters are sometimes inadvertently filed without a reply. (*Tax News*, California Franchise Tax Board, July/August 2005)

• *Use of Form 540A*

California Form 540A is similar to federal Form 1040A. A taxpayer may use Form 540A only if for the taxable year to be reflected in the return the following applies:

— the taxpayer was a full-year resident;

— the taxpayer's only income was from wages, salaries, tips, interest, dividends, tier 1 and tier 2 railroad retirement benefits, unemployment compensation reported on Form 1099-G, paid family leave, U.S. Social Security benefits, taxable scholarships and fellowship grants, fully or partially taxable pensions, annuities, or IRA distributions, and alimony;

— the taxpayer is making California income adjustments to only one or more of the following sources of income: California state income tax refund, unemployment compensation, Social Security and tier 1 and tier 2 railroad retirement benefits, California nontaxable interest and dividends, California IRA distributions (other than Roth IRA distributions), and nontaxable pensions and annuities;

— the taxpayer's adjustments and itemized deductions are the same for state and federal purposes (except for state, local, and foreign taxes);

— the taxpayer does *not* claim any tax credits other than exemption credits, the nonrefundable renter's credit, and the child and dependent care expenses credit;

— only the following payments are made: withholding shown on Form(s) W-2, CA Sch. W-2, and 1099-R, estimated tax payments, payments made with an extension voucher, and excess SDI and VDPI payments;

— no tax is due other than the income tax computed using the tax table, the additional 1% tax on millionaires to support mental health services, and any use tax self-reported on Form 540A.

• *Use of Form 540 2EZ*

Taxpayers who are single, married/registered domestic partner (RDP) joint filers, heads of household, or qualifying widow(er)s and who are not blind may use Form 540 2EZ if, for the taxable year to be reflected in the return, the taxpayer:

— was a full-year resident;

— had income only from wages, salaries, tips, interest, dividends, pensions, taxable scholarships and fellowship grants (only if reported on Form W-2), capital gains from mutual funds (reported on Form 1099DIV, box 2a only), unemployment compensation reported on Form 1099-G, paid family leave, U.S. Social Security benefits, and tier 1 and tier 2 railroad retirement benefits;

— does not claim any itemized deductions, is not required to use a modified standard deduction for dependents, and does not make any adjustments to income;

— does not claim any tax credits other than the personal exemption credit, the senior exemption credit, up to three dependent exemption credits, and the nonrefundable renter's credit;

— does not pay any tax other than withholding shown on Form W-2, CA Sch. W-2, or Form 1099-R;

— had total income consisting of items listed above of $100,000 or less if using the single or head of household filing status or $200,000 or less if using the married/RDP filing joint or qualifying widow(er) filing status;

— did not apply a 2007 overpayment to the tax due in 2008; and

— has no tax due other than the income tax computed using the Form 540 2EZ table and any use tax self-reported on Form 540 2EZ.

Taxpayers who can be claimed as a dependent by another taxpayer cannot file Form 540 2EZ if they have dependents of their own or if their total income is $12,242 or less if single, $24,434 if married/RDP filing jointly or qualifying widow(er), or $17,334 if head of household.

• *Form for nonresidents—Full or part year*

A person who was a nonresident for any part of the year must file a return on Form 540NR or 540NR Short, regardless of status at the end of the year. Any change in residence status should be fully explained on the return or in an attached statement.

A nonresident or part-year resident taxpayer who is a single or joint filer, head of household, or qualifying widower may qualify to file Form 540NR Short if, for the taxable year reflected in the return, the taxpayer:

— had total income of $100,000 or less;

— had income only from wages, salaries, tips, taxable interest, and unemployment compensation;

— does not make any adjustments to income other than adjustments for unemployment compensation, military pay, and paid family leave;

— does not claim any itemized deductions;

— does not claim any tax credits other than the personal exemption credit, up to five dependent exemption credits, and the nonrefundable renter's credit;

— has not made any tax payments other than withholding shown on Form W-2 or CA Sch. W-2;

— does not apply a 2007 overpayment of tax to the tax due for 2008; and

— computes tax only using the tax table.

• *Reproduction of forms*

Most Franchise Tax Board (FTB) forms may be reproduced, along with their supplemental schedules, and the reproductions filed in lieu of the corresponding official forms. Details of specifications and conditions for reproducing forms, and for computer-prepared forms, may be obtained from the Franchise Tax Board, Tax Forms Development and Distribution Section M/S B5, P.O. Box 1468, Sacramento, California 95812-1468; phone (916) 845-3553; e-mail: substituteforms@ftb.ca.gov

• *Whole-dollar reporting*

California law is the same as federal law with respect to whole-dollar reporting (sometimes referred to as "cents-less" reporting). If any amount required to be shown on a return, statement, or other document is other than a whole dollar, the fractional part of a dollar may be rounded to the nearest dollar; that is, amounts under 50¢ are dropped and amounts from 50¢ to 99¢ are increased to the next dollar. (Sec. 18623, Rev. & Tax. Code)

• *Use of address label*

If possible, taxpayers should peel off and use the pre-addressed (piggy-back) address labels that come with their return forms. This assists in expediting return processing. The return form should be filled in completely, including, in particular, all applicable lines on pages 1 and 2. This also assists in return processing and will expedite any refund that may be due.

• *Reporting federal changes*

A California taxpayer filing an amended federal return is required to file an amended California return within six months after filing the federal return if the change increases the amount of California tax due. Also, if any change or correction is made in gross income or deductions by federal authorities, or if gross income or deductions are changed by renegotiation of government contracts or subcontracts, such changes must be reported to the FTB within six months after the final determination of the federal change or correction or renegotiation if any such change increases the amount of California tax due. The "date of a final federal determination" is defined as the date that each adjustment or resolution resulting from an IRS examination is assessed pursuant to IRC Sec. 6203. (Sec. 18622, Rev. & Tax. Code)

The federal determination is presumed to be correct unless the taxpayer overcomes the burden of establishing that the determination is erroneous. This principle has been approved in many appeals decided by the State Board of Equalization (SBE) over the years.

• *Effect of failure to report federal changes*

Failure to comply with the requirements for reporting federal changes may result in extending the statute of limitations on deficiency assessments (¶710).

• *Effect of presumed correctness of federal report*

In *Norman P. Calhoun et al. v. Franchise Tax Board* (1978) (CCH CALIFORNIA TAX REPORTS ¶89-066.20), the FTB assessed California tax on the basis of a federal audit report that showed an understatement of gross income. The federal tax was approved in a U.S. District Court case. Subsequently, the California Supreme Court applied the legal theory of "collateral estoppel" to justify the imposition of the California tax, based on the similarity of California and federal definitions of "gross income."

In *Appeal of M. Hunter and Martha J. Brown* (1974) (CCH CALIFORNIA TAX REPORTS ¶89-206.6792), the SBE held that the FTB—not the taxpayer—must bear the burden of proof where a fraud penalty is proposed based on a federal audit report. The SBE upheld the assessment of California tax because of the presumed correctness of the federal determination, but held that the same presumption does not apply to a fraud penalty. However, the SBE has held in several cases that the presumption of federal correctness does apply to the 5% negligence penalty (¶712); that is, the burden of proof with respect to the negligence penalty is on the taxpayer. See *Appeal of Casper W. and Svea Smith* (1976) (CCH CALIFORNIA TAX REPORTS ¶89-168.25).

¶107 Joint Returns

Law: Secs. 17045-46, 18521-22, 18531.5, 18533-34, 19006 (CCH CALIFORNIA TAX REPORTS ¶15-310, 89-102, 89-210).

Comparable Federal: Secs. 2, 66, 6013, 6015 (CCH U.S. MASTER TAX GUIDE ¶152, 156, 162).

Individuals must generally use the same filing status for California purposes as they use federally. However, registered domestic partners also have the option of filing California joint returns (¶114). (Sec. 18521, Rev. & Tax. Code) Also, for the period from June 16, 2008, until November 4, 2008, California law recognized the right of same-sex couples to enter into legal marriages. On November 4, 2008, California voters approved Proposition 8, which repealed the right of same-sex individuals to enter into legal marriages. Although the Franchise Tax Board (FTB) announced that same-sex married couples (SSMCs) were to be treated as any other married couple for tax purposes, at the time this book went to press the FTB had not yet determined what impact, if any, the passage of Proposition 8 would have on those SSMCs who were married prior to Proposition 8's passage. See ¶119 for details.

• *Joint and several liability of spouses*

Although generally a husband and wife are jointly and severally liable for taxes (including penalties and interest) resulting from filing a joint return, a spouse's liability may be limited as a result of a court decree, an election approved by the FTB for separate liability, the granting of innocent spouse relief by the FTB, or other equitable relief granted by the FTB. (Sec. 19006, Rev. & Tax. Code)

CCH Comment: Innocent Registered Domestic Partner Relief

As registered domestic partners (RDPs) and former RDPs must generally be treated as married taxpayers for California personal income tax purposes (see ¶119), the innocent spouse provisions discussed below apply equally to innocent RDPs beginning with the 2007 taxable year. (FTB Pub. 737, Tax Information for Registered Domestic Partners)

Court decree: Subject to certain conditions and limitations, the joint and several liability for tax on the aggregate income in a joint return may be revised in a court proceeding for dissolution of the marriage. The court order becomes effective when the FTB is served with or acknowledges receipt of the order. A "tax revision clearance certificate" must be obtained from the FTB if the gross income exceeds $150,000 or the tax liability that a spouse is relieved of exceeds $7,500. (Sec. 19006, Rev. & Tax. Code)

Separate liability: An individual who filed a joint return may elect separate liability if the individual is no longer married to, is legally separated from, or for at least for the prior 12 months has been living apart from the person with whom the joint return was filed. This election must be made within two years after the FTB begins collection activities with respect to the individual. (Sec. 18533, Rev. & Tax. Code)

An individual making this election has the burden of proving his or her portion of any deficiency. An election may be partially or completely invalidated if (1) at the time of signing the return, the individual had actual knowledge of any item giving rise to a deficiency or portion thereof or (2) any assets were transferred between joint filers as part of a fraudulent scheme or to avoid tax. (Sec. 18533, Rev. & Tax. Code)

For separate liability purposes, an item giving rise to a deficiency must generally be allocated in the manner it would have been allocated if the taxpayers had filed separate returns. However, an item otherwise allocable to one individual may be allocated to the other individual to the extent the item gave rise to a tax benefit to the other individual. Also, the FTB may provide for a different manner of allocation in the case of fraud on the part of one or both of the individuals. (Sec. 18533, Rev. & Tax. Code)

Practice Tip: Credits and Refunds

Applicable to requests for relief filed after 2007, a taxpayer seeking innocent spouse relief may not claim a credit or refund outside the general statute of limitations period as a result of his or her election to have his or her liability recomputed utilizing the separate income allocation method. (Sec. 18533(e), Rev. & Tax. Code)

The FTB must give notice to a joint filer of the other joint filer's election of separate liability, and the FTB must not make its determination with respect to the election earlier than 30 days after such notification. An individual who is denied a separate liability election may appeal that determination to the State Board of Equalization (SBE). (Sec. 18533, Rev. & Tax. Code)

Federal law contains comparable provisions for electing separate liability.

CCH Example: Separate Liability Election

Joe and Jennifer Jackson, who are separated, file a joint return reporting $60,000 of wage income earned by Joe, $60,000 of wage income earned by Jennifer, and $7,000 of investment income on the couple's jointly owned assets. The FTB assesses a $400 tax deficiency for $5,000 of unreported investment income from assets held in Joe's name. Jennifer knew about a bank account in Joe's name that generated $1,000 of interest income, but she had no actual knowledge of Joe's other separate investments.

If Jennifer properly elects separate liability, she will not be liable for $320 of the tax deficiency, which is the amount attributable to the $4,000 of unreported income of which she had no actual knowledge ($400 × [$4,000 ÷ $5,000]). However, she will be liable for $80 of the tax deficiency, which is the amount attributable to the $1,000 of unreported interest income from the bank account ($400 × [$1,000 ÷ $5,000]).

Innocent spouse relief: Under both California and federal law, an innocent spouse is relieved from tax liabilities (including penalties and interest) in certain cases of wrongdoing in joint return situations. Innocent spouse relief is available if an individual establishes that (1) in signing a joint return, he or she did not know or have reason to know of any understatement on the return attributable to his or her spouse and (2) it would be inequitable to hold the individual liable. Innocent spouse relief is also available on a partial basis if the individual establishes that he or she did not know or have reason to know of the *extent* of an understatement on the return attributable to his or her spouse. (Sec. 18533, Rev. & Tax. Code)

CCH Practice Pointer: Relief Unavailable if No Return Filed

In a nonprecedential opinion, the SBE has taken the position that a taxpayer is ineligible for innocent spouse relief under the rules discussed above if the deficiency arises as a result of the failure to file a timely return rather than as a result of an understatement of income (*Appeal of Clausen* (2001) (CCH CALIFORNIA TAX REPORTS ¶89-226.369)).

An individual seeking innocent spouse relief must elect such relief within two years after the commencement of collection activities with respect to that individual. The FTB must give notice to a joint filer of the other joint filer's election of innocent spouse relief, and the FTB must not make its determination with respect to the election earlier than 30 days after such notification. An individual who is denied an innocent spouse election may appeal that determination to the SBE. (Sec. 18533, Rev. & Tax. Code)

Applicable to tax liabilities that become final after 2003 and before 2009, or to tax liabilities that became final prior to January 1, 2004, and remain unpaid as of that date, unless an individual's liability has been revised by a court in a divorce proceeding, an individual who filed a joint return will automatically be granted innocent spouse relief from California personal income tax liabilities if the individual was granted relief from federal income tax liabilities under the federal innocent spouse provisions provided that the following conditions are satisfied:

— the individual requests relief under the federal innocent spouse provisions;

— the facts and circumstances that apply to the understatement and liabilities for which relief is requested are the same facts and circumstances that applied to the understatement and liabilities for which the individual was granted federal income tax relief; and

— the individual provides the FTB with a copy of the federal determination and any other supporting documentation requested by the FTB. (Sec. 18533, Rev. & Tax. Code)

Within 30 days of notification from the FTB, the non-requesting spouse may provide information to the FTB indicating why the requested relief should not be granted. If, prior to the date the FTB issues its determination with respect to a request for relief, the requesting individual demonstrates to the FTB that a request for federal relief involving the same facts and circumstances has been filed with the IRS, the FTB may not deny relief until there is a final action on the federal request for relief. (Sec. 18533, Rev. & Tax. Code)

CCH Practical Analysis: Separate Liability or Innocent Spouse Relief

The "actual knowledge" standard for separate liability is narrower than the "knew or should have known" standard for innocent spouse relief. This may make separate liability available under circumstances in which innocent spouse relief is not.

Equitable relief: Furthermore, if relief is not specifically available under the separate liability provisions or the innocent spouse provisions, equitable relief may still be provided if, taking into account all the facts and circumstances, it would be inequitable to hold the individual liable. The taxpayer must demonstrate that he or she did not benefit from the income at issue (*Appeal of Clausen* (2001) (CCH CALIFORNIA TAX REPORTS ¶89-226.369)).

The FTB's denial of equitable relief may be appealed to the SBE so long as a taxpayer has requested relief under either the traditional innocent spouse relief or the separate liability election subsections of the innocent spouse relief statute. (*Appeal of Tyler-Griffis*, 2006-SBE-004, CCH CALIFORNIA TAX REPORTS ¶404-120).

• *Effect of mixed residence status*

A nonresident joint California return is required if one spouse/RDP was a resident for the entire taxable year and the other spouse/RDP was a nonresident for all or any portion of the taxable year. However, this rule does not apply to active military personnel and their spouses/RDPs. (Sec. 18521, Rev. & Tax. Code)

• *Returns by surviving spouse/RDP*

A joint return must be filed by a surviving spouse/RDP whose husband, wife, or RDP dies during the taxable year if this status is elected federally. In instances in which spouses/RDPs have different taxable years because of the death of either spouse/RDP, the joint return will be treated as if the taxable years of both spouses/ RDPs ended on the date of closing of the surviving spouse's/RDP's taxable year. (Sec. 18521, Rev. & Tax. Code)

• *Change from separate to joint return*

Spouses/RDPs who have filed separate California and federal returns may refile on a joint California return, provided they meet certain limitations as to the time for refiling and if they refile federally. This change may be made even if all previous separate liabilities of the individuals have not been paid. (Sec. 18522, Rev. & Tax. Code)

Under both California and federal laws, a change from a joint return to separate returns is permitted only if separate returns are filed on or before the due date. (Sec. 18522, Rev. & Tax. Code)

For statute of limitations and delinquency penalty purposes, both California and federal laws provide special rules for determining the date on which a joint return is deemed to be filed in situations where one or both of the spouses/RDPs previously filed a separate return. If only one spouse/RDP previously filed a separate return, the result depends on the amount of income of the spouse/RDP who did not file a separate return. (Sec. 18522, Rev. & Tax. Code)

¶108 Returns—Time and Place for Filing

Law: Secs. 6707, 11003, Government Code; Secs. 6452.1, 18510, 18566-67, 18572, 18621.5, 18621.9, 21027, Revenue and Taxation Code; Reg. 18567, 18 CCR (CCH CALIFORNIA TAX REPORTS ¶89-102, 89-106, 89-110).

Comparable Federal: Secs. 6072, 6081, 6091, 7508A (CCH U.S. MASTER TAX GUIDE ¶118, 119, 122, 2537).

California Forms: Form 540 (California Resident Income Tax Return), Form 540A (California Resident Income Tax Return), Form 540 2EZ (California Resident Income Tax Return), FTB 3519 (Payment for Automatic Extension for Individuals), FTB 3537 (Payment for Automatic Extension for Limited Liability Companies), FTB 3538 (Payment for Automatic Extension for Limited Partnerships, LLPs, and REMICs), FTB 3563 (Payment for Automatic Extension for Fiduciaries), FTB 3582 (Payment Voucher for Individual e-filed Returns), FTB 3587 (Payment Voucher for LP, LLP, and REMIC e-filed Returns), FTB 3588 (Payment Voucher for LLC e-filed Returns), FTB 8453 (California e-file Return Authorization), FTB 8453-OL (California Online e-file Return Authorization), FTB 8454 (e-file Opt-Out Record), FTB 8455 (California e-file Payment Record), FTB 8633 (California Application to Participate in the e-file Program), FTB 8879 (California e-file Signature Authorization).

• *Due dates*

As is the case with the federal return, calendar-year income tax returns are due on April 15 following the close of the calendar year. Fiscal-year returns must be filed by the 15th day of the fourth month following the close of the fiscal year. (Sec. 18566, Rev. & Tax Code; Sec. 19001, Rev. & Tax. Code) California returns of taxpayers residing or traveling abroad are due two months later than the regular due date; that is, calendar-year returns of such taxpayers are due on June 15 (¶109). (Sec. 18567, Rev. & Tax. Code)

• *Final returns*

The final California return of a decedent is due on April 15 following the close of the calendar year in which death occurred or, in the case of a fiscal-year taxpayer, by the 15th day of the fourth month following the close of the decedent's fiscal year. (Reg. 18505-4, 18 CCR) This is the same as the federal rule.

As under federal law, the final California return of an estate or trust is due within 3½ months after the close of the month in which the estate or trust is terminated.

• *Qualified use taxes*

Persons not required to hold a seller's permit or to register with the California State Board of Equalization (SBE) may self-report their qualified use tax liabilities on their timely filed original personal income tax returns. Persons electing to report such taxes are required to report and remit the tax on an income tax return that corresponds to the taxable year in which the use tax liability was incurred. A married individual filing a separate California personal income tax return may elect to report either one-half of the qualified use tax or the entire qualified use tax on his or her separate California personal income tax return. The non-electing spouse is not bound by the other spouse's election. (Sec. 6452.1, Rev. & Tax. Code)

Payments remitted with income tax returns are applied first to income taxes, penalties, and interest and, second, to qualified use tax liabilities. See ¶1510 for details.

Practice Pointer: Amended Use Taxes

Taxpayers that want to revise their use tax previously reported on an income tax return should contact the SBE directly rather than filing an amended income tax return (California Personal Income Tax Booklet).

• *Extensions of time*

The Franchise Tax Board (FTB) may grant an extension or extensions of time for filing any return, declaration, statement, or other document for a period up to six months from the regular due date, or for a longer period in the case of a taxpayer who is abroad (¶109). (Sec. 18567, Rev. & Tax. Code) See ¶110 regarding extensions of time for payment of tax.

The FTB will allow an automatic six-month filing extension if the return is filed within six months of the original due date. No written request is required. The automatic extension does not extend the time for paying tax. Tax payments must accompany FTB 3519 (Payment Voucher for Automatic Extension for Individuals), FTB 3537 (Payment Voucher for Automatic Extension for Limited Liability Companies), FTB 3538 (Payment Voucher for Automatic Extension for Limited Partnerships, LLPs and REMICs), or FTB 3563 (Payment Voucher for Automatic Extension for Fiduciaries). See ¶712 for a discussion of the penalty for failure to pay an adequate amount of tax by the regular due date.

In addition, the FTB may postpone certain tax-related deadlines, including the deadline for filing a return, for a period of up to one year for taxpayers affected by a presidentially-declared disaster (renamed "federally-declared disaster" by the Emergency Economic Stabilization Act of 2008) or a terroristic or militaristic action. (Sec. 18572, Rev. & Tax. Code) The deadlines that may be postponed are the same as those that may be postponed by reason of a taxpayer's service in a combat zone (¶109). See ¶711 for a discussion concerning the abatement of interest available to taxpayers granted such an extension.

Practice Tip: Extensions for Disaster Victims

The FTB will follow the updated federal tax postponement dates for state taxpayers affected by Hurricane Ike, Hurricane Gustav, and the November 2008 Southern California wildfires. Hurricane victims will have until 1 January 5, 2009, to file returns, pay taxes, and perform other time-sensitive acts. The extended deadline for the Southern California fire victims is February 11, 2009. (*Press Releases*, FTB, September 15, 2008, and September 18, 2008; *Press Release*, FTB, November 20, 2008)

An extension of time for filing the California return extends the statute of limitations on assessments to a date four years from the date the return is filed (¶710).

See ¶110 for interest charged during extension periods.

• *Filing by mail*

Returns and requests for extensions of time filed by mail are deemed to be filed on the date they are placed in the U.S. mail, provided they are properly addressed and the postage is prepaid. The date of the postmark is ordinarily deemed to be the date of mailing, although it may be possible to prove that the return was actually mailed on an earlier date. (Sec. 11003, Govt. Code) It is obviously desirable to mail early enough to be sure the postmark is timely. When the due date falls on a Saturday, Sunday, or other legal holiday, returns are due on the next business day. (Sec. 6707, Govt. Code) Federal law provides that the postmark date on a properly mailed return will be deemed to be the delivery date. (Note that a postage meter date is not a "postmark.")

CCH Caution: Returns Sent by Private Delivery Services

Returns sent by a private delivery service should be sent in time to be *received* by the due date.

Returns should be mailed to the FTB in Sacramento, or filed with any of the FTB's regional or district offices. The regular Sacramento address for filing personal income tax returns and the special address for returns that show a refund due, are indicated on the return form.

• *E-file*

The FTB also accepts electronic filing of returns by tax professionals through the e-file program. Detailed information concerning this program is available at the FTB's Web site at http://www.ftb.ca.gov/professionals/efile/proinfo.shtml.

Mandatory electronic filing: Tax return preparers who prepare and file more than 100 California personal income tax returns annually and who prepare at least one personal income tax return using tax preparation software in the current calendar year must file all personal income tax returns for the current calendar year and subsequent calendar years using electronic technology (see ¶712 for related penalties). The requirement ceases to apply to a tax return preparer if, during the previous calendar year, the tax return preparer prepared no more than 25 original personal income tax returns. A taxpayer may also elect to have his/her tax return preparer file a paper, rather than electronic, return by filing Form FTB 8454 (e-file Opt-Out Record for Individuals). (Sec. 18621.9, Rev. & Tax. Code)

E-signatures: The FTB accepts electronic signatures for individual e-filed returns and recognizes the same PIN methods available federally: the Self-Select PIN method, the Practitioner PIN method and the electronic return originator (ERO) PIN. All signature methods, including pen-on-paper using form FTB 8453, will be accepted for all California e-file return types (Forms 540, 540 2EZ, and 540NR Long and Short) throughout the duration of the e-file season. For more information see the FTB's Web site at: http://www.ftb.ca.gov/professionals/efile/esig.shtml

Filing procedures: Personal income tax returns and other documents that are filed using electronic technology must be in a form prescribed by the FTB and are not complete unless accompanied by an acceptable electronic signature. The FTB will accept electronic signatures using the Self-Select PIN and Practitioner PIN methods, in lieu of the e-file Return Authorization (FTB 8453). Tax payments made by check must be accompanied by FTB 3582 (Payment Voucher for Electronically Transmitted Returns).

EROs approved for the Internal Revenue Service (IRS) e-file program are automatically enrolled in the California e-file program. In addition, the FTB will automatically receive any updates made by approved EROs to their IRS accounts. (*Tax News*, California Franchise Tax Board, September 2007, CCH CALIFORNIA TAX REPORTS ¶404-446)

California conforms to federal income tax provisions allowing electronic postmarks as proof of the date electronically filed returns are deemed filed.

• *Magnetic media*

California generally adopts the federal standards in federal Reg. 301.6011-2 for determining which income tax returns must be filed on magnetic media or in other machine-readable form. (Reg. 19524, 18 CCR) The California standards must take into account the ability of the taxpayer to comply at reasonable cost with the filing requirements. The FTB may not require (1) that estates or trusts file any personal income tax returns in any manner other than on paper forms supplied by the FTB or (2) that returns filed on magnetic media contain more information than is required to be included under federal law. A copy of a magnetic media or other machine-readable return filed with the IRS may be filed with the FTB for state tax purposes instead of the return required under state law. (Sec. 18409, Rev. & Tax. Code)

California law, unlike federal law, does not require partnerships having more than 100 partners to file returns on magnetic media.

• *FTB offices*

The FTB has branch offices in principal cities throughout California and also in Chicago and New York.

¶109 Extensions of Time for Persons Outside the United States

Law: Secs. 17142.5, 18567-71 (CCH CALIFORNIA TAX REPORTS ¶17-750).

Comparable Federal: Secs. 6081, 7508 (CCH U.S. MASTER TAX GUIDE ¶120, 2509, 2537).

California Form: FTB 3519 (Payment Voucher for Automatic Extension for Individuals).

• *Taxpayers abroad*

Taxpayers who are "abroad" can ordinarily obtain an unlimited extension of time for filing California returns, to cover the entire period of their absence from the country. A taxpayer who is outside the United States on the return due date is automatically granted a two-month extension of time; thus, the April 15 date for a calendar-year return is extended to June 15. This extension, combined with the automatic six-month paperless extension, extends the due date to December 15. However, interest accrues on any unpaid tax from the original due date of April 15 and late payment penalties may be imposed on any tax still unpaid as of June 15. (Sec. 18567, Rev. & Tax. Code) Payments made prior to filing the return should be accompanied by FTB 3519 (Payment Voucher for Automatic Extension for Individuals).

To obtain further extensions of time, the taxpayer must continue to file timely requests periodically during his or her sojourn abroad. California has not defined "abroad" by regulation. Under comparable federal regulations, "abroad" is defined as outside the United States and Puerto Rico, and taxpayers who are abroad are granted an automatic extension of time to June 15 for calendar-year federal returns.

• *Armed Forces and merchant marines*

California grants automatic extensions of time to members of the U.S. Armed Forces and merchant marines who serve outside the boundaries of the 50 states of the United States and the District of Columbia. The extension also applies to the spouses of such individuals. The extension runs to a date 180 days after a serviceperson or merchant marine returns to the United States, and applies to filing returns, paying taxes, filing protests, filing claims for refund, and filing appeals to the State Board of Equalization. (Sec. 18570, Rev. & Tax. Code)

California conforms to federal law as of the current IRC tie-in date (¶103), which allows members of the Armed Forces who serve in combat zones, overseas contingency operations, or who are hospitalized as a result of injuries received while serving in combat zones or hazardous duty areas to postpone the deadline for filing income tax returns and paying taxes (other than income taxes withheld at the source or employment taxes) by the following periods:

— the amount of time they served in a combat zone,

— the period of time they were hospitalized as a result of injuries sustained in the zone, or

— the period of time they were missing in action from the zone, plus

— 180 days following the end of their service, hospitalization, or missing status. (Sec. 18571, Rev. & Tax. Code)

Taxpayers serving in combat zones who are filing on extension should alert the FTB to this fact when they file by writing in red on the top of their return or payment: "Combat Zone: Operation Iraqi Freedom" (or the name of the specific combat zone served in). They must also indicate the dates they entered and left the combat zone (*News Release,* California Franchise Tax Board, March 27, 2003).

The combat zone/hazardous duty area/contingency operation extension also applies to deadlines for tax assessments, tax collections, levies, the granting of a credit or refund of taxes, filing a claim for a refund or credit, and the filing of a suit for a refund or a credit.

¶110 Payment of Tax

Law: Secs. 18567, 18572, 19001-05, 19008, 19011, 19101; Sec. 415 of the Military and Veterans Code (CCH CALIFORNIA TAX REPORTS ¶17-510, 89-102, 89-108, 89-188).

Comparable Federal: Secs. 6151, 7508A (CCH U.S. MASTER TAX GUIDE ¶2537).

California Form: FTB 3567BK (Installment Agreement Request), FTB 3567BK AMNESTY (Amnesty Installment Agreement Request).

The entire balance of tax due must be paid with the income tax return. Where tax has been withheld or a prepayment has been made during the year, the withholding or prepayment is deducted to arrive at the balance due with the return. See ¶111 regarding payment of estimated tax; see ¶714 and 715 regarding withholding.

• *Extension of time*

The Franchise Tax Board (FTB) may grant a reasonable extension of time for payment of tax whenever, in its judgment, good cause exists. Where an extension of time is granted, interest is charged from the regular due date to the date of payment. The interest rate is the rate charged on deficiencies, as explained at ¶711.

In addition, California incorporates federal law allowing the FTB to postpone certain tax-related deadlines, including the deadline for payment of tax, for a period of up to one year for taxpayers affected by a presidentially-declared disaster (renamed "federally-declared disaster" by the Emergency Economic Stabilization Act of 2008). (Sec. 18572, Rev. & Tax. Code) The deadlines that may be postponed are the same as those that may be postponed by reason of a taxpayer's service in a combat zone (¶109). See ¶711 for a discussion concerning the abatement of interest available to taxpayers granted such an extension.

Practice Tip: Extensions for Disaster Victims

The FTB will follow the updated federal tax postponement dates for state taxpayers affected by Hurricane Gustav, Hurricane Ike, and the November 2008 Southern California wildfires. Hurricane victims will have until January 5, 2009, to file returns, pay taxes, and perform other time-sensitive acts. The extended deadline for the Southern California fire victims is February 11, 2009. (*Press Releases*, FTB, September 5, 2008, September 18, 2008, and November 20, 2008)

• *Installment payments—Generally*

The FTB may allow taxpayers experiencing financial hardships to pay their tax in installment payments. Applicable interest (¶711) and penalties over the life of the installment period apply. The FTB must enter into an agreement to accept payment of an individual's liability in installments if, as of the date the individual offers to enter into the agreement, all of the following apply:

— the aggregate amount of the liability, excluding interest or penalties, does not exceed $10,000;

— the individual and, if the individual has filed a joint return, the individual's spouse or registered domestic partner has not during the preceding five years failed to file a return, failed to pay any tax required to be shown on the return, or entered into an installment agreement for payment of tax;

— the FTB determines that the individual is financially unable to pay the liability in full when due;

— the agreement requires full payment of the liability within three years; and

— the individual agrees to comply with the tax law for the period the agreement is in effect. (Sec. 19008, Rev. & Tax. Code)

CCH Practice Pointer: Installment Program Expanded

The FTB has expanded the statutory installment program to encompass taxpayers who have filed all required personal income tax returns if they (1) owe a balance $25,000 or less and (2) can pay the outstanding balance within 60 months. A taxpayer is not required to submit a financial statement to enter into the agreement. The FTB reserves the right to file a lien as a condition of the installment agreement depending on a taxpayer's compliance history. For further information, taxpayers may contact the FTB's Collection Response and Resolution Section at 1-800-689-4776. (*News Release*, California Franchise Tax Board, January 2007)

A request for an independent administrative review submitted within 30 days of the date of rejection of an offer of an installment agreement or termination of an agreement will stay the collection of tax. (Sec. 19008, Rev. & Tax. Code)

Also, a levy may not be issued on the property or rights to property of any person with respect to any unpaid tax during any period for which an installment offer is pending, an installment agreement is in place, or a review of an installment agreement rejection or termination is pending. However, the levy restrictions do not apply to the following:

— any unpaid tax if the taxpayer waives the restrictions or if the FTB determines that the collection of tax is jeopardized;

— any levy that was first issued before the date that the proceeding commenced; and

— at the discretion of the FTB, any unpaid tax for which the taxpayer makes an offer of an installment agreement subsequent to a rejection of an offer of an installment agreement with respect to that unpaid tax. (Sec. 19008, Rev. & Tax. Code)

The period of limitations for the FTB to bring an action to recover unpaid tax is suspended for the period during which the FTB is prohibited under the above provisions from making a levy.

Taxpayers who owe less than $10,000 may enter into an electronic installment payment agreement on-line on the FTB's Web site at: http://www.ftb.ca.gov/online/eia/index.asp. A taxpayer requesting an installment payment plan agrees to pay the income tax liability in monthly installments by electronic funds transfer. The taxpayer also agrees to (1) ensure that adequate funds are available for the transfers; (2) timely file all future returns; (3) ensure that future tax liabilities are paid in full with the taxpayer's returns; and (4) pay a $20 fee to the FTB for this service. (Sec. 19008, Rev. & Tax. Code) Taxpayers who do not meet the above requirements may also request to enter into an installment agreement by submitting FTB 3567 (Installment Agreement Request) or by calling the FTB at (800) 689-4776.

Generally, any failure by the taxpayer to comply fully with the agreed-upon payment plan, other than for reasonable cause, ends the agreement, provided (1) the FTB notifies the taxpayer of the termination at least 30 days before the termination date and (2) such notice includes an explanation of the reason for the intended termination of the agreement. However, notice is not required if the FTB determines that collection of the tax is in jeopardy or there is mutual consent to terminate, alter, or modify the agreement. Taxpayers may seek administrative review by the Taxpayers' Advocate of any such termination. The administrative review will not stay the collection of tax. (Sec. 19008, Rev. & Tax. Code)

• *Deferment for servicepersons*

The federal Servicemembers Civil Relief Act provides for the deferment of collection of state income taxes from servicepersons if their ability to pay is materially impaired by reason of their entering military service. (Sec. 409.6, Milit. & Vet. Code; Sec. 17140.5, Rev. & Tax. Code) Also, see ¶109 regarding automatic extension of time granted to certain individuals.

A member of the National Guard or an army reservist of the U.S. Military Reserve who is called up for active duty may be eligible for deferral of income tax payments for a period of up to six months after the termination of his or her period of military service if the person's ability to pay the tax is materially impaired by reason of the service. Interest and penalties may not be imposed during the deferment period. (FTB Pub. 1032, Tax Information for Military Personnel)

• *Payment by mail*

A payment is deemed to be made on the date it is mailed, provided it is properly addressed and the postage is prepaid. The federal rule is similar. (Sec. 11003, Govt. Code) See ¶108 for comment regarding the effect of a postmark date.

• *Payment by check*

Payment of personal income tax in the form of a check must be made payable in U.S. funds.

To expedite processing, payments for separate purposes (*e.g.*, balance due on return and estimate payment) should not be combined in one check. The taxpayer's social security number should be shown on each check. Also, returns and payments of estimated tax should be mailed in separate envelopes.

• *Payment by credit card*

Taxpayers may use Discover/NOVUS, MasterCard, Visa, or American Express cards to pay their personal income taxes, including any amounts past due.

• *Electronic payments*

Applicable to all installments due after 2008, personal income taxpayers must make payments electronically, including utilizing a pay by phone option, if their estimated personal income tax installment payment or extension request payment exceeds $20,000 or if their total annual post-2008 tax liability exceeds $80,000. Taxpayers may make a written election to not make their payments electronically if they did not meet the $20,000 or $80,000 threshold requirements for the preceding taxable year.

A penalty of 1% of the tax owed will be imposed against taxpayers who fail to make an electronic payment unless reasonable cause exists. In addition, the FTB may waive the electronic payment requirement if it determines that the particular amounts paid in excess of the threshold amounts were not representative of the taxpayer's tax liability. (Sec. 19011.5, Rev. & Tax. Code)

Upon taxpayer request, the FTB will allow payments to be made by electronic funds transfer. Once permission is granted, a 10% penalty is imposed if payments are not made in this manner (¶712).

• *Payment by Web-pay*

A taxpayer may pay the current amount owed and schedule future payments, such as estimated tax, up to one year in advance through a secure service offered on the FTB's Web site. The taxpayer dictates the amount paid and when he or she would like the payment made and the payment will be deducted from the taxpayer's account on the date indicated. (http://www.ftb.ca.gov/online/payment_choices.html)

¶111 Payment of Estimated Tax

Law: Secs. 19007, 19010, 19136–36.12 (CCH CALIFORNIA TAX REPORTS ¶89-104, 89-204, 89-206, 89-210).

Comparable Federal: Secs. 6315, 6654 (CCH U.S. MASTER TAX GUIDE ¶2679—2691).

California Forms: Form 540-ES (Estimated Tax for Individuals), FTB 5805 (Underpayment of Estimated Tax by Individuals and Fiduciaries), FTB 5805F (Underpayment of Estimated Tax by Farmers and Fisherman).

California law, including the special treatment for farmers and fishermen, is the same as federal law except that California, unlike federal law, imposes no penalty for underpayment, and therefore requires no estimated tax payments, if either the actual tax (after deduction of credits) for the preceding year or the estimated tax for the current year is under $500 ($200 prior to the 2009 taxable year) for a single person or a married couple/registered domestic partnership (RDP) filing jointly, or $250 ($100 prior to the 2009 taxable year) for a married person/RDP filing separately. (Sec. 19136, Rev. & Tax. Code) Federal law does not impose a penalty for underpayment of estimated tax if the actual tax is less than $1,000 after withholding.

• *Dates and amounts of payment*

For calendar-year taxpayers, estimated tax is payable in quarterly installments, on April 15, June 15, September 15, and January 15. If a due date for payment falls on a Saturday, Sunday, or legal holiday, it is extended to the next day that is not a

Saturday, Sunday, or legal holiday. If the individual's tax situation changes during the year, payments for the remaining installments may be revised accordingly. (Sec. 19136, Rev. & Tax. Code)

For fiscal-year taxpayers, estimated tax payments are due by the 15th day of the fourth, sixth, and ninth months of the fiscal year and the first month of the following fiscal year.

Applicable to installments due for each taxable year beginning after 2008, the amount of the estimated tax installment payments for the first and second installments are equal 30% of the estimated amount for the taxable year, and the third and fourth installments are equal to 20% of the estimated amount due for the taxable year. (Sec. 19136.1, Rev. & Tax. Code) For taxable years beginning prior to 2009, the required quarterly installments were generally equal to 25% of the amount due.

Practice Note: Safe Harbor

Except as discussed below, the required estimated tax amount is based on the lesser of (1) 90% of the current year's tax or (2) 100% (110% for taxpayers whose AGI for the current year exceeds $150,000 ($75,000 if married filing separately) of the preceding year's tax, provided the preceding taxable year was a 12-month taxable year. (Sec. 19136, Rev. & Tax. Code) Beginning with the 2009 taxable year, however, individuals with annual adjusted gross incomes of $1 million ($500,000 if married filing separately) or more may no longer base their estimated tax payment on 110% of the preceding year's tax. (Sec. 19136.3, Rev. & Tax. Code)

• *Early return and full payment in place of fourth installment*

If a final return for the year is filed and the full amount of tax is paid by taxpayers generally before February 1, or by farmers or fishermen before March 2, it has the same effect as a payment of estimated tax on January 15. (Sec. 19136, Rev. & Tax. Code)

• *Account information*

To determine what payments a taxpayer has already made, and what payments the FTB has received, the FTB is posting secured tax information on its Web site. Taxpayers and tax preparers may access this information at http://www.ftb.ca.gov/online/myacct/index.html. This service allows taxpayers to view the following:

— estimated tax payments;

— recent payments applied to a balance due;

— a taxpayer's total current balance due; and

— a summary of each balance due by tax year on the taxpayer's account.

• *Penalty for underpayment*

A penalty is imposed for underpayment of estimated tax, computed as a percentage of the underpayment, for the period of the underpayment. The Instructions to Forms 5805 and 5805F state that for purposes of computing the amount of the underpayment, a taxpayer may use the figures listed on his or her amended return only if the amended return was filed on or prior to the due date for the original return. The penalty rate applied is the same as the interest rate on deficiencies and refunds, see ¶711. However, the penalty rate is not compounded. (Sec. 19136, Rev. & Tax. Code)

The amount of underpayment subject to penalty is based on 90% of tax for taxpayers generally and 66²/3% for farmers and fishermen (for definition of "underpayment," see ¶813).

Waivers and abatements.—The underpayment penalty may be waived for newly retired or disabled individuals and in cases of casualties, disasters, or other unusual circumstances. (Sec. 19136, Rev. & Tax. Code) The waiver request is made on Form 5805 or 5805F.

In addition, no penalty will be applied if the underpayment is attributable to any of the following:

— changes made to the laws of other states concerning the allowance of credits for taxes paid to another state (Sec. 19136.5, Rev. & Tax. Code);

— an erroneous levy, erroneous processing action, or erroneous collection action by the FTB (Sec. 19136.7, Rev. & Tax. Code);

— legislation chaptered and operative for the taxable year of the underpayment (Sec. 19136(g), Rev. & Tax. Code);

— legislation enacted in 2006 and 2007 regarding the taxation of registered domestic partners that resulted in an underpayment of the 2007 estimated tax installments (Sec. 19136.13, Rev. & Tax. Code).

Comment: Federal Legislation

The relief for underpayments resulting from legislation chaptered and operative for the taxable year of the underpayment does not apply to federal law changes that may create an underpayment of state tax, because federal law is enacted without being chaptered. (Bill Analysis, Ch. 242 (S.B. 14), Laws 2005, Senate Floor, August 23, 2005)

• *Reporting underpayment penalties*

Where the figures on a return indicate that there has been (or may have been) an underpayment of estimated tax, the taxpayer should attach FTB 5805 or FTB 5805F (for farmers and fishermen) to show computation of the penalty or to explain why no penalty is due. Federal Forms 2210 and 2210F should not be used with California returns.

• *Penalty for failure to pay*

Civil and criminal penalties are imposed for willful failure to make timely payments of estimated tax, see ¶712.

• *New residents, nonresidents, estates and trusts*

New residents and nonresidents are subject to the requirements for paying estimated tax as set forth above. The Instructions to FTB 5805 indicate that if the taxpayer had no California tax liability for the previous year, no estimated tax is due in the first taxable year of residence. Estates and trusts are subject to California estimated tax requirements, as they are under federal law.

¶112 Tax Base

Law: Sec. 17073 (CCH CALIFORNIA TAX REPORTS ¶15-355, 15-505).

Comparable Federal: Sec. 63 (CCH U.S. MASTER TAX GUIDE ¶124, 126).

The income tax rates (except for the alternative minimum tax discussed at ¶117) are applied to the amount of taxable income, which is defined at ¶203.

¶113 Exemption Credits

Law: Secs. 17054, 17054.1, 17056, 17733 (CCH CALIFORNIA TAX REPORTS ¶16-815).

Comparable Federal: Sec. 151 (CCH U.S. MASTER TAX GUIDE ¶133).

California Forms: Form 540 (California Resident Income Tax Return), Form 540A (California Resident Income Tax Return), Form 540 2EZ (California Resident Income Tax Return), Form 540NR (California Nonresident or Part-Year Resident Income Tax Return).

Tax credits are allowed for personal exemptions. (Sec. 17054, Rev. & Tax. Code) The credits are deducted from tax computed on taxable income without benefit of such exemptions. The credit applies to the separate tax on lump-sum distributions.

Following are the credits for the years shown:

	2004	*2005*	*2006*	*2007*	*2008*
Single person	$ 85	$ 87	$ 91	$ 94	$ 99
Married/RDP, separate return	85	87	91	94	99
Married/RDP, joint return	170	174	182	188	198
Head of household	85	87	91	94	99
Surviving spouse	170	174	182	188	198
Dependent	265	272	285	294	309
Blind person—additional	85	87	91	94	99
Estate	10	10	10	10	10
Trust	1	1	1	1	1
Elderly—additional	85	87	91	94	99

• *Disability trusts*

The exemption credit for disability trusts is equal to the personal exemption credit for single individuals and is subject to the limitations for high-income taxpayers discussed below. (Sec. 17733, Rev. & Tax. Code)

• *Dependents*

California, unlike federal, law will allow a dependent credit even if a taxpayer fails to provide an identification number for the dependent on the taxpayer's personal income tax return. (Sec. 17054, Rev. & Tax. Code) See ¶115 for a definition of "dependent."

Practical Analysis: Limitations on Dependent Exemption

An unmarried taxpayer may not claim a dependent exemption on behalf of an unmarried child if the child (1) is 19 years old or older, (2) is not a student, and (3) has gross income equal to or greater than the federal exemption amount ($3,500 for 2008). Additionally, an unmarried taxpayer may not claim a dependent exemption on behalf of an unmarried child if the child (1) is under 19 years old or a student under 24 years old and (2) pays more than half of his or her support. (Instructions, Form 540, California Resident Income Tax Return)

In *Montoya v. Daniele,* (2005), CCH CALIFORNIA TAX REPORTS ¶403-793 (not to be cited as precedent), a California court of appeal held that a family law court properly exercised its discretion in a child support proceeding by allocating California personal income tax exemptions for two dependent children to their noncustodial parent so as to maximize the resources available to the children. It was reasonable for the court to make this allocation because the court had calculated that awarding the exemptions to the noncustodial parent would increase the amount of child support payable by the noncustodial parent to the custodial parent, thereby increasing the total resources available to the children, without adversely affecting the custodial parent's tax liability.

• *Reduction of credits for high-income taxpayers*

The exemption credits are reduced if a taxpayer's federal adjusted gross income exceeds a threshold amount. (Sec. 17054.1, Rev. & Tax. Code) For 2008, with respect to single taxpayers, each credit is reduced by $6 for each $2,500 or fraction thereof by which the taxpayer's federal adjusted gross income exceeds $163,187. For a married/RDP taxpayer filing a joint return or a surviving spouse, each credit is reduced by $12 for each $2,500 or fraction thereof by which the taxpayer's federal adjusted gross income exceeds $326,379. For married/RDP taxpayers filing separately, each credit is reduced by $6 for each $1,250 of federal adjusted gross income over $163,187. For heads of households, each credit is reduced by $6 for each $2,500 of federal adjusted gross income over $244,785.

A worksheet is provided in the Form 540 Instructions to assist taxpayers in determining the amount of the exemption credit reduction.

• *Nonresidents and part-year residents*

Nonresidents and part-year residents are allowed reduced credits for personal exemptions, on the basis of prorated taxable income. (Sec. 17055, Rev. & Tax. Code) The phase-out of exemption credits for high-income taxpayers (discussed above) must be applied before proration of the credits (¶132).

• *Missing children*

California follows federal law (TAM No. 200038059) allowing taxpayers to claim a dependent exemption for missing children.

• *California-federal differences*

California has not incorporated the following federal provisions adopted by the Tax Reform Act of 1986: (1) the repeal of the additional exemption for blind individuals (California retains an additional $99 exemption credit) and (2) the repeal of the additional exemption for the elderly (California allows an additional $99 exemption credit).

Although California conforms in principle to federal law requiring a phase-out of the personal exemption, the reduction computation and the threshold amounts differ from federal law (see above). In addition, California has not incorporated federal amendments made by the Economic Growth and Tax Relief Reconciliation Act of 2001 that reduce and eventually repeal the personal exemption phase-out for higher income taxpayers. The reduction of the phase-out commences with the 2006 tax year and the phase-out is completely eliminated for federal purposes in tax years beginning after 2009.

¶114 Filing Status

Law: Secs. 17021.5, 17042, 18521, 18532 (CCH CALIFORNIA TAX REPORTS ¶15-305, 15-310, 15-315, 15-320, 15-325, 15-330).

Comparable Federal: Secs. 2, 7703 (CCH U.S. MASTER TAX GUIDE ¶152, 173, 175).

For California purposes, with the exception of registered domestic partners (RDPs) and same-sex married couples discussed below, an individual must use the filing status used on his or her federal return for the same taxable year or, if no federal return was filed, the status that the individual would have used on a federal return. (Sec. 18521, Rev. & Tax. Code)

Married taxpayers are also required to use their federal filing status, except that married taxpayers who file a joint federal return may file either joint or separate California returns if (1) either spouse was an active member of the military or (2) one spouse was a nonresident for the entire year and had no California-source income. A joint nonresident income tax return is required of a husband and wife who file a joint federal return if one of the spouses was a California resident for the entire taxable year and the other was a nonresident for all or any part of the tax year and had California-source income. (Sec. 18521, Rev. & Tax. Code)

The determination of whether an individual is married, a "surviving spouse," a "head of household," or blind is made as of the close of the taxable year. (Sec. 18532, Rev. & Tax. Code) A joint return may be filed if one spouse dies during the taxable year. (Sec. 18521, Rev. & Tax. Code) An individual who is legally separated from his or her spouse under a decree of divorce or of separate maintenance is not considered married. (Sec. 18532, Rev. & Tax. Code)

Planning Note: Registered Domestic Partners and Same-Sex Married Couples

Beginning with the 2007 taxable year, taxpayers who are registered as domestic partners by the close of the taxable year must file personal income tax returns jointly or separately by applying the same standards as are applied to married taxpayers under federal income tax law. (Sec. 18521, Rev. & Tax. Code) For additional details concerning the tax treatment of RDPs, see ¶119

Previously, the SBE had taken the position that a domestic partner qualified as a head of household even though the child was not the biological offspring, stepchild, or legally adopted child of the taxpayer. The SBE determined that in the case at hand, the domestic partners jointly decided to rear the child, the taxpayer's domestic partner agreed to undergo donor insemination and to gestate the child conceived, and the taxpayer agreed to support the family unit after the child was born. Because the child would otherwise not exist, acting on this plan indicated the taxpayer's intent to parent and established the requisite parent child relationship necessary to claim head of household filing status (*Hisserich* (2000) (CCH CALIFORNIA TAX REPORTS ¶15-320.30)). However, a California superior court issued a peremptory writ prohibiting the SBE and the FTB from giving effect to the SBE's decision (*Proposition 22 Legal Defense and Education Fund* (2001) (CCH CALIFORNIA TAX REPORTS ¶15-320.201)).

Special rules apply for purposes of determining limitations based on adjusted gross income (¶202). Community property rules also apply (¶239).

In addition, for the period June 16, 2008, until November 4, 2008, California law recognized the right of same-sex individuals to enter into legal marriages and the FTB took the position that same-sex married couples were to be treated as all other spouses for purposes of California taxation. However, on November 4, 2008, California voters passed Proposition 8, which repealed the right of same-sex individuals to enter into a legal marriage. At the time this book went to press, the FTB had not determined what impact, if any, the passage of Proposition 8 would have on the tax treatment of those same-sex individuals who were married prior to the passage of Proposition 8. Consult the FTB's Web site at http://www.ftb.ca.gov for the latest information. For additional details concerning the tax treatment of same-sex married couples, see ¶119.

• *Head of household*

The federal law defining "head of household" is incorporated into California law by reference, as of the current IRC tie-in date (see ¶103). (Sec. 18521, Rev. & Tax. Code)

Head-of-household filing status is granted to unmarried taxpayers maintaining a household for qualifying persons, and to married persons and RDPs who are living apart from their spouse or RDP and who are maintaining a household for their child. (Sec. 17042, Rev. & Tax. Code) An unmarried person's unmarried child does not qualify him or her as a head-of-household if the child (1) is 19 years old or older, (2) is not a student, and (3) has gross income equal to or greater than the federal exemption amount ($3,800 for 2008). Additionally, an unmarried child does not qualify an unmarried taxpayer for the head-of-household filing status if the child (1) is under 19 years old or a student under 24 years old and (2) pays more than half of his or her support. (Instructions, Form 540, California Resident Income Tax Return)

In *Appeal of William Tierny* (1997) (CCH CALIFORNIA TAX REPORTS ¶15-320.65), the State Board of Equalization (SBE) allowed a taxpayer who was not legally married at the end of the taxable year to include one-half of the time that he occupied the same household with his ex-wife and children to determine whether his household was his children's principal place of abode for more than one-half of the taxable year. The SBE reasoned that taxpayers who share their income with their children to the extent that they provide more than half of the children's support during the calendar year and pay for more than half of the expenses necessary to maintain a household are entitled to some relief. In *Appeal of Barbara Godek* (1999) (CCH CALIFORNIA TAX REPORTS ¶15-320.552), the SBE extended the *Tierney* reasoning to a taxpayer who was legally married at the end of the taxable year before her divorce, but was "treated as not married" for the taxable year under the controlling statute.

CCH Example: Married Individual as Head of Household

Barbara and her daughter Monica lived in the same house with Barbara's husband from January 1, 2008, through March 9, 2008 (68 days). During the period from March 10, 2008, through December 31, 2008, Barbara and Monica lived together for an additional 163 days without Barbara's husband. Barbara and her husband were still married at the end of 2008, but they qualified to be "treated as not married" for the year. Barbara may count 34 days (1/2 of the 68 days) plus 163 days in calculating the number of days that her household was the principal place of abode for Monica in 2008. Because the total of 197 days is more than 1/2 of the year, Barbara qualifies for head of household filing status for the year.

In *Appeal of Patrick R. Lobo* (1999) (CCH CALIFORNIA TAX REPORTS ¶15-320.22), the SBE held that a taxpayer's unrelated 37-year old dependent was not a foster child and, thus, was not a qualifying individual for head of household filing purposes, because the foster relationship did not begin until after the dependent became an adult. The SBE noted that although there is no statutory definition of a "foster child" in the California tax laws, the term is intended to refer to an individual who was under the age of 18 at the time the foster child relationship began.

A checklist is included in the Instructions for Form 540 to assist taxpayers in determining whether they qualify for the head of household filing status.

Under federal law, a taxpayer is ineligible to claim head of household status if he or she fails to provide the correct taxpayer identification number for his or her dependent. California does not have a similar requirement.

• *Missing children*

Under both California and federal law, taxpayers are allowed to continue to claim surviving spouse or head of household filing status if their qualifying child has been kidnapped by a nonrelative. This special treatment ends with the first tax year of the taxpayer that begins after the year in which the kidnapped child is determined to be deceased or in which the child would have reached age 18, whichever occurs earlier. (Sec. 17042, Rev. & Tax. Code)

• *Unrelated individuals living together*

As indicated above, both California and federal laws require a specified relationship to qualify for "head of household" classification. This means that unrelated individuals living together do not qualify, even though one may furnish the chief support and be entitled to an exemption credit for a dependent. See *Appeal of Stephen M. Padwa* (1977) (CCH CALIFORNIA TAX REPORTS ¶15-320.40), cited in several later cases.

• *Married individuals treated as "unmarried"*

Certain married individuals may be treated as "unmarried" for purposes of determining their filing status. This applies where the individual lives apart from his or her spouse or RDP for the last six months of the year and maintains a home for a dependent child, under certain limited conditions. (Sec. 17021.5, Rev. & Tax. Code) The principal California advantage of the "unmarried" classification is that it puts the individual in a position where he or she may, under the rules discussed above, get the benefit of the lower rates that go with "head of household" classification. ("Head of household" classification is, of course, also advantageous on the federal return.)

• *Effect of interlocutory decree*

For both federal and California tax purposes, a husband and wife are, by law, deemed *not* to be legally separated during the period between issuance of an interlocutory decree of divorce and issuance of the final decree. They are therefore considered to be married until issuance of the final decree.

¶115 Definition of Dependents

Law: Sec. 17056 (CCH CALIFORNIA TAX REPORTS ¶15-130).

Comparable Federal: Sec. 152 (CCH U.S. MASTER TAX GUIDE ¶137).

California law is the same as federal law as of the current IRC tie-in date (see ¶103). California incorporates the federal definition of a "dependent." (Sec. 17056, Rev. & Tax. Code) However, California does not adopt federal provisions that beginning with the 2009 taxable year (1) require that a qualifying child be younger than the taxpayer; (2) with specified exceptions, prohibit the filing of a joint return by a qualifying child; and (3) clarify the tie-breaker rules that apply when more than one taxpayer can claim the same qualifying child.

• *Multiple-support agreements*

Under federal law, as incorporated by California, a taxpayer may satisfy the requirement of supporting a dependent even though he or she did not furnish over half the support, in certain "multiple support" situations. Under these rules, a taxpayer may claim a dependent for whom the taxpayer contributed less than one-half (but more than 10%) of the support, provided the taxpayer is a member of a group that contributed over one-half the support, and provided the other members of the group can meet the limitations imposed in these special provisions. (Sec. 17056, Rev. & Tax. Code)

• *Support paid from community income*

Where all of the income is community income neither spouse or registered domestic partner (RDP) contributes *over* half of their dependents' support, so technically neither is entitled to the credit for dependents on a separate return. However, as a practical matter, the credit is allowed under such circumstances to either spouse or RDP.

• *Divorced or separated parents*

The law provides detailed rules for determining which spouse or RDP is considered to have furnished over half the support of a child where the parents are divorced or separated. California law is the same as federal law. (Sec. 17056, Rev. & Tax. Code)

A California court of appeal has ruled that federal law did not preempt a family law court from alternating the California dependency exemption between two divorced parents who shared physical custody of their child, even though one parent received slightly more time with the child than the other parent. In the case at issue, the joint legal and custodial arrangement between the parents was, for all intents and purposes, equal, and allocation of the dependency exemption to both parents on an alternating basis was proper. (*Rios v. Pulido* (2002) (CCH CALIFORNIA TAX REPORTS ¶16-815.30))

In Legal Ruling No. 93-3 (1993) (CCH CALIFORNIA TAX REPORTS ¶402-643), the Franchise Tax Board indicated that a divorced, custodial parent who waives the federal dependent exemption deduction is precluded from claiming the corresponding state dependency credit.

• *Effect of classification as "dependent"*

The rules discussed above merely provide the *definition* of a "dependent." A taxpayer may or may not be allowed a *credit* for a person who qualifies as a "dependent," depending on the amount of the dependent's income and other conditions, see ¶113.

Regardless of whether or not a taxpayer is entitled to a credit, classification as a "dependent" may affect the deduction for medical expenses (¶325).

¶116 Tax Rates

Law: Secs. 17008.5, 17041, 17043, 17046, 17048, 17935, 17941, 17946, 17948, 23038 (CCH CALIFORNIA TAX REPORTS ¶10-235, 15-115, 15-355).

Comparable Federal: Sec. 1 (CCH U.S. MASTER TAX GUIDE ¶126).

California personal income tax is imposed on taxable income, as shown in the schedules and tables in Part I of this book. For purposes of determining the tax rate to be applied, taxable income is computed for the taxable year as if the resident were a California resident for the entire taxable year and for all prior taxable years for any carryover items, deferred income, suspended losses, or suspended deductions. For the definition of "taxable income," see ¶203. The current progressive rates range from 1% to 9.3% (10.3% when the additional tax on millionaires, discussed below, is applied). Unlike federal law, California does not tax capital gains or dividend income at reduced rates. (Sec. 17041, Rev. & Tax. Code)

A minimum tax of $800 is imposed on limited partnerships, limited liability partnerships (LLPs), and limited liability companies (LLCs) that are treated as partnerships or that are disregarded and treated as sole proprietorships (¶625), unless a limited partnership, LLP, or LLC did no business in California during the taxable year and its taxable year was 15 days or less. (Secs. 17935, 17936, 17941, 17946, 17948, Sec. 17948.2, Rev. & Tax. Code) In addition, a domestic LLC that has not conducted any business in California and that has obtained a certificate of cancellation within 12 months from the date that the articles of organization were filed is exempt from the minimum tax. However, the LLC will not be entitled to a refund of any taxes or fees already paid. (Sec. 17946, Rev. & Tax. Code)

A limited partnership, LLP, or an LLC is relieved of liability from the minimum tax if it satisfies the following conditions:

— files a timely final annual tax return for a taxable year with the Franchise Tax Board (FTB);

— does not do business in this state after the end of the taxable year for which the final annual tax return was filed; and

— files a certificate of cancellation or notice of cessation or similar document with the Secretary of State's Office before the end of the 12-month period beginning with the date the final annual tax return was filed.

(Sec. 17937, Rev. & Tax. Code, Sec. 17947, Rev. & Tax. Code, Sec. 17948.3, Rev. & Tax. Code)

Practitioner Comment: Entities's Final Year

A corporation, as well as other entities, is no longer required, prior to the dissolution of the entity, to obtain a tax clearance certificate from the FTB. Instead, the Secretary of State must notify the FTB of the dissolution.

In addition, a corporation will not be subject to the minimum tax in the year that a final return is filed if the corporation did not thereafter do business in California and dissolution, surrender or cancellation of the entity is completed before the end of the 12 month period following the date the final tax return was filed. Similar relief from the annual tax will be accorded to a limited partnership, limited liability company or limited liability partnership if these entities: 1) ceased doing business in California prior to the beginning of the taxable year; 2) filed a timely final tax return for the preceding taxable year; and 3) filed a certificate of cancellation with the Secretary of State before the end of the 12 month period beginning with the original due date of the tax return for the preceding taxable year.

Any outstanding tax, penalty or interest for a taxable year beginning after the corporation ceased doing business can be cancelled if:

— the corporation was incorporated prior to January 1, 2006;

— the corporation was suspended for taxable years beginning on or before December 1, 2005 and ceased doing business before January 1, 2006;

— the tax liability for each taxable year to be waived does not exceed the minimum tax due;

— the corporation applied for corporate dissolution; and

— the corporation applied for waiver of tax, penalty and interest. (Ch. 773 (A.B. 2341), Laws 2006)

Bruce Daigh, Chris Whitney, Contributing Editors

Practitioner Comment: Timely Filing of Certificates of Dissolution and Cancellation Certificates for Inactive Entities Can Save Minimum Tax

A limited partnership was found to be liable for the $800 minimum partnership tax for years after it had transferred all of its assets to a limited liability company and ceased operations because the limited partnership failed to file a cancellation certificate, the California State Board of Equalization (SBE) ruled. Under Cal. Sec. 17935, Rev. & Tax Code, every limited partnership that has filed a certificate of limited partnership with the state must pay the annual tax until a certificate of cancellation is filed. As it was undisputed that the limited partnership failed to file a cancellation certificate, the SBE held that the minimum partnership tax was due, notwithstanding the fact that the transferee LLC filed and paid tax as an LLC for the same years [Uncitable Summary Decision, *Appeal of Cinema Plaza Partners, LP.*, Cal. State Bd. of Equal., No 207907, November 18, 2003, CCH St. Tax Rept., ¶ 10-225.30].

Similarly, a corporation was liable for the minimum tax for the year in which it surrendered its operations to another corporation because a certificate of dissolution was not timely filed with the Secretary of State. Despite the fact that the corporation had filed a "final" tax return and had clearly surrendered its business operations, state law provides that a corporation remains subject to the minimum tax until it files a certificate of dissolution with the Secretary of State. In the instant case, the certificate was not filed until more than two years after the "final" return was filed [Uncitable Summary Decision, *Red Bud Industries*, Cal. State Bd. of Equal., No. 224004, March 23, 2004, CCH St. Tax Rept., ¶ 10-215.35]

Bruce Daigh, Chris Whitney, Contributing Editors

In a nonprecedential opinion, the SBE ruled in *Appeal of Wi LV #2* (2005) (CCH CALIFORNIA TAX REPORTS ¶ 403-935) that the FTB was estopped from imposing the minimum tax against a limited partnership because the FTB failed to follow its mandate under Rev. & Tax. Code Sec. 17935(b)(2) to notify the partnership upon its filing of a "final" return that the minimum tax was due annually until a certificate of cancellation was filed with the Secretary of State.

Also, a special tax is imposed on the active conduct of any trade or business by certain grandfathered publicly traded partnerships that elect to continue to be treated as partnerships rather than corporations (¶ 616). (Secs. 17008.5, 23038.5(a), Rev. and Tax Code)

• *Additional tax on millionaires*

An additional 1% tax, referred to as the Mental Health Services Tax, is imposed on the portion of a taxpayer's income in excess of $1 million. Personal income tax credits may not be applied against this additional tax. (Sec. 17043, Rev. & Tax. Code)

• *Inflation adjustment*

Indexing of the rate brackets is based on the amount of inflation, or deflation, as measured by the change in the California Consumer Price Index from June of the prior year to June of the current year. The rate brackets for high-income taxpayers (discussed above) are indexed annually for inflation. (Sec. 17041, Rev. & Tax. Code)

• *Use of tax tables*

The tax rate *schedules* are shown in Part I. Also shown are the tax *tables* used to determine the amount of tax on the return. The tax schedules *must* be used for all California returns on which the taxpayer's taxable income is over $100,000.

Married couples filing joint returns receive "split-income" benefits that are built into the tax tables (Part I).

The rates for estates and trusts are the same as for single individuals.

• *Tax rates for nonresidents*

Tax is imposed on a nonresident's or part-year resident's taxable income as follows. A nonresident's or part-year resident's taxable income is all of the nonresident's or part-year resident's gross income and deductions for the portion of the taxable year that the taxpayer was a California resident and/or the gross income and deductions attributable to California during the period the taxpayer was a nonresident of California. Carryover items, deferred income, suspended losses, or suspended deductions are includible or allowable only to the extent that the carryover item, deferred income, suspended loss, or suspended deduction was derived from sources within this state.

The tax rate applied to the nonresident's or part-year resident's taxable income is computed by first determining the tax on the taxpayer's entire taxable income as if the nonresident or part-year resident were a California resident for the taxable year and for all prior taxable years for purposes of any carryover items, deferred income, suspended losses, or suspended deductions. This amount is divided by the taxpayer's total taxable income and the resultant amount is multiplied by the taxpayer's California-sourced taxable income to arrive at the taxpayer's California tax liability. (Sec. 17041, Rev. & Tax. Code) See FTB Pub. 1100, Taxation of Nonresidents and Individuals Who Change Residency, for more details.

• *Tax rates for servicemembers domiciled outside California*

Military compensation of servicemembers domiciled outside of California, and their spouses, may not be included in gross income for purposes of determining the tax rate on nonmilitary income; see ¶225.

¶117 Alternative Minimum Tax

Law: Secs. 17039, 17039.1, 17062, 17062.3, 17062.5 (CCH CALIFORNIA TAX REPORTS ¶15-405—15-440, 16-805).

Comparable Federal: Secs. 55-59 (CCH U.S. MASTER TAX GUIDE ¶1401—1480).

California Forms: Sch. P (540) (Alternative Minimum Tax and Credit Limitations - Residents), Sch. P (540NR) (Alternative Minimum Tax and Credit Limitations - Nonresidents or Part-Year Residents), Sch. P (541) (Alternative Minimum Tax and Credit Limitations - Fiduciaries).

The alternative minimum tax (AMT), which is in addition to regular tax, is imposed under both California and federal law in an amount equal to the excess (if any) of the tentative minimum tax for the taxable year over regular tax for the taxable year. (Sec. 17062, Rev. & Tax. Code)

• *"Regular tax" defined*

For California AMT purposes, "regular tax" is the personal income tax before reduction for any credits against tax. (Sec. 17062, Rev. & Tax. Code)

• *Federal-California differences*

The California tentative minimum tax rate is 7%. (Sec. 17062, Rev. & Tax. Code) For federal purposes, the tentative minimum tax rate is (1) 26% of the first $175,000 of a taxpayer's alternative minimum taxable income (AMTI) in excess of the exemption amount and (2) 28% of any additional AMTI in excess of the exemption amount. However, the federal, but not California, minimum tax rate is lowered to reflect the reduction in the federal capital gains rate and the reduced rate applied to dividends.

A nonresident's or part-year resident's tentative minimum tax is determined by multiplying the nonresident's or part-year resident's AMTI by a ratio, the numerator of which is the tax determined as if the taxpayer were a California resident for the taxable year and for all prior taxable years for any carryover items, deferred income, suspended losses, or suspended deductions, and the denominator of which is the taxpayer's total AMTI. A nonresident or part-year resident's AMTI includes all items of AMTI during which the taxpayer was a California resident and only those items derived from California sources during any period that the taxpayer was a nonresident. Any carryover items, deferred income, suspended losses, or suspended deductions are allowable only to the extent that the carryover item, suspended loss, or suspended deduction was derived from California sources. There is no equivalent computation for federal purposes. (Sec. 17062(b)(3)(B), Rev. & Tax. Code) Consult FTB Pub. 1100, Taxation of Nonresidents and Individuals Who Change Residency, for detailed explanations and examples.

California, like federal law, includes as an item of tax preference (TPI) an amount equal to one-half of the amount of gain realized from the disposition of certain small business stock excluded from gross income. (Sec. 17062, Rev. & Tax. Code) Federal, but not California, law reduces the amount of tax preference from 50% to 7% of gain on the sale of small business stock excluded from gross income for dispositions of small business stock after May 5, 2003.

California modifies federal law disallowing the standard deduction and the deduction for personal exemptions for AMT computation purposes to disallow only the standard deduction. California also modifies federal law to exclude from AMTI the income, adjustments, or items of tax preference attributable to a trade or business of a taxpayer who (1) owns or has an ownership interest in a trade or business and (2) has aggregate gross receipts, less returns and allowances, of less than $1 million during the taxable year from all trades or businesses owned by the taxpayer or in which the taxpayer has an ownership interest.

For purposes of computing the taxpayer's gross receipts, only the taxpayer's proportionate interest in a trade or business in which the taxpayer has an ownership interest is included. "Aggregate gross receipts, less returns and allowances" is the sum of (1) the gross receipts of the trades or businesses that the taxpayer owns, and (2) the proportionate interest of the gross receipts of the trades or businesses in which the taxpayer has an ownership interest and the pass-through entities in which the taxpayer holds an interest. The term includes gross income from the production of both business income and nonbusiness income. (Sec. 17062, Rev. & Tax. Code)

CCH Practice Tip: $1 Million Threshold

According to the Franchise Tax Board, the $1 million threshold applies regardless of the taxpayer's filing status. Thus, married taxpayers filing jointly are not allowed to increase the $1 million threshold to $2 million (Instructions to Sch. P (540)).

California specifically does not incorporate federal provisions (1) designating tax-exempt interest on specified private activity bonds as a TPI and (2) allowing an alternative minimum tax foreign tax credit. (Sec. 17062, Rev. & Tax. Code) However, California allows certain credits to reduce a taxpayer's regular tax below the tentative minimum tax, after an allowance for the minimum tax credit. The following are the credits that may reduce the regular tax below the tentative minimum tax:

— the former solar energy credits;

— the renter's credit;

— the research credit;

— the former manufacturer's investment credit;

— the former orphan drug research credit;

— the low-income housing credit;

— the credit for excess unemployment compensation contributions;

— the credits for taxes paid to other states;

— the credit for withheld tax;

— the personal, dependent, blind, and senior exemption credits;

— the credits for sales and use tax paid or incurred in connection with the purchase of qualified property used in an enterprise zone, a former program area, the former Los Angeles Revitalization Zone, or the targeted tax area;

— the enterprise zone, former program area, former Los Angeles Revitalization Zone, and targeted tax area hiring credits;

— the former teacher retention credit;

— the natural heritage preservation credit;

— the adoption costs credit;

— the credits for qualified joint custody head of household and a qualified taxpayer with a dependent parent; and

— the senior head of household credit. (Secs. 17039, 17039.1, Rev. & Tax. Code)

Because of California's federal conformity date, California did not incorporate the amendments made to IRC Sec. 56(d)(1)(A) by the Job Creation and Worker Assistance Act of 2002 and the Working Families Tax Relief Act of 2004 (P.L. 108-311) that increased the limits placed on the alternative tax NOL deduction for NOLs generated or claimed in 2001 or 2002.

Finally, California (but not federal) law increases the exemption amounts and the exemption phaseout amounts for taxable years beginning after 1998, and indexes these amounts for inflation beginning with the 2000 taxable year (see discussion below).

• *Computation of AMTI*

For both federal and California purposes, AMTI is regular taxable income after certain adjustments, increased by the amount of TPIs. However, as discussed above, for purposes of calculating AMTI, qualified taxpayers exclude income, adjustments, or items of tax preference from their trade or business. (Sec. 17062, Rev. & Tax. Code)

The following are the applicable adjustments and TPIs:

Adjustments: The following adjustments must be made to the deductions claimed or the methods used in calculating regular taxable income:

— *excess depreciation:* an AMT adjustment is required for depreciation claimed under the MACRS method if the taxpayer does not depreciate the property for regular tax purposes in the same manner prescribed for AMT purposes;

— *capitalizable expenses:* certain expenses that would ordinarily be treated as TPIs if deducted in the current year will not be treated as TPIs if the taxpayer elects to amortize them over a specified amortization period for regular tax purposes;

— *long-term contracts:* the percentage-of-completion method must be substituted for the completed-contract method to determine AMTI; for certain small construction contracts, simplified procedures for allocation of costs must be used;

— *alternative minimum tax NOL deduction:* NOL deductions must be recomputed on the same basis as AMTI (that is, reduced by TPIs and other adjustments); an alternative NOL may not offset more than 90% of the AMTI for a tax year without regard to the NOL deduction (100% for federal purposes only for NOLs attributable to qualified federal disasters and for NOLs generated or taken as carryovers in 2001 and 2002);

CCH Tip: Computation of AMTI NOL Deduction

The Franchise Tax Board's legal division has taken the position that AMTI NOL is computed without reference to the exclusion available to taxpayers involved in a trade or business with gross receipts of $1 million or less (Question and Answer No. 2, 1997, CPA/FTB Liaison Meeting, October 16, 1997).

— *certified pollution control facilities:* the five-year depreciation method must be replaced by the alternative depreciation system specified by federal law (straight-line method, without regard to salvage value); however, a facility placed in service after 1998 is depreciated using the IRC Sec. 168 straight-line method;

— *alternative tax itemized deductions:* in determining AMTI, no deduction is allowed for miscellaneous itemized deductions (including certain interest and medical expenses that are less than 10% of adjusted gross income (AGI); state, local, and foreign real property taxes and state and local personal property taxes are not deductible for AMT purposes, nor are mortgage interest expenses associated with proceeds used for purposes other than buying, building, or improving the taxpayer's principal residence or qualified second home; the overall limitation on itemized deductions of 6% of AGI (3% of AGI for federal purposes) does not apply for AMT purposes;

— *adjusted gain or loss:* gain or loss from the sale or exchange of business property during the tax year or from a casualty to business or income-producing property must be recomputed for AMT purposes by using the AMT adjusted tax basis rather than the regular tax adjusted basis of the property;

— *passive farm tax shelter losses:* taxpayers who are not material participants in a farming business may not deduct passive farming losses from AMTI; however, a loss determined upon the disposition of the taxpayer's entire interest in a tax shelter farming activity is not considered a loss from a tax shelter farm activity and is deductible in computing AMTI;

— *passive nonfarm business activity losses:* the rules limiting deductibility of other passive activity losses for regular tax purposes are subject to the following adjustments: (1) the amount of passive loss denied is reduced by the amount of insolvency; (2) passive activity losses must be computed on the same basis as AMTI (that is, reduced by TPIs and other adjustments, including the adjustment for passive farm losses); and (3) qualified housing interests are not included in computing passive business activity losses;

— *incentive stock options:* a taxpayer must include in AMTI the excess (if any) of (1) the fair market value of an incentive stock option at the time the taxpayer's rights in the option are freely transferable or are no longer subject to a substantial risk of forfeiture over (2) the price paid for the option; the amount of income excluded for regular tax purposes from exercising a California incentive stock option (¶ 207) is added back for purposes of computing AMTI;

— *tax recoveries:* refunds of taxes that are included in computing AGI for regular tax purposes (*e.g.*, state and local personal property taxes and state, local, and foreign real property taxes) are not included in gross income for purposes of determining AMTI; and

— *depreciation of grapevines:* California (but not federal) law provides that if grapevines are replanted as a result of phylloxera infestation or Pierce's disease and are being depreciated over five years instead of 20 years for regular tax purposes, they must be depreciated over 10 years for AMT purposes.

Items of tax preference: The following TPIs must be added back in computing AMTI:

— *excess depreciation on property placed in service prior to 1987:* for nonrecovery real property, leased personal property, pollution control facilities, leased recovery property, 19-year real property, and low-income housing, the excess of accelerated depreciation deductions over normal depreciation is a TPI;

— *excess deductions from oil or mineral operations:* the excess of the depletion deduction claimed by a taxpayer (other than an independent oil and gas producer) for an interest in a mineral deposit over its adjusted basis at the end of the tax year must be added back, as must the amount by which an integrated oil company's excess intangible drilling costs exceed 65% of net income from oil, gas, and geothermal properties; and

— *excluded gain on sale of small business stock:* one-half of the amount of gain excluded from gross income on the sale or disposition of qualified small business stock (as calculated for California personal income tax purposes) is a TPI.

• *Exemption amount*

The California and federal alternative minimum tax is imposed on AMTI minus the exemption amount. For both California and federal purposes, the exemption amounts are reduced by 25¢ for each $1 that AMTI exceeds the beginning phase-out level, until the exemption is completely phased out. (Sec. 17062, Rev. & Tax. Code)

For the 2008 taxable year, the exemption amounts for California purposes are as follows:

	Exemption amount	*Phaseout begins at*	*Phaseout ends at*
Married/RDP filing jointly and surviving spouse . .	$80,017	$300,065	$620,133
Single and head of household	60,014	225,050	465,106
Married/RDP filing separately and estates and trusts	40,007	150,031	310,059

For married individuals filing separately, AMTI is adjusted so that the maximum amount of the exemption phase out is the same for married taxpayers filing jointly. California, but not federal, law requires the Franchise Tax Board to index for inflation both the exemption amounts and the phase-out of exemption amounts.

For federal purposes, the exemption amounts for 2008 are as follows:

	Exemption amount	*Phaseout begins at*	*Phaseout ends at*
Married filing jointly and qualifying spouse	$69,950	$150,000	$429,800
Single and head of household	46,200	112,500	297,300
Married filing separately	34,975	75,000	214,900
Estates and trusts	22,500	75,000	165,000

In the case of a child under 14 years old, the maximum exemption amount is the lesser of (1) the exemption available to an individual taxpayer (for the 2008 tax year, $60,014 for California purposes and $46,200 for federal purposes) or (2) the sum of the child's earned income plus $6,400.

¶118 Children Under 14 with Unearned Income (Kiddie Tax)

Law: Sec. 17041(g) (CCH CALIFORNIA TAX REPORTS ¶15-360).

Comparable Federal: Sec. 1(g) (CCH U.S. MASTER TAX GUIDE ¶114, 706).

California Forms: FTB 3800 (Tax Computation for Children Under Age 14 with Investment Income), FTB 3803 (Parent's Election to Report Child's Interest and Dividends).

California conforms to federal law as of California's current federal conformity date (¶103) for purposes of calculating the amount of income tax for children under 14 years of age who have "investment income" in excess of a certain amount ($1,800 for 2008). (Sec. 17041(g), Rev. & Tax. Code) However, California has not conformed to federal amendments made to IRC Sec. 1(g) by the Tax Increase Prevention and Reconciliation Act of 2005 and the Small Business and Work Opportunity Tax Act of 2007 that (1) increase the age of a child whose unearned income is taxed at the parent's higher tax rate from under age 14 to under age 19, or, if a full time student, under age 24, and (2) exclude from the kiddie tax rules distributions to a child beneficiary from a qualified disability trust.

The "kiddie" tax is computed on Form 3800 (Tax Computation for Children Under Age 14 with Investment Income), which parallels federal Form 8615. California also conforms to the federal provision permitting a parent to report the interest and dividends of a child (more than $900 but less than $9,000 for 2008) on the parent's return. However, see¶217 and ¶226 for a discussion of the adjustments required for parents that include such income on their federal return for children between the ages of 14 and 24.

The tax is designed to prevent parents from shifting investment income to a child in a lower bracket, and equals the greater of:

(1) the income tax on the child's taxable income figured at the child's rates without benefit of a personal exemption; or

(2) the total of:

(a) the "parental tax" (defined below); plus

(b) the income tax figured at the child's rates on the amount of the child's taxable income that remains after subtracting out the child's "net investment income" (defined below).

• *"Investment income," "net investment income," "parental tax" defined*

"Investment income" is all income other than wages, salaries, professional fees, and other amounts received as pay for work actually done.

"Net investment income" is investment income reduced by the greater of:

(1) $1,800 (for 2008); or

(2) $900 (for 2008) plus the child's itemized deductions that are directly connected with the production of his or her investment income.

"Parental tax" is the difference in tax on the parent's income figured with and without the child's net investment income.

• *Election to claim child's unearned income on parent's return*

A parent may elect to include on the parent's return the unearned income of a child whose income in 2008 is more than $900 but less than $9,000 and consists solely of interest, dividends, or Alaska Permanent Fund dividends. The child is treated as having no gross income and does not have to file a tax return if the child's parent makes the election. However, the election is not available if estimated tax payments were made in the child's name and taxpayer identification number for the tax year or if the child is subject to backup withholding. (Sec. 17041, Rev. & Tax. Code)

To report the unearned income of a child on the parent's 2008 return, FTB 3803 (comparable to federal Form 8814) must accompany the parent's return. In addition to the child's gross income in excess of $1,800 being taxed at the parent's highest marginal rate, additional tax liability must be reported equal to 1% (10% for federal purposes) of the lesser of $900 or the child's income exceeding $900. Special rules apply to unmarried taxpayers and married taxpayers filing separate returns, see Instructions to FTB 3803.

¶119 Registered Domestic Partners and Same-Sex Married Couples

Law: Sec. 17021.7 (CCH CALIFORNIA TAX REPORTS ¶15-165).

Comparable Federal: None.

California Forms: Form 540 (California Resident Income Tax Return), Sch. CA (540) California Adjustments - Residents).

California, unlike federal law, recognizes registered domestic partners (RDPs) for tax purposes, and also treated same-sex married couples (SSMCs) as "spouses" for tax purposes as well.

- *Same-sex married couples*

For the period June 16, 2008, until November 4, 2008, California law recognized the right of same-sex couples to enter into legal marriages.

Prior to the passage of Proposition 8 in the November 2008 election, the Franchise Tax Board (FTB) took the position that for purposes of the Revenue and Taxation Code, California would treat same-sex married individuals as spouses. Consequently, such individuals who were legally married on the last day of the taxable year were instructed to file either a joint return or married, filing separate returns. Because same-sex married couples are still required to file their federal tax returns using the single filing status, adjustments may be required to recompute those deductions claimed on the state tax return that are computed using a taxpayer's federal adjusted gross income (AGI) figures. Examples of such deductions include a taxpayer's itemized deductions or a deduction for contributions to an individual retirement account (IRA). Same-sex married individuals must recompute their federal AGI for purposes of computing and claiming these deductions on their state tax returns utilizing the same filing status as that used on their state return. Frequently, this will mean adding each individual's AGI from their federal returns to compute their combined AGI. (FTB Notice 2008-5, California Franchise Tax Board, June 20, 2008 (CCH CALIFORNIA TAX REPORTS ¶404-691))

The FTB has also dedicated a Web page to address tax-related issues concerning same-sex married individuals—see http://www.ftb.ca.gov/individuals/Same_sex_marriage/index.shtml. Included on the Web site is a Draft Pub. 776, Tax Information for Same-Sex Married Couples, which discusses the specific adjustments that SSMCs would be required to make if the FTB treats SSMCs as spouses for personal income tax purposes.

Impact of Proposition 8's Passage

At the time this book went to press, the FTB had not yet determined the tax filing status for those taxpayers who were married between June 16th, 2008, the date upon which the California Supreme Court declared that same-sex couples could be legally married, and November 4, 2008, the date that voters passed Proposition 8, revoking the right of same-sex couples to be legally married. Taxpayers should consult the FTB's Web site at http://www.ftb.ca.gov/ by searching for "SSMC" for the latest information.

• *Registered domestic partners*

Beginning with the 2007 taxable year, registered domestic partners (RDPs) or former RDPs who are qualified and are registered with the California Secretary of State's Office are required to be treated as married taxpayers or former spouses under California income and franchise tax laws, unless specified exceptions apply.

The statutory exceptions relate to business entity classifications, tax-favored accounts, and deferred compensation plans. Consequently, RDPs will not be treated as a single shareholder for purposes of determining whether an S corporation has exceeded the 100 shareholder limitation. In addition, an RDP will not be treated as a spouse if such treatment would result in disqualification of a federally qualified deferred compensation plan or disqualification of tax-favored accounts, such as individual retirement accounts, Archer medical savings accounts, qualified tuition programs, or Coverdell education savings accounts. (Sec. 17021.7, Rev. & Tax. Code)

Other State Unions

The Franchise Tax Board has indicated that if individuals have entered into a same sex legal union, other than a marriage, in another state, and that union has been determined to be substantially equivalent to a California registered domestic partnership, the individuals are required, beginning with the 2007 taxable year, to file using either the married/RDP filing jointly or married/RDP filing separately filing status. More information on what state unions are considered substantially equivalent to a California registered domestic partnership can be found on the FTB's Web site by searching for the term "RDP." (FTB Pub. 737, Tax Information for Registered Domestic Partners)

RDPs must use the same filing status as required for married taxpayers (see ¶114). Special rules apply for purposes of determining limitations based on adjusted gross income (¶202). Community property rules also apply (¶239).

California has allowed an exclusion from gross income beginning with the 2002 taxable year for employer-provided accident, health insurance, and medical expense reimbursements for an RDP and the RDP's dependents if the reimbursements were not previously excluded on the federal return. In contrast, under federal law, a company's contribution to a domestic partner's benefits is treated as taxable income to the employee partner. Self-employed individuals may also claim a deduction for health insurance costs paid for a RDP and the RDP's dependents. (Sec. 17021.7, Rev. & Tax. Code) (FTB Pub. 1001, Supplemental Guidelines to California Adjustments)

Beginning with the 2007 taxable year, additional adjustments are required to reconcile the differences that arise from RDPs using a different filing status on their California and federal personal income tax returns. These adjustments may be made by completing a pro forma federal return or by completing the worksheets provided in FTB Pub. 737, Tax Information for Registered Domestic Partners. RDP adjustments include, but are not limited to:

— division of community property (¶239)

— capital losses (¶526)

— transactions between RDPs (¶502)

— sale of residence (¶229)

— dependent care assistance (¶253)

— investment interest (¶305)

— medical and dental expenses (¶325)

— job expenses and current miscellaneous deductions (¶303)

— qualified residence acquisition loan and equity loan interest (¶305)

— IRA income and deductions (¶206, ¶330)

— expense depreciation limitations (¶311)

— reforestation expenses (¶ 315)

— education loan interest (¶ 305)

— rental real estate passive loss (¶ 340)

— rollover of publicly traded securities gain into specialized small business investment companies (¶ 501).

Estimated Tax Underpayment Penalties

Registered domestic partners (RDPs) who underpaid their 2007 tax liability may be issued a notice for underpayment of estimated tax in error. However, as a result of legislation enacted in 2007, RDPs may not be assessed a penalty for underpayment of estimated tax to the extent that the penalty was assessed as a result of the tax treatment of RDPs. If the penalty was assessed because of filing as an RDP instead of filing as a single taxpayer or head of household, the penalty will be waived. Taxpayers who qualify to have the penalty waived should call (800) 852-7511, or the Tax Practitioner Hotline at (916) 845-7057 to have the penalty waived. (*Tax News*, California Franchise Tax Board, June 1, 2008, CCH CALIFORNIA TAX REPORTS ¶ 404-678)

Registered domestic partners are qualified to register with the Secretary of State's Office if all of the following requirements are met:

— both persons are of the same sex or one or both of the persons is/are over the age of 62 and is/are eligible for old-age insurance benefits under the Social Security program;

— both persons share a common residence;

— neither person is married to someone else or is a member of another RDP;

— the persons are not related by blood in a way that would prevent them from being legally married to each other in California;

— both persons are at least 18 years of age; and

— both persons are capable of consenting to the domestic partnership.

(Sec. 297, Family Code)

PERSONAL INCOME TAX

CHAPTER 1A
CREDITS

¶125 Credits—In General

Law: Secs. 17024.5(b)(10), 17039, 17039.2, 17043, 17055, 19852, 19853 (CCH CALIFORNIA TAX REPORTS, ¶16-805).

Comparable Federal: None.

California Forms: Form 540 (California Resident Income Tax Return), Form 540NR (California Nonresident or Part-Year Resident Income Tax Return), Sch. P (540) (Alternative Minimum Tax and Credit Limitations - Residents), Sch. P (540NR) (Alternative Minimum Tax and Credit Limitations - Nonresidents or Part-Year Residents), Sch. P (541) (Alternative Minimum Tax and Credit Limitations - Fiduciaries), FTB 3540 (Credit Carryover Summary), FTB 3801-CR (Passive Activity Credit Limitations).

In addition to the credits for personal and dependency exemptions (¶113), California law provides a variety of credits that may be used to reduce taxable income. However, as discussed at ¶117, certain credits may not be used to reduce the taxpayer's regular tax, plus the tax imposed on lump-sum distributions from employees' trusts, below the taxpayer's tentative minimum tax.

A taxpayer who claims more than three credits must complete the appropriate form for each credit and the credits must be summarized on Schedule P (Alternative Minimum Tax and Credit Limitations). Three or less credits may be claimed directly on Form 540.

Comment: Millionaire (Mental Health Services) Tax

Credits may not be applied against the mental health services additional tax on a taxpayer's taxable income in excess of $1 million (see ¶116). (Sec. 17043, Rev. & Tax. Code)

Also, some credits may be limited because they arise from passive activities (¶340). The taxpayer must file FTB 3801-CR (Passive Activity Credit Limitations) if the taxpayer claims any of the following credits and the credits arise from passive activities: low-income housing credit (¶138), research and development credit (¶139), orphan drug research credit carryover (see below), or targeted jobs credit generated prior to 1996.

Comment: Temporary Limitation on Credit Amounts

The amount of business credits and business credit carryovers that may be claimed by taxpayers are limited to 50% of a taxpayer's tax during the 2008 and 2009 tax years. Thereafter, the credits may be claimed in full. Any unused credit may be carried over and the carryover period is extended by the number of taxable years the credit, or any portion thereof, was not allowed as a result of the 50% limitation. A taxpayer with net business income of less than $500,000 for the taxable year is exempt from the 50% limitation. For purposes of determining the amount of business credits that may be claimed, nonbusiness credits must be applied before any business credits. (Sec. 17039.2, Rev. & Tax. Code)

Although federal tax credits are not applicable under California law, certain California credits are similar to their federal counterparts. California also has many credits for which there are no comparable federal credits, and there are some federal credits that have no California counterparts.

Practice Note: Employers Required to Provide EITC Information to Employees

Even though California does not have an earned income tax credit, California employers must notify employees covered by the employer's unemployment insurance that they may be eligible for the federal earned income tax credit (EITC). The notice must be provided by handing the notice directly to the employee or mailing the notice to the employee's last-known address within the one week period before or after the employer provides the employee an annual wage summary. (Sec. 19852, Rev. & Tax. Code; Sec. 19853, Rev. & Tax. Code)

• *Carryover credits*

Expired credits for which carryovers may be claimed (and the years for which the credits were available) include the following:

— water conservation credit (1980—1982);

— solar pump credit (1981—1983);

— solar energy credit (1985—1988);

— energy conservation credit (1981—1986);

— ridesharing credits (1981—1986 and 1989—1995);

— political contributions credit (1987—1991);

— commercial solar energy credit (1987—1988);

— residential rental and farm sales credit (1987—1991);

— food donation credit (1989—1991);

— orphan drug research credit (1987—1992);

— qualified parent's infant care credit (1991—1993);

— commercial solar electric system credit (1990—1993);

— recycling equipment credit (1989—1995);

— low-emission vehicle credit (1991—1995);

— Los Angeles Revitalization Zone hiring and sales and use tax credits (1992—1997);

— salmon and steelhead trout habitat credit (1995—1999);

— manufacturer's investment credit (1994—2003);

— joint strike fighter property credit (2001—2005);

— joint strike fighter wage credit (2001—2005);

— solar and wind energy systems credit (2001—2005); and

— rice straw credit (1997—2007).

All of the above credit carryovers may be claimed on FTB 3540. See prior editions of the *Guidebook to California Taxes* for details about these credits.

• *Credit sharing*

Unless a personal income tax credit provision specifies some other sharing arrangement, two or more taxpayers (other than a husband and wife or registered domestic partners (RDPs) may share a tax credit in proportion to their respective shares of the creditable costs. Partners may divide a credit in accordance with a written partnership agreement. In the case of a husband and wife or RDPs filing separately, either may claim the whole of the credit or they may divide it equally between them. (Sec. 17021.7, Rev. & Tax. Code; Sec. 17039, Rev. & Tax. Code)

• *Pass-through entities*

Credits that become inoperative, and that are passed through (in the first tax year after they become inoperative) to a taxpayer who is a partner or shareholder of an eligible pass-through entity may be claimed in the year of the pass-through. An eligible pass-through entity is any partnership or S corporation that files a fiscal year return and is entitled to a credit in the last year that the credit is operative. (Sec. 17039(h), Rev. & Tax. Code)

• *Limitation on credit claimed by taxpayers with interest in a disregarded entity*

If a taxpayer owns an interest in a disregarded business entity, credits claimed for amounts paid or incurred by the business are limited to the difference between the taxpayer's regular tax figured with the income of the disregarded entity and the taxpayer's regular tax figured without the disregarded entity's income. If the disregarded entity reports a loss, the taxpayer may not claim the credit for the year of the loss, but can carry over the credit amount received from the disregarded entity. (Sec. 17039(g), Rev. & Tax. Code)

• *Reduced credits for nonresidents and part-year residents*

Nonresidents and part-year residents are allowed reduced tax credits, with some exceptions. Credits are allowed on the basis of a prorated taxable income formula (see ¶116). If California income is 50% of the total, allowable credits are 50% of total credits. However, different rules apply to the following credits:

— the renter's credit (¶133) is allowed in proportion to the period of residence;

— credits for taxes paid to other states (¶128, 129) are allowed in full; and

— credits that are conditional upon a transaction occurring wholly within California are allowed in full. (Sec. 17055, Rev. & Tax. Code)

¶126 Tax Credits—Priorities

Law: Sec. 17039 (CCH CALIFORNIA TAX REPORTS ¶16-810).

Comparable Federal: None.

The law provides rules for the order in which various tax credits are to be applied. These rules are necessary because of the variety of provisions for carryovers, refundability, etc., in the various credits. Credits are allowed against "net tax" (the regular tax plus the tax on lump-sum distributions less exemption credits, but in no event less than the tax on lump-sum distributions) in the following order:

(1) credits, except the credits in categories 4 and 5, below, with no carryover or refundable provisions;

(2) credits with carryovers that are not refundable, except for those that are allowed to reduce "net tax" below the tentative minimum tax (see ¶117);

(3) credits with both carryover and refundable provisions;

(4) the minimum tax credit;

(5) credits that are allowed to reduce "net tax" below the tentative minimum tax (see ¶117);

(6) credits for taxes paid to other states; and

(7) credits with refundable provisions but no carryover (withholding, excess SDI). (Sec. 17039, Rev. & Tax. Code)

Also, see ¶125 for a discussion of the credit ordering as applied to the business credit limitations applicable to the 2008 and 2009 taxable years.

¶127 Credit for Taxes Paid Other States—General

Law: Secs. 18001-11 (CCH CALIFORNIA TAX REPORTS ¶16-825).

Comparable Federal: Secs. 901-5 (CCH U.S. MASTER TAX GUIDE ¶1311).

California Form: Sch. S (Other State Tax Credit).

In an effort to relieve double taxation, California law allows in some cases a credit against California personal income tax for income tax paid to another state or to a U.S. territory or possession. (Sec. 18001, et. seq., Rev. & Tax. Code) (Note:

Reference to territories or possessions is frequently omitted in the following discussion for the sake of simplicity; "other state" should be understood to include also territories or possessions.) Detailed rules for such credits in different situations are set forth below in ¶128—131, inclusive. General rules applicable to credits in all situations are included in this paragraph.

No credit is allowed for income taxes paid to cities or to foreign countries. However, some foreign taxes on gross receipts may be taken as a *deduction* (¶306).

• *Tax based on net income*

The credit is allowed only for taxes of another state based on *net income* (excluding any tax comparable to the alternative minimum tax). It therefore does not apply to a tax imposed on *gross income.* In *Appeal of Jesson* (1957) (CCH CALIFORNIA TAX REPORTS ¶16-825.20), the State Board of Equalization held that the Alaska gross production tax on gold mining royalties was not based on net income and therefore is not eligible for credit against California personal income tax.

• *Credit to estates and trusts and pass-through entities*

Credit is allowed to estates or trusts as well as to individuals. (Sec. 18004, Rev. & Tax. Code) Credit may be allowed to an individual for taxes that were paid to another state by an estate or trust of which the individual is a beneficiary or by a partnership of which the individual is a partner, an S corporation for which the individual is a shareholder, or a limited liability company of which the individual is a member. (Sec. 18005, Rev. & Tax. Code; Sec. 18006, Rev. & Tax. Code) See ¶130 —131 for details.

• *Timing of credit*

A taxpayer may not take credit for tax paid another state until the tax is actually paid. If the other-state tax has already been paid, the credit may be claimed at the time of filing the California return; if not, it may be claimed later by means of a refund claim. (Reg. 18001-1 (c), 18 CCR) See ¶719 for a discussion of the limitations period to claim a refund.

The claim for credit must be supported by filing Schedule S together with a copy of the return filed with the other state. A copy of the other state's return does not need to be filed with the California return if the taxpayer files electronically. However, the other state's return should be retained by the taxpayer for his or her records. (Instructions, Schedule S, Other State Tax Credit)

• *Effect of joint or separate returns*

In the case of spouses or registered domestic partners (RDPs) who file separate returns in California and a joint return in the other state, each spouse/RDP is allowed a credit based upon the portion of the other-state tax allocable to his or her own income. The total tax paid to the other state is prorated to each on the basis of the income that is included in the joint return and also taxed in the California separate returns. Where a joint return is filed in California, the entire amount of taxes paid by either spouse/RDP or both to the other state may be claimed as a credit, regardless of which spouse/RDP paid the other tax or whether a joint return or separate returns are filed in the other state. (Reg. 18001-1, 18 CCR) (Instructions, Schedule S, Other State Tax Credit)

• *Refunds must be reported*

A taxpayer who obtains a refund or a credit of any portion of tax paid to another state must report the refund or credit immediately to the Franchise Tax Board. The reduction in the credit against California personal income tax must be computed and the resulting increase in the net California personal income tax paid, with interest. (Instructions, Schedule S, Other State Tax Credit)

In *Appeal of Daniel W. Fessler* (1981) (CCH CALIFORNIA TAX REPORTS ¶16-825.251), the taxpayer claimed credit based upon $726 withheld from his wages by the State of New York. The taxpayer's New York return showed a tax of only $130; he had claimed, but not yet received, a New York refund of $596. The State Board of Equalization held that the credit should be based upon the correct New York tax of $130, because the larger amount withheld was only an estimate of the anticipated tax liability.

• *California-federal differences*

There are many differences between the California credits for taxes paid to other states and the foreign tax credit in the federal law. The federal credit is allowed for income taxes generally; the California credit is allowed only for taxes based on *net income* (excluding any tax comparable to the alternative minimum tax). Federal credit is allowed only where the taxpayer elects to take the credit instead of using the foreign tax as a deduction; California requires no election, because it allows no deduction for income taxes under any circumstances.

¶128 Credit for Taxes Paid Other States—Residents

Law: Secs. 18001, 18006 (CCH CALIFORNIA TAX REPORTS ¶16-825).

Comparable Federal: Secs. 901-5 (CCH U.S. MASTER TAX GUIDE ¶1311).

California Forms: Sch. R (Apportionment and Allocation of Income), Sch. S (Other State Tax Credit).

Credit is allowed California residents for *net income* taxes paid to another state (not including any tax comparable to California's alternative minimum tax) on income subject to the California income tax, subject to the conditions discussed below. (Sec. 18001, Rev. & Tax. Code)

Credit is allowed only if the other state does *not* allow California residents a credit for California taxes. The purpose is to prevent the allowance of credits by both states at the same time. Under this rule credit is allowable only for taxes paid to the following states and possessions:

Alabama
American Samoa
Arkansas
Colorado
Connecticut
Delaware
District of Columbia (unincorporated business tax and income tax, the latter for dual residents only—see below)
Georgia
Hawaii
Idaho
Illinois
Iowa
Kansas
Kentucky
Louisiana
Maine
Maryland
Massachusetts
Michigan
Minnesota
Mississippi
Missouri
Montana
Nebraska
New Hampshire (business profits tax)
New Jersey
New Mexico
New York
North Carolina
North Dakota
Ohio
Oklahoma
Pennsylvania
Puerto Rico
Rhode Island
South Carolina
Utah
Vermont
Virginia (dual residents only—see below)
Virgin Islands
West Virginia
Wisconsin

Credit is allowed for District of Columbia and Virginia taxes paid by dual residents. A dual resident is any taxpayer who is defined as a resident under both California law and another jurisdiction's law. A taxpayer who is a dual resident is allowed to claim the other state tax credit for taxes paid to the other jurisdiction on income attributable to that other jurisdiction. Certain U.S. officials and staff are also treated as dual residents if, during their temporary absence from California, they are residents of another jurisdiction. (Instructions, Schedule S, Other State Tax Credit)

California residents who are included in a group nonresident return similar to the return described in Rev. & Tax. Code Sec. 18535 filed with any of the above-listed states or with Arizona, Indiana, Oregon, or Virginia may also claim a credit for their share of income taxes paid to these states, unless any of these states allow a credit for taxes paid to California on the group nonresident return. (Instructions, Schedule S, Other State Tax Credit) In *Appeal of Gregory K. Soukup and Mary Jo Carr* (1994) (CCH CALIFORNIA TAX REPORTS ¶16-825.85), the State Board of Equalization (SBE) held that taxpayers who filed a composite Indiana return were entitled to credit on their California return for income taxes paid to Indiana because their election to file a composite return made them ineligible to claim the credit in Indiana.

Partners, S corporation shareholders, and limited liability company members are allowed a credit for their pro rata share of tax paid to other states (¶131). (Sec. 18006, Rev. & Tax. Code)

• *Nonresident of other state*

Credit is ordinarily allowed only for taxes (not including any tax comparable to California's alternative minimum tax) paid on net income that is taxable by the other state *irrespective* of residence or domicile of the recipient. See below for exceptions. In other words, the income taxed by the other state must be derived from sources within that state, under the California interpretation of what constitutes income from sources within that state. "Income from sources from within that state" is determined by applying the nonresident sourcing rules for determining income from sources within this state, see ¶231. (Sec. 18001, Rev. & Tax. Code)

The credit is intended to apply in a situation in which the California resident is taxed by the other state as a *nonresident* of that state, and not to a situation where the taxpayer is taxed as a resident by both states. The effect of this rule is to deny or limit the credit in cases where the taxpayer is treated as a resident of the other state as well as of California, and to deny credit in almost all cases for tax paid on income from intangible property. Such income (dividends, interest, etc.) is deemed under California law to be attributable to California as the state of residence and therefore not derived from sources in another state, on the theory that intangible property generally has its situs at the domicile of the owner. See below for discussion of cases to this effect. This rule would not apply in the rare case where an intangible asset has acquired a "business situs" outside of California; see ¶231 for explanation of "business situs."

The general requirement that the taxes paid to the other state be imposed without regard to the taxpayer's residence or domicile does not apply to certain U.S. governmental officials, who are considered to be California residents as explained at ¶105. The purpose of this exception presumably is to insure that such officials will not be denied credit if they are treated as residents by the other state as well as by California. (Sec. 18001, Rev. & Tax. Code)

• *"Alternative minimum taxes" do not qualify*

The credit does not apply to any preference, alternative, or minimum tax paid to other states that is comparable to California's alternative minimum tax (¶117). However, the credit may be applied against the taxpayer's alternative minimum tax, if the taxpayer is liable for that tax (¶117).

• *Limitation on amount*

The amount of the credit is limited to the same proportion of the total California tax as the income taxed by both states bears to the total income taxed by California. (Sec. 18001, Rev. & Tax. Code) The purpose of this rule is to ensure that the credit allowed will not be any greater than the California tax actually paid on the income that has been subjected to double taxation. In *Appeal of John and Olivia A. Poole* (1963) (CCH CALIFORNIA TAX REPORTS ¶16-825.87), the SBE held that the word "income" for purposes of this limitation means the equivalent of "adjusted gross income" as defined in the California law.

A taxpayer who has income from a trade or business activity conducted both inside and outside California must use Schedule R for purposes of calculating the income apportionable to California for which the credit may be claimed.

Comment: Temporary Limitation on Credit Amounts

See ¶125 for a discussion of the 50% limitation on the amount of business credits and credit carryovers that may be claimed during the 2008 and 2009 taxable years. (Sec. 17039.2, Rev. & Tax. Code)

• *Procedure to determine credit*

A California resident (or part-year resident) should take the following steps to determine the credit:

— Find out from the list above whether the other state qualifies for the California credit.

— Determine what items of income are taxed to the resident/part-year resident as a *nonresident* by the other state and also taxed by California (called the "double-taxed income"). (As explained above, U.S. officials are not subject to the *nonresident* limitation; they should include at this point all income that is taxed by both states.)

— Determine the net amount of the "double-taxed income" that is actually subject to tax by California after deducting any expenses that apply specifically to that income (such as depreciation, etc.). This computation should be made by applying the California rules for determination of adjusted gross income to the "double-taxed income."

— Apply the limitation described under the heading *"Limitation on amount,"* above.

— The credit is the lower of two amounts: (1) the amount computed under step 4, below, or (2) the actual tax paid to the other state.

CCH Example: Computation of Credit

		California	*State "X"*
(a)	Total gross income	$25,000	$10,000
(b)	Gross income taxed in both states	10,000	10,000
(c)	Deductions directly attributable to income on line (b)	1,000	1,000
(d)	Other deductions, not directly attributable to any income	4,500	3,000
(e)	Taxable income	19,500	6,000
(f)	Tax paid (illustrative amounts)	1,205	285

Step 1—Assume that State "X" qualifies for California credit and that you are being taxed by "X" as a nonresident.

Step 2—"Double-taxed income"	$10,000
Step 3—Net amount of "double-taxed income" taxed by both states	9,000
Step 4—Limitation: $9,000/$24,000 × $1,205 =	452
Step 5—Credit = ¾ actual tax paid to "X"	285

• *Decisions of courts and State Board of Equalization*

In *Appeals of Michael A. DeBenedetti and Frances, Jr., and Joy Purcell* (1982) (CCH CALIFORNIA TAX REPORTS ¶16-825.751), the taxpayers were California stockholders of a corporation that was taxed by Oregon as a "tax-option" (S) corporation. The taxpayers argued that the stock had acquired a "business situs" in Oregon, because it was pledged there to secure indebtedness of another corporation. The SBE held that the source of the dividend income was in California, and denied credit for the Oregon tax.

In *Appeal of Stanley K. and Beatrice L. Wong* (1978) (CCH CALIFORNIA TAX REPORTS ¶16-825.751), the taxpayers were California residents who claimed credit for income tax paid to the state of Hawaii. The income taxed by Hawaii consisted of (1) interest on a note resulting from the sale of a Hawaii condominium and (2) dividends on stock of a family corporation located in Hawaii. The taxpayers argued that the note and the stock certificates were physically located in Hawaii and had acquired a "business situs" there. The SBE held that the source of the income was in California and denied the credit. To the same effect, see *Appeal of Marvin and Alice Bainbridge* (1981) (CCH CALIFORNIA TAX REPORTS ¶16-825.703), involving interest received on a contract for sale of Hawaii land.

The case of *Theo Christman v. Franchise Tax Board* (1976) (CCH CALIFORNIA TAX REPORTS ¶16-825.701) involved a taxpayer who was a California stockholder in a "tax-option" (S) corporation that operated in Georgia. His share of the corporation's income was taxed directly to him under Georgia's "tax-option" rules. He paid Georgia tax on the income and claimed credit against his California tax. A California court of appeal denied the credit on the grounds that the source of the income was California, despite the fact that the corporation was treated—in effect—as a partnership for purposes of federal and Georgia taxes. To the same effect, see *Appeal of Estate of Donald Durham* (1974) (CCH CALIFORNIA TAX REPORTS ¶16-825.701), and *Appeal of Maude Peterson* (1978) (CCH CALIFORNIA TAX REPORTS ¶16-825.25).

In *Appeal of Leland M. and June N. Wiscombe* (1975) (CCH CALIFORNIA TAX REPORTS ¶16-825.98), a California resident received salary from an Alabama corporation for services rendered in California. The salary was taxed by Alabama, and the taxpayer claimed California tax credit for the tax paid to Alabama. The SBE denied the credit on the ground that the income was from a California source and was not properly taxed by Alabama to a nonresident, even though Alabama insisted on taxing it.

In *Appeal of Hugh Livie, et al.* (1964) (CCH CALIFORNIA TAX REPORTS ¶16-825.751), a California resident paid Puerto Rico income tax on the gain realized upon liquidation of a Puerto Rico corporation. The SBE held that the Puerto Rico tax was not allowable as a credit against California tax, since the income was derived from a California source. See also *Appeal of Allan H. and Doris Rolfe* (1978) (CCH CALIFORNIA TAX REPORTS ¶16-825.75), applying the same principle to disallow credit for Iowa tax.

¶129 Credit for Taxes Paid Other States—Nonresidents

Law: Secs. 18002, 18006 (CCH CALIFORNIA TAX REPORTS ¶16-825).

Comparable Federal: Secs. 901-5 (CCH U.S. MASTER TAX GUIDE ¶1311).

California Forms: Sch. R (Apportionment and Allocation of Income), Sch. S (Other State Tax Credit).

• *Conditions for credit*

Credit is allowed nonresidents for *net income* taxes (excluding minimum or preference taxes comparable to California's alternative minimum tax) paid to the taxpayer's state of residence on income that is also taxed by California, subject to the following conditions:

(1) Credit is allowed only where the state of residence either (a) does not tax income of California residents at all, or (b) allows California residents a credit for California taxes. In other words, California does not allow credit to a resident of another state unless the other state provides a similar credit to California residents. This is commonly referred to as the reciprocity requirement. The states that qualify under this rule are listed below.

(2) Credit is allowed only where the other state does *not* allow its residents a credit in the same situation. Where the other state would allow a credit *even though* California also allowed one, this rule prevents the allowance of the credit

by California. The purpose is to keep a taxpayer from getting credits from both states at the same time. (Sec. 18002, Rev. & Tax. Code)

Because of above rules (1) and (2), credit is currently allowable to nonresidents only for taxes paid to the following states and territories (Instructions, Schedule S, Other State Tax Credit):

Arizona

Guam

Indiana

Oregon

Virginia

However, in *Appeal of Daniel Q. and Janice R. Callister* (1999) (CCH CALIFORNIA TAX REPORTS ¶16-825.353), the State Board of Equalization held that nonresidents were entitled to a credit for a portion of the local income tax surcharges they paid to another state because the other state required its counties to impose that portion of the surcharge. The portion of the local surcharges that the state required counties to impose was recognized as a state, rather than local, tax.

• *Limitations on amount*

The maximum credit amount is limited to the lesser of the following two amounts: (1) the same proportion of the total tax paid to the state of residence as the income taxed in both states bears to the total income taxed by the state of residence; or (2) the same proportion of the total California tax as the income taxed in both states bears to the total income taxed by California. The total California tax for this purpose is the tax after deducting credit for personal exemptions. (Sec. 18002, Rev. & Tax. Code)

In computing limitations (1) and (2), follow the principles set forth in the example in ¶128. As with resident individuals, if the taxpayer has income from a trade or business activity conducted both inside and outside California, the taxpayer must use Schedule R for purposes of calculating the income apportionable to California for which the credit may be claimed.

Comment: Temporary Limitation on Credit Amounts

See ¶125 for a discussion of the 50% limitation on the amount of business credits and credit carryovers that may be claimed during the 2008 and 2009 taxable years. (Sec. 17039.2, Rev. & Tax. Code)

• *Nonresident S corporation shareholders, partners, and LLC members*

Nonresident S corporation shareholders, nonresident partners, and nonresident limited liability company members are entitled to this credit for the pro rata share of taxes paid to another state (¶131). The taxes are treated as if paid by the individuals, and thus the conditions discussed above apply in determining this credit. (Sec. 18006, Rev. & Tax. Code) Nonresident beneficiaries are not entitled to this credit (FTB Information Letter No. 89-427, CCH CALIFORNIA TAX REPORTS ¶401-748).

¶130 Credit for Taxes Paid Other States—Estates and Trusts

Law: Secs. 18003-05 (CCH CALIFORNIA TAX REPORTS ¶16-825).

Comparable Federal: Secs. 901-5 (CCH U.S. MASTER TAX GUIDE ¶1311).

California Form: Sch. S (Other State Tax Credit).

Two types of credits are allowed in connection with estates and trusts: (1) credit may be allowed to the estate or trust itself where its income is taxed by two states;

and (2) credit may be allowed to a resident beneficiary for taxes paid by the estate or trust to another state. (Sec. 18004, Rev. & Tax. Code; Sec. 18005, Rev. & Tax. Code)

• *Credit to estate or trust*

Credit is allowed to an estate or trust where it is treated as a "resident" of California and also of another state. (Sec. 18004, Rev. & Tax. Code) For this purpose, it is considered to be a "resident" of any state that taxes its income irrespective of whether the income is derived from sources within that state. (Sec. 18003, Rev. & Tax. Code) There are no reciprocal provisions for granting this credit as there are for resident and nonresident individuals as outlined above in ¶128 and 129, so the credit is allowable against net income taxes imposed by any state. The credit is subject to the following limitations:

— the amount of the credit may not exceed the same proportion of the total tax paid to the other state as the income taxed in both states bears to the total income taxed in the other state; and

— the amount of the credit is limited to the same proportion of the total California tax as the income taxed in both states bears to the total income taxed by California.

In *Appeal of Estate of Marilyn Monroe, Deceased* (1975) (CCH CALIFORNIA TAX REPORTS ¶16-825.45), the estate was taxed on substantial income by both New York State and California. The State Board of Equalization denied the estate's claim for credit for the New York tax, on the ground that the estate was not a "resident" of both states, because Marilyn Monroe was not a California resident at the time of her death and "only estates of resident decedents are residents of California" for tax-credit purposes.

• *Credit to beneficiary*

Credit is also allowed to the *beneficiary* of an estate or trust where a beneficiary who is a California resident pays California tax on income that has been taxed to the estate or trust in another state. (Sec. 18005, Rev. & Tax. Code) The credit is subject to the following limitations:

— the amount of the credit may not exceed the same proportion of the total tax paid to the other state by the estate or trust as the income taxed to the *beneficiary* in California and also to the *estate* or *trust* in the other state bears to the total income taxed by the other state; and

— the amount of the credit is limited to the same proportion of the total California tax paid by the beneficiary as the income taxed to the *beneficiary* in California and also to the *estate* or *trust* in the other state bears to the beneficiary's total income taxed by California.

The purpose of these rules is to limit the credit to the amount of other-state tax and also to the amount of California tax actually paid on the net income that has been subjected to tax by both states. Computation of the limitations is similar in principle to that shown above in the example at ¶128, although it may become somewhat more complicated where credit to a beneficiary is involved.

• *Credit on distribution of accumulated income*

In Legal Ruling No. 375 (1974) (CCH CALIFORNIA TAX REPORTS ¶16-825.375), the Franchise Tax Board discussed the tax credit for accumulated distributions made by a Minnesota trust to California beneficiaries. The ruling held that the beneficiaries were entitled to credit against their California tax for taxes paid to Minnesota by the trust. The credit was the amount that would have been allowed if the trust income had been distributed ratably in the year of distribution and the five preceding years, to conform to the method of taxing the distribution to the beneficiaries.

Comment: Temporary Limitation on Credit Amounts

See ¶125 for a discussion of the 50% limitation on the amount of business credits and credit carryovers that may be claimed during the 2008 and 2009 taxable years. (Sec. 17039.2, Rev. & Tax. Code)

¶131 Credit for Taxes Paid Other States—Partners, S Corporation Shareholders, and LLC Members

Law: Sec. 18006 (CCH CALIFORNIA TAX REPORTS ¶16-825).

Comparable Federal: Secs. 901-5 (CCH U.S. MASTER TAX GUIDE ¶1311).

California Form: Sch. S (Other State Tax Credit).

Resident partners, S corporation shareholders, and limited liability company (LLC) members are allowed a credit for their pro rata share of taxes paid another state by the partnership, S corporation, or LLC itself on income that is also taxed by California; the taxes are treated as if paid by the partners, shareholders, or members. (Sec. 18006, Rev. & Tax. Code) A resident S corporation shareholder may claim the credit only if (1) the other state imposing the taxes does not recognize S corporations or (2) the other state taxes S corporations and the California S corporation has elected to be an S corporation in the other state. The credit is computed using the same formula outlined at ¶128, above, under the heading "Procedure to determine credit."

A nonresident partner, S corporation shareholder, or LLC member is allowed a credit for his or her pro rata share of taxes paid by the partnership, S corporation, or LLC to the nonresident's state of residence on income also taxed by California. The taxes are treated as if paid by the nonresident partner, shareholder, or member. (Sec. 18006, Rev. & Tax. Code) For conditions governing determination of the credit, see ¶129, above.

Taxpayers are required to attach a copy of their Schedule K-1 (100S, 565, or 568) and a schedule showing their share of the net income tax paid to the other states. (Instructions, Schedule S, Other State Tax Credit)

Comment: Temporary Limitation on Credit Amounts

See ¶125 for a discussion of the 50% limitation on the amount of business credits and credit carryovers that may be claimed during the 2008 and 2009 taxable years. (Sec. 17039.2, Rev. & Tax. Code)

¶132 Excess SDI Credit

Law: Sec. 17061, Revenue and Taxation Code; Sec. 1185 Unemployment Insurance Code (CCH CALIFORNIA TAX REPORTS ¶16-826).

Comparable Federal: None.

California Forms: Form 540 (California Resident Income Tax Return), Form 540A (California Resident Income Tax Return).

An income tax credit is allowed for any excess employee contributions for disability insurance under the Unemployment Insurance Code. As explained at ¶1806, an employee who works for more than one employer during the year is entitled to recover any amounts withheld from wages in excess of the tax on the maximum wage limit (amount over $693.58 withheld in 2008), plus interest. An employee who files an income tax return recovers any such excess by claiming credit on the return. If the claim is disallowed, the employee may file a protest within 30 days with the Employment Development Department. Amounts withheld by a single employer that exceed the tax on the maximum wage limit must be recovered from the employer. (Sec. 17061, Rev. & Tax. Code; Sec. 1185, Unemp. Ins. Code)

¶133 Renter's Credit

Law: Sec. 17053.5 (CCH CALIFORNIA TAX REPORTS ¶16-907).

Comparable Federal: None.

California Forms: Form 540 (California Resident Income Tax Return), Form 540A (California Resident Income Tax Return).

A nonrefundable credit is allowed to anyone who is a "qualified renter," as explained below. The credit is not related in any way to the amount of rent paid. For the 2008 taxable year, the amount of the credit is $120 for married couples and registered domestic partners (RDPs) filing joint returns, heads of households, and surviving spouses, provided adjusted gross income is $69,872 or less, and $60 for other individuals, provided adjusted gross income is $34,936 or less. The adjusted gross income limits are adjusted annually for inflation. (Sec. 17053.5, Rev. & Tax. Code)

• *"Qualified renter" defined*

To be a "qualified renter" for purposes of claiming this credit, an individual must be a California "resident," as explained at ¶105, and have rented a principal residence in California for at least one-half of the year. (Sec. 17053.5, Rev. & Tax. Code)

An individual is *not* a "qualified renter" —and, therefore, gets no credit—if any of the following conditions described below exist:

— Someone living with the individual claims the individual as a dependent (¶115) for income tax purposes. (The Franchise Tax Board takes the position that this applies where the individual is claimed as a "dependent" for either California or federal income-tax purposes.)

— Either husband or wife or a RDP has been granted the homeowner's property-tax exemption (¶1704) during the taxable year. This does not apply to a spouse or RDP who is not granted the homeowner's exemption, if both maintain separate residences for the entire year.

— The property rented is exempt from property taxes (¶1704), unless the taxpayer, landlord, or owner pays possessory interest taxes or makes payments that are substantially equivalent to property taxes.

• *Special rules for married couples/RDPs*

The credit for a married couple or RDP that files separate returns may be taken by either spouse or RDP or divided equally between them, except as follows:

— if either spouse or RDP is not a California resident for part of the year, the credit is divided equally and prorated as described below for the period of nonresidency; or

— if both spouses or RDPs are California residents and maintain separate residences for the entire year, the credit must be divided equally between them; there is no option for one to take the full credit. (Sec. 17053.5, Rev. & Tax. Code)

• *Heads of household—Welfare recipients*

In *Appeals of Juanita A. Diaz and Constance B. Watts* (1989) (CCH CALIFORNIA TAX REPORTS ¶16-907.55), the taxpayers were entitled to claim the head of household renter's credit rather than the individual renter's credit, even though more than half the expenses of maintaining their households were paid by Aid to Families with Dependent Children (AFDC).

• *Part-year residents*

A person who is a resident for only part of the year (provided he or she qualifies, as explained above) is allowed 1/12 credit for each full month of California residence during the year. (Sec. 17053.5(e), Rev. & Tax. Code)

• *How to claim credit*

The credit should be claimed on the income tax return, with the appropriate supporting schedule.

¶134 Employers' Credits for Child Care Programs

Law: Secs.17052.17, 17052.18 (CCH CALIFORNIA TAX REPORTS ¶16-910, 16-911).

Comparable Federal: Sec. 45F (CCH U.S. MASTER TAX GUIDE ¶1344C).

California Form: FTB 3501 (Employer Child Care Program/Contribution Credit).

Child care program start-up credit: For tax years beginning before 2012, an employer may take a credit for 30% of start-up costs incurred in establishing a child care program or constructing a facility to be used by the children of the taxpayer's employees. This 30% credit is also available for an employer's contributions to California child care information and referral services, such as those that identify local child care services, offer information describing these resources to employees, and make referrals of employees to child care services when there are vacancies. (Sec. 17052.17, Rev. & Tax. Code)

Additionally, a taxpayer who owns a commercial building and is not required by local law to provide child care services may claim the 30% credit for (1) start-up costs incurred in establishing a child care program to be used primarily by employees of tenants leasing space in the building, or (2) contributions to child care information and referral services that will benefit those same employees. (Sec. 17052.17, Rev. & Tax. Code)

The credit is divided among two or more employers who share in the costs eligible for the credit in proportion to their respective share of the costs claimed. Spouses or registered domestic partners (RDPs) that file separate returns can divide the credit equally or one spouse or RDP may claim the whole credit on his or her return. (Sec. 17052.17, Rev. & Tax. Code)

Any taxpayer wishing to claim a credit for child care program start-up costs must disclose to the Franchise Tax Board the number of children the program will legally accommodate. (Sec. 17052.17, Rev. & Tax. Code)

The credit may not reduce the taxpayer's net tax by more than $50,000 in any one tax year, but excess amounts may be carried over. If the available credit for the current year combined with a credit carryover from a prior year exceeds $50,000, the combined excess amount may be carried over until exhausted. (Sec. 17052.17, Rev. & Tax. Code)

The employer may not take a deduction for the portion of expenses equal to the credit amount. The cost basis of the facility is reduced by the amount of credit. A taxpayer can elect to take depreciation in lieu of claiming the credit. In any event, the taxpayer may take depreciation on the cost of the facility in excess of the credit. (Sec. 17052.17, Rev. & Tax. Code)

A proportionate share of the credit claimed for a child care center that is disposed of or ceases operation within 60 months after completion will be recaptured in the taxable year of the disposition or nonuse. (Sec. 17052.17, Rev. & Tax. Code)

• *Comparison to federal credit*

The California credits are similar to the federal credits for qualified child care expenditures and qualified child care resource and referral expenditures under IRC Sec. 45F, with the following differences:

— California's credit for qualified expenditures is limited to start-up expenditures, whereas the federal credit may also be claimed for operating costs and contractual services.

— The federal credit is limited to 25% of qualified expenditures and 10% for resource and referral expenditures; California has a 30% limit for both components.

— The federal credit for qualified expenditures, unlike the California credit, is limited to the fair market value of such care.

— The federal credit, unlike the California credit, requires that at least 30% of the enrollees of a child care facility located at the taxpayer's principal trade or business be the taxpayer's employees.

— The California credit for qualified child care expenditures is subject to recapture for the initial five years after the facility is constructed; the federal credit, or a percentage thereof, is subject to recapture for up to 10 years after the facility is constructed.

— The federal credit is limited to $150,000 per taxpayer annually; the California limit is $50,000 per taxpayer annually.

• *Child care plan credit*

For tax years beginning before 2012, employers, including self-employed individuals, may take a credit for contributions made to a qualified child care plan on behalf of a qualified dependent of a qualified employee. For purposes of this credit, contributions do not include amounts contributed to a qualified care plan pursuant to a salary reduction agreement to provide benefits under a dependent care assistance program. The amount of the credit is 30% of the cost of plan contributions paid directly to the child care program or provider, up to a maximum credit of $360 per year for each qualified dependent. (Sec. 17052.18, Rev. & Tax. Code)

A qualified dependent must be under the age of 12 years. A "qualified employee" is an employee of the taxpayer who is performing services for the taxpayer in California. The credit may not be claimed for payments made to a person who qualifies as a dependent of the employee or the employee's spouse or who is the employee's child or stepchild under 19 years of age at the close of the taxable year. A qualified plan includes a plan that provides services at the work site, at child care centers, at home, or at a dependent care center (which is a specialized facility for short-term illnesses of an employee's dependents), as long as the facilities meet any applicable state licensing requirements. (Sec. 17052.18, Rev. & Tax. Code)

An employer may claim a prorated portion of the credit if child care is for less than 42 weeks, computed by the ratio of number of weeks of care to 42. The employer may not take a deduction for the portion of expenses equal to the credit amount. Unused credit may be carried forward until exhausted. (Sec. 17052.18, Rev. & Tax. Code)

The basis of the facility for which an employer claims a credit for contributions to a qualified care plan used at a facility owned by the employer must be reduced by a corresponding amount in the taxable year the credit is allowed. (Sec. 17052.18, Rev. & Tax. Code)

Comment: Temporary Limitation on Credit Amounts

See ¶125 for a discussion of the 50% limitation on the amount of business credits and credit carryovers that may be claimed during the 2008 and 2009 taxable years. (Sec. 17039.2, Rev. & Tax. Code)

¶135 Senior Head of Household Credit

Law: Sec. 17054.7 (CCH CALIFORNIA TAX REPORTS ¶16-912).

Comparable Federal: None.

California Form: Form 540 (California Resident Income Tax Return).

California allows a "senior head of household" to claim a credit equal to 2% of taxable income, up to a maximum of $1,203 (for 2008). To qualify, a taxpayer must (1) be at least 65 years old as of the end of the taxable year and (2) have qualified as the head of household (¶114) for either of the two taxable years preceding the current taxable year by maintaining a household for a qualifying individual who died during either of those preceding taxable years. Additionally, the credit is limited to taxpayers whose adjusted gross income does not exceed a statutory maximum that is adjusted annually for inflation. The maximum adjusted gross income for 2008 is $63,831. (Sec. 17054.7, Rev. & Tax. Code)

¶136 Credits for Joint Custody Head of Household, Dependent Parent

Law: Sec. 17054.5 (CCH CALIFORNIA TAX REPORTS ¶16-914a, 16-914b).

Comparable Federal: None.

California Form: Form 540 (California Resident Income Tax Return).

For the 2008 taxable year, the California joint custody head of household credits equal the lesser of 30% of the net tax or $393. The credits cover both dependent children and dependent parents. The credits are subject to the same annual inflation adjustment as the exemption credits (¶113). However, neither may be claimed if the taxpayer used either the head of household or qualifying widow(er) filing status. (Sec. 17054.5, Rev. & Tax. Code)

• *Dependent child*

To claim the credit as "joint custody head of household" for purposes of a dependent child the taxpayer must satisfy the following conditions:

— be unmarried at the end of the year;

— maintain a home that is the principal place of abode of the taxpayer's dependent or descendant for no less than 146 days but no more than 219 days of the year, under a decree of dissolution or separate maintenance, or under a written custody agreement prior to the issuance of such a decree where proceedings have been initiated; and

— furnish over half the cost of household expenses. (Sec. 17054.5, Rev. & Tax. Code)

• *Dependent parent*

A "qualified taxpayer," for purposes of claiming the dependent parent credit, is one who satisfies the following conditions:

— is married but living apart from the spouse for the last half of the tax year,

— files separately,

— furnishes over half of the cost of maintaining the household that is the principal residence of the dependent parent, and

— does not qualify to file as a head of household or as a surviving spouse.

The dependent parent does not have to live in the taxpayer's home for purposes of claiming the dependent care credit. (Sec. 17054.5, Rev. & Tax. Code)

¶137 Farmworker Housing Credit

Law: Sec. 17053.14 (CCH CALIFORNIA TAX REPORTS ¶16-906).

Comparable Federal: None.

California Forms: Form 540 (California Resident Income Tax Return), Sch. P (540) (Alternative Minimum Tax and Credit Limitations - Residents).

Prior to the 2009 taxable year, a credit is allowed for the lesser of (1) up to 50% of eligible costs paid or incurred for the construction or rehabilitation of farmworker housing, or (2) the amount certified by the California Tax Credit Allocation Committee (the "Committee"). The amount of the credit is also subject to the federal low-income housing credit limitations. No other credit or deduction may be claimed for the qualified amounts used to compute the credit. However, unused credit may be carried over until exhausted. The credit is subject to recapture if the Committee determines that certification was obtained as a result of fraud or misrepresentation or if the taxpayer does not comply with program requirements. (Sec. 17053.14, Rev. & Tax. Code)

Comment: Repeal of Credit

Beginning with the 2009 taxable year, the farmworker housing credit is repealed and made part of the low-income housing credit (¶138) A specified set-aside for farmworker housing development is established in the low-income housing credit allocation and certain criteria are eased for purposes of qualifying farmworker housing projects for the low-income housing credit.

"Qualified farmworker housing" means housing located within California that satisfies the requirements of the Farmworker Housing Assistance Program, as outlined in the Health and Safety Code. "Eligible costs" are the total costs for financing, construction, excavation, installation, and permits paid or incurred to construct or rehabilitate qualified farmworker housing. "Eligible costs" include, but are not limited to, costs for improvements to ensure compliance with laws governing access for persons with disabilities and costs related to reducing utility expenses. However, "eligible costs" do not include land and costs financed by grants and below-market financing.

To qualify for the credit, a taxpayer must satisfy the following conditions:

— submit an application for credit certification to the Committee;

— ensure that the construction or rehabilitation of the property is done in conformity with the Farmworker Housing Assistance Program;

— own or operate, or ensure the ownership or operation of, the farmworker housing in compliance with the provisions governing the availability of the credit, including making the housing available to farmworkers for 30 years; and

— enter into a written agreement with the Committee guaranteeing that the program requirements have been satisfied.

Comment: Temporary Limitation on Credit Amounts

See ¶125 for a discussion of the 50% limitation on the amount of business credits and credit carryovers that may be claimed during the 2008 and 2009 taxable years. (Sec. 17039.2, Rev. & Tax. Code)

¶138 Low-Income Housing Credit

Law: Sec. 17058, Reg. 10300 et. seq. (CCH CALIFORNIA TAX REPORTS ¶16-905).

Comparable Federal: Sec. 42 (CCH U.S. MASTER TAX GUIDE ¶1334).

California Form: FTB 3521 (Low-Income Housing Credit).

California provides a credit computed under federal law (as modified) as of the tie-in date (¶103) for investors in qualified low-income housing projects in California. The credit is applied against the net tax, and may reduce tax liability to below the "tentative minimum tax." (Sec. 17058, Rev. & Tax. Code)

The California credit is claimed over a four-year period, rather than over a 10-year period as under federal law. Generally, the percentage of costs for which credit may be claimed in the first three years is the highest percentage allowed federally in the month the building is placed in service. For the fourth year, the percentage is the difference between 30% and the sum of the credit percentage for the first three years. However, for (1) new buildings that are federally subsidized, and (2) existing buildings that are at risk of conversion to market rental rates, the percentage of creditable costs in the first three years is the same as the federal percentage applicable to subsidized new buildings, while for the fourth year the percentage is the difference between 13% and the sum of the credit percentages for the first three years. (Sec. 17058, Rev. & Tax. Code) As a result of California's current IRC conformity date (¶103), California has not adopted an amendment made by the federal Housing Assistance Tax Act of 2008 that provides a minimum applicable percentage of 9% for computing the credit for newly constructed non-federally subsidized buildings placed in service after July 30, 2008 and before December 31, 2013.

The California provisions require a "compliance period" of 30 consecutive tax years, rather than the 15-year federal period. However, unlike federal law, California has no recapture provision (see IRC Sec. 42(i)(1)). If the credit exceeds the taxpayer's net tax for the taxable year, the excess may be carried forward to succeeding years.

When the basis of a building that has been granted a low-income housing tax credit is increased and exceeds the basis at the end of the first year of the four-year credit period, the taxpayer is eligible for a credit on the excess basis. This additional credit is also taken over a four-year period beginning with the taxable year in which the increase in qualified basis occurs.

California does not incorporate a federal provision that allows low-income housing investors, for the first tax year ending after October 24, 1990, to elect to claim 150% of the low-income housing credit otherwise allowable and to accept a corresponding pro rata reduction in the low-income housing credit taken in subsequent tax years. California also does not incorporate the federal provision allowing a taxpayer to reduce the credit for the portion of the first year that the housing remains unoccupied and claim such an amount in the year following the allowable credit period. Further, as a result of California's current IRC conformity date (¶103), California has not adopted federal amendments made by the Mortgage Forgiveness Debt Relief Act of 2007 that clarify that certain full-time students who are single parents and their children are allowed to live in housing units eligible for the low-income housing credit provided that their children are not dependents of another individual, other than the child's parent.

The federal credit was further modified by the Housing Assistance Tax Act of 2008 (HATA). Amendments made by HATA (1) repeal the prohibition against providing the credit for buildings receiving moderate rehabilitation assistance at any time during the 15-year compliance period; (2) modify the definition of related persons for purposes of determining the eligible basis of a building; (3) allow state housing credit agencies to designate a building as located in a difficult development area if the enhanced credit resulting from the increase in eligible basis is necessary for the building to be financially feasible as part of a qualified low-income housing project; (4) increase the maximum amount of the adjusted basis of a community service facility that may be taken into account in determining the adjusted basis of a building located in a qualified census tract; (5) exclude federally funded grants used to finance a low-income building from the eligible basis of the building; (6) increase the minimum amount of rehabilitation expenditures required for such expenditures to be treated as a new building that qualifies for the credit; (7) clarify the general public use requirement that must be met in order to claim the credit; (8) expand the exception to the general rule that a credit allocation be made no later than the close of the calendar year that a building is placed in service; (9) revise the definition of a federally subsidized building; (10) modify the income limitation for determining qualification of a low-income housing project in certain rural areas; (11) provide that students previously under the care and placement of a foster care program governed by the Social Security Act will not disqualify a student housing unit from being a low-income unit; (12) repeal the requirement to post a bond upon disposition of an interest in a qualified low-income building prior to the end of the compliance period to avoid recapture of the credit; and (13) require state allocation plans to take into consideration the energy efficiency of the project and the historic nature of the project when making credit allocations. Taxpayers should consult the California Tax Credit Allocation Committee's Web site (http://www.treasurer.ca.gov/ctcac/) for information on how these amendments might impact allocations of the state low-income housing credit.

Comment: Partnership Allocations

During the 2009 through 2015 taxable years, the credit must be allocated to the partners of a partnership owning the project in accordance with the partnership agreement, regardless of how the federal low-income housing tax credit is allocated to the partners, or whether the partnership agreement's credit allocation has substantial economic effect. If the credit allocation lacks substantial economic effect, losses or deductions attributable to a partnership interest sale or disposition that is made prior to the federal credit's expiration may not be claimed in the taxable year in which the sale or other disposition occurs. The loss or deduction must be deferred until and treated as if it occurred in the first taxable year immediately following the taxable year in which the federal credit period expires.

These rules do not apply to state low-income housing credits allocated for farmworker housing projects that are financed through the farmworker housing set-aside provision (discussed below) unless the project also receives a preliminary reservation of federal low-income housing tax credits.

California, unlike federal law, limits the total amount of low-income housing credits that the California Tax Credit Allocation Committee may allocate for corporation franchise and income tax, personal income tax, and gross premiums tax on insurers to $70 million per year (indexed for inflation) plus any amounts returned and unused for preceding years. Beginning with the 2009 taxable year, the Committee must set aside at least $500,000 of the funds available for the low-income housing credit, plus any unallocated or returned farmworker housing credits that may still be available, for use in promoting farmworker housing projects. Projects applying for the low-income housing credit for farmworker housing under this set-aside provision do not have to have been allocated a federal low-income housing credit to qualify for the state low-income housing credit.

The credit is computed on FTB 3521, which must be attached to the return. A Certificate of Final Award of California Low-Income Housing Tax Credits (FTB 3521A) issued by the California Tax Credit Allocation Committee must be provided to the FTB upon request.

Comment: Temporary Limitation on Credit Amounts

See ¶125 for a discussion of the 50% limitation on the amount of business credits and credit carryovers that may be claimed during the 2008 and 2009 taxable years. (Sec. 17039.2, Rev. & Tax. Code)

¶139 Adoption Costs Credit

Law: Sec. 17052.25 (CCH CALIFORNIA TAX REPORTS ¶16-913).

Comparable Federal: Sec. 23 (CCH U.S. MASTER TAX GUIDE ¶1306).

California Form: Form 540 (California Resident Income Tax Return).

California provides a credit for an amount equal to 50% of the specified costs paid or incurred by a taxpayer for the adoption of any U.S. citizen or legal resident minor child who was in the custody of a state or county public agency. The credit may not exceed $2,500 per child and may be claimed only for specified costs directly related to the adoption. (Sec. 17052.25, Rev. & Tax. Code)

The adoption cost credit may be claimed only for the taxable year in which the decree or order of adoption is entered; however, the costs that are included may have been incurred in previous taxable years. The credit may be carried over until the total credit of $2,500 is exhausted. Any personal income tax deduction for any amount paid or incurred by the taxpayer upon which the credit is based must be reduced by the amount of the adoption cost credit.

The California credit is similar to the federal tax, with the following major exceptions:

— the amount of the California credit is lower (50% of qualifying costs vs. the 100% allowed under the federal credit);

— the dollar cap on the California credit is lower;

— unlike the federal credit, California's credit is not phased out on the basis of the taxpayer's adjusted gross income;

— the expenses that may be claimed for purposes of the federal credit include any reasonable and necessary adoption fees, court costs, attorney fees, and other expenses that are directly related to the adoption proceedings; whereas California specifies that expenses include adoption fees charged by the Department of Social Services or a licensed adoption agency, travel expenses related to adoption, and unreimbursed medical fees related to adoption;

— California's requirements concerning the adoptive child's citizenship, residency, and custodial status do not apply for purposes of claiming the federal credit; and

— California's credit may be carried over until exhausted, whereas there is a five-year carryover limit on the federal credit.

¶140 Disabled Access Expenditures Credit

Law: Sec. 17053.42 (CCH CALIFORNIA TAX REPORTS ¶16-954).

Comparable Federal: Sec. 44 (CCH U.S. MASTER TAX GUIDE ¶1338).

California Form: FTB 3548 (Disabled Access Credit for Eligible Small Businesses).

California allows eligible small businesses a credit in an amount equal to 50% of up to $250 of the eligible access expenditures paid or incurred by those businesses to comply with the federal Americans with Disabilities Act. Thus, a California credit of up to $125 is allowed. Except for the credit amount, the California credit is the same as the credit allowed under federal law. (Sec. 17053.42, Rev. & Tax. Code)

An "eligible small business" is a business that elects to claim the credit and either (1) had gross receipts (less returns and allowances) of $1 million or less for the preceding taxable year or (2) had no more than 30 full-time employees during the preceding taxable year.

"Eligible access expenditures" include all reasonable amounts paid or incurred to perform the following:

— remove architectural, communication, physical, or transportation barriers that prevent a business from being accessible to, or usable by, disabled individuals,

— provide qualified interpreters or other effective methods of making aurally delivered materials available to hearing impaired individuals,

— provide qualified readers, taped texts, or other effective methods of making visually delivered materials available to visually impaired individuals,

— acquire or modify equipment or devices for disabled individuals, or

— provide other similar services, modifications, materials, or equipment.

Amounts paid or incurred in connection with any new facility first placed in service after November 5, 1990, are not eligible access expenditures.

If the credit allowable exceeds "net tax" for the year, the excess may be carried over to succeeding years until exhausted.

Any deduction allowed for the same expenditures for which the credit is claimed must be reduced by the amount of the credit. In addition, amounts for which the credit is claimed may not be used to increase the basis of the property.

Comment: Temporary Limitation on Credit Amounts

See ¶125 for a discussion of the 50% limitation on the amount of business credits and credit carryovers that may be claimed during the 2008 and 2009 taxable years. (Sec. 17039.2, Rev. & Tax. Code)

¶141 Credit for Costs of Transporting Donated Agricultural Products

Law: Sec. 17053.12 (CCH CALIFORNIA TAX REPORTS ¶16-952).

Comparable Federal: None.

California Form: FTB 3547 (Donated Agricultural Products Transportation Credit).

California allows taxpayers engaged in the business of processing, distributing, or selling agricultural products to claim a credit equal to 50% of the costs paid or incurred in connection with the transportation of agricultural products donated to nonprofit charitable organizations. Eligible transportation costs may be determined in either of the following ways: (1) 14¢ per mile or (2) actual transportation expenses, excluding depreciation and insurance (Instructions to FTB 3547). (Sec. 17053.12, Rev. & Tax. Code)

Upon the delivery of donated agricultural products by a taxpayer, the nonprofit charitable organization must provide a certificate to the taxpayer stating the following:

— that the products were donated in accordance with requirements specified in the Food and Agriculture Code;

— the type and quantity of products donated;

— the distance transported;

— the transporter's name;

— the taxpayer donor's name and address; and

— the donee's name and address.

The certification must be provided to the Franchise Tax Board upon request.

If the credit is claimed, any deduction allowed for the same costs must be reduced by the amount of the credit allowed. Unused credit may be carried over until exhausted.

Comment: Temporary Limitation on Credit Amounts

See ¶125 for a discussion of the 50% limitation on the amount of business credits and credit carryovers that may be claimed during the 2008 and 2009 taxable years. (Sec. 17039.2, Rev. & Tax. Code)

¶142 Household and Dependent Care Expense Credit

Law: Sec. 17052.6 (CCH CALIFORNIA TAX REPORTS ¶16-914).

Comparable Federal: Sec. 21 (CCH U.S. MASTER TAX GUIDE ¶1301).

California Form: FTB 3506 (Child and Dependent Care Expenses Credit).

A refundable credit for employment-related household and dependent care expenses is allowed against California personal income tax in an amount determined in accordance with IRC Sec. 21 as of the current conformity date (¶103). (Sec. 17052.6, Rev. & Tax. Code)

• *Credit amount*

The amount of the California credit is a percentage of the allowable federal credit determined on the basis of the amount of federal adjusted gross income earned as follows (Sec. 17052.6, Rev. & Tax. Code):

Adjusted gross income of $40,000 or less	50% of the federal credit
Adjusted gross income over $40,000 but not over $70,000	43% of the federal credit
Adjusted gross income over $70,000 but not over $100,000	34% of the federal credit
Adjusted gross income over $100,000	0%

The credit is allowed only for care provided in California, and only to the extent of earned income subject to California personal income taxation. Earned income includes compensation, other than pensions or retirement pay, received by a member of the Armed Forces for active services as a member of the Armed Forces, whether or not the member is domiciled in California.

For California purposes, registered domestic partners (RDPs) may claim the credit in the same manner as married persons. Generally, married persons and RDPs must file a joint return to claim the credit. However, a married person or RDP may claim the credit on a separate return if he or she (1) lived apart from his or her spouse/RDP at all times during the last six months of the year, (2) had a qualifying person(s) living in his or her home for more than half of the year, (3) provided over half the cost of keeping up the home, and (4) otherwise meets all of the criteria for claiming the credit.

The Instructions to FTB 3506, Child and Dependent Care Expenses Credit, provide useful charts outlining (1) tie-breaker rules in instances in which there is a qualifying child of more than one person and (2) rules for divorced, separated, RDP-terminated, and never married persons.

CCH Comment: Prior Notice Not Required Prior to Adjustment

A denial of the credit or a refund is treated in the same manner as a mathematical error, except that taxpayers denied a credit or portion of the credit have the right of protest and appeal. Consequently, the Franchise Tax Board may adjust the credit/refund amount without providing any prior notice.

¶143 Natural Heritage Preservation Credit

Law: Sec. 17053.30, Rev. & Tax. Code; Secs. 37001–37022, Public Resources Code (CCH CALIFORNIA TAX REPORTS ¶16-900).

Comparable Federal: None.

California Form: FTB 3503 (Natural Heritage Preservation Credit).

Taxpayers may claim a nonrefundable credit equal to 55% of the fair market value of real property donated before July 1, 2008, for qualified conservation purposes to the California Resources Agency (CRA), a local government, or an exempt nonprofit land and water conservation organization designated by the CRA or a local government to accept donations. (Sec. 17053.30, Rev. & Tax. Code; Sec. 37001, Pub. Res. Code; Sec. 37002, Pub. Res. Code; Sec. 37006, Pub. Res. Code)

A donation, which may include the donation of a perpetual interest in property, may consist of land, conservation easements, land that includes water rights, or water rights and must also meet the criteria for a federal charitable contribution deduction. The donated property must help preserve wildlife and wildlife habitat, open space, agricultural land, fish, plants, water, or endangered species as evidenced by meeting specific criteria. However, the credit may not be claimed for property donated as a condition for obtaining use of the property from a public agency through a lease, permit, license, certificate, or other form of entitlement to property use. Unused credit may be carried forward for eight succeeding taxable years.

The California Wildlife Conservation Board must approve the donated real property for purposes of claiming the credit and may award up to $100 million in tax credits from fiscal years 2000—2001 through 2007—2008. The credit is available beginning January 1, 2005, through June 30, 2008. (Instructions, Form 3503, Natural Heritage Preservation Credit).

Information regarding current funding, qualified contributions of property, and the awarding of credits may be obtained from the Wildlife Conservation Board by phone at (916) 445-8448 or on the Internet at http://www.wcb.ca.gov/ .

CCH Practice Pointer: Relationship with Other Credits and Deductions

The credit is in lieu of any other credit or deduction to which the taxpayer may otherwise be allowed with respect to the donated property. (Sec. 17053.30, Rev. & Tax. Code)

Shareholders or partners may claim a partnership or other pass-through entity's credit in proportion to their interest in the pass-through entity as of the date of the qualified contribution.

Comment: Temporary Limitation on Credit Amounts

See ¶125 for a discussion of the 50% limitation on the amount of business credits and credit carryovers that may be claimed during the 2008 and 2009 taxable years. (Sec. 17039.2, Rev. & Tax. Code)

¶144 Tax-Incentive Credit—Sales Tax Equivalent

Law: Secs. 17053.33, 17053.45, 17053.70 (CCH CALIFORNIA TAX REPORTS ¶16-865, 16-866, 16-867).

Comparable Federal: None.

California Forms: FTB 3805Z (Enterprise Zone Deduction and Credit Summary), FTB 3807 (Local Agency Military Base Recovery Area Deduction and Credit Summary), FTB 3809 (Targeted Tax Area Deduction and Credit Summary).

• *Enterprise zones*

An income tax credit is allowed for the amount of sales or use tax paid on the purchase of machinery or parts used for specific purposes in "enterprise zones." (Secs. 17053.70, Rev. & Tax. Code) Detailed rules are provided in the law. Designated enterprise zones are listed at ¶104.

The credit applies to purchases up to a value of $1 million of machinery and parts used for the following:

— fabricating, processing, assembling, and manufacturing;

— production of renewable energy resources;

— pollution control mechanisms;

— data processing and communications equipment; and

— motion picture manufacturing equipment central to production and post-production work.

Practitioner Comment: Capitalization Requirement

The underlying statutes (Secs. 17053.70 and 23612.2) refer only to qualified property that is placed in service in an enterprise zone. Unlike the former California Manufacturers Investment Tax Credit (or "MIC" discussed at ¶818) the statutes do not explicitly state that the qualified costs must be capitalized for tax purposes. Nonetheless, the State Board of Equalization held on September 11, 2007 in the *Appeal of Taiheiyo Cement* that only capitalized costs qualify for the EZ Sales and Use Tax Credit. At the hearing, the State Board of Equalization indicated its intention to publish its decision.

Bruce Daigh, Chris Whitney, Contributing Editors

The total amount of both the enterprise zone sales and use tax credit and the enterprise zone hiring credit (¶145), including any carryover from prior years, is limited to the amount of income tax attributable to income from the enterprise zone. A taxpayer who also operates a business elsewhere must use a special apportionment formula to determine the amount of income attributable to the zone. The amount of the taxpayer's business income attributable to California is first determined by applying the apportionment formula discussed at ¶1305—1309. For purposes of apportioning income to the enterprise zone, however, the sales factor is eliminated from the standard apportionment formula and the business income used in the apportionment formula is limited to California-based income rather than worldwide income.

Credit that exceeds the "net tax" for the year may be carried over and applied against the tax on income from the enterprise zone in succeeding years. Any sales tax claimed as a credit on "qualified property" may not also increase the basis of such property.

The sales and use tax credit may be used to reduce an enterprise zone taxpayer's regular tax below the tentative minimum tax (¶117).

A taxpayer may claim the credit for use tax paid on qualified property only if qualified property of a comparable quality and price is not timely available for purchase in California.

• *Local agency military base recovery areas*

A credit is also allowed for sales or use tax paid or incurred by a local agency military base recovery area (LAMBRA) business for certain property purchased for exclusive use in a recovery area. The credit is substantially similar to the sales tax equivalent credit allowed for property purchased by enterprise zone businesses except that, for purposes of LAMBRA businesses, the credit applies to (1) high technology equipment; (2) aircraft maintenance equipment; (3) aircraft components; or (4) property that is depreciable under IRC Sec. 1245(a)(3). (Sec. 17053.45, Rev. & Tax. Code)

A taxpayer who is allowed a LAMBRA credit for qualified property is limited to only one credit under the Personal Income Tax Law with respect to that property. The credit is subject to recapture in the year of noncompliance if the qualified property is disposed of, or is no longer used by, the taxpayer within the LAMBRA at any time before the close of the second taxable year after the property is placed in service or if the taxpayer has not increased the number of employees by one or more during the first two taxable years after commencing business within a LAMBRA.

The amount claimed by a taxpayer for both of the LAMBRA credits (the sales tax credit and the hiring credit (¶147)) combined may not exceed the amount of tax attributable to income from the area. The special apportionment formula used for purposes of calculating the enterprise zone and targeted tax area sales and use tax credits is also used to calculate the LAMBRA credit.

• *Targeted tax area*

A similar credit is allowed for sales or use tax paid on the purchase of machinery and parts purchased and placed in service after October 31, 1998, and used for the following (see ¶104):

— fabricating, processing, assembling, and manufacturing;

— producing renewable energy resources;

— air or water pollution control mechanisms;

— data processing and communications; and

— motion picture production. (Sec. 17053.33, Rev. & Tax. Code)

The amount that may be claimed for all of a taxpayer's targeted tax area credits combined is limited to the amount of tax that would be imposed on the taxpayer's business income attributable to the area as if that attributable income represented all of the taxpayer's income that was subject to personal income tax. A taxpayer who also operates outside that area must use a special apportionment formula to determine the amount of income attributable to the targeted tax area. The amount of business income attributable to California is first determined by applying the apportionment formula discussed at ¶1305 —1309. For purposes of determining the amount attributable to the targeted tax area, however, the sales factor is eliminated from the standard apportionment formula and the business income used in the formula is limited to California-based income rather than worldwide income.

A taxpayer who is allowed a targeted tax area credit for qualified property is limited to only one credit under the Personal Income Tax Law with respect to that property.

Unused credit may be carried over and added to the credit in succeeding years until the credit is exhausted.

A taxpayer who claims the credit may not also increase the basis of the qualifying property by the amount of sales tax paid or incurred.

Comment: Temporary Limitation on Credit Amounts

See ¶125 for a discussion of the 50% limitation on the amount of business credits and credit carryovers that may be claimed during the 2008 and 2009 taxable years. (Sec. 17039.2, Rev. & Tax. Code)

Practical Analysis: Impact on Basis

The basis of the property for which these credits are claimed may not be increased for the sales and use taxes paid on the property. (Instructions, FTB 3805Z, Enterprise Zone Deduction and Credit Summary)

¶145 Tax-Incentive Credit—Enterprise Zone Employers

Law: Sec. 17053.74 (CCH CALIFORNIA TAX REPORTS ¶16-855).

Comparable Federal: Sec. 1396 (CCH U.S. MASTER TAX GUIDE ¶996C, 1339A).

California Form: FTB 3805Z (Enterprise Zone Deduction and Credit Summary).

A tax credit is allowed to employers for a portion of "qualified wages" paid to certain "qualified employees" who are hired to work in an enterprise zone. General business deductions that are otherwise allowable for wages paid to such individuals must be reduced by the amount of any credit claimed. (Sec. 17053.74, Rev. & Tax. Code) Detailed rules are provided in the law. Designated enterprise zones are listed at ¶104.

• *Definitions*

"Qualified wages" are generally the amounts, not in excess of 150% of the California minimum wage, paid to qualified disadvantaged employees. However, with respect to up to 1,350 otherwise qualified disadvantaged individuals employed in the Long Beach enterprise zone in certain aircraft manufacturing activities, "qualified wages" is expanded to include that portion of hourly wages that does not exceed 202% of the minimum wage. (Sec. 17053.74, Rev. & Tax. Code)

An individual is a "qualified employee" if the following conditions are satisfied:

— 90% of the individual's services in an enterprise zone for the taxpayer during the taxable year are directly related to the conduct of the taxpayer's enterprise zone trade or business;

— the individual performs at least 50% of his or her services for the taxpayer during the taxable year in an enterprise zone;

— the individual was hired after designation of the area as an enterprise zone; and

— immediately preceding the qualified employee's employment with the taxpayer, he or she was a qualified disadvantaged individual, a resident of a targeted employment area, or an employee who qualified the employer for the enterprise zone or program area hiring credits in effect prior to 1997.

A "qualified disadvantaged individual" is an individual who, immediately preceding employment with the taxpayer, was one of the following:

— an individual who was eligible for services under the federal Job Training Partnership Act (JTPA) or its successor, who was receiving, or was eligible to receive, subsidized employment, training, or services funded by the JTPA or its successor;

— an individual who was eligible to be a voluntary or mandatory registrant under the Greater Avenues for Independence (GAIN) Act or its successor;

— an economically disadvantaged individual 14 years of age or older;

— a qualified dislocated worker;

— a disabled individual who was eligible for, enrolled in, or had completed a state rehabilitation plan or was a service-connected disabled veteran, veteran of the Vietnam era, or veteran who was recently separated from military service;

— an ex-offender, including an individual placed on probation without a finding of guilt;

— a person who was eligible for, or a recipient of, benefits from certain specified public assistance programs;

— a member of a federally recognized Indian tribe, band, or other group of Native American descent; a resident of a targeted employment area;

— an employee who qualified the employer for a hiring credit under a former enterprise zone or program area; or

— a member of a targeted group under IRC Sec. 51(d).

Practitioner Comment: SBE Again Rejects FTB Attempt to Limit Senior Eligibility for the Enterprise Zone Hiring Credit

In the Appeal of *Jessica McClintock and Jessica McClintock, Inc.*, ("McClintock") decided on August 14, 2007, the California State Board of Equalization (SBE) rejected the arguments of the Franchise Tax Board (FTB) and ruled that older workers (age 55+) do not need to meet the income limitations of the Older Americans Act (125% of federal poverty level) to qualify under the former federal Jobs Training Partnership Act (JTPA) for purposes of the California enterprise zone hiring credit. As a result, individuals eligible for services under the JTPA, including those who face certain "barriers to employment," are considered "qualified disadvantaged individuals" for purposes of the credit, whether or not they are considered "economically disadvantaged."

The FTB originally indicated it would follow the *McClintock* decision. The FTB, however, subsequently stated in an April 2008 Tax News article that *McClintock* was contrary to California Employment Development Department (EDD) Directive 96-5 and would not be followed

On August 18, 2008, in the *Appeal of DeVry, Inc.*, the SBE again rejected the FTB's position and reaffirmed its decision in *McClintock* that older workers do not need to meet the income limitations of the Older Americans Act. In its briefing for the appeal, the FTB submitted a declaration under penalty of perjury from an employee of the EDD supporting the FTB's position. As in *McClintock*, the SBE found the statutory scheme and the JTPA forms and instructions (prepared by the EDD contemporaneously with the state's implementation of the JTPA program) required the result it reached in both appeals.

The SBE further concluded that the employment applications and questionnaires completed by DeVry's employees at the date of hire provided adequate documentation to support DeVry's claims regarding the credits for employees with disabilities and who experienced job losses due to business closures. The decision reverses the FTB's rejection of all claimed hiring credits still at issue at the time of the appeal.

Other than the direct result of its decision, the SBE's ruling is interesting in several particular aspects. First, it implicitly recognizes and relies on the SBE's Rules for Tax

Appeals section 5523.6, which allows the SBE to accept and consider any relevant evidence. Second, in doing so, it highlights the potential importance of contemporaneous documentation, such as employment applications and other employment forms, prepared without tax considerations. And, third, it shows that the SBE will assign lesser weight to evidence, even a declaration under penalty of perjury, lacking foundation and inconsistent with other reliable evidence.

Bruce Daigh, Chris Whitney, Contributing Editors

• *Amount of credit*

The amount of the credit is 50% of "qualified wages" in the first year of employment, 40% in the second year, 30% in the third year, 20% in the fourth year, and 10% in the fifth year. For purposes of computing the credit, seasonal workers are treated as continuously employed. (Sec. 17053.74, Rev. & Tax. Code)

The total amount of the enterprise zone hiring credit and the enterprise zone sales and use tax credit (¶144), including any carryover from prior years, is limited to the tax attributable to income from the enterprise zone. A taxpayer who also operates outside the zone area must use a special apportionment formula to determine the amount of income attributable to the zone area. The amount of business income attributable to California is first determined by applying the standard apportionment formula discussed at ¶1305—1309. For purposes of determining the amount of income attributable to the enterprise zone, however, the sales factor is eliminated from the standard apportionment formula and the income used in the apportionment formula is limited to California-based income rather than worldwide income.

• *Certification*

A taxpayer must obtain certification on a form HCD EZ1 (hiring voucher) or VoucherApp 10-07 that an individual meets the requirements for a "qualified employee" from the local agency responsible for verifying employee eligibility. (Sec. 17053.74, Rev. & Tax. Code; FTB 3805Z Booklet, Enterprise Zone Business Booklet)

Comment: Top Audit Issue

Invalid hiring vouchers have been identified as one of the FTB top audit issues. (*Tax News*, California Franchise Tax Board, November/December 2005)

Practitioner Comment: Additional Documentation Required

Although the statute only requires that a taxpayer obtain a certification from a local zone administrator in order to claim this credit, the FTB on audit has requested that taxpayers provide it with the underlying documentation that was originally given to the local zone administrator. In many cases, taxpayers may no longer have such records at the time of the audit. In the *Appeal of Deluxe Corp*, 2006-SBE-003, December 12, 2006, CCH CALIFORNIA TAX REPORTS ¶404-121, the State Board of Equalization (SBE) in a formal decision held that the FTB had the authority to request the underlying substantiation supporting the taxpayer's enterprise zone hiring credit vouchers and can deny the hiring credit for employees that it deems are not qualified or for which substantiation is not provided.

Bruce Daigh, Chris Whitney, Contributing Editors

• *Limitations and recapture*

The credit is reduced by any credit allowed under the federal work opportunity credit. Unless specified exceptions apply, the credit is subject to recapture if an involved employee is terminated within a prescribed period (generally, roughly one year). (Sec. 17053.74, Rev. & Tax. Code)

Unused credit may be carried forward and added to the credit in succeeding years.

The hiring credit may be used to reduce an enterprise zone taxpayer's regular tax below the tentative minimum tax (¶117).

Comment: Temporary Limitation on Credit Amounts

See ¶125 for a discussion of the 50% limitation on the amount of business credits and credit carryovers that may be claimed during the 2008 and 2009 taxable years. (Sec. 17039.2, Rev. & Tax. Code)

¶146 Tax-Incentive Credit—Enterprise Zone Employees

Law: Sec. 17053.75 (CCH CALIFORNIA TAX REPORTS ¶16-850).

Comparable Federal: None.

California Form: FTB 3553 (Enterprise Zone Employee Credit).

A limited tax credit is allowed to "qualified employees" for wages received from an enterprise zone business prior to the zone designation's termination or expiration. The amount of the credit is 5% of "qualified wages," defined as wages subject to federal unemployment insurance, up to a maximum of $525 per employee. The maximum amount of qualified wages for 2008 is $10,500. For each dollar of income received by the taxpayer in excess of "qualified wages," the credit is reduced by nine cents. The credit is not refundable and cannot be carried forward. The amount of the credit is further limited to the amount of tax that would be imposed on income from employment in the enterprise zone, computed as though that income represented the taxpayer's entire taxable net income. (Sec. 17053.75, Rev. & Tax. Code)

An individual is a "qualified employee" if he or she meets the following criteria:

— the individual is not an employee of the federal government, the State of California, or any political subdivision of the State;

— 90% of the individual's services in an enterprise zone for the taxpayer during the taxable year are directly related to the conduct of the taxpayer's enterprise zone trade or business; and

— the individual performs at least 50% of his or her services for the taxpayer during the taxable year in an enterprise zone.

Designated enterprise zones are listed at ¶104.

Comment: Temporary Limitation on Credit Amounts

See ¶125 for a discussion of the 50% limitation on the amount of business credits and credit carryovers that may be claimed during the 2008 and 2009 taxable years. (Sec. 17039.2, Rev. & Tax. Code)

¶147 Tax-Incentive Credit—Local Agency Military Base Recovery Area Employers

Law: Sec. 17053.46 (CCH CALIFORNIA TAX REPORTS ¶16-857).

Comparable Federal: None.

California Form: FTB 3807 (Local Agency Military Base Recovery Area Deduction and Credit Summary).

Local agency military base recovery area (LAMBRA) employers are allowed a credit for qualified wages paid to specified disadvantaged individuals or displaced employees. LAMBRAs are discussed at ¶104. (Sec. 17053.46, Rev. & Tax. Code)

Only those employers with a net increase of one or more employees during the first two taxable years after commencing business within a LAMBRA are eligible to claim the credit. A business must obtain certification from either the California Employment Development Department, the local county or city Job Training Partnership Act administrative entity, or the local county Greater Avenues to Independence (GAIN) office or social services agency that the employee meets the qualifications necessary for the employer to claim the credit (see discussion below). The certification must be made available to the California Franchise Tax Board upon request.

The credit that may be claimed during the first year of business operations within a LAMBRA is 50% of "qualified wages," which is defined as that portion of hourly wages that does not exceed 150% of the minimum wage established by the California Industrial Welfare Commission. For the second, third, fourth, and fifth years of operation, the credit is reduced to 40%, 30%, 20%, and 10%, respectively. For purposes of computing the credit, seasonal workers are considered continuously employed. The total amount of wages paid or incurred by a LAMBRA employer for which the credit may be claimed is limited to $2 million.

• *"Disadvantaged individual," "displaced employee" defined*

To qualify as a "displaced employee," a person must be a military base employee who was displaced as a result of a base closure. To qualify as a "disadvantaged individual" a person must be one of the following:

— determined eligible for services under the federal Job Training Partnership Act;

— a voluntary or mandatory registrant under California's Greater Avenues for Independence Act;

— an economically disadvantaged individual age 16 years or older;

— a qualified dislocated worker;

— an individual who is enrolled in or has completed a state rehabilitation plan or is a service-connected disabled veteran, veteran of the Vietnam era, or veteran who is recently separated from military service;

— an ex-offender;

— a recipient of specified federal, state, or local public assistance programs; or

— a member of a federally recognized Indian tribe, band, or other group of Native American descent. (Sec. 17053.46, Rev. & Tax. Code)

A "displaced employee" or "disadvantaged individual" must also be a person hired after the area in which the person's services are performed was designated a LAMBRA, at least 90% of whose services for the employer during the taxable year were directly related to the conduct of the employer's LAMBRA business, and at least 50% of whose services for the employer during the taxable year were performed within the LAMBRA.

• *Limitations on credit, carryover of unused amounts*

A taxpayer who is allowed a LAMBRA credit for qualified wages is limited to only one credit under the Personal Income Tax Law with respect to those amounts paid. The employer's wage payment credit must be reduced by the federal work opportunity credit and by the former state jobs tax credit. (Sec. 17053.46, Rev. & Tax. Code)

The amount of credit claimed for both the LAMBRA sales tax credit (discussed at ¶144) and the LAMBRA credit for qualified wages may not exceed the tax that would be imposed on the income attributed to the taxpayer's business activities within a LAMBRA. A taxpayer whose business also operates outside of the LAMBRA must use a special apportionment formula to determine the amount of income attributable to the LAMBRA. The amount of business income attributable to California is first determined by applying the standard apportionment formula discussed at ¶1305—1309. For purposes of determining the amount of income attributable to the LAMBRA, however, the sales factor is eliminated from the standard apportionment formula and the income used in the apportionment formula is limited to California-based income rather than worldwide income.

Unused credit may be carried over and applied to tax on income from the area in succeeding tax years until the credit is exhausted.

The credit is subject to recapture if an employee is terminated within a prescribed period (generally, roughly one year). In addition, any credit claimed is recaptured in the second taxable year if the employer fails to increase its number of jobs by one or more after commencing business within the LAMBRA. The law provides several exceptions to the recapture rules.

Comment: Temporary Limitation on Credit Amounts

See ¶125 for a discussion of the 50% limitation on the amount of business credits and credit carryovers that may be claimed during the 2008 and 2009 taxable years. (Sec. 17039.2, Rev. & Tax. Code)

¶148 Tax-Incentive Credit—Targeted Tax Area Employers

Law: Sec. 17053.34 (CCH CALIFORNIA TAX REPORTS ¶16-856).

Comparable Federal: None.

California Form: FTB 3809 (Targeted Tax Area Deduction and Credit Summary).

Targeted tax area employers are allowed a credit for qualified wages paid qualified employees. Targeted tax areas are discussed at ¶104. Only those employers involved in the following business activities described in the Standard Industrial Classification Manual (SIC Manual) are eligible to claim the targeted tax area credit: manufacturing; transportation; communications; electric, gas, and sanitary services; and wholesale trade.

The credit that may be claimed for the first year of employment is 50% of "qualified wages," which is defined as that portion of hourly wages that does not exceed 150% of the minimum wage established by the California Industrial Welfare Commission. For the second, third, fourth, and fifth years of operation, the credit is reduced to 40%, 30%, 20%, and 10%, respectively. For purposes of computing the credit, seasonal workers are considered continuously employed. (Sec. 17053.34, Rev. & Tax. Code)

• *Qualified employee*

An individual is a "qualified employee" if (1) he or she was hired after designation of the area as a targeted tax area, (2) 90% of the individual's services for the employer during the taxable year are directly related to the conduct of the employer's trade or business located in the targeted tax area, (3) the individual performs at least 50% of his or her services for the taxpayer during the taxable year in a targeted tax area, and (4) the individual is, or immediately preceding employment with the taxpayer was, any of the following:

— eligible for services under the federal Job Training Partnership Act (JTPA) or its successor, who was receiving, or was eligible to receive, subsidized employment, training, or services funded by the JTPA or its successor;

— eligible to be a voluntary or mandatory registrant under the Greater Avenues for Independence (GAIN) Act or its successor;

— an economically disadvantaged individual 14 years of age or older;

— a qualifying dislocated worker;

— a disabled individual eligible for, enrolled in, or having completed a state rehabilitation plan, or a service-connected disabled veteran, a veteran of the Vietnam era, or a veteran recently separated from military service;

— an ex-offender, including an individual placed on probation without a finding of guilt;

— a person who was eligible for, or a recipient of, benefits from certain specified public assistance programs;

— a member of a federally recognized Indian tribe, band, or other group of Native American descent;

— a resident of a targeted tax area; or

— a member of a targeted tax group for purposes of the federal Work Opportunity Credit, or its successor. (Sec. 17053.34, Rev. & Tax. Code)

• *Limitations and carryovers*

The total amount of the targeted tax area hiring credit and the targeted tax area sales and use tax credit (¶144), including any carryover from prior years, is limited to the tax attributable to income from the area. A taxpayer whose business also operates outside the targeted tax area must use a special apportionment formula to determine the amount of income attributable to the area. The amount of business income attributable to California is first determined by applying the standard apportionment formula discussed at ¶1305—1309. For purposes of determining the amount of income attributable to the targeted tax area, however, the sales factor is eliminated from the standard apportionment formula and the income used in the apportionment formula is limited to California-based income rather than worldwide income. (Sec. 17053.34, Rev. & Tax. Code)

The tax is subject to recapture if an employee is terminated within a prescribed period (generally, roughly one year). The law provides several exceptions to the operation of this recapture rule.

Unused credit may be carried over to succeeding taxable years until exhausted.

Comment: Temporary Limitation on Credit Amounts

See ¶125 for a discussion of the 50% limitation on the amount of business credits and credit carryovers that may be claimed during the 2008 and 2009 taxable years. (Sec. 17039.2, Rev. & Tax. Code)

¶149 Tax-Incentive Credit—Manufacturing Enhancement Area Employers

Law: Sec. 17053.47 (CCH CALIFORNIA TAX REPORTS ¶16-858).

Comparable Federal: None.

California Form: FTB 3808 (Manufacturing Enhancement Area Credit Summary).

Manufacturing enhancement area employers are allowed a credit for qualified wages paid to specified disadvantaged individuals or displaced employees. Manufacturing enhancement areas are discussed at ¶104. Only those employers involved in the following activities are eligible to claim the credit: business activities as described in Codes 2011 to 3999 of the Standard Industrial Classification Manual (SIC Manual); agricultural production; and livestock, animal specialties, or crop preparation services. (Sec. 17053.47, Rev. & Tax. Code)

The credit that may be claimed for the first year of employment is 50% of "qualified wages," which is defined as that portion of hourly wages that does not exceed 150% of the minimum wage established by the California Industrial Welfare Commission. For the second, third, fourth, and fifth years of employment, the credit is reduced to 40%, 30%, 20%, and 10%, respectively. For purposes of computing the credit, seasonal workers are considered continuously employed. The total amount of wages that may be taken into account for purposes of claiming the credit may not exceed $2 million per taxable year.

• *"Qualified taxpayer" and "qualified disadvantaged individual" defined*

A "qualified taxpayer" is a taxpayer engaged in a manufacturing trade or business within the area that, once the area has been designated as a manufacturing enhancement area, hires at least 50% of the business' employees from the county in which the area is located, 30% of whom are qualified disadvantaged individuals. (Sec. 17053.47, Rev. & Tax. Code)

An individual is a "qualified disadvantaged individual" if (1) he or she was hired after designation of the area as a manufacturing enhancement area, (2) 90% of the individual's services for the employer during the taxable year are directly related to the conduct of the employer's trade or business located in the manufacturing enhancement area, (3) the individual performs at least 50% of his or her services for the taxpayer during the taxable year in a manufacturing enhancement area, and (4) immediately preceding employment with the taxpayer, the individual was any of the following:

— determined eligible for services under the federal Job Training Partnership Act (JTPA) or any successor program;

— a voluntary or mandatory registrant under the Greater Avenues for Independence (GAIN) Act or any successor program; or

— certified eligible by the Employment Development Department under the Targeted Jobs Tax Credit Program or any successor program, whether or not the program is in effect.

• *Limitations and carryovers*

The total amount of the credit, including any carryover from prior years, is limited to the tax attributable to income from the manufacturing enhancement area. A taxpayer whose business also operates outside the area must use a special apportionment formula to determine the amount of income attributable to the area. The amount of business income attributable to California is first determined by applying the apportionment formula discussed at ¶1305—1309. For purposes of determining the amount of income attributable to the manufacturing enhancement area, however, the sales factor is eliminated from the standard apportionment formula and the income used in the apportionment formula is limited to California-based income rather than worldwide income. (Sec. 17053.47, Rev. & Tax. Code)

The credit is reduced by the amount of any federal work opportunity credit allowed for the same wages. Unless specified exceptions apply, the tax is subject to recapture if an employee is terminated within a prescribed period (generally, roughly one year).

If the amount of the credit exceeds the employer's tax for the taxable year, the excess may be carried over to succeeding taxable years until exhausted.

Comment: Temporary Limitation on Credit Amounts

See ¶125 for a discussion of the 50% limitation on the amount of business credits and credit carryovers that may be claimed during the 2008 and 2009 taxable years. (Sec. 17039.2, Rev. & Tax. Code)

¶150 Research and Development Credit

Law: Sec. 17052.12 (CCH CALIFORNIA TAX REPORTS ¶16-870).

Comparable Federal: Sec. 41 (CCH U.S. MASTER TAX GUIDE ¶1330).

California Form: FTB 3523 (Research Credit).

California provides a credit for increased research expenditures that is similar to that provided by federal law prior to its amendment by the Energy Tax Incentives Act of 2005, the Gulf Opportunity Zone Act of 2005, the Tax Relief and Health Care Act of 2006 (TRHCA), and the Emergency Economic Stabilization Act of 2008 (EESA), with the following exceptions (Sec. 17052.12, Rev. & Tax. Code):

— The California credit is available indefinitely, whereas the federal credit does not apply to amounts paid or incurred after 2009.

— The applicable California percentage is 15% of the excess of qualified research expenses for the tax year over a specified percentage of the taxpayer's average annual gross receipts for the four preceding taxable years (the "base amount"). The federal percentage is 20% of the excess of qualified expenses over the base amount.

— California uses 1.49%, 1.98%, and 2.48% for the three tiers used to compute the amount of the credit under the alternative incremental computation (AIC) method. The federal percentages are 2.65%, 3.2%, and 3.75%, increased to 3%, 4%, and 5%, respectively, effective generally for tax years ending after 2006. California has not adopted federal amendments enacted by the EESA that repeal the alternative incremental credit effective beginning with the 2009 taxable year. Thus, unless California adopts these federal amendments, taxpayers will still be able to utilize the AIC method for purposes of calculating their California research and development credit.

— California has not conformed to TRHCA amendments that authorize the use of a third method, the alternative simplified credit, generally effective for federal purposes in tax years ending after 2006.

— California does not allow a credit against personal income tax for basic research payments. Under federal law, a credit equal to 20% of basic research payments is allowed.

— Research must be conducted in California to qualify for the California credit. Federal law provides that research must be conducted in the United States, Puerto Rico, or other U.S. possessions.

— The California credit may be carried over. The federal credit is part of the general business credit subject to the limitations imposed by IRC Sec. 38.

— For purposes of determining the base amount under California law, only the gross receipts from the sale of property that is held primarily for sale to customers in the ordinary course of the taxpayer's trade or business and delivered or shipped to a purchaser within California, regardless of F.O.B. point or other conditions of sale, may be taken into account.

— California law, but not federal law, disallows the credit for expenses incurred to purchase property for which a sales and use tax exemption for teleproduction or other postproduction property is claimed (¶1507).

— California did not incorporate the federal suspension periods of July 1, 1999—September 30, 2000, and October 1, 2000—September 30, 2001, that were enacted by the Tax Relief Extension Act of 1999.

— California has not adopted amendments made by the Energy Tax Incentives Act of 2005 that (1) allow a taxpayer to claim 20% of amounts paid or incurred by the taxpayer during the tax year to an energy research consortium and (2) repeal the limitation on contract research expenses paid to eligible small businesses, universities, and federal laboratories for qualified energy research. These amendments are effective for federal purposes for amounts paid or incurred after August 8, 2005, in tax years ending after such date.

— California does not adopt provisions enacted by the EESA that clarify the calculation of the credit in a year of the credit's termination.

For additional details concerning this credit, taxpayers should consult FTB Pub. 1082, *Research and Development Credit: Frequently Asked Questions*, FTB, revised August 2002)

Practitioner Comment: Alternative Simplified Method Not Adopted

California does not conform to the Tax Relief Acts of 2006, which, among other things, increased the rates under the alternative incremental credit (AIC) election as well as established a third method—the Alternative Simplified Credit Method (or "ASCM"). For many taxpayers that are limited under the standard calculation, the ASCM provides a higher credit than under the AIC method.

Bruce Daigh, Chris Whitney, Contributing Editors

• *Alternative incremental research credit election*

If a taxpayer's "base amount" is higher than the taxpayer's current qualified research expenses, the taxpayer may not qualify for the regular research credit, but may be eligible to receive the benefit of the alternative incremental credit (AIC); see third item above. The AIC is elected and claimed on the California return. Taxpayers may want to attach a statement to their California returns indicating that they are making the AIC election, although this is not required.

Once taxpayers make the AIC election, they are required to continue using the AIC for California purposes until they obtain permission from the FTB to revoke the election. They must receive permission from the FTB to revoke the California AIC election even if their federal AIC is revoked.

Revocation of an election can only be granted on a current or prospective basis. Federal Form 3115, Application for Change in Accounting Method, or federal Form 1128, Application to Adopt, Change, or Retain a Tax Year, can be used to request the change. Federal Form 3115 or Federal Form 1128 should be completed using the appropriate California tax information, including the taxpayer's California Corporate Number (CCN) at the top of page 1. Any reference on these forms, or their instructions, to the Internal Revenue Code should be read as referring to the corresponding Revenue and Taxation Code section, if it exists. A cover letter, with the taxpayer's name and CCN, should be attached to the front of Form 3115 or Form 1128, with an indication that a "Change in Accounting Period" or a "Change in Accounting Method" is being requested. Requests should be sent to the Franchise Tax Board, Change in Accounting Periods and Methods Coordinator, P.O. Box 1998, Sacramento, CA 95812. (*Tax News*, California Franchise Tax Board, September 2006)

Practitioner Comment: Federal Election Not Binding

Similar to its federal counterpart (IRC Sec. 41), the California statute imposes a binding election on taxpayers who elect the three-tier alternative incremental credit (AIC), unless the Franchise Tax Board consents to a revocation. However, a state taxpayer is not bound by its federal election. Therefore, a taxpayer could claim the qualified research and development credit under federal law and the three-tier AIC under state law, or vice versa.

Chris Micheli, Esq., Carpenter, Snodgrass & Associates, Sacramento, CA

• *Special rules for start-up companies*

California conforms to federal law providing special rules to determine the fixed-base percentage used in determining the amount of the credit that may be claimed by start-up companies. (Sec. 17052.12, Rev. & Tax. Code)

Comment: Temporary Limitation on Credit Amounts

See ¶125 for a discussion of the 50% limitation on the amount of business credits and credit carryovers that may be claimed during the 2008 and 2009 taxable years. (Sec. 17039.2, Rev. & Tax. Code)

• *Interaction with research deduction*

For both California and federal purposes, taxpayers do not have the option of electing to forego the research and development credit. Accordingly, taxpayers may not avoid the reduction in the research expense deduction that is required whenever the research expense credit is claimed (¶331, 336). (Sec. 17052.12, Rev. & Tax. Code)

¶151 Ultra-Low Sulfur Diesel Fuel Credit

Law: Sec. 17053.62 (CCH CALIFORNIA TAX REPORTS ¶16-887).

Comparable Federal: Secs. 45H (CCH U.S. MASTER TAX GUIDE ¶1344E).

California Form: FTB 3511 (Environmental Tax Credit)

For taxable years beginning before 2018, an environmental tax credit is available for ultra-low sulfur diesel fuel produced by a qualified small refiner at a California facility. (Sec. 17053.62, Rev. & Tax. Code) The credit is similar to the federal credit allowed under IRC Sec. 45H, except for the following differences:

— the credit is limited to ultra-low sulfur diesel fuel produced at a California facility;

— California's definition of a "small refiner" is more restrictive;

— the period in which the costs must be incurred to qualify for the credit is different; and

— the certification procedures may be different (see below).

For purposes of the California credit, the qualified capital costs must be incurred during the period beginning January 1, 2004, and ending on May 31, 2007. (Sec. 17053.62(c)(6), Rev. & Tax. Code) Costs qualify for the federal credit if incurred during the period beginning January 1, 2003, and ending on the earlier of (1) the date that is one year after the date by which the taxpayer must comply with the applicable Environmental Protection Agency (EPA) regulations or (2) December 31, 2009.

Both the California credit and the federal credit may be claimed for diesel fuel with a sulfur content of 15 parts per million or less. In addition, for purposes of the California credit, it may also be rebuttably presumed that ultra-low sulfur diesel fuel for which the credit may be claimed includes vehicular diesel fuel produced and sold by a small refiner (1) after May 31, 2006, and (2) before June 2006 if the refiner proves that the fuel meets applicable California Air Resources Board (CARB) regulations. The presumption that the fuel sold by a small refiner after May 31, 2006, qualifies for the credit may be rebutted by the CARB. (Sec. 17053.62(c)(7), Rev. & Tax. Code)

• *Credit amount*

The credit is equal to five cents for each gallon of ultra-low sulfur diesel fuel produced during the taxable year. (Sec. 17053.62(a), Rev. & Tax. Code) The credit may not exceed 25% of the qualified capital costs certified by the U.S. Treasury Secretary or the CARB that are incurred by the small refiner with respect to each facility, reduced by the aggregate ultra-low sulfur diesel fuel credits for all prior taxable years with respect to that facility. (Sec. 17053.62(b), Rev. & Tax. Code)

Comment: Temporary Limitation on Credit Amounts

See ¶125 for a discussion of the 50% limitation on the amount of business credits and credit carryovers that may be claimed during the 2008 and 2009 taxable years. (Sec. 17039.2, Rev. & Tax. Code)

• *Planning considerations*

Certification.— Prior to claiming the credit, taxpayers must receive certification from the CARB or the U.S. Secretary of the Treasury, in consultation with the EPA, that the qualified capital costs for which the taxpayer is claiming the credit are in compliance with the applicable CARB or EPA regulations. However, certification by the U.S. Secretary of the Treasury may not be sufficient if the CARB demonstrates that the fuel produced does not meet CARB regulations. (Sec. 17053.62(c)(2), Rev. & Tax. Code) The Instructions to the FTB 3511, Environmental Tax Credit, state that the taxpayer must receive certification from the CARB.

Basis.— The increase in basis that results from expenditures for which the credit is claimed must be reduced by the amount of the credit taken. (Sec. 17053.62(d)), Rev. & Tax. Code)

Exclusivity provision.—No other deduction may be claimed for the expenses for which the credit is taken. (Sec. 17053.62(e), Rev. & Tax. Code)

Carryforward provisions.—Unused credit may be carried over for up to 10 years. (Sec. 17053.62(f), Rev. & Tax. Code)

Recapture provisions.—The credit is subject to recapture if a small refiner sells, transfers, or otherwise disposes of a facility within five years of the taxable year during which it first claimed the credit. (Sec. 17053.62(g), Rev. & Tax. Code)

¶152 Credit for Prior Year Minimum Tax

Law: Sec. 17063 (CCH CALIFORNIA TAX REPORTS ¶15-440).

Comparable Federal: Sec. 53 (CCH U.S. MASTER TAX GUIDE ¶1370).

California Form: FTB 3510 (Credit for Prior Year Alternative Minimum Tax - Individuals or Fiduciaries).

California allows a credit in the form of a carryover to taxpayers who have incurred California alternative minimum tax in prior years but not in the current tax year. (Sec. 17063, Rev. & Tax. Code)

The credit is computed in the same manner as the federal credit under IRC Sec. 53 ("credit for prior year minimum tax") with the substitution of certain California figures in place of the federal. In addition, as a result of California's current IRC conformity date (¶103), California does not incorporate amendments made by the Tax Relief and Health Care Act of 2006, the Tax Technical Corrections Act of 2007, and the Emergency Economic Stabilization Act of 2008 that (1) create a refundable AMT credit for individuals with a long-term unused minimum tax credit, applicable for federal purposes to tax years beginning after December 20, 2006, and beginning before January 1, 2013, and (2) allow for an abatement of any outstanding underpayment of tax, including penalties and interest, associated with the exercise of an incentive stock option.

Both the federal and California credits are based on the amount of alternative minimum tax paid on "deferral preferences" (items that defer tax liability) as distinct from "exclusion items" (items that permanently reduce tax liability).

The credit is computed on FTB 3510, and for a taxpayer claiming this credit for the first time, most of the figures needed for the computation come from Schedule P (540) of the prior year's California personal income tax return. The credit is equivalent to the adjusted net minimum tax for all prior taxable years beginning after 1986, reduced by the minimum tax credit for all such prior taxable years. However, the credit may not exceed the excess of the following:

— the California regular tax reduced by all credits except (1) refundable credits without carryover provisions and (2) any credit that reduces the tax below the tentative minimum tax over

— the tentative minimum tax for the taxable year (¶117).

The adjusted net minimum tax for any taxable year is the taxpayer's minimum tax for that year, reduced by a theoretical minimum tax, assuming that only the adjustments and preferences specified in IRC Sec. 53(d)(1)(B)(ii) and, for California tax purposes only, the California items of tax preference relating to small business stock.

Unused credit may be carried forward indefinitely.

Comment: Temporary Limitation on Credit Amounts

See ¶125 for a discussion of the 50% limitation on the amount of business credits and credit carryovers that may be claimed during the 2008 and 2009 taxable years. (Sec. 17039.2, Rev. & Tax. Code)

• *Nonresidents and part-year residents*

Nonresidents and part-year residents prorate the credit on the basis of California taxable income. (Sec. 17055, Rev. & Tax. Code) This ratio is computed on FTB 3510; see ¶116 for a more detailed discussion.

¶153 Enhanced Oil Recovery Credit

Law: Sec. 17052.8 (CCH CALIFORNIA TAX REPORTS ¶16-953).

Comparable Federal: Sec. 43 (CCH U.S. MASTER TAX GUIDE ¶1336).

California Form: FTB 3546 (Enhanced Oil Recovery Credit).

California allows certain independent oil producers a credit equal to 1/3 of the enhanced oil recovery credit allowed under federal law. Thus, a California credit is allowed in an amount equal to up to 5% of the taxpayer's qualified costs attributable to qualified enhanced oil recovery projects. However, California modifies the federal definition of "qualified enhanced oil recovery project" to include only projects located within California. (Sec. 17052.8, Rev. & Tax. Code)

CCH Practice Note: Credit Unavailable in 2006 Through 2008

As a result of current oil prices, the credit is unavailable for both California and federal purposes for the 2006 through 2008 taxable years.

• *"Qualified costs" defined*

Qualified costs include the following:

— amounts paid or incurred for tangible property that is an integral part of a qualified enhanced oil recovery project and for which depreciation or amortization is allowed;

— intangible drilling and development costs that are paid or incurred in connection with a qualified enhanced oil recovery project and that a taxpayer may elect to capitalize and amortize under state law; and

— tertiary injectant expenses paid or incurred with respect to a qualified enhanced oil recovery project. (Sec. 17052.8, Rev. & Tax. Code)

CCH Comment: Current Deduction of Tertiary Injectant Costs

California does not conform to federal law (IRC Sec. 193) allowing taxpayers to currently deduct tertiary injectant costs. Consequently, such costs must be capitalized and deducted through depreciation for California personal income tax purposes (Instructions, FTB 3546, Enhanced Oil Recovery Credit).

• *Limitations*

The credit is not available to certain retailers, refiners, and related persons who are not eligible for the percentage depletion specifically allowed to independent producers and royalty owners. (Sec. 17052.8, Rev. & Tax. Code)

No deduction is allowed for costs for which the credit is allowed. Also, the basis of any property for which a credit is allowed must be reduced by the amount of the credit attributable to the property.

Comment: Temporary Limitation on Credit Amounts

See ¶125 for a discussion of the 50% limitation on the amount of business credits and credit carryovers that may be claimed during the 2008 and 2009 taxable years. (Sec. 17039.2, Rev. & Tax. Code)

• *Federal election binding*

A federal election not to have the credit apply is binding and irrevocable for California purposes. Also, a taxpayer must make an election between credits if the taxpayer's costs qualify for another credit. (Sec. 17052.8, Rev. & Tax. Code)

• *Carryover*

Any amount of the credit exceeding "net tax" for the taxable year may be carried forward for up to 15 years. (Sec. 17052.8, Rev. & Tax. Code)

For the 2006 through 2008 taxable years, when the credit is unavailable, form FTB 3546 will continue to be used for carryover or recapture of the credit.

¶154 Prison Inmate Labor Credit

Law: Sec. 17053.6 (CCH CALIFORNIA TAX REPORTS ¶16-875).

Comparable Federal: None.

California Form: FTB 3507 (Prison Inmate Labor Credit).

California allows a credit equal to 10% of the wages paid to prison inmates employed under a prisoner employment joint venture agreement with the Director of Corrections. The credit is in addition to any other deduction to which the employer is entitled. (Sec. 17053.6, Rev. & Tax. Code) According to the Instructions to FTB 3507, the credit may only be claimed for wages paid to an individual who was hired after the joint venture agreement was executed.

There is no carryover allowed for unused credits.

Comment: Temporary Limitation on Credit Amounts

See ¶125 for a discussion of the 50% limitation on the amount of business credits and credit carryovers that may be claimed during the 2008 and 2009 taxable years. (Sec. 17039.2, Rev. & Tax. Code)

¶155 Community Development Investment Credit

Law: Sec. 17053.57, Rev. & Tax. Code; Sec. 32301, Financial Code (CCH CALIFORNIA TAX REPORTS ¶16-831).

Comparable Federal: Sec. 38 (CCH U.S. MASTER TAX GUIDE ¶1325).

California Forms: Form 540 (California Resident Income Tax Return), Sch. P (540) (Alternative Minimum Tax and Credit Limitations - Residents).

For taxable years beginning before 2012, a nonrefundable credit is available in an amount equal to 20% of each qualified investment made into a community development financial institution. However, the amount that may be claimed by a taxpayer is limited to the amount certified by the California Organized Investment Network (COIN). (Sec. 17053.57, Rev. & Tax. Code)

A "community development financial institution" (CDFI) is a private financial institution located in California that (1) is certified by COIN; (2) has community development as its primary mission; and (3) makes loans in California urban, rural, or reservation-based communities. The State Assistance Fund for Enterprises, Business, and Industrial Development Corporation (SAFE-BIDCO) is a community development financial institution for purposes of this credit.

A "qualified investment" is an investment that does not earn interest, or an equity investment or equity-like investment, of $50,000 or more. The investment must be made for at least 60 months. The entire credit previously claimed is subject to recapture if the qualified investment is withdrawn before the end of the 60-month period and not reinvested in another CDFI within 60 days. If a qualified investment is reduced before the end of the 60-month period, but not below $50,000, an amount equal to 20% of the total reduction will be recaptured.

The aggregate credits against personal income tax, corporation franchise or income tax, and insurance gross premiums tax may not exceed $10 million annually. However, unallowed credits from previous years may be added to the $10 million limit. Furthermore, unused credit may be carried forward for the next four taxable years.

Comment: Temporary Limitation on Credit Amounts

See ¶125 for a discussion of the 50% limitation on the amount of business credits and credit carryovers that may be claimed during the 2008 and 2009 taxable years. (Sec. 17039.2, Rev. & Tax. Code)

PERSONAL INCOME TAX

CHAPTER 2

GROSS INCOME

¶ 201 Gross Income—In General

Law: Secs. 17071, 17072, 17081, 17083, 17087, 17131-36, 17139.5, 17141, 17147.7, 17151, 17153.5, 17154 (CCH CALIFORNIA TAX REPORTS ¶ 15-510, 16-060).

Comparable Federal: Secs. 61, 62, 84-86, 88, 90, 120, 125-27, 129-132, 136, 139A (CCH U.S. MASTER TAX GUIDE ¶ 700, 716, 722, 861, 863, 869, 871, 881, 883, 884, 1005).

California Forms: Sch. CA (540) (California Adjustments - Residents), Sch. CA (540NR) (California Adjustments - Nonresidents or Part-Year Residents), Sch. D (Capital Gain or Loss Adjustment), Sch. D-1 (Sales of Business Property).

California conforms, as a general rule, to most of the federal provisions concerning gross income as of the current IRC tie-in date (¶ 103).

Practice Tip: Treatment of Federal Rebates

The federal economic stimulus payments (rebates) issued to taxpayers beginning in May 2008 are not subject to California personal income taxes. Furthermore, taxpayers who filed federal income tax returns solely to qualify for these rebates were not required to file California personal income tax returns. (*Announcement*, California Franchise Tax Board, March 3, 2008)

The following paragraphs will detail the California-federal differences as to what is included in gross income for the 2008 taxable year.

"Gross income" is broadly defined to include income derived from any source whatever, except as otherwise specifically provided by statute.

Practice Pointer: SBE Audits

Taxpayers who undergo a sales and use tax audit by the State Board of Equalization (SBE) should be aware that the SBE provides the FTB with copies of sales and use tax audit reports for the audits that result in adjustments of additional gross receipts (total sales). The FTB reviews these sales and use tax reports to determine if an income tax adjustment is warranted. (*Tax News*, California Franchise Tax Board, November 2008)

The California law incorporates the federal definition by reference. This means that the same items are included under both laws, unless a specific exception is spelled out. However, even if an item is included in both California and federal gross income, the amounts to be included may differ because of prior law or other differences. The following list highlights differences in California and federal gross income that should be reported on Sch. CA (540) or Sch. CA (540NR) (other relevant forms are indicated):

— California does not include in income the following benefits, which are taxed to some extent under federal law: social security, unemployment, paid family leave, and railroad retirement benefits, which include pensions, ridesharing benefits, and sick pay. (Sec. 17087, Rev. & Tax. Code)

— Income from certain annuities and pension and profit-sharing plans (¶205, ¶206).

— Taxable and nontaxable interest (¶217).

— California does not tax state income tax refunds. (FTB Pub. 1001, Supplemental Guidelines to California Adjustments)

— Nonresident's military compensation attributable to resident spouse (¶225).

— Dividends and other corporate distributions (¶226).

— Patronage allocations from cooperatives (¶232).

— Sales and exchanges (Sch. D, Sch. D-1, Sch. D (541)) (¶229 and ¶501 et seq.).

— Income of nonresidents (Form 540NR, Sch. CA (540NR)) (¶231).

— Certain income received by Native Americans (¶254).

— California does not follow the special federal provisions for Domestic International Sales Corporations (DISCs), personal holding companies, foreign investment companies, foreign trusts, etc. (Sec. 17024.5(b), Rev. & Tax. Code)

— California qualified stock options (¶207).

— Income from investments in depressed areas (FTB 3805Z and FTB 3806) (¶240).

— Compensation received by an employee for participating in a ridesharing arrangement (¶241).

— California provides an exclusion for income derived from an obligation of a Community Energy Authority under certain provisions of the California Government Code.

— Winnings from the California lottery, including amounts received pursuant to an assignment, are exempt from California tax. Such winnings are subject to federal tax as wagering gains, except to the extent that they may be offset by wagering losses (¶307).

However, income taxes are imposed on the income that retailers realize on the sale of lottery tickets. This also includes extra cash bonuses that the Lottery Commission pays to lottery game retailers, according to percentages of lottery prizes, because they are compensation for the sale of lottery tickets (*Letter* , FTB, CCH CALIFORNIA TAX REPORTS ¶16-305.40).

— Any amount received by the consumer for recycling empty beverage containers is exempt from California tax. (Sec. 17153.5, Rev. & Tax. Code)

— Certain water conservation rebates are treated as refunds or price adjustments rather than as income (¶244).

— Rewards received from a government authorized crime hotline (¶246).

— Certain compensation received by Holocaust and internment victims (¶248).

— Compensation paid by California to an individual who sustained pecuniary injury as a result of an erroneous criminal conviction and incarceration is excluded for California purposes, but not federal purposes, provided the individual did not contribute to his or her arrest. (Sec. 17157, Rev. & Tax. Code)

— Health savings accounts (¶219, ¶247).

— Prescription drug subsidies (¶252).

California does not incorporate the domestic production activity deduction (see ¶301).

In addition, California does not incorporate federal incentives available to businesses located in renewal communities, including the gross income exclusion of capital gain from the sale or exchange of a "qualified community asset" held for more than five years and acquired after 2001 and before 2010.

• *Cafeteria plans*

Although California generally incorporates the federal treatment of cafeteria plans, including the treatment and availability of health and dependent flexible spending accounts, as a result of California's current federal conformity date (¶103), California does not follow federal amendments made by the Heroes Earnings Assistance and Relief Tax Act of 2008 that exclude from gross income distributions of all or a portion of the balance in a health flexible spending arrangement if the individual is a reservist who has been called to active duty for a specified period of time. Consequently, such income is included in California gross income.

¶202 Definition of "Adjusted Gross Income"

Law: Sec. 17072 (CCH CALIFORNIA TAX REPORTS ¶15-510).

Comparable Federal: Secs. 62 (CCH U.S. MASTER TAX GUIDE ¶1005, 1006).

The California definition of "adjusted gross income" incorporates the federal definition as of a fixed date (¶103), except that California does not incorporate the federal above-the line deduction for qualified expenses incurred by elementary and secondary school teachers, instructors, counselors, principals, or aides during the 2002 through 2009 tax years. (Sec. 17072, Rev. & Tax. Code)

Practice Pointer: Treatment of Registered Domestic Partners/Same Sex Married Couples

Beginning with the 2007 taxable year, registered domestic partners (RDPs) (see ¶119) must file returns jointly or separately by applying the same standards as are applied to married taxpayers under federal income tax law. (Sec. 18521, Rev. & Tax. Code) For purposes of computing their adjusted gross income (AGI) and limitations based on AGI, a RDP or former RDP should use a pro forma federal return, treating the RDP or former RDP as a spouse or former spouse and using the same filing status that was used on the state tax return for the same taxable year. Alternatively, RDPs may use the worksheets provided in FTB Pub. 737, Tax Information for Registered Domestic Partners. (Sec. 17024.5(h), Rev. & Tax. Code)

At the time this book went to press, the FTB had not yet determined the tax treatment of same-sex couples that married after the California Supreme Court ruled that such couples could legally marry and before the California voters passed Proposition 8 repealing such right. See ¶119 for details.

¶203 Taxable Income

Law: Secs. 17073, 17073.5 (CCH CALIFORNIA TAX REPORTS ¶15-510, 15-535).

Comparable Federal: Sec. 63 (CCH U.S. MASTER TAX GUIDE ¶124, 126).

The federal law defining "taxable income" is incorporated in the California law by reference. With the following exceptions listed below, California law is the same as federal law as of the current IRC tie-in date (¶103):

— California allows no deduction for personal exemptions. Instead, California law allows personal exemption credits (¶113).

— California standard deduction amounts are different from the federal (¶335).

— California has not adopted the federal additional standard deductions for aged and blind individuals (¶335). However, California provides additional personal exemption credits for such taxpayers (¶113).

Taking into account these differences, California "taxable income" may be defined briefly as adjusted gross income reduced either by the standard deduction or by itemized deductions.

¶204 Alimony

Law: Sec. 17081 (CCH CALIFORNIA TAX REPORTS ¶15-610).

Comparable Federal: Sec. 71 (CCH U.S. MASTER TAX GUIDE ¶771).

California Form: Sch. CA (540) (California Adjustments - Residents).

California law is generally the same as federal law as of the current IRC tie-in date (¶103), except with respect to alimony received by a nonresident alien. Generally, alimony and separate maintenance payments received pursuant to a divorce, dissolution, or legal separation are taxable to the spouse who receives the payments. Any amount received for support of minor children is not taxable. (Sec. 17081, Rev. & Tax. Code)

Alimony paid by a California resident to a nonresident is not taxable to the recipient (¶323). Alimony paid either by a nonresident or by a part-year resident during a period of nonresidence is deductible on a prorated basis (¶323, ¶337).

Alimony Received or Paid by Registered Domestic Partners (RDPs)

If a court orders termination of a registered domestic partnership and a California Family Law Court awards spousal support that satisfies the requirements under tax law for alimony, the payments are taxable to the payee and deductible by the payor for California purposes. However, federal treatment of these payments is uncertain. An RDP receiving alimony not included in federal income should include that amount on line 11, column C, of his or her California RDP Adjustments Worksheet. An RDP paying alimony not included in the RDP's adjustments to income for federal purposes should enter that amount on line 31, column C, of his or her California RDP Adjustments Worksheet, as a positive amount. (FTB Pub. 737, Tax Information for Registered Domestic Partners)

In *Appeal of Karapetian* (2004) (CCH CALIFORNIA TAX REPORTS ¶15-610.45), the State Board of Equalization (SBE) followed the IRS's ruling in *Baxter v. Commissioner,* T.C. Memo 1999-190, and held that payment of mortgage interest by a former husband to his ex-wife pursuant to a marital settlement agreement was taxable alimony because the marital settlement agreement provided that the obligation of the former husband to make mortgage payments on the taxpayer's home would cease upon her death. Because the payments were taxable alimony, the ex-wife was not entitled to deduct those payments as qualified residence interest. The payments were deductible only by the former husband.

In *Appeal of Sara J. Palevsky* (1979) (CCH CALIFORNIA TAX REPORTS ¶15-610.205), the SBE held that certain payments received under a property settlement agreement were fully taxable, despite the fact that the payor spouse had agreed to claim an income tax deduction for only two-thirds of the payments.

¶205 Annuities

Law: Secs. 17024.5, 17081, 17085, 17087, 17131 (CCH CALIFORNIA TAX REPORTS ¶15-800, 16-345).

Comparable Federal: Secs. 72, 122 (CCH U.S. MASTER TAX GUIDE ¶817—845, 891).

California law is substantially the same as federal law as of California's current federal conformity date (see ¶103). (Sec. 17081, Rev. & Tax. Code; Sec. 17085, Rev. & Tax. Code) However, California does not incorporate the federal provision governing the basis application rules for amounts contributed to an annuity as part of the compensation for services performed by a nonresident alien, effective for distributions made after October 21, 2004. California does not incorporate IRC provisions related to nonresident aliens. (Sec. 17024.5(b), Rev. & Tax. Code)

In addition, California has not incorporated amendments made to IRC Sec. 72(e) by the Pension Protection Act of 2006 (P.L. 109-280) that exclude from taxable distributions from annuity and life insurance contracts the cost of a qualified long-term care insurance coverage rider that is charged against the cash or cash surrender value of the contract. The amendments are effective for federal purposes for contracts issued after 1996, but only with respect to tax years beginning after 2009.

California and federal law provide, in general, that amounts paid under an annuity contract must be included in gross income. However, amounts representing a return of capital may be excluded. The excludable portion is determined by dividing the cost of the annuity by the expected return and multiplying the result by the annuity payment received. Detailed rules are provided for various special situations.

See ¶215 for a discussion of the rules applicable when an annuity is transferred for consideration. A discussion of the penalty on premature distributions is at ¶206.

• *Self-employed retirement plans, IRAs*

For discussion of treatment of annuities or other payments received under a self-employed retirement plan or an individual retirement account, see ¶206.

• *Annuities received under Railroad Retirement Act*

Annuity or pension payments received under the federal Railroad Retirement Act are exempt from California tax. (Sec. 17087, Rev. & Tax. Code)

• *Inherited annuity*

See ¶405 for discussion of the *Kelsey* case, where annuity income earned by a decedent outside California was taxed to a survivor under the rules for income from annuities, although the income was classified as "income in respect of a decedent" and could not have been taxed to the decedent if he had become a California resident.

• *Annuities held by non-natural persons*

Annuities held by partnerships, trusts, and other non-natural persons are not entitled to the same preferential treatment as are annuities held by individuals. Instead, tax is imposed on the excess of

— the sum of the net surrender value of the contract at the end of the tax year plus any amounts distributed under the contract to date, over

— the investment in the contract (the aggregate amount of premiums paid under the contract minus policyholder dividends or the aggregate amounts received under the contract that have not been included in income).

This special rule applies for both California and federal purposes with respect to amounts invested in annuity contracts after February 28, 1986. (Sec. 17081, Rev. & Tax. Code; Sec. 17085, Rev. & Tax. Code)

¶206 Income from Pension and Profit-Sharing Plans

Law: Secs. 17085, 17501, 17501.5, 17501.7, 17504, 17506, 17507, 17507.6, 17551, 17952.5, 23712 (CCH CALIFORNIA TAX REPORTS ¶16-685, 15-800, 16-345, 16-545).

Comparable Federal: Secs. 72, 401, 402-03, 408-20, 457, 530 (CCH U.S. MASTER TAX GUIDE ¶817 et seq., 898, 2153 et seq.).

California Forms: Sch. G-1 (Tax on Lump-Sum Distributions), FTB 3805P (Additional Taxes on Qualified Plans (Including IRAs) and Other Tax-Favored Accounts).

The general plan of taxing income from pension and profit-sharing plans is the same under California law and federal law as amended to date. California incorporates federal law relating to pension, profit-sharing, stock bonus plans, etc., unless otherwise provided, without regard to taxable year to the same extent as applicable for federal purposes. (Sec. 17501, Rev. & Tax. Code)

CCH Comment: Registered Domestic Partnerships

Although registered domestic partners (RDPs) or former RDPs are generally required to be treated as married taxpayers or former spouses under California income and franchise tax laws, an RDP will not be treated as a spouse if such treatment would result in disqualification of a federally qualified deferred compensation plan or disqualification of tax-favored accounts, such as individual retirement accounts, Archer medical savings accounts, qualified tuition programs, or Coverdell education savings accounts. (Sec. 17021.7, Rev. & Tax. Code)

An RDP may have an adjustment to income if the RDP has a California-only basis in an IRA, which is recoverable from an IRA distribution. For example, an RDP may have a California-only basis in an IRA if the RDP's partner is covered by an employer-provided retirement plan and, based on the RDPs' combined adjusted gross income, the available deduction for an IRA contribution is reduced for California income tax purposes. The amount disallowed for the IRA contribution would create a California-only basis in the IRA. RDPs must keep track of their California-only basis in order to recover it tax-free from IRA distributions reported in future years. (FTB Pub. 737, Tax Information for Registered Domestic Partners)

Because California incorporates the deferred compensation provisions as amended to date, California conforms to post-2005 federal amendments that allow penalty-free early distributions to victims of Hurricane Katrina, allow three-year income averaging for such distributions, increase the allowable amount that may be borrowed, delay loan payment due dates, and treat as a rollover amounts withdrawn for a first-time home purchase before Katrina which purchase could not be completed because of Katrina.

CCH Caution Note: Potential Future Differences

California limits the maximum amount of elective deferrals that may be excluded from gross income under IRC Sec. 402(g), as incorporated, to the maximum amount established under the Economic Growth and Tax Relief Reconciliation Act of 2001 and the Job Creation and Worker Assistance Act of 2002. The basis in any plan, account, or annuity must be increased for California income tax purposes to reflect the amount of elective deferrals not excluded. Any income not excludable as a result of California's limitation will be includible in the gross income of the individual for whose benefit the plan or account was established in the year the income is distributed. Similar limits apply to deferred compensation under IRC Sec. 457, relating to deferred compensation salary reduction plans for state, municipal, and tax-exempt organization employees.

Generally, with the exception of qualified charitable distributions from IRAs made in 2006 through 2009, both California and federal laws tax benefits received under qualified pension or profit-sharing plans to the employee only when actually distributed to the employee. Such distributions are usually taxed as though they were an annuity, under the rules set forth in ¶205, the consideration for which is the amount (if any) contributed by the employee under the plan. Certain nonforfeitable rights to receive annuities are taxed in the year in which the employer pays for the annuity contract. Certain lump-sum distributions are subject to special treatment, as explained below. See also ¶330.

Qualified retirement income received by a former California resident is not taxable by California. (Sec. 17952.5, Rev. & Tax. Code) See ¶405 for a more detailed discussion.

• *Special rules for some organizations*

Special rules are provided for the taxation of employee annuities where the employer is a tax-exempt charitable-type organization or school, where the plan is not subject to the rules discussed above. Such annuities are only partially taxable, under a formula providing for an "exclusion allowance." The California rules are the same as the federal rules. (Sec. 17551, Rev. & Tax. Code)

• *Nonqualified plans*

Both California and federal laws provide special rules for taxing the beneficiary of a *nonqualified* employee pension or profit-sharing plan or annuity, in cases where the employee's rights are forfeitable at the time the employer's contribution is made. The general effect is to tax the employee in the year the employee's rights are no longer subject to a substantial risk of forfeiture. (Sec. 17501, Rev. & Tax. Code) California has not incorporated the federal provision (IRC Sec. 457A) that requires the current inclusion in income of some deferred compensation paid by foreign corporations when there is no substantial risk of forfeiture of the rights to the compensation, applicable for federal purposes to amounts deferred that are attributable to services performed after 2008.

Under both California and federal law, if certain operational or design failures occur in a nonqualified deferred compensation plan, the deferred amounts, including compensation deferred under the plan in prior years and notional or actual income attributable to the deferred compensation, is included in the affected plan participants' gross income immediately unless it is still subject to a substantial risk of forfeiture. The tax on the compensation required to be included is increased by interest on the portion of the compensation that was deferred in prior years and by an amount equal to 20% of the compensation required to be included. The interest is the amount of interest at the underpayment rate plus one percentage point on the underpayments that would have occurred had the deferred compensation been includible in gross income for the tax year in which it was deferred or, if later, the first tax year in which it was not subject to a substantial risk of forfeiture.

Noncompliance With IRC Sec. 409A Requirements

The FTB is following Internal Revenue Service (IRS) Notice 2007-100, which allows taxpayers to correct certain unintentional operational failures of nonqualified deferred compensation plans in order to comply with IRC Sec. 409A. Unlike the IRS requirement that taxpayers submit attachments to their federal income tax returns stating that they are relying upon Notice 2007-100 with respect to a correction of a failure to comply with Sec. 409A, the FTB only requires taxpayers to retain the statements instead of submitting them with their California tax returns. (*Announcement*, California Franchise Tax Board, April 18, 2008)

• *Lump-sum distributions*

If an employee's benefits are paid in one taxable year of the employee because of death or termination of employment, the taxable amount is subject to special treatment as a "lump-sum distribution." The taxable amount is the total distribution less (1) employee contributions and (2) any unrealized appreciation on employer securities included in the distribution. (Sec. 17501, Rev. & Tax. Code)

Both California and federal law have eliminated capital gain treatment for lump-sum distributions made after 1986 that are at least partially attributable to pre-1974 participation in a qualified pension plan. However, a taxpayer who reached age 50 before 1986 may elect to apply an exception that allows capital gain treatment.

For tax years beginning before 2000, both California and federal law allowed five-year averaging for a single lump-sum distribution received by an individual who has attained the age of $59^1/_2$. The five-year averaging method is repealed for tax years beginning after 1999. Prior law rules applicable to individuals who attained age 50 before 1986 remain in effect. (Sec. 17504, Rev. & Tax. Code)

• *Self-employed plans*

For purposes of both federal law and California law, the rules for self-employed plans are generally the same as for employee plans, as set forth above. However, there will be differences in the *amounts* taxable in California and federal returns because of differences in the deductibility of contributions in prior years. As explained at ¶330, for pre-1987 tax years, California allowed smaller deductions than federal. Also, the interest element in the redemption of certain federal retirement bonds issued before 1984 was recoverable tax-free for California purposes. (Sec. 17085, Rev. & Tax. Code; Sec. 17507, Rev. & Tax. Code)

The difference between allowable California and federal contributions is recoverable free of California tax. See below for summary of amounts recoverable tax-free.

As to the *timing* of the tax-free recovery, where distributions are received over a period of years, it has been the Franchise Tax Board's (FTB) policy to treat the amounts involved as part of the "investment in the contract" that is recoverable tax-free under the annuity rules.

For a discussion of the taxability of distributions from self-employed plans when the taxpayer's status changed from resident to nonresident, or vice-versa, see ¶405.

• *Individual retirement accounts*

The California treatment of distributions from IRAs is the same as the federal, except that California permits tax-free recovery of the following:

— Contributions that were not allowed as California deductions (see ¶330).

— Interest earned in 1975 or 1976 on a 1975 contribution, as explained below.

(Sec. 17507, Rev. & Tax. Code)

Practice Note: Distributions from IRAs to Health Savings Accounts

Although California generally conforms to federal deferred compensation provisions as amended to date, because California does not recognize health savings accounts (HSAs) (see ¶247) it does not conform to an amendment made to IRC Sec. 408 that authorizes a one-time tax-free distribution from an IRA to an HSA, effective for tax years beginning after 2006. Consequently, a California taxpayer who makes such a distribution is required to include the distribution in his or her gross income and the distribution is subject to California's penalty on premature withdrawals.

As to the *timing* of the tax-free recovery of amounts contributed prior to 1987 or after 2006, the amount of contributions not allowed as California deductions is considered to be the cost basis of the IRA account and no income is reportable for California purposes until the basis is recovered. Each year, the amount reportable federally is reduced for California purposes by California basis until such basis is recovered.

As for the recovery of post-1986 contributions, or at the election of the taxpayer, contributions made after July 1, 1986, the federal annuity rule is adopted in California and the portion of each distribution recognized federally is recognized for California purposes. Under this rule, the amount invested is recovered ratably, depending on the period of expected return. (Sec. 17501, Rev. & Tax. Code)

Tax-free basis of IRA account of taxpayers who have changed residency: A nonresident is treated as though he or she were a resident for all items of deferred income, including IRAs. (Sec. 17041(i)(3), Rev. & Tax. Code) Thus, only contributions not allowed as a deduction for California purposes are used to determine the tax-free basis of the IRA.

Practice Pointer: Canadian Registered Retirement Savings Plan

The Franchise Tax Board has taken the position that a Canadian Registered Retirement Savings Plan (RRSP) will be treated as a savings account rather than a functional equivalent to an IRA for California personal income tax purposes. This is contrary to federal treatment. Consequently, unlike under federal law, California taxpayers may not elect to defer taxation on RRSP earnings until a taxpayer begins receiving distributions, and must add such earnings to their taxable income. After taxpayers pay tax on these earnings, the earnings will also be treated as a capital investment in the RRSP. When taxpayers receive distributions from their RRSP, the amount consisting of the contributions and the previously taxed earnings is treated as a nontaxable return of capital. Under federal law, such earnings will be subject to tax when distributed. Consequently, taxpayers may subtract these distributions from federal adjusted gross income in the year of distribution. (*Tax News*, California Franchise Tax Board, May/June 2003)

• *1975 contribution to IRA*

For California tax purposes, any 1975 contribution to an IRA is treated, in effect, as a separate grantor trust. Any interest earned on a 1975 contribution in 1975 or 1976 was subject to California tax as earned, and of course will not be subject to California tax when it is distributed at a later time. However, as a result of 1977 legislation, any income earned after 1976 on a 1975 contribution is not taxable until it is distributed. So far as contributions to the account for years subsequent to 1975 are concerned, the account automatically qualifies under California law even though it was established before the California law providing for IRAs was enacted. (Sec. 17507, Rev. & Tax. Code)

• *Roth IRAs*

As explained in further detail at ¶330, both California and federal law recognize a "Roth IRA." For both California and federal purposes, earnings from a Roth IRA are tax-free and qualified distributions are not included in gross income or subject to a penalty on early withdrawals. (Sec. 17501, Rev. & Tax. Code)

Caution: Allowable Roth IRA Contribution for RDPs

For California income tax purposes, if RDPs contribute to a Roth IRA, the RDPs must review the income phase-out limitations. The allowable Roth IRA contribution may be reduced based on the RDPs' combined federal modified AGI. For example, if RDP One made a contribution to his Roth IRA of $5,000 in 2008 and his federal modified AGI is $90,000, and RDP Two made a contribution to his Roth IRA of $5,000 in 2008 and his federal modified AGI is $95,000, the RDPs' combined federal AGI exceeds the $169,000 limitation for an allowable Roth IRA contribution for 2008. Thus, for California purposes, the Roth IRA contributions of both RDPs are treated as excess contributions. However, California does not impose the 6% excise tax that is imposed under federal law on excess contributions to Roth IRAs. If either RDP later receives a qualified distribution from his Roth IRA, the qualified distribution is tax-free and is not includible in their California taxable income. This tax*f*free treatment applies even if the qualified distribution includes earnings attributable to a previous excess contribution for California purposes. (FTB Pub. 737, Tax Information for Registered Domestic Partners)

• *Coverdell Education Savings Accounts (aka Education IRAs)*

As explained in further detail at ¶330, under both California law and federal law, taxpayers with modified adjusted gross income below certain levels may contribute up to $2,000 per child per year to a Coverdell Education Savings Account (called an "Education IRA" prior to the 2002 taxable year). Earnings on contributions will be distributed tax-free provided that they are used to pay the child's post-secondary education expenses and/or elementary or secondary education expenses. (Sec. 23712, Rev. & Tax. Code)

Additional tax on amounts not used for education: An additional tax of 2.5% (10% for federal purposes) is imposed on amounts distributed and not used for qualified higher education expenses. (Sec. 23712, Rev. & Tax. Code) The additional penalty does not apply to the following distributions:

— made to a beneficiary's estate after the beneficiary's death;

— attributable to the beneficiary's being disabled;

— used for the beneficiary's attendance at a U.S. Armed Forces related academy;

— made on account of a scholarship received by the account holder to the extent that the amount of the distribution does not exceed the amount of the scholarship; or

— that constitute the return of excess contributions and earnings therein (although earnings are includable in income).

• *Income attributable to nondeductible contributions to traditional IRAs*

As explained at ¶330, California law provides that any income attributable to the nondeductible portion of contributions to traditional IRAs is not taxable to the beneficiary until the income is distributed.

• *Simplified employee pension (SEP) plans*

As explained at ¶330, California law conforms generally to federal law permitting employer contributions to an employee's individual retirement plan through a "simplified employee pension" (SEP) plan. The employer's contributions to the employee's SEP-IRA are excluded from the employee's gross income. The employee's contributions to the SEP-IRA are separate and apart from the employer's contributions and may be deducted from the employee's gross income in the same manner, and to the same extent, as any IRA contribution (¶330). SEP distributions are subject to tax on the basis of the same rules that apply to distributions from an IRA (see above). (Sec. 17201, Rev. & Tax. Code; Sec. 17501, Rev. & Tax. Code)

• *Savings incentive match plans for employees (SIMPLE plans)*

Certain small employers may establish SIMPLE plans structured as IRAs or as qualified cash or deferred arrangements. Employees are not taxed on account assets until distributions are made, and employers generally may deduct contributions to such plans. SIMPLE plans are not subject to nondiscrimination rules or some of the other complex requirements applicable to qualified plans. (Sec. 17501, Rev. & Tax. Code)

• *Summary of amounts recoverable free of California tax*

SELF-EMPLOYED PLANS

1963-1970: All 1963-1970 contributions recoverable tax-free (no California deduction).

1971-1973: No 1971-1973 contributions recoverable tax-free (California deduction same as federal).

1974-1986: Excess of 1974-1986 federal deduction over California deduction recoverable tax-free.

1987 and subsequent years: No contributions recoverable tax-free (California deduction same as federal).

All years: Interest element in redemption of "retirement bonds" issued before 1984 recoverable tax-free.

DEDUCTIBLE INDIVIDUAL RETIREMENT ACCOUNTS

1975: All 1975 contributions recoverable tax-free (no California deduction).

1975 and 1976: Income from 1975 contributions recoverable tax-free (income was taxed currently).

1976-1981: No 1976-1981 contributions recoverable tax-free (California deduction same as federal).

1982-1986: Excess of 1982-1986 federal deduction over California deduction recoverable tax-free.

1987 and subsequent years: No contributions recoverable tax-free (California deduction same as federal).

2007-2009: Increased contributions made by individuals who participated in a bankrupt employer's 401(k) plan or for active participants in an employer-sponsored retirement plan or whose spouse was an active participant in an employer-sponsored plan. (California did not conform to increased deduction)

All years: Interest element in redemption of "retirement bonds" issued before 1984 recoverable tax-free.

ROTH INDIVIDUAL RETIREMENT ACCOUNTS

1998 and subsequent years: All contributions and earnings recoverable tax free (contributions taxed currently).

SIMPLIFIED EMPLOYEE PENSION PLANS

1979-1986: Excess of 1979-1986 federal deduction over California deduction recoverable tax-free.

1987 and subsequent years: No contributions recoverable tax-free (California deduction same as federal).

NOTE: This summary assumes that the taxpayer was a California resident during the contribution year, as well as during the year of distribution. In case there has been a change of residence, see ¶405.

• *Government and nonprofit pension plans*

California incorporates federal law, generally as amended to date, governing plans maintained for governmental employees; see ¶330. (Sec. 17551, Rev. & Tax. Code)

• *Premature distributions*

Both California and federal laws impose a penalty tax on premature distributions (before age 59½) from self-employed plans, annuity plans, IRAs, and "modified endowment contracts," to the extent the distribution is includible in income. The California penalty is 2.5% of the distribution, while the federal penalty is generally 10% of the distribution. The penalty is inapplicable to premature distributions from IRAs if the distributions are used to pay the following:

— medical expenses in excess of 7.5% of a taxpayer's adjusted gross income;

— health insurance premiums if a taxpayer is unemployed and either received 12 consecutive weeks of unemployment compensation or, if self-employed, would have received such benefits but for the fact that he or she was self-employed;

— qualified first-time home buyer expenses; or

— qualified higher education expenses. (Sec. 17085(c)(1), Rev. & Tax. Code)

Practice Note: Early Distribution to Pay Qualified Expenses of RDPs

Because federal law does not recognize RDPs, a taxpayer may take an early distribution from an IRA or other tax-favored account to pay certain expenses, such as qualified higher education expenses, of an RDP or an RDP's child and may incur premature distribution penalties with respect to that distribution for federal income tax purposes, but not for California income tax purposes. However, for both federal and California tax purposes, the RDP would need to include in taxable income the early distribution from the IRA, unless the RDP has a basis in the IRA that may be recovered tax-free. (FTB Pub. 737, Tax Information for Registered Domestic Partners)

Also, the penalty does not apply to distributions from a qualified retirement plan or IRA if the distribution is made on account of an FTB notice to withhold from the plan or IRA (an IRS levy on the plan or IRA for federal purposes).

As a result of California's current federal conformity date, California has not incorporated post-2005 federal amendments that waive the early withdrawal penalty for certain distributions to (1) qualified public safety employees who separate from service after age 50, applicable for federal purposes to distributions made after August 17, 2006, and (2) to qualified members of the National Guard or the Reserve who are called to active duty, applicable for federal purposes retroactively to September 11, 2001. Consequently, distributions to such taxpayers are subject to the early withdrawal penalty for California tax purposes, but not federal tax purposes.

CCH Practice Pointer: Requirement to File FTB 3805P

A taxpayer that is liable for the penalty tax on premature distributions is required to file form FTB 3805P whether or not he or she meets the threshold individual income tax filing requirements. The return filing deadline is the same for filing the individual income tax return (¶108).

• *Transfer of excess pension assets to retiree health accounts*

California incorporates federal law permitting employers, under strictly limited conditions, to transfer excess pension assets to retiree health accounts without disqualifying either the pension or health plan, and without including the transferred assets in gross income. (Sec. 17501, Rev. & Tax. Code)

Generally, only one such transfer may be made in any tax year.

• *Excess contributions, accumulations, or distributions*

California does not have taxes similar to those imposed under IRC Sec. 4973 (tax on excess contributions to individual retirement arrangements) or IRC Sec. 4974 (tax on excess accumulation in qualified retirement plans).

• *Rollovers*

Both California and federal laws permit tax-free "rollovers" from one tax-qualified retirement plan to another, under certain conditions.

• *Cross references*

See ¶205 regarding taxability of payments received under the Railroad Retirement Act. See ¶330 for deductions available for retirement plan contributions. See ¶405 regarding taxability of distributions from self-employed plans after change of residence.

¶207 Employee Stock Options and Purchase Plans

Law: Secs. 17081, 17501, 17502 (CCH California Tax Reports ¶15-800, 16-345).

Comparable Federal: Secs. 83, 421-24 (CCH U.S. Master Tax Guide ¶1928, 1929).

Except as noted below, California law is substantially the same as federal law as of the current IRC tie-in date (see ¶103). (Sec. 17081, Rev. & Tax. Code; Sec. 17501, Rev. & Tax. Code) For a discussion of the issues arising when a taxpayer changes residency, see ¶405.

• *California qualified stock options*

The favorable tax treatment afforded by federal law to incentive and employee stock options applies for California purposes to California qualified stock options. Accordingly, a taxpayer who exercises a qualifying stock option may postpone paying tax until disposing of the option or the underlying stock. (Sec. 17502, Rev. & Tax. Code)

A "California qualified stock option" is a stock option

— designated by the corporation issuing the stock option as a California qualified stock option at the time the option is granted,

— issued by a corporation to its employees after 1996 and before 2002, and

— exercised by a taxpayer either while employed by the issuing corporation or within three months after leaving the employ of the issuing corporation.

A taxpayer who becomes permanently and totally disabled may exercise the option within one year of leaving the employ of the issuing corporation.

The favorable tax treatment of California qualified stock options is available only to a taxpayer whose earned income from the corporation granting the option does not exceed $40,000 for the taxable year in which the option is exercised, and only to the extent that the number of shares transferable by the taxpayer's exercise of qualified options does not exceed a total of 1,000 shares and those shares have a combined fair market value of less than $100,000 (determined at the time the options are granted). (FTB Pub. 1001, *Supplemental Guidelines to California Adjustments*)

¶208 Services of Child

Law: Sec. 17081 (CCH CALIFORNIA TAX REPORTS ¶15-515).

Comparable Federal: Secs. 73, 6201 (CCH U.S. MASTER TAX GUIDE ¶114).

California law is the same as federal law.

Income from services of a child is includible in the gross income of the child, and not in the income of the parent. All expenditures, by parent or child, attributable to such income are treated as paid or incurred by the child. (Sec. 17081, Rev. & Tax. Code)

Under certain circumstances, an assessment on the child's income is treated as an assessment against the parent as well as the child.

¶209 Prizes and Awards

Law: Sec. 17081 (CCH CALIFORNIA TAX REPORTS ¶15-780).

Comparable Federal: Sec. 74 (CCH U.S. MASTER TAX GUIDE ¶785).

California law is the same as federal law. (Sec. 17081, Rev. & Tax. Code)

Prizes and awards are specifically designated as being includible in taxable income, with two exceptions. The exceptions relate to (1) the value of certain employee achievement awards, and (2) amounts received in recognition of achievement of charitable, scientific, artistic, etc., nature. To be eligible for the charitable award exemption the recipient must be selected without any action on his or her part and must not be required to render substantial future services. Also, the award must be transferred by the payor to a charity designated by the recipient. The federal law is incorporated in California by reference.

See ¶201 for the tax treatment applied to lottery winnings.

¶210 Dealers in Tax-Exempt Securities

Law: Sec. 17081 (CCH CALIFORNIA TAX REPORTS ¶16-075).

Comparable Federal: Sec. 75 (CCH U.S. MASTER TAX GUIDE ¶1970).

California follows the federal rules. (Sec. 17081, Rev. & Tax. Code)

Dealers in tax-free municipal bonds may be required to make an adjustment to gross income with respect to such securities sold during the year. The cost, or other basis, of certain municipal bonds sold by a dealer must be reduced by an amount equivalent to the amortization of bond premiums that would otherwise be allowable as a deduction if the interest on the bonds were fully taxable.

Exceptions are provided for certain cases where the bonds are sold within 30 days after acquisition, or where the bonds mature, or are callable, more than five years after acquisition. Special rules are provided where dealers use different inventory methods.

The federal law is incorporated in California's by reference. However, in view of the fact that certain municipal bond interest is taxable for California but not federal purposes, and interest on U.S. bonds is taxable for federal but not California purposes, there will be cases where the rules apply under one law but not under the other.

¶211 Commodity Credit Loans

Law: Sec. 17081 (CCH CALIFORNIA TAX REPORTS ¶15-515).

Comparable Federal: Sec. 77 (CCH U.S. MASTER TAX GUIDE ¶769).

California follows the federal law. (Sec. 17081, Rev. & Tax. Code)

The taxpayer may elect to treat as income amounts received as loans from the Commodity Credit Corporation.

¶212 Employees' Group Term Life Insurance

Law: Secs. 17020.12, 17081 (CCH CALIFORNIA TAX REPORTS ¶15-515).

Comparable Federal: Secs. 79, 7701(a)(20) (CCH U.S. MASTER TAX GUIDE ¶721).

California follows the federal law. (Sec. 17081, Rev. & Tax. Code)

An employee must include in income an amount equivalent to his or her employer's cost of group term life insurance to the extent the cost exceeds (1) the cost of $50,000 of coverage plus (2) any contribution by the employee to purchase the insurance. Exceptions are provided where the employer, or a charitable organization, is the beneficiary. An exemption is also provided for insurance under a qualified pension or profit-sharing plan (¶206).

The federal law is incorporated in California's by reference, including federal rules concerning the determination of cost under a discriminatory plan.

¶213 Certain Death Benefits

Law: Secs. 17131, 17132.5 (CCH CALIFORNIA TAX REPORTS ¶15-655, 16-036).

Comparable Federal: Sec. 101 (CCH U.S. MASTER TAX GUIDE ¶803, 813).

California generally incorporates federal law as of California's current federal conformity date (¶103). (Sec. 17131, Rev. & Tax. Code)

See ¶225 for the tax treatment of military death benefits and the income tax exemption for terrorist victims.

• *Life insurance*

In general, life insurance proceeds are nontaxable except for the interest element. (However, see ¶215 for an exception to the general rule.) The interest received is fully taxable if proceeds are held by an insurer under an agreement to pay interest. The interest element is also taxable if the proceeds are paid in installments that include an interest element. California law is the same as federal law. (Sec. 17131, Rev. & Tax. Code)

As a result of California's current federal conformity date (¶103), California has not incorporated amendments made by the Pension Protection Act of 2006 that limit the exclusion for employers holding a life insurance policy as a beneficiary that covers the life of an employee (IRC Sec. 101(a) and (j)). The amendments limit the employer's exclusion to an amount equal to the amount paid for the policy as premiums or other payments unless the employer satisfies several requirements, including notice and consent requirements, applicable generally for federal purposes to life insurance contracts issued after August 17, 2006. To the extent the exclusion is limited for federal income tax purposes, taxpayers may subtract the difference between the full amount of the benefits paid, less certain interest, and the amount of the federal exclusion.

• *Survivors of state employees, etc.*

Both California and federal law exclude from gross income certain survivor benefits paid as an annuity to the spouse, former spouse, or child of a public safety officer killed in the line of duty. (Sec. 17131, Rev. & Tax. Code) However, California did not allow the federal exclusion of survivor annuities paid on the death of a public safety officer killed in the line of duty for amounts received in post-2001 tax years with respect to individuals who died prior to 1997. (Sec. 17132.5, Rev. & Tax. Code)

¶214 Life Insurance—Other Than Death Benefits

Law: Secs. 17081, 17085 (CCH CALIFORNIA TAX REPORTS ¶15-800).

Comparable Federal: Sec. 72 (CCH U.S. MASTER TAX GUIDE ¶817 et seq.).

California law conforms to the federal provisions as of California's current federal conformity date (see ¶103), regarding the taxability of amounts received on life insurance contracts other than death benefits, interest, or annuities. (Sec. 17081, Rev. & Tax. Code)

Under these provisions, the proceeds from life insurance or endowment contracts are includible in income subject to an exclusion factor determined by reference to the investment in, and expected return from, such contracts. Lump-sum proceeds will not be deemed to be constructively received if an insured elects within 60 days after maturity of a policy to take the proceeds as an annuity rather than a lump sum.

California also incorporates the federal penalty on premature distributions from "modified endowment contracts," but substitutes a different penalty rate (¶206). (Sec. 17085, Rev. & Tax. Code)

¶215 Life Insurance or Annuity Transferred for Consideration

Law: Secs. 17081, 17131 (CCH CALIFORNIA TAX REPORTS ¶15-655, 15-800).

Comparable Federal: Secs. 72(g), 101(a), 101(g) (CCH U.S. MASTER TAX GUIDE ¶807).

California follows federal law. (Sec. 17081, Rev. & Tax. Code)

Where the recipient of the proceeds has acquired a life insurance contract for a valuable consideration, the general rule is that the proceeds are exempt only to the extent of the consideration given and the premiums subsequently paid. An exception to the general rule exempts life insurance proceeds from taxation in cases where the transferee is the insured, a partner of the insured, or a corporation in which the insured is an officer or shareholder. Also exempt are transfers where basis for the contract is determined by reference to basis in the hands of the transferor.

As a result of California's current federal conformity date (¶103), California has not incorporated amendments made by the Pension Protection Act of 2006 that limit the exclusion for employers holding a life insurance policy as a beneficiary that covers the life of an employee (IRC Sec. 101(a) and (j)). The amendments limit the employer's exclusion to an amount equal to the amount paid for the policy as premiums or other payments unless the employer satisfies several requirements, including notice and consent requirements, applicable generally for federal purposes to life insurance contracts issued after August 17, 2006. To the extent the exclusion is limited for federal income tax purposes, taxpayers may subtract the difference between the full amount of the benefits paid, less certain interest, and the amount of the federal exclusion.

As to annuities transferred for a valuable consideration, the general rule is that the cost of the annuity (determined for purposes of computing the tax-free recovery of cost) is computed by reference to the actual value of the consideration paid on transfer, plus premiums and other sums subsequently paid. An exception is provided for certain tax-free exchanges.

• *Accelerated death benefits*

California conforms to federal law allowing an exclusion from gross income when accelerated death benefits are received under a life insurance contract on the life of a terminally or chronically ill individual or when amounts are received from the sale or assignment to a viatical settlement provider of any portion of the death benefits under a life insurance contract on the life of a terminally or chronically ill individual. In the case of a chronically ill individual (1) the exclusion applies only if amounts are received under a rider or other provision of a contract that is treated as a qualified long-term care insurance contract, and (2) the excludable amount is capped at a specified amount. (Sec. 17131, Rev. & Tax. Code)

¶216 Gifts, Inheritances, Tips, etc.

Law: Sec. 17131 (CCH CALIFORNIA TAX REPORTS ¶15-715).

Comparable Federal: Sec. 102 (CCH U.S. MASTER TAX GUIDE ¶847).

California law incorporates the federal law by reference. The value of property received as a gift, bequest, devise, or inheritance is nontaxable but the income from such property is taxable. (Sec. 17131, Rev. & Tax. Code)

Tips received by a waiter are taxable income and are not exempt as gifts. See *Hugo Rihn v. Franchise Tax Board* (1955) (CCH CALIFORNIA TAX REPORTS ¶15-715.55), decided by the California Court of Appeal.

The State Board of Equalization (SBE) held in *Appeal of Ida A. Rogers* (1956) (CCH CALIFORNIA TAX REPORTS ¶15-715.47) that voluntary payments by a corporation to the widow of one of its employees constituted gifts and were not taxable income. A similar result was reached by the SBE in *Appeal of Irma Livingston* (1956) (CCH CALIFORNIA TAX REPORTS ¶15-715.47), as to voluntary payments to surviving children of a deceased employee.

¶217 Tax-Free Interest

Law: Secs. 17088, 17133, 17143, 17145 (CCH CALIFORNIA TAX REPORTS ¶15-185, 15-720, 16-075, 16-280).

Comparable Federal: Secs. 103, 141-50, 852, 1286 (CCH U.S. MASTER TAX GUIDE ¶729, 731, 1952, 2307).

California Forms: Form 540 (California Resident Income Tax Return), Sch. CA (540) (California Adjustments - Residents).

California's treatment of interest on certain governmental obligations differs from federal rules, as explained below.

See ¶305 for treatment of interest expense related to tax-free interest.

• *Interest exempt*

Interest on the following obligations is exempt from California tax:

(1) Bonds and other obligations of the United States, U.S. territories, and Puerto Rico. (31 U.S.C. 3124) (Interest on Philippine Islands obligations issued on or after March 24, 1934, is not exempt. Interest on District of Columbia obligations issued after December 24, 1973, is not exempt.)

(2) Bonds (not including other obligations) of the State of California or of political subdivisions thereof, issued after November 4, 1902.

(Sec. 17143, Rev. & Tax. Code)

Practitioner Comment: Taxation of Out-of-State Obligations

It should be noted that the constitutionality of taxing out-of-state municipal bond interest under provisions similar to those described above under California law was recently called into question in Kentucky. On January 6, 2006, the Kentucky Court of Appeals in *Davis v. Department of Revenue*, No. 2004-CA-001940-MR, held that these provisions were facially discriminatory in favor of in-state bonds in violation of the Commerce Clause. On August 17, 2006, the Kentucky Supreme Court denied the Kentucky Department of Revenue's motion for discretionary review. On May 21, 2007, the U.S. Supreme Court granted certiorari and on May 19, 2008, upheld the state's preferential tax treatment of interest from in-state bonds, seemingly laying to rest any speculation as to whether taxpayers in other states, including California, might be entitled to refunds on interest from out of state municipal bonds.

Chris Micheli, Esq., Carpenter, Snodgrass & Associates, Sacramento, CA

If there is a separation of the ownership between the tax-exempt bond and the right to receive interest, the payments or accruals on the stripped bond and stripped coupon are treated in the manner provided under the federal law, which requires allocation of basis to prevent artificial losses.

The exemption set forth in (1), above, does not extend to interest received on refunds of U.S. taxes. This point is not covered in the regulations or any published ruling, but it has been the Franchise Tax Board's (FTB) administrative policy to deny the exemption. The Attorney General has ruled (NS 4570, 10-28-42) that interest on postal savings accounts is taxable. Interest on bonds of other States is not exempt.

See ¶513 for the treatment of gain or loss from the sale of such bonds.

Interest on Housing Authority bonds (issued by housing projects created under the Housing Authorities Law) is exempt if the bonds are issued by a project located in California, but is taxable if the bonds are issued by a project located outside the state. Such interest would presumably be exempt from federal tax.

• *California-federal differences*

The above exemptions are quite different from those under federal law, which exempt interest on obligations of *any* state or political subdivision thereof and which extend only limited exemptions to certain U.S. obligations.

Interest on "arbitrage bonds" or private activity bonds issued by state or local governments is subject to federal tax. California has not adopted these provisions so the interest on any such bonds issued in California would be exempt from California tax. (The federal rule would have no effect on California tax so far as interest on bonds of other states is concerned, because California already taxes interest on such bonds.) (Sec. 17143, Rev. & Tax. Code)

• *Status of federal agency obligations*

Whether interest from federal agency obligations is taxable for California purposes is generally governed by federal law.

Practice Note: Taxable Bonds

The following are not considered U.S. obligations for California purposes and, therefore, interest earned on these obligations is subject to tax: Federal National Mortgage Association (Fannie Maes); Government National Mortgage Association (Ginnie Maes); and Federal Loan Home Mortgage Corporation (Freddie Macs) (FTB Pub. 1001, Supplemental Guidelines to California Adjustments).

The FTB has indicated that interest on the following obligations is not subject to tax: Student Loan Marketing Association (SLMA), Federal Home Loan banks, the Resolution Funding Corporation, the Production Credit Association, Federal Farm Credit banks, and the Commodity Credit Corporation. Interest from CATS (Certificates of Accrual on Treasury Securities) and TIGRS (Treasury Investment Growth Receipts) is also exempt because those obligations have been found to be government securities under federal law.

• *Interest on notes*

In *Appeal of M.G. and Faye W. Odenheimer* (1964) (CCH CALIFORNIA TAX REPORTS ¶202-481), the State Board of Equalization held that interest on a promissory note of a California municipality, issued for purchase of land to be used as a parking lot, qualified for exemption from the California personal income tax.

• *Mutual funds*

California generally adopts the federal treatment of regulated investment companies (RICs) and their shareholders as of California's current federal conformity date (¶103). However, California has its own rules governing exempt-interest dividends and does not adopt the federal treatment of undistributed capital gains. (Sec. 17145, Rev. & Tax. Code)

As to the pass-through of tax-exempt income, California provides that the flow-through treatment is allowed if, as of the close of each quarter, at least 50% of the value of a management company's assets consists of obligations that pay interest that is exempt from taxation by California. State and federal tax-exempt obligations may be combined for purposes of meeting the 50% test. (Sec. 17145, Rev. & Tax. Code)

Also, California conforms to a federal provision that limits the amount of a distribution allowable as an exempt-interest dividend. With respect to the company's taxable year, if the aggregate amount designated by the company as an exempt-interest dividend is greater than the excess of

— the amount of interest it received that was exempt from California taxation or excludable from gross income under federal law, over

— the amounts that would be disallowed as deductions for expenses related to exempt income under California or federal law,

the portion of the distribution designated as an exempt-interest dividend that will be allowed as an exempt-interest dividend is only that proportion of the designated amount that the excess bears to the designated amount.

It should be noted that the flow-through treatment applies to interest from federal obligations that would be exempt if held directly by an individual. Therefore, interest received from certain agency bonds (*e.g.*, GNMA, FNMA, etc.) is not exempt interest from federal obligations.

Amounts designated as "exempt-interest dividends" are treated by recipients as nontaxable income.

See ¶206 regarding exemption of interest element upon redemption of individual retirement bonds.

• *Interest income from children*

As a result of California's current federal conformity date (see ¶103), California has not incorporated amendments made by the Tax Increase Prevention and Reconciliation Act of 2005 and the Small Business and Work Opportunity Tax Act of 2007 that allow parents to elect to report a child's interest and dividends on the parents' return as long as the child is under 19 years old or is a full time student over the age of 18, but under age 24, unless the earned income of such individual exceeds half of the individual's support for the year. Because California still limits the election for parents to interest income of children under age 14, parents that included the interest income of children between the ages of 14 and 24 on their federal return must subtract such income from the amount included in their federal adjusted gross income, and the children age 14 and above with interest income must each file a state return if they meet the minimum reporting requirement. (Pub. 1001, *Supplemental Guidelines to California Adjustments*)

¶218 Compensation for Injury or Sickness

Law: ; Secs. 17131, 17132.7, Rev. & Tax. Code (CCH CALIFORNIA TAX REPORTS ¶15-640, 15-650, 16-235).

Comparable Federal: Sec. 104 (CCH U.S. MASTER TAX GUIDE ¶851, 852).

California adopts by reference the federal law as of the current IRC tie-in date (¶103). (Sec. 17131, Rev. & Tax. Code)

Amounts received as accident or health insurance benefits, damages, workers compensation, etc., on account of personal injuries or sickness, are tax-exempt. Payments made to individuals under Sec. 103(c)(10) of the Ricky Ray Hemophilia Relief Act of 1998 are treated as tax-exempt damages. (Sec. 17132.7, Rev. & Tax. Code)

The exemption does not apply to amounts received as reimbursement for medical expenses that were allowed as deductions in prior years. Nor does it apply to (1) punitive damages, whether or not related to a claim for damages from personal injury or sickness, or (2) damages for emotional distress, except to the extent of any amounts received for medical care attributable to the emotional distress or attributable to a physical injury or sickness.

Consequently, the State Board of Equalization has disallowed the deduction for sex discrimination settlement proceeds (*Evenson* (2001) (CCH CALIFORNIA TAX REPORTS ¶15-650.551)) and damages received from an age discrimination suit (*Allison* (2001) (CCH CALIFORNIA TAX REPORTS ¶15-650.25)).

Also, this exemption generally does not cover employer contributions to accident and health plans for *employees;* see ¶219 for discussion of special rules covering such plans. These rules are the same as the federal rules. However, the amount includible in income on account of reimbursed medical expenses may be different because of a difference in the extent to which the expenses were deductible in an earlier year.

¶219 Amounts Received Under Accident and Health Plans

Law: Secs. 17021.7, 17087, 17131, 17131.4 (CCH CALIFORNIA TAX REPORTS ¶15-165, 15-705, 16-100, 16-345).

Comparable Federal: Secs. 105-06, 7702B (CCH U.S. MASTER TAX GUIDE ¶853—859).

California generally conforms to federal law as of California's current federal conformity date. (Sec. 17131, Rev. & Tax. Code) However, California does not incorporate the federal provision requiring that sick pay benefits received under the Railroad Unemployment Insurance Act be included in gross income. (Sec. 17087(c), Rev. & Tax. Code) Nor does California incorporate the exclusion for employer contributions to health savings accounts. (Sec. 17131.4, Rev. & Tax. Code) Finally, California, but not federal law, treats a registered domestic partner as a spouse for purposes of determining the amount that may be excluded. (Sec. 17021.7, Rev. & Tax. Code) See ¶119 for a discussion of California's tax treatment of same-sex married couples.

Certain amounts paid under an employer-financed accident or health plan to reimburse an employee for expenses incurred by the employee for medical care of the employee or the employee's spouse or dependents are excludible from gross income, unless received in reimbursement for medical expenses previously deducted. These rules also cover payments made for loss of use of a member or function of the body, or for disfigurement. Such plans are subject to detailed rules designed to prevent discrimination. (Sec. 17131, Rev. & Tax. Code)

Employer-provided coverage under an accident or health plan (including amounts contributed to an employee's medical savings account) are also excluded from an employee's gross income. However, employer-provided coverage for long-term care service provided through a flexible spending or similar arrangement must be included in an employee's gross income.

In *Appeal of Frank A. Aiello* (1987) (CCH CALIFORNIA TAX REPORTS ¶15-705.40), lump-sum payments made by a former employer to "buy out" its obligations to provide retired employees with group health benefits was taxable income and not an excludable health benefit.

¶220 Rental Value of Parsonages

Law: Sec. 19827.5, Govt. Code; Secs. 17131, 17131.6, Rev. & Tax. Code (CCH CALIFORNIA TAX REPORTS ¶15-155).

Comparable Federal: Sec. 107 (CCH U.S. MASTER TAX GUIDE ¶875).

California Forms: Sch. CA (540) (California Adjustments - Residents).

The California exemption for the rental value of a minister's dwelling is the same as under the federal law as of California's current federal conformity date (¶103). (Sec. 17131, Rev. & Tax. Code) However, unlike federal law, California law does not limit the exclusion to the fair market rental value of the home, including furnishings and appurtenances, plus the cost of utilities. (Sec. 17131.6, Rev. & Tax. Code)

In addition, California allows state-employed members of the clergy to allocate up to 50% of their gross salary to either the rental value of a home furnished to him or her or to the rental allowance paid to him or her to rent a home. (Sec. 19827.5, Govt. Code) The taxpayer may claim a subtraction if, as a result of this provision, the federal exclusion is less than the California exclusion. If the federal exclusion is greater than the California exclusion, the taxpayer is required to make an addition adjustment.

In *Appeal of Nickolas Kurtaneck* (1987) (CCH CALIFORNIA TAX REPORTS ¶15-155.25), the State Board of Equalization (SBE) reviewed applicable federal regulations and rulings and denied the housing exclusion to an ordained minister who taught biblical studies at an independent, nonaffiliated university. The SBE held that the institution was not operated as an integral agency of a church.

¶221 Discharge of Indebtedness

Law: Secs. 17131, 17134, 17144, 17144.5 (CCH CALIFORNIA TAX REPORTS ¶15-680).

Comparable Federal: Secs. 108, 382 (CCH U.S. MASTER TAX GUIDE ¶791, 885).

California Forms: Form 540 (California Resident Income Tax Return), Sch. CA (540) (California Adjustments - Residents).

California generally incorporates federal law as of the current IRC tie-in date (see ¶103), which provides that, if a debt of a taxpayer is canceled or forgiven, the taxpayer must include the canceled amount in gross income. Also, California partially conforms to federal amendments made by the Mortgage Forgiveness Debt Relief Act of 2007 (Mortgage Relief Act) and the Emergency Economic Stabilization Act of 2008 (EESA) (see below). Exceptions to the general conformity rule are provided in bankruptcy situations, where the debtor/taxpayer is insolvent, or where the canceled debt is qualified real property business indebtedness or qualified farm indebtedness. (Sec. 17131, Rev. & Tax. Code)

California has not conformed to federal amendments made by the Emergency Economic Stimulus Act of 2008 that exclude from gross income certain discharged indebtedness of summer 2008 Midwestern storm victims whose principal residence on the applicable disaster date was located in the Midwestern disaster area, applicable to discharges of debt on or after the applicable disaster date and before January 1, 2010.

Under the discharge of indebtedness rules, the income-tax consequences of debt discharge may be deferred—but not permanently avoided—by reducing tax "attributes" such as capital losses or capital loss carryovers and the basis of depreciable property. Certain debt reductions are treated as purchase-price adjustments.

• *Discharge of qualified principal residence indebtedness*

California partially conforms to federal amendments made by the Mortgage Relief Act allowing an exclusion from gross income for discharge of an individual's qualified principal residence indebtedness. However, the California exclusion is limited to indebtedness discharged in the 2007 and 2008 calendar years, while the federal exclusion applies to indebtedness discharged after 2006 and before 2013. Also, qualified principal residence indebtedness is limited for California purposes to $800,000 ($400,000 in the case of a married/RDP taxpayer filing separately), and the amount of the California exclusion is limited to $250,000 ($125,000 in the case of a married/RDP taxpayer filing separately). Under federal law, on the other hand, the amount of qualified principal residence indebtedness is limited to $2 million ($1 million in the case of a married individual filing separately), and there is no limit on the debt relief amount. (Sec. 17144.5, Rev. & Tax. Code)

CCH Practice Tip: Filing for relief

A taxpayer can file for debt relief on an original 2007 or 2008 California return or, if the taxpayer has already filed a 2007 California return, the taxpayer may file for debt relief on an amended California return. If the amount of debt relief for federal purposes is more than the California limit, the taxpayer must include the amount in excess of the California limit on Schedule CA (540/540NR), line 21f, column (C). If the taxpayer files for relief on an original California return, the taxpayer should include a copy of his or her federal return, including Form 982, Reduction of Tax Attributes Due to Discharge of Indebtedness (and Section 1082 Basis Adjustment), with the California return. A taxpayer who files for relief on an amended California return should enter on line 2e, column (B), the amount originally entered on Schedule CA (540/540NR), line 21f, column (C). (*Announcement*, California Franchise Tax Board, October 8, 2008)

Notwithstanding any other law to the contrary, no penalties or interest may be imposed with respect to the discharge of any qualified principal residence indebtedness during the 2007 taxable year, regardless of whether the taxpayer reports the discharge on his or her return for the 2007 taxable year. (Sec. 17144.5, Rev. & Tax. Code)

• *Cancellation of student loans*

California incorporates federal law allowing an exclusion from gross income for income from the discharge of qualified student loans. (Sec. 17131, Rev. & Tax. Code)

The discharge of a loan made pursuant to the California State University's Forgivable Loan Program is excludable from California gross income if the discharge is made in connection with the recipient's performance of services for the California State University. (Sec. 17134, Rev. & Tax. Code)

• *California-federal differences*

Although, as stated above, federal law concerning discharge of indebtedness income has generally been incorporated by California, federal and California results may be quite different because of federal credit carryovers that do not apply to California. For example, federal law requiring the reduction of tax attributes refers to foreign tax credit carryovers, which are not applicable for California tax purposes.

In addition, for purposes of both the reduction of tax attributes and the exclusion of income from the discharge of qualified farm indebtedness, California's treatment of other credit carryovers is slightly modified. Under federal law, a taxpayer who does not elect to reduce the basis of depreciable assets or inventory realty by the amount of a discharged obligation must instead reduce certain listed tax attributes, including general business credit carryover reductions of 33$^{1}/_{3}$¢ for each dollar excluded. California modifies this provision to (1) refer instead to carryovers of credits allowed under California law and (2) require reduction of only 11.1¢ for each dollar excluded. For both federal and California purposes, a taxpayer may elect to apply the amount discharged to reduce the basis of his or her depreciable property in lieu of applying the excluded amount against tax attributes. (Sec. 17144, Rev. & Tax. Code)

Under both California and federal law, income from the discharge of certain farm indebtedness may be excluded even if the farmer is not insolvent or bankrupt, but the amount that may be excluded is limited to the sum of (1) the aggregate adjusted bases of the taxpayer's trade, business, and income-producing property in the year following the discharge year and (2) the taxpayer's "adjusted" tax attributes. For federal purposes, the taxpayer adjusts the general business credit carryover attribute by tripling it. For California purposes, the taxpayer multiplies the credit carryover figure by nine rather than by three. (Sec. 17144(d), Rev. & Tax. Code)

¶222 Lessee Improvements

Law: Sec. 17131 (CCH CALIFORNIA TAX REPORTS ¶ 15-740).

Comparable Federal: Sec. 109 (CCH U.S. MASTER TAX GUIDE ¶ 764).

An exemption is granted to lessors on income derived upon termination of a lease in the form of improvements made by a lessee. The federal law is incorporated into California's by reference. (Sec. 17131, Rev. & Tax. Code)

¶223 Lessee Construction Allowances

Law: Sec. 17131 (CCH CALIFORNIA TAX REPORTS ¶ 15-740).

Comparable Federal: Sec. 110 (CCH U.S. MASTER TAX GUIDE ¶ 764).

Under both California and federal law, certain tenants may exclude from gross income construction allowances received from lessors and used for additions or improvements to retail space. The exclusion applies only with respect to nonresidential real property that is (1) held under a lease of 15 years or less and (2) used in the tenant's retail trade or business. (Sec. 17131, Rev. & Tax. Code)

¶224 Recoveries of Bad Debts, Prior Taxes, etc.

Law: Secs. 17131, 17142 (CCH CALIFORNIA TAX REPORTS ¶15-810, 16-120, 16-327).

Comparable Federal: Sec. 111 (CCH U.S. MASTER TAX GUIDE ¶799).

The federal law is incorporated in California's by reference. (Sec. 17131, Rev. & Tax. Code)

Amounts may be excluded from gross income to the extent they represent recovery of prior-year deductions that did not reduce income tax. The portion of the federal provision dealing with credit and credit carryovers is modified to refer to California credits. (Sec. 17142, Rev. & Tax. Code) Detailed rules are provided.

• *California-federal difference*

The California rule is the same as the federal rule, but the effect of the rule may be different under the two laws because the deduction in the earlier year of the item recovered may have resulted in a tax benefit under one law but not under the other. This could result from a difference in treatment of the item in question in the year of deductibility, or it could be the result of differences in taxable income having no relation to the item in question.

• *Cases decided by State Board of Equalization*

In *Appeal of Boeddeker* (2001) (CCH CALIFORNIA TAX REPORTS ¶15-810.35), the SBE held that taxpayers could exclude from their gross income an amount equal to one-half of the accrued but unpaid interest that they had previously deducted upon the restructuring of a mortgage that resulted in the cancellation of all accrued but unpaid interest and the reduction of principal. Because the taxpayers received a tax benefit, in the form of net operating loss carryovers, for only one-half of the canceled interest that was allocated to them, only that portion of the canceled interest was includible in their gross income for the year. The remaining one-half of the canceled interest was a recovery exclusion, which was nontaxable.

In *Appeal of Percival M. and Katharine Scales* (1963) (CCH CALIFORNIA TAX REPORTS ¶15-810.40), the SBE held that taxes and carrying charges on real property deducted in one period, without a corresponding reduction in tax liability, could not be excluded from income when recovered in a subsequent year upon sale of the property. The SBE said the "tax benefit" rule was not intended to have such broad application. To the same effect, see *Appeal of H.V. Management Corporation* (1981) (CCH CALIFORNIA TAX Reports ¶10-910.50), a case that involved gain on sale of a partnership interest. Also to the same effect, see *Appeal of Argo Petroleum Corporation* (1982) (CCH CALIFORNIA TAX REPORTS ¶10-910.50), which involved sale of an oil and gas lease.

¶225 Military and Terrorist Victims' Compensation

Law: Secs. 17131, 17132.4, 17140.5, 17142.5, 17731 (CCH CALIFORNIA TAX REPORTS ¶15-175).

Comparable Federal: Secs. 112, 122, 134, 692 (CCH U.S. MASTER TAX GUIDE ¶895, 896, 2533).

Except as discussed below, the California exemptions for military pay are the same as the federal as of the current IRC tie-in date (¶103). This applies also to forgiveness of taxes of service members who die as a result of serving in a "combat zone" or "qualified hazardous duty area" (as defined in ¶109). However as a result of the California's IRC conformity date (¶103), California does not incorporate an amendment made by the Heroes Earnings Assistance and Relief Tax Act of 2008 that excludes state or local bonus payments to members of the U.S. uniformed services or their dependents from gross income if the payments were made by reason of the members' service in a combat zone. Such amounts excluded on the federal return must be added back to federal adjusted gross income for purposes of calculating California taxable income.

The following military compensation is exempt from California tax:

— educational benefits received under federal or state law;

— compensation, including reenlistment bonuses, earned by enlisted personnel and warrant officers for active service in a "combat zone" or "qualified hazardous duty area" or while hospitalized as a result of such service; and

— military compensation of a person not domiciled or taxable in California, but attributable to a resident spouse because of community property laws. Members serving on active duty and domiciled in community property states (Arizona, Idaho, Louisiana, Nevada, New Mexico, Texas, Washington, Wisconsin, or Puerto Rico) with California resident spouses may subtract half of their military pay from federal AGI.

(Sec. 17131, Rev. & Tax. Code; Sec. 17140.5, Rev. & Tax. Code)

For commissioned officers, other than commissioned warrant officers, the monthly tax exclusion is capped at the highest enlisted pay, plus any hostile or imminent danger pay received.

Expenses attributable to service pay that is exempt from tax are not deductible (¶336).

• *Victims of terroristic or military actions; astronauts*

Taxpayers who died as a result of injuries or wounds from a terroristic or military action directed against the United States or one of its allies incurred while the individual was a U.S. military or civilian employee are exempt from tax during the taxable year of the taxpayer's death and in any prior taxable year beginning with the last taxable year ending before the taxable year in which the wounds or injury were incurred. Federal law, but not California law, provides a $10,000 minimum tax relief benefit. (Sec. 17731(b), Rev. & Tax. Code)

California law, but not federal law, excludes the entire amount of a $10,000 death benefit paid by the state of California to the surviving spouse of, or a beneficiary designated by, any member of the California National Guard, State Military Reserve, or Naval Militia, who dies or is killed after March 1, 2003, in the performance of duty. (Sec. 17132.4, Rev. & Tax. Code)

• *Effect of residence status on taxability*

Under the federal Servicemembers Civil Relief Act, a nonresident serviceperson may not be taxed by California on service pay received for services in California, even though he or she may be stationed in the state during the entire year, and despite the fact that such income would be considered taxable to a nonresident under the regular rules. (Sec. 17140.5, Rev. & Tax. Code) However, all other income of a nonresident serviceperson from California sources is subject to California tax. Under Legal Ruling No. 300 (CCH CALIFORNIA TAX REPORTS ¶202-877), issued by the Franchise Tax Board in 1965, a person who enters military service from California will be treated as a nonresident when he or she leaves the state under permanent military orders to serve at another post of duty (¶105).

California law conforms to the federal Servicemembers Civil Relief Act (SCRA) (P.L. 108-189). Among the provisions of this legislation are the following:

— The military compensation of a servicemember not domiciled in California may not be used to increase the tax liability imposed on other income earned by that servicemember or that servicemember's spouse.

— The running of the statute of limitations is suspended for the period of a servicemember's military service.

— The interest rate is limited to a maximum of 6% per year on any underpayment incurred before the servicemember enters military service.

— A servicemember not domiciled in California does not become a resident by reason of being present in the state solely in compliance with military orders.

— Military compensation of a servicemember not domiciled in California is not income for services performed or from sources within the state.

— Native American servicemembers whose legal residence or domicile is a federal Indian reservation are treated as living on the federal Indian reservation and the compensation for military service is deemed to be income derived wholly from federal Indian reservation sources.

(Sec. 17140.5, Rev. & Tax. Code)

Prior to California's conformity with the SCRA, although a nonresident's military pay was excluded from gross income subject to California personal income tax, California included a nonresident's military pay in the computation used to determine the tax rate applied to California-source income subject to California personal income tax; see ¶116 for more details (*Brownell* (2001) (CCH CALIFORNIA TAX REPORTS ¶403-171)).

¶226 Dividends and Other Corporate Distributions

Law: Secs. 17024.5(b), 17088, 17321, 17322 (CCH CALIFORNIA TAX REPORTS ¶15-645).

Comparable Federal: Secs. 301-46, 851-60, 951-52, 995 (CCH U.S. MASTER TAX GUIDE ¶733 et seq., 2301 et seq., 2465, 2468).

California Forms: Sch. CA (540) (California Adjustments - Residents), Sch. CA (540NR) (California Adjustments - Nonresidents or Part-Year Residents).

Although California and federal law regarding dividends and other corporate distributions are generally the same as of the current IRC tie-in date (see ¶103), California has not completely conformed to current federal law. (Sec. 17321, Rev. & Tax. Code) In addition, prior differences in California and federal law may still affect the cost basis of property. Both current California-federal differences and prior-year differences are discussed below.

The principal provisions of the federal law to which California conforms may be summarized very briefly as follows:

— Any distribution out of earnings and profits of the current year or out of earnings and profits accumulated after February 28, 1913, is a "dividend" (IRC Sec. 316).

— Certain liquidating distributions are treated as payments in exchange for stock (IRC Sec. 302-03).

— A redemption of stock that is "essentially equivalent to the distribution of a taxable dividend" is to be treated as such. This may apply to acquisition of a corporation's stock by an affiliated corporation (IRC Sec. 304). Detailed rules are provided for some situations. Certain types of redemptions are not to be treated as taxable dividends. These include "disproportionate distributions," termination of a shareholder's interest, and redemption of stock to pay death taxes.

— Certain stock dividends may be nontaxable (IRC Sec. 305).

— Detailed rules are provided for the computation of "earnings and profits" so that a determination can be made regarding the taxability of a corporate distribution in the hands of shareholders (IRC Sec. 312).

• *Distributions from mutual funds*

California adopts the federal tax treatment of regulated investment companies (RICs) and their shareholders (IRC Sec. 852) as of the current IRC tie-in date (¶103), with certain modifications. (Sec. 17088, Rev. & Tax. Code) See ¶217 for a discussion of the pass-through of RIC income that is exempt from California personal income tax.

• *Constructive dividends*

Following federal cases involving the same issue, the State Board of Equalization held in *Appeal of Howard N. and Thelma Gilmore* (1961) (CCH CALIFORNIA TAX REPORTS ¶201-861) that unsupported travel and entertainment expenses disallowed to a closely-held corporation were taxable as constructive dividends to the individual shareholders. Later cases have been decided to the same effect.

• *Current California-federal differences*

Current differences between California and federal law are summarized briefly as follows:

— Federal law provides for "consent dividends" (applicable to "personal holding companies," etc.). There is no comparable California provision.

— Federal limitations periods for waivers of stock attribution are modified for California purposes. (Sec. 17132, Rev. & Tax. Code)

— California has not adopted a special federal rule governing generation-skipping transfers. (Sec. 17024.5(b), Rev. & Tax. Code)

— The federal provision relating to distributions by foreign corporations, foreign investment companies, and foreign personal holding companies is not applicable for California purposes. (Sec. 17024.5(b), Rev. & Tax. Code)

— Under both California and federal law, a corporate distribution may be a nontaxable return of capital if there are no "earnings and profits" out of which the distribution is made. However, the amount of "earnings and profits" of a corporation may be different for California tax purposes than it is for federal tax purposes. Such a difference may result in a particular distribution being nontaxable under one law but a taxable dividend under the other.

— California does not incorporate the special federal provisions for Domestic International Sales Corporations (DISC). Accordingly, a DISC is taxed under California law in the same manner as other corporations, and the special federal treatment of its dividends has no effect for California tax purposes. (Sec. 17024.5(b), Rev. & Tax. Code)

— California, unlike federal law, does not apply a lower tax rate to qualified dividend distributions.

— California does not allow parents to elect to include their child's dividend income on the parents return if the child is between the age of 14 and 24 (see below)

• *Dividend income from children*

As a result of California's current federal conformity date (see ¶103), California has not incorporated amendments made by the Tax Increase Prevention and Reconciliation Act of 2005 and the Small Business and Work Opportunity Tax Act of 2007 that allow parents to elect to report a child's interest and dividends on the parents' return as long as the child is under 19 years old or is a full time student over the age of 18, but under age 24, unless the earned income of such individual exceeds half of the individual's support for the year. Because California still limits the election for parents to interest income of children under age 14, parents that included the dividend income of children between the ages of 14 and 24 on their federal return must subtract such income from the amount included in their federal adjusted gross income, and the children age 14 and above with dividend income must each file a state return if they meet the minimum reporting requirement. (Pub. 1001, *Supplemental Guidelines to California Adjustments*)

• *Prior-year differences*

In addition to the differences listed above, there were prior-year differences that may continue to affect computations of basis. These prior-year differences concern the following:

— federal rules for distributions by World War I "personal service corporations";

— rules for corporate liquidations in 1954, 1955, and 1956;

— special California provisions for 1935 or 1936 distributions by a "personal holding company";

— effective dates (all before 1972) of provisions regarding redemption of stock through an affiliate, and "collapsible corporations";

— various amendments in 1954 and 1955, regarding distribution of stock dividends and rights, etc.;

— various amendments, in 1981 and before, relating to special rules for redemption of stock to pay death taxes;

— 1958 federal amendments to special rules for 12-month liquidations;

— 1964-1978 difference in rules for "sidewise attribution" in stock ownership rules;

— 1954-1961 difference in special rules regarding distributions of property with a government-secured loan; and

— 1969-1971 differences in rules for taxation of stock dividends.

¶227 Scholarship and Fellowship Grants

Law: Secs. 17131 (CCH CALIFORNIA TAX REPORTS ¶15-685).

Comparable Federal: Sec. 117 (CCH U.S. MASTER TAX GUIDE ¶879).

California conforms to federal law as of California's current federal conformity date (see ¶103). (Sec. 17131, Rev. & Tax. Code)

Certain scholarship and fellowship grants and tuition grants are excluded from taxable income, as long as the grant or scholarship does not represent compensation for services performed as a condition of the grant. In the case of graduate teaching or research assistants of exempt educational institutions, the amount of *any* tuition reduction for education at the employing institution may be excluded.

¶228 Meals and Lodging Furnished by Employer

Law: Sec. 17131 (CCH CALIFORNIA TAX REPORTS ¶15-705).

Comparable Federal: Sec. 119 (CCH U.S. MASTER TAX GUIDE ¶873).

California conforms to the federal law as of the current tie-in date (see ¶103). (Sec. 17131, Rev. & Tax. Code)

The value of meals and lodging furnished by an employer for the convenience of the employer is excluded from gross income, provided (1) the meals are furnished on the business premises of the employer and (2) the employee is required to accept the lodging on the employer's premises as a condition of employment.

Under both California and federal law, all meals furnished to employees on the employer's premises are treated as furnished for the convenience of the employer as long as more than 50% of the employees to whom such meals are provided are furnished the meals for the convenience of the employer.

¶229 Gain on Sale or Exchange of Personal Residence

Law: Secs. 17131, 17152 (CCH CALIFORNIA TAX REPORTS ¶15-710, 16-070, 16-270).

Comparable Federal: Sec. 121 (CCH U.S. MASTER TAX GUIDE ¶1705).

Both California and federal law allow an individual taxpayer to exclude from his or her gross income up to $250,000 ($500,000 for married taxpayers or registered domestic partners (RDPs) filing jointly) of gain realized on the sale or exchange of his or her residence if the taxpayer owned and occupied the residence as a principal residence for an aggregate period of at least two of the five years prior to the sale or exchange. Under both California and federal law, if a taxpayer does not meet the two-year ownership and use requirement due to a change in place of employment, health, or unforeseen circumstances, the exclusion may be prorated. (Sec. 17131, Rev. & Tax. Code)

Practice Pointer: Registered Domestic Partners/Same-Sex Married Couples

A registered domestic partner (see ¶119) who was subject to the $250,000 limit discussed above on his or her federal return, would be able to claim up to $500,000 if the registered domestic partner and his or her partner file a married, filing joint California personal income tax return. If the FTB determines that same-sex couples married prior to the passage of Proposition 8 should be treated as other spouses for Revenue and Tax Code purposes, similar treatment would apply to such same-sex married couples. See ¶119 for details.

The exclusion amount is based on federal filing status, and not on California filing status. The exclusion applies only to one sale or exchange every two years. The California rules are generally the same as the federal rules, except that under California law, but not federal, a portion of the two-year ownership and use requirement is waived for individuals who served in the Peace Corps (the period waived is the length of the time of service, up to a maximum of 18 months). (Sec. 17152, Rev. & Tax. Code) In addition, the $500,000 exclusion limit applies to RDPs under California, but not federal law. (Sec. 17021.7, Rev. & Tax. Code)

However, under both California and federal law, uniformed or foreign service personnel called to active duty away from home may elect to suspend the five-year test period for a period of up to five years. A federal election, or lack thereof, is binding for California purposes. (Sec. 17152(e), Rev. & Tax. Code)

California does not incorporate a federal provision that extends eligibility for the exclusion to estates, heirs, and qualified revocable trusts, applicable to estates of decedents dying after 2009. (Sec. 17152(f), Rev. & Tax. Code)

In addition, although California conforms to the federal provision (IRC Sec. 1033(f)(10)) that requires that a personal residence acquired in a like-kind exchange be held for at least five years in order to be eligible for the exclusion, as a result of California's current federal conformity date (see ¶103) California has not adopted an amendment made by the Gulf Opportunity Zone Act of 2005 that extends this requirement to transferees of the property. Nor does California incorporate amendments made by the Tax Relief and Health Care Act of 2006 and the Heroes Earnings Assistance and Tax Relief Act of 2008 that suspend the five-year test period and use period for certain employees of the intelligence community, and, effective for tax years beginning after 2007, for taxpayers serving in the Peace Corps.

Additional adjustments are required as the result of California's nonconformity to amendments made by the Mortgage Forgiveness Debt Relief Act of 2007 that allow an unmarried surviving spouse the $500,000 exclusion available to joint filers if the principal residence is sold or exchanged within two years of the spouse's death, for sales or exchanges after 2007.

Finally, California also does not conform to the federal provision that provides that gain from the sale of a principal residence that is allocable to periods of nonqualified use is not excluded from the taxpayer's income, effective for sales and exchanges after 2008. Unless a conforming amendment is adopted, California taxpayers will be able to claim the full exclusion on their California returns.

See ¶503 concerning a provision that allows nonrecognition of gain in situations involving involuntary conversion.

¶230 Employees of Foreign Country

Law: Sec. 17146 (CCH CALIFORNIA TAX REPORTS ¶15-700).

Comparable Federal: Sec. 893.

Exemption is granted for compensation for services of an employee of a foreign country, provided certain conditions are met. California law incorporates the federal law by reference. (Sec. 17146, Rev. & Tax. Code)

¶231 Gross Income of Nonresidents

Law: Secs. 17041, 17951-17955; Regs. 17951-4, 17951-6 (CCH CALIFORNIA TAX REPORTS ¶15-105, 15-115, 15-120, 15-515, 16-505, 16-510, 16-515, 16-520, 16-525, 16-530, 16-540, 16-545, 16-550, 16-555, 16-560, 16-565, 16-570).

Comparable Federal: Secs. 861-65, 911-12, 931-33 (CCH U.S. MASTER TAX GUIDE ¶2402 et seq., 2429, 2440, 2463).

California Forms: Form 540NR (California Nonresident or Part-Year Resident Income Tax Return), Sch. CA (540NR) (California Adjustments - Nonresidents or Part-Year Residents), Sch. R (Apportionment and Allocation of Income).

For purposes of determining a nonresident's taxable income (¶116) gross income of nonresidents includes only gross income from sources within California. (Sec. 17951, Rev. & Tax. Code)

A nonresident member of a partnership or similar organization must include his or her distributive share of income from California sources. A nonresident beneficiary of an estate or trust must include distributable income of the estate or trust from California sources. (Sec. 17953, Rev. & Tax. Code)

Nonresidents are taxed as though they were residents but with the tax computed on the basis of a prorated taxable income formula. (Sec. 17041, Rev. & Tax. Code) See ¶116 for details. FTB Pub. 1100, Taxation of Nonresidents and Individuals Who Change Residency, ¶403-885, provides extensive discussion and examples of the attribution rules for income from various sources.

A part-year resident is taxed on income regardless of source during the period of California residence and on income from California sources during the period of nonresidency. (Sec. 17041, Rev. & Tax. Code)

• *Pension income*

A former California resident's qualified retirement income received after leaving California is not subject to California income tax, even if accrued while the nonresident resided in California. The current exclusion from gross income encompasses income or distributions received from most tax-exempt trusts, simplified employee pensions, annuity plans and contracts, individual retirement plans, government plans, and deferred compensation plans of state and local governments and tax-exempt organizations, and it also encompasses specified distributions from nonqualified plans. (Sec. 17952.5, Rev. & Tax. Code)

Practice Pointer: Nonresident Partners

P.L. 109-264 (H.R. 4019), Laws 2006, amended 4 U.S.C. Sec. 114 to provide that the prohibition against taxing former resident's pension income applies to the retirement income of a nonresident retired partner, as well as a nonresident retired employee, and that the application of a predetermined formula cap or a cost-of-living adjustment in a nonqualified deferred compensation plan does not make the retirement income of such nonresidents subject to state taxation. These amendments apply retroactively to amounts received after December 31, 1995. Taxpayers should examine their prior year returns to determine if a refund claim is in order.

• *Income from tangible property*

Any income from ownership, control, management, sale or transfer of real or tangible personal property in California is income from California sources. (Reg. 17951-3, 18 CCR) In *Appeal of L.N. Hagood* (1960) (CCH CALIFORNIA TAX REPORTS ¶16-550.77), the State Board of Equalization (SBE) held that since U.S. oil and gas leases of lands in California are real property, the income arising out of the granting of purchase options relative thereto is taxable income from California sources to a nonresident.

• *Income from intangible property*

In general, income of nonresidents from intangible property has its source at the state of residence of the owner and is therefore not taxable by California (but see next paragraph). Alimony income is considered to be derived from an intangible asset and is not taxable to a nonresident. (Sec. 17952, Rev. & Tax. Code)

Income from intangible personal property, including gain on its sale or exchange, is attributable to California if the property has a business situs in the state. Such property is deemed to have a business situs in the state if it is employed as capital in California or its use and value become an asset of a business, trade, or profession in the state. Even if the property does not have a business situs in California, if a nonresident deals in the property in California with sufficient regularity as to constitute doing business in the state, the income from such activity is taxable in California. (Sec. 17952, Rev. & Tax. Code)

The source of gains and losses from the sale or other disposition of intangible personal property is determined at the time of the sale or disposition of that property. Consequently, gain from an installment sale of intangible property made by a California resident taxpayer continues to be sourced to California even if the taxpayer subsequently becomes a nonresident. In addition, a California nonresident who sells intangible personal property that had a business situs in California at the time of the sale would be taxed by California on gain as it is recognized upon receipt of future installment payments. (Regulation 17952, 18 CCR)

In *Appeal of Robert M. and Ann T. Bass et al.* (1989) (CCH CALIFORNIA TAX REPORTS ¶16-565.672), the SBE held that a nonresident's distributive share of income from a limited partnership that was headquartered in California and that was engaged in the acquisition, holding, monitoring, and disposition of stocks and other securities was not subject to California income tax, because the limited partnership was not doing business in California.

Income from qualifying investment securities is not taxable by California if an individual's only contact with the state with respect to the securities is through a broker, dealer, or investment adviser located in California. Special rules apply in the case of income from qualifying investment securities distributed to a nonresident by an investment partnership, a qualifying estate or trust, or a regulated investment company. Income from qualifying investment securities is taxable by California if

— the income is from investment activity that is interrelated with a California trade or business in which the nonresident owns an interest and the primary activities of the trade or business are separate and distinct from the acts of acquiring, managing, or disposing of qualified investment securities and

— the income is from qualifying investment securities that are acquired with the working capital of a California trade or business in which the nonresident owns an interest. (Sec. 17955, Rev. & Tax. Code)

• *Payment for contract termination*

In *Appeal of Edward and Carol McAneeley* (1980) (CCH CALIFORNIA TAX REPORTS ¶16-570.411), the taxpayer, a professional hockey player, was a Canadian resident employed by a California team. He received a $17,500 payment for termination of his California contract. The SBE held that the termination payment was not taxable by California, because the payment was for the sale of an intangible property right that had its situs in Canada.

• *Income from business*

Income of a business, trade, or profession carried on within the state is taxable. If such income is derived from both within and without the state, and if the part conducted outside the state is distinct and separate, only the gross income from the California operations need be reported. However, gross income from the entire business must be reported if there is any business relationship between the parts within and without the state (flow of goods, etc.) so that the net income from sources outside the state cannot be accurately determined. In such cases, a portion of the net income is attributed to California, ordinarily—but not always—by use of the apportionment formula described at ¶1305. (Reg. 17951-4, 18 CCR)

The source of net income of a nonresident sole proprietor, partner, S corporation shareholder, or limited liability company (LLC) member from a business, trade, or profession that is not business income must be determined in accordance with the sourcing rules discussed in Rev. & Tax. Code Secs. 17951 through 17956 and the regulations thereunder, and not by reference to the nonbusiness allocation rules of the Uniform Division of Income for Tax Purposes Act (UDITPA). The business activity of a partnership, LLC, or S corporation will not ordinarily be considered part of a unitary business with another business activity unless the partner, member, or shareholder owns, directly or indirectly, a 20% or more capital or profits interest in a partnership, LLC, or S corporation. In addition, the FTB has discretion to treat business activities as part of a unitary business if it determines such combination is appropriate after conducting a comparable uncontrolled price examination.

Taxpayers complete Sch. R for purposes of determining the amount of business income apportionable to California. See Chapter 13 for discussion of methods of apportionment, what constitutes business income subject to apportionment, etc. Regulation 17951-4 provides detailed explanations concerning sourcing of income for unitary multistate sole proprietorships, partnerships, S corporations, and limited liability companies and clarifies how to determine the 20% threshold discussed above. Special rules apply to professional corporations.

In *Appeal of Chester A. and Mary E. Johnson* (1981) (CCH CALIFORNIA TAX REPORTS ¶16-515.30), the taxpayers were Australian residents whose pet-food business operated in both California and Iowa. The taxpayers computed their income attributable to California by using a federal formula provided by Internal Revenue Code Section 911. The SBE upheld the Franchise Tax Board (FTB) in requiring the use of the three-factor formula required under prior law.

• *Compensation for services*

Compensation (including stock options) for personal services performed in California is considered attributable to California. (Reg. 17951-5, 18 CCR) This includes fees of nonresidents for professional services. However, California may not tax the income received from the following individuals to the extent prohibited under federal law (Amtrak Reauthorization and Improvement Act of 1990 (P.L. 101-322)):

— a nonresident who performs regularly-assigned duties while engaged as a pilot, master, officer, or crewman on a vessel operating on the navigable waters of more than one state;

— a nonresident employee of an airline, if 50% or less of the pay received by the employee is earned in California;

— a nonresident employee of a railroad, if the employee performs services in two or more states;

— a nonresident employee of an interstate motor carrier, if the employee performs services in two or more states; and

— a nonresident member of the U.S. Armed Forces who is stationed in California.

In addition, when a nonresident receives pension income that is based on services rendered in California, the income is not taxable by California (¶405).

In *Appeal of Hearst* (2002) (CCH CALIFORNIA TAX REPORTS ¶16-570.416), athletes' signing bonuses constituted compensation for services subject to apportionment under the duty days apportionment formula, and not true signing bonuses allocable 100% to their state of residence. Because the language of the signing bonus riders obligated the players to repay a proportionate share of the bonuses for any period of time in which they refused to practice or play, the bonuses represented compensation for services, and not mere consideration for signing the contracts.

In *Wilson et al. v. Franchise Tax Board* (1993) (CCH CALIFORNIA TAX REPORTS ¶16-570.415), a nonresident professional football player's income was properly apportioned to California on the basis of the ratio of the athlete's duty days spent in California to the athlete's total duty days. "Duty days" included all days from the beginning of the official preseason training through the last game, including post-season games, in which the team competed during the taxable year.

In *Paul L. and Joanne W. Newman v. Franchise Tax Board* (1989) (CCH CALIFORNIA TAX REPORTS ¶16-570.222), a nonresident actor's income from a motion picture was properly apportioned according to a formula that divided his working days in California by his total working days on the picture, with "working days" including all the days on which, by contract, he was exclusively committed to his employer and on call at the employer's discretion, and not merely those days on which he actually performed.

In *Appeal of Joseph Barry Carroll* (1987) (CCH CALIFORNIA TAX REPORTS ¶16-570.414), compensation paid to a nonresident professional basketball player employed by the Golden State Warriors was apportioned to California on the basis of a "working day" or "duty day" formula that included days spent in training camp, practice sessions, and team travel. The taxpayer argued that he was paid for games only, and not practice or travel days, but produced no evidence to that effect. Accordingly, the SBE computed his California-source income on the basis of the ratio of training camp, practice, travel, and game days spent in California to total training camp, practice, travel, and game days.

In *Appeal of Edwin O. and Wanda L. Stevens* (1986) (CCH CALIFORNIA TAX REPORTS ¶16-570.38), the SBE held that benefits, sick leave, and vacation pay earned while working and residing in California are California-source income and taxable in the state, even though the right to such benefits accrued during employment and residence in another state.

In *Appeal of Karl Bernhardt* (1984) (CCH CALIFORNIA TAX REPORTS ¶400-983), the taxpayer was a member of the Canadian Armed Forces who worked temporarily for Sperry Univac in California as a part of his service training. His salary was paid into a Canadian bank in Canadian funds. The SBE held that the salary was subject to California tax.

In *Appeal of George and Sheila Foster* (1984) (CCH CALIFORNIA TAX REPORTS ¶16-570.413), the taxpayer was an Ohio resident, where he played professional baseball for Cincinnati. He contended that $400,000 of his $985,000 salary for 1979 represented a "signing bonus" for signing a renegotiated contract, and that the "bonus" was not subject to apportionment by California according to the usual "working-days" formula. The SBE held that the $400,000 was a "playing bonus," subject to apportionment, and was not a "signing bonus" attributable to the state of residence.

In *Appeal of Dennis F. and Nancy Partee* (1976) (CCH CALIFORNIA TAX REPORTS ¶16-570.41), the taxpayer was a nonresident professional football player with the San Diego Chargers. Here also, the SBE upheld the FTB's determination of the portion of the taxpayer's total salary allocable to California on the basis of the number of "working days" spent in the State. The taxpayer argued for use of the "games-played" formula used in other sports—see the *Krake* case, discussed below.

In *Appeals of Philip and Diane Krake, et al.* (1976) (CCH CALIFORNIA TAX REPORTS ¶16-570.412), the twelve taxpayers were nonresident members of the Los Angeles Kings professional hockey team. The SBE upheld the FTB's application of the "games-played" formula to total salaries, to determine the portion allocable to California. The taxpayers argued that a portion of their salary should be allocated to off-season activities before applying the "games-played" formula. However, the SBE agreed with the FTB's contention that the "games-played" method, as applied to regular season games, is a practical and reasonable method that produces approximately the same result as the "working-days" method for baseball, basketball, and hockey players.

• *Airline personnel*

Wages of nonresident flight personnel are not taxable by California unless 50% of the employee's schedule flight time is in California. If the 50% threshold is met, then wages are apportioned on the ratio of the time spent in California to total scheduled flight time. (FTB Pub. 1031, Guidelines for Determining Residence Status, revised December 2007)

• *Burden of proof*

Appeal of Robert L. Webber (1976) (CCH CALIFORNIA TAX REPORTS ¶16-570.223), involved an actor who was a New York resident. Part of his earnings for his personal services came from a wholly-owned corporation. The question at issue was the amount of his income for services performed in California. The SBE held that the taxpayer had submitted sufficient evidence to shift the burden of proof to the FTB, concluding that the latter had not borne that burden and holding in favor of the taxpayer. For another case involving similar issues, see *Appeal of Janice Rule* (1976) (CCH CALIFORNIA TAX REPORTS ¶16-570.22). See also *Appeal of Oscar D. and Agatha E. Seltzer* (1980) (CCH CALIFORNIA TAX REPORTS ¶16-570.332); in this case a corporate executive who was an Oregon resident was subjected to California tax on one-third of his income, because he did not overcome the presumption of correctness of the FTB's determination.

• *Royalty income*

In Legal Ruling No. 345 (1970) (CCH CALIFORNIA TAX REPORTS ¶16-570.49), it was held that royalty income received by an author on the sale of books is compensation for personal services and is taxable at the place the services are performed. Where a nonresident author's writing was done in California, his royalties received from a New York publisher were subject to California tax.

• *Covenant not to compete*

Under Reg. 17951-6, 18 CCR, income from a covenant not to compete executed in connection with the sale of a business conducted entirely within California or within and without California is California-source income to the extent the income is assigned to California. Income is assigned to locations within the area covered by the covenant not to compete according to a formula that consists of the average of the property, payroll, and sales factors of the business that was sold, weighted in accordance with the general statutory formula for the apportionment of business income (currently, a double-weighted sales factor formula), as in effect for the tax year of sale.

In general, UDITPA and the applicable statutes and regulations apply, except that for purposes of computing the numerator and the denominator of the sales factor, all sales of tangible personal property are assigned to the state of the purchaser where the property is delivered or shipped, and the statutory throwback provisions do not apply. In addition, the FTB may use apportionment factors for another year or years or employ another method of assigning income if this formula does not accurately reflect the nature of the prohibited activities expressed or reasonably implied from the covenant not to compete, or if they do not accurately represent the location of the recent business activities of the business that was sold, such that there is a gross distortion of income assigned within the covered area.

CCH Comment: Covenant Not Sourced To California

Despite the FTB's regulations and policies, taxpayers should determine whether the covenant not to compete has any true value in California. A California court of appeal reversed the FTB's taxation of a nonresident's covenant not to compete, finding that California's taxation of the covenant violated the U.S. Commerce Clause because none of the payments received on the covenant arose from California activities or from capital located in or associated with California. The record demonstrated that the covenant had no value in California. The business that was sold had 100% of the California market and any potential competitor would have to invest a substantial amount of capital. (*Milhous v. FTB* (2005) (CCH CALIFORNIA TAX REPORTS ¶403-843))

In *Appeal of Stephen D. Bragg* (2003) (CCH CALIFORNIA TAX REPORTS ¶16-525.454), the SBE held that the FTB properly apportioned a taxpayer's income from a covenant-not-to-compete using the three-factor apportionment formula used by the business that made the payments to the taxpayer.

• *Change of residence status*

See ¶405 regarding determination of income subject to California tax when status changes from resident to nonresident or vice versa.

• *California-federal differences*

Although the federal law includes some rules comparable to the California law, the differences are so numerous that no attempt is made here to describe them. Any such comparison would be applicable only to nonresident aliens, because U.S. citizens and resident aliens are taxable for federal purposes on all their income from whatever source, with certain specific exemptions. California law has nothing comparable to the special federal provisions for earned income and deductions of Americans living and working abroad.

¶232 Patronage Allocations from Cooperatives

Law: Sec. 17086 (CCH CALIFORNIA TAX REPORTS ¶15-170).

Comparable Federal: Secs. 1381-83, 1385 (CCH U.S. MASTER TAX GUIDE ¶698).

California Form: Sch. CA (540) (California Adjustments - Residents).

With the exception of its treatment of agricultural cooperative patronage dividends, California's treatment of patronage allocations from cooperatives is the same as federal law. (Sec. 17086, Rev. & Tax. Code)

California provides optional methods of taxing non-cash patronage allocations from farmers' cooperatives and mutual associations. An election must be made to include such allocations in income either in the year the dollar amount of allocations is made known, or in the year the allocation is redeemed or realized. For a detailed discussion of the rules for such elections, see *Appeal of J.H. Johnson and Sons, Inc.* (1979) (CCH CALIFORNIA TAX REPORTS ¶15-170.25).

Generally, the federal rules require that allocations be included in income in the year they are received. The federal rules provide that cooperatives will not be allowed a deduction for patronage dividends and per-unit retain certificates unless the patrons include such amounts in taxable income, whether they are actually received or merely allocated.

¶233 S Corporation Shareholders

Law: Secs. 17087.5, 17951, 18006, 18535, 23800-10 (CCH CALIFORNIA TAX REPORTS ¶15-185, 16-565).

Comparable Federal: Secs. 1361-79 (CCH U.S. MASTER TAX GUIDE ¶309 et seq.).

The California taxation of shareholders of federal S corporations that have elected S corporation status for California purposes is the same as federal law as of the current IRC tie-in date (¶103). (Sec. 17087.5, Rev. & Tax. Code) (See ¶806 for a discussion of S corporations generally). Essentially, S corporation shareholders are treated in the same manner as that of partners in partnerships. (*Valentino et al. v. Franchise Tax Board* (2001) (CCH CALIFORNIA TAX REPORTS ¶15-185.72)

Because of California's current federal conformity date (¶103) California has not adopted amendments made by the Pension Protection Act of 2006 (PPA), as modified and extended by the Tax Technical Corrections Act of 2007 (TTCA) and the Emergency Economic Stabilization Act of 2008, that modify the computation of a shareholder's basis reduction in the S corporation's stock when the S corporation makes a charitable contribution. For federal purposes, except as otherwise provided, the basis reduction equals the shareholder's pro rata share of the adjusted basis of the contributed property rather than the fair market value of the contributed property, applicable to contributions made during the 2006 through 2008 tax years.

Under long-standing federal law, as adopted by California, the shareholders of qualified S corporations report the current corporate income as though they had earned it individually, thus avoiding a tax at the corporate level for federal purposes and most of the corporate tax for California purposes (California imposes a reduced corporate tax rate on S corporation income prior to its pass-through to shareholders) (¶806). Shareholders are entitled to a credit for their pro rata share of taxes paid to another state by the S corporation on income also taxed by California (¶128, ¶129).

CCH Comment: Reporting of Withholding Amounts on Schedule K-1

An S corporation must report withholding payments made from the S corporation that are allocated to all shareholders based on their stock ownership, as well as payments withheld-at-the-source on nonresident shareholders. The total withholding amount must be reported on each shareholder's Schedule K-1 (100S), line 14, and the S corporation must provide each shareholder with a completed Form 592-B, Nonresident Withholding Tax Statement. Shareholders must attach Form 592-B to the front of their California tax returns to claim the withheld amounts. (Instructions, Schedule K-1 (100S), Shareholder's Share of Income, Deductions, Credits, etc.; Instructions, Form 592-B, Nonresident Withholding Tax Statement)

In *Appeal of Merwyn P. Merrick, Sr. and Margaret F. Merrick* (1975) (CCH CALIFORNIA TAX REPORTS ¶15-185.51), the stockholders of a "tax-option" (S) corporation received distributions representing the proceeds of sale of the corporation's plant. The SBE held that the distributions were taxable as ordinary dividends.

See discussion at ¶718 of the *Winkenbach* case, involving the application of the doctrine of "equitable recoupment" where income was erroneously taxed to a corporation and later taxed to the individual stockholders.

CCH Comment: Basis Adjustments Related to Items From Closed Tax Years

The FTB has issued a technical advice memorandum (TAM) that addresses how a shareholder's basis in an S corporation is calculated when some years are closed by the statute of limitations. The TAM concludes that in situations when an S corporation has both items of income and deduction for the closed years and the shareholder failed to report these items on the shareholder's personal income tax return for the closed years, the shareholder's basis is not increased for items of income, but basis is decreased for items of deduction, but not below zero. Because the shareholder has not reported the items of loss or deduction, the shareholder may carry over any items of loss or deduction in excess of basis to future years. In instances when an S corporation has both items of income and deduction for the closed years and the shareholder reports all of these items on the shareholder's personal income tax return, basis is increased for items of income and basis is decreased for items of loss and deduction, but not below zero. Because the shareholder has reported and received the benefit of claiming these items of loss or deduction, the shareholder may not carry over any items of loss or deduction in excess of basis to future years.

The FTB has also taken the position that IRC Sec. 1016, the duty of consistency and/or the tax benefit rule, does not require a shareholder that reported items of loss and deduction in excess of the shareholder's basis in a closed year to increase the shareholder's income in an open year by the amount of the erroneous items of income and loss reported. In addition, a worthless loss deduction claimed in an open tax year generated from income items in an open tax year is not a double deduction, even if a shareholder reported losses in excess of basis in a closed year. The worthless loss deduction is not a double deduction with respect to the previous loss deductions. The basis that permits the taxpayer to take a deduction was generated from the income items in the open year. It is not attributable to any basis that was previously used. (*Technical Advice Memorandum 2003-305*, FTB, June 4, 2005, CCH CALIFORNIA TAX REPORTS ¶404-567)

• *Nonresident shareholders*

Nonresident shareholders are taxed on the portion of their distributive shares of an S corporation's income or loss, as modified for California purposes, that is derived from sources within the state. (Sec. 17951, Rev. & Tax. Code)

S corporations are required to withhold tax at a rate of 7% on distributions of California source income paid to their nonresident shareholders if the annual distributions to a shareholder are at least $1,500. (Sec. 18662, Rev. & Tax. Code; FTB Pub. 1017 (2008), Nonresident Withholding S Corporation and Partnership Guidelines) These shareholders typically must file California Form 540NR, California Nonresident or Part-Year Resident Income Tax Return, to report such income and pay any additional tax due or claim a refund. However, these shareholders may request a waiver of the withholding requirement using Form 588, Nonresident Withholding Waiver Request, or may elect to file a group nonresident return, which is discussed in detail at ¶619. (*Tax News*, California Franchise Tax Board, December 2006) See ¶714 for details.

Practical Analysis: Nonresident Group Returns

Nonresident shareholders should carefully weigh whether it makes sense to file a Form 540NR (California Nonresident Income Tax Return) or elect to file a group return. The group return is much less cumbersome. However, because taxpayers are precluded from claiming the personal exemption credit and a net operating loss on the group return and are also limited to claiming only those credits generated by the S corporation, the tax is often higher on the group return than if the nonresident completes an individual Form 540NR.

• *Part-year resident shareholders*

A part-year resident shareholder's distributive share of S corporation income is taxed based on the shareholder's period of residency and nonresidency during the S corporation's taxable year. The allocation of income between the period of residency and the period of nonresidency must be made in a manner that reflects the actual date of realization. In the absence of information that reflects the actual date of realization, the S corporation income for the corporation's taxable year must be allocated on a proportional basis between the two periods, using a daily pro rata method. (FTB Pub. 1100, Taxation of Nonresidents and Individuals Who Change Residency, CCH CALIFORNIA TAX REPORTS ¶403-885)

Practitioner Comment: Sourcing of Pass-Through Income

In Legal Ruling 2003-1, CCH CALIFORNIA TAX REPORTS ¶403-434, the FTB explains the computation of California income for owners of pass-through entities that change residency status during the year. Ch. 920 (A.B. 1115), Laws 2001, requires owners of pass-through entities to treat the items of income, deduction, and credit earned by such entities as if the items were earned by the owners at the same time and in the same manner as earned by the pass-through entity.

As noted in the ruling, the computation method is a significant shift from the method used in pre-2002 taxable years, which employed an accrual concept of accounting and looked to the individual's residency status on the last day of the pass-through entity's tax year. Under the prior method, if an individual moved out of California before the pass-through entity's year-end, the nonresident individual would only be taxed on his or her distributive share of pass-through entity income derived from California sources.

Taxpayers should keep in mind that the change to the sourcing of pass-through entity income described in the FTB's ruling is by no means clear in the provisions of A.B. 1115, so we may well see some taxpayers challenge the position outlined in the ruling.

Bruce Daigh, Chris Whitney, Contributing Editors

¶234 Merchant Marine Act Exemptions

Law: Sec. 17088.3 (CCH CALIFORNIA TAX REPORTS ¶192-869).

Comparable Federal: Sec. 7518.

California Form: Sch. CA (540) (California Adjustments - Residents).

Under Sec. 607 of the federal Merchant Marine Act, commercial fishermen and carriers can deposit part of their income in a special reserve fund to acquire or construct vessels, and can reduce their federal taxable income accordingly. Federal law, as adopted by California, provides detailed rules for treatment of deposits, withdrawals from the fund, etc. (Sec. 17088.3, Rev. & Tax. Code)

¶235 Cost-of-Living and Peace Corps Allowances

Law: None (CCH CALIFORNIA TAX REPORTS ¶16-060).

Comparable Federal: Sec. 912.

California Form: Sch. CA (540) (California Adjustments - Residents).

California has no provisions comparable to a federal law specifically excluding from income certain cost-of-living allowances of civilian officers and employees of the U.S. Government residing outside the U.S., and certain allowances of Peace Corps volunteers. In *Appeal of Sammie W. and Harriet C. Gillentine* (1975) (CCH CALIFORNIA TAX REPORTS ¶16-060.20), the taxpayer (presumably a California resident) received a cost-of-living allowance as a U.S. Government employee stationed in Hawaii. The State Board of Equalization held that the allowance was subject to California income tax.

¶236 Relocation Payments

Law: Sec. 7269, Government Code (CCH CALIFORNIA TAX REPORTS ¶16-332).

Comparable Federal: Public Law 91-646.

Both California and federal laws provide that a person who is displaced from real property by a public entity may receive tax-exempt governmental assistance in the form of relocation payments.

California law also allows taxpayers to exclude from gross income tenant relocation assistance payments if such payments are required by state law or local ordinance. (Sec. 7269, Govt. Code)

¶237 Income from Original Issue Discount

Law: Secs. 17024.5, 17224, 18151, 18178 (CCH CALIFORNIA TAX REPORTS ¶15-720, 16-075, 16-280).

Comparable Federal: Secs. 163(e), 1271-88, 6706 (CCH U.S. MASTER TAX GUIDE ¶1859 et seq., 1952 et seq.).

California Forms: Sch. CA (540) (California Adjustments - Residents), Sch. CA (540NR) (California Adjustments - Residents or Part-Year Residents).

The reporting of income from original issue discount by the holder of debt instruments is the same under California law as federal as of the current IRC tie-in date (¶103).

"Original issue discount" is the excess of the stated redemption price of a debt instrument at maturity over its issue price.

Although California generally conforms to the federal interest deduction allowed under IRC Sec. 163, an addition adjustment may be required by issuers of original issue discount (OID) for debt instruments issued in 1985 and 1986. Unlike federal law, an issuer is required to deduct the amount of OID attributable to the instrument each year. However, different rules applied in California for debt instruments issued in 1985 or 1986 and California law requires that any differences between state and federal law concerning the OID for these instruments be taken into account in the year that the debt instrument matures, is sold, exchanged, or otherwise disposed of. (Sec. 17224, Rev. & Tax. Code) Consequently, issuers of the debt instruments must make an addition adjustment to the extent that the amount eligible for deduction for California personal income tax purposes exceeds the amount reported on the federal return. A subtraction is allowed if the federal deduction exceeds the California deduction.

California conforms to the federal law used to determine how much original issue discount a purchaser of tax-exempt stripped bonds or coupons must attribute to those bonds or coupons. California also conforms to the federal provision that splits the yield on certain high-yield OID obligations into a deductible interest element and a nondeductible element representing return on equity. (Sec. 18151, Rev. & Tax. Code; Sec. 18178, Rev. & Tax. Code)

The Franchise Tax Board has taken the position that OID on "stripped" U.S. Treasury obligations is interest on U.S. obligations and is exempt from California taxation. Such obligations include securities such as TIGRs and CATs, which are issued by investment firms (¶217).

¶238 Expense Reimbursements

Law: Secs. 17081, 17131 (CCH CALIFORNIA TAX REPORTS ¶15-515, 15-760).

Comparable Federal: Secs. 82, 123, 132 (CCH U.S. MASTER TAX GUIDE ¶877, 1076).

Specific rules are provided for certain types of expense reimbursement. California law incorporates federal law by reference as of the current IRC tie-in date (see ¶103). (Sec. 17081, Rev. & Tax. Code; Sec. 17131, Rev. & Tax. Code)

• *Moving expenses*

California adopts federal law allowing a taxpayer to exclude from gross income as a qualified fringe benefit any amount received by the taxpayer from an employer for moving expenses that would have been deductible by the taxpayer if they had not been reimbursed. (Sec. 17081, Rev. & Tax. Code)

The source of reimbursed moving expenses is the state to which the taxpayer moves, regardless of the taxpayer's place of residence when the reimbursement is made. (FTB Pub. 1031, Guidelines for Determining Residency Status)

Moving expense deductions are discussed at ¶328.

• *Loss on sale of home*

Generally, reimbursement for a loss on sale of a personal residence would be includible in income because the loss would be a personal one and nondeductible. However, where the loss is incurred in another state in connection with a move to California, the taxpayer might take the position that the reimbursement is compensation for services outside California during the period before he or she became a California resident and therefore is not taxable in California (¶405). On the other hand, the Franchise Tax Board (FTB) has taken the position that such a reimbursement is, in effect, a bonus for future services in California and is taxable.

CCH Practical Analysis: Reimbursement of Loss May Be Excludable

Under the FTB's reasoning, it would appear that reimbursement for a loss on the sale of a personal residence in connection with a move from California to another state would not be includible in California income.

Appeal of William H. Harmount and Estate of Dorothy E. Harmount (1977) (CCH CALIFORNIA TAX REPORTS ¶205-777) involved a taxpayer who moved in 1970 from Illinois to California. As an inducement to accept employment in California, the new employer reimbursed the taxpayer for certain expenses, including $5,031 for expenses in connection with the sale of an Illinois home. The State Board of Equalization held that the reimbursement represented compensation for services to be performed in California, subject to California tax. To the same effect, see *Appeal of Peter M. and Anita B. Berk* (1984) (CCH CALIFORNIA TAX REPORTS ¶15-535.33). See also the *Frame* case, discussed at ¶405, holding in effect that the source of the reimbursement income is irrelevant if the income "accrues" after the taxpayer becomes a California resident.

• *Living expenses*

Reimbursement from an insurance company for excess living expenses paid as a result of destruction (or threatened destruction) of the taxpayer's home by fire or other casualty is excluded from gross income under both California (Sec. 17081, Rev. & Tax. Code) and federal law (IRC Sec. 123).

¶239 Community Income

Law: Sec. 771, Family Code (CCH CALIFORNIA TAX REPORTS ¶15-125).

Comparable Federal: Secs. 66, 879 (CCH U.S. MASTER TAX GUIDE ¶710).

In general, in the absence of an agreement to the contrary, earnings of spouses and registered domestic partners (RDPs) who are domiciled in California and are not permanently separated are community property. On separate returns, any community income or deductions must be split equally between the spouses or RDPs. The credit for a dependent supported by community funds may be taken by either spouse or RDP.

Caution Note: Registered Domestic Partners and Same-Sex Married Couples

California's community property tax laws apply to registered domestic partners (RDPs) as well. Consequently, beginning with the 2007 taxable year, RDPs who file separate income tax returns must each report one-half of the combined income earned by both RDPs, as spouses do, rather than their respective individual incomes for the taxable year. (Uncodified Sec. 1, Ch. 802 (S.B. 1827), Laws 2006)

Although California treats income earned by RDPs as community income, the Internal Revenue Service does not. Consequently, RDPs filing married, filing separately should consult the FTB Pub. 1051A, Guidelines for Married/RDP Filing Separate Returns, and utilize the worksheets contained therein for information on how to determine the community income that must be reported on the California return.

At the time this book went to press, the FTB had not yet determined the tax treatment of same-sex individuals who were married prior to Proposition 8's passage, which repealed the rights of such individuals to legally marry. If the FTB recognizes such marriages as valid, community property laws would apply. See ¶119 for details.

FTB Pub. 1031 (Guidelines for Determining Residency Status) provides a useful chart that demonstrates how income should be reported if a spouses or RPDs are residents of different states and how to treat their respective incomes, depending on whether the state of residency is a community property or separate property state.

Where the spouses or RDPs are separated with no intention of resuming the marital relationship, the earnings of each spouse or RDP during the period of separation are his or her separate property. This is the effect of a provision of the Family Code. (Sec. 771, Fam. Code)

Both California and federal law provide relief for the "innocent spouse" in certain community-property situations and empower the Internal Revenue Service/Franchise Tax Board to treat community income as separate under certain conditions (¶107).

Where one spouse is a nonresident alien, community property laws are inapplicable to some extent for federal income tax purposes; California has not conformed to this federal treatment.

Several decisions of the State Board of Equalization (SBE) have held a California-resident wife taxable on one-half of her nonresident husband's earnings, on the ground that the husband was domiciled in California and his earnings were therefore community property. See *Appeal of Annette Bailey* (1976) (CCH CALIFORNIA TAX REPORTS ¶15-125.252), where the husband was a resident of Canada and *Appeal of Nancy*

B. Meadows (1980) (CCH CALIFORNIA TAX REPORTS ¶15-252.259), where the husband was a resident of Alabama.

Also, see *Appeal of George F. and Magdalena Herrman* (1962) (CCH CALIFORNIA TAX REPORTS ¶15-125.25), where the husband was a resident and domiciliary of the State of Washington: the SBE held the wife taxable on one-half of the husband's income because she was entitled to it under Washington law. To the same effect, see *Appeal of Roy L. and Patricia A. Misskelley* (1984) (CCH CALIFORNIA TAX REPORTS ¶15-125.255); in this case the husband was a resident and domiciliary of Nevada.

In *Appeal of Richard and Eva Taylor* (1989) (CCH CALIFORNIA TAX REPORTS ¶15-125.257), a wife was liable for tax on her community share of her husband's foreign earnings, and he was liable for tax on his community share of her California earnings because even though the husband established and maintained foreign residence, both spouses remained California domiciliaries.

¶240 Income from Investments in Depressed Areas

Law: Sec. 17235 (CCH CALIFORNIA TAX REPORTS ¶16-280).

Comparable Federal: None.

California Forms: FTB 3805Z (Enterprise Zone Deduction and Credit Summary).

California allows a deduction for net interest received from loans made to a trade or business located in an enterprise zone (¶104). It does not apply to anyone who has an ownership interest in the debtor. (Sec. 17235, Rev. & Tax. Code)

According to the Instructions to the FTB 3805Z, Enterprise Zone Deduction and Credit Summary, the deduction may only be claimed for payments received on or before the zone's expiration date.

The deduction for interest received from loans made to an enterprise zone business is reported on FTB 3805Z.

¶241 Ridesharing and Employee Commuter Deductions

Law: Secs. 17090, 17149 (CCH CALIFORNIA TAX REPORTS ¶15-705, 16-065, 16-265).

Comparable Federal: Sec. 132 (CCH U.S. MASTER TAX GUIDE ¶863).

California Forms: Sch. CA (540) (California Adjustments - Residents), Sch. CA (540NR) (California Adjustments - Nonresidents or Part-Year Residents).

Compensation or the fair market value of nonwage benefits furnished by an employer to an employee for participation in any employer-sponsored ridesharing program in California is excluded from the employee's California gross income. This includes compensation or benefits received for the following items:

— commuting in a vanpool, subscription taxipool, carpool, buspool, private commuter bus, or ferry;

— transit passes for use by employees or their dependents, other than transit passes for use by dependents who are elementary or secondary school students;

— free or subsidized parking for employees who participate in ridesharing arrangements;

— bicycling to or from work;

— travel to or from a telecommuting facility; or

— use of any other alternative transportation method that reduces the use of a motor vehicle by a single occupant for travel to or from that individual's place of employment.

(Sec. 17149, Rev. & Tax. Code)

Unlike the California gross income exclusion for ridesharing and employee commuter deductions, including the value of parking provided to ridesharing participants, the federal exclusion is subject to a cap.

Cash allowances received by an employee pursuant to a parking cash-out program (¶343), unless used for ridesharing purposes, must be included in the employee's gross income. (Sec. 17090, Rev. & Tax. Code)

¶242 Employee Educational Assistance Plans

Law: Sec. 17151 (CCH CALIFORNIA TAX REPORTS ¶15-685).

Comparable Federal: Sec. 127 (CCH U.S. MASTER TAX GUIDE ¶871).

California law is substantially the same as federal law concerning the exclusion of up to $5,250 of employer-provided educational assistance benefits from an employee's gross income. (Sec. 17151, Rev. & Tax. Code)

¶243 Payments for Conservation and Environmental Protection

Law: Secs. 17131, 17135.5 (CCH CALIFORNIA TAX REPORTS ¶15-690, 16-260).

Comparable Federal: Sec. 126 (CCH U.S. MASTER TAX GUIDE ¶881).

California incorporates the federal exclusion for cost-sharing payments received under certain conservation and environmental protection programs. (Sec. 17131, Rev. & Tax. Code)

• *Payments received by forest landowners*

In addition, California provides a specific exclusion from gross income for cost-share payments received by forest landowners from the Department of Forestry and Fire Protection pursuant to the California Forest Improvement Act of 1978 or from the United States Department of Agriculture, Forest Service, under the Forest Stewardship Program and the Stewardship Incentives Program, pursuant to the federal Cooperative Forestry Assistance Act. The amount of any excluded payment must not be considered for a determination of the basis of property acquired or improved or in computation of any deduction to which the taxpayer may otherwise be entitled. (Sec. 17135.5, Rev. & Tax. Code)

¶244 Water Conservation Rebates and Vouchers

Law: Sec. 17138 (CCH CALIFORNIA TAX REPORTS ¶16-260).

Comparable Federal: None.

California Forms: Sch. CA (540) (California Adjustments - Residents), Sch. CA (540NR) (California Adjustments - Nonresidents or Part-Year Residents).

California law treats certain water conservation rebates and vouchers received by taxpayers from local water or energy agencies or suppliers as excludable refunds or price adjustments rather than as taxable income for personal income tax purposes. To qualify, a rebate/voucher must be for the taxpayer's expenses in purchasing or installing

— water conservation water closets or urinals that meet specified performance standards and use no more than (1) 1.6 gallons per flush in the case of a water closet or (2) 1 gallon per flush in the case of a urinal;

— a water and energy efficient clothes washer; and/or

— a plumbing device necessary to use recycled water for toilet and urinal flushing in structures if required by a state or local agency.

(Sec. 17138, Rev. & Tax. Code)

¶245 Energy Conservation Subsidies

Law: Secs. 17131, 17138.1, Rev. & Tax. Code; Secs. 25433.5 and 25434.5, Public Resources Code (CCH CALIFORNIA TAX REPORTS ¶15-690, 16-260, 112-001).

Comparable Federal: Sec. 136 (CCH U.S. MASTER TAX GUIDE ¶884).

California incorporates the federal gross income exclusion for subsidies received from a public utility for the purchase or installation of an energy conservation measure designed to reduce the consumption of electricity or natural gas or to improve the management of energy demand with respect to a dwelling unit. (Sec. 17131, Rev. & Tax. Code)

Energy-efficienct home improvement grants awarded by the State Energy Resources Conservation and Development Commission to an individual with a gross annual income equal to or less than 200% of the federal poverty level are excluded from the individual's gross income (Sec. 25433.5, Pub. Res. Code).

California specifically excludes from gross income any amount received as a rebate, voucher, or other financial incentive issued by the California Energy Commission, the California Public Utilities Commission, or a local public utility for the purchase or installation of (1) thermal energy systems, (2) solar energy systems, (3) wind energy systems that produce electricity, and (4) fuel cell generating systems that produce electricity. (Sec. 17138.1, Rev. & Tax. Code)

¶246 Crime Hotline Rewards

Law: Sec. 17147.7 (CCH CALIFORNIA TAX REPORTS ¶16-325).

Comparable Federal: None.

California Forms: Sch. CA (540) (California Adjustments - Residents), Sch. CA (540NR) (California Adjustments - Nonresidents or Part-Year Residents).

Rewards received from a crime hotline are excludable from gross income if the hotline is established by a government agency or a California nonprofit charitable organization and is authorized by a government entity. Employees of a government agency or nonprofit charitable organization that contributes reward funds to the crime hotline are ineligible to claim this exclusion. (Sec. 17147.7, Rev. & Tax. Code)

¶247 Medical and Health Savings Accounts

Law: Secs. 17131.4, 17131.5, 17201, 17215, 17215.1 (CCH CALIFORNIA TAX REPORTS ¶15-755, 16-100).

Comparable Federal: Secs. 138, 220, 223 (CCH U.S. MASTER TAX GUIDE ¶860).

California Form: FTB 3805P (Additional Taxes on Qualified Plans (Including IRAs) and Other Tax-Favored Accounts).

Except as noted below, California incorporates federal law concerning medical savings accounts (MSAs), but does not follow the federal treatment of health savings accounts (HSAs).

• *Medical savings accounts*

With the exception of the amount of penalties imposed on unauthorized withdrawals, California law is the same as federal law as of the current IRC tie-in date (¶103). Employer's contributions to an Archer MSA and any interest or dividends earned on an Archer MSA are excluded from a taxpayer's gross income. (Sec. 17201, Rev. & Tax. Code)

Withdrawals made from an Archer MSA are also exempt if used to pay unreimbursed qualified medical expenses of the taxpayer, spouse, and dependents (which are essentially the same as those expenses that qualify for an itemized deduction). Distributions from an Archer MSA for nonmedical purposes are treated as taxable income and are subject to a 10% penalty (15% under federal law), unless the distribution is made after the taxpayer reaches age 65, becomes disabled, or dies. (Sec. 17215, Rev. & Tax. Code) The penalty is reported on FTB 3805P.

CCH Comment: Registered Domestic Partners

Although registered domestic partners (RDPs) or former RDPs are required to be treated as married taxpayers or former spouses under California income and franchise tax laws, an RDP will not be treated as a spouse if such treatment would result in disqualification of an Archer medical savings account. (Sec. 17021.7, Rev. & Tax. Code)

• *Medicare Plus Choice MSAs/Medicare Advantage MSAs*

Under both California and federal law, certain seniors are permitted to establish Medicare Plus Choice MSAs (renamed the Medicare Advantage MSA under federal law). (Sec. 17201, Rev. & Tax. Code) The tax treatment of Medicare Plus Choice MSAs is similar to that of regular MSAs, with the following exceptions:

— tax-free distributions from the Medicare Plus Choice MSA may be used only for the qualified medical expenses of the account holder;

— the Secretary of Health and Human Services, rather than the account holder's employer, makes tax-free contributions to the Medicare Plus Choice MSA; and

— a Medicare Plus Choice MSA may only be used in conjunction with a high deductible Medicare Plus Choice MSA health plan (MSA health plan).

• *Health savings accounts*

California does not incorporate the federal gross income exclusion of employer contributions to HSAs. (Sec. 17131.4, Rev. & Tax. Code; Sec. 17131.5, Rev. & Tax. Code) Nor does California incorporate the federal deduction for taxpayer contributions to an HSA (see ¶326).

Planning Note: Employer Contributions Excluded From W-2 Wages

Because employers are required to exclude HSA contributions made to eligible employees from their W-2 wages, employers must reflect California and federal wage differences on their employees' Form W-2s.

As a result of California's nonconformity to federal law (¶103), interest and dividends earned on HSAs are also subject to California personal income tax. Because such amounts are excluded from federal adjusted gross income, an addition adjustment is required for the excluded interest and dividends.

Finally, amounts rolled over from a medical savings account into an HSA are excluded from federal income tax, but subject to California personal income tax. (Sec. 17215.1, Rev. & Tax. Code) The amount withdrawn from the MSA is subject to California's penalty on nonqualified withdrawals (discussed above).

Practice Note: Treatment of Nonqualified Distributions

Nonqualified distributions from HSAs are subject to federal tax. However, because contributions to and earnings on HSAs are subject to California personal income tax , such distributions are not subject to California personal income taxation. The adjustment is made on Sch. CA (540), line 21f, column B. (Instructions, Sch. CA (540), California Adjustments --Residents)

¶248 Holocaust, Internment, and Genocide Victim Compensation

Law: Secs. 17131.1, 17131.2, 17155, 17155.5, 17156.5 (CCH CALIFORNIA TAX REPORTS ¶16-335).

Comparable Federal: United States-Federal Republic of Germany Income Tax Convention; Sec. 803 of the Economic Growth and Tax Relief Reconciliation Act of 2001 (P.L. 107-16) (CCH U.S. MASTER TAX GUIDE ¶802).

California Form: Sch. CA (540) (California Adjustments - Residents).

California law mirrors federal law (Sec. 803, P.L. 107-16) that excludes from gross income Holocaust restitution payments and related interest received by an eligible individual or the individual's heirs or estate. In addition, California provides exclusions for Canadian government reparation payments paid to persons of Japanese ancestry and to Armenian genocide settlement payments. (Sec. 17131.1, Rev. & Tax. Code)

• *Holocaust restitution payments*

For purposes of the exclusion for Holocaust restitution payments, an eligible individual is a person who was persecuted by Nazi Germany, any other Axis regime, or any other Nazi-controlled or Nazi- allied country on the basis of the person's race, religion, physical or mental disability, or sexual orientation. An excludable restitution payment is a payment or distribution to an individual or the individual's heirs or estate that is one of the following:

(1) payable by reason of the individual's status as an eligible individual;

(2) the direct or indirect return of, or compensation or reparation for, assets stolen or hidden from or otherwise lost to the individual before, during, or immediately after World War II by reason of the individual's status as an eligible individual; or

(3) interest payable as part of any payment or distribution described in (1) or (2), above.

Excludable interest is interest earned from

— escrow accounts or settlement funds established pursuant to the settlement of *In re Holocaust Victim Assets Litigation,* U.S. District Court, Eastern District of New York, C.A. No. 96-4849, August 12, 1998;

— certain funds to benefit individuals or their heirs that are created by the International Commission on Holocaust Insurance Claims; or

— similar funds subject to the administration of the U.S. courts that are created to provide excludable restitution payments to eligible individuals or their heirs or estates.

For purposes of the exclusion, the basis of any property received by an eligible individual or the individual's heirs or estate as part of an excludable restitution payment is the fair market value of the property at the time of receipt. (Sec. 17131.1, Rev. & Tax. Code)

Under California's Holocaust Victim Compensation Relief Act, as under federal law, payments or property received as compensation pursuant to the German Act Regulating Unresolved Property Claims are also excludable from an individual's gross income. The basis of any property received pursuant to the German Act is the fair market value of the property at the time of receipt by the individual. (Sec. 17155, Rev. & Tax. Code)

In addition, California law allows Holocaust victims, or their heirs or beneficiaries, to exclude from gross income settlements received for claims against any entity or individual for any recovered asset. For purposes of the expanded exclusion,

"Holocaust victim" means any person who was persecuted by Nazi Germany or any Axis regime during any period from 1933 to 1945. "Recovered asset" means any asset of any kind, including any bank deposits, insurance proceeds, or artwork owned by a Holocaust victim during any period from 1920 to 1945, inclusive, and any interest earned on the asset, that was withheld from that victim or the victim's heirs or beneficiaries from and after 1945 and that was not recovered, returned, or otherwise compensated to the victim or his or her heirs or beneficiaries until after 1994. Humanitarian reparation payments made to persons required to perform slave or forced labor during World War II are excluded for California, but not federal, income tax purposes. (Sec. 17155.5, Rev. & Tax. Code)

• *Japanese internment reparation payments*

California law, but not federal law, also excludes from gross income reparation payments made by the Canadian government for the purpose of redressing the injustice done to persons of Japanese ancestry who were interned in Canada during World War II. (Sec. 17156.5, Rev. & Tax. Code)

• *Armenian genocide settlement payments*

Settlement payments and related interest received by eligible individuals (or by the heirs or estates of eligible individuals) who were persecuted on the basis of race or religion during the Armenian genocide (1915—1923) are excludable from gross income for California personal income tax purposes. (Sec. 17131.2, Rev. & Tax. Code)

¶249 Adoption Assistance Programs

Law: Sec. 17131 (CCH CALIFORNIA TAX REPORTS ¶15-605).

Comparable Federal: Sec. 137 (CCH U.S. MASTER TAX GUIDE ¶1306).

Under both California and federal law, an employee may exclude from his or her gross income amounts paid or expenses incurred for the employee's qualified adoption expenses as part of an employer's written, nondiscriminatory, adoption assistance program. Under California law and federal law, the maximum amount that may be excluded in 2008 is $11,650 of qualified expenses per eligible child. The $11,650 exclusion is allowed with respect to the adoption of a special needs child, regardless of the amount of qualified expenses. For the 2008 taxable year, the exclusion is phased out ratably for taxpayers with adjusted gross incomes of between $174,730 and $214,730.

¶250 Qualified Tuition Programs

Law: Secs. 17140, 17140.3 (CCH CALIFORNIA TAX REPORTS ¶15-685).

Comparable Federal: Secs. 529, 530 (CCH U.S. MASTER TAX GUIDE ¶697).

California Form: FTB 3805P (Additional Taxes on Qualified Plans (Including IRAs) and Other Tax-Favored Accounts).

California incorporates IRC Sec. 529, as of California's current IRC conformity date (see ¶103), concerning qualified tuition programs, which excludes from the gross income of a beneficiary of, or contributor to, a qualified tuition program, qualified distributions or earnings under such program. To qualify for the exclusion, distributions must be used to pay for a beneficiary's qualified higher education expenses. However, amounts distributed to a contributor (*e.g.*, refunds to a parent or other relative) will be included in the contributor's gross income to the extent that such amounts exceed the contributions made by that person. (Sec. 17140.3, Rev. & Tax. Code)

Distributions are also not taxable under the annuity rules if they are transferred within 60 days to another qualified tuition program for the benefit of the designated beneficiary (limited to once in a 12-month period) or to the credit of another beneficiary under a qualified tuition program who is a family member of the designated beneficiary. Also, a change in beneficiary will not be treated as a distribution if the new beneficiary is a member of the previously designated beneficiary's family.

Practice Note: EGTRRA Amendments Made Permanent

The Pension Protection Act of 2006 (PPA) (P.L. 109-280) made permanent the amendments enacted by the Economic Growth and Tax Relief and Reconciliation Act (EGTRRA) (P.L. 107-16) that affect qualified tuition programs. (Uncodified Sec. 1304 of the PPA) These amendments were originally scheduled to expire at the end of 2010. California incorporates the EGTRRA's sunset date provision "in the same manner and to the same taxable years as it applies for federal income tax purposes." (Sec. 17024.5(a)(2)(B), Rev. & Tax. Code) As the PPA made the sunset provision inapplicable to the EGTRRA amendments that impacted qualified tuition programs, it appears as though California would similarly disregard the sunset provision and make these amendments permanent for California income tax purposes as well.

Distributions not used for qualified education expenses are subject to a 2.5% penalty (10% for federal purposes). (Sec. 17140.3, Rev. & Tax. Code) The penalty is reported on FTB 3805P.

California law contains a provision specifically addressing California's qualified state tuition program, the "Golden State Scholarshare Trust," which generally mirrors the treatment of contributions to, and distributions from, a qualified tuition program. (Sec. 17140, Rev. & Tax. Code)

Practice Pointer: Contributors May Remove Funds from Account

If the beneficiary of a Scholarshare account does not ever attend a qualified educational institution, or if there are still funds in the account after the beneficiary graduates from a qualified educational institution, the funds can be transferred to a Scholarshare account for the benefit of another family member. Alternatively, the contributor to the account may cancel the account and take back the available funds, but must pay taxes on any earnings, as well as a penalty.

¶251 Disaster Relief Payments

Law: Sec. 17131 (CCH CALIFORNIA TAX REPORTS ¶15-675).

Comparable Federal: Secs. 139, 139A (CCH U.S. MASTER TAX GUIDE ¶897).

California Form: Sch. CA (540) (California Adjustments - Residents).

California conforms to federal law, which excludes from gross income qualified disaster relief payments received as a result of terroristic or military actions against the United States or one of its allies, Presidentially-declared disasters (renamed "federally-declared disasters" by the Emergency Economic Stabilization Act), common carrier accidents, other events determined by the Secretary of the Internal Revenue Service to be of a catastrophic nature, or disasters determined to warrant federal, state, or local government assistance. Under federal law, as incorporated by California, these payments are excludable only to the extent the payment is not otherwise compensated for by insurance or otherwise. (Sec. 17131, Rev. & Tax. Code)

In addition, as a result of California's current IRC conformity date¶103), California has not conformed to federal amendments enacted by the Mortgage Forgiveness Debt Relief Act of 2007 that allow qualified volunteer firefighters and emergency medical responders to exclude from their gross income reductions of state and local taxes and limited payments made to such volunteer emergency personnel in exchange for providing services, effective for federal purposes for tax years beginning after 2007 and before 2011. Consequently, taxpayers claiming such an exclusion must make an addition adjustment on their California personal income tax returns.

¶252 Prescription Drug Subsidies

Law: Sec. 17139.6 (CCH CALIFORNIA TAX REPORTS ¶16-100).

Comparable Federal: Sec. 139A (CCH U.S. MASTER TAX GUIDE ¶859).

California does not incorporate the federal exclusion of federal government subsidies provided to employers to compensate them for costs incurred in a qualified retiree prescription drug plan. (Sec. 17139.6, Rev. & Tax. Code)

¶253 Dependent Care Assistance

Law: Secs. 17021.7, 17131 (CCH CALIFORNIA TAX REPORTS ¶15-660).

Comparable Federal: Sec. 129 (CCH U.S. MASTER TAX GUIDE ¶869).

California generally incorporates federal law concerning dependent care assistance programs. Consequently, taxpayers who claim the exclusion of payments of up to $5,000 ($2,500 in the case of a married person filing separately) to an employee for dependent care assistance, when made under an employer's written nondiscriminatory plan, on the federal return are not required to make an adjustment on their California return. However, adjustments may be required by registered domestic partners (RDPs) who claim the deduction on their federal return. (Sec. 17021.7, Rev. & Tax. Code)

For RDPs filing a joint return, an addition adjustment must be made on the California return if the RDPs' combined exclusion exceeded $5,000 on their federal returns. Similarly, an RDP filing separately must make an addition adjustment on his or her California return if he or she excluded more than $2,500 of dependent care assistance benefits on his or her federal return. (FTB Pub. 737, Tax Information for Registered Domestic Partnerships)

¶254 Income Received by Native Americans

Law: (CCH CALIFORNIA TAX REPORTS ¶15-180).

Income received by Native Americans from Indian country sources is exempt from personal income taxation. To be exempt, the taxpayer must be a member of a federally recognized tribe and must live in Indian country. In addition, the income earned must be from the same Indian country source where the taxpayer resides and is a tribal member. Wages earned on an Indian reservation may be subtracted on Schedule CA (540 or 540NR), line 7, column B. Other sources of income should be subtracted on Line 21(f).

A listing of federally recognized California Indian tribes is available by searching for "federally recognized" on the National Conference of State Legislatures Web site at http://www.ncsl.org.

If a P.O. Box is used as a Native American's mailing address, his or her physical residence address must be included in the blank line on Line 21(f). (*FTB Pub. 1001, Supplemental Guidelines to California Adjustments*, CCH CALIFORNIA TAX REPORTS ¶404-588; *FTB Pub. 674, Frequently Asked Questions About the Income Taxation of Native American Indians*, revised August 2007, CCH CALIFORNIA TAX REPORTS ¶404-600)

Planning Note: Proof of Indian Reservation Residency

Taxpayers claiming an exemption based on residency on an Indian reservation need to gather and retain documentation to support their residency claim. A statement from the Indian tribe council stating that an individual has a home on the reservation is not sufficient. Records such as homeowner's or renter's insurance policies, motor vehicle licenses, automobile insurance policies, utility bills etc, showing an Indian reservation address should be maintained. Declarations from an individual's parents, friends, or relatives verifying the individual's Indian reservation residency may also be used to support an individual's Indian reservation residency claim. (*FTB Pub. 674, Frequently*

Asked Questions About the Income Taxation of Native American Indians, revised August 2007, CCH CALIFORNIA TAX REPORTS ¶404-600)

• *Military income*

Military income is exempt if received by an Indian tribe member who is living outside Indian country as a result of military orders. (*FTB Pub. 674, Frequently Asked Questions About the Income Taxation of Native American Indians*, revised December 2006, CCH CALIFORNIA TAX REPORTS ¶404-132)

• *Tribal casino operation distributions*

Although federal law taxes income from tribal casino operations (per capita distributions) regardless of where the tribal member resides, California does not tax per capita distributions received by tribal members who live in Indian country affiliated with their tribe that are sourced from the same Indian country where they are members. Distributions that are exempt under California law may be subtracted from federal income by entering the amount on Sch. CA (540 or 540NR), line 21f, column B. (*FTB Pub. 674, Frequently Asked Questions About the Income Taxation of Native American Indians*, revised August 2007, CCH CALIFORNIA TAX REPORTS ¶404-600)

Practice Tip: Impact of Incarceration on Residency Determination

In a nonprecedential decision, the California State Board of Equalization (SBE) held that per capita distributions received by a Native American while he was incarcerated were subject to tax because the taxpayer was not a resident of the tribal reservation at the time the distributions were received. The SBE rejected the taxpayer's contention that he was still a resident because his incarceration amounted to an involuntary absence from the reservation. (*Appeal of Andrade* (2008) CCH CALIFORNIA TAX REPORTS ¶404-636)

• *Return filing requirements*

Native Americans with income only from the Indian country in which they reside are not required to file a California income tax return. However, if California taxes are withheld, a California resident income tax return must be filed to receive a refund of the amounts withheld. (*FTB Pub. 674, Frequently Asked Questions About the Income Taxation of Native American Indians*, revised August 2007, CCH CALIFORNIA TAX REPORTS ¶404-600)

PERSONAL INCOME TAX

CHAPTER 3

DEDUCTIONS

¶300 Deductions—Generally

Law: Sec. 17201 (CCH CALIFORNIA TAX REPORTS, ¶15-510).

Comparable Federal: Secs. 161-222, 261-280H (CCH U.S. MASTER TAX GUIDE ¶901 et seq., 1001 et seq., 1101 et seq., 1201 et seq.).

California Forms: Sch. CA (540) (California Adjustments - Residents), Sch. CA (540NR) (California Adjustments - Nonresidents or Part-Year Residents), FTB 3526 (Investment Interest Expense Deduction), FTB 3805V (Net Operating Loss (NOL) Computation and NOL and Disaster Loss Limitations - Individuals, Estates, and Trusts), FTB 3885A (Depreciation and Amortization Adjustments), FTB 3885F (Depreciation and Amortization), FTB 3885L (Depreciation and Amortization), FTB 3885P (Depreciation and Amortization).

In general, California conforms to federal law as of the current IRC tie-in date (¶103) regarding deductions that may be taken to reduce taxable income, but there are some differences that are discussed in the following paragraphs. (Sec. 17201, Rev. & Tax. Code) As under federal law, some deductions may be used to reduce gross income and others may be used to reduce adjusted gross income. Any differences between the amounts of the California deductions and the federal deductions must be reported on Sch. CA (540) or Sch. CA (540NR) (¶30, ¶31).

Practice Note: Registered Domestic Partners and Same-Sex Married Couples

California law, unlike federal law, treats registered domestic partners (RDPs) and former RDPs as married taxpayers for California income tax purposes, unless specified exceptions apply. At the time this book went to press, the Franchise Tax Board (FTB) had not yet determined whether same-sex individuals who were married between June 16, 2008, and November 4, 2008, would likewise be treated as spouses for California income tax purposes, see ¶119 for details.

In addition, some deductions may be limited because they arise from passive activities (¶340).

¶301 Trade or Business Expenses

Law: Secs. 17021.7, 17201, 17201.5, 17203, 17269, 17270, 17273, 17278 (CCH CALIFORNIA TAX REPORTS ¶15-165, 15-805, 16-150).

Comparable Federal: Secs. 162, 179C, 179E, 190, 280A (CCH U.S. MASTER TAX GUIDE ¶901 et seq., 961 et seq., 1287).

California Forms: Sch. CA (540) (California Adjustments - Residents), Sch. CA (540NR) (California Adjustments - Nonresidents or Part-Year Residents).

All ordinary and necessary expenses of a trade or business are deductible. The California law is the same as the federal law as of the current IRC tie-in date (see ¶803) (Sec. 17201, Rev. & Tax. Code) except as follows:

— California prohibits deduction of certain types of expenses (illegal activities, etc.), as explained at ¶336.

— California has not adopted special federal rules for travel expenses of state legislators. (Sec. 17270(a), Rev. & Tax. Code)

— Where a federal tax credit is allowed for wages to provide new jobs, the wages are disallowed as a federal deduction; however, such wages are still allowed as a California deduction. (However, wages subject to the various hiring credits available to employers operating in economic incentive areas, described at ¶104, are not allowed as a California deduction.)

— California denies a business expense deduction for expenditures made at, or payments made to, a club that engages in discriminatory practices as explained at ¶336. (Sec. 17269, Rev. & Tax. Code)

— California, but not federal, law treats a taxpayer's registered domestic partner as the taxpayer's spouse for purposes of determining the amount that may be deducted for self-employed individual health insurance and amounts paid or incurred by the taxpayer as to certain group health plans under IRC Sec. 162(n). (Sec. 17021.7, Rev. & Tax. Code) Also, see ¶119 for a discussion of California's tax treatment of same-sex married couples.

— California law, unlike federal law, does not allow a current expense deduction for qualified film and television production costs (¶310). (Sec. 17201.5, Rev. & Tax. Code)

— Because of California's current federal conformity date (see ¶103), California has not adopted federal provisions enacted by the Energy Tax Incentives Act of 2005, the Tax Relief and Health Care Act of 2006, and the Emergency Economic Stabilization Act of 2008 that allow taxpayers to (1) currently expense 50% of the cost of qualified refinery property, effective for properties placed in service after August 8, 2005, and 50% of the advanced mine safety equipment expenses purchased after December 20, 2006, and placed in service prior to 2010, and (2) limit the deduction that may be taken for executive compensation paid to executives in financial institutions participating in the federal troubled asset relief program, effective for tax years ending after October 2, 2008. (Sec. 17024.5, Rev. & Tax. Code)

Deduction for Compensation Paid to Highly Compensated Officers

California conforms to federal law limiting the deduction for compensation paid to chief executive officers and the next four highest compensated officers. The deduction is limited to $1 million per individual. However, there is a "qualified performance-based compensation" exception to the $1 million deduction limit for compensation attributable to the exercise of an option, if the exercise price of the option equals or exceeds the share value on the grant date and certain other requirements are met. Thus, the FTB is conducting a self-compliance program under which employers who may have issued discounted stock options and/or stock appreciation rights (stock rights) to their employees may be contacted with a self-compliance letter, which will include instructions on how to resolve the noncompliance, if the $1 million limitation is applicable. (*Tax News*, California Franchise Tax Board, November 2007, CCH CALIFORNIA TAX REPORTS ¶404-487)

• *"Ordinary" and "necessary" expenses*

It should not be assumed that an item of expense that is allowed under federal law will always be allowed by California, because the interpretations of different taxing authorities concerning what are "ordinary" and "necessary" business expenses are not always uniform. Also, expenses that would normally be deductible under federal law are not allowed by California when they are attributable to income that is not taxed by California (¶336).

• *Principal place of business*

For purposes of claiming a home office expense deduction, a taxpayer's home office qualifies as a "principal place of business" if the following conditions are satisfied:

— the office is used by the taxpayer to conduct business-related administrative or management activities;

— there is no other fixed business location where such activities take place; and

— the office is used by the taxpayer exclusively on a regular basis as a place of business.

Also, if the taxpayer is an employee, the taxpayer's use of the home office must be for the convenience of the taxpayer's employer.

Practice Pointer: Commuting from Home Office Deduction

Although the expenses of commuting from an individual's residence to a local place of business are generally classified as nondeductible commuting expenses, such expenses may be deductible as ordinary and necessary business expenses if the individual uses his or her home as a principal place of business. For example, an anesthesiologist whose residence is her principal place of business may be able to deduct the expenses of traveling between her home and the hospitals at which she performs her primary duties.

• *Self-employed health insurance costs*

For both California and federal purposes, self-employed taxpayers are allowed to deduct 100% of the amounts they have paid for medical insurance for themselves and their families, not to exceed the taxpayer's earned income from the taxpayer's trade or business. California law provides that amounts used as "earned income" for purposes of computing a taxpayer's federal deduction (rather than the earned income computed using California amounts) must be used for purposes of computing the taxpayer's state deduction. (Sec. 17203, Rev. & Tax. Code) In addition, California law, but not federal law, treats a taxpayer's registered domestic partner as the taxpayer's spouse for purposes of determining the amount that may be deducted. (Sec. 17021.7, Rev. & Tax. Code) See ¶119 for a discussion of same-sex married couples.

This deduction may be taken even if the taxpayer does not itemize deductions.

• *Automobile expenses*

The Internal Revenue Service has followed a policy of allowing fixed per diem allowances and automobile mileage rates in lieu of itemized details for certain deductible expenses. For transportation expenses paid or incurred, the rate is 50.5¢ per mile for the period January 1, 2008, through June 30, 2008, and 58.5¢ per mile for the period July 1, 2008, through December 31, 2008. California adopts these rates as well for California income tax purposes.

California also conforms to federal law allowing a U.S. Postal Service rural mail carrier to deduct the amount of qualified reimbursements received for expenses incurred for the use of the mail carrier's vehicle for the collection and delivering of mail on the carrier's route.

• *Physicians' deduction for interindemnity payments*

California conforms to federal law allowing physicians to deduct certain interindemnity payments made to provide protection from malpractice liability. (Sec. 17278, Rev. & Tax. Code)

• *Architectural adaptations to accommodate the handicapped*

Both California and federal law allow a deduction of certain expenditures for the removal of architectural and transportation barriers to the handicapped and the elderly. California and federal law allowing a credit for disabled access expenditures is discussed at ¶140. Amounts for which a credit is claimed may not be deducted.

¶302 Meals, Entertainment, and Travel Expenses

Law: Sec. 17201 (CCH CALIFORNIA TAX REPORTS ¶15-805).

Comparable Federal: Secs. 162, 170, 274 (CCH U.S. MASTER TAX GUIDE ¶910 et seq.).

California law is generally the same as federal law as of the current IRC tie-in date (see ¶103). (Sec. 17201, Rev. & Tax. Code)

• *Meal and beverage expenses*

With certain exceptions, taxpayers may deduct only 50% of business-related meal and beverage expenses, including the cost of meals incurred during business travel away from home. The 50% limit is also applicable to unreimbursed expenses incurred by employees on behalf of their employer (¶329). (Sec. 17201, Rev. & Tax. Code)

Also, the deduction is generally not allowed unless taxpayers establish that (1) the meal and beverage expenses were directly related to the active conduct of their trade or business; or (2) in the case of expenses directly preceding or directly following a bona fide business discussion, that the expenses were associated with the active conduct of their trade or business.

An exception is provided allowing deductions by taxpayers for the cost of their own meals while away on business. Food and beverage expenses deemed lavish or extravagant under the circumstances are not deductible.

The deductible percentage of meals provided to employees subject to Department of Transportation hours-of-service rules is 80% beginning with the 2008 taxable year. In addition, meals provided at an eating facility for employees are fully deductible by the employer, instead of possibly being subject to the 50% limitation. For this purpose, the employee is treated as having paid an amount for the meal equal to the direct operating costs of the facility that are attributable to the meal.

• *Entertainment expenses*

Under both California and federal law, business expense deductions are not allowed with respect to an activity generally considered to be entertainment, amusement, or recreation, unless (1) the taxpayer establishes that the item was directly related or associated with the active conduct of the taxpayer's trade or business, or (2) the facility (e.g., an airplane) for which the deduction is claimed is used in connection with such activity. However, such expenses are deductible if the expenses are reported by the taxpayer as compensation and wages to the employee or if the recipient is not an employee (e.g., nonemployee director) as compensation for services rendered or as a prize or award. (Sec. 17201, Rev. & Tax. Code)

Taxpayers may deduct only 50% of the cost of business entertainment expenses. They must establish that (1) the expenses were directly related to the active conduct of their trade or business; or (2) in the case of entertainment expenses directly preceding or directly following a bona fide business discussion, that the expenses were associated with the active conduct of their trade or business.

Generally, taxpayers may not deduct more than 50% of the face value of entertainment tickets. However, the full amount paid for tickets to sporting events may be deducted if (1) the event benefits a charity; (2) the proceeds go to the charity; and (3) the event uses volunteers to perform substantially all the event's work.

Both California and federal law prohibit deductions for club dues paid or incurred for membership in any business, pleasure, social, athletic, luncheon, sporting, airline, or hotel club.

• *Travel expenses*

Taxpayers may not deduct the cost of travel that in itself constitutes a form of education. For example, a language teacher may not deduct the cost of visiting a foreign country merely for the purpose of maintaining familiarity with the country's language and culture. (Sec. 17201, Rev. & Tax. Code)

In addition, a taxpayer's employment away from home for more than one year will be treated as indefinite, rather than temporary; thus, no deduction for travel expenses will be allowed in connection with such employment. However, both California and federal law allow a deduction to federal employees traveling on temporary duty status in connection with the investigation or prosecution of a federal crime, even if they are away from home for more than one year.

Charitable travel expenses may be deducted only if there is no significant element of personal pleasure, recreation, or vacation in such travel.

Also, taxpayers may not deduct the expenses of attending a convention, seminar, or similar meeting in connection with their investment activities. The convention, meeting, or seminar must relate to the taxpayer's trade or business and must offer significant business related activities, *e.g.*, participation in meetings, workshops, or lectures.

A deduction for travel expenses of a spouse, dependent, or any other individual accompanying a person on a business trip is disallowed unless the following conditions are satisfied:

— the accompanying individual is an employee of the person paying or reimbursing the travel expenses;

— the accompanying individual's travel is also for a bona fide business purpose; and

— the expenses would otherwise be deductible by the accompanying individual.

¶303 Itemized Deductions

Law: Secs. 17024.5, 17073, 17076, 17077, 17201, 17207, 17220 (CCH CALIFORNIA TAX REPORTS ¶15-545).

Comparable Federal: Secs. 63, 67, 68, 163, 164, 165 (CCH U.S. MASTER TAX GUIDE ¶1011 et seq., 1021 et seq., 1047, 1141).

California Forms: Sch. CA (540) (California Adjustments -Residents), Sch. CA (540NR) (California Adjustments - Nonresidents or Part-Year Residents).

Individuals may take the standard deduction or itemize deductions for California purposes, whether or not they itemize federally. (Sec. 17073(c), Rev. & Tax. Code) However, married/registered domestic partner taxpayers who file separate returns must either both itemize or both take the standard deduction for California purposes. (Instructions, Form 540, California Resident Income Tax Return) California has conformed to most of the federal itemized deduction provisions. (Sec. 17201, Rev. & Tax. Code; Sec. 17024.5(b)(12) and (i), Rev. & Tax. Code)

Following are the major differences between California and federal itemized deductions:

— state, local, and foreign income taxes, state disability insurance tax (SDI), and qualified sales and use taxes may be deducted for federal but not California purposes (¶306);

— the contribution carryover from pre-1987 tax years could differ;

— there may be a California-only carryover from a disaster loss (¶307);

— miscellaneous itemized deductions for expenses related to producing income taxed under federal law, but not California law, are not deductible for California purposes, and vice versa (¶ 336);

— the deduction for interest on certain home mortgages may differ (¶ 305);

— deductions including an element of gain or loss may differ because of differences in California and federal bases (¶ 542); and

— itemized deductions for high-income taxpayers must be reduced by 6% of adjusted gross income for California purposes instead of the federal 3% reduction (see below).

Practice Note: Registered Domestic Partners and Same-Sex Married Couples

California law, unlike federal law, treats registered domestic partners (RDPs) and former RDPs as married taxpayers or former spouses for California income tax purposes, unless specified exceptions apply. At the time this book went to press, the FTB had not yet determined whether same-sex couples who were married prior to the passage of Proposition 8 would similarly be treated as "spouses" for California income tax purposes, see ¶ 119 for details.

• *2% floor on miscellaneous itemized deductions*

Certain unreimbursed employee expenses, expenses of producing income, and other qualifying expenses are deducted as miscellaneous itemized deductions federally and for California purposes. For both California and federal purposes, most miscellaneous itemized deductions are subject to a 2% floor. Only the portion of the total amount of such deductions in excess of 2% of the taxpayer's federal adjusted gross income is deductible. (Sec. 17076, Rev. & Tax. Code; Sec. 17201, Rev. & Tax. Code)

Following are the most common expenses subject to the 2% floor:

— professional society dues;

— employment-related educational expenses;

— office-in-the-home expenses;

— expenses of looking for a new job;

— professional books, magazines, journals and periodicals;

— work clothes and uniforms;

— union dues and fees;

— certain unreimbursed employee business expenses;

— safe deposit box rental;

— tax counsel and assistance;

— cost of work-related small tools and supplies;

— investment counsel fees;

— fees paid to an IRA custodian; and

— certain expenses of a partnership, grantor trust, or S corporation that are incurred for the production of income.

Following are the most common expenses *not* subject to the 2% floor:

— certain adjustments when a taxpayer restores amounts held under a claim of right;

— amortizable bond premium;

— gambling losses to the extent of gambling winnings;

— deductions allowable in connection with personal property used in a short sale;

— impairment-related work expenses of a handicapped individual that are for deductible attendant care services at the individual's place of work, and other expenses in connection with the place of work that are necessary for the individual to be able to work;

— mutual fund shareholder expenses;

— nonbusiness casualty losses; and

— interest on public utility-financed loans to purchase energy-efficient equipment.

• *Overall limitation for high-income taxpayers*

California generally conforms to federal law concerning limitations on the amount of itemized deductions claimed by high-income taxpayers. (Sec. 17077, Rev. & Tax. Code) The itemized deductions of taxpayers in high-income brackets must be reduced by the lesser of (1) 6% (3% under federal law) of the excess of adjusted gross income over the threshold amount or (2) 80% of the amount of the itemized deductions otherwise allowable for the tax year.

For 2008, the California threshold amounts are:

— $163,187 for a single taxpayer or a married/RDP taxpayer filing a separate return;

— $244,785 for a head of household; and

— $326,379 for a surviving spouse or a married/RDP taxpayer filing a joint return.

The California threshold amounts are adjusted annually for inflation.

The federal threshold amount for 2008 is $159,950 ($79,975 for married/RDP taxpayers filing separate returns). California does not incorporate the federal five-year phase-out and eventual repeal of the limitation on high-income taxpayers claiming itemized deductions. (Sec. 17077(d) and (e), Rev. & Tax. Code) The federal phase-out begins with the 2007 tax year and the repeal is scheduled to go into effect beginning with the 2010 tax year.

For both California and federal purposes, the limitation does not apply to deductions for medical expenses, casualty and theft losses, wagering losses, or investment interest expenses.

¶304 Expenses for Production of Income

Law: Sec. 17201 (CCH CALIFORNIA TAX REPORTS ¶ 15-730).

Comparable Federal: Sec. 212 (CCH U.S. MASTER TAX GUIDE ¶ 1085).

California Forms: Sch. CA (540) (California Adjustments - Residents), Sch. CA (540NR) (California Adjustments - Nonresidents or Part-Year Residents).

California law is generally the same as federal law. (Sec. 17201, Rev. & Tax. Code) Taxpayers may deduct all ordinary and necessary expenses incurred as follows:

— for the production or collection of income;

— for the management, conservation, or maintenance of property held for the production of income; or

— in connection with the determination, collection, or refund of any tax.

Practice Pointer: Application of 2% Floor

Deductions for the expenses of producing income are generally subject to the 2% floor on miscellaneous itemized deductions. However, expenses attributable to property held for the production of rents or royalties are subtracted from gross income to arrive at adjusted gross income (*i.e.*, as above-the-line deductions) and, thus, their deduction is not subject to the 2% floor.

For California purposes, deductible expenses must relate to income that is taxable by California; see ¶336. Moreover, it should be noted that, although federal and California law are formally the same, different taxing authorities may take different views concerning whether an item of expense is "ordinary" and "necessary." In practice, therefore, deductions allowed under one law may not always be allowed under the other.

In *Appeal of Glenn M. and Phylis R. Pfau* (1972) (CCH CALIFORNIA TAX REPORTS ¶15-730.30), the taxpayers claimed a deduction for campaign expenses in an election for municipal court judge. The State Board of Equalization (SBE) denied the deduction, following a former California regulation and federal cases decided under the comparable federal statute.

In *Appeal of Bernard B. and Dorothy Howard* (1961) (CCH CALIFORNIA TAX REPORTS ¶15-730.53), the SBE held that legal and accounting fees incurred while the taxpayer was a resident of California, but applicable to a federal tax controversy involving years prior to the establishment of California residence, were not deductible under the third item above. The SBE based its decision on the fact that such expenses were connected with income not taxable in California; therefore, they were nondeductible under the rule denying deductions for expenses applicable to tax-exempt income (¶336).

¶305 Interest

Law: Secs. 17072, 17201, 17204, 17208.1, 17224, 17230, 17280 (CCH CALIFORNIA TAX REPORTS ¶15-720, 16-050, 16-075, 16-260, 16-280).

Comparable Federal: Secs. 163, 221, 264, 265(a)(2), 265(a)(6) (CCH U.S. MASTER TAX GUIDE ¶909, 937 et seq., 970, 1043 et seq., 1082, 1094).

California Forms: FTB 3526 (Investment Interest Expense Deduction), Sch. CA (540) (California Adjustments - Residents), Sch. CA (540NR) (California Adjustments - Nonresidents or Part-Year Residents).

California conforms to federal law as of the current IRC tie-in date (¶103) concerning the deductibility of interest expenses, except as discussed below.

• *Tax-exempt interest*

Interest expense incurred to purchase or carry tax-exempt obligations is not deductible under either California or federal law (¶217). The same rule applies to shareholders of mutual funds holding such obligations and distributing tax-exempt interest on them (¶217). However, the amount of nondeductible interest may differ due to differences between California and federal law regarding tax-exempt obligations.

• *Personal interest*

No deduction for personal interest is available.

Qualified residence interest is not subject to the same treatment as personal interest (see below).

• *Investment interest*

A deduction is allowed for investment interest up to the amount of net investment income. (IRC Sec. 163; Sec. 17201, Rev. & Tax. Code) The deduction is calculated on FTB 3526, Investment Interest Expense Deduction. Net capital gain from the disposition of investment property is generally excluded from investment income. However, taxpayers may elect to include as much of their net capital gain investment income as they choose in calculating the investment interest limitation for federal purposes if they also reduce the amount of net capital gain eligible for the special federal capital gain tax. Taxpayers are allowed to make a similar election for California purposes; however, as discussed at ¶523, California treats capital gains as ordinary income.

Any amount not allowed as a deduction for any taxable year because of this limitation may be carried over and treated as deductible investment interest in the succeeding taxable year.

The limitation on itemized deductions for high-income taxpayers does not apply to investment interest expenses (¶303).

• *Mortgage interest*

A deduction is allowed for a limited amount of interest paid or accrued on (1) debts incurred to acquire a principal or second residence and (2) home equity debts. The aggregate amount of acquisition indebtedness must not exceed $1 million, and the aggregate amount of home equity indebtedness must not exceed $100,000. Interest attributable to debt over such limits is nondeductible personal interest. See ¶221 for a discussion of the exclusion available for the discharge of qualified residence indebtedness.

California law provides that payments made to the California Housing Finance Agency by first-time home buyers under a "buy-down mortgage plan" are considered payments of interest for purposes of the interest deduction. Such payments are made under Section 52514 of the Health and Safety Code, to reimburse the agency for its cost of subsidizing the borrower's interest cost. (Sec. 17230, Rev. & Tax. Code) Although there is no comparable provision in the federal law, it might be argued that the payments are made in lieu of interest and therefore should be treated as interest for federal as well as California purposes.

Because of California's IRC conformity date (¶103), California has not yet incorporated federal amendments made by the Tax Relief and Health Care Act of 2006 (TRHCA) and the Mortgage Forgiveness Debt Relief Act of 2007 that treat qualified premiums paid for mortgage insurance in 2007 through 2010 as deductible interest. Taxpayers that claim this interest expense deduction on their federal return must make an adjustment on their California personal income tax return.

• *Energy-efficient equipment loan interest*

Taxpayers may claim a deduction for the amount of interest paid or incurred by a taxpayer on a public utility-financed loan or indebtedness obtained to acquire any energy-efficient product or equipment for installation in a qualified residence located in California. Examples of qualifying equipment include heating, ventilation, air-conditioning, lighting, solar, advanced metering of energy usage, windows, insulation, zone heating products, and weatherization systems. Like the home mortgage interest deduction, this deduction is not subject to the 2% floor on miscellaneous itemized deductions. (Sec. 17208.1, Rev. & Tax. Code)

• *Interest on company-owned life insurance*

An employer is generally precluded from claiming a deduction for interest paid or incurred on money borrowed to fund an insurance policy or an endowment or annuity contract covering the life of *any* individual for whom the taxpayer has an insurable interest. However, an employer may still deduct interest paid or incurred to purchase life insurance policies, annuities, and endowment contracts for a limited number of officers and 20% owners if (1) the aggregate amount of debt with respect to the policies and contracts does not exceed $50,000 per key person and (2) the interest rate does not exceed a specified amount. (Sec. 17201, Rev. & Tax. Code) See ¶301 for limitations on the deductibility of premiums on company-owned life insurance.

• *Student loan interest*

Under both California and federal law, an above-the-line deduction is allowed for interest due and paid on qualified education loans up to a maximum of $2,500. The deduction is subject to gradual phase-outs for individuals with modified adjusted gross income (AGI) of $50,000 or more ($100,000 for joint filers), with complete phase-outs for individuals with modified AGI of $65,000 or more ($130,000 for joint filers). (Sec. 17204, Rev. & Tax. Code)

For purposes of this deduction, modified AGI includes income from social security benefits as well as amounts contributed to an individual retirement account.

• *Miscellaneous interest*

See ¶327 regarding deductibility of interest by tenant-stockholders of cooperative housing corporations. See ¶414 for special rules regarding imputed interest on certain installment contracts. See ¶416 regarding capitalization of interest during the construction period of real property.

¶306 Taxes

Law: Secs. 17201, 17220, 17222 (CCH CALIFORNIA TAX REPORTS ¶15-820, 16-120, 16-145).

Comparable Federal: Secs. 164, 275 (CCH U.S. MASTER TAX GUIDE ¶920 et seq., 1021 et seq.).

California Forms: Form 540 (California Resident Income Tax Return), Form 540A (California Resident Income Tax Return), Sch. CA (540) (California Adjustments - Residents), Sch. CA (540NR) (California Adjustments - Nonresidents or Part-Year Residents).

California law incorporates federal law as of the current IRC tie-in date (see ¶103), except that California specifically prohibits the deduction of "state, local, and foreign income, war profits, and excess profits taxes," and California does not allow the deduction of state or local sales and use taxes or the California SDI tax (see below). (Sec. 17024.5(b)(7), Rev. & Tax. Code; Sec. 17220, Rev. & Tax. Code; Sec. 17222, Rev. & Tax. Code) California also prohibits the deduction for personal income tax purposes of any tax imposed under the bank and corporation tax law. However, some such taxes may be used as the basis for claiming credits (¶125—¶131).

Under both California and federal law, the following taxes may be deducted

— state, local, and foreign real property taxes;

— state and local personal property taxes; and

— other state, local, and foreign taxes relating to a trade or business, or to property held for production of income (except income taxes—see below).

• *Taxes based on gross receipts*

A tax on gross receipts may be deductible under the third item above, if it can avoid classification as an income tax, because it presumably is incurred "for the production or collection of income."

In *Scott Beamer v. Franchise Tax Board* (1977) (CCH CALIFORNIA TAX REPORTS ¶205-694), the California Supreme Court held that the Texas "occupation tax" on oil and gas production is not "on or according to or measured by income or profits" and therefore is deductible.

• *Self-employment tax*

A deduction for one-half of a taxpayer's federal self-employment tax liability for the taxable year is available under both California and federal law.

• *State and foreign taxes*

Numerous rulings and decisions over the years have held specific foreign taxes nondeductible under the income-tax prohibition. Following is a partial listing, in alphabetical order by state or country:

ALASKA—gross production tax on oil royalties—*Appeal of Jesson* (1957) (CCH CALIFORNIA TAX REPORTS ¶16-145.254).

ARGENTINA—tax withheld on royalties—*Appeal of Don Baxter, Inc.* (1964) (CCH CALIFORNIA TAX REPORTS ¶10-561.203).

AUSTRALIA—tax withheld on dividends—*Appeal of Siff* (1975) (CCH CALIFORNIA TAX REPORTS ¶16-145.352).

BRAZIL—same as Argentina, above.

CANADA—tax withheld on dividends, interest, and trust distributions—*Appeal of Bochner* (1974) (CCH CALIFORNIA TAX REPORTS ¶16-145.35), *Appeal of Siff* (1975) (CCH CALIFORNIA TAX REPORTS ¶16-145.352).

HAWAII—gross income tax—*Robinson et al. v. Franchise Tax Board* (1981) (CCH CALIFORNIA TAX REPORTS ¶16-145.253).

ITALY—same as Argentina, above.

JAPAN—tax withheld on royalties and dividends—*Appeal of Everett* (1973) (CCH CALIFORNIA TAX REPORTS ¶16-145.60), *Appeal of Siff* (1975) (CCH CALIFORNIA TAX REPORTS ¶16-145.352).

MEXICO—tax withheld on royalties, dividends, and interest—*Appeal of Don Baxter, Inc.* (1964) (CCH CALIFORNIA TAX REPORTS ¶10-561.203), *Appeal of Mabee* (1966) (CCH CALIFORNIA TAX REPORTS ¶16-145.353), *Appeal of Blankenbeckler* (1969) (CCH CALIFORNIA TAX REPORTS ¶16-145.354).

NETHERLANDS—tax withheld on dividends—*Appeal of Siff* (1975) (CCH CALIFORNIA TAX REPORTS ¶16-145.352).

PHILIPPINES—same as Argentina, above.

SOUTH AFRICA—tax withheld on dividends—*Appeal of Haubiel* (1973) (CCH CALIFORNIA TAX REPORTS ¶16-145.351), *Appeal of Siff* (1975) (CCH CALIFORNIA TAX REPORTS ¶16-145.352).

UNITED KINGDOM—tax withheld on dividends—*Appeal of Siff* (1975) (CCH CALIFORNIA TAX REPORTS ¶16-145.352).

See ¶1006 for similar rulings under the corporate income tax law. Because the personal income tax and corporate income tax provisions governing the deduction for taxes are similar, rulings under the corporate income tax law may likely be applied under the personal income tax law.

• *SDI tax*

California does not allow a deduction for the employees' tax under the unemployment insurance law (commonly referred to as SDI—see ¶1806). (Sec. 17222, Rev. & Tax. Code) A 1977 Tax Court decision *(Trujillo)* allowed a federal deduction for the SDI tax on the ground that it is, in effect, a state income tax; however, as explained above, California denies any deduction for income taxes. See *Appeal of Arnold E. and Mildred H. Galef* (1979) (CCH CALIFORNIA TAX REPORTS ¶16-125.70).

However, California does allow a credit for excess SDI if two or more of the taxpayer's employers withheld more than the maximum amount for the year (¶132).

• *Minimum tax and LLC fees*

The minimum tax imposed on limited partnerships, limited liability partnerships, and limited liability companies (¶116) is not deductible at either the entity or the partnership/shareholder level (Instructions to Form 565). However, at the time this book went to press, the LLC fee may still be deducted (see ¶625).

• *Vehicle license fees*

California motor vehicle license fees listed on vehicle registration billing notices from the Department of Motor Vehicles are deductible as personal property taxes. Other fees listed on the billing notice, such as registration fees, weight fees, county or district fees, special plate fees, and owner responsibility fees are not deductible.

• *Postponed property taxes*

Where payment of property taxes is postponed, as explained at ¶1705 , the taxes are treated as if paid for income tax purposes and are deductible in the taxable year when the required certificate is submitted to the tax assessor.

• *Cross-references*

See ¶327 regarding deductibility of taxes by tenant-stockholders of cooperative housing corporations. See ¶416 regarding capitalization of taxes during the construction period of real property.

¶307 Losses

Law: Secs. 17201, 17207, 17207.4 (CCH CALIFORNIA TAX REPORTS ¶15-745, 16-300).

Comparable Federal: Secs. 165, 470, 1242-44 (CCH U.S. MASTER TAX GUIDE ¶1101 et seq., 1124 et seq., 2395).

California Forms: FTB Pub. 1034 and 1034A series (California Disaster Relief Tax Provisions), FTB 3805V (Net Operating Loss (NOL) Computation and NOL and Disaster Loss Limitations - Individuals, Estates, and Trusts).

California incorporates federal law as of the current IRC tie-in date (¶103) with the modifications noted below. (Sec. 17201, Rev. & Tax. Code) Under both California and federal laws, an ordinary loss deduction is allowed for a loss that is not compensated for by insurance or otherwise. As to individual taxpayers, losses are limited to the following:

— those incurred in a trade or business;

— those incurred in a transaction entered into for profit; or

— those arising from casualty or theft, to the extent the total of such losses, after excluding the first $100 of each loss, exceeds 10% of federal adjusted gross income. Casualty, theft, and wagering losses are not subject to the limitations on high income taxpayers explained at ¶303.

CCH Tip: Disaster-Related Losses

California does not incorporate federal amendments made by the Emergency Economic Stabilization Act of 2008 (EESA) that (1) eliminate the 10% of AGI limitation for casualty losses occurring in 2008 or 2009 that are net disaster losses attributable to federally-declared disasters, (2) temporarily increase the $100 per casualty limitation to $500 for tax years beginning in 2009, and (3) extend enhanced disaster relief to victims of the severe storms, tornadoes, and flooding occurring in the Midwest in the spring and summer of 2008.

Consequently, addition adjustments are required for taxpayers qualifying for the federal deduction as a result of the easing of these limitations

Similarly, California did not incorporate federal amendments made by the Katrina Emergency Tax Relief Act of 2005 (KETRA) that eliminated the 10% of AGI and $100 floor limitations for casualty losses that arose in a Hurricane Katrina disaster area and that were attributable to Katrina after August 24, 2005.

Casualty losses are measured, generally, by the loss in value of the property; but are limited by the amount of the cost or other basis of the property. (See *Appeal of Dominic and Mary Barbaria* (1981) (CCH CALIFORNIA TAX REPORTS ¶15-745.241), where a deduction was denied because the property lost had been fully depreciated.)

Federal law disallows income tax deductions for certain losses if the losses may be claimed as federal estate-tax deductions. Although California law generally provides that references to federal estate tax should be ignored, the Franchise Tax Board has announced that estate administration expenses can be deducted for California income tax purposes or California estate "pickup" tax purposes, but not both. (*Tax News*, FTB, May 1988)

• *Theft losses*

Theft losses are deductible only in the year of discovery, unlike other losses, which are deductible in the year sustained. (Sec. 17201, Rev. & Tax. Code)

• *Disaster losses*

California law (Sec. 17207, Rev. & Tax. Code; Sec. 17207.4, Rev. & Tax. Code) allows losses due to the following causes, including related casualties, to be carried forward for up to 15 years (five years for losses incurred prior to 2004) if they were sustained in Presidentially-designated disaster areas (renamed "federally declared disaster areas" by the EESA) or in California counties or cities proclaimed to be in a state of disaster by the Governor:

— earthquake or aftershocks occurring in 1989 in California;

— fire during 1990 in California;

— the Oakland/Berkeley Fire of 1991;

— storm or flooding occurring in February 1992 in California;

— earthquake or aftershocks occurring in April 1992 in Humboldt County;

— riots or arson occurring in April or May 1992 in California;

— earthquakes occurring in San Bernardino County in June and July 1992;

— the Fountain Fire in Shasta County or the fire in Calaveras County in August 1992;

— storm or flooding occurring in the Counties of Alpine, Contra Costa, Fresno, Humboldt, Imperial, Lassen, Los Angeles, Madera, Mendocino, Modoc, Monterey, Napa, Orange, Plumas, Riverside, San Bernardino, San Diego, Santa Barbara, Sierra, Siskiyou, Sonoma, Tehama, Trinity, and Tulare and the City of Fillmore in January 1993;

— fire in Los Angeles, Orange, Riverside, San Bernardino, San Diego, or Ventura County during October or November 1993;

— earthquake or aftershocks in Los Angeles, Orange, and Ventura counties on or after January 17, 1994;

— fire in San Luis Obispo County in August 1994;

— storms or flooding during 1995;

— storms or flooding during December 1996 or January 1997;

— storms or flooding during February 1998;

— the freeze during the winter of 1998-99;

— the earthquake in Napa County in September 2000;

— the San Simeon earthquake or aftershocks in Santa Barbara and San Luis Obispo counties in December 2003;

— the fires and related floods, mudflows, and debris flows in Los Angeles, Riverside, San Bernardino, San Diego, and Ventura counties in October and November 2003;

— the levee break in San Joaquin County in June 2004;

— the wildfires in Shasta County, commencing August 11, 2004;

— the severe rainstorms, related flooding and slides in Kern, Los Angeles, Orange, Riverside, San Bernardino, San Diego, Santa Barbara, and Ventura counties in December 2004 through March 2005, or June 2005;

— the severe rainstorms, related flooding and landslides, and any other related casualties that occurred in Alameda, Alpine, Amador, Butte, Calaveras, Colusa, Contra Costa, Del Norte, El Dorado, Fresno, Humboldt, Kings, Lake, Lassen, Madera, Marin, Mariposa, Mendocino, Merced, Monterey, Napa, Nevada, Placer, Plumas, Sacramento, San Joaquin, San Luis Obispo, San Mateo, Santa Cruz, Shasta, Sierra, Siskiyou, Solano, Sonoma, Stanislaus, Sutter, Trinity, Tulare, Tuolumne, Yolo, and Yuba counties in December 2005, and January, March, and April 2006;

— the wildfires in San Bernardino County in July 2006;

— the wildfires in Riverside and Ventura counties that occurred during the 2006 calendar year;

— the freeze in El Dorado, Fresno, Imperial, Kern, Kings, Madera, Merced, Monterey, Riverside, San Bernardino, San Diego, San Luis Obispo, Santa Barbara, Santa Clara, Stanislaus, Tulare, Venture, and Yuba counties that occurred in January 2007;

— the wildfires in El Dorado County that occurred in June 2007;

— the Zaca Fire in Santa Barbara and Ventura counties that occurred during the 2007 calendar year;

— the wildfires during the 2007 calendar year in Inyo, Los Angeles, Orange, Riverside, San Bernardino, San Diego, Santa Barbara, and Ventura counties;

— the strong winds in October 2007 in Riverside County;

— the wildfires during May or June of 2008 in Butte, Kern, Mariposa, Mendocino, Monterey, Plumas, Santa Clara, Santa Cruz, Shasta, and Trinity counties;

— the wildfires in July 2008 in Santa Barbara County;

— the severe rainstorms, floods, landslides, or accumulation of debris during July 2008 in Inyo County; and

— the wildfires that started during May 2008 in Humboldt County.

All of these losses may be taken in the year prior to the casualty, pursuant to an adopted federal provision. Also, a loss resulting from a disaster declared by the Governor may be claimed in the year prior to the casualty whether the President has declared the area a disaster or not.

Prior to the September 2000 disaster, 50% of any loss remaining after the five-year carryover period may be carried forward for the next 10 years. Beginning with the September 2000 Napa earthquake disaster, the amount of any loss remaining after the five-year carryover period that may be carried forward for the next 10 years is tied to the amount of the net operating loss deduction (NOL) that may be claimed (55% for losses incurred in the 2000 and 2001 taxable years; 60% for losses incurred in the 2002 and 2003 taxable years, and 100% for loss incurred in post-2003 taxable years); see ¶309 for a discussion of the NOL deduction.

Both the President and the Governor declared a state of disaster in the counties of Los Angeles, Orange, and San Diego as a result of the firestorms that occurred in October 1996. However, California legislation has not been enacted to extend the special disaster loss carryover and carryback provisions to losses resulting from this disaster.

A taxpayer is allowed to carry over only disaster losses that exceed taxable income increased by the sum of

— the personal exemption deduction and

— the lower of (a) $3,000 ($1,500 for married or registered domestic partner taxpayers filing separately) or (b) the amount by which losses from sales or exchanges of capital assets exceed gains from such sales or exchanges.

• *Wagering losses*

Wagering losses are deductible only to the extent of wagering gains. However, see ¶336 regarding disallowance of deductions for expenses of illegal activities or California lottery losses. (Sec. 17201, Rev. & Tax. Code)

• *Worthless securities*

Losses from worthless securities that are capital assets are considered losses from the sale or exchange of the securities on the last day of the taxable year in which the securities become worthless. As under federal law, such losses are therefore subject to the limitations on deduction of capital losses. (Sec. 17201, Rev. & Tax. Code)

In *Appeal of Everett R. and Cleo F. Shaw* (1961) (CCH CALIFORNIA TAX REPORTS ¶15-745.952), the State Board of Equalization held that a worthless stock loss was not deductible in the year claimed, where the company that issued the stock later expressed an intent to continue operations with a possibility of future earnings.

• *Losses on "small business corporation" stock*

Under both California and federal law losses of up to $50,000 ($100,000 on joint returns) on stock of small business investment companies created under the Small Business Investment Company Act of 1958 are deductible from ordinary income. (Sec. 17201, Rev. & Tax. Code) In addition, any loss treated as ordinary loss under this provision must also be treated as attributable to a trade or business of the taxpayer for purposes of applying the net operating loss deduction provisions (discussed at ¶309). Current treatment of gains on small business corporation stock is discussed at ¶525.

• *Tax-exempt lease losses*

California generally follows federal law (IRC Sec. 470), which applies loss deferral rules in the case of property leased to tax-exempt entities. (Sec. 17551, Rev. & Tax. Code) Because of California's current IRC conformity date (¶103), California does not incorporate amendments made by the Tax Technical Corrections Act of 2007 (TTCA), which retroactively make the loss deferral rules for property leased to tax-exempt entities inapplicable to partnerships unless specified conditions are satisfied. However, similar treatment applied during the 2004 through 2006 tax years as a result of IRS notices and bulletins and presumably would be followed by California currently. (*Summary of Federal Income Tax Changes—2007*, California Franchise Tax Board, April 2008)

• *Violation of public policy*

A loss deduction may be disallowed on the ground that the loss is the result of actions that are violative of public policy. See *Appeal of Anthony H. Eredia* (1981) (CCH CALIFORNIA TAX REPORTS ¶15-745.7858), involving a loss of money advanced to a narcotics dealer.

• *Cross references*

See ¶535 for treatment of losses on redemption of U.S. Savings Bonds. See ¶338 for discussion of special rules regarding farm and hobby losses. See ¶339 for "at risk" limitations on deductible losses. See ¶340 for a discussion of passive losses.

See ¶523 regarding losses on "capital assets." See ¶527 regarding disallowance of loss on "wash sales."

¶308 Bad Debts

Law: Sec. 17201 (CCH CALIFORNIA TAX REPORTS ¶15-617).

Comparable Federal: Secs. 166, 271 (CCH U.S. MASTER TAX GUIDE ¶1145 et seq., 1166).

California law is the same as federal law. "Nonbusiness" bad debts are treated as short-term capital losses (one year or less). (Sec. 17201, Rev. & Tax. Code)

In *Hameetman v. California Franchise Tax Board*, (2006) CCH CALIFORNIA TAX REPORTS ¶404-117, a California court of appeal ruled that an individual limited partner of a property management partnership could not claim a bad debt deduction based on a defaulted loan that the individual had made in the name of the partnership, because the business of the partnership could not be imputed to the partner.

¶309 Net Operating Loss Deduction

Law: Secs. 17041, 17276-76.7 (CCH CALIFORNIA TAX REPORTS ¶15-765, 16-105, 16-310).

Comparable Federal: Sec. 172 (CCH U.S. MASTER TAX GUIDE ¶1173 et seq.).

California Forms: FTB 3805D (Net Operating Loss (NOL) Computation and Limitation - Pierce's Disease), FTB 3805V (Net Operating Loss (NOL) Computation and NOL and Disaster Loss Limitations - Individuals, Estates, and Trusts), FTB 3805Z (Enterprise Zone Deduction and Credit Summary), FTB 3806 (Los Angeles Revitalization Zone Deduction and Credit Summary), FTB 3807 (Local Agency Military Base Recovery Area Deduction and Credit Summary), FTB 3809 (Targeted Tax Area Deduction and Credit Summary).

California generally conforms to the federal net operating loss (NOL) deduction for losses incurred in taxable years beginning after 1984, with the exception of the following:

— prior to the 2011 taxable year, California does not allow an NOL carryback to prior years, including the extended NOL carryback deduction enacted by the Job Creation and Worker Assistance Act of 2002, for losses incurred during the 2001 and 2002 tax years, or the extended NOL carryback deduction enacted by the Emergency Economic Stabilization Act of 2008 for NOLs attributable to federally-declared disasters in 2008 and 2009. Furthermore, California limits the NOL carryback for 2011 to 50% of the NOL and for 2012 to 75% of the NOL (Sec. 17276(c), Rev. & Tax. Code);

— although California adopts the federal 20-year carryover period beginning with the 2008 taxable year, previously the carryover period was limited to 10 years (5 years for losses incurred prior to the 2000 taxable year) (Sec. 17276.10, Rev. & Tax. Code);

— for tax years beginning in 2008 and 2009, California does not allow NOL deductions other than for businesses with net business income of less than $500,000 for the taxable year; however, California extends the carryover period by one additional year for an NOL sustained during the 2008 tax year and by two additional years for an NOL sustained in pre-2008 tax years (Sec. 17276.9, Rev. & Tax. Code);

— for NOLs incurred prior to 2004, except for NOLs sustained during the 2002 and 2003 taxable years, California law generally allows a specified percentage of the loss to be carried forward for up to 10 years (five years for losses incurred prior to the 2000 taxable year) rather than the federal 100% carryover for up to 20 years (15 years for NOLs incurred in tax years beginning before August 6, 1997) (Sec. 17276(b), Rev. & Tax. Code);

— for tax years beginning in 2002 and 2003, California did not allow NOL deductions; however, California extends the carryover period (1) by one additional year for an NOL sustained in a tax year beginning in 2002 and (2) by two additional years for an NOL sustained in a tax year beginning before 2002 (Sec. 17276.3, Rev. & Tax. Code);

— special rules apply to NOLs incurred by small businesses, new businesses, bankrupt taxpayers, and qualified enterprise zone, former Los Angeles Revitalization Zone, local agency military base recovery area, and targeted tax area businesses (see below); and

— an NOL sustained by a nonresident or part-year resident is limited to the sum of (1) the portion of the NOL attributable to the part of the year in which the taxpayer is a resident, plus (2) the portion of the NOL that, during the portion of the year when the taxpayer is not a resident, is attributable to California-source income and deductions (Sec. 17041(i), Rev. & Tax. Code).

• *Nonresidents and part-year residents*

As discussed at ¶116, beginning with the 2002 taxable year a nonresident's or part-year resident's NOL carryover losses and suspended losses are includible or allowable only to the extent that the loss was derived from sources within this state. The NOL must be computed as if the nonresident/part-year resident was a full-year resident for the entire year using only California amounts. Taxpayers should consult FTB Pub. 1100, Taxation of Nonresidents and Individuals Who Change Residency, for detailed explanations and examples of how the NOL is computed for nonresidents and part-year residents.

• *Carryover percentages*

For NOLs incurred after 2003, 100% of the NOL incurred may be carried over. For NOLs incurred prior to 2004, the amount of loss that may be carried over is limited to a specified percentage. The specified percentage that may be carried over is 50% for losses incurred in taxable years beginning before 2000; 55% for losses incurred in taxable years beginning after 1999 and before 2002; and 60% for losses incurred in taxable years beginning after 2001 and before 2004. The losses may be carried over for 10 years (five years for losses incurred prior to the 2000 taxable year). (Sec. 17276(b), Rev. & Tax. Code) Federal law allows a 100% carryover of such losses for up to 20 years (15 years for NOLs incurred in tax years beginning before August 6, 1997).

• *Carryover for new and small businesses*

A business that commences activity in this state after 1993 (a new business) or a business that has total receipts of less than $1 million for the tax year (a small business) may deduct 100% of an NOL that is equal to or less than its net loss attributable to the new or small business. "Net loss" means the amount of net loss after application of IRC Sec. 465, which limits deductions to the amount at risk (¶339), and IRC Sec. 469, which limits passive activity losses and credits (¶340). The portion of the taxpayer's NOL that exceeds its net loss attributable to a new or small business is carried over as a general NOL, subject to the applicable percentages discussed above. (Sec. 17276(b)(2), Rev. & Tax. Code)

The carryover period for new or small businesses is as follows:

— for a new business, the carryover period is 10 years for losses incurred after 1999 (for losses incurred in taxable years beginning prior to 2000, eight years if the loss is attributable to its first year of business, seven years if the loss is attributable to its second year of business, and six years if the loss is attributable to its third year of business); and

— for a small business, the carryover period is 10 years for losses incurred after 1999 (five years for losses incurred prior to the 2000 taxable year), regardless of the year to which the loss is attributable.

Taxpayers involved in certain biopharmaceutical or other biotechnology activities that have not received regulatory approval for any product from the U.S. Food and Drug Administration are also eligible for the extended NOL carryover available to new businesses.

Under the analysis provided in FTB Legal Ruling 96-5 (CCH CALIFORNIA TAX REPORTS ¶402-875), an existing business will be considered a "new business" if it undertakes a new activity within California that is classified under a different *division* of the Standard Industrial Classification (SIC) Manual than its existing business activity. If a taxpayer acquires assets of an existing trade or business that is doing business in California, the trade or business thereafter conducted by the taxpayer or related persons will be considered a new business only if the fair market value of the acquired assets is 20% or less of the total assets of the trade or business.

The same divisional approach is used to determine whether a business qualifies for the "small business" NOL deduction. For purposes of determining whether a business's gross receipts are under the $1 million eligibility limit for a small business, each business activity will be examined separately if the activities are classified under different SIC Manual divisions.

CCH Comment: Enhanced Benefits Lapse

Because the NOL for both new and existing businesses is equal to 100% for taxable years beginning after 2003 and the carryover period for both is 10 years, there is no "enhanced" NOL deduction for new businesses or small businesses for NOLs incurred after the 2003 taxable year. Similarly, although the NOL carryover period for businesses in economic development areas discussed below is 15 years, beginning with the 2008 taxable year when the standard NOL carryover period is extended to 20 years, it is questionable what advantage is gained by claiming an economic development area NOL rather than the standard NOL.

• *Carryover for enterprise zone, LARZ, LAMBRA, and targeted tax area businesses*

Enterprise zones, local agency military base recovery areas (LAMBRAs), and the targeted tax area, are economically deprived regions in which the state and local governments provide an array of tax and other incentives for taxpayers (¶104). The Los Angeles Revitalization Zone (LARZ) was also designated as an area in which businesses could receive a variety of tax incentives, including an NOL deduction. Because the LARZ designation was repealed December 1, 1998, qualified taxpayers may claim only NOL carryovers for LARZ losses sustained prior to the 1998 taxable year. However, a taxpayer could receive a LARZ NOL in 1998 as a pass-through NOL from a 1997 fiscal-year partnership, S corporation, or limited liability company. (Sec. 17276, Rev. & Tax. Code; Sec. 17276.1, Rev. & Tax. Code; Sec. 17276.2, Rev. & Tax. Code; Sec. 17276.4, Rev. & Tax. Code; Sec. 17276.6, Rev. & Tax. Code)

The NOL deduction available to taxpayers in these designated areas is the same as California's regular NOL deduction except that 100% of the NOLs incurred by businesses operating in these regions may be carried forward to each taxable year ending before the expiration date for the zone or area or for up to 15 taxable years following the year of the loss, whichever is longer. Taxpayers that also conduct business outside of the designated zone or area must apportion loss to the area by multiplying the business's total loss by a two-factor apportionment formula, comprised of the property and payroll factors.

Because the loss attributable to the area may be claimed only against income attributable to the area, further calculations are also required. The amount of business income is first determined using the standard apportionment formula described in ¶1305 —¶1309. For purposes of determining the amount of business income attributable to the zone or area, however, the sales factor is eliminated from the standard apportionment formula and the income used in the apportionment formula is limited to California-based income rather than worldwide income.

In order to claim the special NOL, a taxpayer must make an irrevocable election designating whether the loss is being claimed for a business located in an enterprise zone, LARZ, LAMBRA, or targeted tax area and attach a copy of the election form to a timely tax return. An enterprise zone, LARZ, LAMBRA, or targeted tax area NOL may be used only to offset income from the zone, area, or former zone for which the NOL is claimed. In addition, if a taxpayer elects to claim an enterprise zone, LARZ, LAMBRA, or targeted tax area NOL, no other type of NOL may be carried over. A worksheet is provided in the FTB 3805Z, FTB 3806, FTB 3807, and FTB 3809 booklets to assist taxpayers in determining the most advantageous NOL.

Forms.—The NOL deduction for enterprise zone businesses is claimed on FTB 3805Z. LARZ businesses claim the NOL carryover deduction on FTB 3806 and the LAMBRA NOL is claimed on FTB 3807. The NOL deduction for targeted tax area businesses is claimed on FTB 3809. The LAMBRA NOL is subject to recapture if the taxpayer does not satisfy the net increase in jobs requirement discussed at ¶104.

• *Carryover for farming businesses impacted by Pierce's disease*

For taxable years beginning after 2000 and before 2003, a person or business that conducted a farming business that was confirmed by the California Department of Food and Agriculture as being directly impacted by Pierce's disease and its vectors could carry forward the entire amount of an NOL to the nine tax years following the tax year of loss. An NOL carryover was allowed only with respect to the taxpayer's farming business income attributable to the area affected by Pierce's disease and its vectors. A loss was apportioned to the area affected by Pierce's disease and its vectors by multiplying the total loss from the farming business by a fraction, the numerator of which was the property factor plus the payroll factor and the denominator of which was two. (Sec. 17276.1, Rev. & Tax. Code; Sec. 17276.7, Rev. & Tax. Code)

A Pierce's disease NOL was claimed on FTB 3805D.

• *Effect of certain deductions and exclusions on computation of NOL*

California generally follows federal law under which certain deductions and exclusions may not be taken into account in computing an NOL deduction. However, California modifies federal law to disallow the California gross income exclusion provided to personal income taxpayers for gain on the sale of certain small business stock (¶525).

¶310 Depreciation and Amortization

Law: Secs. 17201, 17201.5, 17250, 17250.5 (CCH CALIFORNIA TAX REPORTS ¶15-670, 16-040, 16-245).

Comparable Federal: Secs. 167-68, 181, 197, 198, 280F (CCH U.S. MASTER TAX GUIDE ¶903, 1201, 1203, 1206, 1211 et seq., 1216 et seq., 1234, 1236 et seq., 1288).

California Forms: FTB 3885A (540) (Depreciation and Amortization Adjustments), FTB 3885F (541) (Depreciation and Amortization), FTB 3885L (568) (Depreciation and Amortization), FTB 3885P (565) (Depreciation and Amortization), Sch. CA (540) (California Adjustments - Residents), Sch. CA (540NR) (California Adjustments - Nonresidents or Part-Year Residents), Sch. D (California Capital Gain or Loss Adjustment).

California has adopted federal depreciation provisions (the modified accelerated cost recovery system, or MACRS) for personal income tax purposes as of a specified tie-in date (¶103). (Sec. 17201, Rev. & Tax. Code) However, California's asset expense deduction under IRC Sec. 179 may differ depending on the year the property is purchased (¶311).

Assets placed in service before 1987 continue to be depreciated under pre-1987 California rules (see the discussion of assets placed in service before 1987, below). Property placed in service in 1987 in a taxable year which began in 1986 is depreciated under pre-1987 California law, unless the taxpayer elects to have the post-1986 law apply.

California does not incorporate federal provisions that allow a 50% bonus depreciation deduction for property placed in service in 2008. Nor did California allow the 30% first-year bonus depreciation deduction for qualified property purchased after September 10, 2001, and before May 6, 2003, and placed in service before January 1, 2005; the additional 50% first-year bonus depreciation deduction allowed for qualified property purchased after May 5, 2003, and before 2005; nor the additional 30%/50% first-year depreciation allowance for purchases of qualified New York Liberty Zone property (see ¶312). (Sec. 17250(a)(4), Rev. & Tax. Code) In addition, federal law, but not California law, allows special recovery periods that permit faster write-offs for qualified Indian reservation property that is placed in service after 1993 and before 2010. (Sec. 17250(a)(3), Rev. & Tax. Code)

California also does not incorporate federal renewal community incentives that allow a taxpayer who receives a revitalization allocation from a state agency to elect for qualified buildings placed in service prior to 2009 either to (1) deduct one-half of any qualified revitalization expenditures chargeable to capital account with respect to any qualified revitalization building in the tax year that the building is placed in service or (2) amortize all such expenditures ratably over 120 months beginning in the month that the building is placed in service.

In addition, because of California's current federal conformity date (¶103), California has not incorporated amendments made by the Energy Tax Incentives Act (ETIA) of 2005 that allow taxpayers to currently deduct 50% of the cost of any qualified refinery property, effective for properties placed in service after August 8, 2005.

Nor has California incorporated amendments made by the ETIA that require two-year amortization of geological and geophysical expenses under IRC Sec. 167 and provide the following recovery periods under IRC Sec. 168 for property placed in service after April 11, 2005:

— for certain electric transmission property, 15 years;

— for new natural gas gathering lines, seven years; and

— for new natural gas distribution lines, 15 years.

Finally, California has not incorporated amendments made by (1) the Tax Increase Prevention and Reconciliation Act of 2005 (TIPRA) and the Energy Independence and Security Act of 2007 (EISA) that require certain major integrated oil companies to amortize geological and geophysical expenditures over a five-year period (seven years for expenditures paid or incurred after December 19, 2007) instead of a 24-month period for expenditures incurred after May 17, 2006, and (2) the Tax Reform and Health Care Act of 2006 (TRHCA) and the Emergency Economic Stabilization Act of 2008 (EESA) that allow a 50% additional depreciation allowance for

— qualified cellulosic biomass ethanol plant property acquired and placed in service after December 20, 2006, and before January 1, 2013,

— qualified cellulosic biofuel paced in service after October 3, 2008,

— qualified reuse and recycling property acquired and placed in service after August 31, 2008, and

— qualified disaster assistance property placed in service after 2007 with respect to disasters declared during 2008 and 2009.

Unless California incorporates the amendments discussed above, adjustments to the taxpayer's federal depreciation and amortization deductions will be required.

The following summary of MACRS applies to federal and California post-1986 asset acquisitions:

The 1986 Tax Reform Act (TRA) modified the Accelerated Cost Recovery System (ACRS) for property placed in service after 1986, except for property covered by transitional rules. Four classes of property were added:

— 7-year property;

— 20-year property;

— residential rental property (generally, 27.5 years); and

— nonresidential real property (31.5 years).

The Revenue Reconciliation Act of 1993 extended for federal purposes the recovery period for nonresidential real property acquired after May 12, 1993, to 39 years. California conforms to the 39-year recovery period for nonresidential real property, but only for property placed in service after 1996 in taxable years beginning after 1996.

The 3-year, 5-year, and 10-year classes were also revised by the TRA, and more accelerated depreciation was provided within these classes. Property within the 15-year and 20-year classes is depreciated under the TRA modifications by methods that maximize the depreciation deduction. However, commercial real estate and residential rental property are depreciated over longer periods than under pre-TRA provisions.

• *Depreciation methods according to class (IRC Sec. 168)*

Under the federal MACRS method as incorporated by California (Sec. 17201, Rev. & Tax. Code), there are six classes of recovery property: 3-year, 5-year, 7-year, 10-year, 15-year, and 20-year. Prescribed depreciation methods are assigned to each class, as follows:

— for 3-year, 5-year, 7-year, and 10-year classes, depreciation is by the 200% declining-balance method, switching to straight line when the latter yields a larger deduction;

— for 15-year and 20-year property, depreciation is by the 150% declining-balance method, switching to straight line when the latter yields a larger deduction; and

— for residential rental property and nonresidential real property, straight-line depreciation is to be used.

Taxpayers may make an irrevocable election to depreciate personal property using the straight-line ACRS method over the regular recovery period. Taxpayers may also make an irrevocable election to depreciate property qualified for the 200% declining-balance method under the 150% declining-balance method. If the latter election is made, depreciation may be computed over the longer class lives prescribed by the alternative depreciation system of IRC Sec. 168(g) or over *the regular tax recovery period,* applicable to property placed in service after 1998.

The above elections apply to all property in the same class that is placed in service during the same tax year. The election is to be made on the taxpayer's return for the year in which the property is placed in service.

California does not incorporate federal law that classifies "qualified leasehold improvement property" and "qualified restaurant property" placed in service after October 22, 2004, and before January 1, 2010, and qualified retail improvement property placed in service in 2009, as 15-year MACRS property with a 15-year recovery period using the straight-line method unless the MACRS alternative depreciation system (ADS) is elected or otherwise applies. (Sec. 17250(a)(5), (6), and (7), Rev. & Tax. Code) Consequently, leasehold improvement, qualified restaurant property, and qualified retail improvement property must be depreciated using the standard MACRS 39-year recovery period for California personal income tax purposes.

Nor does California incorporate federal provisions that provide a 10-year recovery period for qualified smart electric meters and smart grid systems placed in service after October 3, 2008. Consequently, such property must continue to be depreciated using the 20-year recovery period for California personal income tax purposes. Similarly, California does not allow the shortened recovery periods for the following property as enacted by the Heartland, Habitat, Harvest, and Horticulture Act of 2008 (Farm Act) and the Emergency Economic Stabilization Act of 2008 (EESA):

— 5-year recovery period for qualified farming machinery and equipment placed in service in 2009 that is depreciated under the General Depreciation System (GDS);

— 7-year recovery period for motorsports entertainment complexes placed in service during 2009 or 2010 (although the 7-year recovery period was available for the 2005 through 2007 taxable years); and

— 3-year recovery period for race horses two years or younger placed in service after 2008 and before 2014.

• *Alternative depreciation system (IRC Sec. 168)*

An alternative system is provided for property used predominantly outside the United States, tax-exempt use property, tax-exempt bond-financed property, and certain other property. In addition, the alternative method must be used for computing the portion of the depreciation allowance treated as a tax preference item for purposes of the alternative minimum tax. The allowable depreciation deductions for luxury cars and listed property used 50% or less in business are also determined under the alternative system.

Under this alternative depreciation system, the cost of property is recovered over the property's Asset Depreciation Range (ADR) midpoint life by the straight-line method. In computing the depreciation preference for alternative minimum tax purposes, recovery of the cost of personal property is calculated by the 150% declining-balance method.

An irrevocable election may be made to use the alternative depreciation system for all property in any class.

• *Disease-infested vineyards*

The depreciation period under MACRS for any grapevine replaced in a California vineyard is reduced from the 10-year period normally allowed for fruit-bearing vines to a five-year period if the vine is replaced (1) in a taxable year beginning after 1991 as a direct result of phylloxera infestation or (2) in a taxable year beginning after 1996 as a direct result of Pierce's Disease infestation. If an election is made to use the alternative depreciation method (discussed above), such grapevines will have a 10-year class life rather than the 20-year class life normally specified for such vines. (Sec. 17250, Rev. & Tax. Code)

• *Luxury autos (IRC Sec. 280F)*

There are limits on the allowable recovery deduction for passenger automobiles in a given tax year. For automobiles first placed in service during 2008, the federal and California limits are as follows: $2,960 for the first recovery year ($10,960 if first-year bonus depreciation is claimed); $4,800 for the second year; $2,850 for the third year; and $1,775 for each succeeding tax year in the recovery period. The limits for trucks and vans, including sport utility vehicles (SUVs) and minivans that are built on a truck chassis, first placed in service during 2008, are $3,160 ($11,160 if first-year bonus depreciation is claimed), $5100, $3,050, and $1,875, respectively.

Practice Pointer: Limits Apply to All Auto Depreciation

The limits on depreciation deductions for passenger automobiles used in a trade or business apply to all types of depreciation deductions for automobiles, including IRC Sec. 179 asset expense deductions.

Under both California and federal law, the amount of the deduction that may be claimed for electric passenger vehicles built by an original equipment manufacturer is tripled and the cost of an installed device that equips a nonclean-burning fuel vehicle to be propelled by clean-burning fuel is exempt from the deduction limitations. The higher depreciation limits for clean-fuel vehicles may be claimed for years following the regular depreciation period, as well as during the regular depreciation period.

• *Listed property (IRC Sec. 280F)*

Special depreciation rules apply to property that is classified as "listed property" that is not used more than 50% of the time for business purposes. The depreciation of such property must be determined using the alternative depreciation method discussed above. If the percentage of business use was originally more than 50% and drops below that percentage in a subsequent tax year, the excess depreciation deduction claimed in the years that it was predominantly used in a trade or business must be recaptured.

"Listed property" includes the following:

— a passenger automobile,

— other property used as transportation,

— property that is generally used for purposes of entertainment, recreation, or amusement,

— computers or peripheral equipment (except those used exclusively at regular business establishments), and

— cellular telephones and other similar telecommunications equipment.

• *Effective date differences*

Although California incorporates most of the amendments made by the American Jobs Creation Act of 2004 (AJCA) (P.L. 108-357) that impact the depreciation deduction, different effective dates apply. (Sec. 17024.5, Rev. & Tax. Code; Sec. 17201, Rev. & Tax. Code) Following are the effective date differences:

— The requirement that certain intangible property, including copyright or patent interests, intangible property, and computer software, be amortized over an extended recovery period of not less than 125% of the lease term if it is leased to an exempt entity and would otherwise be considered tax-exempt use property under IRC Sec. 168(h), applies for California purposes to taxable years beginning after 2004 and is generally effective for federal purposes for leases entered into after October 3, 2004.

— The establishment of a seven-year depreciation period for motorsports entertainment complexes, applies for California purposes beginning with the 2005 taxable year and before the 2008 taxable year, and is applicable for federal purposes to property placed in service after October 22, 2004, and before 2010.

— The increase in the cost recovery period from seven to 20 years for initial land clearing and grading costs incurred by electric utilities and from seven to 15 years for costs incurred by gas utilities, applies for California purposes to taxable years beginning after 2004, and is generally effective for federal purposes for property placed in service after October 22, 2004.

— The limits placed on depreciation deductions associated with sale-in, lease-out transactions (SILOs) involving purchases of municipal property and the denial of the deduction of tax-exempt use losses if the lessor does not have sufficient ownership rights in the property are applicable for California purposes beginning with the 2005 taxable year and are generally effective for federal purposes for property placed in service after October 22, 2004.

Assets Placed in Service Before 1987

The California rules for depreciation of assets placed in service before 1987 are the same as the federal rules in effect before the 1981 introduction of ACRS, except for the California prohibition against use of the "ADR" ranges. However, there are differences in the special rules for depreciation (or amortization) for certain classes of property, as explained below. Also, there have been many differences in prior years that may still have an effect on current depreciation; because of this possible effect, the prior-year differences are explained in some detail.

The basic rules for depreciation in the federal law (IRC Sec. 167) were incorporated in the California law by reference. However, California did not adopt the federal ACRS provisions (IRC Sec. 168) that apply to assets placed in service after 1980 and before 1987.

The federal law was amended in 1984, 1985, and 1986 to provide special rules for ACRS depreciation of luxury automobiles and of property not used principally in business. The California law applicable to pre-1987 assets was amended in 1985 to conform in principle to the pre-1986 federal rules; however, the California rules are based on the depreciation allowances under the ADR system, discussed below, rather than on the ACRS system.

• *California depreciation rules for pre-1987 assets*

In general, California depreciation methods and rates for pre-1987 assets are the same as the federal methods and rates applicable to assets placed in service during the years 1971 to 1980, inclusive. California has not conformed for pre-1987 assets to the mandatory federal Accelerated Cost Recovery System (ACRS) that was adopted in 1981 for tangible assets placed in service after 1980, except for certain residential property as explained at ¶318. The federal ACRS allows generally a much faster write-off of tangible depreciable property; however, the pre-1981 rules still apply to current federal depreciation on assets acquired before 1981, and also to depreciation on assets that are not covered by ACRS.

• *Depreciation based on useful life*

Under the California rules for pre-1987 assets, property must be depreciated over its estimated useful life (economic life as well as physical life). The taxpayer could determine the useful life by any means that produced a reasonable result, or could elect to use the useful life that is specified under the Federal Class Life Asset Depreciation Range System (known as ADR). The ADR system was in effect for federal purposes during the years 1971 to 1980, and is still applicable to assets acquired during that period and to assets not covered by ACRS. California adopted the ADR system in 1976, for assets placed in service after 1970, and it is still in effect for assets placed in service before 1987, although California uses only the standard ADR rates and does not permit use of the "ranges" of 20% above or below the standard rate.

• *Useful life under ADR system*

Under the ADR system, the useful life for each class of property is specified in Federal Revenue Procedure 83-35, which superseded Revenue Procedure 77-10. The classes of assets and their prescribed useful life (called the "Asset Guideline Period") are listed in previous editions of the *Guidebook.*

There are no ADR classes for buildings, except for farm buildings. A taxpayer that elected ADR could determine the useful life of buildings by using the old federal guideline lives under Revenue Procedure 62-21 as in effect from 1962 to 1970, or may determine the useful life in some other way that produced a reasonable result. The old guideline lives for buildings were as follows:

Apartment buildings, hotels, theaters	40 years
Factories, garages, machine shops, office buildings, dwellings	45 years
Loft buildings, banks	50 years
Wholesale and retail business buildings, warehouses, grain elevators	60 years

A complete table with guideline lives can be found in Revenue Procedure 83-35, 1983-1 CB 745, or see pre-1988 editions of the *Guidebook To California Taxes.*

In *Appeal of Morris M. and Joyce E. Cohen* (1973) (CCH CALIFORNIA TAX REPORTS ¶16-040.753), the State Board of Equalization (SBE) overruled the FTB and allowed the taxpayers to use a shorter life for 1968 depreciation than the guideline life shown in Rev. Proc. 62-21, discussed above. The taxpayers used a 25-year life for a new apartment building. The FTB used the 40-year life shown in Rev. Proc. 62-21, but offered no explanation or evidence to support the use of the longer life. The SBE stated that Rev. Proc. 62-21 was only a guide and could not be arbitrarily applied with no objective standard, and concluded that the FTB's action in the particular circumstances of this case was "arbitrary and capricious."

• *California depreciation methods*

In accordance with federal rules for property that is not covered by the Accelerated Cost Recovery System, California permits a variety of depreciation methods for assets placed in service before 1987 as follows:

(1) *Straight-line method:* This is the time-honored method, applicable to both tangible and intangible property (other methods, described below, apply only to tangible property). Under this method, the cost basis of the property, less salvage value, is written off ratably over the property's estimated useful life.

(2) *200% declining-balance method:* This method may be used only for new personal property with a useful life of three years or more, and for certain new residential rental property on which at least 80% of the gross rentals come from dwelling units.

(3) *Sum-of-the-years-digits method:* This method may be used wherever the 200% declining-balance method may be used.

(4) *150% declining-balance method:* This method may be applied to used personal property and to new real estate.

(5) *125% declining-balance method:* This method may be applied to used residential rental property having a remaining useful life of 20 years or more.

(6) Other "consistent methods" (*e.g.,* sinking-fund method), with limitations on the total amount deductible during the first two-thirds of the useful life.

In accordance with the federal rules for property not covered by ACRS, California ordinarily allowed only a part of a full year's depreciation in the first year, based on the portion of the year in which the property was in service. A taxpayer that elected the ADR system could also elect to use one of two first-year conventions (1) the half-year convention, or (2) the modified half-year convention. In the year property is sold the depreciation allowable may be reduced or eliminated, in cases where excessive depreciation was taken in prior years; this conforms to a 1962 federal ruling (Rev. Rul. 62-92, 1962-1 C.B. 29).

• ***Salvage value***

In computing California depreciation for pre-1987 asset additions, salvage value must be taken into account in two ways. First, in all methods except declining-balance, salvage value must be deducted from the asset's cost basis in computing the annual write-off based on useful life. Second, regardless of method, no asset may be depreciated below a reasonable salvage value. However, as to depreciable personal property (except livestock) with a useful life of three years or more, the salvage value taken into account may be reduced by up to 10% of the basis of the property.

Generally, salvage value is the amount estimated to be recoverable by the taxpayer at the end of the asset's useful economic life.

• ***Change of depreciation method***

California follows the federal rules for changing depreciation methods for pre-1987 asset additions, as set forth in Revenue Ruling 74-11. Application for permission to change should be made within the same time as the application to the Internal Revenue Service, and a copy of the federal form should be submitted to the FTB. California follows the federal rules in permitting changes from certain accelerated methods to the straight-line method without consent.

• ***Prior-year differences***

There have been many differences over the years between California and federal rules for depreciation. Since these differences may still affect current depreciation computations or the adjusted basis of property, they are summarized briefly in the following comments.

Any such formula is subject to FTB approval. It appears, however, that use of such a formula would not be practicable where federal depreciation is determined under ACRS.

Prior to the introduction of the ADR system in 1971, the federal rules provided guidelines for depreciation rates, published in 1962 in Revenue Procedure 62-21. Assets placed in service after 1970 and before 1987 are governed by the ADR system.

The original federal provisions for accelerated depreciation methods were enacted in 1954, but California did not conform until 1959. During the period 1954-1958 the FTB maintained the position that in failing to adopt conforming legislation in those years the California legislature had issued a mandate that the accelerated depreciation methods were not allowable for California purposes. The FTB was sustained in this position by the SBE in *Appeal of Garrett Freightlines, Inc.* (CCH CALIFORNIA TAX REPORTS ¶200-754) in 1957, and in *Appeal of William S. and Camilla A. Andrews* (CCH CALIFORNIA TAX REPORTS ¶201-442) in 1959. Where this situation created a difference between California and federal depreciation in the years 1954-1958, the FTB permitted taxpayers to eliminate this difference over a period of years on a somewhat arbitrary basis, in order to avoid the necessity of continuing detailed separate computations of depreciation for California tax purposes.

Use of the 200% declining-balance and sum-of-the-years-digits methods was suspended under federal law for the period October 10, 1966, to March 9, 1967. California did not follow this federal suspension.

The California law was amended in 1977 to conform to a 1976 federal amendment permitting a change from accelerated methods to the straight-line method on real estate. The California amendment permitted the change in the first taxable year ending after 1976; the federal amendment applied to the first year ending after 1975. (The corporation tax law was not amended in 1977 to conform to this personal income tax amendment.)

Special Depreciation and Amortization Rules

• ***Motion picture films, books, copyrights, etc.***

Special rules have been applied over the years to the depreciation or amortization of production costs of motion picture films. The major film studios maintaining their own distribution systems amortize such costs over estimated useful lives as have been established by their own experience, or by industry averages.

Independent producers, on the other hand, are permitted to use an estimated receipts method to develop a formula for cost amortization. This formula uses estimated total receipts as the denominator and periodic receipts as the numerator in arriving at the proportion of production cost to be amortized in each period. The use of this formula by independent producers was upheld by the SBE in *Appeal of Filmcraft Trading Corporation* (1957) (CCH CALIFORNIA TAX REPORTS ¶10-905.551). The rule was further clarified in *Appeal of King Bros. Productions, Inc.* (1961) (CCH CALIFORNIA TAX REPORTS ¶10-905.551). Similar treatment is accorded production costs of television films. The federal rules are substantially the same.

Taxpayers may elect to compute depreciation using the income forecast method for property such as film, video tape, sound recordings, copyrights, books, patents, and other property of a similar character approved by federal regulation. If such an election is made, the depreciation claimed must take into account the amount of income expected to be earned in connection with the property before the close of the 10th tax year following the tax year that the property was placed in service, which means that 11 tax years are taken into account.

Depreciation is determined using the income forecast method by multiplying the property's cost (less estimated salvage value) by a fraction, the numerator of which is the income generated by the property during the year and the denominator of which is the total estimated income to be derived from the property during its useful life. The income forecast method may not be used to compute depreciation for intangible property amortizable under IRC Sec. 197 or for consumer durables subject to rent-to-own contracts.

Although California conforms to federal law concerning the income forecast method, unlike federal law, California law does not prohibit taking distribution costs into account for purposes of determining the depreciation deduction using the income forecast method. (Sec. 17250.5(c), Rev. & Tax. Code) Nor does California incorporate the federal provision providing special rules for depreciating participations and residuals, allowing taxpayers to currently deduct participations and residuals rather than depreciate them using the income forecast method. (Sec. 17250.5(d), Rev. & Tax. Code)

As a result of California's current federal conformity date (¶103), California does not incorporate amendments made by TIPRA that allow amortization of expenses paid or incurred in creating or acquiring a musical composition or a copyright to a musical composition over five-years, effective for property placed in service in tax years beginning after 2005 and before 2011.

In addition, California does not conform to federal law that allows film productions to expense the first $15 million ($20 million in specified low-income or distressed communities) of "qualified" film or television production expenses rather than depreciate or amortize such costs. (Sec. 17201.5, Rev. & Tax. Code) The federal election is applicable to qualified film and television productions commencing after October 22, 2004. Consequently, taxpayers that claim the deduction on their federal return, must make an addition adjustment on their California return, but will also be able to increase the depreciation deduction claimed for any depreciable property for which the federal current expense deduction was claimed.

• *"Safe harbor" transactions*

The federal Economic Recovery Act of 1981 permits the transfer of depreciation benefits and investment tax credits between taxpayers under certain conditions. This is accomplished by so-called "safe harbor" rules that treat as a lease what would otherwise be treated as a sale. Because California has not conformed to these federal provisions, California follows prior federal rulings and may treat as a sale a transaction that is treated as a lease under the federal rules. See Legal Ruling 419 (1981) (CCH CALIFORNIA TAX REPORTS ¶206-665) for discussion of the effect of this difference on the taxpayers involved.

¶311 Asset Expense Election (IRC "Sec. 179" Election)

Law: Secs. 17201, 17255 (CCH CALIFORNIA TAX REPORTS ¶16-040).

Comparable Federal: Secs. 179, 1400N (CCH U.S. MASTER TAX GUIDE ¶1208).

California Forms: FTB 3885A (Depreciation and Amortization Adjustments), Sch. D (California Capital Gain or Loss Adjustment).

Although California has adopted the federal asset expense election for assets placed in service after 1986, California does not incorporate post-2002 federal amendments that make the following changes:

— increase the maximum federal deduction amount to at least $100,000 for property placed in service during taxable years after 2002 and before 2011 (see below for specific amounts allowed in specific years) and allow additional increases for property purchased by qualified disaster victims or for qualified disaster property;

— increase the phase-out amount from $200,000 to $400,000 for property placed in service after 2002 and before 2007, $500,000 for property placed in service in 2007, 2009, or 2010, and $800,000 for property placed in service in 2008; and

— allow the deduction to be claimed for off-the-shelf computer software purchased after 2002 and before 2011.

The federal figures are indexed for tax purposes. (Sec. 17201, Rev. & Tax. Code; Sec. 17255, Rev. & Tax. Code)

California's maximum current expense deduction is $25,000 for property placed in service after 2002 and before 2011, as opposed to the federal maximum of $250,000 for property placed in service in 2008 and $125,000 for property placed in service during 2009 and 2010 (absent additional federal amendments, the federal deduction reverts to $25,000 after 2010). However, because federal provisions limit the asset expense deduction to $25,000 for SUVs with loaded weights between 6,000 and 14,000 pounds, applicable to vehicles placed in service after October 22, 2004, the deduction for these vehicles remains the same for both California and federal purposes. SUVs placed in service after 2002 and before October 23, 2004, would qualify for the higher deduction on a taxpayer's federal, but not California, return. California also does not adopt the increased in the expense deduction available for federal purposes for qualified property used in a renewal community.

In addition, although California adopts the federal expense deduction amount for property placed in service after 1998 and before 2003, different deduction amounts applied for earlier taxable years. The following chart lists the maximum deductions for both California and federal purposes for post-1992 tax years:

MAXIMUM CURRENT EXPENSE DEDUCTION

Property placed in service in:	California Law	Federal Law
2008	$25,000	$250,000
2007	$25,000	$125,000
2006	$25,000	$108,000
2005	$25,000	$105,000
2004	$25,000	$102,000
2003	25,000	100,000
2001-2002	24,000	24,000
2000	20,000	20,000
1999	19,000	19,000
1998	16,000	18,500
1997	13,000	18,000
After 1992 and before 1997	10,000	17,500

Because depreciable basis must be reduced by any IRC Sec. 179 deduction, the depreciable basis of property placed in service after 2002 and before 2010 and after 1992 and before 1999 may differ for federal and state purposes.

For both California and pre-2003 federal law purposes, the deduction is reduced, but not below zero, by the excess of the total investment in qualified property over $200,000 in the tax year. (Sec. 17255(b), Rev. & Tax. Code) The $200,000 limit is increased to $400,000 for federal purposes for property placed in service after 2002 and before 2007, $500,000 for property placed in service during 2007, 2009, or 2010, and $800,000 for property placed in service during 2008. Consequently, California's deduction will be further decreased for investments in excess of $200,000 during the 2003 through 2010 taxable years. The $400,000 and $500,000 figures are indexed for inflation. The limit is $800,000 for the 2008 tax year, $500,000 for the 2007 tax year, $430,000 for the 2006 tax year, $420,000 for the 2005 tax year, and $410,000 for the 2004 tax year.

The excess of the deduction over otherwise allowable depreciation is recaptured if the property ceases to be used predominately in the trade or business before the end of its recovery period. The deduction cannot exceed the taxable income derived from the trade or business during the tax year.

In addition, California does not incorporate the federal provision that allows taxpayers to make, revoke, or modify an IRC Sec. 179 election made with respect to property placed in service in the 2003 through 2010 tax years without IRS permission on an amended return. (Sec. 17255(e), Rev. & Tax. Code) Presumably, a taxpayer would be required to obtain the California Franchise Tax Board's permission to make, revoke, or amend an election on the California return.

• *Married and registered domestic partner taxpayers*

Married and registered domestic partner (RDP) taxpayers who file a joint return are to be treated as one taxpayer for purposes of the dollar limitations. For married taxpayers filing separate returns, unless otherwise elected, 50% of the cost of the qualifying property that is to be expensed is allocated to each spouse. Same-sex married couples and RDPs may be required to make adjustments on their California return, see ¶119.

¶312 Additional First-Year Depreciation

Law: Sec. 17250 (CCH CALIFORNIA TAX REPORTS ¶16-040).

Comparable Federal: Sec. 168(k) (CCH U.S. MASTER TAX GUIDE ¶1237).

California Forms: FTB 3885A (Depreciation and Amortization Adjustments), Sch. D (California Capital Gain or Loss Adjustment).

California does not incorporate federal law allowing an additional 50% first-year bonus depreciation deduction for qualified property acquired and placed in service during 2008 (and 2009 for certain property with a long production period, including commercial and noncommercial aircraft). California also did not incorporate federal law that provided a 30% additional first-year bonus depreciation allowance for certain property acquired after September 10, 2001, and before May 6, 2003, and placed in service before 2005, or a 50% additional first-year bonus depreciation allowance for certain property acquired after May 5, 2003, and before January 1, 2005, and placed in service before 2005. (Sec. 17250(a)(4), Rev. & Tax. Code) Consequently, any bonus depreciation deduction claimed on the federal return was required to be added back to federal adjusted gross income, and the basis of property for which the federal bonus deduction was claimed will be different under California law.

For the post-1986 asset expense election that replaced the first-year allowance for personal income tax purposes, see ¶311.

¶313 Amortization of Cost of Acquiring a Lease

Law: Sec. 17201 (CCH CALIFORNIA TAX REPORTS ¶15-615).

Comparable Federal: Sec. 178 (CCH U.S. MASTER TAX GUIDE ¶1234).

California law incorporates the federal law by reference.

For purposes of amortizing the cost of acquiring a lease, the term of the lease includes all renewal options (and any other period for which the parties to the lease reasonably expect the lease to be renewed) if less than 75% of such cost is attributable to the unexpired term of the lease on the date of its acquisition. In determining the unexpired term of the lease, the taxpayer may not take into consideration any period for which the lease may subsequently be renewed, extended, or continued pursuant to an option exercisable by the lessee. (Sec. 17201, Rev. & Tax. Code)

¶314 Amortization of Pollution Control Facilities

Law: Sec. 17250 (CCH CALIFORNIA TAX REPORTS ¶15-615, 16-015).

Comparable Federal: Sec. 169 (CCH U.S. MASTER TAX GUIDE ¶1287).

California Form: FTB 3580 (Application to Amortize Certified Pollution Control Facility).

California incorporates federal law allowing an accelerated (60-month) write-off of pollution control facilities, with the following modifications (Sec. 17250, Rev. & Tax. Code):

— the California deduction is available only for facilities located in California; and

— the "state certifying authority" in cases involving air pollution is the State Air Resources Board and in cases involving water pollution is the State Water Resources Control Board.

Also, California has not conformed to federal amendments made by the Energy Tax Incentives Act of 2005, which expand the amortization deduction for atmospheric pollution control facilities. The amendments allow the amortization deduction to be claimed for qualified air pollution control facilities placed in service after April 11, 2005, even if not used in connection with a plant that was in operation before January 1, 1976. However, the amortization period applicable to taxpayers eligible under the expanded criteria is extended from 60 months to 84 months. To the extent taxpayers may only qualify for the amortization deduction on their federal tax return under the expanded eligibility criteria, the taxpayer is required to make an addition adjustment on the California tax return.

FTB 3580 may be used to file an election with the Franchise Tax Board for an accelerated write-off.

¶315 Amortization of Reforestation Expenditures

Law: Secs. 17201, 17278.5 (CCH CALIFORNIA TAX REPORTS ¶15-690, 16-055).

Comparable Federal: Sec. 194 (CCH U.S. MASTER TAX GUIDE ¶1287).

California Form: FTB 3885A (Depreciation and Amortization Adjustments).

California law is the same as federal as of the current IRC tie-in date (see ¶103), except that California limits the deduction to expenses associated with qualified timber located in California. (Sec. 17201, Rev. & Tax. Code; Sec. 17278.5, Rev. & Tax. Code) Under both California and federal law taxpayers may currently deduct up to $10,000 ($5,000 for married taxpayers or registered domestic partners filing separately) in qualified reforestation expenses and to amortize any remaining costs over a period of 84 months.

¶316 Accelerated Write-Offs for Economic Incentive Areas

Law: Secs. 17266, 17267.2, 17267.6, 17268, 18036 (CCH CALIFORNIA TAX REPORTS ¶16-040).

Comparable Federal: None.

California Forms: FTB 3805Z (Enterprise Zone Deduction and Credit Summary), FTB 3807 (Local Agency Military Base Recovery Area Deduction and Credit Summary), FTB 3809 (Targeted Tax Area Deduction and Credit Summary), Sch. D (California Capital Gain or Loss Adjustment).

Under the tax incentive programs enacted by California, explained at ¶104, accelerated write-offs are allowed for certain property as explained below.

• *Property used in enterprise zones, LAMBRAs, and the targeted tax area*

Taxpayers can expense 40% of the cost of IRC Sec. 1245 property that is purchased for use exclusively in a business conducted in an enterprise zone, a targeted tax area, or, a local agency military base recovery area (LAMBRA). The deduction is claimed in the year the property is placed into service. (Sec. 17267.2, Rev. & Tax. Code; Sec. 17267.6, Rev. & Tax. Code; Sec. 17268, Rev. & Tax. Code)

The cost that may be taken into account is limited to $100,000 for the taxable year that an area is designated as a qualifying zone or area, $100,000 for the first taxable year thereafter, $75,000 for the second and third taxable years after the year of designation, and $50,000 for each taxable year after that. For businesses located in an enterprise zone expansion area, the amount of the deduction is determined using the original zone's designation date.

Practical Analysis: Property Must Be Placed In Service

To qualify for the accelerated write-off, the property must be placed in service within the zone or area prior to the expiration of the zone's or area's designation.

Taxpayers that elect the accelerated write-off for property located in economic incentive areas may not claim the IRC Sec. 179 asset expense election described at ¶311 on their California returns for the same property. The election is not available to estates or trusts or for property acquired from certain related persons.

The expense deduction is recaptured if the property ceases to be used in the zone or area at any time before the close of the second taxable year after the property was placed in service. The deduction claimed by LAMBRA businesses may also be recaptured if the taxpayer does not satisfy the net increase in jobs requirement (¶104).

A taxpayer's basis in the property must be adjusted to reflect the expense deduction. Conversely, if the deduction is subject to recapture, the depreciable basis of the property may be increased by the amount recaptured. (Reg. 17267.1, 18 CCR)

The enterprise zone deduction is claimed on FTB 3805Z, the LAMBRA deduction is claimed on FTB 3807, and the targeted tax area deduction is claimed on FTB 3809; see ¶104. The deduction must be claimed on the original return and may not be claimed on an amended return.

• *Property used in the Los Angeles Revitalization Zone (Prior law)*

Taxpayers could elect to expense the cost of any IRC Sec. 1245 property purchased prior to December 1, 1998, for exclusive use in a trade or business conducted within the Los Angeles Revitalization Zone. (Former Sec. 17266, Rev. & Tax. Code)

Property acquired from certain related persons did not qualify for this treatment. Furthermore, the election was not available to estates and trusts.

¶317 Domestic Production Activities Deduction

Law: Sec. 17201.6 (CCH CALIFORNIA TAX REPORTS ¶16-085).

Comparable Federal: Sec. 199 (CCH U.S. MASTER TAX GUIDE ¶245).

California Forms: Sch. CA (540) (California Adjustments - Residents), Sch. CA (540NR) (California Adjustments - Nonresidents or Part-Year Residents).

California does not incorporate the federal deduction of income from qualified domestic production activities (Sec. 17201.6, Rev. & Tax. Code) Consequently, any deduction claimed on the federal return must be added back for California personal income tax purposes.

¶318 Refiners' Sulfur Rules Compliance Costs

Law: Secs. 17201.4, 17255.5 (CCH CALIFORNIA TAX REPORTS ¶16-055, 16-220).

Comparable Federal: Sec. 179B.

California Forms: Sch. CA (540) (California Adjustments - Residents), Sch. CA (540NR) (California Adjustments - Nonresidents or Part-Year Residents).

California does not incorporate the federal deduction available for capital costs incurred in complying with Environmental Protection Agency (EPA) sulfur regulations. (Sec. 17201.4, Rev. & Tax. Code). However, California does allow small business refiners to elect to deduct up to 75% of qualified capital costs paid or incurred during the taxable year to bring California facilities into compliance with EPA or California Air Resources Board regulations. The California deduction is applicable to qualified capital costs paid or incurred by the taxpayer during any taxable year that includes the period beginning after 2003 and ending on May 31, 2007. California's deduction is similar to the deduction allowed under federal law (IRC Sec. 179B), but differs from federal law concerning its definition of "small refiners" and "qualified capital costs." (Sec. 17255.5, Rev. & Tax. Code).

Taxpayers that claim the deduction must reduce the basis of the property by the amount of the deduction claimed. In addition, if the property is of a character that would be subject to depreciation, the amount of the deduction claimed will be treated as an allowance for depreciation for purposes of IRC Sec. 1245, relating to the gain from dispositions of depreciable property, and related California provisions. (Sec. 17255.5, Rev. & Tax. Code)

Taxpayers that do not elect to claim the deduction may be eligible to claim a credit for the qualified capital costs paid or incurred (see ¶151).

¶319 Depletion and Natural Resources

Law: Secs. 17681, 17681.6 (CCH CALIFORNIA TAX REPORTS ¶15-665, 16-037).

Comparable Federal: Secs. 611-14, 636, 638 (CCH U.S. MASTER TAX GUIDE ¶1289, 1291).

With the exception of the federal extension of the exemption for owners of marginal oil and gas wells, California law is the same as federal as of the current IRC tie-in date (see ¶103) for tax years beginning after 1992. (Sec. 17681, Rev. & Tax. Code)

However, because of California's current federal conformity date (¶103), California has not incorporated amendments made by the Energy Tax Incentives Act of 2005 that increase the refinery limitation on independent producers, effective for federal purposes in tax years ending after August 8, 2005.

• *Percentage depletion*

Both California and federal law allow percentage depletion on specified types of depletable assets. This allowance is computed as a percentage of gross income from the property, with a limitation based on 50% of the taxable income from the property before the depletion allowance (100% in the case of oil and gas properties). However, California does not incorporate the federal suspension of the 100% taxable income limit on percentage depletion deductions for oil and gas production from marginal properties. (Sec. 17681.6, Rev. & Tax. Code) The suspension applies for federal purposes for the 2009 tax year and for tax years beginning after 1997 and before 2008.

• *Oil and gas wells and geothermal deposits*

California fully conforms to the federal law on percentage depletion for oil and gas wells and geothermal deposits. Under the incorporated federal law, the following depletion rates apply:

— 22% for domestic regulated natural gas and natural gas sold under a fixed contract;

— 10% for qualified natural gas from geopressurized brine;

— 15% for domestic crude oil and natural gas from wells of certain independent producers and royalty owners, limited to 65% of the taxpayer's taxable income before the depletion allowance; and

— 15% for geothermal deposits located in the United States.

For taxable years beginning before 1993, instead of conforming to federal law, California provided a 22% depletion rate for oil, gas, and geothermal wells, up to a maximum of 50% of the taxpayer's taxable income from the property before the depletion allowance. California also imposed a limit on depletion, applicable when the accumulated depletion allowed or allowable exceeded the taxpayer's adjusted interest in the property.

• *Depletable assets other than oil, gas, and geothermal*

California also adopts federal percentage depletion provisions for depletable assets other than oil, gas, and geothermal deposits. (17681, Rev. & Tax. Code)

In pre-1987 tax years California law provided its own depletion percentages. See the 1986 and prior editions of this *Guidebook*.

• *Continental shelf areas*

California law conforms to IRC Sec. 638, concerning continental shelf areas. Therefore, natural resources include those located in seabeds and the subsoil of submarine areas adjacent to the territorial waters of the United States over which the United States has exclusive rights, in accordance with international law, in regard to the exploration and exploitation of natural resources. (Sec. 17681, Rev. & Tax. Code)

¶320 Development and Exploration Expenses of Mines, etc.

Law: Secs. 17260, 17681 (CCH CALIFORNIA TAX REPORTS ¶15-665).

Comparable Federal: Secs. 193, 263(c), 616-17 (CCH U.S. MASTER TAX GUIDE ¶987 et seq.).

Development and exploration expenditures in connection with a mine or other mineral deposit (other than an oil, gas, or geothermal wells) may be deducted currently or may be deferred (as to development expenses only), at the taxpayer's election, subject to the following general rules:

— Exploration expenses are those paid or incurred prior to the development period. Deductions for such expenses are subject to "recapture" when the mine reaches the productive stage.

— Development expenses are those paid or incurred after the existence of ores or minerals in commercially marketable quantities has been established. There is no dollar limitation on such deductions.

— Alternatively, development expenses may be capitalized and amortized on a ratable basis over a ten-year period depending on the units of ores or minerals produced and sold. However, the election to capitalize and amortize applies only to the excess of development expenditures paid or incurred during the taxable year over the net receipts during the year from the sale of ores or minerals produced. California has adopted federal rules for post-1986 expenditures.

Both California and federal laws permit the taxpayer to elect to expense intangible drilling and development costs of oil, gas, and geothermal wells. (Sec. 17681, Rev. & Tax. Code)

Unlike federal law, California law does not allow taxpayers to currently deduct expenditures for tertiary injectants. Such expenditures must be depreciated for California personal income tax purposes. (Sec. 17260, Rev. & Tax. Code)

¶321 Contributions

Law: Secs. 17201, 17275.5 (CCH CALIFORNIA TAX REPORTS ¶15-625, 16-220).

Comparable Federal: Secs. 170, 501(k) (CCH U.S. MASTER TAX GUIDE ¶1058 et seq.).

California Forms: Sch. CA (540) (California Adjustments - Residents), Sch. CA (540NR) (California Adjustments - Nonresidents or Part-Year Residents).

The current California contribution deduction is generally the same as the federal deduction as of the current IRC tie-in date (¶103), with the exception of the excise tax on premiums concerning split dollar insurance arrangements (see below). (Sec. 17201, Rev. & Tax. Code)

Because of California's current federal conformity date (¶103) California has not incorporated amendments made to IRC Sec. 170 by the Katrina Emergency Tax Relief Act of 2005 (KETRA) , the Gulf Opportunity Zone Act of 2005, the Pension Protection Act of 2006 (PPA), and the Emergency Economic Stabilization Act of 2008 (EESA). For federal purposes, these amendments make the following changes:

— waive the 50% income limitation for cash donations made through the end of 2005, and exempt them from the phase-out of itemized deductions for high AGI taxpayers;

— provide an enhanced deduction for donations of wholesome food inventory made by businesses prior to 2010 and waive the 10% limitation applicable to such contributions for contributions made by farmers and ranchers after October 2, 2008, and before 2009;

— with certain exceptions, disallow the deduction for donations of clothing or household items unless the items are in good used condition or better;

— limit the amount of the deduction for donations of appreciated tangible personal property to the taxpayer's basis in the property if the donee organization does not make proper certification and disposes of the property within three years of receiving it;

— limit the deduction for donations of taxidermy property to the lesser of the donor's basis in the property or the fair market value of the property;

— tighten the rules regarding (1) contributions of historic structures, and (2) deductions for contributing a facade easement for a building in a registered historic district,

— reduce the deduction for the portion of a qualified conservation contribution attributable to the rehabilitation credit;

— change the rules regarding donations of fractional interests in tangible personal property;

— increase the amount of the charitable deduction to 50% (100% for farmers and ranchers) of a taxpayer's contribution base that may be taken for contributions of qualified conservation real property; and

— with certain exceptions, make qualified contributions to donor advised funds fully deductible, applicable to contributions made after the date which is 180 days after August 17, 2006.

Because California does not incorporate these amendments, taxpayers will be required to make adjustments on their California tax returns.

• *Carryovers*

California follows federal law, which allows a five-year carryover of contributions that exceed the percentage limit and specifies how the carryover is to be absorbed in succeeding tax years. (Sec. 17201, Rev. & Tax. Code)

• *Automobile expense*

California conforms to federal law allowing taxpayers to claim a fixed automobile mileage rate of 14¢ per mile for use of an automobile in activities for the benefit of an organization that qualifies for deductible contributions. (Sec. 17201, Rev. & Tax. Code).

• *Split dollar insurance arrangements*

California incorporates federal law that generally denies a charitable deduction for a transfer of money to a charitable organization if, in connection with the transfer (1) the charitable organization directly or indirectly pays a premium on a life insurance, annuity, or endowment contract and (2) the transferor, any member of the transferor's family, or any other person (other than a charity) chosen by the transferor is a direct or indirect beneficiary under the contract. However, a federal provision requiring payment of an excise tax equal to the amount of nondeductible premiums does not apply for California purposes. (Sec. 17275.5, Rev. & Tax. Code)

• *Substantiation*

California conforms to federal provisions as of the current IRC tie-in date (see ¶103) that allow a deduction for charitable contributions only if the contributions are verified under regulations prescribed by the Secretary of the Treasury (the Franchise Tax Board for California purposes). (Sec. 17201, Rev. & Tax. Code)

Although California incorporates the increased substantiation requirements for deductions claimed for donations of motor vehicles, vessels, and aircraft with a claimed value of $500 or more, different effective dates apply. To claim such a deduction, taxpayers must obtain a contemporaneous written acknowledgment from the donee organization, and if the donee organization sells the property, the deduction may not exceed the gross proceeds received from the sale. In addition, recent federal amendments incorporated by California (1) increase substantiation requirements for other noncash donations of $500 or more, (2) may require a qualified appraisal for donations of $5,000 or more, and (3) require a qualified appraisal for donations of $500,000 or more. (Sec. 17024.5, Rev. & Tax. Code)

Because of California's current federal conformity date (see ¶103), California does not incorporate amendments made by the PPA that require donors of charitable contributions of monetary gifts to retain certain records, regardless of the amount, applicable to contributions made after August 17, 2006. Nor does California incorporate the KETRA amendments that increase the substantiation requirements for donations of vehicles, boats and airplanes, applicable to contributions made after 2004.

In *Appeal of James N. Harger* (2003) (CCH CALIFORNIA TAX REPORTS ¶15-625.704) the California State Board of Equalization upheld the FTB's disallowance of a charitable contribution deduction for a residential structure because the taxpayer failed to prove that he actually delivered the structure to the charity. The charity's acknowledgment of its receipt of the structure, by itself, was insufficient evidence of actual delivery because the charity was providing bogus appraisals to other donors of structures that were to be demolished rather than donated to the charity. In addition, the taxpayer's contention that he observed the disassembling of the residence in preparation for its removal and reassembly elsewhere was too self-serving to be credible.

¶322 Designated Contributions

Law: Secs. 18705—18855 (CCH CALIFORNIA TAX REPORTS ¶89-224).

Comparable Federal: None.

California Form: Form 540 (California Resident Income Tax Return).

California permits taxpayers to make certain contributions by designating the desired amounts (full dollar amounts) on their returns as additions to their tax liability. Thus, the designated amounts increase the balance payable on the return or reduce the refund, if any. The contributions, funds, and accounts listed on the 2008 returns are as follows:

— The Rare and Endangered Species Preservation Program.

— The State Children's Trust Fund for the Prevention of Child Abuse.

— The Alzheimer's Disease and Related Disorders Fund.

— The California Fund for Senior Citizens.

— The California Breast Cancer Research Fund.

— The California Firefighters' Memorial Fund.

— The Emergency Food for Families Fund.

— The California Peace Officer Memorial Foundation Fund.

— The California Military Family Relief Fund.

— The California Sea Otter Fund.

— The California Ovarian Cancer Research Fund.

— The Municipal Shelter Spay/Neuter Fund.

— The California Cancer Research Fund.

— The ALS/Lou Gehrig's Disease Research Fund.

In addition, a taxpayer who is 65 years of age or older and who is entitled to claim an additional personal exemption credit may designate an amount not to exceed the amount of the credit as a contribution to the California Seniors Special Fund. The amount of the contribution need not be reduced to reflect any income-based reduction in the amount of the credit.

All the above designated contributions are permitted as charitable contributions (¶321).

¶323 Alimony

Law: Secs. 17201, 17302 (CCH CALIFORNIA TAX REPORTS ¶15-610, 16-012).

Comparable Federal: Sec. 215 (CCH U.S. MASTER TAX GUIDE ¶771).

California Forms: Sch. CA (540) (California Adjustments - Residents), Sch. CA (540NR) (California Adjustments - Nonresidents or Part-Year Residents).

Alimony payments includible in income of the spouse who receives the payments (¶204) are deductible in computing adjusted gross income of the California resident spouse who makes the payments. (IRC Sec. 215; Sec. 17201, Rev. & Tax. Code) Taxable alimony payments include payments made to a third party, including cash payments to a third party to provide a residence for a former spouse (i.e., rent, mortgage, utilities, etc.), medical cost payments, or other such expenses incurred by the recipient. The following types of payments are not considered alimony: (1) property settlement payments, even if required by the divorce decree or other written instrument or agreement; (2) retirement benefits that the other spouse is entitled to receive; (3) voluntary payments made before they are required by a divorce decree or agreement; and (4) child support payments. (*Alimony—Frequently Asked Questions*, California Franchise Tax Board, February 14, 2008, CCH CALIFORNIA TAX REPORTS ¶404-562) Nonresidents and part-year residents are allowed a deduction for alimony paid in the same ratio that California adjusted gross income for the entire year (computed without regard to the alimony deduction) bears to total adjusted gross income (computed without regard to the alimony deduction). (Sec. 17302, Rev. & Tax. Code)

Questions frequently arise concerning the relationship of alimony with child support payments and family support payments. Payments designated as child support are not deductible. The Franchise Tax Board has taken the position that if the payor is required to pay both alimony and child support, but pays less than the total amount required, the payments are applied first to child support and any remaining amount is considered alimony.

Payments designated as family support in a divorce decree or separation instrument are considered alimony, unless the decree or instrument designates a portion of the payments as child support. (*Alimony—Frequently Asked Questions*, California Franchise Tax Board, February 14, 2008, CCH CALIFORNIA TAX REPORTS ¶404-562)

Alimony Received or Paid by Registered Domestic Partners (RDPs)

If a court orders termination of a registered domestic partnership and a California Family Law Court awards spousal support that satisfies the requirements under tax law for alimony, the payments are taxable to the payee and deductible by the payor for California purposes. However, federal treatment of these payments is uncertain. An RDP receiving alimony not included in federal income should include that amount on line 11, column C, of his or her California RDP Adjustments Worksheet. An RDP paying alimony not included in the RDP's adjustments to income for federal purposes should enter that amount on line 31, column C, of his or her California RDP Adjustments Worksheet, as a positive amount. (FTB Pub. 737, Tax Information for Registered Domestic Partners)

A California-federal difference could arise in a case in which a California court holds a foreign divorce invalid. For federal tax purposes, the deductibility of alimony paid under a state divorce decree is not affected by another state's declaration that the divorce is invalid. The rule is designed to avoid the uncertainty that could arise from conflicting state determinations regarding the validity of divorces.

• *Paid to nonresident*

Alimony paid by a California resident is deductible even if paid to a former spouse who is not a California resident, although the former spouse is not taxable on the income. This has been the policy of the Franchise Tax Board for many years, following two 1951 decisions of the California Court of Appeal. These cases are *Ada Davis Francis, Executrix v. McColgan* (CCH CALIFORNIA TAX REPORTS ¶15-610.65) and *M.B. Silberberg, Executor v. Franchise Tax Board* (CCH CALIFORNIA TAX REPORTS ¶15-610.65).

• *Mortgage payments*

In *Appeal of Karapetian* (2004) (CCH CALIFORNIA TAX REPORTS ¶15-610.45), the State Board of Equalization followed the IRS's ruling in *Baxter v. Commissioner,* T.C. Memo 1999-190, and held that mortgage payments made by a former husband on behalf of his ex-wife pursuant to a marital settlement agreement was taxable alimony because the marital settlement agreement provided that the obligation of her former husband to make mortgage payments on the taxpayer's home would cease upon her death. Because the payments were taxable alimony, the ex-wife was not entitled to deduct those payments as qualified residence interest. The payments were deductible only by the former husband.

¶324 Amortization of Bond Premium

Law: Secs. 17201 (CCH CALIFORNIA TAX REPORTS ¶15-615).

Comparable Federal: Sec. 171 (CCH U.S. MASTER TAX GUIDE ¶1967).

California Forms: FTB 3885A (Depreciation and Amortization Adjustments).

Deduction is allowed at the taxpayer's election for amortization of premium on bonds the income of which is taxable under California law. California law incorporates the federal law by reference. (Sec. 17201, Rev. & Tax. Code) However, the amortization may apply to different bonds because of the differences in taxability of government bond interest. This means that amortization may be deductible on a given bond on the California return and not on the federal, or vice versa. Both federal and California law treat amortizable bond premium deductions as interest.

As to nontaxable bonds, no deduction is allowed but amortization of premium must nevertheless be taken into account in computing the adjusted basis of the bond at time of sale or other disposition. This adjustment may be different for California purposes than for federal because the particular bond involved may be taxable for California purposes but not federal, or vice versa.

In some computations of adjusted basis involving amortization of premium on bonds, the result will be different for California purposes than for federal. This is because California did not conform to certain amendments to federal law affecting the computation of amortization until subsequent years, so that the computations of amortization may be different even though the two laws are now the same.

Amortization is not allowed on any portion of bond premium attributable to conversion features of the bond.

Special rules are provided for dealers in tax-exempt securities. See ¶210.

¶325 Medical Expenses

Law: Secs. 17021.7, 17201 (CCH CALIFORNIA TAX REPORTS ¶15-165, 15-755).

Comparable Federal: Sec. 213 (CCH U.S. MASTER TAX GUIDE ¶1015 et seq.).

California Forms: Sch. CA (540) (California Adjustments - Residents), Sch. CA (540NR) (California Adjustments - Nonresidents or Part-Year Residents).

With the exception of the treatment of registered domestic partners, California law is the same as federal with respect to the deductibility of medical expenses, including the disallowance of a medical expense deduction for unnecessary cosmetic surgery. (Sec. 17201, Rev. & Tax. Code) California, but not federal law, treats a taxpayer's registered domestic partner as the taxpayer's spouse for purposes of determining the amount that may be deducted. (Sec. 17021.7, Rev. & Tax. Code)

A deduction is permitted for medical and dental expenses, not compensated for by insurance or otherwise, to the extent that such expenses paid for medical and dental care of the taxpayer, a spouse, and dependents exceed 7.5% of federal adjusted gross income (10% for purposes of the alternative minimum tax). The definition of "dependent" is the same as for purposes of the exemption credit for dependents (¶115), and is determined without reference to the gross income of the dependent.

The definition of "medical care" includes amounts paid for qualified long-term care services and eligible long-term care premiums paid under qualified long-term care insurance contracts. For the 2008 taxable year, "eligible long-term care premiums" must not exceed the following amounts:

— $310 for persons attaining age 40 or less by the close of the taxable year;

— $580 for persons attaining an age over 40 but not over 50 by the close of the taxable year;

— $1,150 for persons attaining an age over 50 but not over 60 by the close of the taxable year;

— $3,080 for persons attaining an age over 60 but not over 70 by the close of the taxable year; and

— $3,850 for persons attaining an age over 70 by the close of the taxable year.

The limitation on itemized deductions for high-income taxpayers does not apply to medical expenses (¶303).

¶326 Medical and Health Savings Accounts

Law: Secs. 17201, 17215, 17215.4 (CCH CALIFORNIA TAX REPORTS ¶15-755, 16-100).

Comparable Federal: Secs. 138, 220, 223 (CCH U.S. MASTER TAX GUIDE ¶860, 1286).

Although California incorporates federal law concerning medical savings accounts (MSAs), California does not recognize the federal treatment of health savings accounts (HSAs).

• *Medical savings accounts*

California law is the same as federal law concerning MSAs as of the current IRC tie-in date (¶103), with the exception of the penalty amount imposed on withdrawals from an MSA that are used for nonqualified expenses and the imposition by California of penalties on rollovers from MSAs to health savings accounts (see ¶247 for a discussion of the penalty). (Sec. 17201, Rev. & Tax. Code; Sec. 17215, Rev. & Tax. Code)

CCH Comment: Registered Domestic Partners

Although RDPs or former RDPs are generally required to be treated as married taxpayers or former spouses under California income tax laws, an RDP will not be treated as a spouse if such treatment would result in disqualification of an Archer medical savings account. (Sec. 17021.7, Rev. & Tax. Code) See ¶119 for a discussion of adjustments required to be made RDPs and the California tax treatment of same-sex married couples.

Taxpayers that claim a federal deduction for contributions to an Archer MSA or MedicarePlus Choice MSA may claim the same deduction on their California return. The deduction is not subject to the 7.5% floor for itemized medical expense deductions (discussed at ¶325). Under both California and federal law, a contribution made after the end of the taxable year is considered to have been made on the last day of the year, provided that the contribution is on account of such taxable year and is made no later than the due date of the return.

• *Health savings accounts*

Unlike federal law, California does not recognize HSAs. Consequently, an individual's contributions to HSAs that were deducted on the federal tax return, must be added back for California personal income tax purposes. (Sec. 17215.4, Rev. & Tax. Code) Other addition requirements are required as a result of California's nonconformity with federal exclusions of employer contributions to HSAs and interest and dividends earned on HSAs (see ¶247).

¶327 Tenant Expenses—Cooperative Apartment and Housing Corporations

Law: Sec. 17201 (CCH CALIFORNIA TAX REPORTS ¶15-515).

Comparable Federal: Sec. 216 (CCH U.S. MASTER TAX GUIDE ¶1040).

California law is the same as federal as of the current IRC tie-in date (¶103). California does not incorporate amendments made by the Mortgage Forgiveness Debt Relief Act of 2007 that ease the qualification criteria for cooperative housing corporations to qualify for pass-through treatment. The amendments establish alternative tests to the income-based test requiring that 80% of the cooperative's income be received from residents. The alternative tests enable cooperatives to qualify for pass-through treatment based on square footage devoted to residential purposes and expenditures made on behalf of residents, applicable for federal purposes in tax years ending after December 20, 2007.

Deductions are allowed to tenant-stockholders in cooperative apartment and housing corporations for amounts representing taxes and interest paid to such corporations. (Sec. 17201, Rev. & Tax. Code)

¶328 Moving Expenses

Law: Secs. 17072, 17076 (CCH CALIFORNIA TAX REPORTS ¶15-760).

Comparable Federal: Sec. 217 (CCH U.S. MASTER TAX GUIDE ¶1073 et seq.).

California adopts federal provisions that allow an above-the-line deduction for moving expenses incurred in connection with the commencement of work at a new principal place of work. (Sec. 17072, Rev. & Tax. Code; Sec. 17076, Rev. & Tax. Code)

The treatment of an employer's moving expense reimbursements for purposes of calculating an employee's gross income is discussed at ¶238.

¶329 Employee Business Expenses

Law: Secs. 17072, 17076, 17201 (CCH CALIFORNIA TAX REPORTS ¶15-685, 15-805).

Comparable Federal: Secs. 62(a), 67, 68, 162, 274 (CCH U.S. MASTER TAX GUIDE ¶910 et seq., 941, 1011).

California and federal unreimbursed employee business expenses are considered miscellaneous itemized deductions rather than adjustments to gross income. As explained at ¶303, only the total amount of miscellaneous itemized deductions in excess of 2% of the taxpayer's federal adjusted gross income is deductible. (Sec. 17072, Rev. & Tax. Code; Sec. 17076, Rev. & Tax. Code; Sec. 17201, Rev. & Tax. Code)

California also incorporates the 50% limit on deductions for business meals and entertainment expenses (¶302). The 50% limit is computed before the 2% floor is applied. A deduction is allowed even if reimbursement comes from a third party rather than from the employer. Reimbursed employee business expenses that are included in the taxpayer's gross income are deducted from gross income.

¶330 Payments to Pension or Profit-Sharing Plans and Education Savings Accounts

Law: Secs. 17201, 17203, 17501, 17504-09, 17551, 17563.5, 23712 (CCH CALIFORNIA TAX REPORTS ¶15-800, 16-135).

Comparable Federal: Secs. 194A, 219, 402, 404-419A, 457, 530 (CCH U.S. MASTER TAX GUIDE ¶2147 et seq.).

California Forms: Form 5498-ESA (Coverdell ESA Contribution Information), Form 1099-Q (Payments from Qualified Education Programs).

California generally conforms to the federal rules for deduction of contributions to retirement plans by employers, employees, and the self-employed. Unlike California's incorporation of most IRC provisions, which are tied to a specified federal conformity date (¶103), the incorporated federal provisions concerning retirement benefits and deferred compensation plans (IRC Sec. 401—IRC Sec. 420) and governmental deferred compensation plans (IRC Sec. 457) are incorporated into California law without regard to the taxable year, to the same extent as applicable for federal purposes. Consequently, California incorporates the amendments made to IRC Sec. 401 through IRC Sec. 420, and IRC Sec. 457 by the Pension Protection Act of 2006. However, the maximum amount of elective deferrals that may be excluded from gross income under IRC Sec. 402(g) and the maximum amount of deferred compensation that may be excluded under IRC Sec. 457, as applicable for state purposes, is capped at the amount established under federal law as amended by Economic Growth and Tax Relief Reconciliation Act of 2001 and the Job Creation and Worker Assistance Act of 2002. (Sec. 17501, Rev. & Tax. Code)

Although California incorporates Part I of Subchapter D of Chapter 1 of Subtitle A of the Internal Revenue Code (IRC Sec. 401 through IRC Sec. 420), California does not automatically incorporate federal amendments made to Part II of Subchapter D of Chapter 1 of Subtitle A of the Internal Revenue Code. Consequently, the federal provisions governing certain stock options (IRC Sec. 421—IRC Sec. 424) are incorporated by California, but only as of California's current federal conformity date (¶103). Because the new deferred compensation provisions that were enacted by the PPA that address minimum funding rules for single-employer defined benefit plans and multiemployer plans (IRC Sec. 430—IRC Sec. 436) are governed by the federal Employee Retirement Income Security Act (ERISA), federal law preempts state law in this area and presumably California is required to follow these new provisions.

CCH Comment: Registered Domestic Partners and Same-Sex Married Couples

Although registered domestic partners (RDPs) or former RDPs are generally required to be treated as married taxpayers or former spouses under California income tax laws, an RDP will not be treated as a spouse if such treatment would result in disqualification of a federally qualified deferred compensation plan or disqualification of tax-favored accounts, such as individual retirement accounts, Archer medical savings accounts, qualified tuition programs, or Coverdell education savings accounts. (Sec. 17021.7, Rev. & Tax. Code) See ¶119 for a discussion of adjustments required to be made RDPs and the California tax treatment of same-sex married couples.

Beginning with the 1987 taxable year, California law has followed federal law fairly closely. For taxable years beginning before 1987, California law provided important differences, as explained below.

Under both California and federal law, a contribution made after the end of the taxable year is considered to have been made on the last day of the year, provided the contribution is on account of such taxable year and is made no later than the due date of the return. Except for IRAs, the due date for this purpose includes any extensions.

• *Payments by employers*

Detailed rules are provided for deduction of employers' payments made under an employees' trust or annuity plan or other arrangement for deferring compensation. The California rules are the same as the federal, except for the differences explained below.

California has not conformed to federal provisions that impose special excise taxes on insufficient distributions, inadequate funding, prohibited transactions, etc. However, California does impose a penalty tax on premature distributions (before age 59½) from self-employed plans and individual retirement accounts although at a lower rate than under federal law (¶ 206).

See below regarding employer contributions to self-employed retirement plans and to individual retirement accounts.

To the extent the California and federal laws are comparable, it is the stated policy of the FTB to follow all federal rules and regulations. Where the federal rules require advance approval of a plan, California will accept the federal approval and it is not necessary to file a separate application with the state.

• *Self-employed retirement plans (Keoghs)*

Both California and federal laws allow deductions for contributions to self-employed retirement plans, commonly known as "H.R. 10" or "Keogh" plans. California incorporates federal law concerning limits on deductible contributions to Keogh plans. California law requires that amounts used as "earned income" for purposes of computing a taxpayer's federal deduction (rather than the earned income computed using California amounts) must be used for purposes of computing the corresponding state deduction.

For pre-1987 tax years, California had allowed a deduction of 10% of earned income for contributions to these plans, with a maximum of $2,500 and no minimum. The federal law had allowed a deduction with varying limits that have been higher than California's since 1974.

• *Individual retirement accounts—Current law*

Both California and federal laws allow deductions for contributions to individual retirement accounts or for the purchase of individual retirement annuities or bonds. These arrangements are commonly known as "IRAs." The California IRA deduction in taxable years beginning after 1986 is generally the same as the federal. This includes conformity to the provisions of the federal Heroes Earned Retirement Opportunities Act (P.L. 109-227) that allow members of the Armed Forces serving in a combat zone to make contributions to their IRA plans even if the compensation on which such contributions are based is excluded from gross income.

Caution: IRA Deductions for RDPs

For California income tax purposes, if one or both RDPs are covered by an employer-provided retirement plan, then the California deduction for an IRA contribution may be limited. For example, assume RDP One made an IRA contribution of $5,000 in 2008, his federal AGI is $80,000, and he is not covered by an employer-sponsored retirement plan. On his separate federal return, RDP One deducted his entire IRA contribution. RDP Two is covered by an employer-sponsored retirement plan, did not make an IRA contribution in 2008, and his federal AGI is $150,000. The RDPs' combined modified federal AGI exceeds the $169,000 limitation, so they cannot deduct an IRA contribution for California purposes. When they recalculate their federal modified AGI for California purposes, as if they were married, they must make a $5,000 adjustment. (FTB Pub. 737, Tax Information for Registered Domestic Partners)

Practice Pointer: Nonconformity with Catch-Up Contributions and Certain Limitations

Because of California's current federal conformity date (see ¶103), California has not incorporated amendments made to IRC Sec. 219(b) by the Pension Protection Act of 2006 that allow qualifying individuals who participated in a bankrupt employer's 401(k) plan to make additional IRA contributions of up to $3,000 for 2007 through 2009. Nor does California incorporate the PPA's indexing for inflation of the income limits beginning in 2007 for

— deductible contributions to a traditional IRA for active participants in an employer-sponsored retirement plan or whose spouse is an active participant in an employer-sponsored plan; and

— Roth IRA contributions.

Nor does California incorporate amendments made by the Heroes Earnings Assistance and Relief Tax Act of 2008 (HEART Act), which include differential wages in compensation for purposes of determining the annual limitations on contributions to traditional individual retirement arrangements (IRAs) and Roth IRAs, effective beginning with the 2009 taxable year. A differential wage payment is any payment made by an employer to an employee for any period during which the employee is performing qualified military service to compensate the employee for the difference between the employee's military pay and the amount the employee would have received as wages from the employer.

Consequently, taxpayers who are able make additional IRA contributions on their federal return as a result of these amendments, or who qualify to make contributions on their federal return as a result of the increased income limits, are required to make adjustments on their California personal income tax return.

"Roth IRAs" : California law is the same as federal law in its treatment of Roth IRAs.

Deemed IRAs: Under both California and federal laws, if a qualified plan allows employees to make voluntary employee contributions to a separate account or annuity established under the plan and, under the terms of the plan, the account or annuity meets the requirements for a traditional IRA or a Roth IRA, the account or annuity will be deemed an individual retirement plan and not a qualified plan.

• *Individual retirement accounts—Pre-1987 law*

Because of important differences in pre-1987 California and federal deductible contribution limits, there could be a difference in the California and federal taxable amounts of IRA distributions (¶206).

• *Simplified employee pension (SEP) plans*

Under both California and federal law, an employer may provide for a simplified employee pension (SEP) plan for his or her employees. California's treatment of SEP plans is the same as the federal treatment.

• *Savings Incentive Match Plans for Employees (SIMPLE Plans)*

Both California and federal law authorize Savings Incentive Match Plans for Employees (SIMPLE plans). California's treatment of SIMPLE plans is the same as the federal treatment.

"SIMPLE IRAs": Contributions to a SIMPLE IRA are limited to employee elective contributions and required employer matching contributions. Employees may make elective contributions up to the amounts discussed above, even though the maximum amount that may be contributed to a traditional IRA is lower (see traditional IRA discussion above). Employers may adopt a SIMPLE IRA for noncollectively bargained employees, even if the employer also maintains a qualified plan for collectively bargained employees.

• *Contributions to union pension plans*

California conforms to the federal rules regarding deductibility of members' contributions to union pension plans. This means, generally, that the contributions are not deductible, because the employee ordinarily has a vested interest or the right to a return of his or her contributions. See *Appeal of Allen B. Crane* (1978) (CCH CALIFORNIA TAX REPORTS ¶15-805.96) and *Appeal of Allan I. and Ivy L. Berr* (1980) (CCH CALIFORNIA TAX REPORTS ¶15-805.961) (5% of the contributions in question was allowed as a deduction, because that portion was forfeitable upon termination of union membership).

• *Coverdell Education Savings Accounts (formerly known as education IRAs)*

Under both California law and federal law joint filers with modified adjusted gross income below $190,000 ($95,000 for single filers) may contribute up to $2,000 per child per year to a Coverdell education savings account. Earnings on contributions will be excluded from gross income and distributed tax-free provided that they are used to pay the child's post-secondary education expenses or a child's elementary or secondary education expenses. A federal election, or lack thereof, to waive the application of the exclusion is binding for California purposes. (Sec. 23712, Rev. & Tax. Code)

The $2,000 annual contribution is phased out for joint filers with modified adjusted gross income of $190,000 to $220,000, and for single filers with modified adjusted gross income of $95,000 to $110,000. The $2,000 maximum annual contribution is reduced by an amount that bears the same ratio to $2,000 as the excess of the contributor's modified adjusted gross income for the tax year over $190,000, or $95,000, bears to $30,000 for joint filers or $15,000 for single filers.

As a result of California's current IRC conformity date (see ¶103), California does not incorporate amendments made by the Heroes Earnings Assistance and Relief Tax Act of 2008 that allow an individual to contribute a military death gratuity or payment under the Servicemembers' Group Life Insurance (SGLI) program to a Coverdell ESA, notwithstanding the $2,000 annual contribution limit and the income phase-out of the limit that would otherwise apply. The amendments are generally effective for federal purposes with respect to deaths from injuries occurring after June 16, 2008, although the amendments also apply to contributions made from gratuities or payments received for deaths from injuries occurring after October 6, 2001, and before June 17, 2008, if such contribution is made no later than one year after June 17, 2008. Because California has not conformed to these amendments, taxpayers who are allowed to deduct more than $2,000 on their federal return as a result of this expanded contribution limit will be required to make an addition adjustment on their California return.

Taxpayers may make deductible contributions for the tax year up until the time for filing the return (without extensions).

Form 5498-ESA, Coverdell ESA Contribution Information, is used to report Coverdell education savings account contributions. Distributions are reported on Form 1099-Q, Payments from Qualified Education Programs.

CCH Practice Tip: Transfer of Coverdell Education Savings Account Balances

Before a beneficiary reaches age 30, the balance of a Coverdell education savings account may be transferred or rolled over to another Coverdell education savings account for a member of the former beneficiary's family in order to further defer or possibly avoid payment of tax on the earnings in the account.

¶331 Research and Experimental Expenditures

Law: Sec. 17201 (CCH CALIFORNIA TAX REPORTS ¶15-795).

Comparable Federal: Secs. 59(e), 174 (CCH U.S. MASTER TAX GUIDE ¶979).

Research and experimental expenditures may be deducted currently, or may be amortized over a 60-month period at the election of the taxpayer. For both California and federal purposes, the option to deduct or amortize research and experimental expenditures applies only to expenditures that are "reasonable under the circumstances." (Sec. 17201, Rev. & Tax. Code)

Both California law and federal law allow a credit for certain increases in research expenditures (¶148).

¶332 Trademark or Trade Name Expenditures

Law: Sec. 18151 (CCH CALIFORNIA TAX REPORTS ¶15-615, 15-620).

Comparable Federal: Former Sec. 167(e), Sec. 1253 (CCH U.S. MASTER TAX GUIDE ¶1775).

California incorporates special federal rules governing the deductibility of payments made in connection with the transfer of a trademark, trade name, or franchise. Such amounts, when paid or incurred in the conduct of a trade or business during the taxable year, are currently deductible if they satisfy the following conditions:

— they are contingent on the productivity, use, or disposition of the trademark, trade name, or franchise;

— they are paid as part of a series of amounts payable at least annually throughout the term of the transfer agreement; and

— the payments are substantially equal in amount or are to be paid pursuant to a fixed formula. (Sec. 18151, Rev. & Tax. Code)

Transfer payments that do not meet the above requirements are generally subject to amortization over a 15-year period for post-August 10, 1993, transfers (¶310).

¶333 Goodwill and Other Intangibles

Law: Sec. 17279 (CCH CALIFORNIA TAX REPORTS ¶15-615).

Comparable Federal: Sec. 197 (CCH U.S. MASTER TAX GUIDE ¶1288).

California incorporates IRC Sec. 197 as of the current IRC tie-in date (see ¶103), which provides for the amortization, over a 15-year period, of goodwill and certain other intangibles used in a trade or business or for the production of income. (Sec. 17279, Rev. & Tax. Code)

The following intangibles are subject to amortization unless specifically excluded by federal law:

— goodwill, going concern value, and covenants not to compete entered into in connection with the acquisition of a trade or business;

— workforce in place;

— information base;

— know-how;

— any customer-based intangible;

— any supplier-based intangible;

— any license, permit, or other right granted by a governmental unit or agency; and

— any franchise, trademark, or trade name.

¶334 Start-Up Expenditures

Law: Sec. 17201 (CCH California Tax Reports ¶15-805).

Comparable Federal: Sec. 195 (CCH U.S. Master Tax Guide ¶904).

California law incorporates the federal law as of the current IRC tie-in date (¶103). (Sec. 17201, Rev. & Tax. Code)

Under both California and federal law, taxpayers may (1) currently deduct up to $5,000 in start-up expenditures (reduced by the amount by which the expenditures exceed $50,000) in the year the trade or business begins and (2) amortize any remainder over a period of 15 years.

¶335 Standard Deduction

Law: Sec. 17073.5 (CCH California Tax Reports ¶15-540).

Comparable Federal: Sec. 63 (CCH U.S. Master Tax Guide ¶126).

California Forms: Form 540 (California Resident Income Tax Return), Form 540A (California Resident Income Tax Return), Form 540 2EZ (California Resident Income Tax Return).

California conforms to federal law allowing taxpayers to elect a standard deduction in lieu of itemizing deductions, with the exception of the amount of the deduction. (Sec. 17073.5, Rev. & Tax. Code) California does not follow federal law allowing an additional standard deduction for state and local real property taxes or for disaster losses.

For 2008, the California standard deduction for a head of household, surviving spouse, or a married couple or registered domestic partnership filing a joint return is $7,384. For others, the deduction is $3,692.

Both federal and California law limit the standard deduction of a person who is claimed as a dependent. For 2008, the deduction is limited to the greater of (1) $900 or (2) the earned income of the dependent plus $300.

CCH Example: Deduction for Employed Dependent

Matthew, age 16, has $300 of interest income from a savings account and $2,000 of earned income from a summer job in 2008. Assuming Matthew is eligible to be claimed as a dependent on his parents' tax return, his standard deduction is $2,300: the greater of (1) $900 or (2) the $2,000 of earned income plus $300.

Both federal and California law provide for inflation adjustments to the standard deduction.

As under federal law, the following taxpayers may not take the standard deduction:

— a married individual filing separately when the other spouse itemizes (the same applies to registered domestic partners for California purposes only);

— an individual making a short-period return because of a change in the annual accounting period; or

— an estate, trust, common trust fund, or partnership.

Federal law also denies the standard deduction to nonresident aliens, but California does not.

¶336 Items Not Deductible

Law: Secs. 17201, 17269, 17270, 17274-75, 17280-82, 17286, 17299.8-9.9, Rev. & Tax. Code; Sec. 11135, Govt. Code (CCH CALIFORNIA TAX REPORTS ¶15-735, 15-775, 16-110, 16-150, 16-290, 16-315).

Comparable Federal: Secs. 162, 183, 261-68, 273, 274, 276, 280A, 280B, 280C, 280E, 280G (CCH U.S. MASTER TAX GUIDE ¶903, 907, 909, 910, 961, 963, 965, 966, 969, 999, 1044, 1195, 1214, 1286, 1330, 1343, 1527).

California Forms: Sch. CA (540) (California Adjustments - Residents), Sch. CA (540NR) (California Adjustments - Nonresidents or Part-Year Residents).

Federal law making certain items expressly nondeductible is incorporated in California's law by reference as of the current IRC tie-in date (¶103). (Sec. 17201, Rev. & Tax. Code) Because of California's federal conformity date, California does not adopt federal amendments made by the Emergency Economic Stabilization Act of 2008, which expand the golden parachute prohibitions to apply to covered executives that leave the employment of financial institutions that sell troubled assets to the U.S. Treasury Department through the Troubled Asset Relief Program.

In addition, there are several specific differences between California law and federal law that are explained below.

• *California-federal differences*

California provides for the following categories of nondeductible items not provided under federal law:

— expenses of certain illegal activities in addition to those specified federally, or of other activities that directly tend to promote or are otherwise related to such activities (Sec. 17281, Rev. & Tax. Code; Sec. 17282, Rev. & Tax. Code);

— certain expenses attributable to substandard housing, as explained below;

— abandonment fees on open-space easements and timberland tax-recoupment fees, as explained below;

— in connection with the denial of deductions for illegal bribes, etc., California provides for disallowance of certain payments that would be unlawful under U.S. laws (Sec. 17286, Rev. & Tax. Code);

— deductions for remuneration of personal services that are not reported in required statements to employees (¶715) or in required information returns (¶713) may be disallowed at the discretion of the Franchise Tax Board;

— deductions for interest, taxes, depreciation, and amortization are denied to property owners who fail to file proper information returns as explained at ¶713 ; and

— business expense deductions for expenditures made at, or payments paid to, a club that engages in discriminatory practices on the basis of age, sex, race, religion, color, ancestry, national origin, ethnic group identification, sexual orientation, or disability. (Sec. 17269, Rev. & Tax. Code; Sec. 11135, Govt. Code)

Federal law that generally prohibits a current deduction for capital expenditures (IRC Sec. 263(a)) does not apply to expenditures for which a deduction is allowed under California law for enterprise zone property.

• *Illegal activities*

The California law has two quite similar provisions that deny deductions for expenses of illegal activities. The first provision applies to activities defined in Chapters 9, 10, and 10.5 of Title 9, Part 1, of the Penal Code of California. (Sec. 17281, Rev. & Tax. Code; Sec. 17282, Rev. & Tax. Code) Chapter 9 refers to lotteries; Chapter 10 covers gaming; Chapter 10.5 applies to touting, etc., in connection with horse racing. The purpose is to deny deduction of expenses against income from gambling.

The law specifically provides that wagering losses may be deducted as an offset to wagering gains, but it has been held that this does not apply to bookmakers. See *Appeal of M.R. and J.V. Van Cleave* (1955) (CCH CALIFORNIA TAX REPORTS ¶200-346), decided by the State Board of Equalization (SBE), and *Herman E. Hetzel v. Franchise Tax Board* (1958) (CCH CALIFORNIA TAX REPORTS ¶16-150.36), decided by the California District Court of Appeal. These cases disallowed deductions claimed by bookmakers for wagering losses and taxed them on their entire gross winnings. The SBE reached a similar result in cases regarding payouts to pinball machine winners—see *Appeals of C.B. Hall, Sr., et al.* (CCH CALIFORNIA TAX REPORTS ¶16-150.41) and *Appeal of Arnerich et al.* (CCH CALIFORNIA TAX REPORTS ¶16-150.53).

The second provision of this type applies to a variety of activities defined in certain chapters of the Penal Code and the Health and Safety Code. These chapters cover a wide range of criminal activities, including larceny, robbery, burglary, forgery, counterfeiting, lewd conduct, prostitution, drug trafficking, etc. This provision includes a prohibition against deductions for cost of goods sold.

• *Substandard rental housing*

California denies deductions for interest, taxes, depreciation, or amortization attributable to substandard rental housing. This applies to both occupied and unoccupied housing that violates laws or codes relating to health, safety, or building, where (1) the property is not renovated within six months after notice of violation is given or (2) good faith compliance efforts have not been commenced. It also applies to employee housing that has not been brought into compliance with the conditions stated in a written notice of violation issued under the Employee Housing Act within 30 days of the date of such notice or the date prescribed in the notice. (Sec. 17274, Rev. & Tax. Code)

Exceptions to the disallowance of deductions are provided for cases where the substandard condition results from a natural disaster or from a change in standards (unless there is danger to occupants), or where failure to renovate is due to unavailability of credit.

This deduction prohibition was applied to deny deductions for interest, taxes, and depreciation in *Appeal of Robert J. and Vera Cort* (1980) (CCH CALIFORNIA TAX REPORTS ¶16-150.73). Other cases have held to the same effect. In *Appeal of Bryan H. Hillstrom* (1983) (CCH CALIFORNIA Tax Reports ¶15-974.36), deductions were disallowed even though the notice of violation had been issued to a prior owner and the current owner was not aware of the notice or the substandard condition.

• *Fees under environmental laws*

California denies deductions for abandonment fees paid to terminate an open-space easement, and also for tax recoupment fees imposed by the Government Code under the program for timberland preserves (see also ¶559). (Sec. 17275, Rev. & Tax. Code)

• *Expenses for which credits are allowable*

California incorporates the portions of IRC Sec. 280C that (1) disallow a deduction for that portion of qualified research expenses or basic research expenses that is equal to the amount of the credit allowed for such expenses (¶148) and (2) disallow a deduction or credit for that portion of the qualified clinical testing expenses otherwise available as a deduction that is equal to the amount of the clinical testing tax credit allowable under IRC Sec. 28.

California does not incorporate the rest of IRC Sec. 280C, which disallows a deduction for that portion of expenses for which other federal credits, including the federal employment credit, are allowed. Because California law makes federal provisions relating to federal credits inapplicable (Sec. 17024.5(b), Rev. & Tax. Code), unless specifically incorporated, federal provisions that disallow deductions for expenses for which federal credits were claimed are inapplicable. Consequently, California taxpayers may subtract these amounts from federal AGI in computing California taxable income.

• *Other nondeductible items*

Differences between federal and California rules as to what is tax-exempt income may also result in differences in expenses that are nondeductible. For example, California exempts certain interest income, whereas federal does not. Expenses attributable to such income that would be deductible for federal tax purposes would not be deductible for California purposes. Also, California does not permit deduction of expenses attributable to income that was not taxed by California.

CCH Example: Nondeductible Lottery Expenses

California lottery losses may not be deducted from lottery winnings for California purposes, because the expenses are attributable to the production of income not taxed by California.

See the following paragraphs for other possible federal or California nondeductible items:

¶ 305 Interest.

¶ 338 Farm and hobby losses.

¶ 339 "At risk" limitations.

¶ 416 Construction-period interest and taxes.

¶ 532 Gain or loss on options.

¶337 Deductions of Nonresidents

Law: Secs. 17041, 17301-10 (CCH California Tax Reports ¶ 15-105).

Comparable Federal: None.

California Form: Sch. CA (540NR) (California Adjustments - Nonresidents or Part-Year Residents).

As explained at ¶ 116, the tax on nonresidents and part-year residents is determined on the basis of the taxable income of a nonresident or part-year resident. In computing either California adjusted gross income or a nonresident's or part-year resident's taxable income for this purpose, only deductions that are attributable to California are allowable. (Sec. 17041(i), Rev. & Tax. Code)

Nonresidents and part-year residents may prorate their itemized deductions, including, deductions for alimony paid, or the standard deduction by the ratio that California adjusted gross income bears to total adjusted gross income. (Sec. 17301, Rev. & Tax. Code)

A net operating loss carryover (¶ 309) is deductible for California purposes even if the loss was sustained while the taxpayer was not a state resident, as long as the loss was attributable to California sources. (Sec. 17041(i)(2), Rev. & Tax. Code)

In computing the tax that would be payable if the taxpayer were a full-year resident, the usual rules for itemizing deductions are applicable; that is, deductions should normally be itemized if they amount to more than the standard deduction (¶ 335).

¶338 Farm and Hobby Losses

Law: Sec. 17201 (CCH CALIFORNIA TAX REPORTS ¶15-745).

Comparable Federal: Sec. 183 (CCH U.S. MASTER TAX GUIDE ¶1195).

California conforms to federal law (¶103).

California and federal law provide special rules to restrict the tax benefit of farm and hobby losses. These rules disallow loss deductions under certain conditions and "recapture" prior deductions when property is sold. (IRC Sec. 183; Sec. 17201, Rev. & Tax. Code)

¶339 "At Risk" Limitations

Law: Sec. 17551 (CCH CALIFORNIA TAX REPORTS ¶15-745).

Comparable Federal: Sec. 465 (CCH U.S. MASTER TAX GUIDE ¶2045).

California law is the same as federal as of the current IRC tie-in date (¶103). (Sec. 17551, Rev. & Tax. Code)

Detailed rules are provided to limit the deduction of certain losses to the amount of the taxpayer's economic risk. These provisions, which were designed to restrict the use of various types of tax shelters, apply to any activity engaged in as a trade or business or for the production of income. The federal law is incorporated in California's by reference.

In *Haggard and Williams* (1994) (CCH CALIFORNIA TAX REPORTS ¶402-752) the State Board of Equalization held that losses arising from a taxpayer's investment in a tax shelter that involved the purchase and leaseback of computer equipment were not deductible, because the taxpayer was protected against loss by the provisions of his purchase agreement. Although business losses generated by the leasing of depreciable property may be deducted to the extent that a taxpayer is "at risk," a taxpayer is not considered "at risk" with respect to amounts protected against loss through nonrecourse financing, guarantees, stop loss agreements, or similar arrangements.

¶340 Passive Activity Losses and Credits

Law: Secs. 17551, 17561 (CCH CALIFORNIA TAX REPORTS ¶15-745, 16-095).

Comparable Federal: Sec. 469 (CCH U.S. MASTER TAX GUIDE ¶2053 et seq.).

California Forms: Sch. CA (540) (California Adjustments - Residents), Sch. CA (540NR) (California Adjustments - Nonresidents or Part-Year Residents), FTB 3801 (Passive Activity Loss Limitations), FTB 3801-CR (Passive Activity Credit Limitations).

California incorporates, with the changes noted below, the federal law as of the current IRC tie-in date (¶103) that generally prohibits the use of passive losses to reduce nonpassive income. (Sec. 17551, Rev. & Tax. Code)

California makes the following three modifications to the federal rule as incorporated:

(1) under IRC Sec. 469(d)(2), certain federal passive income credits may be carried over to later tax years if they exceed the tax attributable to the passive activity; for California purposes, credits that may be carried over are the credits for research expenses and low-income housing and the former credits for targeted jobs and orphan drug research;

(2) for purposes of California's low-income housing credit, California substitutes a $75,000 limitation in place of the federal $25,000 limitation on use of passive activity losses or credits against nonpassive rental income; and

(3) California has not conformed to federal amendments made by the Revenue Reconciliation Act of 1993 that, for tax years beginning after 1993, ease application of the passive activity loss rules to rental real estate losses suffered

by certain taxpayers who materially participate in a real property trade or business. For California purposes, all rental activities are passive activities, regardless of the level of participation. (Sec. 17561, Rev. & Tax. Code)

• *Computation*

All California taxpayers who engage in passive activities must segregate California adjustments that relate to passive activities from California adjustments that relate to nonpassive activities. On FTB 3801, taxpayers must make adjustments to items of federal adjusted gross income that relate to passive activities and as to which California and federal law differ (*e.g.*, depreciation).

On FTB 3801, the taxpayer first adjusts passive activity losses to reflect any California/federal differences (as in depreciation) and then subjects the modified figure to the passive activity loss limitation rules. The resultant figure, which is the California passive activity loss, is transferred to the form or schedule normally used to report the California adjustment amount. The adjustment is computed and then entered on the appropriate line of Schedule CA (540) or Schedule CA (540NR). If there is no California schedule or form to compute the passive activity loss adjustment (*e.g.*, for rental real estate losses), the adjustment is computed on a special worksheet on FTB 3801 and then transferred directly to the corresponding line in either the subtraction or addition section of Schedule CA (540) or Schedule CA (540NR). To compute passive activity loss adjustment amounts for Schedule CA (540) or Schedule CA (540NR), the taxpayer should use total adjusted gross income amounts and should not start with federal income amounts.

Taxpayers should consult FTB Pub. 1100, Taxation of Nonresidents and Individuals Who Change Residency, for detailed explanations and examples of how the passive activity loss limitations impact nonresidents and part-year residents.

Unallowed (*i.e.*, excess) passive activity losses and credits may be carried forward and subtracted from passive activity income in succeeding tax years.

Practice Tip: Dispositions

Unallowed passive activity credits, unlike passive activity losses, are not allowable when a taxpayer disposes of his or her interest in an activity in a taxable transaction. However, a taxpayer may elect to increase the basis (by the amount of the original basis reduction) to the extent that the credit has not been used. (Instructions to FTB 3801-CR).

¶341 Expenses of Soil Conservation, etc.

Law: Sec. 17201 (CCH CALIFORNIA TAX REPORTS ¶15-170).

Comparable Federal: Secs. 175, 180 (CCH U.S. MASTER TAX GUIDE ¶982, 985).

California law concerning the expensing of soil and water conservation expenses is the same as federal as of the current federal conformity date (see ¶103). (Sec. 17201, Rev. & Tax. Code) California does not incorporate the federal amendment made by the Heartland, Habitat, Harvest, and Horticulture Act of 2008 (Farm Act) that allows farmers to currently expense endangered species recovery expenditures paid or incurred after 2008. Unless conforming legislation is adopted, taxpayers claiming this deduction on their federal return will be required to make adjustments on their California return.

• *Soil and water conservation*

Farmers may deduct expenditures for soil and water conservation and the prevention of erosion on farmland.

• *Expenditures for fertilizer, etc.*

Farmers are permitted to elect to deduct expenditures for fertilizer and other materials designed to improve farm land, where the costs would otherwise be chargeable to capital account.

¶342 Circulation Expenditures of Periodicals

Law: Sec. 17201 (CCH CALIFORNIA TAX REPORTS ¶15-515).

Comparable Federal: Sec. 173 (CCH U.S. MASTER TAX GUIDE ¶971).

Expenditures to "establish, maintain, or increase" the circulation of a periodical are deductible. This provision permits deduction of costs of increasing circulation, which would otherwise have to be capitalized, with elective three-year amortization of such expenditures. California law incorporates the federal law by reference. (Sec. 17201, Rev. & Tax. Code)

¶343 Employee Parking Cash-Out Programs

Law: Sec. 17202 (CCH CALIFORNIA TAX REPORTS ¶16-365).

Comparable Federal: Sec. 162 (CCH U.S. MASTER TAX GUIDE ¶863).

California law allows employers a business expense deduction for expenses incurred in connection with an employee parking cash-out program. Under such a program, an employer provides a cash allowance to an employee in an amount equal to the parking subsidy that the employer would otherwise pay to provide the employee with a parking space. (Sec. 17202, Rev. & Tax. Code)

¶344 Tuition and Related Expenses

Law: Sec. 17204.7 (CCH CALIFORNIA TAX REPORTS ¶16-050).

Comparable Federal: Sec. 222 (CCH U.S. MASTER TAX GUIDE ¶1082).

California Forms: Sch. CA (540) (California Adjustments - Residents), Sch. CA (540NR) (California Adjustments - Nonresidents or Part-Year Residents).

Unlike federal law, California does not allow a deduction for qualified tuition and related expenses incurred by individual taxpayers. (Sec. 17204.7, Rev. & Tax. Code) Federal law allows such a deduction for tax years beginning after 2001 and before 2010. Taxpayers who claim the deduction on their federal return must make an addition adjustment on Sch. CA (540).

¶345 Energy Efficient Commercial Property Costs

Law: None. (CCH CALIFORNIA TAX REPORTS ¶16-055).

Comparable Federal: Sec. 179D (CCH U.S. MASTER TAX GUIDE ¶977D).

California Forms: FTB 3885A (540) (Depreciation and Amortization Adjustments), FTB 3885F (541) (Depreciation and Amortization), FTB 3885L (568) (Depreciation and Amortization), FTB 3885P (565) (Depreciation and Amortization), Sch. CA (540) (California Adjustments - Residents), Sch. CA (540NR) (California Adjustments - Nonresidents or Part-Year Residents), Sch. D (California Capital Gain or Loss Adjustment).

Because of California's current IRC conformity date, California does not incorporate the federal deduction available for a portion of the costs of installing energy-efficient systems in commercial buildings (Code Sec. 179D). The federal deduction is available for qualified commercial property placed in service after 2005 but before 2014.

Taxpayers that claim the federal deduction for such costs must add these amounts to federal adjusted gross income (AGI) when computing their California taxable income. The expenses added back to federal AGI may then be depreciated on the California personal income tax return.

¶346 Expensing of Environmental Remediation Costs

Law: Sec. 17279.4. (CCH CALIFORNIA TAX REPORTS ¶16-055).

Comparable Federal: Sec. 198 (CCH U.S. MASTER TAX GUIDE ¶977D).

California Forms: FTB 3885A (540) (Depreciation and Amortization Adjustments), FTB 3885F (541) (Depreciation and Amortization), FTB 3885L (568) (Depreciation and Amortization), FTB 3885P (565) (Depreciation and Amortization), Sch. CA (540) (California Adjustments - Residents), Sch. CA (540NR) (California Adjustments - Nonresidents or Part-Year Residents), Sch. D (California Capital Gain or Loss Adjustment).

Under federal law, but not California law, taxpayers may elect to currently deduct costs paid or incurred in connection with the abatement or control of hazardous substances at a qualified contaminated site. California allowed the deduction prior to 2004. (Sec. 17279.4, Rev. & Tax. Code)

An addition adjustment is made on Sch. CA (540). Amounts expensed on the federal return must be treated as capitalized costs for California personal income tax purposes; therefore, a depreciation adjustment must also be made (see ¶310).

The federal deduction may only be claimed for expenditures incurred prior to 2010. Once the federal deduction expires, no addition adjustment is required.

¶347 Expensing of Qualified Disaster Costs

Law: None.

Comparable Federal: Sec. 198A (CCH U.S. MASTER TAX GUIDE ¶977D).

California Forms: FTB 3885A (540) (Depreciation and Amortization Adjustments), FTB 3885F (541) (Depreciation and Amortization), FTB 3885L (568) (Depreciation and Amortization), FTB 3885P (565) (Depreciation and Amortization), Sch. CA (540) (California Adjustments - Residents), Sch. CA (540NR) (California Adjustments - Nonresidents or Part-Year Residents), Sch. D (California Capital Gain or Loss Adjustment).

Under federal law, but not California law, taxpayers may elect to currently expense qualified disaster expenses after 2007, rather than capitalizing them.

An addition adjustment is made on Sch. CA (540). Amounts expensed on the federal return must be treated as capitalized costs for California personal income tax purposes; therefore, a depreciation adjustment must also be made (see ¶310).

The federal deduction may only be claimed for expenditures incurred in relation to disasters that occur before 2010. Once the federal deduction expires, no addition adjustment is required.

PERSONAL INCOME TAX

CHAPTER 4
ACCOUNTING METHODS AND BASES, INVENTORIES

¶400 Accounting Periods and Methods—In General

Law: Secs. 17551-70 (CCH CALIFORNIA TAX REPORTS ¶15-455—15-480, 16-070, 89-102).

Comparable Federal: Secs. 441-83 (CCH U.S. MASTER TAX GUIDE ¶1501, 1515).

California generally incorporates federal law governing accounting periods and methods of accounting as of the current tie-in date (¶103). (Sec. 17551, Rev. & Tax. Code) However IRC Sec. 457, relating to deferred compensation plans of state and local governments and tax-exempt organizations, is incorporated by California as amended to date (see ¶206 for details). California's requirements in connection with annualized short-period returns are somewhat different (¶403). In addition, California has a special rule with no federal counterpart authorizing the Franchise Tax Board to allocate income between separately filing spouses (¶412).

• *Taxable year of inclusion*

California incorporates federal law providing that income must be included in the year of receipt unless properly accounted for in another period under an acceptable method of accounting. Amounts accrued only by reason of the death of an accrual-basis taxpayer are not included for the taxable period of the taxpayer's death.

California does not incorporate federal law allowing taxpayers to elect to recognize qualified gain from a qualifying electric transmission transaction over an eight-year period. (Sec. 17551(f), Rev. & Tax. Code) Consequently, taxpayers must recognize the entire gain for California purposes in the year of the transaction. Presumably, this difference is reflected on Sch. D (540 or 540NR).

Production flexibility contracts: California law mirrors Sec. 2012 of the Tax and Trade Relief Extension Act of 1998, which allows farmers to include in their taxable income production flexibility contract payments made under the Federal Agriculture Improvement and Reform Act of 1996 (P.L. 104-127) in the taxable year of actual receipt, even though the contract grants the farmer the option to receive payments earlier. (Sec. 17552.3, Rev. & Tax. Code)

• *Taxable year of deduction*

California incorporates federal law as of California's current federal conformity date (see ¶103) to provide that deductions must be taken in conformance with the method of accounting employed by the taxpayer. (Sec. 17551, Rev. & Tax. Code) However, as a result of California's current federal conformity date, California does not incorporate a federal amendment made by the Heartland, Habitat, Harvest , and Horticulture Act of 2008 (Farm Act) that limits the amount of net Schedule F losses from farming activities that may be claimed by taxpayers, other than C corporations, who receive Commodity Credit Corporation loans or certain other farm subsidies, beginning with the 2010 tax year. If California does not conform to this amendment, taxpayers whose losses were limited on their federal returns as a result of this provision will be able to claim a greater loss on their California returns.

¶401 Accounting Periods

Law: Secs. 17551, 17565 (CCH CALIFORNIA TAX REPORTS ¶15-455, 89-102).

Comparable Federal: Secs. 441, 444, 645 (CCH U.S. MASTER TAX GUIDE ¶1501 et seq.).

California incorporates federal law as of a specified tie-in date (¶103). (Sec. 17551, Rev. & Tax. Code) The taxpayer's tax year must be the same as federal unless a different period is initiated or approved by the Franchise Tax Board. (Sec. 17565, Rev. & Tax. Code)

The taxpayer may report on a calendar year or fiscal year basis, in accordance with the taxpayer's books. If no books are kept, the taxpayer must report on the calendar year basis. A 52-53 week year may be used under certain circumstances; special rules are provided for determining the effective date of law changes in such cases.

If a fiscal year is to be established by a new taxpayer, the year must be adopted on or before the time prescribed by law (not including extensions) for filing the return for that year.

In *Appeal of P.A. Reyff* (1958) (CCH CALIFORNIA TAX REPORTS ¶15-455.25), the State Board of Equalization held that the taxpayer was required to report on a calendar year basis for the particular year in question because he kept no books, even though returns were filed and accepted in later years on a fiscal year basis. The later years were not in question.

¶402 Change of Accounting Period

Law: Secs. 17551, 17556 (CCH CALIFORNIA TAX REPORTS ¶15-455).

Comparable Federal: Sec. 442 (CCH U.S. MASTER TAX GUIDE ¶1513).

California law is essentially the same as federal law, including the provisions on accounting-period changes by partnerships, S corporations, trusts, and personal service corporations (and the effects of the taxable income of partners, S corporation shareholders, etc.).

Federal law regarding changes of accounting period is incorporated in California law by reference. (Sec. 17551, Rev. & Tax. Code)

Generally, a change of accounting period requires the approval of the taxing authorities. However, an estate may change its annual accounting period one time without the approval of the FTB. (Sec. 17556, Rev. & Tax. Code) Application for change should be filed by the 15th day of the second month following the close of the short period. Under the conformity rules, an application for federal purposes is considered an application for California purposes also, and federal approval will apply for California purposes as long as the following conditions are met:

— California has conformed to the underlying law that is being applied;

— the FTB has authority for granting the request; and

— the FTB has not announced that it will decline to follow the federal procedure being relied upon.

However, federal forms must be submitted to the Franchise Tax Board, as prescribed, if the taxpayer cannot rely on a federally approved change request, desires a change different from the federal change, or desires a change for state tax purposes only (FTB Notice 2000-8 (2000) (CCH CALIFORNIA TAX REPORTS ¶ 15-455.321)). Federal Form 3115, Application for Change in Accounting Method, or federal Form 1128, Application to Adopt, Change, or Retain a Tax Year, must be submitted to the FTB by the due date specified in California law or, if none is specified, by the due date for a federal change request if a federal change request has been submitted to the IRS for that change. Other than specified identifying information, the federal forms must be completed using appropriate California tax information and not federal tax information, taking into account differences in federal and California law (e.g., different depreciation methods).

A cover letter must be attached to the front of federal Form 3115 or Form 1128, clearly indicating that a "Change in Accounting Period" or a "Change in Accounting Method" is being requested. The application and the accompanying cover letter should be sent to: Franchise Tax Board, Change in Accounting Periods and Methods, Coordinator, P.O. Box 1998, Sacramento, CA 95812. The FTB will acknowledge receipt of the request within 30 days and will issue a response in writing once the request has been reviewed (FTB Notice 2000-8 (2000) (CCH CALIFORNIA TAX REPORTS ¶ 15-455.321))

See ¶ 616 for a discussion of the taxable year of a partnership.

¶403 Return for Short Period—Annualization of Income

Law: Secs. 17551, 17552 (CCH CALIFORNIA TAX REPORTS ¶ 15-455, 89-102).

Comparable Federal: Sec. 443 (CCH U.S. MASTER TAX GUIDE ¶ 1505).

California law is the same as federal law with minor exceptions noted below. (Sec. 17551, Rev. & Tax. Code)

California law, unlike federal law, requires a short-period return when a taxpayer's year is terminated by the Franchise Tax Board because of a jeopardy assessment. (Sec. 17552, Rev. & Tax. Code)

California requires a proportional reduction in the amount allowed for exemption credits when a short-period return is filed. Federal law requires a similar reduction for exemption deductions.

¶404 Optional Method for Short-Period Returns

Law: Sec. 17551 (CCH CALIFORNIA TAX REPORTS ¶ 15-455, 89-102).

Comparable Federal: Sec. 443 (CCH U.S. MASTER TAX GUIDE ¶ 1515).

California law is the same as federal law (¶ 103). (Sec. 17551, Rev. & Tax. Code)

¶405 Change of Status, Resident or Nonresident

Law: Sec. 17041(b) and (i) (CCH CALIFORNIA TAX REPORTS ¶16-510, 16-535, 16-545, 16-550, 16-555, 16-560, 16-570).

Comparable Federal: None.

For California personal income tax purposes, the term "taxable income of a nonresident or part-year resident" includes the following:

— for any part of the taxable year during which the taxpayer was a resident of this state, all items of gross income and all deductions, regardless of source and

— for any part of the taxable year during which the taxpayer was not a resident of this state, gross income and deductions derived from sources within this state.

(Sec. 17041(i)(1), Rev. & Tax. Code)

Practice Pointer: Attribution and Accrual Rules

Taxpayers should consult FTB Pub. 1100, Taxation of Nonresidents and Individuals Who Change Residency, for the FTB's interpretation of the attribution and accrual rules. The publication provides numerous examples to illustrate how the current attribution and accrual rules apply.

For pre-2002 taxable years, if the status of the taxpayer changed from resident to nonresident, or vice versa, the determination of whether or not income was subject to California tax was made on the accrual basis, even though the taxpayer reported on the cash basis of accounting. The period in which the income was actually to be reported, however, was determined under the regular rules relating to the taxpayer's method of accounting. The purpose of the pre-2002 rules, as interpreted by the State Board of Equalization (SBE) in the cases discussed below, was to treat cash-basis taxpayers the same as accrual-basis taxpayers when a change of residency occurred.

• *Installment sales*

The FTB has taken the position that installment proceeds received by a California resident from the sale of property located outside California are taxable by California. Conversely, installment proceeds received by a former California resident from the sale of California property are not taxable by California (FTB Pub. 1100, Taxation of Nonresidents and Individuals Who Change Residency, revised 11-2007, CCH CALIFORNIA TAX REPORTS ¶404-599).

• *Individual retirement accounts, employer-sponsored retirement plans, and compensation*

Taxpayers who move into California do not receive a stepped-up basis for annual contributions and earnings on individual retirement accounts (IRAs) for contributions made when they are nonresidents. Because part-year residents are treated as residents for all prior years for all items of deferred income, which includes IRAs, taxpayers are allowed a basis for contributions actually made, even if they would not have been allowed under California law before they became California residents.

Compensation received by a California resident is taxable by California, even if it accrued prior to becoming a resident. However, taxpayers may be eligible to claim a credit for taxes paid to the other state (FTB Pub. 1100, Taxation of Nonresidents and Individuals Who Change Residency, revised 11-2007, CCH CALIFORNIA TAX REPORTS ¶404-599).

• *Stock options*

Nonstatutory stock options.—California taxes the wage income received by a nonresident taxpayer from nonstatutory stock options on a source basis, whether the taxpayer was always a nonresident or was formerly a California resident. On the other hand, if a taxpayer is granted nonstatutory stock options while a nonresident and later exercises the options while a California resident, the resulting compensation is taxable by California because the wage income is recognized while the taxpayer is a California resident. The taxable wage income is the difference between the fair market value of the stock on the exercise date and the option price. (FTB Pub. 1004, Stock Option Guidelines, revised 10-2007, CCH CALIFORNIA TAX REPORTS ¶404-589; FTB Pub. 1100, Taxation of Nonresidents and Individuals Who Change Residency, revised 11-2007, CCH CALIFORNIA TAX REPORTS ¶404-599)

> ***Example:*** *Nonresident:* On February 1, 2003, while a California resident, the taxpayer was granted nonstatutory stock options. The taxpayer performed all of his services in California from February 1, 2003, to May 1, 2007, the date he left the company and permanently moved to Texas. On June 1, 2007, he exercised his nonstatutory stock options. The income resulting from the exercise of his nonstatutory stock options is taxable by California because the income is compensation for services having a source in California, the state where he performed all of his services.

> ***Example:*** *Move-in to California:* On March 1, 2003, while a Nevada resident, the taxpayer was granted nonstatutory stock options. On April 1, 2007, the taxpayer retired and permanently moved to California. On May 1, 2007, the taxpayer exercised her options. The compensation resulting from the exercise of her nonstatutory stock options is taxable by California because she was a California resident when the income was recognized.

Statutory stock options.— California taxes the capital gain income received by a former nonresident from the sale of stock in a qualifying disposition of statutory stock options because the stock is sold while the taxpayer is a resident. (FTB Pub. 1004, Stock Option Guidelines, revised 10-2007, CCH CALIFORNIA TAX REPORTS ¶404-589; FTB Pub. 1100, Taxation of Nonresidents and Individuals Who Change Residency, revised 11-2007, CCH CALIFORNIA TAX REPORTS ¶404-599)

> ***Example:*** *Move-in to California:* On February 1, 1998, while a Texas resident, the taxpayer was granted incentive stock options. On February 1, 2004, the taxpayer exercised his options. On December 1, 2004, the taxpayer permanently moved to California, and on March 1, 2005, the taxpayer sold his stock for a gain. The resulting capital gain is taxable by California because the taxpayer was a California resident when he sold the stock.

In the reverse situation, if statutory stock options are granted to a taxpayer while he or she works in California, but are exercised and sold in a qualifying disposition after the taxpayer moves out of California, the capital gain on the sale of the stock would not be taxed by California. (Question 14, California Society of CPAs 2001 Liaison Meeting with FTB, November 14, 2001; FTB Pub. 1004, Stock Option Guidelines, revised 10-2007, CCH CALIFORNIA TAX REPORTS ¶404-589)

• *Rules for application of accrual provision (prior law)*

The purpose and application of this former provision are discussed in some detail in *Appeal of Virgil M. and Jeanne P. Money* (1983) (CCH CALIFORNIA TAX REPORTS ¶16-545.255). The opinion reasons that the purpose was merely to prevent differing treatment of cash- and accrual-basis taxpayers, and concluded that the provision was applicable only if

— California's sole basis for taxation was the taxpayer's residency; and

— taxation would differ depending on whether the taxpayer used the accrual or cash method of accounting.

Applying these criteria to a situation where a California taxpayer received a military pension that started when he was a nonresident, the SBE held that the second condition was not satisfied and, therefore, the pension was taxable by California.

In the *Money* opinion, the SBE stated specifically that it had reversed its earlier reasoning regarding the intent of the law. Cases decided before 1983 should be reconsidered in the light of the rationale of the *Money* case. Some such older cases have been cited in the discussion below, because the conclusions reached in the cited cases would presumably be the same under the *Money* rationale.

• *Distributions from qualified plans for deferred compensation*

In *Appeal of Frank W. and Harriet S. Walters* (1984) (CCH CALIFORNIA TAX REPORTS ¶16-545.256), the SBE applied the rationale of the *Money* case, discussed above, to distributions from a qualified deferred-compensation plan. The taxpayer earned future benefits in Missouri, and moved to California after his retirement. The SBE held that his benefit payments were taxable by California, since there is no distinction between cash- and accrual-basis taxpayers in the treatment of distributions from qualified plans. Also, to the same effect, see *Appeal of Edward A. and Leonora F. Kodyra* (1985) (CCH CALIFORNIA TAX REPORTS ¶16-545.253); in this case, the pension of a retired New York policeman was taxed by California even though it was exempt from state and local taxation under New York law. Similarly, in *Daks v. Franchise Tax Board* (1999) (CCH CALIFORNIA TAX REPORTS ¶16-545.258) a California court of appeal held that pension benefits earned by a taxpayer as a participant in his employer's noncontributory, qualified, defined-benefit pension plan while the taxpayer was a resident of New York were taxable in California because the benefits were received by the taxpayer while he was a resident of California.

The SBE has also cited and followed the *Money* decision in a case involving a lump-sum distribution from a qualified plan. In *Appeal of Lawrence T. and Galadriel Blakeslee* (1983) (CCH CALIFORNIA TAX REPORTS ¶400-716), the taxpayer became entitled to a lump-sum distribution in 1976, before moving to California from Florida; however, she did not receive the distribution until 1978, after she became a California resident. The SBE held that the distribution was taxable by California, on the ground that California makes no distinction between cash- and accrual-basis taxpayers in the treatment of lump-sum distributions; this principle was affirmed in *Appeal of Ralph G. and Martha E. McQuoid* (1989) (CCH CALIFORNIA TAX REPORTS ¶16-545.257).

Similar reasoning was applied by a California court of appeal in *Paine v. Franchise Tax Board* (2004) (CCH CALIFORNIA TAX REPORTS ¶16-545.2591) in determining that deferred compensation payments from a partnership that were received by taxpayers residing in California were subject to California personal income tax even though the payments began before the taxpayers became California residents. The court ruled that the second prong of the *Money* test was not met, because the partnership elected to use a cash method of accounting and the taxpayers were bound by that election. Consequently, the taxpayers were required to recognize the income they received after they became California residents.

It should be observed that California taxation of pensions earned elsewhere does not depend on the rationale of the *Money* case. Many earlier cases held that such pensions were taxable to California residents because the right to receive the pensions was contingent upon the taxpayer's survival and therefore the income had not "accrued" when the change of residence occurred.

Under current law, all income from qualified plans for deferred compensation are taxable by California if received by a California resident, even if the compensation "accrued" prior to the taxpayer's California residency.

• *Sale of out-of-state real estate*

In the *Appeal of Estate of Albert Kahn, Deceased, and Lillian Kahn* (1986) (CCH CALIFORNIA TAX REPORTS ¶401-307), the taxpayers, having established residence in California on May 21, 1976, were not allowed to deduct rental expenses on out-of-state real estate even though the expenses were paid at the escrow for the sale of the property and even though the gain from the sale was taxable. Although binding agreements of sale had been executed prior to the establishment of California residency, escrow closed afterwards, and the gain was realized during the period of residency. The SBE applied the rationale of the *Money* case and held that the rental expenses were accrued prior to the establishment of California residency.

• *Distributions from self-employed (Keogh) or IRA plans*

Retirement income attributable to services performed outside California but received after the taxpayer becomes a resident is taxable in its entirety by California. California does not impose tax on retirement income, including income from a self-employed (Keogh) plan or an individual retirement account (IRA), received by a nonresident. (FTB Pub. 1005, Pension and Annuity Guidelines, CCH CALIFORNIA TAX REPORTS ¶404-590; FTB Pub. 1100, Taxation of Nonresidents and Individuals Who Change Residency, revised November 2007, CCH CALIFORNIA TAX REPORTS ¶404-599)

See ¶206 for a discussion of (1) a possible recoverable tax-free California basis of a self-employed plan resulting from pre-1987 differences between California and federal law on deductibility of contributions to such a plan and (2) how to calculate the California basis of an IRA of a California resident that made nondeductible contributions to an IRA while a nonresident.

• *Income from annuities*

In *Appeal of Preston T. and Virginia R. Kelsey* (1976) (CCH CALIFORNIA TAX REPORTS ¶16-435.41), the taxpayer was the current beneficiary of her deceased father's retirement annuity. The annuity had been earned entirely in Pennsylvania. The SBE held that the taxpayer, as a California resident, was fully taxable under the rules for income from annuities, even though the payments were properly classifiable as "income in respect of a decedent" (¶413).

• *Liquidation of corporation*

The case of *Sweetland et al.* (1961) (CCH CALIFORNIA TAX REPORTS ¶16-550.92) involved a large gain realized by a shareholder upon liquidation of a corporation. The taxpayer contended that his gain was not taxable because it was the result of appreciation in value prior to the time he became a resident (and also prior to the time the California income tax law was enacted in 1935). A California court of appeal held that the entire gain was taxable in the year of liquidation, because there was no realization of income until that year. Other cases have held to the same effect.

• *Installment sales (prior law)*

In cases decided before the *Money* decision, discussed above, the SBE held that installments received by nonresidents on a sale made when they were California residents were subject to California tax. See *Appeal of Sherwood R. and Marion S. Gordon* (1983) (CCH CALIFORNIA TAX REPORTS ¶16-550.47). Presumably these cases are not affected by the *Money* decision, since the income is from a California source and is therefore taxed regardless of residence. As to installments received by a California resident on an out-of-state sale made before becoming a California resident, the installments are not subject to California tax because the right to receive the income accrued during nonresidency. Any interest from installment sales is taxable while the taxpayer is a resident.

• *Disputed or contingent income*

In *Appeal of David D. and Linda D. Cornman* (1984) (CCH CALIFORNIA TAX REPORTS ¶16-825.252), the taxpayer earned income in Alaska during the years 1974-1977 when he was a resident of that state. The amount of the income was subject to litigation, which was settled in 1979 after he had become a California resident. The SBE held that the income was subject to California tax.

In *Appeal of Louis E. and Echite M. Dana* (1979) (CCH CALIFORNIA TAX REPORTS ¶16-570.28), the taxpayer received income after he became a California resident, under a contingent-fee contract executed with other attorneys when he was a Michigan resident. The SBE held that the income was taxable by California, because uncertainty regarding the amount to be received prevented its accrual before the change of residence.

The issue of "disputed" or "contingent" income is moot under current law if the income is received while the taxpayer is a current resident, as all income received by a California resident is subject to tax.

• *Expense reimbursement*

In *Appeal of James H. and Heloise A. Frame* (1979) (CCH CALIFORNIA TAX REPORTS ¶16-535.331), the taxpayer received approximately $50,000 from IBM as reimbursement for expenses of moving to California. The right to receive the reimbursement was clearly established before the taxpayer became a California resident; however, the SBE held that the reimbursement (partly offset by about $11,000 of deductions allowed) was taxable by California, because uncertainty as to the amount prevented accrual before the change of residence. See ¶238 for further discussion of treatment of reimbursed expenses when a taxpayer moves to or from California.

The issue of "disputed" or "contingent" income is moot under current law if the income is received while the taxpayer is a current resident, as all income received by a California resident is subject to tax.

¶406 Tax Rate Change During Taxable Year

Law: Sec. 17034 (CCH CALIFORNIA TAX REPORTS ¶191-645).

Comparable Federal: Sec. 15 (CCH U.S. MASTER TAX GUIDE ¶2561).

California law differs from federal in situations involving rate changes during the taxable year.

The general California rule is that, unless an amending act specifies otherwise, changes affecting the imposition or computation of taxes (including rates), credits, penalties, and additions to tax are applicable to taxable years beginning on or after January 1 of the year in which the amending act takes effect. All other tax-related provisions are applied beginning on the date the act takes effect. (Sec. 17034, Rev. & Tax. Code)

¶407 Accounting Methods—General

Law: Secs. 17201, 17207, 17551, 17564 (CCH CALIFORNIA TAX REPORTS ¶15-460, 15-465, 15-470, 15-745).

Comparable Federal: Secs. 165, 263A, 446-48, 451, 455-56, 458, 460, 461, 464, 467-68B, 481 (CCH U.S. MASTER TAX GUIDE ¶1515 et seq.).

California Form: FTB 3834 (Interest Computation Under the Look-Back Method for Completed Long-Term Contracts).

With minor exceptions, California law is the same as federal law as of the current IRC tie-in date (¶103). (Sec. 17551, Rev. & Tax. Code; Sec. 17564, Rev. & Tax. Code)

• *Automatic consent procedure for accounting method change*

California does not follow federal law that provides for an automatic consent procedure for a change in accounting method for purposes of claiming the full deduction for any previously unclaimed depreciation or amortization allowed—see IRS Rev. Proc. 96-31; FTB Notice 96-3 (CCH CALIFORNIA TAX REPORTS ¶402-880).

• *Timing of excess disaster-loss deductions*

Both California law and federal law allow taxpayers to elect to deduct in the prior year certain excess casualty losses sustained after the end of the year in a disaster area, as determined by the President. (Sec. 17201, Rev. & Tax. Code; Sec. 17207, Rev. & Tax. Code) California law provides similar treatment for specified categories of excess losses sustained in a disaster area declared by the Governor. Under California law, all of these losses may also be carried forward to subsequent years from the year claimed. For a discussion of disaster losses, see ¶307.

• *Special rules for accounting methods*

See ¶310 for special rules regarding production costs of films, books, etc. See ¶416 for special rules regarding construction-period interest and taxes. See ¶620 for special rules regarding partnership accounting.

¶408 Election to Accrue Income on Noninterest-Bearing Obligations Issued at Discount

Law: Secs. 17551, 17553 (CCH CALIFORNIA TAX REPORTS ¶15-465).

Comparable Federal: Sec. 454.

California law is the same as federal as of the current IRC tie-in date (¶103). (Sec. 17551, Rev. & Tax. Code)

A cash-basis taxpayer may elect to accrue the increment in value of noninterest-bearing bonds issued at a discount and redeemable for fixed amounts increasing at stated intervals. The election is binding for subsequent years. On certain short-term obligations issued at a discount, the discount is not considered to accrue until the obligation is disposed of.

Federal law includes a special rule for income from U.S. Savings Bonds. Because interest from such bonds is exempt from California tax (¶217), this rule is not applicable to California. (Sec. 17553, Rev. & Tax. Code)

See also ¶237, regarding special rules for discount bonds.

¶409 Inventories

Law: Secs. 17201, 17551, 17570 (CCH CALIFORNIA TAX REPORTS ¶15-475).

Comparable Federal: Secs. 263A, 471, 475 (CCH U.S. MASTER TAX GUIDE ¶1553 et seq.).

California law is the same as federal law as of the current IRC tie-in date (¶103). (Sec. 17551, Rev. & Tax. Code)

Inventories are required where the production, purchase, or sale of merchandise is an income-producing factor. Valuation must conform to the best practice in the industry and must clearly reflect income. California follows federal regulations that provide detailed rules for inventory valuation.

• *Mark-to-market accounting*

California incorporates federal law requiring securities dealers to use the mark-to-market method of accounting in identifying and valuing inventory. (Sec. 17551, Rev. & Tax. Code ; Sec. 17570, Rev. & Tax. Code)

¶410 Inventories—Last-In, First-Out Method

Law: Sec. 17551 (CCH CALIFORNIA TAX REPORTS ¶15-475).

Comparable Federal: Secs. 472-74 (CCH U.S. MASTER TAX GUIDE ¶1564, 1565).

A taxpayer may elect to use the last-in, first-out (LIFO) method of inventory valuation. California law is the same as federal law (¶103), including the limitation on the election of the simplified dollar-value LIFO method for small businesses. (Sec. 17551, Rev. & Tax. Code)

See ¶806 for special rules concerning the LIFO method of reporting for S corporations.

¶411 Installment Sales

Law: Secs. 17551, 17560 (CCH CALIFORNIA TAX REPORTS ¶15-460).

Comparable Federal: Secs. 453, 453A, 453B (CCH U.S. MASTER TAX GUIDE ¶1801 et seq.).

California Form: FTB 3805E (Installment Sale Income).

California law is the same as federal as of the current IRC tie-in date (¶103). (Sec. 17551, Rev. & Tax. Code) However, income reported federally on the installment basis may differ from that reported for California purposes because of federal/ California differences in basis of property sold and differences in installment reporting rules applicable to the year of sale.

Practitioner Comment: Significant Uncertainty Regarding Contingent Consideration

California adopts IRC Sec. 453A, which imposes an interest charge on tax which is deferred under the installment sale rules. Although expressly called for by the statute, regulations have not been issued to date that explain how these provisions should apply where contingent consideration is concerned. Possibilities would include a "wait and see" approach that retroactively assesses interest based upon the amount ultimately collected and a "fair market value" approach that bases the interest charge upon the fair market value of the contingent note.

In one non-citable letter decision the State Board of Equalization (SBE) held that the interest charge should be based upon the fair market value of the note at the end of each year despite the fact that no amount was ultimately collected. See *Appeal of Kingston Technology Corporation, et al.*, Nos. 286420, 286421 and 288052, August 17, 2006. The SBE similarly held that fair market value should be used in its letter decision in the *Appeal of Rawlings*, No. 343163, June 1, 2007, but subsequently granted a petition for rehearing in the *Appeal of Kingston Technology Corporation, et al.* On February 28, 2008, the SBE issued a letter decision in *Kingston* concluding in that case that the taxpayer's use of the wait and see method was appropriate. Given that the SBE has upheld the use of the fair market value method in *Rawlings* and, on rehearing, has upheld the use of the wait and see method in *Kingston*, until a published decision or regulations are issued, significant uncertainty will persist in this area.

Bruce Daigh, Chris Whitney, Contributing Editors

Income from casual sales of real or personal property other than inventory is reported on FTB 3805E if payments are received in a year after the year of sale.

• *Law applicable when installments received*

The taxation of installment sales is governed by the law in effect at the time each installment is received. To this effect, see *William S. Andrews et al. v. Franchise Tax Board* (1969) (CCH CALIFORNIA TAX REPORTS ¶15-460.24), involving the percent of gain to be taken into account after the law was changed in 1959. See also *Appeal of Herbert J. and Sheila Frankel* (1978) (CCH CALIFORNIA TAX REPORTS ¶15-620.52), holding that the percent of gain to be taken into account on a 1974 installment was governed by the law as amended in 1972, although the installment sale was made in 1970.

• *Change of residence*

See ¶405 for discussion of treatment of installments received after an interstate move, where an installment sale was made before the change of residence.

¶412 Allocation of Income and Deductions—Related Organizations, etc.

Law: Secs. 17201, 17287, 17555 (CCH CALIFORNIA TAX REPORTS ¶15-315, 15-480).

Comparable Federal: Secs. 269A-69B, 482 (CCH U.S. MASTER TAX GUIDE ¶1573, 1575).

California law, otherwise the same as federal law, contains a unique marital provision that applies when spouses file separate returns. This provision empowers the Franchise Tax Board to make any adjustments necessary to reflect the proper income of the spouses. (Sec. 17555, Rev. & Tax. Code) Presumably, this would apply to registered domestic partners as well (see ¶119).

Under both federal and California law, the tax authorities are given broad powers to allocate income or deductions among related organizations, trades, or businesses where necessary to prevent evasion of taxes or to clearly reflect income. (Sec. 17551, Rev. & Tax. Code) Specific authority is given for treatment of personal service corporations formed, or availed of, to avoid or evade income tax.

¶413 Income and Deductions in Respect of Decedents

Law: Secs. 17024.5, 17731 (CCH CALIFORNIA TAX REPORTS ¶15-160).

Comparable Federal: Sec. 691 (CCH U.S. MASTER TAX GUIDE ¶182 et seq.).

Income and deductions of a decedent, not reportable during his or her life, are includible in the return of the decedent's estate or heir when received or paid. (Sec. 17731, Rev. & Tax. Code)

Despite the inclusion of federal law in California law by reference (¶103), California does not allow a deduction for federal death tax attributable to the income reported. Any provision relating to federal estate tax is ignored for California purposes. Also, no deduction is allowed for the California estate tax allowed as a credit against the federal tax. (Sec. 17024.5, Rev. & Tax. Code)

In *Appeal of Estate of Marilyn Monroe, Deceased* (1975) (CCH CALIFORNIA TAX REPORTS ¶16-825.45), the estate received substantial income under contracts providing for payment of a percentage of the earnings of certain films in which the actress Marilyn Monroe had appeared. She was not a California resident when she died. The State Board of Equalization held that to the extent the films were made in California, the income was from a California source and was taxable by California as "income in respect of a decedent."

See ¶405 for discussion of the *Kelsey* case, where annuity income earned by a decedent outside California was classified as "income in respect of a decedent" but was taxed to a survivor under the rules for income from annuities.

¶414 Imputed Interest—Loans with Below-Market Interest

Law: Secs. 17024.5, 17551, 18180 (CCH CALIFORNIA TAX REPORTS ¶15-465).

Comparable Federal: Secs. 483, 7872 (CCH U.S. MASTER TAX GUIDE ¶795, 1868, 1872).

California law generally is the same as federal law as of California's current federal conformity date (see ¶103). (Sec. 17551, Rev. & Tax. Code) California incorporates IRC Sec. 7872, which concerns taxation of "foregone interest" on loans with below-market interest rates. (Sec. 18180, Rev. & Tax. Code)

When property is sold on a deferred payment basis and no provision is made for interest, or an unreasonably low rate of interest is provided, a portion of the deferred payments is treated as interest to the buyer and to the seller.

Because of California's current federal conformity date, California has not incorporated amendments made by the Tax Increase Prevention and Reconciliation Act of 2005 that relax the requirements of exemption from the below-market interest loan rules for loans to continuing care facilities for a five-year period, applicable for federal purposes in calendar years beginning after 2005, with respect to loans made before, on, or after December 31, 2005.

¶415 Claim of Right—Effect of Repayment

Law: Secs. 17049, 17076 (CCH CALIFORNIA TAX REPORTS ¶15-635).

Comparable Federal: Sec. 1341 (CCH U.S. MASTER TAX GUIDE ¶1543).

California allows a claim of right adjustment similar to the adjustment allowed under federal law. Under the claim of right provision, if an individual includes an item of income in his or her gross income for a preceding taxable year(s), and a deduction in excess of $3,000 is allowable for the taxable year based on the repayment of the item by the individual during the taxable year, then the tax imposed on the individual for the taxable year will be the lesser of:

(1) the tax for the taxable year computed without regard to the deduction; or

(2) an amount equal to the tax for the taxable year computed without that deduction, minus the decrease in tax for the prior taxable year(s) that would result solely from the exclusion of the item or portion thereof from the gross income required to be shown on the individual's California return for the preceding taxable year(s).

If the decrease in tax for the preceding taxable year(s) exceeds the tax imposed for the taxable year, computed without the deduction, the excess will be considered a payment of tax on the last day prescribed for the payment of tax for the taxable year, and will be refunded or credited in the same manner as if it were an overpayment for the taxable year. (Sec. 17049, Rev. & Tax. Code)

The above provisions do not apply to any deduction allowable with respect to an item that was included in gross income by reason of the sale or other disposition of stock in trade of the taxpayer, or other property of a kind that would properly have been included in the inventory of the taxpayer if on hand at the close of the prior taxable year, or property held by the taxpayer primarily for sale to customers in the ordinary course of his or her trade or business. (Sec. 17049, Rev. & Tax. Code)

Detailed rules apply if the exclusion of the item for prior taxable years would have resulted in a net operating loss or a capital loss. (Sec. 17049, Rev. & Tax. Code)

Amounts restored under a claim of right are exempt from the 2% floor for miscellaneous itemized deductions; see ¶303. Deductions of $3,000 or less are subject to the 2% adjusted gross income floor for miscellaneous itemized deductions. An individual eligible to claim the adjustment who included the income in prior taxable years when he or she was a nonresident may make the claim of right adjustment only for income that was attributable to California during the preceding years.

See the Instructions to Schedule CA(540), line 41 for details.

¶416 Construction-Period Interest and Taxes

Law: Sec. 17201 (CCH CALIFORNIA TAX REPORTS ¶15-775).

Comparable Federal: Former Sec. 189, Sec. 263A (CCH U.S. MASTER TAX GUIDE ¶1029).

California conforms to federal rules requiring capitalization under the uniform capitalization rules of interest and taxes incurred during the construction period of real property. (Sec. 17201, Rev. & Tax. Code)

PERSONAL INCOME TAX

CHAPTER 5

SALES AND EXCHANGES, GAIN OR LOSS, BASIS

¶501 Gain or Loss—General Rule

Law: Secs. 18031, 18042 (CCH CALIFORNIA TAX REPORTS ¶15-710).

Comparable Federal: Secs. 1001, 1042 (CCH U.S. MASTER TAX GUIDE ¶1601, 1733, 2394).

California Forms: Sch. D (Capital Gain or Loss Adjustment), Sch. D-1 (Sales of Business Property).

Gain or loss on disposition of property is the difference between the adjusted basis and the amount realized. The entire gain or loss is recognized except where specifically exempted or deferred. Exceptions to the general rule are discussed in subsequent paragraphs. (Sec. 18031, Rev. & Tax. Code; Sec. 18042, Rev. & Tax. Code)

Although California law is generally the same as federal law, the *effect* may be different because (1) of a difference in the basis of the property and (2) California law, unlike federal law, does not apply a lower tax rate to capital gains.

¶502 Transfers Between Spouses/Registered Domestic Partners

Law: Secs. 17021.7, 18031 (CCH CALIFORNIA TAX REPORTS ¶15-710).

Comparable Federal: Sec. 1041 (CCH U.S. MASTER TAX GUIDE ¶1693).

California law is the same as federal law with respect to the treatment of transfers between spouses. (Sec. 18031, Rev. & Tax. Code) No gain or loss is recognized on a transfer of property from an individual to, or in trust for the benefit of (1) a spouse or (2) a former spouse if the transfer is incident to a divorce. However, gain is recognized with respect to the transfer of property in trust to the extent that the liabilities assumed, plus the amount of any liabilities to which the property is subject, exceeds the total of the adjusted basis of the property transferred.

However, while California law extends this treatment to transfers of property to registered domestic partners (RDPs) and former RDPs, federal law does not, see ¶119. (Sec. 17021.7, Rev. & Tax. Code) Consequently, a subtraction adjustment may be made by RDPs who are required to recognize such gain on their federal income tax returns. (FTB Pub. 737, Tax Information for Registered Domestic Partners). Presumably, California will also extend this treatment to same-sex married couples, however, at the time this book went to press, the Franchise Tax Board had not yet determined whether they would treat same-sex married couples who had married prior to the passage of Proposition 8 as spouses for California income tax purposes, see ¶119 for details.

¶503 Involuntary Conversion

Law: Secs. 18031, 18037 (CCH CALIFORNIA TAX REPORTS ¶15-710, 16-070).

Comparable Federal: Sec. 1033 (CCH U.S. MASTER TAX GUIDE ¶1713 et seq.).

California Forms: Sch. D (Capital Gain or Loss Adjustment), Sch. D-1 (Sales of Business Property).

California law is generally the same as federal as of the current IRC tie-in date (¶103). (Sec. 18031, Rev. & Tax. Code)

Because of California's current federal conformity date (¶103), California does not conform to post-2004 federal amendments that extend the two-year replacement period (four years for residential property in a federally declared disaster area) to five years for property converted by Hurricane Katrina, the 2007 Kansas tornadoes, or the summer 2008 Midwestern storms, as long as the replacement property purchased is located in the applicable disaster area. For California personal income tax purposes, an addition adjustment will be required for property purchased after the regular two-year or four-year period.

Loss (but not gain) is recognized on involuntary conversion of property due to destruction, theft, condemnation, etc. Gain is recognized, however, to the extent (1) the proceeds are not used to acquire other property similar or related in service or use or (2) the taxpayer purchases the replacement property or stock from related persons. However, a taxpayer, other than a C corporation or a partnership with majority corporate partners, may defer gain recognition if the aggregate of the amount of gain realized on the property is $100,000 or less.

The taxpayer may elect not to recognize gain even though the proceeds of the involuntary conversion are not expended *directly* on the replacement property. In this case the replacement property must be purchased within a limited period of time as specified in the law. A longer period may be allowed upon application by the taxpayer. Replacement property may consist of stock in a corporation owning qualified replacement property, provided control of the corporation is acquired. "Control" for this purpose is defined as 80% of the voting stock, plus 80% of all other classes of stock outstanding.

Special rules limit the amount of gain a taxpayer must recognize on the receipt of insurance proceeds for the taxpayer's principal residence (including a rented residence) or its contents that are involuntarily converted as a result of a federally-declared disaster. In addition, if business or investment property is compulsorily or involuntarily converted as the result of a federally-declared disaster, *any* tangible property of a type held for productive use in a trade or business will be treated for nonrecognition purposes as "similar or related in service or use" to the converted property.

CCH Example: Disaster-Related Involuntary Conversion

Paul's coffee cart was destroyed as a result of a federally-declared disaster. Before the disaster, Paul sold coffee, juices, and pastries from the cart outside a local hospital. Within two months of the cart's destruction, Paul received related insurance proceeds and immediately used all of the proceeds to purchase a computer for use in the word processing business he runs from his home. The computer will be treated as similar or related in use to the coffee cart, and Paul may elect not to recognize gain with respect to the involuntarily converted cart.

¶504 Sale of Residence

Law: Sec. 18031 (CCH CALIFORNIA TAX REPORTS ¶15-710).

Comparable Federal: Sec. 121 (CCH U.S. MASTER TAX GUIDE ¶1705).

California law is generally the same as federal law as of the current IRC tie-in date (¶103). (Sec. 18031, Rev. & Tax. Code) See ¶229 for details.

Gain from the sale or exchange of the taxpayer's own residence is taxable as a capital gain because the residence is a "capital asset" (¶524). Loss from such a sale or exchange is not deductible, either as a capital loss or as an ordinary loss (¶307).

Taxpayers who sell or exchange property that they owned and occupied as a principal residence for at least two of the five years preceding the sale or exchange can elect a $250,000 ($500,000 for joint filers) exclusion from gross income of gain realized on the sale or exchange. However, as discussed at ¶229, certain exceptions apply to the two-year and five-year use and test periods.

¶505 Gain from Sale of Assisted Housing

Law: Sec. 18041.5 (CCH CALIFORNIA TAX REPORTS ¶16-270).

Comparable Federal: Former Sec. 1039.

No gain is recognized on the sale of an assisted housing development to a tenant association, organization, agency, or individual that obligates itself and its successors to make the development affordable to low-income families for (1) 30 years from the date of sale or (2) for the remaining term of existing federal government assistance, whichever is longer. The proceeds from the sale must be reinvested in residential real property, other than a personal residence, within two years of the sale. An "assisted housing development" is a multifamily rental housing development that receives federal government assistance. (Sec. 18041.5, Rev. & Tax. Code)

¶506 Liquidation Under S.E.C. Order

Law: Sec. 18031 (CCH CALIFORNIA TAX REPORTS ¶15-710).

Comparable Federal: Former Sec. 1081 (CCH U.S. MASTER TAX GUIDE ¶2247).

California law is the same as federal law as of the current IRC conformity date (¶103). (Sec. 18031, Rev. & Tax. Code)

California prohibits a shareholder from recognizing gain or loss from distributions in liquidation of a corporation pursuant to an order of the Securities and Exchange Commission under the Public Utility Holding Company Act. California has not incorporated federal amendments that repeal this provision, generally applicable for federal purposes to transactions after February 7, 2006.

¶507 Exchange of Property for Like Property

Law: Sec. 18031 (CCH CALIFORNIA TAX REPORTS ¶15-710).

Comparable Federal: Sec. 1031 (CCH U.S. MASTER TAX GUIDE ¶1721 et seq.).

California law is generally the same as federal law as of the current IRC tie-in date (¶103). (Sec. 18031, Rev. & Tax. Code)

Generally, no gain or loss is recognized if property held for productive use or investment is exchanged for property of a like kind. However, under both federal and state law, an exchange of foreign real property for real property located within the United States may not qualify as a like-kind exchange. This disqualification from nonrecognition of gain extends to exchanges of *personal property* predominantly used outside the United States for personal property predominantly used in the United States.

Like-Kind Exchange of TIC Interest

The Franchise Tax Board has identified a trend that is resulting in many audit adjustments, with respect to like-kind exchanges of tenancy-in-common (TIC) interests. A TIC interest is considered like-kind property for purposes of the like-kind exchange provisions. A partnership interest, however, is not treated as such. The FTB has identified a number of cases in which the property interest exchanged is more closely aligned with a partnership interest than a TIC. If a property interest is found, in substance, to be a partnership interest, then the property is not considered like-kind property, and deferring gain is not allowed. The FTB will continue to consider IRS Rev. Proc. 2002-22 (relating to rental real property), on which taxpayers are relying to support their position that they hold a TIC interest and are entitled to defer gain, but will continue to make determinations based on existing law and the facts and circumstances of each case. (*Tax News*, California Franchise Tax Board, November 2007, CCH CALIFORNIA TAX REPORTS ¶404-487)

• *Exchanges by nonresidents*

The Franchise Tax Board has taken the position that a nonresident's gain or loss from the exchange of real or tangible property located within California for real or tangible property located outside California is sourced to California. Because the taxation will not occur until the gain or loss is recognized, the taxpayer is required to keep track of the deferred California sourced gains and losses to report them to California in the year the property received in the exchange is sold or transferred. California also taxes the gain realized on the sale of California property in a non-deferred transaction, even if the sale is of property that was exchanged for out-of-state property while the taxpayer was a nonresident. However, the taxpayer is eligible for a credit for taxes paid to the other state on any gain that was deferred from the original transaction (FTB Pub. 1100, Taxation of Nonresidents and Individuals Who Change Residency, revised 11-2007, CCH CALIFORNIA TAX REPORTS ¶404-599).

¶508 Exchange of Insurance Policies

Law: Sec. 18031 (CCH CALIFORNIA TAX REPORTS ¶15-710).

Comparable Federal: Sec. 1035 (CCH U.S. MASTER TAX GUIDE ¶1724).

California law is the same as federal law as of California's current federal conformity date (¶103). However, California has not incorporated amendments made to IRC Sec. 1035 by the Pension Protection Act of 2006 that expand the tax-free exchange treatment of certain insurance and annuity contracts to include exchanges involving long-term care insurance contracts, applicable to exchanges occurring after December 31, 2009.

No gain or loss is recognized on (1) the exchange of a life insurance contract for another life insurance contract or (2) certain exchanges involving endowment or annuity contracts. (Sec. 18031, Rev. & Tax. Code)

¶509 Exchange of Stock for Stock

Law: Sec. 18031 (CCH CALIFORNIA TAX REPORTS ¶15-710).

Comparable Federal: Sec. 1036 (CCH U.S. MASTER TAX GUIDE ¶1728).

California law is the same as federal law (¶103). (Sec. 18031, Rev. & Tax. Code)

No gain or loss is recognized on an exchange of a corporation's (1) common stock for common stock of the same corporation or (2) preferred stock for other shares of its preferred stock.

¶510 Exchange of Certain U.S. Obligations

Law: Sec. 18031 (CCH CALIFORNIA TAX REPORTS ¶15-710).

Comparable Federal: Sec. 1037 (CCH U.S. MASTER TAX GUIDE ¶1726, 1925).

California law is the same as federal law (¶103). (Sec. 18031, Rev. & Tax. Code)

Certain designated U.S. obligations (bonds issued under chapter 31, title 31, of the United States Code) may be exchanged tax-free for other obligations issued under the same chapter.

¶511 Reacquisition of Property After Installment Sale

Law: Sec. 18031 (CCH CALIFORNIA TAX REPORTS ¶15-710).

Comparable Federal: Sec. 1038 (CCH U.S. MASTER TAX GUIDE ¶1841, 1843).

California law is the same as federal law (¶103). (Sec. 18031, Rev. & Tax. Code)

Certain limitations are imposed on a seller's recognized gain or loss upon repossession of certain *real* property if the property had previously been sold on the installment method.

¶512 Sale or Exchange of Property for Stock

Law: Sec. 17321 (CCH CALIFORNIA TAX REPORTS ¶15-710).

Comparable Federal: Sec. 351 (CCH U.S. MASTER TAX GUIDE ¶203, 1731, 2205, 2233, 2257).

California law is the same as federal law as of the current IRC tie-in date (¶103). Generally, no gain or loss is recognized on a transfer of property to a corporation in exchange for its stock or securities, when the transferors are in control after the exchange. (Sec. 17321, Rev. & Tax. Code)

¶513 Sale or Exchange of Tax-Exempt Bonds

Law: Sec. 17133.5 (CCH CALIFORNIA TAX REPORTS ¶15-710).

Comparable Federal: None.

The gain or loss from the sale or transfer of bonds yielding tax-exempt interest is not exempt. Federal law is the same regarding state and municipal obligations. (Sec. 17133.5, Rev. & Tax. Code)

¶514 Sale of Stock to ESOPs or Cooperatives

Law: Sec. 18042 (CCH CALIFORNIA TAX REPORTS ¶15-170, 16-070).

Comparable Federal: Sec. 1042 (CCH U.S. MASTER TAX GUIDE ¶1733, 2109).

California generally conforms to federal law allowing taxpayers to sell qualified securities to an employee stock ownership plan (ESOP) or worker-owned cooperative and to replace such securities with other securities without recognition of the gain. However, California does not incorporate the federal provision that allows a taxpayer to defer the recognition of gain from the sale of stock of a qualified agricultural refiner or processor to an eligible farm cooperative. (Sec. 18042, Rev. & Tax. Code)

¶515 Sale of Small Business Stock

Law: Secs. 18038.4, 18038.5, 18152.5 (CCH CALIFORNIA TAX REPORTS ¶15-710, 16-070).

Comparable Federal: Sec. 1045 (CCH U.S. MASTER TAX GUIDE ¶2397).

California law generally mirrors federal law allowing a taxpayer, other than a C corporation, to elect to roll over capital gain from a sale of qualified small business stock held for more than six months, provided that the gain from the sale is used to purchase other qualified small business stock within 60 days from the date of the original sale. The election must be made on an original return filed on or before the due date (including extensions) for filing the income tax return for the taxable year in which the qualified small business stock is sold. (Sec. 18038.4, Rev. & Tax. Code; Sec. 18038.5, Rev. & Tax. Code)

CCH Comment: Replacement Stock Purchases by Partnerships

For purposes of the requirement to acquire replacement stock, effective for transactions after August 13, 2007, a taxpayer may use a partnership other than the one selling the qualified small business stock to acquire the replacement stock, and an individual may use a partnership to acquire replacement stock on his or her behalf. This FTB position is based on final federal Reg. 1.1045-1, which took effect August 14, 2007. For transactions prior to August 14, 2007, a taxpayer may not use a partnership other than the one selling the qualified small business stock to acquire the replacement stock, and an individual may not use a partnership to acquire replacement stock on his or her behalf. This FTB position is based on proposed federal Reg. 150562-03, concerning the application of IRC Sec. 1045 to partnerships and their partners. (*Tax News*, California Franchise Tax Board, October 2007, CCH CALIFORNIA TAX REPORTS ¶404-468)

For California purposes only, a corporation's stock will not qualify for the rollover unless 80% of the corporation's payroll, measured by total dollar value, is attributable to employment located within California (see below).

• *Eighty percent requirement*

California's exclusion of 50% of the gain on qualified small business stock is almost identical to the federal exclusion (IRC Sec. 1202). However, to qualify for the California exclusion, California also requires that the following conditions be satisfied:

— at least 80% of the corporation's payroll, measured by total dollar value, must be attributable to employment located within California and

— at least 80% (by value) of the assets of the corporation must be used by the corporation in the active conduct of one or more qualified trades or businesses in California. (Sec. 18152.5(c)(2)(A), Rev. & Tax. Code)

Planning Note: Time of 80% Payroll and Asset Requirement

The 80% requirement in regard to both payroll and assets in California applies both at the time of the purchase of the stock and at the time of the sale of the stock. The Franchise Tax Board (FTB) reads Sec. 18152.5(c)(2)(A), Rev. & Tax. Code very closely and applies that standard when considering whether the requirement was met. That subsection specifically states "Stock in a corporation shall not be treated as qualified small business stock unless, during *substantially all* of the taxpayer's holding period for the stock, the corporation meets the active business requirements of subdivision (e) and the corporation is a C corporation." (emphasis added)

The FTB understands, according to its Audit Division, that at some times, the amount of payroll and/or assets may fall below the 80% requirement, but in order to qualify as qualified small business stock (QSBS), it must meet the requirement substantially all of the time. There have been attempts to quantify the phrase "substantially all" as a definitive amount so that, for instance, the requirement is met when both (1) the corporation's assets are used in a trade or business in California, and (2) the corporation's payroll is attributable to employment within California, 80% of the time or more. However, although taxpayers have attempted to get a clear definition of "substantially all," there has never been, according to the FTB, any court case or administrative ruling that has decided what constitutes "substantially all" for purposes of the qualified small business stock provision.

There have been many instances in which taxpayers have argued lesser amounts as qualified, but a good guideline to use, according to the FTB, is that stock usually will not be considered QSBS if the amount of time the requirement is met falls below 80% of the time, and stock will definitely not be considered QSBS if the amount of time of compliance falls below 70% of the time. Whether stock is QSBS also depends on circumstances and is decided by the FTB on a case-by-case basis. Courts likewise have been reluctant to place an actual percentage on the term, but have instead ruled "in this instance, 85% of the time qualifies" or "in this instance, 75% does not qualify." (*Telephone interview*, California Franchise Tax Board, Audit Division, May 19, 2005)

Taxpayers that claim the exclusion on the federal return must complete Schedule D (540 or 540NR).

Reporting requirements.—To qualify as a small business, corporations must file a completed Form FTB 3565, Small Business Stock Questionnaire, with the FTB, and mail copies to each of its shareholders. A corporation's failure to complete and file a Form FTB 3565 will not disqualify stockholders from claiming the exclusion. However, the stockholders must prove that the stock satisfies the statutory definition of "small business stock". (*FTB Notice 96-2*, Franchise Tax Board, May 6, 1996, CCH CALIFORNIA TAX REPORTS ¶402-840)

See ¶525 for a discussion of the capital gains exclusion applicable to sales of qualified small business stock.

¶516 Exchange in Connection with Reorganization

Law: Sec. 17321 (CCH CALIFORNIA TAX REPORTS ¶15-710).

Comparable Federal: Secs. 354, 368 (CCH U.S. MASTER TAX GUIDE ¶2205).

California law is the same as federal law as of the current IRC tie-in date (¶103). (Sec. 17321, Rev. & Tax. Code)

No gain or loss is recognized if stock or securities in a corporation that is a party to a reorganization are exchanged solely for other stock or securities in the corporation or for stock or securities in another corporation that is a party to the reorganization (a "B" type reorganization). "Reorganization" and other terms are specifically defined.

¶517 "Spin-Off" Reorganization

Law: Sec. 17321 (CCH CALIFORNIA TAX REPORTS ¶15-710).

Comparable Federal: Sec. 355 (CCH U.S. MASTER TAX GUIDE ¶2201).

California law is the same as federal law as of the current IRC tie-in date (¶103). (Sec. 17321, Rev. & Tax. Code)

No gain is recognized in a "spin-off" type of reorganization, provided certain tests of the business purpose of the transaction are met. This type of reorganization involves the transfer of part of a corporation's assets to a new corporation and the distribution of the new corporation's stock to the shareholders of the old corporation. Both corporations must be engaged in the active conduct of a trade or business that has been operating for at least five years, and it must be shown that the transaction was not used principally as a "device for the distribution of earnings and profits."

Practitioner Comment: California-Federal Differences

California's lagging conformity to the Internal Revenue Code (IRC) may result in certain transactions that qualify as tax-free spin-offs for federal income tax purposes being treated as taxable dividends for California tax purposes. California has conformed to the IRC as of January 1, 2005. However, on May 17, 2006, IRC Sec. 355(b)(3) was enacted in order to simplify the active trade or business test by treating all members of either the distributing and the controlling entity(ies)'s affiliated group as one corporation. Because this enactment was subsequent to the latest conformity date, certain spin-off transactions that are nontaxable for federal purposes may now be taxable for California income tax purposes until California's conformity date is updated.

The Franchise Tax Board in Chief Counsel Ruling 2007-3, July 17, 2007, CCH CALIFORNIA TAX REPORTS ¶404-447, acknowledged that a taxpayer could restructure in order to meet the active trade or business requirements. Further, although such was intended to avoid adverse California tax consequences, the FTB indicated that it would not regard the restructuring as a non-economic substance transaction or "NEST" otherwise subject to potential penalties under RTC Section 19774.

Bruce Daigh, Chris Whitney, Contributing Editors

¶518 Exchanges Not Solely in Kind

Law: Sec. 17321 (CCH CALIFORNIA TAX REPORTS ¶15-710).

Comparable Federal: Sec. 356 (CCH U.S. MASTER TAX GUIDE ¶2237).

California law is the same as federal law as of the current IRC tie-in date (¶103). (Sec. 17321, Rev. & Tax. Code)

Where exchanges would be exempt except for the fact that money or other property ("boot") is received, gain is recognized up to the amount of money or other property, but no loss may be recognized. Where a distribution has the effect of a taxable dividend, it is subject to tax up to the amount of gain recognized on the transaction.

¶519 Exchanges Involving Foreign Corporations

Law: Sec. 17321 (CCH CALIFORNIA TAX REPORTS ¶16-079).

Comparable Federal: Sec. 367 (CCH U.S. MASTER TAX GUIDE ¶2267).

California law is the same as federal law as of the current IRC tie-in date (¶103). (Sec. 17321, Rev. & Tax. Code)

Certain exchanges involving foreign corporations lose their exempt status unless property is transferred to the foreign corporation for use in its active conduct of a trade or business.

¶520 Transfers of Property to Foreign Trusts and Estates

Law: Sec. 17760 (CCH CALIFORNIA TAX REPORTS ¶16-398a).

Comparable Federal: Sec. 684.

California does not incorporate federal law, which provides special gain recognition rules for certain transfers to foreign trusts and estates. (Sec. 17760, Rev. & Tax. Code)

¶521 Foreign Currency Transactions

Law: Sec. 17078 (CCH CALIFORNIA TAX REPORTS ¶15-700, 16-520).

Comparable Federal: Sec. 988 (CCH U.S. MASTER TAX GUIDE ¶2498).

California law is the same as federal law (¶103), except that the federal provision relating to the source of income or loss does not apply for California purposes. Gains and losses resulting from foreign currency transactions are characterized as ordinary income and classified as interest income or expense. (Sec. 17078, Rev. & Tax. Code)

¶522 Liquidation of Corporation

Law: Secs. 17024.5, 17321 (CCH CALIFORNIA TAX REPORTS ¶15-645).

Comparable Federal: Secs. 331-46 (CCH U.S. MASTER TAX GUIDE ¶2253 et seq.).

California law is the same as federal law as of the current IRC tie-in date (¶103), except for provisions relating to domestic international sales corporations (DISCs) that are not recognized by California. (Sec. 17024.5(b), Rev. & Tax. Code; Sec. 17321, Rev. & Tax. Code)

Gain or loss to a stockholder upon liquidation of a corporation is ordinarily a capital gain or loss because it results from the exchange of stock for assets distributed in liquidation (see also ¶226).

• *Relief for minority shareholders*

Relief is provided for minority shareholders in corporate liquidations if the liquidation is tax-free to a parent corporation owning 80% or more of the stock. Accordingly, minority shareholders are protected from the double impact of corporate tax on the sale of appreciated property and a personal income tax on the distribution from the corporate liquidation (see also ¶1216).

¶523 Capital Gains and Losses—General Rules

Law: Secs. 18151, 18152.5, 18155, 18171, 18178, 18181 (CCH CALIFORNIA TAX REPORTS ¶15-620).

Comparable Federal: Secs. 1201-57, 1260 (CCH U.S. MASTER TAX GUIDE ¶1735 et seq.).

California Form: Sch. D (Capital Gain or Loss Adjustment).

California law is the same as federal law as of the current IRC tie-in date (¶103), with the exceptions of the tax rate applied to capital gains and other differences discussed below. (Sec. 18151, Rev. & Tax. Code)

Because California treats capital gains as ordinary income, the amount of California tax is not dependent on the holding period, and the distinction between long-term and short-term capital gains has less significance for California purposes. Because lower capital gains rates apply for federal purposes for long-term capital gains (gain from sales or exchanges of property held for more than 12 months) the concept of long-term capital gains and holding periods still plays a significant role for federal taxation purposes.

Certain gains and losses are classified as "capital" gains and losses and are subject to special rules. Generally, capital losses are subject to restrictions, as explained at ¶525, ¶526. Ordinarily, a gain or loss constitutes a "capital" gain or loss only if

— the asset disposed of is a "capital asset" (¶524) or a noncapital asset that, under a special rule, is treated as a "capital asset" (¶537),

— the gain or loss results from a *sale or exchange,* including a sale or exchange of specified securities futures contracts, or from something that, under a special rule, is treated as a sale or exchange (¶529 , 540), and

— the gain or loss is attributable to the cancellation, lapse, expiration, or other termination of a right or obligation (other than a securities futures contract) with respect to a capital asset or an IRC Section 1256 contract that is a capital asset in the hands of the taxpayer.

The last item does not apply to the retirement of a debt instrument.

• *Special rules*

Worthlessness of securities is arbitrarily treated as a sale or exchange (¶307). A nonbusiness bad debt is treated as a capital loss (¶308). Losses from the destruction or theft of property may also be treated as a sale or exchange under some circumstances (¶537). Gain or loss on liquidation of a corporation is ordinarily capital gain or loss (¶522). Losses on wash sales are not allowable (¶527), and limits are placed on the losses attributable to straddles (¶532).

Losses resulting from abandonment are not subject to capital loss limitations, because they do not result from sale or exchange.

The general rules for capital gains and losses discussed above are provided under federal law incorporated by California. However, there are a number of differences between California and federal law in the numerous special rules. The differences are discussed in later paragraphs. See also ¶226 for special federal capital-gain treatment of dividends from mutual funds.

Taxpayers are allowed to report capital gain distributions from mutual funds on Form 540 2EZ. (Instructions, 2007 Form 540)

• *Federal-California differences*

—California does not incorporate a federal provision that allows a 50% exclusion for gain from the sale of certain small business stock, but has adopted a substantially similar provision (¶525). (Sec. 18152, Rev. & Tax. Code, Sec. 18152.5, Rev. & Tax. Code)

—California does not permit capital loss carrybacks (¶526). (Sec. 18155, Rev. & Tax. Code)

—California renders inoperative for specified periods certain federal rules relating to recapture of excess depreciation (¶539). (Sec. 18171, Rev. & Tax. Code

—As noted above, California does not adopt the special federal tax rates imposed on long-term capital gains.

—California does not incorporate the federal provisions providing special treatment for certain passive foreign investment companies. (Sec. 18181, Rev. & Tax. Code)

—California does not incorporate federal incentives available to businesses located in renewal communities, including the gross income exclusion of capital gain from the sale or exchange of a "qualified community asset" held for more than five years and acquired after 2001 and before 2010.

¶524 Definition of "Capital Assets"

Law: Sec. 18151 (CCH CALIFORNIA TAX REPORTS ¶15-620).

Comparable Federal: Sec. 1221 (CCH U.S. MASTER TAX GUIDE ¶1741).

California law is the same as federal law as of the current IRC tie-in date (¶103).

Under both California and federal law, the term "capital assets" includes all property *except:*

— inventoriable assets;

— property held for sale in the ordinary course of business;

— depreciable business property;

— real property used in business;

— certain copyrights, books, artistic works, etc. (however, see discussion below);

— accounts or notes receivable acquired in the ordinary course of business through sales or services;

— certain government publications;

— most commodities derivative financial instruments held by a commodities derivative dealer;

— hedging transactions; and

— supplies of a type regularly consumed in the ordinary course of business. (Sec. 18151, Rev. & Tax. Code)

As a result of California's federal conformity date (see ¶103), California does not incorporate amendments made by the Tax Increase Prevention and Reconciliation Act of 2005 that allow a taxpayer to elect to treat as a sale or exchange of a capital asset, the sale or exchange of musical compositions or copyrights in musical works created by the taxpayer's personal efforts (or having a basis determined by reference to the basis in the hands of the taxpayer whose personal efforts created the composition or copyrights). The election is available for federal purposes in tax years beginning after May 17, 2006, but before January 1, 2011.

See ¶537 —540 for items that, although they are not actually capital assets, are treated under some circumstances as though they were.

¶525 Capital Gains and Losses—Amount Taken into Account

Law: Secs. 18151, 18152, 18152.5 (CCH CALIFORNIA TAX REPORTS ¶15-620).

Comparable Federal: Secs. 1202, 1222, 1260 (CCH U.S. MASTER TAX GUIDE ¶1740, 1742, 1777).

Both California and federal law measure the amount of capital gains in the same manner, except as noted below. (Sec. 18151, Rev. & Tax. Code)

• *Small business stock*

California generally follows federal law allowing 50% of the gain from the sale or exchange of qualified small business stock held for more than five years to be excluded from gross income under certain conditions, provided the issuing corporation meets specified active business requirements within California. (Sec. 18152, Rev. & Tax. Code; Sec. 18152.5, Rev. & Tax. Code) See ¶515 for a discussion of the rollover of gain allowed for sales of certain small business stock.

In a nonprecedential letter decision, the California State Board of Equalization held in *Appeal of Anderson* (2006) (CCH CALIFORNIA TAX REPORTS ¶15-620.83) that family limited partnerships (FLPs) were ineligible to exclude gain from the sale of qualified small business stock sold by the FLPs. Because the small business stock was acquired at original issue by the founding partners and not by the partnerships, the stock did not constitute qualified small business stock for purposes of the exclusion.

Amounts excluded from gross income are treated as a tax preference item in a computation of the alternative minimum tax (¶117).

¶526 Deductible Capital Losses—Carryovers, Carrybacks

Law: Secs. 18151, 18155 (CCH CALIFORNIA TAX REPORTS ¶15-620).

Comparable Federal: Secs. 1211-12 (CCH U.S. MASTER TAX GUIDE ¶1752, 1754).

California Form: Sch. D (Capital Gain or Loss Adjustment).

Capital losses are deductible in full both federally and for California purposes against capital gain. In addition, up to $3,000 ($1,500 for married or registered domestic partner (see ¶119) taxpayers filing separately) of any excess of capital loss over capital gain is also deductible against ordinary income. (Sec. 18151, Rev. & Tax. Code)

Practice Pointer: Registered Domestic Partners

RDPs who claimed capital losses on their federal returns may need to recompute the amount that may be claimed on their California personal income tax returns to stay within the limits specified above. If California recognizes pre-Proposition 8 same-sex married couples (SSMCs) for California income tax purposes, similar adjustments would presumably be required for SSMCs as well (see ¶119).

• *Current treatment of carryovers*

Any unused net capital loss may be carried forward, indefinitely, to offset capital gains in subsequent years and may be deducted from ordinary income up to the limitation discussed above. The California rule is the same as the federal rule. (Sec. 18151, Rev. & Tax. Code)

• *No carrybacks*

California law does not permit capital loss carrybacks by individuals under any circumstances. (Sec. 18155, Rev. & Tax. Code) Federal law, on the other hand, allows individuals to claim capital loss carrybacks with respect to capital losses from "marked to market" contracts (regulated futures contracts, foreign currency contracts, nonequity options, and dealer equity options).

¶527 Loss from Wash Sales

Law: Sec. 18031 (CCH CALIFORNIA TAX REPORTS ¶15-620).

Comparable Federal: Sec. 1091 (CCH U.S. MASTER TAX GUIDE ¶1935, 1939).

California law is the same as federal law as of the current IRC tie-in date (¶103). (Sec. 18031, Rev. & Tax. Code) Losses on disposition of stock or securities are disallowed where substantially identical property is acquired within 30 days before or after the sale. The wash sale rules apply to a contract or option to acquire or sell stock or securities solely by reason of the fact that the option or contract is, or could be, settled in cash or property other than the stock or securities.

Rules similar to the rules disallowing losses on such wash sales also apply to certain short sales of stock or securities. Any loss realized on the closing of a short sale of stock or securities, including securities futures contracts to sell, is disallowed if within a period beginning 30 days before the date of closing and ending 30 days after that date (1) substantially identical stock or securities were sold or (2) another short sale of substantially identical stock or securities was entered into.

¶528 Holding Period—Special Rules

Law: Secs. 18151, 18155.5 (CCH CALIFORNIA TAX REPORTS ¶15-620).

Comparable Federal: Sec. 1223 (CCH U.S. MASTER TAX GUIDE ¶1777, 1941).

California law as to the character of gain or loss as long or short term is the same as federal law as of the current tie-in date (¶103). (Sec. 18151, Rev. & Tax. Code; Sec. 18155.5, Rev. & Tax. Code)

Special rules are provided for determining the holding period in situations where (1) property was received in a tax-free exchange, and (2) stock was acquired through exercise of rights. Where property is acquired from a decedent and sold within one year after his or her death, the property is considered to have been held for more than one year.

Under both California and federal law, the holding period for the surviving spouse's share of community property dates from the date of original acquisition.

¶529 Gain or Loss on Short Sales

Law: Sec. 18151 (CCH CALIFORNIA TAX REPORTS ¶15-620).

Comparable Federal: Sec. 1233 (CCH U.S. MASTER TAX GUIDE ¶1944).

California law as to the character of gain or loss as capital or ordinary or long-term or short-term is the same as federal law as of the current IRC tie-in date (¶103). (Sec. 18151, Rev. & Tax. Code)

Gains or losses on short sales are treated as capital gains or losses to the extent the property used to close the short sale is a "capital asset." The law regarding short sales includes many special rules for determining holding period, etc., intended to close certain "loopholes" that permitted tax avoidance through conversion of short-term gains into long-term gains.

¶530 Sale or Exchange of Patents

Law: Sec. 18151 (CCH CALIFORNIA TAX REPORTS ¶15-620).

Comparable Federal: Secs. 1235, 1249 (CCH U.S. MASTER TAX GUIDE ¶1741, 1767, 2489).

California law as to the character of gain or loss as (1) capital or ordinary and (2) long-term or short-term is generally the same as federal law as of the current IRC tie-in date (¶103). (Sec. 18151, Rev. & Tax. Code)

Capital gain treatment is accorded investors and certain others on gain from the sale or exchange of patent rights, or interests therein. This treatment pertains even though the transaction has certain characteristics of a license rather than a sale. The provision does not apply to transfers between certain family members, controlled corporations, etc. California law incorporates the federal law by reference, except for the federal provision that denies capital gains treatment on transactions with controlled foreign corporations.

¶531 Transfers of Trademarks, Trade Names, and Franchises

Law: Sec. 18151 (CCH CALIFORNIA TAX REPORTS ¶15-620).

Comparable Federal: Sec. 1253 (CCH U.S. MASTER TAX GUIDE ¶1774, 1775).

California law as to the character of gain or loss as (1) capital or ordinary and (2) long-term or short-term is the same as federal law as of the current IRC tie-in date (¶103). (Sec. 18151, Rev. & Tax. Code)

Detailed rules govern the transfer of a franchise, trademark, or trade name. Generally, the transaction is denied capital gain treatment if the transferor retains any significant power, right, or continuing interest.

¶532 Gain or Loss on Options

Law: Sec. 18151 (CCH CALIFORNIA TAX REPORTS ¶15-620).

Comparable Federal: Secs. 1092, 1234, 1256 (CCH U.S. MASTER TAX GUIDE ¶1919, 1926, 1948).

California law as to the character of gain or loss as capital or ordinary or long-term or short-term is the same as federal law as of the current IRC tie-in date (¶103). (Sec. 18151, Rev. & Tax. Code)

Gain or loss attributable to the sale or exchange of (or loss arising from failure to exercise) a privilege or option to buy or sell property may or may not be a capital gain or loss. The character of the gain or loss depends on the character of the optioned property in the hands of the taxpayer.

The law provides special rules designed to prevent tax avoidance by means of option transactions, including the use of straddle options. Certain futures contracts must be marked to market under these rules and 40% of the gain or loss is treated as short-term while 60% is treated as long-term. The special marked-to-market rules do not apply to hedging transactions.

California incorporates IRC Sec. 1092, as of California's current federal conformity date (¶103), which provides rules relating to the recognition of gain or loss on transactions involving straddles. (Sec. 18031, Rev. & Tax. Code) California has not incorporated amendments made by the Tax Technical Corrections Act of 2007 that amend the basis adjustment provisions of the straddle rules, effective for federal purposes after October 21, 2004, and the straddle identification rules, effective for federal purposes for straddles acquired after December 29, 2007.

¶533 Dealers in Securities

Law: Sec. 18151 (CCH CALIFORNIA TAX REPORTS ¶15-620).

Comparable Federal: Sec. 1236 (CCH U.S. MASTER TAX GUIDE ¶1760).

California law as to the character of gain or loss as capital or ordinary or long-term or short-term is the same as federal law as of the current IRC tie-in date (¶103). (Sec. 18151, Rev. & Tax. Code) For a discussion of the accounting methods applicable to security dealers, see ¶409.

Securities dealers are subject to special rules designed to prevent switching of securities in and out of the capital asset category for the purpose of realizing capital gains and ordinary losses.

¶534 Appreciated Financial Positions

Law: Sec. 18151 (CCH CALIFORNIA TAX REPORTS ¶15-620).

Comparable Federal: Sec. 1259 (CCH U.S. MASTER TAX GUIDE ¶1944).

California incorporates federal law as of the current IRC tie-in date (see ¶103), which treats specified hedging transactions as constructive sales that require the immediate recognition of gain (but not loss). The provision generally applies to "short sales against the box," futures or forward contracts, notional principal contracts, and to any other transactions as prescribed by regulations. (Sec. 18151, Rev. & Tax. Code)

¶535 Retirement of Bonds, etc.

Law: Secs. 17024.5, 18151 (CCH CALIFORNIA TAX REPORTS ¶15-620).

Comparable Federal: Secs. 1271-74 (CCH U.S. MASTER TAX GUIDE ¶1952, 1954, 2431).

California law as to the character of gain or loss as capital or ordinary or long-term or short-term is the same as federal law as of the current IRC tie-in date (¶103). (Sec. 18151, Rev. & Tax. Code)

Amounts received upon retirement of bonds, etc., are ordinarily treated as amounts received in exchange therefore. The purpose of this provision is to permit such transactions to qualify for capital gain treatment. However, capital gain treatment does not apply to any obligation issued before July 2, 1982, if the issuer was neither a corporation nor a governmental unit or political subdivision.

¶536 Real Estate Subdivided for Sale

Law: Sec. 18151 (CCH CALIFORNIA TAX REPORTS ¶15-620).

Comparable Federal: Sec. 1237 (CCH U.S. MASTER TAX GUIDE ¶1762).

California law as to the character of gain or loss as capital or ordinary or long-term or short-term is the same as federal law as of the current IRC tie-in date (¶103). (Sec. 18151, Rev. & Tax. Code)

In general, profits from land subdivision activities will be treated as ordinary income. However, at least a part of the gain may be treated as long-term capital gain if the taxpayer can comply fully with certain very restrictive conditions in the law. Detailed rules are provided, including a requirement that the property be held at least five years, a prohibition against substantial improvements to the property, etc.

¶537 Sales of Property Used in Business, etc.

Law: Sec. 18151 (CCH CALIFORNIA TAX REPORTS ¶15-620).

Comparable Federal: Secs. 1231, 1239 (CCH U.S. MASTER TAX GUIDE ¶1747 et seq.).

California Forms: Sch. D (Capital Gain or Loss Adjustment), Sch. D-1 (Sales of Business Property).

California law as to the character of gain or loss as capital or ordinary or long-term or short-term is the same as federal law as of the current IRC tie-in date (¶103). (Sec. 18151, Rev. & Tax. Code)

Capital gain treatment applies to the disposition of certain property that would not otherwise qualify for such treatment because the property is not a "capital asset" or because it is not sold or exchanged. In applying the rule, the following three classes of transactions are lumped together:

— sales or exchanges of "property used in the trade or business;"

— involuntary conversions (including losses upon destruction, theft, or condemnation) of business property; and

— involuntary conversions of capital assets held for more than one year.

If, during the taxable year, the gains on all three classes of transactions exceed the losses (using 100% of each gain or loss regardless of holding period), all transactions are treated as sales or exchanges of capital assets. This means that all of the gains or losses involved are treated as capital gains or losses, applying the rules discussed in ¶525 in determining the amount to be taken into account in computing taxable income. If the total gains do not exceed the total losses, all gains and losses are treated as "ordinary" gains and losses. Thus, involuntary conversions of *capital assets* resulting in a loss would give rise to a fully-deductible "ordinary" loss if there were no offsetting gains.

Nonresidents net only California source IRC Sec. 1231 gains and losses for purposes of computing California taxable income (FTB Pub. 1100, Taxation of Nonresidents and Individuals Who Change Residency, revised November 2007, CCH CALIFORNIA TAX REPORTS ¶404-599).

• *"Property used in trade or business"*

Federal law is incorporated in California law by reference.

For this purpose "property used in the trade or business" includes:

— depreciable and real property used in a trade or business, held for more than one year;

— cattle and horses held for draft, breeding, dairy, or sporting purposes, provided they are held for two years or longer, and other livestock held for such purposes provided they are held for one year or longer;

— unharvested crops sold with land used in a trade or business and held for more than one year; and

— timber, coal, and iron ore, under certain circumstances (¶540).

However, depreciable and real property used in a business is *not* "property used in the trade or business" for capital gain treatment purposes if it is any of the following:

— inventoriable property;

— property held primarily for sale in the ordinary course of business;

— copyrights, etc., of the type included in the fifth item listed in ¶524; and

— certain government publications.

• *Transactions between related taxpayers*

Capital gain treatment is denied on the sale or exchange, directly or indirectly, of depreciable property between a husband and wife and, for California purposes only, between registered domestic partners and possibly same-sex married couples (see ¶119). This rule applies also to transactions between

— an individual and a corporation that is 50% or more owned by such individual,

— an executor and beneficiary of an estate, except in the case of a sale or exchange in satisfaction of a pecuniary bequest, and

— certain related individuals.

¶538 Sale of Stock of Foreign Investment Companies, etc.

Law: Sec. 17024.5 (CCH CALIFORNIA TAX REPORTS ¶15-515, 15-620).

Comparable Federal: Sec. 1248 (CCH U.S. MASTER TAX GUIDE ¶2487, 2488).

California has not adopted federal provisions that treat as ordinary income, rather than capital gain, the gain arising out of the sale or exchange of certain stock investments in foreign investment companies and other foreign corporations. (Sec. 17024.5, Rev. & Tax. Code)

¶539 Recapture of Excess Depreciation, etc.

Law: Secs. 18151, 18165, 18171, 18171.5 (CCH CALIFORNIA TAX REPORTS ¶15-620).

Comparable Federal: Secs. 1239, 1245, 1250-55 (CCH U.S. MASTER TAX GUIDE ¶1744, 1779).

California law as to the character of gain or loss as capital or ordinary or long-term or short-term is the same as federal law as of the current IRC tie-in date (¶103). (Sec. 18151, Rev. & Tax. Code)

The law contains several "recapture" provisions intended to prevent possible abuse of the capital gain benefits permitted on the sale of various kinds of business property as explained at ¶537. The recapture provisions treat as ordinary income a portion of the gain realized upon disposition of certain property that has been subject to depreciation deductions. The amount "recaptured" depends on (1) the type of property, (2) the method of depreciation used, and (3) the period during which depreciation has been deducted. The types of property subject to this treatment are prescribed in IRC Secs. 1245 and 1250, which are incorporated into California law by reference.

California provides for the following differences from the federal rules:

— special federal rules for Subchapter S corporations do not apply to California for pre-1987 tax years;

— federal provisions for recapture on pollution control facilities do not apply to California;

— federal provisions for recapture of pre-1983 amortization of trademarks do not apply to California;

— California provides for some exceptions to the federal rules for certain low-income housing (for pre-1987 tax years) and historic structures;

— California substitutes different dates for various dates in the federal law, as follows:

— December 31, 1970, for July 24, 1969, and December 31, 1969,

— January 1, 1971, for January 1, 1970,

— December 31, 1976, for December 31, 1975, and

— January 1, 1977, for January 1, 1976; and

— the federal provision treating certain deductions as deductions allowable for amortization is modified for California purposes to also apply to enterprise zone, former Los Angeles Revitalization Zone, local agency military base recovery area, and targeted tax area asset expense allowance deductions (discussed at ¶316). (Sec. 18165, Rev. & Tax. Code ; Sec. 18171, Rev. & Tax. Code; Sec. 18171.5, Rev. & Tax. Code)

In addition, because of California's current federal conformity date (¶103), California does not conform to amendments made by the Energy Tax Incentives Act of 2005 that require recapture as ordinary income on disposal of multiple IRC Sec. 197 assets (intangibles) to the extent amortization deductions were claimed on any of the assets. The recapture provision applies for federal purposes to dispositions after August 8, 2005.

Even where the applicable California and federal recapture provisions are the same, the amount of recapture may of course be different because of differences in amounts deducted in prior years.

¶540 Gain or Loss in the Case of Timber, Coal, or Domestic Iron Ore

Law: Sec. 17681 (CCH California Tax Reports ¶15-620, 15-665).

Comparable Federal: Sec. 631 (CCH U.S. Master Tax Guide ¶1772).

California law as to the character of gain or loss as capital or ordinary or long-term or short-term is the same as federal law as of the current IRC tie-in date (¶103).

Special rules allow a taxpayer to elect to apply capital gain treatment to the cutting of timber held for more than one year or the disposal of coal or domestic iron ore held for more than one year. This is accomplished by including gains or losses from such cutting or disposal in the class of transactions designated the first item in the first list in ¶537, above. (Sec. 17681, Rev. & Tax. Code)

¶541 Cancellation of Lease or Distributor's Agreement

Law: Sec. 18151 (CCH CALIFORNIA TAX REPORTS ¶15-650).

Comparable Federal: Sec. 1241 (CCH U.S. MASTER TAX GUIDE ¶1751).

California law as to the character of gain or loss as capital or ordinary or long-term or short-term is the same as federal law as of the current IRC tie-in date (¶103). (Sec. 18151, Rev. & Tax. Code)

The law provides for capital gain treatment on (1) amounts received by a lessee for the cancellation of a lease and (2) amounts received by a distributor for cancellation of a distributor's agreement, provided the distributor has a substantial capital investment in the distributorship.

¶542 Basis, General Rule

Law: Sec. 18031 (CCH CALIFORNIA TAX REPORTS ¶15-710).

Comparable Federal: Secs. 1012, 1059A (CCH U.S. MASTER TAX GUIDE ¶1701).

Except where otherwise provided, the "basis" of property is its cost. California law is the same as federal law as of the current IRC tie-in date (¶103). (Sec. 18031, Rev. & Tax. Code) California has not incorporated an amendment made by the Emergency Economic Stabilization Act of 2008 that requires that the determination of the basis of securities be done on an account by account basis using existing conventions prescribed by IRS regulations and provides special rules for mutual funds and dividend reinvestment plans, effective for federal purposes on January 1, 2011.

Prior to 1961 for California purposes (and prior to 1954 for federal), certain real property taxes paid by the buyer were not deductible and were required to be capitalized. Any such taxes are includible in the basis of the property.

¶543 Basis, Inventoriable Property

Law: Sec. 18031 (CCH CALIFORNIA TAX REPORTS ¶15-710).

Comparable Federal: Sec. 1013 (CCH U.S. MASTER TAX GUIDE ¶1601).

The basis of inventoriable property is the last inventory value thereof. California law incorporates the federal law by reference as of the current IRC tie-in date (¶103). (Sec. 18031, Rev. & Tax. Code)

¶544 Basis of Property Acquired by Gift

Law: Secs. 17081, 18031 (CCH CALIFORNIA TAX REPORTS ¶15-710).

Comparable Federal: Secs. 84, 1015 (CCH U.S. MASTER TAX GUIDE ¶1630).

California law is the same as federal law as of the current IRC tie-in date (¶103). (Sec. 17081, Rev. & Tax. Code; Sec. 18031, Rev. & Tax. Code)

The basis of property acquired by gift after 1920 is generally determined by reference to the donor's basis, except that for the purpose of determining loss, the basis is limited to the fair market value at the date the gift was made. The basis of property acquired by gift before 1921 is the fair market value at the date the gift was made.

• *Adjustment for gift tax*

The basis may be increased by federal gift tax paid, but there is a limitation on this adjustment. For gifts before 1977, the gift tax adjustment is limited to the excess of fair market value over the donor's adjusted basis. For gifts after 1976, the adjustment is limited to an amount proportionate to the appreciation in value over the donor's adjusted basis. (Sec. 18031, Rev. & Tax. Code)

Prior to 1985, the California limitation on gifts after 1976 was the same as for earlier gifts.

• *Transfers between spouses*

The federal law was amended in 1984 to provide a special rule for transfers between spouses. Such transfers are treated as gifts, with carryover of basis to the transferee and with no limit on the transferee's basis for determining loss. California conformed in 1985. (Sec. 18031, Rev. & Tax. Code) Presumably, California law, but not federal law, extends this treatment to transfers between registered domestic partners and may also extend the treatment to same-sex married couples married prior to Proposition 8's passage in the November 2008 general election (see ¶119).

• *Procedure where facts unknown*

Where the necessary facts for determination of basis are unknown to the donee, the Franchise Tax Board (FTB) is required to obtain the facts. If the FTB can not obtain sufficient facts to make the determination, the basis is the fair market value, as determined by the FTB, as of the date the property was acquired by the donor. (Sec. 18031, Rev. & Tax. Code)

The provision for FTB determination of basis of gift property was applied in *Appeal of Victor and Evelyn Santino* (1975) (CCH CALIFORNIA TAX REPORTS ¶15-710.281). The State Board of Equalization upheld the FTB's finding, based on 1926 records and market values.

¶545 Basis of Property Acquired by Transfer in Trust

Law: Sec. 18031 (CCH CALIFORNIA TAX REPORTS ¶15-710).

Comparable Federal: Sec. 1015 (CCH U.S. MASTER TAX GUIDE ¶1630, 1678).

California law is the same as federal law as of the current IRC tie-in date (¶103). (Sec. 18031, Rev. & Tax. Code)

The basis of property acquired by a transfer in trust (other than by gift, bequest or devise) after 1920 is the grantor's basis adjusted for gain or loss recognized to the grantor on the transfer. For such transfers before 1921, the basis is the fair market value at the date of the transfer.

The federal law was amended in 1984 to provide special basis rules for interspousal transfers in trust, and California conformed in 1985 (¶544).

¶546 Basis of Property Transmitted at Death

Law: Secs. 18031, 18035.6, 18036.6 (CCH CALIFORNIA TAX REPORTS ¶15-710).

Comparable Federal: Secs. 1014, 1022 (CCH U.S. MASTER TAX GUIDE ¶1633).

Federal law regarding basis of property transmitted at death is incorporated by California by reference as of the current IRC tie-in date (¶103). (Sec. 18031, Rev. & Tax. Code) However, the California law provides for important differences from the federal rules as explained below.

— Ordinarily, the basis of property acquired by bequest, devise, or inheritance (or deemed to be so acquired) is the fair market value at date of death.

— If federal estate tax is calculated on the basis of the value of the property at the "optional" valuation date (six months after death), that value becomes the basis. California conformed to the federal law in 1985.

— If family farms or businesses are valued for federal estate tax purposes at less than fair market value, the reduced valuation becomes the basis. California conformed to the federal law in 1985.

— Federal (but not California) law contains special rules for the basis of stock in certain foreign personal holding companies and Domestic International Sales Corporations (DISCs). The federal rule concerning foreign personal holding companies is repealed, effective for tax years of foreign corporations beginning after 2004 and for tax years of U.S shareholders with or within which such tax years of foreign corporations end.

— If death occurred between January 1, 1977, and November 6, 1978, and a carryover basis was elected, the basis is the carryover basis.

— If appreciated property is received by a decedent as a gift within one year before death and the same property reverts to the donor (or spouse), a carryover basis applies.

— The basis of individual retirement accounts and retirement bonds is zero. However, as to the portion attributable to contributions that were not deductible for state purposes, the California basis would be fair market value.

— Special rules are provided for community property, quasi-community property, and joint tenancy property. The California and federal rules are different, as explained below.

— California does not incorporate the federal repeal of the "stepped-up" basis rule and adoption of a modified carryover basis rule with respect to decedents dying after 2009. (Sec. 18035.6, Rev. & Tax. Code; Sec. 18036.6, Rev. & Tax. Code)

• *Community property*

Each spouse has a one-half interest in California community property. With the exception of cases in which a carryover basis was elected (as discussed above), the California basis of the *decedent spouse's* one-half interest in the hands of the surviving spouse (or other party) is fair market value at date of death. Although California applies the community property laws to registered domestic partners (RDPs) beginning with the 2007 taxable year, federal law does not, see ¶119. Consequently, basis adjustments may be required in situations involving the transfer of community property to an RDP upon the death of his or her RDP. The same may be true for same-sex couples married prior to the passage of Proposition 8 in the November 2008 general election (see ¶119).

• *"Quasi-community" property*

In determining the basis of property acquired from a decedent, quasi-community property is treated as community property.

"Quasi-community" property generally refers to property that was acquired while the taxpayer was domiciled outside of California and that would have been community property had the taxpayer been domiciled in California.

• *Interest of surviving spouse*

The basis of the *surviving spouse's* one-half interest varies according to date of death and other circumstances. Under federal law, for deaths occurring after 1947, the basis of a surviving spouse's one-half interest is fair market value. California basis is also fair market value for deaths occurring after 1986. Prior to 1987, the California basis of the surviving spouse's one-half interest was valued at cost.

• *Joint tenancy property*

The basis of joint tenancy property transmitted at death is not covered by the general rule stated at the beginning of ¶546, because such property is not received by "bequest, devise or inheritance." However, federal law provides that, in the case of decedents whose deaths occurred after 1953, such property is considered to have been acquired from the decedent as to the portion of the property that is includible in the estate for federal death-tax purposes. As to that portion, the basis is fair market value, under the rule stated at the beginning of ¶546. As to the survivor's interest, the basis is cost. This federal provision was incorporated in California law by reference so that the California basis is now the same as the federal.

Prior-Year Basis Rules

The many changes in the inheritance tax and income tax laws over the years are reflected in the following summary of the California rules for determining the basis of California community property in the hands of the survivor, covering both the decedent's and the surviving spouse's interests in the property:

(1) **if death occurred prior to April 9, 1953:** basis of decedent's one-half interest is fair market value at date of death and basis of surviving spouse's one-half interest is cost;

(2) **if death occurred after April 8, 1953, and before September 15, 1961:**

(a) if wife was survivor, basis of entire property is fair market value;

(b) if husband was survivor and all of wife's one-half interest went to others, basis of entire property is fair market value; and

(c) if husband was survivor and he received any part of wife's one-half interest, basis of decedent wife's one-half interest is fair market value and basis of surviving husband's one-half interest is cost;

(3) **if death occurred after September 14, 1961, and before January 1, 1987:**

(a) if decedent's entire interest went to others than the surviving spouse (prior to June 8, 1982), basis of entire property is fair market value; and

(b) if any part of decedent's interest went to surviving spouse, basis of decedent's one-half interest is fair market value and basis of surviving spouse's one-half interest is cost (excepted from this rule is the period from January 1, 1981, to June 8, 1982; see below).

(c) **if death occurred after December 31, 1986:** basis of entire property is fair market value—the same as the federal basis.

• *Death 1965-1975—Conversion of separate property*

There is a special rule for community property that was converted from separate property, applicable when death occurred between September 17, 1965, and December 31, 1975. In this case, the basis of the entire property is fair market value. Under the present law, there is no special treatment of such converted property.

• *Decisions of courts and State Board of Equalization*

In *Howard Mel v. Franchise Tax Board* (1981) (CCH CALIFORNIA TAX REPORTS ¶15-710.256), involving four companion cases, the bulk of the deceased husband's one-half interest in community property was left in trust upon his death in 1967, with a lifetime beneficial interest to the surviving wife. The wife claimed a stepped-up basis for her one-half interest when she sold certain items of the community property. A California Court of Appeal applied rule 3(b), above, to deny a stepped-up basis on the items in question. For a later case, citing and following the *Mel* case, see *Appeal of Georgianna Brewer* (1983) (CCH CALIFORNIA TAX REPORTS ¶15-710.257).

In *The Bank of California, N.A., et al. v. Franchise Tax Board* (1978) (CCH CALIFORNIA TAX REPORTS ¶15-710.255), the deceased husband's one-half interest in a substantial estate of community property was left to a testamentary trust. The trust provided for payments of $1,000 per month to the surviving wife for her lifetime. The surviving wife claimed a stepped-up basis for her one-half interest in certain items of the community property. The Franchise Tax Board (FTB) applied rule 3(b), above, and denied the stepped-up basis. However, a California Superior Court overruled the FTB and allowed the stepped-up basis, concluding that it was the legislative intent to conform the California law to the federal. However, see discussion above of the *Howard Mel* case, in which the Court of Appeal overruled the trial court and reached the opposite conclusion.

In *Appeals of Estate of William S. Hatch et al.* (1976) (CCH CALIFORNIA TAX REPORTS ¶15-710.30), community property (a citrus grove) was in escrow when the husband died, under an almost-completed contract of sale. The State Board of Equalization (SBE) held, following federal precedents, that decedent's one-half of the property constituted a right to receive "income in respect of a decedent" and that neither one-half of the property was entitled to a stepped-up California basis.

In *Appeal of Estate of Philip Rosenberg, Deceased* (1975) (CCH CALIFORNIA TAX REPORTS ¶15-710.253), the question was whether the surviving wife was entitled to a stepped-up California basis on her one-half interest in community property. The husband died in 1966, leaving the community property in trust for the surviving wife and children. The situation fell squarely within item (3)(b) of the discussion above. The SBE's opinion deplored the fact that the California result was different from the federal, but upheld the FTB in limiting the survivor's basis to her cost and denying a step-up to the value at date of death. See also *Appeal of Louis (L.M.) Halper Marital Trust* (1977) (CCH CALIFORNIA TAX REPORT ¶15-710.254), to the same effect.

• ***Non-California community property***

The basis provisions of the income tax law apply to property held "under the community property laws of any state, territory or possession of the United States or any foreign country." However, the basis of non-California community property may be different from the basis of California community property as discussed above, because of differing treatment under the inheritance tax law. See the following discussion of quasi-community property.

• ***"Quasi-community" property (prior law)***

"Quasi-community" property is property acquired outside California that would have been California community property if the spouse acquiring the property had been domiciled in California at the time of acquisition. Under the California inheritance tax law from 1957 to 1980, one-half of such property was includible in the estate.

• ***Joint tenancy property***

Prior to 1985 California law provided a rule that was similar in principle to the federal rule, but California permitted a stepped-up basis only on the portion of the property that was subject to California inheritance tax. Since the California inheritance tax was repealed on June 8, 1982, in case of death after that date and subsequent disposition of the property before 1985, it appears that the basis of the entire property would be cost.

• ***Death between January 1981 and June 1982***

Under the California inheritance tax law in effect from January 1, 1981, to June 8, 1982, property transferred to the spouse of the decedent was exempt from the tax. Thus, none of such property has a basis of fair market value, and the basis of the entire property in the hands of the surviving spouse is cost.

• ***Surviving joint tenant other than spouse***

When death occurred during the period January 1, 1955, to June 8, 1982, and the surviving joint tenant is other than the spouse, the basis of the decedent's interest is fair market value. However, when death occurred prior to 1955, the basis of the entire property is cost; this applies also when the surviving joint tenant was the spouse.

• ***Decedent spouse's interest—Death before 1981***

When the surviving joint tenant is the spouse and death occurred prior to 1981, the basis of the decedent's interest is usually fair market value. This applies back to 1955 in cases in which the property was originally separate property of the spouses; the decedent's interest is determined by contribution to the original cost. It applies back to September 15, 1961, in cases where the property was originally "quasi-community" property (as defined in the gift tax law); the decedent is deemed to have had a one-half interest. It applies back to 1976 in cases where the property was originally California community property; the decedent's interest was one-half of the total property. When death occurred prior to 1976 and the property was originally California community property, the basis of the decedent's interest is usually cost; however, there are some exceptions, and it is suggested that the FTB be consulted in case of any question.

• ***Decision of SBE***

Appeal of William F. and Dorothy M. Johnson (1976) (CCH CALIFORNIA TAX REPORTS ¶15-710.331) involved the basis to the survivor of joint tenancy property that had its source in community property, where death occurred in 1967. The SBE held that the basis was original cost, applying the rule set forth above.

• ***California-federal differences***

The federal basis of joint tenancy property in the hands of the survivor may be different from the California basis because of differences in the death tax treatment and differences between the two laws in prior years. Where death occurred prior to 1954, the federal basis of the entire property is cost. Where death occurred after 1953, the federal basis is fair market value for the portion includible in the estate (unless a carryover basis applied under prior law) and cost for the remainder of the property. Note that the decedent's interest is always "includible in the estate" for federal estate tax purposes, even though the property may be completely relieved of tax by the marital deduction. In the case of joint tenancy property of husband and wife, where death occurs after 1981, the decedent's interest is deemed to be one-half of the property regardless of which spouse furnished the consideration.

¶547 Basis of Property Acquired in Tax-Free Exchange

Law: Sec. 17321 (CCH CALIFORNIA TAX REPORTS ¶15-710).

Comparable Federal: Sec. 358 (CCH U.S. MASTER TAX GUIDE ¶2201, 2205).

California law is the same as federal law as of the current IRC tie-in date (¶103).

The basis of property acquired after February 28, 1913, in a tax-free exchange is the same as that of the property exchanged, with adjustment for "boot" received, for any amount treated as a dividend in the exchange, and for any gain or loss recognized upon the exchange. (Sec. 17321, Rev. & Tax. Code)

¶548 Basis of Property Acquired in Corporate Liquidation

Law: Sec. 17321 (CCH CALIFORNIA TAX REPORTS ¶15-645, 15-710).

Comparable Federal: Sec. 334 (CCH U.S. MASTER TAX GUIDE ¶2261).

California law is the same as federal law as of the current IRC tie-in date (¶103). (Sec. 17321, Rev. & Tax. Code)

Generally, the basis of property received by an individual stockholder in a corporate liquidation is the fair market value of the property at the date of liquidation.

¶549 Basis of Stock After "Spin-Off" Reorganization

Law: Sec. 17321 (CCH CALIFORNIA TAX REPORTS ¶15-710).

Comparable Federal: Sec. 358 (CCH U.S. MASTER TAX GUIDE ¶2201, 2205).

California law is the same as federal law as of the current IRC tie-in date (¶103). (Sec. 17321, Rev. & Tax. Code)

When stock of a new corporation is distributed to stockholders of another corporation in a "spin-off" type reorganization (¶517), the adjusted basis of the old stock is allocated between the old and new stocks.

¶550 Basis of Property Acquired upon Involuntary Conversion

Law: Secs. 18031 (CCH CALIFORNIA TAX REPORTS ¶15-710).

Comparable Federal: Sec. 1033 (CCH U.S. MASTER TAX GUIDE ¶1713, 1715).

California law is the same as federal law as of the current IRC tie-in date (¶103). (Sec. 18031, Rev. & Tax. Code)

The basis of property acquired as a result of involuntary conversion (¶503) is the same as that of the property converted, with adjustment for any part of the proceeds not reinvested as required by the law and for any gain or loss recognized upon the conversion.

¶551 Basis of FNMA Stock

Law: Sec. 18031 (CCH CALIFORNIA TAX REPORTS ¶15-710).

Comparable Federal: Sec. 1054.

Basis is reduced for the excess of cost over fair market value (deductible as a business expense) of Federal National Mortgage Association (FNMA) stock issued to an initial holder. California law incorporates the federal law by reference as of the current IRC tie-in date (¶103). (Sec. 18031, Rev. & Tax. Code)

¶552 Redeemable Ground Rents

Law: Sec. 18031 (CCH CALIFORNIA TAX REPORTS ¶15-710).

Comparable Federal: Sec. 1055 (CCH U.S. MASTER TAX GUIDE ¶1611).

Redeemable ground rents are treated as being the equivalent of a mortgage. California law incorporates the federal law by reference as of the current IRC tie-in date (¶103). (Sec. 18031, Rev. & Tax. Code)

¶553 Basis of Securities Acquired in Wash Sale

Law: Sec. 18031 (CCH CALIFORNIA TAX REPORTS ¶15-710).

Comparable Federal: Sec. 1091 (CCH U.S. MASTER TAX GUIDE ¶1939).

The basis of stock or securities acquired in a "wash sale" is the same as that of the securities sold, increased, or decreased, as the case may be, by the difference between the cost of the new securities and the selling price of the securities that were subject to the "wash sale" rules. California law incorporates the federal law by reference as of the current IRC tie-in date (¶103). (Sec. 18031, Rev. & Tax. Code)

¶554 Basis Prescribed by Personal Income Tax Law of 1954

Law: Sec. 18039 (CCH CALIFORNIA TAX REPORTS ¶15-710).

Comparable Federal: Sec. 1052.

The basis of property acquired after February 28, 1913, in certain transactions covered by the California Personal Income Tax Law of 1954, is as prescribed in that Law. (Sec. 18039, Rev. & Tax. Code)

The federal law contains a somewhat comparable provision that refers to federal Revenue Acts of 1932 and 1934. Prior to 1983 California law contained a conforming provision.

¶555 Basis of Partnership Property

Law: Sec. 17851 (CCH CALIFORNIA TAX REPORTS ¶15-185).

Comparable Federal: Secs. 701-61 (CCH U.S. MASTER TAX GUIDE ¶443, 459, 467).

California law is the same as federal law as of the current IRC tie-in date (¶103). (Sec. 17851, Rev. & Tax. Code)

Except as noted above, the basis of property transferred to a partnership is the transferor's basis, adjusted for any gain or loss recognized upon the transfer.

• *Property distributions to a partner*

The rules for determining basis of property distributed by a partnership to a partner may be summarized very briefly as follows:

— generally, the basis of property in the hands of the partner-distributee is the same as the basis in the hands of the partnership;

— the basis of property distributed in liquidation of a partner's interest is the properly allocable part of the basis of the partner's partnership interest;

— special rules to prevent tax avoidance are provided for the treatment of inventories, "unrealized receivables," and depreciable property subject to "depreciation recapture" provisions that are distributed to a partner (there are minor federal-California differences in these rules, as explained at ¶618);

— under some conditions, the partnership may adjust the basis of its assets remaining after the distribution to reflect the step-up or step-down of basis in the transfer from the partnership to the partner; and

— the partnership may elect to adjust the basis of partnership assets to reflect the purchase price paid by a new partner for his or her interest; under some conditions the same type of adjustment may be made by a partner who receives a distribution of partnership property within two years after acquiring an interest.

¶556 Basis of Property Acquired Before March 1, 1913

Law: Sec. 18031 (CCH CALIFORNIA TAX REPORTS ¶15-710).

Comparable Federal: Sec. 1053.

For property acquired before March 1, 1913, when the fair market value at March 1, 1913, was greater than the adjusted basis otherwise determined as of that date, the basis for determining gain is such fair market value. Federal law is incorporated in California law by reference as of the current IRC tie-in date (¶103). (Sec. 18031, Rev. & Tax. Code)

¶557 Basis of Property Acquired Pursuant to S.E.C. Order

Law: Sec. 18031 (CCH CALIFORNIA TAX REPORTS ¶15-710).

Comparable Federal: Sec. 1082.

The basis of securities received in certain liquidations under order of the federal Securities and Exchange Commission is the same as that of the securities exchanged. Federal law is incorporated in California law by reference as of the current IRC tie-in date (¶103). (Sec. 18031, Rev. & Tax. Code)

¶558 Basis of Rights to Acquire Stock

Law: Sec. 17321 (CCH CALIFORNIA TAX REPORTS ¶15-645).

Comparable Federal: Sec. 307 (CCH U.S. MASTER TAX GUIDE ¶1907).

California law is the same as federal law as of the current IRC tie-in date (¶103). (Sec. 17321, Rev. & Tax. Code)

If the fair market value of stock rights is less than 15% of the value of the stock on which the rights are issued, the basis of the rights is zero unless the taxpayer elects to allocate to the rights a portion of the basis of the stock.

As to the following rights, the basis of the stock is allocated between the stock and the rights according to their respective values at the time the rights are issued:

— all rights acquired in a taxable year beginning before 1937, *except* as to certain rights acquired before 1935 (see below); and

— nontaxable rights acquired in a taxable year beginning after December 31, 1936, where the value of the rights is more than 15% or the taxpayer elects to allocate as explained above.

If a stock right was acquired prior to 1935 and it constituted income under the Sixteenth Amendment to the Federal Constitution, the basis of the right is its fair market value when acquired.

If stock rights were acquired and sold in a taxable year beginning after 1934 and prior to 1941 and the entire proceeds were reported as income, the basis of the stock is determined without any allocation to the rights.

California law incorporates the federal law by reference. California has conformed closely to the federal law for many years, although there have been minor differences in the effective dates of prior-year amendments.

¶559 Adjusted Basis

Law: Secs. 17024.5, 18031, 18036 (CCH CALIFORNIA TAX REPORTS ¶ 15-710, 16-020).

Comparable Federal: Secs. 1011, 1016-21 (CCH U.S. MASTER TAX GUIDE ¶ 1604, 1701).

Although California generally incorporates federal law (IRC Sec. 1016) as of California's current federal conformity date (¶ 103), concerning adjustments to basis, many of the federal adjustments are inapplicable for California purposes because California does not incorporate the federal credits or deductions that require the basis adjustments. In addition, when applying the incorporated provisions of IRC Sec. 1016(a) to make California basis adjustments, any references in IRC Sec. 1016 to other IRC provisions must be treated as including California modifications to those other IRC provisions. (Sec. 17024.5(i), Rev. & Tax. Code)

The following federal basis adjustments, although contained in federal law, are inapplicable under California law (Sec. 18036, Rev. & Tax. Code):

— adjustments for amounts related to a shareholder's stock in a controlled foreign corporation (Sec. 17024.5(b)(9), Rev. & Tax. Code);

— adjustments for certain federal investment tax credits (Sec. 17024.5(b)(10), Rev. & Tax. Code); and

— adjustments to the basis of a U.S. taxpayer's stock in a foreign personal holding company to reflect certain undistributed income of the company (Sec. 17024.5(b)(4), Rev. & Tax. Code).

The following basis adjustments required under federal law are examples of provisions technically incorporated by California but that have no practical effect because California does not incorporate the underlying credit or deduction. Thus, for California personal income tax purposes, no adjustments are required for the following:

— adjustments for amounts specified in a shareholder's consent made under IRC Sec. 28 of the 1939 Internal Revenue Code;

— adjustment for amortization under IRC Sec. 811(b) of premium and accrual of discount on bonds and notes held by a life insurance company;

— adjustment for certain carryover basis property acquired from a decedent under IRC Sec. 1023;

— adjustments to the basis of stock required by IRC Sec. 1059, concerning a basis reduction for extraordinary dividends;

— adjustment for adoption costs for which a taxpayer has claimed a federal credit under IRC Sec. 23;

— adjustment with respect to property the acquisition of which resulted in the nonrecognition of gain on the rollover of empowerment zone investments under IRC Sec. 1397B;

— adjustment required with respect to property for which a federal employer-provided child care credit was claimed under IRC Sec. 45F, although California requires a similar basis adjustment for taxpayers who claim the California employer's credit for child care programs (¶ 134); and

— adjustment required under IRC Sec. 1016(d) for certain automobiles for which a taxpayer is required to pay the federal "gas guzzler tax".

Adjustments must also be made for certain deducted enterprise zone, former Los Angeles Revitalization Zone (LARZ), and local agency military base recovery area (LAMBRA) business expenses. No comparable basis adjustments are required under federal law.

Finally, in addition to the adjustments required under IRC Sec. 1016, proper adjustments must be made for the following:

— upon the sale of depreciable property for amounts for which the federal bonus deprecation deduction or increased federal IRC Sec. 179 asset expense election was claimed;

— for amounts that were formerly allowed as deductions as deferred expenses under former Sec. 17689, Rev. & Tax. Code (b) or Sec. 17689.5, Rev. & Tax. Code, relating to certain exploration expenditures, and that resulted in a reduction of the taxpayer's California personal income taxes; and

— for certain deducted enterprise zone, former LARZ, and LAMBRA business expenses (¶316). No comparable basis adjustments are required under federal law. (Sec. 18036, Rev. & Tax. Code)

See ¶221 regarding basis adjustment upon discharge of indebtedness. See ¶561 regarding basis adjustment for lessee improvements.

¶560 Substituted Basis

Law: Sec. 18031 (CCH CALIFORNIA TAX REPORTS ¶15-710).

Comparable Federal: Sec. 1016 (CCH U.S. MASTER TAX GUIDE ¶1607).

"Substituted basis" is defined as the basis determined (1) by reference to the basis in the hands of a transferor or (2) by reference to other property held at any time by the taxpayer. California law incorporates federal law by reference as of the current IRC tie-in date (¶103). (Sec. 18031, Rev. & Tax. Code)

¶561 Lessor's Basis for Lessee's Improvements

Law: Sec. 18031 (CCH CALIFORNIA TAX REPORTS ¶15-710).

Comparable Federal: Sec. 1019 (CCH U.S. MASTER TAX GUIDE ¶1601).

Where the value of improvements by a lessee is excluded from income (¶222), there is no effect on the basis of the property to the lessor. Where the value of such improvements was included in the lessor's income, in a taxable year beginning before 1943, the basis of the lessor's property is adjusted accordingly. California law incorporates federal law by reference as of the current IRC tie-in date (¶103). (Sec. 18031, Rev. & Tax. Code)

¶562 Basis for Depreciation and Depletion

Law: Secs. 17201, 17681 (CCH CALIFORNIA TAX REPORTS ¶15-665).

Comparable Federal: Secs. 167, 612-13 (CCH U.S. MASTER TAX GUIDE ¶1203, 1289).

The basis for depreciation and for cost depletion is the adjusted basis for purposes of determining gain upon sale of the property, except that certain deferred development and exploration expenses includible in basis are disregarded for this purpose (¶320). California law incorporates federal law by reference as of the current IRC tie-in date (¶103). (Sec. 17201, Rev. & Tax. Code; Sec. 17681, Rev. & Tax. Code)

For rules regarding percentage depletion, see ¶319.

¶563 Basis for Player Contracts

Law: Sec. 18031 (CCH CALIFORNIA TAX REPORTS ¶15-710).

Comparable Federal: Sec. 1056.

The basis of player contracts that are acquired in connection with a sports franchise is limited to the basis to the seller plus the gain recognized by the seller on the transfer. California law incorporates federal law by reference (¶103). (Sec. 18031, Rev. & Tax. Code)

¶564 Allocation of Transferred Business Assets

Law: Sec. 18031 (CCH CALIFORNIA TAX REPORTS ¶15-710).

Comparable Federal: Sec. 1060 (CCH U.S. MASTER TAX GUIDE ¶1620).

California has adopted the federal residual method for allocating purchases of assets that constitute a trade or business (¶103). Generally, under the residual method, the purchase price is allocated first to the assets to the extent of their fair market value, and then, if there is any excess, to goodwill and going concern value. However, if a transferor and a transferee agree in writing as to the allocation of consideration for transferred business assets, their agreement will generally be binding for tax purposes. (Sec. 18031, Rev. & Tax. Code)

PERSONAL INCOME TAX

CHAPTER 6

ESTATES AND TRUSTS, PARTNERSHIPS

¶601 Application of Tax to Estates and Trusts

Law: Secs. 17041, 17731, 17731.5, 17734.6, 18505, 18635.5, 19136 (CCH CALIFORNIA TAX REPORTS ¶15-210, 15-215, 15-225, 15-270, 89-104).

Comparable Federal: Secs. 641, 643, 644, 646, 665, 6034A, 6048 (CCH U.S. MASTER TAX GUIDE ¶518, 520 et seq.).

California Forms: Forms 541 (California Fiduciary Income Tax Return), 541-A (Trust Accumulation of Charitable Amounts), 541-B (Charitable Remainder and Pooled Income Trusts), 541-ES (Estimated Tax for Fiduciaries), 541-QFT (California Income Tax Return for Qualified Funeral Trusts), 541-T (California Allocation of Estimated Tax Payments to Beneficiaries).

The personal income tax law applies to the income of estates and to property held in trust, whether the income is accumulated or distributed. The federal law is incorporated by California as of the current IRC tie-in date (¶103). (Sec. 17731, Rev. & Tax. Code) However, California does not incorporate the federal provision that allows an electing Alaska Native Settlement Trust to elect to pay tax on its income at the lowest tax rate applicable to individuals and allows beneficiaries to exclude from their gross income amounts contributed to the electing trust. (Sec. 17734.6, Rev. & Tax. Code)

The tax rates for estates and trusts are the same as for resident individuals. (Sec. 17041(e), Rev. & Tax. Code) The highest individual tax rate is applied to an electing small business trust's income (¶116). (Sec. 17731.5, Rev. & Tax. Code) The alternative minimum tax, discussed at ¶117, applies to estates and trusts as well.

• *Estimated tax*

Generally, trusts and estates make estimated tax payments in the same manner as individuals (¶111). However, under both California and federal law, this general rule is inapplicable to the following:

— private foundations;

— charitable trusts that are taxed on unrelated business income;

— any estate in the first two tax years following the decedent's death; or

— any trust in the first two tax years following the grantor's death if (1) the trust receives the residual of a probate estate under the grantor's will or, (2) the grantor died without a will and the trust is primarily responsible for the estate's taxes, debts, and administrative expenses.

(Sec. 19136, Rev. & Tax. Code)

Under both California and federal law, a trust or, for its final year, a decedent's estate, may elect to have any part of its estimated tax payments treated as made by a beneficiary or beneficiaries. For California purposes, the election is made on Form 541-T, which must be filed by the 65th day after the close of the estate's or trust's taxable year.

• *Consistency rule*

Under both California and federal law, beneficiaries of an estate or trust are required to (1) file their returns in a manner consistent with that reported on the trust's or estate's return or (2) file a notice of inconsistent treatment with the Franchise Tax Board (FTB) (the Secretary for federal purposes) that identifies the inconsistent items. (Sec. 18635.5, Rev. & Tax. Code) If a beneficiary fails to comply with these requirements, any adjustment necessary in order to make the treatment of the items consistent will be treated as a mathematical or clerical error subject to summary assessment procedures. A negligence penalty will also be imposed if the noncompliance was the result of the beneficiary's negligence (¶712).

• *Returns*

Form 541 is used to report the tax information of estates and trusts unless otherwise indicated.

• *Notice of administration*

A personal representative of an estate or an estate attorney must provide notice of administration of an estate subject to California probate law to the FTB within 90 days after the estate's personal representative has been issued letters in probate. (Sec. 9202, Probate Code).

¶602 Effect of Residence upon Taxability

Law: Secs. 17742-45 (CCH CALIFORNIA TAX REPORTS ¶15-205).

Comparable Federal: None.

In the case of an estate, the following rules apply:

— if the decedent was a resident of California at the time of his or her death, all of the estate's net income is taxable, regardless of source;

— if the decedent was a nonresident, only income of the estate from California sources is taxable, unless income is distributed to California beneficiaries; if income is not distributed, it does not matter that either the fiduciary or beneficiary, or both, are California residents ("income in respect of a decedent" may be from a California source and therefore taxable, even though the decedent was a nonresident, where the income arose from personal services in California—see ¶413); and

— any income distributed to a beneficiary who is a California resident is taxable to the beneficiary, regardless of the source of the income.

(Sec. 17742, Rev. & Tax. Code)

See ¶605 for taxation of nonresident and part-year resident beneficiaries.

In the case of a trust, taxability depends on the residence of the fiduciaries and noncontingent beneficiaries (contingent beneficiaries are not relevant). All of the income is taxable, regardless of source, if either the fiduciary (or all fiduciaries, if more than one) or the beneficiary (or all beneficiaries, if more than one) is a California resident. (Sec. 17742, Rev. & Tax. Code) This applies only to any net income that is taxable to the trust, as distinguished from the beneficiaries. It does not apply to distributed (or distributable) income that is taxable to the beneficiaries; see ¶605 for treatment of such income.

Practitioner Comment: Passive Fiduciaries and Contingent Beneficiaries

The California State Board of Equalization (SBE) held in an unpublished decision on October 2, 2007 in the *Appeals of Yolanda King Family Trust and Mary L. Tunney Jr. Trust*, CCH CALIFORNIA TAX REPORTS ¶404-483, that a trust with trustees as well as income beneficiaries who were California residents was nonetheless not subject to tax in California. The SBE agreed that the trustees had delegated all of their authority to an out-of-state bank and should not be considered. Further, the SBE agreed that income beneficiaries of a discretionary trust were contingent beneficiaries which were excluded from consideration under the statute.

Bruce Daigh, Chris Whitney, Contributing Editors

See also *Appeal of The First National Bank of Chicago, Trustee* (1960) (CCH CALIFORNIA TAX REPORTS ¶15-205.201), decided by the State Board of Equalization, in which a nonresident trustee was held taxable on the undistributed income of a trust only because its beneficiaries were California residents. In *Robert P. McCulloch v. Franchise Tax Board* (1964) (CCH CALIFORNIA TAX REPORTS ¶15-235.341), the California Supreme Court held that the tax on income accumulated by a nonresident trust could be collected from a resident trustee-beneficiary in the year of distribution to him.

The residence of a corporate fiduciary is determined by reference to the place where the corporation transacts the major portion of its administration of the trust. (Sec. 17742, Rev. & Tax. Code)

If the taxability of the trust depends on the residence of the fiduciary and there are two or more fiduciaries, not all of whom are residents of California, the taxable income from sources outside California is apportioned to California according to the number of California fiduciaries in relation to the total number of fiduciaries. (Sec. 17743, Rev. & Tax. Code) For example, suppose a trust has two fiduciaries, only one of whom is a California resident, and has net income of $10,000 from property located in New York. One-half of the income of the trust, or $5,000, is taxable for California income tax purposes. This rule has no application to income derived from sources within California (¶231); such income is fully taxable in California regardless of the residence of the fiduciary, beneficiary, or settlor.

If the taxability of the trust depends on the residence of the beneficiary and there are two or more beneficiaries, not all of whom are California residents, the taxable income from sources outside California is apportioned to California to the extent the income will eventually be distributed to beneficiaries who are California residents. (Sec. 17744, Rev. & Tax. Code) To illustrate, suppose A, a resident, and B, a nonresident, are equal beneficiaries of the income of a trust established by a nonresident settlor and having a nonresident fiduciary. Its income of $10,000 is all derived from property located in New York State. All of the income is accumulated in the trust. One-half of the income, or $5,000, is taxable for California income tax purposes. As in the rule discussed in the preceding paragraph, this rule has no application to income derived from California sources.

Where there are multiple fiduciaries and also multiple beneficiaries, some of whom are California residents and some nonresidents, the practice of the Franchise Tax Board has been to apply the above rules consecutively; that is first to the fiduciaries and then to the beneficiaries, or vice versa. For example, suppose there are two fiduciaries, one of whom is a California resident, and two (equal) beneficiaries, one of whom is a California resident. One-half of the income taxable to the trust would be considered attributable to California because of the resident fiduciary. Of the remaining one-half, 50% would then be considered as California income because of the resident beneficiary, the result being that 75% of the total income is attributed to California. This practice is explained in some detail in Legal Ruling No. 238 (1959) (CCH CALIFORNIA TAX REPORTS ¶ 15-205).

Where a nonresident trust has a resident trustee who is also a beneficiary, taxability of the trust's income has been held to be determined only by reference to the resident's status as a trustee. See *Robert P. McCulloch v. Franchise Tax Board*, cited above.

• *Qualified settlement funds*

A fiduciary must file a Form 541 on behalf of a qualified settlement fund (including designated settlement funds) as defined under IRC Sec. 468B, if (1) the court or government agency administering the fund is located in California or (2) the fund receives or expects to receive income from California sources.

¶603 Income of Estate from Community Property

Law: Reg. 17742, 18 CCR (CCH CALIFORNIA TAX REPORTS ¶ 15-215).

Comparable Federal: None.

Franchise Tax Board Reg. 17742, 18 CCR provides that the estate of a deceased spouse is taxable on the income from that part of his or her one-half of the community property that is subject to administration. Income received by the estate, but derived from the surviving spouse's share of the community property, is taxable to the surviving spouse.

Under the California Probate Code, the decedent's share of community property may pass to the surviving spouse without administration. In this case, the entire income is taxable to the surviving spouse. (Secs. 13500 et. seq., Prob. Code)

¶604 Taxable Income of Estate or Trust

Law: Secs. 17076, 17731, 17731.5, 17735-36, 17750, 17751, 18038 (CCH CALIFORNIA TAX REPORTS ¶ 15-215).

Comparable Federal: Secs. 67, 641-45, 651, 661, 1040 (CCH U.S. MASTER TAX GUIDE ¶ 520 et seq., 528 et seq., 537 et seq.).

The taxable income of an estate or trust is computed the same as for individuals, as explained in Chapters 2—5 of this *Guidebook*, inclusive, with the following exceptions:

(1) unlimited deduction is allowed for income paid or set aside by an estate or complex trust under the terms of the will or trust instrument for certain charitable-type purposes (see discussion below);

(2) deduction is allowed for income required to be distributed currently to beneficiaries, the deduction not to exceed the "distributable net income" ; and

(3) deduction is allowed to certain types of trusts ("complex" trusts—see ¶ 605) for other amounts properly paid or credited or required to be distributed.

The federal law is incorporated in California's by reference as of the current IRC tie-in date (¶103). (Sec. 17731, Rev. & Tax. Code) However, California does not incorporate a federal provision that limits the amount of gain that is taxable to an estate or trust that transfers appreciated farm property or closely held business real estate that has been valued for estate tax purposes under the "special-use" valuation method of IRC Sec. 2032A to a "qualified heir." (Sec. 18038, Rev. & Tax. Code)

In the case of an estate, California allows no deduction under items (2) and (3), above, for distributions that are taxable to a nonresident beneficiary if the fiduciary fails to obtain a tax-clearance certificate as explained at ¶613. (Sec. 17735, Rev. & Tax. Code)

• *Expenses of administration*

Expenses of administration of an estate are ordinarily deductible. However, estate administration expenses can be deducted for California income tax purposes or California estate "pickup" tax purposes, but not both (*Tax News*, FTB, May 1988, CCH CALIFORNIA TAX REPORTS ¶15-215.751). For federal purposes, such expenses may be deducted for federal income tax purposes or federal estate tax purposes, but not both.

• *Unlimited deduction*

The deduction described in (1), above, is subject to some restrictions. (Sec. 17736, Rev. & Tax. Code) Generally, the unlimited deduction is reduced or denied where the trust has "unrelated business income" or where it engages in certain "prohibited transactions." The deduction is allowed only for income actually paid out and not for income set aside by a trust. A trust claiming the unlimited deduction presumably would be classified as a charitable trust and treated as a corporation for California tax purposes, as explained at ¶606.

For both federal and California tax purposes, the above deductions are not miscellaneous itemized deductions subject to the 2% floor (¶303). (Sec. 17076, Rev. & Tax. Code)

• *Electing small business trusts*

The portion of a small business trust that consists of stock in one or more S corporations is treated as a separate trust for purposes of computing the income tax attributable to the S corporation stock held by the trust and is taxed at the highest rate applicable to individuals. (Sec. 17731.5, Rev. & Tax. Code) Special rules also apply to the income attributable to the S corporation stock, treatment of capital losses, deductions, exemptions, and credits.

• *Treatment of revocable trust as part of estate*

A qualified revocable trust may make an irrevocable election to be treated for income tax purposes as part of a decedent's estate, provided the election is made jointly by the trustee of the revocable trust and the executor of the decedent's estate by the due date for filing the estate's income tax return for its first tax year. (Sec. 17731, Rev. & Tax. Code) A federal election, or lack thereof, is binding for California purposes. (Sec. 17751, Rev. & Tax. Code)

¶605 Income Taxable to Beneficiaries

Law: Secs. 17731, 17734, 17745, 17779, 18631 (CCH CALIFORNIA TAX REPORTS ¶15-235, 89-104).

Comparable Federal: Secs. 642, 652, 662-68 (CCH U.S. MASTER TAX GUIDE ¶554 et seq., 567).

California Form: FTB 5870A (Tax on Accumulation Distribution of Trusts).

Federal law pertaining to income taxable to beneficiaries is incorporated in California law by reference as of the current IRC tie-in date (¶103). (Sec. 17731, Rev.

& Tax. Code) However, California provides special rules to cover various residence situations, as explained below.

Amounts deductible under (2) and (3) of ¶604 are includible in the income of the beneficiaries.

Income retains the same character (capital gain, exempt income, etc.) in the hands of the beneficiary that it had in the hands of the estate or trust. In other words, the estate or trust is treated as merely a "conduit" for income that is taxable to the beneficiaries. Depreciation is apportioned between the trust or estate and the beneficiaries according to the terms of the trust instrument or on the basis of the income allocable to each.

• *Notice to estate or trust beneficiaries*

The fiduciary of an estate or trust must furnish each beneficiary (or nominee) (1) who receives a distribution from an estate or trust or (2) to whom any taxable item is allocated, a statement (in accordance with IRC Sec. 6034A) containing information necessary for the beneficiary to file his or her California income tax return. (Sec. 18631, Rev. & Tax. Code)

• *Nonresident and part-year resident beneficiaries*

Nonresident beneficiaries are taxed on their distributive shares of estate or trust income only to the extent the income and deductions are derived from sources within California. (Sec. 17734, Rev. & Tax. Code) Thus, four beneficiaries who were residents of Sweden were required to pay California income tax on distributions from their brother's estate because the distributions were from the sale of real estate located in California (*Appeals of Folke Jernberg et al.* (1986), CCH CALIFORNIA TAX REPORTS ¶15-205.302); the accumulated income from these holdings was also taxable.

A part-year resident beneficiary's distributive share of certain trust income is taxed based on the beneficiary's period of residency and nonresidency during the trust's taxable year (¶605). The allocation of income between the period of residency and the period of nonresidency must be made in a manner that reflects the actual date of realization. In the absence of information that reflects the actual date of realization, the annual amount of trust income must be allocated on a proportional basis between the two periods, using a daily pro rata method (FTB Pub. 1100, Taxation of Nonresidents and Individuals Who Change Residency, revised 11-2007, CCH CALIFORNIA TAX REPORTS ¶404-599).

• *Miscellaneous provisions*

In *Estate of Dehgani-Fard* (2006) (CCH CALIFORNIA TAX REPORTS ¶404-038), a California court of appeal ruled that a state university that was among several beneficiaries of a decedent's estate was not liable for any portion of the California personal income tax attributable to the after-discovered assets of the estate, where the income tax on those assets was paid before the income was distributed, and the estate, on its tax returns, had already claimed and received a partial tax exemption based on the university's status as a tax-exempt organization.

In *Appeal of Proctor P. and Martha M. Jones* (1983) (CCH CALIFORNIA TAX REPORTS ¶15-235.342), the taxpayer, a California resident, was one of several beneficiaries of an out-of-state trust. The State Board of Equalization held that tax-exempt California municipal bond income of the trust was properly allocated exclusively to the taxpayer.

Where accumulated income is distributed by a nonresident trust to a resident beneficiary, the distribution is fully taxable to the beneficiary in the year of distribution if it has not previously been taxed in California. If the beneficiary was not a resident during the period of accumulation, the income may or may not be taxable in the year of distribution (¶405). However, credit will be allowed for taxes paid to other states (¶130). California law also provides the following:

(1) where taxes have not been paid on the income of a trust because a resident beneficiary's interest was merely contingent, and not vested, the income is taxable to the resident beneficiary when distributed, or distributable, to the beneficiary;

(2) even though the trust instrument provides that income accumulations are to be added to corpus, the income is nevertheless taxable as distributed, or distributable, to a resident beneficiary, if the trust failed to pay the tax when due, or no tax was paid by the trust because the interest of the resident beneficiary was merely contingent during the period of accumulation;

(3) the tax attributable to the inclusion of trust distributions in income by a resident beneficiary under (1), above, is the total amount of tax that would have been paid by the beneficiary if he or she had included a ratable amount in his or her income for the shorter of the following two periods: (a) the year of distribution and the five preceding years, or (b) the period that the trust acquired or accumulated the income (the "throwback" rules discussed below do not apply in this situation); and

(4) where a resident beneficiary leaves California within 12 months prior to the date of distribution of accumulated income and returns within 12 months after the receipt of such distribution, the beneficiary is presumed to be a resident throughout the entire intervening period of distribution.

(Sec. 17745, Rev. & Tax. Code)

In *Robert P. McCulloch v. Franchise Tax Board* (1964) (CCH CALIFORNIA TAX REPORTS ¶15-235.341), the California Supreme Court held that where income was accumulated by a nonresident trust, and the tax on that income was not paid over to the state when due, it was properly includible in the resident beneficiary's income when distributed in a later year in proportion to the amount that should have been taxed to the trust in prior years.

The law divides trusts into two classes. The first type—commonly known as the "simple" trust—is one that is required to distribute all of its income currently. All other trusts and decedents' estates are included in the other category, commonly called "complex" trusts. Separate rules are provided for the determination of the amount taxable to beneficiaries of "simple" and of "complex" trusts. (Sec. 17731, Rev. & Tax. Code)

Relief is provided to beneficiaries in some cases in the year of termination of an estate or trust. If the deductions of the estate or trust exceed the gross income for the last year, the excess deductions may be carried over and allowed to the beneficiaries. The same procedure applies to unused capital loss carryovers.

If the taxable year of the beneficiary is different from that of the estate or trust, the amount of distributable income that the beneficiary reports is based upon the income of the estate or trust for the taxable year of the estate or trust that ends within the beneficiary's taxable year.

¶606 Charitable Trusts

Law: Secs. 17009, 17731, 18635 (CCH CALIFORNIA TAX REPORTS ¶15-215, 15-235, 89-104).

Comparable Federal: Secs. 501(c)(3), 642(c), 664, 681, 4940-48, 6034 (CCH U.S. MASTER TAX GUIDE ¶590 et seq.).

Under California law, a charitable trust is treated as a corporation. (Sec. 17009, Rev. & Tax. Code) (This is accomplished by including trusts operated for charitable purposes within the definition of "corporation.") This means that a charitable trust should apply for tax exemption under Section 23701d of the corporation tax law and should comply with the reporting requirements discussed at ¶811. (Sec. 18635, Rev. & Tax. Code)

The special federal treatment of "charitable remainder annuity trusts" and "charitable remainder unitrusts" is incorporated in California law by reference. (Sec. 17731, Rev. & Tax. Code)

Although California has conformed in principle to federal law by creating a special category of organizations classified as "private foundations," California has not adopted many of the complicated federal provisions relating to such organizations. California does not impose a tax on the investment income of "private foundations," nor does California impose any of the excise taxes (on self-dealing, income-accumulation, prohibited investments, lobbying, termination, etc.) that are included in the federal law. The California provisions regarding "private foundations" are almost all in the corporation tax law (¶811).

Both California and federal laws require specified trusts, including "private foundations," to include certain provisions in their governing instruments in order to maintain their tax-exempt status, unless a state statute accomplishes the same result. The California Civil Code provides that the required provisions are deemed to be included automatically in the governing instruments of all trusts to which the requirement applies, and further provides that any provisions of trust instruments that are inconsistent or contrary are of no effect.

¶607 Employees' Trusts

Law: Secs. 17501, 17504, 17510, 17631-40, 18506, 19518 (CCH CALIFORNIA TAX REPORTS ¶15-800).

Comparable Federal: Secs. 401-7, 501-14, 4971-75, 6047, 7701 (CCH U.S. MASTER TAX GUIDE ¶2101 et seq.).

California law is generally the same as federal law. (Sec. 17501, Rev. & Tax. Code)

A trust forming part of an employees' stock bonus, pension, or profit-sharing plan is exempt from taxation provided it meets certain requirements as summarized very briefly as follows:

— contributions must be made for the exclusive benefit of employees or their beneficiaries and it must be impossible for any part of the corpus or income to be diverted to any other purpose; and

— the plan must benefit the employees generally, under certain specific rules, and must not discriminate in favor of officers, shareholders, supervisory employees, etc.

The employee benefits under an exempt plan are taxed to the employee only when actually distributed to the employee. See ¶206.

California rules for employees' trusts (including self-employed plans and individual retirement accounts) conform generally to federal rules. See ¶206 and ¶330 for a detailed discussion.

An exempt employees' trust need not file a California return unless it changes its character, purpose, or method of operation, or unless it has unrelated business income. (Sec. 18506, Rev. & Tax. Code) However, both California and federal laws require trustees and insurers to file information returns regarding payments made under self-employed retirement plans. (Sec. 19518, Rev. & Tax. Code) Also, as to individual retirement accounts, California requires trustees and others to file copies of federal reports with the Franchise Tax Board.

¶608 Trusts Taxable to Grantor

Law: Secs. 17731, 17760.5 (CCH CALIFORNIA TAX REPORTS ¶15-215).

Comparable Federal: Secs. 671-79, 685 (CCH U.S. MASTER TAX GUIDE ¶571 et seq.).

California law is the same as federal law as of the current IRC tie-in date (¶103). (Sec. 17731, Rev. & Tax. Code)

Where the grantor retains an interest, as specifically defined in the Code sections cited above, in either corpus or income, the income is taxable to the grantor and not to the trust or the beneficiaries. However, under both California and federal law, qualified pre-need funeral trusts may not be treated as grantor trusts. (Sec. 17760.5, Rev. & Tax. Code) Consequently, the tax on the annual earnings of a funeral trust is payable by the trustee, if a trustee elects this special tax treatment. A federal election to receive such treatment for a qualified pre-need funeral trust is binding for California purposes and a separate California election is not allowed.

Where income of a trust may be used to satisfy the grantor's legal obligation to support a beneficiary, the income is taxed to the grantor to the extent—and only to the extent—that the income is so used.

In *Appeal of Blake and Alice Hale* (1960) (CCH CALIFORNIA TAX REPORTS ¶15-215.907), the State Board of Equalization held that income from a voluntary trust was taxable to the grantor when the trust instrument did not specifically provide that the trust was irrevocable, and partial or total revocations were contemplated in certain provisions.

Where the grantor in a trust of the type under discussion is not a California resident, he or she is taxed on the income of the trust only to the extent it is derived from sources within California.

There are special federal rules for taxing the income of foreign trusts to their U.S. grantors, under certain conditions. In addition, the U.S. beneficiary of a foreign trust may be treated as the grantor of the trust in certain cases in which the grantor trust rules would otherwise be frustrated.

Fiduciaries of certain grantor trusts are not required to file a return for the trust; the income, deductions, and credits of the trust are reported on the grantor's return.

¶609 Real Estate Investment Trusts

Law: Sec. 17088 (CCH CALIFORNIA TAX REPORTS ¶10-360).

Comparable Federal: Secs. 856-60 (CCH U.S. MASTER TAX GUIDE ¶2326 et seq.).

California generally adopts by reference the federal provisions as of the current IRC tie-in date, see ¶805 for additional information. (¶103). (Sec. 17088, Rev. & Tax. Code) California law, unlike federal law, does not apply a lower tax rate to qualified dividend distributions made by a real estate investment trust (REIT).

A REIT is ordinarily treated as a business trust subject to the corporation income tax, as explained at ¶805. The corporation tax law allows such organizations a deduction for income distributed, as explained at ¶1022.

¶610 Financial Asset Securitization Investment Trusts

Law: Sec. 17088 (CCH CALIFORNIA TAX REPORTS ¶10-370).

Comparable Federal: Former Secs. 860H—860L (CCH U.S. MASTER TAX GUIDE ¶2369).

California incorporates federal provisions concerning financial asset securitization investment trusts (FASITs) as of the current IRC tie-in date (¶103). (Sec. 17088, Rev. & Tax. Code) A FASIT is a pass-through entity that may be used to securitize debt obligations such as credit card receivables, home equity loans, and auto loans. Securities issued by a FASIT are treated as debt for federal income tax purposes, regardless of whether instruments with similar terms issued by an entity other than a FASIT would be characterized as equity ownership interests. Consequently, a FASIT may be used to avoid imposition of a corporate level tax on investors' income and to ensure that interest paid to investors will be deductible by the loan pool's sponsor. For a detailed discussion of FASITs, see ¶805.

The FASIT provisions are repealed under both California and federal law, generally effective January 1, 2005. However, the repeal does not apply to any FASIT in existence on October 22, 2004, to the extent that regular interests issued by the FASIT before such date continue to remain outstanding in accordance with the original terms of issuance.

¶611 Alimony Trusts

Law: Secs. 17731, 17737 (CCH CALIFORNIA TAX REPORTS ¶15-215).

Comparable Federal: Sec. 682 (CCH U.S. MASTER TAX GUIDE ¶775).

Income of "alimony trusts" is taxable to the beneficiary and is not taxable to the trustor. (Sec. 17731, Rev. & Tax. Code) This rule does not apply to any part of such income that is payable for the support of minor children. (Sec. 17737, Rev. & Tax. Code)

California law incorporates federal law by reference as of the current IRC tie-in date (¶103).

¶612 Lien for Tax on Trust Income

Law: Secs. 19221, 19223-24 (CCH CALIFORNIA TAX REPORTS ¶89-172).

Comparable Federal: Sec. 6321.

California law provides that under certain conditions the amount of taxes imposed upon the grantor of a trust on the trust income (¶608) constitutes a lien on the trust property. (Sec. 19221, Rev. & Tax. Code) Although federal law contains certain provisions for liens for unpaid taxes, it contains no rule similar to this one.

¶613 Liability of Fiduciary

Law: Secs. 19071-74, 19512-17 (CCH CALIFORNIA TAX REPORTS ¶89-166).

Comparable Federal: Secs. 6501, 6901, 6903, 6905 (CCH U.S. MASTER TAX GUIDE ¶512).

California Forms: Form 541 (California Fiduciary Income Tax Return), FTB 3571 (Request for Estate Income Tax Certificate).

California law is the same as federal law as of the current IRC tie-in date (¶103).

The fiduciary is personally liable for the taxes on an estate or trust under certain conditions. (Sec. 19073, Rev. & Tax. Code; Sec. 19074, Rev. & Tax. Code) Federal law provides for discharge of an executor's liability under certain circumstances. There is no comparable California provision.

If the asset value of an estate exceeds $1 million and assets valued at more than $250,000 are distributable to one or more nonresident beneficiaries, the fiduciary of an estate must file with his or her final accounting a certificate from the Franchise Tax Board (FTB) to the effect that all California income taxes have been paid or otherwise provided for. (Sec. 19513, Rev. & Tax. Code) For purposes of the $1 million threshold, the assets' fair market values are determined as of the decedent's date of death. All assets are included for decedents who were California residents but only assets located in California are included for decedents who were nonresidents of California.

The FTB supplies a form (FTB 3571, Request for Estate Income Tax Clearance Certificate) for applying for such a certificate. The law allows 30 days for processing such requests. (Sec. 19514, Rev. & Tax. Code) There is no similar federal requirement. Issuance of the certificate does not relieve the estate of any taxes due or that might become due from the decedent or the estate, nor does it relieve the fiduciary from personal liability for taxes or expenses. (Sec. 19515, Rev. & Tax. Code; Sec. 19516, Rev. & Tax. Code)

A fiduciary (or other person liable for the tax) of an estate or trust may by written request filed with the FTB shorten the period of limitations on assessment, etc., to 18 months. (Sec. 19517, Rev. & Tax. Code) The comparable federal provision is limited to the fiduciary of an estate.

A fiduciary should give the FTB notice in writing of the assumption of the duties, rights, etc., attaching to the fiduciary capacity. A fiduciary who wishes to be relieved of fiduciary responsibilities must give the FTB a written termination notice, accompanied by evidence of such termination. (Sec. 19512, Rev. & Tax. Code) The California rule is the same as the federal rule.

In *Appeals of Dunham et al.* (1963) (CCH CALIFORNIA TAX REPORTS ¶89-166.40), the State Board of Equalization (SBE) held that the co-executors of an estate remained liable for additional California income tax imposed on the estate after they had been discharged from their duties by a superior court. The SBE held that failure to notify the FTB of discharge by a superior court left them responsible, in their representative capacities, for the additional tax.

¶614 Common Trust Funds

Law: Secs. 17671, 17677 (CCH CALIFORNIA TAX REPORTS ¶15-515).

Comparable Federal: Sec. 584 (CCH U.S. MASTER TAX GUIDE ¶595).

California law is the same as federal law as of the current IRC tie-in date (¶103). (Sec. 17671, Rev. & Tax. Code)

Special rules are provided for common trust funds maintained by banks or trust companies. The general plan is to treat such funds as reporting entities, only the individual shares of income being taxed to the participants, as is the manner for partnerships.

¶615 Real Estate Mortgage Investment Conduits

Law: Secs. 17088, 24874 (CCH CALIFORNIA TAX REPORTS ¶10-365).

Comparable Federal: Secs. 860A—860G (CCH U.S. MASTER TAX GUIDE ¶2343 et seq.).

California law is the same as federal law as of the current IRC tie-in date (¶103) (Sec. 17088, Rev. & Tax. Code), except that California does not impose an excise tax on prohibited transactions, but subjects real estate mortgage investment conduits (REMICs) to a minimum tax. (Sec. 24874, Rev. & Tax. Code)

Trusts or partnerships that meet specified requirements may elect to be treated as a REMIC. A REMIC, which is a fixed pool of mortgages with multiple classes of interests held by investors, is not taxed on its income, but its income is taxable to the holders of its interests.

¶616 Partnerships—Method of Taxing

Law: Secs. 17008, 17008.5, 17551, 17851, 17935, 17941, 17948, 23081, 23097, 24637 (CCH CALIFORNIA TAX REPORTS ¶10-220, 15-455, 15-185).

Comparable Federal: Secs. 444, 701-61, 7701, 7704 (CCH U.S. MASTER TAX GUIDE ¶403, 404, 416).

California Form: Form 565 (Partnership Return of Income).

California law is the same as federal law as of the current IRC tie-in date (¶103) (Sec. 17851, Rev. & Tax. Code), except for a minimum tax imposed by California on limited partnerships, limited liability partnerships (LLPs), and limited liability companies (LLCs) treated as partnerships (¶116) that are organized or registered in California or doing business in California.

The minimum tax must be paid for each taxable year until a certificate of cancellation is filed with the office of the Secretary of State (SOS). (Sec. 17935, Rev. & Tax. Code; Sec. 17941, Rev. & Tax. Code; Sec. 17948, Rev. & Tax. Code) Ceasing operations, filing a "final return", and filing a certificate of dissolution with the Secretary of State's Office, without filing a certificate of cancellation with the Secretary of State's office, was insufficient to relieve a limited partnership from liability for the minimum tax. (Uncitable decision, *Third Pine Associates, L.P. and 1319 Promenade, L.P.* (2006) CCH CALIFORNIA TAX REPORTS ¶89-210.544) See ¶623 for further details.

Partnerships are not taxable as such but are treated as reporting entities only, the distributive shares of the partners being reported and taxed in their individual returns. (Sec. 17851, Rev. & Tax. Code) "Partnership" may include a syndicate, group, pool, joint venture, or other unincorporated organization. (Sec. 17008, Rev. & Tax. Code)

California adopts the federal provision that treats publicly traded partnerships as corporations unless (1) 90% or more of their gross income consists of qualifying passive income or (2) they are grandfathered publicly traded partnerships exempt from corporate treatment. (Sec. 17008.5, Rev. & Tax. Code) However, a grandfathered publicly traded partnership that elects to continue its partnership status is subject to a California tax equal to 1% of its California-source gross income attributable to the active conduct of any trade or business (a 3.5% tax on gross income attributable to the active conduct of any trade or business for federal purposes).

For a detailed discussion of limited liability partnerships, see ¶623. For a discussion of limited liability companies classified as partnerships, see ¶625.

• *Taxable year*

Generally, a partnership must use the same taxable year as the taxable year of a majority of its partners (usually a calendar year). However, certain partnerships may elect to change to a taxable year with a three-month deferral period. (Sec. 17551, Rev. & Tax. Code) Federal law requires an entity making the election federally to make certain "required payments" to the IRS in exchange for deferral of the tax. California does not adopt the "required payments" requirement.

Partnership information is reported on Form 565 unless otherwise indicated.

¶617 Transactions Between Partner and Partnership

Law: Sec. 17851 (CCH CALIFORNIA TAX REPORTS ¶16-417, 16-428).

Comparable Federal: Secs. 704, 707, 721-24, 731-36 (CCH U.S. MASTER TAX GUIDE ¶421, 425, 428, 432, 435, 443, 453 et seq.).

California law generally is the same as federal law as of the current IRC tie-in date (¶103). (Sec. 17851, Rev. & Tax. Code)

In keeping with the theory that a partnership is not a separate taxable entity, it has been the general rule that no gain or loss is recognized when property is transferred from a partner to a partnership or *vice versa.* Special rules applicable to specific situations have, to some extent, eroded that general rule, however. Distributions of money and distributions in liquidation of a partner's interest are subject to special rules under which gain or loss is sometimes recognized. Also, recognition treatment is accorded to distributions of appreciated property contributed by a partner when the property is distributed within seven years of its contribution. See ¶555 for rules regarding basis of property contributed to or distributed by a partnership.

California incorporates federal law that dramatically limits the ability of partners and partnerships to shift or duplicate losses by (1) placing restrictions on certain partnership allocations traceable to built-in loss property and (2) limiting elections not to make partnership basis adjustments under IRC Secs. 743 and 734 in "substantial" loss situations.

When a partner engages in a transaction with the partnership in a non-partner capacity, the partner is generally treated as an outsider. This provision does not apply, however, in the case of losses on such transactions where the partner holds more than a 50% interest in the partnership. Also, capital gain treatment is denied on certain sales or exchanges where a partner holds more than a 50% interest in a partnership or where the same group owns more than a 50% interest in two partnerships.

¶618 Transfer of Partnership Interest

Law: Secs. 17024.5, 17851, 17855-57 (CCH CALIFORNIA TAX REPORTS ¶15-190).

Comparable Federal: Secs. 736, 737, 741-55 (CCH U.S. MASTER TAX GUIDE ¶438, 440, 454).

The sale of a partnership interest is generally considered to be the sale of a capital asset, with exceptions for cases where there are "unrealized receivables" or appreciated inventory.

The federal law is incorporated in California law by reference as of the current IRC tie-in date (¶103). (Sec. 17851, Rev. & Tax. Code) However, there are some specified California differences, as explained below.

The law provides special rules for treatment of "unrealized receivables" and appreciated inventory in the sale or liquidation of a partnership interest. The purpose is to prevent tax avoidance by converting profit on such items from ordinary income to capital gain. The federal definition of "unrealized receivables" includes the following items that are not included in the California definition:

— stock in a Domestic International Sales Corporation (DISC);

— stock in certain foreign corporations; and

— certain oil, gas, and geothermal property.

(Sec. 17024.5(b)(2) and (5), Rev. & Tax. Code; Sec. 17855, Rev. & Tax. Code)

Under both California and federal law, if the partner receiving property in liquidation does not have enough available basis to cover the full amount of the partnership's basis in unrealized receivables and inventory, the shortfall in available basis must be accounted for. The difference between the partnership's basis in the unrealized receivables and inventory and the partner's substituted basis available for allocation is treated as a basis "decrease." The decrease is allocated first to properties with unrealized depreciation. Any remaining decrease is allocated to the properties in proportion to their respective adjusted bases.

For an example of ordinary-income treatment of "unrealized receivables" upon sale of a partnership interest, see *Appeal of Gerald H. and Dorothy A. Bense* (1979) (CCH CALIFORNIA TAX REPORTS ¶15-190.57).

¶619 Nonresident and Part-Year Resident Partners

Law: Secs. 17951, 18535 (CCH CALIFORNIA TAX REPORTS ¶16-565, 89-102).

Comparable Federal: None.

California Forms: Form 540NR (California Nonresident or Part-Year Resident Income Tax Return), Sch. CA (540NR) (California Adjustments - Nonresidents or Part-Year Residents), FTB 3864 (Group Nonresident Return Election).

• *Nonresident partners*

Nonresident partners are taxable on the portion of their distributive share of partnership income that is derived from sources within California. Such partners are taxable on any such income and may deduct their share of any loss attributable to California sources. (Sec. 17951, Rev. & Tax. Code) See ¶231 for a discussion of taxable income of nonresidents and ¶129 for a credit nonresident partners may take on taxes paid other states on income also taxed by California. Withholding requirements for distributions to nonresident partners is discussed at ¶714.

A nonresident partner in an investment partnership is not subject to California taxation on income from qualifying investment securities. However California tax applies to income from an investment activity that is interrelated with a California trade or business in which the nonresident owns an interest and the primary activities of the trade or business are separate and distinct from the acts of acquiring, managing, or disposing of qualified investment securities. Likewise, income from qualifying investment securities that are acquired with the working capital of a California trade or business in which the nonresident owns an interest is taxable by California. (Sec. 17955, Rev. & Tax. Code)

• *Group returns*

An election to file a group nonresident personal income tax return (Form 540NR, California Nonresident or Part-Year Resident Personal Income Tax Return) is available to nonresident partners of California partnerships or partnerships having California source income (this provision also applies to nonresident shareholders of S corporations and nonresident members of a limited liability company; see ¶233 and ¶625, respectively). The election is only available if two or more nonresident partners agree to be part of the return. However, applicable to returns filed after 2009, for taxable years beginning after 2008, the FTB will allow a nonresident group return to be filed on behalf of a single nonresident partner. (Sec. 18535, Rev. & Tax. Code)

An irrevocable election must be made by the partnership each year. Election to file a group return relieves a nonresident partner of the responsibility of filing individually. A nonresident may only participate in the group return if he or she is an individual, was a nonresident for the full year, and has no income from any other California source (other than another business entity that files a nonresident group return on behalf of the individual). Individuals with taxable income in excess of $1 million who are subject to the mental health services tax (see ¶116) may not be included in a group return. (*Tax News*, California Franchise Tax Board, June 2006) However, this limitation is eliminated applicable to returns filed after 2009, for taxable years beginning after 2008. (Sec. 18535, Rev. & Tax. Code)

A calendar year should be used for the group nonresident return, even if the partnership has a fiscal year end. Any estimated tax payments should also be made on a calendar year basis. A Schedule 1067B should be used to authorize the FTB to move estimated tax payments from the group to an individual's account, or from an individual's account to the group. It will take the FTB six to eight weeks to move the estimated tax payments and make them available to be claimed on the group nonresident return. (FTB Pub. 1067, Guidelines for Filing a Group Form 540NR)

The tax rate applicable to each partner's distributive share will be the highest marginal rate, including, when applicable, the additional 1% mental health services tax applied to individuals with taxable income in excess of $1 million. Only distributive deductions, those necessary to determine each partner's distributive share, are permitted (an exception is made for deferred-compensation deductions attributable to the partner's earned income from the partnership, provided this is the only earned income the partner has). Credits are restricted to those directly attributable to the partnership (*e.g.*, as net income taxes paid to other states by the partnership) and do not include credits to which the nonresident may be otherwise entitled as an individual.

Once the group nonresident return is filed, the return cannot be amended to either include or exclude a nonresident member. Similarly, if a nonresident member is included in the group nonresident return, the member may not subsequently file an individual nonresident return.

For more information concerning nonresident group returns, see FTB Pub. 1067, Guidelines for Filing a Group Form 540NR.

The Franchise Tax Board may adjust the income of an electing nonresident taxpayer included in a group return to properly reflect income. (Sec. 18535, Rev. & Tax. Code)

• *Part-year resident partners*

A part-year resident partner's distributive share of partnership income is taxed based on the partner's period of residency and nonresidency during the partnership's taxable year (¶605). The allocation of income between the period of residency and the period of nonresidency must be made in a manner that reflects the actual date of realization. In the absence of information that reflects the actual date of realization, the annual amount of partnership income must be allocated on a proportional basis between the two periods, using a daily pro rata method (FTB Pub. 1100, Taxation of Nonresidents and Individuals Who Change Residency, revised 11-2007, CCH CALIFORNIA TAX REPORTS ¶404-599).

Practitioner Comment: Sourcing of Pass-Through Income

In Legal Ruling 2003-1, the Franchise Tax Board (FTB) explains the computation of California income for owners of pass-through entities that change residency status during the year. Chapter 920 (A.B. 1115), Laws 2001, requires owners of pass-through entities to treat the items of income, deduction, and credit earned by such entities as if the items were earned by the owners at the same time and in the same manner as earned by the pass-through entity.

As noted in the ruling, the computation method is a significant shift from the method used in 2001 and prior years, which employed an accrual concept of accounting and looked to the individual's residency status on the last day of the pass-through entity's tax year. Under the prior method, if an individual moved out of California before the pass-through entity's year-end, the nonresident individual would only be taxed on his distributive share of pass-through entity income derived from California sources.

Taxpayers should keep in mind that the change to the sourcing of pass-through entity income described in the FTB's ruling is by no means clear in the provisions of A.B. 1115, so we may well see some taxpayers challenge the position outlined in the ruling.

Bruce Daigh, Chris Whitney, Contributing Editors

¶620 Computation of Partnership Income

Law: Secs. 17851-54, 17858 (CCH CALIFORNIA TAX REPORTS ¶10-220, 15-190).

Comparable Federal: Secs. 702, 703, 709 (CCH U.S. MASTER TAX GUIDE ¶417, 419, 427).

California law is substantially the same as federal law as of the current IRC tie-in date (¶103), except that California deductions are not allowed to the partnership for state income taxes. (Sec. 17851, Rev. & Tax. Code; Sec. 17853, Rev. & Tax. Code) In addition, California does not incorporate federal law providing special treatment for small partnerships.

Under both California and federal law, the taxable income of a partnership is computed in the same way as that of an individual, except that no deduction is allowed for charitable contributions or for personal items such as medical expenses. The individual partners are permitted to pick up their shares of the partnership contributions in their individual returns. Capital gains and losses of the partnership are segregated from other income so that the individual partners' shares may be picked up and combined with other capital gains and losses on their individual returns.

Guaranteed payments to partners for salary and interest are treated as though paid to an outsider, and are reported by the partners as separate items. For purposes of computing a nonresident's taxable income (¶116), guaranteed payments received by a nonresident are included in gross income from California sources in the same manner as if those payments were a distributive share of that partnership. (Sec. 17854, Rev. & Tax. Code)

A partner's share of a partnership loss may be deducted only to the extent of the adjusted basis of the partner's interest in the partnership at the end of the partnership year. However, such losses may be deducted in a subsequent year when the partner has sufficient basis to offset the loss.

Generally, elections affecting the computation of partnership income, such as depreciation, must be made on the partnership return; thus, the amount of depreciation is not recalculated by individual partners. (Sec. 17858, Rev. & Tax. Code) However, certain elections are made by each partner separately.

See ¶1304 and ¶1305 regarding computation of California partnership income where a partnership is engaged in a unitary business with a corporate partner.

Special rules are provided for determining income of partnerships and partners, as part of the effort to restrict the use of various forms of tax shelters. These provisions include "at risk" limitations on losses (¶339), restrictions on the ability of partners and partnerships to shift or duplicate losses (¶617), limitations on deduction of syndication and organization expenses, specific rules for apportionment of income among partners, restrictions on deductions by farming syndicates, and use of the accrual method of accounting by certain farming partnerships.

Under both California and federal law partnerships may currently deduct up to $5,000 of their organizational expenditures, reduced by the amount by which such expenditures exceed $50,000, for the tax year in which the partnership begins business. The remainder of any organizational expenses can be deducted ratably over the 180-month period beginning with the month in which the partnership begins business.

¶621 Taxable Year in Which Income of Partner Includible

Law: Sec. 17851 (CCH California Tax Reports ¶15-190).

Comparable Federal: Secs. 706, 708 (CCH U.S. Master Tax Guide ¶404, 416).

California law is the same as federal law (¶103). (Sec. 17851, Rev. & Tax. Code)

A partner must report a distributive share of the partnership income for the taxable year (or years) of the partnership ending within or with the partner's taxable year. A partnership is limited in its choice of a taxable year (¶616). In order to adopt a taxable year other than that of its principal partners, the partnership must establish a business purpose. (Sec. 17851, Rev. & Tax. Code)

¶622 Partnership Returns

Law: Secs. 18409, 18633, 19172 (CCH California Tax Reports ¶89-102, 89-206).

Comparable Federal: Secs. 6011(e), 6031, 6698 (CCH U.S. Master Tax Guide ¶404 et seq.).

California Form: Form 565 (Partnership Return of Income).

Partnership returns are made on Form 565 and must be filed by the 15th day of the fourth month after the close of the partnership's taxable year. Automatic extensions of up to six months are available (¶108). (Sec. 18633, Rev. & Tax. Code) Partnership returns may be filed electronically.

CCH Caution Note: Husband and Wife Joint Ventures

Because of California's current federal conformity date (¶103), California does not conform to a federal amendment made to IRC Sec. 761(f) by the Small Business and Work Opportunity Tax Act of 2007 that allows husbands and wives who are the sole members of a joint venture to elect to not file a federal partnership return, beginning with the 2007 taxable year. However, the FTB has stated that because California follows Revenue Procedure 2002-69, which allows a married couple living in a community property state to file as either a Schedule C business or a partnership, California effectively conforms to this federal amendment. (*Summary of Federal Income Tax Changes—2007*, California Franchise Tax Board, released April 10, 2008)

Returns must be filed by all partnerships (including real estate mortgage investment conduits treated as partnerships) having income from sources in California or engaging in a trade or business within California. Regardless of where the trade or business of the partnership is located, a partnership is considered to be doing business in California if any of its partners (general or limited) or other agents is conducting business in California on behalf of the partnership.

CCH Tip: Required signature

Form 565 is not considered a valid return unless it is signed by a general partner.

Pertinent information from the return must be furnished to each partner and to each person who holds a partnership interest as a nominee for another person. The provision is the same as federal law. California also conforms to the federal reporting requirements of a partnership that has one or more exempt partners subject to the unrelated business tax. (Sec. 18633, Rev. & Tax. Code) However, California does not conform to the federal requirement that all partnerships having more than 100 partners file returns on magnetic media. (Sec. 18409, Rev. & Tax. Code)

California law imposes a special penalty, in addition to other penalties discussed at ¶712, for failure to file a timely and proper partnership return. The penalty is $10 per month per partner, for a maximum of five months. (Sec. 19172, Rev. & Tax. Code) This conforms generally to a federal penalty that is imposed at the rate of $50 per month per partner. However, the federal exception to the imposition of penalties for certain small partnerships does not apply for California purposes.

A partnership carrying on no business in California and having no income from sources in California is not required to file a partnership return, even if the partnership consists of one or more California residents. However, if any partner is a California resident, a return must be filed if there is an election required to be made by the partnership, and the partners wish to obtain different California treatment with respect to the election than that chosen for federal purposes (*e.g.*, installment method, exclusion from partnership provisions, etc.).

Even if there are no partnership elections to be made and a return is not filed, a resident partner of a nonresident partnership may be required to submit information to determine whether or not there is any liability for California tax on partnership income; this may include information regarding the apportionment factors discussed in Chapter 13, as well as a copy of federal Form 1065.

Limited partnerships and limited liability partnerships that have a certificate on file or are registered with the Secretary of State must file a return even if they are not doing business in California. However, if the limited partnership has no income from California sources and is not carrying on any business in California, its reporting requirements may be reduced.

For information concerning a partnership's obligation to withhold on payments and distributions to nonresident partners, see ¶714.

¶623 Limited Liability Partnerships

Law: Sec. 12189, Government Code; Secs. 16101, 16951, 16953, 16956, 16959, Corporation Code; Secs. 17948—17948.2, Revenue and Taxation Code (CCH CALIFORNIA TAX REPORTS ¶10-225).

Comparable Federal: None.

California Form: Form 565 (Partnership Return of Income).

The formation of registered limited liability partnerships (LLPs) and the registration of foreign LLPs by legal, accounting, and architectural firms is authorized in California. (Sec. 16951, Corp. Code) A qualifying partnership, other than a limited partnership, may register as an LLP if all of the firm's partners are licensed, registered, or authorized to practice public accountancy, law, or, until January 1, 2012, architecture, either in California or in another jurisdiction. (Sec. 16101, Corp. Code)

A partnership that is related to an LLP and provides services related or complementary to the professional services provided by the LLP or provides services to the LLP may also register as an LLP. A partnership is considered related to an LLP if it meets one of the following requirements:

— at least a majority of the partners in one partnership are also partners in the other partnership;

— at least a majority in interest in each partnership hold interest or are members in another entity and each renders services pursuant to an agreement with that other entity; or

— one partnership controls, is controlled by, or is under common control with the other partnership. (Sec. 16101, Corp. Code)

• *LLPs subject to minimum tax*

An LLP must pay an annual nondeductible minimum tax if the LLP is doing business in California or has had its certificate of registration issued by the Secretary of State and has had a taxable year of more than 15 days. (Sec. 17948, Rev. & Tax. Code ; Sec. 17948.2, Rev. & Tax. Code) An LLP must continue to pay the tax until one of the following requirements are satisfied:

— the LLP files a notice of cessation with the California Secretary of State,

— a foreign LLP withdraws its registration, or

— the registered LLP or foreign LLP dissolves and is finally wound up.

See ¶816 for the minimum tax rate.

In addition, a registered LLP is relieved of liability for the minimum tax if it (1) files a timely final annual tax return for a taxable year with the Franchise Tax Board (FTB), (2) does not do business in California after the end of the taxable year for which the final annual tax return was filed, and (3) files a notice of cessation or similar document with the Secretary of State's Office before the end of the 12-month period beginning with the date the final annual tax return was filed. (Sec. 17948.3, Rev. & Tax. Code)

• *Registration requirements*

To register as an LLP or foreign LLP, a partnership must file a registration statement with the Secretary of State and pay a fee of $70. A foreign LLP that transacts intrastate business in California without registration is subject to a penalty of $20 per day, up to a maximum of $10,000. In addition, as part of the registration requirement, all LLPs are required to provide specified amounts of security against any claims that might arise against the LLP. (Sec. 12189, Gov't. Code; Sec. 16953, Corp. Code; Sec. 16956, Corp. Code; Sec. 16959, Corp. Code)

¶624 Electing Large Partnerships

Law: Sec. 17865 (CCH CALIFORNIA TAX REPORTS ¶10-230).

Comparable Federal: Secs. 771-777 (CCH U.S. MASTER TAX GUIDE ¶482 et seq.).

California does not incorporate the federal provisions that authorize electing large partnerships, which may use simplified reporting systems and significantly reduce the number of items that must be separately reported to their partners. (Sec. 17865, Rev. & Tax. Code) Consequently, such electing large partnerships are required to file California's partnership returns and comply with other California partnership reporting responsibilities (see ¶622).

An "electing large partnership" is any nonservice partnership that elects to apply certain simplified reporting provisions, provided that the number of qualifying partners in the partnership was at least 100 during the preceding tax year. An electing large partnership combines most items of partnership income, deduction, credit, and loss at the partnership level and passes through net amounts to the partners. Netting of capital gains and losses occurs at the partnership level, and passive activity items are separated from capital gains stemming from partnership portfolio income. Special rules apply to partnerships engaging in oil and gas activities.

¶625 Limited Liability Companies

Law: Sec. 17060, Corporations Code; Secs. 17087.6, 17941-46, 18535, 18633.5, 18662, 18666, 19172, 19394, 23038 (CCH CALIFORNIA TAX REPORTS ¶10-240, 89-102, 89-206).

Comparable Federal: Reg. 301.7701-2 (CCH U.S. MASTER TAX GUIDE ¶402A, 402B).

California Forms: Form 568 (Limited Liability Company Return of Income), FTB 3522 (Limited Liability Company Tax Voucher), FTB 3832 (Limited Liability Company Nonresident Members' Consent), Sch. K-1 (568) (Member's Share of Income, Deductions, Credits, etc.).

California authorizes the formation of limited liability companies (LLCs), whether or not for profit, and also allows foreign LLCs to qualify to do business in California. California conforms to federal "check-the-box" rules, and an LLC will be classified for California tax purposes according to the classification the LLC elects for federal purposes. (Sec. 23038, Rev. & Tax. Code)

However, an entity that is a previously existing foreign single member LLC that was classified as a corporation under pre-1997 California law but became a disregarded entity for federal purposes for post-1996 taxable years may continue to be classified differently for California and federal tax purposes. Such an entity may make an irrevocable election to be disregarded for California tax purposes as well, unless specified exceptions apply. The election is made on FTB 3574, Special Election for Business Trusts and Certain Foreign Single Member LLCs. (Reg. 23038, 18 CCR; Instructions, FTB 3574, Special Election for Business Trusts and Certain Foreign Single Member LLCs)

The taxes and fees discussed below apply to LLCs classified as partnerships or that are disregarded and taxed as a sole proprietorship for California tax purposes. LLCs classified as corporations remain subject to the same tax return and tax payment requirements as any other corporation.

California authorizes the formation of single member LLCs and allows a member of an LLC to have alter ego liability for the LLC's debts or other liabilities.

Each series in a Delaware Series LLC is considered a separate LLC and must file its own return and pay its own separate LLC fee and tax. (FTB Pub. 3556, Limited Liability Company Filing Information, July 2008, CCH CALIFORNIA TAX REPORTS ¶404-737)

• *Minimum tax*

An LLC that is classified as a partnership or that is disregarded and treated as a sole proprietorship for California tax purposes must pay an annual minimum tax if the LLC (1) is doing business in California or (2) has had its articles of organization accepted or a certificate of registration issued by the Secretary of State. The LLC is not liable for the tax if it did no business in California during the taxable year and the taxable year was 15 days or less.

CCH Caution: "Doing Business" Threshold Quite Low

In a nonprecedential decision, the State Board of Equalization (SBE) has ruled that the activities undertaken by a foreign LLC's California-resident managers on behalf of the LLC constituted "doing business" and therefore subjected the LLC to the minimum tax even though the LLC, which was formed to acquire and manage real estate, was not registered in California, its primary asset was real estate located in Montana, and the day-to-day management of the real estate was performed by a Montana real estate management company. The property purchasing negotiations conducted by the California-resident members were sufficient for purposes of satisfying the "doing business" threshold requirements, as was a loan transaction between the LLC and one of its members. The SBE held that it is not where property is located that is most germane to determining whether the LLC was conducting business in California, but where the activity of the business that owns that property occurred. (*Appeal of Mockingbird Partners, LLC* (2006) CCH CALIFORNIA TAX REPORTS ¶404-012)

A similar ruling was reached in another nonprecedential SBE decision concerning a Nevada LLC whose sole member was a California resident. The SBE found that the activities undertaken by the member constituted doing business in California because there was no evidence produced to demonstrate that he left California to conduct LLC business. (*International Health Institute, LLC* (2006) CCH CALIFORNIA TAX REPORTS ¶10-240.221)

A tiered entity is considered doing business in California if it is a nonregistered foreign LLC that is a member of an LLC doing business in California or it is a general partner in a limited partnership that is doing business in California. (FTB Pub. 3556, Limited Liability Company Filing Information, July 2008, CCH CALIFORNIA TAX REPORTS ¶404-737)

An LLC is relieved of liability for the minimum tax if it (1) files a timely final annual tax return for a taxable year with the Franchise Tax Board (FTB), (2) does not do business in California after the end of the taxable year for which the final annual tax return was filed, and (3) files a certificate of cancellation (Form LLC-4/7) with the Secretary of State's Office before the end of the 12-month period beginning with the date the final annual tax return was filed. (Sec. 17947, Rev. & Tax. Code)

Also, a domestic LLC that has not conducted any business in California and that files a short-form certificate of cancellation (Form LLC-4/8) with the Secretary of State's Office within 12 months from the date that the articles of organization were filed is exempt from the minimum tax, provided that the following criteria are satisfied:

— the LLC has no debts or liabilities, other than tax liabilities;

— the known assets of the LLC have been distributed to the entitled persons;

— the LLC has filed or will file a final tax return with the FTB;

— the dissolution of the LLC is authorized by a majority of the members or managers, or the person or majority of persons who signed the articles of organization; and

— all payments the LLC has received for interests from investors have been returned to the investors.

However, the LLC will not be entitled to a refund of any taxes or fees already paid. (Sec. 17941, Rev. & Tax. Code) (Instructions, Form 568, Limited Liability Company Return of Income) See ¶816 for the minimum tax rate.

The tax is due by the 15th day of the fourth month after the beginning of the taxable year. (The taxable year of an LLC that was not previously in existence begins when the LLC is organized, registered, or begins doing business in California.) If the 15th day of the fourth month of the taxable year has passed before an existing foreign LLC commences business in California or registers with the Secretary of State, the tax should be paid immediately after commencing business in California or registering with the Secretary of State. The LLC is liable for the tax until it files a certificate of cancellation of registration or of articles of organization with the California Secretary of State.

CCH Example: When to Pay the Annual LLC Tax

DDLLC, a newly formed calendar-year taxpayer, organizes as an LLC in Delaware on June 1. DDLLC registers with the California Secretary of State on August 12, and begins doing business in California on August 13. Because DDLLC's initial tax year began on June 1, it must pay an annual LLC tax by September 15 (the 15th day of the fourth month of its short-period taxable year). Thereafter, its annual LLC tax is due on April 15 of each year.

The minimum tax is submitted with FTB 3522, LLC Tax Voucher and should not be submitted along with the Form 568. (Instructions, Form 568, Limited Liability Company Return of Income)

• *Fee*

Additionally, other than exempt title-holding companies, every LLC classified as a partnership or treated as a sole proprietorship and subject to the minimum tax must pay an annual fee. The fees are permanently set as follows (Sec. 17942, Rev. & Tax. Code):

— $900 if the total income of the LLC from all sources derived from or attributable to California for the taxable year is at least $250,000 but less than $500,000;

— $2,500 if the LLC's total income derived from or attributable to California is at least $500,000 but less than $1 million;

— $6,000 if the LLC's total income derived from or attributable to California is at least $1 million but less than $5 million; and

— $11,790 if the total income derived from or attributable to California is $5 million or more.

For purposes of these provisions, California-source income is determined using the rules for assigning sales under California's apportionment provisions, other than those provisions that exclude receipts from the sales factor. (Sec. 17942, Rev. & Tax. Code)

Excluded from total income derived from or attributable to California are allocations or attributions of income, gain, or distributions to one LLC in its capacity as a member of, or holder of an economic interest in, another LLC if the allocations or attributions are directly or indirectly attributable to income that is included in determining the annual fee payable by the other LLC. If, however, multiple LLCs are formed primarily to reduce the annual fees payable by members of a group of commonly controlled LLCs, the FTB may determine that the total income of a commonly controlled LLC is the aggregate total income of *all* the commonly controlled group members. (Sec. 17942, Rev. & Tax. Code)

Prior to the 2007 taxable year, the fee was based on an LLC's worldwide income rather than on the LLC's California-source income.

CCH Comment: Constitutionality of Former LLC Fee Scheme

A California court of appeal has ruled that California's pre-2007 taxable year LLC fee scheme as applied to an out-of-state LLC that had registered as an LLC with the California Secretary of State's office but that had no income from activities in California amounted to an unfairly apportioned tax in violation of the U.S. Constitution's Commerce and Due Process Clauses. The court ordered a refund of all LLC fees paid by the out-of-state LLC, plus interest and penalties and the FTB did not appeal the portion of the ruling declaring the tax unconstitutional as applied to the taxpayer. (*Northwest Energetic Services, LLC v. California Franchise Tax Board*, (2008) 159 Cal.App. 4th 841, CCH CALIFORNIA TAX REPORTS ¶404-550) Another California court of appeal also found that the LLC fee was an unconstitutional unapportioned tax, but held that in the case of a taxpayer with income from both inside and outside California, the proper remedy to be applied to the unapportioned tax was to refund the difference between the amount of the fee paid by the taxpayer and the amount of the fee that would have been required had the fee been fairly apportioned. (*Ventas Finance I, LLC v. California Franchise Tax Board*, (2008) 165 Cal.App.4th 1207, petition for review denied, California Supreme Court, No. S166870, November 13, 2008, CCH CALIFORNIA TAX REPORTS ¶404-709). Another case that challenges the constitutionality of the LLC fee as applied to an LLC that conducted all of its activities in California is pending in the San Francisco Superior Court (*Bakersfield Mall, LLC v. Franchise Tax Board*, San Francisco Superior Court, No. CGC-07-462728).

The FTB has outlined the procedures that taxpayers with no income from activities in California should follow to have their refunds processed in light of the California Court of Appeal's final decision in *Northwest Energetic Services*, see *FTB Notice 2008-2*, April 14, 2008, CCH CALIFORNIA TAX REPORTS ¶404-656. LLCs with income attributable solely to California or with income attributable to sources both inside and outside California should follow the protective claim procedures outlined by the FTB on its Web site.

Legislation enacted in 2007 (Ch. 381 (A.B. 198), Laws 2007), revised the basis of the fee from one based on the LLC's total income to the LLC's total income apportionable to California, but only on a prospective basis. The Legislature stated its intent that no inference be drawn in connection with the legislative amendments for any taxable year beginning before 2007. However, for refund actions filed after October 10, 2007, or for refund actions filed prior to such date that are not final as of October 10, 2007, if the LLC fee as imposed prior to the 2007 taxable year is finally adjudged to be discriminatory or unfairly apportioned under California or federal law, the fee of any disfavored taxpayer that files a timely claim for refund asserting discrimination or unfair apportionment will be recomputed, but only to the extent necessary to remedy the discrimination or unfair apportionment. Such refunds will be limited to the amount by which the fee paid, plus any interest assessed, exceeds the amount of the fee that would have been assessed if the fee had been determined pursuant to the new provisions. (Sec. 19394, Rev. & Tax. Code)

Payment of fee: The annual fee is due on the original due date of the return, which is the 15th day of the 4th month following the close of the LLC's taxable year. However, beginning with the 2009 taxable year, LLCs are required to make an estimated LLC fee payment by the 15th day of the sixth month of the current taxable year. A 10% underpayment penalty will be imposed if the estimated fee paid by the LLC is less than the amount of the fee actually due and payable with the LLC's return. However, no penalty will be imposed if the estimated fee equals or exceeds the amount of the fee paid by the LLC in the preceding taxable year.

• *Returns*

LLCs classified as partnerships: An LLC classified as a partnership must file a return (Form 568) by the 15th day of the fourth month after the close of its taxable year. (Sec. 18633.5, Rev. & Tax. Code) LLC returns may be filed electronically. The LLC must attach to the return a Schedule K-1 (568) for each member containing the member's name, address, and taxpayer identification number and the amount of the member's distributive share of the LLC's income, deductions, credits, etc. Also, when the LLC files its return, it must do one of the following:

— attach the agreement of each nonresident member to file a return, make timely tax payments, and be subject to personal jurisdiction in this state for purposes of the collection of income taxes (FTB 3832) (see ¶619 for details), or

— pay tax on behalf of each nonconsenting nonresident member, computed by multiplying the member's distributive share of income by the highest marginal tax rate in effect.

The return must be verified by a written declaration that it is made under the penalties of perjury, and it must be signed by one of the LLC members or managers. A copy of each member's Schedule K-1 (568) must be provided to that member. Unrelated business taxable income of an LLC must be separately stated to the members.

Penalties are authorized for the failure to file an LLC return or provide LLC information as required by the FTB. (Sec. 19172, Rev. & Tax. Code) Penalties are discussed in detail at ¶712.

LLCs treated as sole proprietorships: An owner of an LLC that is disregarded and treated as a sole proprietorship is required to file a California return if the LLC is doing business in California, is organized in California, or is registered with the Secretary of State. The return must contain information necessary to verify the tax liability for the minimum tax and LLC fees and must be filed by the 15th day of the fourth month after the close of the owner's taxable year. If the owner fails to comply with the reporting and payment requirements, the LLC will be liable for California tax at an amount equal to the highest marginal tax rate and will be subject to penalties and interest for failure to timely pay the amount due.

LLCs with nonresident members: An LLC with nonresident members must file FTB 3832, Limited Liability Company Nonresident Members' Consent, along with Form 568, when one of its members is a nonresident of California. Form FTB 3832 must be filed for the first taxable period for which the LLC became subject to tax with nonresident members and for any taxable year in which the LLC had a nonresident member not previously listed on form FTB 3832 (Instructions, Form FTB 3832, Limited Liability Company Nonresident Members' Consent). The LLC is required to pay the tax on the member's distributive share of income at that member's highest marginal tax rate if the member fails to sign FTB 3832.

Nonregistered foreign LLCs: Nonregistered foreign LLCs that are not doing business in, but that are deriving income from California or that are filing to report an election on behalf of a California resident, should file Form 565, Partnership Return of Income. Nonregistered foreign LLCs that are members of an LLC doing business in California or general partners in a limited partnership doing business in California are considered doing business in California and are required to file a Form 568, Limited Liability Company Return of Income. (Instructions, Form 568 Booklet, Limited Liability Return of Income)

CCH Comment: LLC Suspension/Forfeiture Program

Beginning in early 2009, the FTB will begin to suspend/forfeit the rights, powers, and privileges of LLCs for nonpayment of taxes, penalties, or interest, and/or failure to file a return. The FTB will send notification to all entities at their last known addresses, 60 days before imposing the suspension/forfeiture. Nonregistered LLCs acting and filing in California will be subject to contract voidability. The reasons for contract voidability are the same as for suspension/forfeiture: failure to file a return, and/or failure to pay taxes, penalties, or interest. (*Tax News*, California Franchise Tax Board, October 2008, CCH CALIFORNIA TAX REPORTS ¶404-769)

• *Withholding*

An LLC may be subject to three different withholding requirements. An LLC is required to withhold on amounts paid to nonresident domestic members, but only if the income paid to the nonresident exceeds $1,500 during the calendar year or the LLC is directed to withhold by the FTB. (Sec. 18662, Rev. & Tax. Code; Reg. 18662-2, 18 CCR) The tax is equal to 7% of the amount actually distributed to the member. (Sec. 18662, Rev. & Tax. Code; Reg. 18662-3, 18 CCR)

Different rules apply to the withholding required for LLCs treated as partnerships for amounts paid to nonresident foreign members. These amounts are subject to withholding at the highest personal income tax rate and are applied to the nonresident's distributive share of income. (Sec. 18666, Rev. & Tax. Code)

Finally, if the LLC fails to file an nonresident member agreement to file a California return, the LLC must pay withholding on behalf of the nonresident member in an amount equal to the highest marginal tax rate in effect multiplied by the member's distributive share of LLC income, and reduced by any withholding amounts previously paid under either of the withholding requirements discussed above. (Sec. 18633.5, Rev. & Tax. Code). This is referred to as the nonconsenting nonresident's (NCNR) withholding tax. Because the NCNR tax is imposed at the same rate and on the same tax base as the foreign nonresident withholding tax, an LLC is not required to pay any additional NCNR withholding tax for nonresident foreign members for whom an agreement to file and pay tax was not filed.

However, an LLC must pay additional NCNR withholding tax on behalf of nonresident domestic members for whom an agreement was not filed. The withholding applies to those domestic nonresident members that do not satisfy the $1,500 threshold requirement of the domestic member withholding tax and also applies to the difference between the highest tax rate (up to 9.3% for individuals and up to 8.84% for corporations) and the 7% tax rate imposed under Sec. 18662. Additional amounts may also be due as a result of the different tax bases. The domestic nonresident member withholding tax is imposed on the amount actually distributed to members, while the NCNR withholding tax is imposed on the nonresident's distributive share of income allocable to California.

Example: Computing the NCNR withholding tax. — A nonresident domestic member had a $1,000 distributive share of income allocable to California, and only $900 was actually distributed. Under the domestic nonresident withholding requirements, the LLC is required to pay the $63 in withholding tax ($900 x 7%). If the LLC does not timely file the agreement, then the LLC is responsible for paying an additional NCNR member's tax of $30. This is equal to the difference between $93 (the tax due by multiplying 9.3% x $1,000) and the $63 previously paid.

For more detailed information concerning an LLC's withholding at source requirements and procedures, see ¶714.

• *Returns of LLC members*

Persons with membership or economic interests in an LLC are required to include in their California taxable income their share of the LLC's California-source income in the same manner as partners must include their distributive share of partnership income in their taxable income (¶619, 620). (Sec. 17087.6, Rev. & Tax. Code) As with nonresident partners of a partnership, nonresident members of an LLC may elect to file a group income tax return in lieu of filing individual returns (¶619). (Sec. 18535, Rev. & Tax. Code) The filing of FTB 3832, Limited Liability Company Nonresident Members' Consent, does not relieve the nonresident member from filing a California tax return.

Planning Note: Inconsistent Items

Generally, members must report tax items shown on their Sch. K-1s and any attached schedules, the same way the LLC treated the items on its tax return. If the treatment on a member's return is inconsistent with the LLC treatment, or the LLC did not file a return, the member is required to attach a statement explaining the difference or to note that an LLC return has not been filed. Failure to attach this statement may result in the imposition of an accuracy-related penalty (see ¶712). (Instructions, Schedule K-1 (568), Members' Share of Income, Deductions, Credits, etc.)

• *Report to Secretary of State*

LLCs are required to file with the Secretary of State a biennial report showing names of managers or members and other information. The first report must be filed within 90 days of filing original articles of organization. Thereafter, reports are due biennially by the date indicated by the Secretary of State on the form mailed to the LLC. LLCs may file a brief statement in lieu of the biennial report in cases where no changes have occurred during the filing period. (Sec. 17060, Corp. Code)

PERSONAL INCOME TAX

CHAPTER 7
ADMINISTRATION, DEFICIENCIES, REFUNDS

¶701 Administration of Tax—General

Law: Secs. 5054 , 22250–22255, Bus. & Prof. Code; Sec. 13943.1, Govt. Code; Secs. 18624-25, 19167, 19501-11, 19525, 19717, 21001-26, Rev. & Tax. Code (CCH CALIFORNIA TAX REPORTS ¶34-601, 89-054—89-060, 89-064, 89-068, 89-222, 89-226).

Comparable Federal: Secs. 6060, 6107, 6109, 6694-96, 7421, 7430, 7811 (CCH U.S. MASTER TAX GUIDE ¶2517, 2518, 2719, 2796, 2707).

California income tax law is administered by the Franchise Tax Board (FTB), composed of the State Controller, the Director of the Department of Finance, and the Chairman of the State Board of Equalization. The chief administrative officer is the Executive Officer of the FTB. The FTB has broad powers to prescribe necessary rules and regulations, etc.

Practice Tip: Taxpayer Information Available on FTB's Web Site

The *My FTB Account* service available on the FTB's Web site enables taxpayers and practitioners to view the following information for a particular taxpayer:

— a taxpayer's last 25 estimated tax payments;

— up to 60 recent payments made by a taxpayer and applied to a balance due and the total current balance due;

— a summary of up to 10 tax years with a balance due;

— a maximum of four years of California wage and withholding information; and

— up to three years of FTB-issued 1099-G and 1099-INT information.

In the future the FTB plans to expand the service to enable taxpayers to make a payment, check a refund status, or check an e-file status from the *My FTB Account* site. To access the information currently available, enter "my account" in the search bar of the FTB's Web site at http://www.ftb.ca.gov.

If an audit of a return is concluded with no change, the FTB will notify the taxpayer to that effect; this procedure is similar to the federal one. For the procedure in case of underpayment or overpayment, see subsequent paragraphs in this chapter.

The FTB and the Internal Revenue Service have exchanged tax-related data for many years. When an audit is conducted by either the FTB or the IRS, the results are reported to the other entity. See ¶106 regarding required California reporting of federal changes by taxpayers.

• *Tax-return preparers*

Tax preparers must do the following:

— maintain a $5,000 bond for each individual preparing tax returns for another person;

— provide in writing to each customer the tax preparer's name, address, telephone number, and evidence of compliance with the bonding requirements before rendering tax return preparation services; and

— meet stringent educational requirements.

(Sec. 22250, Bus. & Prof. Code; Sec. 22252, Bus. & Prof. Code; Sec. 22255, Bus. & Prof. Code)

Conversely, tax preparers are prohibited from doing the following:

— making deposits instead of complying with the bonding requirements;

— making false, fraudulent, or misleading statements;

— having taxpayers sign documents containing blank spaces to be filled in after they have been signed;

— failing to sign taxpayers' returns;

— failing to maintain copies of returns prepared for customers; and

— failing to return taxpayers' records upon request.

(Sec. 22253, Bus. & Prof. Code)

Practice Tip: Signature Requirements

California tax returns, including corporation franchise and income, personal income, and sales and use tax returns, that are prepared by an employee of a tax preparer who is exempt from the California Tax Education Council (CTEC) registration requirements must be signed by a California certified public accountant, attorney, enrolled agent, or a tax preparer who is registered with the CTEC. However, this requirement does not apply to employees who are themselves exempt from the CTEC registration requirements, who are registered with the CTEC, or who are employees of a trust company or financial institution, at least with respect to the returns prepared within the scope of their employment. Tax return preparation includes inputting of tax data into a computer. (Sec. 22258, Bus. & Prof. Code)

Tax preparers must be at least age 18. Currently licensed public accountants, active members of the State Bar, employees of certain trust companies, financial institutions regulated by the state or federal government, and enrolled agents who practice before the IRS are exempt from compliance with the provisions governing tax preparers. (Sec. 22250, Bus. & Prof. Code)

An individual or firm holding a valid and current license, certificate, or permit to practice public accountancy from another state may prepare tax returns for natural persons who are California residents or estate tax returns for the estates of natural persons who were clients at the time of death without obtaining a California permit to practice public accountancy or a practice privilege so long as the individual or firm does not physically enter California to practice public accountancy, does not solicit California clients, and does not assert or imply that the individual or firm is licensed or registered to practice public accountancy in California. (Sec. 5054, Bus. & Prof. Code)

Federal law also provides for the regulation of "income tax preparers." California law conforms to federal requirements for furnishing copies of returns to taxpayers, retaining certain records, and providing identification numbers (social security numbers or IRS-approved alternatives) of preparers on returns and refund claims. (Sec. 18624, Rev. & Tax. Code; Sec. 186245, Rev. & Tax. Code)

Violations.—The FTB is required to notify the California Tax Education Council (CTEC) when it identifies an individual who has violated specific provisions regulating tax preparers. The CTEC is required to notify the Attorney General, a district attorney, or a city attorney of the violation, and the person so notified may do any of the following:

— cite individuals preparing tax returns in violation of provisions governing tax preparers;

— levy a fine on such individuals not to exceed $5,000 per violation; and

— issue a cease and desist order effective until the tax preparer is in compliance with the registration requirement. (Sec. 22253.2, Bus. & Prof. Code)

In addition, the FTB is authorized to impose a penalty of up to $5,000 ($2,500 for first-time offenders) against a tax preparer that fails, without reasonable cause, to register with the CTEC. The penalty must be waived if proof of registration is provided to the FTB within 90 days from the date notice of the penalty is mailed to the tax preparer. The penalty will not be imposed unless there is an appropriation in the FTB's budget to implement the penalty or the CTEC agrees to finance the program. (Sec. 19167, Rev. & Tax. Code)

Other penalties are discussed at ¶712.

Confidentiality.—A tax preparer is prohibited, except in specified circumstances, from disclosing confidential information concerning a client or a prospective client without obtaining the client's written consent. However, tax preparers are allowed to make the following disclosures:

— in compliance with a subpoena or a summons enforceable by an order of court;

— regarding a client or prospective client to the extent the tax preparer reasonably believes it is necessary to maintain or defend himself or herself in a legal proceeding initiated by the client or prospective client;

— in response to an official inquiry from a federal or state government regulatory agency;

— to another tax preparer in connection with a proposed sale or merger of the tax preparer's professional practice;

— to another tax preparer to the extent necessary for purposes of professional consultation;

— to organizations that provide professional standards review and ethics or quality control peer review; and

— when specifically required by law.

(Sec. 22252.1, Bus. & Prof. Code)

• *Issuance of rulings by FTB*

See ¶703 for a discussion.

• *FTB audit and procedure manuals*

The FTB has issued several audit and procedure manuals for the guidance of its staff. These manuals may be purchased from the Technical Analysis Section of the FTB; prices will be quoted upon request. The manuals are also available on-line at http://www.ftb.ca.gov/aboutFTB/manuals/index.shtml.

• *Recovery of litigation costs*

California law follows federal provisions that permit a taxpayer to recover litigation costs in a civil income tax proceeding if the taxpayer has exhausted all available administrative remedies, including the filing of an appeal before the State Board of Equalization, and the State is unable to establish that its position in the proceeding was substantially justified. (Sec. 21021, Rev. & Tax. Code)

Practitioner Comment: Taxpayer is Reimbursed Litigation Costs by California

On August 15, 2005, the California Court of Appeal, Fourth Appellate District, ruled in an unciteable decision that taxpayers were entitled to recover attorney fees incurred in litigation contesting the California FTB's denial of their California personal income tax refund claim. According to the Court, the FTB's position in the litigation was not substantially justified, so reimbursement of the taxpayers' attorney fees incurred during the trial, as well as the fees associated with filing the initial refund claim, participating in settlement negotiations, and opposing the FTB's motion for summary judgment was appropriate. The Court also ruled, however, that the lower court acted within its discretion in denying reimbursement for (1) attorney fees incurred in filing an unsuccessful cross-motion for summary judgment and (2) amounts billed the attorneys for outside paralegal services. (*Milhous v. Franchise Tax Board*, California Court of Appeal, Fourth Appellate District, No. D044362, August 15, 2005, CCH CALIFORNIA TAX REPORTS ¶403-845)

The holding in *Milhous* makes it clear that while the FTB's position does not have to be a winning one, it does have to be justified. The Court stated, "...there is no basis upon which the FTB could attribute the lump sum payment the Milhouses received (at the close of the sale and before the buyers had control of the business) to capital in this state . . . .there was a good deal which undermined the FTB's position that income from the covenant was attributable to activities in this state. In particular, we note the quantum of evidence in the record which demonstrated that the covenant had no value in California because as a practical matter it was not possible to compete here."

Taxpayers should keep in mind that even if they prevail against the FTB, they still must exhaust all administrative remedies and they bear the burden of proving the FTB's position is not "substantially justified."

Attorney fees were also awarded to taxpayers in *American General Realty Investment Corp. v. Franchise Tax Board*, San Francisco Sup. Court, No. CGC-03-425690, April 28, 2005, CCH CALIFORNIA TAX REPORTS ¶403-794, and *Fujitsu IT Holdings, Inc. v. Franchise Tax Board*, California Court of Appeal, First Appellate District, No. A102550, July 7, 2004, CCH CALIFORNIA TAX REPORTS ¶403-655.

Bruce Daigh, Chris Whitney, Contributing Editors

• *Taxpayers' bill of rights*

The legislature provides for the safeguarding of taxpayer privacy and property rights during the tax collection process. See ¶702 for a discussion.

• *Enforcement program*

Additional information returns, including returns of tax-shelter promoters, are required as explained at ¶713 and ¶727. The FTB is empowered to employ private in-state as well as out-of-state collection agencies and add their compensation to the amount of tax due. The FTB may establish a reward program for information leading to the collection of underreported taxes.

• *Discharge of tax debts*

The FTB is authorized to discharge and extinguish the following liabilities for unpaid taxes, fees, or other uncollectible amounts due the state :

— a liability of less than $250;

— a liability of a person who has been deceased for more than four years for whom there is no active probate;

— a liability of a person with a permanent financial hardship; or

— a liability that has been unpaid for more than 30 years.

(Sec. 13943.1, Bus. & Prof. Code)

¶702 Taxpayers' Bill of Rights

Law: Secs. 19225, 21001-28 (CCH CALIFORNIA TAX REPORTS ¶89-222).

Comparable Federal: Sec. 7811 (CCH U.S. MASTER TAX GUIDE ¶2755, 2707, 2708).

Taxpayers dealing with the Franchise Tax Board (FTB) are given a wide range of protections under the "Katz-Harris Taxpayers' Bill of Rights". (Sec. 21001, Rev. & Tax. Code) The provisions contained in the "Bill of Rights" are applicable to both the personal income and corporation franchise and income taxes. Similar "bills of rights" apply to unemployment insurance tax matters involving the Employment Development Department (¶715) and property and sales and use tax matters involving the State Board of Equalization (SBE) (¶1510, ¶1709).

• *Hearing and appeal procedures*

Protest hearings before the FTB's audit or legal staff must be held at times and places that are reasonable and convenient to the taxpayer. Prior to the hearing, the taxpayer must be informed of the right to have a designated agent present. Hearings may be recorded only with prior notice to the taxpayer, who is entitled to receive a copy of any such recording. (Sec. 21001, Rev. & Tax. Code) Protest hearings are discussed further at ¶704.

Taxpayers who appeal to the SBE and who are successful may be awarded reimbursement for reasonable fees and expenses related to the appeal that were incurred after the date of the notice of proposed deficiency assessment. The decision to make such an award is discretionary with the SBE, which must determine, in ruling on a reimbursement claim filed with the SBE, whether action taken by the FTB's staff was unreasonable, and in particular, whether the FTB has established that its position in the appeal was substantially justified. Fees may be awarded in excess of the fees paid or incurred if the fees paid or incurred are less than reasonable fees. (Sec. 21013, Rev. & Tax. Code) See ¶701 for more details.

For appeals to the SBE from an action of the FTB on a deficiency assessment protest or refund claim, the burden of proving the correctness of certain items of income reported by third parties on information returns filed with the FTB also shifts to the FTB if the taxpayer asserts a reasonable dispute with respect to the reported amounts and fully cooperates with the FTB. The items of income to which the shift applies are the same as under federal law. (Sec. 21024, Rev. & Tax. Code)

Appeals to the SBE are discussed further at ¶705 and ¶717.

• *Tax levy protections*

The FTB must send a notice of levy to a taxpayer at least 30 days prior to issuing a levy for unpaid tax. Also, if the FTB holds the collection of unpaid tax in abeyance for more than six months, the FTB is generally required to mail the taxpayer an additional notice prior to issuing a levy. A taxpayer may, within the 30-day period, request an independent administrative review and if a review is requested the levy action will be suspended until 15 days after there is a final determination in the review. (Sec. 21015.5, Rev. & Tax. Code)

Except in the case of property seized as a result of a jeopardy assessment, a previously issued tax levy must be released in the following situations:

— the expense of selling the property levied upon would exceed the taxpayer's liability;

— the proceeds of the sale would not result in a reasonable reduction of the taxpayer's debt;

— a determination is made by the Taxpayer Rights Advocate that the levy threatens the health or welfare of the taxpayer or the taxpayer's family;

— the levy was not issued in accordance with administrative procedures;

— the taxpayer has entered into an installment payment agreement with the FTB to satisfy the tax liability for which the levy was made, and nothing in the agreement or any other agreement allows for the levy;

— the release of the levy will facilitate the collection of the tax liability or will be in the best interest of the taxpayer and the State; or

— the FTB otherwise deems the release of the levy appropriate.

(Sec. 21016, Rev. & Tax. Code)

Certain household and other goods are exempted from levy under California's Code of Civil Procedure. The taxpayer must be notified in writing of these exemptions prior to the sale of any seized property. (Sec. 21017, Rev. & Tax. Code)

The FTB must release a levy on salary or wages as soon as practicable upon agreement with the taxpayer that the tax is not collectible. However, this requirement does not apply to any levy issued with respect to a debt that has been discharged because the tax debtor and/or the tax debtor's assets cannot be located, unless the debt is satisfied. (Sec. 21016, Rev. & Tax. Code)

• *Civil actions against the FTB; litigation costs*

Taxpayers aggrieved by the reckless disregard of the FTB's published procedures on the part of an officer or employee of the FTB may bring a superior court action against the state for actual damages. In determining damages, the court must take into consideration any contributing negligence on the taxpayer's part. A taxpayer who prevails in such an action is entitled to reasonable litigation costs, but there is a penalty of up to $10,000 for filing frivolous claims. (Sec. 21021, Rev. & Tax. Code)

Taxpayers may also file a civil action against the State for direct economic damages and costs totaling up to $50,000 if an officer or employee of the FTB intentionally entices an attorney, certified public accountant, or tax preparer representing the taxpayer into disclosing taxpayer information in exchange for a compromise or settlement of the representative's tax liability. However, the action is not allowed if the information was conveyed by the taxpayer to the representative for the purpose of perpetuating a fraud or crime. The action must be brought within two years after the date the activities creating the liability were discoverable by the exercise of reasonable care. (Sec. 21022, Rev. & Tax. Code)

• *Reimbursement of third-party charges and fees*

A taxpayer may be reimbursed for third-party charges and fees assessed against a person as a result of an erroneous levy, erroneous processing action, or erroneous collection action by the FTB. The charges and fees that may be reimbursed are limited to the usual and customary charges and fees imposed by a business entity in the ordinary course of business. (Sec. 21018, Rev. & Tax. Code)

• *Reliance on FTB written opinions; taxpayers' remedies*

See ¶703 for a complete discussion.

• *Tax liens*

A taxpayer is entitled to preliminary notice of the proposed filing or recording of a tax lien, mailed at least 30 days beforehand, and an opportunity in the interim to demonstrate by substantial evidence that the lien would be in error. Also, at least five business days after the date the notice of lien is filed the FTB must notify taxpayers in writing of the filing or recording of a notice of state tax lien and the taxpayer's right to an independent administrative review. A taxpayer must request a review during the 15-day period beginning on the day after the five-day period described above. (Sec. 21019, Rev. & Tax. Code)

The FTB must mail a release to the taxpayer and the lien recorder within seven working days if it finds that its action was in error. The FTB may also release a lien if it determines that the release will facilitate the collection of tax or will be in the best interest of the taxpayer and the State.

• *Unassociated payments*

If the FTB receives a payment from a taxpayer that the FTB cannot associate with the taxpayer's account, the FTB must make reasonable efforts to notify the taxpayer of this situation within 60 days after receipt of the payment. (Sec. 21025, Rev. & Tax. Code)

• *Annual notice of tax delinquencies*

The FTB must mail an annual notice to each taxpayer who has a delinquent tax account, indicating the amount of the delinquency as of the date of the notice, unless a previously mailed notice has been returned to the FTB as undeliverable or the account has been discharged from accountability. (Sec. 21026, Rev. & Tax. Code)

• *Client/tax practitioner communications*

California conforms until January 1, 2009, to federal law extending the lawyer-client privilege to communications between clients and federally authorized tax practitioners with respect to non-criminal tax matters before the FTB, the SBE, or the Employment Development Department. (Sec. 21028, Rev. & Tax. Code)

• *Other provisions*

The Taxpayers' Bill of Rights also obligates the FTB to undertake extensive taxpayer education and information programs; report annually to the legislature concerning areas of noncompliance with the tax laws; develop simplified written statements of taxpayer rights and FTB procedures; develop and implement an employee and officer evaluation program; and draw up plans to reduce the time required to resolve amended return claims for refunds, protests, and appeals. (Sec. 21001, Rev. & Tax. Code) The FTB is authorized to settle certain civil tax disputes (¶722) and the Taxpayers' Rights Advocate is authorized to abate penalties, interest, fees, and additions to tax under specified circumstances (¶712). FTB officers and employees are prohibited from authorizing, requiring, or conducting an investigation or surveillance of taxpayers for reasons unrelated to tax administration. (Sec. 21014, Rev. & Tax. Code)

¶703 Reliance on FTB's Advice

Law: Sec. 21012 (CCH CALIFORNIA TAX REPORTS ¶89-222, 89-226).

Comparable Federal: Sec. 6404(f) (CCH U.S. MASTER TAX GUIDE ¶2813, 2838).

Under the "Taxpayers' Bill of Rights" (¶702), taxpayers may be relieved from penalties, interest, and even tax liability itself in certain cases in which there was detrimental reliance on written advice from the Franchise Tax Board (FTB). (Sec. 21012, Rev. & Tax. Code)

• *Taxpayer's reliance on FTB rulings*

The following concerns the waiver of tax, penalties, and interest in situations in which the taxpayer relied on the FTB's own written advice (FTB Notice No. 89-277, CCH CALIFORNIA TAX REPORTS ¶89-222.402):

—*Waiver of tax:* If a taxpayer's failure to timely file or pay is due to reasonable reliance on a Chief Counsel Ruling or an Opinion Letter, the taxpayer may be relieved—under the proper conditions (see below)—of having to pay *the tax itself,* as well as any interest, penalty, or addition to the tax.

—*Waiver of penalties, interest, and additions to tax only:* If the taxpayer relies on FTB correspondence other than Chief Counsel Rulings or Opinion Letters, such as standard computer-generated letters issued in response to frequently asked questions, the taxpayer may be relieved—under the proper conditions (see below)—of having to pay any interest, penalty, or addition to the tax. The taxpayer will not be relieved of having to pay the tax itself.

—*Conditions for waiver:* All of the following conditions must be met for the taxpayer to receive a waiver:

— the taxpayer must have made a written request that the FTB indicate whether a particular activity or transaction is taxable and must have described in the request all of the facts and circumstances involved;

— the FTB must have responded in writing, stating whether the activity was taxable or the conditions under which it would be taxable;

— the taxpayer must have failed to remit tax in reliance on the FTB's advice;

— the FTB's ruling must not have been revoked before the taxpayer relied on it; and

— there must have been no change in applicable state or federal law or in the facts or circumstances of the taxpayer's case.

• *How to make a proper advance ruling request*

A written request for an advance ruling must contain the taxpayer's name, identifying number, and a statement of all facts relating to the transaction from which the tax question arises. In addition, the request must disclose if the same question arose in (1) a prior year's return, (2) an ongoing audit, protest, or appeal, or (3) litigation involving the taxpayer (FTB Notice No. 89-277, *supra*).

Practice Tip: How a Taxpayer May Seek Relief

If the FTB acts in a way that appears inconsistent with its written advice to the taxpayer, the taxpayer may seek relief following one of two courses. If the advice was not issued by the FTB's legal division, the taxpayer must file FTB 3910 (Request for Waiver of Tax, Penalty or Interest). If the advice was issued by the FTB's Chief Counsel or another member of the FTB's legal division, the taxpayer must mail a written request for relief to the Chief Counsel, enclosing the following:

— a copy of the original written request for an opinion and the FTB's written response,

— documentation of the adverse action subsequently taken by the FTB, and

— a sworn statement that describes the activity or transaction in which the taxpayer engaged and that states that the failure to remit tax was due to reliance on the FTB's opinion. The request for relief must be made separately from any protest or appeal filed by the taxpayer.

Also, see ¶712 for a discussion of the Taxpayers' Rights Advocate's authority to abate penalties, interest, and additions to tax under specified circumstances.

• *Oral advice*

The FTB may also respond to individual queries with nonbinding oral advice, which is purely advisory. A taxpayer who relies on such advice is not entitled to the relief provisions of the Taxpayers' Bill of Rights (FTB Notice No. 89-277, *supra*).

• *Effect of federal regulations and procedures*

The FTB will generally follow federal regulations, procedures, and rulings in situations in which the California provisions substantially conform to those of federal law. However, federal rulings and procedures are not binding on the FTB if the FTB has publicly indicated in writing that the federal ruling or procedure will not be followed (FTB Notice No. 89-277, *supra*).

¶704 Deficiencies—Procedure, Protests

Law: Secs. 18416, 19031-36, 19041-44, 19050-51, 19133 (CCH CALIFORNIA TAX REPORTS ¶89-164, 89-228, 89-238, 89-240).

Comparable Federal: Secs. 6103, 6201, 6211-13 (CCH U.S. MASTER TAX GUIDE ¶2711—2713).

If the Franchise Tax Board (FTB) determines after examining an original or amended return or related electronically stored return that additional tax is payable, it may proceed in any one of the following ways:

— if the additional tax is due to a mathematical error, the FTB sends the taxpayer a notice and requests payment of the tax; the taxpayer has no right of protest or appeal in such cases (Sec. 19051, Rev. & Tax. Code);

— if the FTB is of the opinion that collection of the deficiency will be jeopardized by delay, it may make a jeopardy assessment (¶707);

— if the taxpayer fails to make a required return after notice and demand by the FTB, the FTB may estimate the income and levy the tax from any available information; in such cases the tax is immediately due and payable, without administrative remedies prior to payment, and a special penalty of 25% of the tax is added (¶712); and

— in other cases the FTB will mail to the taxpayer a notice of proposed deficiency assessment (sometimes referred to as an NPA), which must include an explanation of the adjustments made, a computation of the deficiency, and the date determined by the FTB as the last day on which the taxpayer may file a written protest.

(Sec. 19033, Rev. & Tax. Code)

These procedures may also be followed if the return or data is unavailable and the taxpayer fails to provide the return within 30 days (60 days if good cause exists) of a request by the FTB.

Comment: Notice Procedures

The FTB must mail notices to the taxpayer's last known address, which is defined as the address that appears on the taxpayer's last return filed with the FTB, unless the taxpayer has provided to the FTB clear and concise written or electronic notification of a different address, or the FTB has an address it has reason to believe is the most current address for the taxpayer. (Sec. 18416, Rev. & Tax. Code) In addition, all notices concerning proposed and final deficiencies must include a U.S. postal service postmark. (Sec. 19033, Rev. & Tax. Code, Sec. 19049, Rev. & Tax. Code)

In *Appeal of Holland* (2004) (CCH CALIFORNIA TAX REPORTS ¶89-164.451), a case in which a taxpayer failed to report federal changes made to a tax return filed more than 10 years earlier, the State Board of Equalization (SBE) held that the FTB's estimate of the taxpayer's income that was based on the use of an income figure in the median amount of taxable income corresponding to a zero tax liability was arbitrary and unreasonable given that the federal returns for the corresponding year showed the taxpayer's taxable income to be less than the FTB's estimate by more than $300,000. Because the FTB had access to the federal returns and to electronically stored data concerning the taxpayer's income for the taxable year at issue, the SBE refused to uphold the FTB's estimated income figure.

In *Appeal of Melvin D. Collamore* (1972) (CCH CALIFORNIA TAX REPORTS ¶16-825.89), involving the personal income tax, and in *Appeal of Kung Wo Company, Inc.* (1953) (CCH CALIFORNIA TAX REPORTS ¶89-144.70), involving the franchise tax, the SBE held that the FTB can properly make two deficiency assessments against a taxpayer for the same taxable year.

• *Carryover adjustments*

The FTB may serve a taxpayer with notice of a proposed carryover adjustment in regards to any amount of credit, loss, deduction, or any other item shown on a return, including an amended return reporting federal adjustments, if the FTB determines that the amount disclosed by the taxpayer is greater than that disclosed by the FTB's own examination. The proposed adjustment becomes final 30 days after its determination, unless either the FTB or the taxpayer files a petition for rehearing within that 30-day period. Once final, the FTB's carryover adjustment is binding and conclusive except in certain circumstances. A taxpayer's failure to comply with a final carryover adjustment in subsequent tax years is treated as a mathematical error, precluding a taxpayer from subsequent appeals. (Sec. 19043.5, Rev. & Tax. Code)

• *Protest*

A taxpayer who does not agree with the notice of proposed deficiency assessment may file a protest. The protest must be filed within 60 days from the mailing date of the notice of proposed assessment. Other than extensions available for military personnel serving in combat zones (¶109) and disaster victims (Sec. 18572, Rev. & Tax. Code), there is no provision for extension of time for filing a protest. Any protest filed by the last day for filing the protest, as specified by the FTB in a notice of proposed deficiency assessment, will be treated as timely filed. (Sec. 19041, Rev. & Tax. Code)

The FTB has established internal procedures pursuant to which it will attempt to process all docketed protests filed after July 1, 2006, within a two-year period. Protests will be categorized as 12-month, 18-month, or 24-month protests depending upon whether the protest involves an issue for which the FTB already has an established litigating position, the number and complexity of the legal issues involved, and how much factual development is required. (*FTB Notice 2006-6*, California Franchise Tax Board, October 27, 2006, CCH CALIFORNIA TAX REPORTS ¶404-078) A pilot program has also been established by the FTB to process eligible protests within one year of the filing of a protest. (*FTB Notice 2006-5*, California Franchise Tax Board, October 27, 2006, CCH CALIFORNIA TAX REPORTS ¶404-077)

• *Oral hearing*

A request for an oral hearing must be made in the protest. Unless otherwise specified in the request, the hearing usually will be arranged at the branch office of the FTB nearest to the taxpayer's address. A taxpayer who wishes to be represented by others at the hearing should so state in the written protest; arrangements will be made accordingly. The oral hearings are informal. (Sec. 19044, Rev. & Tax. Code)

• *Power of attorney*

No power of attorney is required as evidence of the authority of the taxpayer's representative to discuss the case, provided the taxpayer has indicated, in the protest or otherwise, a desire to be so represented. However, a representative may not take any definite action on the taxpayer's behalf without a power of attorney definitely authorizing the representative to act. The FTB provides FTB 3520 for this purpose. There is no requirement that representatives be admitted to practice or have particular qualifications to be eligible to represent taxpayers.

¶705 Deficiencies—Appeal to State Board of Equalization

Law: Secs. 19045-48 (CCH CALIFORNIA TAX REPORTS ¶ 89-234).

Comparable Federal: Secs. 6211-15 (CCH U.S. MASTER TAX GUIDE ¶ 2711).

Upon receiving notice of action by the Franchise Tax Board (FTB) on the taxpayer's protest, the taxpayer may appeal to the State Board of Equalization (SBE). The appeal must be filed by the appeal filing date specified in the FTB's notice (within 30 days of the date of the FTB's notice). The FTB's action becomes final at the expiration of the 30-day period if no appeal is filed. (Sec. 19045, Rev. & Tax. Code)

Two copies of the appeal and two copies of any supporting documents must be sent to the SBE in Sacramento, which will send a copy of each document to the FTB. (Sec. 19046, Rev. & Tax. Code)

• *Requirements for appeal*

FTB Regulation 5420 covering hearing procedures before the SBE provides that the appeal must be in writing, should state the fact that an appeal is being made, and should include the following information:

— name of appellant (or appellants);

— the social security number or taxpayer identification number of each appellant;

— the address and telephone number of each appellant and each appellant's authorized representative;

— amounts (including tax, penalties, fees, and interest) and years involved;

— copy of the FTB notice from which the appeal is made;;

— statement of facts;

— points and authorities in support of the taxpayer's position;

— statement of portion of tax the taxpayer concedes is owing; and

— signature of appellant (or appellants) or authorized representative.

The appeal may be supplemented at a later date, provided the original appeal is filed timely. If additional data is requested by the SBE and it is not provided by the taxpayer within the time requested (including reasonable extensions of time granted by the SBE), the appeal may be dismissed. Upon receipt of an appeal, the SBE gives the FTB an opportunity to file an answer, and gives the taxpayer an opportunity to file a reply if desired.

• *Hearing on appeal*

The SBE will set a time and place for hearing on the appeal and will so notify the taxpayer or the taxpayer's representatives. Hearings are more formal than the oral hearings before the FTB, sworn testimony being taken and other formalities observed. Taxpayers' representatives are not required to be admitted to practice before the SBE.

After the hearing, the SBE notifies the taxpayer and the FTB of its determination. (Sec. 19047, Rev. & Tax. Code) Either the taxpayer or the FTB may file a petition for rehearing within 30 days of the time of the determination. If such petition is not filed, the determination becomes final at the expiration of the 30-day period. If a petition is filed, the determination becomes final 30 days after the SBE issues its opinion on the petition. (Sec. 19048, Rev. & Tax. Code)

The SBE has published a booklet entitled "Appeals Procedures" and will supply a copy upon request.

• *Suit to establish residence*

See ¶105 for a description of a special procedure whereby a person who is alleged to be a California resident can file a suit to determine the issue of residency without first paying the tax. Otherwise, there is no provision in California law for filing suit until after the tax is paid. See ¶720 regarding suits for refund.

¶706 Final Assessment of Deficiency

Law: Secs. 19042, 19049 (CCH CALIFORNIA TAX REPORTS ¶89-228).

Comparable Federal: Secs. 6213, 6402 (CCH U.S. MASTER TAX GUIDE ¶2711).

A deficiency assessment becomes final, in the absence of protest, at the expiration of the 60-day period allowed for protest after mailing of the notice of proposed deficiency. (Sec. 19042, Rev. & Tax. Code) If a protest is filed, the assessment becomes final at a later date as explained above in ¶704, ¶705. When the assessment becomes final, the Franchise Tax Board mails to the taxpayer a notice and demand for payment of the tax and interest. Except as noted below, the amount is due and payable within 15 days of the date of the notice and demand. (Sec. 19049, Rev. & Tax. Code)

The IRS may offset past-due, legally enforceable state income tax debts that have been reduced to judgment against any federal tax refunds due to the same taxpayer.

¶707 Jeopardy Assessments

Law: Secs. 19081-86, 19093 (CCH CALIFORNIA TAX REPORTS ¶89-168, 89-178).

Comparable Federal: Secs. 6851, 6861 (CCH U.S. MASTER TAX GUIDE ¶2713).

If the Franchise Tax Board (FTB) finds that the collection of a tax or deficiency for any year will be jeopardized by delay, it may make an immediate assessment. (Sec. 19081, Rev. & Tax. Code) As to the current period, it may declare the taxable period immediately terminated. (Sec. 19082, Rev. & Tax. Code) Any such assessment is immediately due and payable, but the taxpayer may stay collection by filing within 30 days a bond in the amount of the tax and accrued interest, or other security in such amount as the FTB may require. (Sec. 19083, Rev. & Tax. Code) Any jeopardy assessment is also a deficiency assessment, if such an assessment has not already been issued for that tax year and amount. (Sec. 19081, Rev. & Tax. Code)

No jeopardy assessment may be made and no levy may be issued less than 30 days after notice and demand is mailed for payment or for a return and payment, unless the Chief Counsel of the FTB or the Chief Counsel's delegate personally approves, in writing, the assessment or levy. (Sec. 19084, Rev. & Tax. Code)

The taxpayer may file a petition for reassessment within 30 days after the FTB furnishes the taxpayer with a written statement of the information upon which it relied in issuing the notice and demand. If the taxpayer so requests, an oral hearing will be granted, and under certain conditions the taxpayer may appeal to the State Board of Equalization (SBE). If no petition for reassessment is filed, the assessment becomes final at the end of the 30-day period. (Sec. 19084, Rev. & Tax. Code)

The taxpayer or the FTB may file a civil action within 60 days in superior court to appeal the decision of the SBE. If no civil action is commenced, the SBE's determination is final.

In *Pierre Roland Dupuy* (1975) (CCH CALIFORNIA TAX REPORTS ¶89-236.26), the taxpayer sought an injunction against seizure and sale of his property under a jeopardy assessment. The matter reached the California Supreme Court, which discussed the constitutional questions involved and concluded that an injunction may be issued in some circumstances in the interests of "due process."

¶708 Bankruptcy and Receiverships

Law: Secs. 19088-91 (CCH CALIFORNIA TAX REPORTS ¶89-170).

Comparable Federal: Secs. 6871-73 (CCH U.S. MASTER TAX GUIDE ¶2750).

California law is generally the same as federal law.

Special provisions apply to taxpayers in bankruptcy or receivership. In such cases the tax may be assessed immediately. The running of the statute of limitations is suspended under certain circumstances. Claims for tax are adjudicated by the court before which the bankruptcy or receivership procedure is pending, despite any appeal which may be pending before the State Board of Equalization. (Sec. 19088 et seq., Rev. & Tax. Code)

Anyone who is appointed trustee, receiver, assignee, or other fiduciary in a receivership or bankruptcy situation is required to give the Franchise Tax Board (FTB) notice of the appointment. Failure to give timely notice may suspend the running of the period of limitations on assessments. (Sec. 19089, Rev. & Tax. Code)

CCH Comment: Discharge in Bankruptcy

A bankruptcy court may enjoin the FTB from collecting prepetition nonpriority personal income taxes discharged in a bankruptcy proceeding in which the FTB declined to participate (*Goldberg v. Elliott*, U.S. Ct. of Appeals, 9th Cir., No. 00-15128, July 16, 2001, CCH CALIFORNIA TAX REPORTS ¶89-170.27). However, a U.S. District Court overturned a bankruptcy court's discharge of delinquent taxes when the FTB failed to participate in a bankruptcy proceeding as a result of the FTB's reliance on the taxpayer's statement in the bankruptcy notice that the delinquent taxes at issue were less than one-third of the amount actually due and shown on the taxpayer's tax returns filed after the bankruptcy claims bar date for government entities had expired. (*Franchise Tax Board v. Joye*, United States District Court for the Northern District of California, No. C 06-2145 SC, March 23, 2007, CALIFORNIA TAX REPORTS ¶404-248) Similarly, a court of appeal upheld a lower court's decision to not discharge the pre-petition taxes assessed by the FTB finding that the taxpayer failed to provide adequate notice when the taxpayer listed an incorrect Social Security number on the notice provided to the FTB, even though the notice contained the taxpayer's correct name and address. (*Ellett v. Stanislaus*, 506 F.3d 774 (9th Cir. 2007) , CCH CALIFORNIA TAX REPORTS ¶404-485)

¶709 Transferee Liability

Law: Secs. 19006, 19071-74 (CCH CALIFORNIA TAX REPORTS ¶89-166).

Comparable Federal: Secs. 6013, 6901-4 (CCH U.S. MASTER TAX GUIDE ¶2745).

The law contains provisions permitting assessment and collection of tax from persons secondarily liable. The period of limitations is extended for assessments against transferees and fiduciaries. (Sec. 19071, Rev. & Tax. Code; Sec. 19072, Rev. & Tax. Code) California law is the same as federal law.

Both California and federal laws provide for suspension of the running of the period of limitations against the transferee while the taxpayer is exercising an administrative remedy. (Sec. 19073, Rev. & Tax. Code)

California law also provides that the spouse who controls the disposition of, as well as the spouse who is taxable on, community income is liable for the tax on such income. (Sec. 19006, Rev. & Tax. Code) There is no comparable federal provision.

In *Appeal of Robert D. Burch* (1968) (CCH CALIFORNIA TAX REPORTS ¶89-234.25), the Franchise Tax Board held a husband liable for an additional assessment against his former wife, because the husband controlled the disposition of the community income involved, but contended that the husband was not entitled to appeal the wife's assessment. The State Board of Equalization permitted the appeal.

¶710 Statute of Limitations on Assessments

Law: Secs. 17024.5, 18529, 18572, 18622, 19057-67, 19087, 19255, 19371, 19444, 19755, 24672 (CCH CALIFORNIA TAX REPORTS ¶89-144).

Comparable Federal: Secs. 1311-14, 6501-4, 7508A (CCH U.S. MASTER TAX GUIDE ¶2537, 2712, 2726 et seq.).

The California statute of limitations on assessments applies to the date for mailing a notice of proposed deficiency assessment, whereas the federal law applies to the date of the actual assessment of tax. The California rules governing time limits on assessment are summarized below. (The statute of limitations on tax *collection* is discussed below under "Statute of limitations on collections.")

(a) **General rule**—Taxes may be assessed up to four years after the return required to be filed by the taxpayer is filed. A return filed before the "last day prescribed by law for filing," determined without regard to any extension of time for filing, is deemed to have been filed on such last day. The federal limitation period is three years, with the same rule about returns filed before the regular due date. (Sec. 19057, Rev. & Tax. Code; Sec. 19066, Rev. & Tax. Code)

(b) **Waivers**—The taxpayer may agree to an extension of the limitation period. The Franchise Tax Board (FTB) must notify a taxpayer of his or her right to (1) refuse to extend the statute of limitations for assessments or (2) limit the extension to a particular period of time. This is the same as the federal rule. The California law has an additional provision that *automatically* extends the limitation period whenever the taxpayer has signed a waiver extending the statute of limitations for federal purposes. The automatic extension runs to six months after the expiration date of the federal waiver. (Sec. 19065, Rev. & Tax. Code; Sec. 19067, Rev. & Tax. Code)

(c) **Omission of over 25% of income**—Where a taxpayer's return omits gross income in excess of 25% of the gross income stated in the return, the limitation date is six years after the return was filed. This provision is comparable to the federal rule. (Sec. 19058, Rev. & Tax. Code; Sec. 19066, Rev. & Tax. Code)

(d) **False or no return**—Where no return or a false or fraudulent return was filed, there is no period of limitation on assessment or collection of tax. The California rule is the same as the federal one. (Sec. 19057, Rev. & Tax. Code)

(e) **Failure to report changes or amendment of federal returns**—Where the taxpayer fails to report any change of income or deductions made by federal authorities or fails to file an amended California return when required (¶106), a notice of proposed deficiency may be mailed at any time after the change or amended return is reported to or filed with the federal government. This rule applies only to the effect of the adjustments made by the federal authorities, or to the items changed in an amended federal return. (Sec. 19060, Rev. & Tax. Code) The California Supreme Court has ruled that this extended limitation period is an exception to the general four-year limitation period discussed in (a) above. (*Ordlock v. Franchise Tax Board* (2006) (CCH CALIFORNIA TAX REPORTS ¶404-022))

(f) **Amended return filed or federal change reported**—When the taxpayer does file an amended return or otherwise reports a federal change within the required time (¶106), the limitation date for deficiencies "resulting from such adjustments" is two years after the filing of the amended return or report, or the date provided in (a) or (c), above, whichever is later. If an amended return is filed or a federal change is reported by the taxpayer after the prescribed time for doing so has expired, the limitation period for deficiencies is four years from the date the amended return or report is filed. The two-year limitation period applies to notifications made by the IRS, as well as by the taxpayer, within six months of the final federal determination or filing of an amended federal return. (Sec. 18622, Rev. & Tax. Code; Sec. 19059, Rev. & Tax. Code; Sec. 19060, Rev. & Tax. Code)

(g) **Change from separate to joint returns**—Where taxpayers elect to change from separate to joint returns (¶107), the otherwise applicable limitation period includes one additional year after the date of filing on the new basis. (Sec. 18529, Rev. & Tax. Code)

(h) **Involuntary conversion**—If the taxpayer elects not to recognize gain on involuntary conversion where replacement property is purchased (¶503), the limitation period is extended to four years from the date the FTB receives notice from the taxpayer regarding the replacement, etc. The federal period is three years. (Sec. 17024.5(g), Rev. & Tax. Code)

(i) **"Federally registered partnerships"** —The limitation date for assessments against partners is extended under certain conditions. (Sec. 19063, Rev. & Tax. Code)

(j) **Installment sales between related parties**—The limitation period may be extended under certain circumstances. (Sec. 24672, Rev. & Tax. Code)

(k) **Additional tax liability shown within 60 days of limitation date for assessment**—Where, within the 60-day period ending on the limitation date for assessment, the FTB receives from the taxpayer a signed document, other than an amended return or report required to be filed due to a federal change or correction (¶106), showing that the taxpayer owes an additional amount of tax for the taxable year, the period for assessment of that additional amount is extended to 60 days after the document is received by the FTB. (Sec. 19057(c), Rev. & Tax. Code)

(l) **Subpoenaed person's intervention**—The statute of limitations for assessment is suspended in certain cases involving actions by taxpayers to quash subpoenas to other persons. This conforms to federal law. (Sec. 19064, Rev. & Tax. Code)

(m) **Abusive tax shelters**—The statute of limitations for issuing proposed deficiency assessments related to abusive tax avoidance transactions is generally eight years after the return is filed. (Sec. 19755, Rev. & Tax. Code)

CCH Comment: Imposition of Penalties

In a nonprecedential decision, the California State Board of Equalization ruled in *Expert Dealer Services, LLC* (2006) CCH CALIFORNIA TAX REPORTS ¶89-206.352) that the four-year statute of limitations period applies only to the assessment of tax deficiencies and not to the imposition of penalties or interest.

• *Special rules*

In the case of members of the Armed Forces, disaster victims, and certain other taxpayers who are outside the United States for a period of time, the statute of limitations is automatically extended under certain conditions. Collection actions may also be suspended for National Guard members and army reservists called into service (¶109, ¶110).

The limitation period for an estate or trust may be shortened to 18 months (¶613).

The running of the period of limitations is suspended for any period during which the FTB is precluded from action by bankruptcy laws and for 30 days thereafter; the California rule is the same as the federal one. (Sec. 19089, Rev. & Tax. Code) Also, the running of the period of limitations may be suspended where a fiduciary fails to give timely notice of his or her appointment (¶708).

California law contains nothing similar to IRC Secs. 1311-14, which mitigate the effect of the statute of limitations in certain situations where an inconsistent position is maintained.

• *Statute of limitations on collections*

California's statute of limitations on court actions to collect tax deficiencies, penalties, and interest is ten years. The period runs from the time the taxpayer's liability for tax, penalties, or interest is first determined, but does not apply in situations in which a tax lien is properly in force. (Sec. 19371, Rev. & Tax. Code)

A 20-year statute of limitations applies to collections of unpaid income tax liabilities, including penalties and interest. The limitations period runs from (1) the date of the latest tax liability for a taxable year or (2) the date any other liability that is not associated with a taxable year becomes due and payable. The 20-year period is extended for any period during which the FTB pursues a civil action or files a probate claim and does not expire until that liability, probate claim, or judgment against the taxpayer is satisfied or becomes unenforceable. (Sec. 19255, Rev. & Tax. Code)

• *Decisions of State Board of Equalization*

Appeal of Orville H. and Jeanne K. Haag (1977) (CCH CALIFORNIA TAX REPORTS ¶89-144.354) involved the application of rule (c) above. The taxpayers failed to report $67,257 of dividends received from an S corporation. The omitted income exceeded 25% of the gross income on the return. However, the reconciliation in the return between federal and state income showed that S corporation income was reported on the federal but not on the state return. The State Board of Equalization (SBE) held that the reconciling item was sufficient to put the FTB on notice as to the possibility of additional California income; it followed that the statute of limitations was not extended and the proposed assessment was not timely.

In *Appeal of Phillip Yordan* (1958) (CCH CALIFORNIA TAX REPORTS ¶89-144.403), the SBE applied rule (e) above in a situation where the taxpayer did report the federal adjustments but did not do so within the specified time limit. Similarly, see *Appeal of the Pullman Company* (1972) (CCH CALIFORNIA TAX REPORTS ¶89-144.408), involving the comparable provision of the corporation tax law. In the *Pullman* case, state assessments for the years 1938 through 1943 were not made until 1957, based on a Tax Court settlement that became final in 1955. See also *Appeal of Vinemore Company, etc.* (1972) (CCH CALIFORNIA TAX REPORTS ¶11-361.15), holding that notice of a Federal Revenue Agent's Report did not constitute the required notice where the final determination was made later in a Tax Court proceeding.

¶711 Interest on Deficiencies

Law: Secs. 19101-20, 19521, 19738, 19777-78 (CCH CALIFORNIA TAX REPORTS ¶89-192, 89-204, 89-210).

Comparable Federal: Secs. 6404, 6601, 6621, 6622, 6631 (CCH U.S. MASTER TAX GUIDE ¶2838 et seq.).

California Form: FTB 3701 (Request for Abatement of Interest).

Interest is charged upon deficiencies or other delinquent payments of tax (see ¶110 for interest charged during extension periods). Interest is compounded daily. (Sec. 19521, Rev. & Tax. Code) As to certain individuals, the running of interest may be suspended for a period because of their absence from the United States (¶109).

CCH Tip: Tax Amnesty

Amnesty was available during the period beginning February 1, 2005, and ending on April 4, 2005. Under the amnesty program, penalties and fees applicable to nonreporting, nonpayment, or underreporting of taxes for pre-2003 tax liabilities were waived for taxpayers that reported all income and paid all tax and interest due by May 31, 2005 (June 30, 2006, for taxpayers that entered into installment agreements). In addition to the enhanced penalties applied to deficiencies associated with the amnesty program, a 50% interest penalty will be imposed for each period for which amnesty could have been requested for amounts that were due and payable on the last date of the amnesty period, for the period beginning on the date on which the tax was due and ending on the last day of the amnesty period. (Sec. 19777.5, Rev. & Tax. Code) The enhanced interest penalties do not apply to taxpayers that had entered into an installment agreement. (Sec. 19738, Rev. & Tax. Code) Any taxpayer who is the subject of a deficiency assessment for unpaid or underpaid tax for a reporting period eligible for amnesty is also liable for the 50% penalty on the interest on the deficiency. See ¶712 for more details.

California imposes interest on tax underpayments at the federal underpayment rate. However, while the federal rate changes on a quarterly basis, the California rate is adjusted semiannually. In addition, California does not follow the federal provision that eliminates the imposition of interest on overlapping periods of tax overpayments and underpayments.

Interest rates are as follows:

January 1, 2005—June 30, 2005	4%
July 1, 2005—December 31, 2005	5%
January 1, 2006—June 30, 2006	6%
July 1, 2006—December 31, 2006	7%
January 1, 2007—June 30, 2007	8%
July 1, 2007—December 31, 2007	8%
January 1, 2008—June 30, 2008	8%
July 1, 2008—December 31, 2008	7%
January 1, 2009—June 30, 2009	5%

• *Interest is mandatory*

The imposition of interest is not a penalty, but is considered to be compensation for the taxpayer's use of money. The assessment of interest is mandatory, regardless of the reason for the late payment of tax. See *Appeal of Robert M. and Mildred Scott* (1981) (CCH CALIFORNIA TAX REPORTS ¶89-202.37), and other cases involving this point. However, as noted below, under some circumstances interest may be waived.

• *Special rules for related taxpayers or items*

In certain cases involving related taxpayers or related items where overpayments are offset against deficiencies, no interest is charged on the portion of the deficiency extinguished by the credit for overpayment for the period subsequent to the date the overpayment was made. This rule applies in the following situations:

(1) where a deficiency owed by one spouse is offset by an overpayment by the other spouse for the same year; presumably this rule would apply to registered domestic partners (RDPs) as well (see ¶119) (Sec. 19107, Rev. & Tax. Code);

(2) where a deficiency owed by a taxpayer for any year is offset by an overpayment by the same taxpayer for any other year (Sec. 19108, Rev. & Tax. Code); and

(3) in the cases of estates, trusts, parents and children (including in-laws), spouses, or RDPs, where the correction of an error results in a deficiency for one taxpayer and an overpayment for a related taxpayer (Sec. 19110, Rev & Tax. Code).

There are no comparable federal provisions with respect to the first and third items. The second item is somewhat similar to a federal provision whereby interest is not imposed on deficiencies satisfied by overpayment credits under certain conditions.

In *Appeal of John L. Todd* (1952) (CCH CALIFORNIA TAX REPORTS ¶89-202.53), the State Board of Equalization (SBE) considered the effect of this rule in a case where the tax was paid in installments. The case involved a deficiency against the husband and an overpayment of exactly the same amount by the wife. The SBE held that there was no overpayment by the wife until she paid her last installment, so interest was properly chargeable on the husband's deficiency from the due date of the return to the date of the last installment.

• *Potentially abusive tax shelters*

For interest penalties related to abusive tax shelters see ¶727.

• *Rules for imposition of interest*

The law contains detailed rules regarding interest on deficiencies. Principal provisions of these rules are as follows:

— interest is assessed, collected, and paid in the same manner as the tax (Sec. 19101, Rev. & Tax. Code);

— interest is assessed on tax deficiencies from the due date of the tax without regard for any extension of time that may have been granted and without regard to any notice of jeopardy assessment issued prior to the last date prescribed for the payment of such deficiency (Sec. 19101, Rev. & Tax. Code);

— interest is normally assessed on a penalty from the date of notice and demand for payment if the penalty is not paid within 15 days from notice and demand for payment; however, as to certain penalties, interest is imposed from the due date of the return (Sec. 19101, Rev. & Tax. Code);

— if an amount is paid within 15 days following notice and demand for payment, no interest will be charged for the period after the date of the notice and demand (Sec. 19101, Rev. & Tax. Code);

— if tax is satisfied by an overpayment credit, interest is not imposed on such tax for any period during which interest was allowable on the overpayment (Sec. 19113, Rev. & Tax. Code);

— interest may be assessed and collected any time during the period within which the related tax may be collected (Sec. 19114, Rev. & Tax. Code); and

— no interest may be imposed for the period between 45 days after the date of final audit review and the date a notice of proposed assessment is sent to the taxpayer (Sec. 19105, Rev. & Tax. Code).

• *Suspension of interest*

The Franchise Tax Board (FTB) must suspend the imposition of interest if an individual files a timely return and the FTB fails to issue a notice specifically stating the taxpayer's liability and the basis for such liability within 18 months following the later of the original due date of the return or the date on which a timely return is filed. The suspension period commences on the date after the 18-month period expires until 15 days after the FTB sends the required notice. The suspension does not apply to the following:

— penalties for failure to file or failure to pay,

— penalties, additions to tax, or additional amounts involving fraud,

— penalties, additions to tax, or additional amounts shown on the return,

— criminal penalties,

— penalties, additions to tax, or additional amounts related to any gross misstatement,

— penalties, additions to tax, or additional amounts related to reportable transactions for which specified requirements are not met and listed transactions, or

— taxpayers with taxable income greater than $200,000 that have been contacted by the FTB regarding the use of a potentially abusive tax shelter.

(Sec. 19116, Rev. & Tax. Code)

Federal law is similar.

Special rules apply when a taxpayer is required to report a federal change or correction to the state. In that case, the FTB has either one or two years from the date the taxpayer or the IRS reports the federal change or correction to issue a notice before interest is suspended, depending on whether the change or correction is reported within six months or more than six months after the final federal determination.

CCH Example: Suspension of Interest

Ken received an automatic extension of time to file his 2005 California personal income tax return and timely filed on September 1, 2006. Ken inadvertently failed to include $1,000 of interest income on the return. The FTB sends Ken the required notice on June 1, 2008, and Ken pays the tax deficiency on July 15, 2008. Ken owes interest on the tax deficiency from April 15, 2006 (the original due date of the return), through March 1, 2008 (the last day of the 18-month period). Interest is suspended from March 2, 2008, through June 15, 2008. Interest runs again from June 16, 2008 (the 15th day after notice was provided), until July 15, 2008 (the date of payment of the tax deficiency).

• *Notice of interest charges*

Each notice that states an amount of interest required to be paid must include the code section under which the interest is imposed and a description of how the interest is computed. Upon request of the taxpayer, the FTB must also provide a computation of the interest. (Sec. 19117, Rev. & Tax. Code)

• *Waiver and abatement of interest*

Interest may be waived for any period for which the FTB determines that the taxpayer cannot pay because of extreme financial hardship caused by catastrophic circumstance. (Sec. 19112, Rev. & Tax. Code) In addition, the FTB is authorized to abate the assessment of interest whenever the following occurs:

— the interest on a deficiency is attributable at least in part to an unreasonable error or delay of an FTB officer or employee, or

— the interest on a delay in payment is the result of dilatory conduct on the part of an FTB officer or employee performing a ministerial or managerial act in an official capacity, or

— a deficiency is based on a final federal determination of tax for the same period that interest was abated on the related federal deficiency amount, provided that the error or delay to which the deficiency is attributable occurred on or before the issuance of the final federal determination.

(Sec. 19104, Rev. & Tax. Code)

In *Appeal of Medeiros* (2004) (CCH CALIFORNIA TAX REPORTS ¶89-210.32), the SBE determined that the FTB's failure to change a taxpayer's "last-known address" of record after the taxpayer sent an attachment to his return indicating that his address had changed was not an unreasonable error given the volume of returns received by the FTB. Consequently, the SBE therefore refused to abate the interest imposed on a deficiency even though the notice of proposed assessment was sent to the wrong address. Under the law in effect at the time, the taxpayer's last-known address was the address shown on the taxpayer's most recently filed return, unless the FTB is given clear and concise notice of a different address. Under the SBE's ruling, an attachment to a return indicating a change of address did not satisfy the "clear and concise notice of a different address" requirement. However, the SBE did abate the interest imposed for the period after the FTB's "request for a tax return" was returned by the post office as undeliverable, because the FTB was then put on notice that the address they had for the taxpayer was not valid and the FTB had the correct address in its records.

A request for such an abatement may be made by submitting FTB 3701 to the FTB. A taxpayer may appeal an interest abatement denial to the SBE. The appeal must be filed within 30 days in the case of unpaid interest or within 90 days in the case of any paid interest. A taxpayer may treat the FTB's failure to make a determination within six months as a denial. A request for abatement may accompany a written protest or appeal of the underlying deficiency. If a deficiency is final, the interest accruing prior to the deficiency becoming final may not be abated. The FTB may also waive interest in certain cases in which the taxpayer has relied on the FTB's written advice (¶703).

In addition, both California and federal law require the abatement of interest imposed against any taxpayer located in a federally-declared disaster area for any period that the FTB (IRS for federal purposes) (1) extended the taxpayer's period for filing an income tax return and paying income tax with respect to such return and (2) waived any corresponding penalties. (Sec. 19109, Rev. & Tax. Code) California differs from the federal law by (1) extending relief to taxpayers in Governor-declared disaster areas and (2) requiring taxpayers seeking relief to have incurred a loss, in addition to being located in a disaster area.

Finally, see ¶712 for a discussion of the FTB's Taxpayers' Rights Advocate's authority to abate the imposition of interest under specified circumstances.

Practitioner Comment: FTB's Errors and Delays May Justify Abatement

The State Board of Equalization held in a published decision in the *Appeal of Alan and Rita Shugart* (2005) CCH CALIFORNIA TAX REPORTS ¶403-816, on July 1, 2005, that the cumulative effect of multiple documented errors and delays on the part of the FTB during the audit and protest process justified an abatement of interest. Although recent legislation requiring the FTB to suspend the imposition of interest on individual taxpayers if the FTB fails to issue a notice of proposed assessment within 18 months of the tax return being filed may mitigate the need for taxpayers to seek to have some or all of their interest abated, in circumstances when this suspension of interest does not apply, taxpayers who experience delays that they believe are unreasonable at audit or protest should maintain careful records documenting the causes of the delays and consider filing a request for interest abatement.

Bruce Daigh, Chris Whitney, Contributing Editors

• *Interest on erroneous overpayment to taxpayer*

Interest may be assessed and collected if the FTB makes an erroneous overpayment to a taxpayer. Interest accrues from the date the refund is erroneously paid but will be abated for the period from the date the refund is made until 30 days after the FTB makes a demand for repayment if payment is made within the 30-day period. (Sec. 19104, Rev. & Tax. Code; Sec. 19411, Rev. & Tax. Code)

¶712 Penalties

Law: Secs. 17299.8, 17299.9, 18633.5, 19011, 19116, 19131-36.3, 19164, 19166-67, 19169, 19170, 19172-79, 19181-87, 19444, 19701-01.5, 19705-06, 19708-09, 19711-15, 19720-21, 19730-38, 19772-74, 19777.5 (CCH CALIFORNIA TAX REPORTS ¶89-192, 89-206—89-210).

Comparable Federal: Secs. 6111-12, 6404, 6651-53, 6657-58, 6662, 6663, 6671-6674, 6682, 6693-95, 6698, 6700-06, 6707, 6721-24, 7201-07, 7408 (CCH U.S. MASTER TAX GUIDE CHAPTER 28).

California Forms: FTB 2300 PIT (Amnesty Application - Individuals).

[*NOTE:* See ¶703 for a discussion of relief provisions under the Taxpayers' Bill of Rights.]

California imposes a variety of civil and criminal penalties for failure to comply with the personal income tax law. Some of these penalties may be waived for reasonable cause. In addition, a short-term amnesty program was available during the beginning of 2005.

• *Penalties*

Penalties related to abusive tax shelters are discussed at ¶727. Other personal income tax penalties are provided as follows:

(1) failing to report personal services remuneration—disallowance of deduction; unreported amount multiplied by the highest personal income tax rate (Sec. 17299.8, Rev. & Tax. Code; Sec. 19175, Rev. & Tax. Code);

(2) failing to report real estate transaction—disallowance of related deductions (Sec. 17299.8, Rev. & Tax. Code);

(3) failing to comply with requirement to remit payment by electronic funds transfer without reasonable cause—10% of amount paid (Sec. 19011, Rev. & Tax. Code);

(4) failing to file return without reasonable cause—5% per month, up to 25%; for individuals, after 60 days, at least the lesser of $100 or 100% of tax; if fraudulent, 15% per month, up to a 75% maximum (Sec. 19131, Rev. & Tax. Code);

(5) failing to pay amount on return by due date or within 15 days of notice and demand without reasonable cause, or, for limited liability companies, failing to pay the income tax liability of a nonresident member when required to do so—5% of unpaid amount plus 0.5% per month of remaining tax, up to 25% of unpaid amount (Sec. 19132, Rev. & Tax. Code);

(6) failing to furnish requested information or to file return on notice and demand by the FTB without reasonable cause—25% of deficiency or of tax amount for which information was requested (Sec. 19133, Rev. & Tax. Code);

(7) failing to make small business stock report without reasonable cause—$50 per report; $100 if failure due to negligence or intentional disregard (Sec. 19133.5, Rev. & Tax. Code);

(8) dishonored check or electronic funds transfer—the lesser of $15 or amount of check; 2% of amount of check if check is for $750 or more (Sec. 19134, Rev. & Tax. Code);

(9) underpayment of estimated tax (¶111);

(10) negligence, substantial underpayment, etc. without reasonable cause—20% of underpayment attributable to violation; 40% for gross valuation misstatements (see ¶727 for provisions relating to underpayments resulting from abusive tax shelters) (Sec. 19164, Rev. & Tax. Code);

(11) fraud—75% of underpayment attributable to fraud (Sec. 19164, Rev. & Tax. Code);

(12) understatement by return preparer—$250 per return; $1,000 if noncompliance with reportable transaction requirements, listed transaction, or gross misstatement; $5,000 if willful or reckless (Sec. 19166, Rev. & Tax. Code);

(13) failure of tax preparer to give taxpayer copy of return, furnish identifying number, or retain copy or list—$50 for each failure up to $25,000 per return period (Sec. 19167, Rev. & Tax. Code);

(14) negotiation or endorsement of client's refund check by tax preparer—$250 per check plus criminal penalty (misdemeanor) of up to $1,000 and/or up to 1 year in jail, and costs of prosecution (Sec. 19712, Rev. & Tax. Code);

(15) failing to file partnership return—$10 multiplied by number of partners (Sec. 19172, Rev. & Tax. Code);

(16) making false statements in connection with withholding—$500 (Sec. 19176, Rev. & Tax. Code);

(17) aiding or abetting understatement of tax liability—$1,000 (Sec. 19178, Rev. & Tax. Code);

(18) filing frivolous return—$500; $5,000 if noncompliance with reportable transaction requirements, listed transaction, or gross misstatement (Sec. 19179, Rev. & Tax. Code);

(19) failing to meet original issue discount reporting requirements without reasonable cause—1% of aggregate issue price, up to $50,000 per issue (Sec. 19179, Rev. & Tax. Code);

(20) failing to file information return or furnish payee statement— $50 per violation up to $100,000 per year for payee statements or $250,000 per year for information returns; the greater of $100 or 5% or 10% of the items to be reported, depending on the return involved, if intentional disregard of requirements (Sec. 19183, Rev. & Tax. Code);

(21) failing to provide written explanation—$10 per failure up to $5,000 (Sec. 19183, Rev. & Tax. Code);

(22) failing to file information report regarding individual retirement account (IRA) or annuity—$50 per failure (Sec. 19184, Rev. & Tax. Code);

(23) overstatement of nondeductible IRA contributions without reasonable cause—$100 per overstatement (Sec. 19184, Rev. & Tax. Code);

(24) failure to timely file a return concerning medical savings accounts, qualified tuition programs, or education savings accounts—$50 per failure (Sec. 19184, Rev. & Tax. Code);

(25) failing to file return or to furnish information repeatedly over a period of 2 years or more or filing false or fraudulent return or information, resulting in an underpayment of at least $15,000; aiding or abetting tax evasion; willfully failing to pay tax or estimated tax—$5,000 maximum plus criminal penalty (misdemeanor) of up to $5,000 and/or up to 1 year in jail, and costs of prosecution (Sec. 19701, Rev. & Tax. Code)

(26) instituting frivolous protest or refund proceedings—$5,000 maximum (Sec. 19714, Rev. & Tax. Code);

(27) obtaining, endorsing, or negotiating a tax refund generated by the filing of a return knowing the recipient is not entitled to the refund—$5,000 maximum plus criminal penalty (misdemeanor) of up to $10,000 and/or up to 1 year in jail, and costs of investigation and prosecution; $10,000 maximum if done willfully and with intent to defraud plus criminal penalty (misdemeanor/felony) of up to $50,000 and/or up to 1 year in jail or up to 3 years in prison, and costs of investigation and prosecution (Sec. 19720, Rev. & Tax. Code; Sec. 19721, Rev. & Tax. Code);

(28) forging spouse's signature—misdemeanor; up to $5,000 and/or up to 1 year in jail (Sec. 19701.5, Rev. & Tax. Code);

(29) willfully making or signing a return or document containing a declaration made under penalty of perjury that the maker or signer does not believe to

be materially true or correct—felony; up to $50,000 and/or up to 3 years in prison, and costs of investigation and prosecution (Sec. 19705, Rev. & Tax. Code);

(30) willfully aiding preparation or presentation of a false return or document—felony; up to $50,000 and/or up to 3 years in prison, and costs of investigation and prosecution (Sec. 19705, Rev. & Tax. Code);

(31) falsely executing or signing a bond, permit, entry, or required document—felony; up to $50,000 and/or up to 3 years in prison, and costs of investigation and prosecution (Sec. 19705, Rev. & Tax. Code);

(32) removing, depositing, or concealing taxable goods to evade tax—felony; up to $50,000 and/or up to 3 years in prison, and costs of investigation and prosecution (Sec. 19705, Rev. & Tax. Code);

(33) concealing property or destroying or falsifying records in regard to a tax settlement, closing agreement, compromise, or offer in compromise—felony; up to $50,000 and/or up to 3 years in prison, and costs of investigation and prosecution (Sec. 19705, Rev. & Tax. Code);

(34) willfully failing to file return or supply information with intent to defraud—misdemeanor/felony; up to $20,000, and/or up to 1 year in jail or 3 years in prison, and costs of investigation and prosecution (Sec. 19705, Rev. & Tax. Code);

(35) willfully making, signing, or verifying false return or statement with intent to evade tax—misdemeanor/felony; up to $20,000 and/or up to 1 year in jail or 3 years in prison (Sec. 19706, Rev. & Tax. Code);

(36) failing to collect and pay withholding—felony; up to $2,000 and/or up to 3 years in prison (Sec. 19708, Rev. & Tax. Code);

(37) failing to withhold or pay over nonresident withholding—misdemeanor; up to $1,000 and/or up to 1 year in jail, and costs of prosecution (Sec. 19709, Rev. & Tax. Code);

(38) filing false information with employer—misdemeanor; $1,000 and/or up to 1 year in jail (Sec. 19711, Rev. & Tax. Code);

(39) failing to set up withholding account—misdemeanor; up to $5,000 and/or up to 1 year in jail (Sec. 19713, Rev. & Tax. Code);

(40) failing to file mandatory electronic return (¶108)—$50 per non-electronic return (Sec. 19170, Rev. & Tax. Code);

(41) failure of tax preparer to register with California Tax Education Council—$5,000 ($2,500 for first offense) (Sec. 19167, Rev. & Tax. Code);

(42) failure to meet original issue discount reporting requirements—1% of aggregate issue price, up to $50,000 per-issue (Sec. 19181, Rev. & Tax. Code); and

(43) willful failure of check cashing business to file information return (see ¶713)—felony; up to $25,000 ($100,000 for a corporation), and or up to 1 year in prison in a county jail or a state prison, plus costs of prosecution (Sec. 18631.7, Rev. & Tax. Code)

The penalties under (4) and (5), above, may be imposed simultaneously but may not exceed 25% combined.

The FTB is authorized by law to waive or not impose the penalty described in item (3), above, under certain conditions. In Legal Ruling 96-4 (CCH CALIFORNIA TAX REPORTS ¶89-206.64), the FTB provides examples of situations in which it will or will not use this authority.

Item (26), above, refers to Rev. & Tax. Code Sec. 19714 (formerly, Sec. 19414), which conforms to IRC Sec. 6673. In *Appeals of Fred R. Dauberger et al.* (1982) (CCH CALIFORNIA TAX REPORTS ¶89-164.506), the State Board of Equalization (SBE) commented on the flood of California "tax protester" cases and used the following language: "We take this opportunity to advise all individuals who proceed with frivolous cases that serious consideration will be given to the imposition of damages under Section 19414." (This case involved a consolidation of appeals for 32 different taxpayers.) In numerous later decisions involving similar facts, the SBE has imposed the penalty.

Item (40), above, will be waived for reasonable cause, including a taxpayer-client electing not to e-file.

CCH Comment: Zero Returns

The State Board of Equalization has taken the position that returns that do not contain sufficient data from which the FTB can compute and assess the tax liability of a particular taxpayer or that do not demonstrate an honest and genuine endeavor to satisfy the requirements of California's tax law (including "zero returns") are not valid returns and may subject filers of such returns to late filing penalties or penalties for failure to file upon notice and demand (*Appeal of Lavonne A. Hodgson* (2002) (CCH CALIFORNIA TAX REPORTS ¶89-206.6094, ¶89-206.7596)).

• *Effect of automatic extension of time*

Under the automatic-extension procedure (¶108), reasonable cause is assumed and a late-payment penalty will not be imposed if at least 90% of the tax is paid by the regular due date and the balance is paid (with the return) by the extended due date. This conforms to federal practice. (Sec. 19132, Rev. & Tax. Code)

• *Procedures for imposing penalties*

Each notice that imposes a penalty must include the name of the penalty, the code section under which it is imposed, and a description of the computation of the penalty. Upon request of the taxpayer, the FTB must also provide a computation of the penalty imposed. (Sec. 19187, Rev. & Tax. Code)

Further, penalties may not generally be imposed unless the initial determination of the imposition of the penalty receives written approval by an authorized FTB supervisor. However, supervisory approval is not required for any penalty (1) for failure to file or failure to pay, (2) calculated through automated means, or (3) resulting from a federal change or correction required to be reported to the state.

• *Abatement of penalties and interest*

From January 1, 2009, through 2011, and applicable to requests for advocate consideration that are received after 2008, the FTB's Taxpayers' Rights Advocate may abate any penalties, fees, additions to tax, or interest assessed against a taxpayer if (1) relief is not otherwise available, (2) the error or delay was not attributable to the taxpayer, and (3) the advocate determines that the penalties, fees, additions to tax, or interest have been assessed as a result of any of the following:

— the FTB's erroneous action or erroneous inaction in processing the taxpayer's documents or payments;

— the FTB's unreasonable delay; or

— erroneous written advice that does not otherwise qualify for relief by the Chief Counsel.

The relief must be approved by (1) the Chief Counsel if the total reduction in the amounts owed exceeds $500 and (2) the FTB board must be notified if the total relief exceeds $7,500. Refunds resulting from the advocate's granting of relief may only be granted if a written request for relief was filed with the advocate's office within the statute of limitations period for filing a refund claim. (Sec. 21004, Rev. & Tax. Code)

• *Review of noneconomic substance penalties*

The FTB has established a process to determine whether the noneconomic substance penalty (NEST) under Sec. 19774, Rev. & Tax. Code should be reduced or withdrawn. To dispute a NEST penalty, taxpayers should file a protest of the penalty within the required 60-day period and also file a Form FTB 626, Request for Chief Counsel To Relieve Penalties. The Chief Counsel will issue a nonappealable determination on the request for penalty relief. Taxpayers may also contest the penalty after paying the full amount and filing a claim for refund with the FTB, and may appeal to the SBE or file an action in court after the refund claim is denied or deemed denied. (*Tax News*, California Franchise Tax Board, September 2008, CCH CALIFORNIA TAX REPORTS ¶404-742)

• *Suspension of penalties*

If an individual files a timely return and the FTB fails to issue a notice specifically stating the taxpayer's liability and the basis for such liability within 18 months following the later of the original due date of the return or the date on which a timely return is filed, the FTB must generally suspend the imposition of civil penalties, additions to tax, or additional amounts during the period beginning from the date after the 18-month period expires until 15 days after the FTB sends the required notice. The suspension does not apply to any of the following:

— penalty for failure to file or failure to pay;

— penalty, addition to tax, or additional amount involving fraud;

— penalty, addition to tax, or additional amount shown on the return;

— criminal penalties;

— penalty, addition to tax, or additional amounts related to any gross misstatement; or

— penalty, addition to tax, or additional amounts related to reportable transactions for which specified requirements are not met and listed transactions.

(Sec. 19116, Rev. & Tax. Code)

Federal law is similar.

• *Relief for innocent spouse*

Under both California and federal law, in cases involving joint returns an innocent spouse may be relieved from penalties in certain cases of wrongdoing or in divorce settlement decrees. See ¶107 for details.

• *Misdemeanor prosecutions*

The FTB may not pursue misdemeanor prosecution of any person for failing to file a return or furnish required information, aiding another person to evade tax, filing a false or fraudulent return or statement, or supplying false or fraudulent information unless the violations occur over a period of two or more years and result in an estimated delinquent tax liability of $15,000 or more. Also, the FTB may not pursue misdemeanor prosecution of any person for failure to pay any tax, including any estimated tax, if the person is mentally incompetent or suffers from dementia, Alzheimer's disease, or a similar condition. (Sec. 19701, Rev. & Tax. Code)

• *Bankruptcy proceedings*

Both California and federal laws provide for relief from penalties in cases where failure to pay is due to rules applicable in bankruptcy proceedings. (Sec. 19161, Rev. & Tax. Code)

• *Collection and filing enforcement fees*

A collection cost recovery fee will be imposed on any taxpayer who fails to timely pay any amount of tax, penalty, addition to tax, interest, or other liability if the FTB has mailed a notice advising the taxpayer that continued failure to pay that amount may result in a collection action, including the imposition of a collection cost recovery fee. A filing enforcement cost recovery fee will be imposed on any taxpayer who fails to file a required tax return within 25 days after formal legal demand is mailed to the taxpayer by the FTB. The fees for the state's 2008—2009 fiscal year are $187 and $119, respectively. Collection and filing enforcement fees are subject to annual adjustment to reflect actual costs. (Sec. 19254, Rev. & Tax. Code)

• *Decisions of State Board of Equalization*

In *Appeal of Freshman* (2006) (CCH CALIFORNIA TAX REPORTS ¶89-210.243), a summary decision not to be cited as precedent, the SBE abated a penalty imposed for late filing of a California personal income tax return. The SBE determined that the taxpayers' reliance on their previous accountant's advice that they did not have a California personal income tax return filing requirement constituted reasonable cause. The taxpayers immediately filed a California nonresident return when they discovered that they were required to file a return and had an established history of timely filing their federal and resident state tax returns.

In *Appeal of Tuason* (2005) (CCH CALIFORNIA TAX REPORTS ¶89-210.275), a summary decision not to be cited as precedent, the SBE abated a penalty imposed for late payment of California personal income tax by the same percentage that the Internal Revenue Service abated the taxpayer's federal late payment penalty, even though the taxpayer did not provide sufficient evidence to support her claim of reasonable cause and the IRS work papers did not specify that the penalty was abated for reasonable cause.

In several cases the SBE has upheld the presumptive correctness of the FTB's imposition of penalties. For example, in *Appeal of Harold G. Jindrich* (1977) (CCH CALIFORNIA TAX REPORTS ¶89-224.7494), the taxpayer failed to file a return and did not respond to the FTB's notice and demand for a return. The SBE upheld the imposition of two 25% penalties, under items (4) and (6) above, on the income as computed by the FTB.

In *Appeal of Terry L. Lash* (1986) (CCH CALIFORNIA TAX REPORTS New ¶89-206.36), the taxpayer failed to prove to the SBE that the failure to respond to notice and demand to file was due to a reasonable cause and not willful neglect. The taxpayer also failed to prove that not filing a timely return in the subsequent year was due to a reasonable cause. Reasonable cause was tested in both years by the standards of a normally intelligent and prudent businessperson.

In *Appeal of Philip C. and Anne Berolzheimer* (1986) (CCH CALIFORNIA TAX REPORTS ¶89-206.901), the SBE held that an underpayment penalty was properly assessed. A New York law firm, acting as the taxpayers' agent, had filed a timely request for an extension of time for filing the taxpayers' 1981 California income tax return. Due to a programming error in the agent's computer tax software program, the capital gains for the year were incorrectly computed, resulting in an underpayment of the amount required to be paid with the extension request. The FTB assessed an underpayment penalty.

In holding that the underpayment was due to willful neglect and not reasonable cause, the SBE found inapplicable the U.S. Supreme Court rule that it is reasonable for a taxpayer to rely on the advice of an accountant or attorney on a matter of tax law. The underpayment was not due to a mistake of law; it was due to a simple mistake in computation of tax due. It is not "reasonable cause" so as to overcome a presumption of "willful neglect" to rely on an accountant or attorney for a simple computational problem as distinguished from a matter of law.

In *Appeal of Greg L. Dexter* (1986) (CCH CALIFORNIA TAX REPORTS ¶89-206.82), the SBE held that a return with the verification above the signature altered was not filed and signed under penalty of perjury and was an invalid return. Since the taxpayer had not filed a valid return, penalties for negligence and failure to respond were upheld and calculated on the entire tax liability.

Failure to receive a tax form does not constitute reasonable cause for failure to file—see *Appeal of Thomas P.E. and Barbara Rothchild* (1973) (CCH CALIFORNIA TAX REPORTS ¶89-206.566).

In *Appeal of Frank E. and Lilia Z. Hublou* (1977) (CCH CALIFORNIA TAX REPORTS ¶89-206.85), the taxpayers failed to respond to a notice and demand for a return. The return, as filed later, showed a tax liability of $213 which was more than offset by a $419 credit for tax withheld from salary, resulting in a refund. The SBE upheld the FTB in imposing a 25% penalty on the $213 tax liability, under item (6) above. To the same effect, see *Appeal of Sal J. Cardinalli* (1981) (CCH CALIFORNIA TAX REPORTS ¶89-206.60), involving penalties imposed under items (6) and (10) above. In *Appeal of Irma E. Bazan* (1982) (CCH CALIFORNIA TAX REPORTS New ¶89-206.605), the SBE's opinion points out that the penalty described in item (6), above, is properly measured by the FTB's estimate of the tax liability rather than the actual tax as later determined.

In *Appeal of Estate of Marilyn Monroe, Deceased* (1975) (CCH CALIFORNIA TAX REPORTS ¶89-206.80), the estate contended that there was reasonable cause for failure to file California returns, because of uncertainties as to whether the estate was subject to tax and the fact that the executor believed in good faith that no tax was due. The SBE upheld imposition of penalties ($12,810) for failure to file, commenting that "mere uninformed and unsupported belief, no matter how sincere ... is insufficient to constitute reasonable cause ...."

In *Appeal of Horace H. and Mildred E. Hubbard* (1961) (CCH CALIFORNIA TAX REPORTS ¶89-206.6092), the SBE upheld the penalty for failure to file, where the taxpayers had repeatedly ignored the demand of the FTB for a return based on a federal audit report.

In *Appeals of Leonard S. and Frances M. Gordon* (1960) (CCH CALIFORNIA TAX REPORTS ¶89-206.6795), the SBE held that taxpayers, having previously been found guilty of filing fraudulent federal income tax returns, were also subject to the California fraud penalty provisions. (But see the *Brown* case, cited at ¶106, to the opposite effect.)

In *Appeal of Thomas* (1955) (CCH CALIFORNIA TAX REPORTS ¶89-206.80), the SBE held that a new resident of California was subject to a delinquency penalty for failure to file a return for his first year in the state. The taxpayer's income was from salary earned in California; the SBE held that he could reasonably have been expected to make inquiry regarding possible liability for California tax. However, in *Appeal of Estate of Anna Armstrong* (1964) (CCH CALIFORNIA TAX REPORTS ¶89-206.907), the SBE held that the taxpayer's failure to file a timely return was due to reasonable cause when she relied on the advice of competent professional tax advisors.

Both California and federal laws provide special provisions for injunctive relief to prevent taxpayers from engaging in certain conduct (abusive tax shelters, etc.) subject to penalty.

• *Tax Amnesty*

Amnesty was available during the period beginning February 1, 2005, and ending on April 4, 2005. Under the amnesty program, penalties and fees applicable to nonreporting, nonpayment, or underreporting of taxes for pre-2003 tax liabilities were waived for taxpayers that filed all returns and paid taxes and interest due by May 31, 2005 (June 30, 2006, for taxpayers that enter into installment agreements). The full payment requirement was also satisfied if the payment was made within 15 days of notice and demand. (Sec. 19731 et seq., Rev. & Tax. Code)

In addition, no criminal action will be brought against the taxpayer, for the tax reporting periods for which tax amnesty was requested, for the nonreporting or underreporting of tax liabilities unless, as of the first day of the amnesty period (1) the taxpayer was on notice of a criminal investigation or was under a criminal investigation or (2) a court proceeding had already been initiated. Penalties and fees will not be waived for any nonreported or underreported tax liability amounts attributable to tax shelter items that could have been reported under either the California voluntary compliance initiative or the Internal Revenue Service's Offshore Voluntary Compliance Initiative. (Sec. 19732, Rev. & Tax. Code)

The accuracy-related penalty imposed on deficiencies associated with the amnesty program, other than those relating to underreporting of tax shelter items, is increased from 20% to 40%. However, the increased penalty will not apply to any taxable year of a taxpayer beginning prior to the amnesty program if, as of the start date of the amnesty program period, the taxpayer was under an FTB audit, had filed a protest or appeal, was engaged in settlement negotiations, or had a pending judicial proceeding in any California or federal court relating to the tax liability of the taxpayer for that taxable year. (Sec. 19164, Rev. & Tax. Code)

In addition to the enhanced penalties, a 50% interest penalty will be imposed for each period for which amnesty could have been requested for amounts that were due and payable on the last date of the amnesty period, for the period beginning on the date on which the tax was due and ending on the last day of the amnesty period. (Sec. 19777.5, Rev. & Tax. Code)

Practitioner Comment: No Definition of "Due and Payable" for Amnesty Program

California's 50% interest penalty applies to amounts "due and payable" as of March 31, 2005. Although "due and payable" is defined statutorily in three different sections of the California Revenue and Taxation Code, the FTB has not adopted the existing statutory definition of "due and payable" for purposes of determining when the amnesty program's 50% interest penalty applies. FTB staff has taken a position, based on its interpretation of the law and the intent of the Legislature, that the strict liability penalty must be calculated on the amount unpaid as of March 31, 2005, the last day of the amnesty period. Interestingly, "due and payable" is not defined in the tax amnesty provisions. The definition most widely used is Rev. & Tax. Code Sec. 19049, which states that a tax becomes due and payable 15 days after the taxpayer is given notice of the final assessment. This issue will likely need to be resolved through litigation.

Bruce Daigh, Chris Whitney, Contributing Editors

The enhanced interest penalties do not apply to taxpayers that have entered into an installment agreement with respect to amounts payable under the agreement. (Sec. 19738, Rev. & Tax. Code) In addition, for purpose of computing the amount of the interest penalty imposed on personal income tax or corporation franchise or income tax deficiencies that become due and payable after March 31, 2005, taxpayers may offset specified overpayments made in one year against underpayments for another tax year. Overpayments made by specified related parties may similarly offset a taxpayer's underpayments during the same tax year. (Sec. 19777.5(a)(3), Rev. & Tax. Code)

A taxpayer may not file a claim for refund or credit for any amounts paid in connection with the enhanced interest penalty unless the penalty was improperly computed by the FTB. (Sec. 19777.5(e), Rev. & Tax Code)

Practitioner Comment: Amnesty is Over and Penalties Are Now Being Assessed

The Tax Amnesty Program ran from February 1, 2005 through March 31, 2005. Amounts paid under the amnesty program are not eligible for a refund. Effectively, by adopting provisions that prohibit a taxpayer from claiming a refund of the additional penalty assessed on pre-2003 franchise tax liabilities not paid by the last day of the amnesty period, the state essentially adopted a "pay-to-play" regime. Of the $4.4 billion collected, $3.5 billion was essentially paid outside of the amnesty program and was accompanied by protective claims filed to preserve taxpayers' appeal rights.

Taxpayers who did not participate in the amnesty program may now be subject to penalties, as follows:

—For each taxable year for which amnesty could have been requested, the FTB is assessing an additional non-appealable and non-refundable penalty on outstanding liabilities that become due and payable on or after the last day of the amnesty period, March 31, 2005. In general, the additional penalty equals an additional 50% of the interest computed from the due date of the tax through March 31, 2005. Although the penalty is equal to 50% of the specified interest, because this is a penalty it will probably not be deductible for federal and state income tax purposes.

Under Ch. 398 (AB 911), Laws 2005, overpayments and underpayments can be netted to determine if the 50% amnesty interest penalty applies. If the 50% amnesty interest penalty applies after overpayments and underpayments have been netted, the penalty applies only to the net underpayment after application of available overpayments. Prior to this legislation, the 50% interest penalty would have been assessed for any underpayment, even if the taxpayer had offsetting refunds in other years. Taxpayers should also be aware that there is still no reasonable cause exception for the amnesty interest penalty.

—The accuracy-related penalty is doubled—from 20% to 40%—for any proposed deficiency assessment issued after the amnesty period expires for any tax year that was eligible for amnesty, except for taxpayers who are under audit (or in the post-audit administrative process) for pre-2003 years at the start date of the amnesty period.

Bruce Daigh, Chris Whitney, Contributing Editors

The FTB has stated that although a taxpayer cannot file a formal protest of a post-amnesty penalty before payment, and there are no formal prepayment protest rights, the FTB will administratively review and correct a post-amnesty penalty before payment if the taxpayer believes that the penalty was computed incorrectly. (*Tax News*, California Franchise Tax Board, June 2006)

¶713 Information at Source

Law: Secs. 18631-32, 18639-61, 19175, 19182 (CCH CALIFORNIA TAX REPORTS ¶89-104).

Comparable Federal: Secs. 6039, 6039D, 6041-50R, 6052-53, 6111 (CCH U.S. MASTER TAX GUIDE ¶628, 797, 871, 2004, 2565, 2607).

Under California law, the Franchise Tax Board (FTB) *may* require individuals, partnerships, corporations, or other organizations engaged in trade or business in California, making payments in the course of such trade or business, to make information returns and to furnish copies to recipients of the payments. (Sec. 18631, Rev. & Tax. Code) The following payments are covered:

— *as to payees whose last known address is in California:*

— payments of any fixed or determinable income (*i.e.*, group term life insurance, gambling winnings, medical payments, remuneration for personal services, but excludes compensation subject to withholding as explained at ¶715) amounting to $600 or more; "service-recipients" required to make a return under IRC Sec. 6041A must also make a return to California;

— payments of dividends if the payor was required to file an information return (1099) under federal law;

— payments of interest if the payor was required to file an information return (1099) under federal law;

— specified payments of interest and exempt-interest dividends aggregating $10 or more if the interest is from other states' bonds exempt from federal income tax but taxable by California (see discussion below);

— group life insurance benefits provided to employees, to the extent the cost of such benefits exceeds the cost of $50,000 of coverage plus the amount contributed by the employee;

— corporate liquidating distributions amounting to $600 or more to any stockholder;

— patronage dividends of cooperatives amounting to $100 or more; and

— original issue discount paid on a publicly offered debt instrument; and

— *as to payees who are not residents of California,*

— payments of compensation for services rendered in California, and

— payments of rents or royalties on property located in California.

See ¶716 for reporting requirements for dispositions of real property.

Practice Tip: Detailed Information Available

The FTB has produced Publication 4227A, *Guide to Information Returns Filed With California* (2006), CCH CALIFORNIA TAX REPORTS ¶404-170, which provides succinct information concerning what type of payments must be reported on which form, the amounts required to be reported, and the filing deadlines for filing the returns with the state and with the recipient.

• *Reporting not required*

The following payments need not be reported, regardless of amount:

— payments to a corporation, other than payments for attorneys' fees;

— partnership, estate, or trust distributions shown on their returns;

— rent payments to a real estate agent having a place of business in California;

— payments to a nonresident that are reported by the withholding agent on Forms 592 and 592-B (¶714);

— payments of income exempt from California income tax;

— payments by those not engaged in a trade or business;

— payments for merchandise, etc.;

— certain payments to employees of interstate carriers;

— certain payments by bankers acting as collection agents.

(Reg. 18631, 18 CCR)

• *Information on cash received in trade or business*

The FTB *must* require a copy of the federal information return relating to cash received in a trade or business (Form 8300) if a federal information return was required under IRC Sec. 6050I. Under federal law, any person required to be named in the return must be furnished with written notice of the name and address of the person required to file the Form 8300 and the amount of cash required to be specified on Form 8300 as received from the person named. California has not adopted this requirement. (Sec. 18631(c)(10), Rev. & Tax. Code)

• *Information on tax-exempt interest and dividends*

Brokerages and mutual fund companies are required to report to the FTB payments of interest and exempt-interest dividends aggregating $10 or more in any calendar year to any person if the interest and dividends are from other states' bonds that are exempt from federal income taxation but taxable by California. (Sec. 18631(c)(8), Rev. & Tax. Code)

• *Procedure for reporting*

Payments are reported on federal Form 1099. Except as noted below, 1099-B returns must be filed on magnetic tape; other information reports may be made on magnetic tape if the volume exceeds specified limits, conforming to the federal procedure. Reports are for the calendar year and are due generally on February 28th of the following year (March 31 if filed using the Internet). Extension of time for filing may be obtained by written request to the FTB. Copies of individual forms should be furnished to recipients by January 31. (FTB Pub. 4227, Information Returns (Forms 1098, 1099, 5498, W-2G))

Practice Note: Electronic Filing

Beginning January 1, 2009, information returns must be submitted using the FTB's Secure Web Internet Filing Transfer (SWIFT) to submit files if the withholding agent submitted more than 250 information returns electronically or filed 2007 returns using the FTB's e-Information Return program.

Practitioner Comment: Internet Filing

Tax practitioners are encouraged to use Internet filing for their clients' information returns (Forms 1098, 1099, 5498, and W-2G). Internet filing information and applications are available on the FTB website at www.ftb.ca.gov. The FTB has extended the Internet reporting due date from February 28 to March 31 to allow more time for making changes or corrections before submitting files. (*Tax News*, California Franchise Tax Board, September/October 2005, CCH CALIFORNIA TAX REPORTS ¶403-884)

Bruce Daigh, Chris Whitney, Contributing Editors

• *Nontaxable distributions*

In the case of corporate distributions believed to be nontaxable, complete information should be supplied to the FTB not later than February 1, for the preceding year. The FTB will then advise the distributing corporation regarding the taxability of the distribution.

• *Stock options*

Corporations transferring stock under certain stock options are required to furnish statements (by January 31 of the following year) to the individuals involved. California incorporates the federal requirement. (Sec. 18631(c)(2), Rev. & Tax. Code)

• *Tips*

The California recordkeeping and reporting requirements for tips are generally the same as the federal regulations. However, under federal law, certain food or beverage establishments employing ten or more workers on a typical business day in the preceding year are required to file annual information returns for the purpose of increasing taxpayer compliance in reporting income from tips. California has no comparable requirement. (Reg. 4350-1)

• *Tax-shelter promoters*

Tax shelter promoters are subject to stringent reporting requirements; see ¶727 for details.

• *Property owners*

Owners and transferors of real property or a mobilehome assessed by a California assessor, except for property covered by a homeowner's exemption (¶1704), may be required to file returns requested and prescribed by the FTB. The returns include the owner's social security number or other identification number prescribed by the FTB, identification of the property interest, and other information the FTB may request. Owners who fail to file within 60 days of the due date or who file a misleading return will be denied deductions for interest, taxes, depreciation, or amortization paid or incurred with respect to the property. (Sec. 18642, Rev. & Tax. Code)

• *Check cashing businesses*

Any check cashing business that cashes checks other than one-party checks, payroll checks, or government checks totaling more than $10,000 in one transaction or in two or more transactions for the same person within the calendar year must file an information return with the FTB no later than 90 days after the end of the calendar year. (Sec. 18631.7, Rev. & Tax. Code)

• *Penalties*

As stated at ¶712, severe civil and criminal penalties may be imposed for various offenses, including failure to comply with the requirements for information returns. Also, as stated at ¶336, certain deductions may be disallowed in cases where required information returns are not filed.

The failure to file information returns on remuneration for personal services is also penalized under the Unemployment Insurance Code. If the failure to file is punishable under the Revenue and Taxation Code as well as the Unemployment Insurance Code, only the latter penalty will be applied. (Sec. 19175, Rev. & Tax. Code)

¶714 Withholding of Tax at Source—General

Law: Secs. 18536, 18662, 18665, 18666, 18668-77, 19002 (CCH CALIFORNIA TAX REPORTS ¶16-605, 16-635, 16-640, 16-650, 16-655, 89-056, 89-176).

Comparable Federal: Secs. 1445, 1446 (CCH U.S. MASTER TAX GUIDE ¶2329, 2492).

California Forms: Forms 587 (Nonresident Withholding Allocation Worksheet), 588 (Nonresident Withholding Waiver Request), Form 589 (Nonresident Reduced Withholding Request), 590 (Withholding Exemption Certificate), 590-P (Nonresident Withholding Exemption Certificate for Previously Reported Income of Partners and Members), 592 (Quarterly Nonresident Withholding Statement), 592-A (Foreign Partner or Member Quarterly Withholding Remittance Statement), 592-B (Resident and Nonresident Withholding Tax Statement), 592-F (Foreign Shareholder, Partner, or Member Annual Return), 594 (Notice to Withhold Tax at Source), 595 (Entertainment Withholding Reduction).

Below is a discussion of the withholding requirements for payments to nonresidents and foreign partners.

• *Nonresidents*

As to nonresidents, withholding is generally required on payments of compensation for personal services performed in California (including payments to independent contractors), rents, patent royalties, prizes, etc., provided the income is attributable to California (see ¶231 for discussion of income from sources within the state). In addition, the Franchise Tax Board (FTB) requires withholding on payments of pass-through entity income to domestic nonresident owners. (Sec. 18662, Rev. & Tax. Code; Reg. 18662-2, 18 CCR) FTB Pub. 1017, *Nonresident Withholding Guidelines* (revised 12-2007), also specifies that withholding must be made on payments from the following sources:

— payments made to nonresident entertainers for services rendered in California. These payments include, but are not limited to, guaranteed payments, overages, royalties, and residual payments;

— payments received for a covenant not to compete in California;

— payments releasing a contractual obligation to perform services in California;

— income from options received for performing personal services in California;

— bonuses paid for services performed in California; and

— distributions of California source taxable income.

However, under Reg. 18662-2, 18 CCR, withholding is not required unless the income payments to a payee by the same payor exceed $1,500 during the calendar year or the payor is directed to withhold by the FTB.

Nonresidents include nonresident individuals, nonresident estates and trusts, and corporations and pass-through entities that do not have a permanent place of business in California and are not registered with the California Secretary of State's Office (SOS). A corporate payee that is not qualified through the SOS and does not have a permanent place of business in this state, but is included in the combined report of a corporation that does have a permanent place of business in California, is also subject to nonresident withholding, However, the corporation may request a waiver from the FTB by submitting Form 588, Nonresident Withholding Waiver Request. (FTB Pub. 1017, *Nonresident Withholding Guidelines* (revised 12-2007)

The tax to be withheld for nonresident individuals and business entities is generally computed at the rate of 7% of gross income. (Reg. 18662-3, 18 CCR) However, in cases such as those involving entertainers where deductible expenses are likely to be large, the FTB may upon application (through the payor's submission of a Form 588, Nonresident Withholding Waiver Request) waive the withholding requirements in whole or in part. According to the Instructions to Form 588, reasons for a waiver request include the following:

— the vendor/payee has California state tax returns on file for the two most recent taxable years in which the vendor/payee has a filing requirement, and the vendor/payee is considered current on any outstanding tax obligations with the FTB;

— the vendor/payee is making timely estimated tax payments for the current taxable year, and the vendor/payee is considered current on any outstanding tax obligations with the FTB;

— the vendor, S corporation shareholder, partner, or member is a corporation not qualified to do business and does not have a permanent place of business in California but is filing a tax return based on a combined report with a corporation that does have a permanent place of business in California; or

— the shareholder, partner, or member is a newly admitted S corporation shareholder, partner, or LLC member.

If none of the above reasons apply, a taxpayer may still submit a request but must attach a specific reason and a calculation of the reduced rate. Waivers may not be granted for withholding on foreign partners. Different procedures apply to waivers for withholding on sales of California real estate.

CCH Practice Pointer: Partnership Distributions Representing a Return of Capital

Waiver requests are not required if a partnership's distribution represents a return of capital. However, the partnership will be subject to penalties for failure to withhold if, upon audit, the FTB determines that the distribution represented taxable income. (FTB Pub. 1017 (REV 12-2007), Nonresident Withholding S Corporation and Partnership Guidelines)

Waivers are effective for a maximum of two years from the date the waiver is granted.

Domestic nonresidents use Form 589, Nonresident Request for Reduced Withholding, to request a reduction in the standard 7% withholding amount that is applicable to California source payments to nonresidents. The payee must complete Form 589 before receiving payment for services and must complete the form based on expenses, costs, or other special circumstances that would justify a reduced withholding amount; calculate the proposed reduced withholding amount as 7% of the net California source payment, which is the gross payment minus expenses or costs identified on the form; and certify under penalty of perjury that the expenses and resulting reduced withholding calculations are true and correct. After the FTB analyzes Form 589, it will issue a letter to the payee and the withholding agent notifying them of its determination and the amount to be withheld. The FTB has indicated that receiving Form 589 at least 10 business days before the withholding agent pays the nonresident payee will help it meet requests as quickly as possible. (*Tax News*, California Franchise Tax Board, November 2007, CCH CALIFORNIA TAX REPORTS ¶404-487)

Practice Note: Treatment of Withholding on Payments to Pass-Through Entities

As a general rule, withholding on payments to pass-through entities must be passed through and credited against the pass-through entity owners' tax liabilities in proportion to their ownership interests. However, pass-through entities may claim the withholding against any entity level tax or fees that may be owing prior to passing through the withholding credit to its owners. The entity level taxes include the annual tax imposed on partnerships, limited liability companies, and S corporations; the LLC fees; and the 1.5% tax imposed against S corporations. (FTB Pub. 1017, *Nonresident Withholding Guidelines*(revised 12-2007))

Practice Note: Withholding Incentive Program

The FTB will offer a voluntary incentive program where withholding agents, who have not previously withheld, may remit past-due nonresident non-wage withholding for tax year 2008 until March 15, 2009. As an incentive, the FTB will apply reasonable cause to waive penalties for failure to file correct information returns (Forms 592 and 592-B). The FTB's Web site will be updated with news, forms, and detailed instructions on the new voluntary withholding incentive program. This information was not available at the time this book went to press. (*Tax News*, California Franchise Tax Board, November 2008, CCH CALIFORNIA TAX REPORTS ¶404-781)

• *Foreign partners*

California incorporates the federal provision (IRC Sec. 1446) that requires the withholding of tax on all amounts paid by U.S. partnerships to foreign partners that are connected to the partnership's U.S. activities. (Sec. 18666, Rev. & Tax. Code) However, the California tax is withheld at the maximum applicable California rate, rather than at the rate specified in the federal provision, and California's withholding is limited to California-source amounts. The $1,500 minimum filing threshold is not applicable to the withholding for foreign partners.

• *Teachers' Replacement Benefit Program Payments*

Annual benefits payable under the Teachers' Replacement Benefits Program are subject to withholding of California personal income and employment taxes. The disbursements under this program represent amounts in excess of federal limitations on annual benefits applicable to a government plan (Sec. 24260, Education Code).

• *Procedures and returns*

A payor who receives a Nonresident Allocation Worksheet (Form 587) from the payee may rely on that certification to determine if withholding is required provided the form is accepted in good faith. A payor is relieved of the obligation to withhold if he or she obtains a Withholding Exemption Certificate (Form 590) or Nonresident

Withholding Exemption Certificate for Previously Reported Income of Partners and Members (Form 590-P). (Reg. 18662-7, 18 CCR) Foreign (non-U.S.) partners or members may not file a Form 590-P as there is no exemption from withholding available to a foreign partner or member. (Instructions to Form 590-P) Penalties (fine, or imprisonment, or both) are provided for violation of withholding requirements.

Tax withheld on California source payments to domestic nonresidents is remitted to the FTB on a quarterly basis (similar to estimated tax payments, see ¶111) using Form 592, Quarterly Nonresident Withholding Statement. Form 592 includes a schedule of payees section that requires the withholding agent to identify the payment recipients, the income, and the withholding amounts. Withholding agents are not required to submit Form 592-B, Resident and Nonresident Withholding Tax Statement, to the FTB for each payee, but must still provide each payee with a paper Form 592-B to show the total amount withheld for the year.

Partnerships and LLCs withholding on foreign partners or members must file Form 592-A *Foreign Partner or Member Quarterly Withholding Remittance Statement,* along with their withholding. Form 592-A is filed on the 15th day of the fourth, sixth, ninth, and twelfth months of the partnership's or LLCs taxable year. At the close of the taxable year, the partnership or LLC must complete Form 592-F, Foreign Partner or Member Annual Return, to report the total withholding for the year and allocate the income or gain and related withholding to the foreign partners or members. When filing Form 592-F, the withholding agent is not required to submit Form 592-B to the FTB for each partner or member. However, withholding agents must provide the partners or members with paper Forms 592-B.

For realty dispositions, Form 593, Real Estate Remittance Statement, is used to report and transmit the amount withheld, see ¶716. Starting January 1, 2008, the FTB initiated a pilot program for electronic submission of real estate withholding data for real estate withholding agents that submit more than 250 information returns annually. Withholding agents must use the FTB's Secure Web Internet Filing Transfer (SWIFT) to submit the files. Persons with problems or questions concerning the SWIFT program may contact the FTB at WSCS.SWIFT@ftb.ca.gov.

Persons interested in filing these forms electronically should consult FTB Pub. 923, Secure Web Internet File Transfer (SWIFT) Guide for Resident and Nonresident Withholding.

• *Interest on late remittances*

The interest on deficiencies (¶709) applies to delayed remittances of amounts withheld from fixed or determinable gains, profits, and income and from remittances of partnership income to foreign partners. (Sec. 18668, Rev. & Tax. Code)

• *Delinquent taxes*

In addition to withholding from payments of income to nonresidents, the FTB may require withholding of delinquent taxes due from both resident and nonresident taxpayers. The FTB may, by notice and demand, require such withholding and payment to the FTB by anyone, including state agencies, who is in possession or control of credits or property belonging to a delinquent taxpayer or belonging to a person who has failed to withhold as required under the law. (Sec. 18670, Rev. & Tax. Code)

In *Greene v. Franchise Tax Board* (1972) (CCH CALIFORNIA TAX REPORTS ¶89-176.60), the California Court of Appeal upheld the FTB's use of the withholding procedure to collect delinquent tax of $72. In *Franchise Tax Board v. Construction Laborers Vacation Trust for Southern California* (1983) (CCH CALIFORNIA TAX REPORTS, ¶89-176.602), the issue was whether the FTB was precluded by federal law (ERISA) from requiring a union vacation trust fund to withhold for unpaid personal income tax owed by union members. The U.S. Supreme Court held that federal courts did not have jurisdiction in the matter, and referred the case back to California Superior Court. In *Franchise Tax*

Board of California v. United States Postal Service (1984) (CCH CALIFORNIA TAX REPORTS ¶89-176.80), the U.S. Supreme Court held that the Postal Service could be required to withhold delinquent California tax from its employees.

An employer is liable for unremitted amounts, plus interest, if the FTB determines that an employer withheld earnings pursuant to an earnings withholding order for taxes but failed to remit the withheld earnings to the FTB, and the employer also fails to remit the withheld earnings following notice from the FTB. A deficiency assessment may be issued for such amount within seven years from the date that the amount, in the aggregate, was first withheld. When the assessment against the employer becomes final, the taxpayer's account may be credited for that amount. Collection action against the taxpayer is stayed until the earlier of the time the credit is applied or the assessment against the employer is withdrawn or revised and the taxpayer is notified thereof. (Sec. 18673, Rev. & Tax. Code)

• *Date tax deemed paid*

For the purpose of filing claims for refund, any tax withheld under the California withholding provisions is deemed to have been paid on the due date (without regard to extensions of time) of the return for the taxable year with respect to which the withheld tax is allowed as a credit. (Sec. 19002, Rev. & Tax. Code) Under the proposed regulations, special rules would apply to end-of-the year payments and distributions. (Proposed Reg. 19002, 18 CCR)

¶715 Withholding on Wages

Law: Secs. 18408, 18551, 18662-66, 19002, 19009, 19852, 19853; Secs. 1151-1153, 1233—1236, 1870-1875, 13004, 13009, 13020, 13021, 13028, 13059, Unemployment Insurance Code (CCH CALIFORNIA TAX REPORTS ¶16-610, 16-615, 16-620, 16-630, 16-645, 16-660, 89-102, 89-106, 89-186, 89-210).

Comparable Federal: Secs. 31, 3401-05, 3501-05, 6051, 6053 (CCH U.S. MASTER TAX GUIDE ¶2601 et seq.).

California Forms: DE-4 (Employee's Withholding Allowance Certificate), W-2 (Wage and Tax Statement), (FTB 3525 (Substitute for W-2, Wage and Tax Statement, or Form 1099-R, Distributions from Pensions, Annuities, Retirement or Profit-Sharing Plans, IRAs, Insurance Contracts, Etc.).

The California wage withholding system conforms closely to the federal system. For this reason, the following discussion will deal principally with the differences between the California and federal rules.

The wage withholding provisions are administered by the Employment Development Department (EDD). The withholding rules are set forth in Division 6 of the Unemployment Insurance Code (Sec. 13000, Unempl. Ins. Code, through Sec. 13101, Unempl. Ins. Code) and the regulations issued by the EDD.

• *California-federal differences*

Employers are required to withhold on all "wages," as defined below, of California residents and on "wages" of nonresidents for services performed in California. (Sec. 13020, Unempl. Ins. Code) As in the federal rules, "wages" includes all remuneration for services of an employee, with specified exceptions for agricultural labor, domestic service, and other categories. Following are differences between the California and federal rules in what is subject to withholding:

— California excludes wages paid to members of a crew on a vessel engaged in foreign, coastwise, intercoastal, interstate, or noncontiguous trade; federal law has no such exclusion;

— federal law excludes compensation paid under certain bond purchase plans; California has no such exclusion;

— federal law excludes certain foreign service; California has no such exclusion; however, such compensation would be excluded under California law if the employee is not a California "resident," as defined at ¶105;

— California specifies that whether an individual provides equipment shall be ignored in determining whether the individual is an "employee" (Sec. 13004, Unempl. Ins. Code); and

— federal law considers certain payments of gambling winnings as wages, whereas California withholding law does not. (Sec. 13009, Unempl. Ins. Code) However, California does require withholding from prizes and winnings. (Reg. 18662-2, 18 CCR)

The California rules for withholding on pensions, annuities, sick pay, supplemental unemployment benefits, and other deferred income conform generally to the federal rules.

• *Employee vs. independent contractor*

In *Hunt Building Corp. v. Michael S. Bernick* (2000) (CCH CALIFORNIA TAX REPORTS ¶16-615.80), a California court of appeal held that a general contractor was subject to California personal income tax withholding and unemployment compensation fund and disability insurance contribution requirements as if it were the employer of its unlicensed subcontractors' employees. State law defined the unlicensed subcontractors and their employees as employees of the general contractor, rather than independent contractors, because their services required the general contractor to obtain a state contractor license. Although the construction work performed by the unlicensed subcontractors' employees was performed for the U.S. government on federal lands, federal law provided no relief from the state requirements, because federal law deferred to state law defining employer/employee relationships.

• *Withholding methods*

California provides two methods for computing the amount of tax to be withheld, as follows:

Method A—WAGE BRACKET TABLE METHOD (similar to federal "wage bracket" method); and

Method B—EXACT CALCULATION METHOD (similar to the federal "percentage" method).

California permits use of other methods in special situations, upon application. Federal rules also permit alternative methods.

With respect to supplemental wages (bonuses, overtime, commissions, sales awards, back pay including retroactive wage increases, reimbursement of nondeductible moving expenses, and stock options), an employer may either (1) add supplemental wages to regular wages and compute withholding on the whole amount or (2) apply a flat percentage rate to the supplemental wages alone, without allowance for exemptions or credits. California's supplemental withholding rate is 6% (9.3% for stock options and bonus payments that constitute wages). (Sec. 13043, Unempl. Ins. Code; Sec. 18663, Rev. & Tax. Code)

• *Instruction booklet*

Detailed instructions for determining the amount to be withheld, with tables and formulas, are included in a booklet entitled "Employer's Tax Guide for the Withholding, Payment, and Reporting of California Income Tax." This booklet can be obtained from offices of the FTB or the EDD or on the EDD's Web site at: http://www.edd.ca.gov/Payroll_Taxes/Rates_and_Withholding.htm.

• *Employee forms*

California provides a form (Form DE-4) for the employee's exemption certificate to determine the number of California withholding exemptions. The employee has the option of using California Form DE-4. Otherwise, the employee must use federal Form W-4 to determine the number of California exemptions. The employee is considered married if the employer cannot determine the employee's marital status from either Form DE-4 or W-4.

California conforms fully to the federal rules for exemption certificates. Thus, any certificate that complies with the federal rules is accepted also for California purposes. The requirements for complete exemption, based on absence of federal income tax liability, are the same for California as for federal; that is, a certificate that eliminates federal withholding also eliminates California withholding. An employer who makes the required special report to the Internal Revenue Service where a large number of exemptions is claimed need not make a report to the state. The FTB may require employers to submit copies of withholding exemption certificates. The law sets forth procedures to be followed if the FTB determines that the withholding exemption certificate is invalid. (Sec. 13040, Unempl. Ins. Code; Sec. 13041, Unempl. Ins. Code; Sec. 18667, Rev. & Tax. Code; Reg. 4340-1, 22 CCR)

• *Filing of returns*

Withheld tax must be reported and paid monthly or quarterly, depending on the amounts involved, as explained below.

Statements must be furnished to employees, using federal Form W-2, by January 31 and upon termination. The Form W-2 must show the amount of disability insurance contributions (SDI) withheld (¶1806). (Sec. 13050, Unempl. Ins. Code)

Practice Note: Earned Income Tax Credit Information Must Be Provided to Employees

California employers must notify employees covered by the employer's unemployment insurance that they may be eligible for the federal earned income tax credit (EITC). The EITC notice must be provided by handing the notice directly to the employee or mailing the notice to the employee's last-known address within the one week period before or after the employer provides the employee an annual wage summary. In addition, upon an employee's request, an employer must process Form W-5 for advance payments of the EITC. Sec. 19852, Rev. & Tax. Code, Sec. 19853, Rev. & Tax. Code

---

Generally, a report of wages must be submitted each calendar quarter showing the total tax withheld for each employee and the amounts withheld from pensions, annuities, and other deferred compensation. A reconciliation return must be filed annually by January 31 (or within 10 days of termination of business). (Sec. 13021, Unempl. Ins. Code; Sec. 13050, Unempl. Ins. Code) Electronic filing, registration, and payment options are available. Details can be found on the EDD's Web site at.http://www.edd.ca.gov/Payroll_Taxes/Electronic_Filing_Registration_and_Payment_Information.htm

Employers authorized under federal law to file magnetic media returns for federal withholding tax purposes must either

— file by means of magnetic media the reports of wages that must accompany their quarterly payments of state withholding tax or

— establish a lack of automation, severe economic hardship, current exemption from the magnetic media requirement, or other good cause for not filing reports of wages magnetically. (Sec. 1114, Unempl. Ins. Code)

The due date of a withholding return, report, or statement may be extended if an employer's failure to timely file or pay tax is attributable to a state of emergency declared by the Governor. (Sec. 13059, Rev. & Tax. Code)

• *Payment of tax*

An employer who is required to remit withheld federal income taxes pursuant to IRC Sec. 6302 and who has accumulated withheld state income taxes in the amount of

$500 or more must remit the withheld state income taxes within the same number of banking days specified for withheld federal income taxes. The $500 threshold amount is adjusted annually for inflation. For 2008 the threshold amount is $450. An employer who is required to withhold tax, but who is not required to remit payment in accordance with IRC Sec. 6302, must remit the amount withheld during each month of each calendar quarter by the 15th day of the subsequent month if the amount withheld for any month, or cumulatively for two or more months within the quarter, is $350 or more. (Sec. 13021, Unempl. Ins. Code)

Any employer whose cumulative average eighth-monthly (as described in IRC Sec. 6302) payment during any deposit period is $20,000 or more must remit the withheld state income taxes by way of electronic funds transfer within the same number of banking days specified in IRC Sec. 6302, for withheld federal income taxes. The electronic funds transfer requirement may be waived if the average withholding payment exceeding the threshold amount is not representative of the taxpayer's actual tax liability and was the result of an unprecedented occurrence.

Employers not required to pay by electronic means may elect to do so with the approval of the EDD. Payment by electronic means will generally be deemed complete on the date the transfer is initiated.

Any income tax withheld that is not covered by any of the above requirements must be remitted to the state by the last day of the month following the end of the quarter. Any amounts withheld for employees' disability-insurance contributions (¶1808) are due and payable at the same time as the payments for income-tax withholding, regardless of the amounts involved.

Employers who are subject to certain requirements for accelerated payment of withheld federal taxes are required to remit withheld California taxes on the same time schedule.

The law provides detailed rules for collection of tax, liabilities and obligations of employers and employees, penalties, etc. An employer or withholding agent is liable for personal income tax required to be deducted and withheld or, beginning with the 2009 taxable year, withheld and not timely remitted. The employer or withholding agent is generally liable whether or not the tax was collected and withheld. (Sec. 13070, Unempl. Ins. Code; Sec. 18668, Rev. & Tax. Code; Reg. 4370-1, 22 CCR) If the tax for which an employer is liable is paid or if the employee reports the wages to the FTB, the employer is relieved of liability for the tax itself but not for penalties or additions to the tax arising out of the failure to withhold. (Sec. 13071, Unempl. Ins. Code)

Upon sale of a business, the purchaser may be liable for unsatisfied obligations of the seller. (Sec. 18669, Rev. & Tax. Code) EDD Reg. 4320-1, 22 CCR, specifies procedures to be followed when employers are required to withhold other-state taxes from wages paid to California residents. In these cases, where the other state's withholding requirement is greater than the California amount, no California withholding is required.

• *Compromise of withholding tax liability*

The EDD is authorized to accept partial payment in satisfaction of final, nondisputed withholding tax liabilities of certain employers if the amount offered in compromise is more than could reasonably be collected through involuntary means during the four-year period beginning on the date the offer is made. (Sec. 1870 et seq., Unempl. Ins. Code)

Practice Pointer: Making an Offer in Compromise

Form DE 999CA, Multi-Agency Form for Offer in Compromise, may be used by individuals to make an offer in compromise for personal income, sales and use, and other taxes owed to the FTB, SBE, and EDD. Corporations, partnerships, and limited liability companies should continue to use Form FTB 4905BE, Offer in Compromise for Business Entities, for FTB offers, and Form BOE-490-C, Offer In Compromise Application For Corporations, Limited Liability Companies, Partnerships, Trusts, and Unidentified Business Organizations, for SBE offers. (*News Release*, California Tax Service Center, August 23, 2006)

• *Penalties*

As stated at ¶712, severe civil and criminal penalties are imposed on employers, employees, and others for various offenses. Also, as stated at ¶322, deductions for remuneration for personal services may be disallowed for failure to report the payments in required statements to employees or to independent contractors.

• *Settlement authority*

The Director of the EDD may approve the settlement of any civil tax dispute involving a reduction of tax of $7,500 or less on his or her own authority. However, the proposed settlement must be submitted to an administrative law judge for approval if any of the following circumstances apply:

— an appeal has been filed with the Unemployment Insurance Appeals Board;

— the appeal has been assigned to an administrative law judge; and

— a notice of hearing has been issued.

(Sec. 1236, Unempl. Ins. Code)

Proposed settlements of $5,000 or more must be reviewed by the Attorney General prior to final approval, and settlements involving amounts over $7,500 must also be approved by the Unemployment Insurance Appeals Board.

• *Waiver for reliance on written advice*

The EDD is authorized to waive tax assessments, interest, additions to tax, or penalties imposed as a result of a taxpayer's failure to make a timely return or payment if the taxpayer's failure was due to the taxpayer's reasonable reliance on the written advice of a ruling by the Director or the Director's designee. If the taxpayer's action was due to reasonable reliance on written advice other than a ruling by the director or director's designee, the EDD is authorized to waive interest, additions to tax, or penalties. All of the following conditions must be met before the EDD may provide relief:

— the taxpayer must request advice regarding the tax consequences of a particular activity or transaction and the activity or transaction must be fully described;

— the EDD must issue a written ruling or opinion;

— the taxpayer must have reasonably relied on that advice; and

— the tax consequences expressed in the EDD's advice must not have been changed by a later issued opinion, statutory or case law, federal interpretation, or material facts or circumstances relating to the taxpayer.

(Sec. 111, Unempl. Ins. Code)

No relief will be provided if the taxpayer's request for written advice contained a misrepresentation or omission of a material fact.

Nonprofit organizations and governmental agencies are specifically excluded from the relief provisions discussed above. Relief from the assessment of unemployment insurance taxes is conditioned upon approval from the U.S. Secretary of Labor; however, relief from any corresponding interest and penalties may still be provided.

¶716 Withholding on Dispositions of California Realty

Law: Secs. 18662, 18668 (CCH CALIFORNIA TAX REPORTS ¶16-625, 89-102, 89-206).

Comparable Federal: Sec. 1445 (CCH U.S. MASTER TAX GUIDE ¶2442).

California Forms: Forms 593 (Real Estate Withholding Remittance Statement), 593-C (Real Estate Withholding Certificate), 593-I (Real Estate Withholding Installment Sale Agreement), 593-E (Real Estate Withholding - Computation of Estimated Gain or Loss), FTB Pub. 1016 (Real Estate Withholding Guidelines).

Applicable to dispositions of real property interests by resident individuals, nonresident individuals, corporations with no permanent place of business in California, and applicable to real property sales occurring after 2008 by out-of-state partnerships, transferees (including intermediaries or accommodators in a deferred exchange) are required to withhold an amount equal to $3^1/_3$% of the sales price of the California real property conveyed. Alternatively, transferees may to elect to withhold at the corporation franchise tax rate (currently, 8.84%), bank and financial corporation tax rate (currently, 10.84%), or highest personal income tax rate (currently, 9.3%), as applicable, multiplied by the reportable gain on the sale rather than at the current withholding rate of 3 1/3% on the sales price of California real property conveyed. For this purpose, the highest personal income tax rate is determined without regard to the additional 1% surtax (*a.k.a.* the mental health services tax) on income in excess of $1 million.

Applicable to sales occurring after 2008, the alternative withholding rate for S corporations is increased from 1.5% of the gain to 10.8% of the gain (the current S corporation tax rate of 1.5% plus the highest personal income tax rate of 9.3%). For S corporations that are financial corporations, the alternative withholding rate is similarly increased from 3.5% to 12.8%. (Sec. 18662, Rev. & Tax. Code)

However, no withholding is required if any of the following circumstances apply:

— the sales price of the California real property conveyed is $100,000 or less;

— written notification of the withholding requirements was not provided by a real estate escrow person (this exception does not apply to an intermediary or an accommodator in a deferred exchange);

— the transferee acquires the property at a sale pursuant to a power of sale under a mortgage or deed of trust, at a sale pursuant to a decree of foreclosure, or by a deed in lieu of foreclosure;

— the transferor is a bank acting as a trustee other than a trustee of a deed of trust;

— the property being conveyed is (1) the principal residence of the transferor or decedent, or (2) the last use of the property being conveyed was use by the transferor as the transferor's principal residence, even if the transferor does not satisfy the two out of the last five years requirement or other special circumstances;

— the property was the subject of an IRC Sec. 1033 compulsory or involuntary conversion and the transferor intends to acquire property similar or related in service or use so as to be eligible for nonrecognition of gain;

— the transaction will result in either a net loss or a net gain not required to be recognized for California income or franchise tax purposes;

— the property being conveyed is exchanged, or will be exchanged, for IRC Sec. 1031 like-kind property, but only to the extent of the amount of the gain not required to be recognized for California purposes under IRC Sec. 1031;

— the transferor is a partnership (including an LLC treated as a partnership);

— the transferor is a corporation with a permanent place of business in California.

(Sec. 18662, Rev. & Tax Code)

Form 593-E, Real Estate Withholding - Computation of Estimated Gain or Loss, must be used by those claiming an exemption due to a loss or zero gain or electing the optional gain on sale withholding.

Form 593-C, Real Estate Withholding Exemption Certificate, must be used by individual and non-individual sellers to certify that they meet one of the withholding requirement exceptions above.

Tax-exempt entities, insurance companies, IRAs, and qualified pension plans are also exempt from the withholding requirements. (FTB Pub. 1016, Real Estate Withholding Guidelines)

• *Installment sales*

Withholding on the full sales price on installment sales can be deferred if the buyer agrees to withhold $3^{1}/_{3}$% (or the installment withholding percentage specified by the seller on Form 593-I) on the principal of each installment payment. The buyer must complete and sign Form 593-I, Real Estate Withholding Installment Sale Agreement. This form must be sent with a copy of the promissory note, the withholding on the first installment payment, and the seller's certified Form 593. (Instructions, Form 593-I, Real Estate Withholding Installment Sale Agreement)

Applicable to real estate transactions occurring after 2008, the buyer must withhold on each installment sale payment made to a nonresident seller. This amendment does not apply to payments received after 2008 pursuant to a pre-2009 installment sale agreement. (Sec. 18662, Rev. & Tax. Code)

• *Penalties*

Those who fail, without reasonable cause, to withhold required tax in connection with a realty disposition or to timely submit such tax are subject to a penalty equal to the greater of $500 or 10% of the amount that should have been withheld. Any transferor who knowingly executes a false certificate for the purpose of avoiding the withholding requirements is liable for twice this amount. A real estate escrow person who fails to give a transferee (other than a transferee that is an intermediary or accommodator in a deferred exchange) written notice of this withholding requirement is liable for the same penalty if the tax due on the transaction is not paid on time. (Sec. 18668, Rev. & Tax. Code)

• *Procedures and returns*

A payor who in good faith receives a Withholding Exemption Certificate and Waiver Request for Real Estate Sales (Form 590-W) from the payee, is relieved of the obligation to withhold.

For realty dispositions, Form 593, Real Estate Withholding Tax Statement, must be used to report and transmit the amount withheld. For information regarding electronic filing, see FTB Pub. 923, Secure Web Internet File Transfer (SWIFT) Guide for Nonresident and Real Estate Withholding. Funds withheld on individual transactions by real estate escrow persons may, at the option of the real estate escrow person, be remitted by the 20th day of the month following the month in which the transaction occurred, or may be remitted on a monthly basis in combination with other transactions closed during that month. (Sec. 18662, Rev. & Tax. Code)

See ¶714 for a discussion of returns required to be filed.

¶717 Overpayments and Refunds—Procedure

Law: Secs. 19301-19302, 19307, 19321-19323 (CCH CALIFORNIA TAX REPORTS ¶89-224).

Comparable Federal: Secs. 6401-02 (CCH U.S. MASTER TAX GUIDE ¶2759 et seq.).

California Form: Form 540X (Amended Individual Income Tax Return).

Claims for refund must be in writing, signed by the taxpayer or the taxpayer's representative, and must state the specific grounds upon which they are based. They should ordinarily be filed on Form 540X, Amended Individual Income Tax Return. Claims should be filed with the Franchise Tax Board (FTB) at Sacramento, California. (Sec. 19322, Rev. & Tax. Code)

Claims for refund made on behalf of a class of taxpayers must be both authorized in writing and signed by each taxpayer.

Upon examination of a refund claim, the FTB must notify the taxpayer of its action on the claim and state its reasons for disallowing any refund claim. It is the FTB's practice to grant the taxpayer an informal hearing, if desired, before the claim is acted upon or within 90 days after the mailing of a notice of disallowance. The law provides that the FTB may reconsider a disallowed claim at any time within the period allowed for filing a suit for refund (¶720). (Sec. 19324, Rev. & Tax. Code)

A return filed within the statutory period for filing refund claims, showing a credit of more than $1 for estimated tax paid in excess of the tax due, is treated as a claim for refund. At the taxpayer's election, such overpayment may be either refunded or applied on the following year's estimated tax. (Sec. 19307, Rev. & Tax. Code)

Legal Ruling No. 386 (1975) (CCH CALIFORNIA TAX REPORTS ¶89-224.75) discusses the question of what constitutes a valid refund claim. The ruling states that it is not necessary to use a particular form, provided the necessary information is provided. A federal revenue agent's report, filed by the taxpayer or a representative and accompanied by a refund request, will constitute a claim if sufficient explanation is provided in the report or otherwise.

Under some circumstances the FTB may initiate a refund action in the absence of a proper claim. See *Newman v. Franchise Tax Board* (1989) (CCH CALIFORNIA TAX REPORTS ¶89-224.753); in this case, the California Court of Appeal held that a statement entitled "protest" qualified as a sufficient claim for refund because it put the FTB on notice that a right was being asserted with respect to an overpayment of tax.

In FTB Notice 97-4 (CCH CALIFORNIA TAX REPORTS ¶89-224.673), the FTB stated its position that a refund request could be adjudicated only if the tax, together with interest and penalties, had been paid in full. Subsequently, in FTB Notice 97-8 (CCH CALIFORNIA TAX REPORTS ¶89-224.671), the FTB stated that it would continue to process a refund claim at the administrative level if the taxpayer paid the assessed tax, additions to tax, and penalties, but not interest. However, pending a final, controlling appellate court decision, the FTB maintained its position that payment of interest was a prerequisite to judicial review. Thereafter, in *Chen et al. v. Franchise Tax Board* (CCH CALIFORNIA TAX REPORTS ¶89-224.67), a California court of appeal held that payment of interest was not a prerequisite to seeking judicial review.

In case of a joint return, an overpayment may be credited against taxes due from both taxpayers and any balance is refunded to both taxpayers. In *Appeal of Elam* (1997) (CCH CALIFORNIA TAX REPORTS ¶89-224.61), the State Board of Equalization ordered the FTB to refund to a divorced taxpayer her portion of an overpayment from a prior year's tax return filed jointly with her ex-husband, even though the FTB had erroneously refunded the entire overpayment to the ex-husband.

¶718 Refund Claims—Appeal to State Board of Equalization

Law: Secs. 19324-35, 19343, 19348 (CCH CALIFORNIA TAX REPORTS ¶89-234).

Comparable Federal: Secs. 6401-02.

A taxpayer may appeal the Franchise Tax Board's (FTB) disallowance of a refund claim. The appeal must be made to the State Board of Equalization (SBE) within 90 days from the date of mailing of the notice of disallowance. (Sec. 19324, Rev. & Tax. Code; Sec. 19343, Rev. & Tax. Code) A taxpayer may consider a claim disallowed and file an appeal with the SBE if the FTB fails to take action on a claim for six months

(120 days in certain bankruptcy situations) after the claim is filed. (Sec. 19348, Rev. & Tax Code)

Procedure on an appeal to the SBE on a refund claim is the same as on a proposed deficiency, as outlined in ¶705, above. Some proceedings that start out as deficiency appeals are converted into refund appeals because the taxpayer pays the tax while the proceeding is pending. In such cases the proceeding is considered after payment of the tax as an appeal from the denial of a claim for refund.

See ¶720 regarding suits for refund.

¶719 Statute of Limitations on Refund Claims

Law: Secs. 18572, 19041.5, 19052, 19066, 19306-16, 19322.1 (CCH CALIFORNIA TAX REPORTS ¶89-224).

Comparable Federal: Secs. 1311-14, 6511, 6603, 7508A (CCH U.S. MASTER TAX GUIDE ¶2763).

The period of limitation for filing refund claims is outlined below.

(a) **General rule** —Generally, a refund claim must be made by the later of (1) four years after the last day prescribed for filing the return (determined without regard to any extension of time for filing), (2) one year from the date of overpayment, or (3) four years from the date the return was filed, if filed by the prescribed date for filing the return (including extensions). This may be compared with the federal rule of the earlier of three years from the date the return was filed or two years from the date the tax was paid. If a return is filed before the actual due date, it is treated as filed on the due date. (Sec. 19306, Rev. & Tax. Code)

A deposit in the nature of a cash bond made by a taxpayer to stop the running of interest after the Franchise Tax Board (FTB) has mailed a notice of proposed deficiency assessment is not a payment of tax for purposes of determining the limitations period for filing a refund claim or converting an administrative refund claim into a judicial refund action, unless the taxpayer provides a written statement to the FTB specifying that the deposit is a payment of tax or the deposit is actually used to pay a final tax liability. (Sec. 19041.5, Rev. & Tax. Code) The FTB will generally follow federal interpretations and procedures relating to tax deposits. (*FTB Notice 2005-6* (CCH CALIFORNIA TAX REPORTS ¶403-924))

An "informal" refund claim may be made, which allows a taxpayer to file a refund claim without full payment of the assessed or asserted tax. An informal refund claim is deemed filed only for purposes of tolling the four-year statute of limitations. For all other purposes, the claim is deemed filed on the date the tax is paid in full. An "informal" refund claim is deemed perfected for purposes of commencing the formal administrative claims procedure (including the deemed six month denial) when all outstanding tax, penalties, and interest are paid. The informal claim procedure does not apply to deficiency amounts that are not finalized (FTB Notice 2003-5 (2003) (CCH CALIFORNIA TAX REPORTS ¶89-224.451)).

(b) **Waivers** —Where a waiver has been executed, *either* for California tax purposes or for federal tax purposes, extending the running of the statute of limitations on deficiency assessments, the limitation date for refunds is the same as that for mailing notices of proposed additional assessments. This is different from the federal rule, which extends the limitation period for refunds six months beyond the period for deficiency assessments. It should be noted, however, that where the California refund limitation date is based on a federal waiver, the date is six months after the expiration of the period for *federal* deficiency assessments, and not six months after the date for additional *California* assessments. (Sec. 19308, Rev. & Tax. Code; Sec. 19065, Rev. & Tax. Code)

The limitation date for a California refund claim, if based upon a federal waiver, may be the same as that for a federal claim.

(c) **Special seven-year rule**—Where the claim is based on (1) a bad debt loss, (2) a worthless security loss, or (3) erroneous inclusion of certain recoveries of no-tax-benefit deductions, the limitation period is extended to seven years from the last day prescribed for filing the return. As to bad debt and worthless security losses, this is the same as the federal. As to erroneous inclusion of certain recoveries, there is no comparable federal rule. (Sec. 19312, Rev. & Tax. Code)

(d) **Changes or corrections to federal returns**—When a change or correction to the taxpayer's federal return is made or allowed by federal authorities, as explained at ¶106, the limitation period is extended to a date two years after the notice or amended return is filed with the FTB, if such date is later than that set forth in (a) or (b), above, or the extended date established by reason of financial disability as described below. (Sec. 19311, Rev. & Tax. Code) In a nonprecedential summary decision, the SBE applied this extended statute of limitations provision to allow a taxpayer to claim a refund of late filing penalties within two years from the date on which the IRS had abated the corresponding federal late payment penalties, even though the general four-year limitations period had lapsed. The SBE held that because the federal abatement changed the amount of the taxpayer's federal tax liability, the taxpayer had two years from the federal determination to file a state refund claim. (*Appeal of Mart* (2006) CCH CALIFORNIA TAX REPORTS ¶89-224.7482)

(e) **Refunds related to taxes paid to another state**—Applicable to taxes paid to another state after 2008, taxpayers may file claims for refund or credit for taxes paid to other states within one year from the date the tax is paid to the other state even if the standard statute of limitations period has lapsed. (Sec. 19311.5, Rev. & Tax. Code)

• *Taxpayers outside United States; disaster victims*

In the case of members of the armed forces and certain other taxpayers who are outside the United States for a period of time, the statute of limitations is automatically extended under certain conditions (¶109). See ¶110 for a discussion of extensions available to victims of disasters or terroristic or militaristic actions. (Sec. 18570, Rev. & Tax. Code; Sec. 18571, Rev. & Tax. Code)

• *Financially disabled persons*

California follows federal law by suspending the statute of limitations periods discussed above for personal income tax refund claims when an individual is financially disabled, as established under the procedures and requirements specified by the FTB. (Sec. 19316, Rev. & Tax. Code)

An individual is "financially disabled" if that individual is unable to manage his or her financial affairs by reason of a medically determinable physical or mental impairment that is either deemed to be a terminal impairment or is expected to last for a continuous period of not less than 12 months. Receipt of social security disability benefits does not in and of itself establish that a taxpayer is unable to manage his or her financial affairs. (*Appeal of Meek* (2006) (CCH CALIFORNIA TAX REPORTS ¶89-224.395) A suspension is not available if the individual's spouse or any other person is legally authorized to act on that individual's behalf in financial matters.

• *Offset of refund against deficiency*

A refund that is barred under the above rules may be allowed as an offset against a deficiency, where the refund and deficiency both result from the transfer of income or deductions from one year to another. Such offset is also allowed where the refund is for the same year as the deficiency and is due to a related taxpayer. The offset must be made within seven years from the due date of the return on which the refund (overpayment) is determined. (Sec. 19314, Rev. & Tax. Code)

In *Appeal of Paritem and Janie Poonian* (1971) (CCH CALIFORNIA TAX REPORTS ¶89-102.554), the State Board of Equalization (SBE) applied the seven-year limitation strictly to deny an offset (an offset had been allowed earlier in settling the federal tax liability, presumably because the federal limitation period had not yet run).

In *Appeal of Earl and Marion Matthiessen* (1985) (CCH CALIFORNIA TAX REPORTS ¶89-224.7491), the taxpayers claimed a barred refund as an offset to a deficiency for a later year. A refund claim had been filed within the seven-year period, but the offset was not claimed until after the deficiency had been paid. The SBE denied the claim.

In *Appeal of Wilfred and Gertrude Winkenbach et al.* (1975) (CCH CALIFORNIA TAX REPORTS ¶89-102.5592), individuals were taxed on income that had been taxed to a corporation in an outlawed year. The situation did not permit an offset of the barred refund due the corporation against the individuals' deficiency, under the rules discussed above, because the corporation and the individuals were not "related" taxpayers as specifically defined in the law. However, the SBE allowed the offset under the doctrine of "equitable recoupment."

• *Credit refunds*

Adjustments to refundable credits are treated as mathematical errors by the FTB, and a taxpayer may claim a refund of such adjusted amounts within the time limits specified above.

• *Effect of federal litigation*

In *Appeal of Valley Home Furniture* (1972) (CCH CALIFORNIA TAX REPORTS ¶89-224.741), the taxpayer's refund claim was based on the allowable deduction of certain salaries paid to an officer-stockholder. The Tax Court had allowed the deduction for federal tax purposes, and the officer-stockholder had paid both federal and California income tax on the salaries. Nevertheless, the refund was denied because the claim was not filed within the required period of one year after the date of overpayment. The SBE commented that the taxpayer "could easily have filed protective claims for refund pending the outcome of the federal litigation."

• *No California relief provision*

California law contains nothing similar to IRC Secs. 1311-14, which mitigate the effect of the statute of limitations in certain situations where an inconsistent position is maintained. In *Appeal of Skaggs Pay Less Drug Stores* (1959) (CCH CALIFORNIA TAX REPORTS ¶89-144.501), the taxpayer attempted to obtain a refund for an outlawed year to conform with a federal adjustment made under IRC Sec. 1311; the SBE held that no refund could be made.

¶720 Suits for Refund

Law: Secs. 19041.5, 19381-92 (CCH CALIFORNIA TAX REPORTS ¶89-236).

Comparable Federal: Secs. 6532, 6603, 7421-22 (CCH U.S. MASTER TAX GUIDE ¶2790).

Generally, suits for refund may be instituted only after the taxpayer has filed a claim for refund, and they must be based on the grounds set forth in the claim. (Sec. 19382, Rev. & Tax. Code) However, if the FTB is on notice and aware of an issue, a taxpayer will not be precluded from pursing judicial relief for failure to specifically state the issue on the claim for refund (*J.H. McKnight Ranch, Inc. v. Franchise Tax Board* (2003) (CCH CALIFORNIA TAX REPORTS ¶89-236.303). Time limits for bringing suit are the later of the following:

— four years from the due date of the return;

— one year from the date the tax was paid;

— 90 days after notice of action by the Franchise Tax Board (FTB) on a claim for refund; or

— 90 days after notice of action by the State Board of Equalization (SBE) on an appeal from the action of the FTB on a refund claim.

(Sec. 19384, Rev. & Tax. Code)

A deposit in the nature of a cash bond made by a taxpayer to stop the running of interest after the FTB has mailed a notice of proposed deficiency assessment is not a payment of tax for purposes of the limitations period for converting an administrative refund claim into a judicial refund action or filing a suit for refund, unless the taxpayer provides a written statement to the FTB specifying that the deposit is a payment of tax or the deposit is actually used to pay a final tax liability. (Sec. 19041.5, Rev. & Tax. Code). The FTB will generally follow federal interpretations and procedures relating to tax deposits. (*FTB Notice 2005-6* (CCH CALIFORNIA TAX REPORTS ¶403-924)

Practice Pointer: Procedural Issues Addressed

Exhaustion of administrative remedies.—Although a taxpayer is not required to pursue an administrative appeal before the SBE prior to bringing a judicial action challenging a refund denial or deemed denial, a taxpayer is precluded from recovering any litigation costs, including attorney fees, incurred in pursuing a judicial action unless the taxpayer has exhausted administrative remedies, including filing an administrative appeal with the SBE. (*Information Letter 2007-2*, California Franchise Tax Board, August 23, 2007, CCH CALIFORNIA TAX REPORTS ¶404-448)

Payment of proposed assessments.—In *City National Corp. v. Franchise Tax Board*, an appellate court held that payment of proposed assessments of California corporation franchise and income taxes was not a prerequisite for filing a suit for refund of taxes involving the same tax years because the proposed assessments had not yet become final. The California Supreme Court has denied a petition for review of the case. (*City National Corp. v. Franchise Tax Board* (2007), CCH CALIFORNIA TAX REPORTS ¶404-200; pet. for review denied, Cal SCt, No. S150563, April 11, 2007)

Tax deposit forms.—Forms 3576-3579, Tax Deposit Voucher, should be used to designate a remittance as a tax deposit for a specific tax year. Form 3581, Tax Deposit Refund or Transfer Request, should be used to request a tax deposit refund, designate the application of a tax deposit to a different tax year, or apply a tax deposit to convert an administrative protest or appeal to an administrative refund action.

If the tax deposit amount is not enough to pay the final deficiency amount, including penalties, fees, and interest, the claim will become an informal claim, and the taxpayer will receive a bill for the remaining amount due. The FTB cannot act on a claim until it is perfected by full payment. The same procedures apply when a taxpayer has appealed the denial of a protested proposed assessment to the SBE and wishes to convert the deficiency appeal to an appeal from the denial of a refund claim. The "deemed denial" period does not start to run until the claim is perfected by full payment. (*Tax News*, California Franchise Tax Board, September 2006; FTB 3581, Tax Deposit Refund and Transfer Request)

A taxpayer may consider a claim disallowed and bring a suit for refund if the FTB fails to take action on a refund claim within six months (120 days in certain bankruptcy situations) after the claim is filed. (Sec. 19385, Rev. & Tax. Code)

Under the California procedure, the taxpayer may appeal to the SBE and, following an adverse decision, may then appeal to the courts by filing suit for refund. The FTB has no right to appeal an adverse decision of the SBE.

Caution Note: Scope of Liability Issues

The FTB is not limited to the issues raised by a taxpayer in a suit to refund, but may raise any and all liability issues in order to defeat the refund claim (*Marken v. Franchise Tax Board* (2002) (CCH CALIFORNIA TAX REPORTS ¶89-224.79)).

See ¶105 for the special procedure whereby a person who is alleged to be a California resident can file a suit to determine the issue without first paying the tax.

The California rules regarding suits for refund are different from the federal in several respects. Due to the technical nature and limited applicability of these provisions, no attempt is made here to explain the differences.

¶721 Disclosure of Information

Law: Secs. 19195, 19504.5, 19530, 19542.3, 19544-65, Revenue and Taxation Code; Sec. 17530.5, Business and Professions Code (CCH CALIFORNIA TAX REPORTS ¶89-134, 89-222).

Comparable Federal: Secs. 6103-10, 7213-16 (CCH U.S. MASTER TAX GUIDE ¶2892).

Under the California Business and Professions Code, it is a misdemeanor for anyone to disclose any information obtained in the business of preparing federal or state income tax returns or in assisting taxpayers to prepare their returns, unless the disclosure is

— authorized by written consent of the taxpayer,

— authorized by law,

— necessary to the preparation of the return, or

— pursuant to court order.

(Sec. 17530.5, Bus. & Prof. Code)

California and federal laws provide for reciprocal exchange of information in administration of tax laws. The Franchise Tax Board (FTB) and the Internal Revenue Service have a continuing program of informing each other of findings resulting from their examinations of tax returns. To avoid duplication of effort, the two agencies may agree that a particular taxpayer's return will be examined by one or the other. Any improper disclosure or use of such information is a misdemeanor. (Sec. 19551, Rev. & Tax. Code)

State law also authorizes reciprocal exchange programs between the FTB and California cities that assesses a city business tax or that require a city business license. (Sec. 19551, Rev. & Tax. Code—Sec. 19551.5, Rev. & Tax. Code)

The California Revenue and Taxation Code provides rules and procedures regarding personal and confidential information in the files of state agencies; these rules are designed to insure privacy of such information. (Sec. 19545, Rev. & Tax. Code) The FTB is required to redact the first five digits of a Social Security number on personal income and corporation franchise and income tax lien abstracts and any other public records created by the FTB that are disclosable under the Public Records Act. (Sec. 15705, Govt. Code)

CCH Comment: Public Disclosure of Tax Delinquencies

The FTB is authorized to make available as a matter of public record an annual list of the 250 largest uncontested tax delinquencies in excess of $100,000 under the Personal Income Tax Law and the Corporation Tax Law. Before making a delinquency a matter of public record, however, the FTB must provide written notice to the person or persons liable by certified mail and provide an opportunity for the taxpayer to comply. (Sec. 19195, Rev. & Tax Code)

Special safeguards are provided to prevent improper disclosure by the FTB of trade secrets or other confidential information with respect to any software that comes into the FTB's possession or control in connection with a tax return examination. (Sec. 19504.5, Rev. & Tax Code) Computer software source code and executable code are considered return information for disclosure purposes. Any person who willfully makes known to another person any computer software source code or executable code obtained in connection with a tax return examination may be punished by a fine or imprisonment or both. (Sec. 19542.3, Rev. & Tax. Code)

¶722 Interest on Overpayments

Law: Secs. 19325, 19340-51, 19363 (CCH CALIFORNIA TAX REPORTS ¶89-204).

Comparable Federal: Sec. 6611 (CCH U.S. MASTER TAX GUIDE ¶2765).

Interest is paid upon overpayments of tax. The interest rate is the same as the rate for deficiencies, as explained at ¶711. (Sec. 19340, Rev. & Tax. Code) The law contains specific rules regarding the period for which interest will be paid, depending on whether the tax is refunded or allowed as a credit.

With the exception discussed below, no interest will be allowed if refund or credit is made within 45 days of the date of filing a return, or within 45 days after the due date (without regard to extensions of time). In case of a late return, no interest will be allowed for any day before the date of filing. (Sec. 19341, Rev. & Tax. Code)

The law contains a provision to prevent payment of interest on overpayments that are made deliberately for the purpose of obtaining interest. (Sec. 19349, Rev. & Tax. Code) In any case where the Franchise Tax Board disallows interest on a refund, the taxpayer may appeal to the State Board of Equalization (SBE) and may bring suit if the action of the SBE is not favorable. (Sec. 19343, Rev. & Tax. Code) Detailed rules are provided for such appeals. There are no comparable federal provisions.

Where a refund is made under the special seven-year limitation period for claims based on bad debt and worthless security losses, the amount of interest paid is limited.

¶723 Closing Agreements

Law: Secs. 19441, 19442 (CCH CALIFORNIA TAX REPORTS ¶89-186).

Comparable Federal: Sec. 7121 (CCH U.S. MASTER TAX GUIDE ¶2721).

The Franchise Tax Board (FTB) and a taxpayer may enter into a "closing agreement" with respect to the tax for any taxable period. Such an agreement is binding and may not be reopened except upon a showing of fraud, etc. The California provision is substantially the same as the federal. (Sec. 19441, Rev. & Tax. Code)

In addition, the Executive Officer and the Chief Counsel of the FTB may approve the settlement of all tax liabilities for a specified year involving a reduction of tax of $7,500 (adjusted annually for inflation) ($9,200 for 2009, $8,800 for 2008) or less without the Attorney General's review or the FTB's approval. (Sec. 19442, Rev. & Tax. Code) For reduction of tax settlements in excess of the annually adjusted amount, the Executive Officer and the Chief Counsel are required to submit the proposed settlements to the Attorney General for review prior to presenting their recommendations to the FTB. However, an assessment or refund may still be issued as a result of a federal tax change.

FTB Notice No. 2007-02, CCH CALIFORNIA TAX REPORTS ¶404-303, addresses the procedures for initiating and processing a request for a settlement agreement. Taxpayers seeking to initiate the settlement of a civil tax dispute should write to:

Patrick J. Bittner
Director, Settlement Bureau, Mail Stop A270
Franchise Tax Board
P.O. Box 3070

Rancho Cordova, CA 95741-3070
Telephone (916) 845-5624
FAX (916) 845-4747
Message Line (916) 845-5034

Written requests should include the following:

— the taxpayer's name and current address;

— if the taxpayer is represented by another, the representative's name, current address, fax, and telephone number, and a copy of the representative's power of attorney, unless a valid form is already on file with the FTB;

— the taxpayer's Social Security number or taxpayer identification number;

— the taxable year(s) involved;

— the tax amount(s) involved;

— the present status of the dispute (*i.e.*, protest, appeal, or claim for refund);

— a good faith settlement offer, including the factual and legal grounds in support of the offer;

— identification and discussion of all issues in contention, including legal and factual grounds for positions taken by the taxpayer; and

— a listing of all notice(s) of proposed assessment (NPA) and claim(s) for refund for the taxable year(s) involved that are not part of the settlement request, including the present status of each NPA(s) and claim(s) for refund and the amount(s) involved.

Practice Tip: Acceptance by Settlement Bureau

A request for settlement will likely be accepted by the FTB's Settlement Bureau for review if the FTB determines that there is a bona fide factual or legal dispute. However, if the FTB determines that there is a negligible litigation risk to the FTB's position in the case or that the facts have not been sufficiently developed to allow proper settlement consideration, the case will be not be accepted into the settlement program. Such a decision is completely discretionary with the FTB. (*FTB Notice No. 2007-02*, CCH CALIFORNIA TAX REPORTS ¶404-303)

The FTB attempts to reach tentative settlement agreements within nine months of the case being accepted into the program.

If the FTB neither approves nor disapproves a recommendation for settlement within 45 days after receiving the recommendation, the recommendation is deemed approved. Disapproval requires a majority vote of the FTB, and a disapproved settlement may be resubmitted to the FTB. All settlements are final and nonappealable, except upon a showing of fraud or material misrepresentation.

CCH Comment: Evidence of Settlement Negotiations Inadmissible

Applicable to settlement negotiations entered into after 2007, evidence of a settlement offer made during settlement negotiations between a taxpayer and the FTB is inadmissible in any subsequent adjudicative proceeding or civil action, including any appeal to the SBE. In addition, no evidence of any conduct or statements related to the settlement negotiations is admissible to prove liability for any tax, penalty, fee, or interest, except to the extent provided for in Sec. 1152 of the Evidence Code. (Sec. 19442, Rev. & Tax. Code)

In *Appeal of Wesley G. Pope* (1958) (CCH CALIFORNIA TAX REPORTS ¶89-186.20), the State Board of Equalization held that a check marked "payment in full" does not follow the statutory requirements of a closing agreement. Hence, the FTB was justified in making subsequent assessments after the receipt of such a payment.

¶724 Compromise of Tax Liability

Law: Sec. 19443 (CCH CALIFORNIA TAX REPORTS ¶89-186).

Federal: Sec. 7122 (CCH U.S. MASTER TAX GUIDE ¶2723).

The executive officer and chief counsel of the Franchise Tax Board (FTB), or their delegates, jointly, may administratively compromise any final tax liability in which the reduction of tax is $7,500 or less. The FTB, itself, upon recommendation by its executive officer and chief counsel, jointly, may compromise a final tax liability in which the reduction of tax is in excess of $7,500 but less than $10,000. (Sec. 19443, Rev. & Tax. Code)

For an amount to be administratively compromised, the taxpayer must establish the following:

— the amount offered in payment is the most that can be expected to be paid or collected from the taxpayer's present assets or income, and

— the taxpayer has no reasonable prospects of acquiring increased income or assets that would enable the taxpayer to satisfy a greater amount of the liability than that offered.

In addition, the FTB must determine that the acceptance of the offer in compromise is in the best interest of the state.

In the case of joint and several liability, the acceptance of an offer in compromise from one spouse does not relieve the other spouse from paying the liability. However, the amount of the liability must be reduced by the amount of the accepted offer.

Also, it is of course possible under California procedures, as under federal, to negotiate a "compromise" of doubtful items of income, expense, etc., in dealing with representatives of the FTB upon examination of returns or during appeal proceedings or to make a settlement of a suit after litigation has begun.

See ¶715 for a discussion of compromises of withholding tax liabilities.

Practice Pointer: Making an Offer of Compromise

Form DE 999CA, Multi-Agency Form for Offer in Compromise, may be used to make an offer in compromise by individuals for personal income, sales and use, and other taxes owed to the FTB, SBE, and EDD. Corporations, partnerships, and limited liability companies should continue to use Form FTB 4905BE, Offer in Compromise by Business Entities, for FTB offers, and Form BOE-490-C, Offer In Compromise Application For Corporations, Limited Liability Companies, Partnerships, Trusts, and Unidentified Business Organizations, for SBE offers. (*News Release*, California Tax Service Center, August 23, 2006)

¶725 Voluntary Disclosure Agreements and Filing Compliance Agreements

Laws: Secs. 19191-94 (CCH CALIFORNIA TAX REPORTS ¶89-186, 89-210).

Comparable Federal: None.

California Form: FTB 4925 (Application for Voluntary Disclosure).

Two programs are available to encourage taxpayers to comply with California's reporting and registration requirements. The voluntary disclosure program is a statutory program that has very specific requirements and applies to a limited class of eligible applicants. In contrast, the filing compliance program is a Franchise Tax Board (FTB) initiated program based on the FTB's authority to abate penalties for reasonable cause under various statutory provisions. Unlike a voluntary disclosure agreement, a filing compliance agreement is not limited to a specific look-back period.

• *Voluntary disclosure program*

The FTB is authorized to enter into voluntary disclosure agreements with the following:

— qualified business entities that in good faith have previously failed to comply with California's registration and reporting requirements;

— qualified S corporation shareholders who in good faith have failed to comply with California's registration, reporting, and payment requirements;

— qualified trusts and qualified beneficiaries of those trusts; and

— limited liability companies (LLCs) and their qualified members.

(Sec. 19191 et. seq., Rev. & Tax. Code)

Under the terms established in a voluntary disclosure agreement, the FTB may waive penalties for noncompliance with specified reporting and payment requirements for the six taxable years immediately preceding the FTB's signing of the agreement. For taxable years ending more than six years prior to the agreement, the business's income taxes, additions to tax, fees, or penalties may also be waived. However, the FTB may not waive penalties for any of the six years immediately preceding the signing of the agreement in which an S corporation shareholder or LLC member was a California resident required to file a California tax return. In addition, for purposes of qualified shareholders and LLC members, the FTB's waiver authority is limited to penalties or additions to tax attributable to the shareholder's California source income from the S corporation or the LLC member's California source income from the LLC.

A "qualifying business entity" includes any out-of-state bank or non-exempt corporation (including any predecessors to the business entity) that voluntarily comes forward prior to any contact from the FTB and that has never filed a California income tax return or been the subject of an FTB inquiry regarding income tax liability.

A "qualified shareholder" is a nonresident shareholder of an S corporation that has applied for a voluntary disclosure agreement and disclosed all material facts pertaining to the shareholder's liability. A "qualified member" is an individual, corporation, or LLC that is a nonresident individual on the signing date of the voluntary disclosure agreement or a corporation not qualified or registered with the California Secretary of State's office. The LLC of which the individual or entity is a member must have applied for a voluntary disclosure agreement under which all material facts pertinent to the member's liability would be disclosed.

To participate in a voluntary disclosure agreement, an LLC must agree to pay all LLC fees, in addition to any tax, interest, and penalties not waived by the FTB for each of the six taxable years ending immediately preceding the signing date of the written agreement. In addition, LLCs and other entities that participate in the voluntary disclosure program are liable for the minimum tax for their first year of business in California.

A "qualified trust" is a trust that has never been administered in California and that has had no resident beneficiaries in California for six taxable years ending immediately preceding the signing date of the voluntary disclosure agreement, other than a beneficiary whose interest in the trust is contingent. A "contingent beneficiary" is a beneficiary that has not received any distribution from a qualified trust at any time during the six taxable years ending immediately preceding the signing date of the voluntary disclosure agreement. A "qualified beneficiary" is an individual who is a beneficiary of a qualified trust and is a nonresident on the signing date of the voluntary disclosure agreement and for each of the preceding six taxable years.

• *Filing compliance program*

Taxpayers with corporation franchise and income tax and personal income tax liabilities that are ineligible for the voluntary disclosure program (VDP) discussed above but that can show reasonable cause for their failure to file may obtain relief from specified penalties by entering into a filing compliance agreement (FCA) with the FTB.

Taxpayers eligible to enter into an FCA are those taxpayers in the class of taxpayers described in the authorizing statute for the VDP discussed above, but who failed to satisfy an eligibility requirement.

The primary differences between an FCA and the VDP are the following:

— a taxpayer may enter into an FCA even if the taxpayer was first contacted by the FTB, whereas a taxpayer may not enter into the VDP if the taxpayer was contacted by the FTB prior to applying for the program;

— relief from penalties and additions to tax is limited to a six year look-back period under the VDP, whereas there is no specified look-back period under the FCA program; and

— the underpayment of estimated tax penalty may be waived under the VDP, but not under the FCA program.

A taxpayer interested in participating in an FCA should send a written request to the FTB containing the following information: (1) an explanation as to why there is an unfulfilled filing requirement and an unpaid California tax liability for past years; (2) detailed facts as to why the taxpayer's situation qualifies for a waiver of penalties under reasonable cause; and (3) the years for which the taxpayer is seeking relief. The request and supporting documentation should be mailed to Legal Attn: Craig Scott, Franchise Tax Board, PO Box 1720, Rancho Cordova, CA. 95741-1720.

Taxpayers allowed to enter into an FCA must submit the required tax returns and payment by the date specified in the agreement. Full payment is usually due within 30 days from the date of the agreement, unless the taxpayer enters into an installment payment agreement.

The FCA will be voided if at any time the information supplied by the taxpayer is subsequently determined by the FTB to be inaccurate or false. (*Filing Compliance Agreement --Frequently Asked Questions*, California Franchise Tax Board, May 2, 2008, CCH CALIFORNIA TAX REPORTS ¶404-666)

¶726 Recovery of Erroneous Refunds

Law: Secs. 19054, 19368, 19411-13 (CCH CALIFORNIA TAX REPORTS ¶89-190).

Comparable Federal: Secs. 6532, 6602, 7405 (CCH U.S. MASTER TAX GUIDE ¶2738).

The Franchise Tax Board may recover erroneous refunds, with interest, subject to certain conditions. The California law is generally similar to the federal law. (Sec. 19368, Rev. & Tax. Code)

In *Appeal of Albert A. Ellis, Jr.* (1972) (CCH CALIFORNIA TAX REPORTS ¶89-202.671), the State Board of Equalization (SBE) allowed interest on recovery of an erroneous refund, although the tax assessment in question was not a "deficiency" under the law then in effect. In *Appeal of Bruce H. and Norah E. Planck* (1977) (CCH CALIFORNIA TAX REPORTS ¶89-190.301), the SBE held that assessment of an erroneous refund was a "deficiency" and that interest was properly imposed under the rules for interest on deficiencies (¶711).

¶727 Abusive Tax Shelters

Law: Secs. 18407, 18628, 18648, 19164, 19164.5, 19173, 19174, 19177, 19179, 19182, 19751-54, 19772, 19774, 19777, 19778 (CCH CALIFORNIA TAX REPORTS ¶89-102, 89-206, 89-210).

Comparable Federal: Secs. 6011, 6111, 6112 (CCH U.S. MASTER TAX GUIDE ¶2001 et seq.).

California conforms to the federal rules as of the current California federal conformity date (¶103) that govern reporting of abusive tax shelters with the following modifications that:

— expand the definition of a "reportable transaction" to include any transaction of a type that either the IRS or the Franchise Tax Board (FTB) determines as having a potential for tax avoidance or evasion (either federal or state tax), including deductions, basis, credits, entity classification, dividend elimination, or omission of income; and

— expand the definition of a reportable "listed transaction" to include a transaction that is the same as, or substantially similar to, a transaction specifically identified by the IRS or the FTB as a federal or state tax avoidance transaction, including deductions, basis, credits, entity classification, dividend elimination, or omission of income.

(Sec. 18628, Rev. & Tax. Code)

The FTB is required to identify and publish "listed transactions" through the use of FTB notices, other published positions, and the FTB Web site.

Generally, taxpayers that are involved in a reportable transaction and/or a listed transaction must attach a copy of the federal Form 8666 to their original or amended California return. A copy must also be sent to the FTB's Abusive Tax Shelter Unit (ATSU), at ATSU 398 MS: F385, Franchise Tax Board, P.O. Box 1673, Sacramento, California, 95812-9900, the first time a reportable transaction is disclosed on the taxpayer's return. (FTB Notice 2007-3, CCH CALIFORNIA TAX REPORTS ¶404-326; Chapter 656 (SB 614/AB 1601) - General Information: Registration & Reporting Requirements—Reportable Transaction Disclosure Requirements, California Franchise Tax Board, July 19, 2006, CCH CALIFORNIA TAX REPORTS¶404-333)

Practitioner Comment: Reportable Transaction Clarification and Amnesty Initiative

The FTB has clarified that it will follow Internal Revenue Service Notice 2006-6 and no longer require the reporting of transactions with substantial book-tax differences to the extent captured on Federal Schedule M-3 unless the transaction is described in one of the other categories of reportable transactions. For transactions with a California-only substantial book-tax difference, reporting on Schedule M-1 is sufficient disclosure.

The FTB has also launched a reportable transaction initiative which was extended through November 15, 2007, under which taxpayers could report or complete the reporting of reportable transactions. The FTB has announced that it will impose penalties on those taxpayers which have not properly reported their reportable transactions after the close of the initiative period.

Bruce Daigh, Chris Whitney, Contributing Editors

Practitioner Comment: California Includes RIC Transactions and REIT Transactions as "Listed Transactions"

The FTB has issued guidance regarding what transactions are considered "listed" transactions under comprehensive tax shelter legislation enacted in 2003. The guidance, contained in a Chief Counsel Announcement dated December 31, 2003, includes as "listed transactions" for California income and franchise tax purposes all federal listed transactions and certain real estate investment trust (REIT) and regulated investment company (RIC) transactions. With respect to the former transactions, the FTB specifically identified as a listed transaction any "transactions involving [REITs] where the REIT takes a deduction for a consent dividend." The guidance notes that California does not conform to the federal consent dividend regime under IRC Section 565. As noted in the guidance, in applying the federal REIT provisions under California law, the REIT is not entitled to deduct consent dividends and the REIT is subject to California tax for amounts treated as consent dividends under federal tax law. Accordingly, the deduction for dividends paid may differ for federal and California purposes.

It is important to note that the FTB's decision to include REIT consent dividends as a listed transaction is not limited to so-called "captive" REITs. Many publicly held REITs deduct consent dividends for valid business reasons. Under the FTB's guidance, these REITs may have listed transactions under California's tax shelter provisions.

Bruce Daigh, Chris Whitney, Contributing Editors

Practitioner Comment: FTB "Reaches Out" to Taxpayers with California and Federal Listed Transaction

California corporate franchise and individual income taxpayers that participated to any degree in a potentially abusive tax shelter, including a federal or California listed transaction, and that did not participate in the California Voluntary Compliance Initiative may soon receive a notice of intent to audit from the FTB. The notice offers two options for an expedient resolution: (1) admit to the use of a potentially abusive tax shelter, file an amended return, and pay the additional tax, interest and applicable penalties; or (2) choose to be audited subject to all applicable penalties. Under the first alternative, the 100% interest-based penalty will be waived, but all other tax shelter penalties will apply.

The FTB, using information obtained from promoter filings submitted during the California Voluntary Compliance Initiative Program and from the IRS, has identified individual and corporate taxpayers that may have been involved in potentially abusive tax shelters. Based on that information, the FTB has begun sending notices of intent to conduct an examination to select taxpayers. The notices describe the transaction at issue and request extensive information with respect to the transaction, including the business purpose for the transaction; any offering prospectus or other literature that describes the transaction, and the related fees paid to participate or structure the transaction; the federal and state tax treatment of the transaction; and other supporting information. Of note, the notices caution taxpayers to retain all relevant documentation, both physical and electronic.

Bruce Daigh, Chris Whitney, Contributing Editors

Bogus optional basis transactions.—The FTB is closely scrutinizing the use of bogus optional basis (BOB) transactions, in which a partnership uses an IRC §754 election to inappropriately increase the basis of its property. In some cases, the basis of assets is increased before their disposition. In other cases, taxpayers are using the additional basis to claim increased depreciation or amortization deductions. Depending upon the facts and circumstances, a BOB transaction may be disregarded or be recast to properly reflect California income, or the basis step-up might be disallowed. (*Tax News*, California Franchise Tax Board, September 2007, CCH CALIFORNIA TAX REPORTS ¶404-446)

From June 23, 2008, until September 12, 2008, the FTB ran a specialized voluntary disclosure program that allowed taxpayers who participated in specified BOB transactions and certain employee stock ownership plan (ESOP) transactions to enter into a closing agreements with the FTB in order to avoid having the noneconomic substance penalty and other penalties imposed. (*FTB Notice 2008-4*, California Franchise Tax Board, June 6, 2008, CCH CALIFORNIA TAX REPORTS ¶404-682)

• *Information returns*

Information returns.—California incorporates, with modifications, federal law (IRC Sec. 6111) requiring specified material advisors to file information returns disclosing reportable transactions. Material advisors are required to send a duplicate of the federal return or the same information required to be provided on the federal reportable transactions return for California reportable transactions to the Franchise Tax Board (FTB) no later than the date specified by the FTB or the U.S. Secretary of the Treasury. Additional information may be required if specified in an FTB Notice. (Sec. 18628, Rev. & Tax. Code)

Comment: FTB Reporting Requirements

Taxpayers are required to attach IRS Form 8886 to the back of their California return. If this is the first time the reportable transaction is disclosed on the return, a copy of the federal form must also be sent to the FTB at:

Tax Shelter Filing

Franchise Tax Board

P.O. Box 1673

Sacramento, CA 95812-1673

Material advisors are subject to the California reporting requirements if they are:

— organized in California;

— doing business in California;

— deriving income from California sources; or

— providing any material aid, assistance, or advice with respect to organizing, managing, promoting, selling, implementing, insuring, or carrying out any reportable transaction with respect to a taxpayer that is organized in California, does business in California, or derives income from California sources.

In addition, material advisors are required to file returns with the FTB for any transactions that become listed transactions at any time for federal income tax purposes or for any transactions that are identified by the FTB as listed transactions for California corporation franchise or income tax purposes. The returns must be filed within 60 days after (1) entering into the transaction, or (2) the transactions become a listed transaction.

More than one advisor.—If more than one material advisor is required to file a form for the same transaction, the material advisors may designate by agreement a single material advisor to file the required form. The designation agreement should be attached to the form filed with the FTB. The designation of one material advisor to file does not relieve the other material advisors from the obligation to file if the designated material advisor fails to file. (*FTB Notice 2005-7* (2005), CCH CALIFORNIA TAX REPORTS ¶403-941)

Filing of request for letter ruling.—If a material advisor sends the FTB a copy of a request for a letter ruling filed with the IRS on or before the date the information return is due with respect to a particular transaction, the FTB will suspend the due date for disclosing that transaction until 60 days from the date of the IRS ruling that the transaction is a reportable transaction or, if the request is withdrawn, 60 days from the date of the request to withdraw. (*FTB Notice 2005-7* (2005), CCH CALIFORNIA TAX REPORTS ¶403-941)

List of advisees.—California also conforms to federal law, requiring material advisors of reportable transactions to keep lists of advisees. The lists must be maintained for California purposes in the form and manner prescribed by the FTB. The lists must be provided to the FTB by the later of 60 days after entering into the transactions, or 60 days after the transaction becomes a listed transaction. (Sec. 18648, Rev. & Tax. Code)

CCH Tip: If It Looks Like a Tax Shelter . . .

According to the Franchise Tax Board if a taxpayer can answer "yes" to any of the following questions, he or she is likely involved in an abusive tax scheme:

—Is the tax loss, deduction, or credit a significant amount and used to offset income from unrelated transactions?

—Is the taxpayer's economic and out-of-pocket loss minimal compared to the tax benefits realized from the transaction?

—Does the transaction lack a business purpose other than the reduction of income taxes?

— Does the transaction lack a reasonable possibility of making a profit?

—Are multiple entities involved to unnecessarily complicate the transaction?

— Does the tax position ignore the true intent of relevant statutes and regulations?

—Does the transaction produce a tax result that is too good to be true?

Common schemes involve:

—*basis shifting,* in which foreign corporations and instruments are utilized to artificially increase and shift the basis of stock held by a foreign shareholder who is not subject to U.S. taxation to stock owned by U.S. shareholders. The taxpayers ultimately sell their stock and report an inflated loss despite incurring no or minimal economic loss.

—*inflated basis,* in which transactions that are characterized as contingent are utilized to inflate an owner's basis in a pass-through entity investment. Taxpayers contribute cash or securities to a pass-through entity and obtain a basis in the entity equal to the value of the cash or cost of the securities contributed. Simultaneously, taxpayers contribute an alleged liability, obligation, or deferred income item to the entity, which should reduce the taxpayers' basis in the entity for the amount of that liability or deferral. But taxpayers involved in such transactions do not reduce their basis in the pass-through entity, claiming that the liability or income item is contingent or deferred for tax purposes. In this manner, taxpayers create an artificially inflated basis for the pass-through entity interest that is then used to deduct ordinary losses or to compute a large loss on liquidating distributions received from the entity. The most common variations of this type of scheme include the contribution of short sale proceeds and liabilities to a partnership, or the contribution of debt instruments that include contingencies or premiums that taxpayers ignore for purposes of computing basis.

—*commercial domicile,* in which taxpayers are told that they can avoid California income taxes if they incorporate in states such as Delaware or Nevada that do not impose an income tax. Although there are many variations of this scheme, the most conspicuous version has, in the past, involved a business incorporating in Nevada, electing S corporation status for federal purposes, but electing C corporation status for California purposes. Individual business owners contribute a highly appreciated intangible asset, such as stock, to the Nevada corporation tax-free. The corporation then sells the asset, recognizing a gain, and claims that the source of the gain from the intangible asset is Nevada, because the commercial domicile of the corporation is Nevada and the corporation is not doing business in California. The individual business owners ultimately receive the proceeds from the stock sale through shareholder loans or via dividends once the shareholders change their state of residence.

(*Tax News,* California Franchise Tax Board, September 2003).

• *Tax professionals*

Tax professionals are subject to special registration and "list of investors" requirements if they are engaged in any of the following activities:

— participation in the organization of a potentially abusive tax shelter;
— advising a potentially abusive tax shelter;
— providing an opinion on a potentially abusive tax shelter;
— promoting a potentially abusive tax shelter;
— selling a potentially abusive tax shelter; or
— managing a potentially abusive tax shelter.

(*Information Release, E-mail,* California Franchise Tax Board, February 10, 2004)

• *Reporting procedures*

Reporting procedures.—Taxpayers submitting information required by California statutory provisions regarding tax shelter registration must provide the applicable California business entity number. The California business entity number of the key corporation must likewise be provided if a business entity is a corporation included in a group return for a combined reporting group (*FTB Notice 2004-1,* California Franchise Tax Board, Legal Department, January 30, 2004).

Practice Tip: Reporting Electronically

Taxpayers that are required to file IRS Form 8886, Reportable Transaction Disclosure Statement, may not file that form electronically as an attachment to their California e-file return. Taxpayers may, however, file IRS Form 8271, Investor Reporting of Tax Shelter Registration Number, electronically. Taxpayers required to file Form 8886 that wish to electronically file their California income tax return may e-file their California return and send a copy of Form 8886 via postal mail. The form should be sent to the attention of "Tax Shelter Filing" at the Franchise Tax Board, PO Box 1673, Sacramento, CA 95812-1673.

Inquiries relating to abusive tax shelters may be e-mailed to the FTB at TaxShelter@ftb.ca.gov.

• *Penalties*

The following penalties relate to abusive tax shelters:

(1) failure to maintain list of advisees—$10,000 for each day of failure if not provided within 20 days of request (Sec. 19173, Rev. & Tax. Code)

(2) material advisor's failure to maintain list—an additional penalty equal to the greater of (1) $100,000 or (2) 50% of advisor's gross income from activity (Sec. 19173, Rev. & Tax. Code)

(3) failure to maintain records to substantiate tax shelter promoter return—$1,000 multiplied by number of investors (Sec. 19174, Rev. & Tax. Code)

(4) promoting abusive tax shelter—$1,000 or 100% of gross income derived or to be derived from violation, whichever is less; except 50% of gross income derived or to be derived from violation if a person makes or causes another to make a statement that the person knows or has reason to know is false or fraudulent as to a material matter (Sec. 19177, Rev. & Tax. Code);

(5) failing to furnish information concerning a reportable transaction—$50,000 (Sec. 19182, Rev. & Tax Code);

(6) failure to furnish information concerning listed transaction—the greater of (1) $200,000 or (2) 50% (100% if intentional) of gross income derived with respect to transaction (Sec. 19182, Rev. & Tax Code);

(7) failure by taxpayer with taxable income greater than $200,000 to include reportable transaction information with return—$15,000 per failure; $30,000 if listed transaction (Sec. 19772, Rev. & Tax Code);

(8) accuracy-related penalty on reportable transaction understatements (¶727)—$250 per return; $1,000 if noncompliance with reportable transaction requirements, listed transaction, or gross misstatement; $5,000 if willful or reckless (Sec. 19164.5, Rev. & Tax. Code);

(9) deficiency and contacted by FTB concerning reportable transaction noncompliance, listed transaction, or gross misstatement—100% of interest payable for period beginning on the last day of payment (without extensions) until date notice or proposed assessment mailed (Sec. 19777, Rev. & Tax Code); and

(10) noneconomic substance transaction (NEST) penalty—40% of the understatement; 20% for underpayments to which the facts were disclosed in the return (Sec. 19774, Rev. & Tax Code)

The tax shelter penalties under (1) and (2), above, may be assessed within eight years from the date of the failure. (Sec. 19173, Rev. & Tax Code)

• *Penalty waivers and abatements*

No penalty will be imposed for failure to comply with providing information concerning reportable transactions required by the FTB if it was not identified in a FTB notice issued prior to the date the transaction or shelter was entered into. (Sec. 19182(c), Rev. & Tax. Code)

The Chief Counsel of the FTB may rescind all or any portion of the accuracy-related reportable transaction penalty or any penalty imposed for failure to maintain a list of advisees or to provide information concerning reportable transactions, or the penalty applicable to taxpayers with taxable income greater than $200,000 that fail to include reportable transactions information with their return if all of the following apply:

— the violation is with respect to a reportable transaction other than a listed transaction;

— the person on whom the penalty is imposed has a history of complying with the requirements of the California franchise or income tax laws;

— the violation is due to an unintentional mistake of fact;

— imposing the penalty would be against equity and good conscience; and

— rescinding the penalty would promote compliance with the requirements of the California franchise or income tax laws and effective tax administration.

(Sec 19164.5(d), Rev. & Tax. Code; Sec. 19173, Rev. & Tax Code; Sec. 19182(d), Rev. & Tax. Code; Sec. 19772, Rev. & Tax. Code)

Also, the Chief Counsel may rescind all or any portion of any penalty imposed for filing a frivolous return if both of the following apply:

— imposing the penalty would be against equity and good conscience; and

— rescinding the penalty would promote compliance with the requirements of the California franchise or income tax laws and effective tax administration.

(Sec. 19179, Rev. & Tax. Code)

If the notice of proposed assessment of additional tax has been sent with respect to a noneconomic substance transaction understatement, only the Chief Counsel may compromise the penalty or any portion thereof. (Sec. 19774, Rev. & Tax. Code)

The FTB Chief Counsel may rescind the penalties associated with non-listed activities in (1) and (2) and for the omissions listed in (7), above, if the taxpayer has a history of compliance and can demonstrate that the failure/omission was the result of an unintentional mistake of fact.

• *Interest penalties*

A penalty equal to 100% of the accrued interest on the underpayment is assessed against taxpayers contacted by the FTB regarding the use of a potentially abusive tax shelter. The penalty accrues from the due date of the return, without regard to extensions, and ends on the date that the notice of assessment is mailed. (Sec. 19777, Rev. & Tax. Code)

Interest at a rate equal to 150% of the interest rate above applies to understatements of tax related to the use of a reportable transaction by taxpayers who have not previously been contacted by the IRS or FTB regarding their investment in a potentially abusive tax shelter. (Sec. 19778, Rev. & Tax. Code)

PART IV

Taxes on Corporate Income

FEDERAL-CALIFORNIA CROSS-REFERENCE TABLE AND INDEX

Showing Sections of California Bank and Corporation Tax Law (Revenue and Taxation Code) Comparable to Sections of Federal Law (1986 Internal Revenue Code)

Federal	California	Subject	Paragraph
IRC Sec. 11	Secs. 23151, 23501	Tax imposed	¶805, 816
IRC Sec. 15	Secs. 23058, 24251	Tax rate changes during year	¶1105
IRC Sec. 30	....	Low emission motor vehicle credit	....
IRC Sec. 38	....	General business credit	....
IRC Sec. 39	....	Unused credits	....
IRC Sec. 40	....	Alcohol fuel credit	....
IRC Sec. 41	Sec. 23609	Qualified research credit	¶818
IRC Sec. 42	Secs. 23610.4-10.5	Low-income housing credit	¶818
IRC Sec. 43	Sec. 23604	Enhanced oil recovery credit	¶818
IRC Sec. 44	Sec. 23642	Disabled access credit	¶818
IRC Sec. 45(a)	Sec. 23684	Renewable resources credit	¶818
IRC Sec. 45C	....	Clinical testing credit	¶818
IRC Sec. 45D	....	New markets tax credit	....
IRC Sec. 45E	....	Credit for small employer pension plan startup costs	....
IRC Sec. 45F	Sec. 23617	Employer-provided child care credit	¶134
IRC Sec. 45G	....	Railroad track maintenance credit	....
IRC Sec. 45H	Sec. 23662	Low sulfur diesel fuel production credit	¶818
IRC Sec. 45I	....	Marginal well production credit	....
IRC Secs. 46-50	....	Investment in depreciable property	¶818
IRC Secs. 51, 52	Sec. 23621	Work opportunity credit	....
IRC Sec. 53	Sec. 23453	Minimum tax credit	¶817, ¶818
IRC Secs. 55-59	Secs. 23400, 23455-59	Alternative minimum tax	¶817, ¶1011
IRC Sec. 59A	....	Environmental tax	....
IRC Sec. 61	Secs. 24271, 24314, 24308, 24315, 24323	Gross income	¶901
IRC Sec. 63	Sec. 24341	Taxable income defined	¶815
IRC Sec. 64	Sec. 23049.1	Ordinary income defined	....
IRC Sec. 65	Sec. 23049.2	Ordinary loss defined	....
IRC Sec. 72	Secs. 24272.2, 24302	Annuities	¶903, ¶904
IRC Sec. 75	....	Dealers in tax-exempt securities	....
IRC Sec. 77	Sec. 24273	Community credit loans	¶912
IRC Sec. 78	....	Dividends from foreign corporations	¶909
IRC Sec. 80	....	Restoration of value of certain securities	....
IRC Sec. 83	Sec. 24379	Transfer of property in exchange for services	¶1001, ¶1017
IRC Sec. 84	....	Property transferred to political organizations	¶901
IRC Sec. 87	....	Alcohol and biodiesel fuel credits	¶901
IRC Sec. 88	Sec. 24275	Nuclear plant expenses	¶901
IRC Sec. 90	Sec. 24276	Illegal federal irrigation subsidies	....
IRC Sec. 101	Secs. 24301, 24302, 24305	Life insurance proceeds	¶902, ¶904
IRC Sec. 102	....	Gifts and inheritances	....
IRC Sec. 103	Secs. 24272, 24301	Interest on government bonds	¶910
IRC Sec. 108	Secs. 24301, 24307	Income from discharge of indebtedness	¶908
IRC Sec. 109	Secs. 24301, 24309	Improvements by lessee	¶905
IRC Sec. 110	Sec. 24309.5	Lessee construction allowances	¶906
IRC Sec. 111	Secs. 24301, 24310	Recovery of bad debts and prior taxes	¶907
IRC Sec. 114	....	Extraterritorial income	¶825, ¶901

Federal	California	Subject	Paragraph
IRC Sec. 118	Secs. 24324, 24325	Contributions to capital of corporation	¶913
IRC Sec. 126	Secs. 24301, 24308.5	Cost-sharing payments	¶923
IRC Sec. 136	Secs. 24301, 24308.1, 24326	Energy conservation subsidies	¶922
IRC Sec. 139A	. . . .	Prescription drug subsidies	¶901 , ¶926
IRC Secs. 141-50	Sec. 24272	Private activity bonds	¶910
IRC Sec. 161	Secs. 24415, 24436.5, 24441, 24447, 24448	Allowance of deductions	. . . .
IRC Sec. 162	Secs. 24343, 24343.2, 24343.5, 24343.7	Deductions for business expense	¶1001 , ¶1023
IRC Sec. 163	Secs. 24344, 24344.5, 24344.7	Interest expense deduction	¶1004 , ¶1312
IRC Sec. 164	Secs. 24345, 24346	Deduction for taxes	¶1006
IRC Sec. 165	Secs. 24347, 24347.5	Losses-deductions	¶1007 , ¶1010
IRC Sec. 166	Sec. 24347	Deduction for bad debts	¶1009
IRC Sec. 167	Secs. 24349-5.4, 24368.1	Depreciation	¶1011 , ¶1250
IRC Sec. 168	Secs. 24349, 24355.3, 24355.4	Accelerated cost recovery system	¶1011
IRC Sec. 169	Sec. 24372.3	Amortization of pollution control facilities	¶1011
IRC Sec. 170	Secs. 24357-59.1	Charitable contributions	¶1014 , ¶1312
IRC Sec. 171	Secs. 24360-63.5	Amortizable bond premium	¶1015
IRC Sec. 172	Secs. 24416-16.10, 25110	Net operating loss deduction	¶1024
IRC Sec. 173	Sec. 24364	Circulation expenditures	¶1003
IRC Sec. 174	Sec. 24365	Research expenditures	¶1011
IRC Sec. 175	Sec. 24369	Soil and water conservation expenditures	¶1002
IRC Sec. 176	. . . .	Social security payments for employees of foreign subsidiaries	. . . .
IRC Sec. 178	Sec. 24373	Depreciation or amortization of lessee improvements	¶1011
IRC Sec. 179	Secs. 24356, 24356.8	Asset expense election	¶1011
IRC Sec. 179B	Sec. 24356.4	Refiners' sulfur rules compliance costs	¶1026
IRC Sec. 179C	. . . .	Expensing of qualified refinery property	¶1001
IRC Sec. 179D	. . . .	Expensing of energy efficient commercial building costs	¶1027
IRC Sec. 180	Sec. 24377	Farm fertilizer expenses	¶1002
IRC Sec. 181	. . . .	Qualified film and television productions	¶1011
IRC Sec. 183	. . . .	Hobby losses	. . . .
IRC Sec. 186	Secs. 24675, 24677, 24678	Recovery of antitrust damages	¶1106
IRC Sec. 190	Sec. 24383	Architectural adaptations for the handicapped	¶1001
IRC Sec. 192	. . . .	Contributions to black lung benefit trust	¶1014
IRC Sec. 193	. . . .	Tertiary injectants	¶1013
IRC Sec. 194	Sec. 24372.5	Amortization of reforestation expenses	¶1011
IRC Sec. 194A	. . . .	Contributions to employer liability trusts	¶1016
IRC Sec. 195	Sec. 24414	Start-up expenses	¶1018
IRC Sec. 196	Sec. 23051.5	Unused investment credits	. . . .
IRC Sec. 197	Sec. 24355.5	Amortization of goodwill	¶1011
IRC Sec. 198	. . . .	Environmental remediation costs	¶1011
IRC Sec. 198A	. . . .	Qualified disaster expenses	. . . .
IRC Sec. 199	. . . .	Domestic production deduction	¶925
IRC Sec. 216	Sec. 24382	Foreclosure of cooperative housing corporation stock	¶1022
IRC Sec. 220	Sec. 24343.3	Archer MSAs	. . . .
IRC Sec. 241	Sec. 24401	Special deductions	. . . .
IRC Secs. 243-247	Secs. 24401, 24402, 24410, 24411	Dividends received by corporations	¶909 , ¶1020
IRC Sec. 248	Secs. 24407-09	Organizational expenditures	¶1011
IRC Sec. 249	Sec. 24439	Deductions of bond premium on repurchase	¶1004 , ¶1223
IRC Sec. 261	Sec. 24421	Disallowance of deductions	¶1023
IRC Sec. 263	Secs. 24422-23	Capital expenditures	¶1013 , ¶1023
IRC Sec. 263A	Sec. 24422.3	Inventory capitalization—inclusion	¶1106 , ¶1107
IRC Sec. 264	Sec. 24424	Payments on life insurance contracts	¶1004 , ¶1023
IRC Sec. 265	Sec. 24425	Deductions allocable to tax-exempt income	¶1004 , ¶1023
IRC Sec. 266	Sec. 24426	Taxes and carrying charges	¶1023
IRC Sec. 267	Sec. 24427	Transactions between related individuals	¶1023

Federal	California	Subject	Paragraph
IRC Sec. 268	....	Sale of land with unharvested crop	¶1023
IRC Sec. 269	Sec. 24431	Acquisitions made to avoid tax	¶1110
IRC Sec. 269A	....	Personal service corporations formed to evade taxes	¶1110
IRC Sec. 269B	....	Stapled interests	¶1110
IRC Sec. 271	Sec. 24434	Debts owed by political parties	¶1009, ¶1023
IRC Sec. 272	....	Disposal of coal or iron ore	....
IRC Sec. 274	Sec. 24443	Disallowance of entertainment and gift expenses	¶1001, ¶1023
IRC Sec. 275	Sec. 24345	Certain taxes	¶1006
IRC Sec. 276	Sec. 24429	Indirect contributions to political parties	¶1023
IRC Sec. 277	Sec. 24437	Deduction limitation for social clubs	¶1023
IRC Sec. 279	Sec. 24438	Interest deduction on corporate acquisition indebtedness	¶1004
IRC Sec. 280B	Sec. 24442	Demolition of historic structures	¶1023
IRC Sec. 280C	Sec. 24440	Expenses for which credit allowed	¶818, ¶1023
IRC Sec. 280E	Secs. 24436-36.1	Illegal sale of drugs	¶1023
IRC Sec. 280F	Sec. 24349.1	Depreciation-luxury cars	¶1011
IRC Sec. 280G	....	Golden parachutes	¶1023
IRC Sec. 280H	Sec. 24442.5	Amounts paid to employee owners	....
IRC Sec. 291	Sec. 24449	Preference items	¶817
IRC Secs. 301-385	Secs. 24451-81	Corporate distributions and adjustments	¶Various
IRC Secs. 401-424	Secs. 23701p, 24601-12, 24685.5	Deferred compensation	¶909, ¶1016, ¶1017
IRC Sec. 430-436	...	Minimum funding for single-employer and multi-employer plans	¶909, ¶1016
IRC Sec. 441	Secs. 24631, 24632, 24633.5	Accounting periods	¶1101
IRC Sec. 442	Sec. 24633	Change in accounting period	¶1102
IRC Sec. 443	Secs. 23113, 24634-36	Short-period returns	¶1103
IRC Sec. 444	Sec. 24637	Election to keep same tax year—S Corporations	¶806, ¶1104
IRC Sec. 446	Sec. 24651	Accounting methods	¶1106
IRC Sec. 447	Secs. 24652-52.5	Accounting for farm corporations	¶1106
IRC Sec. 448	Sec. 24654	Cash method of accounting restricted	¶1106
IRC Sec. 451	Secs. 24661, 24661.5, 24661.6	Taxable year of inclusion	¶1106
IRC Sec. 453	Secs. 24667, 24668.1	Installment method	¶1109
IRC Sec. 453A	Sec. 24667	Installment method	¶1109
IRC Sec. 453B	Sec. 24667	Installment method	¶1109
IRC Sec. 454	Sec. 24674	Obligation issued at discount	¶1111
IRC Sec. 455	Sec. 24676	Prepaid subscription income	¶1106
IRC Sec. 456	....	Prepaid dues income	¶1106
IRC Sec. 457	....	Deferred compensation plans-state governments	....
IRC Sec. 458	Sec. 24676.5	Returned magazines, paperbacks, records	¶1106
IRC Sec. 460	Secs. 24673, 24673.2	Long-term contracts	¶1106
IRC Sec. 461	Sec. 24681	Taxable year of deduction	¶1004, ¶1106
IRC Sec. 464	Sec. 24682	Farming expenses	¶1106
IRC Sec. 465	Sec. 24691	Deductions limited to amount at risk	¶1023, ¶1025
IRC Sec. 467	Sec. 24688	Deferred rental payments	¶1106
IRC Sec. 468	Sec. 24689	Waste disposal costs	¶1106
IRC Sec. 468A	Sec. 24690	Nuclear decommissioning funds	....
IRC Sec. 468B	Sec. 24693	Designated settlement funds	¶807, ¶1106
IRC Sec. 469	Sec. 24692	Passive losses and credits	¶1005, ¶1106
IRC Sec. 470	24694	Tax-exempt use losses	¶1007
IRC Sec. 471	Sec. 24701	Inventories-general rule	¶1107
IRC Sec. 472	Sec. 24701	Inventories-LIFO	¶1108
IRC Sec. 473	....	Liquidation of LIFO inventories	¶1108
IRC Sec. 474	Sec. 24708	Simplified dollar value LIFO	¶1108
IRC Sec. 475	Sec. 24710	Mark to market accounting	¶1107
IRC Sec. 481	Sec. 24721	Adjustments required by changes in method	¶1106
IRC Sec. 482	Sec. 24725	Allocation of income among taxpayers	¶1106, ¶1110
IRC Sec. 483	Sec. 24726	Imputed interest	¶1106, ¶1112
IRC Sec. 501	Secs. 23701-01y, 23703.5, 23704, 23704.4, 23704.5, 23706	Exempt organizations and trusts	¶808, ¶809

Federal	California	Subject	Paragraph
IRC Sec. 502	Sec. 23702	Feeder organizations	¶809
IRC Sec. 503	Secs. 23736-36.4	Requirements for exemption	¶809
IRC Sec. 504	Sec. 23704.6	Status after disqualification for lobbying	¶808
IRC Sec. 505	Sec. 23705	Special rules—VEBAs, etc.	¶808
IRC Sec. 507	Sec. 23707	Private foundation status terminated	¶808
IRC Sec. 508	Sec. 23708	Presumption that organization is private foundation	¶808
IRC Sec. 509	Sec. 23709	"Private foundation" defined	¶808
IRC Sec. 511	Sec. 23731	Unrelated business income	¶809
IRC Sec. 512	Sec. 23732	Unrelated business taxable income	¶809
IRC Sec. 513	Secs. 23710, 23734	Unrelated trade or business	¶809
IRC Sec. 514	Sec. 23735	Unrelated debt-financed income	¶809
IRC Sec. 515	....	Taxes, possessions, and foreign countries	¶809
IRC Sec. 521	....	Farmers' cooperatives-exemption	¶1021
IRC Sec. 526	....	Shipowners' protection associations	....
IRC Sec. 527	Sec. 23701r	Political organizations	¶808
IRC Sec. 528	Sec. 23701t	Homeowners' associations	¶808, ¶915
IRC Sec. 529	Secs. 18645, 23711, 23711.5, 24306	Qualified state tuition program	¶808, ¶924
IRC Sec. 530	Sec. 23712	Education IRAS	¶250, ¶330
IRC Secs. 531-37	....	Corporations improperly accumulating surplus	....
IRC Secs. 541-47	Sec. 23051.5	Personal holding companies	....
IRC Secs. 561-65	Sec. 24402	Deduction for dividends paid	....
IRC Sec. 581	Sec. 23039	Definition of bank	....
IRC Sec. 582	Sec. 24347	Bad debts, losses, and gains	¶1009
IRC Sec. 585	Sec. 24348	Deduction for bad debts—banks and S and L's	¶1009
IRC Sec. 591	Secs. 24370, 24403	Deduction for dividends paid on deposits	¶1021
IRC Sec. 593	Sec. 24348	Deduction for bad debts—federal mutual savings banks	¶1009
IRC Sec. 594	....	Mutual savings banks conducting life insurance business	....
IRC Sec. 597	Sec. 24322	FSLIC financial assistance	¶913
IRC Secs. 611-12	Sec. 24831	Natural resources	¶1012, ¶1250
IRC Sec. 613	Sec. 24831	Percentage depletion	¶1012, ¶1250
IRC Sec. 613A	Secs. 24831, 24831.6	Oil and gas wells	¶1012
IRC Sec. 614	Sec. 24831	"Property" defined	¶1012
IRC Sec. 616	Sec. 24831	Mine development expenditures	¶1012, ¶1013
IRC Sec. 617	Sec. 24831	Mine exploration expenditures	¶1012, ¶1013
IRC Sec. 631	Sec. 24831	Timber, coal, iron ore	¶1012
IRC Sec. 636	Sec. 24831	Mineral production payments	¶1012
IRC Sec. 638	Sec. 24831	Continental shelf areas	¶1012
IRC Secs. 641-92	Sec. 24271	Estates, trusts, and beneficiaries	....
IRC Secs. 701-777	Secs. 23081, 23083, 23091-99.5, 24271	Partnerships	¶616, ¶1246
IRC Secs. 801-848	....	Insurance companies	....
IRC Secs. 851-855	Secs. 24870, 24872	Regulated investment companies	¶805, ¶1021
IRC Secs. 856-860	Secs. 24870, 24872-72.7	Real estate investment trusts	¶805, ¶1021
IRC Secs. 860A-860G	Secs. 24870, 24873, 24874	Real estate mortgage investment conduits	¶805
IRC Secs. 860H-860L	Secs. 24870, 24875	Financial asset securitization trusts	¶805
IRC Secs. 861-865	Sec. 25110	Income from sources within or without U.S.	¶825, ¶1309
IRC Secs. 871-879	....	Foreign government investment income	....
IRC Secs. 881-882	Sec. 24321	Income of foreign corporations	....
IRC Sec. 883	Sec. 24320	Operation of foreign aircraft or ships	¶916
IRC Secs. 884-891	....	Foreign corporations and nonresident aliens	....
IRC Sec. 892	Sec. 24327	Income of foreign governments and of international organizations	....
IRC Secs. 901-907	....	Foreign tax credit	....
IRC Sec. 908	....	Reduction of credit for international boycott participation	....
IRC Secs. 931-937	....	U.S. possessions	....
IRC Secs. 951-964	Sec. 25110	Controlled foreign corporations	¶825, ¶909

Federal	California	Subject	Paragraph
IRC Sec. 965	. . . .	Temporary dividends received deduction	¶1309
IRC Secs. 970-971	. . . .	Export trade corporations	. . . .
IRC Secs. 985-989	Sec. 24905	Foreign currency transactions	¶1204
IRC Sec. 988	Secs. 24905, 24905.5	Hedging transactions	¶1204 , ¶1222
IRC Secs. 991-996	Sec. 23051.5	DISC corporations	¶909
IRC Sec. 1001	Secs. 24901, 24902, 24955	Determination of gain or loss	¶1201
IRC Sec. 1011	Secs. 24911, 24964	Adjusted basis	¶1247
IRC Sec. 1012	Sec. 24912	Basis of property—cost	¶1226
IRC Sec. 1013	Sec. 24913	Basis of property in inventory	¶1227
IRC Sec. 1014	. . . .	Basis of property acquired from decedent	¶1230
IRC Sec. 1015	Secs. 24914, 24915	Basis of property acquired by gift or transfer in trust	¶1228 , ¶1229
IRC Sec. 1016	Secs. 24916, 24916.2, 24917	Adjustments to basis	¶1247 -48
IRC Sec. 1017	Sec. 24918	Discharge of indebtedness	¶1247 , ¶1251
IRC Sec. 1019	Sec. 24919	Improvements to property by lessee	¶1247 , ¶1249
IRC Sec. 1021	. . . .	Sale of annuities	¶1247
IRC Sec. 1031	Sec. 24941	Exchange of property held for productive use	¶1206
IRC Sec. 1032	Secs. 19061, 24942	Exchange of stock for property	¶1224
IRC Sec. 1033	Secs. 19061, 24941-49.5	Involuntary conversions	¶1202 , ¶1235
IRC Sec. 1035	Sec. 24950	Exchanges of insurance policies	¶1207
IRC Sec. 1036	Sec. 24951	Exchange of stock	¶1208
IRC Sec. 1037	. . . .	Exchanges of U.S. obligations	¶1209
IRC Sec. 1038	Sec. 24952	Reacquisitions of real property	¶1210
IRC Sec. 1042	Secs. 24954-54.1	Securities sales to ESOPs	¶1213
IRC Sec. 1044	Sec. 24956	Rollover of publicly traded securities	¶1222
IRC Sec. 1051	Sec. 24961	Basis of property acquired from affiliated corporation	¶1237
IRC Sec. 1052	Sec. 24962	Basis provisions from prior codes	¶1238
IRC Sec. 1053	Sec. 24963	Basis of property acquired before March 1, 1913	¶1238
IRC Sec. 1054	Sec. 24965	Basis of stock issued by FNMA	¶1240
IRC Sec. 1055	. . . .	Redeemable ground rents	¶1241
IRC Sec. 1056	Sec. 24989	Basis limitation for player contracts	¶1252
IRC Sec. 1057	. . . .	Transfers of property to foreign trust	. . . .
IRC Sec. 1059	Sec. 24966	Basis after extraordinary dividend	¶1226
IRC Sec. 1059A	Sec. 24966.1	Basis of property imported from related persons	¶1226 , ¶1227
IRC Sec. 1060	Sec. 24966.2	Allocation of asset acquisitions	¶1226 , ¶1253
IRC Sec. 1081	Sec. 24981	Exchange or distribution in obedience to SEC orders	¶1205
IRC Sec. 1082	Sec. 24988	Basis for determining gain or loss	¶1245
IRC Sec. 1091	Sec. 24998	Wash sales of stock or securities	¶1008 , ¶1236
IRC Sec. 1092	Sec. 24998	Straddles	¶1225
IRC Secs. 1201-60	Secs. 23051.5, 24990, 24990.4-24990.7	Capital gains and losses	¶1011 , ¶1201 , ¶1217 , ¶1222
IRC Secs. 1271-74A	Sec. 24990	Debt instruments	¶911 , ¶1223
IRC Sec. 1275	Secs. 24990, 24991	Definitions and special rules relating to debt instruments	¶910 , ¶911
IRC Secs. 1276-78	Sec. 24990	Market discount on bonds	¶911 , ¶1222
IRC Secs. 1281-83	Secs. 24990, 24991	Discount on short term obligations as income	¶1222
IRC Secs. 1286-88	Sec. 24990	Miscellaneous provisions	¶1222
IRC Secs. 1291-98	Secs. 24990, 24995	Passive foreign investment companies	¶1222
IRC Secs. 1311-14	. . . .	Mitigation of effect of limitations	¶1409
IRC Sec. 1341	. . . .	Repayment of income received under claim of right	¶1106
IRC Sec. 1351	. . . .	Recovery of foreign expropriation losses	. . . .
IRC Secs. 1361-79	Secs. 23800-11, 23813	"Subchapter S" corporations	¶806
IRC Sec. 1381	Secs. 24404-06	Cooperatives	¶1021
IRC Sec. 1382	Secs. 24404-06	Taxable income of cooperatives	¶1021
IRC Sec. 1383	Secs. 24404-06.5	Nonqualified notices of allocation redeemed by cooperative	¶1021
IRC Sec. 1385	Sec. 24273.5	Amounts includible in patron's gross income	¶914
IRC Sec. 1388	Sec. 24406.6	Net earnings of cooperatives	¶1021

Federal	California	Subject	Paragraph
IRC Sec. 1441	. . . .	Withholding on nonresident aliens	¶1413
IRC Sec. 1445	. . . .	Withholding on U.S. real estate sales	¶1413
IRC Sec. 1501	Secs. 23362, 23364a	Consolidated return of affiliated group	¶812
IRC Sec. 1502	Secs. 23363, 25106.5	Regulations	¶812
IRC Sec. 1503	Sec. 23364	Computation and payment of tax	¶812
IRC Sec. 1504	Sec. 23361	"Affiliated group" defined	¶812
IRC Sec. 4911	Sec. 23740	Excess expenditures to influence legislation	¶1023
IRC Secs. 4940-48	. . . .	Taxes on private foundations	¶808
IRC Secs. 4971-75	. . . .	Tax on failure to meet pension funding requirements	¶1016
IRC Sec. 6011	Sec. 18407	Tax shelter reporting requirements	¶1424
IRC Sec. 6012	Various	Returns required	¶810, ¶811
IRC Sec. 6031	Secs. 18535, 18633-33.5	Return of partnership income	. . . .
IRC Sec. 6033	Sec. 23772	Annual returns by exempt organizations	¶811
IRC Sec. 6037	Sec. 18601	S corporation returns	¶806
IRC Sec. 6038	Sec. 19141.2	Information returns on foreign corporations	¶1413, ¶1414
IRC Sec. 6038A	Sec. 19141.5	Report of 25% foreign-owned corporations	¶1414
IRC Sec. 6038B	Sec. 19141.5	Report on transfers to foreign persons	¶1414
IRC Sec. 6038C	Sec. 19141.5	Report of foreign corporation doing U.S. business	¶1414
IRC Sec. 6039	Sec. 18631	Information returns for foreign interests	¶1412
IRC Sec. 6041	Secs. 18631, 25111	Information at source	¶1412
IRC Sec. 6041A	Sec. 18631	Reporting certain payments	¶1412
IRC Sec. 6042	Sec. 18639	Returns for corporate earnings and profits	¶1412
IRC Sec. 6043	. . . .	Returns for dividends on liquidation	. . . .
IRC Sec. 6044	Sec. 18640	Returns for cooperatives	. . . .
IRC Sec. 6045	Secs. 18631, 18642	Returns for brokers	¶1412
IRC Sec. 6049	Sec. 18630	Returns for payment of interest	¶1412
IRC Sec. 6050A	Sec. 18644	Returns for fishing boat operators	¶1412
IRC Sec. 6050I-50S	Sec. 18631	Information returns	¶1411, ¶1412
IRC Sec. 6062	. . . .	Signing of corporation returns	. . . .
IRC Sec. 6065	Secs. 18606, 18621	Verification of return	¶810
IRC Sec. 6072	Sec. 18566	Time for filing returns	¶810
IRC Sec. 6081	Secs. 18567, 18604	Extension of time for filing return	¶810
IRC Sec. 6091	Sec. 18621	Place for filing returns or other documents	. . . .
IRC Sec. 6102	Sec. 18623	Fractional dollar calculations	¶810
IRC Secs. 6103-04	Secs. 19543-49, 19551-55, 19562, 19565, 21023	Confidentiality of returns	. . . .
IRC Sec. 6107	Sec. 18625	Duties of tax prepares	¶1401
IRC Sec. 6109	Sec. 18624	Identifying numbers required on documents	¶1401
IRC Sec. 6111	Sec. 18628	Reportable transactions	¶1424
IRC Sec. 6112	Sec. 18648	Listed transactions	¶1424
IRC Sec. 6115	Sec. 18648.5	Disclosure related to quid pro quo information	¶1014
IRC Sec. 6151	Secs. 19001, 19004-06	Payment of tax	¶814
IRC Sec. 6155	. . . .	Payment on notice and demand	¶1405
IRC Secs. 6161-64	. . . .	Extensions of time for payment	¶814
IRC Sec. 6201	Sec. 21024	Burden of proof	¶1402
IRC Sec. 6211	. . . .	"Deficiency" defined	¶1403, ¶1404
IRC Sec. 6212	Secs. 19031-36, 19049, 19050	Notice of deficiency	¶1403, ¶1404
IRC Sec. 6213	Secs. 19041-48, 19332-34, 19051	Deficiencies—petition to tax court	¶1403, ¶1404, ¶1405
IRC Sec. 6225	Sec. 19063	SOL for partnership items	¶1409
IRC Sec. 6325	Sec. 19226	Release of liens	. . . .
IRC Sec. 6331	Secs. 19231, 19236, 19262, 21019	Levy to collect tax	. . . .
IRC Sec. 6335	Sec. 19262	Sale of seized property	. . . .
IRC Sec. 6338	Sec. 19263	Certificate of sale	. . . .
IRC Sec. 6342	Sec. 19263	Disposition of proceeds of levy or sale	. . . .
IRC Secs. 6401-08	Secs. 19104, 19107, 19116, 19349, 19354, 19362-63, 19431, 21012	Abatements, credits, and refunds	¶1410, ¶1415, ¶1416

Federal	California	Subject	Paragraph
IRC Sec. 6425	. . . .	Adjustment of overpayment of estimated income tax	¶813
IRC Secs. 6501, 6503(i)	Secs. 19057-58, 19065-67, 19087, 19371	Limitations on assessments	¶1403, ¶1409
IRC Sec. 6511	Secs. 19306, 19308-14	Time limitation on filing claim for credit or refund	¶1417
IRC Sec. 6532	Sec. 19384	Limitation periods on suits	¶1418, ¶1423
IRC Sec. 6601	Secs. 19101, 19104, 19108, 19112-14	Interest on tax due	¶814, ¶1410
IRC Sec. 6602	Sec. 19411	Interest on erroneous refund	¶1423
IRC Sec. 6611	Secs. 19340, 19341, 19349, 19351	Interest on overpayments	¶813, ¶1419
IRC Sec. 6621	Sec. 19521	Determination of rate of interest	¶1410
IRC Sec. 6651	Secs. 19131-32.5	Failure to file return or pay tax	¶1411
IRC Sec. 6652	Secs. 19133.5, 23772	Failure to file return	¶811, ¶1411
IRC Sec. 6653	. . . .	Failure to pay stamp tax	¶1411
IRC Sec. 6655	Secs. 19004, 19010, 19023-27, 19142-51	Estimated tax	¶813
IRC Sec. 6657	Sec. 19134	Bad checks	¶1411
IRC Sec. 6658	Sec. 19161	Timely payments during pending bankruptcy	¶1411
IRC Sec. 6662	Secs. 19164, 19772-74	Accuracy-related penalty	¶1411
IRC Sec. 6663	Secs. 19164, 19772-74	Fraud penalty	¶1411
IRC Sec. 6664	Sec. 19164	Definitions and special rules	¶1411
IRC Sec. 6665	Sec. 19164	Applicable rules	¶1411
IRC Sec. 6673	Sec. 19714	Penalty for delay	¶1411
IRC Sec. 6693	Sec. 19184	Failure to file return	¶1411
IRC Sec. 6694	Sec. 19166	Understatement by preparer	¶1411
IRC Secs. 6695-96	Secs. 19167, 19168, 19712	Tax preparer penalties	¶1411
IRC Sec. 6700	Sec. 19177	Penalty for promoting abusive tax shelters	¶1424
IRC Sec. 6701	Sec. 19178	Penalty for aiding understatement of tax liability	¶1411
IRC Sec. 6702	Sec. 19179	Penalty for frivolous tax returns	¶1411
IRC Sec. 6703	Sec. 19180	Rules for penalties	¶1411
IRC Sec. 6706	Sec. 19181	Original issue discount reporting	¶911, ¶1411
IRC Secs. 6707-08	Secs. 19173, 19182, 19772, 19774	Abusive shelter penalties	¶1424
IRC Sec. 6714	Sec. 19182.5	Penalty for failure to disclose quid pro quo information	. . . .
IRC Secs. 6721-24	Sec. 19183	Penalty for nonfiling	¶1411
IRC Sec. 6751	Sec. 19187	Procedures for penalties	¶1411
IRC Sec. 6861	Secs. 19081, 19086, 19092	Jeopardy assessments	¶1406
IRC Sec. 6863	Sec. 19083	Jeopardy assessments stay of collection	¶1406
IRC Sec. 6867	Sec. 19093	Presumption for large amount of cash not identified	. . . .
IRC Sec. 6871	Secs. 19088, 19090	Receivership—immediate assessment	¶1407
IRC Sec. 6872	Sec. 19089	Suspension of period on assessment	¶1407
IRC Sec. 6873	Sec. 19091	Unpaid claims	¶1407
IRC Secs. 6901-04	Secs. 19071-74	Liability of transferees and fiduciaries	¶1408
IRC Sec. 7121	Sec. 19441	Closing agreements	¶1420
IRC Sec. 7122	Sec. 19441	Compromise of tax liability	¶1421
IRC Sec. 7201	. . . .	Attempt to evade or defeat tax	. . . .
IRC Sec. 7202	Secs. 19708, 19709	Wilful failure to collect or pay over tax	¶1411
IRC Sec. 7203	Sec. 19706	Wilful failure to file return	¶1411
IRC Sec. 7206	Secs. 19701, 19705	Fraud and false statements	¶1411
IRC Sec. 7207	. . . .	Fraudulent returns, statements, or other documents	. . . .
IRC Sec. 7213	Secs. 19542, 19542.3, 19552	Unauthorized disclosure of information	. . . .
IRC Sec. 7405	Sec. 19411	Recovery of erroneous refunds	¶1423
IRC Sec. 7421	Secs. 19081, 19381	Prohibition of suits to restrain assessment	¶1419
IRC Sec. 7422	Secs. 19382, 19383, 19387	Actions for refunds	¶1419
IRC Sec. 7428	. . . .	Exempt status declaratory judgments	¶808
IRC Sec. 7430	Secs. 19717, 21013	Recovery of litigation costs	¶1401
IRC Sec. 7502	Sec. 21027	Mailing/delivery of returns	¶1402
IRC Sec. 7508A	Sec. 18572	Disaster relief extensions	¶810, ¶814, ¶1409, ¶1417
IRC Sec. 7518	Sec. 24272.5	Capital construction funds for vessels	¶917

Federal	California	Subject	Paragraph
IRC Sec. 7524	Sec. 21026	Annual notice of delinquency	¶1402
IRC Sec. 7602	Secs. 19504, 19504.7	Examination of books and witnesses	¶1403
IRC Sec. 7609	Sec. 19064	Third-party summonses	¶1403 , ¶1409
IRC Sec. 7612	Sec. 19504.5	Software trade secrets	¶1401
IRC Sec. 7701	Secs. 23031-38, 23041-51	Definitions	¶805 , ¶1106
IRC Secs. 7702, 7702A	Sec. 23045	Modified endowment contracts	. . . .
IRC Sec. 7704	Sec. 23038.5	Publicly traded partnerships	¶804 , ¶805
IRC Sec. 7806	Secs. 23030, 23051.5, 23060	Construction of title	. . . .
IRC Sec. 7811	Secs. 21001-27	Taxpayers' bill of rights	¶1401 , ¶1402
IRC Sec. 7872	Sec. 24993	Imputed interest	¶1112

CALIFORNIA-FEDERAL CROSS-REFERENCE TABLE AND INDEX

Showing Sections of Federal Law (1986 Internal Revenue Code) Comparable to Sections of California Bank and Corporation Tax Law (Revenue and Taxation Code)

California	Federal	Subject	Paragraph
Secs. 18401-03	....	General application of administrative provisions	....
Sec. 18405	....	Relief upon noncompliance with new provisions	....
Sec. 18405.1	....	Perfection of water's-edge election	¶1311
Sec. 18407	IRC Sec. 6011	Tax shelter reporting	¶1424
Sec. 18408	IRC Sec. 6011	Computerized returns	....
Secs. 18412-17	IRC Sec. 7807	Continuity of provisions with prior law	....
Secs. 18416	...	Last known address	....
Sec. 18510	....	Use tax reporting	¶814
Sec. 18536	...	Group returns for nonresident corporate directors	¶714
Sec. 18572	IRC Sec. 7508A	Disaster relief extensions	¶810, ¶814, ¶1409, ¶1417
Sec. 18601	IRC Secs. 6012(a), 6037, 6072	Annual income or franchise tax return	¶810
Sec. 18602	....	Paying wrong tax	¶810
Sec. 18604	IRC Sec. 6081	Extension of time for filing return	¶810
Sec. 18606	IRC Sec. 6012(b)	Returns by receivers, trustees, or assignees	¶810
Sec. 18621	IRC Secs. 6065, 6091	Verification of return	¶810
Sec. 18621.5	....	Electronic filing verification	¶810
Sec. 18622	....	Change in federal income tax return	¶810
Sec. 18623	IRC Sec. 6102	Fractional dollar calculations	¶810
Sec. 18624	IRC Sec. 6109	Identifying numbers	¶1401
Sec. 18625	IRC Sec. 6107	Copy to taxpayer	¶1401
Sec. 18628	IRC Sec. 6111	Reportable transaction reporting requirements	¶1424
Sec. 18631	IRC Secs. 6034A, 6039, 6039C, 6041, 6041A, 6042, 6045, 6049, 6050H-S, 6052	Information return filing requirements	¶1412
Sec. 18631.7	....	Check cashing business information return	¶1411, ¶1412
Sec. 18633.5	IRC Sec. 6031	Limited liability companies	¶805
Sec. 18639	IRC Secs. 6041-43, 6049	Returns for interest, dividends, collections	¶1412
Sec. 18640	IRC Sec. 6044	Returns by cooperatives	¶1412
Sec. 18642	IRC Sec. 6045	Information returns of property owners	¶1412
Sec. 18644	IRC Sec. 6050A	Fishing boat operators—reporting requirements	¶1412
Sec. 18648	IRC Sec. 6112	Listed transactions	¶1412
Sec. 18648.5	IRC Sec. 6115	Disclosure related to quid pro quo information	¶1014
Sec. 18649	IRC Sec. 1275	Information furnished to FTB	¶1412
Sec. 18661	IRC Sec. 3402	Recipient of income	¶1413
Sec. 18662	IRC Secs. 1445, 3402	Withholding of corporate tax	¶716, ¶1413
Sec. 18665	....	Change in withholding due to legislative enactments	¶1413
Sec. 18667	IRC Sec. 3402	Withholding exemption certificates	¶1413
Sec. 18668	IRC Sec. 3403	Withholding penalties	¶1413
Sec. 18669	....	Sale, transfer, or disposition of business	¶1413
Sec. 18670	....	Notice to withhold	¶1413
Sec. 18670.5	....	Electronic notice to withhold	....
Sec. 18671	....	Withholding—state agencies	¶1413
Sec. 18672	....	Liability for failure to withhold	¶1413
Sec. 18674	....	Requirements for withholding agent	¶1413
Sec. 18675	IRC Sec. 6414	Taxpayer remedies when order to withhold	¶1413
Sec. 18676	....	Notice to withhold to state agencies	¶1413

California	Federal	Subject	Paragraph
Sec. 18677	IRC Sec. 3505	Lender, surety, or other person liable	¶1413
Sec. 19001	IRC Sec. 6151	Payment of tax	¶814
Sec. 19002	IRC Sec. 6513	Credit for amount withheld	¶810
Sec. 19004	IRC Sec. 6151	Early tax payment	¶814
Sec. 19005	IRC Sec. 6151	Tax payable to FTB	¶814
Sec. 19007	IRC Sec. 6315	Payments of estimated taxes	¶813
Sec. 19009	IRC Sec. 7512	Failure to pay collected taxes	¶1413
Sec. 19010	IRC Sec. 6655	Assessing delinquent estimated taxes	¶813
Sec. 19011	IRC Sec. 6302	Electronic funds transfer	¶814
Sec. 19021	. . . .	Bank and financial corporation tax	¶813, ¶814
Sec. 19023	IRC Sec. 6655(g)	"Estimated tax" defined	¶813
Sec. 19025	IRC Sec. 6655(c), (d)	Installment payments of tax	¶813
Sec. 19026	IRC Sec. 6655	Revised estimate of taxes	¶813
Sec. 19027	IRC Sec. 6655	Short-year estimated tax payments	¶813
Sec. 19031	IRC Sec. 6212	Deficiency assessments—FTB authority	¶1403
Sec. 19032	IRC Sec. 6212	FTB authorized to examine return	¶1403
Sec. 19033	IRC Sec. 6212	Notice of additional assessment	¶1403
Sec. 19034	IRC Sec. 6212	Contents of notice	¶1403
Sec. 19036	IRC Sec. 6212	Interest, penalties, additions to tax as deficiency assessments	¶1403
Sec. 19041	IRC Sec. 6213	Filing protest	¶1403
Sec. 19041.5	. . . .	Treatment of deposits	¶1417, ¶1418
Sec. 19042	IRC Sec. 6213	60-day protest period	¶1403, ¶1405
Sec. 19043	IRC Sec. 6211	Deficiency defined	¶1403
Sec. 19043.5	. . . .	Carryover adjustments	¶1403
Sec. 19044	IRC Sec. 6213	Protest hearing	¶1403
Sec. 19045	. . . .	Finality of action upon protest	¶1403
Sec. 19046	IRC Sec. 6213	Appeal to SBE	¶1403, ¶1404
Sec. 19047	IRC Sec. 6213	Determination of appeal	¶1403, ¶1404
Sec. 19048	IRC Sec. 6213	Finality of determination	¶1403, ¶1404
Sec. 19049	IRC Sec. 6212	Notice and demand	¶1403, ¶1405
Sec. 19050	IRC Sec. 6212	Certificate of mailing	¶1403
Sec. 19051	IRC Sec. 6213	Mathematical error	¶1403
Sec. 19054	IRC Sec. 6201	Overstatement of credit	¶1403
Sec. 19057	IRC Sec. 6501	Limitation on assessment	¶1403, ¶1409
Sec. 19058	IRC Sec. 6501(e)	Limitation period extended	¶1403, ¶1409
Sec. 19059	. . . .	Assessment of deficiencies on amended returns	¶1409
Sec. 19060	. . . .	Failure to file amended return	¶1409
Sec. 19061	IRC Secs. 1032, 1033(a)(2)(A)-(a)(2)(D)	Deficiency after involuntary conversion	¶1409
Sec. 19063	IRC Secs. 6501(a), 6225	Items of federally registered partnership	¶1409
Sec. 19064	IRC Sec. 7609	Motion to quash subpoena	¶1403, ¶1409
Sec. 19065	IRC Sec. 6501(c)	Federal extension for assessing deficiencies	¶1403, ¶1409
Sec. 19066	IRC Sec. 6501(b)	Time return deemed filed	¶1403, ¶1409
Sec. 19066.5	IRC Sec. 6501(c)	Suspension of SOL	¶1409
Sec. 19067	IRC Sec. 6501(c)	Extension by agreement	¶1403, ¶1409
Sec. 19071	IRC Sec. 6901	Collection from other than taxpayer	¶1408
Sec. 19072	IRC Sec. 6901	Collection from person secondarily liable	¶1408
Sec. 19073	IRC Sec. 6901	Assessment and collection from transferees and fiduciaries	¶1408
Sec. 19074	IRC Sec. 6901	Limitations period for assessment of transferee or fiduciary	¶1408
Sec. 19081	IRC Secs. 6851, 6861	Jeopardy assessments	¶1406
Sec. 19082	IRC Sec. 6862	Jeopardy assessments	¶1406
Sec. 19083	IRC Sec. 6863	Jeopardy assessments—stay of collection	¶1406
Sec. 19084	IRC Sec. 6863	Jeopardy assessments	¶1406
Sec. 19085	IRC Sec. 6863	Jeopardy assessments	¶1406
Sec. 19086	IRC Sec. 6861	Evidence of jeopardy	¶1406
Sec. 19087	IRC Sec. 6501(c)	Estimated assessments	¶1403
Sec. 19088	IRC Sec. 6871	Receivership—immediate assessment	¶1407
Sec. 19089	IRC Secs. 6036, 6872	Notice by receiver to FTB	¶1407
Sec. 19090	IRC Sec. 6871	Adjudication in receivership proceeding	¶1407
Sec. 19091	IRC Sec. 6873	Unpaid claims	¶1407

California	Federal	Subject	Paragraph
Sec. 19092	IRC Sec. 6861	Regulations	. . . .
Sec. 19101	IRC Sec. 6601(a)	Interest on tax due	¶1410
Sec. 19104	IRC Sec. 6404	Interest on deficiency	¶1410
Sec. 19108	IRC Sec. 6601	Overpayment applied to another year's deficiency	¶1410
Sec. 19109	. . . .	Abatement of interest	¶1410
Sec. 19113	IRC Sec. 6601(f)	Satisfaction by credit	¶1410
Sec. 19114	IRC Sec. 6601(g)	Collection and assessment of interest	¶1410
Sec. 19120	. . . .	Interest on erroneous refunds	¶1410
Sec. 19131	IRC Sec. 6651	Penalty for failure to file return	¶1411
Sec. 19132	IRC Sec. 6651	Penalty for underpayment of tax	¶1411
Sec. 19133	. . . .	Penalty for failure to furnish information	¶1411
Sec. 19134	IRC Sec. 6657	Bad checks	¶1411
Sec. 19135	. . . .	Penalty—unqualified and doing business	¶1411
Sec. 19136.8	. . . .	Waiver of estimated tax underpayment penalty	¶813
Sec. 19138	. . . .	Large corporate underpayment penalty	¶1411
Sec. 19141	. . . .	Failure to file annual statement	¶1411
Sec. 19141.2	IRC Sec. 6038	Information returns on foreign corporations	¶1414
Sec. 19141.5	IRC Secs. 6038A-38C	Information returns on foreign-owned and foreign corporations, transfers to foreign persons	¶1411, ¶1414
Sec. 19141.6	. . . .	Penalty for failure to keep water's-edge records	¶1411
Sec. 19142	IRC Sec. 6655(a)	Underpayment of estimated tax	¶813
Sec. 19144	IRC Sec. 6655(b)	Amount of underpayment	¶813
Sec. 19145	IRC Sec. 6655(e)	Period of underpayment	¶813
Sec. 19147	IRC Sec. 6655(d)	Exceptions to underpayment	¶813
Sec. 19148	IRC Sec. 6655	Underpayment of estimated tax	¶813
Sec. 19149	IRC Sec. 6655	Calculation of addition to tax	¶813
Sec. 19150	IRC Sec. 6655	Underpayment for income years of less than 12 months	¶813
Sec. 19151	IRC Sec. 6655	Underpayment not applicable to exempt corporation until certificate revoked	¶813
Sec. 19161	IRC Sec. 6658	Timely payments during pending bankruptcy	¶813, ¶1411
Sec. 19164	IRC Secs. 6662-65	Accuracy- and fraud-related penalties, special rules	¶1411, ¶1424
Sec. 19164.5	IRC Secs. 6662A	Reportable transaction accuracy-related penalty	¶1424
Sec. 19166	IRC Sec. 6694	Penalty—preparer understatement	¶1411
Sec. 19167	IRC Sec. 6695(a), (c), (d)	Penalty—tax preparers	¶1411
Sec. 19168	IRC Sec. 6696	Penalty—tax preparers	¶1411
Sec. 19169	IRC Sec. 6695(f)	Penalty—negotiating client's refund check	¶1411
Sec. 19173	IRC Sec. 6708	Penalty—tax shelters	¶1411
Sec. 19174	IRC Sec. 6700	Penalty—tax shelters	¶1411
Sec. 19176	IRC Sec. 6682	Penalty—withholding	¶1411
Sec. 19177	IRC Sec. 6700	Penalty—abusive tax shelters	¶1411
Sec. 19178	IRC Sec. 6701	Penalty—aiding and abetting	¶1411
Sec. 19179	IRC Sec. 6702	Penalty—frivolous return	¶1411
Sec. 19180	IRC Sec. 6703	Rules for penalties	¶1411
Sec. 19181	IRC Sec. 6706	Penalty for failure to report original issue discount	¶1411
Sec. 19182	IRC Sec. 6707	Penalty for tax shelter providers	¶1411
Sec. 19182.5	IRC Sec. 6714	Penalty for failure to disclose quid pro quo information	. . . .
Sec. 19183	IRC Secs. 6721-24	Penalty for failure to file information return	¶1411
Sec. 19184	IRC Sec. 6693	Penalty for failure to properly report IRA	¶1411
Sec. 19187	IRC Sec. 6751	Procedures for penalties	¶1411
Secs. 19191-94	. . . .	Voluntary disclosure agreements	¶1423
Secs. 19195	. . .	Public disclosure of large delinquent taxpayers	¶721
Sec. 19201	. . . .	Request for judgment	. . . .
Sec. 19202	. . . .	Judgment for taxes	. . . .
Sec. 19221	IRC Sec. 6321	Perfected tax lien	. . . .
Sec. 19222	IRC Sec. 6311	Lien for dishonored checks	. . . .
Sec. 19225	. . . .	Administrative review	¶1402

California	Federal	Subject	Paragraph
Sec. 19226	IRC Sec. 6325	Release of third-party liens	. . . .
Sec. 19231	IRC Sec. 6331	Warrant for collection of tax	. . . .
Sec. 19232	. . . .	Warrant as writ of execution	. . . .
Sec. 19233	. . . .	Fees for warrant	. . . .
Sec. 19234	. . . .	Fees as obligation of taxpayer	. . . .
Sec. 19235	. . . .	Costs associated with sale of property	. . . .
Sec. 19236	IRC Sec. 6331	Seizure of property	. . . .
Sec. 19251	. . . .	Remedies cumulative	. . . .
Sec. 19252	. . . .	FTB as representative	. . . .
Sec. 19253	. . . .	Priority of tax lien	. . . .
Sec. 19253.5	. . . .	Tax practitioner disbarment; suspension	. . . .
Sec. 19254	. . . .	Collection and filing enforcement fees	¶1411
Sec. 19255	IRC Sec. 6502	Limitations period for collections	¶1409
Sec. 19256	IRC Sec. 7504	Fractional dollar amounts	. . . .
Sec. 19262	IRC Secs. 6331, 6335	Seizure and sale of personal property	¶1411
Sec. 19263	IRC Secs. 6338, 6342	Bill of sale; disposition of excess	. . . .
Sec. 19264	. . . .	Earnings withholding tax orders	. . . .
Sec. 19301	IRC Sec. 6402(a)	Overpayment—credit or refund	¶1415
Sec. 19302	. . . .	Credit and refund approval	¶1417
Sec. 19306	IRC Sec. 6511(a)	Time limitation on filing claim for credit or refund	¶1417
Sec. 19307	. . . .	Return as claim for refund	¶1415, ¶1417
Sec. 19308	IRC Sec. 6511(c)	Effect of assessment extension	¶1415, ¶1417
Sec. 19309	IRC Sec. 6511(c)	Claims file before assessment extension	¶1415, ¶1417
Sec. 19311	IRC Sec. 6511	Time limit following federal adjusted return	¶1415, ¶1417
Sec. 19312	IRC Sec. 6511(d)	Time limit where bad debts or worthless securities	¶1415, ¶1417
Sec. 19313	IRC Sec. 6511(g)	Federally registered partnerships	¶1415, ¶1417
Sec. 19314	. . . .	Overpayment allowed as offset	¶1415, ¶1417
Sec. 19321	. . . .	Refund claim where final action	¶1415
Sec. 19322	. . . .	Claim for refund—grounds	¶1415
Sec. 19322.1	. . . .	Informal refund claim	¶1417
Sec. 19323	. . . .	Notice of disallowance	¶1415
Sec. 19324	. . . .	Finality of action upon claim	¶1415
Sec. 19325	. . . .	Disallowance of interest on claims resulting from change in federal law	¶1419
Sec. 19331	. . . .	Presumption of disallowance	¶1415
Sec. 19332	IRC Sec. 6213	Mailing of appeals	¶1415, ¶1416
Sec. 19333	IRC Sec. 6213	SBE's determination	¶1415, ¶1416
Sec. 19334	IRC Sec. 6213	Petition for rehearing	¶1415, ¶1416
Sec. 19335	. . . .	Appeal as claim for refund	¶1415
Sec. 19340	IRC Sec. 6611(b)	Interest on overpayments	¶1419
Sec. 19341	IRC Sec. 6611(e)	Time period for payment without interest	¶1419
Sec. 19342	. . . .	Notice of disallowance	¶1419
Sec. 19343	. . . .	Finality of notice	¶1419
Sec. 19344	. . . .	Appeal to SBE	¶1419
Sec. 19345	. . . .	Determination of appeal	¶1419
Sec. 19346	. . . .	Finality of determination	¶1419
Sec. 19347	. . . .	Suit to recover interest	¶1419
Sec. 19348	. . . .	Failure of FTB to give notice	¶1419
Sec. 19349	IRC Secs. 6401, 6611	Payments not entitled to refunds	¶1419
Sec. 19350	. . . .	No interest on portion of barred claim	¶1419
Sec. 19351	IRC Sec. 6611(b)	Determining limitation period for interest	¶1419
Sec. 19355	. . . .	Refunding excess	. . . .
Sec. 19361	IRC Sec. 6414	Employer's overpayment	. . . .
Sec. 19362	IRC Sec. 6402	Credits against estimated tax	. . . .
Sec. 19363	IRC Sec. 6402	Interest on overpayments of estimated tax	¶813, ¶1419
Sec. 19364	. . . .	Overpayments of tax	¶813
Sec. 19365	. . . .	S corporation transfer of estimated tax	¶806
Sec. 19368	. . . .	erroneous refunds	¶1423
Sec. 19371	IRC Sec. 6502	Writ of attachment	. . . .
Sec. 19372	. . . .	Suit for tax	. . . .
Sec. 19373	. . . .	Prosecution of suit	. . . .
Sec. 19374	. . . .	Evidence of tax due	. . . .

California	Federal	Subject	Paragraph
Sec. 19375	....	Bringing of action	....
Sec. 19376	....	Collection of tax	¶1401
Sec. 19377	IRC Sec. 6301	Agreements with collection agencies	....
Sec. 19378	IRC Sec. 6301	Collection and transfer of funds	....
Sec. 19381	IRC Sec. 7421	Injunction to prevent assessment prohibited	¶1418
Sec. 19382	IRC Sec. 7422	Action to recover void tax	¶1418
Sec. 19383	IRC Sec. 7422	Credit of overpayment	¶1418
Sec. 19384	IRC Sec. 6532	Time limitation on action	¶1418
Sec. 19385	IRC Sec. 6532	FTB's failure to mail notice	¶1418
Sec. 19387	IRC Sec. 7422	Service upon FTB	¶1418
Sec. 19388	IRC Sec. 6532	Place of action	¶1418
Sec. 19389	IRC Sec. 6532	Defense of action	¶1418
Sec. 19390	....	Bar of action	¶1418
Sec. 19391	IRC Sec. 6612	Interest on judgment rendered for overpayment	¶1418
Sec. 19392	....	Judgment against FTB	¶1418
Sec. 19393	....	Recomputation of discriminatory bank tax	....
Sec. 19411	IRC Secs. 6602, 7405	Action to recover refund erroneously made	¶1423
Sec. 19412	....	Location of trial	¶1423
Sec. 19413	....	Prosecution of action	¶1423
Sec. 19431	IRC Sec. 6404	Cancellation of illegal levy	....
Sec. 19432	....	Cancellation of tax for inactive corporations	....
Sec. 19441	IRC Secs. 7121-23	Closing agreements	¶1420
Sec. 19442	....	Settlement of tax disputes	¶1411, ¶1420
Sec. 19443	....	Offers in compromise	¶1421
Sec. 19501	IRC Sec. 7621(a)	FTB's powers	¶1401
Sec. 19502	IRC Sec. 7621(b)	FTB—establishment of districts	¶1401
Sec. 19503	IRC Sec. 7805	FTB—rules and regulations	¶1401
Sec. 19504	IRC Sec. 7602	FTB—audits	¶1401
Sec. 19504.5	IRC Sec. 7612	Software trade secrets	¶1401
Sec. 19504.7	IRC Sec. 7602	Notice of contact of third parties	¶1401
Sec. 19521	IRC Secs. 6621, 6622	Determination of rate of interest	¶1410
Sec. 19525	IRC Sec. 7623	Reward program	¶1401
Sec. 19530	....	Preservation of returns	¶1401
Sec. 19531	....	Fees for publications	....
Secs. 19532-32.1	....	Priority for application of collected amounts	....
Secs. 19542-42.3	IRC Secs. 6103, 7213	Unauthorized disclosure by FTB	....
Sec. 19543	IRC Sec. 6103(b)	Nondisclosure of extraneous matters	....
Sec. 19544	IRC Sec. 6103(b)	Nondisclosure of audit methods	....
Sec. 19545	IRC Sec. 6103(h)	Disclosure in tax administration proceedings	....
Secs. 19546-46.5	IRC Sec. 6103(f)	Disclosure to legislative committee	....
Sec. 19547	IRC Sec. 6103(h)	Matters represented by Attorney General	....
Sec. 19549	IRC Sec. 6103(b)	Definitions	....
Sec. 19551	IRC Sec. 6103(d)	Disclosure to proper authorities	....
Sec. 19551.1-51.5	....	Disclosure to city officials	....
Sec. 19552	IRC Sec. 7213	Unauthorized disclosure	....
Sec. 19559	....	Disclosure of tourist industry information	....
Sec. 19562	IRC Sec. 6103	Charge for reasonable cost	....
Sec. 19563	IRC Sec. 6108	Publication of statistics	....
Sec. 19565	IRC Sec. 6104	Inspection of exempt organizations' applications	....
Sec. 19570	....	Use of Information Practices Act	....
Sec. 19590-92	....	Tax service fees	....
Sec. 19701	IRC Sec. 7206	Failure to file—aiding and abetting	¶1411
Sec. 19703	....	Evidence of failure to file	¶1411
Sec. 19704	....	Time limit on prosecution	¶1411
Sec. 19705	IRC Sec. 7206	False statements and fraud	¶1411
Sec. 19706	IRC Sec. 7203	Wilful failure to file return	¶1411
Sec. 19707	....	Venue	....
Sec. 19708	IRC Sec. 7202	Failure to collect or pay over tax	¶1411
Sec. 19709	IRC Sec. 7202	Failure to withhold tax as misdemeanor	¶1411
Sec. 19710	....	Writ of mandate	¶1411

California	Federal	Subject	Paragraph
Sec. 19712	IRC Sec. 6695	Endorsing client's refund check as misdemeanor	¶1411
Sec. 19713	IRC Sec. 7215	Failure to collect and pay withholding tax	¶1411
Sec. 19714	IRC Sec. 6673	Delay tactics	¶1411
Sec. 19715	IRC Sec. 7408	Penalties—injunctive relief	¶1411
Sec. 19717	IRC Sec. 7430	Recovery of litigation costs	¶1401
Sec. 19719	...	Penalty for doing business after suspension	¶1412
Secs. 19720-21	...	Fraudulently obtaining refunds	¶1412
Secs. 19730-38	...	Amnesty	¶1411
Secs. 19751-54	...	Abusive tax shelter voluntary compliance initiative	¶1424
Sec. 19755	...	Abusive tax shelter limitations period	¶1409
Sec. 19772	Sec. 6707A	Omission of reportable transaction penalty	¶1424
Secs. 19774	...	Nondisclosure of reportable transactions	¶1424
Sec. 19777	...	Interest-based penalty—abusive tax shelter deficiency	¶1424
Sec. 19777.5	...	Amnesty-enhanced interest penalty	¶1410, ¶1411
Sec. 19778	...	Interest—reportable transaction understatement	¶1410
Secs. 21001-28	IRC Secs. 6103(e)(8), 6201(d)(4), 6323, 6331, 6404(f), 7430, 7433, 7435, 7502, 7521, 7524, 7811	Taxpayers' bill of rights	¶810, ¶1401, ¶1402, ¶1411, ¶1414
Sec. 23002	IRC Sec. 7851	Application of Bank and Corporation Law	...
Sec. 23004	IRC Sec. 7805	Regulation authorization	...
Sec. 23030	IRC Sec. 7806	Definitions	...
Secs. 23031-35	IRC Secs. 7701(a)(10), (11), (24), (25), 7704	Definitions	...
Sec. 23036	IRC Sec. 26	"Tax" defined	¶817, ¶818
Sec. 23036.1	...	Natural heritage preservation credit	¶817, ¶818
Sec. 23036.2	...	2008-2009 credit limitations	¶818
Sec. 23037	IRC Sec. 7701(a)(14)	"Taxpayer" defined	...
Sec. 23038	IRC Sec. 7701(a)(3)	"Corporation" defined	¶804, ¶805
Sec. 23038.5	IRC Sec. 7704	Publicly-traded partnerships	¶804, ¶805
Sec. 23039	IRC Sec. 581	"Bank" defined	...
Sec. 23040	...	"Income from sources within State" defined	¶805, ¶909
Sec. 23040.1	...	Income from qualifying investment securities	¶909
Sec. 23041	IRC Sec. 7701(a)(23)	"Taxable year" defined	...
Sec. 23042	...	"Income year" defined	...
Sec. 23043.5	IRC Sec. 7701(g)	"Fair market value—Property subject to nonrecourse debt	...
Sec. 23044	...	"International banking facility" defined	...
Sec. 23045	IRC Secs. 7702, 7702A-B	Modified endowment contracts	...
Sec. 23045.1	IRC Sec. 7701(a)(42)	"Substituted basis" defined	¶1106
Sec. 23045.2	IRC Sec. 7701(a)(43)	"Transferred basis" defined	¶1106
Sec. 23045.3	IRC Sec. 7701(a)(44)	"Exchanged basis" defined	¶1106
Sec. 23045.4	IRC Sec. 7701(a)(45)	"Nonrecognition transaction" defined	¶1106
Sec. 23045.5	IRC Sec. 7701(a)(19)	"Domestic building & loan association" defined	...
Sec. 23045.6	IRC Sec. 7701(a)(20)	Employee defined	...
Sec. 23046	IRC Sec. 7701(a)(46)	Collective bargaining agreements	...
Sec. 23047	IRC Sec. 7701(e)	Lease vs. service contracts	...
Sec. 23048	IRC Sec. 7701(i)	"Taxable mortgage pools" defined	...
Sec. 23049	IRC Sec. 7701(h)	Motor vehicle operating leases	¶1011
Sec. 23049.1	IRC Sec. 64	"Ordinary income" defined	...
Sec. 23049.2	IRC Sec. 65	"Ordinary loss" defined	...
Sec. 23050	...	Specific definitions	...
Sec. 23051	IRC Sec. 7701(a)(29)	Definition of BCTL of 1954	...
Sec. 23051.5	Various	References to federal law	¶Various
Sec. 23051.7	...	Effect of amendments	¶802, ¶818
Secs. 23052-57	IRC Secs. 7807, 7852	Applications and effects	...
Sec. 23058	IRC Sec. 15	Tax rate changes during year	¶1105
Sec. 23101	...	"Doing business" defined	¶804
Sec. 23101	...	"Doing business" defined	¶804

California	Federal	Subject	Paragraph
Sec. 23101.5	....	Activities not constituting doing business	¶804
Sec. 23102	....	Status of holding companies	¶804
Sec. 23104	....	Convention and trade show activities	¶804
Sec. 23113	IRC Sec. 443	Short year returns	....
Sec. 23114	....	Tax attaches irrespective of short period	¶816
Sec. 23151	IRC Sec. 11	Franchise and corporation income tax rate	¶816
Sec. 23151.1	....	Rate of tax of commencing or ceasing corporations	¶819, ¶820
Sec. 23151.2	....	Franchise tax when corporation dissolves or withdraws	¶821
Sec. 23153	....	Minimum franchise tax	¶816
Sec. 23154	....	Tax imposed in lieu of other taxes	¶816
Sec. 23155	....	Credit for erroneous taxes	....
Sec. 23181	....	Imposition of tax on banks	¶816, ¶819, ¶820
Sec. 23182	....	In lieu of other taxes	¶816
Sec. 23183	....	Annual tax on financial corporation	¶816, ¶819, ¶820
Sec. 23183.1	....	Financial corporations—determination of tax	¶816 -20
Sec. 23183.2	....	Tax when financial corporation dissolves or withdraws	¶821
Sec. 23186	....	Rate of tax on banks	¶816, ¶1411
Sec. 23187	....	Tax receipts	¶816
Sec. 23188	....	Erroneous assessment	¶816
Sec. 23201	....	Determination of credit in year of dissolution	¶821
Sec. 23202	....	Transferees in reorganization	¶821
Sec. 23203	....	Submission of evidence for credit	¶821
Sec. 23204	....	Statute of limitations	¶821
Sec. 23221	....	Minimum tax prepayment	¶819
Sec. 23222	....	Prepayment basis for first and subsequent years	¶819
Sec. 23222a	....	Computation in case of short periods	¶819
Sec. 23223	....	Commencing business in year other than incorporation or qualification	¶819
Sec. 23224	....	Computation basis upon change from corporation income to franchise tax	¶819
Sec. 23224.5	....	Doing business after 12/31/71	¶819
Sec. 23225	....	Due date for payment in excess of minimum	¶819
Sec. 23226	....	FTB may apportion income	¶819
Sec. 23251	IRC Sec. 368	"Reorganization" and "control" defined	¶822
Sec. 23253	IRC Sec. 381	Reorganization—procedure taxable to transferee	¶822
Sec. 23281	....	Resuming business after voluntary discontinuance	¶821
Sec. 23282	....	Computation after suspension or forfeiture	¶821
Sec. 23301	....	Suspension of corporate powers for nonpayment	¶824
Sec. 23301.5	....	Suspension for failure to file	¶824
Sec. 23301.6	....	Application of suspension on foreign corporation	¶824
Sec. 23302	....	Transmittal of names by FTB to Secretary of State	¶824
Sec. 23303	....	Doing business while suspended—taxability	¶824
Sec. 23304.1	....	Contracts made during suspension	¶824
Sec. 23304.5	....	Court order rescission of contract	¶824
Sec. 23305	....	Application for certificate of revivor	¶824
Sec. 23305a	....	Endorsement of corporation's name by Secretary of State	¶824
Sec. 23305b	....	Revival without tax payment	¶824
Sec. 23305c	....	Revival sent to Secretary of State	¶824
Sec. 23305d	....	FTB's certificate as evidence of suspension	¶824
Sec. 23305e	....	Letters of good standing	¶824

California	Federal	Subject	Paragraph
Sec. 23305.1	. . . .	Relief from contract voidability	¶824
Sec. 23305.2	. . . .	Revival with bond or other security	¶824
Sec. 23305.5	. . . .	Suspension of LLC corporate powers	¶824
Sec. 23331	. . . .	Effective date of dissolution or withdrawal	¶821
Sec. 23332	. . . .	Corporations dissolving or withdrawing before 1/1/73	¶820, ¶821
Sec. 23332.5	. . . .	Tax on financial corporations	¶821
Sec. 23333	. . . .	Maximum tax on withdrawal or dissolution	¶821
Sec. 23334	. . . .	Issuance of tax clearance certificate by FTB	¶821
Sec. 23335	. . . .	Request of tax clearance certificate	¶821
Sec. 23361	IRC Sec. 1504	"Affiliated group" defined	¶812
Sec. 23362	IRC Sec. 1501	Consolidated return of affiliated group	¶812
Sec. 23363	IRC Sec. 1502	FTB's regulations	¶812
Sec. 23364	IRC Sec. 1503	Parent and each subsidiary severally liable	¶812
Sec. 23364a	IRC Sec. 1501	Computation of tax	¶812
Secs. 23400, 23453-59	IRC Secs. 55-59	Alternative minimum tax	¶817
Sec. 23453	IRC Sec. 53	Minimum tax credit	¶817, ¶818
Sec. 23455.5	. . . .	AMT exclusion for small corporations inapplicable	¶817
Sec. 23456	IRC Sec. 56	AMT adjustments	¶817
Sec. 23456.5	IRC Sec. 56(g)	Extraterritorial AMT adjustments	¶817
Sec. 23457	IRC Sec. 57	Tax preference items	¶817
Sec. 23459	IRC Sec. 59	AMT special rules	¶817
Sec. 23501	IRC Sec. 11(b)	Rate of tax	¶805, ¶816
Sec. 23503	. . . .	Franchise tax offset	¶805, ¶817
Sec. 23504	. . . .	Change to corporation income tax liability	¶820
Sec. 23561	. . . .	Tax payment before termination	¶821
Sec. 23601.5	. . . .	Energy conservation credit	¶818
Sec. 23604	IRC Sec. 43	Enhanced oil recovery credit	¶818
Sec. 23608	. . . .	Credit for transportation of donated agricultural products	¶818
Sec. 23608.2	. . . .	Farmworker Housing credit	¶818
Sec. 23608.3	. . . .	Credit for farmworker housing development loans	¶818
Sec. 23609	IRC Sec. 41	Reseach expense credit	¶818
Sec. 23610	. . . .	Rice straw credit	¶818
Secs. 23610.4-10.5	IRC Sec. 42	Credit for low-income housing	¶818
Sec. 23612.2	. . . .	Sales tax credit	¶818
Secs. 23617, 23617.5	. . . .	Child care assistance	¶818
Secs. 23621	IRC Secs. 51-52	Jobs tax credit	¶818
Sec. 23622.7	. . . .	Enterprise zone wage credit	¶818
Sec. 23622.8	. . . .	Manufacturing enhancement area wage credit	¶818
Secs. 23624	. . . .	Prison inmate labor credit	¶818
Sec. 23630	. . . .	Natural heritage preservation credit	¶818
Sec. 23633	. . . .	Targeted tax area's qualified property sales and use tax credit	¶818
Sec. 23634	. . . .	Targeted tax area's employer's wages credit	¶818
Sec. 23642	IRC Sec. 44	Disabled access credit	¶818
Sec. 23645	. . . .	Sales tax credit	¶818
Sec. 23646	. . . .	Employers' wage payment credit	¶818
Sec. 23649	. . . .	Manufacturing and research property credit	¶818
Sec. 23657	. . . .	Community development investment credit	¶818
Secs. 23662	IRC Sec. 45H	Low-sulfur diesel fuel production credit	¶818
Secs. 23663	. . . .	Assignment of credits to unitary group members	¶1310
Sec. 23701	IRC Sec. 501(a), (b)	Exemption for employee trusts	¶808
Sec. 23701a	IRC Sec. 501(c)(5)	Labor, agricultural, horticultural organizations	¶808
Sec. 23701b	IRC Sec. 501(c)(8)	Fraternal orders	¶808
Sec. 23701c	IRC Sec. 501(c)(13)	Cemetery companies	¶808
Sec. 23701d	IRC Sec. 501(c)(3), (j)	Religious, charitable, educational organizations	¶808

California	Federal	Subject	Paragraph
Sec. 23701e	IRC Sec. 501(c)(6)	Business leagues, chambers of commerce	¶808
Sec. 23701f	IRC Sec. 501(c)(4)	Civic leagues or organizations	¶808
Sec. 23701g	IRC Sec. 501(c)(7)	Nonprofit recreational clubs	¶808
Sec. 23701h	IRC Sec. 501(c)(2)	Companies holding title for exempt organizations	¶808
Sec. 23701i	IRC Sec. 501(c)(9)	Employees' beneficiary associations	¶808
Sec. 23701j	IRC Sec. 501(c)(11)	Teachers' retirement associations	¶808
Sec. 23701k	IRC Sec. 501(d)	Religious organizations	¶808
Sec. 23701l	IRC Sec. 501(c)(10)	Domestic fraternal societies	¶808
Sec. 23701n	IRC Sec. 501(c)(17)	Supplemental unemployment compensation plan	¶808
Sec. 23701p	IRC Sec. 401	Self-employed individual retirement plans	¶808, ¶1016
Sec. 23701r	IRC Secs. 527, 6012(a)(6)	Political organizations	¶808
Sec. 23701s	IRC Sec. 501(c)(18)	Employee funded pension trust—pre-6/25/59	¶808
Sec. 23701t	IRC Secs. 528, 6012(a)(7)	Homeowners' associations	¶808, ¶915
Sec. 23701u	. . . .	Nonprofit public benefit corporations	¶808
Sec. 23701v	IRC Sec. 501(c)	Mobile home owners	. . . .
Sec. 23701w	IRC Sec. 501(c)(19)	Veterans organizations	. . . .
Sec. 23701x	IRC Sec. 501(c)(25)	Title holding companies	¶808
Sec. 23701y	IRC Sec. 501(c)(14)	Credit unions	¶808
Sec. 23701z	IRC Sec. 501(n)	Nonprofit insurance risk pools	¶808
Sec. 23702	IRC Sec. 502	Feeder organizations	¶808, ¶809
Sec. 23703	. . . .	Failure to file with attorney general	¶808, ¶811
Sec. 23703.5	IRC Sec. 501(p)	Terrorist organizations	¶808
Sec. 23704.3	IRC Sec. 501(o)	Participation in provider-sponsored organization	¶808
Sec. 23704.4	IRC Sec. 501(e)	Child care organizations	¶808
Sec. 23704.5	IRC Sec. 501(h)	Expenditures to influence legislation	¶808
Sec. 23704.6	IRC Sec. 504	Status after disqualification for lobbying	¶808
Sec. 23705	IRC Sec. 505	Nondiscrimination requirement	¶808
Sec. 23706	IRC Sec. 501(c)(1)	Exemptions for state instrumentalities	. . . .
Sec. 23707	IRC Sec. 507	Private foundation status terminated	¶808
Sec. 23708	IRC Sec. 508	Presumption that organization is private foundation	¶808
Sec. 23709	IRC Sec. 509	"Private foundation" defined	¶808
Sec. 23710	IRC Sec. 513	Bingo games	¶808
Sec. 23711	IRC Sec. 529	Qualified state tuition program	¶808, ¶924
Sec. 23711.5	. . . .	Golden State Scholarshare Trust	¶808, ¶924
Sec. 23712	IRC Sec. 530	Coverdell Education Savings Accounts	. . . .
Sec. 23731	IRC Secs. 501(b), 511	Unrelated business income	¶805, ¶809
Sec. 23732	IRC Sec. 512	Unrelated business income	¶809
Sec. 23734	IRC Sec. 513	"Unrelated trade or business" defined	¶809
Sec. 23735	IRC Sec. 514	Unrelated debt-financed income	¶809
Sec. 23736	IRC Sec. 503(a)	Prohibited transactions	¶809
Sec. 23736.1	IRC Sec. 503(b)	"Prohibited transactions" defined	¶809
Sec. 23736.2	IRC Sec. 503(a)(1)	Denial of exemption to organizations engaged in prohibited transactions	¶809
Sec. 23736.3	IRC Sec. 503(a)(2)	Taxable years affected	¶809
Sec. 23736.4	IRC Sec. 503(c)	Future status of organizations denied exemption	¶809
Sec. 23737	. . . .	Grounds for denial of exemption	¶809
Sec. 23740	IRC Sec. 4911	Excess expenditures to influence legislation	¶808
Sec. 23741	. . . .	Churches receiving rental income from other churches	¶809
Sec. 23771	IRC Sec. 6012	Returns required	¶809, ¶811
Sec. 23772	IRC Secs. 6033, 6072(e)	Annual returns by exempt organizations	¶811
Sec. 23774	. . . .	Annual return of exempt corporation	¶811
Sec. 23775	. . . .	Exempt corporation's failure to file return	¶811
Sec. 23776	. . . .	Reinstatement of exempt corporation	¶811

California	Federal	Subject	Paragraph
Sec. 23777	. . . .	Revocation of exemption	¶811
Sec. 23778	. . . .	Reestablishing exemption	¶811
Sec. 23800	IRC Secs. 1361-79	S corp determination	¶806
Sec. 23800.5	IRC Sec. 1361	Application	. . . .
Sec. 23801	IRC Sec. 1362	Election	¶806 , ¶1310
Sec. 23802	IRC Sec. 1363	Tax rate	¶806 , ¶816
Sec. 23802.5	IRC Sec. 1366	Determination of shareholders tax liability	. . . .
Sec. 23803	IRC Sec. 1361	Credit carryover	¶806
Sec. 23804	IRC Sec. 1367	Cross references	¶806
Sec. 23806	IRC Sec. 1371	IRC Sec. 338 election	¶806
Sec. 23807	IRC Sec. 1372	Partnership references	¶806
Sec. 23808	IRC Secs. 1373, 1379	Nonconformity to Federal	¶806
Sec. 23809	IRC Sec. 1374	Substituted California tax rate	¶806
Sec. 23811	IRC Sec. 1375	Tax on passive income	¶806
Sec. 23813	IRC Sec. 1377	Determinations	¶816
Sec. 24251	IRC Sec. 15	Tax rate changes during year	¶1105
Sec. 24271	IRC Secs. 61, 641-92, 701-77	Gross income	¶901
Sec. 24272	IRC Secs. 103, 141-50	Interest on government bonds	¶910
Sec. 24272.2	IRC Sec. 72	Annuities	¶904
Sec. 24272.5	IRC Sec. 7518	Capital construction funds for vessels	¶917
Sec. 24273	IRC Sec. 77	Commodity credit loans	¶912
Sec. 24273.5	IRC Sec. 1385	Noncash patronage allocations from farmers' cooperatives	¶914
Sec. 24275	IRC Sec. 88	Nuclear decommissioning costs	¶901
Sec. 24276	IRC Sec. 90	Illegal federal irrigation subsidies	. . . .
Sec. 24301	IRC Secs. 101-36	Exclusions from gross income	. . . .
Sec. 24302	IRC Secs. 72, 101(a)	Life insurance proceeds	¶903 , ¶904
Sec. 24305	IRC Sec. 101(f)	Life insurance proceeds	¶902
Sec. 24306	IRC Sec. 529	Qualified state tuition program	¶924
Sec. 24307	IRC Sec. 108	Income from discharge of indebtedness	¶908
Sec. 24308	IRC Sec. 61	Forest Service payments	¶901
Sec. 24308.1	IRC Sec. 136	Energy conservation subsidy exclusion	¶922
Sec. 24308.5	IRC Sec. 126	Cost-share payments received by forest landowners	¶923
Sec. 24309	IRC Sec. 109	Improvements by lessee	¶905
Sec. 24309.5	IRC Sec. 110	Qualified lessee construction allowances	¶906
Sec. 24310	IRC Sec. 111	Recovery of bad debts and prior taxes	¶907
Sec. 24314	IRC Sec. 61	Gain or loss from exempt bond	¶1212
Sec. 24315	IRC Sec. 61	Recycling income	¶919
Sec. 24320	IRC Sec. 883	Operation of foreign aircraft or ships	¶916
Sec. 24321	IRC Secs. 881-82	Local governmental units prohibited	¶916
Sec. 24322	IRC Secs. 118, 597	Contributions to capital	¶913
Sec. 24323	IRC Sec. 61	Rebates for water-conservation devices	¶921
Sec. 24324	IRC Sec. 118	Exclusion of utilities	. . . .
Sec. 24325	IRC Sec. 118	Contributions to capital	¶913
Sec. 24326	IRC Sec. 136	Energy conservation subsidies	¶922
Sec. 24327	IRC Sec. 892	Foreign government investment income	. . . .
Sec. 24341	IRC Sec. 63	"Net income" defined	¶815
Sec. 24343	IRC Sec. 162	Deductions for business expenses	¶1001
Sec. 24343.2	IRC Sec. 162	Expenses incurred at discriminatory clubs	. . . .
Sec. 24343.3	IRC Sec. 220	Medical savings account deduction	. . . .
Sec. 24343.5	IRC Sec. 162	Subsidization of employees' ridesharing	¶1019
Sec. 24343.7	IRC Sec. 162	Deductions for business expenses	¶1001 , ¶1023
Sec. 24344	IRC Sec. 163	Interest expense deduction	¶1004 , ¶1311 , ¶1312
Sec. 24344.5	IRC Sec. 163	Deduction for discount bonds	¶911 , ¶1004
Sec. 24344.7	IRC Sec. 163	Limitation on interest expense deduction	¶1004
Sec. 24345	IRC Secs. 164, 275	Deduction for taxes	¶1006
Sec. 24346	IRC Sec. 164	Apportionment of taxes on real property	¶1006
Sec. 24347	IRC Secs. 165, 166, 582	Losses—deductions	¶1007 , ¶1009 , ¶1010
Secs. 24347.4-47.5	IRC Sec. 165	Disaster losses	¶1007
Sec. 24348	IRC Secs. 166, 585, 593	Deduction for bad debts	¶1009
Sec. 24349	IRC Secs. 167(a), 168	Depreciation	¶1011

California	Federal	Subject	Paragraph
Sec. 24349.1	IRC Sec. 280F	Depreciation-luxury cars	¶1011
Sec. 24350	. . . .	Limitations on use of methods and rates	¶1011
Sec. 24351	. . . .	Agreement as to useful life—depreciation	¶1011
Sec. 24352	. . . .	Depreciation—change in method	¶1011
Sec. 24352.5	. . . .	Depreciation—salvage method	¶1011
Sec. 24353	IRC Sec. 167(c)	Basis for depreciation	¶1011 , ¶1250
Sec. 24354	IRC Sec. 167(d)	Life tenants and beneficiaries	¶1011
Sec. 24354.1	. . . .	Rules for Sec. 18212 property	¶1011
Sec. 24355	IRC Sec. 167(f)	Intangibles ineligible for amortization	¶1011
Sec. 24355.3	IRC Sec. 168(i)(16)	Useful life of sports entertainment complex	¶1011
Sec. 24355.4	IRC Sec. 168(i)(16)	Useful life of Alaska natural gas pipeline	¶1011
Sec. 24355.4	IRC Sec. 168	Depreciation of rent-to-own property	¶1011
Sec. 24355.5	IRC Sec. 197	Amortization of goodwill	¶1011
Sec. 24356	IRC Sec. 179	Bonus depreciation	¶1011
Sec. 24356.4	IRC Sec. 179B	Sulfur regulation compliance costs	¶1026
Sec. 24356.6	. . . .	Election to expense 40% of cost in targeted tax property	. . . .
Sec. 24356.7	. . . .	Accelerated write-off for enterprise zone property	¶1011
Sec. 24356.8	IRC Sec. 179	Accelerated write-off	¶1011
Sec. 24357	IRC Sec. 170(a), (f)(8), (9), (j)	Charitable contributions	¶1014 , ¶1312
Sec. 24357.1	IRC Sec. 170(e)	Contributions of ordinary income and capital gain property	¶1014
Sec. 24357.2	IRC Sec. 170(f)(3)	Partial interest in property	¶1014
Sec. 24357.3	IRC Sec. 170(f)(4)	Valuation of remainder interest in real property	¶1014
Sec. 24357.4	IRC Sec. 170(f)(5)	Reduction for certain interest	¶1014
Sec. 24357.5	IRC Sec. 170(f)(1)	Disallowance of deduction	¶1014
Sec. 24357.6	IRC Sec. 170(f)(6)	Out-of-pocket expenditures	¶1014
Sec. 24357.7	IRC Sec. 170(h)	Qualified conservation expenditures	¶1014
Sec. 24357.8	IRC Sec. 170(e)	Scientific property used for research—deduction	¶1014
Sec. 24357.9	IRC Sec. 170	Contribution of computer technology to schools	¶1014
Sec. 24357.10	IRC Sec. 170(l)	Contributions in connection with athletic events	¶1014
Sec. 24358	IRC Sec. 170(b)	Limitations on corporate contributions	¶1014
Sec. 24359	IRC Sec. 170(c)	Charitable contribution defined	¶1014
Sec. 24359.1	IRC Sec. 170(e)	Credit or deduction for scientific equipment donated	¶1014
Sec. 24360	IRC Sec. 171(a)	Amortizable bond premium	¶1015
Sec. 24361	IRC Sec. 171(b)	Determination of bond premium	¶1015
Sec. 24362	IRC Sec. 171(c)	Election as to taxable bonds	¶1015
Sec. 24363	IRC Sec. 171(d)	Bond defined	¶1015
Sec. 24363.5	IRC Sec. 171(e)	Offset to interest payments	¶1015
Sec. 24364	IRC Sec. 173	Circulation expenditures	¶1003
Sec. 24365	IRC Sec. 174	Research expenditures	¶1011
Sec. 24368.1	IRC Sec. 167(e)	Trademark expenditures	¶1011
Sec. 24369	IRC Sec. 175	Soil and water conservation expenditures	¶1002
Sec. 24369.4	IRC Sec. 198	Environmental remediation expenses	¶1011
Sec. 24370	IRC Sec. 591	Deductions for dividends paid on deposits	¶1021
Sec. 24372.3	IRC Sec. 169	Amortization of pollution control facilities	¶1011
Sec. 24372.5	IRC Sec. 194	Amortization of reforestation expenses	¶1011
Sec. 24373	IRC Sec. 178	Depreciation or amortization of lessee improvements	¶1011
Sec. 24377	IRC Sec. 180	Farm fertilizer expenses	¶1002
Sec. 24379	IRC Sec. 83	Transfer of property for services	¶1017
Sec. 24382	IRC Sec. 216	Foreclosure of cooperature housing corporation stock	¶1022
Sec. 24383	IRC Sec. 190	Architectural adaptations for the handicapped	¶1001
Sec. 24384.5	IRC Sec. 163	Interest received-depressed areas	¶918
Sec. 24401	IRC Sec. 241	Special deductions	. . . .

California	Federal	Subject	Paragraph
Sec. 24402	IRC Secs. 243-47, 561-565	Dividends received by corporations taxed by California	¶909, ¶1020
Sec. 24403	IRC Sec. 591	Deductions for credits to withdrawable shares	¶1021
Sec. 24404	IRC Secs. 1381-83	Agricultural cooperatives	¶1021
Sec. 24405	IRC Secs. 1381-83	Other cooperatives	¶1021
Sec. 24406	IRC Secs. 1381-83	Cooperative corporations	¶1021
Sec. 24406.5	IRC Sec. 1381	Gas producers' cooperatives	¶1021
Sec. 24406.6	IRC Sec. 1388	Net earnings of cooperatives	¶1021
Sec. 24407	IRC Sec. 248(a)	Organizational expenditures	¶1011
Sec. 24408	IRC Sec. 248(b)	"Organizational expenditures" defined	¶1011
Sec. 24409	IRC Sec. 248(c)	Organizational expenditures—period of election	¶1011
Sec. 24410	IRC Secs. 243-47	Dividends from subsidiary insurance company	¶909, ¶1020
Sec. 24411	IRC Secs. 243-47	Unitary business water's edge election	¶812, ¶1311
Sec. 24414	IRC Sec. 195	Start-up expenses	¶1018
Sec. 24415	IRC Sec. 161	Interindemnity payments	¶1001
Secs. 24416-16.10	IRC Sec. 172	Net operating loss carryovers	¶806, ¶1024
Sec. 24421	IRC Sec. 261	Disallowance of deductions	¶1011, ¶1023
Sec. 24422	IRC Secs. 263, 263A	Capital expenditures	¶1011, ¶1023, ¶1107
Sec. 24422.3	IRC Sec. 263A	Capitalization of inventory-related expense	¶1023, ¶1107
Sec. 24423	IRC Sec. 263	Drilling and development costs—oil and gas	¶1013, ¶1023
Sec. 24424	IRC Sec. 264	Payments on life insurance contracts	¶1004, ¶1023
Sec. 24425	IRC Sec. 265	Deductions allocable to tax-exempt income	¶1023
Sec. 24426	IRC Sec. 266	Taxes and carrying charges	¶1023
Sec. 24427	IRC Sec. 267	Transaction between related individuals	¶1023
Sec. 24429	IRC Sec. 276	Indirect contributions to political parties	....
Sec. 24431	IRC Sec. 269	Acquisitions made to avoid tax	¶1110
Sec. 24434	IRC Sec. 271	Debts owed by political parties	¶1009
Sec. 24436	IRC Sec. 280E	Illegal business expenses	¶1023
Sec. 24436.1	IRC Sec. 280E	Illegal activities	¶1023
Sec. 24436.5	IRC Sec. 161	Deductions on substandard housing	¶1023
Sec. 24437	IRC Sec. 277	Deduction limitation for social clubs	¶1023
Sec. 24438	IRC Sec. 279	Interest deduction on corporate acquisition indebtedness	¶1004
Sec. 24439	IRC Sec. 249	Deductions of bond premium on repurchase	¶1004, ¶1223
Sec. 24440	IRC Sec. 280C(b), (c)	Federal credits	¶818, ¶1021
Sec. 24441	IRC Sec. 161	Abandonment or tax recoupment fees	¶1023
Sec. 24442	IRC Sec. 280B	Demolition of historic structures	¶1023
Sec. 24442.5	IRC Sec. 280H	Limitation on amounts paid to employee-owners	¶1023
Sec. 24443	IRC Sec. 274	Disallowance of entertainment expenses	¶1001, ¶1023
Secs. 24447-48	IRC Sec. 161	Expenses disallowed	¶1023, ¶1024
Sec. 24449	IRC Sec. 291	Preference items	¶817
Sec. 24451	IRC Secs. 301-85	Corporate distributions and adjustments	Various
Sec. 24452	IRC Sec. 301	Special rule for distributions received by 20% shareholder	¶909
Sec. 24453	IRC Sec. 302	Termination of interest	¶909
Sec. 24456	IRC Sec. 306	Source of gain—IRC Sec. 306(f) inapplicable	¶909
Sec. 24461	IRC Sec. 337	Effective dates of 1986 TRA changes as to liquidations	¶1221
Sec. 24465	....	Gain on transfers to insurance companies	¶1211, ¶1214, ¶1216, ¶1218
Sec. 24471	IRC Sec. 381	Items of distributor or transferor corporation	¶909, ¶1221
Sec. 24472	IRC Sec. 382	Discharge of indebtedness	¶908
Sec. 24473	....	Mutual water company reorganization	....
Sec. 24481	IRC Sec. 383	Special limits on certain excess credits, etc.	¶909, ¶1221

California	Federal	Subject	Paragraph
Secs. 24601-12	IRC Secs. 401-24	Deferred compensation	¶909, ¶1001, ¶1016, ¶1017
Sec. 24631	IRC Sec. 441	Accounting periods	¶1101
Sec. 24632	IRC Sec. 441	Income year	¶1101, ¶1102
Sec. 24633	IRC Sec. 442	Change in accounting period	¶1102
Sec. 24633.5	IRC Sec. 441	Change of accounting period	¶806, ¶1102
Sec. 24634	IRC Sec. 443	Short-period returns	¶1103
Sec. 24636	IRC Sec. 443	Computation of tax in short period return	¶1106
Sec. 24637	IRC Sec. 444	Election to Keep Same Tax Year—S Corporations	¶806, ¶1104
Sec. 24651	IRC Sec. 446	Accounting methods	¶1106
Sec. 24652	IRC Sec. 447	Accounting for farm corporations	¶1106
Sec. 24654	IRC Sec. 448	Cash method of accounting restricted	¶1106
Sec. 24661	IRC Sec. 451	Taxable year of inclusion	¶1106
Sec. 24661.3	. . . .	Production flexibility contracts	¶1106
Sec. 24667	IRC Secs. 453, 453A, 453B	Installment method	¶1109
Sec. 24668.1	IRC Sec. 453	Installment method—property condemnations	¶1109
Sec. 24672	. . . .	Installment income on cessation of business	¶1109
Sec. 24673	IRC Sec. 460	Percentage of completion accounting	¶806, ¶1106
Sec. 24673.2	IRC Sec. 460	Long term contracts	¶1106
Sec. 24674	IRC Sec. 454	Obligations issued at discount	¶1111
Sec. 24675	IRC Sec. 186	Patent infringement damages	¶1106
Sec. 24676	IRC Sec. 455	Prepaid subscription income	¶1106
Sec. 24676.5	IRC Sec. 458	Returned magazines, paperbacks, records	¶1106
Sec. 24677	IRC Sec. 186	Breach of contract award	¶1106
Sec. 24678	IRC Sec. 186	Damages received under Clayton Act	¶1106
Sec. 24679	. . . .	Fractional part of month	¶1106
Sec. 24681	IRC Sec. 461	Taxable year of deduction	¶1006, ¶1106
Sec. 24682	IRC Sec. 464	Farming expenses	¶1106
Sec. 24685	. . . .	Accrual of vacation pay	¶1106
Sec. 24685.5	IRC Sec. 404	Accrued vacation and sick pay	¶1016
Sec. 24688	IRC Sec. 467	Deferred rental payments	¶1106
Sec. 24689	IRC Sec. 468	Waste disposal costs	¶1106
Sec. 24690	IRC Sec. 468A	Nuclear decommissioning funds	¶1106
Sec. 24691	IRC Sec. 465	At risk	¶1023, ¶1025
Sec. 24692	IRC Sec. 469	Passive activity losses	¶1005, ¶1106
Sec. 24693	IRC Sec. 468B	Designated settlement funds	¶807
Sec. 24701	IRC Secs. 471, 472	Inventories—general rule	¶1107, ¶1108
Sec. 24708	IRC Sec. 474	Simplified dollar value LIFO	¶1108
Sec. 24710	IRC Sec. 475	Mark-to-market accounting	¶1107, ¶1222
Sec. 24721	IRC Sec. 481	Adjustments required by changes in method	¶1106
Sec. 24725	IRC Sec. 482	Allocation of income among taxpayers	¶1106, ¶1110
Sec. 24726	IRC Sec. 483	Interest on deferred payments	¶1106, ¶1112
Sec. 24831	IRC Secs. 611-38	Natural resources	¶1012, ¶1013, ¶1250
Sec. 24831.6	IRC Secs. 613A	Percentage depletion for marginal properties	¶1012
Secs. 24870-75	IRC Secs. 851-60L	RICs, REITs, REMICs, and FASITs	¶805, ¶1021
Sec. 24900	. . . .	Deemed dividends for overcapitalized insurance companies	¶909
Sec. 24901	IRC Sec. 1001	Determination of gain or loss	¶1201
Sec. 24902	IRC Sec. 1001	Recognition of gain or loss	¶1201
Sec. 24905	IRC Sec. 988	Foreign currency transactions	¶1204
Sec. 24905.5	IRC Sec. 988	Hedging transactions	. . . .
Sec. 24911	IRC Sec. 1011	Adjusted basis	¶1247
Sec. 24912	IRC Sec. 1012	Basis of property—cost	¶1226
Sec. 24913	IRC Sec. 1013	Basis of property in inventory	¶1227
Sec. 24914	IRC Sec. 1015	Basis of property acquired by gift or transfer in trust	¶1228, ¶1229
Sec. 24915	IRC Sec. 1015	Adjustment for gift taxes paid	¶1228
Sec. 24916	IRC Sec. 1016	Adjustments to basis	¶1247
Sec. 24916.2	IRC Sec. 1016	Abandonment fees, open-space easement	¶1247
Sec. 24917	IRC Sec. 1016	Substituted basis	¶1248
Sec. 24918	IRC Sec. 1017	Discharge of indebtedness	¶1251
Sec. 24919	IRC Sec. 1019	Improvements to property by lessee	¶1249

California	Federal	Subject	Paragraph
Sec. 24941	IRC Sec. 1031	Exchange of property held for productive use	¶1206
Sec. 24942	IRC Sec. 1032	Exchange of stock for property	¶1224
Sec. 24943	IRC Sec. 1033(a)	Involuntary conversions	¶1202
Sec. 24944	IRC Sec. 1033(a)(2), (A), (B)	Conversion into money or unrelated property	¶1202
Sec. 24945	IRC Sec. 1033(a)(2)(C)	Time for assessment of deficiency attributable to gain	¶1202
Sec. 24946	IRC Sec. 1033(a)(2)(D)	Time for assessment of other deficiencies	¶1202
Sec. 24947	IRC Sec. 1033(b)	Basis of property	¶1235
Sec. 24948	IRC Sec. 1033(c)	Property sold pursuant to reclamation laws	¶1202
Sec. 24949	IRC Sec. 1033(d)	Diseased livestock	¶1202
Sec. 24949.1	IRC Sec. 1033(e)	Livestock sold on account of drought	¶1202
Sec. 24949.2	IRC Sec. 1033(g)	Condemnation of real property held for productive use	¶1202
Sec. 24949.3	IRC Sec. 1033(f)	Environmental contamination—replacement of livestock	¶1202
Sec. 24949.5	IRC Sec. 1033(h)	Applicability of federal involuntary conversion rules	¶1202
Sec. 24950	IRC Sec. 1035	Exchanges of insurance policies	¶1207
Sec. 24951	IRC Sec. 1036	Exchange of stock	¶1208
Sec. 24952	IRC Sec. 1038	Reacquisitions of real property	¶1210
Sec. 24954	IRC Sec. 1042	Deferral of gain on roll-over sales of stock to ESOP	¶1213
Sec. 24954.1	IRC Sec. 1042(g)	Sales to agricultural refiners and cooperatives	¶1213
Sec. 24955	IRC Sec. 1001	Rollover sales of low-income housing	¶1203
Sec. 24956	IRC Sec. 1044	Rollover of publicly traded securities gain	¶1222
Sec. 24961	IRC Sec. 1051	Basis of property acquired from affiliated corporation	¶1237
Sec. 24962	IRC Sec. 1052	Basis provisions from prior codes	¶1238
Sec. 24963	IRC Sec. 1053	Basis of property acquired before March 1, 1913	¶1238
Sec. 24964	IRC Sec. 1011	Property received from controlled corporation	¶1243
Sec. 24965	IRC Sec. 1054	Basis of stock issued by FNMA	¶1240
Sec. 24966	IRC Sec. 1059	Basis after extraordinary dividend	¶1226
Sec. 24966.1	IRC Sec. 1059A	Basis of property imported from related persons	¶1226, ¶1227
Sec. 24966.2	IRC Sec. 1060	Allocation of transferred business assets	¶1226, ¶1253
Sec. 24981	IRC Sec. 1081	Exchange or distribution in obedience to SEC order	¶1205
Sec. 24988	IRC Sec. 1082	Basis of stock received under Sec. 24981	¶1245
Sec. 24989	IRC Sec. 1056	Basis limitation for player contracts	¶1252
Secs. 24990, 24990.5	IRC Secs. 1201-97	No capital gains or losses	¶1011, ¶1222, ¶1223
Sec. 24990.6	IRC Sec. 1245	Character of gain or loss	. . . .
Sec. 24990.7	IRC Sec. 1248	Gain on sales in foreign corporations	¶1217
Sec. 24991	IRC Sec. 1275	Definition of tax-exempt obligation	¶910, ¶911
Sec. 24993	IRC Sec. 7872	Imputed interest	¶911, ¶1112
Sec. 24995	IRC Secs. 1291-98	Passive foreign investment companies	¶1222
Sec. 24998	IRC Secs. 1091, 1092	Wash sales of stock or securities	¶1008, ¶1225, ¶1236
Sec. 25101	. . . .	Apportionment	¶823, ¶1302, ¶1313
Sec. 25101.3	. . . .	Property factor—aircraft	¶1307
Sec. 25101.15	. . . .	In-state income of two or more taxpayers	¶1310
Sec. 25102	. . . .	Combined return of controlled taxpayers	¶1110, ¶1310
Sec. 25103	. . . .	Corporate transactions to evade tax	¶1110
Sec. 25104	. . . .	Consolidated report	¶1310
Sec. 25105	. . . .	Determination of control	¶1310
Sec. 25106	. . . .	Income from intercompany dividend distribution	¶909
Sec. 25106.5	IRC Sec. 1502	Affiliated corporations—Combined reporting	¶812, ¶1310

California	Federal	Subject	Paragraph
Sec. 25107	. . . .	Apportionment of income of international banking facility	¶1307, ¶1308, ¶1309
Sec. 25108	IRC Sec. 172	Net operating loss	¶1024
Secs. 25110-16	. . . .	Unitary business water's-edge election	¶1024, ¶1311
Sec. 25120	. . . .	Definitions	¶1302
Sec. 25121	. . . .	Allocation and apportionment of income	¶1302
Sec. 25122	. . . .	Taxability in another state	¶1302
Sec. 25123	. . . .	Nonbusiness income	¶1303
Sec. 25124	. . . .	Rents and royalties from real and tangible personal property	¶1303
Sec. 25125	. . . .	Capital gains and losses from sales of real and personal property	¶1303
Sec. 25126	. . . .	Allocation of interest and dividends	¶1303
Sec. 25127	. . . .	Allocation of patent and copyright royalties	¶1303
Sec. 25128	. . . .	Apportionment formula	¶1304, ¶1305
Sec. 25129	. . . .	Property factor	¶1307
Sec. 25130	. . . .	Property valuation	¶1307
Sec. 25131	. . . .	Average value of property	¶1307
Sec. 25132	. . . .	Payroll factor	¶1308
Sec. 25133	. . . .	Allocation of compensation	¶1308
Sec. 25134	. . . .	Sales factor	¶1309
Sec. 25135	. . . .	Sales of tangible personal property	¶1309
Sec. 25136	. . . .	Sales other than sales of tangible personal property	¶1309
Sec. 25137	. . . .	Adjustment of formula	¶1304, ¶1305, ¶1306
Sec. 25138	. . . .	Purpose of act	. . . .
Sec. 25139	. . . .	Title	. . . .
Sec. 25140	. . . .	Intercompany dividends	. . . .
Sec. 25141	. . . .	Professional sports	¶1306

TAXES ON CORPORATE INCOME

CHAPTER 8

IMPOSITION OF TAX, RATES, EXEMPTIONS, RETURNS

¶801 Overview of Corporation Franchise and Income Taxes

The franchise tax was first imposed in 1929; the corporation income tax in 1937. The law is known as the Corporation Tax Law, and constitutes Part 11 of Division 2 of the Revenue and Taxation Code. Administrative provisions affecting both corporate and personal income taxpayers are in Part 10.2 of Division 2 of the Revenue and Taxation Code.

The Law is administered by the Franchise Tax Board, composed of the State Controller, the Director of the Department of Finance, and the Chair of the State Board of Equalization.

The franchise tax is imposed for the privilege of exercising the corporate franchise in California. It is imposed upon corporations organized in California and upon out-of-state ("foreign") corporations that are doing business in the state.

Special rules are provided for beginning corporations, dissolving corporations, and corporations involved in a reorganization (¶819—¶822). Banks and financial corporations are taxed at a higher rate than other corporations, and in turn are relieved of certain other taxes as explained at ¶816.

The corporation income tax is imposed upon net income, at the basic rate of the franchise tax (¶816). It is intended to be complementary to the franchise tax, to apply to corporations that derive income from California sources but that are not subject to the franchise tax. Because the franchise tax applies in the great majority of cases (¶804), the income tax is applicable only to a relatively small number of corporations (¶805).

The franchise and income tax rate applied to general C corporations is 8.84%. (Sec. 23151(e), Rev. & Tax. Code) For banks and financial corporations, the tax rate is 10.84%. (Sec. 23186, Rev. & Tax. Code) S corporations are taxed at a reduced rate of 1.5% (3.5% for S corporations that are financial corporations). (Sec. 23802, Rev. & Tax. Code) For a discussion of the minimum tax, see ¶816.

The computation of income for both the franchise tax and the income tax generally follows the pattern of the federal income tax, and interpretations of the federal law by the Treasury Department and the courts are usually followed in the administration of comparable provisions of the California law. However, there are many differences between the federal and California laws. See ¶803 for an explanation of the federal conformity program established in 1983. There is also one important difference between the two California laws, as explained at ¶910: interest on obligations of the United States is not taxable for income tax purposes although it is included in the measure of the tax for franchise tax purposes.

Some corporations are exempt from both franchise and income taxes. These include insurance underwriting companies (subject to special taxes—see ¶1902), several categories of nonprofit organizations, and others, as explained at ¶808.

¶802 Scope of Chapter

This chapter discusses the two taxes imposed on, or measured by, corporate income: (1) the bank and corporation franchise tax; and (2) the corporation income tax. It covers the question of who is subject and who is exempt, requirements for filing returns and payment of tax, the base upon which the taxes are imposed, the rates of tax and credits against tax, and the extent to which the taxes apply in certain special situations.

¶803 Federal Conformity Program

Law: Sec. 23051.5 (CCH CALIFORNIA TAX REPORTS ¶10-510, 10-515).

Comparable Federal: None.

The federal conformity program adopted in 1983 for the personal income tax, as explained at ¶103, has not been applied as thoroughly to corporation taxes. However, in a number of areas—including gross income, deductions, and accounting periods and methods—California corporation franchise and income tax law consists largely of incorporated federal provisions.

Comment: Incorporation of Federal Exclusions and Deductions

California's corporation tax law is structured differently than California's personal income tax law as it relates to items of income, exclusions, and deductions. Under California's personal income tax law, Revenue and Taxation Code Sections 17081, 17131, and 17201 incorporate entire subchapters of the IRC that govern the treatment of items of gross income, exclusions, and deductions. The California Revenue and Taxation Code sections that follow these specific provisions then modify or specifically decouple from the IRC provisions within those subchapters. Thus, Sec. 17201 specifically incorporates the part of the IRC that contains all of the provisions governing deductions for individual and corporate taxpayers, including the IRC Sec. 199 deduction for domestic production activities income. However, because California personal income tax law contains another provision, Rev. & Tax. Code Sec. 17201.6, that specifically decouples from the IRC Sec. 199 deduction, California does not allow a deduction for domestic production activities income for personal income tax purposes, and an addition adjustment is required.

In contrast, the corporation tax law governing items of gross income and net income, does not have general provisions analogous to Rev. & Tax. Code Secs. 17081, 17131, and 17201 in the personal income tax law. Consequently, unless the corporate income tax law specifically incorporates a federal provision governing items of income, exclusions, or deductions, California does not incorporate the federal law. Using the example above, because there is no specific corporation tax law provision either directly incorporating IRC Sec. 199, nor mirroring its provisions, California does not follow federal law concerning the deduction for domestic production activities income and taxpayers that use the federal reconciliation method of computing their California tax liability will be required to make an addition adjustment on the corporation tax return.

As under the personal income tax law, with the exception of provisions dealing with retirement and deferred compensation plans, water's-edge elections, and certain S corporation and real estate investment trust (REIT) provisions, which conform to the IRC as amended to date (¶806, ¶1311), references to the Internal Revenue Code (and to uncodified federal laws that relate to Internal Revenue Code provisions) are updated periodically through conforming legislation. Such references in the California law are now updated to January 1, 2005 (for taxable years beginning after 2004). (Sec. 23051.5, Rev. & Tax. Code)

Planning Note: EGTRRA Sunset Provision Incorporated

California incorporates the federal provision of the Economic Growth and Tax Relief and Reconciliation Act of 2001 (P.L. 107-134) that provides that all provisions of, and amendments made by, the 2001 Act will not apply to taxable, plan, or limitation years beginning after 2010. However, to the extent that any of these provisions are extended or the sunset date repealed, California will incorporate the extension of these amendments, whether the extension is temporary or permanent (Sec. 23051.5(a)(2), Rev. & Tax. Code)

California has not adopted federal amendments made by the Energy Tax Incentives Act of 2005, the Katrina Emergency Tax Relief Act of 2005, the Gulf Opportunity Zone Act of 2005, the Tax Increase Prevention and Reconciliation Act of 2005, the Tax Relief and Health Care Act of 2006, the U.S. Troop Readiness, Veterans' Care, Katrina Recovery, and Iraq Accountability Appropriations Act of 2007, the Energy Independence & Security Act of 2007, the Tax Increase Prevention Act of 2007, the Tax Technical Corrections Act of 2007, the Economic Stimulus Act of 2008, the Heartland, Habitat, Harvest, and Horticulture Act of 2008, the Heroes Earnings Assistance and Relief Tax Act of 2008, the Housing Assistance Tax Act of 2008, and the Emergency Economic Stimulus Act of 2008. In addition, California does not incorporate many of the amendments made by the Pension Protection Act of 2006 , the Small Business and Work Opportunity Tax Act (Small Business Tax Act), and the Mortgage Forgiveness Debt Relief Act of 2007. However, because California incorporates most IRC provisions relating to deferred compensation and retirement plans and S corporation and REIT elections, qualifications, and terminations as currently amended (¶806, ¶909, ¶1016), California generally adopts post-2004 amendments made to these provisions.

California adopts both temporary and final federal regulations to the extent that the federal regulations do not conflict with California law or California regulations.

• *Federal elections*

A proper election, application, or consent filed in accordance with the Internal Revenue Code is effective for California purposes, unless otherwise specified. To obtain different California treatment than federal treatment, a California taxpayer must file a separate election, application, or consent with the Franchise Tax Board. (Sec. 23151(e), Rev. & Tax. Code)

Federal income tax elections, or lack thereof, made before becoming a California taxpayer are binding for California corporation franchise and income tax purposes, unless a separate election is specifically authorized by a California law or regulation.

• *Taxable income computation methods*

California gives corporations the option of choosing how to compute their net income. Under the federal reconciliation method, the starting point for computing California corporation franchise or income tax is the federal taxable income from federal Form 1120 or Form 1120A, the corporation's federal tax return, before claiming the net operating loss and special deductions. (Instructions, Form 100, California Corporation Franchise or Income Tax Return) The federal amount, after required California additions and subtractions, constitutes the corporation's net income subject to California taxation. (Sec. 24341, Rev. & Tax. Code) The necessary additions and subtractions are discussed in the following chapters.

In lieu of the federal reconciliation method, corporations that are not required to file a federal return or that maintain separate records for state purposes may compute their net income using the California computation method on California Form 100, Schedule F, Computation of Net Income. Generally, if ordinary income is computed under California law, no state adjustments are necessary. (Instructions, Form 100, California Corporation Franchise or Income Tax Return)

Corporations using the California computation method to compute net income must transfer the amount from Schedule F, line 30, to Form 100, Side 1, line 1. Corporations should complete Form 100, Side 1, line 2 through line 17, only if applicable. (Instructions, Form 100, California Corporation Franchise or Income Tax Return)

¶804 Corporations Subject to Franchise Tax

Law: Sec. 191, Corporations Code; Secs. 23038, 23038.5, 23101-04, 23151, Rev. & Tax. Code (CCH CALIFORNIA TAX REPORTS ¶10-075, 10-210, 10-235, 10-240).

Comparable Federal: Sec. 7704 (CCH U.S. MASTER TAX GUIDE ¶403).

California Form: Form 100 (California Corporation Franchise or Income Tax Return).

Every corporation doing business in California is subject to the franchise tax, unless specifically exempted as set forth in ¶808. (Sec. 23151, Rev. & Tax. Code) A corporation incorporated in California or qualified to do business in California, but not actually doing business in the state, and not expressly exempt, is subject only to the minimum franchise tax (¶816). However, if such a corporation has income from California sources, it is subject to the income tax, as explained at ¶805. If there is income from both within and without the state, a portion of the total is assigned to California as explained in Chapter 13.

For purposes of the franchise tax, a corporation includes associations (including nonprofit associations that perform services, borrow money, or own property), other than banking associations, and Massachusetts or business trusts. (Sec. 23038, Rev. & Tax. Code)

• *What is "doing business"*

The law defines "doing business" as "actively engaging in any transaction for the purpose of financial or pecuniary gain or profit." It also provides that certain corporations, the activities of which are limited to the receipt and disbursement of dividends and interest on securities, are not to be considered as doing business. (Sec.

23101, Rev. & Tax. Code) A corporation is not "doing business" in California for franchise tax purposes if the following apply:

— it is not incorporated under the laws of California;

— its sole activity in California is engaging in convention and trade show activities for seven or fewer calendar days during the taxable year; and

— it derives no more than $10,000 of gross income reportable to California from convention and trade show activities during the taxable year.

(Sec. 23104, Rev. & Tax. Code)

In addition, an out-of-state corporation is not considered to be transacting intrastate business and will not be required to obtain a certificate of qualification from the California Secretary of State merely because it is a shareholder in a corporation, a limited partner in a limited partnership, or a member or manager of a limited liability company that is transacting intrastate business in California. (Sec. 191, Corp. Code)

In *Appeal of Amman & Schmid Finance AG et al.* (1996) (CCH CALIFORNIA TAX REPORTS ¶10-210.262), foreign corporations with interests in limited partnerships were not subject to the California franchise tax, because the corporations' only contact with the state was the receipt of distributive shares of the limited partnerships' California source income. Accordingly, they did not meet the active participation requirement for "doing business" in the state.

The Franchise Tax Board (FTB) has taken the position that an out-of-state limited partner in a limited partnership is not subject to the California minimum tax simply because it holds an interest in a limited partnership that is doing business in California. The FTB's position, in effect, extends the holding in *Amman & Schmid Finance AG et al.* to all limited partners, including corporate and limited partnership limited partners. In addition, the FTB has indicated that it will apply this holding to a limited liability company (LLC) to the extent that the LLC is a limited partner in a limited partnership (*Tax News*, FTB, January 1997).

FTB Reg. 23101, 18 CCR, provides, generally, that a foreign corporation that has stocks of goods in California and that makes deliveries in California pursuant to orders taken by employees in California is doing business in the state and is subject to the franchise tax. On the other hand, Regulation 23101 provides that a foreign corporation engaged wholly in interstate commerce is not subject to the franchise tax. (Note that these rules apply to the *franchise* tax. For the application of the corporation *income* tax, see ¶805).

In *Appeal of Hugo Neu-Proler International Sales Corporation* (1982) (CCH CALIFORNIA TAX REPORTS ¶400-444), the taxpayer was a Domestic International Sales Corporation (DISC) subject to special treatment under federal income tax law. The corporation had no employees or physical assets in California. The SBE held that the corporation was doing business in California and subject to the franchise tax, because "the exercise of appellant's corporate powers and privileges was essential to the performance of the various transactions it entered into" in California.

In *Appeal of Putnam Fund Distributors Inc., et al.* (1977) (CCH CALIFORNIA TAX REPORTS ¶11-520.8291), the SBE held that a Massachusetts corporation engaged in promoting California sales of mutual fund shares by brokers was doing business and was subject to the franchise tax. The SBE approved the imposition of 25% failure-to-file penalties (¶1411) for a period of 10 years.

In *Appeal of Kimberly-Clark Corp.* (1962) (CCH CALIFORNIA TAX REPORTS ¶10-210.239), the SBE held that a foreign corporation qualified to do business in California was subject to the franchise tax even though it did not maintain a stock of goods within the State. It conducted extensive activities and had substantial stocks of samples, displays, and sales promotion materials in the state.

A corporation may be "doing business" even though it is in the process of liquidation. The SBE held to this effect in the case of *Appeal of Sugar Creek Pine Co.* (1955) (CCH CALIFORNIA TAX REPORTS ¶10-210.51). The corporation's activities involved principally perfecting title to properties that it had previously contracted to sell.

In *Appeal of American President Lines, Ltd.* (1961) (CCH CALIFORNIA TAX REPORTS ¶10-075.56), the SBE held that a corporation that is principally engaged in interstate and foreign commerce is nevertheless subject to the *franchise* tax on the basis of its entire income attributable to sources within the state when it engages in some *intrastate* business in California.

• *Foreign lending institutions*

The Corporations Code specifies the activities in which a foreign lending institution may engage in California without being deemed to be "doing business" in the state. The permissible activities include purchasing or making loans, making appraisals, enforcement of loans, etc., provided the activities are carried on within the limitations set forth in the law. (Sec. 191, Corp. Code)

• *Exemption for limited activities*

The law authorizes the FTB to determine that a corporation is not subject to franchise or income tax if its only activities in California are within specified limits. A corporation may petition the FTB for such a determination. The limited activities are the following:

— purchasing of personal property or services in California for its own or its affiliate's use outside the state if (1) the corporation has no more than 100 employees in California whose duties are limited to specified activities, or (2) the corporation has no more than 200 employees in California whose duties are limited, as specified, and the items purchased are used for the construction or modification of a physical plant or facility located outside the state; however, the combined number of employees in this state for purposes of both (1) and (2) may not exceed 200; and/or

— presence of employees in California solely for the purpose of attending school.

(Sec. 23101.5, Rev. & Tax. Code)

• *Certain organizations treated as corporations*

The tax law includes "professional corporations" within the definition of "corporation" for franchise tax purposes. Charitable trusts are also treated as "corporations" (¶606). (Sec. 23038, Rev. & Tax. Code)

Under both federal and California law, publicly traded partnerships are treated as "corporations" for income tax purposes unless 90% or more of their gross income consists of qualifying passive activities or they are grandfathered publicly traded partnerships exempt from corporate treatment. However, a grandfathered publicly traded partnership that elects to continue its partnership status is subject to a California tax equal to 1% of its California-source gross income attributable to the active conduct of any trade or business (a 3.5% tax on gross income attributable to the active conduct of any trade or business for federal purposes). The tax is due from the partnership at the time the partnership return is filed (see ¶622). Otherwise, the tax is paid, collected, and refunded in the same manner as corporate franchise and income taxes. (Sec. 23038.5, Rev. & Tax. Code)

Limited liability companies classified as corporations are discussed at ¶805.

¶805 Corporations Subject to Income Tax

Law: Secs. 18633.5, 23038, 23038.5, 23501, 23503, 23731, 24870-75 (CCH CALIFORNIA TAX REPORTS ¶10-015, 10-075, 10-210, 10-235, 10-240, 10-245, 10-355, 10-360, 10-365, 10-370).

Comparable Federal: Secs. 851-860G, 7701, 7704, Former Secs. 860H-860L (CCH U.S. MASTER TAX GUIDE ¶403, 2301—2323, 2326—2340, 2343—2367, 2369).

California Form: Form 100 (California Corporation Franchise or Income Tax Return).

Generally, the corporation income tax applies to those corporations (including associations, Massachusetts or business trusts, and real estate investment trusts) that derive income from sources within California but are not subject to the franchise tax. If there is income from both within and without the state, a portion of the total is assigned to California as explained in Chapter 13. (Sec. 23501, Rev. & Tax. Code)

• *Application of income tax*

The most common application of the income tax is to foreign corporations that engage in some business activity in California but that are not "doing business" in the state so as to subject them to the franchise tax. One example is a corporation that maintains a stock of goods in California from which deliveries are made to fill orders taken by independent dealers or brokers. Another example might be a corporation that has employees operating in California but has no stock of goods or other property in the state; however, the state's right to tax in such a situation may be limited under the federal legislation discussed below. Where a corporation maintains only a stock of samples in California, having no other property or agents or other activity in the state, it has generally been considered not subject to tax in California.

The income tax, rather than the franchise tax, is imposed on the unrelated business income of an exempt organization. (Sec. 23731, Rev. & Tax. Code)

• *Limited activities—Application of P.L. 86-272*

The scope of the California income tax is limited by federal legislation enacted in 1959. This legislation was intended to overcome the effect of two decisions of the U.S. Supreme Court earlier in 1959: *Northwestern States Portland Cement Co. v. Minnesota* and *Williams v. Stockham Valves and Fittings, Inc.*, 358 U.S. 450, 79 S.Ct. 357. These cases ruled that individual states had broad powers to levy taxes on the income of foreign state corporations even though the business conducted within the state was exclusively in interstate commerce. The federal law (P.L. 86-272) prohibits a state from imposing a tax on income derived from interstate commerce, provided:

— the activities within the state are limited to the solicitation of orders for sales of tangible personal property by employees or other representatives;

— orders are sent outside the state for approval; and

— orders are filled from stocks of goods maintained outside the state.

The prohibition against tax applies also to a corporation that sells through a sales office maintained within the state by independent contractors whose activities consist solely of making sales or soliciting orders.

The Franchise Tax Board (FTB) has issued a guide to its interpretation of P.L. 86-272 (FTB 1050, Application and Interpretation of Public Law 86-272). The guide discusses various types of activity that will, or will not, cause a business to lose its state-tax immunity. Activities that will subject a corporation to California taxation include property repairs, credit investigations, and collection of delinquent accounts. Certain activities that are incidental to the solicitation of sales will not cause a business to lose its state-tax immunity. However, if at any time during the taxable year, a company conducts activities that are not protected, all sales in this state or income earned by the company attributed to this state during any part of the taxable year are subject to California taxation.

The guide also discusses various other problems, including use of display rooms, use of independent contractors, maintaining facilities in the state, and application of the throwback rule. It states that the protection of P.L. 86-272 does not apply to California or foreign-nation corporations or to California residents or domiciliaries. The guide can be found at the FTB's Web site at the following address: http://www.ftb.ca.gov/forms/misc/1050.pdf.

In *The Reader's Digest Assoc., Inc. v. Franchise Tax Board*, 94 Cal. App.4th 1240 (2001) (CCH CALIFORNIA TAX REPORTS ¶10-210.26), the court ruled that an out-of-state corporation was doing business in California and subject to tax in the state as a result of activities provided by an in-state affiliate because the in-state affiliate was not an independent contractor to the out-of-state corporation. The court's conclusion that a subsidiary cannot be an independent contractor when the parent has a right to exercise control over the subsidiary may signal a new approach that states may take in challenging a taxpayer's claim of P.L. 86-272 protection.

In Legal Ruling No. 372 (1974) (CCH CALIFORNIA TAX REPORTS ¶16-851.20), the FTB held that the protection of P.L. 86-272 does not extend to salesmen soliciting orders in California; such salesmen are subject to withholding of California income tax.

As explained at ¶804, the FTB may determine that a corporation is subject to neither franchise nor income tax if its only activities in California are within specified limits.

Appeal of Riblet Tramway Co. (1967) (CCH CALIFORNIA TAX REPORTS ¶10-075.97) involved a Washington state manufacturer of ski lift facilities that were installed in California by others. The company usually inspected the facilities after they were installed. The State Board of Equalization (SBE) held that this inspection activity went beyond "solicitation" and subjected the company to California tax.

Similarly, in *Brown Group Retail, Inc. v. Franchise Tax Board* (1996) (CCH CALIFORNIA TAX REPORTS ¶10-075.216), an out-of-state shoe manufacturer and distributor that had no facilities or property in the state was not immune from California franchise tax under P.L. 86-272, because services performed by the taxpayer's employees went beyond the mere solicitation of orders. Although the taxpayer made no direct sales in the state, the presence in California of two of the taxpayer's employees who assisted current and potential customers with financial analysis, lease and loan negotiations, site selection, store design, marketing, etc., established a sufficient nexus with the state to subject the taxpayer to California's franchise tax.

• *Cases decided favorably to taxpayer*

In *Appeal of John H. Grace Co.* (1980) (CCH CALIFORNIA TAX REPORTS ¶10-075.51), the taxpayer was an Illinois corporation that leased railroad cars to industrial companies. The cars sometimes passed into or through California in interstate commerce, and the taxpayer paid the private car tax (¶1905) on the average number of cars per day in California. The SBE held that the corporation was not subject to California income tax, because it had no "activities" within the state and the railroad cars were not under its control when they were in the state.

In *Appeal of E.F. Timme & Son, Inc.* (1969) (CCH CALIFORNIA TAX REPORTS ¶10-075.98), the FTB contended that P.L. 86-272 was not applicable because the taxpayer did not own the goods it was selling in California. The SBE overruled the FTB and held that the taxpayer was exempt from California tax.

• *Cases unfavorable to taxpayer*

In *William Wrigley, Jr., Co. v. Wisconsin Department of Revenue* (1992) (CCH CALIFORNIA TAX REPORTS ¶10-075), the U.S. Supreme Court held that an Illinois-based corporation that had sales representatives in Wisconsin to store goods, replace goods, and restock retailers' display racks was not immune from Wisconsin franchise taxes under P.L. 86-272, because those activities went beyond mere "solicitation."

In *Appeal of Aqua Aerobic Systems, Inc.* (1985) (CCH CALIFORNIA TAX REPORTS ¶10-075.93), the SBE held that an Illinois manufacturer's warranty repairs exceeded "solicitation" and went beyond the protection of P.L. 86-272.

In *Appeal of Ramfjeld and Co., Inc.* (1981) (CCH CALIFORNIA TAX REPORTS ¶10-075.67), the taxpayer warehoused in California canned fish that it sold to U.S. military installations in California and Asia. The taxpayer was a New York corporation, with no office or employees in California. The SBE held that the corporation was subject to California income tax.

In *Appeal of CITC Industries, Inc.* (1979) (CCH CALIFORNIA TAX REPORTS ¶10-075.94), the taxpayer was the U.S. sales representative for a Japanese manufacturer and maintained a sales office in California. The SBE held that the taxpayer's activities went beyond the protection of P.L. 86-272. See also *Appeal of Schmid Brothers, Inc.* (1980) (CCH CALIFORNIA TAX REPORTS ¶10-075.991), to the same effect.

In *Appeal of Kelsey-Hayes Company* (1978) (CCH CALIFORNIA TAX REPORTS ¶11-525.59), the taxpayer corporation had an active California division that admittedly subjected the corporation to the franchise tax. The corporation also had limited activity in California in an entirely unrelated business. The SBE held that P.L. 86-272 was not applicable and the limited activity could be taxed on a unitary basis with related out-of-state operations, because P.L. 86-272 must be applied to the totality of the corporation's California activities.

In *Appeal of Knoll Pharmaceutical Company, Inc.* (1977) (CCH CALIFORNIA TAX REPORTS ¶10-075.32), an out-of-state manufacturer had employees soliciting sales in California. The sales were approved and filled by a California consignee from a stock of goods maintained in the state. The SBE held that the corporation's activities went beyond the protection of P.L. 86-272. See also *Consolidated Accessories Corp. v. Franchise Tax Board* (1984) (CCH CALIFORNIA TAX REPORTS ¶10-075.22), to the same effect.

In *Appeal of Nardis of Dallas, Inc.* (1975) (CCH CALIFORNIA TAX REPORTS ¶10-075.99), an out-of-state corporation sold clothing through a California showroom. The SBE held that the corporation was not protected from California tax under P.L. 86-272, because the California salesman was an employee—not an independent contractor—and the showroom was maintained by the company, even though it was leased in the salesman's name.

In *Appeal of Snap-On Tools Corporation* (1958) (CCH CALIFORNIA TAX REPORTS ¶10-075.34), the SBE held that where an out-of-state corporation operated in California solely through independently owned distributorships, it was not doing business in the state so as to be subject to the franchise tax. However, because the corporation maintained consigned stocks of goods in California from which withdrawals were made by the independent distributors, it was held subject to the income tax.

• *Noncorporate organizations subject to tax*

California adopts IRC Sec. 7704 as of the current IRC tie-in date (see ¶803), under which publicly traded partnerships are taxed as corporations, unless 90% or more of their gross income is qualifying passive income or they are grandfathered publicly traded partnerships exempt from corporate treatment. However, a grandfathered publicly traded partnership that elects to continue its partnership status is subject to a California tax equal to 1% of its California-source gross income attributable to the active conduct of any trade or business (a 3.5% tax on gross income attributable to the active conduct of any trade or business for federal purposes). The tax is due from the partnership at the time the partnership return is filed (see ¶622). Otherwise, the tax is paid, collected, and refunded in the same manner as corporate franchise and income taxes. (Sec. 23038.5, Rev. & Tax. Code)

The income tax applies to certain other organizations that may be said generally to have the characteristics of a corporation. It applies to certain associations, to Massachusetts or business trusts, and to some non-publicly traded limited partnerships. FTB Reg. 23038 (a), 18 CCR, and Reg. 23038 (b), 18 CCR, contain detailed rules in this regard.

Note that a business trust that was classified as a corporation for California corporation franchise tax purposes but was classified as a partnership for federal purposes prior to January 1, 1997, may make an irrevocable election to be classified as a partnership for California tax purposes as well, unless specified exceptions apply. The election is made on FTB 3574, Special Election for Business Trusts and Certain Foreign Single Member LLCs. (Reg. 23038, 18 CCR; Instructions, FTB 3574, Special Election for Business Trusts and Certain Foreign Single Member LLCs)

• *Regulated investment companies*

California adopts federal provisions dealing with regulated investment companies (RICs) (commonly known as "mutual funds") as of the current IRC tie-in date (¶803), with exceptions that (1) allow RICs to deduct exempt interest dividends distributed to shareholders to the extent that the interest was included in gross income and (2) modify the provisions concerning the computation of investment company taxable income taxable to RIC shareholders. (Sec. 24870, Rev. & Tax. Code; Sec. 24871, Rev. & Tax. Code)

At the federal level, the deduction for exempt interest dividends is denied because interest from state and local bonds is excluded from federal gross income; however, because such interest is included in gross income for California purposes (¶910), California permits the deduction. California taxes a RIC the same as a taxable C corporation, except that its California "net income" is the same as its federal "investment company taxable income" with specified modifications.

For purposes of calculating a RIC's investment company taxable income, California incorporates federal law except that

(1) California, unlike federal law, does not exclude a RIC's net capital gain from its taxable income,

(2) California denies the California net operating loss (NOL) deduction rather than the federal NOL deduction,

(3) California disallows the former California dividends received deduction for corporations taxed by California rather than the federal dividends received deduction,

(4) California denies the deductions for (a) an intercompany dividend received from corporations that are members of the unitary group, (b) patronage refunds from certain cooperative corporations, and (c) dividends received from insurance companies;

(5) California, unlike federal law, includes a deduction for capital gain and exempt interest dividends for purposes of computing the deduction for dividends paid;

(6) federal law, but not California, allows taxpayers to pass on the foreign tax credit to its shareholders; and

(7) federal law, but not California, provides for reduced rates for qualified dividend income distributed to investors by RICs.

(Sec. 24871, Rev. & Tax. Code)

In addition, because of California's current IRC conformity date (¶803), California does not conform to amendments made by the Tax Increase Prevention and Reconciliation Act of 2005 that made several changes related to the Foreign Investment in Real Property Tax Act (FIRPTA). These changes include expansion of the

FIRPTA distribution rules, extension of the regularly traded securities exception to publicly traded RIC U.S. Real Property Holding Corporations (USRPHCs), modification of the RIC termination date, required withholding on RIC USRPHC distributions, and treatment of certain RIC capital gain distributions as dividends. The changes generally apply for federal purposes retroactively to tax years of qualified investment entities beginning after 2005.

• *Real estate investment trusts*

An organization that qualifies as a "real estate investment trust" (REIT) for federal income tax purposes is treated as a business trust subject to the corporation income tax. California generally follows federal law as of the current IRC tie-in date (¶803), except that a REIT's California "net income" is the same as its federal "real estate investment company taxable income" with specified modifications. (Sec. 24870, Rev. & Tax. Code; Sec. 24872, Rev. & Tax. Code, through Sec. 24872.7, Rev. & Tax. Code)

Federal law, but not California law, provides for reduced rates for qualified dividend income distributed to investors by REITs. In addition, unlike federal law, California law does not impose tax on income from foreclosure property or prohibited transactions. Nor does California impose a tax in the case of a failure to meet certain requirements. (Sec. 24872, Rev. & Tax. Code)

A federal election, or lack thereof, to qualify as a REIT is binding for California corporation franchise and income tax purposes. The same applies to a federal election to treat certain REIT property as foreclosure property. (Sec. 24872.4, Rev. & Tax Code; Sec. 24872.6, Rev. & Tax. Code) Although California law technically only adopts federal amendments adopted prior to California's IRC conformity date, because California recognizes any federal REIT election or termination thereof, California effectively conforms to all amendments to the federal REIT provisions impacting eligibility, elections, and terminations, even those enacted after California's latest conformity date. Thus, California follows the amendments made to IRC Sec. 856 by the Tax Technical Corrections Act of 2007, the Heartland, Habitat, Harvest, and Horticulture Act of 2008, and the Housing Assistance Tax Act of 2008.

The FTB has identified transactions that involve REIT consent dividends as a "listed transaction"; see ¶727 for details.

• *Real estate mortgage investment conduits*

California follows federal law as of the current IRC tie-in date (¶803), exempting from income or franchise taxation corporations that qualify as "real estate mortgage investment conduits" (REMICs). The income of such an entity is taxable to the holders of its interests. There are two separate interests in a REMIC, with each taxed under a different set of complex rules. California does not incorporate the federal provision that imposes a 100% tax on the net income from prohibited transactions. A REMIC is subject to the minimum tax, but not to the franchise tax, and a REMIC's income is taxable to the holders of its interests (¶804). (Sec. 24870, Rev. & Tax. Code; Sec. 24873, Rev. & Tax. Code; Sec. 24874, Rev. & Tax. Code)

• *Financial asset securitization investment trusts*

California incorporates the former federal provisions concerning financial asset securitization investment trusts (FASITs) as of the current IRC tie-in date (¶803), with modifications. California also incorporates the federal repeal of the FASIT provisions, effective January 1, 2005, including the exceptions to the federal repeal that are applicable to FASITs in existence on October 22, 2004, to the extent that regular interests issued by the FASIT before October 22, 2004, continue to remain outstanding in accordance with the original terms of issuance. (Sec. 24870, Rev. & Tax. Code; Sec. 24875, Rev. & Tax. Code)

• *Limited liability companies*

A limited liability company (LLC) that is classified as a corporation for California tax purposes is subject to the same tax return and tax payment requirements as any other corporation. LLCs that are classified as partnerships or that are disregarded and treated as sole proprietorships are discussed at ¶625.

Note that an entity that was a previously existing foreign single member LLC that was classified as a corporation under California law but elected to be treated as a disregarded entity for federal purposes for pre-1997 taxable years may continue to be classified differently for California and federal tax purposes. However, such an entity, may make an irrevocable election to be disregarded for California tax purposes as well, unless specified exceptions apply. The election is made on FTB 3574, Special Election for Business Trusts and Certain Foreign Single Member LLCs. (Reg. 23038, 18 CCR; Instructions, FTB 3574, Special Election for Business Trusts and Certain Foreign Single Member LLCs) (Sec. 18633.5(h), Rev. & Tax. Code; Sec. 23038, Rev. & Tax. Code)

• *Credit for franchise tax*

A corporation subject to the income tax is allowed a credit for any franchise tax imposed for the same period. (Sec. 23503, Rev. & Tax. Code)

¶806 S Corporations

Law: Secs. 18535, 19365, 23153, 23800-13, 24416, 24633.5, 24637 (CCH CALIFORNIA TAX REPORTS ¶10-215).

Comparable Federal: Secs. 1361-79 (CCH U.S. MASTER TAX GUIDE ¶301—349).

California Form: Form 100S (California S Corporation Franchise or Income Tax Return).

California conforms to federal S corporation provisions as of the current IRC tie-in date (see ¶803), with substantial modifications. (Sec. 23800, Rev. & Tax. Code)

Caution Note: Conformity Traps

Although California only technically incorporates federal law as of California's current conformity date (see ¶803), because S corporations that have a valid S corporation election for federal purposes are treated as S corporations for California corporation franchise and income tax purposes (Sec. 23801(a), Rev. & Tax. Code), California essentially incorporates the IRC provisions governing S corporation qualifications, elections, and terminations (IRC Sec. 1361 and IRC Sec. 1362) as currently amended. Consequently, California incorporates many amendments made by the Small Business and Work Opportunity Tax Act of 2007, even though it was enacted after California's current federal conformity date.

However, California does not conform to other amendments made to the federal S corporation provisions by the Small Business Act that

— allow a bank changing from the reserve method of accounting for bad debts for its first tax year for which it is an S corporation to elect to take into account all IRC Sec. 481 adjustments in the last tax year it was a C corporation, effective for federal purposes beginning with the 2007 tax year;

— provide that an S corporation's sale of a qualified subchapter S subsidiary's (QSub's) stock is treated as a sale of an undivided interest in the QSub's assets followed by a deemed creation of the subsidiary in an IRC Sec. 351 transaction, effective for federal purposes beginning with the 2007 tax year; and

— eliminate a corporation's accumulated earnings and profits that arose during its pre-1983 S corporation years even if the corporation was not an S corporation for its first tax year beginning after 1996, applicable for federal purposes to taxable years beginning after May 25, 2007.

Also, California's conformity to federal provisions recognizing S corporations as pass-through entities is partial in that

— California imposes both a 1.5% tax and the minimum tax at the corporate level, and

— California imposes a minimum tax on qualified subchapter S subsidiaries. (Sec. 23802, Rev. & Tax. Code; Sec. 23153, Rev. & Tax. Code)

Practice Tip: Net Income (Loss) Reconciliation for S Corporations with Total Assets of $10 Million or More

The Internal Revenue Service requires S corporations with total assets of $10 million or more on the last day of the year to complete Schedule M-3 (Form 1120S), instead of Schedule M-1 (Form 1120S). However, for California purposes, the S corporation must still complete the California Schedule M-1 and do one of the following: (1) attach a copy of the Schedule M-3 (Form 1120S) and related attachments; (2) attach a complete copy of the federal return; or (3) provide Schedule M-3 (Form 1120S) in a spreadsheet format. (Instructions, Form 100S)

• *Character of pass-through entity*

Under federal law, small ("S") corporations (limited by the number of shareholders) enjoy the tax advantages of partnerships while at the same time benefiting from the corporate characteristic of limited liability. Tax is not paid by the corporation, as such. Generally, items of income, loss, and credits are passed through to shareholders on a pro-rata basis. California has adopted a hybrid version of the S corporation in which both a reduced corporate tax is paid at the corporate level and income and tax attributes are passed through to shareholders. (Sec. 23800, et. seq., Rev. & Tax. Code)

• *Nonresident shareholders*

S corporations are required to remit California income tax withholding on behalf of their nonresident shareholders (see ¶714).

S corporations are allowed to file group (composite) returns and to make composite tax payments on behalf of electing nonresident shareholders. A single 100% nonresident S corporation may also file a group return. (Sec. 18535, Rev. & Tax. Code)

• *S corporation's taxable year*

California incorporates IRC Sec. 444, under which S corporations may elect a fiscal year that is the same as the corporation used in its last tax year. (Sec. 24637, Rev. & Tax. Code) See ¶1104.

• *Reduced tax at corporate level*

S corporations that are not financial corporations compute the corporate franchise or income tax on Form 100S, but pay this tax at the rate of 1.5% instead of the normal corporate tax rate discussed at ¶816. For purposes of the 1.5% tax, S corporations compute depreciation and amortization deductions using MACRS (see ¶310). (Sec. 23802, Rev. & Tax. Code)

In *Handlery Hotels, Inc.* (1995) (CCH CALIFORNIA TAX REPORTS ¶10-215.217), a California court of appeal held that a corporation that made a valid election to be treated as an S corporation was not entitled to apply the lower S corporation franchise tax rate until the first income year following the corporation's valid election.

As under federal law, S corporations are not subject to the alternative minimum tax (¶817). However, they are subject to the minimum tax (¶816). (Sec. 23153, Rev. & Tax. Code)

• *Financial S corporation*

The tax rate for S corporations that are also financial corporations is 3.5%. (Sec. 23802, Rev. & Tax. Code)

• *Qualified subchapter S subsidiaries*

Under both California and federal law an S corporation may own a qualified subchapter S subsidiary (QSub). However, under California (but not federal) law, a QSub is subject to the California corporate minimum tax if it is incorporated in California, qualified to transact business in California, or doing business in California. In addition, the activities of a QSub are imputed to the S corporation for purposes of determining whether the S corporation is "doing business" in California. An S corporation's federal election to treat a corporation as a QSub is binding for California purposes and no separate election is allowed. (Sec. 23800.5, Rev. & Tax. Code)

In a nonprecedential decision, the SBE ruled that an S corporation was liable for $1,600 in minimum tax imposed on its two QSubs for the two days of the S corporation's taxable year remaining when it acquired the QSubs, even though each of the QSubs had already paid an $800 minimum franchise tax or QSub tax for their short taxable year ending the day before they were acquired by the S corporation. The SBE ruled that the QSubs became new entities, with a new taxable year, when they were acquired by the S corporation, and the taxes in question were payable per entity, per taxable year. (*Appeal of The Greystone Group, Inc.* (2006) (CCH CALIFORNIA TAX REPORTS ¶10-380.451))

• *Separate tax on excess net passive investment income*

A separate tax is imposed on excess net passive investment income from California sources, using the full tax rate that applies to general corporations, but only when the taxpayer has excess net passive income for federal purposes. This tax is not reduced by any tax credits; however, the amount of the income subject to this tax is deductible from net income for purposes of computing the 1.5% tax. (Sec. 23811, Rev. & Tax. Code)

• *NOL deductions*

An S corporation is allowed to deduct a net operating loss incurred during a year in which it is treated as an S corporation. An S corporation may pass the full amount of such loss through to its shareholders in the year the loss is incurred. If a shareholder is unable to use the full amount of the loss in the year it is incurred, the shareholder may carry over or carry back the NOL deduction as allowed for C corporations (see ¶1024). (Sec. 23802(d), Rev. & Tax. Code)

S corporations may also qualify for the 100% NOL carryover deduction available to (1) taxpayers engaged in the conduct of qualified businesses in enterprise zones, the former Los Angeles Revitalization Zone, local agency military base recovery areas, and the targeted tax area; and (2) "new" and "small" businesses (¶1024).

According to the Instructions to FTB 3805Q, an S corporation that converted from a C corporation may apply an NOL carryover from a period in which it was a C corporation only against the tax on built-in gains and not against the standard 1.5% tax imposed on S corporations.

• *Combined reporting of members of a unitary business*

A corporation that elects to be treated as an S corporation is, by virtue of its election, required to be excluded from a combined report of the unitary group. However, the law contains enforcement provisions to help the FTB prevent tax avoidance or evasion (¶1110). (Sec. 23801, Rev. & Tax. Code)

• *Separate tax on built-in capital gains*

A "built-in gains" tax is imposed on gains from sales of assets, as determined under IRC Sec. 1374. The tax applies only to gains from California source income. The tax is not reduced by any credits except credits carried over from years prior to an S election. The full corporate tax rate (¶816) is applied to this income. (Sec. 23809, Rev. & Tax. Code)

For corporations required to convert to S corporations for California tax purposes as a result of their federal S corporation election (see the discussion under "S corporation election, termination of status" below), the effective date of the S corporation election for purposes of determining the California tax on built-in gains is the same as the federal S corporation election date.

• *Credits available to S corporations*

Corporate credits may be claimed against the 1.5% (or 3.5% for financial S corporations) tax, with no pass-through to shareholders. The credits are reduced to one-third of their total value because the tax rate is much lower than the regular corporate tax rate discussed at ¶816. Unused portions of the credit, but not the two-thirds that is denied, may be carried forward. Credit carryovers from years prior to making an S election are also subject to the one-third limitation, but not in subsequent years. Shareholders, however, are able to take the full amount of credits to which they may be entitled as individual taxpayers. (Sec. 23803, Rev. & Tax. Code)

For California purposes, credits and credit carryovers may not reduce the minimum franchise tax, built-in gains tax, excess net passive income tax, credit recaptures, the increase in tax imposed for the deferral of installment sale income, or an installment of last-in first-out (LIFO) recapture tax.

• *Passive activity losses and at-risk rules*

The federal limitations on losses and credits from passive activities (IRC Sec. 469) and the at-risk rules (IRC Sec. 465) are applied in the same manner as if the corporation were an individual (see ¶339 and ¶340). For this purpose, "adjusted gross income" of the S corporation is its "net income," as modified for California purposes, but without any charitable contributions deduction. However, the material participation rules apply as if the S corporation was a closely held corporation. (Sec. 23802, Rev. & Tax. Code)

See the discussion under "Qualified subchapter S subsidiaries," above, for special provisions concerning the disposition of S corporation stock by a QSub for purposes of applying the passive activity loss and at-risk limitations.

Practitioner Comment: California Conforms to Federal LIFO Recapture Income for Estimated Payments

California conforms to federal law by excluding a last-in, first-out (LIFO) recapture amount from estimated tax payments in any taxable year that an annual installment of LIFO recapture is due. For federal tax purposes, a corporation that uses the LIFO method of accounting for its inventory for the taxable year before its election to become an S corporation takes effect must include the LIFO recapture amount in its taxable income and report and pay tax on the recaptured income in four equal annual installments. However, the recapture amount is not included in the amount of federal quarterly estimated tax payments that are made during the years in which an installment payment is due. Previously, California required that corporations include the LIFO recapture amount in determining estimated tax payments. According to a legislative notice issued by the FTB on October 5, 2004, the legislation is operative for tax years beginning on or after January 1, 2006, and, therefore, applies to estimated tax payments that were made during 2005.

Bruce Daigh, Chris Whitney, Contributing Editors

• *S corporation election; termination of status*

A corporation that has in effect a valid federal S corporation election is treated as an S corporation for California tax purposes and no separate election is allowed. (Sec. 23801, Rev. & Tax. Code)

The federal election date is deemed to be the California S corporation election date for corporations that elect to be S corporations after 2001. The federal election applies for purposes of determining shareholders' California income tax liability, even if the corporation is not qualified to do business in California or is not incorporated in California. A termination of a federal S corporation election that is not an inadvertent termination simultaneously terminates the corporation's S corporation status for California tax purposes.

The Secretary for federal purposes (Franchise Tax Board (FTB) for California purposes) has the authority to validate invalid elections that have resulted from the following:

— an entity's inadvertent failure to qualify as a small business corporation;

— failure to obtain required shareholder consents; or

— late filing of an election with reasonable cause.

A corporation may also perfect an S corporation election for California purposes in instances when the corporation merely failed to timely file a federal S corporation election. The corporation and its shareholders must have filed with the IRS for relief and received notification from the IRS of the acceptance of an untimely filed S corporation election.

Under both federal and California law, once a valid election for S corporation treatment has been filed, S corporation status continues for as long as the corporation remains in existence, unless the election is terminated. Termination of a federal election occurs when an S corporation

(1) ceases to qualify as a small business corporation;

(2) has passive investment income that amounts to more than 25% of its gross receipts for each of three consecutive tax years, and has accumulated earnings and profits at the end of each of those years; or

(3) deliberately revokes its S corporation election by filing a revocation statement to which the majority of the shareholders consent.

The termination under (2), above, is not recognized in California unless the election is terminated for federal income tax purposes. Dividends received by an S corporation from a C corporation subsidiary are not treated as passive investment income to the extent such dividends are attributable to the earnings and profits of the C corporation derived from the active conduct of a trade or business.

If an S corporation terminates its election, it is ineligible to make another S corporation election for five years.

• *Other differences from federal treatment*

The federal provisions dealing with coordination with the investment credit recapture are inapplicable as are the provisions dealing with foreign (non-U.S.) income. (Sec. 23051.5, Rev. & Tax. Code) A C corporation resulting from an S corporation termination must annualize its taxable income for the short taxable year under both California and federal law. However, taxpayers must annualize their income on a monthly basis for California corporation franchise and income tax purposes and on a daily basis for federal income tax purposes. (Sec. 23801(f), Rev. & Tax. Code)

• *Taxation of shareholders*

Taxation of shareholders is discussed at ¶ 233.

¶807 Designated Settlement Funds

Law: Sec. 24693 (CCH CALIFORNIA TAX REPORTS ¶ 10-520).

Comparable Federal: Sec. 468B (CCH U.S. MASTER TAX GUIDE ¶ 1539).

California follows IRC Sec. 468B as of California's current federal conformity date (¶ 803), relating to the taxation of designated settlement funds, except that the tax imposed is at the regular California income tax rate, see ¶ 602. The tax is in lieu of any other income tax. (Sec. 24693, Rev. & Tax. Code)

Because of California's current federal conformity date (see ¶ 103), California has not incorporated amendments made by the Tax Increase Prevention and Reconciliation Act of 2005 (TIPRA) that exempt from federal income tax certain escrow accounts, settlement funds, or similar funds established to resolve claims brought under the Comprehensive Environmental Response, Compensation, and Liability Act of 1980 (CERCLA) (P.L. 96-510) by designating these funds as being beneficially owned by the United States. The federal exemption is applicable to accounts and funds established after May 17, 2006.

¶808 Exempt Corporations

Law: Secs. 23701-11.5, 23740, 23741 (CCH CALIFORNIA TAX REPORTS ¶ 10-245, 10-250, 10-525).

Comparable Federal: Secs. 501, 504-05, 507-09, 527-29, 4940-48, 7428 (CCH U.S. MASTER TAX GUIDE ¶ 601—698).

California Form: FTB 3500 (Exemption Application), FTB 3500A (Submission of Exemption Request).

The following organizations are exempt from both corporation franchise and income taxes:

(1) labor, agricultural, or horticultural organizations, with some exceptions (see comment below) (Sec. 23704, Rev. & Tax. Code);

(2) fraternal organizations providing insurance benefits to their members or devoting earnings exclusively to certain charitable-type and fraternal purposes (Sec. 23701b, Rev. & Tax. Code);

(3) nonprofit cemetery or crematory companies (Sec. 23701c, Rev. & Tax. Code);

(4) nonprofit religious, charitable, scientific, literary, or educational organizations (including certain cooperative hospital service organizations and certain amateur athletic associations) (Sec. 23701d, Rev. & Tax. Code);

(5) nonprofit business leagues, chambers of commerce, etc. (Sec. 23701f, Rev. & Tax. Code);

(6) nonprofit civic leagues, etc. (Sec. 23701u, Rev. & Tax. Code);

(7) nonprofit social and recreational clubs (Sec. 23701g, Rev. & Tax. Code);

(8) nonprofit title holding corporations (Sec. 23701h, Rev. & Tax. Code);

(9) voluntary employees' beneficiary associations (Sec. 23704, Rev. & Tax. Code);

(10) teachers' retirement associations (Sec. 23701j, Rev. & Tax. Code);

(11) certain religious or apostolic organizations, provided the income is reported by the individual members (Sec. 23701k, Rev. & Tax. Code);

(12) certain employee-funded pension plans created before June 25, 1959 (Sec. 23701s, Rev. & Tax. Code);

(13) organizations providing child care to the general public (Sec. 23704.4, Rev. & Tax. Code);

(14) insurance underwriting companies (this is a constitutional exemption; see discussion below. Insurance companies are subject to special taxes—see ¶1902);

(15) nonprofit corporations engaged in port and terminal protection and development (Sec. 10703, Corp. Code);

(16) trusts that provide for the payment of supplemental unemployment compensation benefits (Sec. 23701n, Rev. & Tax. Code);

(17) trusts or plans that meet the requirements of the federal Self-Employed Individual Tax Retirement law, if not otherwise exempt as an employees' trust (Sec. 23701p, Rev. & Tax. Code);

(18) political organizations (see discussion below) (Sec. 23701r, Rev. & Tax. Code);

(19) homeowners' associations (¶915) (Sec. 23701t, Rev. & Tax. Code);

(20) tenant organizations established to purchase mobile home parks for conversion into condominiums, stock cooperatives, or other resident ownership interests (Sec. 23701v, Rev. & Tax. Code);

(21) veterans' organizations (Sec. 23701w, Rev. & Tax. Code);

(22) nonprofit public benefit organizations (Sec. 23701u, Rev. & Tax. Code);

(23) nonprofit insurance risk pools (Sec. 23701z, Rev. & Tax. Code);

(24) qualified tuition programs (Sec. 23711, Rev. & Tax. Code); and

(25) state-chartered and federally chartered credit unions (Sec. 23701y, Rev. & Tax. Code).

• *California-federal comparisons*

The California exemptions are largely the same as the federal exemptions as of the current IRC tie-in date (¶803), although there are several differences.

The following exemptions are the same as the federal:

Item above	California law	Federal law
(1)	23701a	501(c)(5)
(2)	23701b, 23701 *l*	501(c)(8), (c)(10)
(3)	23701c	501(c)(13)
(4)	23701d, 23704	501(c)(3), 501(e), 501(j)
(7)	23701g	501(c)(7)
(8)	23701h, x	501(c)(2), (c)(25)
(9)	23701i	501(c)(9)
(10)	23701j	501(c)(11)
(11)	23701k	501(d)
(12)	23701s	501(c)(18)
(13)	23704.4	501(k)
(16)	23701n	501(c)(17)
(17)	23701p	401(a)
(21)	23701w	501(c)(19)
(24)	23711	529
(25)	23701y	501(c)(14)

Item (1) above (Sec. 23701a) is substantially the same as IRC Sec. 501(c)(5). The California exemption for agricultural cooperatives applies only if the organization is determined by the Internal Revenue Service to be exempt (see also ¶1021).

Item (5) above (Sec. 23701e) is the same as IRC Sec. 501(c)(6) except that the federal provision includes professional football leagues and California does not.

Item (6) above (Sec. 23701f) is the same as IRC Sec. 501(c)(4) except that the California law requires that the organization's assets be irrevocably dedicated to exempt purposes.

Item (12) above (Sec. 23701s) is the same as IRC Sec. 501(c)(18) except that California does not impose a tax on excess contributions to employee-funded pension plans.

Item (23) above (Sec. 23701z) applies to any organization established pursuant to the Nonprofit Corporation Law by three or more corporations to pool self-insurance claims or losses of those corporations. Federal law provides a similar exemption to "qualified charitable risk pools" organized under state law.

Item (25) above (Sec. 23701y) applies to California state-chartered credit unions only. Federally-chartered unions are exempt from California taxation by operation of the Federal Credit Union Act.

The federal law contains a number of exemptions not included in the California law. On the other hand, there are no specific exemptions in the federal law comparable to California items (14), (15), (20), and (22), above.

In addition, because of California's current federal conformity date (¶803), California has not incorporated amendments made by the Pension Protection Act of 2006 (PPA) that tighten the requirements for credit counseling organizations to qualify as exempt social welfare organizations or charitable or educational organizations, generally applicable to taxable years beginning after August 17, 2006.

• *Political organizations*

The California exemption for political organizations—item (18) above—with minor exceptions, is the same as the federal exemption. However, the California definition of "political organization" is slightly different from the federal. Also, California has not conformed to federal provisions that tax a nonpolitical organization on certain amounts when such organization engages in political activity. (Sec. 23701r, Rev. & Tax. Code)

An unincorporated political organization is automatically exempt, and is not required to file the usual application for exemption. Likewise, an *incorporated* political organization is not required to file the usual application for exemption. As explained at ¶811, an exempt political organization is required to file an income tax return if it has taxable income in excess of $100.

• *Insurance companies*

The gross premiums tax imposed on insurance companies is "in lieu" of all other state and local taxes and licenses, including the franchise tax (see ¶1902).

• *Title holding companies*

Federally exempt title holding companies that are limited liability companies classified as a partnership or as a disregarded entity are exempt from income taxes, including the fees imposed on LLCs under the personal income tax law (¶625). (Sec. 23701x, Rev. & Tax. Code)

• *Dedication of assets required*

Under California law, a charitable organization is not eligible for exemption under item (4) above unless its assets are irrevocably dedicated to exempt purposes. The California law (Sec. 23701d, Rev. & Tax. Code) provides specific rules for determining whether the assets are so dedicated, and requires a provision to that effect in the articles of organization. Federal law does not include this requirement; however, the governing instrument of a charitable organization must include specific provisions regarding distribution of income, prohibited acts, etc.

• *Use of accumulated income defeated exemption*

The State Board of Equalization (SBE) held in *Appeal of Boys Incorporated of America* (1960) (CCH CALIFORNIA TAX REPORTS ¶10-245.92) that the organization was not operated exclusively for exempt purposes, where it was shown that accumulated income had been used to liquidate indebtedness rather than for its avowed charitable purposes.

• *Application for exemption*

Charitable trusts are treated as corporations for California corporation income and franchise tax purposes (see also ¶606).

IRC Sec. 501(c)(3) organizations that are granted tax-exempt status under federal law may submit FTB 3500A, Submission of Exemption Request, along with a copy of their IRS issued tax-exempt status notice to the FTB to establish their California tax-exempt status. The effective date of an organization's California tax-exempt status will be no later than the effective date of that organization's federal tax-exempt status. An organization that incorporated prior to receiving its federal exempt status and that wants to receive state-exempt status retroactively in order to avoid the imposition of the minimum franchise or annual tax should file FTB 3500, Exemption Application, and not Form FTB 3500A, to request exemption retroactive to its date of incorporation.

Organizations that are not issued a 501(c)(3) federal tax-exempt status notice must file an application (FTB 3500) with the FTB, along with a $25 filing fee. This does not apply to insurance underwriting companies, which are exempt under the state constitution. Neither does it apply to political organizations except that an *incorporated* political organization must either pay the minimum tax (¶816) or obtain a certificate of exemption. (Sec. 23701d, Rev. & Tax. Code)

IRC Sec. 501(c)(3) organizations must still fulfill California's exemption law requirements to receive the FTB's affirmation of federal tax exemption. This includes California's filing requirements for FTB Form 199, California Exempt Organization Annual Information Return; FTB Form 109, California Exempt Organization Business Income Tax Return; or FTB Form 100, Corporation Tax Return. Furthermore, an inactive organization is not entitled to exemption. Organizations seeking to obtain and retain California exempt status must meet requirements that they are organized and operating for nonprofit purposes within the provisions of their exempt code section. (Sec. 23701d, Rev. & Tax. Code) (*FTB Notice 2008-3, May 30, 2008*, CCH CALIFORNIA TAX REPORTS ¶404-679; *Tax News*, FTB, December 2007, CCH CALIFORNIA TAX REPORTS ¶404-503)

Planning Note: Effect of Federal Exemption/Suspension/Revocation

The FTB may still revoke an organization's exempt status if the organization is not organized or operated in accordance with state or federal law. Taxpayers are required to notify the FTB of any federal tax-exempt status suspension or revocation. Upon receipt of such notice, the FTB may suspend or revoke the organization's state tax-exempt status.

Planning Note: Expedited Services

For a fee of $100, the FTB will expedite an application for exempt status. Qualified entities requesting tax exempt status must submit Form FTB 3500 (Exemption Application), along with all necessary documentation, to the Sacramento or Los Angeles FTB district office. (Reg. 15951, 18 CCR; *FTB Notice 2004-09*, California Franchise Tax Board, December 17, 2004, CCH CALIFORNIA TAX REPORTS¶403-722)

Certain organizations are required by federal law to give notice that they are applying for tax-exempt status. In these cases, the organizations are required to file a copy of the federal notice with the FTB.

California law provides that an exempt organization shall not be disqualified on the basis that it conducts bingo games authorized by law, provided the proceeds are used exclusively for charitable purposes. (Sec. 23710, Rev. & Tax. Code) Federal law provides for exemption of income from bingo games under certain conditions (¶809).

• *Retroactivity of exemption*

The FTB may grant exempt status retroactively to years that the organization can prove it satisfied the exemption requirements. (Sec. 23701, Rev. & Tax. Code) All applications for refunds must be timely filed (¶1417).

• *Private foundations*

Although California has conformed in principle to federal law by creating a special category of charitable organizations classified as "private foundations," California has not adopted many of the complicated federal provisions relating to such organizations. Also, whereas federal law imposes a tax on the investment income of such organizations and a series of excise taxes on self-dealing, income-accumulation, prohibited investments, lobbying, termination, etc., California imposes no special taxes on "private foundations" as such. (Sec. 23707, Rev. & Tax. Code)

Corporations classified as "private foundations" are required to include certain provisions in their governing instruments in order to maintain their tax-exempt status, unless a state statute accomplishes the same result. The California Corporations Code imposes the restrictions of federal law on every corporation that is deemed to be a "private foundation" under federal law. The law further provides that any provisions of a corporation's governing instruments that are inconsistent or contrary are of no effect.

Organizations exempt under Sec. 23701d of the law (item (4), above) may lose their exemption by engaging in certain "prohibited transactions" or by accumulating income under certain conditions.

In *Appeal of Vinemore Company, etc.* (1972) (CCH CALIFORNIA TAX REPORTS ¶10-245.40), the SBE revoked a hospital corporation's charitable exemption retroactively six years after the exemption was granted; the FTB had not been informed earlier of the corporation's improper activities.

• *Permissible lobbying activities*

Both California and federal laws provide for permissible levels of lobbying activities that a tax-exempt organization, which elects to apply these provisions, can engage in without losing its exempt status. (Sec. 23704.5, Rev. & Tax. Code) However, California has not conformed to the federal provisions imposing a 25% tax on "excess expenditures." (Sec. 23740, Rev. & Tax. Code; Sec. 23741, Rev. & Tax. Code)

• *No California provision for court review*

The federal law provides for court review of Internal Revenue Service rulings regarding tax-exempt status under certain conditions; there is nothing comparable in the California law.

¶809 Taxation of Business Income of Exempt Corporations

Law: Secs. 23702, 23731-37, 23741, 23771 (CCH CALIFORNIA TAX REPORTS ¶10-245).

Comparable Federal: Secs. 501-03, 511-15 (CCH U.S. MASTER TAX GUIDE ¶655—685).

California law concerning the taxation of unrelated business income of exempt organizations is substantially the same as federal law as of the current IRC tie-in date (¶803), except that certain rentals received by one exempt church from another are exempt from California tax. Unrelated business income is subject to California income tax, rather than franchise tax. (Sec. 23731 et seq., Rev. & Tax. Code) California has not incorporated amendments made by the Pension Protection Act of 2006 (PPA) that (1) specify that, after 2005, only excess qualifying specified payments from a controlled entity are included in an exempt organization's unrelated business taxable income and (2) treat debt management plan services provided by an organization that does not qualify as an as a tax exempt credit counseling organization as an exempt organization's unrelated trade or business, effective generally for federal purposes for tax years beginning after August 17, 2006.

A U.S. circuit court of appeals has held that the California statute that imposed tax on the unrelated business taxable income (UBTI) of otherwise tax-exempt trusts was not preempted by the federal Employee Retirement Income Security Act of 1974 (ERISA). (*Hattem v. Schwarzenegger* (2006) (CCH CALIFORNIA TAX REPORTS ¶15-215.91))

California adopts by reference federal law for treatment of "unrelated debt-financed income" as of the current IRC tie-in date (¶803). Under the rule, tax-exempt organizations in partnership with taxable entities treat income from debt-financed real property as unrelated business taxable income if partnership allocations are neither (1) qualified allocations nor (2) permissible disproportionate allocations. The purpose of the federal rule is to prevent the allocation of tax losses to the taxable partner.

Income from bingo games conducted by exempt organizations is exempt from California tax (Sec. 23710, Rev. & Tax. Code); however, income from games of chance is subject to the federal tax on unrelated business income.

• *Return required for business income*

Organizations otherwise exempt that are subject to tax on unrelated business income are required to file returns reporting their income from taxable activities and to pay tax on such income, under the rules applicable to organizations that are not exempt (¶811).

¶810 Returns—Time and Place for Filing

Law: Secs. 1502, 1502.1, 2117, 2117.1, Corporations Code; Secs. 18510, 18572, 18601-23, 21027, Rev. & Tax. Code (CCH CALIFORNIA TAX REPORTS ¶3-015, 3-020, 89-102—89-112).

Comparable Federal: Secs. 6065, 6072, 6081, 6102, 7508A (CCH U.S. MASTER TAX GUIDE ¶211, 2460, 2505, 2537, 2557).

California Forms: Form 100 (California Corporation Franchise or Income Tax Return), Form 100S (California S Corporation Franchise or Income Tax Return), Form 100X (Amended Corporation Franchise or Income Tax Return), FTB 3539 (Payment for Automatic Extension for Corps and Exempt Orgs), FTB 3586 (Payment Voucher for Corporation E-filed Returns), FTB 8453-C (California e-file Return Authorization for Corporations), FTB 8633 (California Application to Participate in the e-file Program).

Corporations subject to tax are required to file an annual income or franchise tax return by the 15th day of the third month after the close of the taxable year. This is the same as the federal due date and is one month earlier than the date for filing individual income tax returns. The filing date for farmers' cooperative associations is the 15th day of the ninth month after the close of the taxable year. (Sec. 18601, Rev. & Tax. Code)

Practice Tip: Extensions for Hurricane Ike, Hurricane Gustav, and Southern California Fire Victims

The FTB will follow the updated federal tax postponement dates for state taxpayers affected by Hurricane Ike, Hurricane Gustav, and the November 2008 southern California wildfires. Hurricane victims will have until January 5, 2009, to file returns, pay taxes, and perform other time-sensitive acts. The extended deadline for southern

California wildfire victims is February 11, 2009.. (*Press Release* s, California Franchise Tax Board, September 5, 2008, September 18, 2008, and November 20, 2008)

Information returns are discussed at ¶1412. See ¶811 for a discussion of exempt organization returns. Group returns that may be filed by corporations on behalf of their nonresident directors are discussed at ¶714.

• *Short-period returns*

A California short-period return is due the same day as the federal short-period return, which is the 15th day of the third calendar month following the close of the short period. If a federal short-period return is not required, the California short-period return is due within two months and 15 days after the close of the short period. (Sec. 18601, Rev. & Tax. Code)

• *Qualified use taxes*

Operative for returns filed for taxable years ending before 2010, corporations not required to hold a seller's permit or to register with the California State Board of Equalization may self-report their qualified use tax liabilities on their timely filed original corporation franchise or income tax returns. Persons electing to report such taxes are required to report and remit the tax on an income tax return that corresponds to the taxable year in which the use tax liability was incurred. Payments remitted with income tax returns are applied first to income taxes, penalties, and interest and, second, to qualified use tax liabilities. (Sec. 6452.1, Rev. & Tax. Code) See ¶1510 for details.

• *Extensions of time*

The Franchise Tax Board (FTB) has authority to grant extensions of time, not to exceed seven months, for filing any return, declaration, statement, or other document. An automatic extension will be granted for filing franchise or income tax returns (unless the corporation is suspended on the original due date for the return), if the return is filed by the 15th day of the 10th month following the close of the taxable year (October 15 for calendar-year taxpayers). The extended due date for exempt organizations filing a Form 199 or Form 109 is the 15th day of the 12th month following the close of the taxable year (December 15 for calendar-year taxpayers). Employees' trusts and IRAs filing Form 109 must file by the 15th day of the 11th month following the close of the trusts' taxable year (November 15 for calendar-year taxpayers). (Sec. 18604, Rev. & Tax. Code)

An extension of time for filing does not extend the time for paying the underlying tax. Interest and late payment penalties will still accrue from the date the original return was due.

Tax payments must be accompanied by FTB 3539 (Payment for Automatic Extension for Corps and Exempt Orgs). A single FTB 3539 may be filed for all affiliated corporations filing a combined report (¶1313). Corporations required to pay their tax liability by electronic funds transfer (EFT) (¶814) must remit all payments by EFT to avoid penalties and, thus, do not submit FTB 3539.

California incorporates federal law that extends filing deadlines for victims of Presidentially-declared disasters or terroristic or militaristic actions for a period of up to one year. (Sec. 18572, Rev. & Tax. Code)

The deadlines that may be postponed are the same as those that may be postponed by reason of a taxpayer's service in a combat zone (¶109).

• *Interest on late payments*

Interest is charged from the regular due date of the return to the date of payment, if the amount paid by the regular due date of the return (without regard to extensions) is less than the tax payable with the return. However, interest is abated for late payments made by corporations located in disaster areas (¶711). Interest is charged on late payments, at the rate charged on deficiencies as explained at ¶1410. See ¶1411 regarding the penalty for failure to pay by the regular due date, in cases where an extension is granted for filing.

• *Filing by mail*

Returns and requests for extension of time filed by mail are deemed to be filed on the date they are placed in the U.S. mail, provided they are properly addressed and the postage is prepaid. When the due date falls on a Saturday, Sunday, or other legal holiday, returns may be filed on the following business day. The date of the postmark is ordinarily deemed to be the date of mailing. Although it may be possible to prove that the return was actually mailed on an earlier date, it is obviously desirable to mail early enough to be sure the postmark is timely. (Note that a postage meter date is not a "postmark.") If private delivery services are used, items should be sent in time to be *received* by the deadline. (Sec. 1103, Govt. Code)

Returns should be mailed to the FTB in Sacramento, or filed with any area or district office. The Sacramento mailing address is shown in the return instructions.

• *Filing using electronic technology*

Although not mandated, many corporate and business entity forms may be filed electronically, including Forms 100, 100S, 100W, 568 (LLC return), and combined reports. The federal tax return must be e-filed along with the state tax return.

Corporation franchise and income tax returns and other documents that are filed using electronic technology must be in a form prescribed by the FTB. To participate in the business e-file program, a business must be accepted into the Internal Revenue Service and California e-file programs. In addition, taxpayers are required to complete and retain an electronic filing declaration, form FTB 8453-C, California e-file Return Authorization for Corporations, which must be furnished to the FTB upon request. Providers approved for the IRS Electronic Filing (e-file) Program are automatically enrolled in the California e-file Program. All of the information needed for business e-filing, including publications, rules, and a list of approved software providers, may be obtained by going to the FTB's Web site at www.ftb.ca.gov and searching for the term "Business e-file."

FTB 3586, Payment Voucher for Corporation E-filed Returns, must be used to remit payment for e-filed corporation franchise and income tax returns. The mailing address for payments with FTB 3586 is: Franchise Tax Board, P.O. Box 942857, Sacramento, CA 94257-0531.

California conforms to federal income tax provisions allowing electronic postmarks as proof of the date electronically filed returns are deemed filed.

• *Alternative signatures*

Unlike the IRS, the FTB does not offer an electronic signature option for its business e-file program. The business taxpayer, electronic return originator, and paid preparer must sign the California e-file Return Authorization Form (FTB 8453-C, FTB 8453-P, or FTB 8453-LLC) prior to the transmission of the e-file return. This form may be retained by the preparer or business taxpayer or be scanned and included as an attachment to the business e-file return. (*Frequently Asked Questions*, FTB, http://www.ftb.ca.gov/professionals/busefile/profaq.shtml#9)

• *Form for return*

Form 100 is used to file a California corporation franchise or income tax return. Schedules on the California return provide for adjustments and other information needed for state purposes. Corporations may substitute federal schedules for California schedules as long as they attach all supporting federal schedules and reconcile any differences between federal and California figures.

Corporations with total assets or $10 million or more as of the last day of the taxable year must attach either: (1) a copy of the Schedule M-3 (Form 1120); (2) a complete copy of the federal return; or (3) the Schedule M-3 (Form 1120) in a spreadsheet format. Corporations using the federal reconciliation method must transfer the amount from line 28 of Form 1120 to line 1, side 1, of Form 100, and attach the federal return and all pertinent schedules, or copy the information from page 1 of Form 1120 onto Schedule F and transfer the amount from line 30, Schedule F, to line 1, side 1, of Form 100. (Instructions, Form 100, Corporation Franchise or Income Tax Return)

Caution Note: FTB Developing California Schedule M-3

The FTB is currently working with interested parties to develop a California Schedule M-3 for the purpose of capturing information not reflected on the federal M-3 as a result of differences between California and federal tax laws, including differences between the federal consolidated reporting requirements and California's combined reporting requirements. Issues currently being examined by the FTB include what information, if any, would be required of foreign affiliates not included in a water's-edge combined report, the threshold income filing requirement, and the cost and time commitment for taxpayers and software developers to revise financial accounting systems and tax forms to capture the information that would be required by a California Schedule M-3.

Taxpayers should use, if possible, the return forms they receive from the FTB with their name, address, and corporate number already imprinted on the label; this is important to the FTB's handling of returns. If reproduced forms are used in lieu of the forms supplied by the FTB, the gummed label should be affixed to the reproduced form. Details of specifications and conditions for reproducing forms, and for computer-prepared forms, may be obtained from the FTB's Web site at http://www.ftb.ca.gov.

S corporations file Form 100S.

CCH Comment: Attaching Letters To Forms Inadvisable

The FTB advises tax practitioners against attaching letters to their clients' corporation franchise and income tax returns, stating that in most cases tax practitioners will get faster results by calling the FTB's Tax Practitioner Hotline at (916) 845-7057 to ask specific questions regarding their clients' tax returns or other issues requiring timely action. The Tax Practitioner Hotline is open from 8 a.m. to 5 p.m., Monday through Friday. Questions may also be sent by fax to (916) 845-6377, 24 hours a day, seven days a week. Often letters attached to returns are not answered until they have traveled through the FTB's entire return processing system and are ultimately rerouted to the FTB's Taxpayer Service Center for a reply, which may take many weeks. Also, letters are sometimes inadvertently filed without a reply. (*Tax News*, California Franchise Tax Board, July/August 2005)

• *Whole dollar reporting*

The California law conforms to federal law with respect to whole dollar reporting (sometimes referred to as "cents-less" reporting). Under these rules, if any amount required to be shown on a return, statement, or other document is other than a whole dollar, the fractional part of a dollar may be rounded to the nearest dollar; that is, amounts under 50¢ are dropped and amounts from 50¢ to 99¢ increased to the next dollar. (Sec. 18623, Rev. & Tax. Code)

• *Reporting federal changes*

A taxpayer filing an amended federal return is required to file an amended California return within six months if the change increases the amount of California tax due. Corporate taxpayers are required to report changes or corrections to any item required to be reported on a federal tax return within six months of the federal determination of the change or correction, regardless of whether the change or correction increases the amount of tax due. The "date of the final federal determination" is defined as the date that each adjustment or resolution resulting from an IRS examination is assessed pursuant to IRC Sec. 6203. (Sec. 18622, Rev. & Tax. Code)

The taxpayer is required to concede the accuracy of the federal determination or state where the determination is erroneous. Failure to comply with these requirements may result in extending the running of the statute of limitations on deficiency assessments (¶1409).

• *Exempt organizations*

If an exempt-organization return (¶811) is filed in good faith and the organization is later held to be taxable, the return filed is deemed a valid taxable return for the organization. Receivers, trustees in bankruptcy, or assignees operating the property or business of a corporation are required to file returns.

• *Report to Secretary of State*

Sections 1502 and 2117 of the Corporations Code require domestic and foreign corporations to file with the Secretary of State an annual report showing names of officers and directors and other information. The first report must be filed within 90 days of incorporation. Thereafter, reports are due annually by the date indicated by the Secretary of the State on the form mailed to the corporation. The tax law provides for assessment by the FTB of a penalty for failure to file this report (¶1411). Corporations may file a brief statement in lieu of the biennial report in cases where no changes have occurred during the filing period.

In addition to the annual report, publicly traded corporations and foreign corporations must annually file a sworn statement on a form provided by the Secretary of State that contains certain information, including the following:

— the name of the independent auditor that prepared the most recent report on the corporation's annual financial statements;

— a description of any other services performed for the corporation during its two most recent fiscal years and the period between the end of its most recent fiscal year and the date of the statement by the independent auditor, its parent corporation, or a subsidiary or corporate affiliate of the independent auditor or its parent corporation;

— the compensation for the corporation's most recent fiscal year that is paid to each member of the board of directors and paid to each of the five most highly compensated executive officers who are not members of the board, including any shares issued, options for shares granted, and similar equity-based compensation; and

— a description of any loan, including the loan amount and terms, made to any corporate board member during the corporation's two most recent fiscal years.

(Sec. 1502, Corp. Code; Sec. 1502.1, Corp. Code; Sec. 2117, Corp. Code; Sec. 2117.1, Corp. Code)

The statement is due within 150 days after the end of the corporation's fiscal year and will be open for public inspection.

• *Effect of failure to file or pay*

A corporation that fails to file a return or to make required payments may have its corporate rights suspended (¶824).

• *Filing date for DISCs*

California has nothing comparable to the special federal provisions for Domestic International Sales Corporations (DISCs). (Sec. 23051.5, Rev. & Tax. Code) Accordingly, the special federal filing date for such corporations has no application to California returns. See *Appeal of CerwinVega International* (1978) (CCH CALIFORNIA Tax Reports ¶ 89-202.40), in which penalties were imposed on a DISC for underpayment of estimated tax and late payment of tax.

¶811 Returns of Exempt Organizations

Law: Secs. 23703, 23771-78 (CCH CALIFORNIA TAX REPORTS ¶ 10-245).

Comparable Federal: Secs. 6012(a), 6033, 6652 (CCH U.S. MASTER TAX GUIDE ¶ 537, 625, 2145).

California Forms: Form 109 (California Exempt Organization Business Income Tax Return), Form 199 (California Exempt Organization Annual Information Return), FTB 3539 (Payment for Automatic Extension for Corps and Exempt Orgs).

Exempt organizations (including charitable trusts) are required to file annual information returns (Form 199). (Sec. 23771, Rev. & Tax. Code)

• *Exceptions to filing requirement*

The filing of information returns is not required for the following organizations and activities:

— churches;

— religious orders; and

— exempt organizations, except private foundations, with gross receipts of $25,000 or less.

(Sec. 23772, Rev. & Tax. Code)

According to the Instructions to Form 199, a three-year average is used to compute the $25,000 threshold discussed in the third item above. New organizations must file Form 199 if their gross receipts are $37,500 or less for their first year of existence or if their average gross receipts are $30,000 or less for their first two years of existence.

Some other organizations are excepted under discretionary authority of the Franchise Tax Board (FTB).

A religious organization that refuses to file because of religious convictions may be permitted to submit a notarized statement instead. (Sec. 23774, Rev. & Tax. Code)

• *Requirements for returns*

Although the California requirements for information returns are generally similar to the federal requirements, there are some differences and the FTB should be consulted in case of any question.

• *Private foundations*

California private foundations file Form 199 as do other exempt organizations. Instead of completing certain parts of the form, a private foundation may submit a completed copy of the current Form RRF-1, Registration/Renewal Fee Report (including federal Form 990) or a completed copy of federal Form 990-PF with appropriate schedules.

• *Filing with Registrar of Charitable Trusts*

In addition to the information return requirements discussed above, a charitable corporation, association, or a trustee holding property for charitable purposes is required to register with the Registrar of Charitable Trusts, in the office of the

Attorney General in Sacramento, and to file an annual report (RRF-1) with the Registry. (Some types of organizations, including churches, schools, and hospitals, are specifically exempted from this requirement.) An organization that fails to file a required registration or annual report with the Registry on or before the due date (four months and fifteen days after the close of the organization's calendar or fiscal year) or extended due date is subject to assessment of the minimum tax (¶816) and loss of its tax exemption for the period of noncompliance.

Charities with gross receipts or total assets of $25,000 or more must also file a copy of IRS Form 990, 990-EZ, or 990-PF and attachments with the Registry of Charitable Trusts (Instructions to Form RRF-1).

• *Filing fees*

The information returns discussed above (Form 199), with limited exceptions, must be accompanied by a $10 fee if filed on time (including extensions), or by a $25 fee if filed later. (Sec. 23772, Rev. Tax. Code)

• *Time for filing/penalties*

The due date for information returns and statements, including statements from Coverdell education savings accounts, is the 15th day of the fifth month (fourth month for Coverdell education savings accounts) following the end of the organization's taxable year. Employees' trusts and IRAs must file by the 15th day of the fourth month following the close of the taxable year. (Sec. 23771, Rev. & Tax. Code) An exempt organization that fails to timely file an information return without reasonable cause is subject to a penalty for late filing, at the rate of $5 per month, with a maximum of $40. Also, a special penalty of $5 per month, with a $25 maximum, may be imposed where a private foundation fails to respond to a demand for filing. (Sec. 23772, Rev. & Tax. Code)

• *Organizations penalized for failure to file*

In *Appeal of Young Women's Christian Association of Santa Monica* (1971) (CCH CALIFORNIA TAX REPORTS ¶10-245.75), the SBE upheld the imposition under prior law of the $100 minimum tax, plus interest, for failure to file annual information returns, despite the fact that the Internal Revenue Service did not require federal information returns for the years involved. The organization did not come within the exception for filing of returns by charitable organizations, because it did not establish compliance with the exception's requirement that the organization be "primarily supported by contributions of the general public."

• *Effect of failure to file or pay*

An exempt organization that fails to file required reports or to pay any tax due within 12 months from the close of its taxable year may have its corporate rights suspended or forfeited. Provision is made for relief from such suspension under certain conditions. Further, the FTB may revoke the organization's exemption if it fails to file any corporation franchise or income tax return or pay any tax due. (Sec. 23775 et. seq., Rev. & Tax. Code)

• *Extensions of time*

The FTB may grant a reasonable extension of time for filing a return or report of an exempt organization. Exempt organizations will be granted an automatic seven-month "paperless" extension. The extended due date is the 15th day of the twelfth month following the close of the taxable year (fiscal year filers) or December 15 (calendar year filers). An extension of time for filing does not extend the time for paying tax. Tax payments must be accompanied by FTB 3539 (Payment for Automatic Extension for Corps and Exempt Orgs). (Reg. 25402, 18 CCR)

• *Organizations with nonexempt income*

Exempt political organizations are not required to file the annual information returns or statements discussed above. (Sec. 23701r, Rev. & Tax. Code) However, such organizations that have more than $100 of income from sources other than contributions, dues, and political fund-raising ("exempt function income") should file a corporation income tax return. (See ¶808 for discussion of exemption for political organizations.)

Exempt homeowners' associations that have more than $100 of income from sources other than membership dues, fees, and assessments should file a corporation income tax return (¶915). (Sec. 23701t, Rev. & Tax. Code)

An exempt organization, other than a political organization, a homeowner's association, or an organization controlled by the state carrying out a state function, must file an exempt organization business income tax return (Form 109) in addition to its annual information return (Form 199) if it has gross income of $1,000 or more from an unrelated trade or business. The electronic funds transfer requirements discussed at ¶814 also apply to nonprofit corporations with nonexempt income.

• *Filing with Secretary of State*

Sections 6210 and 8210 of the California Nonprofit Corporation Law require nonprofit corporations to file with the Secretary of State an annual report showing names of officers and other information. The tax law provides for assessment by the FTB of a penalty for failure to file this report (¶1411).

¶812 Consolidated Returns

Law: Sec. 23361-64a (CCH CALIFORNIA TAX REPORTS ¶89-102).

Comparable Federal: Sec. 1501-4 (CCH U.S. MASTER TAX GUIDE ¶295).

The law contains provision for filing of consolidated franchise tax returns by certain groups of railroad corporations, where the degree of affiliation through a common parent corporation is 80% or more. Unlike federal law, California law contains no general provisions allowing affiliated groups of corporations other than railroads the privilege of making consolidated returns. However, the Franchise Tax Board may require any affiliated corporations to file a consolidated return to prevent tax evasion or to clearly reflect income earned by the corporations from business in this state (¶1110). (Sec. 23361 et seq., Rev. & Tax. Code)

Although California permits only railroad corporations to file *consolidated returns,* California does permit or require *combined reports* by corporations owned or controlled by the same interests, under some conditions. See ¶1310 for further discussion of combined reporting.

Because California does not incorporate IRC Sec. 1504, which defines affiliated groups, California does not adopt amendments to IRC Sec. 1504, that allowed corporations to offset their income with net operating losses incurred by an Alaska Native Corporation. (*The Pillsbury Co. v. Franchise Tax Board* (2004) (CCH CALIFORNIA TAX REPORTS ¶10-515.61))

¶813 Estimated Tax

Law: Secs. 19010, 19021-27, 19136.8, 19142-61, 19363-64, 26081.5 (CCH CALIFORNIA TAX REPORTS ¶89-104, 89-206, 89-210).

Comparable Federal: Secs. 6611, 6655 (CCH U.S. MASTER TAX GUIDE ¶225 et seq., 2765, 2890).

California Forms: Form 100-ES (Corporation Estimated Tax), FTB 5806 (Underpayment of Estimated Tax by Corporations).

All corporations and exempt organizations subject to franchise or income tax, other than REMICs, are required to pay estimated tax during the taxable year. The estimated tax of a corporation subject to the franchise tax cannot be less than the minimum tax (¶816). (Sec. 19025, Rev. & Tax. Code) Instructions to FTB 5806 state that a newly formed or qualified corporation is required to make estimated tax payments based on its estimated tax liability after credits for its first taxable year. To avoid a penalty, the taxpayer should use its annualized current year income.

If an S corporation has a qualified subchapter S subsidiary (QSub) (discussed at ¶806), the S corporation's estimated tax payments must not be less than the S corporation's minimum tax plus the subsidiary's minimum tax. (Reg. 25562, 18 CCR) California law does not require corporations to file declarations, but they must file their estimated tax with payment vouchers (Form 100-ES). Banks and financial corporations should compute their estimated tax at the special rate for such taxpayers explained at ¶816. California has not adopted the federal provision that waives the underpayment penalty if the tax shown on the return is less than $500.

See ¶814 for a discussion of taxpayers required to submit estimated tax payments through electronic funds transfer. Such corporations do not submit a Form 100-ES.

• *Computation of estimated tax payments*

Practice Note: "Tax" Defined

For purposes of the estimated tax requirements, "tax" includes the alternative minimum tax, taxes from Schedule D, excess net passive income tax, and the minimum franchise tax. (Instructions, FTB 5806, Underpayment of Estimated Tax by Corporations).

If the estimated tax is not over the minimum tax, the entire amount is payable on the 15th day of the fourth month of the corporation's taxable year. For S corporations, this includes the minimum tax for a QSub incorporated in California, qualified to do business in California, or doing business in California. If the QSub is acquired after the due date for the first installment, the minimum tax for the QSub is due with the next required installment. (Sec. 19025, Rev. & Tax. Code) (Instructions, Form 100-ES, Corporation Estimated Tax)

Estimated tax over the minimum tax is payable in installments on the 15th day of the fourth, sixth, ninth, and 12th months of the taxable year, respectively. Applicable to installments due for each taxable year beginning after 2008, the amount of the installment payments is equal to 30% of the estimated amount due for the first two installments, decreased to 20% of the estimated amount due for the last two installments. However, an exception applies if the corporation is not required to make the first installment payment, in which case the corporation is required to make the subsequent installment payments as follows: 40% of the estimated tax liability for the second installment and 30% of the estimated tax liability for the third and fourth installments. (Instructions, FTB 5806, Underpayment of Estimated Tax by Corporations) Previously, estimated tax was payable in four equal installments of 25% of the estimated amount due. The first installment generally may not be less than the minimum tax, unless the taxpayer is a newly formed or qualified corporation, has been granted an exemption by the Franchise Tax Board, or is subject to income tax only (rather than franchise tax) under California law.

***Practitioner Comment:* 2008 Budget Legislation Makes Significant Changes in the Estimated Tax Payment Area**

SB X1 28, enacted on October 1, 2008, made several changes in the estimated tax payment area. For example, the tax payment installments were accelerated to 30% of total tax liability for the first two installments (and 20% of liability for the third and fourth installment) for tax years beginning in 2009. Taxpayers will need to carefully consider the impact of law changes, such as the net operating loss (NOL) suspension and 50% of liability credit limitation applicable in 2008 and 2009 in determining their estimated tax payments in 2009.

In addition, AB 1452 requires that the LLC fee be estimated and paid by the 15th day of the six month of the current taxable year beginning in 2009. Formerly the fee was due by the original due date of the LLC return (generally April 15 of the following year). It appears that the law change does not affect the timing of the payment of $800 minimum tax.

Bruce Daigh, Chris Whitney, Contributing Editors

Practice Tip: Extensions for Hurricane Ike, Hurricane Gustav, and Southern California Fire Victims

The FTB will follow the updated federal tax postponement dates for state taxpayers affected by Hurricane Ike, Hurricane Gustav, and the Southern California fires that occurred in November 2008. Hurricane victims have until January 5, 2009, to file returns, pay taxes, and perform other time-sensitive acts. The extended deadline for Southern California fire victims is February 11, 2009. (*Press Releases*, California Franchise Tax Board, September 5, 2008, September 18, 2008, and November 20, 2008)

If the requirements for making payments of estimated tax are first met after the first day of the fourth month, the payments are spread over the appropriate remaining quarters, depending on the quarter in which the requirements are first met, as in the case of the federal tax.

Practice Pointer: TIPRA Amendments Not Followed

California does not conform to the change in timing of certain corporate estimated tax installment payments enacted by the federal Tax Increase Prevention and Reconciliation Act of 2005. (*Instructions*, Form 5806, Underpayment of Estimated Tax by Corporations)

• *Accounting periods less than 12 months*

When the first accounting period is less than 12 months, the estimated tax payments should be made as follows (for calendar-year taxpayers; others should adjust dates accordingly) (Reg. 19027, 18 CCR). [Note that the regulation and the information noted below has not yet been updated to reflect the change in the estimated tax installment percentages from equal installments of 25% to 30% for the first two installments and 20% for the last two installments, applicable to installments due for the 2009 taxable year. Taxpayers should consult the FTB's latest forms and information for the appropriate figures] :

Taxable Year Begins	*Number of Installments*	*Percent to Be Paid*	*Due Date-15th*
Jan. 1-Jan. 16	4	25%	Apr.-June-Sept.-Dec.
Jan. 17-Mar. 16	3	$33^1/_3$	June-Sept.-Dec.
Mar. 17-June 15	2	50	Sept.-Dec.
June 16-Sept. 15	1	100	Dec.
Sept. 16-Dec. 31	None		

• *Penalty for underpayment*

A penalty, in the form of an addition to the tax, is imposed when there has been an underpayment of estimated tax. (Sec. 19142, Rev. & Tax. Code) The additional tax is computed as a percentage of the amount of the underpayment, for the period of underpayment. (Sec. 19144, Rev. & Tax. Code)

The penalty rate is the same as the interest rate on deficiencies and refunds, which is established semiannually (see ¶711 for rates). However, the penalty rate is not compounded.

An underpayment is defined as the excess of the amount that would be required to be paid on each installment of estimated tax if the estimated tax were equal to 100% of the tax shown on the return, over the amount actually paid on or before the due date of each installment. The tax shown on an amended return filed after the original due date, including extensions, or the tax as finally determined, is not to be used in computing underpayment penalties. If the tax due is the minimum tax and the corporation is not a "large corporation" (see discussion below), then the addition to the tax because of underpayment of any installment is calculated on the amount of the minimum tax. (Sec. 19144, Rev. & Tax. Code; Sec. 19147, Rev. & Tax. Code)

The period of underpayment runs from the due date of each installment to the normal due date of the return, or to the date on which the underpayment was paid, if payment was made prior to the due date of the return. (Sec. 19145, Rev. & Tax. Code)

• *Exceptions to underpayment penalty*

No penalty may be imposed for underpayment of estimated tax to the extent the underpayment was created or increased as the direct result of the following:

— an erroneous levy, erroneous processing action, or erroneous collection action by the FTB (Sec. 19136.7, Rev. & Tax. Code); or

— legislation chaptered and operative for the taxable year of the underpayment. (Sec. 19142(b), Rev. & Tax. Code).

CCH Comment: Federal Legislation

The relief discussed above does not apply to federal law changes that may create an underpayment of state tax, because federal law is enacted without being chaptered. (Bill Analysis, Ch. 242 (S.B. 14), Laws 2005, Senate Floor, August 23, 2005)

CCH Comment: No Excuses

Except as noted above, the estimated tax underpayment penalty is mandatory and will be imposed unless one of the six exceptions below applies. There is no good cause or lack of willful neglect exception. (Sec. 19147, Rev. & Tax. Code; Sec. 19148, Rev. & Tax Code)

California shields a corporation from penalty if the following conditions are satisfied:

— total payments equal or exceed the tax shown on the prior year's return, prorated to each installment (this exception has limited application to "large corporations");

— the installment meets the required percentage of the tax due, computed by placing the taxpayer's net income (or alternative minimum taxable income, if applicable) on an annualized basis as outlined by statute;

— the required percentage of the tax for the taxable year was paid by withholding;

— the required percentage of the net income for the taxable year consisted of items subject to withholding and the amount of the first installment was at least equal to the minimum tax.

(Sec. 19147, Rev. & Tax. Code)

Practitioner Comment: Upon Challenge—Exception to Annualized Income Exception

In a non-citable summary decision, the State Board of Equalization abated a corporation's penalty for underpayment of estimated tax for the first and fourth quarters, when it met the "annualized income" exception. The corporation was still liable for the penalty in the second and third quarters. Under Cal. Rev. & Tax. Code Sec. 19147, taxpayers claiming the "annualized income" exception must meet the applicable percentages in all four quarters. Accordingly, where the FTB imposes a material estimated tax penalty, taxpayers may want to consider an appeal if the annualized income exception is met in one or more of the quarters. (*Howard Hughes Medical Institute*, California State Board of Equalization, No. 246269, August 24, 2004, CCH CALIFORNIA TAX REPORTS ¶ 89-206.33)

Bruce Daigh, Chris Whitney, Contributing Editors

For corporations going through bankruptcy proceedings, an underpayment penalty will not apply if

— the tax was incurred by the estate and the failure to pay the tax occurred pursuant to a court finding of the probable insufficiency of funds of the estate to pay administrative expenses; or

— the tax was incurred by the debtor before a court order for relief or the appointment of a trustee, and the petition was filed before the date of the tax. (Sec. 19147, Rev. & Tax. Code)

Practice Tip: California/Federal Difference

Under California law, the exceptions are computed on a cumulative basis. This differs from federal law, which requires only 25% of the annual payment for each installment (Instructions, FTB 5806, Underpayment of Estimated Tax by Corporations).

Finally, as under IRC Sec. 6655(e), corporations that earn seasonal income are not subject to an underpayment penalty if they have seasonal income for any six consecutive months of the taxable year and if they had in the preceding three taxable years taxable income for the same six-month period that averaged 70% or more of the total income for the taxable year. Such corporations may annualize their income by assuming that the income is earned in the current year in the same pattern as in the preceding taxable years. Estimated income taxes would be required to be paid in the same seasonal pattern in which earned. (Sec. 19148, Rev. & Tax. Code)

• *Special rules for large corporations*

For both California and federal purposes, a corporation that had taxable income of at least $1 million in any of its three immediately preceding taxable years is subject to an underpayment penalty if it fails to make estimated tax payments satisfying the required percentage of the current year's tax liability, even if the corporation's payments equal or exceed the amount of tax shown on its return for the prior year. A large corporation's tax liability for the prior year may, however, be used to determine the first installment of estimated tax for the current year, provided any difference is made up in the next installment. (Sec. 19147, Rev. & Tax. Code)

• *Reporting of underpayment*

Where the figures on the return indicate that there has been an underpayment of estimated tax, FTB 5806 should be attached to show the computation of penalty or to explain why no penalty is due. (Federal forms should not be used with California returns.)

To request a waiver of underpayment penalties created or increased by a provision of law chaptered and operative for the taxable year of the underpayment, taxpayers should:

— use FTB 5806 to compute the full underpayment penalty that would normally be due;

— write "Waiver" across the top of FTB 5806;

— attach an explanation to FTB 5806 giving the specific law change that caused the underpayment and showing the computation and the amount of penalty to be waived; and

— attach FTB 5806 to the face of the return.

A second form FTB 5806, clearly marked "Second form FTB 5806" may be used to show the computation of any penalty not related to a change in the law. (Instructions, FTB 5806, Underpayment of Estimated Tax by Corporations)

• *Penalty strictly applied*

In *Appeal of Bechtel Incorporated* (1978) (CCH CALIFORNIA TAX REPORTS ¶89-210.301), the taxpayer made estimated-tax payments in irregular amounts, totaling $495,000, against an ultimate liability of $1,059,849. The taxpayer claimed relief from penalty on the ground that the total payments exceeded the tax of $459,795 shown on its return for the preceding year. The State Board of Equalization (SBE) held that an underpayment penalty of $13,547 was properly imposed on the first two installments, because they did not meet the specific requirements for avoidance of penalty based on the preceding year's tax.

In *Appeal of Decoa, Inc.* (1976) (CCH CALIFORNIA TAX REPORTS ¶89-210.302), the taxpayer was a Florida corporation that began doing business in California in 1973. The corporation failed to pay estimated tax for its 1973 income year. The SBE held that the underpayment penalty was mandatory and could not be excused because of "extenuating circumstances." Relief was not available under the rules based on the preceding year's return, because such a return had not been filed and was not required to be filed. See also *Appeal of International Business Machines Corporation* (1979) (CCH CALIFORNIA TAX REPORTS ¶89-210.303) and *J.F. Shea Co., Inc.* (1979) (CCH CALIFORNIA TAX REPORTS ¶89-210.302); in the latter case an underpayment of $1,100 resulted in a penalty of $8,500.

In *Appeal of Uniroyal, Inc.* (1975) (CCH CALIFORNIA TAX REPORTS ¶89-206.58), the taxpayer could have avoided an underpayment penalty by timely payment of estimated tax of $100 (based on preceding year's tax, before the minimum was increased to $200). However, because the corporation was unable to prove it had filed or paid estimated tax, the penalty was based on the actual tax of $77,895, in accordance with the definition of "underpayment" set forth above. See also *Appeal of Lumbermans Mortgage Company* (1976) (CCH CALIFORNIA TAX REPORTS ¶89-210.302), to the same effect.

• *Refund/credit of overpayment*

Where payments of estimated tax are made and the total amount of tax due on the completed return is subsequently determined to be less than the estimated tax payments, the balance will be refunded or will be credited against other taxes. An overpayment from a prior year return will be credited as of the first estimated installment due date or the date of payment, whichever is later. No interest is payable on overpayments for the period prior to the due date of the return. Further, no interest will be payable if the refund or credit is made within 90 days after the due date or 90 days after the return is filed, whichever is later. See also ¶1419.

If any overpayment of tax is claimed as a credit against estimated tax for the succeeding taxable year, that amount shall be considered as payment of the tax for the succeeding taxable year (whether or not claimed as a credit in the return of estimated tax for the succeeding taxable year), and no claim for credit or refund of that overpayment will be allowed for the taxable year in which the overpayment occurred. (Sec. 19002(e), Rev. & Tax. Code)

• *Combined reports*

In the case of corporations entitled or required to file a combined report, a combined payment of estimated taxes may be made for the group by the parent or other designated "key" corporation, under the procedure described at ¶1313. Alternatively, each member may make its own payments and have its payments applied against the ultimate tax liability of the combined group. (FTB Pub. 1061, Guidelines for Corporations Filing a Combined Report)

• *DISCs required to file*

California has nothing comparable to the special federal provisions for Domestic International Sales Corporations (DISCs). (Sec. 23051.5, Rev. & Tax. Code) Accordingly, such corporations are subject to the regular California rules for payment of estimated tax. See *Appeal of Cerwin-Vega International* (1978) (CCH CALIFORNIA TAX REPORTS ¶89-206.481), in which penalties were imposed on a DISC for underpayment of estimated tax and late payment of tax.

¶814 Payment of Tax

Law: Secs. 18572, 18604, 19001, 19004, 19005, 19008, 19011, 19021; Reg. 19591, 18 CCR (CCH CALIFORNIA TAX REPORTS ¶89-108).

Comparable Federal: Secs. 6151, 6161, 6601, 7508A (CCH U.S. MASTER TAX GUIDE ¶215, 2529, 2537).

Unless a taxpayer enters into an installment agreement (see below), taxpayers, including banks and financial corporations, must pay, on or before the due date of the return, the entire balance of tax due after applying the advance payments made under the estimated tax procedure outlined at ¶813. (Sec. 19001, Rev. & Tax. Code) Payment in the form of a check must be payable in U.S. funds. (Sec. 19005, Rev. & Tax. Code) To expedite processing, it is suggested that payments for balance due and for estimated payments should not be combined in one check. The corporation number should be shown on each check.

• *Extension of time*

An extension of time for filing the return does not extend the time for payment of the tax (¶810). (Sec. 18604, Rev. & Tax. Code) However, various filing and payment deadlines may be extended for victims of federally-declared disasters or terroristic or militaristic actions for a period of up to one year. The deadlines that may be postponed are the same as those that may be postponed by reason of a taxpayer's service in a combat zone (¶109). (Sec. 18572, Rev. & Tax. Code)

• *Payment by mail*

Under Sec. 11002, Govt. Code, a payment is deemed to be made on the date it is mailed, provided the envelope is properly addressed and the postage is prepaid. The federal rule is similar.

• *Payment by electronic funds transfer*

The Franchise Tax Board must allow payments to be made by electronic funds transfer (EFT). Such payments will generally be deemed complete on the date the transfer is initiated. A taxpayer whose estimated tax liability exceeds $20,000 or more with respect to any installment, or whose total tax liability exceeds $80,000 in any taxable year must remit payment by such electronic means. (Sec. 19011, Rev. & Tax. Code)

Once a taxpayer is required to make payments by EFT, all subsequent payments must be made by EFT regardless of the taxable year to which the payments apply. However, a taxpayer may elect to discontinue making payments in this manner if the threshold amounts set forth above were not met for the preceding taxable year.

A taxpayer required to remit estimated tax payments electronically may satisfy the requirement by means of an international funds transfer.

A penalty of 10% is imposed if mandated payments are made by other means, unless it is shown that failure to use EFT was for reasonable cause.

• *Installment agreement*

The FTB may enter into an agreement with a taxpayer that allows the taxpayer to pay the full or partial amount of outstanding corporation franchise or income taxes, interest, and penalties due in installments if the FTB determines that the taxpayer's situation is one of financial hardship. (Sec. 19008, Rev. & Tax. Code)

Comment: Business Entity Applications

Business entities may request an installment payment arrangement for the payment of unpaid California corporation franchise or income taxes by calling the FTB at 1-888-635-0494. (*FTB Notice 2005-5*, California Franchise Tax Board, October 7, 2005, CCH CALIFORNIA TAX REPORTS ¶403-903) The fee for business entities to enter into an installment payment plan is $35. (Reg. 19591, 18 CCR)

¶815 Tax Base

Law: Sec. 24341 (CCH CALIFORNIA TAX REPORTS ¶10-505).

Comparable Federal: Sec. 63 (CCH U.S. MASTER TAX GUIDE ¶126).

The California franchise tax and income tax are imposed generally upon net income. "Net income" is defined as the gross income less the deductions allowed. (Sec. 24341, Rev. & Tax. Code) For a discussion of "gross income," see Chapter 9; for "deductions," see Chapter 10.

For taxpayers using the federal reconciliation method (¶803), a corporation begins its net income computation with its federal taxable income, modifies it to account for differences between California and federal law, and, if the corporation also does business in other states, allocates and apportions the modified amount to determine the portion taxable by California.

¶816 Tax Rates

Law: Secs. 17942, 23114, 23151-54, 23181-88, 23501, 23802 (CCH CALIFORNIA TAX REPORTS ¶10-215, 10-340, 10-380).

Comparable Federal: None.

The rate of franchise tax and income tax on corporations other than banks and financial corporations or S corporations is 8.84%. (Sec. 23151, Rev. & Tax. Code; Sec. 23501, Rev. & Tax. Code)

• *S corporation rate*

California subjects all S corporations, other than financial corporations, to franchise and income tax at a special 1.5% rate. Financial corporations that are S corporations are taxed at a higher rate of 3.5%. (Sec. 23802, Rev. & Tax. Code)

• *Bank and financial corporation rate*

Financial institutions pay a higher rate, commonly called the "bank rate," designed to equalize the tax burden between financial institutions and other taxpayers. The bank rate is simply equal to the franchise tax rate on nonfinancial corporations plus 2%. Currently, the rate is 10.84%. (Sec. 23802, Rev. & Tax. Code; Sec. 23186, Rev. & Tax. Code)

The reason for the special bank rate is that banks and financial corporations are not subject to personal property taxes and license fees. The additional tax imposed by the bank rate is in lieu of the personal property taxes and license fees that are paid by nonfinancial corporations.

• *Constitutionality of bank rate upheld*

In *Security-First National Bank of Los Angeles, et al. v. Franchise Tax Board* (1961) (CCH CALIFORNIA TAX REPORTS ¶10-105.30), the California Supreme Court upheld the constitutional right of the state to tax banks at the special bank rate. The court held that, because the purpose of the special rate is to equalize tax burdens within the state, it is within the power of the legislature to authorize such taxing procedure and the tax is constitutional.

• *Minimum tax*

The amount of the minimum tax is $800, with some exceptions. The minimum tax is $25 for (1) corporations engaged in gold mining that have been inactive since 1950, and (2) corporations engaged in quicksilver mining that have been inactive since 1971 or have been inactive for a period of 24 consecutive months. In addition, credit unions and nonprofit cooperative associations that are certified by their local board of supervisors are exempt from any minimum tax. However, a credit union must prepay a tax of $25 when it incorporates under the laws of California or when it qualifies to transact business in California. (Sec. 23153, Rev. & Tax. Code)

A domestic bank or corporation that files a certificate of dissolution with the Secretary of State and does no business thereafter is not subject to minimum tax for taxable years beginning on or after the date of the filing. (Sec. 23153, Rev. & Tax. Code)

A corporation is also not subject to the minimum tax if it did no business in the state during the taxable year and its taxable year was 15 days or less. (Sec. 23114, Rev. & Tax. Code) In addition, a domestic limited liability company (LLC) that has not conducted any business in California and that has obtained a certificate of cancellation within 12 months from the date that the articles of organization were filed is exempt from the minimum tax. However, the LLC will not be entitled to a refund of any taxes or fees already paid. (Sec. 17941, Rev. & Tax. Code)

Liability for the tax commences with the earlier of the date of incorporation, qualification, or commencing to do business within California, until the effective date of dissolution or withdrawal, or, if later, the date the corporation ceases to do business within California. (Sec. 23153, Rev. & Tax. Code) Once articles of incorporation are filed with the California Secretary of State, a corporation is subject to the franchise tax unless it is specifically exempt—see *Appeal of Mammouth Academy* (1973) (CCH CALIFORNIA TAX REPORTS ¶10-210.27).

See also *Appeal of Mission Valley East* (1974) (CCH CALIFORNIA TAX REPORTS ¶10-380.47). In this case the Secretary of State permitted the filing of articles of incorporation, but there was a conflict of corporate name and the corporation was not permitted to pursue its business activity. The State Board of Equalization (SBE) held that the corporation was nevertheless subject to the franchise tax. If the foreign corporation is qualified in the state, it is required to pay the minimum franchise tax even though it does not engage in business in the state; see *Appeal of Tip Top Delights, Inc.* (1970) (CCH CALIFORNIA TAX REPORTS ¶10-380.261).

Final year.— A corporation is not required to pay the minimum tax if it does the following:

— files a timely final franchise tax return for a taxable year with the Franchise Tax Board (FTB);

— does not do business in this state after the end of the taxable year for which the final franchise tax return was filed; and

— files a certificate of dissolution or surrender with the Secretary of State's Office before the end of the 12-month period beginning with the date the final franchise tax return was filed. (Sec. 23332, Rev. & Tax. Code)

Taxpayers do not need to provide a tax clearance certificate from the FTB prior to obtaining a certificate of dissolution or surrender.

Practitioner Comment: Timely Filing of Certificates of Dissolution for Inactive Entities Can Save Minimum Tax

A limited partnership was found to be liable for the $800 minimum partnership tax for years after it had transferred all of its assets to a limited liability company and ceased operations because the limited partnership failed to file a cancellation certificate, the California State Board of Equalization (SBE) ruled. Under Cal. Rev. & Tax Code Sec. 17935, every limited partnership that has filed a certificate of limited partnership with the state must pay the annual tax until a certificate of cancellation is filed. As it was undisputed that the limited partnership failed to file a cancellation certificate, the SBE held that the minimum partnership tax was due, notwithstanding the fact that the transferee LLC filed and paid tax as an LLC for the same years [Uncitable Summary Decision, *Appeal of Cinema Plaza Partners, LP.*, Cal. State Bd. of Equal., No 207907, November 18, 2003 (CCH CALIFORNIA TAX REPORTS ¶10-225.30)].

Similarly, a corporation was liable for the minimum tax for the year in which it surrendered its operations to another corporation because a certificate of dissolution was not timely filed with the Secretary of State. Despite the fact that the corporation had filed a "final" tax return and had clearly surrendered its business operations, state law provides that a corporation remains subject to the minimum tax until it files a certificate of dissolution with the Secretary of State. In the instant case, the certificate was not filed until more than two years after the "final" return was filed (*Red Bud Industries*, Cal. State Bd. of Equal., No. 224004, March 23, 2004 (CCH CALIFORNIA TAX REPORTS ¶10-215.35)).

Bruce Daigh, Chris Whitney, Contributing Editors

Corporations that incorporate or qualify to do business in California are not subject to the minimum franchise tax for the corporations' first taxable year. (Sec. 23153, Rev. & Tax. Code) This exemption does not apply to limited partnerships, LLCs, limited liability partnerships, regulated investment companies, real estate investment trusts, real estate mortgage investment conduits, financial asset securitization investment trusts, and qualified Subchapter S subsidiaries.

The minimum tax should not be confused with the alternative minimum tax (¶817).

• *What is a "financial corporation"*

Franchise Tax Board (FTB) Reg. 23183, 18 CCR, defines a "financial corporation" as one that deals predominantly in money or moneyed capital in substantial competition with the business of national banks. (The definition explicitly excludes corporations that are principally engaged in the business of leasing tangible personal property.) A corporation deals "predominantly" in money or moneyed capital if over 50% of its gross income is attributable to such dealings. However, a corporation's status does not change as a result of an occasional year in which its gross income from money dealings goes over or under the 50% level.

A corporation's classification as a financial (or nonfinancial) corporation changes only if there is a shift in the predominant character of its gross income for two consecutive years and the average of its gross income in the current and two immediately preceding years satisfies (or fails) the predominance test. Substantial amounts of gross income arising from incidental or occasional asset sales (such as the sale of a headquarters building) are excluded for these purposes.

In Legal Ruling 94-2 (CCH CALIFORNIA TAX REPORTS ¶10-340.98), the FTB stated its position that corporations whose principal business activity is the finance leasing of tangible personal property are properly classified as financial corporations because such corporations predominantly deal in money or moneyed capital in substantial competition with the business of national banks. A "finance lease" is a lease that is of the type permitted to be made by national banks and is the economic equivalent of an extension of credit.

In Chief Counsel Ruling 2007-1 (CCH CALIFORNIA TAX REPORTS ¶404-330), the FTB stated that income from nonfinancial activities did not equate to "financial income" for purposes of satisfying the 50% gross income threshold. At issue was whether interest income and gains on sales from intangibles generated from a nonfinancial activity could be considered financial income if it was of the same character as income earned from a bank. However, the FTB concluded that the gross measurement test focuses on the activity that generated the income, not the character of the income generated.

Financial classification may result when only a portion of a corporation's income is derived from financial activities, but the financial corporation rate will nevertheless apply to its entire taxable income.

• *Decisions of courts and State Board of Equalization*

For a discussion of the principal factors that have been considered by the courts and the State Board of Equalization (SBE) in determining financial-corporation status, see *Appeals of Delta Investment Co., Inc. and Delta Investment Research Corporation* (1978) (CCH CALIFORNIA TAX REPORTS ¶10-340.82). In that case the taxpayers were held to be taxable as financial corporations, although their loans were made primarily to affiliated corporations and they contended that their financial activities did not constitute the major aspect of their operations.

In *Appeal of Southern Securities Corporation* (1977) (CCH CALIFORNIA TAX REPORTS ¶10-340.81), the taxpayer was engaged in several activities, including use of surplus funds for real estate loans. The SBE held that the taxpayer was taxable as a "financial corporation."

In *Appeal of Cal-West Business Services, Inc.* (1970) (CCH CALIFORNIA TAX REPORTS ¶10-340.84), the SBE held that a corporation that purchased small retail customers' accounts and performed credit, billing, and bookkeeping services on the purchased accounts was taxable as a financial corporation. The SBE found that the taxpayer was in "substantial competition" with national banks in its locality, although testimony showed that the banks generally would not be interested in purchasing the same accounts. See also *Appeal of Atlas Acceptance Corporation* (1981) (CCH CALIFORNIA TAX REPORTS ¶10-340.97), to the same effect; this case involved the purchase and the collection of health spa membership contracts.

In *Appeal of the Diners' Club, Inc.* (1967) (CCH CALIFORNIA TAX REPORTS ¶10-340.91), the SBE held that a credit card company was taxable as a financial corporation because the corporate business was to deal in money and was in substantial competition with national banks.

In *Appeal of Stockholders Liquidating Corp.* (1963) (CCH CALIFORNIA TAX REPORTS ¶10-340.90), the SBE held that a mortgage loan correspondent, servicing mortgages it placed with an insurance company, was taxable as a financial corporation. It was determined that the taxpayer dealt in money and competed with national banks. To the same effect, see *Marble Mortgage Co. v. Franchise Tax Board* (1966) (CCH CALIFORNIA TAX REPORTS ¶10-340.79), decided by the California District Court of Appeal.

In *Appeal of Humphreys Finance Co., Inc.* (1960) (CCH CALIFORNIA TAX REPORTS ¶10-340.692), the SBE held that a corporation engaged solely in the purchase of conditional sales contracts arising out of the sale of personal property by a corporation affiliated with it through common control was properly classified as a financial corporation. It was determined that the taxpayer met the two tests for classification as a financial corporation: (1) it dealt primarily in money, as distinguished from other commodities; and (2) it was in substantial competition with national banks.

In *Appeal of Motion Picture Financial Corporation* (1958) (CCH CALIFORNIA TAX REPORTS ¶10-340.94), the SBE held that a corporation organized to finance motion pictures was a "financial corporation," even though it made loans which a national bank would not make and such loans were made only to a controlling shareholder.

¶817 Alternative Minimum Tax

Law: Secs. 23036, 23036.1, 23400, 23453, 23455, 23455.5, 23456, 23456.5, 23457, 23459, 24449 (CCH CALIFORNIA TAX REPORTS ¶10-385).

Comparable Federal: Secs. 53, 55-59, 291 (CCH U.S. MASTER TAX GUIDE ¶1370, 1401—1480).

California Form: Sch. P (100) (Alternative Minimum Tax and Credit Limitations—Corporations).

California imposes an alternative minimum tax (AMT) on corporations, other than S corporations, in substantial conformity to the federal AMT. (Sec. 23400, Rev. & Tax. Code)

The California AMT is calculated in the same manner as the federal AMT, except California requires modifications to the federal adjustments made in computing alternative minimum taxable income (AMTI) and items of tax preference. For California purposes, "regular tax," used in the calculation of the AMT, means either the California corporation franchise tax, the California corporate income tax, or the California tax on unrelated business income of an exempt organization or trust, before application of any credits. (Sec. 23455, Rev. & Tax. Code)

California does not conform to the federal law providing an AMT exemption for small corporations. (Sec. 23455.5, Rev. & Tax. Code)

The tentative minimum tax, used for the calculation of the California AMT, is equal to 6.65% (the federal rate is 20%) of the amount by which AMTI for the taxable year exceeds the exemption amount.

In computing AMTI California makes the following modifications:

— for purposes of the alternative tax net operating loss deduction, federal references to December 31, 1986, and January 1, 1987, are modified to refer to December 31, 1987, and January 1, 1988, respectively (also, California has not incorporated an increase in the limits placed on the alternative tax net operating loss deduction by the Job Creation and Worker Assistance Act of 2002);

— adjustments for mining exploration/development costs are applicable only to years beginning after 1987 (after 1986 for federal purposes);

— the adjustment available for pollution control facilities may be made for California purposes only if the facility is located in California and certified by the State Air Resources Board or the State Water Resources Control Board; and

— California (but not federal) law requires that if a corporation elected to depreciate a grapevine that was replanted in a vineyard as a result of phylloxera or Pierce's Disease infestation over 5 years instead of 20 years for regular tax purposes (¶1011), it must depreciate the grapevine over 10 years for AMT purposes. (Sec. 23456, Rev. & Tax. Code)

California adopts the federal adjustments on the basis of adjusted current earnings, as specified in IRC Sec. 56(g), with the following modifications:

— although California adopts federal provisions enacted under the Revenue Reconciliation Act of 1993 that eliminate the depreciation adjustment to adjusted current earnings for corporate property placed in service after December 31, 1993, the adjustment is applicable for California purposes in taxable years beginning after 1997;

— depreciation allowed on non-ACRS property placed in service after 1980 and before 1987 is the amount that would have been allowable had the taxpayer depreciated the property under the straight-line method for each year of the useful life for which the property had been held; depreciation allowed on non-MACRS property placed in service after 1986 and before 1990 is the amount determined under the Alternate Depreciation System of IRC Sec. 168(g);

— California does not follow IRC Sec. 56(g)(4)(C)(ii), (iii), and (iv) relating to the federal dividend deduction;

— California follows IRC Sec. 56(g)(4)(D)(ii) in disallowing the current deduction of circulation expenditures and the amortization of organizational expenditures; however, such deduction or amortization could be different under federal and California law, and an appropriate modification must be made to reflect the difference;

— corporations subject to the income tax and, therefore, not subject to the minimum franchise tax, limit the interest income included in adjusted current earnings to the amount included for purposes of the regular tax;

— the interest expense deducted in determining adjusted current earnings is the same as the interest deduction for purposes of the regular California tax; a modification must be made to reflect any differences between the California and federal interest deductions in computing the regular taxes;

— California law requires corporations whose income is subject to allocation and apportionment to calculate their adjustments based on adjusted current earnings by allocating and apportioning adjusted current earnings in the same manner as net income is allocated and apportioned for purposes of the regular tax;

— Although California technically conforms to the provisions of IRC Sec. 56(g)(4)(C) that allow deductions for purposes of computing adjusted current earnings for amounts deductible under IRC Sec. 199 (domestic production deduction) and under IRC Sec. 965 (temporary special dividends received deduction allowed to U.S. shareholders from controlled foreign corporations), because California does not allow any IRC Sec. 199 or IRC Sec. 965 deductions generally, there is no IRC Sec. 199 or IRC Sec. 965 deduction allowed for purposes of determining California adjusted current earnings. In addition, although California technically conforms to the provisions of IRC Sec. 56(g)(4)(B)(i) that allow an exclusion for purposes of computing adjusted current earnings for amounts excludable under IRC Sec. 139A for subsidies allowed for prescription drugs provided under a qualified retiree prescription drug plan and under IRC Sec. 1357 for income subject to the federal tonnage tax, because California does not allow any IRC Sec. 139A or IRC Sec. 1357 exclusions generally, there is no IRC Sec. 139A or IRC Sec. 1357 exclusion allowed for purposes of determining California adjusted current earnings.

(Sec. 23456, Rev. & Tax. Code)

California modifies federal items of tax preference as follows:

— federal treatment of tax-exempt interest as a tax preference item is inapplicable; and

— the excess of depreciation taken on IRC Sec. 1250 property (real property) placed in service before 1987 over the amount allowable under the straight-line method is an item of tax preference. (Sec. 23457, Rev. & Tax. Code)

The AMT applies to commencing and dissolving corporations that are subject to special rules as discussed at ¶819 and ¶820.

• *Exemption amount*

For both federal and California purposes, the first $40,000 of alternative minimum taxable income is exempt from the AMT. However, the exemption amount is reduced (but not below zero) by an amount equal to 25% of the amount by which the taxpayer's alternative minimum taxable income exceeds $150,000. (Sec. 23400, Rev. & Tax. Code)

• *Ten-year writeoff of certain tax preferences*

For both federal and California purposes, certain enumerated expenditures that would otherwise constitute tax preferences may be deducted ratably over an extended period instead of being deducted in the taxable year of the expenditure. The expenditures covered include:

— circulation expenses—three year period;

— research expenses—10 year period; and

— intangible drilling costs—five year period.

(Sec. 24365, Rev. & Tax. Code; Sec. 24423, Rev. & Tax. Code; Sec. 24364, Rev. & Tax. Code)

• *Credits against AMT*

Under federal law as incorporated by California, the AMT is equal to the excess, if any, of the tentative minimum tax over the regular tax for the taxable year. If the regular tax exceeds the tentative minimum tax so that the AMT does not apply, the taxpayer may not then apply tax credits to reduce the regular tax below the tentative minimum tax. For California purposes, an exception is made so that certain credits may reduce the regular tax below the tentative minimum tax, after the allowance of the minimum tax credit. (Sec. 23453, Rev. & Tax. Code)

The following credits discussed at ¶818, may reduce the regular tax below the tentative minimum tax:

— solar energy, commercial solar energy, or commercial solar electric system (carryovers);

— research and development expenditures;

— clinical testing expenses (carryovers);

— low-income housing;

— sales and use tax paid or incurred in connection with the purchase of qualified property used in an enterprise zone, targeted tax area, local agency military base recovery area (LAMBRA), or the former Los Angeles Revitalization Zone (LARZ);

— qualified hiring within an enterprise zone, targeted tax area, LAMBRA, or the former LARZ;

— the former manufacturing investment credit; and

— the natural heritage preservation credit.

Practitioner Comment: Most Credits Can Reduce Regular Tax Below Tentative Minimum Tax But Can Not Reduce the Alternative Minimum Tax Itself

Unlike under federal law, the California AMT is determined separately before the application of credits as the excess of Tentative Minimum Tax (TMT) over regular tax. In contrast to federal law, California credits can not reduce the AMT in California. However, because the California AMT is in addition to the regular tax, most credits can still be used to reduce regular tax below the TMT.

For example, assume a corporation has TMT of $120 and regular tax of $100, before credits, and a $50 research credit. The corporation's tax liability (ignoring the $800 minimum tax) would be $70, consisting of $20 of AMT ($120 TMT - $100 regular tax before credits) and $50 of regular tax ($100 regular tax before credits - $50 research credit).

Bruce Daigh, Chris Whitney, Contributing Editors

• *Credit for prior year minimum tax*

California incorporates the federal credit provisions applicable to taxpayers who have incurred California AMT in prior years but not in the current tax year. (Sec. 23455, Rev. & Tax. Code) See ¶818 for a discussion.

• *Short taxable year*

The AMT for a short taxable year is computed on an annual basis, in the same manner as under federal law. (Sec. 24636, Rev. & Tax. Code)

¶818 Credits Against Tax

Law: Secs. 23036, 23051.7, 23453, 23601.5, 23604, 23608-25, 23630, 23633, 23634, 23642-46, 23649, 23657, 23684; former Secs. 23601, 23601.3, 23601.4, 23603, 23605, 23606, 23606.1, 23607, 23608, 23612.5, 23662, 23666, 23803, 24440; 18 CCR Regs. 23636-0—23636-9, 23637-0—23637-11 (CCH CALIFORNIA TAX REPORTS ¶12-001—12-150).

Comparable Federal: Secs. 38, 41, 42, 45(a), 45C, 48, 53, 280C (CCH U.S. MASTER TAX GUIDE ¶1323, 1326, 1330, 1334, 1339, 1343, 1344, 1353).

California Forms: FTB 3501 (Employer Child Care Program/Contribution Credit), FTB 3507 (Prison Inmate Labor Credit), FTB 3503 (Natural Heritage Preservation Credit), FTB 3508 (Solar or Wind Energy System Credit), FTB 3511 (Environmental Tax Credit), FTB 3521 (Low Income Housing Credit), FTB 3523 (Research Credit), FTB 3534 (Joint Strike Fighter Credits), FTB 3540 (Credit Carryover Summary), FTB 3546 (Enhanced Oil Recovery Credit), FTB 3547 (Donated Agricultural Products Transportation Credit), FTB 3548 (Disabled Access Credit for Eligible Small Businesses), FTB 3802 (Corporate Passive Activity Loss and Credit Limitations), FTB 3805Z (Enterprise Zone Deduction and Credit Summary), FTB 3807 (Local Agency Military Base Recovery Area Deduction and Credit Summary), FTB 3808 (Manufacturing Enhancement Area Credit Summary), FTB 3809 (Targeted Tax Area Deduction and Credit Summary), Sch. C (100S) (S Corporation Tax Credits).

• *Tax credits—In general*

As in the personal income tax law (¶126), the corporation tax law provides rules for the order in which various tax credits are to be applied. The law provides that credits shall be allowed against "tax" (defined as the franchise or income tax, the tax on unrelated business taxable income, and the tax on S corporations).

The priority for claiming credits is as follows:

(1) credits, except the credits in categories 4 and 5, below, with no carryover or refundable provisions;

(2) credits with carryovers that are not refundable, except for those that are allowed to reduce "net tax" below the tentative minimum tax (see ¶117);

(3) credits with both carryover and refundable provisions;

(4) the minimum tax credit;

(5) credits that are allowed to reduce "net tax" below the tentative minimum tax (see ¶117);

(6) credits for taxes paid to other states; and

(7) credits with refundable provisions but no carryover (withholding, excess SDI).

(Sec. 23036, Rev. & Tax. Code)

As discussed at ¶817, only certain specified credits may reduce a taxpayer's regular tax below the tentative minimum tax.

Also, some credits may be limited because they arise from passive activities. The taxpayer must file FTB 3802 (Corporate Passive Activity Loss and Credit Limitations) if the taxpayer claims any of the following credits from passive activities: the orphan drug research credit carryover; the low-income housing credit; or the research and development credit.

• *S corporations*

An S corporation is limited to one-third of the amount of any credit against corporation franchise (income) tax, see ¶806. (Sec. 23036, Rev. & Tax. Code)

• *Pass-through entities*

Credits that become inoperative that are passed through (in the first tax year after they become inoperative) to a taxpayer who is a partner or shareholder of an eligible pass-through entity may be claimed in the year of the pass-through. An eligible pass-through entity is any partnership or S corporation that files a fiscal year return and is entitled to a credit in the last year that the credit is operative. (Sec. 23036, Rev. & Tax. Code)

Caution Note: Temporary Limitation on Credit Amounts

The amount of credits and credit carryovers that may be claimed by taxpayers on a corporation franchise and income tax return are limited to 50% of a taxpayer's tax during the 2008 and 2009 tax years. Thereafter, the credits may be claimed in full. Any unused credit may be carried over and the carryover period is extended by the number of taxable years the credit, or any portion thereof, was not allowed as a result of the 50% limitation. A taxpayer with net business income of less than $500,000 for the taxable year is exempt from the 50% limitation. (Sec. 23036.2, Rev. & Tax. Code)

• *Unitary groups*

For a discussion of the treatment of credits claimed by unitary group members, see ¶1310.

• *Research and development credit*

California provides a credit for research and development expenditures that is generally the same as that provided by federal law (Sec. 41), with the following exceptions:

—The California credit applies to expenses paid or incurred in taxable years beginning after 1986 and is available indefinitely thereafter. The federal credit does not apply to amounts paid or incurred after December 31, 2009.

—The applicable California percentage is 15% of the excess of qualified expenses over a specified percentage of the taxpayer's average annual gross receipts for the four preceding taxable years (the "base amount") and 24% of basic (university) research payments (the federal percentage is 20% of the excess of qualified expenses over a base amount and 20% of basic research payments).

—California substitutes 1.49%, 1.98%, and 2.48% for the federal alternative incremental credit (AIC) method percentages. The federal AIC percentages are 2.65%, 3.2%, and 3.75%, respectively, increased to 3%, 4%, and 5%, respectively, effective generally for tax years ending after 2006. California does not adopt the repeal of the AIC by the Emergency Economic Stabilization Act of 2008, applicable to taxable years beginning after 2008.

—California does not incorporate Tax Relief and Health Care Act of 2006 amendments that authorize the use of a third method, the alternative simplified credit, generally effective for federal purposes in tax years ending after 2006.

—Research must be conducted in California (federal law requires that it be conducted within the United States, Puerto Rico, or other U.S. possessions).

—The California credit may be carried over (the federal credit is part of the general business credit subject to the limitations imposed by Sec. 38).

—The California credit for basic research payments includes payments for applied research. Also, for California purposes only, the credit is extended to payments that are made by taxpayers engaged in specified biopharmaceutical or biotechnology activities for university hospitals and special cancer research facilities.

—For purposes of determining the base amount under California law, only the gross receipts from the sale of property that is held primarily for sale to customers in the ordinary course of the taxpayer's trade or business and delivered or shipped to a purchaser within California, regardless of F.O.B. point or other conditions of sale, may be taken into account.

—California law, unlike federal law, prohibits a taxpayer from claiming the credit for expenses paid or incurred for property for which a sales and use tax exemption for teleproduction or other postproduction services may be claimed.

(Sec. 23609, Rev. & Tax. Code)

Because of California's current IRC conformity date (see ¶803), California has not adopted amendments made by the Energy Tax Incentives Act of 2005 that (1) allow a taxpayer to claim 20% of amounts paid or incurred by the taxpayer during the tax year to an energy research consortium for energy research and (2) repeal the limitation on contract research expenses paid to eligible small businesses, universities and federal laboratories for qualified energy research. These amendments are effective for federal purposes for amounts paid or incurred after August 8, 2005, in tax years ending after such date.

California has adopted the portion of IRC Sec. 280C that bars taxpayers from taking a business deduction for that portion of the research expenditures that is equal to the amount of the allowable credit (¶1023). (Sec. 24440, Rev. & Tax. Code)

Combined groups.— For taxpayers filing on a combined group basis, all members of the combined group must use the same method. To compute either the regular research credit or the AIC, all members of a controlled group are treated as a single taxpayer. The credit amount is then divided and proportionately allocated to each member of the controlled group. (*Tax News*, California Franchise Tax Board, September 2006)

Practitioner Comment: Treatment of R&D Credit Allocation

On August 17, 2006, the California Supreme Court in *General Motors Corp. v. Franchise Tax Board*, 39 Cal. 4th 773 (2006), (CCH CALIFORNIA TAX REPORTS ¶404-044) held that only the taxpayer that incurred the research and development expenses may use the research and development credit so generated. In so holding, the Court's decision was consistent with an earlier State Board of Equalization decision (*Appeal of Guy F. Atkinson Company*, No. 96R-0051, March 19, 1997, CCH CALIFORNIA TAX REPORTS ¶403-307) as well as the unpublished Court of Appeal decision, *Guy F. Atkinson Company v. Franchise Tax Board*, (No. A985075). [CCH Note: Legislation enacted in 2008 allows combined group members to assign credits to other group members, see ¶1310 for details]

Bruce Daigh, Chris Whitney, Contributing Editors

• *Credit for prior year minimum tax*

California allows a credit in the form of a carryover to corporate taxpayers who have incurred California alternative minimum tax in prior years but not in the current tax year. (Sec. 23453, Rev. & Tax. Code)

The credit is computed in the same manner as the federal credit with the substitution of certain California figures in place of the federal. The credit is taken against the "regular tax" but may not reduce liability to less than the "tentative minimum tax." Both the federal and California credits are based on the amount of alternative minimum tax paid on "deferral preferences" (items that defer tax liability) as distinct from "exclusion items" (items that permanently reduce tax liability).

• *Low-income housing credit*

Corporations may qualify for a low-income housing credit, based upon federal law (IRC Sec. 42). The credit is the same as under personal income tax law and is discussed at ¶138. (Sec. 23610.5, Rev. & Tax. Code)

A corporation that is entitled to the low-income housing credit may elect to assign any portion of the credit to one or more affiliated banks or corporations for each taxable year in which the credit is allowed.

• *Credits for establishing child care program or facilities*

In taxable years beginning before 2012, credits are available to employers for establishing child care programs or facilities, for contributing to child care information and referral services, and for contributions to qualified child care plans. The credits are the same as those available under the personal income tax law and are more fully discussed at ¶134. (Sec. 23617, Rev. & Tax. Code; Sec. 23617.5, Rev. & Tax. Code)

• *Prison inmate job tax credit*

Employers may claim a credit equal to 10% of the wages paid to each prison inmate hired under a program established by the Director of Corrections. This credit is identical to the one provided under the personal income tax law (¶154). (Sec. 23624, Rev. & Tax. Code)

• *Tax-incentive credit—Sales tax equivalent*

The corporation tax law allows a tax credit for the amount of sales or use tax paid on the purchase of "qualified property" by businesses located in an enterprise zone, local agency military base recovery area (LAMBRA), or the targeted tax area. The conditions for allowance of the credit are the same as those for the personal income tax credit, as explained at ¶144, except that the corporate credit applies to purchases up to a value of $20 million. (Sec. 23612.2, Rev. & Tax. Code; Sec. 23633, Rev. & Tax. Code; Sec. 23645, Rev. & Tax. Code)

• *Tax-incentive credit—Employers' hiring credit*

Employers may claim a credit for a portion of "qualified wages" paid to certain disadvantaged individuals who are hired to work in an enterprise zone, LAMBRA, targeted tax area, or a manufacturing enhancement area. The conditions for allowance of the credit are the same as those for the personal income tax, as explained at

¶ 145 and ¶ 147 through ¶ 149, respectively. (Sec. 23622.7, Rev. & Tax. Code; Sec. 23646, Rev. & Tax. Code; Sec. 23634, Rev. & Tax Code; Sec. 23622.8, Rev. & Tax. Code)

• *Disabled access expenditures credit*

California allows eligible small businesses a credit for 50% of up to $250 of the disabled access expenditures paid or incurred by those businesses to comply with the federal Americans with Disabilities Act. The conditions for allowance of the credit are the same as those for the personal income tax, as explained at ¶ 140. (Sec. 23642, Rev. & Tax. Code)

• *Enhanced oil recovery credit*

California allows certain independent oil producers an enhanced oil recovery credit equal to 1/3 of the federal credit allowed under IRC Sec. 43 as of the current IRC tie-in date (see ¶ 803), provided the costs for which the credit is claimed are attributable to projects located within California. The conditions for the allowance of the credit are the same as those for the personal income tax, as explained at ¶ 153. The credit is not available during the 2008 taxable year. (Sec. 23604, Rev. & Tax. Code)

• *Credit for costs of transporting donated agricultural products*

California allows a credit against net tax for 50% of the costs paid or incurred in connection with the transportation of agricultural products donated to nonprofit charitable organizations. The conditions for the allowance of the credit are the same as those for the personal income tax, as explained at ¶ 141. (Sec. 23608, Rev. & Tax. Code)

• *Farmworker housing credits*

Prior to the 2009 taxable year, California allows a credit for certain qualified costs associated with the construction or rehabilitation of farmworker housing located in California. The credit is substantially similar to the personal income tax credit discussed at ¶ 137. (Sec. 23608.2, Rev. & Tax. Code)

Also prior to the 2009 taxable year, banks and financial institutions may claim a credit for low-interest loans made to finance qualified expenditures associated with construction or rehabilitation of farmworker housing. The amount of the credit that may be claimed is 50% of the difference between the amount of interest income that could have been collected had the loan rate been one point above prime (or any other index used by the lender) and the lesser amount of interest income actually due for the term of the loan. (Sec. 23608.3, Rev. & Tax. Code)

The credit may not be taken until the first taxable year in which construction or rehabilitation is completed and the housing is actually occupied by eligible farmworkers, and it must be taken in equal installment amounts over a 10-year period or for the term of the loan, whichever is less. Unused credit may not be carried over.

The credit may not be taken for the following:

— interest income on any loan with a term of less than three years;

— interest income on any loan funded prior to 1997;

— loan fees or other charges collected by the bank or financial institution with respect to a loan; or

— interest income on any loan that did not receive prior certification by the California Tax Credit Allocation Committee.

Beginning with the 2009 taxable year, these credits are repealed. However, the low-income housing credit is revised to ease certain eligibility requirements and provide a set-aside of the credit allocation to support the development of farmworker housing projects.

• *Community development investment credit*

For taxable years beginning before 2012, California allows a credit in an amount equal to 20% of each qualified investment made into a community development financial institution. The conditions for the allowance of the credit are the same as those for the personal income tax, as explained at ¶156. (Sec. 23657, Rev. & Tax. Code)

• *Natural heritage preservation credit*

A taxpayer may claim a credit equal to 55% of the fair market value of qualified real property donated before July 1, 2008, for conservation to the California Resources Agency (CRA), a local government, or a nonprofit land and water conservation organization designated by the CRA or local government to accept donations. The corporation franchise and income tax credit is identical to the personal income tax credit discussed at ¶143. (Sec. 23630, Rev. & Tax. Code)

• *Ultra-low sulfur diesel fuel production credit*

A credit is available for ultra low-sulfur diesel fuel produced by a qualified small refiner at a California facility, effective for taxable years beginning before 2018. The corporation franchise and income tax credit is identical to the personal income tax credit discussed at ¶151. (Sec. 23662, Rev. & Tax. Code)

• *Carryover credits*

Expired credits for which carryovers may be claimed (and the years for which the credits were available) include the following:

— solar pump credit (1981—1983);

— solar energy credit (1985—1988);

— energy conservation credit (1981—1986);

— ridesharing credits (1981—1986 and 1989—1995);

— credit for donation of computer or scientific equipment (1983—1986);

— credit for donation of computer software (1986—1987);

— commercial solar energy credit (1987—1988);

— credit for donation of agricultural products (1989—1991);

— orphan drug research credit (1987—1992);

— commercial solar electric system credit (1990—1993);

— recycling equipment credit (1989—1995);

— low-emission vehicles credit (1991—1995);

— Los Angeles Revitalization Zone hiring and sales and use tax credits (1992—1997);

— salmon and steelhead trout habitat credit (1995—1999);

— manufacturer's investment credit (1994—2003);

— joint strike fighter property credit (2001—2005);

— joint strike fighter wage credit (2001—2005);

— solar and wind energy systems credit (2001—2005); and

— rice straw credit (1997—2007).

All of the above credit carryovers may be claimed on FTB 3540. See prior editions of the *Guidebook* for details about these credits.

¶819 Franchise Tax on Commencing Corporations

Law: Secs. 23151.1, 23153, 23181, 23183, 23221-26 (CCH CALIFORNIA TAX REPORTS ¶10-210, 10-240, 10-340, 10-380).

Comparable Federal: None.

New corporations are exempt from the minimum franchise tax for their first taxable year. However, a credit union that incorporates in or qualifies to transact intrastate business in California must prepay a tax equal to $25. (Sec. 23153, Rev. & Tax. Code)

However, a corporation is still liable for the regular tax for it's first taxable year. The tax is computed according to or measured by its net income for the taxable year. (Sec. 23151.1(c)(2), Rev. & Tax. Code)

Franchise Tax Board Reg. 23222, 18 CCR, provides that where a commencing corporation is in existence or is qualified in California for no more than one-half month prior to the end of its accounting period, such period may be disregarded provided the corporation was not doing business in and received no income from sources within the state during the period. The corporation is not required to file a return or pay a tax for such a period, but may be required to file affidavits to establish its right to come under this special rule. This rule does not apply to limited partnerships, which are subject to a minimum franchise tax (¶616).

CCH Example: Corporation Not Required to File or Pay

ABC Corporation files its articles of incorporation with the Secretary of State on December 17, and elects to file on a calendar year basis. However, ABC does no business in California and receives no income from California sources for the period from December 17 through December 31. In this case, no return would be required and no tax would be due for the period from December 17 through December 31. However, if ABC had filed its articles on December 10th, it would be required to file a return, even if it remained inactive and received no income during the period from December 10 through December 31.

• *Cross references*

Special rules apply when a reorganization is involved (¶822).

¶820 Franchise Tax on Corporations Discontinuing Business

Law: Secs. 23151.1, 23181, 23183, 23332, 23504; Reg. 23334, 18 CCR (CCH CALIFORNIA TAX REPORTS ¶10-210, 10-340).

Comparable Federal: None.

The tax for a corporation's taxable year of cessation is imposed on the corporation's net income for the taxable year, which may not be less than the minimum tax discussed at ¶816. (Sec. 23151.1, Rev. & Tax. Code)

A corporation that commenced to do business before 1972 may be allowed a credit, in the year of dissolution or withdrawal, for tax paid during its commencing period (¶821).

A corporation that discontinues business but does not dissolve or withdraw until a later year is subject to the minimum franchise tax until it dissolves or withdraws. See ¶821.

¶821 Franchise Tax upon Dissolution or Withdrawal

Law: Secs. 23151.2, 23201-04, 23223, 23281-82, 23331-35, 23561 (CCH CALIFORNIA TAX REPORTS ¶10-210, 10-340).

Comparable Federal: None.

California Form: FTB 3555A (Request for Tax Clearance Certificate—Exempt Organizations).

The franchise tax for the year of dissolution or withdrawal is based on the income of the year of discontinuing business, unless that income was previously taxed. (Sec. 23151.2, Rev. & Tax. Code) In the usual situation where dissolution or withdrawal occurs in the same year as discontinuance of business, there is of course no additional tax beyond that described at ¶820. In any event, the minimum tax is applicable unless certain conditions are satisfied (see below). Credit may be allowable for tax paid during the corporation's commencing years, as explained below.

• *Effective date of dissolution*

The effective date of dissolution is the date on which a "Certificate of Winding Up," if necessary, and the "Certificate of Dissolution," or certified copy of a court order of dissolution, is filed with the Secretary of State. The effective date of withdrawal is the date on which a certificate of withdrawal is filed with the Secretary of State. (Sec. 23331, Rev. & Tax. Code) See *Appeal of Mount Shasta Milling Company* (1960) (CCH CALIFORNIA TAX REPORTS ¶10-210.452); also, *Appeal of Air Market Travel Corporation* (1978) (CCH CALIFORNIA TAX REPORTS ¶10-210.452).

The California Attorney General has taken the position that the California Secretary of State is not required to accept for filing a certificate of voluntary dissolution of a nonprofit corporation that contains facsimile signatures rather than original signatures of the directors (*Opinion No. 02-514,* Office of the California Attorney General, September 5, 2002 (CCH CALIFORNIA TAX REPORTS ¶10-210.454).

In *Appeal of Rogers* (1950) (CCH CALIFORNIA TAX REPORTS ¶10-210.56), the State Board of Equalization (SBE) considered the question of the date on which a certificate of dissolution was "filed" for purposes of the rule described above. In that case the corporation offered a proper and adequate certificate to the Secretary of State on October 14, 1948, but the Secretary returned the certificate to the corporation for more information. The certificate was sent back to the Secretary, with the information requested, and was accepted for filing on November 1, 1948. The SBE held that the certificate was "filed" on October 14, the date it was first offered to the Secretary of State.

Practitioner Comment: 2006 Legislation Eases California Dissolution Procedures

A corporation, as well as other entities, is no longer required, prior to the dissolution of the entity, to obtain a tax clearance certificate from the Franchise Tax Board (FTB). Instead, the Secretary of State shall notify the FTB of the dissolution.

In addition, a corporation will not be subject to the minimum tax in the year that a final return is filed if the corporation did not thereafter do business in California and dissolution, surrender, or cancellation of the entity is completed before the end of the 12-month period following the date the final tax return was filed. Similar relief from the annual tax will be accorded to a limited partnership, limited liability company, or limited liability partnership if these entities: 1) ceased doing business in California prior to the beginning of the taxable year; 2) filed a timely final tax return for the preceding taxable year; and 3) filed a certificate of cancellation with the Secretary of State before the end of the 12-month period beginning with the original due date of the tax return for the preceding taxable year. Any outstanding tax, penalty, or interest for a taxable year beginning after the corporation ceased doing business can be cancelled if:

— the corporation was incorporated prior to January 1, 2006;

— the corporation was suspended for taxable years beginning on or before December 1, 2005, and ceased doing business before January 1, 2006;

— the tax liability for each taxable year to be waived does not exceed the minimum tax due;

— the corporation applied for corporate dissolution; and

— the corporation applied for waiver of tax, penalty, and interest.

(Ch. 773 (A.B. 2341), Laws 2006)

Bruce Daigh, Chris Whitney, Contributing Editors

• *Shareholders' assumption of liability*

In *Appeal of B.&C. Motors, Inc.* (1962) (CCH CALIFORNIA TAX REPORTS ¶10-210.455), the SBE held that an assumption of liability executed by shareholders of a dissolving corporation imposes an obligation on the shareholders for all franchise taxes of the corporation, even though (1) the taxes apply to a period prior to the time the shareholders acquired their stock, and (2) the tax liability was not disclosed until after the assumption was executed.

• *Special rules*

When a corporation is suspended in one year and is not revived in the same year, but is revived in a later year, its tax for the year of revivor is computed as though it were a new corporation (¶819). (Sec. 23282, Rev. & Tax. Code)

• *Credit for prepaid tax*

A corporation that commenced to do business before 1972 is allowed a credit in the year of dissolution or withdrawal for tax paid during the commencing period. The credit allowed is the excess of the tax paid over the minimum tax, for the first taxable year that constituted a full 12 months of doing business. The reason for this is that under the old commencing-corporation rules tax was paid twice on some income of the commencing years; this doubling up usually applied to the income of the first full year of doing business. (The doubling up was justified by the fact that under the old rules there was no tax on income of the corporation's final year.) (Sec. 23223, Rev. & Tax. Code)

The law provides that the credit is allowable only upon submission by the taxpayer of evidence establishing the amount paid. If the taxpayer does not have a copy of the tax return or other competent evidence that shows the commencing-corporation tax it paid, the FTB will—upon request, and for a fee—supply the necessary information from its files if available.

Corporations that first became subject to the franchise tax before 1933 may encounter special problems in determining the credit; these issues are discussed in Legal Ruling No. 382 (1975) (CCH CALIFORNIA TAX REPORTS ¶205-238).

The credit may be allowed to a transferee corporation for tax paid by a transferor, where there is a "reorganization" as explained at ¶822. In this case the credit is not allowed to the transferor.

¶822 Franchise Tax on Reorganized Corporations

Law: Secs. 23251-53.

Comparable Federal: Secs. 338, 368, 381(b) (CCH U.S. MASTER TAX GUIDE ¶2209, 2277).

In cases involving certain types of reorganizations, the transferor and transferee corporations are treated in effect as one continuing corporation for franchise tax purposes. For this purpose the term "reorganization" is defined in IRC Sec. 368. (Sec. 23251 et. seq., Rev. & Tax. Code)

Practice Note: Apportionment of IRC Sec. 338 deemed asset sales

The Franchise Tax Board's *Legal Ruling 2006-03*, May 6, 2006, CCH CALIFORNIA TAX REPORTS ¶10-540.21, provides information regarding how to apportion the gains resulting from an IRC Sec. 338(h)(1) or IRC Sec. 338(g) election to treat the sale or purchase of stock as a sale or purchase of assets for California corporation franchise and income tax purposes.

• *Procedure after reorganization*

In the case of a reorganization, IRC Sec. 381(b) shall apply in determining the close of the taxable year. This federal law provides that the taxable year of the transferor shall end on the date of the transfer.

• *Effect of insurance-company exemption*

In *First American Title Insurance and Trust Company v. Franchise Tax Board* (1971) (CCH CALIFORNIA TAX REPORTS ¶10-540.803), the transferee corporation took over four subsidiary corporations that were in the escrow business. The transaction was a "reorganization" as described in this paragraph. The transferee was exempt from franchise tax (¶808), except for its trust business. The court of appeal overruled the Franchise Tax Board and held that the transferee was not required to include the transferors' income for the preceding year in the measure of its tax, because the income came within the protection of the transferee's insurance-company exemption.

• *Transferee's credit for transferor's tax*

Under the system for taxing the income of a corporation's final year, as explained at ¶820 and ¶821, a transferee corporation may be allowed credit for tax paid by a transferor. Where there has been a "reorganization," as defined above, the transferee is allowed credit for tax that was paid by the transferor during the commencing period of the transferor. The credit is allowed in a later year when the transferee dissolves or withdraws, under the rules outlined at ¶821—it is not allowed in the year of the reorganization. This conforms to the idea of treating transferor and transferee as though they were one continuing corporation for franchise tax purposes. Thus, when the transferee corporation dissolves or withdraws, it gets the benefit of a credit for the transferor's commencing-corporation tax as well as for its own.

¶823 Tax on Corporations Having Income from Within and Without the State

Law: Secs. 25101, 25120-40 (CCH CALIFORNIA TAX REPORTS ¶10-800, 11-510 et seq.).

Comparable Federal: None.

Corporations having income from both within and without the state are taxed only on the income attributable to California. See Chapter 13 for full discussion of this subject. (Sec. 25101, Rev. & Tax. Code)

Because income from sources outside the state is not subject to California tax, it is presumed that no income will be subject to tax by California and also by another state. Accordingly, California does not allow credit against the California tax for taxes paid to other states or countries. This is contrary to the treatment in the California personal income tax (¶127 —¶131), and is also unlike the federal treatment of domestic corporations that have income from foreign sources.

¶824 Suspension and Revivor of Corporate Powers

Law: Secs. 23301-23305.5 (CCH CALIFORNIA TAX REPORTS ¶10-210).

Comparable Federal: None.

California Forms: FTB 3557BC (Application for Certificate of Revivor), FTB 3557LLC (Application for Certificate of Revivor).

Except for the purpose of amending the articles of incorporation to change the corporate name or filing an application for exempt status, all of the powers, rights, and privileges of a corporation or limited liability company (LLC) may be suspended (or, in the case of a foreign corporation or LLC, forfeited) for failure to file a return or for nonpayment of taxes, penalties, or interest. Generally, these nonpayment provisions come into play if payment is not made within the following time limitations: (1) tax shown on return, by close of year following taxable year and (2) tax payable upon notice and demand, by close of 11th month after due date. (Sec. 23301, Rev. & Tax. Code; Sec. 23301.5, Rev. & Tax. Code)

A corporation or LLC desiring to be relieved of the suspension described above may apply to the Franchise Tax Board (FTB) for a certificate of revivor. The application must be accompanied by payment of all delinquent amounts, unless the FTB determines that prospects for collection will be improved by not imposing this requirement. (Sec. 23305, Rev. & Tax. Code; Sec. 23305b, Rev. & Tax. Code)

Practitioner Comment: Expedited Requests for Corporate Revivor

The fee for submitting expedited service requests for corporation revivor requests is $100 and must be paid by certified checks, money orders, or cash. Personal checks will not be accepted. Corporation revivor requests are made by submitting Form FTB 3557A (Application for Certificate of Revivor—Walk-Through) along with the necessary returns and payments at one of the FTB district offices that accept walk through applications, including the Los Angeles, Oakland, Sacramento, San Diego, San Francisco, or Santa Ana district offices. (Reg. 19591, 18 CCR; *FTB Notice 2004-09*, (2004) CCH CALIFORNIA TAX REPORTS ¶403-722)

Bruce Daigh, Chris Whitney, Contributing Editors

Corporations or LLCs may also be relieved of the contract voidability and penalty provisions imposed for failure to comply with reporting and payment requirements by entering into a voluntary disclosure agreement with the FTB (¶1422).

The FTB is authorized to provide entity status letters verifying the status of a corporation or LLC with the FTB and may charge a fee for the reasonable costs of responding to requests for such letters. (Sec. 23305e, Rev. & Tax. Code)

The law provides that even though a corporation may be suspended, it remains taxable on any income received during the period of suspension. (Sec. 23303, Rev. & Tax. Code)

In *Appeal of Lomita Plaza, Inc.* (1961) (CCH CALIFORNIA TAX REPORTS ¶10-210.854), the State Board of Equalization (SBE) held that a corporation could not file a valid appeal against a proposed assessment of franchise tax at a time when the corporation was under suspension, even though the corporation was kept in existence for the sole purpose of defending against the proposed assessment and was subsequently revived. Similarly, in *Appeal of RJ Standard Corp.* (2004) (CCH CALIFORNIA TAX REPORTS ¶10-210.55), the SBE held that a formerly suspended corporation could not pursue a refund claim that was filed during the period of its suspension after the corporation was revived. The statute of limitations had lapsed during the suspension period and the limitations period was not "tolled" during such period.

A California court of appeal has held that an assignee was not precluded from pursuing a court action to enforce an agreement against a third party even though the assignor's corporate powers were suspended subsequent to the assignment. The rights of an assignor are measured at the time of the assignment, and the rights of the assignee are independent of, and unaffected by, the incapacity of its assignor subsequent to the assignment (*Fidelity Express Network, Inc. v. Mobile Information Systems, Inc.*, (2004) (CCH CALIFORNIA TAX REPORTS ¶89-206.946).

Reference should be made to the law or regulations for detailed rules relating to this subject and the effect on the voidability of a contract of a corporation or LLC during suspension.

¶825 DISCs and FSCs

Law: Sec. 23051.5(b) (CCH CALIFORNIA TAX REPORTS ¶10-515).

Comparable Federal: Sec. 114 (CCH U.S. MASTER TAX GUIDE ¶2471).

California law specifically disallows any application of the IRC provisions on FSCs (Foreign Sales Corporations) or DISCs (Domestic International Sales Corporations). (Sec. 23051.5(b), Rev. & Tax. Code) For California purposes, FSCs and DISCs are treated in the same manner as other corporations.

The federal provisions governing FSCs were repealed by the FSC Repeal and Extraterritorial Income Act of 2000 and replaced with an exclusion for extraterritorial income attributable to foreign trading gross receipts, which in turn was repealed for transactions after 2004 with transitional rules for transactions during 2005 and 2006 (see ¶925 for details). California has not adopted this exclusion.

TAXES ON CORPORATE INCOME

CHAPTER 9
GROSS INCOME

¶901 Gross Income—In General

Law: Sec. 3294.5, Civ. Code; Secs. 24271, 24275, Rev. & Tax. Code (CCH CALIFORNIA TAX REPORTS ¶10-505, 10-515).

Comparable Federal: Secs. 61, 87, 114, 139A, 199 (CCH U.S. MASTER TAX GUIDE ¶71, 2471).

California Form: Form 100 (California Corporation Franchise or Income Tax Return).

"Gross income" is generally the same as under federal law as of the current IRC tie-in date (see ¶103), except that California law specifically includes all interest on federal, state, and municipal bonds for franchise tax purposes (¶910). (Sec. 24271, Rev. & Tax. Code) However, it may not be assumed from this that the items to be included are always the same under federal and California laws. For one thing, the exclusions are different in several respects, as set forth in succeeding paragraphs. It is also possible for the law to be interpreted differently for California purposes than for federal. Any case involving a specific item of income should be checked against the exclusions listed in this chapter and, if there appears to be any question as to its status, should be checked further against the regulations or a more detailed reference work.

Gross income is reported on Form 100, unless otherwise indicated.

Practice Pointer: SBE Audits

Taxpayers who undergo a sales and use tax audit by the State Board of Equalization (SBE) should be aware that the SBE provides the FTB with copies of sales and use tax audit reports for the audits that result in adjustments of additional gross receipts (total sales). The FTB reviews these sales and use tax reports to determine if an income tax adjustment is warranted. (*Tax News*, California Franchise Tax Board, November 2008)

¶902 Life Insurance—Death Benefits

Law: Sec. 24305 (CCH CALIFORNIA TAX REPORTS ¶10-515).

Comparable Federal: Sec. 101 (CCH U.S. MASTER TAX GUIDE ¶803).

Although California law mirrors federal law (IRC Sec. 101) concerning the exclusion from gross income of life insurance benefits paid upon the death of an insured, other than certain interest, California's provision has not been amended to reflect changes made to federal law by the Pension Protection Act of 2006 (PPA). (Sec. 24305, Rev. & Tax. Code)

Amendments made by the PPA limit the exclusion for employers holding a life insurance policy as a beneficiary that covers the life of an employee. The amendments limit the employer's exclusion to an amount equal to the amount paid for the policy as premiums or other payments unless the employer satisfies several requirements, including notice and consent requirements, applicable generally for federal purposes to life insurance contracts issued after August 17, 2006. To the extent the exclusion is limited for federal income tax purposes, taxpayers may subtract the difference between the full amount of the benefits paid, less certain interest, and the amount of the federal exclusion.

¶903 Life Insurance—Other Than Death Benefits

Law: Sec. 24302 (CCH CALIFORNIA TAX REPORTS ¶10-708, 10-906).

Comparable Federal: Sec. 72 (CCH U.S. MASTER TAX GUIDE ¶817 et seq.).

California Form: Form 100 (California Corporation Franchise or Income Tax Return).

Amounts received, other than death benefits, on life insurance, endowment, or annuity contracts are nontaxable until the amount received exceeds the aggregate premiums or other consideration paid. This is different from federal law. See also ¶214. (Sec. 24302, Rev. & Tax. Code)

¶904 Life Insurance, Endowment, or Annuity Contract Transferred for Consideration—Other Than Death Benefits

Law: Secs. 24272.2, 24302 (CCH CALIFORNIA TAX REPORTS 10-708, 10-906).

Comparable Federal: Secs. 72, 101 (CCH U.S. MASTER TAX GUIDE ¶803, 817 et seq.).

California law is substantially the same as federal law.

California law is substantially the same as federal law. Generally, when amounts are received other than by reason of the death of the insured under a life insurance, endowment, or annuity contract that has been acquired for valuable consideration, they are includible in income to the extent that they exceed the consideration paid, plus any subsequent premiums. When the cost basis of such contracts carries over from the transferor to the transferee, or when the transferee is a corporation in which the insured is an officer or shareholder, the basis carried over, plus subsequent premiums, may be recovered tax-free. However, annuities held by corporations and other nonnatural persons are not entitled to the same preferential treatment as annuities held by individuals. Instead, a corporate annuity holder is taxed on the excess of

— the sum of the net surrender value of the contract at the end of the tax year plus any amounts distributed under the contract to date over

— the investment in the contract (the aggregate amount of premiums paid under the contract minus policyholder dividends or the aggregate amounts received under the contract that have not been included in income).

(Sec. 24272.2, Rev. & Tax. Code)

¶905 Lessee Improvements

Law: Sec. 24309 (CCH CALIFORNIA TAX REPORTS ¶10-515).

Comparable Federal: Sec. 109 (CCH U.S. MASTER TAX GUIDE ¶764).

Same as personal income tax (¶222).

¶906 Lessee Construction Allowances

Law: Sec. 24309.5 (CCH CALIFORNIA TAX REPORTS ¶10-515).

Comparable Federal: Sec. 110 (CCH U.S. MASTER TAX GUIDE ¶764).

Same as personal income tax (¶223).

¶907 Recoveries of Bad Debts, Prior Taxes, etc.

Law: Sec. 24310 (CCH CALIFORNIA TAX REPORTS ¶10-703, 10-911).

Comparable Federal: Sec. 111 (CCH U.S. MASTER TAX GUIDE ¶799).

California Form: Form 100 (California Corporation Franchise or Income Tax Return).

Same as personal income tax (¶224).

¶908 Discharge of Indebtedness

Law: Secs. 24307, 24472 (CCH CALIFORNIA TAX REPORTS ¶10-701).

Comparable Federal: Sec. 108 (CCH U.S. MASTER TAX GUIDE ¶791).

Same as personal income tax (¶221).

¶909 Dividends and Other Corporate Distributions

Law: Secs. 23040, 23040.1, 24402, 24410, 24451-481, 24601, 24611, 24900, 25106 (CCH CALIFORNIA TAX REPORTS ¶10-540, 10-630, 10-810, 11-515, 11-520, 11-540, 11-550).

Comparable Federal: Secs. 78, 243-47, 301-46, 404, 951-52 (CCH U.S. MASTER TAX GUIDE ¶237, 733 et seq., 742 et seq., 2101, 2465).

California Forms: Form 100 (California Corporation Franchise or Income Tax Return), Sch. H (100) (Dividend Income Deduction).

Except for the provisions discussed below regarding deduction of dividends where the income has been subjected to tax in the hands of the payor, the corporation tax provisions regarding dividends and other corporate distributions are generally the same as in the personal income tax law as outlined at ¶226. As under the personal income tax law, federal law governing corporate distributions is generally incorporated by reference for corporate tax purposes. (Sec. 24451 et seq., Rev. & Tax. Code)

• *Use of appreciated property to redeem stock*

California incorporates the federal provision (IRC Sec. 311) under which, with some exceptions, a corporation is taxed on the appreciation of value of property used to redeem its own stock. (Sec. 24451, Rev. & Tax. Code)

• *Distributions in kind*

When property is distributed in kind, it is valued in the hands of the recipient at its fair market value. California incorporates the federal rule in this area with minor modifications.

• *IRC Sec. 78 gross-up of dividends*

The California Corporation Tax Law has no provision comparable to IRC Sec. 78, which requires a domestic corporation that elects the foreign tax credit for a proportionate part of foreign taxes paid by a foreign corporation from which the domestic corporation has received dividends to include in gross income not only the actual dividends received from such foreign corporation, but also the foreign taxes it is deemed to have paid. Consequently, California corporations may deduct from gross income the amount of their IRC Sec. 78 gross-up of dividends (*Letter to CCH*, FTB, March 25, 1987, CCH CALIFORNIA TAX REPORTS ¶ 401-491).

• *Deduction for dividends received*

California's dividends received deduction was struck down as unconstitutional (see below). The information discussed below provides insight into California's prior dividends received deduction and discusses remedies that may be available to taxpayers that previously claimed the deduction.

In *Farmer Brothers Co. v. Franchise Tax Board* (2003) (CCH CALIFORNIA TAX REPORTS ¶ 403-464) a California court of appeal found Rev. & Tax. Code Sec. 24402, which tied the California general corporation dividends received deduction to the payor's level of California in-state activity, created an unconstitutional burden on interstate commerce and was, therefore, invalid. The ruling adopts in large part the court's reasoning in *Ceridian Corp. v. Franchise Tax Board* (2000) (CCH CALIFORNIA TAX REPORTS ¶ 403-121), which held that former Rev. & Tax. Code Sec. 24410, which limited the deduction for dividends received from an insurance company based on the insurer's level of California business activity, was discriminatory on its face in violation of the Commerce Clause. The California Supreme Court denied the California Franchise Tax Board's (FTB) petition for review, and the U.S. Supreme Court denied the FTB's petition for certiorari.

The appropriate remedy for taxpayers for whom the dividend deduction was denied under Rev. & Tax. Code Sec. 24402 is still an open question. The California Legislative Counsel has taken the position that under Rev. & Tax. Code Sec. 19393, the FTB has the authority to recompute a taxpayer's tax liability if a statute has been declared invalid (Legislative Counsel Opinion, No. 24420, March 21, 2002 (CCH CALIFORNIA TAX REPORTS¶ 403-271). Following this reasoning, the FTB has issued a resolution stating its intention to retroactively deny all dividend deductions under Sec. 24402 for all taxpayers for all open tax years.

In *Ceridian Corp. v. Franchise Tax Board* (2000) (CCH CALIFORNIA TAX REPORTS ¶ 403-121), which declared the dividends deduction under Sec. 24410 unconstitutional, the court of appeal held that refunds were appropriate because Sec. 24410 could not be "reformed" and the tax years at issue were beyond the statute of limitations. The superior court in *Farmer Bros.* ordered a refund, even for the open tax years at issue, despite the FTB's resolution. Both the *Farmer Bros.* and *Ceridian* courts noted that it is debatable whether Sec. 19393 applies only to discriminatory taxes involving national banking associations. The *Farmer Bros.* court noted that "any retroactive collection of taxes would doubtless be the subject of intense litigation undertaken by the affected parties." The appellate court in *Farmer Bros.* did not address the remedy issue as the FTB failed to appeal this issue.

Practitioner Comment: Taxpayers Should Review Options Under Farmer Brothers

The California Court of Appeals ruling in *Farmer Brothers Co. v. Franchise Tax Board* (2003) (CCH CALIFORNIA TAX REPORTS ¶403-464) is a mixed decision for California corporate taxpayers that earned dividend income in open tax years. The decision struck down as unconstitutional the California dividend received deduction (Rev. & Tax. Code Section 24402) that tied the deduction to the payor's level of activity in the state. The ruling obligates the FTB to apply the provisions of the Due Process Clause and provide "meaningful backward-looking relief" to rectify an unconstitutional deprivation.

The FTB has announced that it will allow a dividend received deduction to all qualified corporate taxpayers for tax years ending before December 1, 1999, but will disallow the deduction for all later tax years.

For tax years ending prior to December 1, 1999, most taxpayers will be well advised to file timely refund claims. For tax years ending after December 1, 1999, taxpayers should expect to receive an assessment notice. Taxpayers should carefully evaluate their situation and decide whether to pay the deficiency and file a refund claim for a full dividend received deduction or protest the assessment.

Any dividend income that has not already been deducted under one of California's other dividend provisions (*i.e.*, Sec. 24410, 24411, or 25106) may give rise to a 70%, 80%, or 100% deduction under Sec. 24402. However, taxpayers will also need to carefully consider the implications of the interest disallowance rules of Sec. 24425 (discussed at ¶1023). In *American General Realty Investment Corp., Inc. v. Franchise Tax Board* (2005) CCH CALIFORNIA TAX REPORTS ¶403-794, the Court held that the FTB erred in disallowing a portion of a taxpayer's interest expense deduction, because all of the interest expense was directly traceable to the active conduct of the taxpayer's consumer finance and real estate businesses, both of which generated taxable income.

Notably, in this decision, the Court found that, under the rules of statutory construction, Section 24344(b) is applied before 24425. In other words, if there is no excess of business interest expense over business interest income, there is simply nothing to disallow. Before *Ceridian*, the FTB's administrative position was that Section 24344(b) applies first, as outlined in FTB Legal Ruling 374, FTB Legal Ruling 424, and FTB Notice 2000-9. After the Ceridian decision, the FTB argued the opposite—that Section 24425 applies first.

The FTB alternately argued that IRC Sec. 265(a)(2) and Rev. Proc. 72-18 would apply to disallow the interest expense as well. The Court rejected both positions. With respect to Rev. Proc. 72-18, the Court firmly rejected the FTB's assertions and held that the taxpayer had met its burden of proving that no debt was incurred for the purposes of receiving exempt income.

American General Realty Investment Corp. is not binding precedent. However, in a letter decision, the SBE has ruled that FTB improperly disallowed a portion of the interest expense deductions claimed by a taxpayer's unitary group. The SBE ruled for the taxpayer and allowed the full deduction. The SBE did not give an explanation of its decision. However, the result in the letter decision is consistent with *American General Realty Investment Corp.* (*Appeal of Beneficial California, Inc.* (2005) CCH CALIFORNIA TAX REPORTS ¶403-851)

It is not clear at this point whether the FTB will follow the decision in *American General.* In any event, the case does not resolve the issue of how to apply Section 24425 to other expenses that the FTB may attempt to allocate to insurance company dividend income, as Section 24344(b) only applies to interest.

It is possible that the FTB may attempt to disallow an amount of interest expense that actually exceeds the dividend deduction, or to disallow interest expense in years when no dividend income was received.

Practitioners should also keep in mind that for tax years beginning before January 1, 1990, there were no ownership limitations on the Sec. 24402 deduction, so the dividend received deduction would be equal to 100% of all qualifying dividends received by the taxpayer.

Finally, it should be also be noted that the State Board of Equalization in a letter decision dated September 12, 2006 in the *Appeal of River Garden Retirement Home* (No. 297405) (CCH CALIFORNIA TAX REPORTS ¶404-055) held that a taxpayer was not entitled to deduct dividends it received in 1999 and 2000 from corporations previously taxed in California. In essence, the SBE upheld the FTB's above-mentioned policy in this area. Both Abbott Labs and River Garden Retirement Home are currently litigating this issue. See *Abbott Labs v. FTB*, Los Angeles Superior Court Civil Case No. BC369808.

Bruce Daigh, Chris Whitney, Contributing Editors

FTB's internal policy outlined.—In an internal memorandum sent to the FTB's audit staff, the FTB outlined its policies for dealing with returns in which a dividends received deduction was claimed under Sec. 24402 since it was declared unconstitutional in *Farmer Bros.* (*Memorandum*, California Franchise Tax Board, Multistate Audit Program Bureau, May 17, 2004, CCH CALIFORNIA TAX REPORTS ¶403-646).

The FTB has taken the position that California law requires that the deduction be disallowed for all open tax years (*CCH Note:* The *Farmer's Bros.* lower court ordered a refund, even for open tax years, but the FTB did not appeal this portion of the ruling; therefore, the appropriate remedy was not addressed in the appellate court's ruling). For tax years ending after November 30, 1999, the FTB disallows all Sec. 24402 deductions. Expenses associated with the dividend income that were previously added back, because the dividend income was not included in the measure of tax, should be subtracted.

For tax years ending prior to December 1, 1999, all dividends received from noninsurance corporations are deductible, subject to the statutory ownership limitations. For example, prior to the *Farmer Bros.* decision, a taxpayer with a 15% dividends received deduction percentage, computed on the basis of the percentage of the dividends that had previously been subject to corporation franchise or income tax, was required to limit the dividends received deduction to 15% of the dividends paid, multiplied by the applicable statutory ownership limitation (see below for an explanation of the ownership limitation). After the *Farmer Bros.* decision, for tax years ending prior to December 1, 1999, the first limitation may not be applied and, if otherwise qualified, the taxpayer may claim a 100% dividends received deduction, subject to the applicable statutory ownership limitation. However, expenses associated with the dividend income must be added back to federal taxable income for purposes of computing California taxable income (see ¶1023 for a discussion of this addback provision).

The exclusion of 75% of qualified dividends received from foreign subsidiaries by taxpayers filing a water's-edge election will not generally be available to taxpayers for tax years ending prior to December 1, 1999, because such dividends will likely be fully deductible under Sec. 24402. Consequently, the foreign investment interest offset will not be applicable in most cases for tax years ending prior to December 1, 1999.

Prior law.—Prior to being declared unconstitutional, Sec. 24402 excluded from taxable income a portion of dividends received that were paid out of income that had been subject to either the franchise tax, the alternative minimum tax, or the corporation income tax in the hands of the paying corporation. In order for the recipient corporation to claim such a deduction, the paying corporation must have had income from sources in California that required the filing of a California income or franchise tax return.

One hundred percent of dividends received from a more than 50%-owned corporation that was subject to California tax was excluded; also excluded were 80% of dividends from a 20%-owned corporation, and 70% of dividends from a less-than-20%-owned corporation. The percentage owned referred to the percentage of stock owned by vote and value by the taxpayer. Preferred stock was not considered in determining the percentage of stock owned.

• *Intercompany dividends*

Intercompany dividends between members of a controlled group filing a combined report are excluded from income, to the extent such dividends are paid out of unitary income. (Sec. 25106, Rev. & Tax. Code) Dividends received from noncontrolled affiliated corporations may be treated as "business" income, apportionable within and without the state as described in Chapter 13 (¶1302).

Practice Pointer: Dividends Paid Up the Corporate Chain

The FTB Chief Counsel has taken the position that distributions paid up the corporate chain from lower tier subsidiaries to the ultimate parent of a unitary group each constituted dividends, creating unitary income to the respective payees within the meaning of Rev. & Tax. Code Sec. 25106, so that the third in the series of three distributions qualified for the intercompany dividend elimination from income. Furthermore, the Chief Counsel clarified that for purposes of the dividend elimination provision, California follows an earnings and profits ordering rule for dividend payments similar to the federal rules, whereby dividends are deemed paid out of current earnings and profits first and then layered back on a last-in, first-out basis. (*Chief Counsel Ruling 2007-4*, California Franchise Tax Board, January 3, 2008, CCH CALIFORNIA TAX REPORTS ¶404-710)

Dividend elimination is available whether or not the members of the group are California taxpayers. Dividends paid by a group member may be eliminated even if no group members were subject to California taxation at the time the income was earned as long as the income would have been included in a California combined report had any of the group members been subject to California taxation at the time that the income was earned. (Sec. 25106, Rev. & Tax. Code)

For taxable years beginning after 2007, the law provides that intercompany dividends may also be eliminated if paid from the unitary group's income to a newly formed corporation if the recipient corporation was part of the unitary group from the time it was formed until the time the dividends were received. (Sec. 25106, Rev. & Tax. Code)

Tax evasion.—Beginning with the 2009 taxable year, the FTB may deny the elimination of intercompany dividends available to members of a unitary combined reporting group if the FTB determines that the transaction is entered into or structured with a principal purpose of evading California corporation franchise or income taxes. (Sec. 25106, Rev. & Tax. Code)

• *Dividends from insurance subsidiary*

Practitioner Comment: Ceridian Dividends Received Deduction Issue Resolved

Under A.B. 263, Laws 2004, Rev. & Tax. Code Section 24410 is amended to allow a deduction for dividends received (DRD) from an insurance company in which the taxpayer owns at least 80% of each class of stock. This deduction is available irrespective of the location of the insurance company or the source of its income.

This legislation resolves the confusion that ensued following the 2001 Court of Appeals decision in *Ceridian Corp. v. Franchise Tax Board,* 85 Cal.App.4th 875 (2001), which held that a California franchise tax deduction for dividends paid by insurance companies to their non-insurance parent companies unlawfully discriminated in favor of domestic corporations. Following the decision, FTB legal staff had taken the position that *Ceridian* invalidated Section 24410 in its entirety and that no dividends received deduction was available for years following the decision. Taxpayers, on the other hand, believed that the portions of Section 24410 invalidated by *Ceridian* are severable from the remainder of the statute, which remained in effect and provides a full dividends received deduction.

The legislation, while providing a DRD for current and future years, also provided an opportunity for taxpayers to claim a dividends received deduction for taxable years ending on or after December 1, 1997, and beginning before January 1, 2004. During these years, a deduction of 80% of the qualifying dividends would generally be allowed provided that the taxpayer made an irrevocable election by March 28, 2005, and remitted any amounts due for the qualifying years as a result of that election. An electing taxpayer may not pursue any refund claims requesting a greater DRD than the amount allowed under the election.

In exchange for allowing the dividends received deduction for tax years beginning after 2003, the legislation contains complex "anti-stuffing" provisions designed to prevent the use of insurance companies to shelter income from California franchise tax. Although these anti-abuse provisions are aimed at captive insurers, the provisions are very broad and may impact non-captive insurers as well. These anti-stuffing rules may result in a reduction (or elimination) of the allowable DRD as well as disallowance of other deductions attributable to intercompany transactions with insurance subsidiaries.

Bruce Daigh, Chris Whitney, Contributing Editors

A deduction is allowed for a portion of the qualified dividends received by a corporation or by members of the corporation's commonly controlled group (if any) from an insurance company subsidiary, regardless of whether the insurance company is engaged in business in California, if at the time of each dividend payment, at least 80% of each class of stock of the insurer was owned by the corporation receiving the dividend. The deduction is equal to 85% (80% prior to the 2008 taxable year) of the qualified dividends received. (Sec. 24410, Rev. & Tax. Code)

Disincentives to overcapitalization of insurance company subsidiaries.—Dividends qualifying for the deduction must be reduced on the basis of an overcapitalization percentage. The overcapitalization percentage is calculated by dividing the five-year average of net written premiums for all insurance companies in the insurance company's commonly controlled group by the five-year average of total income for all insurance companies in the insurance company's commonly controlled group. The dividends qualifying for the deduction will not be reduced if the overcapitalization percentage is 70% or greater (60% prior to 2008). If the overcapitalization percentage is greater than 10% and less than 70% (60% prior to 2008), the dividends qualifying for the deduction will be ratably reduced for each percentage point by which the overcapitalization percentage falls below 70% (60% prior to 2008). The dividends qualifying for the reduction will be reduced to zero if the overcapitalization percentage is 10% or less. (Sec. 24410, Rev. & Tax. Code)

Special rules for dividends from self-insurance companies.—Special rules apply to dividends received from an insurance company that insures risks of a member of its commonly controlled group. Premiums received or accrued from another member of the insurance company's commonly controlled group will not be included in the overcapitalization ratio calculation. Furthermore, dividends attributable to premiums received or accrued by the insurance company from a member of the insurance company's commonly controlled group will not qualify for the dividends received deduction. (Sec. 24410, Rev. & Tax. Code)

Legislative intent.—The provisions of Sec. 24410 set forth above are intended to provide equitable tax treatment for insurance company dividends in light of the California court of appeal's decision in *Ceridian Corp. v. Franchise Tax Board*, 85 Cal.App.4th 875 (2000) (see below). The legislature has declared that the tax treatment of insurance company dividends under Section 24410 is unrelated to and distinguishable from the tax treatment of general corporation dividends under Section 24402 and from the application of Section 24425 to deductions allocable to those dividends, and that no inference should be drawn with respect to Section 24402 (see above) or the application of Section 24425 (see ¶1023) from the changes with respect to Section 24410. (Uncodified Sec. 6, Ch. 868 (A.B. 263), Laws 2004)

Prior law.—Rev. & Tax. Code Sec. 24410 previously allowed only California-domiciled corporations a deduction for dividends received from a California subsidiary insurance company that was subject to the gross premiums tax. A California appellate court determined that the deduction allowed to California-domiciled corporations for dividends received by a California subsidiary insurance company was unconstitutional because it facially discriminated against interstate commerce without compelling justification, in violation of the Commerce Clause of the U.S. Constitution. According to the court, the statute unconstitutionally favored domestic corporations over foreign competitors by disallowing deductions based on property owned and people employed outside California by a dividend-declaring insurer (*Ceridian Corp. v. Franchise Tax Board*, (2000) CCH CALIFORNIA TAX REPORTS ¶403-121; *aff'g* SuperCt, No. 983377, May 7, 1998, CCH CALIFORNIA TAX REPORTS ¶402-996).

Deemed dividends.—The FTB may include a deemed dividend from an insurance company subsidiary in the gross income of the parent corporation (or a member of the corporation's combined reporting group), if all insurance companies in the commonly controlled group have a capitalization percentage not exceeding 15% (10% for taxable years beginning prior to 2008) and the earnings and profits of the insurance company subsidiary have been accumulated to avoid income taxes of any state. The deemed dividend equals the corporation's pro rata share (or the combined reporting group member's pro rata share) of the insurance companies' earnings and profits for the taxable year. However, the amount of the deemed dividend is limited to a particular insurance company's net income attributable to investment income less that insurance company's net written premiums received for the year. The amount included is treated as a dividend received from an insurance company during the taxable year, which may be deductible under Sec. 24410, above. (Sec. 24900, Rev. & Tax. Code)

• *Expenses attributable to dividend income*

The FTB has taken the position in some cases that general and administrative expenses attributable to dividend income are not deductible. This is on the ground that expenses attributable to tax-exempt income are nondeductible. (Sec. 24425, Rev. & Tax. Code) See ¶1021 and ¶1023.

• *Dividends paid to employee stock ownership plan*

California conforms to federal law (IRC Sec. 404(k)) allowing a deduction for specified dividends paid on stock held by an employee stock ownership plan. The deduction is unavailable to S corporations under both California and federal law. (Sec. 24601, Rev. & Tax. Code)

• *Income from qualifying investment securities*

A corporation's distributive share of interest, dividends, and gains from qualifying investment securities that are sold or exchanged by an investment partnership in which the corporation is a partner is not income derived from sources within California and thus is not subject to the corporation income tax, provided that the following conditions are satisfied:

(1) the income is the corporation's only income derived from sources within California;

(2) the corporation does not participate in the management of the investment partnership's investment activities; and

(3) the corporation is not engaged in a unitary business with another corporation or partnership that does not meet the requirements of (1) and (2), above.

Income, gain, or loss from stocks or securities received by an alien corporation is also exempt if the corporation's sole activity in California involves trading stocks or securities for its own account. The exemption does not apply to an alien corporation that has income attributable to California sources or that is engaged in a unitary business with another corporation that has California source income other than the income, gain, or loss from stocks or securities described above. Dealers in stocks and securities are also ineligible to claim this exemption. (Sec. 23040.1, Rev. & Tax. Code)

• *Special rules for liquidations*

See ¶1220 for special rules regarding certain corporate liquidations.

¶910 Interest on Government Bonds

Law: Sec. 24272 (CCH CALIFORNIA TAX REPORTS ¶10-610).

Comparable Federal: Secs. 103, 141-150 (CCH U.S. MASTER TAX GUIDE ¶729 et seq.).

California Form: Form 100 (California Corporation Franchise or Income Tax Return).

Although federal law generally prohibits states from taxing obligations issued by the U.S. government, this prohibition does not apply to the imposition of a nondiscriminatory corporate franchise tax. Accordingly, corporations that are subject to the California franchise tax must include in gross income all interest received from federal obligations. Interest income from state, municipal, or other bonds must also be included in gross income for franchise tax purposes. (Sec. 24272, Rev. & Tax. Code)

However, because the California corporate income tax is subject to the federal prohibition described above, corporations subject to the corporate income tax may exclude U.S. bond interest from gross income. Income from bonds issued by the state of California or by a local government within the state are similarly exempt from the corporate income tax.

The exemption of U.S. obligations does not extend to interest received on refunds of federal taxes (¶217). See ¶1212 for the treatment of gain or loss on the sale of government bonds.

Under federal law, interest on the obligations of a state or its political subdivisions and on obligations issued by the federal government are generally exempt from state tax.

¶911 Income from Bond Discount, etc.

Law: Secs. 23051.5, 24344.5, 24991-93 (CCH CALIFORNIA TAX REPORTS ¶10-640, 10-815).

Comparable Federal: Secs. 1271-88, 6706 (CCH U.S. MASTER TAX GUIDE ¶1952 et seq.).

California Forms: Form 100 (California Corporation Franchise or Income Tax Return), Sch. D (100) (California Capital Gains and Losses), Sch. D-1 (Sales of Business Property).

Same as personal income tax (¶237).

¶912 Commodity Credit Loans

Law: Sec. 24273 (CCH CALIFORNIA TAX REPORTS ¶10-515).

Comparable Federal: Sec. 77 (CCH U.S. MASTER TAX GUIDE ¶769).

As under federal law, a taxpayer may elect for California purposes to treat as income amounts received as loans from the Commodity Credit Corporation. (Sec. 24273, Rev. & Tax. Code)

¶913 Contributions to Capital of a Corporation

Law: Secs. 24322, 24325 (CCH CALIFORNIA TAX REPORTS ¶10-340, 10-515).

Comparable Federal: Sec. 118

California incorporates federal law that excludes a contribution to capital from a corporate taxpayer's income. (Sec. 24325, Rev. & Tax. Code)

Where property is contributed to capital by someone other than a shareholder, the corporation is required to reduce the basis of property by the amount of the contribution (¶1234).

¶914 Patronage Allocations from Cooperatives

Law: Sec. 24273.5 (CCH CALIFORNIA TAX REPORTS ¶10-250).

Comparable Federal: Sec. 1385 (CCH U.S. MASTER TAX GUIDE ¶698).

Same as personal income tax (¶232).

¶915 Condominiums and Co-ops

Law: Sec. 23701t (CCH CALIFORNIA TAX REPORTS ¶10-245, 89-102).

Comparable Federal: Sec. 528 (CCH U.S. MASTER TAX GUIDE ¶699).

California Form: Form 100 (California Corporation Franchise or Income Tax Return).

Nonprofit homeowners' associations, such as condominium management associations and timeshare associations, are usually tax-exempt. However, any income from sources other than membership dues, fees, and assessments ("exempt-function income") is taxable if it exceeds $100 a year. Associations that have such taxable income should file a corporation income tax return, in addition to the usual information return or statement as explained at ¶811. The California law conforms generally, but not completely, to the federal law. (Sec. 23701t, Rev. & Tax. Code)

As one of the conditions required for exemption, California requires that any "exempt-function income" not expended for association purposes during the taxable year be "transferred to and held in trust" for proper use in the association's operations. There is nothing comparable in the federal law.

¶916 Income from Foreign Aircraft or Ships

Law: Secs. 24320-21 (CCH CALIFORNIA TAX REPORTS ¶10-704, 10-913).

Comparable Federal: Sec. 883 (CCH U.S. MASTER TAX GUIDE ¶2455).

California Form: Form 100 (California Corporation Franchise or Income Tax Return).

Income from the operation of foreign aircraft or ships is exempt under certain conditions. The aircraft or ships must be registered or documented in a foreign country, and the income of the corporation must be exempt from national income taxes under a reciprocal agreement between the United States and the foreign country. The federal law contains a similar exemption. (Sec. 24320, Rev. & Tax. Code; Sec. 24321, Rev. & Tax. Code)

In *Appeals of Learner Co. et al.* (1980) (CCH CALIFORNIA TAX REPORTS ¶11-520.43), the State Board of Equalization held that this exemption did not apply where the ship involved was documented in Liberia, because there was no reciprocal agreement between the United States and Liberia.

¶917 Merchant Marine Act Exemption

Law: Sec. 24272.5 (CCH CALIFORNIA TAX REPORTS ¶10-515).

Comparable Federal: Sec. 7518.

California conforms to federal law. U.S. citizens that own or lease qualified vessels may establish tax-deferred reserve funds, called capital construction funds, under Section 607 of the Merchant Marine Act of 1936, for the replacement or addition of vessels. Generally, amounts deposited into a capital construction fund are deductible from taxable income, and earnings from the investment of amounts held in the fund are not taken into account.

Withdrawals made for the acquisition, construction, or repair of a qualified vessel are "qualified withdrawals" and do not generate income. Nonqualified withdrawals generate income and are taxed in the year they are made. (Sec. 24272.5, Rev. & Tax. Code)

¶918 Income from Investments in Depressed Areas

Law: Sec. 24384.5 (CCH CALIFORNIA TAX REPORTS ¶10-845).

Comparable Federal: None.

California Form: Form 100 (California Corporation Franchise or Income Tax Return).

The corporation tax law allows a deduction for net interest received from loans made to a trade or business located in an enterprise zone (¶104). It does not apply to any taxpayer that has an ownership interest in the debtor. (Sec. 24384.5, Rev. & Tax. Code)

¶919 Income from Recycled Beverage Containers

Law: Sec. 24315 (CCH CALIFORNIA TAX REPORTS ¶10-860).

Comparable Federal: None.

California Form: Form 100 (California Corporation Franchise or Income Tax Return).

Same as personal income tax (¶201).

¶920 Relocation Payments

Law: Sec. 7269, Government Code (CCH CALIFORNIA TAX REPORTS ¶10-912).

Comparable Federal: Public Law 91-646 (CCH U.S. MASTER TAX GUIDE ¶702).

California Form: Form 100 (California Corporation Franchise or Income Tax Return).

Same as personal income tax (¶236).

¶921 Rebates for Installation of Water Conservation Devices

Law: Sec. 24323 (CCH CALIFORNIA TAX REPORTS ¶10-860).

Comparable Federal: None.

California Form: Form 100 (California Corporation Franchise or Income Tax Return).

Under California law, but not federal law, certain water conservation rebates received by taxpayers from local water agencies or suppliers for the purchase or installation of specified water closets are treated as excludable refunds or price adjustments rather than as taxable income. (Sec. 24323, Rev. & Tax. Code)

¶922 Energy Conservation Subsidies

Law: Secs. 24308.1, 24326 (CCH CALIFORNIA TAX REPORTS ¶10-860).

Comparable Federal: Sec. 136 (CCH U.S. MASTER TAX GUIDE ¶884).

California Form: Form 100 (California Corporation Franchise or Income Tax Return).

Same as personal income tax (¶245).

¶923 Cost-Share Payments Received by Forest Landowners

Law: Sec. 24308.5 (CCH CALIFORNIA TAX REPORTS ¶10-860).

Comparable Federal: Sec. 126 (CCH U.S. MASTER TAX GUIDE ¶881).

California Form: Form 100 (California Corporation Franchise or Income Tax Return).

California provides an exclusion from gross income for cost-share payments received by forest landowners from the Department of Forestry and Fire Protection pursuant to the California Forest Improvement Act of 1978 or from the U.S. Department of Agriculture, Forest Service, under the Forest Stewardship Program and the Stewardship Incentives Program, pursuant to the federal Cooperative Forestry Assistance Act. The amount of any excluded payment must not be considered when determining the basis of property acquired or improved or when computing any deduction to which the taxpayer may otherwise be entitled. (Sec. 24308.5, Rev. & Tax. Code)

¶924 Earnings on Qualified Tuition Programs

Law: Secs. 23711, 23711.5, 24306 (CCH CALIFORNIA TAX REPORTS ¶10-245, 10-515).

Comparable Federal: Sec. 529 (CCH U.S. MASTER TAX GUIDE ¶697).

California incorporates federal law excluding from a contributor's gross income any earnings under a qualified tuition program. Distributions to a corporation as a result of a refund or credit on the qualified tuition program or savings account is includible in the corporation's gross income to the extent the distribution exceeds the amounts actually contributed. See ¶250 for more details. (Sec. 23711, Rev. & Tax. Code)

California has established a qualified state tuition program entitled the Golden State Scholarshare Trust.

¶925 Foreign Source Income

Law: None (CCH CALIFORNIA TAX REPORTS ¶10-707).

Comparable Federal: Secs. 114, 199 (CCH U.S. MASTER TAX GUIDE ¶245, 2471).

Unlike federal law, California does not provide any special treatment for foreign source income. Foreign source income is treated as ordinary income for California corporation franchise and income tax purposes. In addition, California does not incorporate the federal domestic production activities deduction (IRC Sec. 199).

Taxpayers that use the federal reconciliation method (¶803) must make an adjustment on their California corporation franchise or income tax return, adding back any amounts excluded.

¶926 Federal Prescription Drug Subsidies

Law: None (CCH CALIFORNIA TAX REPORTS ¶10-709).

Comparable Federal: Sec. 139A.

California does not incorporate and does not have any provision similar to IRC Sec. 139A, which allows taxpayers to exclude special federal subsidies for prescription drug plans received under Sec. 1860D-22 of the Social Security Act. Taxpayers that use the federal reconciliation method (¶803) must make an addition adjustment to the extent such amounts are excluded from federal taxable income.

TAXES ON CORPORATE INCOME

CHAPTER 10
DEDUCTIONS

¶1001 Trade or Business Expenses

Law: Secs. 24343, 24343.7, 24383, 24415, 24443, 24602 (CCH CALIFORNIA TAX REPORTS ¶10-515, 10-595, 10-645, 10-830, 10-880).

Comparable Federal: Secs. 83, 162, 190, 274 (CCH U.S. MASTER TAX GUIDE ¶713, 901—999, 1287).

California Form: Form 100 (California Corporation Franchise or Income Tax Return).

Same as personal income tax, as explained at ¶301 and ¶302, except for provisions that, by their terms, do not apply to corporations. (Sec. 24343, Rev. & Tax. Code; Sec. 24343.7, Rev. & Tax. Code; Sec. 24383, Rev. & Tax. Code; Sec. 24415, Rev. & Tax. Code; Sec. 24443, Rev. & Tax. Code; Sec. 24602, Rev. & Tax. Code)

Corporations are specifically precluded by California law from claiming business expense deductions for granting California qualified stock options (see ¶207 for a discussion of the favorable tax treatment afforded to California qualified stock options).

¶1002 Expenses of Soil Conservation, etc.

Law: Secs. 24369, 24377 (CCH CALIFORNIA TAX REPORTS ¶10-515).

Comparable Federal: Secs. 175, 180 (CCH U.S. MASTER TAX GUIDE ¶982, 985).

Same as personal income tax (¶341).

¶1003 Circulation Expenditures of Periodicals

Law: Sec. 24364 (CCH CALIFORNIA TAX REPORTS ¶10-515).

Comparable Federal: Sec. 173 (CCH U.S. MASTER TAX GUIDE ¶971).

Same as personal income tax (¶342).

¶1004 Interest

Law: Secs. 24344, 24344.5, 24344.7, 24424, 24438-39, 24451 (CCH CALIFORNIA TAX REPORTS ¶10-210, 10-515, 10-540, 10-815, 11-515).

Comparable Federal: Secs. 163, 249, 264, 265, 279, 385, 461(g) (CCH U.S. MASTER TAX GUIDE ¶341, 533, 909, 940, 970, 1044, 1055, 1056).

California Form: Form 100 (California Corporation Franchise or Income Tax Return).

California incorporates by reference as of the current IRC tie-in date (¶803) the federal rule generally providing a deduction for all interest paid or accrued on business debts. (Sec. 24344, Rev. & Tax. Code) In *Hunt-Wesson, Inc. v. Franchise Tax Board* (2000) (CCH CALIFORNIA TAX REPORTS ¶403-071), the U.S. Supreme Court held that a California interest offset provision that reduced a non-California corporation's interest expense deduction by the amount of the corporation's nonbusiness income not allocable to California was unconstitutional because it imposed tax on income outside California's jurisdictional reach. According to the Court, the state's attribution of all taxpayer borrowing first to nonunitary investment, even if none of the funds borrowed were actually invested in the nonunitary business, was not a reasonable allocation of taxpayer expense deductions to the income that the expense generated.

• *FTB clarification of post-**Hunt-Wesson** interest expense deductions*

The California Franchise Tax Board has issued *FTB Notice 2000-9* (CCH CALIFORNIA TAX REPORTS ¶403-120) to explain the limitations on the deductibility of interest expense in light of the U.S. Supreme Court decision in *Hunt-Wesson.* The FTB policy is that the interest-offset provision invalidated in *Hunt-Wesson* will not be applied to nondomiciliary corporations, but that all other provisions in the interest-offset rules will continue to be applied.

FTB Notice 2000-9 explains the treatment of interest expense deductions and the interest offset in the aftermath of *Hunt-Wesson.* Based on the notice, domestic and foreign corporations must compute their allowable interest expense deduction differently. Foreign (*i.e.,* non-California) corporations allocate their interest expense between apportionable and nonapportionable income as follows:

(1) A deduction for interest expense equal to business interest income may be claimed in computing income subject to apportionment.

(2) A deduction for interest expense in excess of business interest income may be claimed in computing income subject to apportionment in an amount equal to the amount of nonbusiness interest and dividend income.

(3) Any interest expense in excess of interest income and nonbusiness dividend income may be assigned to other types of nonbusiness income, such as rents and royalties, under authority of Reg. 25120 (d), 18 CCR. Interest expense assigned to such nonbusiness income items would not be deductible in determining apportionable income. Note, however, that the FTB will not apply Reg. 25120 (d), 18 CCR to

assign interest expense to assets that have the potential to generate interest and dividend income. In other words, the FTB will not use the regulation to assign interest expense to capital gains or losses from sales or other exchanges of stocks, bonds and similar instruments.

(4) Any remaining interest expense (after applying steps 1 through 3) is deductible against apportionable income.

For domestic (*i.e.,* California) corporations, interest expense is allocated in the same manner, except that step 2 is modified to provide that interest expense in excess of business interest income may reduce nonbusiness interest and dividend income allocable to California in an amount equal to the amount of nonbusiness interest and dividend income. In other words, California corporations continue to enjoy a full offset of interest expense against nonbusiness interest and dividend income.

Practitioner Comment: Interest Offset Provisions Continue to Benefit In-State Companies

As noted above, FTB policy after *Hunt-Wesson* is to require the dollar-for-dollar offset of interest expense against nonbusiness interest and dividend income only with respect to such nonbusiness income items that are allocable to California. This approach can provide a substantial benefit for taxpayers domiciled in California. A.B. 1618, which passed the legislature in 2007, would have repealed the interest offset provisions of Cal. Rev. & Tax. Code Sec. 24344(b). The Governor vetoed this legislation on October 11, 2007. As a result, for the time being these provisions will continue to benefit California domiciled businesses.

Bruce Daigh, Chris Whitney, Contributing Editors

• *Pre-**Hunt-Wesson** decisions*

In *Appeal of F.W. Woolworth Co. et al.* (1998) (CCH CALIFORNIA TAX REPORTS ¶10-815.33), a California court of appeal held that the interest expense deducted by a parent corporation and its wholly owned subsidiary was properly reduced by the amount of its nonunitary dividend income. However, the U.S. Supreme Court has remanded this case in light of the *Hunt-Wesson, Inc.* case (discussed above).

The exclusion of dividends deductible under former Sec. 24402 applied to foreign domiciliary corporations as well as to California corporations—see Legal Ruling No. 379 (1975) (CCH CALIFORNIA TAX REPORTS ¶11-520.55).

Application of the rule limiting deductibility of interest expense was discussed in *Appeal of Kroehler Mfg. Co.* (1964) (CCH CALIFORNIA TAX REPORTS ¶11-520.53). The rule (as it stood prior to the 1967 amendment relating to intercompany dividends) was also discussed at length in the 1972 decision of the California Supreme Court, in *The Pacific Telephone and Telegraph Company v. Franchise Tax Board* (1972) (CCH CALIFORNIA TAX REPORTS ¶11-515.352).

In *Appeal of Sears, Roebuck and Co., et al.* (1970) (CCH CALIFORNIA TAX REPORTS ¶11-520.532), the State Board of Equalization (SBE) held that carrying charges on installment sales may not be treated as interest income in applying the rules set forth above. The SBE held that the special provisions permitting the buyer to treat a portion of carrying charges as interest (¶305) had no application to the seller.

The Franchise Tax Board ruled in Legal Ruling No. 59 (1958) (CCH CALIFORNIA TAX REPORTS ¶10-815.92) that interest on federal tax deficiencies was subject to the foregoing limitations.

• *Prepaid interest*

Both California and federal law require cash-basis taxpayers to deduct prepaid interest over the period to which it applies. (Sec. 24681, Rev. & Tax. Code)

• *Interest on company-owned life insurance*

California incorporates federal law, disallowing a deduction by an employer for interest expenses paid or accrued that are associated with debt incurred by the employer to purchase life insurance policies or endowment or annuity contracts for *any* individual for whom the employer has an insurable interest. However, an employer may still deduct interest paid or incurred on debt to purchase life insurance policies, annuities, and endowment contracts for a limited number of officers and 20% owners if (1) the aggregate amount of debt with respect to the policies and contracts does not exceed $50,000 per person and (2) the interest rate does not exceed a specified amount. (Sec. 24424, Rev. & Tax. Code)

• *California-federal differences*

California and federal rules regarding deduction of interest differ in that:

— Federal law has nothing comparable to the special California rules for multistate corporations, discussed above.

— Federal law disallows interest on indebtedness incurred or continued to carry tax-exempt obligations. California has no comparable provision regarding interest, although the same result presumably would be achieved under the California provision disallowing expenses allocable to tax-exempt income (¶1023). Such interest is deductible generally by financial institutions as a business expense. However, federal deductions for such interest are reduced as a result of a provision reducing the benefits of certain tax preferences. For private activity bonds and certain other obligations not meeting federal qualifications issued after August 7, 1986, interest indebtedness expense is not deductible under federal law.

— California has not conformed to special federal rules regarding bond registration requirements.

— Because of California's conformity date (¶803), California does not incorporate federal amendments made by the Tax Increase Prevention and Reconciliation Act of 2005 (TIPRA), which revised the federal earnings stripping rules to provide that a corporate partner's interest and expenses for purposes of the limitation on the interest expense deduction for disqualified interest is to be treated as that of the corporation and not the partnership. Consequently, taxpayers may have greater limits placed on the interest deduction claimed on their federal return than on their California return.

California conforms to the federal law regarding computation of deductions for original issue discount (OID) as of the current IRC tie-in date (see ¶803).

¶1005 Passive Activity Losses and Credits

Law: Sec. 24692 (CCH CALIFORNIA TAX REPORTS ¶10-635).

Comparable Federal: Sec. 469 (CCH U.S. MASTER TAX GUIDE ¶2053 et seq.).

California Form: FTB 3802 (Corporate Passive Activity Loss and Credit Limitations).

Same as personal income tax (¶340).

¶1006 Taxes

Law: Secs. 24345-46 (CCH CALIFORNIA TAX REPORTS ¶10-515, 10-615, 10-840, 11-515).

Comparable Federal: Sec. 164 (CCH U.S. MASTER TAX GUIDE ¶532).

California Form: Form 100 (California Corporation Franchise or Income Tax Return).

The California deduction for taxes is the same as the federal deduction as of the current IRC tie-in date (¶803), except for the following differences:

— unlike federal law, California does not permit deduction of the California franchise or income tax, or of any other tax based on income or profits and levied by any foreign country or by any state, territory, or taxing subdivision thereof; neither are such taxes allowed as a credit against the California tax (¶823);

— California law permits deduction of water or irrigation district general assessments levied on all lands within the district; there is nothing comparable under federal law; and

— California does not permit an increase in basis for sales tax for which a credit is claimed by enterprise zone, former Los Angeles Revitalization Zone, local agency military base recovery area, and targeted tax area taxpayers, as explained at ¶818.

(Sec. 24345, Rev. & Tax. Code; Sec. 24346, Rev. & Tax. Code)

The prohibition against deduction of income taxes is the same as under the personal income tax law. See the discussion at ¶306, including cases holding that the prohibition does not apply to some taxes based on *gross receipts.* However, the prohibition does apply to taxes based on *gross income.* See *MCA, Inc. v. Franchise Tax Board* (1981) (CCH CALIFORNIA TAX REPORTS ¶10-561.202), in which the Court of Appeal disallowed deductions for foreign taxes paid on film rentals and record royalties. The Court's opinion makes a careful distinction between "gross receipts" and "gross income."

• *Treatment of various taxes*

The following outlines the treatment of various state, federal, and foreign taxes. Addition adjustments are only necessary for those taxes that are nondeductible under California law.

Canadian mining taxes.—Nondeductible (*Alloys, Inc.* (1984) (CCH CALIFORNIA TAX REPORTS ¶400-493)

Federal minimum tax.—Nondeductible (*Coachella Valley Savings and Loan Assn.* (1987) (CCH CALIFORNIA TAX REPORTS ¶401-499)

Federal social security taxes paid by employers —Deductible (Reg. 24345-5, 18 CCR)

Foreign income taxes.—Nondeductible (*California Response to CCH Multistate Corporate Income Tax Survey,* California Franchise Tax Board, July 21, 2003, CCH CALIFORNIA TAX REPORTS ¶403-506)

Kentucky license tax.—Deductible (*California Response to CCH Multistate Corporate Income Tax Survey,* California Franchise Tax Board, July 21, 2003, CCH CALIFORNIA TAX REPORTS ¶403-506)

Libyan petroleum tax surcharge.—Deductible (*Occidental Petroleum Corp.* (1983) CCH CALIFORNIA TAX REPORTS ¶403-394)

Michigan single business tax (MSBT).—Deductible (*Kelly Service, Inc.* (1997) CCH CALIFORNIA TAX REPORTS ¶402-935; *Dayton Hudson Corp.* (1994) CCH CALIFORNIA TAX REPORTS ¶402-678)

New Hampshire business profits tax.—Nondeductible (*California Response to CCH Multistate Corporate Income Tax Survey,* California Franchise Tax Board, July 21, 2003, CCH CALIFORNIA TAX REPORTS ¶403-506)

New York franchise taxes.—Nondeductible (*Coro, Inc.* (1955) CCH CALIFORNIA TAX REPORTS ¶200-306)

Ohio franchise tax - net worth portion.—Deductible (*California Response to CCH Multistate Corporate Income Tax Survey,* California Franchise Tax Board, July 21, 2003, CCH CALIFORNIA TAX REPORTS ¶403-506)

Texas franchise tax - net worth portion.—Deductible (*California Response to CCH Multistate Corporate Income Tax Survey,* California Franchise Tax Board, July 21, 2003, CCH CALIFORNIA TAX REPORTS ¶403-506)

Unemployment insurance tax contributions paid by employers.—Deductible (Reg. 24345-5, 18 CCR)

Washington business and occupation tax.—Deductible (*California Response to CCH Multistate Corporate Income Tax Survey,* California Franchise Tax Board, July 21, 2003, CCH CALIFORNIA TAX REPORTS ¶403-506)

West Virginia business and occupation tax.—Deductible (*California Response to CCH Multistate Corporate Income Tax Survey,* California Franchise Tax Board, July 21, 2003, CCH CALIFORNIA TAX REPORTS ¶403-506)

¶1007 Losses

Law: Secs. 24347-47.5, 24694 (CCH CALIFORNIA TAX REPORTS ¶10-515, 10-685, 10-820, 10-875).

Comparable Federal: Secs. 165, 198A, 470, 582 (CCH U.S. MASTER TAX GUIDE ¶1101—1195).

California Form: Form 100 (California Corporation Franchise or Income Tax Return).

California incorporates federal law as of the current IRC tie-in date (¶803), which allows a deduction for losses sustained and not compensated for by insurance or otherwise. (Sec. 24347, Rev. & Tax. Code)

California also incorporates federal law disallowing deductions for losses associated with tax-exempt use property to the extent the losses exceed the income from the leases of the property. Amounts disallowed as tax-exempt use losses are carried over to the next year and are treated as a federal deduction with respect to the property, again limited to the income received from the property leases. (Sec. 24694, Rev. & Tax. Code) As a result of California's current IRC conformity date, California does not incorporate the Tax Technical Corrections Act of 2007 amendments made to IRC Sec. 470 that retroactively make the loss deferral rules for property leased to tax-exempt entities inapplicable to partnerships unless specified conditions are satisfied. However, similar treatment applied during the 2004 through 2006 tax years as a result of IRS notices and bulletins and presumably would be followed by California currently. (*Summary of Federal Income Tax Changes—2007,* Franchise Tax Board, April 2008)

Also, California has not conformed to a provision of the federal Emergency Economic Stabilization Act of 2008 that allows certain financial institutions to take ordinary gain or loss on the sale or exchange of preferred stock in the Federal National Mortgage Association (Fannie Mae) or the Federal Home Loan Mortgage Corporation (Freddie Mac), applicable to sales or exchanges occurring after December 31, 2007, in tax years ending after that date.

The corporate provisions regarding the deduction and carryover of disaster losses are the same as the provisions for personal income (¶307). (Sec. 24347.4, Rev. & Tax. Code; Sec. 24347.5, Rev. & Tax. Code)

See Chapter 12 of this *Guidebook* for a discussion of capital losses.

See ¶1223 for treatment of losses on redemption of U.S. Savings Bonds. See ¶1023 regarding disallowance of certain losses.

¶1008 Wash Sales

Law: Sec. 24998 (CCH CALIFORNIA TAX REPORTS ¶10-640).

Comparable Federal: Sec. 1091 (CCH U.S. MASTER TAX GUIDE ¶2361).

Same as personal income tax (¶527).

¶1009 Bad Debts

Law: Secs. 24347, 24348, 24434 (CCH CALIFORNIA TAX REPORTS ¶10-340, 10-515, 10-685, 10-875).

Comparable Federal: Secs. 166, 271, 582, 593, 595 (CCH U.S. MASTER TAX GUIDE ¶1128, 1157—1163).

California law governing the deduction of bad debts is the same as federal law as of the current IRC tie-in date (see ¶803) with the following modifications:

— with respect to partially worthless debts, if a portion of a debt is deducted in any year, no deduction is allowable in a subsequent year for any portion of the debt that was charged off in a prior year, whether claimed as a deduction in the prior year or not; and

— California incorporates federal law relating to bad debts with respect to securities held by financial institutions, but modifies a federal limitation on foreign corporations so that the limitation applies only to foreign corporations that have a water's-edge election in effect for the taxable year.

(Sec. 24347, Rev. & Tax. Code; Sec. 24348, Rev. & Tax. Code; Sec. 24434, Rev. & Tax. Code)

California allows banks, at the discretion of the FTB, to claim a deduction for bad debt reserves in conformance with federal law. (Sec. 24348, Rev. & Tax. Code)

• *Bad debt vs. capital contribution*

For a loan to qualify as a bad debt deduction, the taxpayer must have a reasonable expectation of repayment and a debtor-creditor relationship must exist. If a purported advance of funds is essentially a capital investment placed at the risk of the business, it does not qualify as a loan for a bad debt deduction.

• *Decisions of State Board of Equalization*

In *Appeal of Southwestern Development Company* (1985) (CCH CALIFORNIA TAX REPORTS ¶10-875.24), the State Board of Equalization (SBE) upheld the FTB's position that items deducted by the taxpayer as bad debts were actually capital contributions and, hence, not deductible. Funds placed at the risk of the business with no reasonable expectation of repayment were capital contributions. Advances made during the formation period of a business and later funds to protect the initial investment were also capital contributions. The SBE also held that losses from a business could not be claimed as totally worthless in a year when the business continued in operation beyond that particular year.

In *Appeal of San Fernando Valley Savings and Loan Association* (1975) (CCH CALIFORNIA TAX REPORTS ¶10-340.23), the taxpayer made inadequate additions to its bad-debt reserve in 1968 and 1969, resulting in a debit balance in the reserve. Adequate additions would have resulted in net operating losses for those years. In 1970 the taxpayer claimed a deduction for an addition to the reserve to reduce the debit balance built up in 1968 and 1969. The SBE upheld the FTB's disallowance of the 1970 deduction, pointing out that the taxpayer's accounting had the effect of a net operating loss carryover, which was not allowed under California law in effect at that time.

In *Appeal of Culver Federal Savings and Loan Association* (1966) (CCH CALIFORNIA TAX REPORTS ¶10-340.57), the SBE held that a reserve for bad debts entered on its books by the taxpayer and deducted for federal income tax purposes, but not for California, could nevertheless be claimed later to obtain a refund of California tax. The FTB applied the rationale of this case in Legal Ruling No. 417 (1981) (CCH CALIFORNIA TAX REPORTS ¶10-340.261), which provides that a savings and loan association may retroactively increase its bad debt deduction up to the amount of the year's addition to the reserve as shown on the association's books, but not beyond that amount.

¶1010 Worthless Securities

Law: Sec. 24347 (CCH CALIFORNIA TAX REPORTS ¶10-340, 10-515, 10-685, 10-820).

Comparable Federal: Sec. 165 (CCH U.S. MASTER TAX GUIDE ¶1764).

Same as personal income tax (¶307).

¶1011 Depreciation and Amortization

Law: Secs. 24349-56.8, 24365, 24368.1, 24369.4, 24372.3-73, 24407-09, 24421-22, 24990 (CCH CALIFORNIA TAX REPORTS ¶10-385, 10-515, 10-640, 10-670, 10-680, 10-690, 10-800, 10-845, 10-900, 10-915).

Comparable Federal: Secs. 59, 167-69, 174, 178, 179, 181, 194, 197, 198, 248, 280F (CCH U.S. MASTER TAX GUIDE Chapter 12).

California Forms: FTB 3580 (Application to Amortize Certified Pollution Control Facility), FTB 3805Z (Enterprise Zone Deduction and Credit Summary), FTB 3807 (Local Agency Military Base Recovery Area Deduction and Credit Summary), FTB 3809 (Targeted Tax Area Deduction and Credit Summary), FTB 3885 (Corporation Depreciation and Amortization), Sch. B (100S) (S Corporation Depreciation and Amortization).

A corporate taxpayer is permitted a deduction for depreciation of real or personal property used in a trade or business or held for the production of income. (Sec. 24349, Rev. & Tax. Code) The California depreciation provisions are generally the same as those contained in the pre-1987 personal income tax law (see "Assets Placed in Service Before 1987" at ¶310). However, beginning with the 2005 taxable year, the useful life of motor sports entertainment complexes and Alaska natural gas pipelines is seven years. (Sec. 24355.3, Rev. & Tax. Code; Sec. 24355.4, Rev. & Tax. Code)

Except as discussed below, the federal accelerated cost recovery system (ACRS) depreciation method for assets placed in service after 1980 and the federal modified accelerated cost recovery system (MACRS) depreciation method for assets placed in service after 1986 have not been adopted into the California corporation tax law.

Practitioner Comment: Corporate Partners Need Not Recompute Their Distributive Share of Income for Depreciation Items

While California does not conform to IRC Sec. 168 (so called "MACRS" depreciation) under the Bank and Corporate Tax Law, it does so in the Personal Income Tax Law. The Franchise Tax Board's longstanding view has been that corporate partners need not recompute their share of partnership income, even though such may have been based on federal depreciation methods not adopted under the Bank and Corporate Tax Law. See *FTB Notice 89-129* (CCH CALIFORNIA TAX REPORTS ¶401-175.

Bruce Daigh, Chris Whitney, Contributing Editors

Written agreements may be made between the taxpayer and the Franchise Tax Board (FTB) as to the useful life and depreciation rate of a particular property. (Sec. 24351, Rev. & Tax. Code; Sec. 24352, Rev. & Tax. Code)

• *ACRS depreciation allowed for S corporations*

An S corporation's deduction for depreciation and amortization is computed under the personal income tax law (¶310, ¶311). (Sec. 17201, Rev. & Tax. Code)

• *IRC Sec. 179 asset expense election*

Taxpayers may elect to claim an IRC Sec. 179 asset expense election for corporation income and franchise tax purposes in lieu of the first-year additional bonus depreciation deduction discussed below. California's asset expense election is limited to $25,000 per taxable year, rather than the $250,000 federal maximum available during the 2008 taxable year ($125,000 federal maximum during 2007, 2009, and 2010 tax years; $100,000 federal maximum for the 2003 through 2006 tax years). The federal maximum, unlike the California maximum limit, is subject to inflation adjustments. (Sec. 24356(b), Rev. & Tax. Code) The federal maximum amount as adjusted for inflation was $108,000 for property placed in service in 2006, and $105,000 for 2005.

Other differences between California and federal law are as follows:

— the phase-out threshold for the cost of the qualified property is $200,000 for California purposes in contrast to the federal phase-out threshold of $800,000 during the 2008 tax year, $500,000 during 2007, 2009, and 2010 tax years, $400,000 during the 2003 through 2006 tax years, subject to an inflation adjustment). The federal phase-out threshold amounts as adjusted for inflation were $430,000 for the 2006 tax year, and $420,000 for the 2005 tax year;

— federal law, unlike California law, allows the election to be made for purchases of off-the-shelf computer property; and

— California does not allow taxpayers to make, modify, or revoke the election without the consent of the FTB, whereas taxpayers may unilaterally make, modify, or revoke the election during the 2003 through 2010 tax years for federal purposes; and

— California law, unlike federal law, does not raise the deduction amount for disaster-related purchases.

If a taxpayer elects this deduction, the depreciable basis of the subject property must be reduced by the IRC Sec. 179 expense. (Instructions, FTB 3885F, Corporation Depreciation and Amortization) Because the maximum California deduction differs from the maximum federal deduction, the depreciable basis of property will differ for federal and state purposes.

Prior to the 2005 taxable year, the asset expense election was not available to corporation franchise and income taxpayers, other than S corporations. C corporation taxpayers were limited to claiming the additional first-year bonus depreciation deduction discussed below.

• *Residential rental property*

Although California does not incorporate MACRS or ACRS, California allows the use of these federal depreciation methods to determine a reasonable depreciation allowance for California purposes. Accordingly, under federal law as incorporated by California, corporate taxpayers are permitted to treat residential rental property on which construction began after 1986, and before July 1, 1988, as either 18-year real property, 27.5-year residential rental property, or asset depreciation range property. (*Letter*, FTB, September 13, 1988, CCH CALIFORNIA TAX REPORTS ¶401-662)

• *Phylloxera infested vineyards*

The useful life for any grapevine replaced in a California vineyard is five-years if the grapevine was replaced as a direct result of (1) phylloxera infestation or (2) Pierce's Disease infestation. However, a taxpayer may elect to use the federal alternative depreciation system (¶310). If the taxpayer chooses to use this method and if the taxpayer elected not to capitalize the costs of replacing the infested vines, the replacement vines will have a class life of 10 years rather than the 20-year class life normally specified under federal law for fruit-bearing vines. (Sec. 24349(c), Rev. & Tax. Code)

• *Luxury automobiles and listed property*

For corporate income tax purposes, California adopts a modified version of IRC Sec. 280F, which imposes a limitation on depreciation deductions for luxury automobiles and other listed property, including computers and peripheral equipment. The limitation is similar to that imposed under the personal income tax law (¶310), except that for corporate purposes, the terms "deduction" or "recovery deduction" relating to ACRS mean amounts allowable as a deduction under the bank and corporation tax law. (Sec. 24349.1, Rev. & Tax. Code)

• *Property leased to tax-exempt entities*

California has adopted the IRC 168(h) limitation on deductions for property leased to tax-exempt entities for taxable years after 1986. For taxable years beginning after 1990, the amount of such deductions is limited to the amount determined under IRC Sec. 168(g), concerning the alternative depreciation system. (Sec. 24349(d), Rev. & Tax. Code)

• *Salvage reduction*

The amount of salvage value to be taken into consideration in computing the amount subject to depreciation may be reduced by up to 10% of the depreciable basis of the property, except with respect to property for which California allows the use of the current federal depreciation methods. (Sec. 24352.5, Rev. & Tax. Code)

• *Additional first-year depreciation*

Planning Note: Additional 30%/50% First-Year Bonus Depreciation Not Allowed

California does not incorporate the IRC Sec. 168(k) 50% bonus depreciation deduction for property purchased in 2008, nor did California allow the IRC Sec. 168(k) additional 30% or 50% bonus depreciation deduction for property purchased after September 10, 2001, and before 2005. California also does not incorporate the additional 30% first-year bonus depreciation deduction allowed for qualified New York Liberty Zone property. However, California does allow a limited 20% first-year bonus depreciation deduction as discussed below.

California does allow a corporate taxpayer to take an additional 20% first-year (bonus) depreciation deduction on personal property having a useful life of six years or more. It is limited to 20% of the cost of such property, and may be claimed only with respect to $10,000 of property additions each year and is taken in lieu of the IRC Sec. 179 deduction discussed above. (Sec. 24356, Rev. & Tax. Code ; Reg. 24356-1, 18 CCR; Reg. 24356(d), 18 CCR)

The limitation is applied to each taxpayer, and not to each taxpayer's trade or business. In determining the allowable first-year depreciation bonus, all members of an affiliated corporation are treated as one taxpayer. The basis of the property used for regular depreciation purposes must be reduced by the amount of bonus depreciation claimed.

• *Safe-harbor leases*

California recognizes safe harbor leases under former IRC Sec. 168(f). (*California Response to CCH Multistate Corporate Income Tax Survey*, California Franchise Tax Board, July 21, 2003, CCH CALIFORNIA TAX REPORTS ¶403-506).

• *Pollution control facilities*

Same as personal income tax (¶314). (Sec. 24372.3, Rev. & Tax. Code)

CCH Practice Tip: Preference Item Reduction

Because California incorporates the IRC Sec. 291 tax preference item treatment for C corporations and for elections made during the first three taxable years following a C corporation conversion to an S corporation, only 80% of the facility's adjusted basis may be amortized over 60 months. Accordingly, for corporations, the amortizable basis for such facilities for which a rapid amortization election is made must be reduced by 20%. (Instructions, FTB 3580, Application to Amortize Certified Pollution Control Facility)

• *Trademark, trade name, and franchise transfer payments*

Same as personal income tax (¶332). (Sec. 24368.1, Rev. & Tax. Code)

• *Films, video tapes, sound recordings, and similar property*

Same as personal income tax (¶310). (Sec. 24349(f), Rev. & Tax. Code ; Sec. 24355.4, Rev. & Tax. Code)

• *Indian reservation property*

Same as personal income tax (¶310).

• *Environmental remediation expenses*

Same as personal income tax (¶346).

• *Reforestation expenses*

A corporate taxpayer may elect to currently deduct up to $10,000 of qualified reforestation expenses in the year paid and to capitalize and amortize any remaining amount over a seven-year period. This applies to direct costs of forestation or reforestation, including seeds, labor, equipment, etc. The amortization period begins on the first day of the second half of the taxable year of the expenditures. The deduction is taken from adjusted gross income and is limited to $10,000 per taxable year. (Sec. 24372.5, Rev. & Tax. Code)

• *Research and experimental expenditures*

Same as personal income tax (¶331). (Sec. 24365, Rev. & Tax. Code; Reg. 24365-24368(a) --Reg. 24365-24368(d), 18 CCR)

• *Amortization of cost of acquiring a lease*

Same as personal income tax (¶313). (Sec. 24373, Rev. & Tax. Code)

• *Organizational expenditures*

As under federal law, taxpayers may currently deduct up to $5,000 in start-up expenses and amortize any remainder over a 15-year period. (Sec. 24407, Rev. & Tax. Code)

• *Term property interests*

California adopts federal law, under which no depreciation or amortization deduction is allowed for any term property interest (such as a life interest, an interest for a term of years, or an income interest in a trust) for any period during which the remainder interest is held, directly or indirectly, by a related person. The basis of such property for which a depreciation or amortization deduction has been allowed must be reduced by the amount of the disallowed deduction, and the basis of the remainder interest in such property must be increased by the same amount. (Sec. 24368.1, Rev. & Tax. Code)

• *Accelerated write-offs for depressed areas*

Same as personal income (¶316), except that in addition to disallowing the IRC Sec. 179 asset expense election if the write-offs are claimed by enterprise zone, local agency military base recovery area, targeted tax area, or former Los Angeles Revitalization Zone businesses, the additional first-year depreciation is disallowed. (Sec. 24356.7, Rev. & Tax. Code; Sec. 24356.8, Rev. & Tax. Code; Former Sec. 24356.4, Rev. & Tax. Code)

• *Goodwill and other intangibles*

Same as personal income tax (¶ 333). (Sec. 24355.5, Rev. & Tax. Code)

¶1012 Depletion

Law: Secs. 24831, 24831.6 (CCH CALIFORNIA TAX REPORTS ¶ 10-515, 10-850).

Comparable Federal: Secs. 611-38 (CCH U.S. MASTER TAX GUIDE ¶ 1289 et seq.).

California Form: Form 100 (California Corporation Franchise or Income Tax Return).

Same as personal income tax (¶ 319, ¶ 540).

¶1013 Development and Exploration Expenses of Mines, etc.

Law: Secs. 24423, 24831 (CCH CALIFORNIA TAX REPORTS ¶ 10-515, 10-850).

Comparable Federal: Secs. 193, 263(c), 263(i), 616-17 (CCH U.S. MASTER TAX GUIDE ¶ 987—990, 1779).

California Form: Form 100 (California Corporation Franchise or Income Tax Return).

Except for minor technical differences, the corporation tax law is the same as the personal income tax law, as explained at ¶ 320. The corporation tax law also specifically provides for deduction of intangible drilling and development costs of oil and gas wells. (Sec. 24423, Rev. & Tax. Code; Sec. 24831, Rev. & Tax. Code)

California has no provision comparable to the federal provision that provides a deduction for expenses incurred for tertiary injectants.

¶1014 Contributions

Law: Secs. 18648.5, 24357-59.1 (CCH CALIFORNIA TAX REPORTS ¶ 10-650, 10-705, 10-880, 10-900).

Comparable Federal: Secs. 170, 6115 (CCH U.S. MASTER TAX GUIDE ¶ 1058—1071).

California Form: Form 100 (California Corporation Franchise or Income Tax Return).

Corporations are allowed a California deduction for contributions paid to certain organizations, up to a limit of 10% of net income computed without the benefit of this deduction or certain other special deductions (dividends received, building and loan dividends paid, certain deductions of cooperatives, etc.). Contributions in excess of the 10% limit may be carried over to the next five succeeding taxable years. (Sec. 24357, Rev. & Tax. Code; Sec. 24358, Rev. & Tax. Code)

• *California-federal differences*

—There are differences in the adjustments to income for purposes of computing the limitation. For federal purposes, income is adjusted for net operating loss carryovers and other special deductions not applicable to California. For California purposes, income is adjusted, as shown above, for special deductions not applicable to the federal computation. (Sec. 24357, Rev. & Tax. Code)

—There are slight differences in the rules for contributions of appreciated property. California ordinarily reduces the contribution by the amount of the untaxed gain; in effect, the deduction is limited to the cost basis of the property. The federal law similarly limits the deduction to the donor's basis in the property. However, federal law retains an exception for donations of appreciated stock to certain private foundations. (Sec. 24357.1, Rev. & Tax. Code)

—Federal law, unlike California law, allows a deduction for certain contributions of research property to a California college or university, the amount being the basis of the property plus one-half of the appreciation, limited to twice the basis.

—California allows a deduction for charitable contributions only if the contributions are verified under regulations prescribed by the Franchise Tax Board. For federal purposes, charitable contributions may be deducted only if the contributions are verified under regulations prescribed by the Secretary of the Treasury. (Sec. 24357, Rev. & Tax. Code)

—Under federal law prior to the 2010 tax year, certain gifts of computer technology and equipment by C corporations to specified organizations qualified for an augmented charitable deduction. California allowed a similar deduction for qualified computer contributions made during the 2002 and 2003 taxable years.

—California has no provision similar to the federal provision disallowing the deduction for transfers made in split-dollar insurance arrangements.

—California does not adopt federal provisions that limit the charitable contributions deduction for patents and most other intellectual property donated to a charitable organization to the lesser of the donor's basis in the property or its fair market value, but allow limited additional deductions for such contributions if the donee has income attributable to the donation during the 12 years after the property is donated. Nor has California conformed to the limits placed on the amount of deductions that may be claimed for vehicles, boats, and aircraft and the increased substantiation requirements for such property (see ¶321 for details).

—California has not adopted federal provisions that allow an enhanced deduction for donations of food and books from the taxpayer's inventory, applicable for federal purposes to donations made between August 28, 2005, and December 31, 2009.

—California did not adopt amendments made by the Gulf Opportunity Zone Act of 2005 that waived the 10% of taxable income limitation for corporations for qualified cash donations related to Hurricanes Katrina, Rita, and Wilma or the Emergency Economic Stabilization Act of 2008 that waives the 10% limitation for the 2008 Midwest storm victims.

Finally, California also has not enacted amendments similar to those made by the PPA that:

— increase the amount of the charitable contributions deduction that may be claimed for qualified conservation real property for corporate farmers and ranchers, applicable to contributions made in tax years beginning after 2005;

— limit the deduction for donations of taxidermy property to the lesser of the donor's basis in the property or the fair market value of the property, applicable to contributions made after July 25, 2006;

— require donors of charitable contributions of monetary gifts to retain certain records, regardless of the amount, applicable to contributions made after August 17, 2006;

— with certain exceptions, make qualified contributions to donor advised funds fully deductible, applicable to contributions made after the date that is 180 days after August 17, 2006; and

— change the rules regarding donations of fractional interests in tangible personal property, applicable to contributions made after August 17, 2006.

Because the contribution deduction is limited to the adjusted basis of the assets being contributed and the income from which the contributions are deducted, taxpayers must add back the federal contributions deduction and recalculate the amount that may be deducted for California corporation franchise and income tax purposes. The computation is completed on a separate worksheet, using the Form 100, California Corporation Franchise or Income Tax Return, as a format and adding in any federal contribution deduction on Line 8, Form 100. An additional worksheet is also provided in the Form 100, Instructions to Line 14, to complete the computation. (Instructions, Form 100, California Corporation Franchise or Income Tax Return)

The California limitation may also be affected by the apportionment of income within and without the state (¶1312).

¶1015 Amortization of Bond Premium

Law: Secs. 24360-63.5 (CCH CALIFORNIA TAX REPORTS ¶10-610).

Comparable Federal: Sec. 171 (CCH U.S. MASTER TAX GUIDE ¶1967).

California Form: Form 100 (California Corporation Franchise or Income Tax Return).

Deduction is allowed, at the taxpayer's election, for amortization of premium on bonds owned. (Sec. 24360, Rev. & Tax. Code through 24363.5, Rev. & Tax. Code) The general rule is the same as the federal rule, but there may be a difference in its application because of differences in taxability of government bond interest or because the taxpayer may elect to amortize for California purposes and not for federal, or vice versa. This may result in a difference in the adjusted cost basis, and consequently a difference in gain or loss, when bonds are sold. For California purposes, the premium of a taxable bond is allocated to the interest from the bond. In lieu of being deducted, the premium is applied against (and reduces) interest income from the bond.

No amortization is allowable on any portion of bond premium attributable to conversion features of the bond.

The federal law provides that the amortization period is to be determined with reference to the maturity date of the bonds, except that if use of an earlier call date results in a smaller amortization deduction, then the call date is to be used.

The California law contains nothing comparable to the federal provision that requires securities dealers to amortize premium paid on certain short-term municipal bonds. Because of the difference in treatment of interest on municipal bonds for franchise tax purposes, there would be no point in having such a provision in the California law.

¶1016 Payments to Pension or Profit-Sharing Plans

Law: Secs. 24601-12, 24685.5 (CCH CALIFORNIA TAX REPORTS ¶10-515, 10-520, 10-595).

Comparable Federal: Secs. 194A, 401-20, 4971-75 (CCH U.S. MASTER TAX GUIDE Chapter 21).

Same as personal income tax, except that the corporation tax law incorporates by reference only those federal provisions that deal with employer deductions (¶330, ¶607). (Sec. 24601 et. seq., Rev. & Tax. Code; Sec. 24685.5, Rev. & Tax. Code)

¶1017 Employee Stock Options

Law: Secs. 24379, 24601-12 (CCH CALIFORNIA TAX REPORTS ¶10-515, 10-520, 10-595, 10-645).

Comparable Federal: Secs. 83, 421-24 (CCH U.S. MASTER TAX GUIDE ¶1919— 1934A).

Except with respect to California qualified stock options, the California rules regarding an employer's treatment of employee stock options and other transfers of property for services are the same as federal. (Sec. 24379, Rev. & Tax. Code; Sec. 24601 et. seq., Rev. & Tax. Code)

An employer corporation is precluded by California law from claiming a business expense deduction for granting a California qualified stock option (see ¶207 for a discussion of the favorable tax treatment afforded California qualified stock options). (Sec. 24602, Rev. & Tax. Code)

¶1018 Start-Up Expenditures

Law: Sec. 24414 (CCH CALIFORNIA TAX REPORTS ¶10-210, 10-515).

Comparable Federal: Sec. 195 (CCH U.S. MASTER TAX GUIDE ¶481, 984).

Same as personal income tax (¶334).

¶1019 Subsidization of Employees' Ridesharing and Parking

Law: Sec. 24343.5 (CCH CALIFORNIA TAX REPORTS ¶10-830).

Comparable Federal: None.

California Form: Form 100 (California Corporation Franchise or Income Tax Return).

The corporation tax law permits employers to claim a business expense deduction for specific benefits paid or incurred relating to employee ridesharing and parking. These benefits are the following:

— subsidizing employees commuting in buspools, private commute buses, carpools, and subscription taxipools;

— subsidizing monthly transit passes to employees and their dependents;

— compensating employees who do not require free parking;

— providing free or preferential parking to carpools, vanpools, and any other vehicle used in a ridesharing arrangement;

— making facility improvements to encourage employees to participate in ridesharing arrangements, to use bicycles, or to walk (corporations are allowed a 36-month depreciation deduction for these improvements);

— providing company commuter van or bus service to employees for commuting to and from their homes; improvements (capital costs) to the vehicle are not allowed as a business expense deduction;

— providing employee transportation services that are required as part of the employer's business activities, if the employee is not reimbursed and there is no available ridesharing incentive program; and

— providing cash allowances to employees in amounts equal to the parking subsidies that the employer would otherwise pay to secure parking spaces for those employees.

(Sec. 24343.5, Rev. & Tax. Code)

¶1020 Deduction for Dividends Received

Law: Secs. 24402, 24410 (CCH CALIFORNIA TAX REPORTS ¶10-810).

Comparable Federal: Secs. 243-47 (CCH U.S. MASTER TAX GUIDE ¶237 et seq.).

California law provided a deduction for dividends received when the income distributed had been subjected to tax in the hands of the paying corporation. However, as discussed at ¶909, this deduction was held unconstitutional as applied to non-California corporations. (Sec. 24402, Rev. & Tax. Code) California does allow a deduction for dividends paid from insurance company subsidiaries (¶909). California also allows an intercompany dividend elimination for members of a combined unitary group (¶909).

¶1021 Deductions Allowed to Special Classes of Organizations

Law: Secs. 24370, 24403-06.6, 24870-74 (CCH CALIFORNIA TAX REPORTS ¶10-250, 10-340, 10-355, 10-360, 10-365, 10-370, 10-701).

Comparable Federal: Secs. 521, 591, 851-60, 1381-83 (CCH U.S. MASTER TAX GUIDE ¶698, 2301, 2317, 2320, 2323, 2326, 2329, 2337, 2339, 2383,).

California Form: Form 100 (California Corporation Franchise or Income Tax Return).

The California law allows special deductions to certain classes of organizations, as follows:

— building and loan associations: dividends on shares allowed as a deduction (Sec. 24403, Rev. & Tax. Code);

— agricultural cooperative associations: income from nonprofit activities allowed as a deduction (Sec. 24404, Rev. & Tax. Code);

— other cooperative associations: income from certain nonprofit activities allowed as a deduction (see below) (Sec. 24405, Rev. & Tax. Code);

— retail cooperatives: certain allocated patronage refunds allowed as a deduction (see below) (Sec. 24406, Rev. & Tax. Code);

— mutual savings banks: certain interest on deposits allowed as a deduction for franchise tax purposes (Sec. 24370, Rev. & Tax. Code);

— real estate investment trusts (REITs): income distributed during the year, or within a certain period after the year, is allowed as a deduction (see also ¶805);

— regulated investment companies (RICs): exempt interest dividends distributed to shareholders allowed as a deduction (see also ¶805) (Sec. 24870 et. seq., Rev. & Tax. Code);

— gas producers' cooperatives: patronage refunds paid to patrons allowed as a deduction (Sec. 24406, Rev. & Tax. Code); and

— credit unions: income arising from business with credit union members and income from investments of surplus member savings capital (see *Christian Community Credit Union* (2003) (CCH CALIFORNIA TAX REPORTS ¶10-250.24) for the formula established by the SBE for computing this deduction) and income resulting from reciprocal transactions with member credit unions are allowed as a deduction.

Income allocations to members of agricultural cooperatives may be made within $8^1/_2$ months after the close of the taxable year and still be considered as having been made on the last day of the taxable year, provided the members are advised of the dollar amount of such allocations.

Income earned by credit unions from third-party investments are not exempt from tax as income from business done for credit union members, and share dividends paid by the credit unions to their members are not deductible as patronage dividends, interest, or ordinary and necessary business expenses. (*Educational Employees Credit Union v. Franchise Tax Board* (2006) CCH CALIFORNIA TAX REPORTS ¶10-250.4191)

Agricultural cooperatives are permitted to deduct all income, regardless of source, that is properly allocated to members. See Legal Ruling No. 389 (1975) (CCH CALIFORNIA TAX REPORTS ¶10-250.25) and Legal Ruling No. 418 (1981) (CCH CALIFORNIA TAX REPORTS ¶10-250.34).

Retail cooperatives are permitted to deduct patronage refunds allocated to their patrons, provided the refunds are made and allocated within specific restrictions set forth in the law. (Sec. 24406, Rev. & Tax. Code)

In *Appeal of Certified Grocers of California, Ltd.* (1962) (CCH CALIFORNIA TAX REPORTS ¶10-250.35), the State Board of Equalization (SBE) held that a wholesale grocery cooperative could deduct patronage dividends and interest on members' accounts, following long-standing federal practice, irrespective of the fact that the California law did not provide specifically to this effect in the year involved.

California law, like federal law, allows a cooperative to pay a dividend on capital stock or other proprietary capital interest of the organization without reducing net earnings, to the extent that the organizational documents provide that the dividend is in addition to amounts otherwise payable to patrons. (Sec. 24406.6, Rev. & Tax. Code)

• *Some expenses not deductible*

In Security-First National Bank v. Franchise Tax Board (1961) (CCH CALIFORNIA TAX REPORTS ¶10-210.361), it was held that a cooperative association could not deduct expenses allocable to income for which special deductions discussed above were allowable. To the same effect, see *Anaheim Union Water Company v. Franchise Tax Board* (1972) (CCH CALIFORNIA TAX REPORTS ¶10-250.393), involving the deductibility of operating losses of a nonprofit mutual water company against income from certain profit-making activities. The Court of Appeal held that the losses in question were nondeductible because they were allocable to exempt income. Also, to the same effect, see *Appeal of Los Angeles Area Dodge Dealers Association* (1978) (CCH CALIFORNIA TAX REPORTS ¶10-250.55), involving interest on short-term certificates of deposit. See also ¶1023.

In *Appeal of San Antonio Water Company* (1970) (CCH CALIFORNIA TAX REPORTS ¶10-250.39), the SBE held that gain on sale of land to a member of a cooperative was not deductible under the third item above.

For a good discussion of the accounting rules applicable to organizations covered by the other cooperative associations, above, see *Appeal of Redwood Mutual Water Company* (1980) (CCH CALIFORNIA TAX REPORTS ¶10-250.391).

In *Appeal of Imperial Hay Growers' Association* (1970) (CCH CALIFORNIA TAX REPORTS ¶10-250.27), the SBE held that a loss on plant abandonment was outside the scope of the special provisions described above and was deductible against income derived from nonmembers.

The federal law allows some special deductions somewhat comparable, in a general way, to the California deductions described above. In view of the many differences, no attempt is made here to compare the two laws.

¶1022 Tenant Expenses—Cooperative Apartment and Housing Corporations

Law: Sec. 24382 (CCH CALIFORNIA TAX REPORTS ¶10-515).

Comparable Federal: Sec. 216 (CCH U.S. MASTER TAX GUIDE ¶1028, 1040).

California law is generally the same as federal law in allowing certain expenses of tenant-stockholders to be deducted. (Sec. 24382, Rev. & Tax. Code) However, as a result of California's current IRC conformity date (see ¶803), California does not adopt federal amendments made by the Mortgage Forgiveness Debt Relief Act of 2007 that add alternative tests based on square footage devoted to residential purposes, and expenditures made on behalf of residents for purposes of determining whether a housing cooperative qualifies for pass-through treatment, applicable to tax years ending after December 20, 2007.

¶1023 Items Not Deductible

Law: Secs. 24343.2, 24343.7, 24421-29, 24436-37, 24441-48, 24691 (CCH CALIFORNIA TAX REPORTS ¶10-250, 10-515, 10-520, 10-525, 10-595, 10-645, 10-665, 10-800, 10-810).

Comparable Federal: Secs. 162, 261-68, 271, 274, 276-77, 280B, 280C, 280E, 280G (CCH U.S. MASTER TAX GUIDE ¶293, 673, 901, 903, 907, 909, 910 et seq., 969, 970, 972, 990 et seq., 1029, 1122, 1166, 1330, 1343, 1551, 1553, 1717, 1747, 2028, 2257).

California Form: Form 100 (California Corporation Franchise or Income Tax Return).

Certain items are made expressly nondeductible, the principal items being:

(a) capital expenditures, certain life insurance premiums, interest on indebtedness incurred in connection with certain life insurance and annuity contracts, expenses allocable to tax-exempt income, carrying charges that the taxpayer elects to capitalize, etc. (Sec. 24422, et seq., Rev. & Tax. Code);

(b) losses on transactions between certain related interests (Sec. 24427, Rev. & Tax. Code);

(c) accrued expenses and interest payable to a person or corporation related to the payor, under certain circumstances (generally, the payor is required to report such items on the cash basis of accounting) (Sec. 24427, Rev. & Tax. Code);

(d) expenses of certain illegal activities or of other activities that tend to promote or are otherwise related to such illegal activities, as explained at ¶336;

(e) illegal bribes, kickbacks, etc., and certain other expenses, as explained at ¶336;

(f) certain expenses attributable to substandard housing, as explained at ¶336;

(g) abandonment fees on open-space easements and timberland tax-recoupment fees, as explained at ¶336;

(h) certain expenses in connection with entertainment activities, business gifts, and foreign conventions, as explained at ¶302;

(i) deductions for remuneration of personal services that are not reported in required statements to employees (¶715) or in required information returns (¶713) may be disallowed at the discretion of the Franchise Tax Board (FTB);

(j) deductions for interest, taxes, depreciation, and amortization are denied to property owners who fail to file proper information returns as explained at ¶713;

(k) business expenses incurred at a discriminatory club, as explained at ¶336; and

(l) expenses of advertising in political programs or for admission to political fundraising functions and similar events (Sec. 24429, Rev. & Tax. Code).

• *California-federal differences*

(a) There are no federal provisions comparable to items (d), (f), (g), and (k), above, except for a federal provision that prohibits deductions and credits for illegal drug trafficking. Otherwise, the California rules are generally similar to the federal rules, as they relate to corporations.

(b) The federal law provides that certain "golden parachute" payments are not deductible by the payor corporation. (An excise tax is imposed on the recipient.) California corporation tax law has not conformed to this provision.

(c) Federal law contains a special provision disallowing expenses attributable to the production of an unharvested crop in certain cases when the land is sold after having been used in a trade or business. There is no necessity for a comparable California rule, because California has no special alternative method of computing the tax on capital gains.

(d) Federal law that generally prohibits a current deduction for capital expenditures does not apply for California purposes to expenditures for which a deduction is allowed under California law for enterprise zone, local agency military base recovery area, or targeted tax area property.

• *Entertainment and gifts*

California law is the same as federal law. (Sec. 24443, Rev. & Tax. Code)

• *Shipping company and oil/gas drilling rig employee's meal expenses*

Both California and federal law allow a 100% deduction (rather than 50%) of meals to employees on offshore oil or gas rigs and to employees who are crew members of certain commercial vessels (¶302).

• *Expenses allocable to exempt income*

Like federal law (IRC Sec. 265(a)), a California deduction of expenses allocable to tax-exempt income is not allowed. (Sec. 24425, Rev. & Tax. Code) Under the allocation and apportionment provisions (see ¶1301 *et seq.*), if some income is not included within a corporation's measure of tax, any deductions in connection with the production of such income may not be deducted from income attributable to such sources. (Reg. 25120, 18 CCR)

Also, under California law, no deduction is allowed for specified interest and other expenses paid or incurred to an insurer, if the insurer is a member of the taxpayer's commonly controlled group and the amount paid or incurred would constitute income to the insurer if the insurer were subject to California corporation franchise or income tax (see Sec. 24425(b) for details).

There may be a difference between federal and California treatment of expenses allocable to tax-exempt income, as referred to in item (a), above, in that certain items may be excludable or deductible from income for California purposes, but not for federal. Examples include interest earned by certain cooperative associations, income from bonds exempt under California law, but not federal law, etc. See ¶1021 for cases involving credit unions and cooperative associations, and ¶1004 regarding unallowable interest on indebtedness incurred to acquire property from which the income is allocable to sources outside California. Also see ¶909 for a discussion of this in relation to the dividends received deduction.

In *Appeal of Mission Equities Corporation* (1975) (CCH CALIFORNIA TAX REPORTS ¶10-800.402), the State Board of Equalization (SBE) followed the *Great Western Financial* case, below, in disallowing expenses allocable to dividends received from California subsidiaries. The SBE approved the FTB's allocation of indirect expenses between taxable and nontaxable income in proportion to the amount of each, the same formula having been approved by the Supreme Court in the *Great Western Financial* case.

In *Great Western Financial Corporation v. Franchise Tax Board* (1971) (CCH CALIFORNIA TAX REPORTS ¶204-497), the FTB disallowed deductions for interest and for general and administrative expenses of a parent corporation, on the ground that the deductions were allocable to income from dividends received from subsidiary California corporations and that such dividends were "exempt" income because they were deducted as explained in ¶909. The California Supreme Court held for the FTB, and concluded that "expenses incurred by a taxpayer in producing or receiving dividend income are properly deductible only when that taxpayer's dividend income is taxable."

Practitoner Comment: Deemed Intention

In *American General Realty Investment Corp., Inc. v. Franchise Tax Board,* California Superior Court for the City and County of San Francisco, No. CGC-03-425690, April 28, 2005, CCH CALIFORNIA TAX REPORTS ¶403-794, the Court held that the California Franchise Tax Board (FTB) erred in disallowing a portion of a taxpayer's interest expense deduction, because all of the interest expense was directly traceable to the active conduct of the taxpayer's consumer finance and real estate businesses, both of which generated taxable income.

Notably, in this decision the Court found that, under the rules of statutory construction, Section 24344(b) is applied before 24425. In other words, if there is no excess of business interest expense over business interest income, there is simply nothing to disallow. Before *Ceridian* the FTB's administrative position was that Section 24344(b) applies first, as outlined in FTB Legal Ruling 374, FTB Legal Ruling 424, and FTB Notice 2000-9. After the *Ceridian* decision, the FTB argued the opposite—that Section 24425 applies first.

The FTB alternately argued that IRC Sec. 265(a)(2) and Rev. Proc. 72-18 would apply to disallow the interest expense as well. The Court rejected both positions. With respect to Rev. Proc. 72-18, the Court firmly rejected the FTB's assertions and held that the taxpayer had met its burden of proving that no debt was incurred for the purposes of receiving exempt income.

American General Realty Investment Corp. is not binding precedent. However, in a letter decision the SBE has ruled that the FTB improperly disallowed a portion of the interest expense deductions claimed by a taxpayer's unitary group. The SBE ruled for the taxpayer and allowed the full deduction. The SBE did not give an explanation of its decision. However, the result in the letter decision is consistent with *American General Realty Investment Corp.* (*Appeal of Beneficial California, Inc.* (2005) CCH CALIFORNIA TAX REPORTS ¶403-851)

It is not clear at this point whether the FTB will follow the decision. In any event, the case does not resolve the issue of how to apply Section 24425 to other expenses that the FTB may attempt to allocate to insurance company dividend income, as Section 24344(b) only applies to interest.

It is possible that the FTB may attempt to disallow an amount of interest expense that actually exceeds the dividend deduction, or to disallow interest expense in years when no dividend income was received.

As to the disallowance of expenses other than interest expenses, the Superior Court on July 1, 2008 rejected the FTB's attempt to disallow certain overhead expenses which were charged by a corporate parent to its insurance company subsidiaries under the theory that "but for" such expenses the insurance companies would have been unable to conduct business and hence pay dividends to their parent. Instead, the court agreed that the expenses were directly traceable to the management fees received the subsidiaries and should be allowed. See *Mercury General Corporation v. Franchise Tax Board*, Superior Court, San Francisco Case No. CGC-07-462688. It is not known at this time whether the FTB will appeal this decision and it should be noted that Superior Court decisions are not citable and cannot be relied on as precedent.

Bruce Daigh, Chris Whitney, Contributing Editors

In *Appeal of Zenith National Insurance Corporation* (1998) (CCH CALIFORNIA TAX REPORTS ¶10-800.40), the FTB determined that the income from the taxpayer's sale of debentures and purchase of preferred stock contributed to both the taxpayer's taxable and nontaxable activities and, therefore, utilized a general formula to allocate the interest expense in accordance with the ratio of the taxpayer's tax-exempt income to the taxpayer's gross income. However, the SBE found that the taxpayer incurred the expense for the purpose of producing taxable income for three of the four income years at issue and, thus, could claim the full deduction for those three years.

• *Expenses for which credits are allowable*

California incorporates, as of the current IRC tie-in date (see ¶803), the portion of IRC Sec. 280C that disallows a deduction for (1) qualified clinical testing expenses that were otherwise available, to the extent that such expenses were claimed for the federal clinical testing tax credit, and (2) that portion of qualified research expenses or basic research expenses that equals the credit amount allowed for such expenses under IRC Sec. 41 (¶818).

California does not incorporate the rest of IRC Sec. 280C, which disallows a deduction for expenses for which other federal credits are claimed, such as the federal work opportunity credit and the low sulfur diesel fuel production credit.

Because federal provisions dealing with federal credits are inapplicable under California law (Sec. 23051.5(b), Rev. & Tax. Code), these provisions are inapplicable and taxpayers utilizing the federal reconciliation method (¶803) would be allowed to subtract such expenses on their federal return.

See ¶1004 regarding deduction of prepaid interest. See ¶1106 regarding certain deductions of farming corporations.

¶1024 Net Operating Loss Carryover and Carryback

Law: Secs. 24416, 24416.1-16.10, 25108, 25110 (CCH CALIFORNIA TAX REPORTS ¶10-385, 10-805, 11-550).

Comparable Federal: Sec. 172 (CCH U.S. MASTER TAX GUIDE ¶1173—1188).

California Forms: FTB 3805Q (Net Operating Loss (NOL) Computation and Disaster Loss Limitations - Corporations), FTB 3805Z (Enterprise Zone Deduction and Credit Summary), FTB 3806 (Los Angeles Revitalization Zone Deduction and Credit Summary), FTB 3807 (Local Agency Military Base Recovery Area Deduction and Credit Summary), FTB 3809 (Targeted Tax Area Deduction and Credit Summary).

Same as personal income tax (¶309), except as discussed below. (Sec. 24416 et. seq., Rev. & Tax. Code)

Practitoner Comment: Consider Deferral Strategies in Light of 2008 and 2009 NOL Suspension and New NOL Carry Back Provisions

Under AB 1452, enacted September 30, 2008, net operating loss (NOL) deductions are suspended for tax years beginning on or after January 1, 2008 and before January 1, 2010. As with the previous times that California NOLs were suspended (i.e., 2002 and 2003 and 1991 and 1992), taxpayers may incur substantial California corporate franchise tax liabilities during the suspension period. Taxpayers may consider strategies to defer income until years beginning on or after January 1, 2010 such as via permissible accounting method changes.

In addition, it should be noted that the legislation will allow the carry back of NOLs for tax years beginning on or after January 1, 2011 to the two immediately preceding years. It appears that NOLs generated in 2011 can be carried back and utilized in 2009 despite the NOL suspension applicable in 2009 to NOL carryovers generated in prior years. However, only 50% of NOLs attributable to tax year 2011 and 75% of NOLs attributable to tax year 2012 can be carried back.

Bruce Daigh, Chris Whitney, Contributing Editors

• *Water's-edge corporations*

A multinational corporation that has made a water's-edge election for the current taxable year may not fully deduct a net operating loss (NOL) carryover from a prior taxable year in which it had no water's-edge election in effect. Rather, the deduction is denied to the extent that the NOL carryover reflects income and apportionment factors of affiliated entities that would not have been taken into account had a water's-edge election been in effect for the year of the loss. (Sec. 24416(c), Rev. & Tax. Code)

In Legal Ruling 99-2 (1999) (CCH CALIFORNIA TAX REPORTS ¶10-805), the Franchise Tax Board clarified that, despite a prior legal ruling stating the contrary, in determining whether a water's-edge taxpayer is an "eligible small business" or a "new business" for NOL purposes, the procedures for computing business assets and gross receipts do not deviate from the procedures used for other taxpayers.

• *Corporations subject to allocation and apportionment*

California modifies federal law by providing that for multistate corporations subject to allocation and apportionment and corporations electing intrastate combined reporting, an NOL may be deducted from the sum of the net income or loss of a corporation apportionable or allocable to California. The effect of this modification is to limit the deduction to the amount specifically allocable to the company that generated the loss. (Sec. 25108, Rev. & Tax. Code)

• *Combined reporting*

Corporations that are members of a unitary group filing a single return must use intrastate apportionment, separately computing the loss carryover for each corporation in the group using its individual apportionment factors and completing a separate FTB 3805Q for each taxpayer included in the combined report. Unlike the loss treatment for a federal consolidated return, a California loss carryover for one member in a combined report may not be applied to the income of another member included in the combined report. (Instructions, Form 3805Q, Net Operating Loss (NOL) Computation and NOL and Disaster Loss Limitations—Corporations)

¶1025 "At Risk" Limitations

Law: Sec. 24691 (CCH CALIFORNIA TAX REPORTS ¶10-060).

Comparable Federal: Sec. 465 (CCH U.S. MASTER TAX GUIDE ¶2045).

California conforms to federal law (¶803). (Sec. 24691, Rev. & Tax. Code) A brief explanation of the federal provisions is covered at ¶339.

¶1026 Refiners' Sulfur Rules Compliance Costs

Law: Sec. 24356.4 (CCH CALIFORNIA TAX REPORTS ¶10-860).

Comparable Federal: Sec. 179B (CCH U.S. MASTER TAX GUIDE ¶1285).

Same as personal income tax (¶318).

¶1027 Energy Efficient Commercial Building Costs

Law: None (CCH CALIFORNIA TAX REPORTS ¶10-665).

Comparable Federal: Sec. 179D (CCH U.S. MASTER TAX GUIDE ¶977D).

Same as personal income tax (¶345).

TAXES ON CORPORATE INCOME

CHAPTER 11

ACCOUNTING METHODS AND BASES, INVENTORIES

¶1100 Accounting Periods and Methods—In General

Law: Secs. 24631-726 (CCH CALIFORNIA TAX REPORTS ¶10-520).

Comparable Federal: Secs. 441-83 (CCH U.S. MASTER TAX GUIDE Chapter 15).

California generally conforms to, and in some cases incorporates, federal law governing accounting periods, accounting methods, year of inclusion and deduction, inventories, and adjustment. Differences are noted in the following paragraphs. (Sec. 24631 et seq., Rev. & Tax. Code)

¶1101 Accounting Periods

Law: Secs. 24631, 24632 (CCH CALIFORNIA TAX REPORTS ¶10-520).

Comparable Federal: Sec. 441 (CCH U.S. MASTER TAX GUIDE ¶1501).

Same as personal income tax (¶401).

¶1102 Change of Accounting Period

Law: Secs. 24632, 24633, 24633.5 (CCH CALIFORNIA TAX REPORTS ¶10-520).

Comparable Federal: Sec. 442 (CCH U.S. MASTER TAX GUIDE ¶1513).

The taxable year of a corporation must be the same as the tax year used by the corporation for federal income tax purposes, unless a change in accounting period is initiated or approved by the Franchise Tax Board. (Sec. 24632, Rev. & Tax. Code; Sec. 24633, Rev. & Tax. Code; Sec. 24633.5, Rev. & Tax. Code)

¶1103 Return for Short Period—Annualization of Income

Law: Secs. 24634-36 (CCH CALIFORNIA TAX REPORTS ¶10-520).

Comparable Federal: Sec. 443 (CCH U.S. MASTER TAX GUIDE ¶1505).

California law incorporates federal law, except that California still requires a short-period return when a taxpayer's year is terminated for jeopardy by the Franchise Tax Board. (Sec. 24634, et seq., Rev. & Tax. Code)

¶1104 Change of Taxable Year—S Corporations

Law: Sec. 24637 (CCH CALIFORNIA TAX REPORTS ¶10-520).

Comparable Federal: Sec. 444 (CCH U.S. MASTER TAX GUIDE ¶1501).

California incorporates federal law by reference (¶803) with one modification relating to "required payments." (Sec. 24637, Rev. & Tax. Code)

Both federal and California law allow S corporations to elect to change to a taxable year with a three-month deferral period, or its previous taxable year deferral period, whichever is shorter.

Federal law requires that such an entity making the election federally must make certain "required payments" on April 15th of each calendar year following the calendar year in which the election begins (IRC Sec. 444(c)). California does not adopt the "required payments" requirement.

¶1105 Tax Rate Change During Taxable Year

Law: Secs. 23058, 24251 (CCH CALIFORNIA TAX REPORTS ¶10-380).

Comparable Federal: Sec. 15 (CCH U.S. MASTER TAX GUIDE ¶2561).

The general rule is the same as for personal income tax (¶406). (Sec. 23058, Rev. & Tax. Code)

The corporation tax law also specifies that, except as otherwise provided, the tax of a fiscal year taxpayer in a year in which the law is changed equals the sum of

— a portion of a tax computed under the law applicable to the first calendar year, based on the portion of the fiscal year falling in the first calendar year, and

— a portion of a tax computed under the law applicable to the second calendar year, based on the portion of the fiscal year falling in the second calendar year.

(Sec. 24251, Rev. & Tax. Code)

¶1106 Accounting Methods—General

Law: Secs. 24633, 24651-54, 24661, 24661.3, 24661.6, 24673, 24673.2, 24675-79, 24681-82, 24685, 24688-90, 24692, 24693, 24701, 24721, 24725, 24726 (CCH CALIFORNIA TAX REPORTS ¶10-520, 10-706, 10-915).

Comparable Federal: Secs. 186, 263A, 446-48, 451, 455-56, 458, 460-61, 464, 467-69, 481-83, 1341, 7701 (CCH U.S. MASTER TAX GUIDE ¶759, 1029, 1515 et seq., 1531, 1533 et seq., 1541, 1543, 1551, 1553, 1573, 1868, 2053 et seq.).

California Form: FTB 3834 (Interest Computation Under the Look-Back Method for Completed Long-Term Contracts).

With minor exceptions, California incorporates by reference federal accounting methods and definitions, including limitations on the cash method of accounting (IRC Sec. 448), as of the current IRC tie-in date (¶803). (Sec. 24651, Rev. & Tax. Code)

California does not incorporate federal law allowing a taxpayer to elect to recognize qualified gain from a qualifying electric transmission transaction over an eight-year period beginning in the tax year of the transaction applicable to transactions before 2008 (2010 for qualified electric utilities). (Sec. 24661.6, Rev. & Tax. Code) Consequently, taxpayers must recognize the total gain in the year of the transaction for California income tax purposes.

Also as a result of California's current IRC conformity date, California does not incorporate an amendment made to IRC Sec. 461 by the Farm Act of 2008 that limits the amount of net Schedule F losses from farming activities that may be claimed by taxpayers, other than C corporations, who receive Commodity Credit Corporation loans or certain other farm subsidies, beginning with the 2010 tax year. If California does not conform to this amendment, taxpayers whose losses were limited on the federal return as a result of this provision will be able to claim a greater loss on their California return.

The corporation tax rules for accounting methods generally are the same as those for personal income tax (¶407) except for those provisions which, by their nature, are applicable only to individuals. The differences between California and federal laws discussed at ¶407 are applicable to corporation tax as well as to personal income tax. Provisions applicable only to corporations are discussed below.

• *Change in accounting periods and methods*

Although California law specifies that a taxpayer must receive approval from the Franchise Tax Board (FTB) for a change in accounting periods or methods (Sec. 24633, Rev. & Tax. Code; Sec. 24651, Rev. & Tax. Code), the FTB has taken the position that it will automatically accept an IRS approved change as long as the following conditions are met:

— California has conformed to the underlying law that is being applied;

— the authority for granting the request is within the FTB's authority; and

— the FTB has not announced that it will not follow the federal procedure being relied upon.

(*FTB Notice 2000-8* (2000) CCH CALIFORNIA TAX REPORTS ¶403-112)

If a California taxpayer (1) cannot rely on a federally approved request for permission to change an accounting period or method, (2) desires to obtain a change different from the federal change, or (3) desires a change for California tax purposes only, a federal Form 3115, Application for Change in Accounting Method, or federal Form 1128, Application to Adopt, Change, or Retain a Tax Year, must be submitted to the FTB. The application must be submitted by the due date specified in California law or, if none is specified, by the due date for a federal change request if a federal change request had been submitted to the IRS for that change. Other than specified identifying information, the federal forms must be completed using appropriate California tax information and not with federal tax information, taking into account differences in federal and California law (e.g., different depreciation methods).

A cover letter must be attached to the front of the federal Form 3115 or Form 1128, clearly indicating that a "Change in Accounting Period" or a "Change in Accounting Method" is being requested. The application and the accompanying cover letter should be sent to: Franchise Tax Board, Change in Accounting Periods and Methods, Coordinator, P.O. Box 1998, Sacramento, CA 95812. The FTB will acknowledge receipt of the request within 30 days and will issue a response in writing once the request has been reviewed. (*FTB Notice 2000-8* (2000) CCH CALIFORNIA TAX REPORTS ¶403-112)

CCH Note: Subsidiary Must Obtain Consent To Change Period

Subsidiaries included in a consolidated return must obtain the FTB's consent for a change of accounting period for California corporation franchise or income tax purposes, even though no such consent is required under federal law. The California State Board of Equalization (SBE) has ruled that the exemption available to corporate subsidiaries from obtaining IRS consent prior to changing accounting periods for purposes of filing a consolidated return does not apply for California corporation franchise and income tax purposes. California, unlike federal law, does not permit the filing of consolidated returns; therefore, the rules governing the filing of consolidated returns are inapplicable for California income tax purposes. (*NIF Liquidating Co.* (1980) CCH CALIFORNIA TAX REPORTS ¶206-429)

California does not follow IRS Rev. Proc. 96-31 allowing an automatic consent procedure for a change of accounting method involving previously unclaimed allowable depreciation or amortization (see *FTB Notice 96-3* (1996), CCH CALIFORNIA TAX REPORTS ¶10-520.204).

• *"Spreadback" relief*

Special rules providing "spreadback" relief in certain cases for income attributable to several years, repealed for federal purposes in 1964 and replaced by the allowance of deductions (IRC Sec. 186), are still in effect for California purposes. These rules apply to the following:

— income from patent infringement awards (Sec. 24675, Rev. & Tax. Code);

— damages received for breach of contract, or breach of fiduciary relationship (Sec. 24677, Rev. & Tax. Code); and

— lump sum antitrust awards under the Clayton Act (Sec. 24678, Rev. & Tax. Code).

• *Prepaid subscription income*

California has a special provision that treats prepaid subscription income, not previously reported when a corporation ceases to do business, as includible in the measure of tax in the last year the corporation is subject to tax. (Sec. 24676, Rev. & Tax. Code)

• *Farm corporations*

Under California and federal law, corporations engaged in farming must use the accrual method of accounting and capitalize preproductive-period expenses. (Sec. 24652, Rev. & Tax. Code; Sec. 24652.5, Rev. & Tax. Code) However, the following are exempt from the accrual method rule:

— S corporations;

— corporations operating nurseries or sod farms or raising or harvesting trees other than fruit and nut trees;

— family farm corporations with gross receipts of $25 million or less in each taxable year; and

— all other corporations with gross receipts of $1 million or less in each taxable year.

Under both California and federal law, a corporation is required to change from the cash method to the accrual method of accounting in a year in which gross receipts exceed $1 million (or, in the case of a family farm corporation, $25 million).

• *Production flexibility contracts*

California law mirrors Sec. 2012 of the Tax and Trade Relief Extension Act of 1998, which allows farmers to include in their taxable income production flexibility contract payments made under the Federal Agriculture Improvement and Reform Act of 1996 (P.L. 104-127) in the taxable year of actual receipt, even though the contract grants the farmer the option to receive payments earlier. (Sec. 24661.3, Rev. & Tax. Code)

• *Long-term contracts*

California incorporates IRC Sec. 460, which generally requires the use of the percentage-of-completion method of accounting for long-term contracts. A look-back rule is generally applied to correct errors in estimates of contract price or costs. A taxpayer may elect not to apply the look-back rule if, for each prior contract year, the cumulative taxable income or loss under the contract, as determined using estimated contract price and costs, is within 10% of the cumulative taxable income or loss, as determined using actual contract price and costs. (Sec. 24673, Rev. & Tax. Code; Sec. 24673.2, Rev. & Tax. Code)

California has a special provision (Sec. 24673, Rev. & Tax. Code) authorizing the FTB to require that income from a contract be reported on the percentage-of-completion basis if the contract period exceeds one year, even if the corporation regularly uses the completed contract basis of accounting. The corporation may prevent such action by furnishing security guaranteeing the payment of a tax measured by the income received upon completion of the contract, *even though* the corporation is not doing business in California in the year subsequent to the year of completion. The principal purpose of this provision is to prevent avoidance of tax by foreign corporations that perform contracts in California.

• *Inventory shrinkage*

Under both California and federal law, a business may determine its year-end closing inventory by taking a reasonable deduction for shrinkage, even if a year-end inventory has not been taken to measure the actual amount of shrinkage. (Sec. 24701, Rev. & Tax. Code)

Shrinkage is generally inventory loss due to undetected theft, breakage, or bookkeeping errors. In order to claim the deduction for estimated shrinkage, a business must normally take a physical count of its inventories at each business location on a regular, consistent basis. It also must make proper adjustments to its inventories and to its estimating methods to the extent its estimates are more or less than the actual shrinkage.

• *Nuclear decommissioning reserve funds and designated settlement funds*

Although California incorporates federal law (IRC Sec. 468A and IRC Sec. 468B), concerning deductible payments to designated settlement funds and nuclear decommissioning reserve funds, respectively, California modifies the provisions to (1) substitute California's franchise tax rate rather than the highest federal tax rate and (2) specify that the California franchise tax is in lieu of any other tax that may be imposed under either the Personal Income Tax Law or the Corporation Tax Law. (Sec. 24690, Rev. & Tax. Code; Sec. 24693, Rev. & Tax. Code)

In addition, California has not incorporated an amendment made by the Energy Tax Incentives Act of 2005 (P.L. 109-58), which limits the amount a taxpayer may pay into the nuclear decommissioning reserve fund to the ruling amount applicable to the taxable year, effective for federal purposes in tax years beginning after 2005. Nor has California incorporated amendments made by the Tax Increase Prevention and Reconciliation Act of 2005 (TIPRA) that exempt from federal income tax certain escrow accounts, settlement funds, or similar funds established to resolve claims brought under the Comprehensive Environmental Response, Compensation, and Liability Act of 1980 (CERCLA) by designating these funds as being beneficially owned by the United States (IRC Sec. 468B). The exemption is applicable to accounts and funds established after May 17, 2006.

• *Other California-federal differences*

There is no California corporation franchise or income tax statute comparable to IRC Sec. 1341, which permits adjustment of income in certain situations where income received under a "claim of right" is later refunded. However, it is clear from the case law that California does apply the claim-of-right doctrine. See *Appeal of J.H. McKnight Ranch, Inc.* (1986) (CCH CALIFORNIA TAX REPORTS ¶ 10-520.85). See also ¶ 415.

• *Accrual basis required in final return*

In *Appeal of Williams & Glass Accountancy Corporation* (1982) (CCH CALIFORNIA TAX REPORTS ¶ 10-520.39), a cash-basis taxpayer distributed in liquidation accounts receivable that represented earned income. The State Board of Equalization upheld the FTB in its use of the accrual method of accounting in the corporation's final return.

¶1107 Inventories

Law: Secs. 24422.3, 24701 (CCH CALIFORNIA TAX REPORTS ¶10-515, 10-520).

Comparable Federal: Secs. 263A, 471, 475 (CCH U.S. MASTER TAX GUIDE ¶475, 1553, 1561, 1564).

Same as personal income tax (¶409).

¶1108 Inventories—Last-In, First-Out Method

Law: Secs. 24701, 24708 (CCH CALIFORNIA TAX REPORTS ¶10-520).

Comparable Federal: Secs. 472-74 (CCH U.S. MASTER TAX GUIDE ¶1565, 1567).

California incorporates by reference IRC Sec. 472, authorizing the use of the last-in, first-out (LIFO) method of inventory identification, and IRC Sec. 474, permitting eligible small business to elect to use a simplified dollar-value LIFO method to account for their inventories. However, California has not incorporated IRC Sec. 473, which prescribes accounting procedures to be employed when qualified liquidations of LIFO inventories are made. (Sec. 24701, Rev. & Tax. Code; Sec. 24708, Rev. & Tax. Code)

¶1109 Installment Sales

Law: Secs. 24667-72 (CCH CALIFORNIA TAX REPORTS ¶10-520).

Comparable Federal: Secs. 453, 453A, 453B, former Sec. 453C (CCH U.S. MASTER TAX GUIDE ¶1801 et seq.).

The same as under the personal income tax law (¶411). (Sec. 24667 et seq., Rev. & Tax. Code)

• *Installment obligations in liquidation of subsidiary*

Both California and federal laws provide that no gain or loss will be recognized if installment obligations are distributed in a complete liquidation of a subsidiary into its parent corporation (¶1216); however, there is a difference between the two laws where the parent corporation is tax-exempt under California law.

The State Board of Equalization held in *Appeal of C.M. Ranch Co.* (1976) (CCH CALIFORNIA TAX REPORTS ¶10-520) that a tax-exempt corporation technically is not a "corporation" under the corporation tax law. Consequently it cannot qualify as a parent "corporation" so as to enable the distributing corporation to avoid recognition of gain or loss on distribution of installment obligations. This reasoning is not applicable under federal law, because the federal definition of "corporation" does not exclude a tax-exempt corporation.

• *Repossession of installment obligations*

See ¶511 regarding limitations on recognition of gain on installment sales of real property where repossession occurs in a subsequent year.

¶1110 Related Taxpayers, Acquisitions to Avoid Tax, etc.

Law: Secs. 24431, 24725, 25102-03 (CCH CALIFORNIA TAX REPORTS ¶10-515, 10-520, 10-835, 11-550).

Comparable Federal: Secs. 269, 269A, 269B, 482 (CCH U.S. MASTER TAX GUIDE ¶273, 1573, 1575).

California law, incorporating by reference IRC Sec. 482, gives the Franchise Tax Board (FTB) broad power to distribute or allocate income or deductions among related taxpayers—if the FTB determines that it is necessary to do so in order to prevent evasion of taxes or clearly reflect income. (Sec. 24725, Rev. & Tax. Code) In addition, the FTB may require combined or consolidated reports and adjust the income or tax of related taxpayers. (Sec. 25102, Rev. & Tax. Code; Sec. 25103, Rev. & Tax. Code) See Chapter 13 for discussion of the apportionment formula as it relates to business done within and without the state.

In *Appeal of Baldwin and Howell* (1968) (CCH CALIFORNIA TAX REPORTS ¶10-520.702), the State Board of Equalization upheld an increase made by the FTB in the income of a parent corporation that was accomplished by transferring certain income from a subsidiary to the parent and by increasing the parent's charge to the subsidiary for the services of loaned employees.

California law is the same as federal law providing for the disallowance of tax benefits upon the acquisition of the stock or property of a corporation when the principal purpose of the acquisition is to evade or avoid tax. (Sec. 24431, Rev. & Tax. Code)

California has not conformed to federal loophole-closing provisions regarding personal service corporations (IRC Sec. 269A) and "stapled interests" (IRC Sec. 269B). Nor does California conform to federal law and regulations (Treasury Regulation 1.482-1 (h)(3)(ii)) that allow taxpayers that make an election under IRC Sec. 936 to use the profit-split method to allocate income and deductions of a possessions corporation affiliate. Under the water's-edge rules, the FTB is specifically directed to use IRC Sec. 482 to make income adjustments among affiliates within and without a water's-edge combined group (FTB Legal Ruling 2003-2 (2003) CCH CALIFORNIA TAX REPORTS ¶11-550.28).

¶1111 Election to Accrue Income on Noninterest-Bearing Obligations Issued at Discount

Law: Sec. 24674 (CCH CALIFORNIA TAX REPORTS ¶10-520).

Comparable Federal: Sec. 454 (CCH U.S. MASTER TAX GUIDE ¶1537).

A cash-basis taxpayer may elect to accrue the increment in value of noninterest-bearing bonds issued at a discount and redeemable for fixed amounts increasing at stated intervals. The election is binding for subsequent years. This rule is the same as the federal one, except that California law does not conform to a federal provision relating to the inclusion in income of the accrued increment in value of obligations owned at the beginning of the year in which the election is made. (Sec. 24674, Rev. & Tax. Code)

See also ¶911, regarding special rules for discount bonds.

¶1112 Imputed Interest

Law: Secs. 24726, 24993 (CCH CALIFORNIA TAX REPORTS ¶10-520, 10-640).

Comparable Federal: Secs. 483, 7872 (CCH U.S. MASTER TAX GUIDE ¶795, 1859, 1868).

California law adopts by reference (¶803) federal provisions concerning both imputed interest on certain deferred payment contracts and "foregone interest" on loans with below-market interest rates. (Sec. 24726, Rev. & Tax. Code; Sec. 24993, Rev. & Tax. Code)

TAXES ON CORPORATE INCOME

CHAPTER 12

SALES AND EXCHANGES, GAIN OR LOSS, BASIS

¶1201 Gain or Loss—General Rule

Law: Secs. 24901-02 (CCH CALIFORNIA TAX REPORTS ¶10-640, 10-825).

Comparable Federal: Secs. 1001, 1221-57 (CCH U.S. MASTER TAX GUIDE ¶1601, 1735 et seq.).

California Forms: Form 100 (California Corporation Franchise or Income Tax Return), Schedule D (100) (California Capital Gains and Losses), Sch. D-1 (Sales of Business Property).

Gain or loss on the disposition of property is the difference between the property's adjusted basis and the amount realized. In general, California has adopted federal general and special rules for determining capital gains and losses. (Sec. 24901, Rev. & Tax. Code; Sec. 24902, Rev. & Tax. Code) However, unlike federal law, California has not adopted lower capital gains tax rates.

For California corporation franchise and income tax purposes, a taxpayer's gain or loss is computed on Schedule D (100), California Capital Gains and Losses, and Schedule D-1, Sales of Business Property. The actual amount of gain recognized is transferred to Form 100, California Corporation Franchise or Income Tax Return.

¶1202 Involuntary Conversion

Law: Secs. 24943-49.5 (CCH CALIFORNIA TAX REPORTS ¶10-640).

Comparable Federal: Sec. 1033 (CCH U.S. MASTER TAX GUIDE ¶1713 et seq.).

California has its own corporate tax provisions governing computation of gain and loss on involuntary conversions and does not generally incorporate the federal law in this area for corporate tax purposes, as it does for personal income tax purposes. However, the rules are generally the same (¶503). (Sec. 24943 et. seq, Rev. & Tax. Code)

Because of California's current federal conformity date (¶803), California does not incorporate amendments made by the Katrina Emergency Tax Relief Act of 2005 that extend the IRC Sec. 1033 replacement period for nonrecognition of gain as a result of an involuntary conversion of business property from two years to five years for property converted as a result of Hurricane Katrina after August 25, 2005. The replacement property must be located in the disaster area.

¶1203 Gain from Sale of Assisted Housing

Law: Sec. 24955 (CCH CALIFORNIA TAX REPORTS ¶10-640).

Comparable Federal: Former Sec. 1039.

Same as personal income tax (¶505).

¶1204 Foreign Currency Transactions

Law: Sec. 24905 (CCH CALIFORNIA TAX REPORTS (¶10-640).

Comparable Federal: Sec. 988 (CCH U.S. MASTER TAX GUIDE ¶2498).

Same as personal income tax (¶520).

¶1205 Liquidation Under S.E.C. Order

Law: Sec. 24981 (CCH CALIFORNIA TAX REPORTS ¶10-640, 10-690).

Comparable Federal: Sec. 1081 (CCH U.S. MASTER TAX GUIDE ¶2247).

Same as personal income tax (¶506).

¶1206 Exchange of Property for Like Property

Law: Sec. 24941 (CCH CALIFORNIA TAX REPORTS ¶10-640).

Comparable Federal: Sec. 1031 (CCH U.S. MASTER TAX GUIDE ¶1721 et seq.).

Same as personal income tax (¶507).

¶1207 Exchange of Insurance Policies

Law: Sec. 24950 (CCH CALIFORNIA TAX REPORTS ¶10-640).

Comparable Federal: Sec. 1035 (CCH U.S. MASTER TAX GUIDE ¶1724).

Same as personal income tax (¶508).

¶1208 Exchange of Stock for Stock

Law: Sec. 24951 (CCH CALIFORNIA TAX REPORTS ¶10-640).

Comparable Federal: Sec. 1036 (CCH U.S. MASTER TAX GUIDE ¶1728).

Same as personal income tax (¶509).

¶1209 Exchange of Certain U.S. Obligations

Law: None (CCH CALIFORNIA TAX REPORTS ¶10-640).

Comparable Federal: Sec. 1037 (CCH U.S. MASTER TAX GUIDE ¶1726, 1925).

The California corporation tax law has nothing comparable to the federal provisions for the tax-free exchange of obligations of the United States issued under the Second Liberty Bond Act.

¶1210 Reacquisition of Property After Installment Sale

Law: Sec. 24952 (CCH CALIFORNIA TAX REPORTS ¶10-640).

Comparable Federal: Sec. 1038 (CCH U.S. MASTER TAX GUIDE ¶1841, 1843).

California has its own corporate tax provisions governing computation of gain and loss upon a seller's repossession of real property following an installment sale and does not incorporate the federal law in this area for corporate tax purposes, as it does for personal income tax purposes. However, the rules are generally the same (¶511). (Sec. 24952, Rev. & Tax. Code)

¶1211 Exchange of Property for Stock

Law: Secs. 24451, 24465 (CCH CALIFORNIA TAX REPORTS ¶10-210, 10-540).

Comparable Federal: Sec. 351 (CCH U.S. MASTER TAX GUIDE ¶203, 1731, 2205, 2233, 2257).

California Form: Form 3725 (Assets Transferred From Parent Corporation to Insurance Company Subsidiary)

Same as personal income tax (¶512), except as noted below. (Sec. 24451, Rev. & Tax. Code)

• *Transfers to insurance companies*

The nonrecognition rules do not apply and gain is recognized on property transferred from a corporation to an insurance company in an IRC Sec. 332 exchange, unless an exception applies. An exception does not apply if the transfer or exchange has the effect of removing the property from the corporation tax base. (Sec. 24465, Rev. & Tax. Code) Form 3725, Assets Transferred From Parent Corporation to Insurance Company Subsidiary, is used to track the assets transferred from a parent corporation to an insurance company subsidiary.

¶1212 Sale or Exchange of Tax-Exempt Bonds

Law: Sec. 24314 (CCH CALIFORNIA TAX REPORTS ¶10-640).

Comparable Federal: None.

The gain or loss from the sale or transfer of bonds yielding tax-exempt interest is not exempt. Federal policy is the same as to state and municipal obligations. (Sec. 24314, Rev. & Tax. Code)

¶1213 Sale of Stock to ESOPs or Cooperatives

Law: Sec. 24954.1 (CCH CALIFORNIA TAX REPORTS ¶10-640).

Comparable Federal: Sec. 1042 (CCH U.S. MASTER TAX GUIDE ¶1733, 2109).

Same as personal income tax (¶514).

¶1214 Exchange in Connection with Reorganization

Law: Secs. 24451, 24465 (CCH CALIFORNIA TAX REPORTS ¶10-210, 10-540).

Comparable Federal: Secs. 354, 355, 357, 361, 368 (CCH U.S. MASTER TAX GUIDE ¶203, 1789, 2205 et seq., 2229, 2233).

California Form: Form 3725 (Assets Transferred From Parent Corporation to Insurance Company Subsidiary)

California incorporates federal law governing computation of gain and loss in connection with corporate reorganizations as of the current IRC tie-in date (¶803). (Sec. 24451, Rev. & Tax. Code)

No gain or loss is recognized if stock or securities in a corporation that is a party to a reorganization are exchanged solely for stock or securities in such corporation, or in another corporation that is a party to the reorganization. Also, no gain or loss is recognized if a corporation exchanges property solely for stock or securities in connection with a reorganization. "Reorganization" and other terms are specifically defined.

In addition, the assumption of liabilities in connection with certain types of tax-free reorganizations is not considered to be money or property and does not prevent the exchange from being tax-free, unless the assumption of liabilities is a device to avoid tax on the exchange, or if the transfer is not made for a bona fide business purpose.

Nonqualified preferred stock received in exchange for stock other than nonqualified preferred stock is treated as "boot" rather than stock, and gain, but not loss, is recognized on such an exchange.

• *Transfers to insurance companies*

Generally, the nonrecognition rules do not apply and gain is recognized on property transferred from a corporation to an insurance company in an exchange governed by IRC Sec. 354 or 361, unless an exception applies. An exception does not apply if the transfer or exchange has the effect of removing the property from the corporation tax base. (Sec. 24465, Rev. & Tax. Code) Form 3725, Assets Transferred

From Parent Corporation to Insurance Company Subsidiary, is used to track the assets transferred from a parent corporation to an insurance company subsidiary.

¶1215 "Spin-Off" Reorganization

Law: Sec. 24451 (CCH CALIFORNIA TAX REPORTS ¶10-210, 10-540).

Comparable Federal: Sec. 355 (CCH U.S. MASTER TAX GUIDE ¶2201).

California incorporates federal law under which certain distributions of the stock or securities of a corporation controlled by the distributor in connection with a "spin-off," "split-up," or "split-off" reorganization may be received by distributees without recognition of gain or loss. (Sec. 24451, Rev. & Tax. Code)

California also incorporates the federal rules governing the taxability of the distributing corporations, including a provision under which distributing corporations may be required to recognize gain on certain distributions resembling outright sales of subsidiaries.

Practitioner Comment: California-Federal Differences

California's lagging conformity to the Internal Revenue Code (IRC) may result in certain transactions that qualify as tax-free spin offs for federal income tax purposes being treated as taxable dividends for California tax purposes. California has conformed to the IRC as of January 1, 2005. However, on May 17, 2006, IRC Sec. 355(b)(3) was enacted in order to simplify the active trade or business test by treating all members of either the distributing and the controlling entity(ies)'s affiliated group as one corporation. Because this enactment was subsequent to the latest conformity date, certain spin-off transactions that are nontaxable for federal purposes may now be taxable for California income tax purposes until California's conformity date is updated.

The Franchise Tax Board in Chief Counsel Ruling 2007-3 acknowledged that a taxpayer could restructure in order to meet the active trade or business requirements. Further, although such was intended to avoid adverse California tax consequences, the FTB indicated that it would not regard the restructuring as a non-economic substance transaction or "NEST" otherwise subject to potential penalties under Cal. Rev. & Tax. Code Section 19774.

Bruce Daigh, Chris Whitney, Contributing Editors

¶1216 Complete Liquidation of Subsidiary

Law: Secs. 24451, 24456 (CCH CALIFORNIA TAX REPORTS ¶10-210, 10-540).

Comparable Federal: Sec. 332 (CCH U.S. MASTER TAX GUIDE ¶2241, 2261).

California Form: Form 3725 (Assets Transferred From Parent Corporation to Insurance Company Subsidiary)

No gain or loss is recognized upon the receipt by a corporation of property distributed in complete liquidation of a subsidiary corporation; 80% ownership is required and other conditions must be satisfied. California incorporates the IRC provisions as of the current IRC tie-in date (¶803). (Sec. 24451, Rev. & Tax. Code)

Under federal law, as incorporated by California, any amount that a liquidating regulated investment company (RIC) or real estate investment trust (REIT) takes as a deduction for dividends paid with respect to an otherwise tax-free liquidating distribution must be included in the income of the corporation receiving the distribution.

In *C.M. Ranch Co.,* discussed at ¶1109, it was held that the California provision for tax-free liquidation does not apply where the parent corporation is tax-exempt, because such a corporation is technically not a "corporation" under the corporation tax law.

• *Transfers to insurance companies*

Generally, the nonrecognition rules do not apply and gain is recognized on property transferred from a corporation to an insurance company in an exchange governed by IRC Sec. 332, unless an exception applies. An exception does not apply if the transfer or exchange has the effect of removing the property from the corporation tax base. (Sec. 24456, Rev. & Tax. Code) Form 3725, Assets Transferred From Parent Corporation to Insurance Company Subsidiary, is used to track the assets transferred from a parent corporation to an insurance company subsidiary.

¶1217 Exchanges of Stock in 10%-Owned Foreign Corporations

Law: Sec. 24990.7 (CCH CALIFORNIA TAX REPORTS ¶10-640).

Comparable Federal: Sec. 1248 (CCH U.S. MASTER TAX GUIDE ¶2488).

California does not currently adopt the federal provision that taxes as a dividend the portion of gain on the sale or exchange of stock in a 10%-owned foreign corporation attributable to earnings and profits of the corporation accumulated in taxable years beginning after 1962, and during the period or periods the stock was owned by the taxpayer. (Sec. 24990.7, Rev. & Tax. Code)

¶1218 Exchanges Not Solely in Kind

Law: Secs. 24451, 24456 (CCH CALIFORNIA TAX REPORTS ¶10-210, 10-540).

Comparable Federal: Sec. 356 (CCH U.S. MASTER TAX GUIDE ¶2237).

California Form: Form 3725 (Assets Transferred From Parent Corporation to Insurance Company Subsidiary)

Same as personal income tax (¶518). (Sec. 24451, Rev. & Tax. Code)

• *Transfers to insurance companies*

Generally, the nonrecognition rules do not apply and gain is recognized on property transferred from a corporation to an insurance company in an exchange governed by IRC Sec. 356, unless an exception applies. An exception does not apply if the transfer or exchange has the effect of removing the property from the corporation tax base. (Sec. 24456, Rev. & Tax. Code) Form 3725, Assets Transferred From Parent Corporation to Insurance Company Subsidiary, is used to track the assets transferred from a parent corporation to an insurance company subsidiary.

¶1219 Exchanges Involving Foreign Corporations

Law: Sec. 24451 (CCH CALIFORNIA TAX REPORTS ¶10-210, 10-540).

Comparable Federal: Sec. 367 (CCH U.S. MASTER TAX GUIDE ¶2267).

Same as personal income tax (¶519).

¶1220 Liquidation of Corporation

Law: Sec. 24451 (CCH CALIFORNIA TAX REPORTS ¶10-210, 10-540).

Comparable Federal: Secs. 331, 334, 336-38 (CCH U.S. MASTER TAX GUIDE ¶2253, 2257, 2261, 2265).

Gain or loss is ordinarily recognized to a corporate stockholder upon liquidation of a corporation, the gain or loss being measured by the difference between the basis of the stock and the value of the property received. California incorporates the federal law (¶803). (Sec. 24451, Rev. & Tax. Code)

• *Liquidation of subsidiary*

See ¶1216 for special rules applying to the complete liquidation of a subsidiary.

• *California-federal differences*

Federal law contains special provisions for treatment of liquidating distributions by certain types of corporations, where corporate income has been taxed directly to shareholders. This applies particularly to Domestic International Sales Corporations and successor entities. Because such special corporations have no counterparts in the California law (Sec. 23051.5(b), Rev. & Tax. Code), their liquidating distributions are subject to the regular rules for California tax purposes.

¶1221 Carryovers in Corporate Acquisitions

Law: Secs. 24451, 24471, 24481 (CCH CALIFORNIA TAX REPORTS ¶10-210, 10-540).

Comparable Federal: Secs. 381-84 (CCH U.S. MASTER TAX GUIDE ¶2277, 2281).

California incorporates federal provisions regarding carryover of certain corporate attributes in reorganizations and in liquidations of subsidiaries, with minor modifications substituting certain California credits for those enumerated in the federal law. (Sec. 24451, Rev. & Tax. Code; Sec. 24471, Rev. & Tax. Code; Sec. 24481, Rev. & Tax. Code)

¶1222 Capital Gains and Losses

Law: Former Sec. 24905.5, Secs. 24956, 24990, 24990.5, 24990.7, 24995 (CCH CALIFORNIA TAX REPORTS ¶10-640).

Comparable Federal: Secs. 988, 1044, 1201-88 (CCH U.S. MASTER TAX GUIDE ¶1735 et seq., 2498).

California Form: Sch. D (Capital Gain or Loss Adjustment).

California law adopts by reference as of the current IRC tie-in date (¶803) the federal treatment of capital gains and losses except for the following differences:

— the federal alternative tax on corporations is inapplicable (Sec. 24990(a), Rev. & Tax. Code);

— California allows a five-year carryover, but no carryback, of capital losses; federal law provides for a three-year carryback in addition to a five-year carryover (Sec. 24990.5, Rev. & Tax. Code);

— the provisions dealing with the treatment of certain passive foreign investment companies do not apply for California purposes (Sec. 24995, Rev. & Tax. Code); and

— provisions relating to gain from certain foreign stock sales or exchanges do not apply for California purposes. (Sec. 24990.7, Rev. & Tax. Code)

In addition, as a result of California's current federal conformity date (see ¶803), California does not incorporate amendments made to IRC Sec. 1245 by the Energy Tax Incentives Act of 2005 that require recapture as ordinary income on disposal of multiple IRC Sec. 197 assets (intangibles) in a single transaction or series of transactions to the extent amortization deductions were claimed on any of the assets. The recapture provision is effective for federal purposes for dispositions of property after August 8, 2005.

Nor does California incorporate amendments made by the Tax Increase Prevention and Reconciliation Act of 2005 and the Tax Relief and Health Care Act of 2006 that allow a taxpayer to elect to treat as a sale or exchange of a capital asset, the sale or exchange of musical compositions or copyrights in musical works created by the taxpayer's personal efforts (or having a basis determined by reference to the basis in the hands of the taxpayer whose personal efforts created the composition or copyrights). The federal election may be made in tax years beginning after May 17, 2006.

• *"Small business" stock*

The limited exclusion for gain on the sale of small business stock that is available for personal income tax purposes (¶525) is not available for corporation franchise or income tax purposes. (Sec. 24956, Rev. & Tax. Code)

¶1223 Retirement of Bonds, etc.

Law: Secs. 24439, 24990 (CCH CALIFORNIA TAX REPORTS ¶10-515, 10-640).

Comparable Federal: Secs. 249, 1271-74A (CCH U.S. MASTER TAX GUIDE ¶1952, 1954, 2431).

Except for U.S. Savings Bonds, gain on retirement of bonds is taxable income and loss is fully deductible. There is a difference between the franchise tax and the income tax in the treatment of gain or loss on redemption of savings bonds, resulting from the difference in the treatment of interest income as explained at ¶910.

Under the corporation income tax, a gain on redemption of Savings Bonds is not taxable and a loss is not deductible, as outlined at ¶535 for the personal income tax. Under the franchise tax, however, such a gain is fully taxable and such a loss is fully deductible, because interest on U.S. obligations is fully taxable for franchise tax purposes. (Sec. 24990, Rev. & Tax. Code)

Where a corporation redeems bonds that were issued at a discount after May 27, 1969, a corporate holder's California gain may be different from the federal gain, because the federal gain will reflect the fact that the federal cost basis of the bonds has been increased by the amount of discount that has been reported as income as explained at ¶911. Although current California law provides for the same addition to basis, it did not become effective for taxable years before 1987.

California law is the same as federal in restricting the amount of deduction for premium paid by a corporation on the repurchase of bonds convertible into stock. The deduction is limited to the amount of a normal call premium. (Sec. 24439, Rev. & Tax. Code)

Original issue discount on bonds is discussed at ¶911.

¶1224 Corporation Dealing in Own Stock

Law: Sec. 24942 (CCH CALIFORNIA TAX REPORTS ¶10-640).

Comparable Federal: Sec. 1032 (CCH U.S. MASTER TAX GUIDE ¶203, 1729).

Under both California and federal law, no gain or loss is recognized to a corporation on the receipt of money or other property in exchange for the corporation's stock, including treasury stock. In addition, a corporation is not required to recognize gain or loss upon any acquisition of an option, or with respect to a securities futures contract, to buy or sell its stock (including treasury stock) or when an option to buy its stock lapses. (Sec. 24942, Rev. & Tax. Code)

In *Federal Employees Distributing Company v. Franchise Tax Board* (1968) (CCH CALIFORNIA TAX REPORTS ¶10-015.20), the California District Court of Appeals held that fees collected for memberships by a nonprofit nonstock corporation were the corporation's sole source of equity capital and therefore were exempt under Sec. 24942 from franchise tax.

¶1225 Limitation of Straddle Losses

Law: Sec. 24998 (CCH CALIFORNIA TAX REPORTS ¶10-640).

Comparable Federal: Sec. 1092 (CCH U.S. MASTER TAX GUIDE ¶1948).

California law is the same as federal law as of the current IRC tie-in date (see ¶803), which prevents taxpayers from using various tax-motivated straddles (positions in a transaction that balance or offset each other) to defer income or to convert short-term capital gain into long-term capital gain. Losses from actively traded personal property are deferred to the extent that the taxpayer had gains in offsetting positions that were not closed out by year-end. Straddle rules deal with "contracts" (including securities futures contracts), "options," or "rights" involving possible price fluctuations as the result of future events and a taxpayer's attempts to reduce the risk of loss on such investments, but do not apply to hedging transactions. (Sec. 24998, Rev. & Tax. Code)

Because of California's current IRC conformity date, California has not incorporated an amendment made by the Tax Technical Corrections Act of 2007, which amended the basis adjustment provisions of the straddle rules effective for federal purposes after October 21, 2004, and the straddle identification rules, effective for federal purposes for straddles acquired after December 29, 2007.

¶1226 Basis, General Rule

Law: Secs. 24912, 24966-66.2 (CCH CALIFORNIA TAX REPORTS ¶10-640).

Comparable Federal: Secs. 1012, 1059, 1059A, 1060 (CCH U.S. MASTER TAX GUIDE ¶237, 315, 1611, 1743).

Same as personal income tax (¶542). California law parallels and in some instances incorporates federal law in this area. The general rule is that the basis of an item of property is its cost. Exceptions are discussed in the following paragraphs. (Sec. 24912, Rev. & Tax. Code; Sec. 24966, Rev. & Tax. Code; Sec. 24966.1, Rev. & Tax. Code; Sec. 24966.2, Rev. & Tax. Code)

¶1227 Basis, Inventoriable Property

Law: Secs. 24913, 24966.1 (CCH CALIFORNIA TAX REPORTS ¶10-640).

Comparable Federal: Secs. 1013, 1059A (CCH U.S. MASTER TAX GUIDE ¶1553 et seq.).

Same as personal income tax (¶543).

¶1228 Basis of Property Acquired by Gift

Law: Secs. 24914-15 (CCH CALIFORNIA TAX REPORTS ¶10-640).

Comparable Federal: Sec. 1015 (CCH U.S. MASTER TAX GUIDE ¶1630, 1678).

Same as personal income tax (¶544) except that the corporation tax law does not provide for property acquired before 1921. (Sec. 24914, Rev. & Tax. Code; Sec. 24915, Rev. & Tax. Code)

¶1229 Basis of Property Acquired by Transfer in Trust

Law: Sec. 24914 (CCH CALIFORNIA TAX REPORTS ¶10-640).

Comparable Federal: Sec. 1015 (CCH U.S. MASTER TAX GUIDE ¶1630, 1678).

Same as personal income tax (¶545) except that the corporation tax law does not provide for property acquired before 1921. (Sec. 24914, Rev. & Tax. Code)

¶1230 Basis of Property Transmitted at Death

Law: None (CCH CALIFORNIA TAX REPORTS ¶11-869).

Comparable Federal: Sec. 1014 (CCH U.S. MASTER TAX GUIDE ¶1633 et seq.).

The California corporation tax law has no provision for basis of property transmitted at death.

¶1231 Basis of Property Acquired in Tax-Free Exchange

Law: Sec. 24451 (CCH CALIFORNIA TAX REPORTS ¶10-210, 10-540).

Comparable Federal: Sec. 358 (CCH U.S. MASTER TAX GUIDE ¶2201, 2205).

Same as personal income tax (¶547).

¶1232 Basis of Stock After "Spin-Off" Reorganization

Law: Sec. 24451 (CCH CALIFORNIA TAX REPORTS ¶10-210, 10-540).

Comparable Federal: Sec. 358 (CCH U.S. MASTER TAX GUIDE ¶2201, 2205).

Same as personal income tax (¶549).

¶1233 Basis of Property Acquired in Reorganization

Law: Sec. 24451 (CCH CALIFORNIA TAX REPORTS ¶10-210, 10-540).

Comparable Federal: Sec. 362 (CCH U.S. MASTER TAX GUIDE ¶1666).

In the case of property acquired by a corporation in a "reorganization," the property takes the transferor's basis, with adjustment for gain recognized upon the transfer. California incorporates federal law as of the current IRC tie-in date (¶803). (Sec. 24451, Rev. & Tax. Code)

¶1234 Basis of Property Acquired by Issuance of Stock or Contribution to Capital

Law: Sec. 24551 (CCH CALIFORNIA TAX REPORTS ¶10-210, 10-540).

Comparable Federal: Sec. 362 (CCH U.S. MASTER TAX GUIDE ¶1660).

In the case of property acquired by a corporation by issuance of stock in a tax-free transaction under IRC Sec. 351 (¶512), or as a contribution to capital, the basis of the property is the transferor's basis, with adjustment for gain recognized on the transfer. However, if a contribution to capital is received from other than a shareholder, the corporation is required to reduce the basis of property by the amount of the contribution.

The California law is the same as the federal law. (Sec. 24451, Rev. & Tax. Code)

¶1235 Basis of Property Acquired upon Involuntary Conversion

Law: Sec. 24947 (CCH CALIFORNIA TAX REPORTS ¶10-640).

Comparable Federal: Sec. 1033 (CCH U.S. MASTER TAX GUIDE ¶1713, 1715).

California has its own corporate tax provision regarding the basis of property acquired upon an involuntary conversion and does not generally incorporate the federal law in this area for corporate tax purposes, as it does for personal income tax purposes. However, the rules are generally the same (¶550). (Sec. 24947, Rev. & Tax. Code)

¶1236 Basis of Securities Acquired in Wash Sale

Law: Sec. 24998 (CCH CALIFORNIA TAX REPORTS ¶10-640).

Comparable Federal: Sec. 1091 (CCH U.S. MASTER TAX GUIDE ¶1939).

Same as personal income tax (¶553).

¶1237 Basis of Property Acquired During Affiliation

Law: Sec. 24961 (CCH CALIFORNIA TAX REPORTS ¶10-640).

Comparable Federal: Sec. 1051.

In the case of property acquired by a corporation from an affiliated corporation during a period of affiliation, the basis of the property is determined under special rules, the general effect of which is to disregard the transfer from the affiliate. The California provision contains several references to federal law and is generally the same as the federal provision. (Sec. 24961, Rev. & Tax. Code) There are some differences, however, and there may be important differences in the effect of the two laws because the periods of affiliation may be different under one law than under the other. Reference should be made to the law or regulations or to a more detailed reference work in case of any question involving this provision.

¶1238 Basis Prescribed by Revenue Acts of 1932 or 1934

Law: Sec. 24962 (CCH CALIFORNIA TAX REPORTS ¶10-640, 10-690).

Comparable Federal: Sec. 1052.

The basis of property acquired after February 28, 1913, in an income year beginning prior to 1937, where the basis was prescribed by the federal Revenue Acts of 1932 or 1934, is as prescribed in those Acts. The California provision parallels the federal one, except that the federal provision applies only to transfers in tax years beginning prior to 1936. (Sec. 24962, Rev. & Tax. Code)

¶1239 Basis of Property Acquired Before March 1, 1913

Law: Sec. 24963 (CCH CALIFORNIA TAX REPORTS ¶10-640, 10-690).

Comparable Federal: Sec. 1053.

Same as personal income tax (¶556).

¶1240 Basis of FNMA Stock

Law: Sec. 24965 (CCH CALIFORNIA TAX REPORTS ¶10-640).

Comparable Federal: Sec. 1054.

The basis of stock issued by the Federal National Mortgage Association to an original holder is cost, reduced by the amount of any premium paid above face value. The premium may be deducted as an ordinary business expense in the year of purchase. The California provision parallels the federal one. (Sec. 24965, Rev. & Tax. Code)

¶1241 Basis Under Redeemable Ground Rents

Law: None (CCH CALIFORNIA TAX REPORTS ¶10-640).

Comparable Federal: Sec. 1055 (CCH U.S. MASTER TAX GUIDE ¶1611).

The California corporate tax law contains nothing comparable to a federal provision that treats redeemable ground rents as being the equivalent of a mortgage. Presumably, California would treat redeemable ground rents as regular leases.

¶1242 Basis of Property Acquired in Corporate Liquidation or Acquisition

Law: Secs. 23051.5, 23806, 24451 (CCH CALIFORNIA TAX REPORTS ¶10-210, 10-540).

Comparable Federal: Secs. 334, 338 (CCH U.S. MASTER TAX GUIDE ¶2261, 2265).

In an ordinary corporate liquidation, the basis of property received by a corporate stockholder is the fair market value of the property at the date of liquidation. California incorporates federal law as of the current IRC tie-in date (¶803). (Sec. 24451, Rev. & Tax. Code)

• *Liquidation in plan to purchase assets*

Upon the complete liquidation of a subsidiary under IRC Sec. 332 (¶1216) the property received by the parent corporation ordinarily takes the same basis it had in the hands of the subsidiary (transferor). However, a different result occurs if the corporation elects under IRC Sec. 338 to treat its acquisition of another business through purchase of a controlling interest (80%) in stock as the purchase of the assets of the acquired corporation. In this case, the buyer receives a fair market value basis in each asset and is entitled to claim depreciation and investment tax credit on a stepped-up basis. The tax attributes of the acquired (target) corporation disappear. In turn, the target corporation is subject to recapture tax liability.

Reg. 24519, 18 CCR permits a California taxpayer to elect out of the federal election of IRC Sec. 338(g), which allows the purchasing corporation to have a stock purchase treated as an acquisition of assets.

CCH Caution Note: Impact of Federal Election Extensions

A taxpayer making a proper federal election under IRC Sec. 338, concerning qualified stock purchases, that makes the election using an automatic extension pursuant to federal Rev. Proc. 2003-33, is entitled to the election for purposes of California corporation franchise or income tax. However, a taxpayer making a separate California election may not rely on the federal revenue procedure to extend the time for filing the separate state election (*FTB Notice 2003-9* (2003) CCH CALIFORNIA TAX REPORTS ¶10-540).

An IRC Sec. 338(h)(10) election is available when an affiliated group sells the stock of a subsidiary. Under this election, the acquired corporation must recognize any gain or loss on the deemed asset sale; however, the selling group does not recognize any gain or loss on the stock sale. Although California incorporates IRC Sec. 338, without modification, under California's general election provisions discussed at ¶803, taxpayers may make a separate election on their California return. (Sec. 23051.5(e), Rev. & Tax. Code) However, a separate election is not allowed if the target corporation is an S corporation. (Sec. 23806, Rev. & Tax. Code) In an informational letter provided to CCH, the Franchise Tax Board (FTB) stated that, for purposes of an IRC Sec. 338(h)(10) election, the FTB requires both the purchasing and selling corporations to be California taxpayers in order

— for a federal election to automatically apply for California corporation franchise income tax purposes,

— to make a separate California election, or

— to elect out of a federal election for California corporation franchise (income) tax purposes. (*Informational Letter,* Franchise Tax Board, October 28, 2003 (CCH CALIFORNIA TAX REPORTS ¶403-566).

See ¶1304 for a discussion of the apportionment rules applicable to IRC Sec. 338 deemed asset sales.

¶1243 Basis of Property Acquired upon Transfers from Controlled Corporations

Law: Sec. 24964 (CCH CALIFORNIA TAX REPORTS ¶10-640).

Comparable Federal: None.

Where a corporation subject to the franchise tax received property after 1927, from a controlled corporation, and where gain or loss was realized but was not taken into account for franchise tax purposes, the property takes the transferor's basis. There is no comparable federal provision. (Sec. 24964, Rev. & Tax. Code)

¶1244 Basis of Rights to Acquire Stock

Law: Sec. 24451 (CCH CALIFORNIA TAX REPORTS ¶10-210, 10-540).

Comparable Federal: Sec. 307 (CCH U.S. MASTER TAX GUIDE ¶1907).

Where the fair market value of stock rights is less than 15% of the value of the stock on which the rights are issued, the basis of the rights is zero unless the taxpayer elects to allocate to the rights a portion of the basis of the stock. This rule dates from 1954 in federal law and from 1955 in California law. (Sec. 24451, Rev. & Tax. Code)

• *Allocation of basis*

As to the following rights, the basis of the stock is allocated between the stock and the rights according to their respective values at the time the rights are issued:

— all rights acquired in an income year beginning before 1937, *except* as to certain rights acquired before 1928 (see below); and

— nontaxable rights acquired in an income year beginning 1936, where the value of the rights is more than 15% or the taxpayer elects to allocate as explained above.

If a stock right was acquired prior to 1928, and it constituted income under the Sixteenth Amendment to the Federal Constitution, the basis of the right is its fair market value when acquired.

• *Pre-1943 transactions*

Where stock rights were acquired and sold in an income year beginning prior to 1943 and the entire proceeds were reported as income, the basis of the stock is determined without any allocation to the rights.

• *California-federal differences*

California law now incorporates the federal law, but, as discussed below, there have been the following differences in effective dates in prior years:

— In the first item listed above under "Allocation of basis," the federal dates are January 1, 1936, in both cases instead of January 1, 1937, and January 1, 1928. As to both dates, the federal refers to *years beginning* before January 1, 1936, instead of to the *period prior* to the date specified.

— In the second item listed above under "Allocation of basis," the federal date is December 31, 1935, instead of December 31, 1936.

— In the rule stated above regarding rights acquired prior to January 1, 1928, the federal law refers to rights acquired in a taxable year beginning prior to January 1, 1936. Also, the federal rule is different in that it applies only if the value of the rights was included in gross income in the year acquired, whereas the prior California rule applies to all cases where the acquisition of the rights constituted income under the Sixteenth Amendment.

— In the rule stated above regarding rights acquired and sold prior to 1943, the federal law refers to rights acquired in any tax year beginning prior to 1939.

¶1245 Basis of Property Acquired Pursuant to S.E.C. Order

Law: Sec. 24988 (CCH CALIFORNIA TAX REPORTS ¶10-640).

Comparable Federal: Sec. 1082.

Special rules are provided for determination of basis in cases involving an order of the Securities and Exchange Commission under the Public Utility Holding Company Act. California incorporates the federal law. (Sec. 24988, Rev. & Tax. Code)

¶1246 Basis of Property Acquired from Partnership

Law: None (CCH CALIFORNIA TAX REPORTS ¶10-220).

Comparable Federal: Sec. 732 (CCH U.S. MASTER TAX GUIDE ¶456).

The corporation tax law contains no provision regarding basis of property distributed in kind by a partnership. However, California law provides that a corporation receiving *income* from an interest in a partnership is to treat that income in the same manner as under the Personal Income Tax Law. (Sec. 73, Ch. 35 (A.B. 1122) and Ch. 34 (S.B. 657), Laws 2002, CCH CALIFORNIA TAX REPORTS ¶201-802) Also, see ¶555 for a discussion of the basis of corporate stock distributed by a partnership to a corporate partner that has control of the distributed corporation after the distribution.

¶1247 Adjusted Basis

Law: Secs. 24911, 24916, 24916.2 (CCH CALIFORNIA TAX REPORTS ¶10-690).

Comparable Federal: Secs. 1011, 1016-21 (CCH U.S. MASTER TAX GUIDE ¶1604, 1701).

The adjusted basis for determining gain or loss on the sale of property is the basis of the property, as adjusted by specific California provisions. (Sec. 24911, Rev. & Tax. Code) The provision is the same as IRC Sec. 1011, as of the current California conformity date (¶803), except that, as discussed below, the federal basis adjustments are in some cases different from those provided by California law. Special rules apply to California's treatment of gains and losses and its general basis rules.

In computing gain or loss on the sale or exchange of assets, adjustments to basis must be made for depreciation allowed or allowable, for various deferred expenses taken as deductions, and for many other factors, which are discussed below. (Sec. 24916, Rev. & Tax. Code)

California law also requires that adjustments be made for certain deducted enterprise zone, LAMBRA, targeted tax area, or former LARZ business expenses (¶316, 1011). No comparable basis adjustments are required under federal law.

Corporate taxpayers may be prohibited from making basis adjustments authorized by federal provisions that have not been adopted by California. For instance, in *Appeal of CRG Holdings, Inc.* (1997) (CCH CALIFORNIA TAX REPORTS ¶11-875.201), a taxpayer was not allowed to adjust its basis in the stock of its subsidiaries based on a consent dividend that was properly reported on the taxpayer's federal return, because California has never adopted the federal provision authorizing consent dividends.

Similarly, in *Appeal of Rapid-American Corporation* (1997) (CCH CALIFORNIA TAX REPORTS ¶11-875.20), a taxpayer that sold its stock in its unitary subsidiaries was prohibited from increasing the basis of stock by the amount of earning and profits held in the subsidiaries that had previously been reported to California on the taxpayer's combined unitary report and that had not been distributed as dividends prior to the sales of stock. Although the disputed adjustment was authorized under federal law, California has never recognized earnings and profits as an appropriate basis adjustment.

• *Identical federal and California treatment*

The treatment of the following basis adjustments is identical for both California and federal law:

— tax free stock distributions (Sec. 24916(c), Rev. & Tax. Code; IRC Sec. 1016(a)(4))

— property pledged to the Commodity Credit Corporation (Sec. 24916(d)(3), Rev. & Tax. Code; IRC Sec. 1016(a)(8))

— deferred mine development expense (Sec. 24916(e), Rev. & Tax. Code; IRC Sec. 1016(a)(9))

— deferred research and experimental expenses (Sec. 24916(g), Rev. & Tax. Code; IRC Sec. 1016(a)(14))

— rollover of gain into a specialized small business investment company (SSBIC) (Sec. 24916(j), Rev. & Tax. Code; IRC Sec. 1016(a)(23))

— lessee-made improvements to real property (Sec. 24919, Rev. & Tax. Code; IRC Sec. 1019)

— the former deduction for clean-fuel vehicles and certain refueling property allowed under IRC Sec. 179A (Sec. 24916(i), Rev. & Tax. Code)

[*CCH Note:* California incorporates the federal basis adjustment for clean fuel vehicles and refueling property even though California no longer incorporates the IRC Sec. 179A deduction]

Although California does not include the following adjustments in its provision requiring basis adjustments, California does incorporate the underlying federal provision that requires a taxpayer to make a basis adjustment. Thus, as under federal law, taxpayers under California law must make adjustments for the following: (1) adjustments to the basis of a shareholder's stock in an S corporation that are required by IRC Sec. 1367, to reflect the shareholder's portion of various items of income, nontaxable return-of-capital distributions by the S corporation, etc. (Sec. 23800, Rev. & Tax. Code); and (2) a reduction in basis in qualified employer securities to employee stock ownership plans (ESOPs) or qualified worker-owned cooperatives purchased by the taxpayer for which nonrecognition of gain is available under IRC Sec. 1042 (Sec. 24954, Rev. & Tax. Code)

Also, although California does not directly incorporate federal provisions that require basis adjustments for capital costs currently deducted by small business refiners under IRC Sec. 179B and facilities for which a production of low sulfur diesel fuel credit was claimed under IRC Sec. 45H, California requires basis adjustments for the equivalent California deduction and credit available to small business refiners. (Sec. 23662(d), Rev. & Tax. Code; Sec. 24356.4(b), Rev. & Tax. Code)

• *Federal basis adjustments not followed under California law*

Under IRC Sec. 1016, but not under California law, basis adjustments must be made for the following items discussed below:

— disallowed deductions on the disposal of coal or domestic iron ore;

— amounts related to a shareholder's stock in a controlled foreign corporation;

— the amount of gas guzzler tax on an automobile;

— for pre-2005 tax years, certain amounts that must be included in the gross income of a United States shareholder in a foreign personal holding company;

— municipal bond premiums required to be amortized under federal law;

— property for which a federal investment tax credit is claimed;

— amounts specified in a shareholder's consent made under IRC Sec. 28 of the 1939 Internal Revenue Code;

— disallowed deductions on the sale of unharvested crops;

— amortization of premium and accrual of discount on bonds and notes held by a life insurance company;

— certain amounts deducted under IRC Sec. 59(e) that are not treated as tax preference items if so deducted;

— property for which a federal credit for qualified electric vehicles was claimed under the federal credit for qualified electric vehicles;

— facilities for which a federal employer-provided child care credit was claimed; and

— railroad track for which a federal credit was claimed under IRC Sec. 45G.

In addition, California has not incorporated amendments made by the Energy Tax Incentives Act of 2005 (ETIA) that require adjustments for expenses for which an IRC Sec. 179D energy efficient commercial buildings deduction was claimed. Other adjustments required under amendments made by ETIA relating to expenses for which federal credits were claimed are inapplicable for California purposes. (Sec. 23051.5(b), Rev. & Tax. Code)

¶1248 Substituted Basis

Law: Sec. 24917 (CCH CALIFORNIA TAX REPORTS ¶10-640, 10-690).

Comparable Federal: Sec. 1016 (CCH U.S. MASTER TAX GUIDE ¶1607).

Same as personal income tax (¶560).

¶1249 Lessor's Basis for Lessee's Improvements

Law: Sec. 24919 (CCH CALIFORNIA TAX REPORTS ¶10-690).

Comparable Federal: Sec. 1019 (CCH U.S. MASTER TAX GUIDE ¶1601).

When the value of improvements by a lessee is excluded from income (¶905) there is no effect on the basis of the property to the lessor. When the value of such improvements was included in the lessor's gross income for any taxable year beginning before 1942, the basis of the lessor's property is adjusted accordingly. The California provision is the same as the federal one except for the effective date for California income tax purposes. (Sec. 24919, Rev. & Tax. Code)

¶1250 Basis for Depreciation and Depletion

Law: Secs. 24353, 24831 (CCH CALIFORNIA TAX REPORTS ¶10-515, 10-850, 10-900).

Comparable Federal: Secs. 167, 612-13 (CCH U.S. MASTER TAX GUIDE ¶1203, 1289).

Same as personal income tax (¶562).

For rules regarding percentage value depletion, see ¶319.

¶1251 Reduction of Basis—Income from Discharge of Indebtedness

Law: Sec. 24918 (CCH CALIFORNIA TAX REPORTS ¶10-690).

Comparable Federal: Sec. 1017 (CCH U.S. MASTER TAX GUIDE ¶1672).

When the taxpayer has elected to exclude from gross income gain from discharge of indebtedness, the amount excluded is applied to reduce the basis of property held by the taxpayer. Federal references to affiliated groups are applied to unitary members under California law. The California rules generally are the same as the federal rules. (Sec. 24918, Rev. & Tax. Code)

California conforms to the federal requirement that the amount of income realized from the discharge of qualified real property business indebtedness that a taxpayer excludes from gross income must be applied to reduce the basis of business real property held by the taxpayer at the beginning of the taxable year following the taxable year in which the discharge occurs.

¶1252 Basis for Player Contracts

Law: Sec. 24989 (CCH CALIFORNIA TAX REPORTS ¶10-640).

Comparable Federal: Sec. 1056.

Same as personal income tax (¶563).

¶1253 Allocation of Transferred Business Assets

Law: Sec. 24966.2 (CCH CALIFORNIA TAX REPORTS ¶10-640).

Comparable Federal: Sec. 1060 (CCH U.S. MASTER TAX GUIDE ¶1620).

California has adopted the federal residual method for allocating purchases of assets that constitute a trade or business (¶803). Generally, under the residual method, the purchase price is allocated first to the assets to the extent of their fair market value, and any excess is allocated to goodwill and going concern value. However, if a transferor and a transferee agree in writing concerning the allocation of consideration for transferred business assets, their agreement will generally be binding for tax purposes. (Sec. 24966.2, Rev. & Tax. Code)

TAXES ON CORPORATE INCOME

CHAPTER 13
ALLOCATION AND APPORTIONMENT

¶1301 Scope of Chapter

The California taxes on corporate income are measured by income derived from or attributable to sources within California only. This applies both to corporations organized in California and to out-of-state ("foreign") corporations.

Where income is derived from sources both within and without the state, it is necessary to determine the income attributable to sources within the state. This chapter discusses the method of making this determination and points out some of the problems encountered. It covers not only situations where the income of only one corporation is involved, but also situations involving affiliated corporations. As pointed out in ¶1310, apportionment of all of the income of an affiliated group may be required even where only one of the affiliated corporations is engaged in any activity in California.

• *Uniform Division of Income for Tax Purposes Act*

California adopted the Uniform Division of Income for Tax Purposes Act (commonly referred to as UDITPA), effective in 1967; the Act has also been adopted by many other states. The California law deviates slightly from the original UDITPA draft, the principal differences being that (1) California does not exclude financial corporations and public utilities from the operation of the Act and (2) California's standard apportionment formula (¶1305) includes a double-weighted sales factor.

In *Appeal of American Telephone and Telegraph Co.* (1982) (CCH CALIFORNIA TAX REPORTS ¶11-530.70), discussed at ¶1305 and ¶1307, the State Board of Equalization (SBE) stated that "UDITPA'S fundamental purpose is to assure that 100%, and no more and no less, of a multistate taxpayer's business income is taxed by the states having jurisdiction to tax it." The SBE cites decisions of courts of other states that have adopted UDITPA, and says that in each of those cases "the court sought to avoid an interpretation of UDITPA which would create a gap in the taxation of the taxpayer's income."

Franchise Tax Board Reg. 25121, 18 CCR, through Reg. 25137, 18 CCR, interpret UDITPA and provide detailed rules for application of the law. Regulation 25121 requires that the taxpayer be consistent in reporting to California and to other states to which the taxpayer reports under UDITPA; if the taxpayer is not consistent in its reporting, it must disclose in its California return the nature and extent of the inconsistency.

• *Multistate Tax Compact*

California has adopted the Multistate Tax Compact, which was developed by the Council of State Governments to promote uniformity among the States and to avoid duplicate taxation. The Compact includes the allocation and apportionment rules of UDITPA, discussed above. The constitutionality of the Compact was upheld by the U.S. Supreme Court in *United States Steel Corp. et al. v. Multistate Tax Commission et al.* (1978) (CCH CALIFORNIA TAX REPORTS ¶ 10-105).

¶1302 Apportionment of Business Income—General

Law: Secs. 25101, 25120-22 (CCH CALIFORNIA TAX REPORTS ¶ 10-800, 11-520, 11-540, 11-550).

Comparable Federal: None.

California Forms: Form 100 (California Corporation Franchise or Income Tax Return), Sch. R (Apportionment and Allocation of Income).

Subject to the limitations pointed out in ¶ 804 and ¶ 805, any corporation deriving income from California sources is subject to California tax. If all of the income is from California, it is all subject to tax and there is, of course, no problem of apportioning a portion of the total net income to the state. However, the corporation may have income from sources outside California if (1) it is "doing business" outside of California, (2) it has property outside the state, or (3) it carries on some other activity outside the state.

If an activity generates both income that is included in the measure of tax and excluded income, only factors related to the production of income should be utilized to apportion that income. (*FTB Legal Ruling 2006-01* (2006) CCH CALIFORNIA TAX REPORTS ¶ 404-006)

• *When apportionment required*

Apportionment of income is required where business activities are *taxable* inside and outside California. (Sec. 25121, Rev. & Tax. Code) For this purpose, a taxpayer is deemed to be taxable outside California if one of the following two specific qualifications is met:

(1) the taxpayer is subject to a net income tax, a franchise tax measured by net income, a franchise tax for the privilege of doing business, or a corporate stock tax in another state; or

(2) another state has jurisdiction to levy a net income tax on the taxpayer, *whether or not* the other state actually subjects the taxpayer to the tax.

(Sec. 25122, Rev. & Tax. Code; Reg. 25122, 18 CCR)

The other state is deemed to have jurisdiction to levy a net income tax if it would be permitted to levy a tax under the limitations imposed by the federal law (P.L. 86-272) pertaining to corporations engaged solely in interstate commerce. See ¶ 805.

As used in these qualification tests, "another state" also means the District of Columbia, Puerto Rico, U.S. territories and possessions, and any foreign country or political subdivision.

Franchise Tax Board (FTB) Reg. 25122, 18 CCR, provides rules for determining whether a taxpayer is taxable in another state, and gives several examples. The FTB may require proof that the taxpayer has filed a return and paid tax of the required type in another state.

• *Procedure to determine taxable income*

Where income is to be apportioned within and outside the state under the rule set forth above, the taxable income is determined by the following steps:

(1) eliminate from the total net income any "nonbusiness" income attributable to intangible assets or to other property not connected with the operation of the principal or unitary business (such items are considered allocable either wholly to California or wholly outside California, as explained in ¶1303);

(2) apportion the remaining net income, described as "business income," within and outside the state by means of a formula or otherwise, as explained in ¶1304 and ¶1305; and

(3) the income taxable is the amount of business income apportioned to California in step 2 plus the income (less the losses) determined in step 1 to be wholly attributable to California.

FTB Reg. 25120, 18 CCR, provides that a single corporate entity may have more than one "trade or business." In this case the income of each business is separately apportioned inside and outside the state. Examples are provided to illustrate the determination of whether the taxpayer's activities constitute a single business or more than one. See ¶1304 for decisions of the State Board of Equalization (SBE) involving use of separate formulas.

• *Distinction between "business" and "nonbusiness" income*

Under FTB Reg. 25120, 18 CCR, income is deemed to be "business" income, subject to apportionment, unless it is clearly classifiable as "nonbusiness" income. A series of examples is provided to illustrate the rules to be applied in determining whether income is "business" or "nonbusiness." In general, all income—including all of the types listed in ¶1303—is "business" income if it arises from the conduct of trade or business operations.

Practitioner Comment: FTB Explains When Income From Interim Investment of IRC. Sec. 965 Dividends Apportionable

The FTB issued a ruling explaining when income earned on the investment of IRC Sec. 965 cash dividends pending domestic reinvestment is considered apportionable business income for California tax purposes. (Legal Ruling 2005-02, California Franchise Tax Board, July 8, 2005, CCH CALIFORNIA TAX REPORTS ¶403-814) Although California has not conformed to IRC Sec. 965, California law allows dividends to be deducted under certain circumstances. The FTB noted that IRC Sec. 965 does not affect the characterization of dividends as business or nonbusiness income, but its requirement that the dividends be used in certain types of investments may affect the characterization of income earned on the dividends after the dividends are paid but before they are used in a qualified investment.

The FTB explained that when the dividends are not immediately reinvested and generate income while waiting to be reinvested, the earmarking of the dividends (as evidenced by the plan of reinvestment) for a particular purpose would control the characterization of the income. It is notable that the ruling never mentions the fact that existing California regulations create a presumption in favor of business income. Under Reg. Sec. 25120(a), "...the income of the taxpayer is business income unless clearly classifiable as nonbusiness income". It is hard to reconcile the regulation with this ruling, which implies one must affirmatively do something (earmark the Section 965 dividends in a certain way), or else income from the portfolio will be nonbusiness income. The resolution of this issue could have significant consequences for taxpayers, with the positive or negative tax consequences depending on whether the taxpayer is headquartered inside or outside of California.

Bruce Daigh, Chris Whitney, Contributing Editors

In *Hoechst Celanese Corp. v. Franchise Tax Board*, (2001) (CCH CALIFORNIA TAX REPORTS ¶11-520.67), the California Supreme Court reversed a decision of the Court of Appeal and held that income attributable to a reversion of surplus pension plan assets constituted business income under the functional test because the pension plan assets were created to retain and attract new employees who materially contributed to its production of business income. The decision marked the first time that the California Supreme Court addressed the question of whether the business income definition contains a functional test as well as a transactional test.

Practitioner Comment: "Cessation of Business" Concept for Classifying Income from Sale of Subsidiary Fails to Pass Muster with Court of Appeal

In what is arguably the first California appellate court decision addressing the "cessation of business" and "partial liquidation" exception concepts, the California Court of Appeal, First Appellate District, held that the complete sale of a subsidiary corporation engaged in a unitary business with the taxpayer resulted in business income under the functional test. (*Jim Beam Brands Co. v. Franchise Tax Board* (2005) CCH CALIFORNIA TAX REPORTS ¶403-904, pet. for review denied, Cal SCt, No. S139031, January 4, 2006) As part of its analysis, the court rejected the concept—advanced by the taxpayer and contained in court decisions of other states—that where the sale of an asset of a unitary business results in the cessation of that line of business activity, the proceeds from that sale are treated as nonbusiness income.

The court initially objected to the taxpayer's portrayal of the partial liquidation exception as an issue of first impression for the court, finding that a 1980 Court of Appeal case (*Times Mirror Co. v. Franchise Tax Board* (1980) CCH CALIFORNIA TAX REPORTS ¶11-520.726) and prior SBE decisions had held that sales of subsidiary stock yielded business income. In addition, relying on the decision in *Hoechst Celanese*, the court stated that focusing on the disposition of the property, as opposed to the income-producing property itself, "is contrary to California decisional law, for it focuses on the nature of the transaction, rather than on the relationship between the property sold and the taxpayer's regular trade or business operations."

Bruce Daigh, Chris Whitney, Contributing Editors

In *Appeal of Consolidated Freightways, Inc.* (2000) (CCH CALIFORNIA TAX REPORTS ¶11-520.561), the SBE held that interest and dividends earned by a California-domiciled taxpayer from investments in long-term securities constituted business income under the functional test because the taxpayer had "earmarked" the funds for acquisition of a target in the same general line of business as the taxpayer.

In Legal Ruling 98-5 (1998) (CCH CALIFORNIA TAX REPORTS ¶11-515.28), the FTB ruled that interest and dividend income generated from liquid assets in excess of current business needs and identified future business needs could not properly be characterized as business income. The fact that the excess income was available for business use did not make the income business income when neither the transactional nor functional test for business income was satisfied.

In *Appeal of Bank of Tokyo, Limited, and Union Bank* (1995) (CCH CALIFORNIA TAX REPORTS ¶11-520.303), a California bank and a Japanese bank engaged in a unitary business were required to treat the Japanese bank's capital gains and dividends from investments in unrelated nonbanking companies as business income, even though a California bank could not have made the same type of investments, because the investment income was earned through a common practice in Japan in which banks own stock in companies to whom they lent funds.

In *Appeal of R.H. Macy & Co., Inc.* (1988) (CCH CALIFORNIA TAX REPORTS ¶11-520.562), the SBE held that interest from short-term marketable securities bought by a New York corporation engaged in retail operations in California was business income. The securities were bought with working capital awaiting use.

In the *Appeal of Inco Express, Inc.* (1987) (CCH CALIFORNIA TAX REPORTS ¶11-520.542), the interest earned on short-term working capital investments by a Washington-based trucking corporation was held to be business income by the SBE in the absence of a showing that the funds were earmarked for nonbusiness purposes.

In *Appeal of American Medical Buildings, Inc.* (1986) (CCH CALIFORNIA TAX REPORTS ¶11-520.563), the short-term investment income of a unitary construction business based in Wisconsin and engaged in business in California was held to be business income by the SBE. The income was intended to help finance the corporation's construction of medical buildings and was therefore integral to the company and apportionable to California.

In *Appeal of Louisiana-Pacific Corporation* (1986) (CCH CALIFORNIA TAX REPORTS ¶11-520.721), gain on the sale of a noncontrolling 50% stock interest in a raw materials supply affiliate was apportionable business income.

In *Appeal of Standard Oil Co. of California* (1983) (CCH CALIFORNIA TAX REPORTS ¶11-520.372), the taxpayer received substantial dividends from noncontrolled affiliated joint venture corporations. The joint venture corporations (Aramco and CPI) were major sources of supply for the taxpayer's worldwide activities. The SBE, in a lengthy and detailed opinion, held that the dividend income was integrally related to the taxpayer's business activities and was apportionable as part of the unitary income.

In *Appeal of Occidental Petroleum Corporation* (1983) (CCH CALIFORNIA TAX REPORTS ¶11-520.72), a California corporation contended that gains and losses on sale of stocks of five subsidiaries were business income, subject to apportionment. The SBE held that three of the subsidiaries were integrated parts of the unitary business, but that two of the subsidiaries were not; it followed that the gains on the latter two were nonbusiness income.

In *Appeal of Johns-Manville Sales Corporation* (1983) (CCH CALIFORNIA TAX REPORTS ¶11-515.571), the taxpayer contended that a loss suffered upon disposition of its 48% interest in a Belgian corporation was a business loss subject to apportionment. The SBE held that the taxpayer had not borne the burden of proving an integral relationship between its stockholding and its unitary business.

In *Appeal of Joy World Corporation* (1982) (CCH CALIFORNIA TAX REPORTS ¶11-520.705), the taxpayer was one of a number of subsidiaries of a Japanese corporation. The taxpayer's principal activity was the purchase of raw cotton for sale to its parent. The business of the affiliated group was admittedly unitary. The FTB included in unitary income the gain realized by the affiliated group on the sale of certain of its securities and fixed assets; the taxpayer objected to this, using as one argument the assertion that the income involved was nonbusiness income under Japanese accounting principles. The SBE upheld the FTB.

In *The Times Mirror Co. v. Franchise Tax Board* (1980) (CCH CALIFORNIA TAX REPORTS ¶206-294), the parent corporation realized a capital gain on sale of stock of a subsidiary in 1969. The subsidiary was one of several that had been included in a combined return with the parent and had been treated for many years as parts of a unitary business for California tax purposes. The Court of Appeal held that the capital gain was "business" income, to be apportioned within and without the state along with other income of the unitary business.

Appeal of General Dynamics Corporation (1975) (CCH CALIFORNIA TAX REPORTS ¶205-274) involved gain on the sale of certain stock in 1967. The stock had been acquired in a complicated series of transactions that arose in the course of the unitary business. The SBE held that the gain was unitary "business income" rather than "nonbusiness income" attributable to its out-of-state situs. The SBE's opinion included this significant comment: "In determining whether the income from intangibles constitutes business or nonbusiness income, the classifications normally given income, such as interest, dividends, or capital gains are of no assistance. The relevant inquiry is whether the income arises in the main course of the taxpayer's business operations." To the same effect, see *Appeal of Pacific Telephone and Telegraph Co.* (1978) (CCH CALIFORNIA TAX REPORTS ¶11-525.80), involving business income gained on the sale of stock of an affiliated corporation that was received in a reorganization, and *Robert Half International, Inc. v. Franchise Tax Board* (1998) (CCH CALIFORNIA TAX REPORTS ¶11-515.592), involving a nonbusiness loss incurred on the acquisition of a warrant for stock.

• *Pertinent cases under prior law*

Under pre-1967 law, there were many decisions of the SBE and the courts dealing with the question of whether certain income was "unitary" income subject to "allocation" or was nonunitary income that was attributable entirely to a particular State. The reasoning of these cases should apply, generally, under present law, to the question of whether income is "business" or "nonbusiness." (However, as pointed out in the opinion in the *Times Mirror* case, discussed above, such prior-law cases cannot be used as *precedents* under the current law; also, as pointed out in the *Standard Oil* case, the pre-1967 law regarding dividends was different from current law.)

Appeal of Capital Southwest Corporation (1973) (CCH CALIFORNIA TAX REPORTS ¶204-818) involved a "small business investment company," with its head office outside California and a small office within the State. The SBE held that the taxpayer's income from dividends and capital gains was part of its unitary business income from long-term investments and was subject to apportionment.

In *Appeal of the Western Pacific Railroad Company* (1972) (CCH CALIFORNIA TAX REPORTS ¶11-530.38), the SBE held in 1972 that gains and losses on sales of land were not includible in unitary income subject to apportionment. The land was sold to prospective shippers to increase rail traffic, but it was never used in the unitary operations.

In *Appeal of W.J. Voit Rubber Company* (1964) (CCH CALIFORNIA TAX REPORTS ¶11-520.70), a California corporation sold an entire manufacturing plant located in another state. The out-of-state plant had previously been operated as part of a unitary business, and gain arising out of its sale was held to be unitary income subject to allocation within and without California. To the same effect, involving the out-of-state sale of motion pictures that had been produced in prior years in a unitary business, see *Appeal of Paramount Pictures Corp.* (1969) (CCH CALIFORNIA TAX REPORTS ¶11-525.31).

In *Appeal of the United States Shoe Corporation* (1959) (CCH CALIFORNIA TAX REPORTS ¶11-520.661), the SBE held that license fees received from licensees in foreign countries for technical information, services, advice, and manufacturing "know-how" were includible in unitary income, since the taxpayer's ability to furnish such advice and "know-how" arose out of its unitary business.

In *Appeal of Union Carbide & Carbon Corporation* (1957) (CCH CALIFORNIA TAX REPORTS ¶11-520.42), the SBE held that certain government project fees were part of unitary income to be allocated by formula. These fees were received for services of a managerial and technical nature, the services having been rendered at the Oak Ridge atomic energy plant and other locations outside of California. The SBE's decision was based on the reasoning that the fees were received for the use of skills developed in the taxpayer's regular business operations.

In *Appeal of International Business Machines Corp.* (1954) (CCH CALIFORNIA TAX REPORTS ¶11-520.661), the SBE held that royalty income of a foreign corporation was part of its unitary income and subject to allocation. In this case the corporation received large royalties for the use of its patents in foreign countries. The patents had been developed and were used in the corporation's regular business operations in this country. To the same effect, see *Appeal of National Cylinder Gas Company* (1957) (CCH CALIFORNIA TAX REPORTS ¶11-520.66) and *Appeal of Rockwell Manufacturing Company* (1958) (CCH CALIFORNIA TAX REPORTS ¶11-520.66).

• *Cases decided under UDITPA*

Later cases, involving the Uniform Division of Income for Tax Purposes Act that became effective in 1967, follow the pattern of the prior-law cases discussed above. In *Appeal of New York Football Giants, Inc.* (1977) (CCH CALIFORNIA TAX REPORTS ¶11-525.512), the SBE held that compensation to an out-of-state corporation for loss of a franchise was part of unitary "business income" to be allocated by formula. In *Appeal of Borden, Inc.* (1977) (CCH CALIFORNIA TAX REPORTS ¶11-520.701), the SBE held that losses on sale of a California plant and goodwill were "business income" subject to formula apportionment. The SBE refused to recognize a liquidation exception to the functional test for determining whether income is business income.

In *Appeal of Calavo Growers of California* (1984) (CCH CALIFORNIA TAX REPORTS ¶11-520.703), it was held that gain on the sale of Florida citrus groves was "business income"; the groves had been acquired in an earlier year upon default of a company to which the taxpayer had made loans. In *Appeal of Triangle Publications, Inc.* (1984) (CCH CALIFORNIA TAX REPORTS ¶11-520.702), the SBE cited and followed the *Borden* and *Calavo Growers* cases. In *Appeal of Kroehler Manufacturing Co.* (1977) (CCH CALIFORNIA TAX REPORTS ¶11-520.721), the SBE held that rebates received upon liquidation of the pension plan of a predecessor corporation were "business income" subject to formula apportionment. In *Appeal of Thor Power Tool Company* (1980) (CCH CALIFORNIA TAX REPORTS ¶203-306), the SBE held that gain on sale of land (former plant site) was "business income." In *Appeal of Fairchild Industries, Inc.* (1980) (CCH CALIFORNIA TAX REPORTS ¶11-520.662) the SBE held that gain on sale of patent rights was "business income."

The cases have held that the present law provides two alternative tests for determining what is "business income": the "transactional test" and the "functional test." For a discussion of these tests, see the decision of the SBE in *Appeal of DPF, Inc.* (1980) (CCH CALIFORNIA TAX REPORTS ¶11-520.48). In that case the SBE decided that gain on repurchase of debentures was "business income." On the other hand, in *Appeal of Beck Industries* (1982) (CCH CALIFORNIA TAX REPORTS ¶11-520.805) the SBE applied the two tests and found that interest received on certificates of deposit was nonbusiness income; in that case the deposited funds arose from selling discontinued business interests during a bankruptcy reorganization. However, interest income from short-term investment of excess funds was held to be business income in *Appeal of A. Epstein and Sons, Inc.* (1984) (CCH CALIFORNIA TAX REPORTS ¶11-520.837).

In two 1977 decisions involving UDITPA, the SBE held that real estate rentals were "business income" subject to formula allocation. See *Appeal of Isador Weinstein Investment Co.* (CCH CALIFORNIA TAX REPORTS ¶11-520.692) and *Appeal of O.K. Earl Corp.* (CCH CALIFORNIA TAX REPORTS ¶11-520.691).

¶1303 Allocation of Nonbusiness Income—General

Law: Secs. 25123-27 (CCH CALIFORNIA TAX REPORTS ¶11-515).

Comparable Federal: None.

As explained at ¶1302, most income is deemed to be "business" income—regardless of the form or type of income involved—but some income is clearly classifiable as "nonbusiness." The law provides the following specific rules for the treatment of certain types of income, to the extent that the income constitutes "nonbusiness" income:

— Net rents and royalties from real property, and gains and losses from the sale thereof, are allocable to the state in which the property is located. (Sec. 25124, Rev. & Tax. Code)

— Net rents and royalties from tangible personal property are allocable to the state in which the property is utilized. However, if the taxpayer was not organized in, or is not taxable in, the state in which the property is utilized, such income is taxable in the state of the owner's commercial domicile. For tangible personal property utilized in more than one state, the income is allocated on the basis of the number of days of physical location within and without California during the rental or royalty period of the taxable year. If the physical location during the period is unknown or unascertainable by the taxpayer, the property is deemed utilized in the state in which the property is located at the time the payer of the rent or royalty obtained possession. (Sec. 25124, Rev. & Tax. Code)

— Gains and losses from sale of tangible personal property are allocable to the state where the property is located at the time of sale. However, if the taxpayer is not taxable in the state in which the property is located at the time of sale, the gain or loss is allocable to the state of the taxpayer's commercial domicile. (Sec. 25125, Rev. & Tax. Code)

— Interest and dividends, as well as gains and losses from sale of intangible personal property, are allocable entirely to the state of the taxpayer's commercial domicile. (Sec. 25125, Rev. & Tax. Code; Sec. 25126, Rev. & Tax. Code)

— Patent and copyright royalties are allocable to the state in which the patent or copyright is utilized by the payer of the royalties. However, if the taxpayer is not taxable in the state in which the property is utilized, the royalty income is allocable to the state of commercial domicile. Royalty income from a patent that is utilized in more than one state in production, fabrication, manufacturing, etc., or a patented product that is produced in more than one state is allocable to the states of utilization on the basis of gross royalty receipts. However, if the taxpayer fails to maintain accounting records to reflect the states of utilization, the entire amount is allocable to the state of the taxpayer's commercial domicile. A copyright is deemed to be utilized in the state in which printing or other publication originates. (Sec. 25127, Rev. & Tax. Code)

• *What is "commercial domicile"?*

The law defines "commercial domicile" as "the principal place from which the trade or business of the taxpayer is directed or managed." (Sec. 25120, Rev. & Tax. Code) This is generally similar to the pre-1967 law, so the reasoning of the 1955 decision of the California District Court of Appeal in *Pacific Western Oil Corp. v. Franchise Tax Board* (CCH CALIFORNIA TAX REPORTS ¶11-515.301) presumably would be applicable under present law. In that case, the taxpayer was a Delaware corporation and received income from dividends, interest, and gains from sale of securities at its offices in New Jersey. However, it was held that the taxpayer's commercial domicile was in California and, therefore, the income from the intangibles was includible in the measure of the franchise tax. Important factors influencing the decision were:

— revenue from sales of products was greater in California than in all other states combined,

— the value of the fixed assets in California was several times greater than those located in other states,

— over 90% of the employees were performing services in California,

— the principal accounting records were kept in California,

— the income from the intangibles had not been taxed by any other state, and

— the federal income tax returns were filed in California.

In *Appeal of Vinnell Corporation* (1978) (CCH CALIFORNIA TAX REPORTS ¶11-515.453), the taxpayer (a predecessor corporation) was a wholly-owned subsidiary of a California corporation. The taxpayer was incorporated in Panama and was engaged in the construction business entirely outside the United States. The State Board of Equalization (SBE) held that the taxpayer's commercial domicile was not in California, although there were some contacts with California. The SBE dismissed the contacts as "artificial and lacking in substance" and commented that the concept of commercial domicile that has been developed by the courts is an "intensely practical" one.

In *Appeal of Norton Simon, Inc.* (1972) (CCH CALIFORNIA TAX REPORTS ¶11-515.45), the SBE held that the commercial domicile of a predecessor corporation (Harbor Plywood) was in California. The SBE held that "the essence of the concept of commercial domicile is that is the place where the corporate management functions, the place where real control exists . . . "

In *Appeal of Bristol-Myers Company* (1972) (CCH CALIFORNIA TAX REPORTS ¶11-515.26), a New York company suffered losses on its investment in a nonunitary subsidiary located in California. The corporation claimed deduction of the losses for franchise tax purposes, contending that it had commercial domiciles in both New York and California. The SBE held that the losses were attributable to New York, the state of the parent corporation's only domicile, and were not deductible.

• *Share of out-of-state partnership loss*

In *Appeal of The National Dollar Stores, Ltd.* (1986) (CCH CALIFORNIA TAX REPORTS ¶11-515.59), losses from an oil and gas drilling partnership in Colorado incurred by a California clothing retailer were nonbusiness income, unrelated to the retailer's unitary retail sales business. The losses were attributable to Colorado and not deductible.

In *Appeal of Custom Component Switches, Inc.* (1977) (CCH CALIFORNIA TAX REPORTS ¶11-515.48), a California corporation was a manufacturer of electrical equipment and was a member of a real estate partnership. The SBE held that partnership losses attributable to out-of-state property were from sources outside California and were not deductible.

• *Intercompany dividends*

Dividends received by one member from another member of a group of affiliated corporations filing a combined California report are excluded from income, to the extent such dividends are paid out of unitary income, see ¶909 for details. In *Appeal of Louisiana-Pacific Corporation* (1987) (CCH CALIFORNIA TAX REPORTS ¶11-515.404), the exclusion for intercompany dividends paid from unitary income did not apply to distributions made prior to the time the payor corporation became a member of the unitary business.

• *Royalty income*

In the *Appeal of Masonite Corporation* (1987) (CCH CALIFORNIA TAX REPORTS ¶11-515.59), income derived from the production of oil and gas from reserves underlying taxpayer's Mississippi timberlands was nonbusiness income. The SBE held that income was unrelated to the taxpayer's unitary wood-products business because the oil production activities were, in fact, detrimental to the timberlands.

• *Allocation of gain or loss on sale of partnership interests*

An interstate or international corporation that sells a partnership interest must use an allocation formula to determine the portion of capital gain or loss realized from the sale that must be attributed to California taxable income. The allocation formula is based on the relationship that the original cost of the partnership's tangible property located in California bears to the original cost of all the partnership's tangible property. In the event that more than 50% of the partnership's assets consists of intangible property, the allocation to California income of the gain or loss realized must be determined by using the ratio of the partnership's California sales to the partnership's total sales during the first full tax period preceding the sale of the partnership interest. (Sec. 25125, Rev. & Tax. Code)

¶1304 Methods of Apportioning Business Income

Law: Secs. 25128, 25137 (CCH CALIFORNIA TAX REPORTS ¶11-520, 11-550).

Comparable Federal: None.

The law provides detailed rules for apportionment of business income by formula. It also provides for use of separate accounting where apportionment by formula does not fairly reflect the extent of the taxpayer's business activity in the state, and permits the taxpayer to petition for use of separate accounting.

• *FTB policy on apportionment, separate accounting, and decombination*

Until the early 1990s, it was the consistent policy of the Franchise Tax Board (FTB) to find business operations unitary (and thus require apportionment or, if separate affiliates were involved, combined reporting) if sufficient, minimum unitary criteria were met. For example, operations were generally considered unitary if there was any flow of goods or benefits between the part of the business within and the part outside the state, or where one part contributed directly or indirectly to the other. Examples of such relationships would be one division purchasing materials or merchandise from another; insurance or pension plans handled jointly; advertising done on a cooperative basis; centralized purchasing, selling, engineering accounting, financing, etc.

In August 1992, however, the FTB issued revised audit guidelines with respect to the unitary combination of diverse businesses (*FTB Notice No.* 92-4, CCH CALIFORNIA TAX REPORTS ¶11-520.35). According to the revised guidelines, there is no unique test for evaluating unity in diverse business cases. Unity may be established under any of the judicially acceptable tests (the three unities, contribution or dependency, and flow of value tests) and may not be denied merely because another of those tests does not simultaneously apply, *i.e.*, the tests are not mutually exclusive. In addition, a lack of functional integration will not prevent a finding of unity. On the other hand, the fact that functionally integrated businesses may be found to be unitary does not mean that functional integration is a *requirement* for unity.

Also, presumptions of unity under Reg. 25120(b), 18 CCR, which states that the activities of a taxpayer will be considered a single business if there is evidence to indicate that the segments under consideration are integrated with, depend on, or contribute to, each other and the operations of the taxpayer as a whole, although important considerations, are not conclusive in determining unity.

Finally, the guidelines state that *Mole-Richardson*, *Dental Insurance Consultants*, and *Tenneco West, Inc.* (all discussed below) are controlling of the diverse business issue and that State Board of Equalization (SBE) decisions that are not in accord with these cases should not be relied upon.

If the operations of a business are "unitary" in nature, it makes no difference whether there is only one corporation or an affiliated group. Consolidation and income-apportionment of a large group of corporations may be required even where only one of the corporations is subject to California tax. See *Edison California Stores* and other cases discussed below. See also ¶1310.

The FTB has issued a legal ruling containing guidelines for determining whether the "unity of ownership" requirement for unitary treatment is satisfied (see below) (*FTB Legal Ruling No.* 91-1, CCH CALIFORNIA TAX REPORTS ¶11-520.954).

CCH Practice Tip: Apportionment of IRC Sec. 338 deemed asset sales

For information regarding how to apportion the gains resulting from an IRC Sec. 338(h)(1) or IRC Sec. 338(g) election to treat the sale or purchase of stock as a sale or purchase of assets, see the FTB's *Legal Ruling 2006-03*, May 6, 2006, CCH CALIFORNIA TAX REPORTS ¶10-540.21.

• *Leading cases*

The courts have developed the following three general tests for determining whether a business is "unitary:

— the three unities test, in the *Butler Brothers* case,

— the contribution and dependency test, in the *Edison California Stores* case, and

— the functional integration test, in the *Container* case.

The existence of a unitary business is established if any of the three tests is met.

In *Butler Brothers v. McColgan* (1942) (CCH CALIFORNIA TAX REPORTS ¶11-520.2096), the U.S. Supreme Court upheld use of the allocation formula (equivalent to the "apportionment" formula under present law) in preference to separate accounting. In that case the taxpayer corporation operated a number of stores throughout the country, one of which was in California. The unitary nature of the business was held to have been definitely established by the presence of the following factors:

— unity of ownership;

— unity of operation as evidenced by central purchasing, advertising, accounting, and management divisions; and

— unity of use in its centralized executive force and general system of operation.

Separate accounting showed a large loss for the California store, whereas application of the formula resulted in a substantial profit allocable to California. Nevertheless, the court upheld the use of the formula, because the taxpayer did not demonstrate convincingly that the formula produced a clearly unreasonable result and that separate accounting fairly and accurately reflected the income properly allocable to California.

In *Container Corporation of America v. Franchise Tax Board* (1983) (CCH CALIFORNIA TAX REPORTS ¶11-520), the U.S. Supreme Court upheld the application of the standard three-factor apportionment formula to a domestic corporation and several foreign subsidiaries. The court held that the parent and subsidiaries were unitary because they were linked by common managerial or operational resources that produced economies of scale and transfers of value. The court stated that whether businesses are unitary is determined by whether contributions to income result from functional integration, centralization of management, and economies of scale. Other issues in *Container Corporation of America* are discussed at ¶1310.

In *Edison California Stores, Inc. v. McColgan* (1947) (CCH CALIFORNIA TAX REPORTS ¶11-520.803), the California Supreme Court held that the allocation formula (equivalent to the "apportionment" formula under present law) was properly applicable to the combined income of a California corporation and its foreign parent corporation and other subsidiaries. The taxpayer produced evidence to show that its separate accounting for the subsidiary was reasonable and proper, but the court held that the taxpayer had not met the burden of proving that the consolidation and the allocation formula produced an unreasonable result. The court stated clearly its test of whether or not a business is unitary: "If the operation of the portion of the business done within the state is dependent upon or contributes to the operation of the business without the state, the operations are unitary . . . ."

• *Other cases holding business to be unitary*

Over the years there have been many decisions of the courts and the SBE that have followed the lead of the *Butler Brothers* and *Edison* cases and have held that businesses were unitary. The following brief summaries of these cases will provide a "feel" for the trend of the decisions.

For a later case that followed *Butler Brothers* in a somewhat similar situation, see the SBE opinion in *Appeal of Ohrbach's, Inc.* (1961) (CCH CALIFORNIA TAX REPORTS ¶11-520.836). The taxpayer operated department stores in New York and California. The reasoning applied in *Edison* was applied by a California court of appeal in *Yoshinoya West, Inc. v. Franchise Tax Board* (2006) (CCH CALIFORNIA TAX REPORTS ¶11-520.8396). The court ruled that a U.S. corporation that operated fast-food restaurants was unitary with its Japanese parent corporation because the U.S.-based business depended upon and contributed to the business conducted by the Japanese parent company.

In *Appeal of PBS Building Systems, Inc., and PKH Building Systems* (1994) (CCH CALIFORNIA TAX REPORTS ¶11-520.491), the SBE held that a "passive" holding company was engaged in a unitary business with its operating subsidiary for combined reporting purposes, as evidenced by a complete overlap of officers and directors and extensive intercompany financing consisting of loans, loan guarantees, debt refinancing, debt reduction, and a covenant not to compete that was purchased by the holding company for the benefit of its subsidiary. Because "passive" holding companies are fully capable of providing and receiving a flow of value to or from an operating subsidiary, the factors to consider in determining whether a holding company is unitary with its operating subsidiaries are the same factors that must be considered with respect to any other business enterprise.

In *Dental Insurance Consultants, Inc. v. State Franchise Tax Board* (1991) (CCH CALIFORNIA TAX REPORTS ¶11-520.351), a court of appeal held that a dental insurance consulting corporation and its wholly owned farming subsidiary were engaged in a unitary enterprise. Although the FTB argued that the three unities test should be abandoned in favor of the functional integration test, the court determined that application of both tests was proper because they were not mutually exclusive. The court held that under both the three unities test and the functional integration test, the corporations were unitary. In addition, the court held that application of the dependency and contribution test was unnecessary because its use would result in the same conclusion yielded by the three unities test.

In *Mole-Richardson v. Franchise Tax Board* (1990) (CCH CALIFORNIA TAX REPORTS ¶11-520.353), a court of appeal held that a group of commonly owned and centrally managed corporations that did business both inside and outside of California constituted a unitary business even though the business they engaged in inside California was primarily the manufacture and sale of lighting equipment and the business they engaged in outside of California was primarily ranching. The court rejected the FTB's argument that the corporations constituted two distinct business groups because they were not "functionally integrated." In doing so, the court stated that "functional integration" was not a new concept by which business enterprises must be evaluated to justify unitary treatment. Moreover, the court held that the presence of strong centralized management and economies of scale was evidence that the corporations were functionally integrated.

In *Appeal of Capital Industries—EMI, Inc.* (1989) (CCH CALIFORNIA TAX REPORTS ¶11-520.8098), a California corporation that produced and sold recorded music, sheet music, and blank audio tapes was engaged in a unitary business with its British parent, which conducted similar activities on a worldwide basis. Factors considered by the SBE as supporting unity were intercompany matrix agreements, intercompany sales, transfers of key personnel, common directors, joint use of key labels, intercompany financing, mutual international promotional activities, and exercise of parental control over the distribution of the music of the parent's artists.

In *Appeal of Trails End, Inc.* (1986) (CCH CALIFORNIA TAX REPORTS ¶11-520.838), the SBE denied rehearing an earlier decision that a California plastics manufacturer, a California vitamin manufacturer, and a Michigan corporation were in a unitary business relationship. The plastics manufacturer was a subsidiary of the vitamin manufacturer, which was itself a subsidiary of and engaged in a unitary business with the Michigan corporation. It is necessary in establishing unity only that the business within California is dependent upon or contributes to the business outside California, and it is the aggregate effect of one company on another that determines unity. The relationship between the plastics manufacturer and the Michigan corporation did not need to be direct to establish a unitary relationship; it was sufficient for franchise tax purposes if the unitary business relationship was indirect. Thus, because the plastics manufacturer was found to be engaged in a unitary business with the vitamin manufacturer, its operations could not justifiably be separated from the unitary operation of the Michigan corporation and the vitamin manufacturer.

In *Appeal of Atlas Hotels, Inc., et al.* (1985) (CCH CALIFORNIA TAX REPORTS ¶11-520.8197), the taxpayer was in the hotel business and its subsidiary was in the restaurant business. The SBE found that the subsidiary became "instantly unitary" with the parent's unitary business from the date of its acquisition when there was evidence that many of the managerial and operational changes that demonstrated the subsidiary's integration with its parent not only were implemented immediately upon acquisition, but were planned or commenced well before the actual acquisition date.

In *Appeal of Allstate Enterprises, Inc., et al.* (1984) (CCH CALIFORNIA TAX REPORTS ¶11-520.8197), the taxpayer and several affiliated corporations were engaged in providing vehicle financing and motor club services. Another subsidiary was engaged in the mortgage banking business, and the taxpayer contended that this corporation should not be included in the unitary group. The SBE held that the mortgage banking business was a part of a unitary operation.

In *Appeal of Lancaster Colony Corporation and August Barr, Inc.* (1984) (CCH CALIFORNIA TAX REPORTS ¶11-520.82), there were seven divisions and fourteen subsidiaries engaged in a wide variety of industrial and consumer businesses. The SBE held that the operations constituted a single unitary business, based on flow of goods, supplying of administrative and technical services, interlocking officers and directors, and other indications of unity.

Appeal of Data General Corporation (1982) (CCH CALIFORNIA TAX REPORTS ¶11-520.806) involved a Delaware corporation that conducted a worldwide business in computers and related products with four domestic and twelve foreign subsidiaries. The SBE held that the group met both the "unity" and "dependency" tests for a unitary operation: the SBE referred to the taxpayer's public reports as one indication of the centralization and integration of management and operations.

In *Appeal of Kikkoman International, Inc.* (1982) (CCH CALIFORNIA TAX REPORTS ¶11-520.825), the taxpayer was a 70% owned California subsidiary of a prominent Japanese company. The taxpayer contended that the income attributable to California could be determined fairly only by separate accounting, because the property and payroll factors did not account for the disparity between California and Japan in property costs and wages. The SBE held that the companies were "a classic example of the type of vertically integrated enterprise to which the unitary concept has been applied" and required use of the standard apportionment formula.

See ¶1310 for discussion of other cases involving foreign operations, including the 1983 decision of the U.S. Supreme Court in the case of *Container Corporation of America.*

In *Appeal of Beck/Arnley Corporation of California* (1981) (CCH CALIFORNIA TAX REPORTS ¶11-520.805), the taxpayer was the wholly-owned subsidiary of a New York corporation. Both corporations were engaged in the sale of automobile parts and accessories. The SBE held that the operations were unitary under either the "unity" test or the "contribution and dependency" tests.

In *Appeal of Credit Bureau Central, Inc.* (1981) (CCH CALIFORNIA TAX REPORTS ¶11-520.827), a California corporation was one of 14 wholly owned subsidiaries of a Georgia corporation. All of the subsidiaries operated as collection agencies. The SBE held that the operations were unitary, based largely on centralized executive and management services.

In *Appeal of National Silver Co.* (1980) (CCH CALIFORNIA TAX REPORTS ¶11-520.813), the taxpayer was engaged in the marketing of houseware products. The corporation had various relationships with two affiliated out-of-state corporations and purchased 10% of the output of one of the affiliates. The SBE held that the businesses of the three corporations were unitary.

In *Appeal of L&B Manufacturing Co.* (1980) (CCH CALIFORNIA TAX REPORTS ¶11-520.812), the taxpayer was a member of an affiliated group of seven corporations engaged in the restaurant and hotel furnishings business. The SBE held that the business was unitary, since the taxpayer did not carry the burden of proof to the contrary under either the "unity" or the "dependency" test.

In *Appeal of Wynn Oil Company* (1980) (CCH CALIFORNIA TAX REPORTS ¶206-308), the taxpayer was engaged primarily in the manufacture and distribution of petrochemical products. The corporation supplied active management direction and services to a subsidiary that operated student dormitories on college campuses. The SBE held that, despite their diverse nature, the businesses of the parent and subsidiary were unitary. However, a 1990 decision of the SBE ruled that this decision has "no continuing validity as precedent" because the test following the U.S. Supreme Court decision in *Container Corporation v. FTB* requires an analysis on evidence of a functionally integrated enterprise (see *Appeal of Meadows Realty Co.* (1990), CCH CALIFORNIA TAX REPORTS ¶12-500.90).

In *Allright Cal., Inc.* (1979) (CCH CALIFORNIA TAX REPORTS ¶11-520.808), the taxpayer was one of 95 subsidiaries of a Texas corporation. The affiliated corporations operated a nationwide network of automobile parking lots. The SBE cited the *John Deere Plow Co.* case, discussed below (and others), and held that the operations were unitary and subject to formula apportionment. Principal unitary factors were ownership, interlocking officers and directors, centralized overhead functions, common pension plan, and parent-supplied financing and other services.

In *Appeals of Cascade Dental Laboratory, Inc., et al.* (1978) (CCH CALIFORNIA TAX REPORTS ¶11-520.828), the taxpayers were dental-laboratory subsidiaries of a health-service company that had its headquarters in Texas. The SBE held that the business was not unitary in the first year at issue, but that the character of the operation changed to the point that the business was unitary in later years.

In *Appeal of Parador Mining Co., Inc.* (1977) (CCH CALIFORNIA TAX REPORTS ¶11-520.8292), the taxpayer was a closely held corporation engaged in mineral exploration. Most of its business was conducted in the home of the president and chief stockholder. The SBE held that the business was unitary and that its California income must be determined by formula rather than by separate accounting.

In *Appeal of Isador Weinstein Investment Co.* (1977) (CCH CALIFORNIA TAX REPORTS ¶11-520.692), the taxpayer's principal activity was real estate rentals. The SBE held that the operation was unitary and was subject to formula allocation. To the same effect, see *Appeal of O.K. Earl Corp.* (1977) (CCH CALIFORNIA TAX REPORTS ¶ 11-520.809), involving a variety of related activities in addition to real estate rentals.

Appeal of Beecham, Inc. (1977) (CCH CALIFORNIA TAX REPORTS ¶ 11-520.8293) involved a large conglomerate with an English parent company. The SBE held that the business was unitary and that the income of the entire group was subject to allocation by formula. Although the propriety of including the foreign parent and its foreign subsidiaries was not a primary issue in the case, the SBE pointed out that in earlier cases the income of foreign subsidiaries has been held to be includible in a combined report and commented: "We are unable to discern any difference when the foreign corporation is the parent rather than the subsidiary."

In *Appeal of Putnam Fund Distributors, Inc., et al.* (1977) (CCH CALIFORNIA TAX REPORTS ¶ 11-520.8291), the SBE held that a Massachusetts mutual-fund-management company was engaged in a unitary operation with a 51% owned California corporation and other subsidiaries; the subsidiaries were engaged principally in sales activities.

In *Appeal of Automated Building Components, Inc.* (1976) (CCH CALIFORNIA TAX REPORTS ¶ 11-520.8298), the taxpayer was a Florida corporation that had an operation in California and had foreign subsidiaries. The SBE held that the group was engaged in a unitary operation that required a combined report as discussed in ¶ 1310. The SBE's opinion discusses the general tests established in the *Butler Brothers* and *Edison California Stores* cases, and concludes that "a unitary business exists if *either* the three unities or the contribution or dependency tests are satisfied" (emphasis supplied).

In *Appeal of Grolier Society, Inc.* (1975) (CCH CALIFORNIA TAX REPORTS ¶ 11-520.8299), the SBE held that five Canadian subsidiaries and four Latin American subsidiaries were engaged in a unitary business with the taxpayer, its parent, and other subsidiaries.

In *Appeal of Harbison-Walker Refractories Company* (1972) (CCH CALIFORNIA TAX REPORTS ¶ 11-520.83), the SBE decided that a Pennsylvania corporation and its Canadian subsidiary were engaged in a unitary business. The corporations had common officers and directors, common purchases, intercompany purchases and sales, and an intercompany management fee.

In *Appeal of Anchor Hocking Glass Corporation* (1967) (CCH CALIFORNIA TAX REPORTS ¶ 11-520.8193), the SBE held that the use of common trademarks and patents and the interchange of "know-how" were significant factors in determining the existence of a unitary business between a U.S. parent and its foreign and domestic subsidiaries.

In *Appeal of Cutter Laboratories* (1964) (CCH CALIFORNIA TAX REPORTS ¶ 11-520.8194), the SBE held that a parent corporation manufacturing and selling vaccines and pharmaceuticals for both human and animal consumption was engaged in a unitary business with its wholly owned subsidiary operating in another State in the manufacture and sale of veterinary instruments and animal vaccines. The taxpayer's contention that the corporations were engaged in different types of business was rejected when the two corporations were found to be closely related through common officers and directors, interstate flow of products, and joint participation in insurance, retirement, and automobile leasing plans.

In *Appeal of Youngstown Steel Products Company of California* (1952) (CCH CALIFORNIA TAX REPORTS ¶ 11-520.213), the SBE upheld the application of the allocation formula to the combined income of three corporations, only one of which operated in California, despite the fact that the California corporation operated under an "arm's-length" contractual arrangement similar to a previous arrangement with an unrelated corporation.

In *John Deere Plow Co. v. Franchise Tax Board* (1951) (CCH CALIFORNIA TAX REPORTS ¶11-520.202), the California Supreme Court upheld the FTB in applying the allocation formula to the combined income of a parent corporation and 84 subsidiaries, only one of which was doing business in California. The taxpayer contended unsuccessfully that use of the allocation formula was unreasonable because the income of the California branch was overstated rather than understated by the use of separate accounting. The taxpayer's argument was based partly on the fact that no charge had been made to the California branch for services rendered to it by the central office of the affiliated group.

• *Unity of ownership*

The FTB has issued detailed guidelines for determining whether ownership of a group of corporations satisfies the "unity of ownership" standard (*FTB Legal Ruling No.* 91-1, *supra*). Generally, unity of ownership is established only when the same interests directly or indirectly own or control more than 50% of the voting stock of all members of the purported unitary group. "Indirect ownership" may include direct ownership and control of more than half the voting stock of a corporation that in turn directly owns and controls the requisite amount of voting stock in another corporation. Likewise, "indirect control" includes control exercised through ownership or control of an intermediary corporation. "Direct control" of voting stock includes ownership of the voting rights alone, pursuant to a binding and permanent legal transfer of those rights.

The requisite control may also be exercised by a group of shareholders acting in concert. In *Rain Bird Sprinkler Mfg. Corp. v. FTB* (1991) (CCH CALIFORNIA TAX REPORTS ¶11-520.8092), seventeen corporations that were operated as a single business enterprise constituted a unitary business even though no *single* individual or entity held a majority interest in all of the corporations. The court held that "unity of ownership" existed because members of the same family held the majority of the voting stock in each of the corporations, and all of the stock of each corporation was subject to written stock purchase agreements prohibiting transfer to outsiders.

According to the FTB, application of the "concerted ownership or control" principle of *Rain Bird* is not limited to members of the same family. Factors to be considered in determining whether a group of shareholders exercises concerted ownership or control of several corporations include the business relationships of the corporations involved, the relationships between the shareholders, the degree of common ownership, common voting patterns, and each shareholder's relative percentage of ownership or control. A similar conclusion was reached in *Appeal of AMP, Inc.* (1996) (CCH CALIFORNIA TAX REPORTS, ¶11-520.95).

• *Cases holding business to be nonunitary*

In *Appeal of F.W. Woolworth Co. et al.* (1998) (CCH CALIFORNIA TAX REPORTS ¶11-520.60), a California court of appeal held that a parent corporation was not engaged in a unitary business with its wholly owned subsidiary, because they were not in the same general line of business. The parent conducted a mass merchandising business in apparel and general merchandise and the subsidiary was engaged primarily in the manufacture and sale of shoes and there was not strong centralization of the management of the two corporations.

In *Appeal of Hearst Corporation* (1992) (CCH CALIFORNIA TAX REPORTS ¶11-520.6091), a domestic corporation that was engaged in various business activities, including publication of newspapers, books, and magazines, was not engaged in a unitary business with its wholly owned foreign subsidiary, which published books and magazines in the United Kingdom. The taxpayer rebutted the presumption that the businesses were unitary by providing evidence that they had separate editorial, writing, and photographic staffs and that intercompany sales and use of material were extremely minimal. Additionally, the SBE found that no phase of the subsidiary's operations was actually integrated with the taxpayer's operations.

In *Tenneco West, Inc. v. Franchise Tax Board* (1991) (CCH CALIFORNIA TAX REPORTS ¶11-520.352), a court of appeal held that the taxpayer, which was in the oil and gas business, and its subsidiaries, which were in the business of shipbuilding, packaging, manufacturing automotive parts, manufacturing equipment used in construction, and farming, were not unitary. The court determined that there was no strong centralized management and that the subsidiaries were engaged in diverse activities unrelated to the parent's business and thus lacked integration.

In *Appeal of Meadows Realty Company et al.* (1990) (CCH CALIFORNIA TAX REPORTS ¶11-520.45), unity did not exist between a parent corporation's oil refining activities and its subsidiary's realty development activities even though the subsidiary received financial assistance and management services from the parent corporation. The SBE indicated that "functional integration" was required to establish the existence of a unitary business.

In *Appeal of Postal Press* (1987) (CCH CALIFORNIA TAX REPORTS ¶11-520.609), the SBE held that a 68.3% ownership of a subsidiary's stock by a taxpayer was insufficient to prove that it was engaged in a unitary business. The taxpayer specialized in commercial printing and its subsidiary specialized in instant printing. The SBE found that, despite the stock ownership and use of similar trademarks and names, other indications of unity, such as common management and operations, were absent.

In *Appeal of Nevis Industries, Inc.,* (1985) (CCH CALIFORNIA TAX REPORTS ¶11-520.952), ownership of a Nevada corporation and eight affiliated companies was shared equally (never exceeding 50%) by two brothers. The California Supreme Court held that the businesses were not unitary because no single entity owned more than 50% and had controlling interest in any of the involved companies. Stock owned directly or indirectly by family members is not attributed to other family members, for purposes of determining unity of ownership.

In *Appeal of Coachmen Industries of California* (1985) (CCH CALIFORNIA TAX REPORTS ¶11-520.8197), the SBE found that a California company's evidence of independence from its Indiana parent was insufficient to prove it was not engaged in a unitary business. A number of factors, when taken in the aggregate, indicated that the two companies were involved in a single economic enterprise. The connections that indicated a unitary relationship included almost identical businesses, interlocking officers and directors, intercompany product flow, shared purchasing, exclusively intercompany financing, and shared group life and health insurance.

Appeal of The Grupe Company et al. (1985) (CCH CALIFORNIA TAX REPORTS ¶11-520.604) was another case in which the taxpayer contended that two businesses were unitary but was overruled by the SBE. In this case, land development operations were conducted in California and an alfalfa farm was operated on leased land in Nevada.

In *Appeal of Vidal Sassoon of New York, Inc.* (1984) (CCH CALIFORNIA TAX REPORTS ¶11-520.607), the taxpayer and 19 affiliated corporations operated hairdressing salons in the United States, Canada, and Europe under the common name "Sassoon." The SBE held that the operations in Europe were not unitary with those in the United States.

In *Appeals of Dynamic Speaker Corporation* and *Talone Packing Company* (1984) (CCH CALIFORNIA TAX REPORTS ¶11-520.607), the parent company of the taxpayers and six subsidiaries were engaged in a variety of diverse businesses. Although there were some unitary factors, the SBE held that the operations were not unitary. To the same effect, see also *Appeal of P and M Lumber Products, Inc.* (1984) (CCH CALIFORNIA TAX REPORTS ¶11-520.357) and *Appeal of Berry Enterprises, Inc.* (1986) (CCH CALIFORNIA TAX

REPORTS ¶11-520.952). In these cases, the taxpayers had contended that the businesses were unitary.

In *Appeals of Santa Anita Consolidated, Inc., et al.* (1984) (CCH CALIFORNIA TAX REPORTS ¶11-520.6094), the taxpayer and its four subsidiaries were engaged in a variety of activities including operation of a racetrack, transportation of automobiles, real estate development, etc. Although there were some unitary factors in management and operation, the SBE held that the business did not constitute a "functionally integrated enterprise" and was not unitary.

To the same effect, see *Appeal of Bredero California, Inc., Bredero Consulting, Inc., and Best Blocks, Inc.* (1986) (CCH CALIFORNIA TAX REPORTS ¶11-520.612). Also to the same effect, see *Appeals of Andreini & Company and Ash Slough Vineyards, Inc.* (1986) (CCH CALIFORNIA TAX REPORTS ¶11-520.608), in which an agricultural insurance brokerage was found not to constitute a unitary business with its vineyard subsidiary.

In *Appeal of Holloway Investment Company* (1983) (CCH CALIFORNIA TAX REPORTS ¶11-520.521), the taxpayer held a variety of apparently unrelated property interests in California and Illinois. Citing some of the cases discussed below and also the U.S. Supreme Court decision in *Container Corporation* (¶1310), the SBE held that the business was not unitary.

In *Appeal of Unitco, Inc.* (1983) (CCH CALIFORNIA TAX REPORTS ¶11-520.69), the taxpayer was a closely held corporation that owned rental properties in California and three other states. The FTB contended that the operations were unitary, based largely on the similarity of activities in the four states and the personal participation of the three owner-officers in policy decisions. The SBE held that the business was not unitary, commenting that "at best, the suggested unitary connections are superficial and trivial."

In *Bay Alarm Company* (1982) (CCH CALIFORNIA TAX REPORTS ¶11-520.601), a California corporation had a burglar alarm business in California, an investment portfolio, and a cattle ranch in New Mexico. The SBE upheld the FTB in holding that the activities did not constitute a unitary business. To the same effect, see *Appeal of Myles Circuits, Inc.* (1982) (CCH CALIFORNIA TAX REPORTS ¶11-520.601), in which the taxpayer and its subsidiaries had a circuit breaker factory in California and a cattle ranch in Texas.

In *Appeal of Mohasco Corp.* (1982) (CCH CALIFORNIA TAX REPORTS ¶11-520.607), the taxpayer and its Mexican subsidiaries were engaged in the manufacture and sale of carpets and related products. Although there were some intercompany relationships and transactions, the SBE found that these were insignificant in the situation as a whole and held that the operations were not unitary.

In *Appeal of Hollywood Film Enterprises, Inc.* (1982) (CCH CALIFORNIA TAX REPORTS ¶11-520.602), the taxpayer operated wholly within California. It was a wholly owned subsidiary of a Delaware corporation with headquarters in New York and some operations in California. The two corporations were involved in diverse lines of business (although both involved motion picture films), but there were several intercompany activities of various kinds. In this case the taxpayer contended that the two businesses *should* be treated as unitary, while the FTB took the position that they should not. The SBE held that the taxpayer had not borne the required burden of proof that the businesses were unitary.

• *Use of separate accounting*

Despite the general preference for use of the allocation or apportionment formula, separate accounting may be permitted (or required) in some cases. The following are the principal situations where it may be used:

— businesses that by their nature permit accurate determination of results by separate accounting; and

— cases where a corporation is in entirely different businesses within and without the state, with no unitary factors present. (Sec. 25137, Rev. & Tax. Code)

FTB Reg. 25137, 18 CCR provides that exceptions to the regular allocation formula will be permitted only where "unusual fact situations . . . produce incongruous results" under the regular rules. The regulation mentions specific industries that are subject to special treatment (¶1306). See ¶1307 for a more detailed explanation of deviations from the standard UDITPA formula.

• *Cases upholding use of separate accounting*

In *Appeal of The National Dollar Stores, Ltd.* (1986) (CCH CALIFORNIA TAX REPORTS ¶11-520.607), a California clothing retail corporation was not unitary with a wholly owned subsidiary that imported and marketed Asian films. The SBE held that, though there was 100% unity of ownership, the unities of use and operation did not exist between the two. There was no evidence that either business contributed to or was dependent on the other.

In *Appeal of The Amwalt Group* (1983) (CCH CALIFORNIA TAX REPORTS ¶11-520.6094), a closely-held California architectural firm owned 100% of a leasing subsidiary and 80% of a heavy equipment dealership. Fiscal management was centralized and there were some intercompany transactions, and the corporations filed a combined report on a unitary basis. The FTB took the position that the operations were not unitary and required separate accounting for the three corporations; the SBE agreed.

In *Appeal of Carl M. Halvorson, Inc.* (1963) (CCH CALIFORNIA TAX REPORTS ¶11-520.70), the SBE held that separate accounting more clearly reflected income attributable to California by a heavy construction contractor engaged in construction projects located within and without the State. It was further held that overhead expenses were properly allocated to such projects on the basis of direct costs incurred. However, it is the policy of the FTB to require use of the apportionment formula in the construction business "where the usual tests of unitary business are met." The FTB has issued detailed regulations for apportionment of income from long-term contracts, and also detailed rules for corporate partners in joint ventures—see below and ¶1306.

In *Appeal of Highland Corporation* (1959) (CCH CALIFORNIA TAX REPORTS ¶11-520.358), the SBE held that a business is not unitary when the only unitary factor is centralized management. The corporation operated a lumber business in Oregon, had oil interests in New Mexico, and was in the construction business and owned rental properties in California. All activities were controlled and supervised by executives who operated out of the corporation's head office, which was in California. In this case the FTB took the position that the business was not unitary and that separate accounting should be used, and the SBE agreed. To the same effect, see *Appeal of Allied Properties, Inc.* (1964) (CCH CALIFORNIA TAX REPORTS ¶11-520.357), involving a cattle ranch in Nevada and real estate investments in California.

• *Oil and gas operators*

The FTB for many years required oil and gas operators to use separate accounting in some situations, particularly where a profitable segment of an oil business was conducted in California while an extensive exploratory program was carried on in an out-of-state location of such magnitude as to produce deductions that offset or materially reduced the California income. However, the FTB was overruled by the SBE in a 1959 decision involving a situation of this type. In *Appeal of Holly Development Company* (CCH CALIFORNIA TAX REPORTS ¶11-520.835), it was held that a unitary business existed where the corporation was engaged in the acquisition and development of oil properties in both California and Texas, and the evidence showed centralized management, accounting, financing, and purchasing. To the same effect, see *Superior Oil Co. v. Franchise Tax Board* (CCH CALIFORNIA TAX REPORTS ¶11-520.201) and *Honolulu Oil Co. v. Franchise Tax Board* (CCH CALIFORNIA TAX REPORTS ¶11-520.201), both cases decided by the California Supreme Court in 1963.

Legal Ruling No. 366 (1973) (CCH CALIFORNIA TAX REPORTS ¶11-520.2091) deals with allocation questions of unitary oil operations beyond the 3-mile continental limit. The ruling states that use of the standard allocation formula is appropriate, and provides that factors relating to offshore operations should be reflected only in the denominators of the formula; thus, no income from such operations is apportioned to California. Legal Ruling No. 396 (1976) (CCH CALIFORNIA TAX REPORTS ¶10-075.73) modifies the portion of Legal Ruling No. 366 pertaining to operations of drilling barges.

In the case of partnership interests in oil and gas properties that are deemed to be "tax shelters" and not part of the unitary business, income or loss has been held to be nonbusiness income allocated to the state where the oil or gas property is located. *Appeal of The National Dollar Stores, Ltd.* (1986) (CCH CALIFORNIA TAX REPORTS ¶11-520.607).

• *Combination of separate accounting and formula*

Where a taxpayer has more than one trade or business as discussed at ¶1302, it is possible to use a combination of separate accounting and the apportionment formula. One example under prior law may be found in *Appeal of Industrial Management Corporation* (1959) (CCH CALIFORNIA TAX REPORTS ¶11-520.358). In this case the corporation was engaged in the insecticide business both within and without California, and also was engaged in two businesses (sale of street improvement bonds and rental of real estate) solely within California. The principal office was in California. There was no unitary relationship between the insecticide business and the other two. The insecticide business showed a loss and the other two showed a profit. The SBE upheld the contention of the FTB that only the insecticide business was unitary and subject to allocation by formula; thus, the entire income of the two California businesses was taxed, with an offset for only an allocated portion of the loss on the unitary business.

In *Appeal of Hunt Foods & Industries, Inc.* (1965) (CCH CALIFORNIA TAX REPORTS ¶11-520.8194), the FTB contended that, where the taxpayer operated a match manufacturing business and a food processing business, the income of each should be computed and allocated separately. However, the SBE held that a single allocation formula applied to the entire income of both businesses was proper, since there was common management, the products were sold in the same markets, they shared common warehouses, and other unitary factors were present.

In *Appeal of Simco, Incorporated* (1964) (CCH CALIFORNIA TAX REPORTS ¶11-520.52), the SBE permitted a combination of separate accounting and the allocation formula. The income of fruit orchards operated entirely in California was determined by separate accounting, and the allocation formula was applied to a farming and cattle business operated in both California and Nevada. The SBE held that centralization of management and of accounting, legal, and tax services did not mean that the entire business was unitary.

In *Appeal of Halliburton Oil Well Cementing Co.* (1955) (CCH CALIFORNIA TAX REPORTS ¶11-520.831), the taxpayer was turned down in its attempt to use a combination of separate accounting and an allocation formula. The company used separate accounting for its income from service activities and from sale of purchased goods and used a (nonstandard) formula for income from sale of its own manufactured goods. The SBE upheld the FTB in requiring the use of the standard formula for both service and merchandising activities.

In *Appeal of American Writing Paper Corporation* (1952) (CCH CALIFORNIA TAX REPORTS ¶11-520.8392), the SBE upheld the FTB in applying the allocation formula to the entire income of a foreign corporation that sold in California the products of some—but not all—of its plants. The taxpayer was unsuccessful in its contention that the income of the plants manufacturing the product sold in California should be determined by separate accounting and the allocation formula applied only to that income instead of to the entire income from operations of all plants.

• *Use of separate formulas*

As explained at ¶1302, separate apportionment formulas may sometimes be used for different portions of a taxpayer's business. In *Appeal of Lear Siegler, Inc.* (1967) (CCH CALIFORNIA TAX REPORTS ¶11-520.6095), a single corporation had six separate manufacturing divisions, each operating within and without California. The SBE permitted the taxpayer to apply six separate apportionment formulas to the various divisions.

In *Appeal of United Parcel Service* (1986) (CCH CALIFORNIA TAX REPORTS ¶11-540.75), the taxpayer was a unitary business with package delivery cars that ordinarily operated within the state and tractor-trailer rigs that operated both within and without the state. The SBE, in reversing the FTB's application of separate apportionment formulas to the two classes of equipment, held that the special interim formula developed by the FTB for truckers applied to all the taxpayer's trucks whether in interstate or intrastate commerce.

• *Treatment of partnership interests*

FTB Reg. 25137-1, 18 CCR outlines the appropriate method for apportionment and allocation of partnership income in unitary situations where a corporation has an interest in a partnership and one or both have income from sources within and without the State. The corporation is not required to own any particular percentage of the partnership for this regulation to apply. The partnership income and apportionment factors are included in determining unitary income only to the extent of the corporation's percentage of ownership interest.

In *Appeal of Powerine Oil Company* (1985) (CCH CALIFORNIA TAX REPORTS ¶11-520.591), the taxpayer was engaged in oil refining and distribution and also had a 50% interest in a joint venture engaged in copper mining in California. The SBE cited the *Pittsburgh-Des Moines Steel Company* case, above, and held that the taxpayer's share of joint-venture losses could be included in determining the unitary income allocable to California.

In *Appeal of A. Epstein and Sons, Inc.* (1984) (CCH CALIFORNIA TAX REPORTS ¶11-520.837), the taxpayer was a member of a group of closely-held affiliated corporations under common control of two brothers. The brothers also owned a New York partnership that had been formed (because of legal requirements) to render architectural services at cost to the corporations. The SBE held that the affiliated group of corporations was engaged in a unitary business, subject to formula allocation, but denied inclusion of the partnership in the computation. See also *The National Dollar Stores, Ltd.*, under "Oil and Gas Operators," above.

In *Appeal of Pittsburgh-Des Moines Steel Company* (1983) (CCH CALIFORNIA TAX REPORTS ¶11-520.59), the taxpayer corporation was engaged in a unitary business involving various aspects of the steel business. The corporation had a 50% interest in a joint venture with a real-estate operator; the joint venture was formed to build and lease two office buildings in California. The SBE held that the corporation's share of the income and apportionment factors of the joint venture should be included in the corporation's combined report. To the same effect, see *Appeal of Willamette Industries, Inc.* (1987) (CCH CALIFORNIA TAX REPORTS ¶11-520.373).

In *Appeal of Saga Corp.* (1982) (CCH CALIFORNIA TAX REPORTS ¶11-520.821), the taxpayer corporation and subsidiaries supplied food service to colleges, hospitals, and other organizations throughout the United States. The corporation owned 50.51% of another corporation that developed and managed off-campus student dining and housing facilities in California and elsewhere; the subsidiary employed the taxpayer (or other subsidiaries) to provide food services in these facilities. The corporation also owned 50% of a partnership that owned and constructed a dormitory complex for which the two corporations provided management and food services. The SBE held that the subsidiary and the partnership were both parts of a unitary operation with the taxpayer, and that the partnership's income and apportionment factors should be taken into account to the extent of the taxpayer's 50% interest.

In *Appeal of Albertson's, Inc.* (1982) (CCH CALIFORNIA TAX REPORTS ¶11-520.65), the taxpayer corporation operated a multistate chain of supermarkets selling principally food items. The corporation owned 50% of a partnership that operated a chain of supermarkets selling both food items and general merchandise. The corporation shared, with the other 50% owner, the overall control and direction of the partnership's management policies and also provided some financial and management assistance. The SBE held that the partnership was engaged in a unitary business with the taxpayer, and that the partnership factors should be taken into account to the extent of the taxpayer's 50% ownership interest.

In *Appeal of Pup 'n' Taco Drive Up* (1977) (CCH CALIFORNIA TAX REPORTS ¶11-520.8297), the taxpayer was a California fast-food corporation with a majority interest in two out-of-state partnerships. The SBE held that the corporation and the partnerships were engaged in a unitary business and were subject to formula allocation.

¶1305 Apportionment Formula

Law: Secs. 25128, 25137 (CCH CALIFORNIA TAX REPORTS ¶11-520, 11-550).

Comparable Federal: None.

California Form: Sch. R (Apportionment and Allocation of Income).

The apportionment formula is used only to compute a percentage, which is then applied to the total "business" income to determine the portion taxable in California. It should be kept in mind throughout the discussion of the formula that the items attributed to California in computing the various factors are not taxed directly, but are only used in the computation of a percentage to be applied to the net income. This point was illustrated in *Appeal of North American Aviation, Inc.* (1952) (CCH CALIFORNIA TAX REPORTS ¶11-525.27). Under the peculiar facts in that case title to certain goods sold had passed twice and technically there were two "sales." The State Board of Equalization (SBE) sustained the Franchise Tax Board (FTB) in eliminating the duplication in computing the sales factor in the allocation formula. The SBE's opinion pointed out that to include both sales would be unreasonable, in view of the purpose of the sales factor as a measure of the taxpayer's activity within and without California.

• *Standard apportionment formula*

The standard apportionment formula applied in California is a double-weighted sales factor formula consisting of the following factors:

— property, both real and tangible personal property, owned or rented by the taxpayer (¶1307);

— payroll, including all forms of compensation paid to employees (¶1308); and

— sales, meaning all gross receipts of the taxpayer from the sale of tangible and intangible property (¶1309).

(Sec. 25128, Rev. & Tax. Code)

The double-weighted sales factor formula is applied by determining the ratios of the property, payroll, and two times the sales factors within California to the property, payroll, and sales factors everywhere. The sum of the ratios is divided by four and the resulting factor is applied to the total income of the taxpayer to arrive at California taxable income. The California double-weighted sales factor formula may be depicted graphically as:

$$\left(\frac{\text{Calif. Prop.}}{\text{Total Property}} + \frac{\text{Calif. Payroll}}{\text{Total Payroll}} + \frac{2 \times \text{Calif. Sales}}{\text{Total Sales}}\right) / 4 = \text{Calif. factor}$$

However, an equally-weighted apportionment formula applies in California to taxpayers that derive more than 50% of their "gross business receipts" from (1) extractive or agricultural business activity, (2) savings and loan activity, or (3) banking or financial business activity. The equally weighted apportionment formula is the same as the above formula except that the California sales factor is not multiplied by two and the sum of the ratios is divided by three instead of four. (Sec. 25128, Rev. & Tax. Code)

If the income and apportionment factors of two or more affiliated banks or corporations must be included in a combined report (¶1310), the above apportionment formulas apply to the combined income of those banks or corporations.

• *Deviations from standard formula*

The Uniform Division of Income for Tax Purposes Act (UDITPA) provides for deviation from the standard formula, where necessary to fairly reflect the extent of the taxpayer's business activity in California. This may be accomplished by excluding, adding, or modifying one or more factors, or by other means, as indicated in the cases discussed below. (Some of these cases were decided under pre-1967 law, but their reasoning is applicable generally under the present law.) The FTB may require such special treatment or the taxpayer may petition for it, in which case the FTB may grant a hearing. (Sec. 25137, Rev. & Tax. Code)

Deviation is only allowed where unusual fact situations, which ordinarily will be unique and nonrecurring, produce incongruous results (Reg. 25137, 18 CCR). In *Appeal of Crisa Corp.* (2002) (CCH CALIFORNIA TAX REPORTS ¶11-540.25), the SBE rejected the taxpayer's contention that Mexican hyperinflation distorted the calculation of both net income and the property factor of the apportionment formula. In ruling in favor of the FTB, the SBE focused on whether an unusual fact situation existed and rejected the use of a quantitative comparison for purposes of whether there was sufficient distortion to justify deviation from the standard UDITPA formula. Stating that there is no bright line rule that can be used, the SBE summarized the following five examples from previous cases that may justify deviation from the standard formula:

— A corporation does substantial business in California, but the standard formula does not apportion any income to California. For example, the employees of a professional sports franchise render services in California while playing "away" games, but the standard formula apportions all income to the team's home state (see *Appeal of New York Football Giants; Appeal of Milwaukee Professional Sports and Services, Inc.* (1979), (CCH CALIFORNIA TAX REPORTS ¶11-525.514)).

— The factors in the standard formula are mismatched to the time during which the income is generated. For example, a construction contractor reports income when long-term contracts are completed, but the standard formula requires income to be reported currently (see *Appeal of Donald M. Drake Company* (1977) (CCH CALIFORNIA TAX REPORTS ¶11-540.651)).

— The standard formula creates "nowhere income" that does not fall under the taxing authority of any jurisdiction. For example, a company owns equipment, the value of which is attributed to the high seas or outer space, where it cannot be taxed by any jurisdiction (see *Appeal of American Telephone and Telegraph Company* (1982) (CCH CALIFORNIA TAX REPORTS ¶ 11-530.70)).

— One or more of the standard factors is biased by a substantial activity that is not related to the taxpayer's main line of business. For example, the taxpayer continuously reinvests a large pool of "working capital," generating large receipts that are allocated to the site of the investment activity. However, the investments are unrelated to the services provided by the taxpayer as its primary business (see *Appeal of Pacific Telephone and Telegraph Company* (1978) (CCH CALIFORNIA TAX REPORTS ¶ 11-535.37)).

— A particular factor does not have material representation in either the numerator or denominator, rendering that factor useless as a means of reflecting business activity. For example, because a company does not own or rent any tangible or real personal property, the numerator and denominator of the property factor are zero (see *Appeal of Oscar Enterprises, LTD* (1987) (CCH CALIFORNIA TAX REPORTS ¶ 11-540.20)).

CCH Practice Tip: Prior Approval Required

An original return that is inconsistent with California's standard allocation and apportionment rules that is filed without having obtained prior approval from the FTB will be treated as erroneous and the FTB may impose an accuracy-related penalty, including an increased penalty for substantial understatement (see ¶ 1411). Prior approval to file an original return that is inconsistent with the standard allocation and apportionment rules will be deemed to have been provided, without having to actually obtain prior approval, only if the inconsistent treatment meets the following criteria:

—is a variation permitted in an audit manual that was operative during the taxable year or that is currently operative, and the taxpayer's facts are substantially the same as those described in the manual;

—is a variation specifically permitted in a published opinion of the California State Board of Equalization, a California court of appeal, or the California Supreme Court, and the taxpayer's facts are substantially the same as those described in the opinion;

—has been approved in writing in a prior year petition that specifically states that the variation also applies to the taxable year in question; or

—has been approved in a prior year closing agreement that by its terms also applies to the taxable year in question.

For tax returns with a due date before October 15, 2004 (determined without regard to extensions), a statement in or attached to the return that adequately discloses that the taxpayer's return is inconsistent with the standard allocation and apportionment rules, or that the taxpayer has relied, for its filing position, upon the statutory provision authorizing variations from the standard allocation and apportionment rules, will be considered adequate disclosure for purposes of California's accuracy-related penalty provisions.

The FTB will not impose an accuracy-related penalty if the taxpayer's position is adequately disclosed, provided the taxpayer's self-assessed position is one that would have a realistic possibility of being granted by the FTB as fairly representing the extent of the taxpayer's business activity in the state. Merely entering data on California Schedule R, Apportionment and Allocation of Income, using an alternative method of allocation and apportionment will not, by itself, be considered adequate disclosure, because that cannot reasonably be expected to apprise the FTB of the nature of the potential controversy (*FTB Notice 2004-5*, (2004) (CCH CALIFORNIA TAX REPORTS ¶ 403-663)).

In *Appeal of Evergreen Marine Corporation (Calif.), Ltd.* (1986) (CCH CALIFORNIA TAX REPORTS ¶ 11-520.2095), the taxpayer, its parent corporation, and affiliates were engaged in various aspects of the ocean freighter business. In upholding the FTB's application of the standard formula to the unitary income of the corporate group, the SBE held that methods other than the standard formula may be used only in exceptional circumstances where UDITPA's provisions do not fairly represent the extent of the taxpayer's business activity in the state. The challenge to the formula must attack each element of the formula equation, and show that the formula as a whole unfairly apportions net income to California. Furthermore, deviations from the formula are not permitted simply because there is a better approach. If the standard formula fairly represents the extent of in-state activity it must be used.

In *American Telephone and Telegraph Co.* (1982) (CCH CALIFORNIA TAX REPORTS ¶11-530.70), discussed at ¶1307, the FTB adjusted the California property factor by including property located in outer space and on the high seas. The SBE upheld the FTB, and expressed the belief that the law authorizes the FTB to deviate from UDITPA's standard provisions "in order to prevent some . . . business income from escaping taxation entirely."

Appeal of Universal C.I.T. Credit Corporation (1972) (CCH CALIFORNIA TAX REPORTS ¶11-530.85) involved a large finance company with a Delaware parent corporation and more than fifty subsidiaries. The taxpayer agreed to the three-factor formula used in the finance company cases cited above, but contended that receivables originating in California had a business situs outside the State and therefore could not properly be attributed to California in computing the "property" factor (loans outstanding). The SBE held that the loans were a proper measure of the portion of the business emanating from California, citing as support a court decision dealing with tangible property in the property factor and expressing the belief that the same principles apply to intangible property.

In *Appeal of Public Finance Company, et al.* (1958) (CCH CALIFORNIA TAX REPORTS ¶11-520.834), the corporations involved were engaged in the small loan business. The FTB used an allocation formula consisting of the factors of (1) average loans outstanding, (2) payroll, and (3) interest earned. The taxpayers contended that their income should be determined by separate accounting. The SBE held that the business was unitary and approved the formula used. See also *Appeal of Beneficial Finance Co. of Alameda and Affiliates* (1961) (CCH CALIFORNIA TAX REPORTS ¶11-520.208). A similar result was reached in *Appeal of Tri-State Livestock Credit Corporation* (1960) (CCH CALIFORNIA TAX REPORTS ¶11-530.464). In this case the taxpayer's only office was in California, but many loans were made outside the State. The SBE apportioned the factor of average loans outstanding entirely to California, on the theory that a loan has a business situs where it is serviced. The interest-earned factor, being somewhat comparable to the sales factor in the usual formula, was developed by assigning interest income to the places where employees solicited the loans.

• *Omission of one or more factors*

Where property is a negligible factor in the business, as in the case of some service corporations, the property factor might be omitted; the computation would then be made by averaging only the other two factors. The same procedure may occasionally be applied also to the wages or sales factor, in special cases where use of the factor would be meaningless or impracticable or would result in distortion. For example, in the case of a gold mining operation the sales factor might be omitted, because all gold must be sold to the U.S. Government and there is no sales activity in the usual sense.

In *Appeal of Twentieth Century-Fox Film Corporation* (1962) (CCH CALIFORNIA TAX REPORTS ¶11-540.80), the SBE held that a taxpayer could not use a single factor formula (gross receipts) to determine the California portion of one segment of its income, *i.e.*, distribution of films for unrelated producers, and another formula (the usual 3-factor formula) to determine California income from distribution of its self-produced films.

In *Appeal of Farmers Underwriters Association* (1953) (CCH CALIFORNIA TAX REPORTS ¶11-530.83), the taxpayer was a service corporation and contended that the property factor should be omitted from the allocation formula. The SBE sustained the FTB in requiring inclusion of the property factor, because the taxpayer used a substantial amount of property (land, buildings, furniture, office equipment, supplies, and motor vehicles) in its business. However, in *Appeal of Woodward, Baldwin & Co., Inc.* (1963) (CCH CALIFORNIA TAX REPORTS ¶11-530.25), it was held that where a manufacturer's sales agent employed a relatively small amount of owned property in its business, the property factor should be ignored, and income allocated according to the remaining two factors of payroll and sales.

• *Cases involving professional sports*

Two 1977 decisions of the SBE involved questions of deviating from the standard formula in special situations. *Appeal of Danny Thomas Productions* (CCH CALIFORNIA TAX REPORTS ¶11-540.55) involved production of television shows; *Appeal of New York Football Giants* (CCH CALIFORNIA TAX REPORTS ¶11-525.512) involved a professional football team. The SBE allowed some deviations (too complicated for discussion here) and commented that the party desiring to deviate from the standard formula must bear the burden of proving that it does not produce a fair result. See also *Appeal of Milwaukee Professional Sports and Services, Inc.* (1979) (CCH CALIFORNIA TAX REPORTS ¶11-525.514), involving a professional basketball team, and *Appeal of Boston Professional Hockey Association, Inc.* (1979) (CCH CALIFORNIA TAX REPORTS ¶11-525.511), involving a professional hockey team. See ¶1306 for discussion of special statutory rules for professional sports teams.

¶1306 Apportionment Rules for Specialized Industries

Law: Secs. 25107, 25137, 25141 (CCH CALIFORNIA TAX REPORTS ¶11-525, 11-530, 11-540).

Comparable Federal: None.

Over the years the Franchise Tax Board (FTB) has provided modified apportionment rules for a number of specialized industries, and for specialized types of business such as foreign operations and partnerships. Some of these rules have been issued as official regulations. In addition, FTB Reg. 25137, 18 CCR sets forth the circumstances under which it will permit a taxpayer to use an apportionment method other than that prescribed by law. Following is a listing of special industries and other groups (in alphabetical order) for which modified apportionment rules apply, with a brief summary for each category.

Practitioner Comment: Special Industry Apportionment Regulations are Under Review

On September 5, 2007, the FTB approved staff's request to hold interested parties meetings that would consider the revision of the print media, motion picture and television producers and broadcasters, and airline industry apportionment regulations. The concern with the print media and motion picture regulations is primarily that they may be out of date in that they do not address new media forms and the impact of technology in general on these industries. Revisions to the airline industry regulation are deemed necessary in light of the State Board of Equalization's March 1, 2007 letter decision in the *Appeal of Alaska Airlines* in which it rejected the FTB's attempt to regroup the taxpayer's aircraft by make and model for apportionment purposes. Interested parties meetings were held in January 2008 and as yet no changes to the special industry apportionment regulations have been finalized.

Bruce Daigh, Chris Whitney, Contributing Editors

• *Airlines*

The law (Sec. 25101.3, Rev. & Tax. Code) provides a special formula for the property factor, as explained at ¶1307. FTB Reg. 25137-7, 18 CCR provides detailed rules for computation of all three of the standard factors.

• *Banks and financial corporations*

FTB Reg. 25137-4.2, 18 CCR, provides detailed rules for computation of the property and sales factors. Loans, receivables, and other intangible assets are included in the property factor. The regulation is substantially similar to a Multistate Tax Commission model regulation, under which banks and financial corporations apportion their income using a three-factor formula consisting of equally-weighted sales, property, and payroll factors.

FTB Reg. 25137-10, 18 CCR, details the rules regarding the computation of income of a unitary business consisting of a bank or financial corporation and a general corporation.

An international banking facility maintained by a bank within California is to be treated for purposes of the apportionment formula as though it were doing business outside the state. (Sec. 25107, Rev. & Tax. Code)

See ¶1305 for a discussion of *Appeal of Universal C.I.T. Credit Corporation* and other cases involving apportionment of income of financial corporations.

• *Commercial fishing*

FTB Reg. 25137-5, 18 CCR, provides special rules for computation of the three standard-formula factors. Allocations are based largely on the ratio of California port days to total port days. Port days represent time spent either in port or at sea while a ship is "in operation."

• *Construction, manufacturing, and fabrication contractors*

FTB Reg. 25137-2, 18 CCR, provides detailed rules and examples for apportioning income from long-term contracts under the completed-contract method and the percentage-of-completion method of accounting. The rule applies to long-term construction contracts and manufacturing and fabrication contracts. The three standard-formula factors are used, but special rules apply to the computation of each factor. The regulation also covers the application of the special rules for corporations that discontinue doing business in California (¶819).

FTB Reg. 25137-1, 18 CCR, regarding partnerships (see below), provides special rules for apportionment where a corporation is a member of a construction-contractor partnership. See also *Appeal of Donald M. Drake Company* (1977) (CCH CALIFORNIA TAX REPORTS ¶11-540.651), involving a construction contractor reporting income on the completed-contract basis. The State Board of Equalization (SBE) held that the taxpayer's share of joint ventures' property, payroll, and sales should be included in the allocation formula in the years the project is in progress rather than in the year the contract is completed.

In *Appeal of Robert E. McKee, Inc.* (1983) (CCH CALIFORNIA TAX REPORTS ¶11-540.652), the taxpayer was engaged in numerous construction projects in California and other States. The SBE applied the methodology specified in the regulations, and cited, with approval, the *Drake* case.

• *Franchisors*

FTB Reg. 25137-3, 18 CCR, provides rules for corporations engaged in the business of franchising. Special rules are provided for the payroll and sales factors.

• *Motion picture and television producers and broadcasters*

FTB Reg. 25137-8, 18 CCR, provides rules for the apportionment of income of motion picture and television producers and television network broadcasters. Topical film properties are included in the denominator of the property factor at full value for one year and other film properties are included at full value for twelve years. All other film properties are included at eight times the receipts generated in an amount not to exceed the original cost of such properties. Special rules are also provided for other situations peculiar to the industry.

• *Mutual fund service providers*

,Reg. 25137-14, 18 CCR requires mutual fund service providers to apportion their receipts from mutual fund services utilizing a shareholder location sales factor approach with a throwback provision using the methodology employed in *Appeal of Finnigan Corp.* (1990) (CCH CALIFORNIA TAX REPORTS ¶11-525.813). Similarly, a mutual fund service provider's receipts from performing asset management services are assigned to California if the asset's beneficial owner's domicile is located in California. However, a shareholder's or beneficiary's receipts will be disregarded in computing the shareholder ratio in instances when a shareholder of record's domicile cannot reasonably be obtained.

• *Offshore drilling companies*

Legal Ruling No. 366 (1973) (CCH CALIFORNIA TAX REPORTS ¶11-520.2091) deals with allocation questions of unitary oil operations beyond the 3-mile continental limit. The ruling states that use of the standard allocation formula is appropriate, and provides that factors relating to offshore operations should be reflected only in the denominators of the formula; thus, no income from such operations is apportioned to California. Legal Ruling No. 396 (1976) (CCH CALIFORNIA TAX REPORTS ¶10-075.73) modifies the portion of Legal Ruling No. 366 pertaining to operations of drilling barges.

• *Partnerships*

FTB Regulation 25137-1, 18 CCR, provides detailed rules for apportionment where a corporation is a partner. Special rules are provided for long-term contracts, intercompany transactions, etc. See also ¶1304.

• *Personal service companies*

See *Appeal of Farmers Underwriters Association* and *Appeal of Woodward, Baldwin & Co., Inc.*, discussed at ¶1305, involving questions of which factors should be used in apportioning income of service corporations.

• *Professional sports teams*

The law (Sec. 25141, Rev. & Tax. Code) provides rules for calculating the apportionment formula for all professional sports teams.

Section 25141 applies to any "professional athletic team" that

— has at least five participating members,

— is a member of a league of at least five teams,

— has paid attendance of at least 40,000 for the year, and

— has gross income of at least $100,000 for the year.

Section 25141 provides rules for computation of each of the three standard factors in the allocation formula. The basic approach is that *all* property, payroll, and sales are to be allocated to the state or country in which the team's operations are based. The base of operations is in the state in which the team derives its territorial rights under the league's rules. Special rules are provided for cases where the team is subject to an apportioned tax in another state or country.

Entities that operate a professional sports organization are treated as corporations for purposes of the minimum franchise tax on corporations. The liability of any corporation owning a sports organization is satisfied by the minimum tax if that corporation is not otherwise doing business in the state.

See cases discussed at ¶1305 that involve question of deviating from the standard allocation formula by sports organizations.

• *Publishers of print media*

FTB Reg. 25137-12, 18 CCR, provides rules for the apportionment of income of taxpayers in the business of publishing, selling, licensing, or distributing newspapers, magazines, periodicals, trade journals, or other printed material. A special circulation factor is used to determine the amount of the taxpayer's gross receipts from advertising and the sale, rental, or use of customer lists that must be included in the numerator of the sales factor.

• *Trains*

FTB Reg. 25137-9, 18 CCR, provides special rules for computation of income from railroad operations. Generally the three standard-formula factors are used, but special rules apply to the computation of each factor.

• *Trucking companies*

FTB Reg. 25137-11, 18 CCR, provides special rules for computation of income from trucking companies. Special rules are provided for the property and sales factor.

Practitioner Comment: Significant Uncertainty Surrounds Application of Special Apportionment Provisions to Mixed Combined Groups in Light of Recent SBE Decision

As noted above, California has a number of regulations that set forth specialized apportionment rules for industries ranging from long term construction contractors to mutual fund service providers. Certain of these regulations provide specific rules for apportioning income of mixed combined groups which contain members in special industries. See for example CCR Section 25137-10 dealing with mixed financial and nonfinancial groups. Most of the regulations do not contain provisions regarding mixed groups, raising some uncertainty as to how the special apportionment regulations should be applied in such instances. It has generally been thought that absent a specific rule, and consistent with California's general "separate entity" approach to combined reporting group members, that the special apportionment regulations would only be applied to specific members who are engaged in special industry operations. (See CCR Section 25106.5(c)(7)(B))

Some doubt has been raised as to this view as a result of the SBE's letter decision in the *Appeal of Swift Transportation Co., Inc. and Swift Transportation Corporation*, (2008), CCH CALIFORNIA TAX REPORTS, ¶404-616. In *Swift*, the SBE held that all members of a combined reporting group were required to use the special apportionment regulations applicable to trucking companies because that was the overall nature of Swift's unitary business even though certain members of the group did not operate as carriers of freight but instead solicited and procured customers or leased trucking equipment to the actual carrier.

Bruce Daigh, Chris Whitney, Contributing Editors

¶1307 Property Factor in Apportionment Formula

Law: Secs. 25101.3, 25107, 25129-31 (CCH CALIFORNIA TAX REPORTS ¶11-530, 11-540).

Comparable Federal: None.

California Form: Sch. R (Apportionment and Allocation of Income).

In computing the property factor, all real estate and tangible personal property owned or rented by the corporation and used in the business is included. (Sec. 25129, Rev. & Tax. Code) Property used to produce "nonbusiness" income is excluded from the factor, but property used to produce both "nonbusiness" and "business" income is included to the extent it is used to produce "business" income. Property owned by the corporation that is in transit between states is generally considered to be located at its destination. Franchise Tax Board (FTB) Reg. 25129, 18 CCR, gives examples that show what to include in the property factor in unusual situations such as a plant under construction, closing of a plant, etc., and provides specific rules for property in transit, movable property, etc.

• *Closing of plant*

In *Appeal of Ethyl Corporation* (1975) (CCH CALIFORNIA TAX REPORTS ¶11-530.581), the taxpayer closed its California plant and started to sell its equipment in 1963 and contended that the property was permanently removed from the unitary business in that year. The State Board of Equalization (SBE) held that the plant was includible in the property factor until it was dismantled in 1965.

• *Property under construction*

In *Appeal of O.K. Earl Corp.* (1977) (CCH CALIFORNIA TAX REPORTS ¶11-530.561), the taxpayer questioned the regulations regarding inclusion of costs of construction in progress in the property factor of construction contractors. The SBE upheld the provision that such costs are to be included only to the extent they exceed progress billings.

• *In-transit inventory*

In *Appeal of Craig Corporation* (1987) (CCH CALIFORNIA TAX REPORTS ¶11-530.661), goods ceased to be "in transit" and entered the taxpayer's unitary business when received from Japan at the taxpayer's California facility for customs inspection, repackaging, and shipment to the taxpayer's regional warehouses in other states. The SBE held that within the context of a multistate unitary business it was too restrictive to interpret "destination" as the goods' ultimate storage place prior to sale. The imported goods were properly included in the California property factor numerator.

• *Property in outer space*

In *Appeal of American Telephone and Telegraph Co.* (1982) (CCH CALIFORNIA TAX REPORTS ¶11-530.70), the FTB revised the California property factor by including the following property not physically located in the State: (1) the high-seas portion of certain jointly-owned California-Hawaii cables, and (2) a portion of certain leased satellite circuits in outer space. The FTB first contended that the property was "used" in California within the intent of the law, but the SBE rejected this argument. However, the SBE permitted the same result to be achieved by applying the provision of the law (discussed at ¶1305) that provides for deviation from the standard formula to fairly reflect the extent of California business activity. To the same effect, see the Court of Appeal decision in *Communications Satellite Corporation v. Franchise Tax Board* (1984) (CCH CALIFORNIA TAX REPORTS ¶11-540.53); this case applied the same reasoning to the sales factor.

• *Property neither owned nor rented*

In *Appeal of Union Carbide Corporation* (1984) (CCH CALIFORNIA TAX REPORTS ¶11-540.421), the taxpayer operated rent-free a government-owned nuclear gas-separation plant outside California. The SBE held that, under FTB Regulation 25137 regarding deviations from the standard formula for exceptional circumstances, the property in question was properly includible in the denominator of the property factor.

• *Transportation companies*

Transportation companies present unusual problems in the property factor, and special procedures have been developed for them. The law provides a statutory formula for airlines and air taxis, based on time in California, number of arrivals and departures, etc. (Sec. 25101.3, Rev. & Tax. Code; Reg. 25137-7, 18 CCR)

Although the law does not provide specific formulas for other transportation companies, the FTB has developed a special formula for railroads and trucking companies based on "revenue miles" and a formula for sea transportation companies based on "voyage days" within and without California.

• *Use of original federal cost basis*

Property owned by the taxpayer is included in the property factor at its original cost ("basis") for *federal* income tax purposes. This means that depreciation is ignored. (Sec. 25130, Rev. & Tax. Code) However, certain adjustments are allowed, including adjustments for any subsequent capital additions or improvements, special deductions, and partial deductions because of sale, exchange, abandonment. Inventory is included in accordance with the method of valuation for *federal* income tax purposes. FTB Reg. 25130, 18 CCR provides specific rules and examples for determining "original cost" in unusual situations such as corporate reorganizations, inherited property, etc.; in each case, the determination relates to the *federal* cost basis of the property. Leasehold improvements are included at their original cost. In the case of property acquired as a result of involuntary conversion or exchange, the original federal cost is carried over to the replacement property—see Legal Ruling No. 409 (1977) (CCH CALIFORNIA Tax Reports ¶11-530.97).

In *Appeal of Pauley Petroleum, Inc.* (1982) (CCH CALIFORNIA TAX REPORTS ¶11-530.591), the taxpayer had elected to expense intangible drilling and development costs for federal income tax purposes, but included them as costs in the property factor of the State apportionment formula. The SBE held that the costs could not be included in the property factor, since they were not included in the federal tax basis of the property.

• *Rental property and royalties*

Rental property is included in the property factor at eight times the net annual rental rate. (Sec. 25130, Rev. & Tax. Code) Any subrentals received—provided they constitute "nonbusiness" income—are ordinarily deducted from rentals paid to determine the net annual rate; however, FTB Reg. 25137, 18 CCR, provides for special treatment in exceptional cases where deduction of subrentals would produce a distorted result. FTB Reg. 25130, 18 CCR, and Reg. 25137, 18 CCR, give examples to illustrate treatment of this and other unusual situations, and also provide rules and examples for determining the "net annual rental" in cases of short-term leases, reorganizations, payments in lieu of rent, nominal rental rates, etc.

Under both Reg. 25130, 18 CCR and Reg. 25137, 18 CCR, and FTB Legal Ruling 97-2 (1997) (see CCH CALIFORNIA TAX REPORTS ¶11-530.44), royalty payments made by a corporation with respect to the corporation's oil and gas and/or timber rights are treated as equivalents to rental payments to the extent that the property for which the royalty payments are made is actually used.

• *Averaging for year*

The amount to be included in the property factor is the average value for the year. This is usually determined by averaging the values at the beginning and end of the year. However, the FTB may require or allow averaging by monthly values, where substantial fluctuations occur during the year or large amounts of property are acquired or disposed of during the year or where membership in the unitary group changes during the year. (Reg. 25131, 18 CCR) The FTB was sustained in this position by the SBE in *Appeal of Craig Corporation* (1987) (CCH CALIFORNIA TAX REPORTS ¶11-530.661).

¶1308 Payroll Factor in Apportionment Formula

Law: Secs. 25107, 25132-33, 25137 (CCH CALIFORNIA TAX REPORTS ¶11-535, 11-540).

Comparable Federal: None.

California Form: Sch. R (Apportionment and Allocation of Income).

The payroll factor includes all salaries, wages, commissions, and other compensation to employees. (Sec. 25132, Rev. & Tax. Code; Reg. 25132, 18 CCR) Officer compensation and 401(k) deferred earnings are also included in the payroll factor (California Response to CCH Multistate Corporate Income Tax Survey, California Franchise Tax Board, July 21, 2003, CCH CALIFORNIA TAX REPORTS ¶403-506). The test of whether a person is an employee is the way the person is treated for payroll tax purposes; if the person is not considered to be an employee for payroll taxes the person's compensation is not included. Compensation is attributable to California under the following scenarios:

— the employee performs services entirely within California;

— the employee performs services both within and without the state, but the services performed outside the state are merely incidental to those performed within the state;

— the employee performs some services within the state, and the base of operations is in the state, or if there is no base of operations, the place from which services are directed or controlled is in California; or

— the employee performs some services within the state and the base of operations, or the place from which services are directed or controlled, is not in any state in which some part of the services are performed, but the employee's residence is in California.

(Sec. 25133, Rev. & Tax. Code; Reg. 25133e, 18 CCR)

In *Appeal of Photo-Marker Corporation of California* (1986) (CCH CALIFORNIA TAX REPORTS ¶11-535.60), wages paid principal corporate officers residing in California were includible in the California numerator because the base of operations for the officers was in California even though the corporation was headquartered in New York.

Compensation attributable to "nonbusiness" income (¶1303) should be excluded from the payroll factor. Capitalized payroll costs (*e.g.*, plant construction) should be included in the payroll factor, even though they also become part of the property factor.

Special rules have been developed over the years for determining the payroll factor in unusual industry situations. For example, in the case of transportation companies, payroll of traveling personnel may be apportioned according to "revenue miles" or "voyage days" as discussed in ¶1307.

The California payroll of an international banking facility is to be treated for purposes of the apportionment formula as payroll outside the state. (Sec. 25137, Rev. & Tax. Code)

¶1309 Sales Factor in Apportionment Formula

Law: Secs. 25107, 25134-37 (CCH CALIFORNIA TAX REPORTS ¶11-525, ¶11-540).

Comparable Federal: None.

California Form: Sch. R (Apportionment and Allocation of Income).

For purposes of the sales factor, the term "sales" generally means gross receipts from operations that produce "business" income, less returns and allowances. (Sec. 25134, Rev. & Tax. Code) Franchise Tax Board (FTB) Reg. 25134, 18 CCR, through Reg. 25136, 18 CCR, provide specific rules for determining what should be included. The following are excluded from the sales factor:

— substantial amounts of gross receipts from an occasional sale of a fixed asset or other property held or used in the regular course of a taxpayer's trade or business, such as a sale of a factory or plant, and

— insubstantial amounts of gross receipts arising from incidental or occasional transactions or activities unless such exclusion would materially affect the amount of income apportioned to California.

"Substantial amount" means a decrease of 5% or more in the sales factor denominator.

The law provides specific rules for determining which sales are attributable to California. Sales of tangible personal property are deemed to be California sales if the property is delivered or shipped to a purchaser, other than the U.S. government, located in California; this applies regardless of the f.o.b. point or other conditions of sale. Such sales are also attributable to California if shipped from an office, warehouse, store, factory, or other storage facility in California, where the purchaser is the U.S. government or where the seller is not taxable in the state or country where the purchaser is located. (Sec. 25135, Rev. & Tax. Code) See *Appeal of Chromalloy American Corporation* (1977) (CCH CALIFORNIA TAX REPORTS ¶12-525.53), in which the SBE approved this rule as it applies to sales to the U.S. government.

A sale is a California sale if a seller transfers possession of goods to a purchaser at the purchaser's place of business in California. (Sec. 25135, Rev. & Tax. Code)

• *Sales to U.S. government*

Sales to the U.S. government include only sales for which the government makes direct payment to the seller under a contract with the seller; in other words, only prime contracts are included and subcontract sales are excluded. (Sec. 25135(b), Rev. & Tax. Code)

• *Effect of Public Law 86-272*

If the other state, territory, or country could tax the seller but does not actually do so, the seller is nevertheless deemed to be "taxable" there and sales shipped there from California are not attributable to California. On the other hand, when P.L. 86-272 (¶805) would preclude taxing of the seller by the other state, sales shipped from California are attributable ("thrown back") to California.

In Legal Ruling 99-1 (1999) (CCH CALIFORNIA TAX REPORTS ¶10-105.75), the FTB ruled that a corporation's sales of tangible personal property shipped from California into Puerto Rico should be included in the corporation's sales factor for apportionment purposes because Puerto Rico had no authority to impose a tax on the corporation. The corporation was protected from Puerto Rico taxation under P.L. 86-272 because its activity there was limited to the solicitation of orders. Although a commonwealth, Puerto Rico was a destination state for purposes of P.L. 86-272.

In *McDonnell Douglas Corporation v. Franchise Tax Board* (1994) (CCH CALIFORNIA TAX REPORTS ¶11-525.45), a California court of appeal held that an aircraft manufacturer was permitted to exclude from the California sales factor numerator of the apportionment formula its sales of aircraft that were destined for use outside California but that were delivered to purchasers in California.

However, in *Appeal of Mazda Motors of America, Inc.* (1994) (CCH CALIFORNIA TAX REPORTS ¶11-525.451), the SBE held that an automobile importer's sales receipts for vehicles that the importer stored, assembled, serviced, repaired, and subsequently shipped to the purchaser in Texas were properly included in the numerator of the apportionment formula's sales factor for purposes of calculating the taxpayer's California taxable income. Unlike the situation in *McDonnell Douglas Corp.*, where the purchaser merely picked up the goods in this state for shipment to an out-of-state destination, the taxpayer exercised sufficient possession and control over the vehicles while they were in California to subject the goods to taxation by the state.

In *Appeal of Schwinn Sales West, Inc.* (1988) (CCH CALIFORNIA TAX REPORTS ¶11-520.2099), the nonsolicitation activities in California of a regional sales manager of an Illinois bicycle manufacturer, along with the company's conducting of service schools for its California dealers, indicated that the company's activities were regular and systematic, exceeding protected solicitation.

In *Appeals of Foothill Publishing Co. and the Record Ledger, Inc.* (1986) (CCH CALIFORNIA TAX REPORTS ¶11-525.818), the income derived by two California publishers for printing Nevada and Arizona publications was "thrown back" under prior law to California because under P.L. 86-272 neither Nevada nor Arizona could tax the publishers. The only business activity in those states was the solicitation of orders that were sent outside the state for approval and then delivered from California.

In *Appeal of Union Carbide Corporation* (1984) (CCH CALIFORNIA TAX REPORTS ¶11-525.8192), the taxpayer's subsidiaries sold its products in various foreign countries. The taxpayer contended that it would have been taxable in those countries except for certain tax treaties; however, it did not offer any evidence that the foreign activities were extensive enough to subject it to the tax jurisdiction of the foreign countries. The SBE held that the foreign sales were properly "thrown back" to California under prior law.

In *Appeal of The Olga Company* (1984) (CCH CALIFORNIA TAX REPORTS ¶11-525.8191), the taxpayer shipped its products from California to more than 30 other states. Although the taxpayer did not pay income taxes in the other states, it contended that the other states had jurisdiction to tax because of the taxpayer's extensive sales activities. The SBE held that the sales in other states should be "thrown back" to California under prior law.

In *Appeal of Dresser Industries* (1982) (CCH CALIFORNIA TAX REPORTS ¶11-525.817), the taxpayer sold its products in Japan through several subsidiaries. The SBE held that these sales could not be attributed ("thrown back") to California under prior law, because the FTB did not show that Japan lacked jurisdiction to tax the parent corporation. The SBE held that the criteria of P.L. 86-272 could not be applied, because P.L. 86-272 does not apply to foreign commerce. See also the opinion on rehearing in this case.

In *Appeals of Learner Co. et al.* (1980) (CCH CALIFORNIA TAX REPORTS ¶11-520.43), the taxpayer shipped scrap metal to customers in Japan. The taxpayer contended that it would have been taxable by Japan if the standards of P.L. 86-272 had been applicable there. The SBE held that the taxpayer would not have been taxable by Japan, and that the sales to Japan were properly assigned to California for purposes of the allocation formula.

In *Hoffmann-La Roche, Inc. v. Franchise Tax Board* (1980) (CCH CALIFORNIA TAX REPORTS ¶11-525.57), the taxpayer questioned the constitutionality of the rule involving P.L. 86-272 discussed above. The FTB attributed to California sales that were shipped from California to certain other states, in which states the taxpayer (seller) was not taxable. A federal appellate court upheld the constitutionality of the rule.

• *Throwback rule in context of combined unitary group*

See ¶1310 for a discussion of the throwback rule in connection with unitary group apportionment.

• *Sales other than of tangible personal property; sales of services*

Receipts from sources other than tangible personal property sales are included in the sales factor if the receipts are derived from a taxpayer's income-producing activity, including income from intangible property used in the taxpayer's business. (Reg. 25136, 18 CCR)

"Income producing activity" means transactions and activity directly engaged in by the taxpayer in the regular course of its trade or business for the ultimate purpose of obtaining gains or profit. Such activity does not include transactions and activities performed on behalf of a taxpayer, such as those conducted on its behalf by an independent contractor (see Chief Counsel Ruling 2007-2, California Franchise Tax Board, CCH CALIFORNIA TAX REPORTS ¶404-331).

Practitioner Comment: Treatment of Combined Reporting Group Members

In FTB *Legal Ruling 2006-02*, May 3, 2006, CCH CALIFORNIA TAX REPORTS ¶404-008, the FTB explained that the activities performed by one member of a combined reporting group "on behalf of" another member of the same combined reporting group will be considered in determining the income producing activity of the other member of the combined reporting group for sales factor purposes.

Although Reg. 25136(b), 18 CCR, has always excluded from the definition of the term "income producing activity" those activities performed on behalf of a taxpayer, such as those performed by an independent contractor, the FTB takes the position that the "on behalf of" rule cannot exclude all possible actors who perform services on behalf of a taxpayer. Because a corporation is an artificial legal entity that can only act through its members, officers, or agents, someone must perform acts on its behalf.

For many years the FTB has argued that the term "taxpayer" refers to a specific legal entity, not the combined reporting group as a whole. However, in this ruling, the FTB acknowledges that the several elements of a unitary business are treated as one unit for taxation purposes. According to the FTB, it would be inconsistent to disregard the activity of one member of the combined reporting group in determining the income producing activity of another because such activities are directly proximate to the generation of the business income by the group.

However, for water's-edge elections, with respect to transactions with entities that are fully or partially excluded from the combined reporting group, the "on behalf of" rule would operate to exclude activities performed by such entities for purposes of determining where the greater costs of performance occurred.

Bruce Daigh, Chris Whitney, Contributing Editors

"Income-producing activity" includes, but is not limited to, the following:

— the rendering of personal services by employees or the utilization of tangible and intangible property by the taxpayer in performing a service;

— the sale, rental, leasing, licensing or other use of real property;

— the rental, leasing, licensing or other use of tangible personal property; and

— the sale, licensing or other use of intangible personal property.

The mere holding of intangible personal property is not, of itself, an income-producing activity (Reg. 25136, 18 CCR).

Practitioner Comment: "Personal Services" Defined for Sales Factor Purposes

The FTB issued Legal Ruling 2005-1, March 21, 2005, CCH CALIFORNIA TAX REPORTS ¶403-772, explaining that the term "personal services" for purposes of apportioning gross receipts, using an income-producing activity standard, includes any service performed where capital is not a material income-producing factor. Furthermore, personal services are not limited to professional services or to specialized services performed by one individual.

As the ruling explains, California regulations generally require a taxpayer to apportion receipts using a "time spread" method where the contract between a taxpayer and its customer calls for a personal service, where capital is not a material income-producing factor, and where the corporation performs the contracted-for services utilizing the labor of its employees with little or no utilization of tangible or intangible property. The time spread method requires a taxpayer to treat the time each employee, including the project manager, spends in each state as a separate income-producing activity for purposes of determining the numerator of the sales factor.

In a situation in which capital is a material income-producing factor, the special time-spread rule does not apply. Instead, the standard cost of performance rule would assign the receipts to the state with the greatest cost of performance.

Bruce Daigh, Chris Whitney, Contributing Editors

According to the FTB, business income dividends constitute gross receipts that are generally includible in the recipient's sales factor. However, dividends are includible in the sales factor only when the holder engages in an activity that constitutes more than the mere holding of intangible property. Income-producing activity with respect to a dividend exists when there is participation in the management and/or the operations of the dividend payor. The exercise of voting rights conferred by ownership of stock, the receipt and review of material normally supplied to a stockholder, and accounting for the receipt of dividend income do not constitute participation in the management and/or operations of the dividend payor. Consequently, such actions do not constitute income-producing activity with respect to a dividend (*FTB Legal Ruling 2003-3* (2003), (CCH CALIFORNIA TAX REPORTS ¶403-576)).

Sales of other than tangible personal property are attributable to California if the activity that produced the sale is performed in California. If the income-producing activity is performed both within and without the state, then the sale is attributed to California only if a greater portion of the income-producing activity is performed in California than in any other state, based on costs of performance. These rules apply to income from personal services and any income from property that does not come within the category of "sales of tangible personal property." FTB Reg. 25136, 18 CCR provides specific rules and examples for treatment of income of these types. The regulation provides that income from personal services is to be attributed to California to the extent the services are performed in California.

In *Appeal of PacifiCorp.* (2002) (CCH CALIFORNIA TAX REPORTS ¶11-525.34), the SBE ruled that the generation and transmission of electricity sold to California customers was the sale of a service excluded from the numerator of the apportionment sales factor, where the services were performed for the most part outside the state. In reaching this conclusion, the SBE found that, "for purposes of California tax law, electricity is intangible."

In *Appeal of Mark IV Metal Products, Inc.* (1982) (CCH CALIFORNIA TAX REPORTS ¶11-525.531), the taxpayer fabricated metal products in California for a customer in Texas. The SBE held that the taxpayer was selling services, and sales to the Texas customer were attributable to California for purposes of the sales factor.

In *Appeal of The Babcock and Wilcox Company* (1978) (CCH CALIFORNIA TAX REPORTS ¶11-525.58), the taxpayer was engaged in the design, manufacture, and sale of steam generating systems. The taxpayer contended that sales of these systems were sales of "other than tangible personal property" and therefore were subject to the rules for such property rather than to the rules for tangible personal property. The SBE held that the sales in question were of tangible personal property, attributable entirely to California; the SBE pointed out that the property and payroll factors fairly reflected the out-of-state activity in planning, engineering, etc.

• *Installment sales*

In Legal Ruling No. 413 (1979) (CCH CALIFORNIA TAX REPORTS ¶12-525.35), the FTB ruled that an apportioning corporation reporting a sale on the installment basis should include the total sales price in the sales factor in the year of sale, and should apportion the installment income each year according to the apportionment percentage of the year of sale.

• *Cost-plus contracts*

In *Appeal of Bechtel Power Corporation, et al.* (1997) (CCH CALIFORNIA TAX REPORTS ¶11-525.71), the SBE ruled that in order to accurately reflect the taxpayer's economic activities in California, client-furnished materials used to fulfill a "cost-plus" contract were required to be included in the taxpayer's sales factor for apportionment purposes.

• *Special rules and decisions*

The FTB has developed special rules for the sales factor in some unusual industry situations. In the case of sea transportation companies, income from carrying cargo is attributed to California under a formula based on "voyage days" (see also ¶1307).

In *Appeal of Royal Crown Cola Co.* (1974) (CCH CALIFORNIA TAX REPORTS ¶12-525.54), the taxpayer argued for a novel computation of the sales factor. The taxpayer contended that to avoid a distorted result, the sales of certain subsidiaries should be excluded from the sales factor and intercompany sales of the parent to the subsidiaries (normally eliminated) should be included instead. The SBE held against the taxpayer, citing several of the cases discussed above at ¶1304 and emphasizing the broad discretion vested in the FTB in apportionment matters.

• *Sales of securities*

The issue of how to treat short-term investments made by a multi-state corporation's treasury department has generated a host of recent litigation, with taxpayers contending that all income from such investments, including return of principal, should be included in the sales factor denominator. The California Supreme Court has weighed in on this issue, holding that the sales factor includes all gross receipts from sales and redemptions of securities, but includes only the interest income from repurchase agreements. In reaching its decisions, the Court looked to the economic reality of the transactions to determine whether the total proceeds should be included in gross receipts. In situations in which the money is received in exchange for a commodity, such as the redemption of a security, the full price is to be treated as gross receipts. (*Microsoft Corp. v. Franchise Tax Board* (2006) (CCH CALIFORNIA TAX REPORTS ¶404-043)) In contrast, if the income is received in exchange for the use of money, such as in the case of a repurchase agreement, only the interest, not the principal, is a gross receipt. (*General Motors Corp. v. Franchise Tax Board,* (2006) (CCH CALIFORNIA TAX REPORTS ¶404-044) A California appellate court reached a similar conclusion in *The Limited Stores, Inc. v. Franchise Tax Board* (2005) (CCH CALIFORNIA TAX REPORTS ¶403-819).

Although the California Supreme Court determined that total proceeds received from redemptions of securities should be included in gross receipts for sales factor purposes, the Court found that in the *Microsoft* case the FTB met its burden of establishing that an alternate formula that excludes the return of principal from the redemption should be used to calculate the taxpayer's tax liability. In so holding, the Court stated that "the party attempting to invoke the Revenue and Taxation Section 25137 alternative apportionment provision has the burden of proving by clear and convincing evidence that (1) the approximation provided by the standard formula is not a fair representation, and (2) its proposed alternative is reasonable." Microsoft's short-term investments produced less than 2% of the company's income, but 73% of its gross receipts. Inclusion of these receipts in the sales factor resulted in severely diminishing the impact of Microsoft's activities in those states in which the treasury department was not located and overemphasizing the impact of the business's activities in the state where its treasury department was located.

In its decision in *Microsoft Corp.*, the Court fell short of ruling that equitable apportionment would be proper in all instances involving short-term treasury investments and called on the California Legislature to address this issue. The court noted that absent a global redefinition of gross receipts to exclude such returns, smaller distortions insufficient to trigger a reappraisal under the equitable apportionment provision may slip through the cracks, resulting in underestimation of the tax owed California. In fact, in its decision in *General Motors Corp.*, the Court remanded this issue to the appellate court to determine if there was indeed unreasonable distortion and if the FTB's approach was reasonable.

Practitioner Comment: FTB Modifies Regulation to Exclude Treasury Receipts

The FTB amended California Code of Regulation Sec. 25137(c)(1)(D), which now excludes "treasury function" income and receipts from the sales factor. This includes interest, dividends, gross receipts and net gains, as well as receipts and gains from foreign currency hedging activity (but not hedging related to price risk of products consumed or produced by the taxpayer). A "treasury function" is defined as any pooling, managing and investing of or intangible assets for the purpose of satisfying the cash flow needs of the business. Taxpayers principally engaged in an intangible activity such as registered broker dealers and financial institutions are excluded. The amendments are effective for years beginning on or after January 1, 2007.

Bruce Daigh, Chris Whitney, Contributing Editors

The California Supreme Court has instructed two California courts of appeal to vacate their prior decisions in *Toys "R" Us, Inc. v. Franchise Tax Board* (2006) (CCH CALIFORNIA TAX REPORTS ¶403-996) and *The Limited Stores, Inc. v. Franchise Tax Board* (2005) (CCH CALIFORNIA TAX REPORTS ¶403-819), and to reconsider the cases in light of the decisions in *Microsoft* and *General Motors*. (*Toys "R" Us, Inc. v. Franchise Tax Board*, California Supreme Court, No. S143422, November 15, 2006; *The Limited Stores. v. Franchise Tax Board*, California Supreme Court, No. S136922, November 15, 2006) On remand, the court of appeals in the *Limited Stores, Inc.* applied reasoning similar to the California Supreme Court's reasoning in *Microsoft Corp.* to find that an alternative apportionment calculation should be applied and should only include the net income from the taxpayer's short term investments in the sales factor calculation. (*The Limited Stores, Inc. v. Franchise Tax Board* (2007) (CCH CALIFORNIA TAX REPORTS ¶404-295)

Practical Analysis: Taxpayers' Next Steps

Corporations that have out-of-state treasury departments that have generated large amounts of income from short-term investments should definitely consider filing refund claims if they have income apportionable to California. As the law currently stands, the FTB will have to establish that exclusion of the total receipts from the sales factor is reasonable on a case-by-case basis.

In light of the California Supreme Court's decisions, corporations with treasury departments located in California must include income from redemption of securities in both the numerator and denominator of the corporation's sales factors. Taxpayers that failed to previously do so must file amended returns to report this change in their sales factor. This will undoubtedly dramatically increase a corporation's tax liability. Taxpayers should consider filing Section 25137 petitions, but must keep in mind that the taxpayer invoking Section 25137 relief has the burden of proving both that application of the standard apportionment formula is unfair and that the proposed alternative is reasonable. These taxpayers may also want to consider relocating their treasury departments to other states to decrease their tax liability in the future.

In *General Mills, Inc. & Subsidiaries v. Franchise Tax Board*, (2007) (CCH CALIFORNIA TAX REPORTS ¶404-475), the San Francisco Superior Court ruled that receipts from a taxpayer's sales transactions in the commodity futures market could not be included as "gross receipts" in calculating the taxpayer's sales factor. The court reasoned that because futures contracts had no value at inception and did not create a binding obligation, they could not be said to be supported by money or consideration in the same way as trading in other goods or commodities. Although in deciding that the receipts did not constitute gross receipts for apportionment purposes the court did not have to address the issue of distortion, the court indicated that should they be included in gross receipts "that great potential exists for a finding of distortion under Cal. Rev. & Tax. Code Sec. 25137."

• *Patent infringement awards*

In an informal decision that cannot be cited as precedent, the SBE followed the North Carolina Supreme Court's ruling in *Polaroid Corp. v. Offerman*, 349 N.C. 290 (1998), and held that the proceeds from a patent infringement lawsuit constituted unrealized lost profits that were apportionable business income rather than nonbusiness income allocable to the taxpayer's state of domicile. In so ruling, the SBE adopted the North Carolina Supreme Court's reasoning that it was irrelevant whether the income was received in the courtroom vs. the marketplace (*Appeal of Polaroid Corp.* (2003) (CCH CALIFORNIA TAX REPORTS ¶10-075.92)). The SBE granted the appellant's petition for rehearing in this case (*Appeal of Polaroid Corp.* (2004) (CCH CALIFORNIA TAX REPORTS ¶11-525.60)), but the appeal was dismissed and a stipulated agreement was entered on August 25, 2004.

• *International banking facility*

The California sales of an international banking facility are to be attributed outside the state for purposes of the apportionment formula. (Sec. 25137, Rev. & Tax. Code)

¶1310 Affiliated Corporations—Combined Reporting

Law: Secs. 23801, 25101.15, 25102, 25104-05, 25106.5 (CCH CALIFORNIA TAX REPORTS ¶10-640, 11-520, 11-540, 11-545, 11-550).

Comparable Federal: None.

California Forms: Form 100 (California Corporation Franchise or Income Tax Return), FTB 3726 (Deferred Intercompany Stock Account (DISA) and Capital Gains Information).

As explained at ¶812, the California law specifically provides for the filing of consolidated franchise tax returns only by certain railroad corporations. However, when a group of corporations conducts a unitary business (discussed at ¶1304), members of the group are generally required to file a combined report if the unitary activities are carried on within and without California. (Sec. 25102, Rev. & Tax. Code)

The combined report shows the manner in which the unitary business apportions and allocates its income to California and to other states in which it does business, but should not be equated with a combined group return (discussed at ¶1313). Members of a unitary group deriving income solely from California sources may elect to file a combined return, but are not required to do so; such an election must be made annually. When computing the elements of sales, property, and payroll for a combined report, some intercompany transactions must be eliminated (see discussion below).

While Franchise Tax Board (FTB) Publication 1061, Guidelines for Corporations Filing a Combined Report, indicates that combined reporting is required whenever a unitary business conducts unitary activities both within and without the state, the applicable statutes state that combined reporting is generally required only if the corporations are members of a "commonly controlled group." A "commonly controlled group" is any of the following:

— a group of corporations connected through stock ownership (or constructive ownership) if the parent corporation owns stock possessing more than 50% of the voting power of at least one corporation and, if applicable, the parent or one or more of the other corporations own stock cumulatively representing more than 50% of the voting power of each of the corporations (other than the parent);

— any two or more corporations if stock representing more than 50% of the voting power of the corporations is owned (or constructively owned) by one person;

— any two or more corporations if more than 50% of the ownership or beneficial ownership of the stock possessing voting power in each corporation consists of stapled interests; or

— any two or more corporations if stock representing more than 50% of the voting power of the corporations is cumulatively owned (without regard to constructive ownership) by, or for the benefit of, members of the same family.

(Sec. 25105, Rev. & Tax. Code)

A corporation eligible to be a member of more than one commonly controlled group must elect to be a member of a single group. Such membership will be terminated when stock of the corporation is sold, exchanged, or otherwise disposed of, unless the corporation meets the requirements for being a member of the same commonly controlled group within a two-year period.

A corporation that is a partner in a partnership that is part of a unitary business is not required to own more than 50% of the partnership before the partnership may be included in a combined report. Because the partnership is not a separate taxable entity, its income and apportionment factors are included only to the extent of the corporate partner's percentage of ownership interest. See cases cited at ¶1304.

Practitioner Comment: Partnership's Apportionment Factors Included in Year of Liquidation

In a nonprecedential decision, the State Board of Equalization held in the *Appeal of Eli Lilly & Co.*, (2007) (CCH CALIFORNIA TAX REPORTS ¶404-213), that when a taxpayer liquidates its interest in a limited liability company (LLC) treated as a partnership for federal and state tax purposes, the taxpayer must include its proportionate share of the LLC's apportionment factors on its California corporate franchise tax return for the year in which the interest was liquidated.

Bruce Daigh, Chris Whitney, Contributing Editors

S corporations are generally prohibited from being included in a combined report. (Sec. 23801, Rev. & Tax. Code) However, in some cases, the FTB may use combined reporting methods to clearly reflect income of an S corporation.

Under California's water's-edge law, taxpayers may elect to exclude certain foreign affiliates from a combined report. For further details, see ¶1311.

CCH Comment: Corporation Numbers Must Be Listed on Schedule R-7

Tax return preparers are reminded that when their client is the designated key corporation for a combined reporting group for California corporation franchise and income tax purposes, they should list, on Part 1 of Schedule R-7, Election to File a Unitary Taxpayers' Group Return and List of Affiliated Corporations, the California corporation numbers for the client and every member of the client's combined reporting group. In addition, when a client is a designated key corporation, tax return preparers must list, on Part 2 of Schedule R-7, any members of the client's commonly controlled group that are not listed on Part 1 of Schedule R-7 as making an election to file a single unitary group return. It is not enough to provide federal employer identification numbers. The California corporation numbers are critical because they provide the Franchise Tax Board (FTB) with the most effective and reliable way to verify information on returns, and they allow the FTB to process returns faster and more accurately. (*Tax News*, California Franchise Tax Board, May/June 2005)

For taxable years beginning on or after January 1, 2008, the FTB has revised Schedule R-7 to add a new Part I, Section B, List of Taxpayers No Longer Included in the Single Group Tax Return After the Last Filing. Each taxpayer's name, California corporation number or federal employer identification number (FEIN), and effective date of removal from the single group tax return should be included in the spaces provided. (Instructions, Schedule R, Apportionment and Allocation of Income)

• *Combination of general and financial corporations*

FTB Reg. 25137-10, 18 CCR, sets forth in detail how a unitary business that consists of at least one bank or financial corporation and at least one general corporation whose predominant activity is not financial, allocates and apportions income in a combined report.

• *Insurance affiliates*

In Legal Ruling No. 385 (1975) (CCH CALIFORNIA TAX REPORTS ¶205-232), the FTB ruled that a California corporate insurer engaged in a unitary business must be excluded from a combined report for apportionment of unitary income, because the state constitution exempts such organizations from franchise and income taxes.

However, in a nonprecedential decision, the SBE refused to extend this finding and held that a taxpayer's combined report was required to include its wholly owned unitary insurance subsidiary that conducted a non-insurance business within California and was not subject to California's gross premiums tax but conducted an insurance business in Texas and was classified as an insurance company under Texas law. The SBE also went on to hold that the calculation of the sales factor properly included the premiums received by the subsidiary during the course of its Texas insurance activities. (*Appeal of Electronic Data Systems Corp.* (2008) CCH CALIFORNIA TAX REPORTS, ¶404-727)

• *Parent company excluded*

Legal Ruling No. 410 (1979) (CCH CALIFORNIA TAX REPORTS ¶206-100) involved a situation where three subsidiaries were engaged in a unitary business but their parent was not involved. The ruling concluded that the subsidiaries must be included in a combined report but the parent corporation should be excluded.

• *FTB policy*

The FTB requires combined reporting of multistate operations wherever a "unitary" business is operated within and without California. As discussed more fully at ¶1304 , there are three judicially acceptable tests for determining whether a business is unitary. These are (1) the three unities test, (2) the contribution and dependency test, and (3) the flow of value test.

The FTB has issued audit guidelines with respect to the unitary combination of diverse businesses (*FTB Notice No. 92-4*, CCH CALIFORNIA TAX REPORTS ¶402-432). According to the guidelines, there is no unique test for evaluating unity in diverse business cases. Unity may be established under any of the judicially acceptable tests and may not be denied merely because another of those tests does not simultaneously apply, *i.e.*, the tests are not mutually exclusive. In addition, a lack of functional integration will not prevent a finding of unity. On the other hand, the fact that functionally integrated businesses may be found to be unitary does not mean that functional integration is a *requirement* for unity.

Also, presumptions of unity under Reg. 25120 (b), 18 CCR, which states that the activities of a taxpayer will be considered a single business if there is evidence to indicate that the segments under consideration are integrated with, depend upon, or contribute to, each other and the operations of the taxpayer as a whole, although important considerations, are not conclusive in determining unity.

Finally, the guidelines state that *Mole-Richardson, Dental Insurance Consultants,* and *Tenneco West, Inc.* (each discussed at ¶1304), are controlling of the diverse business issue and that State Board of Equalization (SBE) decisions that are not in accord with these cases should not be relied upon.

• *Corporations under common control*

In *Rain Bird Sprinkler Mfg. Corp. v. Franchise Tax Board* (1991) (CCH CALIFORNIA TAX REPORTS ¶11-520.8092), a California court of appeal allowed seventeen corporations to file a combined report even though no single individual or entity held a majority interest in all of the corporations. The court, rejecting what it called "a host" of SBE decisions requiring ownership by a single individual or entity, held that "unity of ownership" existed because members of the same family held the majority of the voting stock in each of the corporations, and all of the stock of each corporation was subject to written stock purchase agreements prohibiting transfer to outsiders.

• *Other cases involving questions of control*

In *Appeal of Armco Steel Corp.* (1984) (CCH CALIFORNIA TAX REPORTS ¶11-540.63), the taxpayer owned exactly 50% of the stock of a "captive mining corporation" that supplied iron ore to the taxpayer at cost. The captive corporation was treated as a partnership for federal tax purposes. The SBE followed the *Revere Copper and Brass* case (below) in holding that the taxpayer could not include the captive corporation's factors in its computation of unitary income, even though the factors could have been included if the captive corporation had been a partnership (see also ¶1304).

In *Appeal of Revere Copper and Brass Inc.* (1977) (CCH CALIFORNIA TAX REPORTS ¶205-752), the taxpayer was admittedly engaged in a unitary business. The taxpayer bought a substantial portion of its raw material requirements from a subsidiary that was 50% owned by the taxpayer. The SBE held that the subsidiary was not includible in a combined return, since the taxpayer's ownership in the subsidiary was not more than 50%. To the same effect, see *Appeal of Standard Brands, Inc.* (1977) (CCH CALIFORNIA TAX REPORTS ¶11-520.952). However, in *Appeal of Signal Oil and Gas Co.* (1970), the SBE held that a 50% owned German subsidiary of a Swiss subsidiary of a California parent should be included in the computation of unitary income, since the 50% stock ownership carried with it decisive control over the subsidiary's operations.

• *Apportionment of tax within group*

Where income of an affiliated group is combined and there are two or more corporations having activity in California, there may be a question of how the total tax on the combined income taxed by California should be divided between the corporations having income from California sources. Legal Ruling No. 234 (1959) (CCH CALIFORNIA TAX REPORTS ¶11-520.206) prescribes the method of apportionment to be used. The apportionment is based upon the California income attributable to each member of the affiliated group, such income being assigned to each corporation on the basis of the average ratio of the California factors of each corporation to the total factors of the group. This method is illustrated in the ruling as follows:

	Corp. A	Corp. B	Corp. C	Total
Totals within and without the State:				
Property	$ 500,000	$ 64,000	$ 36,000	$ 600,000
Payroll	300,000	74,000	26,000	400,000
Sales	4,000,000	600,000	400,000	5,000,000
Totals within the State:				
Property	24,000	—0—	36,000	60,000

	Corp. A	Corp. B	Corp. C	Total
Payroll	14,000	—0—	26,000	40,000
Sales	150,000	450,000	400,000	1,000,000
Allocating fractions:				
Property	4.0%	—0—	6.0%	10.0%
Payroll	3.5	—0—	6.5	10.0
Sales	3.0	9.0%	8.0	20.0
Total	10.5%	9.0%	20.5%	40.0%
Average	3.5 %	3.0%	$6.83\frac{1}{3}\%$	$13\frac{1}{3}\%$

Applying the foregoing fractions to a combined business income of $1,000,000 would result in $133,333 being attributed to California sources. This amount would then be allocated to each corporation, and the tax computed at the appropriate rate, as follows:

Corp. A (3.5% of $1,000,000)	$ 35,000
Corp. B (3% of $1,000,000)	30,000
Corp. C ($6.83\frac{1}{3}\%$ of $1,000,000)	68,333
Total	$133,333

• *Significance of apportionment within group*

Practitioner Comment: Joyce Vs. Finnegan Approach to Sourcing Receipts of Combined Reporting Group Members

In general, sales of tangible personal property are sourced on a destination basis but are *thrown back* to the state of origin in situations where the corporation shipping the product from California lacks nexus in the destination state. The application of these rules to combined reporting groups where unitary affiliates may have nexus in the destination state has evolved over the years. For example, in 1966, the State Board of Equalization in the *Appeal of Joyce, Inc.*, 66-SBE-070 (Nov. 23, 1966), held that sales of a Florida corporation shipping product to California could not be sourced to the state because the corporation lacked nexus in California, despite the fact that its unitary affiliates had nexus in the state. However, in 1990, the State Board of Equalization in *Appeal of Finnegan Corp.*, 88-SBE-022-A (Jan. 24, 1990), held that a corporation's sales shipped from California to states where it lacked nexus could not be thrown back to California because its unitary affiliates had nexus in the destination states. In 1999, the State Board of Equalization held in *Appeal of Huffy Corp.*, 99-SBE-005 (Apr. 22, 1999) that it returned to the *Joyce* approach on a prospective basis for income years beginning on or after April 22, 1999, the date of the opinion. This prospective application was affirmed on rehearing at 99-SBE-005-A (Sep. 1, 1999).

The *Joyce* approach seems to be consistent with the separate entity approach to utilizing credits endorsed by the California Supreme Court in *General Motors*—see Practitioner Comment at ¶1310. The FTB in recent years has made exceptions to the separate entity approach in the apportionment area. See for example the Practitioner Comment above regarding FTB Legal Ruling 2006-2. Also, as noted in ¶1306, the FTB has promulgated a regulation first effective in 2007 that provides special apportionment rules for the mutual fund service industry that use a *Finnegan* approach to sourcing mutual fund service receipts.

Bruce Daigh, Chris Whitney, Contributing Editors

CCH Comment: Planning Opportunities in Light of the Readoption of the Joyce *Rule*

The readoption of the *Joyce* rule has given unitary business groups opportunities to achieve favorable tax consequences through careful planning. By limiting activities that could give rise to taxable nexus in California (such as servicing and installing products or collecting accounts) to certain affiliates, other members of the unitary group may be able to exclude their California destination sales from the sales factor numerator of the group's combined report, thus reducing the unitary group's income subject to taxation in California. Of course, these sales may be "thrown back" to the state from which the products were shipped.

Conversely, with the abandonment of the *Finnigan* rule, taxpayers shipping products from California can no longer rely on the activities of unitary affiliates in other states to avoid throwback of those sales to California. When conducting tax planning, taxpayers need to bear in mind that there are many other issues to be considered when trying to manage nexus by using multiple entity structures, including attributional nexus based on an agency relationship (see discussion of *Reader's Digest Assoc., Inc.* at ¶805).

• *Minimum tax applies to each corporation*

The minimum tax (discussed at ¶816) is imposed on *each* corporation in the combined group that is incorporated or qualified to do business in California, even though the combined report shows a net loss or shows taxable income that would produce a lower tax. (Instructions, Form 100, California Corporation Franchise or Income Tax Return)

• *Allocation of credits and capital gains and losses*

Unless otherwise provided by statute, specific credit(s) are only available to the taxpayer corporation that incurred the expense that generated the credit(s). Reg. 25106.5-2, 18 CCR allows capital gains attributable to one member of a unitary group to be offset by capital losses incurred by another member.

Practitioner Comment: Treatment of Credits

On August 17, 2006, the California Supreme Court in *General Motors Corp. v. Franchise Tax Board* (2006) (CCH CALIFORNIA TAX REPORTS ¶404-044) held that only the taxpayer that incurred the research and development expenses may use the research and development credit so generated. In so holding, the Court's decision was consistent with an earlier State Board of Equalization decision (*Appeal of Guy F. Atkinson Company* (1997) CCH CALIFORNIA TAX REPORTS ¶403-307) as well as the unpublished Court of Appeal decision, *Guy F. Atkinson Company v. Franchise Tax Board* (2000) (CCH CALIFORNIA TAX REPORTS ¶403-097).

Bruce Daigh, Chris Whitney, Contributing Editors

However, beginning with the 2010 taxable year, members of a unitary group included in a combined report may assign tax credits to other eligible members of the unitary group. The members may assign any credit earned by the taxpayer in a taxable year beginning after 2007 or any credit earned in any taxable year beginning before July 1, 2008, that is eligible to be carried forward to the taxpayer's first taxable year beginning after June 30, 2008.

To be eligible to receive the credit, the assignee must have been a member of the assigning taxpayer's unitary combined group on (1) the last day of the first taxable year in which the credit was allowed to the taxpayer (June 30, 2008, in the case of credits earned in taxable years beginning before July 1, 2008), and (2) the last day of the taxable year of the assigning taxpayer in which the eligible credit is assigned.

The taxpayer must make an irrevocable election on its original return for the taxable year in which the assignment is made. Any credit limitations that would apply to the assigning taxpayer in the absence of an assignment also apply to the same extent to the assignee. (Sec. 23663, Rev. & Tax. Code)

An assignee may pay consideration to the assigning taxpayer for the credit transfer. However, the assignee may not claim any deduction with respect to any amounts so paid and the assigning taxpayer may not include in its gross income any amounts received as consideration. (Sec. 23663(d), Rev. & Tax. Code)

Practitioner Comment: Newly Enacted Assignment of Credit Provisions Can Be Used to Circumvent California's Separate Entity Application of Credits

AB 1452, signed into law on September 30, 2008, allows "eligible credits" to be assigned to other members of a combined reporting group for tax years beginning on or after July 1, 2008. Assignment can be made both with respect to credits generated in years beginning after that date as well as to carryovers from prior years. The assignee, however, can only use the assigned credits in a tax year beginning on or after January 1, 2010. The assignment must be made on the original return for the year of assignment. Once the election is made the credit "belongs" to the other member and can not be reassigned nor can the election be revoked. With proper planning these provisions can be used to circumvent the separate entity limitations endorsed by the California Supreme Court's 2006 decision in "General Motors", discussed above.

It is the FTB's position that any limitations on the assignor's use of the credit will also apply to the assignee however. For example, enterprise zone credits assigned to other members would still need to meet the enterprise zone activity limitations imposed under those provisions.

Bruce Daigh, Chris Whitney, Contributing Editors

• *Adjustments for intercompany transactions*

FTB Pub. 1061, Guidelines for Corporations Filing a Combined Report, discusses the adjustments necessary to properly reflect intercompany transactions among unitary affiliates included in the combined report. The adjustments concern inventories, intangible assets, fixed assets and capitalized items, dividends (see ¶909), and other factor adjustments.

Reg. 25106.5-1, 18 CCR generally conforms to Treasury Regulation Sec. 1.1502-13, concerning the treatment of intercompany transactions between seller members and buyer members of combined reporting groups. The regulation does not conform, however, to federal sourcing rules. Instead, California treats intercompany items as current apportionable business income.

Deferred Intercompany Stock Account (DISA) Disclosures

FTB 3726, Deferred Intercompany Stock Account (DISA) and Capital Gains Information, must be used to annually disclose the balance of any deferred intercompany stock account (DISA) and to report the capital gains from a DISA due to the occurrence of a triggering event. Failure to disclose the existing DISA balance for any tax year may result in the current recognition of capital gain. The corporation that must complete the form is the corporation that received the distribution. When filing a combined return, if there is more then one corporation that has a DISA, a separate form FTB 3726 must be completed for each corporation and must be attached to Form 100 or 100W. If the FTB has not contacted the corporation for an audit and the corporation needs to disclose DISA information for a prior taxable year, the corporation should file an amended return. (Instructions to FTB 3726, Deferred Intercompany Stock Account (DISA) and Capital Gains Information)

• *Accounting methods and periods*

Reg. 25106.5 et seq., 18 CCR, provide detailed rules concerning the accounting methods and periods to be used by a unitary group and its individual members. Under these rules, each member of a combined reporting group has its own accounting methods and elections. However, the unitary group is authorized to make an election on behalf of an individual member if that member has not otherwise made an election on a California or federal return.

The principal member's accounting period is used as a reference period for all members of the combined reporting group to aggregate and apportion combined report business income of the group. The regulations also address fiscalization issues, clarify how to incorporate/exclude a business's income that joins/leaves the unitary group mid-year, and govern the preparation of combined reports that include operations in foreign countries (see *Appeal of Crisa Corp.* (2002) (CCH CALIFORNIA TAX REPORTS ¶11-540.25)) for a discussion of the functional currency to be used in a combined report with unitary businesses in different countries).

¶1311 Water's-Edge Election for Multinational Unitary Businesses

Law: Secs. 18405.1, 24344, 24411, 25110-16 (CCH CALIFORNIA TAX REPORTS ¶10-815, 11-515, 11-550).

Comparable Federal: None.

California Forms: Form 100W (California Corporation Franchise or Income Tax Return - Water's Edge Filers), Form 100-WE (Water's-Edge Election), FTB 1115 (Request for Consent for a Water's-Edge Re-Election), FTB 1117 (Request to Terminate Water's-Edge Election).

Multinational taxpayers have an option to compute their California tax base on a water's-edge basis. Taxpayers that make such an election are taxed on income from sources solely within the United States. (Sec. 25110, Rev. & Tax. Code; Reg. 25110, 18 CCR)

• *Pre-water's-edge contract intercompany sales*

The California State Board of Equalization (SBE) upheld a water's-edge group member's nonrecognition of profits realized from its sale to a third party of inventory that it had purchased from its foreign parent company the year before the water's-edge filing election, even though the unitary group's worldwide combined report for that year properly eliminated the parent seller's intercompany inventory property. Consequently, the taxpayer only had to report as income the difference between the price it had paid its parent for the inventory, including the parent's profit, and the sales price it received from the third parties rather than recognizing income equal to the difference between the parent's acquisition price and the company's sales price. Without guidance from contradictory authority, profits from selling the inventory to a third party could be excluded from the water's-edge group's combined report (*Yamaha Motor Corp., U.S.A.* (2000) (CCH CALIFORNIA TAX REPORTS ¶12-650.60)).

• *IRC conformity*

Except as specifically provided in the statutory provisions governing water's-edge elections, when any of the statutory provisions governing water's-edge elections refers to a provision of the Internal Revenue Code (IRC), the reference is to the IRC, including all amendments, in effect for federal purposes for the taxable period. This overrides the general incorporation date for IRC provisions (see ¶803) so that relevant changes to federal law are applied in computing the income and deductions of a water's-edge group for California purposes. (Sec. 25116, Rev. & Tax. Code)

• *Qualifying entities*

Under the water's-edge election, California taxable income is computed based on the income and apportionment factors of only the following entities:

— any corporation (other than a bank) the average of whose U.S. property, payroll, and sales is 20% or more;

— U.S.-incorporated entities (excluding those making an election under IRC Secs. 931-936), , if, generally for water's-edge elections made before January 1, 2006, more than 50% of their stock is controlled by the same interest;

— DISCs, FSCs, and Export Trade Corporations;

— a "controlled foreign corporation" (CFC) as defined in IRC Sec. 957 that, generally for water's-edge elections made before January 1, 2006, is an affiliated corporation, and has "Subpart F income" as defined in IRC Sec. 952 (the income and apportionment factors of a CFC are multiplied by a fraction representing the ratio of Subpart F income to earnings and profits. A CFC is treated as having no Subpart F income if such income is less than $1 million and represents less than 5% of the CFC's earnings and profits); and

— any entity not described above, to the extent that its income is derived from or attributable to U.S. sources.

(Sec. 25110, Rev. & Tax. Code; Reg. 25110, 18 CCR) For taxable years beginning after 2005, the FTB is required to issue regulations to prevent the double taxation of income when a CFC has both U.S.-source income and Subpart F income. (Sec. 25110, Rev. & Tax. Code)

Practitioner Comment: U.S. Source Income Definition Modified for Water's Edge Taxpayers

As noted above, foreign corporations are includible in the water's edge combined group to the extent of their U.S. source income. In 2007, the FTB modified its regulations to redefine the definition of U.S. source income for this purpose. As currently defined, U.S. source income includes only effectively connected income ("ECI"). Non-effectively connected income ("NECI") is not included unless a principal purpose of tax avoidance exists. NECI includes such items as interest, dividends, and royalties received from U.S. corporations.

Bruce Daigh, Chris Whitney, Contributing Editors

Practitioner Comment: CFC Dividends

In *Fujitsu IT Holdings Inc. v. Franchise Tax Bd.*, Cal.Ct.App., 120 Cal. App. 4th (2004), CCH CALIFORNIA TAX REPORTS ¶403-655, the court held that dividends paid from one controlled foreign corporation (CFC) to its parent CFC are eliminated in determining the amount of CFC income to be included in the income of the unitary group, to the extent that the lower-tier CFC paid the dividends out of income that was included in combined income. The court also found that where the CFC receives dividends from a lower-tier subsidiary whose income and factors are fully included in the combined return of the water's-edge group, the dividends subsequently paid by the CFC are deemed first to be distributed from unitary group earnings and profits (E&P), and to that extent are completely eliminated.

The main point made by this decision is that intercompany dividends paid from a lower-tier CFC to an upper-tier CFC are not taken into account in determining the upper-tier CFC's water's-edge inclusion ratio (to the extent the dividends were paid out of combined income of the unitary group). The SBE reached a similar result in its unpublished decision in *Appeal of Baxter Healthcare Corporation* (August 1, 2002).

Another important point made by the court is that dividends paid by a partially included first-tier CFC from current E&P are treated as first coming out of the E&P eligible for elimination under Cal. Rev. & Tax. Code Sec. 25106 with any excess coming out of the E&P that was excluded from the water's-edge group (*e.g.*, E&P eligible for Cal. Rev. & Tax. Code Sec. 24411 DRD). This is significant, because of the application of the 100% dividends received deduction under Cal. Rev. & Tax. Code Sec. 25106 rather than the 75% deduction under Cal. Rev. & Tax. Code Sec. 24411. Further, dividends eligible for Cal. Rev. & Tax. Code Sec. 25106 elimination are not subject to the foreign investment interest offset rules.

The court's conclusion appears to overturn the pro-rata ordering method contained in the regulations promulgated under Cal. Rev. & Tax. Code Sec. 24411. The court did not specifically address the ordering rule for distributions from prior year accumulated E&P. However, the conceptual basis for the court's decision supports the position that a dividend should not be considered paid out of excluded E&P until after all combined

E&P is exhausted (*e.g.*, both current and any accumulated E&P that had been included in a California combined report). The FTB has not yet announced how it will apply the court's decision.

The court rejected Fujitsu's constitutional challenge to the 75% reduction under Cal. Rev. & Tax. Code Sec. 24411, agreeing with the superior court's finding that "this scheme actually provides better tax treatment for foreign subsidiaries' income." The superior court explained that, while 100% of domestic dividends are eliminated, the income from which the dividends are paid is included 100% on the combined report. Where the income of a foreign subsidiary has been excluded from the combined report through the use of the water's-edge election, only 25% of the dividends paid by the subsidiary are subject to apportionment.

Finally, the court noted that under a treaty with the United Kingdom, U.S. corporations that own 10% or more of the stock of a U.K. corporation are entitled, when the corporation pays a dividend, to a payment from the United Kingdom of half of the amount of the tax credit that an individual U.K. shareholder would receive. The court found that this U.K. "Advance Corporation Tax" (ACT) credit received with respect to dividends from its U.K. subsidiaries should be taxable as additional dividend income, either subject to elimination under Cal. Rev. & Tax. Code Sec. 25106 or a partial deduction under Sec. 24411.

The FTB has issued discussion drafts of proposed amendments to existing Regulations Secs. 24411 and 25106.5-1. As explained in the FTB's Notice and Request for Public Comment, the proposal "would apply the ordering rules of section 316 of the Internal Revenue Code, and if a distribution from a given year's earning and profits are not sufficient to exhaust the earning and profits of that year, the distribution will be considered drawn from each class of potential dividend on a pro rata basis." The proposal seeks to "clarify" these regulations after *Fujitsu* , deeming dividends to be paid first out of unitary group income and thus fully eliminated, with only the remainder being subject to partial deduction. (Notice 2005-1, California Franchise Tax Board, March 4, 2005, CCH CALIFORNIA TAX REPORTS ¶403-766)

Taxpayers that followed the FTB's rule for determining the partial inclusion ratio for controlled foreign corporations with subpart F income, or that adhered to the FTB's regulatory pro rata scheme for dividends should consider filing refund claims for open years.

It should be noted that on November 20, 2006, the SBE rendered a formal opinion in the *Appeal of Apple Computer, Inc.*, in which it held that foreign dividends should be considered to be paid from current year Earnings and Profits ("E&P") first and then from accumulated E&P on a last-in-first-out or "LIFO" basis. Further, the SBE upheld the FTB's regulatory pro rata scheme and specifically rejected the portion of the California Court of Appeals' decision in *Fujitsu,* in which the court had held that foreign dividends should be considered paid from included earnings first and eligible for elimination.

The *Apple* decision is the first and only SBE decision involving a California corporate income and franchise tax matter of which the contributing editors are aware in which the SBE refused to follow a published California Court of Appeal decision that the SBE acknowledged was on point. It is expected that the FTB will continue to deny all refund claims filed pursuant to this portion of the *Fujitsu* decision and that the resolution of such claims will remain uncertain unless and until subsequent litigation finally and favorably resolves this matter.

In January 2008, Apple filed a complaint in the San Francisco Superior Court (the same court which had favorably decided *Fujitsu*).

Bruce Daigh, Chris Whitney, Contributing Editors

CCH Practice Tip: U.S.-Located Income

Taxpayers that elect water's-edge treatment are only required to include income that is effectively connected with a U.S. trade or business or that is treated as effectively connected under the provisions of the Internal Revenue Code. However, because California is not a party to federal tax treaties, the immunity provisions of federal tax treaties do not apply for California purposes. Any income satisfying the definition of effectively connected income that is excluded from federal taxable income due to a tax treaty is included for California purposes. (Instructions, California 100W, California Corporation Franchise or Income Tax Return - Water's-Edge Filers).

• *Deduction of dividends*

A qualifying water's-edge group may deduct up to 75% of dividends received from a 50% owned corporation or bank if the average of the payor's U.S. property, payroll, and sales is less than 20%. The dividend deduction is computed on Schedule H of Form 100W. A special provision permits a 100% deduction of dividends from foreign construction projects whose locations are not subject to the groups' control, provided certain other water's-edge conditions are met. (Sec. 24411, Rev. & Tax. Code; Reg. 24411, 18 CCR)

To qualify for water's-edge treatment, the taxpayer must agree that dividends received by *other* unitary group members are business income if received from (1) an entity that is engaged in the same general business and that is more than 50% owned by members of the group, and (2) an entity that purchases, supplies, or sells 15% or more of either input or output from or to the unitary business. Dividends received from any other entity will be classified as business or nonbusiness income under existing provisions.

The deductible amount of qualifying foreign dividends is reduced by the amount of any interest expense incurred for purposes of foreign investment.

• *Elections and terminations*

A water's-edge election must be made on an original, timely filed return for the year of election, in the same manner as any other election. An election on an original, timely filed return will be considered valid if the tax is computed in a manner consistent with a water's-edge election and a Form 100-WE (Water's-Edge Election) is attached to the return. (Sec. 25113, Rev. & Tax. Code; Instructions Form 100W, California Corporation Franchise or Income Tax Return—Water's Edge Filers)

CCH Practice Tip: Perfecting an Election

Water's-edge elections may, at the election of the FTB, be perfected during the applicable period of limitations for mailing a notice of proposed deficiency assessment or allowing a credit or refund. The statute of limitations for all taxpayers in the water's-edge group whose taxable year falls, in whole or in part, within the period of the election will remain open to receive adjustments, under claim of deficiency, consistent with the perfection of the election.

Generally, an election will be effective only if made by every member of the self-assessed combined reporting group that is subject to California corporation franchise or income tax. An election on a group return will constitute an election by each member included in the group return, unless one of the members files a separate return in which no election is made and the nonelecting member is not otherwise deemed to have elected water's-edge treatment. A group member that does not make a water's-edge election on its own return will be deemed to have made such an election if either of the following applies:

— the income and apportionment factors of the nonelecting member are included in the self-assessed combined reporting group on an electing parent corporation's original, timely filed return, including a group return; or

— the income and apportionment factors of the nonelecting member are reflected in the self-assessed combined reporting group on an electing taxpayer's original, timely filed return, and the written notification of election filed with the return is signed by an officer or other authorized agent of a parent corporation or another corporation with authority to bind the nonelecting member to an election.

For purposes of water's-edge elections, a "parent corporation" is a corporation that owns or constructively owns stock possessing more than 50% of the voting power of the taxpayer.

Members of a unitary group that are not subject to California corporation franchise or income taxation when the election is made, but subsequently become subject to the tax, are deemed to have made a water's-edge election with the other members of the combined reporting group.

A corporation engaged in more than one apportioning trade or business may make a separate election for each apportioning trade or business

Special rules apply to taxpayers that become members of a new unitary group when at least one member has previously made a water's-edge election.

Practitioner Comment: "Deemed Elections"

If a water's-edge taxpayer becomes unitary with a non-water's-edge taxpayer, it is necessary to determine whether a water's-edge election will apply to the newly constituted unitary group. Generally, the filing status of the group having the largest net book value of business assets, as measured by the taxpayer members of the group, will control for determining whether the new combined filing group will be on the water's-edge or the worldwide method. It is important to note that there is not an opportunity for automatic termination of a water's-edge election following an acquisition. In order to get a result different from the "larger taxpayer prevails" result, the taxpayer will need to get FTB permission to terminate based on good cause.

Bruce Daigh, Chris Whitney, Contributing Editors

Water's-edge election period: A water's-edge election on an original, timely filed return remains in effect until terminated. Except as otherwise provided, if one or more electing members becomes disaffiliated or otherwise ceases to be included in the combined reporting group, the water's-edge election will remain in effect as to both the departing members and any remaining members. (Sec. 25113, Rev. & Tax. Code)

CCH Comment: Commencement Date of Election

If a taxpayer would have been required to file on a water's-edge basis for its first taxable year beginning after 2002 pursuant to a water's-edge election contract made in a prior year, the taxpayer will be deemed to have made an election under the revised water's-edge election provisions applicable to taxable years beginning after 2002, but the commencement date of the election made in a prior year will continue to be treated as the commencement date of the election for purposes of applying the revised water's-edge election provisions.

Effect of different fiscal years: In cases involving taxpayers with different fiscal years, each member of the water's-edge group must make the election on its timely filed original return for the taxable year for which the election is being made. The election becomes effective as of the beginning of the taxable year of the last member of the water's-edge group to file its return and election. Each taxpayer in the group must compute its tax on a worldwide basis for that portion of the taxable year between the beginning of its taxable year and the date the election becomes effective, and must compute its tax on a water's-edge basis for the remaining portion of the taxable year (*FTB Notice 2004-2* California Franchise Tax Board, May 3, 2004 (CCH CALIFORNIA TAX REPORTS ¶ 11-550.85)).

Election termination: A water's-edge election may be terminated on an original, timely filed return without the consent of the FTB after the election has been in effect for at least 84 months. Termination is accomplished by filing a return on a worldwide basis. To be effective, the termination must be made by every member of the water's-edge group in the same manner as a water's-edge election. (Sec. 25113, Rev. & Tax. Code)

An election may be terminated for good cause before the expiration of the 84-month period only with the consent of the FTB. A request to terminate for good cause must be in writing and must state how the taxpayer meets the requirements provided in Treasury Reg. Sec. 1.1502-75(c), which governs the good cause determinations for electing to discontinue filing on a consolidated basis. A taxpayer must file FTB 1117, Request to Terminate Water's-Edge Election, with the FTB no later than 120 days prior to the due date, including extensions, of the return for which the termination would be effective. FTB 1117 must be filed separately from any other return (*FTB Notice 2004-2*, California Franchise Tax Board, May 3, 2004 (CCH CALIFORNIA TAX REPORTS ¶11-550.85)).

FTB 1117 outlines the conditions to which a taxpayer seeking an early termination might have to consent, unless the taxpayer can explain why the conditions are unnecessary or inapplicable:

— Dividends received during the remaining period of the election from affiliated banks or corporations not included in the water's-edge report will be considered to have been paid first out of the E&P not included in the combined report of a unitary business for purposes of computing any allowable dividend exclusion under Rev. & Tax. Code Sec. 25106. To the extent the dividends exceed such E&P, they may be subject to the exclusion.

— Gains on distribution with respect to stock that is not a dividend or from the sale or other disposition of assets received during the remaining period of the election from affiliated banks or corporations not included in the water's-edge report will not be deferred or eliminated. Losses from the sale or worthlessness of stock or from the sale or other disposition of assets of affiliated banks or corporations not included in the water's-edge report will be allowed only to the extent of dividend income or other gain recognized as a result of the change in election.

— Gains or losses on the disposition of an affiliated bank's or corporation's stock or assets that was included in a combined report prior to the election and that was excluded from the water's-edge combined report will be included in income in the first return filed after permission is granted. Losses will be included only to the extent of gain recognized as a result of the change in election.

The FTB may also terminate an election upon request by all members of a water's-edge group, if the purpose of the request is to permit the state to contract with an expatriate corporation, or its subsidiary.

Except in cases involving deemed elections, once a taxpayer terminates its water's-edge election and returns to filing on a worldwide basis, the taxpayer may not make another water's-edge election for any taxable year beginning with the 84-month period following the last day of the election period that was terminated, unless the FTB waives the application of this prohibition for good cause. FTB 1115, Request for Consent for a Water's-Edge Re-Election, must be used by the taxpayer to request a re-election for good cause. If the taxpayer's request is approved by the FTB, a taxpayer is still required to attach a Form 100-WE, Water's-Edge Election, to a timely filed Form 100W to perfect the new election. (*Instructions*, FTB 1115, Request for Consent for a Water's Edge Re-Election)

CCH Practice Tip: When Consent Not Required

The FTB's consent for a water's-edge election termination or re-election is not required if the election is being or was terminated as a result of an affiliation change as provided in Rev. & Tax. Code Sec. 25113. (Instructions, FTB 1115, Request for Consent for a Water's-Edge Re-Election; Instructions, FTB 1117, Request to Terminate Water's-Edge Election)

• *Recordkeeping requirements*

A taxpayer electing water's-edge treatment must retain and make available upon request by the FTB various kinds of information and documents relating to, among other things, pricing policy, methods of allocating income and expense, apportionment factors, assignment of income to the United States or to foreign jurisdictions, information filed with the IRS, and tax returns from other states. Furthermore, the taxpayer must also consent to the taking of depositions from key employees or officers of the members of the water's edge group and to the acceptance of subpoenas duces tecum requiring the reasonable production of documents.

The FTB is given broad auditing powers with respect to a water's-edge group. Applicable to examinations commenced after 2007, the FTB is allowed to apply discretion in deciding when to conduct a detailed examination of a water's-edge taxpayer's returns for noncompliance issues, including transfer pricing, based on an analysis of all factors, including the relative levels of noncompliance and materiality. Previously, the FTB was mandated to conduct audits of all water's-edge taxpayers if there was the potential for noncompliance. (Sec. 25112, Rev. & Tax. Code)

¶1312 Deductions for Interest and Contributions

Law: Secs. 24344, 24357 (CCH CALIFORNIA TAX REPORTS ¶10-815, 11-515).

Comparable Federal: Secs. 163, 170 (CCH U.S. MASTER TAX GUIDE ¶533, 1058—1071).

Adjustment of deductions for interest and contributions may be required where income is allocated within and without the State. (Sec. 24344, Rev. & Tax. Code; Sec. 24357, Rev. & Tax. Code)

The deduction for interest expense may be limited where income from interest or dividends is allocated outside California—see ¶1004 for details.

• *Limit on deduction for contributions*

As explained at ¶1014, the deduction for contributions is limited to 10% of the net income; this deduction may require adjustment in some cases where a portion of the total net income is allocated outside of California. The usual practice is to treat contributions as one of the deductions entering into the computation of the net income from unitary operations that is subject to allocation within and without the state. If this is done where the total contributions exceed 10% of total net income (and the total deduction has been limited accordingly) and where all the income and deductions relate to the unitary operations, the adjustment of the effective contributions deduction to 10% of the net income used as the measure of the tax is automatic. On the other hand, in a case where the total contributions amount to less than 10% of the net income allocated to California, there is no problem of limitation of the deduction. Under some other circumstances, however, the contributions deduction may require special treatment to limit the deduction to 10% of the net income that is used as the measure of the tax after allocation. (Sec. 24357, Rev. & Tax. Code)

¶1313 Allocation and Apportionment—Administration

Law: Secs. 25101, 25106.5; Regs. 25106.5, 25106.5-11, 18 CCR (CCH CALIFORNIA TAX REPORTS ¶11-520, 11-540, 11-550).

Comparable Federal: None.

California Forms: Sch. R (Apportionment and Allocation of Income).

The return form contains a separate schedule (Schedule R) for allocation of income, with instructions for its use. The schedule provides for the use of the allocation formula described above.

• *Information required from affiliated group*

Where an affiliated group of corporations is involved, the taxpayer is required by the Franchise Tax Board (FTB) to submit information regarding income and business of the group. (Sec. 25106.5, Rev. & Tax. Code: Reg. 25106.5, 18 CCR, Reg. 25106.5-11, 18 CCR) The information submitted should include, in columnar form, profit and loss statements, a combined apportionment formula disclosing for each corporation the total amount of property, payroll, and sales and the amount of California property, payroll, and sales, and schedules disclosing for each corporation:

— the various adjustments necessary to convert the combined profit and loss statement to the combined income subject to apportionment;

— any items of nonbusiness income or expense allocated to California;

— computations of the amount of the interest offset and the charitable contributions adjustment;

— the alternative minimum tax calculation;

— information required by Form 100; and

— the computation of income apportionable and allocable to California and the computation of each member's tax credits and tax liability.

The combined apportionment schedule must reflect the elimination of intercompany sales and other intercompany revenue items, intercompany rent charges, intercompany dividends, and intercompany profits in inventories, if any.

• *Corporations separate entities for some purposes*

Despite the combined reporting approach discussed above, members of the combined group are treated as separate entities for some purposes. Thus, elections to report sales on the installment basis or to use the completed-contract method of accounting should be made individually for each corporation involved. Use of accelerated depreciation methods is based upon the experience of individual group members. (Reg. 25106.5, 18 CCR)

• *Instruction booklet available*

A booklet entitled "Guidelines for Corporations Filing a Combined Report" (FTB Pub. 1061) is available from the FTB. It outlines the rules and schedule format to be followed in preparing such reports.

• *Filing of single combined return*

The FTB permits taxpayers to elect to file one combined return for all the corporations in a unitary group, in lieu of separate returns for each corporation. The parent, or other designated "key" corporation, files the return and pays the entire tax. If the parent corporation is not a California taxpayer, the key corporation should be the taxpayer with the largest value of assets in California. The election is made on Schedule R-7 (part of Sch. R). Each corporation included in the group return must satisfy the following conditions:

— be a taxpayer required to file a return in this state;

— be a member of a single unitary group for the entire taxable year; and

— have the same taxable year as the key corporation or a taxable year that is wholly included within the taxable year of the key corporation, and have the same statutory filing date as the key corporation for the taxable year.

(Reg. 25106.5, 18 CCR)

• *Separate returns for group members*

If a unitary group does not elect the combined-return procedure, a separate return must be filed for each subject corporation. Each such return should carry a notation stating that a combined report has been filed and referring to the inclusion of the necessary supporting schedules in the return of the appropriate corporation. The return of each corporation should reflect the tax on the income allocated to that corporation in the supporting schedules; or, alternatively, the minimum tax may be assessed on all returns except one, and the balance of the entire tax of the affiliated group assessed on the return of one of the group. (Reg. 25106.5, 18 CCR)

• *Reporting should be consistent*

Once a determination has been made as to whether the income should be reported on a combined basis or by separate accounting, the returns should thereafter be prepared on the agreed basis until conditions change so that the method is no longer proper. (Reg. 25106.5, 18 CCR)

TAXES ON CORPORATE INCOME

CHAPTER 14
ADMINISTRATION, DEFICIENCIES, REFUNDS

¶1401 Administration of Tax—General

Law: Sec. 10286, Public Contracts Code; Secs. 18624-25, 19376, 19501-04.7, 19525, 19530, 19717, 21001-26, Rev. & Tax. Code (CCH CALIFORNIA TAX REPORTS ¶10-015, 89-054—89-060, 89-064, 89-068, 89-222).

Comparable Federal: Secs. 6107, 6109, 7430, 7811 (CCH U.S. MASTER TAX GUIDE ¶2517, 2707, 2796).

Same as personal income tax (¶701).

• *Expatriate corporations*

California state agencies are prohibited from entering into contracts with publicly held expatriate corporations, or any of their subsidiaries, if the corporations have reincorporated overseas in countries in which they have no substantial business activities to avoid paying their fair share of California corporation franchise and/or income taxes. Exceptions apply if the taxpayer was an expatriate corporation before 2004 and provides adequate shareholder protections and uses worldwide combined reporting or if the state has a compelling public interest to contract with the corporation. (Sec. 10286, Public Contracts Code)

¶1402 Taxpayers' Bill of Rights

Law: Secs. 19225, 21001-28 (CCH CALIFORNIA TAX REPORTS ¶89-222).

Comparable Federal: Sec. 7811 (CCH U.S. MASTER TAX GUIDE ¶2707).

Taxpayers dealing with the Franchise Tax Board (FTB) are given a wide range of protections under the "Katz-Harris Taxpayers' Bill of Rights." The provisions contained in the "Bill of Rights" govern the FTB's administration of both the personal income and corporation franchise and income taxes. (Sec. 21001 et seq., Rev. & Tax. Code)

• *Suspension of corporate powers*

The FTB may not suspend a taxpayer's corporate powers for failure to pay taxes, penalties, or interest, or for failure to file required returns or statements, without mailing the taxpayer a written notice of the suspension at least 60 days in advance. The notice must indicate the date on which the suspension will occur and the statute under which the action is being taken. (Sec. 21020, Rev. & Tax. Code)

• *Hearing and appeal procedures*

Protest hearings before the FTB's audit or legal staff must be held at times and places that are reasonable and convenient to the taxpayer. Prior to the hearing, the taxpayer must be informed of the right to have an attorney, accountant, or other agent present. Hearings may be recorded only with prior notice, and the taxpayer is entitled to receive a copy of any such recording. Further information on protest hearings is at ¶1403.

Taxpayers who appeal to the State Board of Equalization (SBE) and who are successful may be awarded reimbursement for reasonable fees and expenses related to the appeal that were incurred after the date of the notice of proposed deficiency assessment. The decision to make such an award is discretionary with the SBE, which must determine, in ruling upon a reimbursement claim filed with the SBE, whether action taken by the FTB's staff was unreasonable and, in particular, whether the FTB has established that its position in the appeal was substantially justified. Fees may be awarded in excess of the fees paid or incurred if the fees paid or incurred are less than reasonable fees. (Sec. 21013, Rev. & Tax. Code)

For appeals to the SBE from an action of the FTB on a deficiency assessment protest or refund claim, the burden of proving the correctness of certain items of income reported by third parties on information returns filed with the FTB also shifts to the FTB if the taxpayer asserts a reasonable dispute with respect to the reported amounts and fully cooperates with the FTB. The items of income to which the shift applies are the same as under federal law.

Further information on appeals to the SBE is at ¶1404 and ¶1416. (Sec. 21024, Rev. & Tax. Code)

• *Tax levy protections*

The FTB is generally required to send a notice of levy to a taxpayer at least 30 days prior to issuing a levy for unpaid tax. Also, if the FTB holds the collection of unpaid tax in abeyance for more than six months, the FTB must mail the taxpayer an additional notice prior to issuing a levy. If a taxpayer requests an independent administrative review within the 30-day period, the levy action will be suspended until 15 days after there is a final determination in the review. (Sec. 21015.5, Rev. & Tax. Code)

Except in the case of property seized as a result of a jeopardy assessment, a previously issued tax levy must be released whenever the following occur:

— the state's expenses in selling the property levied upon would exceed the taxpayer's liability;

— the proceeds of the sale would not result in a reasonable reduction of the taxpayer's debt;

— the levy was not issued in accordance with administrative procedures;

— the release of the levy will facilitate the collection of the tax liability or will be in the best interest of the taxpayer and the State; or

— the FTB otherwise deems the release of the levy appropriate.

(Sec. 21016, Rev. & Tax. Code) Certain goods are exempt from levy under California's Code of Civil Procedure; the taxpayer must be notified in writing of these exemptions prior to the sale of any seized property. (Sec. 21017, Rev. & Tax. Code)

• *Civil actions against the FTB; litigation costs*

Taxpayers aggrieved by the reckless disregard of the FTB's published procedures on the part of an officer or employee of the FTB may bring a Superior Court action against the State for actual damages. In determining damages, the court must take into consideration any contributing negligence on the taxpayer's part. A taxpayer prevailing in such an action is entitled to reasonable litigation costs, but there is a penalty of up to $10,000 for filing frivolous claims. (Sec. 21021, Rev. & Tax. Code)

A taxpayer may also file a civil action against the State for direct economic damages and costs totaling up to $50,000 if an officer or employee of the FTB intentionally entices an attorney, certified public accountant, or tax preparer representing the taxpayer into disclosing taxpayer information in exchange for a compromise or settlement of the representative's tax liability. However, the action is not allowed if the information was conveyed by the taxpayer to the representative for the purpose of perpetuating a fraud or crime. The action must be brought within two years after the date the activities creating the liability were discoverable by the exercise of reasonable care. (Sec. 21022, Rev. & Tax. Code)

Practitioner Comment: Taxpayer is Reimbursed Litigation Costs by California

On August 15, 2005, the California Court of Appeal, Fourth Appellate District, ruled in an uncitable decision that taxpayers were entitled to recover attorney fees incurred in litigation contesting the California FTB's denial of their California personal income tax refund claim. According to the Court, the FTB's position in the litigation was not substantially justified, so reimbursement of the taxpayers' attorney fees incurred during the trial, as well as the fees associated with filing the initial refund claim, participating in settlement negotiations, and opposing the FTB's motion for summary judgment was appropriate. The Court also ruled however, that the lower court acted within its discretion in denying reimbursement for (1) attorney fees incurred in filing an unsuccessful cross-motion for summary judgment and (2) amounts billed the attorneys for outside paralegal services. (*Milhous v. Franchise Tax Board*, California Court of Appeal, Fourth Appellate District, No. D044362, August 15, 2005, CCH CALIFORNIA TAX REPORTS ¶403-845)

The holding in *Milhous* makes it clear that while the FTB's position does not have to be a winning one, it does have to be justified. The Court stated, "..there is no basis upon which the FTB could attribute the lump sum payment the Milhouses received (at the close of the sale and before the buyers had control of the business) to capital in this state . . . .there was a good deal which undermined the FTB's position that income from the covenant was attributable to activities in this state. In particular, we note the quantum of evidence in the record which demonstrated that the covenant had no value in California because as a practical matter it was not possible to compete here."

Taxpayers should keep in mind that even if they prevail against the FTB, they still must exhaust all administrative remedies and they bear the burden of proving the FTB's position is not "substantially justified".

Attorney fees were also awarded to taxpayers in *American General Realty Investment Corp. v. Franchise Tax Board*, San Francisco Sup. Court, No. CGC-03-425690, April 28,

2005, CCH CALIFORNIA TAX REPORTS ¶403-794, and *Fujitsu IT Holdings, Inc. v. Franchise Tax Board*, California Court of Appeal, First Appellate District, No. A102550, July 7, 2004, CCH CALIFORNIA TAX REPORTS ¶403-655.

Bruce Daigh, Chris Whitney, Contributing Editors

• *Reliance on FTB written opinions; taxpayers' remedies*

Under certain circumstances, taxpayers may be relieved of penalties, interest, or tax liability itself when the taxpayers relied to their detriment on written rulings from the FTB. (Sec. 21019, Rev. & Tax. Code)

The discussion at ¶703 generally applies to corporate taxpayers, with some differences regarding requests for advance rulings. The FTB will not issue advance rulings to corporate taxpayers under the following circumstances (FTB Notice No. 89-277, CCH CALIFORNIA TAX REPORTS ¶89-222.402):

— the question is of a type that the IRS has announced it will not rule on in advance (*e.g.*, hypothetical questions, alternative plans of proposed transactions);

— the taxpayer's name or identifying number is omitted from the request;

— the requester is a professional preparer or taxpayer representative who has not provided the FTB with his or her own legal analysis and conclusion;

— the law is already clear or is the same as federal law;

— the question is primarily one of fact (*e.g.*, whether a business is unitary);

— the issue arises in an ongoing audit, appeal, or protest involving the requesting taxpayer; or

— the issue is currently pending in an appeal or court decision.

Also, see ¶712 for a discussion of the Taxpayers' Rights Advocate's authority to abate penalties, interest, and additions to tax under specified circumstances.

• *Tax liens*

A taxpayer is entitled to preliminary notice of the proposed filing or recording of a tax lien, mailed at least 30 days beforehand; in the interim, the taxpayer may prevent the filing or recording by presenting substantial evidence that the lien would be in error. Also, the FTB must notify taxpayers in writing of the filing or recording of a notice of state tax lien at least five business days after the date the notice of lien is filed. The FTB must mail the taxpayer an additional notice prior to filing or recording a notice of state tax lien if the FTB has held the collection of unpaid tax in abeyance for more than six months. An independent administrative review with the FTB is available if the taxpayer makes a request within the 15-day period beginning on the day after the five-day period described above. (Sec. 21015.5, Rev. & Tax. Code; Sec. 21019, Rev. & Tax. Code)

The FTB must mail a release to the taxpayer and the lien recorder within seven working days if it finds that its action was in error. The FTB may also release a lien if it determines that the release will facilitate the collection of tax or will be in the best interest of the taxpayer and the State.

• *Reimbursement of third-party charges and fees*

A taxpayer may be reimbursed for third-party charges and fees assessed against the taxpayer as a result of an erroneous levy, erroneous processing action, or erroneous collection action by the FTB. The charges and fees that may be reimbursed are limited to the usual and customary charges and fees imposed by a business entity in the ordinary course of business. (Sec. 21018, Rev. & Tax. Code)

• *Unassociated payments*

If the FTB receives a payment from a taxpayer that the FTB cannot associate with the taxpayer's account, the FTB must make reasonable efforts to notify the taxpayer of this situation within 60 days after receipt of the payment. (Sec. 21025, Rev. & Tax. Code)

• *Annual notice of tax delinquencies*

The FTB must mail an annual notice to each taxpayer who has a delinquent tax account, indicating the amount of the delinquency as of the date of the notice, unless a previously mailed notice has been returned to the FTB as undeliverable or the account has been discharged from accountability. (Sec. 21026, Rev. & Tax. Code)

• *Client/tax practitioner communications*

California conforms until January 1, 2009, to the federal IRS Restructuring and Reform Act of 1998 provision extending the lawyer-client privilege to communications between clients and federally authorized tax practitioners with respect to noncriminal tax matters before the FTB, the SBE, or the Employment Development Department. (Sec. 21028, Rev. & Tax. Code)

• *Other provisions*

The Taxpayers' Bill of Rights also requires the FTB to undertake extensive taxpayer education and information programs; report annually to the legislature concerning areas of noncompliance with the tax laws; develop simplified written statements of taxpayer rights and FTB procedures; develop and implement an employee and officer evaluation program; and draw up plans to reduce the time required to resolve amended return claims for refunds, protests, and appeals. As under the personal income tax law (¶723), the FTB is authorized to settle certain civil tax disputes. FTB officers and employees are prohibited from authorizing, requiring, or conducting the investigation or surveillance of taxpayers for reasons unrelated to tax administration.

¶1403 Deficiencies—Procedure, Protests

Law: Secs. 19031-34, 19036-51, 19054, 19057-58, 19064-67, 19087 (CCH CALIFORNIA TAX REPORTS ¶89-164, 89-228, 89-240).

Comparable Federal: Secs. 6211-13, 6501, 7609 (CCH U.S. MASTER TAX GUIDE ¶2709, 2711, 2726, 2778).

Same as personal income tax (¶704).

¶1404 Deficiencies—Appeal to State Board of Equalization

Law: Secs. 19045-48 (CCH CALIFORNIA TAX REPORTS ¶89-234).

Comparable Federal: Secs. 6211-13 (CCH U.S. MASTER TAX GUIDE ¶2711, 2778, 2838).

Same as personal income tax (¶705).

The California State Board of Equalization (SBE) has taken the position that a nonqualified foreign corporation may file an appeal with the SBE to determine the corporation's California tax filing requirements and appropriate tax liability. However, the case will be dismissed if the SBE determines that the nonqualified foreign corporation transacted intrastate business in California and, therefore, should have obtained a certificate of qualification from the California Secretary of State (*Reitman Atlantic Corp.* (2001) (CCH CALIFORNIA TAX REPORTS ¶2-020.30). A domestic corporation that has had its corporation powers suspended is ineligible to initiate an appeal before the SBE.

¶1405 Final Assessment of Deficiency

Law: Secs. 19042, 19049 (CCH CALIFORNIA TAX REPORTS ¶89-228).

Comparable Federal: Secs. 6155, 6213 (CCH U.S. MASTER TAX GUIDE ¶2711, 2778).

Same as personal income tax (¶706).

¶1406 Jeopardy Assessments

Law: Secs. 19081-86 (CCH CALIFORNIA TAX REPORTS ¶89-168).

Comparable Federal: Secs. 6861, 6863 (CCH U.S. MASTER TAX GUIDE ¶2713).

Same as personal income tax (¶707).

¶1407 Bankruptcy and Receiverships

Law: Sec. 19088 (CCH CALIFORNIA TAX REPORTS ¶89-170).

Comparable Federal: Secs. 6871-73 (CCH U.S. MASTER TAX GUIDE ¶2736).

Same as personal income tax (¶708).

¶1408 Transferee Liability

Law: Secs. 19071-74 (CCH CALIFORNIA TAX REPORTS ¶89-166).

Comparable Federal: Secs. 6901-04 (CCH U.S. MASTER TAX GUIDE ¶2745, 2782).

The law contains provisions permitting assessment and collection of tax from persons secondarily liable. The period of limitations is extended for assessments against transferees and fiduciaries. California law is the same as federal law. (Sec. 19071 et seq., Rev. & Tax. Code)

Both California and federal laws provide for suspension of the running of the period of limitations against the transferee while the taxpayer is exercising an administrative remedy.

¶1409 Statute of Limitations on Assessments

Law: Secs. 18572, 19057-67, 19255, 19755 (CCH CALIFORNIA TAX REPORTS ¶89-144).

Comparable Federal: Secs. 1311-14, 6501-4, 7508A, 7609 (CCH U.S. MASTER TAX GUIDE ¶2726, 2735, 2736, 2756).

Same as personal income tax, as explained at ¶710, except that the corporation tax law extends the limitation period under certain circumstances as to transferees and fiduciaries whereas the personal income tax law does not. The running of the statute of limitations is also suspended until a taxpayer reports required information to the FTB concerning foreign corporations or transfers to foreign persons (see ¶1414 for a discussion of the reporting requirements). (Sec. 18572, Rev. & Tax. Code; Sec. 19057 et seq., Rev. & Tax. Code; Sec. 19255 Rev. & Tax. Code; Sec. 19755, Rev. & Tax. Code)

California law has no provision for a shortened period of limitations for dissolving corporations; federal law does.

Practitioner Comment: Relying on Federal Waiver of Statute of Limitations Can Create a Trap for the Unwary

A waiver to extend the federal statute of limitations for a consolidated return does not extend the California statute of limitations for foreign affiliates that were included in the California combined return but excluded from the federal consolidated return. (Uncitable Summary Decision, *Appeal of Magnetek, Inc.*, SBE, No. 198051 (2004) CCH CALIFORNIA TAX REPORTS ¶89-224.83) This decision highlights the fact that there are often significant differences between the composition of a California combined report and a federal consolidated return. Although the California statute provides that a federal waiver extends the California statute of limitations, it only does so for the specific entities covered by the federal waiver.

A separate California waiver would be required for any California taxpayers that aren't included in the federal consolidated return (*e.g.*, taxpayers owned more than 50% and less than 80%, brother/sister corporations directly owned by a foreign parent, etc.).

Bruce Daigh, Chris Whitney, Contributing Editors

¶1410 Interest on Deficiencies

Law: Secs. 19101, 19104, 19108, 19109, 19112-14, 19120, 19521, 19777-78 (CCH CALIFORNIA TAX REPORTS ¶89-192, 89-204).

Comparable Federal: Secs. 6404, 6601, 6621 (CCH U.S. MASTER TAX GUIDE ¶2813, 2838).

Interest is charged on deficiencies, other delinquent payments of tax, and on extensions of payment of tax and penalties. (Sec. 19101, Rev. & Tax. Code) The rules are generally the same as for the personal income tax, as outlined at ¶711. However, there is a special higher interest rate applicable to large corporate underpayments (see below).

Interest rates are as follows:

January 1, 2005—June 30, 2005	4%
July 1, 2005—December 31, 2005	5%
January 1, 2006—June 30, 2006	6%
July 1, 2006—December 31, 2006	7%
January 1, 2007—June 30, 2007	8%
July 1, 2007—December 31, 2007	8%
January 1, 2008—June 30, 2008	8%
July 1, 2008—December 31, 2008	7%
January 1, 2009—June 30, 2009	5%

The rate is determined semiannually and compounded daily, as explained at ¶711.

Both federal and California law allow the abatement of all or any portion of interest that results from errors or delays in the performance of ministerial acts by the respective taxing agencies, as explained at ¶711. (Sec. 19104, Rev. & Tax. Code) Abatement of interest is also available to victims of disasters, also discussed at ¶711. (Sec. 19109, Rev. & Tax. Code)

There is a special rule that applies to certain cases involving related items where overpayments are offset against deficiencies. In such cases, no interest is charged on the portion of the deficiency extinguished by the credit for overpayment for the period subsequent to the date the overpayment was made. (Sec. 19108, Rev. & Tax. Code)

• *Interest on large corporate underpayments*

Both California and federal law require all corporations except S corporations to pay interest on large underpayments at 2% above the regular rate. A large underpayment is one that exceeds $100,000 for any taxable period. Under federal law, the 2% interest rate increase generally applies to periods after the 30th day following the date the IRS sends either a "30-day letter" or a deficiency notice, whichever is earlier. California modifies this provision so that the increased interest rate applies to periods after the 30th day following either the date on which a proposed assessment is issued or the date when the notice and demand is sent, whichever is earlier. (Sec. 19521, Rev. & Tax. Code)

Under both California and federal law, interest does not begin to accrue until after the mailing of a letter or notice of deficiency, proposed deficiency, assessment, or proposed assessment shows an amount exceeding $100,000. FTB Notice 98-6 (1998) addresses the calculation of the additional interest imposed against unitary corporate members filing a group return (see CCH CALIFORNIA TAX REPORTS ¶89-202.451).

¶1411 Penalties

Law: Secs. 18631.7, 19131-36, 19141-41.6, 19164, 19166-69, 19176-81, 19183, 19187, 19254, 19262, 19442, 19701-06, 19708-15, 19719-21, 19730-38, 19772-4, 19775.5, 21015, 23186 (CCH CALIFORNIA TAX REPORTS ¶10-059, 89-192, 89-206—89-210).

Comparable Federal: Secs. 6050I, 6651-53, 6657-58, 6662-65, 6673, 6694, 6700-03, 6706, 6721-24, 7201-06 (CCH U.S. MASTER TAX GUIDE ¶510, 537, 625, 2011, 2145, 2518, 2521, 2579, 2801, 2805, 2811, 2814, 2816, 2823, 2833, 2854, 2856, 2858, 2860, 2862, 2866).

California Form: FTB 2300 BE (Franchise and Income Tax Amnesty Application - for Business Entities).

[*NOTE:* See ¶1402 for a discussion of possible relief after detrimental reliance on advice from the Franchise Tax Board (FTB).]

Same as personal income tax, including the amnesty program, as explained at ¶712, except as noted below.

The corporation tax law does not include provisions for the penalties listed at items (1), (2), (7), and (15) at ¶712.

The corporation tax law contains provisions similar to those described at items (29), (30), (31), (32), and (33) at ¶712, but the possible fines are higher, reaching a maximum of $200,000. Similarly, the maximum fine for the penalty described at item (43) at ¶712, may reach a maximum of $100,000 for corporate taxpayers.

For purposes of the accuracy-related penalty imposed under item (10) at ¶712 for substantial understatements, a substantial understatement exists for a corporation, other than an S corporation, if the amount of the understatement for the taxable year exceeds the lesser of: (1) 10% of the tax required to be shown on the return for the taxable year (or, if greater, $2,500), or (2) $5 million. For all other taxpayers, a substantial understatement exists if the amount of the understatement exceeds the greater of (1) 10% of the tax required to be shown on the return, or (2) $10,000. (Sec. 19164, Rev. & Tax. Code)

For purposes of the enhanced penalty for substantial underpayments, the "excess" is determined without regard to items to which the reportable transaction accuracy-related penalty or the noneconomic substance transaction understatement penalty is imposed. (Sec. 19164, Rev. & Tax. Code)

The corporation tax law provides the following penalties in addition to those described at ¶712 :

(1) failing without reasonable cause to file return if corporation is doing business in the state without being qualified—$2,000 per taxable year (Sec. 19135, Rev. & Tax. Code);

(2) failing to file corporate organization statement—$250 ($50 for nonprofit corporation) (Sec. 19141, Rev. & Tax. Code);

(3) failing to furnish information concerning foreign-controlled corporation—$10,000 per year of failure (Sec. 19141.5, Rev. & Tax. Code);

(4) failing to furnish information concerning transfers to foreign persons—25% of gain on transaction (Sec. 19141.5, Rev. & Tax. Code);

(5) failing to report transactions between foreign corporations and foreign investors—$10,000 per year of failure (Sec. 19141.5, Rev. & Tax. Code);

(6) failing to keep water's edge records—$10,000 per year; if 90 days after notice by the FTB, $10,000 per 30-day period (Sec. 19141.6, Rev. & Tax. Code);

(7) failing to file copy of federal information return concerning large cash transactions—$50 per return, up to $100,000 maximum per year; if intentional

disregard, $100 per return, or, if greater, 5% of the aggregate amount of items required to be reported (Sec. 19183, Rev. & Tax. Code);

(8) failing to provide information that is required to determine rate of bank and franchise tax—$5,000 and disallowance of specified deductions (Sec. 23186, Rev. & Tax. Code); and

(9) exercising the powers of a corporation suspended for nonpayment of taxes or transacting interstate business of a forfeited foreign corporation—misdemeanor; $250 to $1,000 and/or up to one year in jail (however, the penalty does not apply to any insurer, or counsel retained by an insurer, who provides a defense for a suspended or forfeited corporation in a civil action for personal injury, property damage, or economic losses, and who prosecutes, in conjunction with that defense, any subrogation, contribution, or indemnity rights against other persons or entities in the name of the suspended or forfeited corporation) (Sec. 19179, Rev. & Tax. Code).

CCH Caution: Large Underpayment

Business entities that underpay their tax liability by more than $1 million for any taxable year are subject to a 20% underpayment penalty, in addition to any other penalty that may be imposed. Taxpayers required or allowed to be included in a combined report must aggregate the group members' underpayments for purposes of determining whether the $1 million threshold has been reached. The penalty applies retroactively to each taxable year beginning after 2002, for which the statute of limitations on assessment has not expired. However, taxpayers will have until March 1, 2009, to report and pay outstanding taxes in order to avoid the imposition of this penalty. The Revenue and Taxation Code provisions governing deficiency assessment notices and hearing rights are inapplicable to the assessment and collection of this penalty. Furthermore, credits and refunds of the penalty are limited to the amount improperly calculated by the FTB. (Sec. 19138, Rev. & Tax. Code)

Practitioner Comment: Limited Safe Harbors Exist with Respect to the Newly Enacted 20% Penalty for Large Corporate Underpayments

As noted above, S.B. X1 28, signed into law on October 1, 2008, imposes a new 20% penalty applicable to corporate franchise tax understatements in excess of $1 million for taxable years beginning on or after January 1, 2003. The new penalty applies in addition to other penalties (e.g., accuracy related, noneconomic substance transaction, underpayment penalties etc). There is no reasonable cause exception to the penalty, although the penalty will not be applied for tax years beginning before January 1, 2008, to the extent the tax is paid with an amended return filed on or before May 31, 2009. Otherwise the penalty will apply unless attributable to a change in law (including regulation changes and rulings) that becomes final after the taxpayer has timely filed its return or if the taxpayer reasonably relied on a Chief Counsel Ruling. Thus, while an amnesty program was not enacted as part of the 2008 budget legislation, the 20% penalty can be avoided if taxes relating to years prior to 2008 are paid by the end of May 2009. Unlike the 2005 amnesty program, however, there is no ability to avoid the penalty by making a tax deposit. Instead the FTB has indicated that an amended return disclosing the nature of the adjustments would need to be filed and the taxes paid by May 31, 2009, to avoid the penalty. Taxpayers may claim a refund after May 31, 2009, for amounts paid with those amended returns.

Bruce Daigh, Chris Whitney, Contributing Editors

See ¶811 for penalties imposed for late filing of returns of exempt organizations.

A penalty for the failure to file a federal information return regarding large cash transactions is imposed in accordance with federal law. (Sec. 19183, Rev. & Tax. Code)

• *Penalties imposed under Corporations Code*

The corporation tax law imposes a penalty of $250 for failure to file with the Secretary of State an annual statement required by California Corporations Code Sec. 1502 (¶810). The tax law also imposes a penalty of $50 for failure of a nonprofit corporation to file with the Secretary of State a statement required by Sec. 6210, Corp. Code, or Sec. 8210, Corp. Code (¶811). (Sec. 19141, Rev. & Tax. Code)

• *Collection and filing enforcement fees*

Collection and filing enforcement fees similar to those discussed at ¶712 are imposed under the corporation tax law, but the applicable fees for the state's 2008—2009 fiscal year are $352 and $203, respectively. The fees do not apply to exempt organizations.

• *Relief from penalties*

Relief from the penalties listed in items (3), (4), and (5), above, may be granted, provided that the taxpayer's failure to furnish the required information neither jeopardized the best interests of the state nor resulted from the taxpayer's willful neglect or an intent not to comply. (Sec. 21015, Rev. & Tax. Code)

• *Cases and rulings*

Appeal of BSR USA, Ltd., and BSR North America, Ltd. (1996) (CCH CALIFORNIA TAX REPORTS ¶89-206.6191) involved the imposition of the 25% penalty for failure to furnish information on notice and demand by the FTB. The corporate taxpayers failed to respond to repeated requests by the FTB for information concerning the income and apportionment factors of the taxpayers' foreign affiliates. The penalty was not subject to abatement, because the taxpayers' conduct indicated a pattern of delay and misdirection that belied their contention that the requested information was either not available or too costly to obtain.

In *Appeal of Vidal Sassoon, Inc.* (1986) (CCH CALIFORNIA TAX REPORTS ¶89-206.24), the reasonable cause exception was not applicable to late extension requests and the State Board of Equalization (SBE) upheld the late-filing penalty.

In *Appeal of Krofft Entertainment, Inc.* (1984) (CCH CALIFORNIA TAX REPORTS ¶89-206.74), the taxpayer claimed that its failure to file a timely franchise tax return was due to reasonable cause. The SBE upheld the imposition of a $17,436 penalty, despite the fact that the Internal Revenue Service had removed a similar federal penalty upon a finding of reasonable cause.

In *Appeal of Avco Financial Services, Inc.* (1979) (CCH CALIFORNIA TAX REPORTS ¶89-206.48), a late payment penalty was imposed in a case where 84% of the tax was paid by the regular due date. The SBE upheld the penalty, noting that the difficulty of estimating the tax on worldwide income did not constitute reasonable cause for the underpayment. To the same effect, see *Appeal of Diebold, Incorporated* (1983) (CCH CALIFORNIA TAX REPORTS ¶89-206.773); in this case, the taxpayer's extensive operations required the filing of approximately 350 state and local tax returns.

¶1412 Information at Source

Law: Secs. 18631, 18639-44, 18648-49 (CCH CALIFORNIA TAX REPORTS ¶89-104).

Comparable Federal: Secs. 6041, 6041A, 6042, 6050I, 6050L (CCH U.S. MASTER TAX GUIDE ¶2565, 2607).

Same as personal income tax (¶713).

¶1413 Withholding of Tax at Source

Law: Secs. 18661-62, 18665, 18667-77, 19009 (CCH CALIFORNIA TAX REPORTS ¶12-705, 89-056, 89-176).

Comparable Federal: Secs. 1441, 1445 (CCH U.S. MASTER TAX GUIDE ¶2442, 2492).

The corporation tax law gives the Franchise Tax Board broad power to require the withholding of tax on payments to payees subject to either franchise or income tax. (Sec. 18661, Rev. & Tax. Code; Sec. 18662, Rev. & Tax. Code) Withholding of tax is required on income paid to corporations that do not have a permanent place of business in this state. A corporation has a permanent place of business in this state if it is organized under the laws of this state or if it is a foreign corporation qualified to transact business in this state.

Corporations, among others, are required to withhold tax on certain payments to nonresidents, to withhold amounts due from delinquent taxpayers, to withhold tax on dispositions of California real estate, and to withhold tax from wages (¶714, ¶715, ¶716).

¶1414 Reports on Foreign and Foreign-Owned Corporations, Transfers to Foreign Persons

Law: Secs. 19141.2, 19141.5, 21015 (CCH CALIFORNIA TAX REPORTS ¶89-104).

Comparable Federal: Secs. 6038, 6038A, 6038B, 6038C (CCH U.S. MASTER TAX GUIDE ¶2466, 2491A, 2565).

Corporations that are incorporated in California or doing business in the state and that are more than 25% foreign owned must file a copy of the information return required by IRC Sec. 6038A (federal Form 5472) with respect to transactions with related parties. Special record-keeping requirements are also imposed. Failure to comply subjects a corporation to a $10,000 penalty. (Sec. 19141.5, Rev. & Tax. Code)

In addition, California has adopted the information reporting requirements of IRC Secs. 6038B and 6038C. However, California does not incorporate the penalty imposed under IRC Sec. 6038B against a person that fails to notify the Franchise Tax Board (FTB) regarding a transfer of property to a foreign partnership in exchange for a partnership interest. IRC Sec. 6038B requires the filing of information returns with respect to certain transfers of property to foreign corporations and other foreign persons and, in cases of failure to report, imposes a penalty equal to 25% of the amount of gain realized on the exchange. IRC Sec. 6038C requires foreign corporations engaged in U.S. business to file information returns and imposes a $10,000 penalty for noncompliance.

Relief from these penalties may be granted, provided that the taxpayer's failure to furnish the required information neither jeopardized the best interests of the state nor resulted from the taxpayer's willful neglect or an intent not to comply. (Sec. 21015, Rev. & Tax. Code)

Domestic corporations subject to California corporation franchise or income tax that own more than 50% of the combined voting power, or the value, of all classes of stock of a foreign corporation are required to file with the FTB a copy of the information return required by IRC Sec. 6038 with respect to interests in a foreign corporation (federal Form 5471). If a taxpayer fails to comply without reasonable cause and not due to willful neglect, the taxpayer is subject to a penalty equal to $1,000 for each annual accounting period in which the information is not supplied and an additional $1,000 for each 30-day period (or fraction thereof) beyond the first 90 days, up to a maximum penalty of $24,000. The penalty may be waived if (1) a copy of the information return is filed with the FTB within 90 days after notification and the taxpayer agrees to attach a copy of the information to the taxpayer's original return for subsequent taxable years or (2) the taxpayer enters into a voluntary disclosure agreement with the FTB (¶1422). (Sec. 19141.2, Rev. & Tax. Code)

¶1415 Overpayments and Refunds—Procedure

Law: Secs. 19301-24, 19331-35 (CCH CALIFORNIA TAX REPORTS ¶89-224).

Comparable Federal: Secs. 6401-08 (CCH U.S. MASTER TAX GUIDE ¶2759 et seq.).

California Form: Form 100X (Amended Corporation Franchise or Income Tax Return).

Same as personal income tax, as explained at ¶717, except that refund claims should be filed on Form 100X (Amended Corporation Franchise or Income Tax Return).

A corporation that overpays its tax under the estimated-tax procedure may obtain a refund before the return is filed (¶813).

¶1416 Refund Claims—Appeal to State Board of Equalization

Law: Secs. 19332-34 (CCH CALIFORNIA TAX REPORTS ¶89-234).

Same as personal income tax (¶718).

¶1417 Statute of Limitations on Refund Claims

Law: Secs. 19041.5, 19306-14, 19322.1 (CCH CALIFORNIA TAX REPORTS ¶89-224).

Comparable Federal: Secs. 6511, 7508A (CCH U.S. MASTER TAX GUIDE ¶2482, 2537, 2763).

Same as personal income tax, as explained at ¶719, except that the special seven-year rule (item (c)) does not apply to worthless securities losses. (Sec. 19041.5, Rev. & Tax. Code; Sec. 19306 et seq., Rev. & Tax. Code; Sec. 19322.1, Rev. & Tax. Code)

The law permits a barred refund of one taxpayer to be offset against a deficiency of an affiliated taxpayer in cases where the tax is determined on a combined basis as discussed at ¶1310. This provision also permits a similar offset where items of income or deductions have been transferred from one year to another. However, an offset will not be allowed in either case where more than seven years have elapsed from the due date of the return on which the overpayment is determined. (Sec. 19314, Rev. & Tax. Code)

¶1418 Suits for Refund

Law: Secs. 19041.5, 19381-92 (CCH CALIFORNIA TAX REPORTS ¶89-224).

Comparable Federal: Sec. 6532 (CCH U.S. MASTER TAX GUIDE ¶2738, 2792).

Same as personal income tax (¶720).

¶1419 Interest on Overpayments

Law: Secs. 19325, 19340-51, 19363, 19521 (CCH CALIFORNIA TAX REPORTS ¶89-204).

Comparable Federal: Sec. 6611 (CCH U.S. MASTER TAX GUIDE ¶2765).

The corporation tax rules for interest on overpayments are generally the same as for personal income tax, as explained at ¶722. The adjusted annual interest rate on overpayments of corporation franchise and income taxes is the lesser of 5% or the bond equivalent rate of a 13-week U.S. Treasury bill. (Sec. 19521, Rev. & Tax. Code)

Interest rates are as follows:

July 1, 2006—December 31, 2006	4%
January 1, 2007—June 30, 2007	5%
July 1, 2007—December 31, 2007	5%
January 1, 2008—June 30, 2008	5%
July 1, 2008—December 31, 2008	3%
January 1, 2009—June 30, 2009	2%

In *Appeal of MCA, Inc.* (1967) (CCH CALIFORNIA TAX REPORTS ¶89-202.57), the State Board of Equalization allowed interest on an overpayment of franchise tax although the Franchise Tax Board had contended that such interest was not payable because the overpayment was not made "incident to a bona fide and orderly discharge of an actual liability."

¶1420 Closing Agreements

Law: Secs. 19441-42 (CCH CALIFORNIA TAX REPORTS ¶89-186).

Comparable Federal: Sec. 7121 (CCH U.S. MASTER TAX GUIDE ¶2721).

Same as personal income tax (¶723).

¶1421 Compromise of Tax Liability

Law: Sec. 19443 (CCH CALIFORNIA TAX REPORTS ¶89-186).

Comparable Federal: Sec. 7122 (CCH U.S. MASTER TAX GUIDE ¶2723).

Same as personal income tax (¶724).

¶1422 Voluntary Disclosure Agreements

Laws: Secs. 19191-94 (CCH CALIFORNIA TAX REPORTS ¶89-186).

Comparable Federal: None.

California Form: FTB 4925 (Application for Voluntary Disclosure).

Same as personal income tax (¶725).

¶1423 Recovery of Erroneous Refunds

Law: Secs. 19054, 19368, 19411-13 (CCH CALIFORNIA TAX REPORTS ¶89-190).

Comparable Federal: Secs. 6532, 6602, 7405 (CCH U.S. MASTER TAX GUIDE ¶2738).

Same as personal income tax (¶726).

¶1424 Abusive Tax Shelters

Law: Secs. 18407, 18628, 18648, 19164, 19751-54 (CCH CALIFORNIA TAX REPORTS ¶89-102, 89-104, 89-206, 89-210).

Comparable Federal: Secs. 6011, 6111 (CCH U.S. MASTER TAX GUIDE ¶2001 et seq.).

Same as personal income tax (¶727).

Practitioner Comment: FTB Ruling Holds That Noneconomic Substance Tax Penalty Will Not Apply to Taxpayer Restructuring in Order to Meet IRC 355 Requirements

California imposes a noneconomic substance tax or "NEST" penalty on transactions lacking a "valid non-tax California business purpose." Since its enactment there has been significant uncertainty as to what constitutes a "non-tax California business purpose" and when the penalty might be applied. Taxpayers recently received some guidance in the case of a restructuring that was undertaken in an effort to qualify a distribution of subsidiary stock as tax free under California's adoption of IRC 355. Due to California's January 1, 2005 IRC conformity date, California continues to be out of conformity with 2006 federal amendments made to IRC Section 355(b) (3), see the Practitioner Comment at ¶517. The Franchise Tax Board in Chief Counsel Ruling 2007-3, July 17, 2007, held that a taxpayer's attempts to restructure in order to satisfy California's conformity to the IRC 355 provisions prior to the 2006 amendments, although having the effect of avoiding the imposition of California corporate franchise taxes, would not be regarded as a NEST transaction to which the penalties under RTC 19774 could be applied. In reaching this conclusion, the ruling observed that the IRS has consistently held that a taxpayer can engage in a tax-free structuring for the purpose of qualifying for the active business requirement under the pre-2006 version of IRC 355.

Bruce Daigh, Chris Whitney, Contributing Editors

PART V

SALES AND USE TAXES

CHAPTER 15

SALES AND USE TAXES

¶ 1501 Overview of Sales and Use Taxes

Law: Secs. 6025-31, 6051-51.5, 6201-01.5, 7200-12, 7251.1 (CCH CALIFORNIA TAX REPORTS ¶ 60-010, 60-020, 60-110, 61-720).

The California sales tax was first imposed in 1933; the use tax in 1935. These taxes, which are administered by the State Board of Equalization, have become a major source of the state's revenue.

The sales tax is imposed upon retailers for the privilege of selling tangible personal property at retail. (Sec. 6051, Rev. & Tax. Code) Although the tax is not levied directly on the consumer, it is ordinarily passed on to the consumer. The use tax, enacted as a complement to the sales tax, is imposed upon the storage, use, or other consumption in California of tangible personal property purchased from a retailer without being subjected to the sales tax. (Sec. 6202, Rev. & Tax. Code)

The sales or use tax payable in connection with any given transaction is the sum of three components: (1) the basic state sales and use tax, (2) the Bradley-Burns local tax, and (3) additional local "transactions and use" taxes, if any (¶ 1503).

¶ 1502 Imposition of Tax—Constitutional Limitations

Law: Secs. 2-4, Art. XIIIA, Cal. Constitution; Secs. 23027, 50075 et seq., Government Code; Sec. 99550, Public Utility Code (CCH CALIFORNIA TAX REPORTS ¶ 61-710).

Counties, cities, and special districts are prohibited from imposing "special taxes" (those levied to fund a specific governmental project or program) unless two-thirds of the local electorate approves. (Sec. 4, Art. XIIIA, Cal. Const.) In *Richard J. Rider et al. v. County of San Diego et al.* (1991) (CCH CALIFORNIA TAX REPORTS ¶ 61-710.46), the California Supreme Court invalidated a transactions and use tax imposed by the San Diego County Regional Justice Facility Financing Agency with the approval of a bare majority of the district's voters, because the agency was a "special district" and the tax it imposed was a "special tax."

The *Rider* court determined that the term "special district" includes any taxing agency created to raise funds for city or county purposes to replace revenues lost because of Proposition 13's restrictions on property taxation (see ¶1702 for a discussion of Proposition 13). Approval by a two-thirds vote was similarly required in *Howard Jarvis Taxpayers' Association et al. v. State Board of Equalization* (1993) (CCH CALIFORNIA TAX REPORTS ¶61-710.464) for any local sales and use tax imposed by a county justice facilities financing agency in Orange, Humboldt, Los Angeles, Riverside, San Bernardino, Stanislaus, or Ventura county.

In *Hoogasian Flowers, Inc., et al. v. State Board of Equalization* (1994) (CCH CALIFORNIA TAX REPORTS ¶61-730.39), a California court of appeal held that a local sales and use tax imposed by the San Francisco Educational Financing Authority for the general purpose of providing financial assistance to schools was invalid because it was not approved by two-thirds of the electorate voting on the measure, as required under *Rider.*

In *Santa Clara County Local Transportation Authority v. Carl Guardino et al.* (1995) (CCH CALIFORNIA TAX REPORTS ¶61-710.465), the California Supreme Court upheld a majority vote approval requirement for "general taxes" proposed by local governments. In 1996, California voters approved a measure that specifically prohibits *all* local governments, including charter cities, from imposing, extending, or increasing any general tax after November 5, 1996, without the approval of a majority of the local electorate.

¶1503 Rate of Tax

Law: Secs. 6025-31, 6051-51.5, 6201-01.5, 7200-12, 7251.1 (CCH CALIFORNIA TAX REPORTS ¶60-110, 61-735).

The sales or use tax payable in connection with any given transaction is the sum of three components: (1) the basic state sales and use tax, (2) the Bradley-Burns local tax, and (3) additional local transactions and use taxes, if any.

The basic state sales and use tax rate, which applies to all taxable transactions, is 6%. In addition, beginning July 1, 2004, an additional temporary 0.25% tax is imposed to repay state deficit financing bonds. (Secs. 6051, 6051.2, 6051.3, 6051.4, 6201, 6201.2, 6201.3, 6201.4, Rev. & Tax. Code)

The Bradley-Burns Uniform Local Sales and Use Tax Law authorizes counties to impose an additional 1.25% tax on all transactions that are subject to state sales and use taxes, and every California county does so. Accordingly, if a transaction is taxable at all, it is subject to a combined rate of at least 7.25%—the basic 6% state rate plus the 1.25% Bradley-Burns rate. (Sec. 7202, Rev. & Tax. Code) Effective July 1, 2004, the 1.25% rate is automatically reduced to 1.0% while the temporary 0.25% state tax increase is in effect. Consequently, the combined rate of 7.25% remains in effect.

State law also authorizes municipalities to impose local transactions and use taxes for various purposes. The per-county cap on combined transactions and use taxes is 2.0%. (Sec. 7251.1, Rev. & Tax. Code)

Sourcing rules.—For purposes of determining which local taxes apply to a transaction, all retail sales are deemed to occur at the place of business of the seller. This rule applies regardless of the physical location of the property sold and regardless of where title to the property passes to the buyer. (Sec. 7205, Rev. & Tax. Code) If a retailer has more than one place of business involved in a sale, the transaction is regarded as having taken place where the principal negotiations are carried on or where the order is taken. As long as title passes within the state, it is immaterial that it passes outside the taxing jurisdiction in which the retailer's business is located. (Regs. 1802, 1822, 18 CCR)

The place of sale of an out-of-state retailer that does not have a permanent place of business in this state, other than a stock of tangible personal property, is the place from which delivery or shipment is made. This rule also applies if a retailer has a permanent place of business in California if the sale is negotiated out-of-state and there is no participation in the sale by the retailer's permanent place of business in this state. (Regs. 1802, 1822, 18 CCR)

For transactions of $500,000 or more, if a seller is required to collect local use tax on a transaction the seller must report the local use tax revenues derived therefrom directly to the participating jurisdiction where the first functional use is made. Out-of-state businesses who voluntarily register with the state to collect use tax have the option of reporting such a transaction to the participating jurisdiction. (Reg. 1802, 18 CCR)

Special rules apply (1) to determine the place of use of leased vehicles for purposes of reporting and transmitting local use tax and (2) for sales of jet fuel. (Sec. 7205, Rev. & Tax Code; Sec. 7205.1, Rev. & Tax. Code)

California is a voting member of the Streamlined Sales Tax Project (SSTP) but has not yet enacted any conforming amendments. California will not sign onto the SSTP agreement unless the conditions outlined in Sec. 6029, Rev. & Tax. Code are satisfied. (Sec. 6025, Rev. & Tax. Code, et. seq.)

CCH Comment: City and County Tax Rates

For the latest tax rates in specific cities and counties, see http://www.boe.ca.gov/cgi-bin/rates.cgi. For the rates in effect as of October 2008, see below.

• *Local sales and use tax rates*

The following table indicates city and county tax rates. Special taxing jurisdiction tax rates are not listed. The tables are derived from information provided by the California State Board of Equalization (SBE) and are current as of October 2008. (Publication 71, California City and County Sales and Use Tax Rates, California State Board of Equalization, October 2008)

Local and district taxes collected within each county are reported on Form BOE-401-A2 (State, Local and District Sales and Use Tax Return) and Schedule A (Computation Schedule for District Tax).

City	Tax	County
Acampo	7.75%	San Joaquin
Acton	8.25%	Los Angeles
Adelaida	7.25%	San Luis Obispo
Adelanto*	7.75%	San Bernardino
Adin	7.25%	Modoc
Agoura Hills*	8.25%	Los Angeles
Agua Caliente	7.75%	Sonoma
Agua Caliente Springs	7.75%	San Diego
Agua Dulce	8.25%	Los Angeles
Aguanga	7.75%	Riverside
Ahwahnee	7.75%	Madera
Al Tahoe	7.25%	El Dorado
Alameda*	8.75%	Alameda
Alamo	8.25%	Contra Costa
Albany*	8.75%	Alameda
Alberhill (Lake Elsinore*)	7.75%	Riverside
Albion	7.25%	Mendocino
Alderpoint	7.25%	Humboldt
Alhambra*	8.25%	Los Angeles
Aliso Viejo*	7.75%	Orange
Alleghany	7.25%	Sierra
Almaden Valley	8.25%	Santa Clara
Almanor	7.25%	Plumas
Almondale	8.25%	Los Angeles
Alondra	8.25%	Los Angeles
Alpaugh	7.25%	Tulare
Alpine	7.75%	San Diego
Alta	7.25%	Placer
Alta Loma (Rancho Cucamonga*)	7.75%	San Bernardino
Altadena	8.25%	Los Angeles
Altaville*	7.25%	Calaveras
Alton	7.25%	Humboldt
Alturas*	7.25%	Modoc

City	Tax	County
Alviso (San Jose*)	8.25%	Santa Clara
Amador City*	7.25%	Amador
Amargosa (Death Valley)	7.75%	Inyo
Amboy	7.75%	San Bernardino
American Canyon*	7.75%	Napa
Anaheim*	7.75%	Orange
Anderson*	7.25%	Shasta
Angels Camp*	7.25%	Calaveras
Angelus Oaks	7.75%	San Bernardino
Angwin	7.75%	Napa
Annapolis	7.75%	Sonoma
Antelope	7.75%	Sacramento
Antelope Acres	8.25%	Los Angeles
Antioch*	8.25%	Contra Costa
Anza	7.75%	Riverside
Apple Valley*	7.75%	San Bernardino
Applegate	7.25%	Placer
Aptos	8.00%	Santa Cruz
Arbuckle	7.25%	Colusa
Arcadia*	8.25%	Los Angeles
Arcata*	7.25%	Humboldt
Argus	7.75%	San Bernardino
Arleta (Los Angeles*)	8.25%	Los Angeles
Arlington (Riverside*)	7.75%	Riverside
Armona	7.25%	Kings
Army Terminal	8.75%	Alameda
Arnold	7.25%	Calaveras
Aromas	7.25%	Monterey
Arrowbear Lake	7.75%	San Bernardino
Arrowhead Highlands	7.75%	San Bernardino
Arroyo Grande*	7.75%	San Luis Obispo
Artesia*	8.25%	Los Angeles
Artois	7.25%	Glenn
Arvin*	7.25%	Kern
Ashland	8.75%	Alameda
Asti	7.75%	Sonoma
Atascadero*	7.25%	San Luis Obispo
Athens	8.25%	Los Angeles
Atherton*	8.25%	San Mateo
Atwater*	7.25%	Merced
Atwood	7.75%	Orange
Auberry	7.975%	Fresno
Auburn*	7.25%	Placer
Avalon*	8.75%	Los Angeles
Avenal*	7.25%	Kings
Avery	7.25%	Calaveras
Avila Beach	7.25%	San Luis Obispo
Azusa*	8.25%	Los Angeles
Badger	7.25%	Tulare
Bailey	8.25%	Los Angeles
Baker	7.75%	San Bernardino
Bakersfield*	7.25%	Kern
Balboa (Newport Beach*)	7.75%	Orange
Balboa Island (Newport Beach*)	7.75%	Orange
Balboa Park (San Diego*)	7.75%	San Diego
Baldwin Park*	8.25%	Los Angeles
Ballard	7.75%	Santa Barbara
Ballico	7.25%	Merced
Ballroad	7.75%	Orange
Bangor	7.25%	Butte
Banning*	7.75%	Riverside
Banta	7.75%	San Joaquin
Bard	7.75%	Imperial
Barrington	8.25%	Los Angeles
Barstow*	7.75%	San Bernardino
Bartlett	7.75%	Inyo
Barton	7.975%	Fresno
Base Line	7.75%	San Bernardino
Bass Lake	7.75%	Madera
Bassett	8.25%	Los Angeles
Baxter	7.25%	Placer
Bayside	7.25%	Humboldt
Baywood Park	7.25%	San Luis Obispo
Beale A.F.B.	7.25%	Yuba
Bear River Lake	7.25%	Amador
Bear Valley	7.25%	Alpine
Bear Valley	7.75%	Mariposa
Beaumont*	7.75%	Riverside
Beckwourth	7.25%	Plumas

City	Tax	County
Bel Air Estates	8.25%	Los Angeles
Belden	7.25%	Plumas
Bell Gardens*	8.25%	Los Angeles
Bell*	8.25%	Los Angeles
Bella Vista	7.25%	Shasta
Bellflower*	8.25%	Los Angeles
Belmont*	8.25%	San Mateo
Belvedere*	7.75%	Marin
Ben Lomond	8.00%	Santa Cruz
Benicia*	7.38%	Solano
Benton	7.25%	Mono
Berkeley*	8.75%	Alameda
Bermuda Dunes	7.75%	Riverside
Berry Creek	7.25%	Butte
Bethel Island	8.25%	Contra Costa
Betteravia	7.75%	Santa Barbara
Beverly Hills*	8.25%	Los Angeles
Bieber	7.25%	Lassen
Big Bar	7.25%	Trinity
Big Basin	8.00%	Santa Cruz
Big Bear City	7.75%	San Bernardino
Big Bear Lake*	7.75%	San Bernardino
Big Bend	7.25%	Shasta
Big Creek	7.975%	Fresno
Big Oak Flat	7.25%	Tuolumne
Big Pine	7.75%	Inyo
Big River	7.75%	San Bernardino
Big Sur	7.25%	Monterey
Biggs*	7.25%	Butte
Bijou	7.25%	El Dorado
Biola	7.975%	Fresno
Biola College (La Mirada*)	8.25%	Los Angeles
Birds Landing	7.38%	Solano
Bishop*	7.75%	Inyo
Black Hawk	8.25%	Contra Costa
Blairsden	7.25%	Plumas
Blocksburg	7.25%	Humboldt
Bloomington	7.75%	San Bernardino
Blossom Hill	8.25%	Santa Clara
Blossom Valley	8.25%	Santa Clara
Blue Jay	7.75%	San Bernardino
Blue Lake*	7.25%	Humboldt
Blythe*	7.75%	Riverside
Bodega	7.75%	Sonoma
Bodega Bay	7.75%	Sonoma
Bodfish	7.25%	Kern
Bolinas	7.75%	Marin
Bolsa	7.75%	Orange
Bombay Beach	7.75%	Imperial
Bonita	7.75%	San Diego
Bonny Doon	8.00%	Santa Cruz
Bonsall	7.75%	San Diego
Boonville	7.25%	Mendocino
Boron	7.25%	Kern
Borrego Springs	7.75%	San Diego
Bostonia	7.75%	San Diego
Boulder Creek	8.00%	Santa Cruz
Boulevard	7.75%	San Diego
Bouquet Canyon (Santa Clarita*)	8.25%	Los Angeles
Bowman	7.25%	Placer
Boyes Hot Springs	7.75%	Sonoma
Bradbury*	8.25%	Los Angeles
Bradford	8.75%	Alameda
Bradley	7.25%	Monterey
Branscomb	7.25%	Mendocino
Brawley*	7.75%	Imperial
Brea*	7.75%	Orange
Brents Junction	8.25%	Los Angeles
Brentwood (Los Angeles*)	8.25%	Los Angeles
Brentwood*	8.25%	Contra Costa
Briceland	7.25%	Humboldt
Bridgeport	7.75%	Mariposa
Bridgeport	7.25%	Mono
Bridgeville	7.25%	Humboldt
Brisbane*	8.25%	San Mateo
Broderick (West Sacramento*)	7.75%	Yolo
Brookdale	8.00%	Santa Cruz
Brookhurst Center	7.75%	Orange
Brooks	7.25%	Yolo

City	Tax	County
Browns Valley	7.25%	Yuba
Brownsville	7.25%	Yuba
Bryn Mawr	7.75%	San Bernardino
Bryte (West Sacramento*)	7.75%	Yolo
Buellton*	7.75%	Santa Barbara
Buena Park*	7.75%	Orange
Burbank*	8.25%	Los Angeles
Burlingame*	8.25%	San Mateo
Burney	7.25%	Shasta
Burnt Ranch	7.25%	Trinity
Burrel	7.975%	Fresno
Burson	7.25%	Calaveras
Butte City	7.25%	Glenn
Butte Meadows	7.25%	Butte
Buttonwillow	7.25%	Kern
Byron	8.25%	Contra Costa
Cabazon	7.75%	Riverside
Cabrillo	8.25%	Los Angeles
Cadiz	7.75%	San Bernardino
Calabasas Highlands	8.25%	Los Angeles
Calabasas Park	8.25%	Los Angeles
Calabasas*	8.25%	Los Angeles
Calexico*	7.75%	Imperial
Caliente	7.25%	Kern
California City*	7.25%	Kern
California Hot Springs	7.25%	Tulare
California Valley	7.25%	San Luis Obispo
Calimesa*	7.75%	Riverside
Calipatria*	7.75%	Imperial
Calistoga*	7.75%	Napa
Callahan	7.25%	Siskiyou
Calpella	7.25%	Mendocino
Calpine	7.25%	Sierra
Calwa	7.975%	Fresno
Camarillo*	7.25%	Ventura
Cambria	7.25%	San Luis Obispo
Cambrian Park	8.25%	Santa Clara
Cameron Park	7.25%	El Dorado
Camino	7.25%	El Dorado
Camp Beale	7.25%	Yuba
Camp Connell	7.25%	Calaveras
Camp Curry	7.75%	Mariposa
Camp Kaweah	7.25%	Tulare
Camp Meeker	7.75%	Sonoma
Camp Nelson	7.25%	Tulare
Camp Pendleton	7.75%	San Diego
Camp Roberts	7.25%	Monterey
Campbell*	8.25%	Santa Clara
Campo	7.75%	San Diego
Campo Seco	7.25%	Calaveras
Camptonville	7.25%	Yuba
Canby	7.25%	Modoc
Canoga Annex	8.25%	Los Angeles
Canoga Park (Los Angeles*)	8.25%	Los Angeles
Cantil	7.25%	Kern
Cantua Creek	7.975%	Fresno
Canyon	8.25%	Contra Costa
Canyon Country (Santa Clarita*)	8.25%	Los Angeles
Canyon Lake*	7.75%	Riverside
Canyondam	7.25%	Plumas
Capay	7.25%	Yolo
Capistrano Beach (Dana Point*)	7.75%	Orange
Capitola*	8.25%	Santa Cruz
Cardiff By The Sea (Encinitas*)	7.75%	San Diego
Cardwell	7.975%	Fresno
Carlotta	7.25%	Humboldt
Carlsbad*	7.75%	San Diego
Carmel Rancho	7.25%	Monterey
Carmel Valley	7.25%	Monterey
Carmel*	7.25%	Monterey
Carmichael	7.75%	Sacramento
Carnelian Bay	7.25%	Placer
Carpinteria*	7.75%	Santa Barbara
Carson*	8.25%	Los Angeles
Cartago	7.75%	Inyo
Caruthers	7.975%	Fresno
Casitas Springs	7.25%	Ventura
Casmalia	7.75%	Santa Barbara
Caspar	7.25%	Mendocino

City	Tax	County
Cassel	7.25%	Shasta
Castaic	8.25%	Los Angeles
Castella	7.25%	Shasta
Castle A.F.B.	7.25%	Merced
Castro Valley	8.75%	Alameda
Castroville	7.25%	Monterey
Cathedral City*	7.75%	Riverside
Catheys Valley	7.75%	Mariposa
Cayucos	7.25%	San Luis Obispo
Cazadero	7.75%	Sonoma
Cecilville	7.25%	Siskiyou
Cedar	8.25%	Los Angeles
Cedar Crest	7.975%	Fresno
Cedar Glen	7.75%	San Bernardino
Cedar Ridge	7.38%	Nevada
Cedarpines Park	7.75%	San Bernardino
Cedarville	7.25%	Modoc
Central Valley	7.25%	Shasta
Century City	8.25%	Los Angeles
Ceres*	7.875%	Stanislaus
Cerritos*	8.25%	Los Angeles
Challenge	7.25%	Yuba
Chambers Lodge	7.25%	Placer
Charter Oak	8.25%	Los Angeles
Chatsworth (Los Angeles*)	8.25%	Los Angeles
Cherry Valley	7.75%	Riverside
Chester	7.25%	Plumas
Chicago Park	7.38%	Nevada
Chico*	7.25%	Butte
Chilcoot	7.25%	Plumas
China Lake NWC (Ridgecrest*)	7.25%	Kern
Chinese Camp	7.25%	Tuolumne
Chino Hills*	7.75%	San Bernardino
Chino*	7.75%	San Bernardino
Chiriaco Summit	7.75%	Riverside
Cholame	7.25%	San Luis Obispo
Chowchilla*	7.75%	Madera
Chualar	7.25%	Monterey
Chula Vista*	7.75%	San Diego
Cima	7.75%	San Bernardino
Citrus Heights*	7.75%	Sacramento
City of Commerce*	8.25%	Los Angeles
City of Industry*	8.25%	Los Angeles
City Terrace	8.25%	Los Angeles
Claremont*	8.25%	Los Angeles
Clarksburg	7.25%	Yolo
Clayton*	8.25%	Contra Costa
Clear Creek	7.25%	Siskiyou
Clearlake Highlands	7.25%	Lake
Clearlake Oaks	7.25%	Lake
Clearlake Park (Clearlake*)	7.75%	Lake
Clearlake*	7.75%	Lake
Clements	7.75%	San Joaquin
Clinter	7.975%	Fresno
Clio	7.25%	Plumas
Clipper Mills	7.25%	Butte
Cloverdale*	7.75%	Sonoma
Clovis*	7.975%	Fresno
Coachella*	7.75%	Riverside
Coalinga*	7.975%	Fresno
Coarsegold	7.75%	Madera
Cobb	7.25%	Lake
Cohasset	7.25%	Butte
Cole	8.25%	Los Angeles
Coleville	7.25%	Mono
Colfax*	7.25%	Placer
College City	7.25%	Colusa
College Grove Center	7.75%	San Diego
Colma*	8.25%	San Mateo
Coloma	7.25%	El Dorado
Colorado	7.75%	Mariposa
Colton*	7.75%	San Bernardino
Columbia	7.25%	Tuolumne
Colusa*	7.25%	Colusa
Commerce*	8.25%	Los Angeles
Comptche	7.25%	Mendocino
Compton*	8.25%	Los Angeles
Concord*	8.25%	Contra Costa
Cool	7.25%	El Dorado

City	Tax	County
Copperopolis	7.25%	Calaveras
Corcoran*	7.25%	Kings
Cornell	8.25%	Los Angeles
Corning*	7.25%	Tehama
Corona Del Mar (Newport Beach*)	7.75%	Orange
Corona*	7.75%	Riverside
Coronado*	7.75%	San Diego
Corralitos (Watsonville*)	8.00%	Santa Cruz
Corte Madera*	7.75%	Marin
Coso Junction	7.75%	Inyo
Costa Mesa*	7.75%	Orange
Cotati*	7.75%	Sonoma
Cottonwood	7.25%	Shasta
Coulterville	7.75%	Mariposa
Courtland	7.75%	Sacramento
Covelo	7.25%	Mendocino
Covina*	8.25%	Los Angeles
Cowan Heights	7.75%	Orange
Coyote	8.25%	Santa Clara
Crannell	7.25%	Humboldt
Crenshaw	8.25%	Los Angeles
Crescent City*	7.25%	Del Norte
Crescent Mills	7.25%	Plumas
Cressey	7.25%	Merced
Crest Park	7.75%	San Bernardino
Cresta Blanca	8.75%	Alameda
Crestline	7.75%	San Bernardino
Creston	7.25%	San Luis Obispo
Crockett	8.25%	Contra Costa
Cromberg	7.25%	Plumas
Cross Roads	7.75%	San Bernardino
Crowley Lake (Mammoth Lake*)	7.25%	Mono
Crows Landing	7.38%	Stanislaus
Cucamonga (Rancho Cucamonga*)	7.75%	San Bernardino
Cudahy*	8.25%	Los Angeles
Culver City*	8.25%	Los Angeles
Cummings	7.25%	Mendocino
Cupertino*	8.25%	Santa Clara
Curry Village	7.75%	Mariposa
Cutler	7.25%	Tulare
Cutten	7.25%	Humboldt
Cuyama	7.75%	Santa Barbara
Cypress*	7.75%	Orange
Daggett	7.75%	San Bernardino
Dairy Farm	7.38%	Solano
Daly City*	8.25%	San Mateo
Dana Point*	7.75%	Orange
Danville*	8.25%	Contra Costa
Dardanelle	7.25%	Tuolumne
Darwin	7.75%	Inyo
Davenport	8.00%	Santa Cruz
Davis Creek	7.25%	Modoc
Davis*	7.75%	Yolo
Death Valley	7.75%	Inyo
Death Valley Junction	7.75%	Inyo
Deer Park	7.75%	Napa
Del Kern (Bakersfield*)	7.25%	Kern
Del Mar Heights (Morro Bay*)	7.25%	San Luis Obispo
Del Mar*	7.75%	San Diego
Del Monte Park (Monterey*)	7.25%	Monterey
Del Rey	7.975%	Fresno
Del Rey Oaks*	8.25%	Monterey
Del Rosa	7.75%	San Bernardino
Del Sur	8.25%	Los Angeles
Delano*	8.25%	Kern
Deleven	7.25%	Colusa
Delhi	7.25%	Merced
Denair	7.38%	Stanislaus
Denny	7.25%	Trinity
Descanso	7.75%	San Diego
Desert Center	7.75%	Riverside
Desert Hot Springs*	7.75%	Riverside
Di Giorgio	7.25%	Kern
Diablo	8.25%	Contra Costa
Diamond Bar*	8.25%	Los Angeles
Diamond Springs	7.25%	El Dorado
Dillon Beach	7.75%	Marin
Dinkey Creek	7.975%	Fresno
Dinuba*	8.50%	Tulare

City	Tax	County
Dixon*	7.38%	Solano
Dobbins	7.25%	Yuba
Dollar Ranch	8.25%	Contra Costa
Dorris*	7.25%	Siskiyou
Dos Palos*	7.25%	Merced
Dos Rios	7.75%	Mendocino
Douglas City	7.25%	Trinity
Douglas Flat	7.25%	Calaveras
Downey*	8.25%	Los Angeles
Downieville	7.25%	Sierra
Doyle	7.25%	Lassen
Drytown	7.25%	Amador
Duarte*	8.25%	Los Angeles
Dublin*	8.75%	Alameda
Ducor	7.25%	Tulare
Dulzura	7.75%	San Diego
Duncans Mills	7.75%	Sonoma
Dunlap	7.975%	Fresno
Dunnigan	7.25%	Yolo
Dunsmuir*	7.25%	Siskiyou
Durham	7.25%	Butte
Dutch Flat	7.25%	Placer
Eagle Mountain	7.75%	Riverside
Eagle Rock (Los Angeles*)	8.25%	Los Angeles
Eagleville	7.25%	Modoc
Earlimart	7.25%	Tulare
Earp	7.75%	San Bernardino
East Highlands (Highland*)	7.75%	San Bernardino
East Irvine (Irvine*)	7.75%	Orange
East Los Angeles	8.25%	Los Angeles
East Lynwood (Lynwood*)	8.25%	Los Angeles
East Nicolaus	7.25%	Sutter
East Palo Alto*	8.25%	San Mateo
East Porterville (Porterville*)	7.25%	Tulare
East San Pedro (Los Angeles*)	8.25%	Los Angeles
Eastgate	8.25%	Los Angeles
Easton	7.975%	Fresno
Eastside	7.75%	San Bernardino
Echo Lake	7.25%	El Dorado
Echo Park (Los Angeles*)	8.25%	Los Angeles
Edgemont (Moreno Valley*)	7.75%	Riverside
Edgewood	7.25%	Siskiyou
Edison	7.25%	Kern
Edwards	7.25%	Kern
Edwards A.F.B.	7.25%	Kern
El Cajon*	8.25%	San Diego
El Centro*	7.75%	Imperial
El Cerrito*	8.75%	Contra Costa
El Dorado	7.25%	El Dorado
El Dorado Hills	7.25%	El Dorado
El Granada	8.25%	San Mateo
El Macero	7.25%	Yolo
El Modena	7.75%	Orange
El Monte*	8.25%	Los Angeles
El Nido	7.25%	Merced
El Portal	7.75%	Mariposa
El Segundo*	8.25%	Los Angeles
El Sobrante	8.25%	Contra Costa
El Toro (Lake Forest*)	7.75%	Orange
El Toro M.C.A.S.	7.75%	Orange
El Verano	7.75%	Sonoma
El Viejo	7.38%	Stanislaus
Eldridge	7.75%	Sonoma
Elizabeth Lake	8.25%	Los Angeles
Elk	7.25%	Mendocino
Elk Creek	7.25%	Glenn
Elk Grove*	7.75%	Sacramento
Elmira	7.38%	Solano
Elmwood	8.75%	Alameda
Elverta	7.75%	Sacramento
Emeryville*	8.75%	Alameda
Emigrant Gap	7.25%	Placer
Empire	7.38%	Stanislaus
Encinitas*	7.75%	San Diego
Encino (Los Angeles*)	8.25%	Los Angeles
Enterprise	7.25%	Shasta
Escalon*	7.75%	San Joaquin
Escondido*	7.75%	San Diego
Esparto	7.25%	Yolo

City	Tax	County
Essex	7.75%	San Bernardino
Etiwanda (Rancho Cucamonga*)	7.75%	San Bernardino
Etna*	7.25%	Siskiyou
Ettersburg	7.25%	Humboldt
Eureka*	7.25%	Humboldt
Exeter*	7.25%	Tulare
Fair Oaks	7.75%	Sacramento
Fairfax*	7.75%	Marin
Fairfield*	7.38%	Solano
Fairmount	8.25%	Contra Costa
Fall River Mills	7.25%	Shasta
Fallbrook	7.75%	San Diego
Fallbrook Junction	7.75%	San Diego
Fallen Leaf	7.25%	El Dorado
Fallon	7.75%	Marin
Fancher	7.975%	Fresno
Farmersville*	8.25%	Tulare
Farmington	7.75%	San Joaquin
Fawnskin	7.75%	San Bernardino
Feather Falls	7.25%	Butte
Fellows	7.25%	Kern
Felton	8.00%	Santa Cruz
Fenner	7.75%	San Bernardino
Fernbridge (Fortuna*)	7.25%	Humboldt
Ferndale*	7.25%	Humboldt
Fiddletown	7.25%	Amador
Fields Landing	7.25%	Humboldt
Fig Garden Village (Fresno*)	7.975%	Fresno
Fillmore*	7.25%	Ventura
Finley	7.25%	Lake
Firebaugh*	7.975%	Fresno
Fish Camp	7.75%	Mariposa
Five Points	7.975%	Fresno
Flinn Springs	7.75%	San Diego
Flintridge (LaCanada/ Flintridge*)	8.25%	Los Angeles
Florence	8.25%	Los Angeles
Floriston	7.38%	Nevada
Flournoy	7.25%	Tehama
Folsom*	7.75%	Sacramento
Fontana*	7.75%	San Bernardino
Foothill Ranch	7.75%	Orange
Forbestown	7.25%	Butte
Forest Falls	7.75%	San Bernardino
Forest Glen	7.25%	Trinity
Forest Knolls	7.75%	Marin
Forest Park	8.25%	Los Angeles
Forest Ranch	7.25%	Butte
Foresthill	7.25%	Placer
Forestville	7.75%	Sonoma
Forks of Salmon	7.25%	Siskiyou
Fort Bidwell	7.25%	Modoc
Fort Bragg*	7.75%	Mendocino
Fort Dick	7.25%	Del Norte
Fort Irwin	7.75%	San Bernardino
Fort Jones*	7.25%	Siskiyou
Fort Ord (Seaside*)	7.25%	Monterey
Fort Seward	7.25%	Humboldt
Fortuna*	7.25%	Humboldt
Foster City*	8.25%	San Mateo
Fountain Valley*	7.75%	Orange
Fowler*	7.975%	Fresno
Frazier Park	7.25%	Kern
Freedom	8.00%	Santa Cruz
Freeport	7.75%	Sacramento
Freestone	7.75%	Sonoma
Fremont*	8.75%	Alameda
French Camp	7.75%	San Joaquin
French Gulch	7.25%	Shasta
Freshwater	7.25%	Humboldt
Fresno*	7.975	Fresno
Friant	7.975%	Fresno
Friendly Valley (Santa Clarita*)	8.25%	Los Angeles
Frontera	7.75%	Riverside
Fullerton*	7.75%	Orange
Fulton	7.75%	Sonoma
Galt*	7.75%	Sacramento
Garberville	7.25%	Humboldt
Garden Grove*	7.75%	Orange
Garden Valley	7.25%	El Dorado

City	Tax	County
Gardena*	8.25%	Los Angeles
Garey	7.75%	Santa Barbara
Garnet	7.75%	Riverside
Gasquet	7.25%	Del Norte
Gaviota	7.75%	Santa Barbara
Gazelle	7.25%	Siskiyou
George A.F.B.	7.75%	San Bernardino
Georgetown	7.25%	El Dorado
Gerber	7.25%	Tehama
Geyserville	7.75%	Sonoma
Giant Forest	7.25%	Tulare
Gillman Hot Springs	7.75%	Riverside
Gilroy*	8.25%	Santa Clara
Glassell Park (Los Angeles*)	8.25%	Los Angeles
Glen Avon	7.75%	Riverside
Glen Ellen	7.75%	Sonoma
Glenburn	7.25%	Shasta
Glencoe	7.25%	Calaveras
Glendale*	8.25%	Los Angeles
Glendora*	8.25%	Los Angeles
Glenhaven	7.25%	Lake
Glenn	7.25%	Glenn
Glennville	7.25%	Kern
Gold River (Rancho Cordova*)	7.75%	Sacramento
Gold Run	7.25%	Placer
Golden Hills	7.25%	Kern
Goleta*	7.75%	Santa Barbara
Gonzales*	7.25%	Monterey
Goodyears Bar	7.25%	Sierra
Gorman	8.25%	Los Angeles
Goshen	7.25%	Tulare
Government Island	8.75%	Alameda
Graeagle	7.25%	Plumas
Granada Hills (Los Angeles*)	8.25%	Los Angeles
Grand Terrace*	7.75%	San Bernardino
Granite Bay	7.25%	Placer
Grass Valley*	7.38%	Nevada
Graton	7.75%	Sonoma
Green Valley	8.25%	Los Angeles
Green Valley Lake	7.75%	San Bernardino
Greenacres	7.25%	Kern
Greenbrae (Larkspur*)	7.75%	Marin
Greenfield*	7.25%	Monterey
Greenview	7.25%	Siskiyou
Greenville	7.25%	Plumas
Greenwood	7.25%	El Dorado
Grenada	7.25%	Siskiyou
Gridley*	7.25%	Butte
Grimes	7.25%	Colusa
Grizzly Flats	7.25%	El Dorado
Groveland	7.25%	Tuolumne
Grover Beach*	7.75%	San Luis Obispo
Guadalupe*	7.75%	Santa Barbara
Gualala	7.25%	Mendocino
Guasti (Ontario*)	7.75%	San Bernardino
Guatay	7.75%	San Diego
Guerneville	7.75%	Sonoma
Guinda	7.25%	Yolo
Gustine*	7.25%	Merced
Hacienda Heights	8.25%	Los Angeles
Halcyon	7.25%	San Luis Obispo
Half Moon Bay*	8.25%	San Mateo
Hamilton A.F.B. (Novato*)	7.75%	Marin
Hamilton City	7.25%	Glenn
Hanford*	7.25%	Kings
Happy Camp	7.25%	Siskiyou
Harbor City (Los Angeles*)	8.25%	Los Angeles
Harmony	7.25%	San Luis Obispo
Harris	7.25%	Humboldt
Hat Creek	7.25%	Shasta
Hathaway Pines	7.25%	Calaveras
Havasu Lake	7.75%	San Bernardino
Hawaiian Gardens*	8.25%	Los Angeles
Hawthorne*	8.25%	Los Angeles
Hayfork	7.25%	Trinity
Hayward*	8.75%	Alameda
Hazard	8.25%	Los Angeles
Healdsburg*	7.75%	Sonoma
Heber	7.75%	Imperial

City	Tax	County
Helena	7.25%	Trinity
Helendale	7.75%	San Bernardino
Helm	7.975%	Fresno
Hemet*	7.75%	Riverside
Herald	7.75%	Sacramento
Hercules*	8.25%	Contra Costa
Herlong	7.25%	Lassen
Hermosa Beach*	8.25%	Los Angeles
Herndon	7.975%	Fresno
Hesperia*	7.75%	San Bernardino
Heyer	8.75%	Alameda
Hickman	7.38%	Stanislaus
Hidden Hills*	8.25%	Los Angeles
Highgrove	7.75%	Riverside
Highland Park (Los Angeles*)	8.25%	Los Angeles
Highland*	7.75%	San Bernardino
Highway City (Fresno*)	7.975%	Fresno
Hillcrest (San Diego*)	7.75%	San Diego
Hillsborough*	8.25%	San Mateo
Hillsdale (San Mateo*)	8.25%	San Mateo
Hilmar	7.25%	Merced
Hilt	7.25%	Siskiyou
Hinkley	7.75%	San Bernardino
Hobergs	7.25%	Lake
Hollister*	8.25%	San Benito
Hollywood (Los Angeles*)	8.25%	Los Angeles
Holmes	7.25%	Humboldt
Holt	7.75%	San Joaquin
Holtville*	7.75%	Imperial
Holy City	8.25%	Santa Clara
Homeland	7.75%	Riverside
Homestead	7.25%	Kern
Homestead	7.75%	Riverside
Homewood	7.25%	Placer
Honby	8.25%	Los Angeles
Honeydew	7.25%	Humboldt
Hood	7.75%	Sacramento
Hoopa	7.25%	Humboldt
Hope Valley (Forest Camp)	7.25%	Alpine
Hopland	7.25%	Mendocino
Hornbrook	7.25%	Siskiyou
Hornitos	7.75%	Mariposa
Horse Creek	7.25%	Siskiyou
Horse Lake	7.25%	Lassen
Hughson*	7.38%	Stanislaus
Hume	7.975%	Fresno
Huntington	7.75%	Orange
Huntington Beach*	7.75%	Orange
Huntington Lake	7.975%	Fresno
Huntington Park*	8.25%	Los Angeles
Huron*	7.975%	Fresno
Hyampom	7.25%	Trinity
Hyde Park (Los Angeles*)	8.25%	Los Angeles
Hydesville	7.25%	Humboldt
Idria	7.25%	San Benito
Idyllwild	7.75%	Riverside
Ignacio (Novato*)	7.75%	Marin
Igo	7.25%	Shasta
Imola (Napa*)	7.75%	Napa
Imperial Beach*	7.75%	San Diego
Imperial*	7.75%	Imperial
Independence	7.75%	Inyo
Indian Wells*	7.75%	Riverside
Indio*	7.75%	Riverside
Industry*	8.25%	Los Angeles
Inglewood*	8.75%	Los Angeles
Inverness	7.75%	Marin
Inyo	7.75%	Inyo
Inyokern	7.25%	Kern
Ione*	7.25%	Amador
Iowa Hill	7.25%	Placer
Irvine*	7.75%	Orange
Irwindale*	8.25%	Los Angeles
Isla Vista	7.75%	Santa Barbara
Island Mountain	7.25%	Trinity
Isleton*	7.75%	Sacramento
Ivanhoe	7.25%	Tulare
Ivanpah	7.75%	San Bernardino
Jackson*	7.25%	Amador

City	Tax	County
Jacumba	7.75%	San Diego
Jamacha	7.75%	San Diego
Jamestown	7.25%	Tuolumne
Jamul	7.75%	San Diego
Janesville	7.25%	Lassen
Jenner	7.75%	Sonoma
Johannesburg	7.25%	Kern
Johnsondale	7.25%	Tulare
Johnstonville	7.25%	Lassen
Johnstown	7.75%	San Diego
Jolon	7.25%	Monterey
Joshua Tree	7.75%	San Bernardino
Julian	7.75%	San Diego
Junction City	7.25%	Trinity
June Lake	7.25%	Mono
Juniper	7.25%	Lassen
Kagel Canyon	8.25%	Los Angeles
Kaweah	7.25%	Tulare
Keddie	7.25%	Plumas
Keeler	7.75%	Inyo
Keene	7.25%	Kern
Kelsey	7.25%	El Dorado
Kelseyville	7.25%	Lake
Kelso	7.75%	San Bernardino
Kensington	8.25%	Contra Costa
Kentfield	7.75%	Marin
Kenwood	7.75%	Sonoma
Kerman*	7.975%	Fresno
Kernville	7.25%	Kern
Keswick	7.25%	Shasta
Kettleman City	7.25%	Kings
Keyes	7.38%	Stanislaus
King City*	7.25%	Monterey
Kings Beach	7.25%	Placer
Kings Canyon National Park	7.25%	Tulare
Kingsburg*	7.975%	Fresno
Kinyon	7.25%	Siskiyou
Kirkwood	7.25%	Alpine
Kit Carson	7.25%	Amador
Klamath	7.25%	Del Norte
Klamath River	7.25%	Siskiyou
Kneeland	7.25%	Humboldt
Knights Ferry	7.38%	Stanislaus
Knights Landing	7.25%	Yolo
Knightsen	8.25%	Contra Costa
Korbel	7.25%	Humboldt
Korbel	7.75%	Sonoma
Kyburz	7.25%	El Dorado
L.A. Airport (Los Angeles*)	8.25%	Los Angeles
La Canada-Flintridge*	8.25%	Los Angeles
La Crescenta	8.25%	Los Angeles
La Cresta Village	7.25%	Kern
La Grange	7.38%	Stanislaus
La Habra Heights*	8.25%	Los Angeles
La Habra*	7.75%	Orange
La Honda	8.25%	San Mateo
La Jolla (San Diego*)	7.75%	San Diego
La Mesa*	7.75%	San Diego
La Mirada*	8.25%	Los Angeles
La Mirada*	8.25%	Los Angeles
La Palma*	7.75%	Orange
La Porte	7.25%	Plumas
La Puente*	8.25%	Los Angeles
La Quinta*	7.75%	Riverside
La Selva Beach	8.00%	Santa Cruz
La Verne*	8.25%	Los Angeles
La Vina	8.25%	Los Angeles
Ladera	8.25%	San Mateo
Ladera Heights	8.25%	Los Angeles
Ladera Ranch	7.75%	Orange
Lafayette*	8.25%	Contra Costa
Laguna Beach*	8.25%	Orange
Laguna Hills*	7.75%	Orange
Laguna Niguel*	7.75%	Orange
Lagunitas	7.75%	Marin
Lake Alpine	7.25%	Alpine
Lake Arrowhead	7.75%	San Bernardino
Lake City	7.25%	Modoc
Lake City	7.38%	Nevada

City	Tax	County
Lake Elsinore*	7.75%	Riverside
Lake Forest (El Toro*)	7.75%	Orange
Lake Hughes	8.25%	Los Angeles
Lake Isabella	7.25%	Kern
Lake Los Angeles	8.25%	Los Angeles
Lake Mary	7.25%	Mono
Lake San Marcos	7.75%	San Diego
Lake Shastina	7.25%	Siskiyou
Lake Sherwood	7.25%	Ventura
Lakehead	7.25%	Shasta
Lakeport*	7.75%	Lake
Lakeshore	7.975%	Fresno
Lakeside	7.75%	San Diego
Lakeview	7.75%	Riverside
Lakeview Terrace (Los Angeles*)	8.25%	Los Angeles
Lakewood*	8.25%	Los Angeles
Lamont	7.25%	Kern
Lancaster*	8.25%	Los Angeles
Landers	7.75%	San Bernardino
Landscape	8.75%	Alameda
Lang	8.25%	Los Angeles
Larkfield	7.75%	Sonoma
Larkspur*	7.75%	Marin
Larwin Plaza	7.38%	Solano
Lathrop	7.75%	San Joaquin
Laton	7.975%	Fresno
Lawndale*	8.25%	Los Angeles
Laws	7.75%	Inyo
Laytonville	7.25%	Mendocino
Le Grand (Also Legrand)	7.25%	Merced
Lebec	7.25%	Kern
Lee Vining	7.25%	Mono
Leggett	7.25%	Mendocino
Leisure World	7.75%	Orange
Leisure World (Seal Beach*)	7.75%	Orange
Lemon Grove*	7.75%	San Diego
Lemoncove	7.25%	Tulare
Lemoore*	7.25%	Kings
Lennox	8.25%	Los Angeles
Lenwood	7.75%	San Bernardino
Leona Valley	8.25%	Los Angeles
Leucadia (Encinitas*)	7.75%	San Diego
Lewiston	7.25%	Trinity
Liberty Farms	7.38%	Solano
Likely	7.25%	Modoc
Lincoln Acres	7.75%	San Diego
Lincoln Village	7.75%	San Joaquin
Lincoln*	7.25%	Placer
Linda	7.25%	Yuba
Linden	7.75%	San Joaquin
Lindsay*	7.25%	Tulare
Linnell	7.25%	Tulare
Litchfield	7.25%	Lassen
Little Lake	7.75%	Inyo
Little Norway	7.25%	El Dorado
Little Valley	7.25%	Lassen
Littleriver	7.25%	Mendocino
Littlerock (Also Little Rock)	8.25%	Los Angeles
Live Oak*	7.25%	Sutter
Livermore*	8.75%	Alameda
Livingston*	7.25%	Merced
Llano	8.25%	Los Angeles
Loch Lomond	7.25%	Lake
Locke	7.75%	Sacramento
Lockeford	7.75%	San Joaquin
Lockheed	8.00%	Santa Cruz
Lockwood	7.25%	Monterey
Lodi*	7.75%	San Joaquin
Loleta	7.25%	Humboldt
Loma Linda*	7.75%	San Bernardino
Loma Mar	8.25%	San Mateo
Loma Rica	7.25%	Yuba
Lomita*	8.25%	Los Angeles
Lompoc*	7.75%	Santa Barbara
London	7.25%	Tulare
Lone Pine	7.75%	Inyo
Long Barn	7.25%	Tuolumne
Long Beach*	8.25%	Los Angeles
Longview	8.25%	Los Angeles

City	Tax	County
Lookout	7.25%	Modoc
Loomis*	7.25%	Placer
Lorre Estates	8.25%	Santa Clara
Los Alamitos*	7.75%	Orange
Los Alamos	7.75%	Santa Barbara
Los Altos Hills*	8.25%	Santa Clara
Los Altos*	8.25%	Santa Clara
Los Angeles*	8.25%	Los Angeles
Los Banos*	7.75%	Merced
Los Gatos*	8.25%	Santa Clara
Los Molinos	7.25%	Tehama
Los Nietos	8.25%	Los Angeles
Los Olivos	7.75%	Santa Barbara
Los Osos	7.25%	San Luis Obispo
Los Padres	7.25%	San Luis Obispo
Los Serranos (Chino Hills*)	7.75%	San Bernardino
Lost Hills	7.25%	Kern
Lost Lake	7.75%	Riverside
Lotus	7.25%	El Dorado
Lower Lake	7.25%	Lake
Loyalton*	7.25%	Sierra
Lucerne	7.25%	Lake
Lucerne Valley	7.75%	San Bernardino
Lucia	7.25%	Monterey
Ludlow	7.75%	San Bernardino
Lugo	8.25%	Los Angeles
Luther Burbank (Santa Rosa*)	8.0%	Sonoma
Lynwood*	8.25%	Los Angeles
Lytle Creek	7.75%	San Bernardino
Macdoel	7.25%	Siskiyou
Maclay	8.25%	Los Angeles
Mad River	7.25%	Trinity
Madeline	7.25%	Lassen
Madera*	7.75%	Madera
Madison	7.25%	Yolo
Magalia	7.25%	Butte
Malaga	7.975%	Fresno
Malibu*	8.25%	Los Angeles
Mammoth Lakes*	7.75%	Mono
Manhattan Beach*	8.25%	Los Angeles
Manteca*	8.25%	San Joaquin
Manton	7.25%	Tehama
Manzanita Lake	7.25%	Shasta
Mar Vista	8.25%	Los Angeles
Marcelina	8.25%	Los Angeles
March A.F.B.	7.75%	Riverside
Mare Island (Vallejo*)	7.38%	Solano
Maricopa*	7.25%	Kern
Marin	7.75%	Marin
Marin City	7.75%	Marin
Marina Del Rey	8.25%	Los Angeles
Marina*	7.25%	Monterey
Marine Corps (Twentynine Palms)	7.75%	San Bernardino
Mariner	7.75%	Orange
Mariposa	7.75%	Mariposa
Markleeville	7.25%	Alpine
Marsh Manor	8.25%	San Mateo
Marshall	7.75%	Marin
Martell	7.25%	Amador
Martinez*	8.25%	Contra Costa
Marysville*	7.25%	Yuba
Mather	7.25%	Tuolumne
Mather A.F.B.	7.75%	Sacramento
Maxwell	7.25%	Colusa
Maywood*	8.25%	Los Angeles
McArthur	7.25%	Shasta
McClellan A.F.B.	7.75%	Sacramento
McCloud	7.25%	Siskiyou
McFarland*	7.25%	Kern
McKinleyville	7.25%	Humboldt
McKittrick	7.25%	Kern
Mead Valley	7.75%	Riverside
Meadow Valley	7.25%	Plumas
Meadow Vista	7.25%	Placer
Meadowbrook	7.75%	Riverside
Mecca	7.75%	Riverside
Meeks Bay	7.25%	El Dorado
Meiners Oaks	7.25%	Ventura
Mendocino	7.25%	Mendocino

City	Tax	County
Mendota*	7.975%	Fresno
Menifee	7.75%	Riverside
Menlo Park*	8.25%	San Mateo
Mentone	7.75%	San Bernardino
Merced*	7.75	Merced
Meridian	8.25%	Sutter
Mettler	7.25%	Kern
Meyers	7.25%	El Dorado
Middletown	7.25%	Lake
Midland	7.75%	Riverside
Midpines	7.75%	Mariposa
Midway City	7.75%	Orange
Milford	7.25%	Lassen
Mill Creek	7.25%	Tehama
Mill Valley*	7.75%	Marin
Millbrae*	8.25%	San Mateo
Millville	7.25%	Shasta
Milpitas*	8.25%	Santa Clara
Mineral	7.25%	Tehama
Mineral King	7.25%	Tulare
Mint Canyon	8.25%	Los Angeles
Mira Loma	7.75%	Riverside
Mira Vista	8.25%	Contra Costa
Miracle Hot Springs	7.25%	Kern
Miramar (San Diego*)	7.75%	San Diego
Miramonte	7.975%	Fresno
Miranda	7.25%	Humboldt
Mission Hills (Los Angeles*)	8.25%	Los Angeles
Mission Viejo*	7.75%	Orange
Mi-Wuk Village	7.25%	Tuolumne
Moccasin	7.25%	Tuolumne
Modesto*	7.38%	Stanislaus
Moffett Field	8.25%	Santa Clara
Mojave	7.25%	Kern
Mokelumne Hill	7.25%	Calaveras
Moneta	8.25%	Los Angeles
Mono Hot Springs	7.975%	Fresno
Mono Lake	7.25%	Mono
Monolith	7.25%	Kern
Monrovia*	8.25%	Los Angeles
Monta Vista	8.25%	Santa Clara
Montague*	7.25%	Siskiyou
Montalvo (Ventura*)	7.25%	Ventura
Montara	8.25%	San Mateo
Montclair*	8.0%	San Bernardino
Monte Rio	7.75%	Sonoma
Monte Sereno*	8.25%	Santa Clara
Montebello*	8.25%	Los Angeles
Montecito	7.75%	Santa Barbara
Monterey Bay Academy	8.00%	Santa Cruz
Monterey Park*	8.25%	Los Angeles
Monterey*	7.25%	Monterey
Montgomery Creek	7.25%	Shasta
Montrose	8.25%	Los Angeles
Mooney	7.25%	Tulare
Moonridge	7.75%	San Bernardino
Moorpark*	7.25%	Ventura
Moraga*	8.25%	Contra Costa
Moreno Valley*	7.75%	Riverside
Morgan Hill*	8.25%	Santa Clara
Morongo Valley	7.75%	San Bernardino
Morro Bay*	7.75%	San Luis Obispo
Morro Plaza	7.25%	San Luis Obispo
Moss Beach	8.25%	San Mateo
Moss Landing	7.25%	Monterey
Mount Hamilton	8.25%	Santa Clara
Mount Hebron	7.25%	Siskiyou
Mount Hermon	8.00%	Santa Cruz
Mount Laguna	7.75%	San Diego
Mount Shasta*	7.25%	Siskiyou
Mount Wilson	8.25%	Los Angeles
Mountain Center	7.75%	Riverside
Mountain Mesa	7.25%	Kern
Mountain Pass	7.75%	San Bernardino
Mountain Ranch	7.25%	Calaveras
Mountain View*	8.25%	Santa Clara
Mt. Aukum	7.25%	El Dorado
Mt. Baldy	7.75%	San Bernardino
Murphys	7.25%	Calaveras

City	Tax	County
Murrieta*	7.75%	Riverside
Muscoy	7.75%	San Bernardino
Myers Flat	7.25%	Humboldt
Napa*	7.75%	Napa
Naples	8.25%	Los Angeles
Nashville	7.25%	El Dorado
National City*	8.75%	San Diego
Naval (Port Hueneme*)	7.25%	Ventura
Naval (San Diego*)	7.75%	San Diego
Naval Air Station (Alameda*)	8.75%	Alameda
Naval Air Station (Coronado*)	7.75%	San Diego
Naval Air Station (Lemoore*)	7.25%	Kings
Naval Hospital (Oakland*)	8.75%	Alameda
Naval Hospital (San Diego*)	7.75%	San Diego
Naval Supply Center (Oakland*)	8.75%	Alameda
Naval Training Center (San Diego*)	7.75%	San Diego
Navarro	7.25%	Mendocino
Needles*	7.75%	San Bernardino
Nelson	7.25%	Butte
Nevada City*	7.875%	Nevada
New Almaden	8.25%	Santa Clara
New Cuyama	7.75%	Santa Barbara
New Idria	7.25%	San Benito
Newark*	8.75%	Alameda
Newberry	7.75%	San Bernardino
Newberry Springs	7.75%	San Bernardino
Newbury Park (Thousand Oaks*)	7.25%	Ventura
Newcastle	7.25%	Placer
Newhall (Santa Clarita*)	8.25%	Los Angeles
Newman*	7.38%	Stanislaus
Newport Beach*	7.75%	Orange
Nicasio	7.75%	Marin
Nice	7.25%	Lake
Nicolaus	7.25%	Sutter
Niland	7.75%	Imperial
Nipomo	7.25%	San Luis Obispo
Nipton	7.75%	San Bernardino
Norco*	7.75%	Riverside
Norden	7.38%	Nevada
North Edwards	7.25%	Kern
North Fork	7.75%	Madera
North Gardena	8.25%	Los Angeles
North Highlands	7.75%	Sacramento
North Hills (Los Angeles*)	8.25%	Los Angeles
North Hollywood (Los Angeles*)	8.25%	Los Angeles
North Palm Springs	7.75%	Riverside
North San Juan	7.38%	Nevada
North Shore	7.75%	Riverside
Northridge (Los Angeles*)	8.25%	Los Angeles
Norton A.F.B. (San Bernardino*)	7.75%	San Bernardino
Norwalk*	8.25%	Los Angeles
Novato*	7.75%	Marin
Nubieber	7.25%	Lassen
Nuevo	7.75%	Riverside
Nyeland Acres	7.25%	Ventura
Oak Park	7.25%	Ventura
Oak Run	7.25%	Shasta
Oak View	7.25%	Ventura
Oakdale*	7.38%	Stanislaus
Oakhurst	7.75%	Madera
Oakland*	8.75%	Alameda
Oakley	8.25%	Contra Costa
Oakville	7.75%	Napa
Oasis	7.75%	Riverside
Oban	8.25%	Los Angeles
O'Brien	7.25%	Shasta
Occidental	7.75%	Sonoma
Oceano	7.25%	San Luis Obispo
Oceanside*	7.75%	San Diego
Ocotillo	7.75%	Imperial
Ocotillo Wells	7.75%	San Diego
Oildale	7.25%	Kern
Ojai*	7.25%	Ventura
Olancha	7.75%	Inyo
Old Station	7.25%	Shasta
Olema	7.75%	Marin
Olinda	7.25%	Shasta
Olive View (Los Angeles*)	8.25%	Los Angeles
Olivehurst	7.25%	Yuba

City	Tax	County
Olivenhain (Encinitas*)	7.75%	San Diego
Olympic Valley	7.25%	Placer
Omo Ranch	7.25%	El Dorado
O'Neals	7.75%	Madera
Ono	7.25%	Shasta
Ontario*	7.75%	San Bernardino
Onyx	7.25%	Kern
Opal Cliffs	8.00%	Santa Cruz
Orange Cove*	7.975%	Fresno
Orange*	7.75%	Orange
Orangevale	7.75%	Sacramento
Orcutt	7.75%	Santa Barbara
Ordbend	7.25%	Glenn
Oregon House	7.25%	Yuba
Orick	7.25%	Humboldt
Orinda*	8.25%	Contra Costa
Orland*	7.25%	Glenn
Orleans	7.25%	Humboldt
Oro Grande	7.75%	San Bernardino
Orosi	7.25%	Tulare
Oroville*	7.25%	Butte
Otay (Chula Vista*)	7.75%	San Diego
Oxnard*	7.25%	Ventura
Pacheco	8.25%	Contra Costa
Pacific Grove*	8.25%	Monterey
Pacific House	7.25%	El Dorado
Pacific Palisades (Los Angeles*)	8.25%	Los Angeles
Pacifica*	8.25%	San Mateo
Pacoima (Los Angeles*)	8.25%	Los Angeles
Paicines	7.25%	San Benito
Pajaro	7.25%	Monterey
Pala	7.75%	San Diego
Palermo	7.25%	Butte
Pallett	8.25%	Los Angeles
Palm City	7.75%	Riverside
Palm City (San Diego*)	7.75%	San Diego
Palm Desert*	7.75%	Riverside
Palm Springs*	7.75%	Riverside
Palmdale*	8.25%	Los Angeles
Palo (Vista*)	7.75%	San Diego
Palo Alto*	8.25%	Santa Clara
Palo Cedro	7.25%	Shasta
Palo Verde	7.75%	Imperial
Palomar Mountain	7.75%	San Diego
Palos Verdes Estates*	8.25%	Los Angeles
Palos Verdes/Peninsula	8.25%	Los Angeles
Panorama City (Los Angeles*)	8.25%	Los Angeles
Paradise*	7.25%	Butte
Paramount*	8.25%	Los Angeles
Parker Dam	7.75%	San Bernardino
Parkfield	7.25%	Monterey
Parlier*	7.975%	Fresno
Pasadena*	8.25%	Los Angeles
Paskenta	7.25%	Tehama
Paso Robles*	7.25%	San Luis Obispo
Patterson*	7.38%	Stanislaus
Patton	7.75%	San Bernardino
Pauma Valley	7.75%	San Diego
Paynes Creek	7.25%	Tehama
Pearblossom	8.25%	Los Angeles
Pearland	8.25%	Los Angeles
Pebble Beach	7.25%	Monterey
Pedley	7.75%	Riverside
Peninsula Village	7.25%	Plumas
Penn Valley	7.38%	Nevada
Penngrove	7.75%	Sonoma
Penryn	7.25%	Placer
Pepperwood	7.25%	Humboldt
Permanente	8.25%	Santa Clara
Perris*	7.75%	Riverside
Perry (Whittier*)	8.25%	Los Angeles
Pescadero	8.25%	San Mateo
Petaluma*	7.75%	Sonoma
Petrolia	7.25%	Humboldt
Phelan	7.75%	San Bernardino
Phillipsville	7.25%	Humboldt
Philo	7.25%	Mendocino
Pico Rivera*	8.25%	Los Angeles
Piedmont*	8.75%	Alameda

City	Tax	County
Piedra	7.975%	Fresno
Piercy	7.25%	Mendocino
Pilot Hill	7.25%	El Dorado
Pine Grove	7.25%	Amador
Pine Valley	7.75%	San Diego
Pinecrest	7.25%	Tuolumne
Pinedale (Fresno*)	7.975%	Fresno
Pinetree	8.25%	Los Angeles
Pinole*	8.75%	Contra Costa
Pinon Hills	7.75%	San Bernardino
Pioneer	7.25%	Amador
Pioneertown	7.75%	San Bernardino
Piru	7.25%	Ventura
Pismo Beach*	7.75%	San Luis Obispo
Pittsburg*	8.25%	Contra Costa
Pixley	7.25%	Tulare
Placentia*	7.75%	Orange
Placerville*	7.50%	El Dorado
Plainview	7.25%	Tulare
Planada	7.25%	Merced
Plaster City	7.75%	Imperial
Platina	7.25%	Shasta
Playa Del Rey (Los Angeles*)	8.25%	Los Angeles
Pleasant Grove	7.25%	Sutter
Pleasant Hill*	8.25%	Contra Costa
Pleasanton*	8.75%	Alameda
Plymouth*	7.25%	Amador
Point Arena*	7.75%	Mendocino
Point Mugu	7.25%	Ventura
Point Pittsburg (Pittsburg*)	8.25%	Contra Costa
Point Reyes Station	7.75%	Marin
Pollock Pines	7.25%	El Dorado
Pomona*	8.25%	Los Angeles
Pond	7.25%	Kern
Pondosa	7.25%	Siskiyou
Pope Valley	7.75%	Napa
Poplar	7.25%	Tulare
Port Costa	8.25%	Contra Costa
Port Hueneme*	7.25%	Ventura
Porter Ranch (Los Angeles*)	8.25%	Los Angeles
Porterville*	8.25%	Tulare
Portola Valley*	8.25%	San Mateo
Portola*	7.25%	Plumas
Portuguese Bend (Rancho Palos Verdes*)	8.25%	Los Angeles
Posey	7.25%	Tulare
Potrero	7.75%	San Diego
Potter Valley	7.25%	Mendocino
Poway*	7.75%	San Diego
Prather	7.975%	Fresno
Presidio (San Francisco*)	8.50%	San Francisco
Presidio of Monterey (Monterey*)	7.25%	Monterey
Priest Valley	7.25%	Monterey
Princeton	7.25%	Colusa
Proberta	7.25%	Tehama
Project City	7.25%	Shasta
Prunedale	7.25%	Monterey
Pt. Dume	8.25%	Los Angeles
Pulga	7.25%	Butte
Pumpkin Center	7.25%	Kern
Quail Valley	7.75%	Riverside
Quartz Hill	8.25%	Los Angeles
Quincy	7.25%	Plumas
Rackerby	7.25%	Yuba
Rail Road Flat	7.25%	Calaveras
Rainbow	7.75%	San Diego
Raisin City	7.975%	Fresno
Ramona	7.75%	San Diego
Ranchita	7.75%	San Diego
Rancho Bernardo (San Diego*)	7.75%	San Diego
Rancho California	7.75%	Riverside
Rancho Cordova*	7.75%	Sacramento
Rancho Cucamonga*	7.75%	San Bernardino
Rancho Dominguez	8.25%	Los Angeles
Rancho Mirage*	7.75%	Riverside
Rancho Murieta	7.75%	Sacramento
Rancho Palos Verdes*	8.25%	Los Angeles
Rancho Park (Los Angeles*)	8.25%	Los Angeles
Rancho Santa Fe	7.75%	San Diego
Rancho Santa Margarita	7.75%	Orange

City	Tax	County
Randsburg	7.25%	Kern
Ravendale	7.25%	Lassen
Ravenna	8.25%	Los Angeles
Raymond	7.75%	Madera
Red Bluff*	7.25%	Tehama
Red Mountain	7.75%	San Bernardino
Red Top	7.75%	Madera
Redcrest	7.25%	Humboldt
Redding*	7.25%	Shasta
Redlands*	7.75%	San Bernardino
Redondo Beach*	8.25%	Los Angeles
Redway	7.25%	Humboldt
Redwood City*	8.25%	San Mateo
Redwood Estates	8.25%	Santa Clara
Redwood Valley	7.25%	Mendocino
Reedley*	8.475%	Fresno
Refugio Beach	7.75%	Santa Barbara
Represa (Folsom Prison)	7.75%	Sacramento
Requa	7.25%	Del Norte
Rescue	7.25%	El Dorado
Reseda (Los Angeles*)	8.25%	Los Angeles
Rheem Valley (Moraga*)	8.25%	Contra Costa
Rialto*	7.75%	San Bernardino
Richardson Grove	7.25%	Humboldt
Richardson Springs	7.25%	Butte
Richfield	7.25%	Tehama
Richgrove	7.25%	Tulare
Richmond*	8.75%	Contra Costa
Richvale	7.25%	Butte
Ridgecrest*	7.25%	Kern
Rimforest	7.75%	San Bernardino
Rimpau (Los Angeles*)	8.25%	Los Angeles
Rio Bravo (Bakersfield*)	7.25%	Kern
Rio Dell*	7.25%	Humboldt
Rio Linda	7.75%	Sacramento
Rio Nido	7.75%	Sonoma
Rio Oso	7.25%	Sutter
Rio Vista*	7.38%	Solano
Ripley	7.75%	Riverside
Ripon*	7.75%	San Joaquin
River Pines	7.25%	Amador
Riverbank*	7.38%	Stanislaus
Riverdale	7.975%	Fresno
Riverside*	7.75%	Riverside
Robbins	7.25%	Sutter
Rocklin*	7.25%	Placer
Rodeo	8.25%	Contra Costa
Rohnert Park*	7.75%	Sonoma
Rohnerville	7.25%	Humboldt
Rolling Hills Estates*	8.25%	Los Angeles
Rolling Hills*	8.25%	Los Angeles
Romoland	7.75%	Riverside
Rosamond	7.25%	Kern
Rose Bowl (Pasadena*)	8.25%	Los Angeles
Roseland (Santa Rosa*)	7.75%	Sonoma
Rosemead*	8.25%	Los Angeles
Roseville*	7.25%	Placer
Ross*	7.75%	Marin
Rossmoor	7.75%	Orange
Rough and Ready	7.38%	Nevada
Round Mountain	7.25%	Shasta
Rowland Heights	8.25%	Los Angeles
Royal Oaks	7.25%	Monterey
Rubidoux	7.75%	Riverside
Ruby Valley	7.25%	Humboldt
Rumsey	7.25%	Yolo
Running Springs	7.75%	San Bernardino
Ruth	7.25%	Trinity
Rutherford	7.75%	Napa
Ryde	7.75%	Sacramento
Sacramento*	7.75%	Sacramento
Saint Helena*	7.75%	Napa
Salida	7.38%	Stanislaus
Salinas*	7.75%	Monterey
Salton City	7.75%	Imperial
Salyer	7.25%	Trinity
Samoa	7.25%	Humboldt
San Andreas	7.25%	Calaveras
San Anselmo*	7.75%	Marin

City	Tax	County
San Ardo	7.25%	Monterey
San Benito	7.25%	San Benito
San Bernardino*	8.0%	San Bernardino
San Bruno*	8.25%	San Mateo
San Carlos*	8.25%	San Mateo
San Clemente*	7.75%	Orange
San Diego*	7.75%	San Diego
San Dimas*	8.25%	Los Angeles
San Fernando*	8.25%	Los Angeles
San Francisco*	8.50%	San Francisco
San Gabriel*	8.25%	Los Angeles
San Geronimo	7.75%	Marin
San Gregorio	8.25%	San Mateo
San Jacinto*	7.75%	Riverside
San Joaquin*	7.975%	Fresno
San Jose*	8.25%	Santa Clara
San Juan Bautista*	8.0%	San Benito
San Juan Capistrano*	7.75%	Orange
San Juan Plaza (San Juan Capistrano)	7.75%	Orange
San Leandro*	8.75%	Alameda
San Lorenzo	8.75%	Alameda
San Lucas	7.25%	Monterey
San Luis Obispo*	7.75%	San Luis Obispo
San Luis Rey (Oceanside*)	7.75%	San Diego
San Marcos*	7.75%	San Diego
San Marino*	8.25%	Los Angeles
San Martin	8.25%	Santa Clara
San Mateo*	8.25%	San Mateo
San Miguel	7.25%	San Luis Obispo
San Pablo*	8.25%	Contra Costa
San Pedro (Los Angeles*)	8.25%	Los Angeles
San Quentin	7.75%	Marin
San Rafael*	8.25%	Marin
San Ramon*	8.25%	Contra Costa
San Simeon	7.25%	San Luis Obispo
San Tomas	8.25%	Santa Clara
San Ysidro (San Diego*)	7.75%	San Diego
Sand City*	7.75%	Monterey
Sanger*	8.725%	Fresno
Santa Ana*	7.75%	Orange
Santa Barbara*	7.75%	Santa Barbara
Santa Clara*	8.25%	Santa Clara
Santa Clarita*	8.25%	Los Angeles
Santa Cruz*	8.50%	Santa Cruz
Santa Fe Springs*	8.25%	Los Angeles
Santa Margarita	7.25%	San Luis Obispo
Santa Maria*	7.75%	Santa Barbara
Santa Monica*	8.25%	Los Angeles
Santa Nella	7.25%	Merced
Santa Paula*	7.25%	Ventura
Santa Rita Park	7.25%	Merced
Santa Rosa*	8.0%	Sonoma
Santa Ynez	7.75%	Santa Barbara
Santa Ysabel	7.75%	San Diego
Santee*	7.75%	San Diego
Saratoga*	8.25%	Santa Clara
Saticoy	7.25%	Ventura
Sattley	7.25%	Sierra
Saugus (Santa Clarita*)	8.25%	Los Angeles
Sausalito*	7.75%	Marin
Sawtelle (Los Angeles*)	8.25%	Los Angeles
Sawyers Bar	7.25%	Siskiyou
Scotia	7.25%	Humboldt
Scott Bar	7.25%	Siskiyou
Scotts Valley*	8.50%	Santa Cruz
Sea Ranch	7.75%	Sonoma
Seabright	8.00%	Santa Cruz
Seal Beach*	7.75%	Orange
Seaside*	8.25%	Monterey
Sebastopol*	8.0%	Sonoma
Seeley	7.75%	Imperial
Seiad Valley	7.25%	Siskiyou
Selby	8.25%	Contra Costa
Selma*	8.475%	Fresno
Seminole Hot Springs	8.25%	Los Angeles
Sepulveda (Los Angeles*)	8.25%	Los Angeles
Sequoia National Park	7.25%	Tulare
Shafter*	7.75%	Kern
Shandon	7.25%	San Luis Obispo

City	Tax	County
Sharpe Army Depot	7.75%	San Joaquin
Shasta	7.25%	Shasta
Shaver Lake	7.975%	Fresno
Sheepranch	7.25%	Calaveras
Shell Beach (Pismo Beach*)	7.25%	San Luis Obispo
Sheridan	7.25%	Placer
Sherman Island	7.75%	Sacramento
Sherman Oaks (Los Angeles*)	8.25%	Los Angeles
Sherwin Plaza	7.25%	Mono
Shingle Springs	7.25%	El Dorado
Shingletown	7.25%	Shasta
Shively	7.25%	Humboldt
Shore Acres	8.25%	Contra Costa
Shoshone	7.75%	Inyo
Sierra City	7.25%	Sierra
Sierra Madre*	8.25%	Los Angeles
Sierraville	7.25%	Sierra
Signal Hill*	8.25%	Los Angeles
Silver Lake	7.25%	Amador
Silverado Canyon	7.75%	Orange
Simi Valley*	7.25%	Ventura
Sisquoc	7.75%	Santa Barbara
Sites	7.25%	Colusa
Sky Valley	7.75%	Riverside
Skyforest	7.75%	San Bernardino
Sleepy Valley	8.25%	Los Angeles
Sloat	7.25%	Plumas
Sloughhouse	7.75%	Sacramento
Smartville	7.25%	Yuba
Smith River	7.25%	Del Norte
Smithflat	7.25%	El Dorado
Smoke Tree (Palm Springs*)	7.75%	San Bernardino
Snelling	7.25%	Merced
Soda Springs	7.38%	Nevada
Solana Beach*	7.75%	San Diego
Soledad*	7.25%	Monterey
Solemint	8.25%	Los Angeles
Solvang*	7.75%	Santa Barbara
Somerset	7.25%	El Dorado
Somes Bar	7.25%	Siskiyou
Somis	7.25%	Ventura
Sonoma*	7.75%	Sonoma
Sonora*	7.75%	Tuolumne
Soquel	8.00%	Santa Cruz
Soulsbyville	7.25%	Tuolumne
South Dos Palos	7.25%	Merced
South El Monte*	8.25%	Los Angeles
South Fork	7.25%	Humboldt
South Gate *	9.25%	Los Angeles
South Laguna (Laguna Beach*)	7.75%	Orange
South Lake Tahoe*	7.75%	El Dorado
South Pasadena*	8.25%	Los Angeles
South San Francisco*	8.25%	San Mateo
South Shore (Alameda*)	8.75%	Alameda
South Whittier	8.25%	Los Angeles
Spanish Flat	7.75%	Napa
Spreckels	7.25%	Monterey
Spring Garden	7.25%	Plumas
Spring Valley	7.75%	San Diego
Springville	7.25%	Tulare
Spyrock	7.25%	Mendocino
Squaw Valley	7.975%	Fresno
St. Helena*	7.75%	Napa
Standard	7.25%	Tuolumne
Standish	7.25%	Lassen
Stanford	8.25%	Santa Clara
Stanislaus	7.25%	Tuolumne
Stanton*	7.75%	Orange
Steele Park	7.75%	Napa
Stevinson	7.25%	Merced
Stewarts Point	7.75%	Sonoma
Stinson Beach	7.75%	Marin
Stirling City	7.25%	Butte
Stockton*	8.0%	San Joaquin
Stonyford	7.25%	Colusa
Storrie	7.25%	Plumas
Stratford	7.25%	Kings
Strathmore	7.25%	Tulare
Strawberry	7.25%	Tuolumne

City	Tax	County
Strawberry Valley	7.25%	Yuba
Studio City (Los Angeles*)	8.25%	Los Angeles
Sugarloaf	7.75%	San Bernardino
Suisun City*	7.38%	Solano
Sulphur Springs	8.25%	Los Angeles
Sultana	7.25%	Tulare
Summerland	7.75%	Santa Barbara
Summit	7.75%	San Bernardino
Summit City	7.25%	Shasta
Sun City	7.75%	Riverside
Sun Valley (Los Angeles*)	8.25%	Los Angeles
Sunland (Los Angeles*)	8.25%	Los Angeles
Sunnymead (Moreno Valley*)	7.75%	Riverside
Sunnyside	7.75%	San Diego
Sunnyvale*	8.25%	Santa Clara
Sunol	8.75%	Alameda
Sunset Beach	7.75%	Orange
Sunset Whitney Ranch	7.25%	Placer
Surfside (Seal Beach*)	7.75%	Orange
Susanville*	7.25%	Lassen
Sutter	7.25%	Sutter
Sutter Creek*	7.25%	Amador
Sylmar (Los Angeles*)	8.25%	Los Angeles
Taft*	7.25%	Kern
Tagus Ranch	7.25%	Tulare
Tahoe City	7.25%	Placer
Tahoe Paradise	7.25%	El Dorado
Tahoe Valley	7.25%	El Dorado
Tahoe Vista	7.25%	Placer
Tahoma	7.25%	Placer
Talmage	7.25%	Mendocino
Tamal (San Quentin)	7.75%	Marin
Tarzana (Los Angeles*)	8.25%	Los Angeles
Taylorsville	7.25%	Plumas
Tecate	7.75%	San Diego
Tecopa	7.75%	Inyo
Tehachapi*	7.25%	Kern
Tehama*	7.25%	Tehama
Temecula*	7.75%	Riverside
Temple City*	8.25%	Los Angeles
Templeton	7.25%	San Luis Obispo
Terminal Island (Los Angeles*)	8.25%	Los Angeles
Termo	7.25%	Lassen
Terra Bella	7.25%	Tulare
Thermal	7.75%	Riverside
Thornton	7.75%	San Joaquin
Thousand Oaks*	7.25%	Ventura
Thousand Palms	7.75%	Riverside
Three Rivers	7.25%	Tulare
Tiburon*	7.75%	Marin
Tierra Del Sol	7.75%	San Diego
Tierrasanta (San Diego*)	7.75%	San Diego
Tipton	7.25%	Tulare
Tollhouse	7.975%	Fresno
Toluca Lake (Los Angeles*)	8.25%	Los Angeles
Tomales	7.75%	Marin
Toms Place	7.25%	Mono
Topanga (Los Angeles*)	8.25%	Los Angeles
Topanga Park (Los Angeles*)	8.25%	Los Angeles
Topaz	7.25%	Mono
Torrance*	8.25%	Los Angeles
Town Center	7.25%	Tulare
Trabuco Canyon	7.75%	Orange
Tracy*	7.75%	San Joaquin
Tranquillity	7.975%	Fresno
Traver	7.25%	Tulare
Travis A.F.B. (Fairfield*)	7.38%	Solano
Tres Pinos	7.25%	San Benito
Trinidad*	8.25% (7.25% eff. 1/1/09)	Humboldt
Trinity Center	7.25%	Trinity
Trona	7.75%	San Bernardino
Trowbridge	7.25%	Sutter
Truckee*	7.88%	Nevada
Tujunga (Los Angeles*)	8.25%	Los Angeles
Tulare*	8.25%	Tulare
Tulelake*	7.75%	Siskiyou
Tuolumne	7.25%	Tuolumne
Tuolumne Meadows	7.75%	Mariposa
Tupman	7.25%	Kern

City	Tax	County
Turlock*	7.38%	Stanislaus
Tustin*	7.75%	Orange
Twain	7.25%	Plumas
Twain Harte	7.25%	Tuolumne
Twentynine Palms*	7.75%	San Bernardino
Twin Bridges	7.25%	El Dorado
Twin Peaks	7.75%	San Bernardino
Two Rock Coast Guard Station	7.75%	Sonoma
U.S.Naval Postgrad School (Monterey*)	7.25%	Monterey
Ukiah*	7.75%	Mendocino
Union City*	8.75%	Alameda
Universal City	8.25%	Los Angeles
University	7.75%	Santa Barbara
University Park (Irvine*)	7.75%	Orange
Upland*	7.75%	San Bernardino
Upper Lake/ Upper Lake Valley	7.25%	Lake
Vacaville*	7.38%	Solano
Val Verde Park	8.25%	Los Angeles
Valencia (Santa Clarita*)	8.25%	Los Angeles
Valinda	8.25%	Los Angeles
Vallecito	7.25%	Calaveras
Vallejo*	7.38%	Solano
Valley Center	7.75%	San Diego
Valley Fair	8.25%	Santa Clara
Valley Ford	7.75%	Sonoma
Valley Home	7.38%	Stanislaus
Valley Springs	7.25%	Calaveras
Valley Village	8.25%	Los Angeles
Valyermo	8.25%	Los Angeles
Van Nuys (Los Angeles*)	8.25%	Los Angeles
Vandenberg A.F.B	7.75%	Santa Barbara
Vasquez Rocks	8.25%	Los Angeles
Venice (Los Angeles*)	8.25%	Los Angeles
Ventucopa	7.75%	Santa Barbara
Ventura*	7.25%	Ventura
Verdugo City (Glendale*)	8.25%	Los Angeles
Vernalis	7.75%	San Joaquin
Vernon*	8.25%	Los Angeles
Veteran's Hospital (Los Angeles*)	8.25%	Los Angeles
Victor	7.75%	San Joaquin
Victorville*	7.75%	San Bernardino
Vidal	7.75%	San Bernardino
View Park	8.25%	Los Angeles
Villa Grande	7.75%	Sonoma
Villa Park*	7.75%	Orange
Vina	7.25%	Tehama
Vincent	8.25%	Los Angeles
Vineburg	7.75%	Sonoma
Vinton	7.25%	Plumas
Virgilia	7.25%	Plumas
Visalia*	8.0%	Tulare
Vista Park	7.25%	Kern
Vista*	8.25%	San Diego
Volcano	7.25%	Amador
Volta	7.25%	Merced
Wallace	7.25%	Calaveras
Walnut Creek*	8.25%	Contra Costa
Walnut Grove	7.75%	Sacramento
Walnut Park	8.25%	Los Angeles
Walnut*	8.25%	Los Angeles
Warm Spring (Fremont*)	8.75%	Alameda
Warner Springs	7.75%	San Diego
Wasco*	7.25%	Kern
Waterford*	7.38%	Stanislaus
Watsonville*	8.25%	Santa Cruz
Watts	8.25%	Los Angeles
Waukena	7.25%	Tulare
Wawona	7.75%	Mariposa
Weaverville	7.25%	Trinity
Weed*	7.25%	Siskiyou
Weimar	7.25%	Placer
Weldon	7.25%	Kern
Wendel	7.25%	Lassen
Weott	7.25%	Humboldt
West Covina*	8.25%	Los Angeles
West Hills (Los Angeles*)	8.25%	Los Angeles
West Hollywood*	8.25%	Los Angeles
West Los Angeles (Los Angeles*)	8.25%	Los Angeles
West Pittsburg	8.25%	Contra Costa

City	Tax	County
West Point	7.25%	Calaveras
West Sacramento*	7.75%	Yolo
Westchester (Los Angeles*)	8.25%	Los Angeles
Westend	7.75%	San Bernardino
Westhaven	7.25%	Humboldt
Westlake (Los Angeles*)	8.25%	Los Angeles
Westlake Village (Thousand Oaks*)	7.25%	Ventura
Westlake Village*	8.25%	Los Angeles
Westley	7.38%	Stanislaus
Westminster*	7.75%	Orange
Westmorland*	7.75%	Imperial
Westport	7.25%	Mendocino
Westside	7.38%	Stanislaus
Westwood	7.25%	Lassen
Westwood (Los Angeles*)	8.25%	Los Angeles
Wheatland*	7.25%	Yuba
Wheeler Ridge	7.25%	Kern
Whiskeytown	7.25%	Shasta
Whispering Pines	7.25%	Lake
White Pines	7.25%	Calaveras
Whitethorn	7.25%	Humboldt
Whitewater	7.75%	Riverside
Whitlow	7.25%	Humboldt
Whitmore	7.25%	Shasta
Whittier*	8.25%	Los Angeles
Wildomar	7.75%	Riverside
Wildwood	7.25%	Shasta
Williams*	7.75%	Colusa
Willits*	7.75%	Mendocino
Willow Creek	7.25%	Humboldt
Willow Ranch	7.25%	Modoc
Willowbrook	8.25%	Los Angeles
Willows*	7.25%	Glenn
Wilmington (Los Angeles*)	8.25%	Los Angeles
Wilseyville	7.25%	Calaveras
Wilsona Gardens	8.25%	Los Angeles
Wilton	7.75%	Sacramento
Winchester	7.75%	Riverside
Windsor Hills	8.25%	Los Angeles
Windsor*	7.75%	Sonoma
Winnetka (Los Angeles*)	8.25%	Los Angeles
Winterhaven	7.75%	Imperial
Winters*	7.25%	Yolo
Winton	7.25%	Merced
Wishon	7.75%	Madera
Witter Springs	7.25%	Lake
Wofford Heights	7.25%	Kern
Woodacre	7.75%	Marin
Woodbridge	7.75%	San Joaquin
Woodfords	7.25%	Alpine
Woodlake*	7.25%	Tulare
Woodland Hills (Los Angeles*)	8.25%	Los Angeles
Woodland*	7.75%	Yolo
Woodleaf	7.25%	Yuba
Woodside*	8.25%	San Mateo
Woodville	7.25%	Tulare
Woody	7.25%	Kern
Wrightwood	7.75%	San Bernardino
Yankee Hill	7.25%	Butte
Yermo	7.75%	San Bernardino
Yettem	7.25%	Tulare
Yolo	7.25%	Yolo
Yorba Linda*	7.75%	Orange
Yorkville	7.25%	Mendocino
Yosemite Lodge	7.75%	Mariposa
Yosemite National Park	7.75%	Mariposa
Yountville*	7.75%	Napa
Yreka*	7.25%	Siskiyou
Yuba City*	7.25%	Sutter
Yucaipa*	7.75%	San Bernardino
Yucca Valley*	7.75%	San Bernardino
Zamora	7.25%	Yolo
Zenia	7.25%	Trinity

¶1504 Transactions Subject to Sales Tax

Law: Secs. 6001-6294; Regs. 1524, 1526, 18 CCR (CCH California Tax Reports ¶60-230—60-760).

The sales tax applies to the gross receipts of retailers from the sale of tangible personal property, with the exceptions listed in ¶1509. (Sec. 6051, Rev. & Tax. Code) A "retail sale" is defined as a sale of tangible personal property for any purpose other than for resale in the regular course of business. (Sec. 6007, Rev. & Tax. Code) The tax applies to certain rental transactions, and to many occasional and non-recurring sales by persons who ordinarily would not be thought of as "retailers" (¶1507, 1510). Sales tax also applies to certain fabrication services and to certain services that are a part of the sale or lease of tangible personal property; see discussion below under "Services." (Sec. 6006, Rev. & Tax. Code)

Anyone who makes more than two retail sales within a 12-month period is a "retailer" and therefore subject to tax. (Sec. 6019, Rev. & Tax. Code) This rule has been held applicable to liquidating sales made by a federal bankruptcy trustee—see *California State Board of Equalization v. Sierra Summit, Inc.* (1989) (CCH CALIFORNIA TAX REPORTS ¶60-020.21). Where the customer furnishes the material, the tax applies to charges for fabrication labor (but not for installation, repairs, or alterations).

The sale of tangible personal property at auction is deemed to be a taxable transaction, irrespective of the fact that the sale is made with the understanding that (1) the property will not be delivered to the successful bidder, or (2) any amount paid for the property by the successful bidder will be returned to the bidder. The tax is applied to the amount of the successful bid. (Sec. 6015, Rev. & Tax. Code; Reg. 1565, 18 CCR)

The "true object" test determines whether a transaction involves a taxable sale of tangible personal property or the transfer of property incidental to the performance of a nontaxable service. If the true object sought by the purchaser is a nontaxable service, tax does not apply to the transaction, even if some property is transferred. (Reg. 1501, 18 CCR)

In *Navistar International Transportation Corp. et al. v. State Board of Equalization et al.* (1994) (CCH CALIFORNIA TAX REPORTS ¶60-310.611), a library of custom computer programs produced in-house for use by a taxpayer was subject to sales tax when sold as part of the taxpayer's business because the true object of the transaction was to sell the computer programs as tangible personal property and not to provide a service. Although the service of developing or designing custom computer programs is exempt from sales tax, once the computer programs were designed for the taxpayer's in-house use, the service had been completed, and the subsequent sale involved only the transfer of tangible personal property.

In *State Board of Equalization v. Los Angeles International Airport Hotel Associates* (1996) (CCH CALIFORNIA TAX REPORTS ¶60-020.25), a U.S. bankruptcy appellate court held that a hotel owner was required to pay sales tax on complimentary beverages and breakfasts provided to guests because the money paid by guests for their rooms was consideration for the hotel's duty to provide not only rooms but also beverages and breakfasts. The complimentary beverages and breakfasts had been offered to induce travelers to rent a room at the hotel. However, in *Petitions of Embassy Suites Inc., et al.* (1996) (CCH CALIFORNIA TAX REPORTS ¶60-020.251), the State Board of Equalization (SBE) took the opposite position, ruling that complimentary beverages and breakfasts provided by hotels to their guests were not subject to sales tax, because the retail value of the beverages and breakfasts was *de minimis* , equaling 10% or less of the average daily rate charged for rooms. The SBE has incorporated its ruling in *Embassy Suites, Inc.* into its regulation governing taxable sales of food products. (Reg. 1603, 18 CCR)

Special rules are provided for various nonprofit organizations, to the effect that under certain conditions they are not considered to be "retailers." (Sec. 6375, Rev. & Tax. Code) Special rules are provided for vending machine operators (Sec. 6359(d), Rev. & Tax. Code; Sec. 6359.2, Rev. & Tax. Code; Sec. 6359.4, Rev. & Tax. Code), flea market or swap meet operators, and special event operators (Sec. 6073, Rev. & Tax.

Code). Special rules are also provided for sales of mobile homes and manufactured homes. (Sec. 6012.8, Rev. & Tax. Code; Sec. 6012.9, Rev. & Tax. Code)

Sale and leaseback transactions are not subject to sales tax if (1) the tax was paid by the person selling (and leasing back) the property, and (2) the acquisition sale and leaseback is consummated within 90 days of that person's first functional use of the property. (Sec. 6010.65, Rev. & Tax. Code) Until January 1, 2009, the sale and leaseback of qualified equipment by a public transit agency was exempt from tax, without the 90-day requirement, provided the public transit agency paid tax on its purchase or acquisition of the qualified equipment. The subsequent purchase of qualified equipment by a public transit agency at the end of a lease or sublease that was part of an exempt sale and leaseback transaction was also exempt. (Sec. 6368.8, Rev. & Tax. Code)

• *Technology transfer agreements*

Tax applies to amounts received for any tangible personal property transferred in a technology transfer agreement. However, tax does not apply to amounts received for the assignment or licensing of a patent or copyright interest as part of the agreement. The gross receipts or sales price attributable to the transfer of tangible personal property as part of the agreement is equal to the following:

— the separately stated sales price for the property, so long as this price represents a reasonable fair market value for the property;

— the separate price at which the property or similar property was previously sold, leased, or offered for sale or lease to an unrelated third party, if there is no separately stated price; or

— 200% of the combined costs of materials and labor used to produce the property, if there is no separately stated sales price and the property or similar property has not been previously sold, leased, or offered for sale or lease to an unrelated third party.

(Sec. 6011(c)(10), Rev. & Tax. Code; Sec. 6012(c)(10), Rev. & Tax. Code; Reg. 1507, 18 CCR)

A technology transfer agreement is a written agreement for the following:

— assignment or license of a copyright interest in tangible personal property for the purpose of reproducing and selling other property subject to the copyright interest (including artwork);

— assignment or license of a patent interest for the right to manufacture and sell property subject to the patent interest; or

— assignment or license of the right to use a process subject to a patent interest.

However, a technology transfer agreement is neither an agreement for the transfer of tangible personal property manufactured pursuant to a technology transfer agreement nor an agreement for the transfer of any property derived, created, manufactured, or otherwise processed by property manufactured pursuant to a transfer technology agreement. Moreover, it is not an agreement for the transfer of prewritten software.

CCH Tip: Mobile Telecom Sourcing Act

California adopts the provisions of the federal Mobile Telecommunications Sourcing Act. Under the Act, mobile telecommunications services are taxable in the state and locality where the customer resides or maintains its primary business address and any other state or locality is prohibited from taxing the services, regardless of where the services originate, terminate, or pass through. The Act does not apply to prepaid telephone calling services or air-ground service. (Sec. 41020, Rev. & Tax. Code)

Furthermore, the Act provides that a state or a company designated by the political subdivisions of a state may provide an electronic database identifying the proper taxing jurisdiction for each street address in that state. If the provider of mobile telecommunications services uses such a database, it will be held harmless from any tax otherwise due solely as a result of an error in the database. If no such database exists, then a provider employing an enhanced zip code and exercising due diligence in assigning a street address to a taxing jurisdiction will be held harmless for any incorrect assignment.

• *Services*

Because sales tax is imposed on sales of tangible personal property, service transactions are generally not subject to tax. However, the tax is specifically imposed on certain fabrication services and on incidental services performed in the sale or lease of tangible personal property. Services performed for nontaxable sales, including sales for resales, are not subject to tax. (Sec. 6006, Rev. & Tax. Code; Sec. 6011, Rev. & Tax. Code; Sec. 6012, Rev. & Tax. Code)

California taxes charges for producing, fabricating, processing, printing, or imprinting tangible personal property for consumers who themselves have furnished, either directly or indirectly, the materials used in those procedures. (Sec. 6006(b), Rev. & Tax. Code) SBE Publication 108 states that charges for fabrication are generally taxable, whether or not the consumer supplies the materials.

***Practitioner Comment: Court of Appeal Finds Sales Tax Inapplicable to Non-Separately Stated Services in** Mixed Transactions*

The California Court of Appeal held in *Dell, Inc. vs. San Francisco Superior Court,* Cal. Ct. App. (1st District, Div. 4, No. A118657, January 31, 2008) that charges for optional customer service contracts embedded within the overall price charged for the sale of computers were exempt from sales tax. The Court distinguished bundled transactions in which goods and services are sold together yet are readily separable from "mixed transactions" such as those at issue in the case. Dell had increased the lump sum sales price of its products based upon customer-requested changes to the package configuration.

Two Dell customers brought suit alleging that Dell had improperly applied sales tax to the entire charge and Dell filed a cross complaint to allow it to recover the taxes paid in the event Dell lost the case. Dell and the SBE, while conceding that the services at issue were nontaxable, contended that taxation was justified because there was no separately stated charge for the services. The court rejected the argument of administrative convenience, noting that whether or not the charges were separately stated did not change the fact that the services were nontaxable.

This is another in a series of decisions that have eroded California's long standing policy of generally subjecting to tax the entire amount charged for "bundled transactions." The State's arguments in this case demonstrate that California will most likely continue to take an aggressive approach in such circumstances; however, taxpayers should be encouraged with the favorable treatment received in situations where the parties can demonstrate that the amount subjected to tax includes exempt components. Because bundled transactions including services appear to be 'in play' as a result of this case, we should expect to see an attempt to apply this decision to other types of bundled transactions.

Bruce Daigh, Chris Whitney, Contributing Editors

In determining whether tax applies, "producing, fabricating, and processing" include any operation resulting in, or any step in a process or series of operations resulting in, the creation or production of tangible personal property. (Reg. 1526(b), 18 CCR) For example, tax generally applies to charges for alterations to new clothing, whether or not the alterations are performed by the seller of the garment or by another person (however, special rules apply to dry cleaners). (Reg. 1524, 18 CCR) Charges for painting, polishing, and otherwise finishing tangible personal property in connection with the production of a finished product are also subject to tax, whether the article to be finished is supplied by the customer or by the finisher. Gift-wrapping services are also subject to tax.

Charges for repair or reconditioning of property to refit it for the use for which it was originally produced are exempt, if separately stated, and tax applies only to the retail value of the parts used. The labor charge for assembling an article or piece of equipment, as distinguished from its installation, is taxable. (Reg. 1546, 18 CCR)

Many services performed on customer-furnished goods are but one step in the final production of an article of personal property; as a part of the fabrication, they are subject to tax. For example, charges for firing ceramics, cutting lumber, carving and dressing meats, printing or painting textiles, or laminating or fireproofing an article of personal property are taxable. However, tax applies to the service only if it is performed for the consumer. Consequently, a service performed by a subcontractor is not a taxable fabrication service. (SUTA Series 435, Producing, fabricating, and processing property furnished by consumers --General rules.)

CCH Tip: Computer Maintenance Contracts

Sales tax applies to half of any sum charged for optional maintenance contracts sold with the sale or lease of canned software. While one-half of the transaction is deemed a sale of tangible personal property subject to sales tax, the other half of the transaction is treated as receipts from nontaxable repairs (Reg. 1502, 18 CCR).

However, a California court of appeal has held that optional computer service contracts sold with computers for a single lump-sum price were not subject to California sales and use taxes because the transactions were mixed transactions that involved separately identifiable transfers of goods and services. According to the court, both the computers and the contracts were distinct consumer items, each was a significant object of the transaction, and the service contracts had readily ascertainable values even without itemized invoices. In addition, there was no state statute or regulation that required service contract charges to be separately stated in order to avoid taxation. (*Dell, Inc. v. The Superior Court of the City and County of San Francisco* (2008) (CCH CALIFORNIA TAX REPORTS ¶60-310.55)

¶1505 Transactions Subject to Use Tax

Law: Secs. 6201-94, Rev. & Tax. Code, Sec. 10295.1 Public Contract Code; Reg. 1620, 18 CCR (CCH CALIFORNIA TAX REPORTS ¶60-020, 60-025, 60-570, 60-740, 61-450).

The use tax is imposed on the storage, use, or other consumption in California of property purchased from a retailer for such storage, use, or other consumption. (Sec. 6202, Rev. & Tax. Code) It applies to certain rental transactions and to out-of-state fabrication of customer-furnished materials. Because the use tax does not apply to cases where the sale of the property is subject to the sales tax (Sec. 6401, Rev. & Tax. Code) (except when the purchase is in a district with a lower rate than the district in which the property is purchased to be used and is actually used, and in certain lease transactions—see ¶1507), the use tax generally applies to purchases made outside of California for use within the state. Although this tax is imposed upon the purchaser, any retailer engaged in business in the state is required to collect the tax and remit it to the state.

A "retailer" that has any kind of an establishment in California or representatives conducting any kind of sales activity in the state is deemed to be "engaged in business" in the state. The law applies whether the retailer is involved directly or through a subsidiary or agent. (Sec. 6005, Rev. & Tax. Code; Sec. 6015, Rev. & Tax. Code)

In *Appeal of B & D Litho, Inc.* (2001) (CCH CALIFORNIA TAX REPORTS ¶61-460.90), an out-of-state corporation that held a California use tax registration certificate was required to collect California use tax on sales of property to California customers, even if it did not have nexus with the state.

• *Nexus*

In any sale or other taxable transaction that crosses state lines in any fashion, there has to be a determination of whether the transaction has sufficient nexus with the state to empower the state to impose its taxes. In *National Bellas Hess, Inc. v. Department of Revenue of Illinois*, 386 US 753 (1967) (CCH CALIFORNIA TAX REPORTS ¶60-025), the U.S. Supreme Court held that a vendor had to have a physical presence in a state in order for that state to require the vendor to collect sales and use taxes on mail-order purchases. Physical presence within the state was required regardless of the degree to which the vendor may have availed itself of the benefits and protections of the taxing state.

Although the U.S. Supreme Court, in *Quill Corporation v. North Dakota* (1992) (CCH CALIFORNIA TAX REPORTS ¶60-075.341), upheld the test of physical presence established in *National Bellas Hess, Inc.*, stating that physical presence is still required by the Commerce Clause of the U.S. Constitution to bring out-of-state retailers within the jurisdiction of a state's sales and use tax laws, such physical presence is not required to satisfy the Due Process Clause. The court held that the Due Process Clause by itself would permit a state's enforcement of its use tax against an out-of-state retailer who had an "economic presence" within the state (*i.e.*, continuous and widespread solicitation of business in the state).

A taxpayer's physical presence in a state need not be directly related to the taxed activity to establish nexus. In *National Geographic Society v. California Board of Equalization*, 430 US 551 (1977) (CCH CALIFORNIA TAX REPORTS ¶60-075.82), the U.S. Supreme Court held that the presence in California of advertising sales offices owned by the society provided sufficient nexus for California to require that the society collect use tax on mail-order sales made to California residents by another division of its society. Although the activities conducted by the two advertising sales offices were unrelated to the mail-order sales, the sales offices benefited from California services and, thus, established nexus with the state. The Court applied similar reasoning in *D.H. Holmes Co. v. MacNamara*, 486 US 24 (1988) (CCH CALIFORNIA TAX REPORTS ¶60-025), in which a company with retail outlets in the state had to pay use tax on catalogs ordered from an out-of-state printer and sent by mail to the company's customers.

Furthermore, an Internet business may establish nexus as a result of activities by its "brick-and-mortar" affiliate. An out-of-state retailer of tangible personal property via the Internet was obligated to collect and remit California sales and use tax because the willingness of its authorized representative within the state to accept returned merchandise created for the retailer a substantial physical presence within the state. In *Borders Online, LLC v. State Board of Equalization* (2005) (CCH CALIFORNIA TAX REPORTS ¶60-025.32), a California court of appeal held that the representative's activity on behalf of the retailer was sufficient to consider the retailer as being engaged in business in the state because such activity constituted "selling" and was an integral part of the retailer's selling efforts.

Practitioner Comment: Companies Doing Business Online

Borders Online's returns policy was posted on its Website for less than 11 months of the 18-month audit period. However, that was sufficient for the court to find nexus for the entire audit period, noting that the question for purposes of the Commerce Clause is the "nature and extent" of the activities in the taxing state. The fact that Borders Online changed its policy did not appear to matter to the court, which found that once Borders Online entered the California market, it had nexus for the whole period. Borders Online's policy change did not "break" nexus.

Further, the court appeared to focus on the economic environment created by Borders Inc. for Borders Online, and found nexus despite an arguably slight or tenuous physical presence. In so ruling, the court extensively cited New York's highest court's decision in *Orvis Co. v. Tax Tribunal*, 86 N.Y.2d 165 (1995), and its conclusion that while physical presence is required, it need not be substantial. Rather, it must be demonstrably more than a "slightest presence," the court said, and it may be manifested by the presence in the taxing state of the vendor's property or the conduct of economic activities in the taxing state performed by the vendor's personnel or on its behalf.

Other courts have disagreed with this interpretation, but the court said that *Orvis* is more in keeping with the realities of 21st century marketing and technology, which, in the words of the court, "increasingly affords opportunities for out-of-state vendors to establish a strong economic presence in California by using California's 'legal-economic environment' while maintaining only a minimal or vicarious presence in the state."

Bruce Daigh, Chris Whitney, Contributing Editors

Conversely, in *Barnesandnoble.com LLC v. State Board of Equalization* (2007) (CCH CALIFORNIA TAX REPORTS ¶404-488), the San Francisco Superior Court held that the use by a brick-and-mortar company of coupons in its shopping bags that provided a discount on any one online purchase from its Internet retailer sister company did not create nexus sufficient to impose California use tax registration, collection and remittance obligations on the Internet retailer. In granting summary judgment in favor of the taxpayer, the court rejected the contention of the State Board of Equalization (SBE) that by using the shopping bags with the pre-inserted coupons issued by the taxpayer, the retail stores were acting as the taxpayer's agents or representatives. According to the court, the concept of agency requires something significantly more than the passive distribution of coupons. On May 29, 2008, the SBE approved a global settlement with Barnes & Noble.com that resolves all disputes between Barnes & Noble.com and the State of California for sales and use taxes, including pending litigation in the U.S. District Court for the Eastern District of California and the California Court of Appeal (First District). Under the settlement, two tax determinations against Barnes & Noble.com, plus all interest and penalties, were canceled by the SBE. In addition, the SBE waived all claims for sales and use taxes, interest, and penalties through November 1, 2005, the date on which Barnes & Noble.com voluntarily commenced collecting and remitting sales and use taxes to California.

CCH Comment: Nexus for Online Retailers

The SBE conducted an informational hearing regarding nexus and the collection of use tax by online retailers in light of nexus issues that have arisen in New York and Texas. In New York, a rebuttable presumption is created that any person making taxable sales of tangible personal property or services (seller) is a vendor subject to New York sales and compensating use tax when the seller enters into an agreement with a New York resident to directly or indirectly refer customers to the seller, whether by a link on an Internet Web site or otherwise, for a commission or other consideration, and the agreement generates sales of over $10,000 in the prior four quarterly reporting periods.

SBE staff does not believe that a link on a retailer's affiliate's Web site is enough to establish that the affiliate is an authorized salesperson of the out-of-state retailer and does not establish a sufficient business presence (nexus) in California to warrant a use tax collection responsibility on sales made to California consumers. Consequently, under the current provisions of California law, SBE staff does not require out-of-state companies to collect tax based solely on such links on affiliates' Web sites. Other California activities an affiliate may engage in to promote the link, however, may suffice to establish that the affiliate is an authorized salesperson of the out-of-state retailer.

If the SBE staff's analysis of New York law is accurate, the main difference between New York's approach and California's approach is in regard to who has the burden to prove (or disprove) that other activities in support of the link exist that are sufficient to create nexus. Because New York's approach involves a rebuttable presumption, it is the position of SBE staff that under New York law, as under California law, the existence of a link on an affiliate's Web site does not, on its own, conclusively create nexus. (*Business Taxes Committee Meeting Minutes*, SBE, July 8, 2008; *Information Paper, Nexus and Online*

Retailers; Recent Actions in New York and Texas, Tax Policy Division, Sales and Use Tax Department, SBE, June 19, 2008)

A regulation provides that an out-of-state retailer whose only contact with California is the use of a computer server on the Internet to create or maintain a Web page or site is not "engaged in business" in the state for use tax purposes and, consequently, is not required to collect or remit tax. The regulation also excludes from use tax collection requirements any out-of-state retailer whose contact with California is limited to use of an in-state independent contractor to perform warranty or repair services on tangible personal property that the retailer sells. (Reg. 1684, 18 CCR)

Among others, retailers soliciting orders by mail are considered to be engaged in business in California and, thus, are obligated to collect and remit use tax if the solicitations are substantial and recurring and the retailer benefits from various in-state services (*i.e.*, banking, financing, debt collection, authorized installation services). However, this provision becomes operative only upon the enactment of a congressional act that authorizes states to compel out-of-state retailers to collect state sales and use taxes. (Sec. 6203, Rev. & Tax. Code)

CCH Comment: State Contracts

A California department or agency may not enter into a contract for the purchase of tangible personal property from any vendor, contractor, or affiliate of a vendor or contractor unless the vendor, contractor, and all affiliates that make sales for delivery into California have a valid seller's permit or are registered with the SBE for California sales and use tax purposes. Every vendor, contractor, or affiliate of a vendor or contractor offered such a contract is required to submit a copy of its, and any affiliate's, seller's permit or certificate of registration. Exceptions are allowed if necessary to meet a compelling state interest.

• *Computer telecommunications networks*

A retailer who takes orders from customers in California through a computer telecommunications network located in the state is not required to collect and remit use tax, provided that

— the telecommunications network is not owned by the retailer when orders are taken,

— the orders result from the electronic display of products on the network, and

— the network consists substantially of on-line communications services other than displaying and taking orders for products.

(*Response to CCH Internet/Electronic Commerce Survey*, SBE, September 10, 1999, CCH CALIFORNIA TAX REPORTS ¶403-060)

• *Convention or trade show participation*

A retailer whose sole physical presence in California is to engage in convention or trade show activities is not generally required to collect sales and use tax provided that the retailer and its representatives do not engage in California convention and trade show activities for more than 15 days during any 12-month period and did not derive more than $100,000 of net income from those activities in California during the prior calendar year. However, the retailer is required to collect use tax with respect to any sale occurring during or at California convention or trade show activities, including orders taken during such activities. (Sec. 6203(e), Rev. & Tax. Code; Reg. 1684(b), 18 CCR)

• *Interstate transactions*

In *Montgomery Ward & Co., Inc. v. State Board of Equalization* (1969) 272 CA2d 728, 78 CRptr 373, cert. den. 396 US 1040, 90 SCt 688, the state attempted to force out-of-state stores to collect use tax on over-the-counter sales in Oregon and Nevada that were billed to California residents. The Court of Appeal held that the stores could not be required to collect use tax where the goods were delivered outside the state.

In *National Geographic Society v. California State Board of Equalization* (1977) (CCH CALIFORNIA TAX REPORTS ¶60-020.74, 60-075.82), the U.S. Supreme Court held that the Society could be required to collect use tax on out-of-state mail order sales to California residents. The Society had two small offices in California.

In *Matter of Hewlett Packard Co.* (2000) (CCH CALIFORNIA TAX REPORTS ¶60-450.522), the SBE ruled that donations of electronic equipment and software to out-of-state universities were not subject to use tax.

The law provides that the terms "storage" and "use" do not apply to

— cases where property is brought into the state to be transported outside the state, or to be processed or fabricated into property which is to be transported outside the state, for use outside the state, or

— the rental of certain cargo containers for use in interstate or foreign commerce.

Consequently, such transactions are exempt from use tax.

Property purchased out of state is subject to use tax if its first functional use occurs in California. If the first functional use occurs outside California but the property is brought into California within 90 days of its purchase, the property is presumed to have been purchased for use in California. The presumption may be overcome if the property is used or stored outside the state for at least one-half of the six-month period immediately following its entry into California. Use tax is also not imposed if the property is used out of state for more than 90 days prior to its entry into the state. (Reg. 1620(b)(3), 18 CCR)

• *Imports*

Use tax is not imposed on property that is purchased for use in, and actually used in, interstate or foreign commerce prior to its entry into California and that is thereafter used continuously in interstate or foreign commerce both within and without California but not exclusively in California. (Reg. 1620(b)(2), 18 CCR) In addition, the storage, use, or other consumption in California of the first $800 of tangible personal property purchased in a foreign country by an individual from a retailer and personally hand-carried into California from the foreign country within any 30-day period is exempt from use tax; the exemption does not apply to property sent or shipped to California. (Sec. 6405, Rev. & Tax. Code) The SBE and the U.S. Customs Office have an information exchange program.

• *Drop shipments*

Anyone who delivers tangible personal property, either to a California consumer or to a person for redelivery to a California consumer pursuant to a retail sale made to the consumer by a retailer that does not do business in California, is the retailer of the property for California sales and use tax purposes. The deliverer must include the retail selling price of the property in the gross receipts or sales price of the property. (Sec. 6007, Rev. & Tax. Code) This rule applies to out-of-state wholesalers as well as California wholesalers. (*Mason Shoe Manufacturing Co. v. California State Board of Equalization*, (2005) CCH CALIFORNIA TAX REPORTS ¶60-340.50)

As a general rule, a drop shipper calculates the taxable retail selling price of its drop shipments based on the selling price from the true retailer to the consumer plus a mark-up of 10%. However, if the drop shipper can show that a lower mark-up percentage accurately reflects the retail selling price charged by the true retailer, that lower percentage can be used. (Reg. 1706, 18 CCR)

• *Commerce Clause requirements*

In *National Railroad Passenger Corporation v. State Board of Equalization* (1986) (CCH CALIFORNIA TAX REPORTS ¶ 60-450.62), the state attempted to impose a tax on railroad passenger cars that was not imposed on other passenger vehicles used by common carriers. A federal district court held that such imposition was discriminatory and, therefore, prohibited.

• *Purchases of automobiles, boats, or airplanes*

A purchaser acquiring an automobile without the payment of sales or use tax is required to pay use tax to the Department of Motor Vehicles when applying for transfer of registration, unless the seller is a close relative (parent, grandparent, child, grandchild, spouse, registered domestic partner, or minor brother or sister) of the purchaser and is not in the automobile business. A similar rule applies to the purchase of a boat or airplane.

Vehicles entering California after being purchased outside California are deemed to have been purchased for use in California if the vehicle's first functional use is in California. (Reg. 1620, 18 CCR)

A vehicle, vessel, or aircraft bought outside of California that is brought into California within 12 months from the date of its purchase is presumptively subject to California use tax if the vehicle, vessel, or aircraft:

— was purchased by a California resident;

— is subject to California registration or property tax laws during the first 12 months of ownership, or

— is used or stored in California more than half the time during the first 12 months of ownership.

The presumption is inapplicable to any vehicle, vessel, or aircraft used in interstate or foreign commerce, and any aircraft or vessel brought into California for the purpose of repair, retrofit, or modification. Also, the presumption may be controverted by documentary evidence. (Sec. 6248, Rev. & Tax. Code)

Aircraft or vessels brought into California for the purpose of repair, retrofit, or modification are not subject to California use tax unless, during the period following the time the aircraft or vessel is brought into California and ending when the repair, retrofit, or modification of the aircraft or vessel is complete, more than 25 hours of airtime or sailing time are logged on the aircraft or vessel by the aircraft's or vessel's registered owner or by an authorized agent operating the aircraft or vessel. The return trip to a point outside California is not counted.

• *Insurance companies*

Although insurance companies are exempt under the California Constitution from all taxes other than the gross receipts tax, the California Supreme Court ruled in *Occidental Life Insurance Company v. State Board of Equalization* (1982) (CCH CALIFORNIA TAX REPORTS ¶ 60-440.65), that retail sales of personal property to insurance companies are subject to California sales tax because the incidence of the tax is on the retailer, not the purchaser. Insurance companies are also liable for the collection of the use tax from their customers as held in *Beneficial Standard Life Insurance Company v. State Board of Equalization* (1962) (CCH CALIFORNIA TAX REPORTS ¶ 60-440.15, 60-440.25), decided by a California district court of appeal. In that case, an insurance company was required to pay use tax on purchases of automobiles and furniture from (or through) the company by its employees.

¶1506 Sales for Resale

Law: Secs. 6012, 6051, 6091-95, 6201, 6241-45 (CCH CALIFORNIA TAX REPORTS ¶ 61-020).

A sale for resale is exempt from tax. (Sec. 6051, Rev. & Tax. Code; Sec. 6201, Rev. & Tax. Code) However, it is presumed that all gross receipts are subject to tax until the contrary is established. (Sec. 6091, Rev. & Tax. Code) To be relieved from liability, a seller must obtain a "resale certificate" from the purchaser. To be effective, the resale certificate must be taken in good faith from a person who holds a seller's permit and is engaged in the business of selling tangible personal property. (Sec. 6092, Rev. & Tax. Code) If a resale certificate is not obtained, the seller may still be able to prove by other evidence that the sale was for resale. (Reg. 1668, 18 CCR)

If tax is paid on a purchase of property that is resold prior to any use, the amount of the purchase may be deducted on the purchaser's sales tax return. (Sec. 6012(a)(1), Rev. & Tax. Code; Reg. 1701, 18 CCR) On the other hand, a taxpayer who buys property tax-free with the intention of reselling it but uses it instead (other than for demonstration, display, etc.) must report and pay a tax on the purchase price. Even if the property is later resold, the tax on self-consumption must be paid if the property is used for anything except demonstration or display at any time before it is resold. However, if the use is limited to an accommodation loan to a customer while awaiting property purchased or leased, the tax is imposed only on the fair rental value for the duration of the loan. Also, the tax on property used for demonstration or display or for loans during repairs is measured by the rental value. (Sec. 6094(a), Rev. & Tax. Code , Reg. 1669, 18 CCR)

• *Resale certificates*

A resale certificate may be in any form, such as a note, letter, or memorandum. Although the State Board of Equalization (SBE) does not furnish resale certificates, the form approved by the SBE is reproduced in Reg. 1668, 18 CCR. California will also accept a Border State "Sale for Resale" Certificate from businesses operating within Arizona, California, New Mexico, Oklahoma, Texas, Utah, or Mexico that buy goods for resale that will be transported across state and/or national borders. Possession of the border state certificate will relieve the seller from California sales and use tax liability. (*Tax Information Bulletin*, SBE, September 1996)

¶1507 Rental Transactions

Law: Secs. 6006-18.8, 6094.1, 6365, 6368.7, 6381, 6390, 6406, 7205.1; Reg. 1803.5, 18 CCR (CCH CALIFORNIA TAX REPORTS ¶ 60-460, 60-570).

The tax is applicable to a lease of tangible personal property, except the following:

— motion picture films and tapes, other than video cassettes, videotapes, and videodiscs for private use;

— linen supplies under a continuing laundry or service contract;

— household furniture included in a lease of living quarters;

— mobile transportation equipment for use in for-hire transportation of persons or property, except one-way rental trucks;

— other tangible personal property leased in substantially the same form as acquired by the lessor, where the lessor has paid the sales or use tax on the purchase price of the property;

— certain leases involving the U.S. government or its agencies; and

— leases of original works of art from one tax-exempt nonprofit organization to another for 35 years or more and leases of public art by the state or a local governmental entity from another such entity for display in public places.

(Sec. 6006(g), Rev. & Tax. Code; Sec. 6010(e), Rev. & Tax. Code; Sec. 6365, Rev. & Tax. Code; Reg. 1660(b)(1), 18 CCR)

Special rules apply to mobile home leases. If a mobile home was originally purchased by a retailer without payment of sales or use tax and first leased before July 1, 1980, its lease is taxable unless the mobile home becomes subject to local property taxation, in which case it is exempt from sales and use tax. The lease of a *used* mobile home that was first sold new in California after July 1, 1980, is not subject to sales or use tax. The lease of a mobile home that was originally purchased by a retailer without payment of sales or use tax and first leased on or after July 1, 1980, is not subject to sales tax, but the lessor's use of the property is subject to use tax. (Reg. 1660(d)(8), 18 CCR)

"Lease" is defined to exclude the use of tangible personal property for less than one day for a charge of less than $20, where the use of the property is restricted to the business location of the seller. (Sec. 6006.3, Rev. & Tax. Code)

A contract designated as a lease is considered a sale under a security agreement rather than a lease if the lessee is bound for a fixed term and obtains title after making the required payments or has the option to purchase the property for a nominal amount. (Sec. 6006.3, Rev. & Tax. Code; Reg. 1660(a), 18 CCR)

A lease of tangible personal property is deemed to be a continuing sale by the lessor and a continuing purchase by the lessee for the entire period that the leased property is located in California. (Sec. 6006.1, Rev. & Tax. Code; Sec. 6010.1, Rev. & Tax. Code)

If a lease of tangible personal property covers property that is in substantially the same form as when it was acquired by the lessor, and the lessor has paid the sales or use tax on its acquisition, the rental receipts are not subject to tax. (Sec. 6006(g), Rev. & Tax. Code; Reg. 1660(b)(1)(E), 18 CCR) This rule does not apply to chemical toilets, and their rentals are therefore taxable. (Sec. 6010.7, Rev. & Tax. Code) As indicated above, the tax does apply where the leased property is *not* in substantially the same form as when acquired by the lessor, or where the property was acquired by the lessor in a transaction not subject to sales or use tax; *e.g.*, in an "occasional sale" transaction.

• *Local taxes*

The local use tax from long-term leases of tangible personal property is generally allocated to the lessee's residence, as that is the place where the property is used. However, the place of use for reporting and transmittal of the local use tax for leases of passenger vehicles and small pick-up trucks is

(1) the lessor's place of business at which the lease is negotiated, if the lessor is a California new motor vehicle dealer or leasing company;

(2) the place of business of the new motor vehicle dealer or leasing company from which the vehicle is purchased, if the lessor is not a California new motor vehicle dealer or leasing company; or

(3) the place of the lessee's residence, if the lessor is not a California new motor vehicle dealer or leasing company and the lessor purchases either a new motor vehicle from a person other than a new motor vehicle dealer or a used motor vehicle from any source.

(Sec. 7205.1, Rev. & Tax. Code)

Generally, the place of use, once determined, is the place of use for the duration of the lease. The lessor's sale of the vehicle, assignment of the lease contract to a third party, or, in the case of (1) or (2), above, change of residence will not affect the place of use.

¶1508 Basis of Tax

Law: Secs. 6011, 6012, 6012.3, 6055, 6203.5; Regs. 1641, 1642, 1654, 1671, 18 CCR (CCH CALIFORNIA TAX REPORTS ¶ 61-110—61-180).

Tax is imposed upon "gross receipts" for sales tax purposes and "sales price" for use tax purposes, which are defined as the total amount for which tangible personal property is sold, leased, or rented, valued in money (whether paid in money or otherwise). Excluded from the terms "gross receipts" and "sales price" is the portion of the sales price returned to a used vehicle purchaser or the purchase price of a contract cancellation option agreement. No deduction may be claimed for the following:

(1) the cost of the property sold;

(2) the cost of materials used, labor or service costs, interest paid or charged, losses, or any other expenses; or

(3) the cost of transporting the property, except as otherwise provided.

(Sec. 6011, Rev. & Tax. Code; Sec. 6012, Rev. & Tax. Code)

The "total amount for which property is sold, leased, or rented" includes the following:

(1) any services that are a part of the sale;

(2) any amount for which credit is given to the purchaser by the seller; and

(3) in the definition of "gross receipts," all receipts, cash, credits, and property of any kind.

(Sec. 6011, Rev. & Tax. Code; Sec. 6012, Rev. & Tax. Code)

• *Bad debt deduction*

California permits a deduction for whatever portion of a tax-paid account is found to be worthless, provided that the account has been charged off for federal income tax purposes or, if the taxpayer is not required to file a federal return, the account is charged off under generally accepted accounting principles. The deduction may not include tax-exempt charges such as interest, insurance, repair, installation, or other charges, or collection expenses.

The tax must be repaid if a recovery is made on a charged-off account. In the case of a repossession, a bad debt deduction is allowed to the extent that the seller has sustained a net loss on tax-paid gross receipts. If the tax has previously been paid, the worthless accounts may be deducted from other taxable sales in the quarter in which they are determined to be worthless and charged off, or a refund may be claimed. If there is a subsequent recovery on such accounts, the amount collected must be included in the first return filed after such collection and the tax must be paid accordingly. (Sec. 6055, Rev. & Tax. Code; Sec. 6203.5, Rev. & Tax. Code; Reg. 1642(a), 18 CCR)

The original retailer, a business successor, or specified lenders are eligible to claim the deduction. If a worthless account on which a retailer previously paid tax is held by a lender, the retailer and lender may file an election with the State Board of Equalization (SBE) to designate which party is entitled to claim the deduction or a refund of the tax, but only if (1) the contract between the retailer and lender contains an irrevocable relinquishment of all rights to the account from the retailer to the lender and (2) the account has been found to be worthless and written off by the lender.

• *Coupons, premiums, and cash discounts*

The amount subject to tax does not include cash discounts allowed and taken on sales. The discounts are deductible only if allowed directly to the purchaser. (Sec.

6011(c)(1), Rev. & Tax. Code; Sec. 6012(c)(1), Rev. & Tax. Code; Reg. 1654(b)(2), 18 CCR)

Sellers that issue trading stamps may deduct from taxable receipts the amount that they pay to third parties that redeem the stamps (normally, trading-stamp redemption centers) for furnishing premiums to the seller's customers. The delivery of merchandise in exchange for trading stamps is a taxable retail sale, provided that the merchandise is of a kind normally subject to the sales tax. The amount subject to tax is the average amount that the "third party" (usually, a trading-stamp redemption center) charged the retailer for the stamps, *i.e.*, the per-book value of the stamps. The delivery of premium merchandise by a retailer to a customer in exchange for indicia required by the retailer constitutes a taxable retail sale of such merchandise. The applicable sales tax is measured by the retailer's cost to purchase the merchandise. (Reg. 1671, 18 CCR)

Detailed rules regarding the tax treatment of discounts, coupons, rebates and other incentives can be found in Reg. 1671.1, 18 CCR.

• *Trade-ins*

The value of a trade-in may not be deducted from the sales price of the property for purposes of computing the applicable sales tax. If the SBE finds that the trade-in allowance stated in the sales agreement is less than the fair market value of the property, the agreed upon allowance is presumed to be the fair market value. Although cash discounts are normally excludable from the amount subject to tax, if a transaction involves both a trade-in and a discount, the contract of sale must specify that the parties contracted for both; otherwise, the claimed discount will be treated as an overallowance on the trade-in and will not be excludable from the measure of tax. (Sec. 6011(b)(2), Rev. & Tax. Code; Sec. 6012(b)(3), Rev. & Tax. Code; Reg. 1654, 18 CCR)

The SBE's legal division has commented that a like-kind exchange of property held for productive use in a trade or business or for investment is a sale subject to sales and use tax even if no gain or loss is recognized on the exchange for income tax purposes.

• *Transportation and handling charges*

Separately stated charges for transportation from the retailer's place of business or other point from which shipment is made directly to the purchaser is excluded from the tax base, but the exclusion may not exceed a reasonable charge for transportation. However, if the transportation is provided by a third party hired by the retailer, or if the property is sold for a delivered price, this exclusion is limited to transportation that occurs after the purchase of the property is made. (Sec. 6011(c)(7), Rev. & Tax. Code; Sec. 6012(c)(7), Rev. & Tax. Code; Reg. 1628(a), 18 CCR) Handling charges are taxable. (Pamphlet 73, Your California Seller's Permit: Your Rights and Responsibilities under the Sales and Use Tax Law, California State Board of Equalization, January 1996)

• *Installation charges*

Installation charges are not subject to tax. (Sec. 6011(c)(3), Rev. & Tax. Code; Sec. 6012(c)(3), Rev. & Tax. Code; Reg. 1546(a), 18 CCR)

• *Taxes*

California excludes from the tax base specified federal excise taxes imposed on gasoline, diesel, or jet fuel. California also excludes from the amount subject to tax diesel fuel excise tax and state motor vehicle fees and taxes that are added to or measured by the vehicle's price. (Sec. 6011, Rev. & Tax. Code; Sec. 6012, Rev. & Tax. Code; Reg. 1617, 18 CCR)

Tribal taxes imposed on a stated percentage of the sales or purchase price are excluded from the California sales and use tax base, provided that the tribe is in substantial compliance with California's sales and use tax laws.

• *Installment, layaway, and credit sales*

Tax applies to the entire amount of an installment, lay-away (including any fees charged), or credit sale. Finance, interest, and carrying charges, however, as well as insurance charges, are excludable from the tax base, provided that the taxpayer's records segregate the charges. (Reg. 1641(a), 18 CCR)

CCH Tip: Layaway Fees

Layaway sales, including any layaway fees charged, are reported at the time the purchaser takes possession of the item purchased. Although layaway fees are generally taxable, if a layaway sale is canceled and the layaway fee is forfeited, the fee is not taxable because there is no sale (*Tax Information Bulletin*, SBE, September 2003).

¶1509 Exempt Transactions

Law: Secs. 6351-6423; Regs. 1521, 1618, 18 CCR (CCH CALIFORNIA TAX REPORTS ¶60-360, 60-420, 60-445, 60-510, 60-590, 60-640, 61-010—61-020).

California law allows full or partial sales and use tax exemptions for a very large number of items, transactions, and organizations. The main sales and use tax exemption categories are the following:

admission charges (Sec. 6006, Rev. & Tax. Code; Sec. 6016, Rev. & Tax. Code)

aircraft gasoline and certain aircraft sales (Sec. 6357, Rev. & Tax. Code, Sec. 6366, Rev. & Tax. Code; Sec. 6366.1, Rev. & Tax. Code; Sec. 6480(b), Rev. & Tax. Code; Reg. 1593(a), 18 CCR; Reg. 1598, 18 CCR)

animal life, feed, and medication (Sec. 6358, Rev. & Tax. Code; Sec. 6358.4, Rev. & Tax. Code; Reg. 1587, 18 CCR)

carbon dioxide packing (Sec. 6359.8, Rev. & Tax. Code; Reg. 1630(b), 18 CCR)

cash discounts (excluded from the measure of tax) (Sec. 6011(c)(1), Rev. & Tax. Code; Sec. 6012(c)(1), Rev. & Tax. Code; Reg. 1654(b)(2), 18 CCR)

charitable organizations, goods made, goods donated (Sec. 6375, Rev. & Tax. Code; Reg. 1570, 18 CCR)

common carriers, certain sales (Sec. 6357.5, Rev. & Tax. Code, Sec. 6385, Rev. & Tax. Code, Sec. 6396, Rev. & Tax. Code)

custom computer programs (Sec. 6010.9, Rev. & Tax. Code)

farm equipment and machinery (applicable only to the general state sales and use tax rate) (Sec. 6356.5, Rev. & Tax. Code)

food products and containers (however, prepared food and dietary supplements are taxable) (Sec. 6358, Rev. & Tax. Code, Sec. 6359, Rev. & Tax. Code, Sec. 6359.1, Rev. & Tax. Code, Sec. 7282.3, Rev. & Tax. Code)

food stamp purchases (Sec. 6373, Rev. & Tax. Code)

fuel or petroleum (Sec. 6357, Rev. & Tax. Code, Sec. 6357.5, Rev. & Tax. Code, Sec. 6358.1, Rev. & Tax. Code)

ground control stations, limited (Sec. 6366, Rev. & Tax. Code)

installation charges (excluded from the measure of tax) (Sec. 6011(c)(3), Rev. & Tax. Code; Sec. 6012(c)(3), Rev. & Tax. Code; Reg. 1546(a), 18 CCR)

insurers, sales by (sales tax exemption only) (Sec. 12204, Rev. & Tax. Code

interstate and foreign commerce (Sec. 6396, Rev. & Tax. Code)

leases, various items (¶1507)

liquefied petroleum gas for agricultural or residential use (Sec. 6353, Rev. & Tax. Code)

lodging

lottery tickets (Sec. 8880.68, Govt. Code)

meals delivered to homebound elderly or disabled persons (Sec. 6363.7, Rev. & Tax. Code)

meals served by religious organizations or social clubs (Sec. 6361, Rev. & Tax. Code, Sec. 6363.5, Rev. & Tax. Code, Sec. 6374, Rev. & Tax. Code)

meals served in health care and residential facilities or boarding houses (Sec. 6363.6, Rev. & Tax. Code, Sec. 6363.7, Rev. & Tax. Code)

meals served to low-income elderly persons or students (Sec. 6363, Rev. & Tax. Code , Sec. 6363.7, Rev. & Tax. Code, Sec. 6374, Rev. & Tax. Code, Sec. 6376.5, Rev. & Tax. Code)

meals and food served by nonprofit veterans' organizations for fund-raising purposes (Sec. 6363.8, Rev. & Tax. Code)

medical devices and equipment (Sec. 6018.7, Rev. & Tax. Code, Sec. 6369.1, Rev. & Tax. Code, Sec. 6369.2, Rev. & Tax. Code, Sec. 6369.5, Rev. & Tax. Code)

mobile homes, used (Sec. 6379, Rev. & Tax. Code)

newspapers and periodicals (see below) (Sec. 6362.7, Rev. & Tax. Code, Sec. 6362.8, Rev. & Tax. Code)

occasional sales (see below) (Sec. 6006.5, Rev. & Tax. Code)

prescription medicines (Sec. 6359(c), Rev. & Tax. Code, Sec. 6369, Rev. & Tax. Code, Sec. 6369.1, Rev. & Tax. Code)

realty (Sec. 6051, Rev. & Tax. Code)

resales (Sec. 6092, Rev. & Tax. Code)

returned merchandise (Reg. 1573, 18 CCR)

"safe harbor" sale and leaseback arrangements (Sec. 6010.11, Rev. & Tax. Code, Sec. 6018.8, Rev. & Tax. Code, Sec. 6368.7, Rev. & Tax. Code)

seeds, plants, and fertilizer (Sec. 6358, Rev. & Tax. Code)

space flight property (Sec. 6380, Rev. & Tax. Code)

stocks, bonds, and securities (Sec. 50026.5, Govt. Code)

telegraph and telephone lines (Sec. 6016.5, Rev. & Tax. Code)

teleproduction and postproduction property (applicable only to the general state sales and use tax rate) (Sec. 6378, Rev. & Tax. Code)

timber harvesting equipment and machinery (applicable only to the general state sales and use tax rate) (Sec. 6356.5, Rev. & Tax. Code)

United States purchases, sales (Sec. 6381, Rev. & Tax. Code, Sec. 6402, Rev. & Tax. Code)

utilities' charges (Sec. 6353, Rev. & Tax. Code)

vehicles purchased by family members or foreigners (Sec. 6366.2, Rev. & Tax. Code)

vessels and watercraft, limited (Sec. 6356, Rev. & Tax. Code, Sec. 6368, Rev. & Tax. Code, Sec. 6368.1, Rev. & Tax. Code)

CCH Comment: Impact of Temporary Rate Increase

As a result of the passage of Proposition 57, which authorized the temporary increase of the state's portion of the sales and use tax rate by 0.25% while simultaneously decreasing the local sales and use tax rate by 0.25% (see ¶1501), the following exemptions from the state portion of the sales and use taxes increased from 5.0% to 5.25%, effective July 1, 2004:

— the rural investment tax exemption for purchases and uses of machinery and equipment by eligible entities,

— the teleproduction or other postproduction service equipment exemption for personal property purchased by persons primarily engaged in teleproduction or other postproduction services,

— the farm equipment and machinery exemption,

— the timber harvesting equipment and machinery exemption,

— the exemption for diesel fuel used in farming activities and food processing, and

— the racehorse breeding stock exemption.

• *Internet Tax Freedom Act*

The federal Internet Tax Freedom Act (ITFA) and its amendments (P.L. 105-277, 112 Stat. 2681, 47 U.S.C. 151 note, amended by P.L. 107-75, P.L. 108-435, P.L. 110-108) bar state and local governments from imposing multiple or discriminatory taxes on electronic commerce and taxes on Internet access for the period beginning on October 1, 1998, and ending on November 1, 2014. However, the moratorium imposed by the Act does not apply to Internet access taxes generally imposed and actually enforced prior to October 1, 1998, as long as the state has not, more than 24 months prior to the enactment of P.L. 110-108, repealed its tax on Internet access or issued a rule that it no longer applies such a tax. A second grandfather provision permitted the taxation of certain types of "telecommunications services" until June 30, 2008.

"Internet access" means a service that enables users to connect to the Internet to access content, information, or other services, including the purchase, use, or sale of telecommunications by an Internet service provider to provide the service or otherwise enable users to access content, information, or other services offered over the Internet. It also includes incidental services such as home pages, electronic mail, instant messaging, video clips, and personal electronic storage capacity, whether or not packaged with service to access the Internet. However, "Internet access" does not include voice, audio or video programming, or other products and services using Internet protocol for which there is a charge, regardless of whether the charge is bundled with charges for "Internet access."

• *Newspapers and periodicals*

An exemption applies to newspapers and periodicals issued at regular intervals that are

— distributed free of charge,

— distributed by nonprofit organizations to their members,

— published or purchased by organizations qualifying for tax-exempt status under IRC Sec. 501(c)(3), or

— sold by subscription and delivered by mail.

(Sec. 6362.7, Rev. & Tax. Code; Sec. 6362.8, Rev. & Tax. Code) In each instance, the exemption covers the sale, storage, use, or consumption of the newspaper or periodical, as well as the sale, storage, use, or consumption of tangible personal property that becomes an ingredient or component of the newspaper or periodical.

A nonprofit organization's membership publication qualifies for exemption only if it is distributed to members at least partly in return for membership fees and the costs of printing it are less than 10% of membership fees for the distribution period. An IRC Sec. 501(c)(3) organization's publication qualifies for exemption only if it either (1) accepts no commercial advertising or (2) is distributed to contributors or to members in return for payment of membership fees. (Sec. 6362.8, Rev. & Tax. Code)

All other newspapers and periodicals are subject to sales and use tax. For purposes of the tax on newspapers, a newspaper's publisher or distributor, rather than the newspaper carrier, is considered the retailer of the newspaper. Accordingly, the publisher or distributor is responsible for payment of the tax, which is measured by the price charged to the customer by the newspaper carrier. (Sec. 6015, Rev. & Tax. Code)

• *Occasional sales*

So-called occasional sales are exempt; however, this does not apply to boats or airplanes, or to automobiles required to be registered under the Motor Vehicle Code. (Sec. 6006.5, Rev. & Tax. Code) This exemption is strictly applied in practice. It may or may not apply to the sale of a going business (¶1510).

A regulation (Reg. 1595(a), 18 CCR) provides that a service enterprise's first two sales during any 12-month period of substantial amounts of tangible personal property used in the enterprise are exempt from tax as occasional sales. For subsequent sales in substantial amounts during the 12-month period, the enterprise operator is required to hold a sales and use tax permit; gross receipts from these sales are subject to tax, unless otherwise exempt.

• *Interstate transactions*

California exempts sales of property to be delivered to out-of-state destinations if under the sales contract the property is required to be and is actually shipped by the seller to an out-of-state destination by means of either (1) facilities operated by the seller or (2) delivery by the seller to a carrier, customs broker, or forwarding agent, whether hired by the purchaser or not, for shipment to the out-of-state destination. (Sec. 6396, Rev. & Tax. Code) See ¶1505 for a discussion of interstate transactions exempt from use tax.

CCH Comment: Videocassettes Shipped to Foreign Airline Found Taxable

The California Court of Appeal held in an unpublished decision that videocassettes sold to an export packer for delivery to a foreign airline were not exempt from sales tax under the Import-Export clause because of the export packer's quality control and testing activities in California. Nor did the transaction fall under the statutory exemptions discussed above because (1) there was no evidence of a contract requiring that the videocassettes be shipped to a point outside the state by specified means and (2) at the time of the sale, the export packer was contractually required to test and inspect the videocassettes prior to commencement of the export process. (*National Film Laboratories, Inc. v. California State Board of Equalization*, (2007) CCH CALIFORNIA TAX REPORTS ¶404-471)

• *Government agency transactions*

A statutory exemption applies to sales to

— the U.S. government and its unincorporated agencies and instrumentalities;

— any incorporated agency or instrumentality of the United States that is wholly owned by the United States or by a corporation wholly owned by the United States;

— the American National Red Cross; and

— incorporated federal instrumentalities not wholly owned by the United States (unless federal law permits taxation of the instrumentality).

(Sec. 6381, Rev. & Tax. Code; Sec. 6402, Rev. & Tax. Code)

The use tax may not be imposed on the storage, use, or other consumption of property by the government unless specifically allowed under federal law. (Reg. 1614, 18 CCR) Sales to state or local governmental units are subject to the tax.

Federal contractors: Federal contractors are consumers of materials and fixtures that they furnish and install in performing their contracts. Thus, either the sales tax or the use tax applies to sales of tangible personal property—including materials, fixtures, supplies, and equipment—to contractors for use in performing their contracts with the United States for constructing improvements on or to real property or for repairing fixtures. Sales tax, but not use tax, applies when the contractor purchases property as the agent of the federal government. Federal contractors are retailers of machinery and equipment furnished in connection with construction contracts with the United States. Thus, sales of such property to federal contractors are exempt sales for resale, provided that title passes to the United States before the contractor uses the property. (Sec. 6384, Rev. & Tax. Code; Reg. 1521, 18 CCR)

There are special provisions regarding contracts with the U.S. government to furnish, or fabricate and furnish, tangible personal property when title to items purchased by the contractor for use in performing the contract passes to the United States pursuant to title provisions contained in the contract before the contractor uses the items. (Reg. 1618, 18 CCR) A federal government contractor's purchase of "direct consumable supplies" or "overhead materials" qualifies as a sale for resale to the federal government, provided that the federal government takes title pursuant to a U.S. government supply contract before the contractor uses the property for the purpose it was manufactured. Whether title to direct consumable supplies or overhead materials passes to the United States under a U.S. government supply contract, and the time at which title passes, is determined according to contractual title provisions, if any exist.

See also the U.S. Supreme Court decision in *United States of America v. California State Board of Equalization* (1993) (CCH CALIFORNIA TAX REPORTS ¶61-520.75).

¶1510 Sale of a Business

Law: Secs. 6006.5, 6281, 6292, 6367 (CCH CALIFORNIA TAX REPORTS ¶60-590).

The sale of an entire business and other sales of machinery, equipment, etc., used in a business is usually subject to sales tax. The "occasional sales" exemption ordinarily does not apply to such transactions. The tax may even apply to cases where the principal activity of the business does not involve the sale of tangible personal property and where the seller does not hold a sales tax permit. (Reg. 1595, 18 CCR)

The tax would not ordinarily apply to merchandise inventory included in the sale of a business, because the inventory is sold for resale. Neither does the tax apply to any property that is attached to a building in such a way that it is classified as "real property" rather than "personal property." The tax may apply to machinery, equipment, etc., in some cases.

• *Exemption where no real change of ownership*

Tax does not apply to the sale of a business where the "real or ultimate ownership" of the business is substantially the same after the sale as it was before. Unusual problems may arise in "reorganization" transactions that are tax-free under the income tax laws. The State Board of Equalization (SBE) has ruled that statutory mergers (qualifying under IRC Sec. 368(a)(1)(A)) are not subject to sales tax, whereas the same transaction accomplished in an "assets for stock" exchange (under IRC Sec. 368(a)(1)(C)) would be taxable, at least as to those assets deemed to be "tangible personal property sold at retail."

In *Simplicity Pattern Co. v. State Board of Equalization* (1980) (CCH CALIFORNIA TAX REPORTS ¶60-020.60, 60-590.33), the taxpayer sold its subsidiary's business to another company in exchange for common stock. The California Supreme Court held that the transaction was not exempt from sales tax, even though it presumably would have been exempt if cast in the form of a statutory merger.

An example where the "real or ultimate ownership" test applies to exempt the transaction from sales tax is the incorporation of an existing business by the transfer of assets from a predecessor partnership or proprietorship to the new corporation in exchange for its stock. In *Pacific Pipeline Construction Co. v. State Board of Equalization* (1958) (CCH CALIFORNIA TAX REPORTS ¶60-590.24), the California Supreme Court held that a transfer of certain machinery and equipment in a corporate reorganization was not exempt under the "occasional sale" rule, even though the seller was not engaged in an activity normally requiring the holding of a seller's permit.

• *Other cases involving sale of business*

In *Beatrice Company v. State Board of Equalization* (1993) (CCH CALIFORNIA TAX REPORTS ¶60-590.211), the California Supreme Court held that a parent corporation's transfer of all of the assets of one of its divisions to a commencing subsidiary corporation in exchange for stock in the subsidiary and an assumption by the subsidiary of the division's liabilities was a taxable retail sale.

In *Ontario Community Foundation, Inc. v. California State Board of Equalization* (1984) (CCH CALIFORNIA TAX REPORTS ¶60-590.34), the California Supreme Court held that the sale of hospital equipment as part of the sale of an entire hospital was exempt as an "occasional sale," since the equipment sold had not been used in operations subject to sales tax.

In *Davis Wire Corporation v. State Board of Equalization* (1976) (CCH CALIFORNIA TAX REPORTS ¶60-020.39, 60-590.28), the California Supreme Court cited the *U.S. Industries* case, among others, and held that the sale of the entire business of certain manufacturing businesses was subject to sales tax. The sellers had made no retail sales in the ordinary course of their business. The Court distinguished the *Glass-Tite* case, cited below, on the ground that in *Glass-Tite* the seller's products were component parts of a type that could not have been sold at retail, whereas in *Davis Wire* the seller's products were finished products suitable for sale at retail. To the same effect, see the decision of the District Court of Appeal in *Santa Fe Energy Co. v. The Board of Equalization of California* (1984) (CCH CALIFORNIA TAX REPORTS ¶60-590.30).

In *Hotel Del Coronado Corporation v. State Board of Equalization* (1971) (CCH CALIFORNIA TAX REPORTS ¶60-590.20), a California District Court of Appeal held that the sale of hotel equipment, as part of a sale of the entire property, was subject to the sales tax.

In *Glass-Tite Industries, Inc. v. State Board of Equalization* (1968) (CCH CALIFORNIA TAX REPORTS ¶60-590.26), the seller was a manufacturer of electronic components. The District Court of Appeal held that the sale of the business was exempt from sales tax as an "occasional sale," because it was an isolated transaction and the taxpayer was not really required to have a seller's permit even though it actually had one.

In *U.S. Industries, Inc., et al. v. State Board of Equalization* (1962) (CCH CALIFORNIA TAX REPORTS ¶60-590.25), a California District Court of Appeal held that the sales tax was applicable to the sale of all the tangible assets used in operating a business, in conjunction with the sale of the business. Consideration for the sale included stock and debentures, as well as cash.

• *Liability of purchaser and seller*

The purchaser of a business is personally liable for any sales or use tax liability of the seller, unless the purchaser withholds enough of the purchase price to cover the liability or obtains from the seller evidence from the SBE to the effect that any liability has been paid or that no amount is due. (Sec. 6811, Rev. & Tax. Code; Sec. 6812, Rev. & Tax. Code) For a discussion of this provision, see *Knudsen Dairy Products Co. v. State Board of Equalization* (1970) (CCH CALIFORNIA TAX REPORTS ¶61-470.88), in which the provision was held applicable to the acquisition of a business in return for cancellation of indebtedness.

The seller of a business who fails to surrender a sales tax permit to the SBE upon transfer of the business is liable for any sales tax liability incurred by the purchaser if the seller has knowledge that the purchaser is using the permit. The seller's liability is generally limited to the quarter in which the business is transferred, plus the three subsequent quarters.

¶1511 Permits, Returns, Payment, and Records

Law: Secs. 6066-74, 6451-80.23, 6591, 7053-54; Regs. 1698, 1699, 1707, 18 CCR (CCH CALIFORNIA TAX REPORTS ¶61-210—61-260, 61-805—61-810).

Anyone in the business of selling tangible personal property of the type subject to tax, other than certain sellers of animal feed, must obtain a sales tax permit. (Sec. 6066, Rev. & Tax. Code) Permits are also required for locations at which merchandise is stored when the retailer negotiates sales out of state but fulfills such sales from stocks of goods located within the state. (Reg. 1699, 18 CCR)

CCH Tip: Buying Companies Ineligible for Permits

A buying company formed for the sole purpose of purchasing tangible personal property ex-tax for resale to the entity that owns or controls it, or to which it is otherwise related, in order to re-direct local sales tax from the location(s) of the vendor(s) to the location of the buying company will not be issued a seller's permit separate from the company controlling it. A company will not be treated as formed for the sole purpose of redirecting local sales tax if it adds a markup to its cost of goods sold in an amount sufficient to cover its operating and overhead expenses or issues an invoice or otherwise accounts for the transaction. However, the absence of any of these elements is not indicative of a sole purpose to redirect local sales tax (Reg. 1699, 18 CCR).

• *Direct payment permits*

A qualified big business may obtain a sales tax direct payment permit that allows the business to give a seller an exemption certificate when making a purchase, thereby shifting the duty to pay sales tax from the seller to the business holding the permit. A business may obtain a sales tax direct payment permit only if it had gross receipts from sales of tangible personal property of at least $75 million and purchases of taxable tangible personal property of at least $75 million in each calendar quarter during the 12 months preceding the application. Use tax direct payment permits, which allow taxpayers to self-assess and pay state and local use tax directly to the State Board of Equalization (SBE), may be issued to (1) businesses that purchase or lease tangible personal property valuing $500,000 or more in the aggregate during the calendar year immediately preceding the application for the permit and (2) county and/or city governments and redevelopment agencies. (Sec. 7051.1, Rev. & Tax. Code; Reg. 1669.5, 18 CCR)

• *Qualified use taxes*

For taxable years beginning before 2010, persons not required to hold a seller's permit or to register with SBE may self-report their qualified use tax liabilities on their timely filed original personal income or corporation franchise (income) tax returns. Persons electing to report such taxes are required to report and remit the tax on an income tax return that corresponds to the taxable year in which the use tax liability was incurred. Payments remitted with income tax returns are applied first to income taxes, penalties, and interest, and second to qualified use tax liabilities. Notwithstanding a person's election to self-report, the SBE is still entitled to make determinations for understatement of use tax. (Sec. 6452.1, Rev. & Tax. Code)

"Qualified use tax" does not include use tax imposed on a vehicle, vessel, or aircraft; a mobile home or commercial coach that is required to be registered annually; an off-highway vehicle; a trailer qualified under the permanent trailer identification program; or a lessee of tangible personal property.

• *Prepayments of tax*

Generally, returns must be filed and the tax paid quarterly. However, if the SBE determines that the taxpayer's taxable transactions average $17,000 or more per month, quarterly prepayments of tax must be made. (Sec. 6471, Rev. & Tax. Code; Sec. 6472, Rev. & Tax. Code)

Alternative I prepayment schedule: In the first, third, and fourth calendar quarters, the taxpayer must prepay no less than 90% of the state and local tax liability for each of the first two months of each quarter. In the second calendar quarter, the taxpayer must make a first prepayment of 90% of the state and local tax liability for the first month of the quarter and a second prepayment of either (1) 90% of the state and local tax liability for the second month of the quarter plus 90% of the state and local tax liability for the first 15 days of the third month of the quarter, or (2) 135% of the state and local tax liability for the second month of the quarter. (Sec. 6471, Rev. & Tax. Code)

Alternative II prepayment schedule: Persons in business during the corresponding quarter of the previous year or who are successors to a business in operation during that corresponding quarter may satisfy the prepayment requirements for the first, third, and fourth quarters by paying an amount equal to one-third of the taxable receipts reported on the return filed for the previous year's corresponding quarter multiplied by the current tax rate in effect during the month for which the prepayment is made. The prepayment requirements for the second calendar quarter may be satisfied by a first prepayment equal to one-third of the taxable receipts reported and a second prepayment equal to one-half of the taxable receipts reported on the return filed for the previous year's corresponding quarter multiplied by the current tax rate. (Sec. 6472, Rev. & Tax. Code)

In the first, third, and fourth quarters, prepayments and reports are due by the 24th day following the end of the first two months of the quarter. In the second quarter, the first prepayment and report are due by the 24th day of the second month of the quarter; the second prepayment is due by the 24th day of the third month.

• *Prepayment of tax on motor vehicle fuel*

Distributors and brokers of motor vehicle fuel, after being notified by the SBE, must collect prepayment of the retail sales tax from anyone to whom they distribute or transfer any fuel subject to the motor vehicle fuel license tax, except aviation gasoline and fuel sold to bonded distributors. (Sec. 6480.1, Rev. & Tax. Code) From April 1, 2008, through March 31, 2009, the rates of prepayment per gallon are 16.5¢ for motor vehicle fuel, 12.5¢ for aircraft jet fuel, and 15.5¢ for diesel and other qualifying fuels. Provision is made for annual adjustment or re-adjustment of the rates.

Returns and payments must be filed and paid on or before the 25th day of the calendar month following the prepayment. An exemption applies to motor vehicle fuel sold to qualified purchasers who resell the same fuel to the state or its instrumentalities if certain delivery and possession requirements are satisfied.

The SBE is also authorized to collect retail sales tax prepayments from fuel producers, importers, and jobbers.

• *Alternative method of reporting use tax program*

Under the Alternative Method of Reporting Use Tax (AMRUT) program, taxpayers may report California use tax using a formula based on the percentage of their sales for which the use tax typically applies, rather than on a transaction-by-transaction basis. However, SBE approval of the type of purchase and percentage allowed is required prior to the use of the percentage formula. In addition, an Audit Sampling

Plan (Form BOE-472) must be completed prior to using the percentage reporting method. (See Alternative Method of Reporting Use Tax (AMRUT) Program Guidelines, SBE, Public Information and Administration Section, CCH CALIFORNIA TAX REPORTS ¶403-355).

To participate in this program, a taxpayer must submit a written application, have an account that is in good standing, and maintain acceptable accounting records and internal controls.

• *Installment payments*

A taxpayer may enter into a written installment payment agreement with the SBE for the payment of any taxes, penalties, and interest. The SBE may terminate the agreement if the taxpayer fails to comply with the terms of the agreement. (Sec. 6832, Rev. & Tax. Code)

• *Penalty for failure to pay*

A penalty is imposed if prepayments are not made when required. The penalty is 6% of the prepayment if the prepayment is actually made after its due date (but no later than the due date of the quarterly return). The penalty is 6% of the amount of the actual tax liability for each month for which a prepayment should have been made if the prepayment is not made, but the quarterly return and payment are timely. The penalty is 10% if the failure to prepay is due to negligence or intentional disregard of the rules. The penalty for failure to prepay on time may be waived if a showing of reasonable cause is made. (Sec. 6477, Rev. & Tax. Code; Sec. 6479.3, Rev. & Tax. Code; Sec. 6478, Rev. & Tax. Code; Reg. 1703(c)(5), 18 CCR)

Interest is imposed on any person who is granted relief from the penalties for late prepayments. The interest rate is the same as that charged on sales and use tax deficiencies (¶1512). The SBE may relieve a person from such interest if the person's failure to make timely prepayments was due to a disaster rather than negligence or willful neglect. (Sec. 6591.5, Rev. & Tax. Code; Sec. 6592.5, Rev. & Tax. Code; Sec. 6593, Rev. & Tax. Code; Sec. 6593.5, Rev. & Tax. Code)

• *Time for filing returns; penalty for late filing*

Returns must be filed quarterly, on or before the last day of the month following the quarterly period. (Sec. 6451, Rev. & Tax. Code) The law authorizes the requirement of more frequent returns if deemed necessary to insure payment or facilitate collection; in practice this has resulted in monthly returns being required in some cases. (Sec. 6455, Rev. & Tax. Code)

The tax is payable in full with the return, to the extent not previously paid under the prepayment procedure. Also as discussed above, taxpayers may be eligible to report and pay qualified use taxes directly on their personal income or corporation franchise (income) tax return.

The due date for returns or payments may be extended for not more than one month, upon the filing of a request showing good cause. An extension of more than one month may be granted if the taxpayer requesting the extension is a creditor of the state who has not been paid because the Legislature failed to adopt a budget for the State by July 1 of the tax year in question. Such an extension expires on the last day of the month following the month in which the budget is adopted or one month from the due date of the return or payment, whichever is later. (Sec. 6459, Rev. & Tax. Code; Sec. 6459.1, Rev. & Tax. Code)

A 10% penalty is imposed against taxpayers that fail to file a sales and use tax return in a timely fashion. (Sec. 6591, Rev. & Tax. Code)

• *Form for return*

The sales tax return and the use tax return are combined in one form. A return showing information relating only to one tax is deemed to be a return also for the tax for which no information is shown. The California Supreme Court held to this effect in *People v. Universal Film Exchanges, Inc.* (1950) (CCH CALIFORNIA TAX REPORTS ¶ 61-520.37); the case involved the question of whether the "return" sufficed to start the running of the limitation period on a deficiency assessment of use tax.

In July 2008, more than 90,000 taxpayers were notified that they would no longer be receiving paper returns from the SBE, and they would be expected to file online instead. The first group of existing taxpayers that were scheduled to transition to e-filing included single location quarterly prepayment accounts comprised of medium to large size businesses that file and make prepayments 12 times per year. These taxpayers were expected to e-file rather than use a paper return with the reporting of third quarter 2008 returns, due October 31. In addition to existing accounts, beginning July 1, 2008, all new businesses applying for a seller's permit are set up for e-filing. The majority of existing sales and use tax accounts will be transitioned from paper to e-filing, phased in based on account type and reporting basis. Taxpayers may request a one-year exemption from online filing. (*News Release 46-08-C*, California State Board of Equalization, June 27, 2008)

• *E-filing*

Although e-filing is not mandatory, electronic filing of sales and use tax returns is available via third-party paid service providers or free through BOE-file. Single-outlet retail taxpayer accounts, including temporary accounts, may only currently e-file forms BOE-401-EZ and BOE-401-A with Schedule A and T via the BOE-file program. Taxpayers are ineligible to use the BOE-file program if they:

— are fuel retailers or distributors;

— are filing amended or corrected returns;

— are in bankruptcy;

— are required to report on schedules other than Schedules A, B, or C;

— have voluntary Certificate of Registration – Use Tax (SC) accounts;

— have confidential or "Safe at Home" filing status;

— have accounts registered to a permanent place of business that make sales from temporary locations (does not include those who receive Schedule B); or

— claim the aircraft adjustments for local tax purposes.

For more information, see the SBE's Web site at http://www.boe.ca.gov/elecsrv/efiling/boefile.htm.

E-filers have the option to pay by check in addition to using other electronic forms of payment.

• *Other provisions*

A credit against California use tax is allowed for sales or use tax paid to another state on property purchased in another state prior to its use in California. (Sec. 6901, Rev. & Tax. Code)

Where retailers collect sales and use taxes from customers in excess of amounts legally due, such excess amounts must be returned to the customers; otherwise, the excess collections become obligations due to the state and the customers may then recover such amounts directly from the state. (Sec. 6901.5, Rev. & Tax. Code; Reg. 1700, 18 CCR)

Retailers who engage in business without a permit or after a permit has been revoked are guilty of a misdemeanor. (Sec. 6071, Rev. & Tax. Code)

• *Payment by credit card*

Taxpayers may make current sales and use tax payments using credit cards issued by NOVUS (*e.g.*, NOVUS/Discover card), American Express, MasterCard, or

VISA. Payments by credit card are authorized only for taxes that are due with the taxpayer's sales and use tax return, including prepayment forms. Delinquent taxes or taxes required to be paid by electronic funds transfer may not be charged to a credit card. The SBE has established a special phone number for taxpayers desiring to make payments by credit card. The phone number is 1-800-2PAY-TAX (1-800-272-9829). Alternatively, credit card payments may be made over the Internet at http://www.boe.ca.gov/elecsrv/payinternet.htm .

• *Electronic funds transfer payment requirement*

Anyone whose estimated sales and use tax liability averages $10,000 or more per month must remit amounts due by electronic funds transfer (EFT). A business successor must continue to make payments by EFT if its predecessor was a mandatory participant. Taxpayers not required to participate in the program may, with the SBE's approval, voluntarily remit payments electronically. Taxpayers whose monthly liability falls below the $10,000 threshold must continue to make EFT payments until they receive written SBE approval to discontinue EFT payments. (Sec. 6479.3, Rev. & Tax. Code)

The electronic funds transfer payment requirement does not apply to taxpayers who collect use taxes voluntarily.

• *Records*

All pertinent records must be retained for at least four years (10 years in the case of taxpayers participating in the amnesty program discussed at ¶1512) unless the SBE gives written authorization for their destruction. The required records include the normal books of account together with all bills, receipts, invoices, cash register tapes, or other documents of original entry that support the entries in the books of account, as well as all schedules and working papers used in preparing tax returns. Resale and exemption certificates should also be retained to document claimed nontaxable sales. The records must be made available to the SBE or its authorized representative on request. (Sec. 7053, Rev. & Tax. Code ; Reg. 1698, 18 CCR)

¶1512 Administration, Deficiencies, and Refunds

Law: Secs. 6481-88, 6511-96, 6811-14, 6829, 6901-63, 7051-99, 7070-78 (CCH CALIFORNIA TAX REPORTS ¶61-410, 61-420, 61-440, 61-460, 61-470, 61-520, 61-530, 61-610—61-640, 89-210).

The tax is administered by the State Board of Equalization (SBE). The SBE maintains a staff of field auditors who examine the books of taxpayers.

• *Auditing procedures*

The SBE's auditors have commonly used a procedure known as the "test-check." For example, one or more supposedly typical periods are checked to determine the extent to which sales are improperly reported as being for resale. The percentage of error found in the test period is then assumed to run through the entire period under audit and the same percentage of error is applied to the sales of the whole period and a tax deficiency is assessed accordingly.

Another type of test-check is used where the sales appear to be too low in relation to the cost of goods sold. In such cases the auditor may test the gross profit percentage by computing the mark-up on typical items of merchandise; the percentage of mark-up computed on these items may then be applied to the total costs for the period under audit to determine the taxable sales. This procedure was approved in 1950 by the California District Court of Appeal in the case of *Maganini v. Quinn* (CCH CALIFORNIA TAX REPORTS ¶61-410.21).

Auditors will frequently rely on SBE sales and use tax annotations (SUTAs) when examining a particular transaction. These annotations consist of a compilation of replies by the SBE's legal staff to questions posed by auditors and taxpayers concerning the taxability of particular transactions. In *Yamaha Corporation of America v. State Board of Equalization* (1999) (CCH CALIFORNIA TAX Reports ¶60-030), the California Supreme Court reversed an appellate court's decision in which the appellate court relied on an SBE annotation. The Supreme Court determined that because the annotation was merely an agency's statutory interpretation it could not be equated with an agency rule to which the courts must give judicial deference. However, on remand, and consistent with the California Supreme Court's instructions, a California court of appeal assigned "great weight" to two SBE annotations in support of its opinion because of the SBE's consistency and expertise and evidence of legislative concurrence.

• *Managed audit program*

If selected by the SBE, taxpayers may participate in a managed audit program, in which taxpayers self-audit their books and records under the SBE's guidance. (Sec. 7076, Rev. & Tax. Code) To be eligible to participate in the program, a taxpayer must meet the following criteria:

— have a business that has few or no statutory exemptions and has a small number of clearly identified tax issues;

— agree to participate; and

— have the resources to comply with SBE instructions.

Taxpayers who participate in the program are entitled to a reduced interest rate of one-half the regular rate on liabilities covered by the audit period. Participation in the managed audit program does not limit the SBE's authority to otherwise audit a taxpayer.

See ¶1511 for a discussion of the alternative method of reporting use tax program.

• *Procedure for deficiencies*

The SBE must give written notice of a deficiency determination. (Sec. 6486, Rev. & Tax. Code) A petition for redetermination may be filed within 30 days of service of such notice, and an oral hearing will be granted if requested. The determination becomes final if no petition is filed by the end of the 30-day period. If a petition is filed, the SBE's order or decision on the petition becomes final 30 days after service of notice of such order or decision. (Sec. 6561, Rev. & Tax. Code;Sec. 6562, Rev. & Tax. Code) Provision is also made for jeopardy assessments when collection of the tax will be jeopardized by delay. (Sec. 6536, Rev. & Tax. Code)

The limitation period for assessing deficiencies, generally, is three years. The limitation period for taxpayers that elect to report and remit qualified use taxes on their income tax returns (¶1505) is three years (six years if qualified use taxes are underreported by 25% or more) after the last day for which an acceptable tax return is due or filed, whichever occurs later. The period is eight years when no return is filed. There is no limitation in case of fraud. The limitation period may be extended by waiver agreement and also may be extended for a redetermination of tax under certain conditions. (Sec. 6487, Rev. & Tax. Code)

• *Deficiency procedures for out-of-state retailers and "qualifying purchasers"*

The limitation period for assessing deficiencies for "qualifying" out-of-state retailers that failed to file a return or report is three years. A "qualifying" out-of-state retailer is a retailer doing business in California that, never having previously registered with the SBE, voluntarily registers prior to being contacted by the SBE. In addition, if the SBE determines that the retailer's failure to file is due to reasonable cause, the SBE may waive any corresponding penalties. (Sec. 6487.05, Rev. & Tax. Code)

The statute of limitations is similarly reduced to three years for the collection of unreported use tax by non-California retailers for specified purchases if it was determined that the failure to report and pay the tax was due to reasonable cause. "Qualifying purchaser" means a person who voluntarily filed an individual use tax return for tangible personal property that was purchased out of state for storage, use, or other consumption in California and who never previously (1) registered with the SBE, (2) filed an individual use tax return, (3) reported an amount on his or her individual California income tax return, (4) engaged in business in California as a retailer, or (5) was contacted by the SBE regarding failure to report use tax. The reduced limitations period does not apply to purchases of vehicles, vessels, or aircraft. (Sec. 6487.06, Rev. & Tax. Code)

CCH Comment: Public Disclosure of Large Tax Delinquencies

The SBE is required to make available as a matter of public record a quarterly list of the 250 largest uncontested sales and use tax delinquencies in excess of $100,000. Before making a delinquency a matter of public record, however, the SBE must provide written notice to the person or persons liable by certified mail and provide an opportunity for the person(s) to comply. If the amount due is not remitted or payment arrangements are not made within 30 days after issuance of the notice, the delinquency will be included on the list. (Sec. 7063, Rev. & Tax Code)

• *Amnesty*

Amnesty was available during the period beginning February 1, 2005, and ending on March 31, 2005. Under the amnesty program, penalties and fees applicable to nonreporting, nonpayment, or underreporting of taxes for pre-2003 tax liabilities were waived. In addition, no criminal action will be brought against the taxpayer, for the tax reporting periods for which tax amnesty was requested, for the nonreporting or underreporting of tax liabilities unless, as of the first day of the amnesty period (1) the taxpayer was on notice of a criminal investigation or was under a criminal investigation or (2) a court proceeding had already been initiated. (Sec. 7070, Rev. & Tax. Code; Sec. 7071, Rev. & Tax. Code; Sec. 7072, Rev. & Tax. Code)

Sales and use tax penalties equal to 20% (or 50% in cases involving fraud) will be imposed against taxpayers for deficiency determinations based upon a return filed under the amnesty program, or upon any other nonreporting or underreporting of tax liability by any person who could have otherwise been eligible for amnesty. Such deficiency determinations may be issued within 10 years from the last day of the calendar month following the quarterly period for which the amount is proposed to be determined and taxpayers are required to maintain their records for any period for which they've been granted relief under the amnesty program for 10 years. (Sec. 7073, Rev. & Tax. Code; Reg. 1698, 18 CCR)

CCH Comment: Application of 10-year Statute of Limitations

The 10-year statute of limitations applies to reporting periods beginning before January 1, 2003, which were still open to issue a notice of determination as of August 16, 2004 (the day the amnesty legislation was enacted). The extended statute of limitations does not reopen reporting periods which were closed to issue a notice of determination prior to August 16, 2004. If a taxpayer did not file sales and use tax returns, the Third Quarter 1996 would be the first quarterly reporting period subject to the 10-year statute. Third Quarter 1996 reporting was due on October 31, 1996. The SBE could issue a notice of determination for this reporting period prior to November 1, 2006, for any nonreporting of tax. (*Sales and Use Tax Amnesty Program Frequently Asked Questions* , SBE, February 1, 2005, CCH CALIFORNIA TAX REPORTS ¶403-761)

In addition to the enhanced penalties, a 50% interest penalty will be imposed for amounts that are due and payable on the last date of the amnesty period, for the period beginning on the date on which the tax was due and ending on the last day of the amnesty period. The enhanced interest penalties do not apply to taxpayers that have entered into an installment agreement. Any taxpayer who is the subject of a deficiency assessment for unpaid or underpaid tax for a reporting period eligible for amnesty is also liable for a 50% penalty on the interest on the deficiency. Taxpayers may file a refund claim for the amnesty-related interest penalty. (Sec. 7074, Rev. & Tax. Code)

Although audits generally cover a three-year period, the SBE will consider the following factors in determining whether to extend an audit to cover a longer period of time:

— participation in the amnesty program;

— whether amnesty-eligible periods have already been audited;

— whether the standard three-year audit period starts immediately after or overlaps the amnesty-eligible periods;

— whether the SBE's initial review of the taxpayer's records indicates a reporting error in the amnesty-eligible periods; and

— whether the SBE has other specific or direct information that indicates the taxpayer may owe tax for amnesty-eligible periods.

(*Special Notice*, SBE, December 2005 (CCH CALIFORNIA TAX REPORTS ¶ 61-530.202))

• *Interest and penalties*

In connection with deficiencies, a penalty of 10% is imposed for negligence or intentional disregard of the rules, and a penalty of 25% is imposed where fraud is involved. Fraud must be established by clear and convincing evidence. (Sec. 6484, Rev. & Tax. Code; Sec. 6485, Rev. & Tax. Code) A taxpayer that is required to make payments by electronic transfer funds, who is issued a deficiency determination after failing to remit the tax in a timely fashion, will be assessed an additional 10% penalty of the amount of tax due. This penalty is exclusive of other penalties that might be imposed for delinquencies applicable to other payment methods. (Sec. 6479.4, Rev. & Tax. Code)

Any person who knowingly collects California sales tax reimbursement or use tax and who fails to timely remit those amounts to the SBE is liable for a penalty of 40% of the amount not timely remitted. However, the penalty is inapplicable to any person whose liability for unremitted tax averages $1,000 or less per month or does not exceed 5% of the total amount of tax liability for which the tax reimbursement was collected for the period in which tax was due, whichever is greater. (Sec. 6597, Rev. & Tax. Code)

CCH Comment: Assessment of 40% Penalty

The 40% penalty will not be assessed if:

— the taxpayer failed to remit tax only once within the last three years in business;

— the unreported tax averages less than $1,000 per month;

— the unreported tax is less than 5% of the total tax liability for the reporting period;

— the taxpayer voluntarily reported or corrected errors prior to being contacted by the SBE; or

— the failure to file and pay is due to reasonable cause or circumstances beyond the taxpayer's control.

(*Special Notice L-176*, SBE, August 2007)

Interest is charged on deficiencies at a rate established semiannually. The following chart indicates the rates of interest in effect for the designated periods:

From	*To*	*Modified Adjusted Annual Rate*
July 1, 2004	June 30, 2005	7%
July 1, 2005	December 31, 2005	8%
January 1, 2006	June 30, 2006	9%
July 1, 2006	December 31, 2006	10%
January 1, 2007	June 30, 2007	11%
July 1, 2007	December 31, 2007	11%
January 1, 2008	June 30, 2008	11%
July 1, 2008	December 31, 2008	10%
January 1, 2009	June 30, 2009	8%

The SBE may abate all or part of the interest imposed on tax liabilities resulting from (1) an SBE employee's unreasonable error or delay or (2) the Department of Motor Vehicle's error in calculating the use tax on a vehicle or vessel. (Sec. 6594, Rev. & Tax. Code) Interest will also be abated for late payment or filing if the lateness was due to a natural disaster. (Sec. 6593, Rev. & Tax. Code) In addition, if the SBE finds that neither the person liable for payment of tax nor any person related to that person caused the erroneous refund, no interest will be imposed on the amount of the erroneous refund until 30 days after the date on which the SBE mails a notice of determination for repayment of the erroneous refund. The act of filing a claim for refund will not be considered as causing the erroneous refund. (Sec. 6964, Rev. & Tax. Code)

Criminal penalties may be imposed for a variety of reasons, including giving a resale certificate to a seller with knowledge that the property is not to be resold. (Sec. 6094.5, Rev. & Tax. Code) A penalty of 50% of the tax is imposed upon anyone who registers a vehicle, vessel, or aircraft outside California for the purpose of tax evasion. (Sec. 6485.1, Rev. & Tax. Code, Sec. 6514.1, Rev. & Tax. Code) The state is empowered to employ out-of-state collection agencies and to add their compensation to the amount of tax due. The state may establish a reward program for information leading to the collection of underreported taxes.

A $50 penalty is imposed on paid preparers of sales and use tax returns for each failure to enter their name, Social Security number, and business name and address on a return. (Sec. 6452, Rev. & Tax. Code)

• *Taxpayers' bill of rights*

A "bill of rights" has been enacted to protect taxpayers' privacy and property rights during the sales and use tax collection process. (Sec. 7080, Rev. & Tax. Code through Sec. 7099, Rev. & Tax. Code) It is substantially identical to the one described briefly at ¶702, relating to taxpayer rights in connection with personal income and corporate tax collections, except that the agency involved is the SBE rather than the Franchise Tax Board.

• *Refunds*

The limitation period for filing refund claims, generally, is three years from the due date of the return or, in the case of a deficiency or jeopardy determination or nonfiling of a return, the later of six months from the date a deficiency determination becomes final or within six months of the overpayment. However, a taxpayer has three years from the date of overpayment to file a refund claim if the overpayment was collected as a result of the SBE's collection of an outstanding tax liability through issuance of a levy, lien, or other enforcement procedure. (Sec. 6902, Rev. & Tax. Code; Sec. 6902.3, Rev. & Tax. Code; Sec. 6905, Rev. & Tax. Code)

In *Dan J. Agnew v. California State Board of Equalization* (1999) (CCH CALIFORNIA TAX REPORTS ¶61-620.25), the California Supreme Court held that a taxpayer is *not* required to pay the accrued interest on a tax deficiency in addition to the tax claimed to be due and owing as a prerequisite to administrative review of a claim for refund of an alleged overpayment of sales and use tax.

The limitations period for filing a refund claim is suspended during any period that a person is unable to manage his or her financial affairs because of a physical or mental impairment that is life threatening or that is expected to last for at least 12 months. This waiver does not apply to individuals who are represented in their financial matters by their spouses or by other persons. (Sec. 6902.4, Rev. & Tax. Code)

A claimant may bring suit within 90 days after the SBE mails a notice of disallowance. (Sec. 6933, Rev. & Tax. Code) If the SBE fails to act on the claim within six months after the claim is filed, the claimant may consider the claim disallowed and proceed to bring suit. (Sec. 6934, Rev. & Tax. Code)

Interest is payable by the State on refunds at the modified adjusted rate per month, which is the modified adjusted rate per annum divided by 12. Interest is payable on refunds from the first day of the calendar month following the month during which the overpayment was made to (1) the last day of the calendar month in which the taxpayer is notified that the claim may be filed or (2) the date the claim is approved by the SBE, whichever is earlier. Interest may be waived for a period, in cases where the taxpayer requests deferred action on a refund claim. (Sec. 6591.5, Rev. & Tax. Code)

The following chart indicates the rates of interest for the designated periods.

From	*To*	*Applicable Period Interest Rate*
July 1, 2004	June 30, 2005	1%
July 1, 2005	December 31, 2005	2%
January 1, 2006	June 30, 2006	3%
July 1, 2006	December 31, 2006	4%
January 1, 2007	June 30, 2007	5%
July 1, 2007	December 31, 2007	5%
January 1, 2008	June 30, 2008	5%
July 1, 2008	December 31, 2008	3%
January 1, 2009	June 30, 2009	2%

• *Special refund procedure for invalid local taxes*

Retailers who reside or conduct business in a taxing district in which an invalid tax was imposed must report sales and use tax at the currently effective combined state and local rate but may claim a 0.75% credit against the total amount of taxes reported. A corresponding 0.75% reduction must be made in the amount of sales or use taxes that retailers collect from purchasers. The 0.75% credit may be claimed for taxes due on the first day of the first calendar quarter beginning at least 120 days after a final court determination that a local sales and use tax is invalid. (Sec. 7275, Rev. & Tax. Code; Sec. 7276, Rev. & Tax. Code)

A nonretailer who pays a local sales and use tax that is subsequently held invalid may file a claim for refund of the invalid tax, provided the claim states in writing the specific ground upon which it is made and is accompanied by proof of payment. However, only claims for a single purchase or aggregate purchases of $5,000 or more will be eligible for refund, and any such claim must be filed within one year of the first day of the first calendar quarter after a local sales and use tax has been held invalid. (Sec. 7277, Rev. & Tax. Code)

A California court of appeal held, in *Kuykendall v. State Board of Equalization et al.* (1994) (CCH CALIFORNIA TAX REPORTS ¶61-610.353), that the statutory scheme of reimbursing consumers for the local sales and use tax declared unconstitutional in *Rider* (¶1502) through a sales tax rollback and through direct refunds for claims involving documented purchases of $5,000 or more did not violate constitutional guarantees of due process and equal protection.

• *Officer/shareholder liability*

Upon termination or dissolution of a partnership, limited liability partnership, corporation, or limited liability company, certain officers, members, managers, or other persons may be held personally liable for unpaid sales and use taxes. (Sec. 6829, Rev. & Tax. Code; Reg. 1702.5, Rev. & Tax. Code)

A California court of appeal held, in *State Board of Equalization v. Wirick* (2001) (CCH CALIFORNIA TAX REPORTS ¶ 61-460.40), that a former officer was personally liable for a corporation's unpaid California sales tax when the corporation ceased business because he had responsibility for paying the tax when due.

Caution Note: Returns, Statute of Limitations for Determinations

The SBE has held that a responsible person must file a return in his or her own name for the Sec. 6829, Rev. & Tax. Code liability. Such return must cover the quarter during which the business was terminated. (*In the Matter of the Petition for Redetermination under the Sales and Use Tax Law of McKoon* (2007) CCH CALIFORNIA TAX REPORTS ¶ 404-292)

The limitation period for issuing a determination under Sec. 6829 is three years from the last day of the month following the quarter in which the SBE obtains actual knowledge, through its audit or compliance activities, or by written communication by the business or its representative, of the termination, dissolution, or abandonment of the business, or eight years from the last day of the month following the quarter of termination, dissolution, or abandonment, whichever period expires later. (Sec. 6829, Rev. & Tax. Code)

• *Business successor liability*

The purchaser of a business on which sales and use tax is outstanding must withhold a sufficient portion of the purchase price to cover the unpaid tax until the former owner produces a receipt from the SBE showing that the tax has been paid, unless the SBE issues the purchaser a certificate stating that all liability has been paid or that no amount is due. Noncompliance with this requirement renders the purchaser personally liable for any unpaid taxes incurred by the seller or any former owner, as well as for interest and penalties. Relief from penalties otherwise due may also be available if the SBE finds that the failure to withhold resulted from reasonable cause and circumstances beyond the purchaser's control. (Sec. 6811, Rev. & Tax. Code; Sec. 6812, Rev. & Tax. Code; Sec. 6814, Rev. & Tax. Code)

• *Primary retailer's liability for tax due on concessionaire's sales*

A primary retailer is jointly and severally liable for any sales and use tax imposed or unreported during the period that a retailer operates on the primary retailer's premises as a concessionaire. The primary retailer is relieved of this liability, however, during the period that the concessionaire holds a seller's permit to operate at the primary retailer's location or if the primary retailer takes in good faith the concessionaire's written affirmation that the concessionaire holds a seller's permit for the primary retailer's location. (Reg. 1699, 18 CCR)

• *Relief for innocent spouse/registered domestic partner*

If two spouses' or registered domestic partners' (RDPs) names appear on an application for a seller's permit and sales and use tax liability is understated by one spouse or RDP, the innocent spouse or RDP may be relieved of liability for tax, including interest, penalties, and other amounts attributable to the understatement, if the following conditions are satisfied:

— the underpayment or nonpayment is attributable to the other spouse or RDP;

— the innocent spouse or RDP can establish a lack of knowledge that was reasonable; and

— relief from liability is deemed to be equitable under the circumstances. (Sec. 6456, Rev. & Tax. Code; Reg. 1705.1, 18 CCR)

Relief is not available for either underreporting or nonpayment in any calendar quarter that is

— more than five years from the final date on an SBE determination,

— more than five years from the return due date for nonpayment on a return,

— more than one year from the first contact with the innocent spouse or RDP claiming relief, or

— closed by *res judicata* , whichever is later.

• *Settlement of civil tax disputes*

The Executive Officer of the SBE, or his or her designee, may settle any civil tax dispute involving amounts of $5,000 or less. For civil tax disputes involving amounts in excess of $5,000, the SBE may approve the settlement recommendations made by its Executive Officer (or Chief Counsel if authorized by the Executive Officer) and reviewed by the Attorney General. (Sec. 7093.5, Rev. & Tax. Code)

• *Offers in compromise*

The Executive Director and Chief Counsel of the SBE, or their delegates, may compromise a final sales and use tax liability in which the reduction in tax is $7,500 or less ($10,000 or less if the board delegates such authority). Amounts in excess of $7,500 may be compromised by the Board. (Sec. 7093.6, Rev. & Tax. Code)

Generally, offers in compromise will be considered only for liabilities generated from a business that has been discontinued or transferred, where the taxpayer making the offer no longer has a controlling interest or association with the transferred business or a controlling interest or association with a similar type of business as the transferred or discontinued business. However, through 2012, offers in compromise can be made for a "qualified final tax liability" regardless of whether the taxpayer's business has been discontinued or transferred, or whether the taxpayer has a controlling interest or association with a business similar to the discontinued or transferred business. A "qualified final tax liability" includes (along with related interest, additions to tax, penalties, and other amounts assessed), (1) assessments in which no tax, fee, or surcharges were collected, (2) business successor liabilities, and (3) consumers' use tax liabilities. Taxpayers with previous compromise agreements are ineligible.

For amounts to be compromised, the taxpayer must establish that

— the amount offered is the most that can be expected to be paid or collected from the taxpayer's present assets or income and

— the taxpayer does not have reasonable prospects of satisfying a greater amount of the liability within a reasonable period of time. Furthermore, the SBE must determine that acceptance of the offer is in the best interest of the state. The SBE's determination is not appealable.

When more than one taxpayer is liable for the debt, the acceptance of an offer in compromise from one liable taxpayer does not relieve the other taxpayers from paying the entire liability. However, the amount of the liability will be reduced by the amount of the accepted offer.

CCH Practice Tip: Making an Offer in Compromise

The SBE, the Franchise Tax Board (FTB), and the Employment Development Department (EDD) have developed a single form that individuals can use to apply for offers in compromise of nondisputed final California tax liabilities. Form DE 999CA, Multi-Agency Form for Offer in Compromise, may be used by individuals for personal income, sales and use, and other taxes owed to the FTB, SBE, and EDD. Corporations, partnerships, and limited liability companies should continue to use Form BOE-490-C, Offer In Compromise Application For Corporations, Limited Liability Companies, Partnerships, Trusts, and Unidentified Business Organizations, for SBE offers. (*News Release*, California Tax Service Center, August 23, 2006)

PART VI

DEATH TAXES

CHAPTER 16
DEATH TAXES

¶1601 Scope of Chapter

Comment: California Death Taxes Expire

Because California's death taxes were based on the federal state death tax credit and this credit is repealed for estates of decedents dying after 2004, California does not currently impose any death taxes on estates of decedents dying after 2004. The discussion following summarizes the law for estates of decedents dying prior to 2005. The pre-2005 law may be reinstated in 2011 if federal law is not amended or may be reinstated earlier if future California legislation decouples from the repeal of the federal state death tax credit.

California imposes two death taxes, which are discussed in this chapter: (1) the estate "pick-up" tax, and (2) the generation skipping transfer tax. Neither of these taxes imposes an extra tax burden, because both are so-called "pick-up" taxes that simply collect a tax that would otherwise go to the federal government. The California taxes obtain for the State the maximum benefit for the federal credits that are allowed for State taxes.

The generation skipping transfer tax constitutes Part 9.5 of Division 2 of the Revenue and Taxation Code.

For details of any repealed inheritance or gift taxes, see 1984 or prior editions of the *Guidebook.*

¶1602 Rates and Exemptions

Comment: California Death Taxes Expire

Because California's death taxes were based on the federal state death tax credit and this credit is repealed for estates of decedents dying after 2004, California does not currently impose any death taxes on estates of decedents dying after 2004. The discussion following summarizes the law for estates of decedents dying prior to 2005. The pre-2005 law may be reinstated in 2011 if federal law is not amended or may be reinstated earlier if future California legislation decouples from the repeal of the federal state death tax credit.

• *Estates of decedents dying on or after June 9, 1982*

An estate tax is assessed in an amount equal to the state death tax credit under the federal estate tax laws. Under amendments made to the federal estate tax law by the Economic Growth and Tax Relief Reconciliation Act of 2001 (EGTRRA) (P.L. 107-16), this credit is reduced by 25% in the case of estates of decedents dying during 2002, by 50% in the case of estates of decedents dying during 2003, and by 75% in the case of estates of decedents dying during 2004. In the case of estates of decedents dying in 2005 and afterwards, the credit is eliminated and is replaced by a federal estate tax deduction. This is as follows:

Maximum Federal Credit

Applicable to estates of decedents dying on or after January 1, 1981.

Total Amount of Beneficiaries' Interest Before Exemption		Class A: Surviving Spouse (All transfers except limited powers of appointment are exempt)		Class A: Minor Child (1st $40,000 Exempt)		Class A: Lineal Ancestor, Mutually Acknowledged Child or Lineal Issue of the Decedent (1st $20,000 Exempt)	
I Amount Equal to	II Amount Not in Excess of	Tax on Amount in Col. I	Rate on Excess Over Amount In Col. I (Percent)	Tax on Amount in Col. I	Rate on Excess Over Amount In Col. I (Percent)	Tax on Amount In Col. I	Rate on Excess Over Amount In Col. I (Percent)
$0	$20,000	....	3	....	...	....	...
20,000	25,000	$600	3	....	...	....	3
25,000	40,000	750	4	....	...	$150	4
40,000	50,000	1,350	4	....	4	750	4
50,000	100,000	1,750	6	$400	6	1,150	6
100,000	200,000	4,750	8	3,400	8	4,150	8
200,000	300,000	12,750	10	11,400	10	12,150	10
300,000	400,000	22,750	12	21,400	12	22,150	12
400,000	....	34,750	14	33,400	14	34,150	14

Total Amount of Beneficiaries' Interest Before Exemption		Class B: Brother, Sister, Descendants of Brother or Sister, Wife or Widow of Son, Husband or Widower of Daughter (1st $10,000 Exempt)		Class C: Any Person Not Mentioned Before; Includes Organizations, Stranger, Uncle, Aunt, or Descendant of Either (First $3,000 Exempt)	
I Amount Equal to	II Amount Not in Excess of	Tax on Amount in Col. I	Rate on Excess Over Amount In Col. I (Percent)	Tax on Amount in Col. I	Rate on Excess Over Amount In Col. I (Percent)
$0	$3,000	....	....	....	......
3,000	10,000	....	....	....	10
10,000	25,000	....	6	$700	10
25,000	50,000	$900	10	2,200	14
50,000	100,000	3,400	12	5,700	16
100,000	200,000	9,400	14	13,700	18
200,000	300,000	23,400	16	31,700	20
300,000	400,000	39,400	18	51,700	22
400,000	....	57,400	20	73,700	24

• ***Charitable exemption***

Charitable, religious, etc., exemptions provided in the federal law are allowable under the California law.

¶1603 Computation of Tax

Comment: California Death Taxes Expire

Because California's death taxes were based on the federal state death tax credit and this credit is repealed for estates of decedents dying after 2004, California does not currently impose any death taxes on estates of decedents dying after 2004. The discussion following summarizes the law for estates of decedents dying prior to 2005. The pre-2005 law may be reinstated in 2011 if federal law is not amended or may be reinstated earlier if future California legislation decouples from the repeal of the federal state death tax credit.

Whenever a federal estate tax is payable to the United States, there is imposed a California estate tax equal to the portion, if any, of the maximum allowable amount of the credit for state death taxes, allowable under the applicable federal estate tax law, which is attributable to property located in California. However, in no event shall the estate tax imposed result in a total death tax liability to California and the U.S. in excess of the death tax liability which would result if this provision were not in effect. The threshold for filing a federal estate tax return is $1 million, in the case of decedents dying during 2002 and 2003, and $1.5 million, in the case of decedents dying in 2004.

Where a decedent leaves property having a situs in California, and leaves other property having a situs in another state, or other states, the portion of the maximum state death tax credit allowable against the federal estate tax on the total estate by the federal estate tax law which is attributed to the property having a situs in California is to be determined in the following manner:

(1) For the purpose of apportioning the maximum state death tax credit, the gross value of the property shall be that value finally determined for federal estate tax purposes.

(2) The maximum state death tax credit allowable is to be multiplied by the percentage which the gross value of property having a situs in California bears to the gross value of the entire estate subject to federal estate tax.

(3) The product determined pursuant to (2) above shall be the portion of the maximum state death tax credit allowable which is attributable to property having a situs in California.

¶1604 Additional Estate Tax

Comment: California Death Taxes Expire

Because California's death taxes were based on the federal state death tax credit and this credit is repealed for estates of decedents dying after 2004, California does not currently impose any death taxes on estates of decedents dying after 2004. The discussion following summarizes the law for estates of decedents dying prior to 2005. The pre-2005 law may be reinstated in 2011 if federal law is not amended or may be reinstated earlier if future California legislation decouples from the repeal of the federal state death tax credit.

Since the California estate tax is designed to absorb the federal estate tax credit for state death taxes paid, there is no additional estate tax credit.

¶1605 Taxable Transfers

Comment: California Death Taxes Expire

Because California's death taxes were based on the federal state death tax credit and this credit is repealed for estates of decedents dying after 2004, California does not currently impose any death taxes on estates of decedents dying after 2004. The discussion following summarizes the law for estates of decedents dying prior to 2005. The pre-2005 law may be reinstated in 2011 if federal law is not amended or may be reinstated earlier if future California legislation decouples from the repeal of the federal state death tax credit.

• *Residents*

Transfers are taxable when made by:

— will;

— intestate law;

— gift to take effect in possession or enjoyment at or after death, as an advancement or by a revocable trust.

• *Special property interests*

Special types of property interests are treated as follows:

— Property taken by virtue of the homestead laws is taxable;

— Property in which the decedent had a general power of appointment at the time of his death is taxable;

— Jointly held property is taxable to the extent that the surviving owners cannot show original ownership in themselves;

— Bequests to an executor or trustee in lieu of commissions are taxable to the extent that they exceed reasonable compensation;

— Insurance payable to the estate or executor is taxable; insurance payable to named beneficiaries or to a trustee (except to the extent that the trust requires the proceeds to be used to pay the debts, funeral expenses, expenses of administration, or the taxes due by reason of the insured's death).

• *Nonresidents*

The class of transfers taxable in the estate of a resident decedent is likewise taxable in the estate of a nonresident decedent.

¶1606 Settlement of Domiciliary Disputes

Comment: California Death Taxes Expire

Because California's death taxes were based on the federal state death tax credit and this credit is repealed for estates of decedents dying after 2004, California does not currently impose any death taxes on estates of decedents dying after 2004. The discussion following summarizes the law for estates of decedents dying prior to 2005. The pre-2005 law may be reinstated in 2011 if federal law is not amended or may be reinstated earlier if future California legislation decouples from the repeal of the federal state death tax credit.

Provision is made for compromise and arbitration of state death taxes in cases where there is a dispute over the question of the decedent's domicile.

¶1607 Property Subject to Tax

Comment: California Death Taxes Expire

Because California's death taxes were based on the federal state death tax credit and this credit is repealed for estates of decedents dying after 2004, California does not currently impose any death taxes on estates of decedents dying after 2004. The discussion following summarizes the law for estates of decedents dying prior to 2005. The pre-2005 law may be reinstated in 2011 if federal law is not amended or may be reinstated earlier if future California legislation decouples from the repeal of the federal state death tax credit.

• *Residents*

All real property and tangible personal property within the state and all intangible personal property wherever situated is taxable if it is made the subject of a taxable transfer.

• *Nonresidents*

Real property within the state and tangible personal property having an actual situs within the state are taxable. Intangible personal property of nonresident decedents who live in the United States is not subject to tax. There is provision for the reciprocal exemption of intangibles of nonresident decedents who do not reside in the United States.

¶1608 Deductions

Comment: California Death Taxes Expire

Because California's death taxes were based on the federal state death tax credit and this credit is repealed for estates of decedents dying after 2004, California does not currently impose any death taxes on estates of decedents dying after 2004. The discussion following summarizes the law for estates of decedents dying prior to 2005. The pre-2005 law may be reinstated in 2011 if federal law is not amended or may be reinstated earlier if future California legislation decouples from the repeal of the federal state death tax credit.

The following items are deductible:

— property equal in amount to the clear market value of the decedent's separate property, if it is transferred to a surviving spouse;

— debts of the decedent;

— funeral expenses and expenses of the last illness;

— state, county and municipal taxes and assessments which are a lien at the date of death;

— expenses of administration, including ordinary fees and extraordinary fees of executors and administrators and their attorneys and extraordinary fees of accountants for tax work; however, amounts allowed for deduction of administration expenses and attorney fees in determining inheritance tax are not allowed as a deduction for income tax purposes unless a statement is filed indicating that the amounts have not been allowed as a deduction for inheritance taxes and a waiver of the right to have such deduction is filed;

— loss to property caused by fire, earthquake, landslide or other casualty not compensated by insurance or otherwise, which occurred after the decedent's death but prior to the order fixing the tax or prior to one year from the time of the decedent's death, whichever is earlier.

¶1609 Return and Assessment

Comment: California Death Taxes Expire

Because California's death taxes were based on the federal state death tax credit and this credit is repealed for estates of decedents dying after 2004, California does not currently impose any death taxes on estates of decedents dying after 2004. The discussion following summarizes the law for estates of decedents dying prior to 2005. The pre-2005 law may be reinstated in 2011 if federal law is not amended or may be reinstated earlier if future California legislation decouples from the repeal of the federal state death tax credit.

• *Jurisdiction*

The Superior Court of the county in which decedent last resided has jurisdiction to hear and determine all inheritance tax questions.

• *Return*

Copies of the will and inventory are the only returns required and are to be filed with the State Controller.

• *Final determination*

The Superior Court having jurisdiction of the estate assesses the tax. Upon finding that no tax is due, the court may make an order so decreeing. Where it appears that the tax has not been determined and that no court proceeding to determine the tax is pending or is likely to be filed, the Controller may determine the tax.

• *Compromise of tax*

In the case of the taxation of a contingent or conditional transfer or a transfer of property of a nonresident, a compromise and settlement of the tax may be entered into between the State Controller and executor, etc., but such compromise is not legally effective until it is approved by the Superior Court having jurisdiction, by an order of confirmation of that court.

¶1610 Payment and Refund

Comment: California Death Taxes Expire

Because California's death taxes were based on the federal state death tax credit and this credit is repealed for estates of decedents dying after 2004, California does not currently impose any death taxes on estates of decedents dying after 2004. The discussion following summarizes the law for estates of decedents dying prior to 2005. The pre-2005 law may be reinstated in 2011 if federal law is not amended or may be reinstated earlier if future California legislation decouples from the repeal of the federal state death tax credit.

• *Time for payment*

The tax is due and payable to the State Treasurer at the date of death of the decedent.

• *Receipt for payment*

A receipt of the County Treasurer, signed in triplicate, is made upon payment of the tax. The original and one copy are sent by the County Treasurer to the State Controller; the second copy is delivered by the treasurer to the taxpayer. The original is countersigned by the Controller, or by an employee designated in writing by the Controller, and forwarded for filing to the clerk of the Superior Court having jurisdiction of the estate.

• *Interest and discount*

If the tax is not paid within nine months from the date of death, interest at the rate under IRC Sec. 6621(a)(2) is levied against the deficiency. Currently, the rate is set at 4% per annum.

• *Liability for payment*

The executor or administrator, the trustee and the transferee of property are liable for the tax until it is paid.

In the absence of a direction in a will to the contrary, the federal estate taxes are apportioned among the beneficiaries.

• *Reciprocity*

Reciprocity with other states as to the collection of inheritance and estate taxes in nonresident estates, imposed by the state of domicile, is provided for.

• *Refund*

A refund is provided for where:

(1) There has been a reversal or modification of orders fixing the tax or the Controller's determination of the tax;

(2) The tax on the actual contingency which occurs is less than the tax assessed on the highest contingency;

(3) The federal credit for state death taxes is less than the estate taxes assessed to take advantage of such credit;

(4) The order fixing the tax fails to allow an armed services exemption in the proper situation;

(5) Contingent encumbrances occur; and

(6) Debts allowable as inheritance tax deductions are established and paid after the order fixing the tax is made.

Refunds include interest at the same rate that is applicable to tax underpayments. Currently, the rate is set at 4% per annum.

¶1611 Notice and Waivers

Comment: California Death Taxes Expire

Because California's death taxes were based on the federal state death tax credit and this credit is repealed for estates of decedents dying after 2004, California does not currently impose any death taxes on estates of decedents dying after 2004. The discussion following summarizes the law for estates of decedents dying prior to 2005. The pre-2005 law may be reinstated in 2011 if federal law is not amended or may be reinstated earlier if future California legislation decouples from the repeal of the federal state death tax credit.

• *Residents*

Waivers are not required.

• *Nonresidents*

Waivers are not required.

¶1612 Generation-Skipping Transfer Tax

Comment: California Death Taxes Expire

Because California's death taxes were based on the federal state death tax credit and this credit is repealed for estates of decedents dying after 2004, California does not currently impose any death taxes on estates of decedents dying after 2004. The discussion following summarizes the law for estates of decedents dying prior to 2005. The pre-2005 law may be reinstated in 2011 if federal law is not amended or may be reinstated earlier if future California legislation decouples from the repeal of the federal state death tax credit.

California imposes a generation-skipping transfer tax equal to the federal credit.

PART VII

PROPERTY TAXES

CHAPTER 17

PROPERTY TAXES

¶1701 Scope of Chapter

California does not impose a general ad valorem tax on real and personal property. However, local governmental units throughout the state do impose such a tax. Because of the statewide character of this tax and the fact that its provisions are included in the state Revenue and Taxation Code, this chapter is included for the sake of completeness, despite the fact that the tax is not, strictly speaking, a "state tax."

The purpose of this chapter is to give a very general picture of the nature and application of the property tax and the manner of its administration. It is not intended to provide detailed coverage. It covers, generally, the questions of what property is subject to tax, the base and rate of tax, the requirements for filing returns and making payment, collections, and appeals.

¶1702 Imposition of Tax

Law: Secs. 1-2, Art. XIIIA, Sec. 2, Art. XIIIC, Cal. Constitution; Secs. 51, 61-75.80, 110.1, 170, 401-405, Revenue and Taxation Code, Rule 462.240, 18 CCR (CCH CALIFORNIA TAX REPORTS ¶20-010, 20-070, 20-105, 20-405, 20-610, 20-665, 20-710, 20-715).

The impact of property taxes in California was drastically reduced by the passage of Proposition 13 adding Article XIIIA to the State Constitution. Following is a brief overview of the provisions of Article XIIIA:

— The overall rate of property taxation is limited to 1% of "full cash value" as specifically defined for this purpose (see ¶1706 for discussion of permissible additions to the 1% limit) and also a potential adjustment for a decline in value. (Sec. 1, Art. XIII A, Cal. Const.)

— Valuations of real property are frozen at the value of the property in March 1975, with an allowable adjustment of up to 2% per year for inflation. However, property is assessed at its current value when it is purchased or newly constructed or a "change of ownership" occurs, with subsequent annual adjustment (up to 2%) for inflation. Valuations of personal property are not frozen; they are determined annually as of January 1. (Sec. 2, Art. XIII A, Cal. Const.)

— No new property, sales, or transaction taxes may be imposed on real property. (Sec. 3, Art. XIII A, Cal. Const.)

— A two-thirds vote of the legislature is required for any increases in other state taxes. (Sec. 3, Art. XIII A, Cal. Const.)

— A two-thirds vote of qualified electors is required for the imposition of special taxes by local governments. A majority vote of qualified electors is required for the imposition of any new or higher general taxes by local governments. (Sec. 4, Art. XIII A, Cal. Const.)

• *Transfers of base-year value for seniors and disabled persons*

Homeowners who are over the age of 55 or who are severely and permanently disabled may transfer the adjusted base-year value of their original residence (including an interest in a resident-owned mobilehome park) to a replacement residence (including an interest in a resident-owned mobilehome park) of equal or lesser fair market value in the same county, provided the purchase of the replacement principal residence is within two years of the sale of the original home. According to a California court of appeal, a transfer of a residence's base year value to partial interest in another property does not qualify for relief (see *Bennion v. County of Santa Clara* (2007), CCH CALIFORNIA TAX REPORTS ¶404-445)

Property tax relief is also available for moves between counties if the county where the replacement home is located has adopted an ordinance permitting the valuation transfer. (Sec. 69.5, Rev. & Tax. Code; Sec. 2, Art. XIII A, Cal. Const.) As of April 2007, the counties that authorize the transfer of base-year value are Alameda, Los Angeles, Orange, San Diego, San Mateo, Santa Clara, and Ventura. (*Letter to County Assessors*, No. 2007/020, California State Board of Equalization, April 9, 2007, CCH CALIFORNIA TAX REPORTS ¶20-715.34) The California State Board of Equalization (SBE) has issued a Letter to County Assessors that provides answers to frequently asked questions concerning this program (*Letter to County Assessors*, No. 2006/010, SBE, February 6, 2006, CCH CALIFORNIA TAX REPORTS ¶20-610.24)

Generally, the carryover of a residence's base-year value by a person over the age of 55 or a severely and permanently disabled person is available one-time only. However, a person over the age of 55 who previously transferred the base-year value of a former residence to a replacement residence may utilize the base-year value transfer provisions a second time if the person subsequently becomes severely and permanently disabled.

Taxpayers who transfer their adjusted base-year value from an original residence to a replacement home are not reassessed for subsequent improvements to the replacement residence, so long as the sum of the fair market value of the replacement property and any improvements to the replacement property does not exceed the fair market value of the original home. This applies to improvements completed within two years of (before or after) the sale of the original property and only for replacement dwellings purchased or newly constructed after 1990.

CCH Tip: Applications for Base-Year Value Transfer

Although taxpayers generally must file applications for base-year value transfer within three years after the purchase or construction of the replacement property, assessors are now required to consider transfer applications filed after expiration of the three-year period. (Sec. 69.5(f), Rev. & Tax. Code)

Taxpayers over the age of 55 or disabled are also allowed a base year value transfer if they would otherwise have been eligible for a base year value transfer, except for the fact that their residence was substantially damaged or destroyed by misfortune or calamity and, therefore, the value of their replacement residence exceeds the value of their original residence in its damaged condition. See below under "Damaged property" for a discussion of the transfer of base-year value for damaged or destroyed property.

Businesses are not eligible to transfer original base-year values.

• *Contaminated property*

An owner of qualified contaminated property may transfer the base year value of that property to replacement property located within the same county or within a different county if the other county authorizes such transfers. Alternatively, an owner of qualified property may rebuild a structure substantially destroyed or damaged by environmental remediation on qualified contaminated property without incurring a property tax reassessment for new construction.

The repaired or replacement structure must be similar in size, utility, and function to the original structure. To qualify for the base-year value transfer or the exemption from new construction reassessment, the fair market value of the replacement property must be equal to or less than the fair market value of the qualified contaminated property if the property were not contaminated. Additionally, the replacement property must be acquired or newly constructed within five years after ownership of the qualified contaminated property is sold or otherwise transferred. "Equal or lesser value" means the amount of the full cash value of the original property increased by 5% for each year during the five-year period in which replacement property may be purchased or constructed. To the extent that replacement property, or any portion thereof, is not similar in function, size, and utility, the property, or portion thereof, that is dissimilar will be reassessed and a new base year value assigned.

Once the base-year value is transferred to the replacement property, the county assessor must determine a new base-year value for the original contaminated property. If the original property is not subjected to reappraisal, the original base-year value may not be transferred. In addition, the base-year value may not be transferred to replacement property if (1) property tax relief for damaged or destroyed property or for property transferred by seniors or disabled individuals is available or (2) the claimant has excluded from a new construction reappraisal, structures or buildings reconstructed as a result of damage stemming from qualified contaminated property remediation efforts.

A claimant must file a claim within three years of the date the replacement property was purchased or the new construction of the replacement property was completed. A claimant must submit proof that (1) the claimant did not participate or acquiesce in any act or omission that rendered the real property uninhabitable or unusable and (2) the property has been designated as a toxic or environmental hazard or as an environmental cleanup site by a California or federal agency.

• *New construction*

New construction requiring revaluation includes site development of land, improvements erected on land, additions to existing improvements, and new fixtures (*e.g.*, store fixtures, machinery) that relate directly to the function of the structure. The value of new construction, including construction in progress, is added to the base-year value. (Sec. 69.4, Rev. & Tax. Code)

The law provides relief for certain cases where reconstruction or improvement is required to comply with local ordinances on seismic safety. In these cases, revaluation is deferred for 15 years.

New construction, for purposes of reassessment, does not include the following:

— earthquake safety improvements,

— fire protection improvements,

— access improvements for the disabled,

— for the 1999-2000 through 2015-2016 fiscal years, active solar energy system improvements,

— underground storage tank upgrades, and

— newly created month-to-month leases or other possessory interests in publicly owned real property having a full cash value of $50,000 or less.

• *Change of ownership*

The law provides detailed definitions of what constitutes a change of ownership that will trigger a revaluation of real property. The following is a very brief summary of transactions that are not considered to be changes of ownership:

— Interspousal transfers, including those made in divorce settlements. Sale of an undivided interest results in a revaluation of the portion transferred; however, there is no revaluation if the interest transferred is less than 5% and its value is under $10,000. (Sec. 2, Art. XIIIA, Cal. Const.; Sec. 63, Rev. & Tax. Code; Reg. 462.220, 18 CCR)

— Transfers of partnership interests, or addition or deletion of partners, unless a controlling interest is acquired. (Sec. 64, Rev. & Tax. Code; Reg. 462.180, 18 CCR)

— Transfers of property among members of an affiliated group of corporations, as specifically defined. (Sec. 64, Rev. & Tax. Code)

— A transfer into a trust, if the transferor is the beneficiary or the trust is revocable. (Sec. 62(d), Rev. & Tax. Code)

— Transfers of joint tenancies that do not result in changes of beneficial ownership. (Sec. 62(f), Rev. & Tax. Code)

— An acquisition of property as a replacement for property that was condemned. However, where the value of the property acquired exceeds the value of the property replaced by more than 20%, the excess is revalued and added to the base-year value of the replaced property. (Sec. 63.1, Rev. & Tax. Code; Sec. 68, Rev. & Tax. Code; Sec. 1, Art. XIII A, Cal. Const.)

— Certain transfers of residences to children (including foster children) or wards upon death of parents or guardians. To qualify, the children or wards must have (1) been disabled for at least five years prior to the transfer, (2) lived in the property at least five years, and (3) family income of $20,000 or less. (Sec. 62(n), Rev. & Tax. Code; Reg. 462.240, 18 CCR)

— Transfers of the principal residence and up to $1 million in other property between parents and their children (including foster children) or between grandparents and their grandchildren when the parents of the children who are the blood relative of the grandparent(s) are deceased. The exclusion does not apply to transfers from foster children to their biological parents. (Sec. 2, Art. XIIIA, Cal. Const.; Sec. 63.1, Rev. & Tax. Code; Reg. 462.240, 18 CCR)

— Certain transfers of mobilehome parks to nonprofit entities. This also applies to transfers of rental spaces to tenants under certain conditions. (Sec. 62.1, Rev. & Tax. Code; Reg. 462.240, 18 CCR)

— The acquisition by an employee benefit plan of indirect or direct control of the employer corporation. (Sec. 66, Rev. & Tax. Code; Reg. 462.240, 18 CCR)

— Newly created possessory interests established by month-to-month agreements in publicly owned real property that have a full cash value of $50,000 or less. (Sec. 75.5, Rev. & Tax. Code)

— The transfer of separate property inherited by a surviving domestic partner by intestate succession upon the death of a registered domestic partner. (Reg. 462.240(k), 18 CCR)

— The recordation of a certificate of sale, relating to property sold subject to the right of redemption, for the period in which the right of redemption exists. (Sec. 62.11, Rev. & Tax. Code)

— Transfers between registered domestic partners. (Sec. 62(p), Rev. & Tax. Code)

Planning Note: Estate Planning Pitfalls

Taxpayers should carefully think through the consequences of forming partnerships, limited liability companies, etc., to hold real property that may be transferred to their children or grandchildren upon their death. When real property was transferred into a family partnership, the characterization of a living trust's asset was consequently changed from an interest in real property to an interest in a limited partnership. As a consequence, when the grantor passed away, a change of ownership reassessment was triggered because the taxpayer no longer qualified for the parent/child exclusion available for transfers of real property. The property interest transferred was an interest in the limited partnership, not an interest in the real property. (Unpublished opinion, *Wade v. County of San Luis Obispo* (2005), CCH CALIFORNIA TAX REPORTS ¶20-955.82)

Practical Analysis: Registered Domestic Partners

Ch. 555 (S.B. 559), Laws 2007, made the change in ownership exclusion of transfers between registered domestic partners (RDPs) that was enacted in 2006, and applicable to transfers occurring after 2005, retroactive to eligible transfers that were reassessed between January 1, 2000, and January 1, 2006. In 2007, the 3rd District Court of Appeal upheld the RDP change in ownership exclusion after a challenge by the California Assessors' Association. (See *Strong v. State Board of Equalization* (2007), CCH CALIFORNIA TAX REPORTS ¶404-469)

RDPs have until June 30, 2009, to apply for reversal of reassessments for property that was transferred during calendar years 2000-2005. Any reassessment reversal would apply commencing with the lien date of the assessment year in which a claim is filed, and the county may charge a related fee for the reversals. (Sec. 62(p)(2), Rev. & Tax. Code)

California's passage of The California Domestic Partner Rights and Responsibilities Act of 2003 (DPRRA) raises many interesting property tax issues. The State Board of Equalization (SBE) has taken the position that because the DPRRA cannot change the legal definition of "spouse," the DPRRA does not impact the interspousal exclusion from change-of-ownership reassessments. (As noted above, legislation has been enacted which does allow transfers between registered domestic partners without triggering a reassessment.) However, transfers between parents and their child and the child's domestic partner and transfers from a domestic partner to his or her partner's child would not trigger a reassessment. The SBE has also addressed the impact of the DPRRA on a variety of other property tax exclusions and exemptions. (*Letter to County Assessors*, No. 2005/017, SBE, March 3, 2005, CCH CALIFORNIA TAX REPORTS ¶20-715.48)

Practice Note: Life Estate Conveyance Not Reassessable Change of Ownership

A California court of appeal has held that a taxpayer's acquisition of a life estate in real property upon the death of her sister did not constitute a change of ownership so as to trigger a property tax reassessment, because the transfer of the present interest in the property did not have a value substantially equal to the value of a fee interest. In so ruling, the court held that an SBE property tax rule (Rule 462.060(a)) that was inconsistent with the "substantial equivalency test" could not be enforced because it exceeded the Legislature's grant of authority. (*Steinhart v. County of Los Angeles* (2007), CCH CALIFORNIA TAX REPORTS ¶404-467) This decision conflicts with a 1998 decision by the 4th District (See *Leckie* (1998), CCH CALIFORNIA TAX REPORTS ¶402-999), and a 2006 decision by the 1st District. (See *Reilly* (2006), CALIFORNIA TAX REPORTS ¶404-046)

New owners are required to notify the assessor of a change of ownership and may be penalized for failure to do so. (Sec. 480, Rev. & Tax. Code; Sec. 90, Rev. & Tax. Code; Sec. 482, Rev. & Tax. Code) As a part of the effort to enforce the change-of-ownership rules, corporation and partnership income tax return forms require reporting of changes in property ownership.

• *Constitutionality of acquisition value assessment*

In *Nordlinger v. Hahn* (1992) (CCH CALIFORNIA TAX REPORTS ¶21-930.203), the U.S. Supreme Court concluded that the acquisition value assessment method mandated by Proposition 13 does not violate the principles of the Equal Protection Clause of the Fourteenth Amendment, even though the method may result in significant assessment disparities between similar properties acquired at different times. The same conclusion was reached by a California court of appeal in *R.H. Macy v. Contra Costa County* (1990) (CCH CALIFORNIA TAX REPORTS ¶21-930.202), which involved commercial property. The taxpayer's commercial premises, which were acquired before Proposition 13 was adopted, were held to have been properly assessed at full value (*i.e.*, market price) for the 1987 tax year, when the taxpayer underwent a corporate reorganization that constituted a change of ownership triggering reassessment under Proposition 13.

• *Damaged property*

Detailed rules are provided for reduction in the assessed valuation where property is damaged or destroyed by a "misfortune or calamity." County boards of supervisors may enact an ordinance allowing taxpayers to apply for reassessment of any taxable property that has been damaged or destroyed by a misfortune or calamity through no fault of their own. (Sec. 170, Rev. & Tax. Code)

If an ordinance is adopted, a local assessor must determine separately the full cash value of the land, improvements, and personalty immediately before and after the damage. The assessor must separately determine the percentage reduction in value for each element of the property if the total decrease in value exceeds $10,000.

An ordinance may also allow assessor-initiated reductions in the assessed value of property when the assessor determines the property has been damaged or destroyed by a major misfortune or calamity within the preceding 12 months. After reassessment, taxes remaining due for the assessment year may be prorated, and any excess paid before the reassessment may be refunded.

If real property is damaged or destroyed by disaster, misfortune, or calamity and no ordinance providing for reassessment of the property has been adopted by the county board of supervisors, or if the taxpayer has voluntarily removed real property from land, the taxable value of the property is the sum of (1) the adjusted base year value or full cash value of the land, whichever is less, and (2) the adjusted base year value or full cash value of the improvements, whichever is less. (Sec. 51, Rev. & Tax. Code)

Practical Analysis: Physical Damage Requirement

A California court of appeal has held that property that has declined in value due to the owner's restricted physical access to the property, in the absence of any physical damage, does not qualify as damaged or destroyed property within the meaning of the law. (*Slocum v. State Board of Equalization* (2005) (CCH CALIFORNIA TAX REPORTS ¶403-930))

The base-year value of property damaged or destroyed in an area declared a disaster by the Governor may be transferred to comparable replacement property acquired or constructed within the same county or to comparable replacement property in a *different* county, provided the replacement property is a replacement principal residence located in a county whose board of supervisors has authorized such a transfer prior to the taxpayer's relocation. (Sec. 2, Art. XIIIA, Cal Const.; Sec. 69, Rev. & Tax. Code; Sec. 69.3, Rev. & Tax. Code) As of March 2006, Contra Costa, Los Angeles, Modoc, San Francisco, Santa Clara, Solano, Sutter, and Ventura counties have informed the SBE that they have adopted such an ordinance. (*Letter to County Assessors*, No. 2006/015, SBE, March 1, 2006, CCH CALIFORNIA TAX REPORTS ¶20-150.48))

The time period during which a base-year value transfer may be made for property damaged or destroyed by a disaster is (1) five years from the date of the disaster for intracounty transfers and (2) three years from the date the replacement property is purchased or constructed for intercounty transfers.

Damaged or destroyed property is reassessed at current market value but retains its old base-year value if that value is lower than the reassessed value, notwithstanding the transfer of the base-year value to replacement property. Restoration or repair of the property is considered to be new construction, triggering a reassessment at that time.

In counties that have adopted an ordinance that allows assessees whose property was damaged or destroyed to apply for reassessment of the property, the assessees must file an application for reassessment within 12 months of the damage to the property. (Sec. 170, Rev. & Tax. Code)

• *Purchase price as value*

Reg. 2, 18 CCR, provides that the value of property for revaluation purposes in the case of a change of ownership is the purchase price paid unless there is substantial and convincing evidence that the property would not have transferred for such price in an open market transaction.

• *Effective date of revaluation*

The annual lien date and valuation date for locally assessed property taxes is January 1; this date applies to taxes for the fiscal year beginning on the following July 1. (Sec. 401.3, Rev. & Tax. Code; Sec. 405, Rev. & Tax. Code; Sec. 404, Rev. & Tax. Code; Sec. 2192, Rev. & Tax. Code)

The law provides that new construction or change of ownership will result in revaluation in the following month and a consequent increase in tax liability. Thus, new construction or change of ownership in July increases taxes for the fiscal year beginning in July by $^{11}/_{12}$ths of a full year's tax attributable to the increased valuation. A change in August increases the current tax by $^{10}/_{12}$ths of the tax for a full year, and so on through the fiscal year. (Sec. 75.11, Rev. & Tax. Code)

New construction or a change of ownership occurring on or after the lien date but on or before May 31 results in an increase in taxes both for the current fiscal year and for the following fiscal year. If new construction or a change of ownership occurs on or after June 1 and on or before the next lien date, the assessor will need to determine only one supplemental assessment. (Sec. 75.11, Rev. & Tax. Code)

New construction is exempt from the supplemental assessment explained above until certain events occur (sale, rental, occupancy), provided the owner gives the assessor prescribed notice and requests exemption within specified time limits. (Sec. 75.12, Rev. & Tax. Code)

¶1703 Property Subject to Tax

Law: Secs. 201, 229, 1150-54, 5801-15 (CCH CALIFORNIA TAX REPORTS ¶20-105, 20-190, 20-260, 20-295, 20-325).

All real and tangible personal property in the state is subject to tax unless specifically exempt. (Sec. 201, Rev. & Tax. Code; Sec. 1, Art. XIII, Cal. Const.) There is no tax on intangible property. "Possessory interests" of lessees in tax-exempt public property are subject to tax if they are independent, durable, and exclusive of rights held by others in the property. (Sec. 107, Rev. & Tax. Code; Reg. 20, 18 CCR) Examples of possessory interests are leases of oil and gas properties, homesites, and boat berths.

States may not tax property interests held by the federal government, unless, in cases in which the United States is the owner of land within a state, the United States has merely proprietary interests in the land, and not exclusive jurisdiction over the land (*Coso Energy Developers v. County of Inyo* (2004) (CCH CALIFORNIA TAX REPORTS ¶20-190.31)).

In *United States v. County of San Diego et al.* (1995) (CCH CALIFORNIA TAX REPORTS ¶20-330.303), a federal court of appeals held that the taxpayer, a private research firm that conducted nuclear fusion research for the U.S. Department of Energy (DOE), had a taxable possessory interest in a nuclear device belonging to the DOE because the taxpayer was entitled to exclusive and independent use of the device. Moreover, the property tax assessment was properly calculated using the value of the nuclear device because tax was assessed on the possessory interest of the taxpayer rather than on the United State's ownership interest.

Certain types of property are subject to special taxes "in lieu" of property taxes and therefore are not subject to the general property tax. This applies to motor vehicles and private cars, as explained at ¶1903 and ¶1905.

Airplanes used by domestic airlines and air taxis operated in scheduled air taxi operations are assessed in proportion to the time they are in California. Aircraft owned by foreign airlines are exempt. (Sec. 5331, Rev. & Tax. Code) Special rules apply to the valuation of certificated aircraft, airline possessory interests, and fractionally-owned aircraft. (Sec. 107.9, Rev. & Tax. Code; Sec. 441, Rev. & Tax. Code; Secs. 1150 et. seq., Rev. & Tax. Code; Secs. 1160 et seq., Rev. & Tax. Code)

Special rules are provided for manufactured homes. Those on a permanent foundation are taxed as real property. Others are subject either to vehicle license fees or to property taxes, depending on date of purchase and other factors. (Sec. 5801, Rev. & Tax. Code; Sec. 5810, Rev. & Tax. Code)

Floating homes are taxed as real property, with 1979 (rather than 1975) used as the valuation base for purposes of Proposition 13 (¶1702). A floating home does not include a vessel.

¶1704 Exemptions

Law: Secs. 201-61 (CCH CALIFORNIA TAX REPORTS ¶20-505—20-515).

Many categories of property and property owners are partially or fully exempt under the property tax law. There have been numerous changes in the exemptions over the years. Detailed listing and discussion are beyond the scope of this book.

Property tax is not imposed on the following categories of property:

— business inventories (including livestock held for sale) (Sec. 219, Rev. & Tax Code);

— household goods and personal effects not held or used in a trade or business (Sec. 3(m), Art. XIII, Cal. Const.; Sec. 224, Rev. & Tax. Code),

— employee-owned hand tools (up to $20,000) (Sec. 241, Rev. & Tax. Code);

— intangible property (Sec. 212, Rev. & Tax. Code);

— nonprofit cemetery property (Sec. 204, Rev. & Tax. Code);

— cargo containers (Sec. 232, Rev. & Tax. Code); and

— certain vessels and aircraft. (Sec. 209, Rev. & Tax. Code; Sec. 209.5, Rev. & Tax. Code; Sec. 217.1, Rev. & Tax. Code; Sec. 220, Rev. & Tax. Code; Sec. 220.5, Rev. & Tax. Code; Sec. 228, Rev. & Tax. Code; Sec. 5331, Rev. & Tax. Code; Sec. 5332, Rev. & Tax. Code)

In *Hahn v. State Board of Equalization* (1999) (CCH CALIFORNIA TAX REPORTS ¶20-150.80), a California court of appeal upheld a State Board of Equalization rule that basic operational computer programs (although intangible property) are not exempt from property tax when sold bundled with computer hardware but are exempt when sold separately. However, in *Cardinal Health 301, Inc. v. County of Orange* (2008) (CCH CALIFORNIA TAX REPORTS ¶20-135.27), a California court of appeal noted that not all bundled software is taxable. Where there is no evidence to the contrary, assessors can value computer equipment sold or leased at a single price not segregated between taxable property and nontaxable programs. However, taxpayers have the option and the burden of presenting evidence to rebut the taxability presumption by showing that some of the bundled software at the time of purchase or lease of the computer did not constitute basic operational programs and, therefore, was not subject to tax.

CCH Tip: Business Inventory

To qualify for the business inventory exemption, the inventory must be used for a legitimate business reason and not for an officer's or shareholder's pleasure. Thus, in *Orange County Sunbird Aviation v. County of Orange* (2002) (CCH CALIFORNIA TAX REPORTS ¶20-263.50), a California court of appeal held that an aircraft owned by a limited partnership was not exempt from personal property tax as business inventory because lease of the aircraft to the partnership's sole shareholder evidenced the fact that the corporate entity was a tax evasion device. The shareholder's practice in giving himself preferential rates when he leased the aircraft, coupled with his ability to personally approve or disapprove all other leases based on any conflicts with his schedule, demonstrated that the partnership was the shareholder's alter ego operated for his personal benefit rather than for legitimate business purposes, and justified piercing of the corporate veil.

In addition, in *Amdahl Corp. v. County of Santa Clara* (2004) (CCH CALIFORNIA TAX REPORTS ¶20-240.55), spare parts held by a computer company for purposes of servicing and repairing customers' equipment was not exempt business inventory because it was not held for sale or lease.

A property tax exemption is provided for $7,000 of the value of a homeowner's dwelling. (Sec. 3, Art. XIII, Cal. Const.; Sec. 218, Rev. & Tax. Code; Reg. 464, 18 CCR)

CCH Tip: Damaged/Destroyed Property

Homes destroyed or damaged in the disasters listed in Sec. 218, Rev. & Tax. Code, remain eligible for the homeowners' exemption.

Partial exemptions are also allowed for certain agricultural products, immature timber, fruit and nut trees, and grapevines. (Sec. 3, Art. XIII, Cal. Const.; Sec. 202(a)(1), Rev. & Tax. Code; Sec. 211(a), Rev. & Tax. Code; Sec. 105(b), Rev. & Tax. Code; Sec. 436, Rev. & Tax. Code; Reg. 131, 18 CCR) These exemptions are in addition to constitutional exemptions for property in interstate and international commerce. (Reg. 203, 18 CCR)

In addition, California's property tax law provides full or partial exemptions for qualified property held by the following entities:

— religious institutions and organizations (Sec. 217, Rev. & Tax. Code);

— governments and their agencies (Sec. 3, Art. XIII, Cal. Const.; Sec. 202(a)(4), Rev. & Tax. Code);

— Native American tribes (Sec. 237, Rev. & Tax. Code);

— educational institutions (Sec. 3(d), Art. XIII, Cal. Const.; Sec. 202(a), Rev. & Tax. Code; Sec. 203(a), Rev. & Tax. Code);

— charitable, scientific, and hospital organizations (Sec. 214, Rev. & Tax. Code);

— certain veterans and their surviving spouses (Sec. 3, Art. XIII, Cal. Const.; Sec. 205, Rev. & Tax. Code);

— veterans organizations (Sec. 215, Rev. & Tax. Code);

— banks and insurance companies (personal property only) (Sec. 27, Art. XIII, Cal. Const.; Sec. 28, Art. XIII, Cal. Const.); and

— volunteer fire departments (Sec. 213.7, Rev. & Tax. Code; Sec. 254.6, Rev & Tax. Code).

Some exemptions require the filing of an annual return or claim. In case of any question about exemptions or filing requirements, the assessor's office should be consulted.

Practical Analysis: Housing Finance Agency Exempt From Tax on Foreclosed Homes

In a *Letter to County Assessors*, No. 2008/017, February 25, 2008, the California State Board of Equalization indicated that property held by the California Housing Finance Agency (CHFA) as a result of deed foreclosure proceedings is exempt from the state's property tax. The state constitution exempts property owned by the state, and the CHFA is a public instrumentality and a political subdivision of the state. There also is express statutory language stating that the agency will not be required to pay any tax or assessment on any property it owns or upon the income from that property.

¶1705 Senior Citizens and Disabled Persons Property Tax Assistance

Law: Secs. 20501-641 (CCH CALIFORNIA TAX REPORTS ¶20-155, 20-315).

Some property tax relief has previously been provided for "senior citizens" and disabled persons in the form of "property tax assistance" payments made by the Franchise Tax Board (FTB) to reimburse qualified homeowners for property taxes paid on their primary residence located in California. (Sec. 20501 Rev. & Tax. Code, et. seq.) This program includes manufactured homes and floating homes, and also applies to renters, based upon a property tax equivalent presumed to be paid by renters. To qualify, a homeowner or renter must be age 62 or older or blind or disabled and must have "household income" within specified limits.

CCH Caution: Assistance Payments Not Funded for 2008

Funding for the property tax assistance payments under the Homeowner and Renter Assistance Program was deleted from the 2008/2009 California budget. The FTB will continue to accept 2008 claims and will hold them in the event that funding later becomes available. However, at this time there is no expectation that there will be any funds available to pay those claims. Questions on the program should be directed to the

FTB at (800) 868-4171, Monday through Friday, between 8:00 a.m. and 5:00 p.m. (*Important Notice*, California Franchise Tax Board, September 24, 2008)

CCH Tip: Length of Disability

A taxpayer claiming eligibility on the basis of a disability must present proof that the disability will last at least one year. (*Appeal of Wilson* (2001) (CCH CALIFORNIA TAX REPORTS ¶20-358.25))

"Household income" consists of taxable income plus nontaxable income such as social security, public assistance payments, etc. (Sec. 20503, Rev. & Tax. Code) A regulation addresses specific eligibility and application requirements for resident aliens. (Reg. 20561, 18 CCR)

The amount of relief to a homeowner is a portion of the tax, excluding special or direct assessments, on the first $34,000 of the full value of the home, the percentage varying in inverse ratio to the household income. (Sec. 20542, Rev. & Tax. Code) If funding for payments later becomes available, for 2008, the percentage is 139% where the income for 2007 was $11,022 or less, decreasing by steps to 6% where the income is more than $42,259 but not more than $44,096. All these figures are adjusted for inflation.

Also, if funding for payments later becomes available, the maximum amount of relief to a renter for 2008 is $347.50 for household incomes from $0 to $11,022. The maximum household income limit is $44,096. The claimant must pay rent of at least $50 per month to qualify for assistance. (Sec. 20542, Rev. & Tax. Code)

Relief may not be claimed for tax-exempt property, except those premises on which the owner pays possessory interest taxes, or makes payments in lieu of property taxes (PILOT), which are substantially equivalent to property taxes paid on properties of comparable market value. (Sec. 20509, Rev. & Tax. Code) In *Appeal of Helen Cantor, et al.* (2002) (CCH CALIFORNIA TAX REPORTS ¶20-358.252), the California State Board of Equalization concluded that "substantially equivalent" meant that PILOT payments equaled at least 80% of the property taxes paid on properties of comparable assessed values.

The blank forms necessary to claim assistance are distributed by the FTB. Claims should be filed with the Property Tax Assistance Division annually after June 30 but before October 16 of the next succeeding fiscal year. (Sec. 20563, Rev. & Tax. Code) (Homeowner and Renter Assistance Claim Booklet)

• *Property tax postponement*

Persons age 62 or over and disabled and blind persons may postpone payment of property taxes on their home under certain conditions. The claimant must own (including possessory interests) and occupy the property involved, which may be a manufactured home, houseboat, or floating home, and may be in cooperative housing or in a multipurpose or multiunit structure. The claimant must have at least a 20% equity, based on property-tax valuation. "Ownership" includes an interest in residential property that is held in a type of trust in which the transfer of title does not constitute a change of ownership, provided the Controller determines that the state's interest is adequately protected. (Sec. 20601, Rev. & Tax. Code; Sec. 8.5, Art. XIII, Cal. Const.; Sec. 20505, Rev. & Tax. Code; Sec. 20508, Rev. & Tax. Code; Sec. 20582, Rev. & Tax. Code; Sec. 20585, Rev. & Tax. Code)

To be eligible, the claimant must have "household income" of no more than $35,500 for 2008 ($31,500 in 2007, except for claimants who participated in the program continuously since 1983, for whom the household income limit was $34,000 for 2007). The household income level is increased for all claimants to $39,900 in 2009 and adjusted for inflation thereafter. (Sec. 20585, Rev. & Tax. Code)

"Household income" consists of taxable income plus nontaxable income such as Social Security, public assistance payments, etc., earned by all persons of the household while members of the household. (Sec. 20582, Rev. & Tax. Code; Sec. 20503, Rev. & Tax. Code; Sec. 20504, Rev. & Tax. Code)

The postponed taxes are covered by a lien on the property. They become payable, generally, if the claimant disposes of the property or dies without leaving a spouse living in the home. (Sec. 16190, Govt. Code; Sec. 16191, Govt. Code)

Application for postponement should be filed with the State Controller, who will supply forms and information upon request. (Sec. 20621, Rev. & Tax. Code)

¶1706 Basis and Rate of Tax

Law: Sec. 3, Art. XIII, Sec. 1, Art. XIIIA, Cal. Constitution; Secs. 93, 109, 208-12, 401.17, 402.95, Revenue and Taxation Code (CCH CALIFORNIA TAX REPORTS ¶20-405, 20-610).

As explained at ¶1702, the overall rate of property tax is 1% of "full cash value." This may be increased by any amount necessary to pay interest and redemption charges on any indebtedness approved by the voters before July 1, 1978, or bonded indebtedness for the acquisition or improvement of real property approved on or after July 1, 1978, by two-thirds of those voting in a local election (55% if related to school bonds). (Sec. 1, Art. XIII A, Cal. Const.)

The value of intangible assets and rights relating to the going concern value of a business or the exclusive nature of a concession, franchise, or similar agreement must not enhance or be reflected in the value of taxable property. However, taxable property may be assessed and valued by assuming the presence of intangible assets or rights necessary to put the taxable property to beneficial or productive use. (Sec. 212, Rev. & Tax. Code; Sec. 3(n), Art. XIII, Cal. Const.) Intangible attributes of real property such as zoning, location, and other such attributes that relate directly to the real property must be reflected in the value of the real property. (Sec. 110, Rev. & Tax. Code)

Additionally, in any case in which the cost approach method of valuation is used to value special use property, a component for entrepreneurial profit may not be added unless there is market-derived evidence that such profit exists and has not been fully offset by physical deterioration or economic obsolescence. (Sec. 401.6, Rev. & Tax. Code) Assessors must also exclude from income the benefit from federal and state low-income housing tax credits allocated by the California Tax Credit Allocation Committee when they value property under the income method of appraisal. (Sec. 402.95, Rev. & Tax. Code)

The "assessed value" of property, generally, is the full cash value as modified by Proposition 13 (¶1702). The assessed value may be retroactively reduced when a disaster occurs after the assessment date (¶1707). The base-year value of certain property damaged by a disaster may be transferred to replacement property (¶1702).

Special rules are provided for reduced valuation of several categories of property, including the following:

— certain vessels engaged in fishing or research (Sec. 227, Rev. & Tax. Code);

— "enforceably restricted" open-space land (Sec. 8, Art. XIII, Cal. Const.),

— motion pictures (Sec. 988, Rev. & Tax. Code);

— computer software programs (Sec. 995, Rev. & Tax. Code); and

— business or professional records (Sec. 997, Rev. & Tax. Code).

Effective for fiscal years 2005-2006 through 2010-2011, the value of certificated aircraft is based on the lesser of (1) the historical cost basis or (2) prices listed in the Airliner Price Guide.

In *Auerbach v. Assessment Appeals Board No. 2 for the County of Los Angeles* (2008) (CCH CALIFORNIA TAX REPORTS ¶404-780), a California court of appeal held that a property tax assessment on a business jet aircraft improperly included a theoretical sales tax on the value of the aircraft as an element of value, where the aircraft owner was eligible for a common carrier exemption from sales or use tax on the lien date.

Although Article XIIIA of the Constitution (Proposition 13) refers only to real property, the 1% rate limitation also applies to personal property. (Sec. 2, Art. XIII, Cal. Const.)

The law provides that personal property shall be treated as "secured" only if located upon real property of the same owner at the lien date. Personal property not so located may be treated as "secured" under certain conditions. (Sec. 607, Rev. & Tax. Code; Sec. 608, Rev. & Tax. Code; Sec. 609, Rev. & Tax. Code) In order for such property to be treated as "secured" where it is not located upon real property of the same owner, the property must be located in the same county and the taxpayer must record a certificate from the assessor to the effect that the real property is sufficient to secure the payment of the tax.

¶1707 Assessment Procedure and Equalization

Law: Secs. 108, 170, 401-05, 441-60, 532, 721-59, 1601-45.5 (CCH CALIFORNIA TAX REPORTS ¶20-605 et seq.).

Property is assessed annually as of 12:01 a.m. on the first day of January. (Sec. 401.3, Rev. & Tax. Code; Sec. 405, Rev. & Tax. Code; Sec. 404, Rev. & Tax. Code; Sec. 2192, Rev. & Tax. Code)

Each taxpayer must file a personal property statement with the county assessor during any year the aggregate cost of his or her taxable personal property is $100,000 or more. Others must file a statement if requested by the assessor. The statement must include a description of all taxable property owned, claimed, possessed, controlled or managed by the individual, firm, or corporation involved. (Sec. 441, Rev. & Tax. Code; Sec. 442, Rev. & Tax. Code; Sec. 445, Rev. & Tax. Code)

Practice Note: Audits

Effective January 1, 2009, county assessors must annually conduct a significant number of audits of the books and records of non-exempt business taxpayers with taxable property in the county. A significant number of audits means at least 75% of the fiscal year average of the total number of audits the assessor was required to conduct during the period from fiscal year 2002-2003 through fiscal year 2005-2006. Under the new process, 50% of the audits required annually must be performed on taxpayers selected from a pool of those taxpayers that have the largest assessments of trade fixtures and business tangible personal property in the county. Each taxpayer in the pool must be audited at least once every four years. The selection of businesses for the other 50% of audits performed annually must be conducted in a fair and equitable manner and may be based on evidence of underreporting. (Sec. 469, Rev. & Tax. Code)

The board of supervisors of each county acts as a board of equalization to equalize valuations of the county assessor. (Sec. 1601, Rev. & Tax. Code; Sec. 16, Art. XIII, Cal. Const.; Sec. 119, Rev. & Tax. Code; Sec. 1610.8, Rev. & Tax. Code) Boards of supervisors of certain counties may create assessment appeals boards to handle their equalization duties. (Sec. 16, Art. XIII, Cal. Const.; Sec. 1620, Rev. & Tax. Code) With the exception of state-assessed property, property owners may appear before the county board of equalization or assessment appeals board to protest their assessments (¶1709). The State Board of Equalization (SBE) reviews the valuation of a public utility's state-assessed property where a petition for reassessment has been made. (Sec. 741, Rev. & Tax. Code)

The law authorizes the board of supervisors of any county to provide by ordinance for the reassessment of property damaged or destroyed by a "misfortune or calamity" such as earthquake, fire, flood, or landslide. (Sec. 51, Rev. & Tax. Code; Sec. 15, Art. XIII, Cal. Const.)

The SBE assesses property, as of 12:01 a.m. on the first day of January, of certain classes of public utilities and other inter-county property, even though the property is taxed by local jurisdictions. (Sec. 19, Art. XIII, Cal. Const.) However, land and rights-of-way through which intercounty pipelines run are subject to assessment by county assessors. (Sec. 401.8, Rev. & Tax. Code)

• *Escape assessments*

The period within which an escape assessment for willful tax evasion can be made is eight years from July 1 of the assessment year in which the property escaped assessment or was underassessed. Other escape assessments generally must be made within four years after July 1 of the assessment year in which the property escaped assessment or was underassessed. However, if the escape assessment results from a failure to file a change of ownership statement or a preliminary change in ownership report, an escape assessment may be issued within eight years from July 1 of the year the property escaped assessment or was underassessed. If the escape assessment or underassessment was the result of a taxpayer's fraudulent activities or the result of the taxpayer's failure to file a statement of change of ownership or control of a corporation, partnership, or other legal entity, then an escape assessment may be made at any time for any year in which the property escaped taxation or was underassessed. (Sec. 532, Rev. & Tax. Code)

• *Cancellation of erroneous assessments*

Erroneous property tax assessments paid after the four-year statute of limitations for correction of assessments has elapsed may be canceled by the county auditor if the cancellation is initiated within 120 days of the payment of those erroneous assessments. (Sec. 4986, Rev. & Tax. Code; Sec. 4986.2, Rev. & Tax. Code)

¶1708 Returns and Payment

Law: Secs. 194-4.9, 441-60, 2605-19, 2701-05.5 (CCH CALIFORNIA TAX REPORTS ¶89-102).

As explained above at ¶1707, taxpayers may be required to file annually with the county assessor a written statement of property owned, claimed, possessed, or controlled. (Sec. 442, Rev. & Tax. Code; Sec. 445, Rev. & Tax. Code) The statement must be filed between January 1 and April 1. (Sec. 443, Rev. & Tax. Code) In cases where the cities do their own assessing, a separate statement should be filed with the city.

Owners of a cooperative housing corporation, community apartment project, condominium, planned unit development, or other residential subdivision complex with common areas and facilities in which units or lots are transferred without the use of recorded deeds might be required to file an ownership report with the local assessor by the next February 1 following the local assessor's request. If a report is not filed, the assessor will send a change in ownership statement to every occupant of each individual unit or lot with instructions for any occupant who does not have an ownership interest in the unit or lot to forward the statement to the owner or shareholder of the property. Failure to file the statement could result in penalties of up to $2,500. (Sec. 480.8, Rev. & Tax. Code)

As noted at ¶1704, owners of certain classes of exempt property must file an annual return or affidavit claiming the exemption.

A county tax collector must consolidate all of a requesting taxpayer's property tax obligations into a single tax bill. Consolidated property tax bills may be obtained only in counties in which an authorizing memorandum is recorded with the county recorder and only with respect to property listed on the secured property tax roll. (Sec. 2611.7, Rev. & Tax. Code)

Except in a few cities, the following property taxes are payable:

— **on real property:** first installment (one-half) due and payable November 1 and delinquent after December 10; second installment due and payable February 1 and delinquent after April 10

— **on personal property:** if secured by real estate, payable (in full) with the *first* installment of real estate tax, by December 10; if unsecured, due on first day of March and delinquent after August 31.

(Sec. 2605, Rev. & Tax. Code; Sec. 2606, Rev. & Tax. Code; Sec. 2617, Rev. & Tax. Code; Sec. 2681, Rev. & Tax. Code; Sec. 2701, Rev. & Tax. Code; Sec. 2702, Rev. & Tax. Code; Sec. 2704, Rev. & Tax. Code; Sec. 2705, Rev. & Tax. Code)

If the delinquency date falls on Saturday, Sunday, or a holiday, the taxes do not become delinquent until 5 p.m. or the close of business, whichever is later, on the next business day. (Sec. 2619, Rev. & Tax. Code; Sec. 2705.5, Rev. & Tax. Code) If a county board of supervisors, by adoption of an ordinance or resolution, closes the county's offices for business prior to the time of delinquency on the "next business day" or for a whole day, that day will be considered a legal holiday for purposes of establishing the delinquency date.

A few cities that do their own assessing do not use the payment dates shown above; there is no uniformity in the dates used in such cases.

Practice Tip: Date of Receipt of Electronic Payment

A remittance made using an electronic payment option such as wire transfer, telephoned credit card, or the Internet is deemed received on the date that the taxpayer completes the transaction. The taxpayer must provide proof of the date of the completed transaction in the form of a confirmation number or other convincing evidence. This provision does not apply to payments made by electronic fund transfer. (Sec. 2512, Rev. & Tax. Code)

An owner of property that has sustained substantial damage as the result of a disaster in a county declared by the Governor to be in a state of disaster may apply for deferral of the first post-disaster installment of regular secured property taxes. Real property is considered substantially damaged if the damage amounts to at least 10% of its fair market value or $10,000, whichever is less. Other property qualifies if the damage equals at least 20% of its fair market value immediately preceding the disaster causing the damage. A claim for reassessment of the disaster-damaged property must be filed, or the property must have been otherwise reassessed, in conjunction with any such application for deferral. Taxpayers that were participating in an installment payment agreement prior to the disaster may qualify to defer tax payments for one year. (Sec. 194, Rev. & Tax. Code; Sec. 194.1, Rev. & Tax. Code)

• *Payment on supplemental assessments*

Where supplemental assessments are made in cases of new construction or changes of ownership, as explained at ¶1702 , a supplemental tax bill is mailed by the tax collector. The additional tax is due on the date the bill is mailed, but may be paid in two installments that become delinquent according to the month in which the bill is mailed. If the bill is mailed in the period July-October, the delinquency dates are as follows:

— first installment, December 10;

— second installment, April 10.

If the bill is mailed in the period November-June, the delinquency dates are as follows:

— first installment, last day of month following the month the bill is mailed;

— second installment, last day of the fourth calendar month following the date the first installment is delinquent. (Sec. 75.52, Rev. & Tax. Code)

¶1709 Appeals

Law: Secs. 170, 620.5, 1542, 1603, 1603.5, 1605, 5141 (CCH CALIFORNIA TAX REPORTS ¶20-720, 89-236).

Taxpayers wanting a reduction in assessment must file a timely written application with the county board of supervisors meeting as a county board of equalization or an assessment appeals board. Counties may also authorize the use of electronic applications. (Sec. 1603, Rev. & Tax. Code)

The filing of an appeal does not excuse a taxpayer from making timely payments. Failure to do so will result in the imposition of penalties and interest charges, regardless of the outcome of the appeal (¶1711).

The assessment reduction application must generally be filed between July 2 and September 15 in order to be timely. However, if a taxpayer does not receive a notice of assessment at least 15 calendar days prior to the deadline for filing an application for an assessment reduction, such application may be filed within 60 days of the receipt of the notice of assessment or within 60 days of the mailing of the tax bill, whichever is earlier. Furthermore, the application may be filed within 12 months following the month in which the assessee is notified of an assessment if the assessee and the assessor stipulate that there is an error in the assessment. Purchasers of real property acquired after the lien date and before the first day of the fiscal year may file for reduction by November 15. (Sec. 1603, Rev. & Tax. Code)

Practice Note: Multiple Years

An application must be filed for each year a residential assessment is contested, even if an identical appeal is still pending for a prior year (*Publication 30,* California State Board of Equalization).

An application appealing a supplemental or escape assessment must be filed within 60 days of the later of the date printed on the notice, the tax bill, or the postmark date. (Sec. 75.31, Rev. & Tax. Code)

Counties may allow a reduction application to be filed within 60 days of the mailing of the notice of the assessor's response to a request for reassessment due to a decline in value, provided the following conditions are met:

— the reassessment request was submitted to the assessor in writing on a completed form prescribed by the State Board of Equalization;

— the reassessment request was made on or before the preceding March 15;

— the assessor's response was mailed after August 31;

— the assessor did not reduce the assessment in the full amount requested;

— the assessment reduction application is filed by December 31 of the year in which the reassessment request was filed; and

— the assessment reduction application is accompanied by a copy of the assessor's response.

(Sec. 1603, Rev. & Tax. Code)

A county assessment appeals board must hear and decide a taxpayer's application for reduction of an assessment within two years of the application. If the appeals board fails to act within two years, the taxpayer's opinion of value becomes the assessed value, both for the year listed in the application and for subsequent years until the board makes a final determination on the application. The two-year limitation period may be extended if the taxpayer and the county assessment appeals board agree in writing to extend the time for the hearing or if the application is consolidated for hearing with another application for which an extension of time has been granted. The taxpayer's opinion of market value will not prevail if the taxpayer has failed to provide full and complete information as required by law or when litigation is pending directly relating to the issues involved in the application. (Sec. 1604, Rev. & Tax. Code)

Certain county boards of supervisors may adopt a resolution providing that an assessment hearing officer's decision constitutes the county board of equalization's or county assessment appeals board's decision. (Sec. 1641.1, Rev. & Tax. Code)

An appeal of a reassessment resulting from a disaster or calamity must be filed within six months of the date that the reassessment notice was mailed. (Sec. 170(c), Rev. & Tax. Code)

Special rules apply to state-assessed property.

• *Judicial appeals*

Generally, a civil action for a refund of an improper property tax payment may not be brought unless the taxpayer has filed a timely application for reduction of assessment with the county board of equalization or assessment appeals board, paid the tax (including penalties), and then filed a claim for tax refund. (Sec. 1605, Rev. & Tax. Code) However, prior administrative review has not been required under the following circumstances:

— the facts are undisputed and the property is tax exempt;

— the property is nonexistent;

— the property is outside the taxing jurisdiction;

— the taxpayer does not own the property;

— the assessment is void for failure to follow statutory procedures;

— the questions are solely those of law; or

— there is a correction of deficiencies in assessment procedures rather than individual parcel assessments.

The prior filing of a refund claim is not required with respect to refunds of state assessed taxes. (Sec. 5148, Rev. & Tax. Code)

Refund suits may be brought within six months of the date the refund claim is rejected. If a claim is not acted upon by the authorities within six months, the taxpayer may consider the claim disallowed and file suit. (Sec. 5141, Rev. & Tax. Code) In this case, a taxpayer has four years from the expiration of the six months to commence a suit for refund (*Geneva Towers Limited Partnership v. City and County of San Francisco* (2000) (CCH CALIFORNIA TAX REPORTS ¶21-565.63)). If the taxpayer designates an application for a reduction of assessment to be a claim for refund, the refund claim is deemed denied on the date the equalization board makes its final decision on the application or on the date the final installment of taxes becomes delinquent, whichever is later. (Sec. 5141, Rev. & Tax. Code)

¶1710 Collections

Law: Secs. 760, 2187, 2191.3-91.6, 2602, 2951, 3003, 3101-03, 3436, 3691, 3706, 3794.3, 4505, 4511; Sec. 30, Art. XIII, Cal. Const. (CCH CALIFORNIA TAX REPORTS ¶89-162 et. seq.).

All property taxes are collected by the county tax collector. Unpaid taxes on real property, penalties, and interest automatically become a lien on the property as of January 1 each year. (Sec. 2187, Rev. & Tax. Code; Sec. 2192, Rev. & Tax. Code) After 30 years, unless released sooner, the lien expires and the tax is conclusively presumed to have been paid. (Sec. 30, Art. XIII, Cal. Const.; Sec. 2195, Rev. & Tax. Code)

When a taxpayer defaults in paying property taxes, the property is designated "tax-defaulted" property at the end of the fiscal year as a preliminary step in the actual enforcement of the tax lien against the land. (Sec. 3351, Rev. & Tax. Code; Sec. 75.53, Rev. & Tax. Code; Sec. 3438, Rev. & Tax. Code; Sec. 3353, Rev. & Tax. Code; Sec. 3436, Rev. & Tax. Code) The tax collector may sell tax certificates giving the certificate holder the right to receive the delinquent taxes, assessments, and penalties collected in connection with certain tax-defaulted property. (Sec. 4511, Rev. & Tax. Code)

The declaration of default by the tax collector starts the running of the five-year period (three years for nonresidential commercial property and specified non-owner occupied residential property) during which the taxpayer may redeem the property by payment of taxes and interest, and at the expiration of which the tax collector may sell legal title to the property to the highest bidder. (Sec. 3691, Rev. & Tax. Code) During the redemption period, taxes continue to be assessed and the owner is liable for current, as well as delinquent, payments. (Sec. 4104, Rev. & Tax. Code) The tax collector is required to follow specific notification rules prior to declaring the property "tax defaulted" and to selling the property. (Sec. 3361, Rev. & Tax. Code et seq.) A county tax collector must receive approval from the county board of supervisors prior to selling tax-defaulted property. (Sec. 3694, Rev. & Tax. Code)

• *Unsecured property tax roll collections*

Delinquent taxes on property on the unsecured roll may be collected by the seizure and sale of the taxpayer's personal property, improvements, or possessory interests. (Sec. 2951, Rev. & Tax. Code) Alternatively, the taxes may be collected through court action (Sec. 3003, Rev. & Tax. Code), by placing a judgment lien on the owner's real property in the county through a certificate of delinquency (Sec. 2191.3, Rev. & Tax. Code et. seq.), or by obtaining a judgment against the taxpayer by summary proceedings (Sec. 3101, Rev. & Tax. Code et seq.).

The tax collector can utilize procedures for the collection of taxes on the unsecured roll to collect any amount assessed by the board that becomes delinquent on the secured roll. The collector must send a notice of delinquency stating the board's intent to enforce collection at least 60 days before initiating collection procedures.

¶1711 Administration—Penalties and Refunds

Law: Secs. 461-82, 501-33, 2617, 3691, 4833.1, 4985.3, 5096-97.2, 5367, 5901-09 (CCH CALIFORNIA TAX REPORTS ¶20-265, 89-202 et. seq., 89-222).

Severe penalties may be imposed for failing to supply required information or giving false information. A taxpayer may be fined up to $1,000 and may be imprisoned for not more than six months; a corporate taxpayer is subject to an additional fine of $200 a day, up to a maximum of $20,000. In addition, civil penalties may be imposed. (Sec. 462, Rev. & Tax. Code)

A taxpayer who fails to file a required property statement (¶1707) is subject to a 10% penalty assessment on the unreported property. (Sec. 463, Rev. & Tax. Code; Sec. 5367, Rev. & Tax. Code) A taxpayer who willfully fails to supply information or conceals property is subject to a 25% penalty assessment. (Sec. 502, Rev. & Tax. Code; Sec. 504, Rev. & Tax. Code) These penalties may be abated upon a showing of reasonable cause. For cases involving a fraudulent act, omission, or concealment of property, the taxpayer is subject to a 75% penalty assessment. (Sec. 503, Rev. & Tax. Code)

New owners who fail to file the required notification of change of ownership (¶ 1702) are subject to a penalty of $100 or 10% of the current year's tax. (Sec. 482, Rev. & Tax. Code) Life insurance companies that own real property in a separate account and fail to file the required property statement (¶ 1707) or fail to file a required statement of transfer (¶ 1702) are subject to a penalty of $1,000 in addition to any other penalty prescribed by law. (Sec. 480.7, Rev. & Tax. Code)

A 10% penalty is imposed on delinquent payments. (Sec. 2617, Rev. & Tax. Code; Sec. 2618, Rev. & Tax. Code; Sec. 2704, Rev. & Tax. Code; Sec. 2705, Rev. & Tax. Code; Sec. 2922, Rev. & Tax. Code; Sec. 75.52, Rev. & Tax. Code) An additional 1.5% per month penalty is added for continued delinquency. (Sec. 2922, Rev. & Tax. Code) See ¶ 1708 for delinquency dates. Delinquency penalties may be canceled under certain conditions. (Sec. 75.52, Rev. & Tax. Code; Sec. 4985.2, Rev. & Tax. Code)

In the case of assessment corrections and cancellations, a taxpayer will be relieved of only those penalties for failure to pay tax that apply to the difference between the county board of equalization's final determination of value and the assessed value that was appealed, unless the taxpayer has paid at least 80% of the final assessed value. (Sec. 4833.1, Rev. & Tax. Code; Sec. 4985.3, Rev. & Tax. Code)

Property may be sold to satisfy liens for delinquent taxes. The law provides detailed rules for such sales, redemptions, etc.

State law provides for refunds of property taxes (including benefit assessments; see *Hanjin International Corp. v. Los Angeles County Metropolitan Transportation Authority* (2003) (CCH CALIFORNIA TAX REPORTS ¶ 89-224.82)), on order of the board of supervisors, under certain conditions. (Sec. 5096, Rev. & Tax. Code; Sec. 5097.2, Rev. & Tax. Code; Sec. 533, Rev. & Tax. Code) Generally, a claim for refund must be filed within four years from the date of payment or within one year from the date of mailing of the assessor's notice of overpayment. However, effective January 1, 2009, if a qualifying application has been filed for a reduction in a property tax assessment and the applicant does not state that the application is intended to constitute a claim for a refund, the applicant must request a refund within one year of the earlier of (1) the county notifying the applicant of an assessment reduction without advising the applicant to seek a refund or (2) the expiration of the time period for the county to make a final determination. If a qualifying application has been filed for a reduction in a property tax assessment and the applicant does not state that the application is intended to constitute a claim for a refund, and the applicant is notified of both a reduction in assessment and the right to file a claim for refund, the applicant will have six months within which to file a refund claim. (Sec. 5097, Rev. & Tax. Code) (Refunds of city property taxes may be subject to different limitations.) See also ¶ 1709 concerning judicial appeals.

• *Local rebate programs*

Capital investment incentive programs: Additionally, the governing body of any county, city and county, or city, is authorized to adopt a local ordinance establishing a capital investment incentive program (CIIP), under which the local government may "rebate" to certain large manufacturers an amount up to the amount of California property tax revenues derived from the taxation of the assessed value in excess of $150 million of any qualified manufacturing facility that a manufacturer has elected to locate in the local government's jurisdiction. (Sec. 51298, Govt. Code)

To be a "qualified manufacturing facility," each of the following criteria must be met:

— the manufacturer must have made an initial investment in the facility, in real and personal property, that exceeds $150 million;

— the facility must be located within the jurisdiction of the local government authorizing the rebate;

— the facility must be operated either by a business described in Codes 3500 to 3599 of the federal Standard Industrial Classification Manual, or by a business engaged in the recovery of minerals from geothermal resources, including the proportional amount of geothermal electric generating plants providing electricity as an integral part of the recovery process; and

— the manufacturer must be currently engaged in commercial production, or in the perfection of a manufacturing process or product with intent to manufacture.

Capital investment incentive payments are issued beginning with the first fiscal year after the date a qualified facility is certified for occupancy, or in the absence of such certification, the first fiscal year after the date such a facility commences operations. Also, the manufacturer of the facility must enter into a community services agreement with the local government, under which the manufacturer agrees to pay a community services fee equal to 25% of the rebate, but not to exceed $2 million annually, and sets forth a job creation plan.

• *Taxpayers' bill of rights*

A "bill of rights" for property taxpayers permits county assessors to respond to taxpayer requests for written rulings on certain property tax issues and may relieve a taxpayer from penalties and interest assessed or accrued as a direct result of the taxpayer's reasonable reliance on such a written ruling. (Sec. 5902, Rev. & Tax. Code et. seq.)

Additional protections extended to property taxpayers

— require notice of proposed escape assessments, hearings before a county board of equalization, or judgment liens on taxpayers' unsecured property;

— extend the limitations period for certain escape assessment refund claims;

— authorize taxpayers to inspect and copy assessors' market data and assessment information; and

— provide a procedure for making stipulations with respect to property tax refund claims.

PART VIII

MISCELLANEOUS TAXES

CHAPTER 18

UNEMPLOYMENT INSURANCE TAX

¶1801 Employment Development Department

The California Unemployment Insurance Code is administered by the Director of the Employment Development Department, P.O. Box 826880, Sacramento, California 94280-0001.

¶1802 Unemployment Insurance—Coverage

Employer.— Employing unit having 1 or more employees in employment within current or preceding calendar year if wages paid in any calendar quarter exceed $100. Employers may elect coverage for themselves. Coverage includes movie, radio, or TV contracts where the obligation for payment of remuneration has been taken over by an employer other than the one for whom the services were originally performed.

If an individual or entity contracts to supply an employee to perform services for a customer or client, and is a leasing employer or temporary services employer, he is the employer of the employee who performs the services; if he is not a leasing or temporary services employer, the client or customer is the employer. An individual or entity that contracts to supply an employee to perform services for a customer or client and pays wages to the employee, but is not a leasing or temporary services employer, pays the wages as the agent of the employer. Special circumstances are provided where an employee is loaned from one employer to another.

If two or more business enterprises are united by factors of control, operation, and use, they may be considered one employing unit.

Employment.— Service, including service in interstate commerce, performed by an employee for wages or under any contract of hire, written or oral, express or implied, and including service performed for the state, its political subdivisions and public entities, service performed for an Indian tribe, service performed in the employ of nonprofit organizations described in IRC 501(c)(3), service covered by FUTA on American vessels, or aircraft directed or controlled from California, and certain artistic or literary service under agreement with employer and a theatrical, etc. union. Most services in agricultural labor are also included. Exceptions are set forth below (elective coverage is generally permitted for exempt employments).

Employee.—"Employee" is defined to include: corporation officers; common-law employees; agent- and commission-drivers distributing meat, milk, vegetables, fruits, bakery goods, beverages, or laundry or dry-cleaning, provided such agents or drivers do not have a substantial investment in the business other than in a vehicle; full-time travelling or city salesmen taking orders from wholesalers, retailers, contractors, or hotel-or restaurant-operators, for merchandise for resale or for supplies; individuals performing artistic or literary service under contract; and homeworkers performing work according to specifications furnished by the person for whom the services are performed on materials or goods which must be returned to such person. A director of a corporation or association is not an employee, unless otherwise covered by the law.

Exemptions.—The following are not "employees" for purposes of the unemployment compensation law:

— Baseball players performing on a profit-sharing and expenses basis rather than for a fixed salary.

— Consultant performing professional services as independent contractor—a rebuttable presumption exists that services provided by an individual engaged in work requiring specialized knowledge and skills attained through completion of recognized courses of instruction or experience are rendered as an independent contractor.

— Service not in the course of employer's trade or business if cash remuneration is less than $50 per quarter or employee works on less than 24 days in that or preceding quarter.

— Officers and directors who are sole shareholders of a corporation not subject to FUTA, officers and directors who are also shareholders of a tax exempt corporation engaged in agricultural labor, and an officer of a corporation who is the sole shareholder or the only shareholder other than his or her spouse and the service is not subject to the FUTA.

— Election campaign services performed in employ of candidate for public office or committee.

— Family employment, i.e., service for son, daughter, or spouse, or by child under 18 in employ of parent, except to the extent employer and employee have elected disability coverage for themselves.

— Foreign athletes coming to State for occasional or incidental professional engagements.

— Free-lance jockeys or exercise boys regularly licensed by the California Horse Racing Board.

— Full-time students employed by organized camps, under certain conditions.

— Golf caddies.

— Government employees, either federal, state or foreign, including employees of state instrumentalities and of instrumentalities wholly owned by foreign governments, but see "Government and nonprofit employees," below. Federal instrumentalities are covered to the extent permitted by federal law.

— Hospital employment performed by a patient of the hospital.

— Interns in employ of hospital if they have completed 4-year course in state-chartered or approved medical school.

— Newspaper, shopping news, or magazine carriers under 18 unless engaged in full-time work and attendance at school is incidental thereto, and newspaper or magazine vendors whose remuneration consists of difference between purchase and sale price.

— Officers of nonprofit fraternal organizations during quarter if not covered under federal act and if remuneration does not exceed $100 a month.

— Organizations exempt from income tax, with respect to service performed in calendar quarter if remuneration is less than $50; more specifically, the organizations referred to are various nonprofit organizations, clubs, business associations, etc. (but not pension, profit-sharing, and stock bonus plans) and farmers' cooperatives.

— Broker (real estate, mineral, oil, gas or cemetery, and yacht) or real estate, cemetery, direct sales or yacht salesperson if (1) licensed or engaged in the trade or business of primarily in-person demonstration and sales presentation of consumer products in the home or sales to any buyer on a buy-sell, deposit-commission or similar basis, for resale in the home or other than from a retail or wholesale establishment; (2) substantially all of the remuneration is directly related to sales or other output rather than to the number of hours worked; and (3) the services are performed pursuant to a contract providing that the individual will not be treated as an employee for state tax purposes.

— Service under any unemployment compensation system established by a law of the U.S.

— Student nurses in the employ of a hospital or training school who are attending a state-chartered or approved training school.

— Students in employ of school they are attending. Exemption also applies to service performed by student's spouse if such employment is furnished by the school as financial aid to the student, and if the employment will not be covered by any program of unemployment or disability compensation. Exemption applies to individuals under age 22 at nonprofit or public educational institutions that combine training and work experience (but not if program is established for an employer or group of employers).

— Transcribers of depositions, court proceedings and hearings performed away from the office of the person, firm or association obligated to produce a transcript of proceedings.

— Vessels or aircraft if such are non-American, and if the worker is employed on or in connection with such vessel or aircraft when it is outside the U.S.

Agricultural and domestic employers.— Most agricultural labor is covered. Domestic service in a private home, local college club or local chapter of a college fraternity or sorority is covered if performed for an employer who paid $1,000 in wages for such service in any quarter of the current or preceding calendar year.

Domestic workers for whom an employment agency procures, offers, refers, provides, or attempts to provide domestic work in a private home are excluded from coverage if certain factors exist, including the existence of a written contract between the agency and the worker containing provisions that specify that the agency will assist the worker in securing work, how the agency's referral fee is to be paid, and that the domestic worker is free to sign an agreement with other agencies and to perform domestic work for persons not referred by the agency.

Government and nonprofit employees.— Coverage is provided on a compulsory basis for nonprofit organizations as described in IRC Sec. 501(c)(3). Compulsory coverage is also provided for most employees of the state or any of its political subdivisions or public entities, including Indian tribes.

All service performed by an individual (including the blind and otherwise handicapped) for the state or a state public entity, including an Indian tribe, is covered. "Public entity" includes the State of California (including the Trustees of the California State University and Colleges, and the California Industries for the Blind, any instrumentality of this state (including the Regents of the University of California), any political subdivisions of this state or their instrumentalities, counties, cities, districts (including the governing board of any school district or community college district, any county board of education, any county superintendent of schools, or any personnel commission of a school district or community college district which has a merit system under the Education Code), entities which receive state money to conduct county and agricultural fairs, and public authorities, agencies and corporations.

Not included are the following:

— Service in the employ of a church or convention or association of churches, or in the employ of an organization operated primarily for religious purposes and operated, supervised, controlled, or principally supported by a church, church convention, or church association.

— Service by a minister or member of a religious order in connection with his religious duties.

— Service for a rehabilitation or sheltered-workshop agency by a recipient of the services of the agency.

— Service that is part of an unemployment work-relief or work-training program, by the person receiving the relief or training.

— Elected officials.

— Members of a legislative body or the judiciary, and members of a tribal council.

— Members of the tribal council of an Indian tribe.

— Members of the State National Guard or Air National Guard.

— Employees serving on a temporary basis in case of fire, storm, snow, earthquake, flood or similar emergency.

— Service in major nontenured policymaking or advisory positions.

— Election officials or election workers if the amount of remuneration reasonably expected to be received during the calendar year is less than $1,000 (previously, $200). Note that this exception becomes effective only if a similar exception is enacted under the FUTA.

— Inmates of custodial or penal institutions.

— Inmates of state prison under the jurisdiction of the Department of Corrections or individuals who are otherwise in the custody of such Department and wards in the custody of the Department of the Youth Authority, when services are performed for any public entity, nonprofit or for-profit entity.

— Substitute employee whose employment does not increase the size of the employer's normal work force, is required by law and does not occur on more than 60 days during the base period (this exclusion is inoperative unless and until the U.S. Secretary of Labor finds it in conformity with federal law).

— Individuals under 18 engaged in delivery or distribution of newspapers or shopping news, and individuals engaged in sale of newspapers or magazines where compensation consists of difference between purchase and sale prices.

— Service performed for another state or an instrumentality of another state.

— Also not included are most of the other general exclusions under the regular provisions of the law.

Reimbursement financing is available to nonprofit organizations and state public entities, including Indian tribes, on an elective basis. Reimbursement financing may be accomplished by making payments based on estimates made by the Director, or on the basis of charges to the employer's regular account. In the case of financing on the basis of charges to the employer's account, payment of a bond may be required. School districts are required to make reimbursement payments based on estimates of amounts owed the fund. Special provisions apply to school districts with respect to the levying of taxes to pay for benefits received by classified school employees.

Wages.— Term "wages" means remuneration payable to an employee for personal services, whether by private agreement or consent or by force of statute, including commissions and bonuses, and cash value of remuneration payable in medium other than cash. "Wages" includes all tips received while performing services that constitute employment and included in a written statement furnished to the employer pursuant to IRC Sec. 6053(a). Payments for holiday pay for any holiday occurring in a week during which the individual was unemployed are wages received for the week in which the individual returns to work, if holiday pay is not paid until such return.

In determining whether an individual has been paid as much as the annual taxable limit, the employer includes remuneration paid for services in another state and reported to that state. However, remuneration does not include payments for employee benefits, payments by third-party payors, disability payments, trust fund payments, payments of the employee's social security or unemployment insurance taxes, certain payments for casual labor, moving expenses, payments received under a qualified group legal services plan, payments upon termination of employment by death or retirement, or educational assistance or dependent care assistance program payments when paid by the employer in another state. Wages paid by a predecessor employer may also be included. The annual taxable limit is set in the law at $7000.

Taxable wages include various kinds of deferred compensation, such as IRC §401(k) cash or deferred pay arrangements, non-qualified deferred compensation payments, employer contributions under a state "pickup" plan, IRC §403(b) annuity payments other than through salary reductions, exempt governmental deferred compensation plans, supplemental pension benefits, and employer payments to a SEP-IRA.

For benefit purposes only, "wages" includes compensation for services as a juror or a witness.

"Wages" does not include:

— Remuneration over $7,000 paid to an individual in any calendar year.

— Payments made by an employer to a survivor or the estate of a former employee after the calendar year in which he or she died.

— Payments for sickness or accident disability made over 6 months after separation.

— Remuneration paid in a medium other than cash for services not in the course of an employer's trade or business (unless paid for covered domestic service or agricultural labor).

— Payments to individuals under plan or system established by employer for purpose of supplementing unemployment benefits.

— Expenses incurred in connection with an employer's business.

— Payments received by a member of the National Guard or reserve component of the armed forces for inactive duty training, annual training, or emergency state active duty.

— Vacation pay (including sick leave or holiday pay) earned but not paid for services performed prior to termination of employment.

— Sickness or accident disability payments received under a workers' compensation law.

— Medical or hospitalization expenses in connection with sickness or accident disability.

— Payments made on account of death or retirement for disability.

— Payments made from or to a trust described in IRC Sec. 401(a) or Sec. 403(a) annuity plans.

— Payments under a simplified employee pension other than any contribution described in IRC Sec. 408(k)(6).

— Payments made to, or on behalf of, an employee or his or her beneficiary under a simple retirement account, as described in IRC §408, other than any elective contributions under IRC §408(p)(2)(A)(i).

— Any benefit provided to or on behalf of an employee if at the time provided it is reasonable to believe that the employee will be able to exclude the benefit from income under IRC Sec. 74(c), 117, or 132.

— Any benefit under a cafeteria plan, as described in IRC Sec. 125, if the benefit is excludable from wages.

— Payments under an annuity contract described in IRC Sec. 403(b), other than a payment for the purchase of the contract that is made by reason of a salary reduction agreement.

— Moving expenses, if at the time of payment it is reasonable to believe that a corresponding deduction is allowable under IRC Sec. 217.

— Any payment excludable from gross income under IRC Sec. 120, relating to amounts received under a qualified group legal services plan.

Comment: Leave-based donations to Hurricane relief

The California Employment Development Department has announced that the value of any vacation, sick, or personal leave donated by an employee through an employer's leave-based donation program, whereby the employer provides cash payments to a qualified charitable organization providing relief to Hurricane Katrina victims, will not be considered "wages" subject to California unemployment insurance and disability insurance taxes. (*Tax Branch News*, California Employment Development Department, September 20, 2005.)

¶1803 Unemployment Insurance—Tax Rates

Standard rate.— 3.4%. Maximum possible basic rate is 5.4%. Employees pay tax for disability benefits purposes (see below).

Experience rates.— Employer contribution rates are assigned on a calendar-year basis under one of seven schedules in the law, depending on various factors. However, until the employer has the required "experience"—i.e., until its reserve account has been subject to benefit charges during 12 consecutive completed calendar quarters ending on June 30—its rate will be 3.4% plus any applicable additional contribution. For the employer with the required experience, its individual rate is determined by the ratio of its reserve balance on June 30 to its individual average annual taxable payroll for the past three calendar year. "Reserve balance" is the excess of contributions paid by July 31 over benefits charged.

New employers pay 3.4% (plus the 0.1% employment and training tax) until their accounts have been subject to charges during 12 consecutive completed calendar *months* ending on June 30. Average annual taxable payroll for a new employer is the average taxable payroll for the past two calendar years, or the taxable payroll for the past calendar year.

Employer contribution rates will be determined from one of seven schedules in the law.

(1) If the balance in the fund on September 30 is greater than 1.8% of the wages in covered employment paid during the 12-month period ending on the computation date, the most favorable schedule, AA, will be in effect and will range from 3.7% to 5.4% for negative-balance employers and from 0.1% to 3.4% for positive-balance employers.

(2) Schedule A, ranging from 3.8% to 5.4% for negative-balance employers and from 0.3% to 3.6% for positive-balance employers, is in effect if the fund balance is equal to or less than 1.8% and greater than 1.6%.

(3) Schedule B, ranging from 4.1% to 5.4% for negative-balance employers and from 0.5% to 3.9% for positive-balance employers, will be in effect if the fund balance is equal to or less than 1.6%, but greater than 1.4%.

(4) Schedule C, ranging from 4.4% to 5.4% for negative-balance employers and from 0.7% to 4.2% for positive-balance employers, is in effect if the fund balance is equal to or less than 1.4%, but greater than 1.2%.

(5) Schedule D, ranging from 4.7% to 5.4% for negative-balance employers and from 0.9% to 4.5% for positive-balance employers, will be in effect if the fund balance is equal to or less than 1.2%, but greater than 1.0%.

(6) Schedule E, ranging from 5.0% to 5.4% for negative-balance employers and from 1.1% to 4.8% for positive-balance employers, will be in effect if the fund balance is equal to or less than 1.0%, but greater than 0.8%.

(7) Schedule F, requiring all negative balance employers to pay 5.4% and ranging from 1.3% to 5.1% for positive-balance employers, will be in effect if the fund balance is equal to or less than 0.8%.

If the fund balance on September 30 of any calendar year is less than 0.6%, employers will pay at an emergency solvency surcharge rate for the next tax year. The emergency solvency surcharge rate is 15% of the rate the employer would otherwise have paid in Schedule F, rounded to the nearest 0.1%. Note that, for 2005 and 2006-2009, this special Schedule F+ is in effect.

Schedule F+ is in effect for 2008 and 2009. Rates for 2006 and 2007 (not including the 0.1% special contribution to the Employment and Training Fund by certain employers—see "Additional Taxes") may be determined from the following schedule:

Employer's Reserve Ratio	2005-2009 Rate (%)
Less than –20%	6.2
–20% to –18%	6.2
–18% to–16%	6.2
–16% to –14%	6.2
–14% to –12%	6.2
–12% to –11%	6.2
–11% to –10%	6.2
–10% to –9%	6.2
– 9% to –8%	6.2
– 8% to –7%	6.2
– 7% to –6%	6.2
– 6% to –5%	6.2
– 5% to –4%	6.2
– 4% to –3%	6.2
– 3% to –2%	6.2
– 2% to –1%	6.2
– 1% to zero	6.2
zero to 1%	5.9
1% to 2%	5.6
2% to 3%	5.4
3% to 4%	5.2
4% to 5%	4.9
5% to 6%	4.7
6% to 7%	4.5
7% to 8%	4.3
8% to 9%	4.0
9% to 10%	3.8
10% to 11%	3.6
11% to 12%	3.3
12% to 13%	3.1
13% to 14%	2.9
14% to 15%	2.6
15% to 16%	2.4
16% to 17%	2.2
17% to 18%	2.0
18% to 19%	1.7
19% to 20%	1.6
20% or more	1.5

On the computation date each year, the amount each employer's net balance of reserve is more negative than 21% of its average base payroll will be canceled from its reserve balance.

Additional taxes.— Any contributing employer other than a negative-balance employer, and certain agricultural and domestic employers, is required to pay into the Employment and Training Fund contributions at the rate of 0.1%.

SUTA dumping.— The California UI Code now requires that the Director establish procedures to identify the transfer or acquisition of a business that is undertaken for the purpose of obtaining a lower contribution rate ("SUTA dumping").

In addition, the Director is required to assign an employer the maximum contribution rate plus two percent for specified rating periods if that employer has previously obtained a favorable rate of contributions due to deliberate ignorance, reckless disregard, fraud, intent to evade, misrepresentation or willful nondisclosure. Voluntary contribution payments are also forbidden in such cases.

New law provisions also provide that a transfer of the predecessor's reserve account to the successor employer will not be allowed if the acquisition of the predecessor occurred for the purpose of obtaining a more favorable rate of contributions for the successor employer. Moreover, in the case where an employer transfers all or part of its business or payroll to another employer, and both employers, at the time of transfer, are under common ownership, management or control, the reserve account of the transferred business must be combined with the reserve account of the transferee employer.

Note that a penalty of either $5,000 or 10% of the amount of any resulting underreporting of contributions, penalties and interest, whichever is greater, on a person or business entity that knowingly advises another person to violate any provision of the UI is imposed, and it is now a violation for any person to willfully counsel, advise, procure or coerce anyone to willfully make a false statement or representation, or knowingly fail to disclose a material fact for the purpose of lowering or avoiding any required contribution, or to avoid being or remaining subject to specific requirements.

Voluntary payments.— Most contributing employers are allowed to submit voluntary contributions in order to reduce their contribution rates. Payments must be submitted on or before the last working day of March of the calendar year to which the reduced rate would apply. No redetermination may reduce an employer's rate by more than three rates in the applicable schedule for the year. Voluntary contributions will not be allowed for any year in which Schedule E or F is in effect or any year in which the emergency solvency surcharge is required. New employers, negative-balance employers, and delinquent employers are not allowed to make voluntary contributions. No refund unless the payment is made by an exempt employer or the amount paid is less than or more than the amount needed to reduce the rate. Note that any employer whose eligibility for a contribution rate determination is redetermined to make it eligible to submit voluntary contributions may submit such a voluntary contribution within 30 days of the date of notification of the redetermination. Note that this program is not in effect in 2009 since Schedule F+ is in effect.

¶1804 Unemployment Insurance—Returns and Reports

Form DE 1 Registration Form for Commercial Employers.— All employers conducting business in California are subject to the employment tax laws of the California Unemployment Insurance Code. Once a business hires an employee, the business is considered an employer and must complete and submit a registration form to the EDD within 15 days after paying wages in excess of $100 per quarter. The form used by most commercial employers is Form DE 1. However, the State of California also provides registration forms for specific industries. These forms include, but are not limited to, Registration Form for Agricultural Employers (Form DE 1AG), Registration Form for Household Employers (Form DE 1HW) and Registration Form for Nonprofit Employers (Form DE 1NP).

Form DE 6 Quarterly Wage and Withholding Report.— Form DE 6 Quarterly Wage and Withholding Report: Employers use Form DE 6 to report employee wages subject to unemployment insurance, the employment training tax and state disability insurance. It is also used to report the amount of personal income tax (PIT) withheld and PIT wages. This form is due four times a year April 1, July 1, October 1 and January 1 and becomes delinquent on the last day of each of those four months. An employer must file a DE 6 every quarter even if it paid no wages during that quarter. A wage item penalty of $10 per employee will be charged for late reporting or unreported employee wages. Employers with more than 250 employees must file their reports via magnetic media. Note that employers that are unable to obtain a copy of DE 6 prior to the delinquency date may file an informal report to avoid penalty and interest charges. Form DE 7, Annual Reconciliation Statement, is used to reconcile an employer's payroll tax payments and the total subject wages reported for the year. It must be filed by January 31 of the following year to be considered timely.

¶1805 Unemployment Insurance—Benefits

Base period.— 4 calendar quarters ending in June, September, December, or March depending upon the month in which the particular benefit year begins.

Benefit year.— The 52-week period beginning with first day of week in which individual first files valid claim for benefits.

Weekly benefit amount.— For years beginning on or after January 1, 2003, the weekly benefit amount of an individual whose highest wages in the quarter of the base period exceed $1,832.99 will be determined as 50% of these wages divided by 13, not to exceed $370 for 2003, $410 for 2004, or $450 beginning January 1, 2005. Benefit amounts are reduced by the lesser of the amount of wages in excess of $25 payable to worker for services rendered during the week or the amount of wages in excess of 25% of the amount of wages payable to him during the week. Benefit amounts are computed to next higher multiple of $1.

Claimants may now elect to have income taxes voluntarily withheld from their unemployment compensation payments.

Vacation pay earned but not paid before separation or before unemployment caused by disability will not operate to restrict benefits. Note, however, that deductions may be made to satisfy child support obligations.

Maximum total benefits.— 26 times weekly benefit amount, but not more than one-half individual's total base period wages, computed to next higher multiple of $1.

Claimants, during certain periods of high unemployment, may receive federal-state extended benefits at their regular weekly benefit rates. Federal-state extended benefits will be reduced by state extended benefits previously received in benefit year. Right to receive extended state benefits cancelled if claimant eligible for federal-state benefits; but, if right to federal-state benefits expired, may receive state extended benefits under certain conditions.

There is also an additional benefit program applicable during certain periods of plant closure or substantial reduction in employment at the employee's most recent workplace.

A claimant may receive a shared work weekly benefit amount equal to the percentage of reduction (at least 10%) in his or her wages resulting from reduced hours or days of work multiplied by his or her regular weekly benefit amount, for up to 20 weeks, if his or her employer has elected to participate in a shared work program designed to reduce the hours or days of work of certain employees in order to reduce unemployment and stabilize the work force.

Benefit eligibility.— Requirements—Claimant eligible if he or she—

(1) has met one of the following conditions: (1) has been paid high-quarter wages of at least $900 and been paid base period wages equal to 1.25 × his or her high-quarter wages or (2) been paid high quarter wages of at least $1,300;

(2) serves 1-week waiting period (waived if strict compliance would prevent the mitigation of the effects of any state-of-war emergency or state of emergency);

(3) is able and available for work and searches for work as directed by employment office (however, if an individual becomes unable to work due to a physical or mental illness or injury for one or more days of a week, benefits equal to 1/7 of his or her weekly benefit amount are payable for each day of the week on which he or she is available and able to work—no benefits payable on any day on which he or she is unable to work due to such illness or injury).

Wages used in the determination of benefits payable to an individual during one benefit year may not be used in determining such individual's benefits in any subsequent benefit year. "Lag period" wages (wages paid in the period after the claimant's base period and before the benefit year) may be used in computing benefits in a subsequent benefit year only if within the year following the first valid claim he or she has been paid enough to be able to meet the regular qualifying requirements and has had some work (special considerations apply if individual received disability benefits, or workmen's compensation in the year since his or her first valid claim). The benefit eligibility of longshoremen is preserved during weeks in which, under the terms of a collective bargaining agreement, they are allowed not more than one uncompensated day off.

Persons taking approved training or retraining are not generally subject to the requirements as to availability for work or search for work, to the disqualifications for refusal of suitable work or, if continuing his or her most recent work would require him or her to terminate his or her training, for voluntary leaving.

An individual will not be deemed unavailable for work or disqualified solely because he or she

— is serving on a grand or petit jury or because he or she is serving as a witness under subpoena;

— is before any court of the United States or any state pursuant to a lawfully issued summons to appear for jury duty or is hospitalized for treatment of an emergency or life-threatening condition;

— is available only for part-time work, if his claim is based on the part-time employment, the individual is actively seeking and is willing to accept work under essentially the same conditions as existed while the wage credits were accrued, and the individual imposes no other restrictions and is in a labor market in which a reasonable demand exists for the part-time services offered; or

— cannot reasonably be expected to work up to two day in any week in which there has been a death in his or her immediate family in the state in which he resides, or, for not exceeding four working days, he or she cannot be expected to work because there has been a death in his or her immediate family outside the state of his or her residence.

Work will not be deemed suitable and benefits may not be denied to otherwise qualified individual if offer of work is from employer who

(1) does not possess state license to engage in his or her business, trade, or profession,

(2) does not carry workmen's compensation or possess certificate of self-insurance, or

(3) does not withhold employees' disability contributions or transmit such contributions to EDD.

Disqualifications—Period.— Discharge for misconduct connected with most recent work and voluntary leaving without good cause—for the week in which the disqualifying act occurs and until claimant has, subsequent to the disqualification and his registration for work, received remuneration in excess of five times his weekly benefit amount. An individual will be deemed to have left his most recent work with good cause if he

(1) leaves to accompany his spouse to a place from which it is impractical to commute;

(2) elects to be laid off in place of an employee with less seniority pursuant to a collective bargaining agreement;

(3) leaves because of sexual harassment, provided he has taken reasonable steps to preserve the working relationship; or

(4) leaves to protect his or her children, or himself or herself, from domestic violence abuse.

Refusal of suitable work—2 to 10 weeks.

Labor dispute—duration of dispute.

An individual is disqualified if he is discharged for chronic absenteeism due to intoxication or reporting to work while intoxicated or using intoxicants on the job, gross neglect of duty while intoxicated or otherwise leaving his most recent job for reasons caused by an irresistible compulsion to use or consume intoxicants, including alcoholic beverages. Disqualification continues until he has performed service for which remuneration equal to or in excess of 5 times his weekly benefit amount is received or until it is certified that he has entered into and is continuing or has completed a treatment program for his condition and is able to return to work.

False statement or representation or failure to disclose material fact—2 to 15 weeks if no benefit payments result and 5 to 15 weeks if benefits are paid as a result.

False statement or failure to disclose fact in order to obtain or increase benefits, if convicted by court—week in which criminal complaint was filed and following 14 weeks and forfeiture of benefits for 52 weeks.

24-hour absence from work due to incarceration is a voluntary-leaving disqualification.

Receipt of benefits under another state or federal unemployment compensation law—period of payment. Supplemental unemployment benefits (SUB), or special SUB "separation payments," do not reduce state benefits.

Receipt of payments because of an employer's violation of the WARN Act—no denial or reduction of benefits.

Receipt of cash payments for temporary *total disability* indemnity under workmen's compensation law or employer's liability law of California, any other state, or the federal government—UI benefits reduced by amount of payment.

Unemployment benefits that are payable to an individual for any week that begins in a period with respect to which he is receiving a governmental or other pension, retirement or retired pay, or any other similar periodic payment based on the previous work of the individual are reduced, but not below zero, by the amount of the pension, etc., that is reasonably attributable to that week. No reduction if the individual has made any contribution to the pension, retirement or retired pay, annuity, or other similar periodic payment. Reduction is required only in the case of pensions that are paid under a plan maintained or contributed to by a base period or chargeable employer. Furthermore, in the case of a pension payment other than social security or railroad retirement benefits, reduction will occur only if services performed for a base period or chargeable employer by the individual after the beginning of his base period (or remuneration for the services) affect eligibility for, or increase the amount of, the pension.

Special provisions.—A person discharged from military service and otherwise eligible is not deemed ineligible for any compensated unexpired leave time. Persons in instructional, research, or principal administrative capacity for educational institutions are ineligible in the interim between two successive academic years, or between two regular terms.

Nonprofessional employees of educational institutions are disqualified during periods between academic years or terms if there is reasonable assurance of reemployment in the second year or term. If such assurance is given and the individual has no opportunity to work in the second year or term, retroactive payments of benefits may be claimed. A similar disqualification applies to individuals performing services in an educational institution while in the employ of an educational service agency.

Benefits are not payable to professional athletes for periods between sport seasons if there is a reasonable assurance that the individual will perform services in both seasons.

Benefits are not payable to an alien unless he has been lawfully admitted or is otherwise permanently residing in the United States under color of law.

¶1806 Disability Benefits—Coverage

The definitions of the terms "employer," "employment," "employee," and "wages," contained in the unemployment insurance provisions are also applicable under the disability benefit provisions. Any local public entity may elect coverage for all of its employees, including those with civil service or tenure positions.

> (1) the term "employer" also includes an employing unit having 1 or more individuals performing services in agricultural labor within current or preceding year, if wages paid in any calendar quarter for such services exceed $100, and includes certain nonprofit or local district hospitals; and
>
> (2) the term "employment" also includes service in agricultural labor and service for certain nonprofit or local district hospitals.

An individual who adheres to a faith which depends for healing upon prayer in the practice of religion is exempt from contributions upon filing of proper statement.

The term "employment" also includes domestic service, including in-home supportive services, in a private home, local college club, or local chapter of a college fraternity or sorority if cash wages of at least $750 are paid for such services in any quarter of the current or preceding calendar year.

An exclusion applies to certain intermittent or adjunct instructors at postsecondary educational institutions.

A written election may be filed to cover as "employment" for disability benefits purposes service performed by a child under age 18 in the employ of his father or mother, or service performed by a person in the employ of his son, daughter, or spouse.

Employers and employees participating in an approved voluntary plan are, generally, not liable for disability contributions, except that voluntary plans are liable for 14% of an amount obtained by multiplying the rate of worker contributions in effect for the year by the amount of the taxable wages paid to employees covered by the plan, for the Disability Fund. Voluntary plan employers may require of employees covered by the plan contributions at the same rate as those paid by other (state plan) employees.

If an employer voluntarily withdraws from a voluntary plan due to the plan contributions being in excess of plan costs, all deductions from an employee's wages remaining in the possession of the employer that are not disposed of pursuant to applicable regulations must be remitted to the department and deposited in the Disability Fund.

Any employee contributions and income arising therefrom received or retained by the employer under an approved voluntary plan are trust funds that are not part of an employer's assets. Therefore, the employer must either keep a separate, specifically identifiable account for voluntary plan trust funds in a financial institution, or the employer may send voluntary plan trust funds, including any earned interest or income, directly to the admitted disability insurer. If the employer, with prior approval from the Director of Employment Development, invests voluntary plan trust funds in securities purchased through a commercial bank, the securities account must be separately identifiable from any other securities accounts kept by the employer. If the employer commingles the voluntary plan trust funds with its own assets, or if the employer becomes bankrupt or insolvent, or if a receiver is appointed for the employer's business, such voluntary plan trust funds are entitled to the same preference as are the claims of the state.

An employer for unemployment insurance purposes, or a self-employed individual who is not an employer and who receives the major part of his income from a trade, business, or occupation, can elect disability benefits coverage. Regardless of actual earnings, such employer or self-employed person is deemed to have received remuneration in highest amount needed to qualify for maximum weekly disability benefit and must pay taxes on this amount. This rate may be reduced or increased by a factor estimated to maintain, as nearly as practicable, a cumulative zero balance in funds contributed. This rate is determined by multiplying the current year's rate by the ratio of 1.10 times the current year disbursements divided by contributions for the same period. If in any calendar year, the cumulative balance of contributions minus disbursements equals or exceeds 20% of annual disbursements, the contribution rate for the succeeding year is adjusted to a level necessary to maintain revenues at no more than 20% over annual disbursements. The rate for 2006 is 2.25%.

¶1807 Disability Benefits—Wages

Wages includes all tips that are received while performing covered services and included in a written statement furnished to the employer.

The annual taxable limitation on employees' wages in effect for disability benefit purposes is determined as an amount equal to 4 × the maximum weekly benefit amount for each calendar year multiplied by 13 and divided by 55%. This amount is $86,698 for 2008 and $90,669 for 2009. Wages subject to unemployment insurance law of another state cannot be included in taxable wage limitation.

¶1808 Disability Benefits—Tax Rates

Employees pay contributions under the disability benefits law at a rate equal to 1.45 × the amount disbursed from the Disability Fund during the 12-month period ending September 30 and immediately preceding the calendar year for which the rate is to be effective, less the amount in the Disability Fund on that September 30, with the resulting figure divided by total wages paid during the same 12-month period. The rate may not be less than 0.1% or more than 1.3%. The employee tax may not decrease from the previous year's rate by more than 0.2%. The employee contribution rate is 0.8% for 2008 and 1.1% for 2009.

For 2008, the contribution rate for self-employed individuals and those electing coverage is 2.26%. The rate for 2007 was 1.97%.

Employees may obtain a refund if, because they worked for more than one employer during the year, they have paid excess taxes. The employer must either withhold the contributions required of his employees from their wages, or hold in trust the amount of the contributions if he has agreed to pay the contributions required of his employees without deductions from their wages.

¶1809 Disability Benefits—Returns and Report

Disability insurance (DI) contributions are to be remitted with the personal income tax (PIT) deposit on Form DE 88. An employer that is required to make federal next banking day deposits and has accumulated more than $400 in California PIT during one or more payroll periods must also make California next banking day deposits. (Note that the PIT deposit threshold may be adjusted annually.) Banking days do not include Saturdays, Sundays or legal holidays.

An employer is required to make semi-weekly DI and PIT deposits if it is required to make federal semi-weekly deposits and has accumulated more than $400 in PIT during one or more payroll periods. The semi-weekly deposit schedule requires deposits for paydays on Wednesday, Thursday and Friday to be made by the following Wednesday. For paydays on Saturday, Sunday, Monday, or Tuesday, deposit must be made by the following Friday. Semi-weekly depositors always have three business days after the end of the semi-weekly period to make a deposit. If any of the three business days after the end of a semi-weekly period is a legal holiday, one additional business day is provided to make the deposit.

An employer is required to make monthly deposits of DI and PIT if it is required to make federal annual, quarterly or monthly deposits and accumulates more than $350 in California PIT during one or more months of a quarter. The monthly deposit schedule requires deposits to be made by the 15th of the following month.

Note that an employer is required to make monthly DI and PIT deposits if it is required to make federal semi-weekly or next banking day deposits and accumulates $350-$400 in California PIT during one or more months of a quarter.

Quarterly tax payments are due and delinquent on the same dates as the Quarterly Wage and Withholding Report (Form DE 6), above.

¶1810 Disability Benefits—Benefits

Base period.— For individual who does not have an unexpired benefit year for unemployment benefits, 4 calendar quarters ending in June, September, December, or March, depending upon month in which benefit period begins. For individual who does have unexpired benefit year for unemployment benefits, same base period which was used to establish benefit year for unemployment benefit purposes. Base period will be same as that of an individual who does not have an unexpired benefit year, if individual has sufficient qualifying earnings.

Calendar quarters during which an unemployed individual performed no services for 60 or more days and during which he was actively seeking work may be excluded from his base period. For all quarters so excluded there will be substituted an equal number of quarters immediately preceding the commencement of the normal disability base period.

Base period of "industrially disabled" individual will also exclude quarters during which individual was so disabled for 60 days or more. Substituted for quarters excluded will be equal number of quarters immediately preceding commencement of disability. Quarter in which disability commenced will be counted as completed quarter if more equitable for claimant. "Industrially disabled" individual means person eligible for workmen's compensation who is unable to perform regular job for 60 consecutive days or more, but not to exceed 2 calendar years from date of disability.

Benefit period.— Continuous period of unemployment and disability beginning with first day with respect to which individual files valid claim. Two consecutive periods of disability due to same or related cause and separated by not more than 14 days are considered one disability benefit period.

Weekly benefit amount.— Weekly benefit amount depends on high-quarter wages. Minimum weekly benefit amount is $50. The maximum weekly benefit amount is $917 for 2008. A claimant is paid benefits for any seven-day week or partial week in an amount not to exceed the maximum weekly amount.

Disabled veterans are entitled to state disability benefits until federal payments begin.

Maximum total benefits.— 52 times weekly benefit amount, but not more than 100% of the claimant's base period wages.

Benefit eligibility.— Requirements—Claimant eligible if—

(1) serves 7-day waiting period; after one day's confinement in a hospital, any unexpired full days of the waiting period are waived;

(2) files doctor's certificate unless receiving workmen's compensation);

(3) has at least $300 in base period wages; and

(4) submits to examination, if required by Director.

Family temporary disability insurance benefits (Paid Family Leave).— Family TDI benefits are to be known as Paid Family Leave. Coverage begins on July 1, 2004. Paid Family Leave insurance must provide up to six weeks of wage replacement benefits to workers who take time off work to care for a seriously ill child, spouse, parent, domestic partner or to bond with a new minor child. An individual is eligible to receive Paid Family Leave benefits equal to one-seventh of his or her weekly benefit amount for each full day during which he or she is unable to work due to caring for a seriously ill or injured family member or bonding with a new minor child.

Employee contributions. On or before November 30th of each calendar year, the Director must prepare a statement announcing the employee contribution rate for the next calendar year to all covered employers and self-employed individuals. The rate will be determined by dividing the estimated benefits and administrative costs paid in the prior year by the product of the annual remuneration deemed to have been received and the estimated number of persons who were covered at any time in the previous year. The resulting rate is rounded to the next higher one-hundredth percentage point. The rate may also be decreased or increased by a factor estimated to maintain as nearly as practicable a cumulative zero balance in the funds contributed. Estimates may be made on the basis of statistical sampling, or another method determined by the Director.

Note that the overall rate may not exceed 1.5% or be less than 0.1%, and may not decrease from the rate in the previous year by more than 0.2%.

Maximum benefit amount.— The maximum amount of Paid Family Leave benefits payable to an individual will be six times his or her weekly benefit amount, except that the total benefits amount may not exceed the total wages paid to the individual during his or her disability base period. If the benefit is not a multiple of $1, it must be computed to the next higher multiple of $1. No more than six weeks of Paid Family Leave benefits will be paid within any 12-month period.

Eligibility requirements.—An individual is eligible for Paid Family Leave benefits on any day in which the individual is unable to perform regular or customary work because he or she is caring for a new child during the first year after the birth or placement of the child or a seriously ill child, parent, spouse, or domestic partner, subject to a waiting period of one week during which no benefits are paid.

Exemptions.—An individual is not entitled to Paid Family Leave benefits with respect to any day that he or she has received unemployment compensation benefits, other cash benefits, state disability insurance benefits or on any day that another family member is able and available to provide the required care. An individual who is entitled to leave under the Family and Medical Leave Act and California's Family Rights Act must take Paid Family Leave concurrent with leave taken under those Acts.

Disqualifications—Period.— Receipt of unemployment benefits under California Act or law of another state or the federal government;

Receipt of temporary disability cash payments under workers' compensation law, employer's liability law of California, any other state or the federal government. If such payments are less than state disability benefit, state benefit will be reduced by amount of such other payment;

Receipt of wages (disabled individual receiving wages may be paid disability benefits for any day in an amount not to exceed his maximum daily amount which, together with the wages, does not exceed for such day one-seventh of his weekly wage, exclusive of wages paid for overtime work, immediately prior to commencement of disability);

Disqualification from unemployment benefits by reason of leaving work due to trade dispute not disqualifying.

Disqualification for unemployment benefits by reason of voluntary leaving, discharge for misconduct, false statement or representation, or refusal of suitable employment, unless claimant is suffering bona fide illness and Director finds good cause for paying benefits;

False statement or representation—7-35 days;

Confinement in institution as dipsomaniac, drug addict, or sexual psychopath—period of confinement, except that individuals confined in alcoholic recovery homes or drug-free residential facilities are entitled to limited amounts of benefits.

No disqualification on day of death if otherwise eligible.

Disqualification during any day of incarceration in federal, state, or municipal penal institution, jail, medical facility, public or private hospital, or any other place because of a criminal violation of federal, state, or other municipal law or ordinance.

Commission of crime—disqualified if illness or injury is caused by, or arising out of, the commission of, arrest for, investigation of, or prosecution of any crime that results in a felony conviction.

CHAPTER 19

OTHER STATE TAXES

¶1901 Scope of Chapter

Law: Secs. 7080-99 (CCH CALIFORNIA TAX REPORTS ¶61-620).

This chapter outlines generally and very briefly certain California state taxes and fees that have not already been covered in the text. No effort is made to explain these taxes and fees in detail or to discuss the detailed rules applicable to them. The purpose is merely to indicate in general terms the basis of each tax or fee, by whom it is administered, and where further information may be obtained if desired.

• *Enactment of taxes and fees*

Regulatory fees, such as certain environmental fees, may be enacted by a majority vote of the legislature, unlike taxes which require a two-thirds vote of either the legislature or the electorate (see *Sinclair Paint Co. v. State Board of Equalization* (1997) (CCH CALIFORNIA TAX REPORTS ¶33-050.30)).

• *Taxpayers' bill of rights*

A "bill of rights" has been enacted to protect the privacy and property rights of taxpayers who are subject to the following State Board of Equalization (SBE) administered taxes and fees: motor vehicle fuel license tax (Sec. 8260, Rev. & Tax. Code et. seq.), use fuel tax (Sec. 9260, Rev. & Tax. Code et seq.), underground storage tank maintenance fees (Sec. 50156, Rev. & Tax. Code et. seq.), hazardous substances tax (Sec. 43511, Rev. & Tax. Code et seq.), solid waste disposal site cleanup and maintenance fees, alcoholic beverages tax (Sec. 32460, Rev. & Tax. Code), and cigarette and tobacco products taxes (Sec. 30458, Rev. & Tax. Code). A similar "bill of rights" has been enacted for taxpayers who are subject to various state and local excise taxes and fees. Both are substantially similar to the "bill of rights" described at ¶702, relating to personal income and corporate tax collections, except that the agency involved is the SBE rather than the Franchise Tax Board.

¶1902 Insurance Taxes

Law: Secs.12201-84 (CCH CALIFORNIA TAX REPORTS ¶88-100—88-600).

A gross premiums tax is imposed upon insurance companies (other than ocean marine insurers). (Sec. 12201, Rev. & Tax. Code; Sec. 12204, Rev. & Tax. Code) This tax is in lieu of all other state and local taxes and licenses, with the exception of real estate taxes and motor vehicle license fees. The rate of tax on insurers in general is 2.35% of gross premium income. The rate is 1/2% on premiums received under pension and profit-sharing plans that are qualified under the income tax provisions of the Internal Revenue Code. (Sec. 12102, Rev. & Tax. Code) Ocean marine insurers are taxed at the rate of 5% on their underwriting income. (Sec. 12101, Rev. & Tax. Code) Surplus line brokers and taxpayers that purchase insurance from nonadmitted insurers, with some exceptions, are taxed at the rate of 3% of gross premiums, less return premiums. (Sec. 1775.5, Ins. Code; Sec. 13210, Rev. & Tax. Code)

The administration of the gross premiums tax is divided among the Insurance Commissioner, the State Board of Equalization (SBE), the State Controller, and the Franchise Tax Board (FTB). Insurance companies other than nonadmitted insurers must file an annual tax return with the Commissioner, as shown below. A copy is transmitted to the SBE, which assesses the taxes imposed on insurers for the preceding calendar year, and notifies them of any excess or deficiency. Examination of the return by the Commissioner may result in a deficiency assessment.

Returns and annual payments are due as follows:

	Returns	*Payments*
Insurance companies generally	April 1	April 1
Ocean marine insurance	June 15	June 15
Retaliatory taxes	April 1	April 1
Surplus line brokers	March 1	March 1

(Sec. 1774, Ins. Code; Sec. 1775.5, Ins. Code; Sec. 12281, Rev. & Tax. Code; Sec. 12287, Rev. & Tax. Code; Sec. 12301, Rev. & Tax. Code; Sec. 12302, Rev. & Tax. Code)

Taxpayers that procure insurance from nonadmitted insurers must file a return with the FTB by the first day of the third month following the close of the calendar quarter during which a taxable insurance contract took effect or was renewed. (Sec. 13220, Rev. & Tax. Code)

Insurers transacting business in California whose annual tax for the preceding calendar year was $5,000 or more must prepay their tax for the current calendar year, except that no prepayments are required of ocean marine insurers tax or any retaliatory tax. (Sec. 12251, Rev. & Tax. Code) Prepayments are due on or before April 1, June 1, September 1, and December 1 of the current year. (Sec. 12253, Rev. & Tax. Code) Surplus line brokers, with some exceptions, whose tax liability for the preceding year was $5,000 or more, are required to make monthly installment payments. (Sec. 1775.1, Ins. Code) In addition, any insurer whose annual insurance tax exceeds $20,000 must remit all tax payments by electronic funds transfer. A penalty of 10% of the taxes due will be imposed for failure to comply with the electronic funds transfer requirement. (Sec. 1531, Ins. Code; Sec. 1775.8, Ins. Code; Sec. 12602, Rev. & Tax. Code)

Insurance companies may qualify for a low-income housing credit or, effective for tax years beginning before 2012, a credit for qualified investments made into a community development financial institution. (Sec. 12206, Rev. & Tax. Code; Sec. 12209, Rev. & Tax. Code) These credits are the same as those allowed under the personal income tax law and are discussed at ¶138 and ¶156, respectively. An insurer may also claim a credit equal to the amount of the gross premiums tax due from the insurer on account of pilot project insurance issued to provide low-cost insurance to qualified low-income residents of San Francisco and Los Angeles. (Sec. 12208, Rev. & Tax. Code)

¶1903 Motor Vehicle Taxes

Law: Secs. 1936.3, Civil Code; Sec. 8880.68, Government Code; Secs. 5003.1-03.2., 5136, 5328, Public Utility Code; Secs. 7232-36, 10752-58, Revenue and Taxation Code; Secs. 4601-02, 6262, 9250, 9400, Vehicle Code (CCH CALIFORNIA TAX REPORTS ¶50-050, 50-150, 50-210, 50-270, 50-290).

The following motor vehicle taxes are imposed:

— registration and weight fees (Secs. 4601, Veh. Code et. seq.; Secs. 9400, Veh. Code, et. seq.);

— automobile "in lieu" tax (Sec. 17052, Rev. & Tax. Code);

— motor carrier fees (Sec. 7232 et seq., Rev. & Tax. Code); and

— fees on household goods carriers (Sec. 5003.2, Pub. Util. CodeSec. 5003.2, Pub. Util. Code).

These taxes are discussed in the paragraphs below.

Registration and weight fees: Motor vehicles are required to be registered annually. (Sec. 4601, Veh. Code; Sec. 4602, Veh. Code) The general annual state registration fee is $31, but miscellaneous additional fees may be imposed by the state and certain local jurisdictions. (Sec. 9250, Veh. Code) In addition, there are annual weight fees for the operation of certain commercial vehicles, the amount depending on the weight of the vehicle and other factors. (Sec. 9400, Veh. Code; Sec. 9400.1, Veh. Code) Trailer coaches are also subject to registration and licensing. The administrative agency is the Department of Motor Vehicles.

Automobile "in lieu" tax: The "in lieu" tax, so called because it is a form of property tax that is imposed in lieu of local property taxation of automobiles, including automobiles awarded in a state lottery, is in effect a license fee in addition to the registration fee discussed above. The tax is imposed at 0.65% of the "market value" of the make and model involved, computed under a formula provided by law. (Sec. 17052, Rev. & Tax. Code) The license fee is paid at the same time as the registration fee. The above information regarding administration of registration and weight fees is equally applicable to this tax.

A vehicle license transaction fee is imposed on rental car transactions. The statutory formula used to calculate the amount of the fee is based on the vehicle license fee.

Motor carrier fees: For-hire motor carriers other than household goods carriers or motor carriers of property engaged in interstate or foreign transportation of property must pay an annual permit fee consisting of the following amounts: a safety fee (ranging from $60 to $1,030) and a uniform business license tax fee (ranging from $60 to $2,000). (Sec. 7232, et seq., Rev. & Tax. Code)

In *U-Haul Co. v. Gourley* (2004) (CCH CALIFORNIA STATE TAX REPORTER ¶50-050.28), a California appellate court struck down a hybrid assessment formula used by the California Department of Motor Vehicles (DMV) to determine California motor vehicle license fees for a motor vehicle leasing company because it did not comport with the language of the International Registration Program.

Household goods carriers: Household goods carriers must pay an annual permit fee of $500. (Sec. 5136, Pub. Util. Code) A regulatory fee is also imposed on household goods carriers owning or operating motor vehicles and transporting property for hire on the public highways. The fee is $15 plus 1/3 of 1% of gross operating revenue, payable quarterly to the Public Utilities Commission, if the carrier is under the regulatory jurisdiction of the Commission. However, if the carrier is not under the regulatory jurisdiction of the Commission or is transporting used office, store, and/or institution furniture or fixtures, the fee is $15 plus 1/10 of 1% of gross operating revenue. (Sec. 5003.2, Pub. Util. Code) In addition, household goods carriers are subject to a license fee of 1/10 of 1% of gross operating revenue, payable quarterly to the Commission. (Sec. 5328, Pub. Util. Code)

Copies of pertinent laws and regulations may be obtained from the State Board of Equalization.

¶1904 Alcoholic Beverage Taxes

Law: Secs. 23954.5, 23396.3, Business and Professions Code; Secs. 32151, 32201, Revenue and Taxation Code (CCH CALIFORNIA TAX REPORTS ¶35-100— 35-300).

All those engaged in the production, distribution, or handling of alcoholic beverages in California must be licensed by the Department of Alcoholic Beverage

Control. Licenses are issued for a period of one year, and license fees are payable annually. (Sec. 24045, Bus & Prof. Code) There is a long schedule of annual license fees for various classifications and additional fees and surcharges apply. (Sec. 23320, Bus & Prof. Code; Sec. 23358.3, Bus & Prof. Code; Sec. 23396.3, Bus & Prof. Code)

The application fee for an original on-sale or off-sale general license is $12,000.

An excise tax is imposed upon the sale of alcoholic beverages within the State. The rates are as follows:

Beverage	*Rate*
Beer	20¢ per gallon
Still wines	20¢ per gallon
Champagne, sparkling wine	30¢ per gallon
Sparkling hard cider	20¢ per gallon
Distilled spirits (proof strength or less)	$3.30 per gallon
Nonliquid distilled spirits containing 50% or less alcohol by weight	2¢ per ounce

Distilled spirits in excess of proof strength and nonliquid distilled spirits containing more than 50% alcohol by weight are taxed at double the above rate.

Generally, returns of excise tax must be filed and the tax paid monthly to the State Board of Equalization (SBE). However, the SBE may require returns and payments for quarterly or annual periods. (Sec. 32202, Rev. & Tax. Code; Sec. 32251, Rev. & Tax. Code)

¶1905 Special Taxes in Lieu of Property Tax

Law: Secs. 5701-22, 11251-406 (CCH CALIFORNIA TAX REPORTS ¶20-125, 20-305).

A form of property tax is levied by the state upon the value of racehorses and upon the value of private cars operated on railroads within California. The railroad car tax is in lieu of local taxation of such property, and is imposed at the average rate of general property taxation for the preceding year as determined by the State Board of Equalization (SBE). Persons owning private railroad cars must make an annual report to the SBE. The tax is payable annually on or before December 10. (Sec. 11251 et seq., Rev. & Tax. Code)

Racehorses are taxed annually by the head in three classes, stallions (the rate is based on the stud fees), brood mares, and racehorses (the rate is based on the amount of winnings). (Sec. 5701 et. seq., Rev. & Tax. Code)

¶1906 Cigarette and Tobacco Products Tax

Law: Secs. 30008-123 (CCH CALIFORNIA TAX REPORTS ¶55-100—55-400).

A state tax is imposed on cigarettes. The tax rate applied to cigarettes is 87¢ per pack. (Sec. 30101, Rev. & Tax. Code; Sec. 30123, Rev. & Tax. Code) Tobacco products are taxed at an equivalent rate, determined annually by the State Board of Equalization (SBE). Effective July 1, 2007, through June 30, 2009, the tobacco products tax rate for taxable distributions of all tobacco products other than cigarettes is 45.13% of the wholesale cost of the tobacco products. (Sec. 30123, Rev. & Tax. Code)

Monthly reports must be filed by distributors and others by the 25th of the month for the preceding calendar month. (Sec. 30182 et. seq., Rev. & Tax Code) Distributors are allowed a stamping or metering cost allowance of .85% of the tax. (Sec. 30166, Rev. & Tax. Code) Sales to members of the armed forces in exchanges and commissaries, to state veterans' homes, and to law enforcement agencies for authorized use in a criminal investigation are exempt. (Sec. 30102 —Sec. 30105.5, Rev. & Tax. Code)

Cigarette and other tobacco products tax distributors who elect to remit tax on a twice-monthly basis must remit their first monthly payment by the 5th day of the month for those distributions that occur between the 1st and the 15th of the preceding month, and they must remit their second payment by the 25th day of the month for those distributions that occur between the 16th day and the last day of the preceding month. Distributors who elect to remit tax on a monthly basis must remit payment by the 25th day of the month following the month during which the tobacco products were distributed. (Sec. 30181, Rev. & Tax. Code)

However, the cigarette tax may be prepaid by the use of stamps and metering machines. (Sec. 30161, Rev. & Tax. Code) Cigarette distributors that defer payment for stamps and meter register settings and that elect to remit tax on a twice-monthly basis must remit their first monthly payment by the 5th day of the month; their first monthly payment must equal the greater of one half the tax due on purchases made during the preceding month or the total tax due on purchases made between the 1st and the 15th of the preceding month. The second monthly payment must be remitted by the 25th day of the month for the remainder of the prior month's purchases. Cigarette distributors that defer payment for stamps and meter register settings and that elect to remit tax on a monthly basis must remit their monthly payment by the 25th day of each month. (Sec. 30168, Rev. & Tax. Code)

Persons whose estimated tax liability averages $20,000 or more per month, as determined by the California State Board of Equalization (SBE), must remit amounts due by electronic funds transfer. (Sec. 30190, Rev. & Tax. Code)

The tax is administered by the SBE.

¶1907 Other Taxes and Fees

Law: Secs. 13430-34, Business and Professions Code; Secs. 13244.5, 25299.41-99.43, Health and Safety Code; Secs. 3263, 3402, 48650-71, Public Resources Code; Sec. 4458, Public Utility Code; Secs. 7306-56, 7380-81, 8604-55, 38115, 40016, 41020, Revenue and Taxation Code (CCH CALIFORNIA TAX REPORTS ¶33-100, 40-110—40-730, 45-110, 45-210, 80-110—80-140).

The following is a very brief statement of other taxes imposed by the state:

Motor vehicle fuel taxes: A tax is imposed upon the privilege of distributing motor fuel, and a complementary use tax applies to gasoline and other fuels. The state rate on gasoline is 18¢ per gallon. If the federal license or use tax is reduced below specified levels, then the state rate will be increased by the amount of the federal reduction. (Sec. 7361, Rev. & Tax. Code; Sec. 8651, Rev. & Tax. Code) Returns by persons distributing motor vehicle fuel must be made monthly to the State Board of Equalization (SBE), and returns by vendors and users must generally be made quarterly to the SBE. (Sec. 7338, Rev. & Tax. Code; Sec. 7651, Rev. & Tax. Code; Sec. 8735, Rev. & Tax. Code; Sec. 8752, Rev. & Tax. Code)

A separate tax is imposed for the privilege of storage, removal, entry, or use of diesel fuel. (Sec. 60110 et. seq., Rev. & Tax. Code) The state rate is 18¢ per gallon of diesel fuel, subject to adjustment should the federal fuel tax rate be reduced. (Sec. 60050, Rev. & Tax. Code; Sec. 60050.1, Rev. & Tax. Code; Sec. 60115, Rev. & Tax. Code) An additional surcharge is imposed on interstate users of diesel fuel purchased outside California and used in California. Returns and payments are generally made on a quarterly basis. (Sec. 60115, Rev. & Tax. Code)

Some local jurisdictions are also authorized to impose a limited per gallon tax on the sale, storage, or use of motor vehicle fuel, if approved by the voters.

Aircraft jet fuel tax: A license tax is imposed on aircraft jet fuel dealers at the rate of 2¢ per gallon. (Sec. 7392, Rev. & Tax. Code) Monthly returns are required. (Sec. 7393, Rev. & Tax. Code)

Public utilities: "Public utilities" are not specially taxed as such. However, some companies so classified are subject to special license taxes or fees. These include certain transportation companies (see also ¶1903), and operators of toll bridges, toll roads, toll ferries, street railroads, and private wharves. Information may be obtained from the Public Utilities Commission.

Oil and gas severance tax and fee: A small regulatory tax and a production fee are imposed on the production of oil and sale of gas. (Sec. 3402 et. seq., Rev. & Tax. Code) Information may be obtained from the state Department of Conservation.

Business license taxes: License fees are imposed on many businesses, occupations, and professions. The fees range from nominal amounts to very large amounts (*e.g.*, in the case of horse racing). As there are over 100 categories of license taxes, a listing of them is beyond the scope of this book. Information may be obtained from the various state boards, commissions, etc., involved, or from the Department of Consumer Affairs in Sacramento.

Energy resources surcharge: A nominal surcharge is imposed on electrical energy purchased from an electric utility. (Sec. 40016, Rev. & Tax. Code)

Timber yield tax: Forest trees on privately and publicly-owned land are subject to a severance tax at the time of harvest, at rates to be determined from time to time. (Sec. 38115, Rev. & Tax. Code) Information may be obtained from the SBE.

Emergency telephone users' surcharge: A nominal surcharge is imposed on intrastate telephone services, to finance the state's emergency telephone system. (Sec. 41020, Rev. & Tax. Code)

Motor oil fee: A fee is imposed on certain producers and dealers for the purchase or sale of motor oil. The maximum rate is 2¢ per gallon. (Sec. 13430—Sec. 13434 Bus. & Prof. Code)

Lubricating oil tax: Manufacturers of lubricating oil sold or transferred in California must pay a tax at the rate of 4¢ per quart. (Sec. 48650, Pub. Res. Code)

Underground storage tank fee: Certain underground storage tank owners must pay a fee in the amount of 14 mills for each gallon of petroleum placed in the tank. Quarterly returns are required. (Sec. 25299.41, Hlth. & Sfty. Code; Sec. 25299.43, Hlth. & Sfty. Code)

Propane fees: A nominal surcharge is imposed on sales of propane by operators of propane distribution systems. Also, a fee not to exceed $250 is imposed on owners of propane storage systems.

¶1908 Realty Transfer Tax

Law: Sec. 11911 (CCH CALIFORNIA TAX REPORTS ¶34-701).

Cities and counties are authorized to impose a tax on transfers of interests in real estate with a value of more than $100. The county tax is at the rate of 55¢ for each $500, and the noncharter city rate is one-half of the county rate. The tax is payable to the county recorder at the time the instrument transferring the property is recorded. (Sec. 11911, Rev. & Tax. Code)

Practitioner Comment: Certain Cities and Counties Are Imposing Transfer Taxes in Equity/Stock Transactions

As noted above, cities and counties generally impose a tax on transfers of interests in real estate, payable to the county recorder at the time the instrument transferring the property is recorded. In general, transfer tax is not due when a controlling interest in an entity that owns real property is transferred. One exception to this is transfers of partnership interests that result in technical terminations of the partnership under the Internal Revenue Code. In addition, certain cities, mainly so-called "charter cities," such as San Francisco and Santa Clara, have begun to assess tax under nonconforming municipal and/or county ordinances on transfers of interests in legal entities in general that result in a change in control or change in ownership for property tax reassessment purposes.

Bruce Daigh, Chris Whitney, Contributing Editors

¶1909 Environmental Taxes and Fees

Law: Secs. 25205.1-05.12, 42464, Health and Safety Code; Secs. 43053-152.15, Revenue and Taxation Code (CCH CALIFORNIA TAX REPORTS ¶34-465).

California imposes a variety of fees in connection with the generation, storage, treatment, disposal, and cleanup of waste, including hazardous waste disposal fees; covered electronic waste recycling fees; facility, generator, permit, and hauler fees; fees imposed on solid waste landfill operators; tire disposal fees; various oil spill and medical waste fees; and a general "environmental fee" payable by virtually all businesses/organizations employing 50 or more persons, each employed more than 500 hours in California during the prior calendar year (see below).

• *Environmental fee*

Every corporation, limited liability company, limited partnership, limited liability partnership, general partnership, and sole proprietorship with an SIC (Standard Industrial Classification) code for any industry that uses, generates, or stores hazardous materials or conducts activities in California related to hazardous materials is subject to an annual environmental "fee," whether or not the organization is actually conducting activities related to hazardous materials. (Sec. 25205.6, Hlth. & Sfty. Code) Only those doing business as private households are excluded. The fee is based on the number of employees in California during the previous calendar year. For 2009, the fee schedule is as follows:

Number of employees	*Fee*
1–49	$ 0
50–74	284
75–99	500
100–249	998
250–499	2,139
500–999	3,894
1,000 or more	13,556

Planning Note: Businesses May Qualify for Refunds

The California Department of Toxic Substance Control (DTSC) previously took the position that all in-state corporations with 50 or more employees used, generated, stored, or conducted activities in the state related to hazardous materials and were subject to an environmental fee. The California Supreme Court determined in *Morning Star Co. v. State Board of Equalization* that the position of the DTSC constituted an invalid regulation because Administrative Procedure Act (APA) rulemaking procedures were not followed. However, the Court granted the DTSC a reasonable opportunity to develop and adopt new regulations to define which business are subject to the fee, and the Court allowed the DTSC to continue collecting the fee until the new regulations are adopted. If the new regulations determine that certain business are not subject to the fee, those businesses may be entitled to refunds. Because claims for refunds must be filed within three years of the due date of the return on which the overpayment was made, businesses that have previously paid the fee should consider filing protective claims for refund. (*Morning Star Co. v. State Board of Equalization* (2006) CCH CALIFORNIA TAX REPORTS ¶34-455.211; *Special Notice*, California State Board of Equalization, October 2006)

PART IX

DIRECTORY/RESOURCES

CHAPTER 20

CALIFORNIA RESOURCES

Addresses and other contact information for various state taxing agencies are listed below.

Franchise Tax Board (FTB)

P.O. Box 942840
Sacramento, CA 94240-0040
Phone: (800) 852-5711 or (916) 845-6500
(916) 845-7057 (Tax Practitioner Hotline)
(800) 822-6268 (TDD phones)
Internet: http://www.ftb.ca.gov
There are 6 FTB field offices located throughout California.
Los Angeles—300 S. Spring St, Suite 5704, Los Angeles, CA 90013-1265
Oakland—1515 Clay St, Suite 305, Oakland, CA 94612-1431
Sacramento—3321 Power Inn Rd. Suite 250, Sacramento, CA 95826-3893
San Diego—7575 Metropolitan Dr, Suite 201, San Diego, CA 92108-4421
San Francisco—121 Spear St, Suite 400, San Francisco, CA 94105-1584
Santa Ana—600 W. Santa Ana Blvd, Suite 300, Santa Ana, CA 92701-4532

Members of the Board

Chair	John Chiang, State Controller
Member	Betty Yee, Chair, State Board of Equalization
Member	Michael C. Genest, Director of Finance

Executive Officer	Selvi Stanislaus
FTB on the Internet	**www.ftb.ca.gov**

Tax Practitioner Services

✓	Hotline (not toll-free)	(916) 845-7057
✓	Hotline (Fax)	(916) 845-6377
✓	Personal Income Tax Collection (Fax)	(916) 845-0494
✓	Business Entity Tax Collections (Fax)	(916) 845-0145
✓	e-file	(916) 845-0353

Interactive Voice Response (IVR)/Automated Telephone Service

FTB's automated telephone system provides services in both English and Spanish to callers with touch-tone telephones. Callers may listen to recorded answers to frequently asked questions about state income taxes, 24 hours a day, seven days a week. Callers may order personal income tax forms, verify the status of their personal income tax refund, check their balance due, and confirm recent payment amounts and dates, 24 hours a day, except 10 p.m. Sunday to 5 a.m. Monday. Callers may order business entity tax forms 6 a.m. to 8 p.m., Monday through Friday and 6 a.m. to 4 p.m. Saturdays.

From within the United States, call	(800) 338-0505
From outside the United States, call (not toll-free)	(916) 845-6600

Homeowner and Renter Assistance Toll-Free Telephone Service

Callers may listen to recorded answers to frequently asked questions about homeowner and renter assistance 24 hours a day, seven days a week. Callers may order homeowner and renter assistance claim forms or verify the status of their homeowner and renter assistance payment 24 hours a day, except 10 p.m. Sunday to 5 a.m. Monday.

From within the United States, call . . . . (800) 868-4171
From outside the United States, call (not toll-free) . . . . (916) 845-6600

General Toll-Free Telephone Service (Taxpayer Services Center)

Telephone assistance is available year-round from 7 a.m. until 6 p.m. Monday through Friday. We may modify these hours without notice to meet operational needs.

From within the United States, call . . . . (800) 852-5711
From outside the United States, call (not toll-free) . . . . (916) 845-6500

Assistance for Persons with Disabilities

We comply with the Americans with Disabilities Act. Persons with hearing or speech impairments call:

From TTY/TDD . . . . (800) 822-6268

Where to Call or Write

Note - If an address is not shown use:

UNIT NAME
FRANCHISE TAX BOARD
PO BOX 1468
SACRAMENTO CA 95812-1468

A

Accounting Period/Method Change . . . . (916) 845-7057
Change of Accounting Method/Period
Franchise Tax Board
PO Box 1998
Rancho Cordova CA 95741-1998

Application for Revivor . . . . (916) 845-7057

Audit Division
www.ftb.ca.gov/aboutFTB/ftb_overview.html

B

Bankruptcy, Personal Income Tax . . . . (916) 845-4750
Fax . . . . (916) 845-9799
(Personal Income Tax - Chapters 7/11 & 13)
Bankruptcy Mail Stop PIT A340
PO Box 2952
Sacramento CA 95812-2952

Bankruptcy, Business Entities . . . . (916) 845-4375
Fax . . . . (916) 845-4389
(Business Entities - Chapters 7 & 11)
Bankruptcy Mail Stop BE A345
PO Box 2952
Sacramento CA 95812-2952

Business Entities Filing Enforcement . . . . (800) 478-7194
Email: filing.enforcement@ftb.ca.gov

C

Claims for Refund . . . . (916) 845-7057

Collections
Business Entities
Practitioner Hotline Fax . . . . (916) 845-0145
Collection Contact Center . . . . (888) 635-0494
OR . . . .
Corporations . . . . (916) 845-7033

Exempt Corporations . . . . (916) 845-7163
Partnerships . . . . (916) 845-7165
Limited Liability Corporations (LLC) (916) 845-7166

Personal Income Tax
Practitioner Hotline . . . . (916) 845-7057
Hotline Fax . . . . (916) 845-6377
Collection Contact Center . . . . (800) 689-4776
(916) 845-4470

Court-Ordered Debt Collections . . . . (916) 845-4064
Court-Ordered Debt Collections
Franchise Tax Board
PO Box 1328
Rancho Cordova CA 95741-1328

Industrial Health and Safety Debt Collections . . . . (916) 845-7222
Industrial Health and Safety Collections
Franchise Tax Board MS A-112
PO Box 1146
Rancho Cordova CA 95741-1146

Vehicle Registration Debt Collections (DMV) . . . . (888) 355-6872
(916) 845-6872
Vehicle Registration Collections
Franchise Tax Board
PO Box 419001
Rancho Cordova CA 95741-9001

D

Decedents, General Information . . . . (916) 845-7057
Deductible Dividends, Percent of . . . . (916) 845-4138
Disclosure Section . . . . (916) 845-3226
Dishonored Checks, Status of . . . . (800) 338-0505

E

Economic & Statistical Research Bureau . . . . (916) 845-3400
Tax Policy Research Section . . . . (916) 845-3375
Revenue Analysis Section . . . . (916) 845-7476
Statistical Research Section . . . . (916) 845-3403
Fax . . . . (916) 845-5472
Education and Outreach . . . . (916) 845-7565
e-Programs Customer Service . . . . (916) 845-0353
e-file . . . . (916) 845-0353
EFT . . . . (916) 845-4025
Fax . . . . (916) 845-0287
e-Programs Customer Service
Franchise Tax Board
PO Box 1468
Sacramento CA 95812-1468
Email: e-file@ftb.ca.gov

Equal Employment Opportunity . . . . (916) 845-3652
Estate Income Tax Clearance Certificate . . . . (916) 845-4210
Estates, General Information . . . . (916) 845-7057
Exempt Organizations/Status/Applying for . . . . (916) 845-4171

F

Federal and State Special Audit Section . . . . (916) 845-4028
Fax . . . . (916) 843-2269
RAR/VOL
Franchise Tax Board MS F310
PO Box 1998
Rancho Cordova CA 95741-1998

Filing Enforcement notice Information
Personal Income Tax . . . . (866) 204-7902
Fax . . . . (916) 845-0494
Business Entities Tax . . . . (866) 204-7902
Fax . . . . (916) 845-0145
Filing Enforcement Fax . . . . (916) 855-5646
email: filing.enforcement@ftb.ca.gov

Financial Institution Data Match . . . . (916) 845-6304
FIDM
Franchise Tax Board
PO Box 460
Rancho Cordova CA 95741-0460

H

Head of Household . . . . (800) 555-4005
Homeowner and Renter Assistance
From within the United States . . . . (800) 868-4171
From outside the United States . . . . (916) 845-6600

I

Information Returns . . . . (916) 845-6304
Innocent Spouse Program . . . . (916) 845-7072
Innocent Spouse Program
Franchise Tax Board
PO Box 2966
Sacramento CA 95741-2966
Installment Agreements
Practitioner Hotline . . . . (916) 845-7057
Practitioner Hotline Fax . . . . (916) 845-6377
Personal Income Tax . . . . (800) 689-4776
(916) 845-4470
Business Entities Tax . . . . (888) 635-0494
(916) 845-7033
Practitioner Hotline Fax . . . . (916) 845-0145
Interagency Intercept
From within the United States . . . . (800) 852-5711
From outside the United States . . . . (916) 845-6500
Investigations . . . . (916) 845-4037
Involuntary Conversions, Ext./Time . . . . (916) 845-7057
IRS Reporting/Tax Examination Change . . . . (916) 845-4028
Fax . . . . (916) 843-2269
RAR/VOL
Franchise Tax Board MS F310
PO Box 1998
Rancho Cordova CA 95741-1998

J

Jeopardy Assessments . . . . (916) 845-6175

L

Legal Rulings/notices (requests for) . . . . (916) 845-3306
Legal Department
Franchise Tax Board
PO Box 1720
Rancho Cordova CA 95741-1720
Legislation, Obtain a Specific Bill
www.leginfo.ca.gov
Legislative Bill Room
State Capitol Rm B-32
Sacramento CA 95814
Legislation, Policy/Administrative
Issues . . . . (916) 845-4326
Letter of Good Standing (request for) . . . . (916) 845-7057
Liens Desk . . . . (916) 845-4350
Fax . . . . (916) 845-4389
PO Box 2952
Sacramento CA 95812-2952

M

Magnetic Tape Coordination . . . . (916) 845-3778
Mortgage Interest Filing Enforcement . . . . (800) 262-0512

O

Offers in Compromise . . . . (916) 845-4787

P

Package x . . . . (916) 845-7070
Package x
Franchise Tax Board
PO Box 2708
Rancho Cordova CA 95741-2708
Personal Income Taxes . . . . (916) 845-7057
Political Reform Audit . . . . (916) 845-4802
Power of Attorney (Fax) . . . . (916) 845-0523
Power of Attorney
Franchise Tax Board
PO Box 2828
Rancho Cordova CA 95741-2828
Public Affairs . . . . (916) 845-4800
Public Records Act . . . . (916) 845-3226
Franchise Tax Board
Disclosure Office MS A181
PO Box 1468
Sacramento CA 95812-1468

R

Real Estate Withholding Services and Compliance Section
Toll-free from the United States . . . . . . (888) 792-4900
Withholding Services and Compliance Section Tax Practitioner Hotline (not toll-free) . . . . . . (916) 845-7315
Local or international (not toll-free) . . . . . . (916) 845-4900
Fax your forms . . . . . . (916) 845-9512
Research, Economic & Statistical — See Economic
Returns, Request for Copies (Prior Years)
Personal Income Tax . . . . . . (916) 845-5375
Business Entity Tax . . . . . . (916) 845-5116
FTB Data Services and Storage-RID
Franchise Tax Board
PO Box 1468
Sacramento CA 95812-1468
Revivor/Restoration . . . . . . (916) 845-7057
Fax . . . . . . (916) 845-6377

S

S Corporation — Termination of S Corporation Election . . . . . . (916) 845-7057
Franchise Tax Board
PO Box 942857
Sacramento CA 94257-0540
Secretary of State
www.ss.ca.gov
Corporation Status . . . . . . (916) 657-5448
Corporate name Availability . . . . . . (916) 657-5448
Corporate Officers . . . . . . (916) 657-5448
Secretary of State
1500 11th Street
Sacramento CA 95814
Settlement Bureau . . . . . . (916) 845-4933
Fax . . . . . . (916) 845-4747
Settlement Bureau
Franchise Tax Board
PO Box 3070
Rancho Cordova CA 95741-3070
Small Business Liaison . . . . . . (916) 845-4669
Fax . . . . . . (916) 845-5047
Speakers' Bureau
(Requests for speakers) . . . . . . (916) 845-7565
Email: speakersbureau@ftb.ca.gov
Speakers' Bureau
Franchise Tax Board
PO Box 520
Rancho Cordova CA 95741-0520
Suspended Corporation . . . . . . (916) 845-7057
Fax . . . . . . (916) 845-6377

T

Tax Forms Development & Distribution . . . . . . (916) 845-3442
Order forms by phone: . . . . . . (800) 338-0505
Download from the Internet:
www.ftb.ca.gov
Mail: Tax Forms Request
Franchise Tax Board
PO Box 307
Rancho Cordova CA 95741-0307
Tax Informant Hotline . . . . . . (800) 540-3453
www.ftb.ca.gov/aboutftb/txinform.html
Tax news
Email: taxnews@ftb.ca.gov
Tax news Editor
Franchise Tax Board
PO Box 2708
Rancho Cordova CA 95741-2708
Tax Practitioner Hotline . . . . . . (916) 845-7057
Fax . . . . . . (916) 845-6377
Tax Shelter Hotline . . . . . . (916) 845-4300
Email: taxshelter@ftb.ca.gov
www.ftb.ca.gov/law/tax_shelter/hotline.html
Taxpayer Advocate . . . . . . (800) 883-5910
Fax . . . . . . (916) 845-6614
Taxpayer Advocate Bureau
Franchise Tax Board

PO Box 157
Rancho Cordova CA 95741-0157
Trusts, General Information . . . . (916) 845-7057

V

Voluntary Disclosure Program . . . . (916) 845-3294
Franchise Tax Board
PO Box 942857
Rancho Cordova CA 94257-0540
Voluntary RAR Program . . . . (916) 845-4028
Fax . . . . (916) 843-2269
RAR/VOL
Franchise Tax Board MS F310
PO Box 1998
Rancho Cordova CA 95741-1998

W

Water's-Edge . . . . (916) 845-3940
PO Box 1779
Rancho Cordova CA 95741-1779
Water's-Edge Elections/Termination . . . . (916) 845-5568
PO Box 1779
Rancho Cordova CA 95741-1779
Withholding Services and Compliance Section
Toll-free from the United States . . . . (888) 792-4900
Withholding Services and Compliance
Section Tax Practitioner Hotline (not toll-free) . . . . (916) 845-7315
Local or international (not toll-free) . . . . (916) 845-4900
Fax your forms . . . . (916) 845-9512
Email: wscs.gen@ftb.ca.gov
Withholding Services and Compliance Section
Franchise Tax Board
PO Box 942867
Sacramento CA 94267-0651

State Board of Equalization (SBE)

450 N Street
P.O. Box 942879
Sacramento, CA 94279-0001
Phone: (800) 400-7115 or (916) 324-2926
(800) 735-2929 (TDD phones)
(800) 735-2922 (TDD assistance/voice phones)
Internet: http://www.boe.ca.gov
There are 25 SBE field offices for in-state accounts.

Bakersfield—1800 30th St, Suite 380, PO Box 1728, 93302-1728; (661) 395-2880
Chula Vista—590 3rd Avenue, Suite 202, 91910; (619) 409-7440
Culver City—5901 Green Valley Circle, Suite 200, PO Box 3652, 90230-3652; (310) 342-1000
El Centro—1550 W. Main St, 92243-2832; (760) 352-3431
Eureka—(707) 576-2100
Fresno—5070 N. Sixth St, Suite 110, 93710-7504; (559) 248-4219
Laguna Hills—23141 Moulton Parkway, Suite 100, 92653-1242; (949) 461-5711
Norwalk—12440 E. Imperial Hwy, Suite 200, PO Box 409, 90651-0409; (562) 466-1694
Oakland—1515 Clay St, Suite 303, 94612-1432; (510) 622-4100
Rancho Mirage—35-900 Bob Hope Dr, Suite 280, 92270-1768; (760) 770-4828
Redding—2881 Churn Creek Rd, PO Box 492529, 96049-2529; (530) 224-4729
Riverside—3737 Main St, Suite 1000, 92501-3395; (909) 680-6400
Sacramento—3321 Power Inn Rd, Suite 210, 95826-3889; (916) 227-6700
Salinas—111 E. Navajo Dr, Suite 100, 93906-2452; (831) 443-3003
San Diego—1350 Front St, Rm 5047, 92101-3698; (619) 525-4526
San Francisco—121 Spear St, Suite 460, 94105-1584; (415) 356-6600
San Jose—250 South Second St, 95113-2706; (408) 277-1231
San Marcos—334 Via Vera Cruz, Suite 107, 92078-2637; (760) 510-5850
Santa Ana—28 Civic Center Plaza, Rm 239, 92701-4011; (714) 558-4059
Santa Rosa—50 D St, Rm 230, PO Box 730, 95402-0730; (707) 576-2100
Suisun City—333 Sunset Ave, Suite 330, 94585-2003; (707) 428-2041

Van Nuys —15350 Sherman Way, Suite 250, PO Box 7735, 91409-7735; (818) 904-2300
Ventura —4820 McGrath St, Suite 260, 93003-7778; (805) 677-2700
West Covina —1521 W. Cameron Ave, Suite 300, PO Box 1500, 91793-1500; (626) 480-7200

There are four SBE field offices for out-of-state accounts.

Sacramento, CA —3321 Power Inn Rd, Suite 130, PO Box 188268, 95818-8268; (916) 227-6600
Chicago, IL —120 N. La Salle, Suite 1600, 60602-2412; (312) 201-5300
New York, NY —205 E. 42nd St, Suite 1100, 10017-5706; (212) 697-4680
Houston, TX —1155 Dairy Ashford, Suite 550, 77079-3007; (281) 531-3450

Employment Development Department

800 Capitol Mall, MIC 83
Sacramento, CA 95814
Phone: (888) 745-3886 or (916) 464-3502
(800) 547-9565 (TTY users)
Internet: http://www.edd.ca.gov

Secretary of State

1500 11th Street
Sacramento, CA 95814
Phone: (916) 653-6814
Internet: http://www.ss.ca.gov

State Controller

P.O. Box 942850
Sacramento, CA 94250-5872
Phone: (916) 445-2636
Internet: http://www.sco.ca.gov

County property tax assessors

County assessors are the source of specific property tax information and appropriate forms. County assessor addresses and telephone numbers are as follows:

California County Assessors

ALAMEDA COUNTY ASSESSOR
1221 Oak Street, Room 145
Oakland, CA 94612-4288
(510) 272-3755
ALPINE COUNTY ASSESSOR
99 Water Street
P.O. Box 155
Markleeville, CA 96120-0155
(530) 694-2283
AMADOR COUNTY ASSESSOR
810 Court Street
Jackson, CA 95642
(209) 223-6351
BUTTE COUNTY ASSESSOR
25 County Center Drive
Oroville, CA 95965-3382
(530) 538-7721
CALAVERAS COUNTY ASSESSOR
891 Mountain Ranch Road
San Andreas, CA 95249-9709
(209) 754-6356
COLUSA COUNTY ASSESSOR

547 Market Street, Suite 101
Colusa, CA 95932-2452
(530) 458-0450
CONTRA COSTA COUNTY ASSESSOR
2530 Arnold Drive, Suite 400
Martinez, CA 94553-4359
(925) 313-7500
DEL NORTE COUNTY ASSESSOR
981 H Street, Suite 120
Crescent City, CA 95531-3415
(707) 464-7200
EL DORADO COUNTY ASSESSOR
360 Fair Lane
Placerville, CA 95667-4103
(530) 621-5719
FRESNO COUNTY ASSESSOR
2281 Tulare Street, Rm. 201
P.O. Box 1146
Fresno, CA 93715-1146
(559) 488-3514
GLENN COUNTY ASSESSOR
516 West Sycamore Street, 2nd Floor
Willows, CA 95988
(530) 934-6402
HUMBOLDT COUNTY ASSESSOR
825 Fifth Street, Rm. 300
Eureka, CA 95501-1153
(707) 445-7663
IMPERIAL COUNTY ASSESSOR
940 West Main Street, Suite 115
El Centro, CA 92243-2874
(760) 482-4244
INYO COUNTY ASSESSOR
168 North Edwards Street, Drawer "J"
Independence, CA 93526-0609
(760) 878-0302
KERN COUNTY ASSESSOR
1115 Truxtun Avenue, 3rd Floor
Bakersfield, CA 93301-4617
(661) 868-3485
KINGS COUNTY ASSESSOR
1400 West Lacey Blvd
Hanford, CA 93230-5997
(559) 582-3211
LAKE COUNTY ASSESSOR
255 North Forbes Street
Lakeport, CA 95453-5997
(707) 263-2302
LASSEN COUNTY ASSESSOR
220 South Lassen Street, Suite 4
Susanville, CA 96130-4324
(530) 251-8241
LOS ANGELES COUNTY ASSESSOR
500 W. Temple Street, Rm. 320
Los Angeles, CA 90012-2770

(213) 974-3211
MADERA COUNTY ASSESSOR
200 W. 4th St.
Madera, CA 93637-3548
(559) 675-7710
MARIN COUNTY ASSESSOR
3501 Civic Center Drive, Rm. 208
P.O. Box C
San Rafael, CA 94913-3902
(415) 499-7215
MARIPOSA COUNTY ASSESSOR
4982 Tenth Street
P.O. Box 35
Mariposa, CA 95338-0035
(209) 966-2332
MENDOCINO COUNTY ASSESSOR
501 Low Gap Road, Rm. 1020
Ukiah, CA 95482
(707) 463-4311
MERCED COUNTY ASSESSOR
2222 M Street
Merced, CA 95340-3780
(209) 385-7631
MODOC COUNTY ASSESSOR
204 South Court Street, Rm. 106
Alturas, CA 96101-4064
(530) 233-6218
MONO COUNTY ASSESSOR
25 Bryant Street
P.O. Box 456
Bridgeport, CA 93517-0456
(760) 932-5510
MONTEREY COUNTY ASSESSOR
240 Church Street. Rm. 202
P.O. Box 570
Salinas, CA 93902-0570
(831) 755-5035
NAPA COUNTY ASSESSOR
1127 First Street, Rm. 128
Napa, CA 94559-2931
(707) 253-4467
NEVADA COUNTY ASSESSOR
950 Maidu Lane
Nevada City, CA 95959-8600
(530) 265-1232
ORANGE COUNTY ASSESSOR
12 Civic Center Plaza, 630 N. Broadway, Rm. 142
Santa Ana, CA 92702-0149
(714) 834-2727
PLACER COUNTY ASSESSOR
2980 Richardson Drive
Auburn, CA 95603-2640
(530) 889-4300
PLUMAS COUNTY ASSESSOR
1 Crescent Street

Quincy, CA 95971
(530) 283-6380
RIVERSIDE COUNTY ASSESSOR
4080 Lemon Street
P.O. Box 12004
Riverside, CA 92502-2204
(951) 955-6200
SACRAMENTO COUNTY ASSESSOR
3701 Power Inn Road, Suite 3000
Sacramento, CA 95826-4329
(916) 875-0760
SAN BENITO COUNTY ASSESSOR
440 Fifth Street, Room 108
Hollister, CA 95023-3893
(831) 636-4030
SAN BERNARDINO COUNTY ASSESSOR
172 W. Third Street
San Bernardino, CA 92415-0310
(909) 387-8307
SAN DIEGO COUNTY ASSESSOR
1600 Pacific Highway, Rm. 110
San Diego, CA 92101-2480
(619) 531-5507
SAN FRANCISCO COUNTY ASSESSOR
1 Dr. Carlton B. Goodlett Place, Rm 190
San Francisco, CA 94102-4698
(415) 554-5596
SAN JOAQUIN COUNTY ASSESSOR
24 South Hunter Street #303
Stockton, CA 95202-3273
(209) 468-2630
SAN LUIS OBISPO COUNTY ASSESSOR
1050 Monterey Street, Ste. D360
San Luis Obispo, CA 93408-2070
(805) 781-5643
SAN MATEO COUNTY ASSESSOR
555 County Center, 3rd Floor
Redwood City, CA 94063-1655
(650) 363-4500
SANTA BARBARA COUNTY ASSESSOR
105 East Anapamu Street, Rm. 204
P.O. Box 159
Santa Barbara, CA 93101-0159
(805) 568-2550
SANTA CLARA COUNTY ASSESSOR
70 West Hedding Street, East Wing
San Jose, CA 95110-1705
(408) 299-5500
SANTA CRUZ COUNTY ASSESSOR
701 Ocean Street, Rm. 130
Santa Cruz, CA 95060-4073
(831) 454-2002
SHASTA COUNTY ASSESSOR
County Courthouse
1450 Court Street, Suite 208-A

Redding, CA 96001-1667
(530) 225-3600
SIERRA COUNTY ASSESSOR
100 Courthouse Square, Rm. B1
P.O. Box 8
Downieville, CA 95936-0008
(530) 289-3283
SISKIYOU COUNTY ASSESSOR
311 Fourth Street, Room 108
Yreka, CA 96097-2984
(530) 842-8036
SOLANO COUNTY ASSESSOR
675 Texas Street, Suite 2700
Fairfield, CA 94533-6338
(707) 784-6200
SONOMA COUNTY ASSESSOR
585 Fiscal Drive, Rm. 104F
Santa Rosa, CA 95403-2872
(707) 565-1888
STANISLAUS COUNTY ASSESSOR
1010 10th St., Ste. 2400
Modesto, CA 95354-0847
(209) 525-6461
SUTTER COUNTY ASSESSOR
1160 Civic Center Blvd.
P.O. Box 1555
Yuba City, CA 95992-1555
(530) 822-7160
TEHAMA COUNTY ASSESSOR
444 Oak Street, #B
P.O. Box 428
Red Bluff, CA 96080-0428
(530) 527-5931
TRINITY COUNTY ASSESSOR
11 Court Street, 1st Fl.
P.O. Box 1255
Weaverville, CA 96093-1255
(530) 623-1257
TULARE COUNTY ASSESSOR
221 S. Mooney Blvd, Room 102-E
Visalia, CA 93291-4593
(559) 733-6361
TUOLUMNE COUNTY ASSESSOR
2 South Green Street
Sonora, CA 95370-4618
(209) 533-5535
VENTURA COUNTY ASSESSOR
800 South Victoria Avenue
Ventura, CA 93009-1270
(805) 654-2181
YOLO COUNTY ASSESSOR
625 Court Street, Room 104
Woodland, CA 95695-3495
(530) 666-8135
YUBA COUNTY ASSESSOR

915 8th Street, Suite 101
Marysville, CA 95901-5273
(530) 749-7820

California Department of Housing and Community Development, 1800 Third Street, Sacramento, CA 95814

General Information 916-445-4782

Internet: http://www.hcd.ca.gov/

California Department of Insurance, Producer Licensing Bureau, 320 Capitol Mall, Sacramento, CA 95814

General Information 800-967-9331

. 916-322-3555

Internet: http://www.insurance.ca.gov/

California Department of Motor Vehicles, Office of the Director, 2415 First Avenue Mail Station F101, Sacramento, CA 95818

General Information 800-777-0133

Internet: http://www.dmv.ca.gov/

California Department of Alcoholic Beverage Control, 3927 Lennane Drive, Suite 100, Sacramento, CA 95834

Headquarters 916-419-2500

Internet: http://www.abc.ca.gov/

PART X

DOING BUSINESS IN CALIFORNIA

CHAPTER 21

FEES AND TAXES

¶2101 Domestic Corporation Costs

Law: Secs. 12183-86, 12196, 12199, 12200-02, 12203.7, 12205-08, 12210-10.5, 26850-51, Government Code; Sec. 23221, Revenue and Taxation Code (CCH CALIFORNIA TAX REPORTS, ¶1-121).

• *Initial fees and taxes*

The following fees are charged by the Secretary of State:

Service Performed	*Fee*
Substituted service of process	$ 50.00
Annual statement of officers	20.00
Articles of incorporation (nonprofit)	30.00
Articles of incorporation (business)	100.00
Certificate of conversion (prior to 2005)	250.00
Certificate of conversion (after 2004)	150.00
Certificate of dissolution	No fee
Certificate of official character	20.00
Change of address	No fee
Miscellaneous filing fee	30.00
Registration of corporate name	50.00
Reservation of corporate name	10.00
Certification of a document	5.00
Issuing certificate of status or filing	5.00

The filing fee for a certificate of merger is ordinarily $100; if the merger involves corporations with one or more other types of business entities, the filing fee is $150.

For filing a certificate of amendment converting a nonprofit corporation to a business corporation, the fee is $70.

A certificate of information is $10 if the request is communicated in writing, or $5 if the request is communicated by another authorized medium.

For a document not otherwise specified, the fee is $30.

A fee of $2.25 is charged by a county clerk for the filing of any document or the issuance of any certificate relating to a corporation.

Fees pertaining to foreign corporations are discussed below at ¶2102.

¶2102 Foreign Corporation Costs

Law: Secs. 12186, 12199, 12204, 12210-10.5, 12212, Government Code; Sec. 23221, Revenue and Taxation Code (CCH CALIFORNIA TAX REPORTS, ¶2-230).

• *Initial fees and taxes*

The following fees are imposed on foreign corporations by the Secretary of State:

— Annual statement by foreign corporation, $20;

— Registration of a corporate name, $50;

— Reservation of a corporate name, $10; and

— Statement of address by nonqualified foreign lending institution, $50.

Miscellaneous fees applicable to domestic corporations also apply to foreign corporations (¶2101).

PART XI

UNCLAIMED PROPERTY

CHAPTER 22
UNCLAIMED PROPERTY

¶2201 Unclaimed Property

Comment: Federal court injunction—2007

In June 2007, the U.S. District Court for the Eastern District of California enjoined the State of California from taking title to or control of property as well as from selling or converting property that it already had obtained under the law. However, following enactment of new legislation later in the year, the injunction was dissolved.

In issuing the injunction, the federal district court ruled that until constitutionally adequate notice was provided for under California unclaimed property law, the state could not take title to or control of property and could not sell or convert property that it already had obtained under the law. In addition, the state controller had to submit any new proposed regulations concerning administration of the unclaimed property law to the court. The action was taken the day after the U.S. Court of Appeals for the Ninth Circuit had remanded the case with directions to issue the injunction. (*Taylor v. Westly*, U.S. Court of Appeals for the Ninth Circuit, No. 05-16763, May 31, 2007, *Taylor v. Chiang*, United States District Court for the Eastern District of California, No. Civ. S-01-2407 WBS GGH, June 1, 2007.)

However, following enactment of S.B. 86, Laws 2007, the court dissolved the injunction. The new law, as it was implemented by the Controller, provided constitutionally adequate notice to property owners of the state's intent to take title to, possess, sell, convert, or destroy unclaimed property, the court determined. (*Taylor v. Chiang*, U.S. District Court, Eastern District of California, No. CIV. S-01-2407 WBS GGH, October 17, 2007.)

Bruce Daigh, Chris Whitney, Contributing Editors

"Unclaimed property" is all property that:

— is presently unclaimed, abandoned, escheated, permanently escheated, or distributed to the state;

— will become unclaimed, abandoned, escheated, permanently escheated, or distributed to the state; or

— will become the possession of the state, if not claimed within the time allowed by law, even if there is no judicial determination that the property is unclaimed, abandoned, escheated, permanently escheated, or distributed to the state.

(Sec. 1300, Code of Civ. Proc.)

"Escheat" is the vesting in the state of property whose known owner has refused to accept it or whose owner is unknown. (Sec. 1300, Code of Civ. Proc.) Escheat is essentially a state process; procedures for federal unclaimed property are not as clearly set out as those of the states.

CCH Comment: Potential federal/state conflict

Escheat is an area of potential federal/state conflict. A federal statute may preempt state escheat provisions. For instance, it has been federal policy that the Employee Retirement

Income Security Act of 1974 (ERISA) (particularly Sec. 514(a)) generally preempts state laws relating to employee benefit plans. Thus, funds of missing participants in a qualified employee benefit plan stay in the plan pursuant to the federal executive policy that state escheat laws are preempted by ERISA. (*Advisory Opinion 94-41A*, Department of Labor, Pension and Welfare Benefit Administration, Dec. 7, 1994) However, some states have challenged the federal position on this and similar narrowly delineated situations. Thus, practitioners are advised that a specific situation where federal and state policy cross on the issue of escheat may, at this time, be an area of unsettled law.

With respect to federal tax refunds, IRC Sec. 6408 disallows refunds if the refund would escheat to a state.

California compliance with the procedures required to deal with abandoned property is briefly covered in the following paragraphs. In addition, The State Controller's Office has issued a newsletter that, among other things, highlights the holder notice report requirements and process following the 2007 legislation. (*Unclaimed Property Division Holder Outreach Newsletter*, California State Controller's Office, Fall 2008)

• *Abandoned property*

Generally, all tangible and intangible personal property that is held, issued, or owing in the ordinary course of a holder's business and that has remained unclaimed by the owner for more than three years after it became payable or distributable is presumed abandoned. (Sec. 1520, Code of Civ. Proc.) Such property includes:

— savings accounts;

— contents of safe deposit boxes;

— proceeds of insurance policies;

— dividends, profits, interest, payment on principal, distribution, or other sum by business associations;

— fiduciary property; and

— property held by any government, governmental subdivision or agency.

(Sec. 1513, Code of Civ. Proc.; Sec. 1514, Code of Civ. Proc.; Sec. 1515, Code of Civ. Proc.; Sec. 1516, Code of Civ. Proc.; Sec. 1518, Code of Civ. Proc.; Sec. 1519, Code of Civ. Proc.)

Other presumptive periods for abandonment apply to certain types of property, as discussed below.

Gift certificates, gift cards .—Generally, gift certificates are exempt from reporting requirements in California. However, gift certificates having an expiration date that are given in exchange for money or other things of value are presumed abandoned if left unclaimed by the owner for more than three years after it became payable or distributable. (Sec. 1520, Code of Civ. Proc.; Sec. 1520.5, Code of Civ. Proc.; Sec. 1749.5, Code of Civ. Proc.) Gift cards are treated the same as gift certificates for unclaimed property purposes. (Sec. 1749.45, Civ. Code)

• *Presumption of abandonment*

Actual abandonment of property may be proved at any time, but since unclaimed property is usually held under circumstances in which the ownership of the property is unknown or uncertain, California provides the following presumptive periods for abandonment:

— three years (five years, prior to January 1, 2004) for drafts or certified checks;

— 15 years for traveler's checks;

— six months for distributions in liquidation of a business association;

— seven years for a money order issued by a business association;

— three years for intangible property payable or distributable in the course of the demutualization of an insurance corporation; and

— one year for sums held by a business association for which a refund has been ordered by a court or public agency.

(Sec. 1513, Code of Civ. Proc.; Sec. 1515.5, Code of Civ. Proc.; Sec. 1517, Code of Civ. Proc.; Sec. 1519.5, Code of Civ. Proc.)

• *Report requirements*

Information reports are required of persons holding property (*e.g.*, banks and insurance companies) that has escheated to the state by reason of a presumption of abandonment, as described above. The report is made to the State Controller on forms prescribed by that officer and is due before November 1 for each year ending as of June 30 or earlier. Insurance companies must file by May 1 of each year ending as of December 31 or earlier. The report requires identification of the property and its former owner and dates when the property became payable and when the last transaction with the owner occurred. (Sec. 1530, Code of Civ. Proc.)

• *Existence of identified unclaimed property*

Effective August 24, 2007, in order to inform owners about the possible existence of identified unclaimed property, the Controller is required to mail, within 165 days after the final date for filing the report of escheated funds or property, a notice to each person having an address listed in the report who appears to be entitled to property with a value of $50 or more that has been escheated. If the report includes a social security number, the Controller is required to request that the California Franchise Tax Board (FTB) provide a current address for the apparent owner on the basis of that number. (Sec. 1531, Code of Civ. Proc.)

The Controller must mail the notice to the apparent owner for whom a current address is obtained if the address is different from the address previously reported to the Controller. If the FTB does not provide an address or a different address, then the Controller must mail the notice to the address listed in the report. The mailed notice must contain: (1) a statement that, according to a report filed with the Controller, property is being held to which the addressee appears entitled; (2) the name and address of the person holding the property and any necessary information regarding changes of name and address of the holder; (3) a statement that, if satisfactory proof of claim is not presented by the owner to the holder by the date specified in the notice, the property will be placed in the custody of the Controller and may be sold or destroyed, and all further claims concerning the property or, if sold, the net proceeds of its sale, must be directed to the Controller. (Sec. 1531, Code of Civ. Proc.)

• *Notification program*

Effective August 24, 2007, the Controller is required to establish and conduct a notification program designed to inform owners about the possible existence of unclaimed property that has been received. Upon the request of the Controller, a state or local governmental agency may furnish to the Controller from its records the address or other identification or location information that could reasonably be used to locate an owner of unclaimed property. If the address or other information requested is deemed confidential under any California laws or regulations, it shall nevertheless be furnished to the Controller. However, neither the Controller nor any officer, agent, or employee of the Controller shall use or disclose that information except as may be necessary in attempting to locate the owner of the unclaimed property. (Sec. 1531.5, Code of Civ. Proc.)

The Controller must publish a notice listing the names of the apparent owners, together with their last known address, within one year of the payment or delivery of the unclaimed property. (Sec. 1531, Code of Civ. Proc.)

• *Delivery of unclaimed property*

Effective August 24, 2007, every person who files a report is required to, no sooner than seven months and no later than seven months and 15 days after the final date for filing the report, pay or deliver to the Controller all escheated property specified in the report. If a person establishes his or her right to receive any property specified in the report to the satisfaction of the holder before that property has been delivered to the Controller, or it appears that for any other reason the property may not be subject to escheat, the holder is not required to pay or deliver the property to the Controller but is instead required to file a report with the Controller that contains information regarding the property not subject to escheat. Any property not paid or delivered that is later determined by the holder to be subject to escheat is subject to interest, as provided. (Sec. 1532, Code of Civ. Proc.)

Property reported as unclaimed must be delivered to the State Controller with the report. However, a holder of securities may register the securities in uncertificated form in the name of the Controller. (Sec. 1532, Code of Civ. Proc.) The Controller may decline to take custody of certain tangible property. (Sec. 1533, Code of Civ. Proc.)

Comment: Court Holds State Not Required to Pay Interest on Unclaimed Property

On June 3, 2008, the Second District Court of Appeal in *Morris v. Chiang*, No. B194764 (2nd District. June 3, 2008), held that the State Controller could lawfully retain interest on temporarily held unclaimed property. The property owner had contended that as title to her property had never transferred to the State she was entitled to all interest earned by the State while her funds were held by the State. The court disagreed, finding that the State holds temporary title to the property and is entitled to the interest earned on such. Morris has appealed this decision to the California Supreme Court. It should be noted that this Second District Court of Appeal decision is not consistent with *Suever v. Connell* (October 12, 2007), where the U.S. District Court ruled that the state must pay interest on assets that are reclaimed by owners from the state. The State has filed a motion to stay the court's order in *Suever v. Connell.*

Bruce Daigh, Chris Whitney, Contributing Editors

Interest, penalties, and interest amnesty.— Holders that fail to report and deliver unclaimed property, as required, are subject to annual interest payments of 12%, as well as to penalties, unless the failure is due to reasonable cause. (Sec. 1577, Code of Civ. Proc.)

Interest may be waived if reasonable cause exists. "Reasonable cause" means the exercise of ordinary business care and prudence. Specifically, interest will be waived if (1) in the absence of willful neglect, the failure was due to circumstances beyond the holder's control or (2) the delay or failure to file was due to erroneous information given to the holder of unclaimed property by an employee of the California Controller's office, unless the reliance was not reasonable cause for late reporting, payment or delivery. The burden is on the property holder to establish reasonable cause. The property holder must submit a sworn affidavit to the Comptroller's office attesting to the circumstances establishing reasonable cause. (Reg. 1172.90, 2 CCR; Reg. 1172.92, 2 CCR)

Interest was not imposed for unclaimed property paid and delivered before 2003, provided that all of the following conditions were satisfied:

— on or before January 1, 2003, the property holder was not under investigation by the California Attorney General;

— on or before January 3, 2000, the property holder was not under audit by, or in litigation with, the Controller in regard to the property;

— the required report was due on or before November 1, 1999;

— the property was surrendered directly to the state or its authorized agent;

— reports were submitted electronically, or by paper from holders reporting fewer than 50 accounts or other items;

— property reported after January 1, 2000, was reported separately from currently reportable property, and was not reported with property ineligible for the program;

— property was paid or delivered to the Controller when the report was submitted;

— securities remittances complied with statutory requirements; and

— records were satisfactorily maintained.

(Sec. 1577.5, Code of Civ. Proc.)

The amnesty program does not affect liability for false claims, and amnesty program extensions are not available. Interest paid to the Controller before 2001 is not refundable. (Sec. 1577.5, Code of Civ. Proc.)

• *Sale of escheated property*

Effective August 24, 2007, no sale of escheated property may be made until 18 months after the final date for filing the report. Securities listed on an established stock exchange and other securities may be sold by the Controller no sooner than 18 months, but no later than 20 months, after the final date for filing the report. Any property delivered to the Controller that has no apparent commercial value must be retained by the Controller for a period of not less than 18 months from the date the property is delivered to the Controller. (Sec. 1563, Code of Civ. Proc.)

• *Claims for recovery*

A period of five years is provided to make claims for the recovery of abandoned property. (Sec. 1351, Code of Civ. Proc.) The claim is filed with the State Controller on a form designated by that officer. The Controller must investigate the claim and render a decision within 180 days (90 days for claims for which the Controller has made a decision by August 11, 2003). The state officer must notify the claimant by mail and, for claims for which the Controller has made a decision by August 11, 2003, must pay interest on unclaimed property when it is returned to owners. (Sec. 1540, Code of Civ. Proc.)

• *Claimant remedies*

Claims denied or not decided by the Controller within 180 days after the claim was filed (90 days after the claim was filed for claims for which the Controller has made a decision by August 11, 2003) may be appealed by filing an action naming the State Controller as defendant in the superior court of any county or city in which the California Attorney General has an office. (Sec. 1541, Code of Civ. Proc.) The action must be brought within 90 days of the Controller's decision or within 90 days after the deadline for the Controller's decision.

Practitioner Comment: California Abandoned and Unclaimed Property Reforms

On June 1, 2007, the Ninth Circuit Court of Appeals granted a preliminary injunction in *Taylor v. Westly*, 488 F.3d 1197 (9th Cir. 2007) (*Taylor*) prohibiting the State from accepting, taking title to or possession of unclaimed property until methods for notifying owners of such property were resolved to satisfy due process requirements. On August 24, 2007, S.B. 86 was enacted, amending the State's process of notifying property owners at risk of having their property transferred to the State. On October 18, 2007, the injunction was lifted as a result of S.B. 86, which satisfactorily rectified the notification problems.

S.B. 86 provides for holders to file a preliminary report without remittance of property commencing with the report due before November 1, 2007, or, for life insurance companies, before May 1, 2008. The State must send notices to owners listed in the reports with a property value of $50 or more within 165 days, in an effort to reunite the property with the owners, before property is seized. Holders must then file a second report and remit the unclaimed property between June 1 and June 15, 2008, or, for life insurance companies, between December 1 and December 15, 2008.

In another decision on October 12, 2007, a U.S. District Court judge ruled in *Suever v. Connell* that the State must pay interest on assets that are reclaimed by owners from the State. The impact of this ruling is unclear at this time.

Bruce Daigh, Chris Whitney, Contributing Editors

Table of Cases Cited

References are to paragraph (¶) numbers.

C

D

E

F

Table of Franchise Tax Board

Legal Rulings

References are to paragraph (¶) numbers.

Table of Franchise Tax Board Notices

References are to paragraph (¶) numbers.

CALIFORNIA TAX FORMS AND RELATED FEDERAL FORMS

State of California—Franchise Tax Board

The **CALIFORNIA TAX FORMS AND RELATED FEDERAL FORMS—FTB Pub. 1006** follows. The list of California Tax forms starts on page 774; the federal forms list starts on page 780.

State of California — Franchise Tax Board FTB Pub. 1006

CALIFORNIA TAX FORMS AND RELATED FEDERAL FORMS

CALIFORNIA FORM NUMBER	CALIFORNIA FORM – Title or Description	RELATED FEDERAL FORM	MAY USE FEDERAL FORM See Notes
DE 1	Employer Registration Form**	SS-4	No
DE 4	Employee's Withholding Allowance Certificate	W-4	Yes
DE 4P	Withholding Certificate for Pension or Annuity Payments	W-4P	Yes
DE 4S	Request for State Income Tax Withholding From Sick Pay	W-4S	Yes
DE 6	Quarterly Wage and Withholding Report	941	No
DE 7	Annual Reconciliation Statement	W-3	No
DE 166	Magnetic Media — Submittal Sheet Quarterly Wage and Withholding Information	4804	No
100	California Corporation Franchise or Income Tax Return	1120, 1120F,	No
		1120-FSC, 1120-H,	No
		1120-POL, 1120-RIC	No
		1120-REIT, 990-C	No
		Sch D (1120)	No
Sch H (100)	Dividend Income Deduction	None	Not applicable
Sch P (100)	Alternative Minimum Tax and Credit Limitations — Corporations	4626	No
Sch R	Apportionment and Allocation of Income	None	Not applicable
Sch R-7	Election to File a Unitary Taxpayers' Group Return	851	No
100-ES	Corporation Estimated Tax	1120-W	No
100-ES "Scannable"	Corporation Estimated Tax	None	Not applicable
FTB 3539	Payment for Automatic Extension for Corps and Exempt Orgs	None	Not applicable
FTB 3539 "Scannable"	Payment for Automatic Extension for Corps and Exempt Orgs	None	Not applicable
FTB 3565	Small Business Stock Questionnaire	None	Not applicable
FTB 3805Q	Net Operating Loss (NOL) Computation and NOL and Disaster Loss Limitations — Corporations	None	Not applicable
FTB 3577	Pending Audit Tax Deposit Voucher for Corporations	None	Not applicable
FTB 3586	Payment Voucher for Corp e-filed Returns	None	Not applicable
FTB 3586 "Scannable"	Payment Voucher for Corp e-filed Returns	None	Not applicable
FTB 3885	Corporation Depreciation and Amortization	4562	No
100S	California S Corporation Franchise or Income Tax Return	1120S	No
Sch B (100S)	S Corporation Depreciation and Amortization	None	Not applicable
Sch C (100S)	S Corporation Tax Credits	None	Not applicable
Sch D (100S)	S Corporation Capital Gains and Losses and Built-In Gains	Sch D (1120S)	No

Sch H (100S)	S Corporation Dividend Income Deduction	None	Not applicable
Sch K-1 (100S)	Shareholder's Share of Income, Deductions, Credits, etc.	Sch K-1 (1120S)	No
100W	California Corporation Franchise or Income Tax Return — Water's-Edge Filers	None	Not applicable
Sch H (100W)	Dividend Income — Water's-Edge Filers	None	Not applicable
Sch P (100W)	Alternative Minimum Tax and Credit Limitations — Water's-Edge Filers	None	Not applicable
100-WE	Water's-Edge Election	None	Not applicable
FTB 1115	Request for Consent for a Water's-Edge Re-Election	None	Not applicable
FTB 1117	Request to Terminate Water's-Edge Election	None	Not applicable
FTB 2416	Schedule of Included Controlled Foreign Corporations (CFC)	None	Not applicable
FTB 2424	Water's-Edge Foreign Investment Interest Offset	None	Not applicable
100X	Amended Corporation Franchise or Income Tax Return	1120X	No
109	California Exempt Organization Business Income Tax Return	990-T	No
199	California Exempt Organization Annual Information Return	{ 990, 990EZ, 990-PF,	No
		Sch A (990)	No
540	California Resident Income Tax Return	1040	No
540 "Scannable"	California Resident Income Tax Return	None	Not applicable
540-ES	Estimated Tax for Individuals	1040-ES	No
540-ES "Scannable"	Estimated Tax for Individuals	None	Not applicable
540-V "Scannable"	Payment Voucher for 540 Returns	1040V	No
FTB 3519	Payment for Automatic Extension for Individuals	None	Not applicable
FTB 3519 "Scannable"	Payment for Automatic Extension for Individuals	None	Not applicable
FTB 3885A (540)	Depreciation and Amortization Adjustments	4562	No
Sch CA (540)	California Adjustments — Residents	None	Not applicable
Sch D (540)	California Capital Gain or Loss Adjustment	Sch D (1040)	No
Sch D-1	Sales of Business Property	4797	No
Sch G-1	Tax on Lump-Sum Distributions	4972	No
Sch P (540)	Alternative Minimum Tax and Credit Limitations — Residents	6251	No
Sch S	Other State Tax Credit	None	Not applicable
Sch W-2	Wage and Withholding Summary	None	Not applicable
FTB 3525	Substitute Wage and Withholding Summary	None	Not applicable
540A	California Resident Income Tax Return	1040A	No
540 2EZ	California Resident Income Tax Return	1040EZ	Not applicable
540NR	California Nonresident or Part-Year Resident Income Tax Return — (Long and Short Forms)	{ 1040, 1040A,	No
		1040NR, 1040NR-EZ	No

CALIFORNIA FORM NUMBER	CALIFORNIA FORM – Title or Description	RELATED FEDERAL FORM	MAY USE FEDERAL FORM See Notes
FTB 3576	Pending Audit Tax Deposit Voucher for Individuals	None	Not applicable
FTB 3885A (540NR)	Depreciation and Amortization Adjustments	4562	No
Sch CA (540NR)	California Adjustments — Nonresidents or Part-Year Residents	None	Not applicable
Sch D (540NR)	California Capital Gain or Loss Adjustment	Sch D (1040)	No
Sch P (540NR)	Alternative Minimum Tax and Credit Limitations — Nonresidents or Part-Year Residents	6251	No
540X	Amended Individual Income Tax Return	1040X	No
541	California Fiduciary Income Tax Return	1041	No
Sch D (541)	Capital Gain or Loss	Sch D (1041)	No
Sch J (541)	Trust Allocation of an Accumulation Distribution	Sch J (1041)	No
Sch K-1 (541)	Beneficiary's Share of Income, Deductions, Credits, etc.	Sch K-1 (1041)	No
Sch P (541)	Alternative Minimum Tax and Credit Limitations — Fiduciaries	Sch I (1041)	No
541-A	Trust Accumulation of Charitable Amounts	1041-A	No
541-B	Charitable Remainder and Pooled Income Trusts	5227	No
541-ES	Estimated Tax for Fiduciaries	1041-ES	No
541-ES "Scannable"	Estimated Tax for Fiduciaries	None	Not applicable
541-QFT	California Income Tax Return for Qualified Funeral Trusts	1041-QFT	No
541-T	California Allocation of Estimated Tax Payments to Beneficiaries	1041-T	No
FTB 3885F (541)	Depreciation and Amortization — Fiduciaries	4562	No
565	Partnership Return of Income	1065	No
Sch D (565)	Capital Gain or Loss	Sch D (1065)	No
Sch K-1 (565)	Partner's Share of Income, Deductions, Credits, etc.	Sch K-1 (1065)	No
FTB 3579	Pending Audit Tax Deposit Voucher for LPs, LLPs, and REMICs	None	Not applicable
FTB 3885P (565)	Depreciation and Amortization — Partnerships	4562	No
568	Limited Liability Company Return of Income	None	Not applicable
Sch D (568)	Capital Gain or Loss	Sch D (1065)	No
Sch K-1 (568)	Member's Share of Income, Deductions, Credits, etc.	Sch K-1 (1065)	No
FTB 3578	Pending Audit Tax Deposit Voucher for LLCs	None	Not applicable
FTB 3832	Limited Liability Company Nonresident Members' Consent	None	Not applicable
FTB 3885L (568)	Depreciation and Amortization — Limited Liability Companies	4562	No
570	Nonadmitted Insurance Tax Return	None	Not applicable
587	Nonresident Withholding Allocation Worksheet	None	Not applicable
588	Nonresident Withholding Waiver Request	None	Not applicable
589	Nonresident Request for Reduced Withholding	None	Not applicable
590	Withholding Exemption Certificate	None	Not applicable

590-P	Nonresident Withholding Exemption Certificate for Previously Reported Income	None	Not applicable
592	Quarterly Nonresident Withholding Statement	1042, 8804	No
592-A	Foreign Partner or Member Quarterly Withholding Remittance Statement	8813	No
592-B	Nonresident Withholding Tax Statement	1042S, 8805	No
592-F	Foreign Partner or Member Annual Return	1042, 8804	No
593	Real Estate Withholding Tax Statement	8288, 8288-A	No
593-C	Real Estate Withholding Certificate	None	Not applicable
593-E	Real Estate Withholding — Computation of Estimated Gain or Loss	None	Not applicable
593-I	Real Estate Withholding Installment Sale Agreement	None	Not applicable
593-V	Voucher for Real Estate Withholding Electronic Submission	None	Not applicable
FTB 3500	Exemption Application	1023, 1024	No
FTB 3500A	Affirmation of Internal Revenue Code Section 501(c)(3)	None	Not applicable
FTB 3501	Employer Child Care Program/Contribution Credit	None	Not applicable
FTB 3503	Natural Heritage Preservation Credit	None	Not applicable
FTB 3506	Child and Dependent Care Expenses Credit	2441	No
FTB 3507	Prison Inmate Labor Credit	None	Not applicable
FTB 3509	Political or Legislative Activities by Section 23701d Organizations	None	Not applicable
FTB 3510	Credit for Prior Year Alternative Minimum Tax — Individuals or Fiduciaries	8801	No
FTB 3511	Environmental Tax Credit	None	Not applicable
FTB 3516 (Side 1)	Request for Copy of Personal Income Tax or Fiduciary Return	4506	No
FTB 3516 (Side 2)	Request for Copy of Corporation, Exempt Organization, Partnership, or Limited Liability Company	4506	No
FTB 3519	Payment for Automatic Extension for Individuals	None	Not applicable
FTB 3519 "Scannable"	Payment for Automatic Extension for Individuals	None	Not applicable
FTB 3520	Power of Attorney	2848, 8821	Yes
FTB 3521	Low-Income Housing Credit	8586	No
FTB 3522	LLC Tax Voucher	None	Not applicable
FTB 3522 "Scannable"	LLC Tax Voucher	None	Not applicable
FTB 3523	Research Credit	6765	No
FTB 3525	Substitute for Form W-2, Wage and Tax Statement, or Form 1099-R, Distributions From Pensions, Annuities, Retirement or Profit-Sharing Plans, IRAs, Insurance Contracts, etc.	4852	No
FTB 3526	Investment Interest Expense Deduction	4952	No
FTB 3533	Change of Address	8822	Yes
FTB 3536	Estimated Fee for LLCs	None	Not applicable
FTB 3536 "Scannable"	Estimated Fee for LLCs	None	Not applicable

CALIFORNIA FORM NUMBER	CALIFORNIA FORM – Title or Description	RELATED FEDERAL FORM	MAY USE FEDERAL FORM See Notes
FTB 3537	Payment for Automatic Extension for LLCs	None	Not applicable
FTB 3537 "Scannable"	Pament for Automatic Extension for LLCs	None	Not applicable
FTB 3538	Payment for Automatic Extension for LPs, LLPs, and REMICs	None	Not applicable
FTB 3538 "Scannable"	Payment for Automatic Extension for LPs, LLPs, and REMICs	None	Not applicable
FTB 3539	Payment for Automatic Extension for Corps and Exempt Orgs	None	Not applicable
FTB 3539 "Scannable"	Payment for Automatic Extension for Corps and Exempt Orgs	None	Not applicable
FTB 3540	Credit Carryover Summary	None	Not applicable
FTB 3546	Enhanced Oil Recovery Credit	8830	No
FTB 3547	Donated Agricultural Products Transportation Credit	None	Not applicable
FTB 3548	Disabled Access Credit for Eligible Small Businesses	8826	No
FTB 3553	Enterprise Zone Employee Credit	None	Not applicable
FTB 3561	Installment Agreement Financial Statement	433-D	No
FTB 3563	Payment for Automatic Extension for Fiduciaries	None	Not applicable
FTB 3563 "Scannable"	Payment for Automatic Extension for Fiduciaries	None	Not applicable
FTB 3567	Installment Agreement Request	9465	No
FTB 3570	Waiver Extending Statute of Limitations	None	Not applicable
FTB 3571	Request for Estate Income Tax Clearance Certificate	None	Not applicable
FTB 3574	Special Election for Business Trusts and Certain Foreign Single Member LLCs	None	Not applicable
FTB 3580	Application and Election to Amortize Certified Pollution Control Facility	None	Not applicable
FTB 3581	Tax Deposit Refund and Transfer Request	None	Not applicable
FTB 3582	Payment Voucher for Individual e-filed Returns	None	Not applicable
FTB 3582 "Scannable"	Payment Voucher for Individual e-filed Returns	None	Not applicable
FTB 3587	Payment Voucher for LP, LLP, and REMIC e-filed Returns	None	Not applicable
FTB 3587 "Scannable"	Payment Voucher for LP, LLP, and REMIC e-filed Returns	None	Not applicable
FTB 3588	Payment Voucher for LLC e-filed Returns	None	Not applicable
FTB 3588 "Scannable"	Payment Voucher for LLC e-filed Returns	None	Not applicable
FTB 3601	Transmittal of Annual 1098, 1099, 5498, W-2G Information for Tax Year ____	4804	No
FTB 3604	Transmittal of Paperless Schedules K-1 (565 or 568) on CD or Diskette	None	Not applicable
FTB 3725	Assets Transferred from Parent Corporation to Insurance Company Subsidiary	None	Not applicable
FTB 3726	Deferred Intercompany Stock Account (DISA) and Capital Gains Information	None	Not applicable

FTB 3800	Tax Computation for Children Under Age 14 with Investment Income	8615	No
FTB 3801	Passive Activity Loss Limitations	8582	No
FTB 3801-CR	Passive Activity Credit Limitations	8582-CR	No
FTB 3802	Corporate Passive Activity Loss and Credit Limitations	8810	No
FTB 3803	Parents' Election to Report Child's Interest and Dividends	8814	No
FTB 3805A	Information to Support Exemption Claimed for Dependent	None	Not applicable
FTB 3805D	Net Operating Loss (NOL) Carryover Computation and Limitation – Pierce's Disease	None	Not applicable
FTB 3805E	Installment Sale Income	6252	No
FTB 3805P	Additional Taxes on Qualified Plans (including IRAs) and Other Tax-Favored Accounts	None	Not appllicable
FTB 3805Q	Net Operating Loss (NOL) Computation and NOL and Disaster Loss Limitations — Corporations	None	Not applicable
FTB 3805V	Net Operating Loss (NOL) Computation and NOL and Disaster Loss Limitations — Individuals, Estates, and Trusts	None	Not applicable
FTB 3805Z	Enterprise Zone Deduction and Credit Summary	None	Not applicable
FTB 3806	Los Angeles Revitalization Zone Deduction and Credit Summary	None	Not applicable
FTB 3807	Local Agency Military Base Recovery Area Deduction and Credit Summary	None	Not applicable
FTB 3808	Manufacturing Enhancement Area Credit Summary	None	Not applicable
FTB 3809	Targeted Tax Area Deduction and Credit Summary	None	Not applicable
FTB 3834	Interest Computation Under the Look-Back Method for Completed Long-Term Contracts	8697	No
FTB 4092	Media Filing Application	4419	Yes
FTB 5805	Underpayment of Estimated Tax by Individuals and Fiduciaries	2210	No
FTB 5805F	Underpayment of Estimated Tax by Farmers and Fishermen	2210F	No
FTB 5806	Underpayment of Estimated Tax by Corporations	2220	No
FTB 5870A	Tax on Accumulation Distribution of Trusts	4970	No
FTB 8453	California e-file Return Authorization for Individuals	8453	No
FTB 8453-C	California e-file Return Authorization for Corporations	8453-C	No
FTB 8453-LLC	California e-file Return Authorization for Limited Liability Companies	None	No
FTB 8453-OL	California Online e-file Return Authorization for Individuals	8453-OL	No
FTB 8453-P	California e-file Return Authorization for Partnerships	8453-P	No
FTB 8454	e-file Opt-Out Record for Individuals	None	Not applicable
FTB 8455	California e-file Payment Record for Individuals	None	Not applicable
FTB 8879	California e-file Signature Authorization for Individuals	8879	No
FTB 9000H	Homeowner Assistance Claim	None	Not applicable
FTB 9000R	Renter Assistance Claim	None	Not applicable

FEDERAL FORM NUMBER	FEDERAL FORM – Title or Description	RELATED CALIFORNIA FORM	MAY USE FEDERAL FORM See Notes
SS-4	Application for Employer Identification Number	DE 1	No**
T (Timber)	Forest Activity Schedule	None	Yes
W-2	Wage and Tax Statement	None	Yes
W-3	Transmittal of Wage and Tax Statements	DE 7	No
W-4	Employee's Withholding Allowance Certificate	DE 4	Yes
W-4P	Withholding Certificate for Pension or Annuity Payments	DE 4P	Yes
W-4S	Request for Federal Income Tax Withholding From Sick Pay	DE 4S	Yes
W-9	Request for Taxpayer Identification Number and Certification	None	Yes
56	Notice Concerning Fiduciary Relationship	None	Yes
433-D	Installment Agreement	FTB 3567	No
851	Affiliations Schedule	Sch R-7 (100)	No
872	Consent to Extend the Time to Assess Tax	FTB 3570	No
875	Acceptance of Examiner's Findings By a Partnership, Fiduciary, S Corporation or Interest Charge Domestic International Sales Corporation	None	Yes
907	Agreement to Extend the Time to Bring Suit	None	Yes
926	Return by a U.S. Transferor of Property to a Foreign Corporation	None	Yes
941	Employer's Quarterly Federal Tax Return	DE 6	No
966	Corporate Dissolution or Liquidation	None	Yes
970	Application to Use LIFO Inventory Method	None	Yes
982	Reduction of Tax Attributes Due to Discharge of Indebtedness (and Section 1082 Basis Adjustment)	None	Yes
990	Return of Organization Exempt from Income Tax	199	No
990 (Sch A)	Organization Exempt Under (Section 501(c)(3))	199	No
990-C	Farmers' Cooperative Association Income Tax Return	100	No
990EZ	Short Form Return of Organization Exempt From Income Tax	199	No
990PF	Return of Private Foundation or Section 4947(a)(1) Nonexempt Charitable Trust Treated As a Private Foundation	199	No
990T	Exempt Organization Business Income Tax Return	109	No
1023	Application for Recognition of Exemption Under Section 501(c)(3) of the Internal Revenue Code	FTB 3500	No
1024	Application for Recognition of Exemption Under Section 501(a)	FTB 3500	No
1040	U.S. Individual Income Tax Return	540	No
Sch A (1040)	Itemized Deductions	None	Yes
Sch B (1040)	Interest and Ordinary Dividends	None	Yes
Sch C (1040)	Profit or Loss From Business	None	Yes

Sch C-EZ (1040)	Net Profit From Business	None	Yes
Sch D (1040)	Capital Gains and Losses	Sch D (540)	No
		Sch D (540NR)	No
Sch E (1040)	Supplemental Income and Loss	None	Yes
Sch F (1040)	Profit or Loss From Farming	None	Yes
Sch R (1040)	Credit for the Elderly or the Disabled	Not applicable	Not applicable
1040A	U.S. Individual Income Tax Return	540A	No
1040-ES	Estimated Tax for Individuals	540-ES	No
1040EZ	Income Tax Return for Single and Joint Filers With No Dependents	540 2EZ	No
1040NR	U.S. Nonresident Alien Income Tax Return	540NR (Long)	No
1040NR-EZ	U.S. Income Tax Return for Certain Nonresident Aliens With No Dependents	540NR (Short)	No
1040-V	Payment Voucher	540-V	No
1040X	Amended U.S. Individual Income Tax Return	540X	No
1041	U.S. Income Tax Return for Estates and Trusts	541	No
Sch D (1041)	Capital Gains and Losses	Sch D (541)	No
Sch I (1041)	Alternative Minimum Tax — Fiduciaries	Sch P (541)	No
Sch J (1041)	Accumulation Distribution for Certain Complex Trusts	Sch J (541)	No
Sch K-1 (1041)	Beneficiary's Share of Income, Deductions, Credits, etc.	Sch K-1 (541)	No
1041-ES	Estimated Income Tax for Estates and Trusts	541-ES	No
1041-A	U.S. Information Return on Trust Accumulation of Charitable Amounts	541-A	No
1041-T	Allocation of Estimated Tax Payments to Beneficiaries	541-T	No
1041-QFT	U.S. Income Tax Return for Qualified Funeral Trusts	541-QFT	No
1042	Annual Withholding Tax Return for U.S. Source Income of Foreign Persons	592-A, 592-F	No
1042S	Foreign Person's U.S. Source Income Subject to Withholding	592-B	No
1065	U.S. Return of Partnership Income	565	No
Sch D (1065)	Capital Gains and Losses	Sch D (565)	No
Sch K-1 (1065)	Partner's Share of Income, Credits, Deductions, etc.	Sch K-1 (565)	No
1078	Certificate of Alien Claiming Residence in the United States	590	No
1096	Annual Summary and Transmittal of U.S. Information Returns	None	Yes
1098	Mortgage Interest Statement	None	Yes
1099-A	Acquisition or Abandonment of Secured Property	None	Yes
1099-B	Proceeds From Broker and Barter Exchange Transactions	None	Yes
1099-C	Cancellation of Debt	None	Yes
1099-DIV	Dividends and Distributions	None	Yes

FEDERAL FORM NUMBER	FEDERAL FORM – Title or Description	RELATED CALIFORNIA FORM	MAY USE FEDERAL FORM See Notes
1099-G	Certain Government Payments	None	Yes
1099-INT	Interest Income	None	Yes
1099-LTC	Long-Term Care and Accelerated Death Benefits	None	Yes
1099-MISC	Miscellaneous Income	None	Yes
1099-SA	Distributions From an HSA, Archer MSA, or Medicare Advantage MSA	None	Yes
1099-OID	Original Issue Discount	None	Yes
1099-PATR	Taxable Distributions Received From Cooperatives	None	Yes
1099-R	Distributions From Pensions, Annuities, Retirement or Profit-Sharing Plans, IRAs, Insurance Contracts, etc.	None	Yes
1120	U.S. Corporation Income Tax Return	100	No
Sch D (1120)	Capital Gains and Losses	100	No
1120F	U.S. Income Tax Return of a Foreign Corporation	100	No
1120-FSC	U.S. Income Tax Return of a Foreign Sales Corporation	100	No
1120-H	U.S. Income Tax Return for Homeowners' Associations	100	No
1120-POL	U.S. Income Tax Return for Certain Political Organizations	100	No
1120-REIT	U.S. Income Tax Return for Real Estate Investment Trusts	100	No
1120-RIC	U.S. Income Tax Return for Regulated Investment Companies	100	No
1120S	U.S. Income Tax Return for an S Corporation	100S	No
Sch D (1120S)	Capital Gains and Losses and Built-In Gains	Sch D (100S)	No
Sch K-1 (1120S)	Shareholder's Share of Income, Credits, Deductions, etc.	Sch K-1 (100S)	No
1120-W	Estimated Tax for Corporations	100-ES	No
1120X	Amended U.S. Corporation Income Tax Return	100X	No
1128	Application to Adopt, Change, or Retain a Tax Year	None	Yes
1310	Statement of Person Claiming Refund Due a Deceased Taxpayer	None	Yes
2106	Employee Business Expenses	None	Yes
2106-EZ	Unreimbursed Employee Business Expenses	None	Yes
2120	Multiple Support Declaration	None	Yes
2210	Underpayment of Estimated Tax by Individuals, Estates and Trusts	FTB 5805	No
2210F	Underpayment of Estimated Tax by Farmers and Fishermen	FTB 5805F	No
2220	Underpayment of Estimated Tax by Corporations	FTB 5806	No
2350	Application for Extension of Time to File U.S. Income Tax Return	Not applicable	Not applicable
2441	Child and Dependent Care Expenses	FTB 3506	No
2678	Employer/Payer Appointment of Agent	None	Yes
2848	Power of Attorney and Declaration of Representative	FTB 3520	Yes
3115	Application for Change in Accounting Method	None	Yes

3468	Investment Credit	Not applicable	Not applicable
3903	Moving Expenses	None	Yes
4137	Social Security and Medicare Tax on Unreported Tip Income	Not applicable	Not applicable
4255	Recapture of Investment Credit	Not applicable	Not applicable
4419	Application for Filing Information Returns Magnetically/Electronically	FTB 4092	Yes
4461	Application for Approval of Master or Prototype or Volume Submitter Defined Contribution Plan	None	Yes
4466	Corporation Application for Quick Refund of Overpayment of Estimated Tax	Not applicable	Not applicable
4506	Request for Copy of Tax Return	FTB 3516	No
4562	Depreciation and Amortization	FTB 3885	No
		FTB 3885A (540)	No
		FTB 3885A (540NR)	No
		FTB 3885F (541)	No
		FTB 3885L (568)	No
		FTB 3885P (565)	No
4626	Alternative Minimum Tax — Corporations	Sch P (100)	No
4669	Statement of Payments Received	None	Yes
4670	Request for Relief from Payment of Income Tax Withholding	None	Yes
4684	Casualties and Thefts	None	Yes
4797	Sales of Business Property	Sch D-1	No
4804	Transmittal of Information Returns Reported Magnetically	FTB 3601	No
4835	Farm Rental Income and Expenses	None	Yes
4852	Substitute for Form W-2, Wage and Tax Statement or Form 1099-R, Distributions From Pensions, Annuities, Retirement or Profit-Sharing Plans, IRAs, Insurance Contracts, Etc.	FTB 3525	No
4868	Application for Automatic Extension of Time to File U.S. Individual Income Tax Return	Not applicable	Not applicable
4952	Investment Interest Expense Deduction	FTB 3526	No
4970	Tax on Accumulation Distribution of Trusts	FTB 5870A	No
4972	Tax on Lump-Sum Distributions	Sch G-1	No
5227	Split-Interest Trust Information Return	541-B	No
5329	Additional Taxes on Qualified Plans (including IRAs) and Other Tax-Favored Accounts		
5471	Information Return of U.S. Persons With Respect to Certain Foreign Corporations	None	Yes
5472	Information Return of a 25% Foreign-Owned U.S. Corporation or a Foreign Corporation Engaged in a U.S. Trade or Business	None	Yes
5498	Individual Retirement Arrangement Information	None	Yes

FEDERAL FORM NUMBER	FEDERAL FORM – Title or Description	RELATED CALIFORNIA FORM	MAY USE FEDERAL FORM See Notes
5500	Annual Return/Report of Employee Benefit Plan	Not applicable	Not applicable
5754	Statement by Person(s) Receiving Gambling Winnings	None	Yes
5884	Work Opportunity Credit	None	No
6198	At-Risk Limitations	None	Yes
6251	Alternative Minimum Tax — Individuals	Sch P (540),	No
		Sch P (540NR)	No
6252	Installment Sale Income	FTB 3805E	No
6765	Credit for Increasing Research Activities	FTB 3523	No
7004	Application for Automatic 6-Month Extension of Time To File Certain Business Income Tax, Information, and Other Returns	Not applicable	Not applicable
8023	Elections Under Section 338 for Corporations Making Qualified Stock Purchases	None	Yes
8275	Disclosure Statement	None	Yes
8275-R	Regulation Disclosure Statement	None	Yes
8288	U.S. Withholding Tax Return for Dispositions by Foreign Persons of U.S. Real Property Interests	593	No
8288-A	Statement of Withholding on Dispositions by Foreign Persons of U.S. Real Property Interests	593	No
8300	Report of Cash Payments Over $10,000 Received in a Trade or Business	None	Yes
8453	U.S. Individual Income Tax Declaration for Electronic Filing	FTB 8453	No
8453-OL	U.S. Individual Income Tax Declaration for an IRS e-file Online Return	FTB 8453-OL	No
8453-C	U.S. Corporation Income Tax Declaration for an IRS e-file Return	FTB 8453-C	No
8453-P	U.S. Partnership Declaration and Signature for Electronic Filing	FTB 8453-P	No
8582	Passive Activity Loss Limitations	FTB 3801	No
8582-CR	Passive Activity Credit Limitations	FTB 3801-CR	No
8586	Low-Income Housing Credit	FTB 3521	No
8615	Tax for Children Under Age 18 With Investment Income of More Than $1800	FTB 3800	No
8633	Application to Participate in the IRS e-file Program	Not applicable	Yes
8697	Interest Computation Under the Look-Back Method for Completed Long-Term Contracts	FTB 3834	No
8801	Credit for Prior Year Minimum Tax — Individuals, Estates and Trusts	FTB 3510	No
8804	Annual Return for Partnership Withholding Tax (Section 1446)	592, 592-A, 592-F	No
8805	Foreign Partner's Information Statement of Section 1446 Withholding Tax	592-B	No
8810	Corporate Passive Activity Loss and Credit Limitations	FTB 3802	No
8813	Partnership Withholding Tax Payment (Section 1446)	592-A	No
8814	Parent's Election To Report Child's Interest and Dividends	FTB 3803	No

8821	Tax Information Authorization	FTB 3520	Yes
8822	Change of Address	FTB 3533	Yes
8824	Like-Kind Exchanges	None	Yes
8826	Disabled Access Credit	FTB 3548	No
8827	Credit for Prior Year Minimum Tax — Corporations	Sch P (100), Part III	No
8830	Enhanced Oil Recovery Credit	FTB 3546	No
8839	Qualified Adoption Expenses	FTB 5123	No
8842	Election to Use Different Annualization Periods for Corporation Estimated Tax	None	Yes
8869	Qualified Subchapter S Subsidiary Election	None	Yes
9465	Installment Agreement Request	FTB 3567	No

Notes

No California form must be used.

** Form number may vary based on industry-specific registration.

Yes If there is no difference between California and federal amounts, you may use a copy of the federal form. If there is a difference between California and federal amounts, use the California form. If there is no California form, complete the federal form using California amounts and attach it to your California tax return.

Not applicable Federal form is not applicable to California tax or California form is not applicable for federal tax.

Yes[1] Copies of paper information returns (1099 series, 1098, and 5498) filed with the Internal Revenue Service are not required to be filed with the Franchise Tax Board (FTB). However, if federal and California amounts differ, information returns may be attached to Form 1096 and filed with the FTB.

When to attach a copy of a complete federal return to the California return.

Short Form 540NR, Form 540A, and Form 540 2EZ: Do not attach the federal return.

Form 540: Attach a copy of the complete federal return when federal forms and schedules other than Schedule A or Schedule B are attached to the federal return.

Long Form 540NR: Always attach a copy of the complete federal return.

INDEX

References are to paragraph (¶) numbers.

C

E

F

S